# ENGLISH · PORTUGUESE
# PORTUGUESE · ENGLISH
# DICTIONARY

# DICIONÁRIO
# INGLÊS · PORTUGUÊS
# PORTUGUÊS · INGLÊS

COLLINS
**GEM**
DICTIONARY

# ENGLISH · PORTUGUESE
# PORTUGUESE · ENGLISH

# INGLÊS · PORTUGUÊS
# PORTUGUÊS · INGLÊS

---

*General Editor/Organizador*
**Mike Harland B.A., M.A.**

*Brazilian Consultant/Assessora Brasileira*
Dr Euzi Rodrigues Moraes

---

*completely revised edition*
*completamente revisada*

**Collins**
*London and Glasgow*

*first published in this edition 1986*

**ISBN 0 00 458666 2**

© **William Collins Sons & Co. Ltd. 1986**

*contributors/colaboradores*
Betty Wilson, Ana Lúcia Campbell,
Mark Dinneen, Lata Jamieson

*consultants/assessores*
David Treece, Antonio Fornazaro

*editorial staff/redação*
Susan Dunsmore

*Printed in Great Britain*
**Collins Clear-Type Press**

## INTRODUÇÃO

**Quem** quiser ler e compreender a língua inglesa encontrará neste dicionário um extenso léxico moderno que abrange uma ampla variedade de locuções de uso corrente. Encontrará também, por ordem alfabética, as abreviaturas, as siglas, os nomes geográficos mais conhecidos e ainda as formas verbais irregulares mais comuns, apontando-se as respectivas raízes, sendo então feita a tradução.

A pessoa que aspirar a comunicar e a expressar-se em língua estrangeira, encontrará uma explicação clara e pormenorizada das palavras fundamentais, sendo utilizado um sistema de indicadores que a remeterão para a tradução mais precisa e lhe assinalarão o seu uso correcto.

## INTRODUCTION

**The user** whose aim is to read and understand Portuguese will find a comprehensive and up-to-date wordlist including numerous phrases in current use. He will also find listed alphabetically the main irregular forms with a cross-reference to the basic form where a translation is given, as well as some of the most common abbreviations, acronyms and geographical names.

The user who wishes to communicate and to express himself in the foreign language will find clear and detailed treatment of all the basic words, with numerous indicators pointing to the appropriate translation, and helping him to use it correctly.

# ABREVIATURAS

# ABBREVIATIONS

| | | |
|---|---|---|
| abreviatura | **abr/abbr** | abbreviation |
| adjetivo | **adj** | adjective |
| advérbio | **adv** | adverb |
| administração | **ADMIN** | administration |
| aeronáutica | **AER/AVIAT** | aeronautics/aviation |
| agricultura | **AGR** | agriculture |
| anatomia | **ANAT** | anatomy |
| arquitetura | **ARQ/ARCH** | architecture |
| artigo | **art** | article |
| astronomia/astrologia | **ASTRO** | astronomy/astrology |
| atributivo | **atr** | attributive |
| automobilismo | **AUTO/AUT** | automobile |
| biologia | **BIO/BIOL** | biology |
| botânico | **BOT** | botany |
| brasileiro | **Br** | Brazilian |
| da Grã-Bretanha | **Brit** | British |
| química | **CHEM** | chemistry |
| coloquial | **col/fam** | colloquial/familiar |
| comércio | **COM/COMM** | commerce |
| composto | **comp** | compound |
| conjunção | **conj** | conjunction |
| construção | **CONSTR** | construction |
| cozinha | **CULIN** | cookery |
| economia | **ECON** | economics |
| educação | **EDUC** | education |
| eletricidade | **ELET/ELEC** | electricity |
| especialmente | **esp** | especially |
| exclamação | **excl** | exclamation |
| feminino | **f** | feminine |
| ferrovia | **FERRO** | railway |
| figurado | **fig** | figurative |
| fotografia | **FOTO** | photography |
| (verbo inglês) do qual a partícula é invariável | **fus** | (phrasal verb) where the particle is inseparable |
| geografia/geologia | **GEO** | geography/geology |
| geralmente | **ger/gen** | generally |
| invariável | **inv** | invariable |
| irregular | **irr** | irregular |
| jurídico | **JUR/LAW** | legal |
| linguística | **LING** | linguistics |
| literário | **LIT** | literary |
| masculino | **m** | masculine |
| matemática | **MAT/MATH** | mathematics |

| | | |
|---|---|---|
| mecânica | **MEC/MECH** | mechanical |
| medicina | **MED** | medicine |
| militar | **MIL** | military |
| música | **MÚS/MUS** | music |
| nome | **n** | noun |
| náutico | **NÁUT/NAUT** | nautical |
| negativo | **neg** | negative |
| numeral | **num** | numeral |
| objeto | **obj** | object |
| a si mesmo | **o.s.** | oneself |
| pejorativo | **pej** | pejorative |
| fotografia | **PHOT** | photography |
| plural | **pl** | plural |
| política | **POL** | politics |
| particípio passado | **pp** | past participle |
| prefixo | **pref** | prefix |
| preposição | **prep** | preposition |
| pronome | **pron** | pronoun |
| psicologia | **PSICO/PSYCH** | psychology |
| pretérito | **pt** | past tense |
| português | **Pt** | Portuguese |
| química | **QUÍM** | chemistry |
| ferrovia | **RAIL** | railway |
| religião | **REL** | religion |
| alguém | **sb** | somebody |
| ensino | **SCOL** | schools, universities |
| singular | **sg** | singular |
| algo | **sth** | something |
| subjuntivo | **subj** | subjunctive |
| sufixo | **suf** | suffix |
| tecnologia | **TEC/TECH** | technology |
| telecomunicações | **TEL** | telecommunications |
| televisão | **TV** | television |
| tipografia | **TYP** | typography |
| dos Estados Unidos | **US** | American |
| verbo | **vb** | verb |
| verbo intransitivo | **vi** | verb intransitive |
| verbo reflexivo | **vr** | verb reflexive |
| verbo transitivo | **vt** | verb transitive |
| verbo transitivo/ intransitivo | **vt/i** | verb transitive/ intransitive |
| marca registada | ® | registered trademark |
| equivalente cultural | ≈ | cultural equivalent |

# PORTUGUESE PRONUNCIATION

The rules given below refer to Portuguese as spoken in the city and surrounding region of Rio de Janeiro, Brazil.

## Consonants

| | | | |
|---|---|---|---|
| c | [k] | café | c before a, o, u is pronounced as in cat |
| ce, ci | [se, sɪ] | cego | c before e or i, as in receive |
| ç | [s] | raça | ç is pronounced as in receive |
| ch | [ʃ] | chave | ch is pronounced as in shock |
| d | [d] | data | As in English EXCEPT: |
| de, di | [dʒɪ] | difícil | d before i and final unstressed e is |
| | | cidade | pronounced as in judge |
| g | [g] | gado | g before a, o or u, as in gap |
| ge, gi | [ʒɪ] | gíria | g before e or i, as in leisure |
| h | | humano | h is always silent in Portuguese |
| j | [ʒ] | jogo | j is pronounced as in leisure |
| l | [w] | total | l after a vowel tends to become w |
| lh | [ʎ] | trabalho | lh is pronounced like the lli in million |
| m | [ãw] | cantam | final m preceded by a vowel nasalises |
| | [ĩ] | sim | the preceding vowel |
| nh | [ɲ] | tamanho | nh is pronounced like the ni in onion |
| q | [k] | queijo | q is pronounced as in kick |
| qu | [kw] | quanto | qu before a or o is pronounced as in quoits |
| -r- | [r] | compra | r preceded by a consonant (except n) and followed by a vowel is pronounced with a single trill |
| r-, -r, | [x] | rato | initial r, final r, r preceded by a vowel |
| rr | [x] | bezerro | or n, and rr are pronounced similar to the Scottish ch in loch |
| s- | [s] | sol | As in English EXCEPT: |
| -s- | [z] | mesa | intervocalic s is pronounced as in rose |
| -s-, -s | [ʃ] | escada | s preceded or followed by a consonant |
| | | livros | or finally is pronounced as in sugar |
| t | [t] | todo | As in English EXCEPT: |
| te, ti | [tʃɪ] | amante | t followed by i and final unstressed |
| | | tipo | e is pronounced as in cheer |
| x- | [ʃ] | xarope | initial x is pronounced as in sugar |
| -x- | [ʃ] | rixa | x in any other position may be |
| | [ks] | fixo | pronounced as in sugar, axe or sail |
| | [s] | auxiliar | according to the individual word |
| z-, -z- | [z] | zangar | As in English EXCEPT: |
| -z | [ʃ] | cartaz | final z is pronounced as in sugar |

## Vowels

| | | | |
|---|---|---|---|
| a, ã, á, â | [a] | m*a*t*a* | *a* is normally pronounced as in f*a*t |
| ã | [ã] | irm*ã* | *ã* is pronounced as in s*ang* |
| e | [e] | v*e*jo | *e* is pronounced either as in Scottish |
| | [ɛ] | dir*e*ta | gr*e*at or as in b*e*t, usually depending |
| | [ɪ] | fom*e* | upon the following sound. Final *e* is pronounced as in mon*ey* |
| é | [ɛ] | mis*é*ria | *é* is pronounced as in b*e*t |
| ê | [e] | p*ê*lo | *ê* is pronounced as in Scottish gr*e*at |
| i | [ɪ] | v*i*da | *i* is pronounced as in m*ea*n |
| o | [u] | livr*o* | *o* is pronounced as in f*oo*d when |
| | [ɔ] | l*o*ja | unstressed, otherwise either as in r*o*ck |
| | [o] | gl*o*bo | or as in Scottish l*ow*, usually depending upon the next sound |
| ó | [ɔ] | *ó*leo | *ó* is pronounced as in r*o*ck |
| ô | [o] | col*ô*nia | *ô* is pronounced as in Scottish l*ow* |
| u | [u] | l*u*va | *u* is pronounced as in r*u*de. It is silent |
| | [w] | á*gu*a | in *que, qui, gue* and *gui*. It is pronounced |
| | | a*gü*entar | *w* in *qua, quo* and *gua* and when marked with a dieresis |

## Diphthongs

| | | | |
|---|---|---|---|
| ãe | [ãj] | m*ãe* | nasalised, approximately as in fl*ying* |
| ai | [aj] | v*ai* | as in r*i*de |
| ao, au | [aw] | *ao*s, *au*xílio | as in sh*ou*t |
| ão | [ãw] | v*ão* | nasalised, approximately as in r*ou*nd |
| ei | [ej] | f*ei*ra | as in Scottish gr*ea*t |
| eu | [eu] | d*eu*sa | both elements pronounced |
| oi | [oj] | b*oi* | as in t*oy* |
| õe | [õj] | avi*õe*s | nasalised, approximately as in 'b*oing*!' |

## Stress

The rules of stress in Portuguese are as follows:

(a)  when a word ends in *a, e, o, m* (except *im, um*) or *s* (except *ns*), the second last syllable is stressed: camar*a*da, camar*a*das, p*a*rte, p*a*rtem

(b)  when a word ends in *ã, i, u, im, um, ns* or a consonant other than *m* or *s*, the stress falls on the last syllable: vend*i*, alg*um*, alg*uns*, fal*ar*

(c)  when the rules set out in a and b are not applied, an acute or circumflex accent appears over the stressed vowel: *ó*tica, *â*nimo, ingl*ê*s

In the phonetic transcription, the symbol ['] precedes the syllable on which the stress falls.

# PRONÚNCIA INGLESA

## Vogais e ditongos

| | Exemplo Inglês | Explicação |
|---|---|---|
| a: | f*a*ther | Entre o *a* de p*a*dre e o *o* de n*ó* |
| ʌ | b*u*t, c*o*me | Aproximadamente como o primeiro *a* de c*a*ma |
| æ | m*a*n, c*a*t | Som entre o *a* de l*á* e o *e* de p*é* |
| ə | f*a*ther, *a*go | Som parecido com o *e* de qu*e* |
| ə: | b*i*rd, h*ea*rd | Entre o *e* aberto e o *o* fechado |
| ɛ | g*e*t, b*e*d | Como em p*é* |
| I | *i*t, b*i*g | Mais breve do que em s*i* |
| i: | t*ea*, s*ee* | Como em f*i*no |
| ɔ | h*o*t, w*a*sh | Como em p*ó* |
| ɔ: | s*aw*, *a*ll | Como o *o* de p*o*rte |
| u | p*u*t, b*oo*k | Som breve e mais fechado do que em b*u*rro |
| u: | t*oo*, y*ou* | Som aberto como em *u*m |
| aI | fl*y*, h*i*gh | Como em b*ai*le |
| au | h*ow*, h*ou*se | Como em c*au*sa |
| ɛə | th*ere*, b*ear* | Como *o* e de a*ero*porto |
| eI | d*ay*, ob*ey* | Como o *ei* de l*ei* |
| Iə | h*ere*, h*ear* | Como *ia* de companh*ia* |
| əu | g*o*, n*o*te | [ə] seguido de um *u* breve |
| ɔI | b*oy*, o*il* | Como em b*ói*a |
| uə | p*oor*, s*ure* | Como *ua* em s*ua* |

# Consoantes

| | Exemplo Inglês | Explicação |
|---|---|---|
| d | men*ded* | Como em con*d*e, an*d*ar |
| g | *g*et, bi*g* | Como em *g*rande |
| dʒ | *g*in, *j*udge | Como em a*dj*etivo |
| ŋ | si*ng* | Como em ci*n*co |
| h | *h*ouse, *h*e | *h* aspirado |
| j | *y*oung, *y*es | Como em *i*ogurte |
| k | *c*ome, mo*ck* | Como em Es*c*ócia |
| r | *r*ed, t*r*ead | *r* como em pa*r*a, mas pronunciado no céu da boca |
| s | *s*and, ye*s* | Como em *s*ala |
| z | ro*s*e, æbra | Como em æ*b*ra |
| ʃ | *sh*e, ma*ch*ine | Como em *ch*apéu |
| tʃ | *ch*in, ri*ch* | *t* seguido por um *ch* |
| w | *w*ater, *wh*ich | Como o *u* em q*u*arto |
| ʒ | vi*s*ion | Como em *j*á |
| θ | *th*ink, my*th* | Sem equivalente, aproximadamente como um *s* pronunciado entre os dentes |
| ð | *th*is, *th*e | Sem equivalente, aproximadamente como um *s* pronunciado entre os dentes |

b, f, l, m, n, p, t, v pronunciam-se como em português.

O signo * indica que o r final escrito pronuncia-se apenas em inglês britânico quando a palavra seguinte começa por uma vogal. O signo ['] indica a sílaba acentuada.

# ENGLISH - PORTUGUESE
## INGLÊS - PORTUGUÊS

## A

**a, an** [eɪ, ə, æn] *art* um(a); **3 a day/week** 3 por dia/semana; **10 km an hour** 10 km por hora.

**A.A.** *n abbr of* **Automobile Association; Alcoholics Anonymous.**

**aback** [ə'bæk] *adv*: **to be taken ~** ficar surpreendido, sobressaltar-se.

**abandon** [ə'bændən] *vt* abandonar, deixar; (*renounce*) renunciar // *n* abandono, desamparo; (*wild behaviour*) desenfreamento.

**abashed** [ə'bæʃt] *adj* envergonhado.

**abate** [ə'beɪt] *vi* abater; (*lessen*) diminuir; (*calm down*) acalmar-se.

**abattoir** ['æbətwɑ:*] *n* matadouro.

**abbey** ['æbɪ] *n* abadia, mosteiro.

**abbot** ['æbət] *n* abade *m*.

**abbreviate** [ə'bri:vɪeɪt] *vt* abreviar, resumir; **abbreviation** [-'eɪʃən] *n* (*short form*) abreviatura; (*act*) abreviação *f*.

**abdicate** ['æbdɪkeɪt] *vt* abdicar, renunciar // *vi* abdicar, renunciar ao trono; **abdication** [-'keɪʃən] *n* abdicação *f*.

**abdomen** ['æbdəmən] *n* abdómen *m*.

**abduct** [æb'dʌkt] *vt* raptar; **~ion** [-'dʌkʃən] *n* rapto, seqüestro.

**aberration** [æbə'reɪʃən] *n* aberração *f*.

**abet** [ə'bet] *vt* (*incite*) incitar; (*aid*) ser cúmplice de.

**abeyance** [ə'beɪəns] *n*: **in ~** (*law*) em desuso; (*matter*) suspenso.

**abhor** [əb'hɔ:*] *vt* detestar, odiar; **~rent** *adj* detestável, repugnante.

**abide** [ə'baɪd], *pt, pp* **abode** *or* **abided** *vt* agüentar, suportar; **to ~ by** *vt fus* cumprir, ater-se a.

**ability** [ə'bɪlɪtɪ] *n* habilidade *f*, capacidade *f*; (*talent*) talento.

**ablaze** [ə'bleɪz] *adj* em chamas, ardendo; (*Pt*) em chamas, a arder.

**able** ['eɪbl] *adj* capaz; (*skilled*) talentoso; **to be ~ to do sth** poder fazer alguma coisa; **~-bodied** *adj* são/sã; **ably** *adv* habilmente.

**abnormal** [æb'nɔ:məl] *adj* anormal; **~ity** [-'mælɪtɪ] *n* anormalidade *f*.

**aboard** [ə'bɔ:d] *adv* a bordo // *prep* a bordo de.

**abode** [ə'bəud] *pt, pp of* **abide** // *n* residência, domicílio.

**abolish** [ə'bɔlɪʃ] *vt* abolir, suprimir; **abolition** [æbəu'lɪʃən] *n* abolição *f*, supressão *f*.

**abominable** [ə'bɔmɪnəbl] *adj* abominável, detestável.

**aborigine** [æbə'rɪdʒɪnɪ] *n* aborígene *m*, primitivo.

**abort** [ə'bɔ:t] *vt* abortar; **~ion** [ə'bɔ:ʃən] *n* aborto; **to have an ~ion** fazer um aborto; **~ive** *adj* abortivo, fracassado.

**abound** [ə'baund] *vi* abundar.

**about** [ə'baut] *prep* (*subject*) acerca de, sobre; (*place*) em redor de, por // *adv* quase, mais ou menos; **to walk ~ the town** andar pela cidade; **it takes ~ 10 hours** leva mais ou menos 10 horas; **at ~ 2 o'clock** aproximadamente às duas; **to be ~ to** estar a ponto de; **what** *or* **how ~ doing this?** que tal se fizermos isso?; **~ turn** *n* meia-volta.

**above** [ə'bʌv] *adv* em/por cima, acima // *prep* sobre, acima de, por cima de; **mentioned ~** acima mencionado; **~ all** sobretudo; **~ board** *adj* legítimo, limpo.

**abrasion** [ə'breɪʒən] *n* (*on skin*) esfoladura; **abrasive** [ə'breɪzɪv] *adj* abrasivo.

**abreast** [ə'brest] *adv* lado a lado; **to**

**keep ~ of** estar a par de.

**abridge** [ə'brɪdʒ] vt resumir, abreviar.

**abroad** [ə'brɔːd] adv (to be) no estrangeiro; (to go) ao estrangeiro.

**abrupt** [ə'brʌpt] adj (sudden) brusco, inesperado; (gruff) áspero; **~ly** adv bruscamente.

**abscess** ['æbsɪs] n abscesso.

**abscond** [əb'skɔnd] vi fugir, esconder-se.

**absence** ['æbsəns] n ausência.

**absent** ['æbsənt] adj ausente; **~ee** [-sən'tiː] n ausente m/f; **~eeism** [-'tiːɪzəm] n absenteísmo; **~-minded** adj distraído.

**absolute** ['æbsəluːt] adj absoluto; **~ly** [-'luːtli] adv absolutamente.

**absolve** [əb'zɔlv] vt: **to ~ sb (from)** absolver or perdoar alguém (de).

**absorb** [əb'zɔːb] vt absorver; **to be ~ed in a book** estar absorvido num livro; **~ent** adj absorvente; **~ing** adj absorvente, cativante.

**abstain** [əb'steɪn] vi: **to ~ (from)** abster-se (de).

**abstention** [əb'stenʃən] n abstenção f, desistência.

**abstinence** ['æbstɪnəns] n abstinência, sobriedade f.

**abstract** ['æbstrækt] adj abstrato (Pt: -ct-) // n resumo.

**absurd** [əb'sɜːd] adj absurdo, ridículo; **~ity** n absurdo, disparate m.

**abundance** [ə'bʌndəns] n abundância; **abundant** [-dənt] adj abundante.

**abuse** [ə'bjuːs] n (insults) insultos mpl, injúrias fpl; (misuse) abuso // vt [ə'bjuːz] (ill-treat) maltratar; (take advantage of) abusar de; **abusive** adj ofensivo.

**abysmal** [ə'bɪzməl] adj abismal; (ignorance etc) profundo, abissal.

**abyss** [ə'bɪs] n abismo.

**academic** [ækə'demɪk] adj acadêmico, universitário; (pej: issue) teórico.

**academy** [ə'kædəmɪ] n (learned body) academia; (school) instituto, academia, colégio.

**accede** [æk'siːd] vi: **to ~ to** (request) consentir (em), aceder a; (throne) subir a.

**accelerate** [æk'sɛləreɪt] vt acelerar // vi apressar-se; **acceleration** [-'reɪʃən] n aceleração f; **accelerator** n acelerador m.

**accent** ['æksənt] n (gen) acento; (pronunciation) sotaque m.

**accept** [ək'sɛpt] vt aceitar; (approve) aceitar, (permit) admitir; **~able** adj aceitável, admissível; **~ance** n aceitação f, aprovação f.

**access** ['æksɛs] n acesso, entrada; **to have ~ to** ter acesso para; **~ible** [-'sɛsəbl] adj acessível.

**accessory** [æk'sɛsərɪ] n acessório; **toilet accessories** npl artigos mpl de toilette.

**accident** ['æksɪdənt] n acidente m; (chance) casualidade f; **by ~** (unintentionally) sem querer; (by coincidence) por acaso; **~al** [-'dɛntl] adj acidental; **~ally** [-'dɛntəlɪ] adv sem querer, casualmente; **~-prone** adj com tendência para sofrer/causar acidente.

**acclaim** [ə'kleɪm] vt aclamar, aplaudir // n aclamação f, aplausos mpl.

**acclimatize** [ə'klaɪmətaɪz] vt: **to become ~d** aclimatar-se, habituar-se.

**accommodate** [ə'kɔmədeɪt] vt acomodar, alojar, hospedar; (reconcile) conciliar; (oblige, help) comprazer; (adapt) to **~ one's plans** to acomodar seus projetos a; **accommodating** adj complacente, serviçal.

**accommodation** [əkɔmə'deɪʃən] n, **accommodations** (US) [əkɔmə'deɪʃənz] npl alojamento, acomodação f; (space) lugar m; (Pt) sítio.

**accompaniment** [əˈkʌmpənɪmənt] n acompanhamento;

**accompany** [-nɪ] vt acompanhar.

**accomplice** [əˈkʌmplɪs] n cúmplice m/f.

**accomplish** [əˈkʌmplɪʃ] vt (finish) acabar, alcançar; (achieve) realizar, levar a cabo; **~ed** adj ilustre, talentoso; **~ment** n (ending) conclusão f; (bringing about) realização f; (skill) talento, habilidade f.

**accord** [əˈkɔːd] n acordo // vi conceder // vi concordar; **of his own ~** por sua iniciativa; **~ance** n: **in ~ance with** de acordo com; **~ing** to prep segundo; (in accordance with) conforme; **~ingly** adv (thus) por conseguinte, consequentemente.

**accordion** [əˈkɔːdɪən] n acordeão m.

**accost** [əˈkɒst] vt dirigir-se a.

**account** [əˈkaʊnt] n (COMM) conta; (report) relato; **of little ~** sem importância; **on his own ~** por sua conta; **on no ~** de modo nenhum; **~ of** por causa de; **to take into ~**, **take ~ of** levar em conta; **to ~ for** prestar contas de; (answer for) justificar; (explain) explicar; **~able** adj responsável.

**accountancy** [əˈkaʊntənsɪ] n contabilidade f; **accountant** [-tənt] n contador(a); (Pt) contabilista m/f.

**accumulate** [əˈkjuːmjuleɪt] vt acumular, amontoar // vi acumular-se; **accumulation** [-ˈleɪʃən] n acumulação f.

**accuracy** [ˈækjurəsɪ] n exatidão (Pt: -ct-) f, precisão f; **accurate** [-rɪt] adj (number) exato (Pt: -ct-); (answer) correto (Pt: -ct-); (shot) exato (Pt: -ct-), preciso.

**accusation** n acusação f; **accuse** [əˈkjuːz] vt acusar; (blame) culpar; **accused** [əˈkjuːzd] n culpado a.

**accustom** [əˈkʌstəm] vt acostumar; **~ed** adj: **~ed to** acostumado a.

**ace** [eɪs] n ás m.

**ache** [eɪk] n dor f // vi doer; **my head ~s** doi-me a cabeça.

**achieve** [əˈtʃiːv] vt (reach) alcançar; (realize) realizar; (victory, success) obter; **~ment** n (completion) realização f; (success) sucesso.

**acid** [ˈæsɪd] adj ácido; (bitter) azedo // n ácido; **~ity** [əˈsɪdɪtɪ] n acidez f.

**acknowledge** [əkˈnɒlɪdʒ] vt reconhecer; (letter) acusar o recebimento de; (Pt) acusar a recepção de; (fact) admitir; **~ment** n reconhecimento, notificação f de recebimento.

**acne** [ˈæknɪ] n acne f.

**acorn** [ˈeɪkɔːn] n bolota.

**acoustic** [əˈkuːstɪk] adj acústico; **~s** npl acústica sg.

**acquaint** [əˈkweɪnt] vt: **to ~ sb with sth** (warn) avisar alguém de alguma coisa; (inform) pôr alguém ao corrente de alguma coisa; **to be ~ed with** (person) conhecer; (fact) saber; **~ance** n conhecimento; (person) conhecido/a.

**acquiesce** [ækwɪˈes] vi: **to ~ in** aquiescer em, concordar com.

**acquire** [əˈkwaɪə*] vt adquirir; (achieve) alcançar; **acquisition** [ækwɪˈzɪʃən] n aquisição f; **acquisitive** [əˈkwɪzɪtɪv] adj cobiçoso.

**acquit** [əˈkwɪt] vt absolver; **to ~ o.s. well** desempenhar-se bem; **~tal** n absolvição f.

**acre** [ˈeɪkə*] n acre m.

**acrimonious** [ækrɪˈməʊnɪəs] adj (remark) mordaz; (argument) acrimonioso.

**acrobat** [ˈækrəbæt] n acrobata m/f; **~ics** [ækrəʊˈbætɪks] npl acrobacia sg.

**across** [əˈkrɒs] prep (on the other side of) no outro lado de; (crosswise) através de // adv transversalmente, de um lado ao outro; **to run/swim**

~ atravessar correndo/a nado; ~ **from** em frente de.

**act** [ækt] n ação (Pt: -cç-) f; (THEATRE) ato (Pt: -ct-); (in music-hall etc) número; (LAW) lei f // vi (machine) funcionar; (person) agir; (THEATRE) representar; (pretend) fingir; (take action) tomar medidas // vt (part) representar; **to ~ as** fazer-se de; **~ing** adj interino // n: **to do some ~ing** ser ator/atriz.

**action** [ˈækʃən] n ação (Pt: -cç-) f; (MIL) batalha, combate m; (LAW) processo judicial; **to take ~** proceder.

**activate** [ˈæktɪveɪt] vt (mechanism) ativar (Pt: -ct-).

**active** [ˈæktɪv] adj ativo (Pt: -ct-); (volcano) em atividade; **activity** [-ˈtɪvɪtɪ] n atividade f.

**actor** [ˈæktə*] n ator (Pt: -ct-) f.

**actress** [-trɪs] n atriz (Pt: -ct-) f.

**actual** [ˈæktjuəl] adj real, existente; **~ly** adv realmente, de fato (Pt: -ct-).

**acupuncture** [ˈækjupʌŋktʃə*] n acupuntura.

**acute** [əˈkjuːt] adj (gen) agudo.

**ad** [æd] n abbr of **advertisement**.

**A.D.** adv abbr of **Anno Domini** d.C. (depois de Cristo).

**Adam** [ˈædəm] n Adão; **~'s apple** n pomo-de-Adão; (Pt) maçã-de-Adão f.

**adamant** [ˈædəmənt] adj inflexível.

**adapt** [əˈdæpt] vt adaptar; (reconcile) acomodar // vi: **to ~ (to)** adaptar-se (a); **~able** adj (device) ajustável; (person) adaptável; **~ation** [ædæpˈteɪʃən] n adaptação f, ajustamento; **~er** n (ELEC) adaptador m.

**add** [æd] vt acrescentar; (figures: also: ~ **up**) somar // vi: **to ~ to** (increase) acrescentar, aumentar; **it doesn't ~ up** isto não faz soma.

**adder** [ˈædə*] n víbora.

**addict** [ˈædɪkt] n (enthusiast) dedicado/a; (to drugs etc) viciado/a; **~ed** [əˈdɪktɪd] adj: **to be(come) ~ed**

to entregar-se a; **addiction** [əˈdɪkʃən] n (enthusiasm) dedicação f; (dependence) vício.

**adding machine** [ˈædɪŋməʃiːn] n máquina de somar.

**addition** [əˈdɪʃən] n (adding up) adição f; (thing added) soma; **in ~** além disso; **in ~ to** além de; **~al** adj adicional.

**additive** [ˈædɪtɪv] n aditivo.

**address** [əˈdrɛs] n endereço; (speech) discurso // vt (letter) endereçar; (speak to) dirigir-se a, dirigir a palavra a; **~ee** [ædrɛˈsiː] n destinatário/a.

**adenoids** [ˈædɪnɔɪdz] npl adenóides fpl.

**adept** [ˈædɛpt] adj: **~ at** hábil or competente em.

**adequate** [ˈædɪkwɪt] adj (apt) adequado; (enough) suficiente.

**adhere** [ədˈhɪə*] vi: **to ~ to** aderir a; (fig: abide by) manter-se fiel a; (: hold to) apegar-se a; **adherent** n partidário/a.

**adhesive** [ədˈhiːzɪv] adj, n adesivo.

**adjacent** [əˈdʒeɪsənt] adj: **~ to** adjacente a, contíguo a.

**adjective** [ˈædʒɛktɪv] n adjetivo (Pt: -ct-).

**adjoining** [əˈdʒɔɪnɪŋ] adj adjacente, contíguo.

**adjourn** [əˈdʒɜːn] vt adiar; (session) suspender // vi encerrar a sessão.

**adjudicate** [əˈdʒuːdɪkeɪt] vi adjudicar; **adjudicator** n juiz m, árbitro.

**adjust** [əˈdʒʌst] vt (change) ajustar; (arrange) arranjar; (machine) regular // vi: **to ~ (to)** adaptar-se (a); **~able** adj ajustável; **~ment** n regulação f; (engine) regulagem f; (of prices, wages) ajustamento.

**adjutant** [ˈædʒətənt] n ajudante m.

**ad-lib** [ædˈlɪb] vt/i improvisar; **ad lib** adv à vontade.

**administer** [ədˈmɪnɪstə*] vt dirigir; (justice) administrar; **ad-ministration** [-ˈtreɪʃən] n

administração f; (government)
governo; **administrative** [-trətɪv] adj
administrativo; **administrator**
[-treɪtə\*] n administrador(a) m/f.

**admirable** [ˈædmərəbl] adj
admirável.

**admiral** [ˈædmərəl] n almirante m;
**A~ty** n Ministério da Marinha,
Almirantado.

**admiration** [ædməˈreɪʃən] n
admiração f.

**admire** [ədˈmaɪə\*] vt admirar;
**admirer** n admirador(a) m/f.

**admission** [ədˈmɪʃən] n (entry)
entrada; (enrolment) admissão f;
(confession) confissão f.

**admit** [ədˈmɪt] vt admitir; (permit)
permitir; (acknowledge) reconhecer; (accept) aceitar; **to ~ to**
confessar; **~tance** n entrada;
**~tedly** adv evidentemente.

**admonish** [ədˈmɒnɪʃ] vt
repreender; (advise) avisar.

**ado** [əˈduː] n: **without (any) more ~**
sem mais cerimônias.

**adolescence** [ædəʊˈlɛsns] n
adolescência; **adolescent** [-lɛsnt]
adj, n adolescente m/f.

**adopt** [əˈdɒpt] vt adotar (Pt: -pt:);
**~ed** adj adotivo (Pt: -pt:); **~ion**
[əˈdɒpʃən] n adoção (Pt: -pç-) f.

**adore** [əˈdɔː\*] vt adorar.

**adorn** [əˈdɔːn] vt adornar, enfeitar.

**adrenalin** [əˈdrɛnəlɪn] n
adrenalina.

**Adriatic** [eɪdrɪˈætɪk] n: **the ~ (Sea)**
o (Mar) Adriático.

**adrift** [əˈdrɪft] adv à deriva; **to come
~** desprender-se.

**adult** [ˈædʌlt] n (gen) adulto.

**adulterate** [əˈdʌltəreɪt] vt
adulterar.

**adulterer** n adúltero; **adulteress** n
adúltera; **adultery** [əˈdʌltərɪ] n
adultério.

**advance** [ədˈvɑːns] n (gen) avanço;
(money) adiantamento, empréstimo; (MIL) avançada // vt (develop)
desenvolver, promover; (lend)

emprestar // vi avançar; **in ~**
adiantamente; **~d** adj avançado;
(EDUC. studies) adiantado; **~d in
years** entrado em anos; **~ment** n
avanço, progresso; (in rank)
promoção f, ascenção f.

**advantage** [ədˈvɑːntɪdʒ] n
vantagem f; (tennis) a favor de; **to
take ~ of** (use) aproveitar-se de;
(gain by) tirar proveito de; **~ous**
[ædvənˈteɪdʒəs] adj vantajoso,
favorável.

**advent** [ˈædvənt] n vinda, chegada;
**A~** Advento.

**adventure** [ədˈvɛntʃə\*] n aventura;
**adventurer** n aventureiro;
**adventurous** [-tʃərəs] adj venturoso.

**adverb** [ˈædvɜːb] n advérbio.

**adversary** [ˈædvəsərɪ] n
adversário/a.

**adverse** [ˈædvɜːs] adj adverso,
contrário; **~ to** contrário a.

**adversity** [ədˈvɜːsɪtɪ] n adversidade
f.

**advert** [ˈædvɜːt] n abbr of
**advertisement** anúncio.

**advertise** [ˈædvətaɪz] vi anunciar,
fazer propaganda; (in newspaper
etc) publicar um anúncio // vt
anunciar; **~ment** [ədˈvɜːtɪsmənt] n
anúncio; **advertising** n publicidade
f, anúncios mpl.

**advice** [ədˈvaɪs] n conselhos mpl; (a
piece of ~) conselho; (notification)
aviso; **to take legal ~** consultar um
advogado.

**advisable** [ədˈvaɪzəbl] adj
aconselhável.

**advise** [ədˈvaɪz] vt aconselhar;
(inform) informar; **adviser** n
conselheiro; (business adviser)
consultor m; **advisory** adj
consultivo.

**advocate** [ˈædvəkeɪt] (argue for)
defender; (give support to) advogar,
recomendar // n [-kɪt] advogado.

**aerial** [ˈɛərɪəl] n antena // adj
aéreo.

**aeronautics** [ɛərə'nɔːtɪks] n aeronáutica sg.

**aeroplane** ['ɛərəpleɪn] n avião m.

**aerosol** ['ɛərəsɔl] n aerossol m.

**aesthetic** [iːs'θetɪk] adj estético; ~s estética sg.

**afar** [ə'fɑː*] adv: from ~ de longe.

**affable** ['æfəbl] adj afável, simpático.

**affair** [ə'fɛə*] n negócio; (also: love ~) caso amoroso, romance m; that is my ~ isso é comigo.

**affect** [ə'fekt] vt afetar (Pt: -ct-), tocar; (move) comover; ~ation [æfek'teɪʃən] n afetação (Pt: -ct-) f; ~ed adj afetado (Pt: -ct-).

**affection** [ə'fekʃən] n afeto (Pt: -ct-), afeição f; ~ate adj afetuoso (Pt: -ct-), carinhoso.

**affiliated** [ə'fɪlɪeɪtɪd] adj filial.

**affinity** [ə'fɪnɪtɪ] n afinidade f.

**affirmation** [æfə'meɪʃən] n afirmação f.

**affirmative** [ə'fɜːmətɪv] adj afirmativo.

**affix** [ə'fɪks] vt (signature) apor; (stamp) afixar, colar.

**afflict** [ə'flɪkt] vt afligir; to be ~ed with sofrer de; ~ion [ə'flɪkʃən] n aflição f, dor f.

**affluence** ['æfluəns] n riqueza, opulência; **affluent** [-ənt] adj rico, opulento.

**afford** [ə'fɔːd] vt (provide) fornecer, dar; can we ~ it? temos dinheiro para comprar isso?

**affront** [ə'frʌnt] n afronta, ofensa.

**afield** [ə'fiːld] adv: far ~ muito longe.

**afloat** [ə'fləut] adv (floating) flutuando; (at sea) no mar.

**afoot** [ə'fut] adv: there is something ~ está acontecendo algo; (Pt) algo está-se a passar.

**aforesaid** [ə'fɔːsed] adj supracitado, referido.

**afraid** [ə'freɪd] adj: to be ~ of (person) ter medo de; (thing) recear; to be ~ to ter medo de,

temer; I am ~ that lamento que.

**afresh** [ə'freʃ] adv de novo, outra vez.

**Africa** ['æfrɪkə] n África; ~n adj, n africano/a.

**aft** [ɑːft] adv a ré.

**after** ['ɑːftə*] prep (time) depois de; (place, order) atrás de; ~ day day dia após dia; time ~ time repetidas vezes // adv depois, atrás // conj depois que; what are you ~? o que você quer?; who are you ~? quem procura?; to ask ~ sb perguntar por alguém; ~ all afinal de contas; ~ you! passe primeiro!; ~birth n placenta; ~effects npl conseqüências, resultados; ~life n vida após a morte; ~math n consequências fpl, resultados mpl; ~noon n tarde f; ~shave (lotion) n loção f para depois de barbear; ~thought n reflexão f; ~wards adv depois, mais tarde; immediately ~wards logo depois.

**again** [ə'gen] adv outra vez, de novo; to do sth ~ voltar a fazer algo; ~ and ~ repetidas vezes; now and ~ de vez em quando.

**against** [ə'genst] prep (opposed) contra, em oposição a; (close to) junto de/a.

**age** [eɪdʒ] n (gen) época, idade f; (old ~) velhice f; (period) época; to be under ~ ser menor de idade // vi envelhecer-se // vt envelhecer; to come of ~ atingir a maioridade; it's been ~s since ... há muito tempo que não ...; ~d adj ['eɪdʒɪd] velho, ancião/anciã // adj [eɪdʒd]: ~d 10 com 10 anos de idade; ~group n: to be in the same ~ group ter a mesma idade; ~less adj (eternal) eterno; (ever young) sempre jovem; ~limit n idade f mínima/máxima.

**agency** ['eɪdʒənsɪ] n agência; through or by the ~ of por meio de.

**agenda** [ə'dʒendə] n ordem f do dia, programa m.

**agent** ['eɪdʒənt] n (gen) agente m/f;

(*representative*) representante *m/f*.

**aggravate** ['ægrəveɪt] *vt* agravar; (*annoy*) irritar; **aggravation** [-'veɪʃən] *n* irritação *f*.

**aggregate** ['ægrɪgeɪt] *n* (*whole*) conjunto; (*collection*) agregado.

**aggression** [ə'greʃən] *n* agressão *f*; **aggressive** [ə'gresɪv] *adj* agressivo; (*zealous*) ativo (*Pt*: -ct-).

**aggrieved** [ə'griːvd] *adj* ofendido, aflito.

**aghast** [ə'gɑːst] *adj* horrorizado; **to be ~** espantar-se.

**agile** ['ædʒaɪl] *adj* ágil.

**agitate** ['ædʒɪteɪt] *vt* (*shake*) agitar; (*trouble*) perturbar; **to ~ for** fazer agitação em prol de *or* a favor de; **agitation** [-ʃən] *n* agitação *f*; **agitator** *n* agitador(a) *m/f*.

**ago** [ə'gəʊ] *adv*: **2 days ~** há 2 dias; **not long ~** há pouco tempo; **how long ~?** há quanto tempo?

**agog** [ə'gɒg] *adj* (*anxious*) ansioso; (*excited*) excitado.

**agonizing** ['ægənaɪzɪŋ] *adj* (*pain*) agudo; (*suspense*) angustiante.

**agony** ['ægənɪ] *n* (*pain*) dor *f*; (*distress*) angústia; **to be in ~** sofrer dores terríveis.

**agree** [ə'griː] *vt* (*price*) combinar, ajustar // *vi* (*statements etc*) combinar; **to ~ (with)** (*person*) concordar (com), estar de acordo (com); **to ~ to do** aceitar fazer; **to ~ that** (*admit*) admitir; **garlic doesn't ~ with me** não me dou bem com o alho; **~able** *adj* agradável; (*person*) simpático; (*willing*) disposto; **~d** *adj* (*time, place*) combinado; **~ment** *n* acordo; (*COMM*) contrato; **in ~ment** de acordo, conforme.

**agricultural** [ægrɪ'kʌltʃərəl] *adj* agrícola; **agriculture** ['ægrɪkʌltʃə*] *n* agricultura.

**aground** [ə'graʊnd] *adv*: **to run ~** encalhar.

**ahead** [ə'hed] *adv* adiante; **~ of** à frente de; (*fig: schedule etc*) antes

de; **~ of time** antes do tempo; **to go ~ (with)** prosseguir (com); **to be ~ of sb** (*fig*) ter vantagem sobre alguém; **go right** *or* **straight ~** continue sempre em frente.

**aid** [eɪd] *n* ajuda, auxílio // *vt* ajudar, auxiliar; **in ~ of** em benefício de; **to ~ and abet** (*JUR*) ser cúmplice de.

**aide** [eɪd] *n* (*person*) ajudante *m/f*.

**ailment** ['eɪlmənt] *n* doença, achaque *m*.

**aim** [eɪm] *vt* (*gun, camera*) apontar; (*missile, remark*) dirigir; (*blow*) apontar // *vi* (*also*: **take ~**) apontar // *n* pontaria; (*objective*) propósito, meta; **to ~ at** (*objective*) visar; **to ~ to do** pretender fazer; **~less** *adj* sem propósito; **~lessly** *adv* ao acaso, sem rumo.

**air** [ɛə*] *n* ar *m*; (*appearance*) aparência, aspeto (*Pt*: -ct-) // *vt* arejar; (*grievances, ideas*) discutir // *cmp* (*currents, attack etc*) aéreo; **~borne** *adj* (*in the air*) no ar; (*MIL*) aéreo; **~conditioned** *adj* com ar condicionado; **~ conditioning** *n* ar condicionado; **~craft**, *pl inv* avião *m*; **~craft carrier** *n* porta-aviões *m inv*; **A~ Force** *n* Força Aérea, Aviação *f*; **~gun** *n* espingarda de ar comprimido; **~ hostess** *n* aeromoça; (*Pt*) hospedeira; **~letter** *n* carta aérea; **~lift** *n* ponte aérea; **~line** *n* linha aérea; **~liner** *n* avião *m* de passageiros; **~lock** *n* entupimento de ar; **~mail** *n*: **by ~mail** por avião, via aérea; **~plane** (*US*) *n* avião (*Pt*); **~port** *n* aeroporto; **~ raid** *n* ataque *m* aéreo; **~sick** *adj*: **to be ~sick** enjoar-se (no avião); **~strip** *n* pista (de aterrissar); **~tight** *adj* hermético; **~y** *adj* (*room*) arejado, ventilado; (*manners*) ligeiro, delicado.

**aisle** [aɪl] *n* (*of church*) nave *f*; (*of theatre*) corredor *m*, coxia.

**ajar** [ə'dʒɑː*] *adj* entreaberto.

**akin** [ə'kɪn] *adj*: **~ to** parecido com.

**alarm** [ə'lɑ:m] n alarme m;
(anxiety) inquietação f // vt
alarmar, inquietar; ~ **clock** n
despertador m; ~**ing** adj alarmante.
**Albania** [æl'beiniə] n Albânia.
**album** ['ælbəm] n álbum m;
(record) L.P., álbum f.
**alcohol** ['ælkəhɔl] n álcool m; ~**ic**
['hɔlik] adj n alcoólico; ~**ism** n
alcoolismo.
**alcove** ['ælkəuv] n alcova.
**alderman** ['ɔːldəmən] n, pl -**men**
vereador m.
**ale** [eil] n cerveja.
**alert** [ə'lə:t] adj atento; (sharp)
esperto // n alerta, alarme m; **to be
on the** ~ estar de sobreaviso or
alerta // vt espertar, alertar.
**algebra** ['ældʒibrə] n álgebra.
**Algeria** [æl'dʒiəriə] n Algéria; ~**n**
adj, n argelino.
**alias** ['eiliəs] adv também chamado
// n outro nome, pseudónimo.
**alibi** ['ælibai] n álibi m.
**alien** ['eiliən] n estrangeiro // adj:
~ **to** estranho a, alheio a; ~**ate** vt
alienar; ~**ation** ['neiʃən] n
alienação f.
**alight** [ə'lait] adj aceso // vi apear.
**align** [ə'lain] vt alinhar; ~**ment** n
alinhamento.
**alike** [ə'laik] adj igual, parecido //
adv igualmente, do mesmo modo; **to
look** ~ parecer-se.
**alimony** ['æliməni] n (payment)
pensão f alimentícia, sustento.
**alive** [ə'laiv] adj (gen) vivo; (lively)
ativo (Pt: -ct-).
**alkali** ['ælkəlai] n álcali m.
**all** [ɔːl] adj todo; (pl) todos/as // pron
tudo; (pl: pessoas) todos // adv tudo,
completamente; ~ **alone**
completamente só; **not at** ~ em
absoluto, absolutamente não; ~ **the
time/his life** todo o tempo/toda a
sua vida; ~ **five** todos os cinco; ~
**of them** todos eles; ~ **of us went**
todos nós fomos; **not as hard as** ~
**that** não tão difícil como isso; ~ **in**

~ ao todo; **it's** ~ **the same** dá no
mesmo.
**allay** [ə'lei] vt (fears) acalmar;
(pain) aliviar.
**allegation** [æli'geiʃən] n alegação f,
afirmação f.
**allege** [ə'ledʒ] vt alegar, afirmar.
**allegiance** [ə'li:dʒəns] n lealdade f.
**allegory** ['æligəri] n alegoria.
**allergic** [ə'lə:dʒik] adj: ~ **to**
alérgico a; **allergy** ['ælədʒi] n
alergia.
**alleviate** [ə'li:vieit] vt aliviar.
**alley** ['æli] n (street) viela, beco; (in
garden) passeio.
**alliance** [ə'laiəns] n aliança; **allied**
['ælaid] adj aliado; (related)
aparentado.
**alligator** ['æligeitə*] n aligátor m,
jacaré m.
**all-in** ['ɔːlin] adj (also adv: charge)
tudo incluído; ~ **wrestling** n luta
livre.
**alliteration** [əlitə'reiʃən] n
aliteração f.
**all-night** ['ɔːl'nait] adj (café) aberto
toda a noite; (party) que dura toda a
noite.
**allocate** ['æləkeit] vt (share out)
distribuir; (devote) designar;
**allocation** [-'keiʃən] n (of money)
repartição f; (distribution)
distribuição f.
**allot** [ə'lɔt] vt distribuir, repartir;
~**ment** n distribuição f, partilha;
(garden) lote m.
**all-out** ['ɔːlaut] adj (effort etc)
máximo; **all out** adv com todas suas
forças; (speed) a toda a velocidade.
**allow** [ə'lau] vt (practice, behaviour)
permitir, deixar; (sum to spend etc)
dar, conceder; (a claim) admitir;
(sum, time estimated) (concede): **to** ~ **that** reconhecer
que; **to** ~ **sb to do** permitir a
alguém fazer; **to** ~ **for** vt fus levar
em conta; ~**ance** n (gen) concessão
f; (payment) pensão f, subsídio;
(discount) desconto; **family** ~**ance**

abono de família; **to make ~ances for** levar em consideração.

**alloy** ['ælɔɪ] *n* liga; (*mix*) mistura.

**all: ~ right** *adv* (*well*) bem; (*correct*) correto (*Pt: -ct-*); (*as answer*) está bem!; **~-round** *adj* (*gen*) completo; (*view*) geral, amplo; (*person*) consumado; **~-time** *adj* (*record*) de todos os tempos.

**allude** [ə'luːd] *vi*: **to ~ to** aludir a.

**alluring** [ə'ljuərɪŋ] *adj* tentador(a), sedutor(a).

**allusion** [ə'luːʒən] *n* alusão *f*.

**ally** ['ælaɪ] *n* aliado // *vr* [ə'laɪ]: **to ~ o.s. with** aliar-se com.

**almighty** [ɔːl'maɪtɪ] *adj* onipotente (*Pt: -mn-*), todo-poderoso.

**almond** ['ɑːmənd] *n* (*fruit*) amêndoa; (*tree*) amendoeira.

**almost** ['ɔːlməust] *adv* quase.

**alms** [ɑːmz] *npl* esmolas *fpl*, esmola *sg*.

**aloft** [ə'lɔft] *adv* em cima, no alto.

**alone** [ə'ləun] *adj* só, sozinho // *adv* só, somente; **to leave sb ~** deixar alguém em paz; **to leave sth ~** não tocar em algo; **let ~** sem falar em.

**along** [ə'lɔŋ] *prep* por, ao longo de // *adv*: **is he coming ~ with us?** ele vem co(n)osco?; **he was limping ~** ia coxeando; **~ with** junto com, em companhia de; **~side** *prep* ao lado de // *adv* (*NAUT*) encostado.

**aloof** [ə'luːf] *adj* afastado, separado // *adv*: **to stand ~** afastar-se.

**aloud** [ə'laud] *adv* em voz alta.

**alphabet** ['ælfəbet] *n* alfabeto; **~ical** [-'betɪkəl] *adj* alfabético.

**alpine** ['ælpaɪn] *adj* alpino, alpestre.

**Alps** [ælps] *npl*: **the ~** os Alpes.

**already** [ɔːl'redɪ] *adv* já.

**alright** [ɔːl'raɪt] *adv* = **all right.**

**also** ['ɔːlsəu] *adv* também.

**altar** ['ɔːltə*] *n* altar *m*.

**alter** ['ɔːltə*] *vt* alterar, modificar // *vi* alterar-se, modificar-se; (*worsen*) alterar-se; **~ation** [ɔːltə'reɪʃən] *n* alteração *f*, modificação *f*.

**alternate** [ɔl'təːnɪt] *adj* alternado; **on ~ days** em dias alternados // *vi* ['ɔltəːneɪt] alternar-se; **~ly** *adv* alternadamente; **alternating** [-'neɪtɪŋ] *adj* (*current*) alternado.

**alternative** [ɔl'təːnətɪv] *adj* alternativo // *n* alternativa; **~ly** *adv*: **~ly one could ...** por outro lado se podia ...

**alternator** [ɔltə'neɪtə*] *n* (*AUT*) alternador *m*.

**although** [ɔːl'ðəu] *conj* embora; (*given that*) se bem que.

**altitude** ['æltɪtjuːd] *n* altitude *f*.

**alto** ['æltəu] *n* (*female*) contralto *f*; (*male*) alto.

**altogether** [ɔːltə'geðə*] *adv* totalmente, de todo; (*on the whole, in all*) no total, ao todo.

**aluminium** [ælju'mɪnɪəm], **aluminum** [ə'luːmɪnəm] (*US*) *n* alumínio.

**always** ['ɔːlweɪz] *adv* sempre.

**am** [æm] *vb see* **be.**

**a.m.** *adv abbr of* **ante meridiem** da manhã.

**amalgamate** [ə'mælgəmeɪt] *vi* amalgamar-se, unir-se // *vt* amalgamar, unir; **amalgamation** [-'meɪʃən] *n* (*COMM*) amalgamação *f*, união *f*.

**amass** [ə'mæs] *vt* acumular, amontoar.

**amateur** ['æmətə*] *n* amador(a) *m/f*.

**amaze** [ə'meɪz] *vt* assombrar, espantar; **~ment** *n* assombro, espanto.

**Amazon** ['æməzən] *n* (*GEO*) o Amazonas *m*.

**ambassador** [æm'bæsədə*] *n* embaixador *m*.

**amber** ['æmbə*] *n* âmbar *m*; **at ~** (*AUT*) em amarelo.

**ambidextrous** [æmbɪ'dekstrəs] *adj* ambidestro.

**ambiguity** [æmbɪ'gjuɪtɪ] *n* ambigüidade *f*; (*of meaning*) duplo sentido; **ambiguous** [-'bɪgjuəs] adj ambíguo.

**ambition** [æm'bɪʃən] n ambição f; **ambitious** [-ʃəs] adj ambicioso; (plan) grandioso.

**ambivalent** [æm'bɪvələnt] adj ambivalente; (pej) equívoco.

**amble** ['æmbl] vi (gen: ~ along) andar a furta-passo, caminhar.

**ambulance** ['æmbjuləns] n ambulância.

**ambush** ['æmbuʃ] n emboscada // vt emboscar; (fig) atacar de surpresa.

**amenable** [ə'miːnəbl] adj: ~ to (advice etc) acessível a.

**amend** [ə'mend] vt (law, text) emendar; (habits) corrigir; ~ment n emenda, correção (Pt: -cç-); ~s n sg: to make ~s (for) compensar; reparar.

**amenities** [ə'miːnɪtɪz] npl atrações (Pt: -cç-) fpl, comodidades fpl.

**America** [ə'merɪkə] n América, os Estados Unidos mpl; ~n adj, n americano/a.

**amiable** ['eɪmɪəbl] adj (kind) amável, simpático; (hearty) caloroso.

**amicable** ['æmɪkəbl] adj amigável, amigo.

**amid(st)** [ə'mɪd(st)] prep entre, no meio de.

**amiss** [ə'mɪs] adv: to take sth ~ levar alguma coisa a mal.

**ammonia** [ə'məunɪə] n amoníaco.

**ammunition** [æmju'nɪʃən] n munição f.

**amnesia** [æm'niːzɪə] n amnésia.

**amnesty** ['æmnɪstɪ] n anistia (Pt: -mn-).

**amok** [ə'mɔk] adv: to run ~ enlouquecer-se.

**among(st)** [ə'mʌŋ(st)] prep entre, no meio de.

**amoral** [æ'mɔrəl] adj amoral.

**amorous** ['æmərəs] adj amoroso; (in love) apaixonado, enamorado.

**amount** [ə'maunt] n (gen)

quantidade f; (of bill etc) quantia, importância, montante m // vi: to ~ to (reach) chegar a; (total) montar a; (be same as) equivaler a, significar.

**amp(ere)** ['æmp(cə*)] n ampère m.

**amphibian** [æm'fɪbɪən] n anfíbio; **amphibious** [-bɪəs] adj anfíbio.

**amphitheatre** ['æmfɪθɪətə*] n anfiteatro.

**ample** ['æmpl] adj (spacious) amplo, extenso; (abundant) abundante; (enough) suficiente.

**amplifier** ['æmplɪfaɪə*] n amplificador m.

**amplify** ['æmplɪfaɪ] vt amplificar, aumentar; (explain) explicar.

**amputate** ['æmpjuteɪt] vt amputar, cortar.

**amuck** [ə'mʌk] adv = **amok**.

**amuse** [ə'mjuːz] vt divertir; (distract) distrair, entreter; ~ment n diversão f, divertimento; (pastime) passatempo; (laughter) riso.

**an** [æn, ən, n] art see **a**.

**anaemia** [ə'niːmɪə] n anemia; **anaemic** [-mɪk] adj anêmico; (fig) insípido.

**anaesthetic** [ænɪs'θetɪk] n anestésico; **anaesthetist** [æ'niːsθɪtɪst] n anestesista m/f.

**analgesic** [ænæl'dʒiːsɪk] adj, n analgésico.

**analogy** [ə'nælədʒɪ] n analogia.

**analyse** ['ænəlaɪz], **analyze** (US) vt analizar; **analysis** [ə'næləsɪs], pl **-ses** [-siːz] n análise f; **analyst** ['ænəlɪst] n analista m/f; **analytic(al)** [-'lɪtɪk(əl)] adj analítico.

**anarchist** ['ænəkɪst] adj, n anarquista m/f; **anarchy** [-kɪ] n anarquia.

**anatomy** [ə'nætəmɪ] n anatomia.

**ancestor** ['ænsɪstə*] n antepassado; **ancestry** [-trɪ] n ascendência, linhagem f.

**anchor** ['æŋkə*] n âncora f // n ancorar, fundear // vt (fig) segurar, amarrar; **to weigh** ~ levantar âncoras; ~age *n* ancoradouro.

**anchovy** ['æntʃəvɪ] *n* enchova.

**ancient** ['eɪnʃənt] *adj* ancião/ciã, velho.

**and** [ænd] *conj* e; ~ **so on** e assim por diante; **try** ~ **come** tente vir; **better** ~ **better** cada vez melhor.

**Andes** ['ændɪːz] *npl*: the ~ os Andes.

**anecdote** ['ænɪkdəʊt] *n* anedota.

**anemia** (*US*) *n* see **anaemia**.

**anesthetic** (*US*) *n* see **anaesthetic**.

**anew** [ə'njuː] *adv* de novo, outra vez.

**angel** ['eɪndʒəl] *n* anjo.

**anger** ['æŋgə*] *n* cólera, zanga // *vt* irritar, zangar.

**angina** [æn'dʒaɪnə] *n* angina (de peito).

**angle** ['æŋgl] *n* ângulo; **from their** ~ do ponto de vista deles.

**angler** ['æŋglə*] *n* pescador *m* de vara; (*Pt*) pescador *m* à linha.

**Anglican** ['æŋglɪkən] *adj*, *n* anglicano/a.

**angling** ['æŋglɪŋ] *n* pesca à vara; (*Pt*) pesca à linha.

**Anglo-** ['æŋgləʊ] *pref* anglo-; ~**Saxon** *adj* anglo-saxão.

**angrily** ['æŋgrɪlɪ] *adv* com zanga, zangadamente.

**angry** ['æŋgrɪ] *adj* zangado; **to be** ~ **with sb/at sth** estar zangado com alguém/algo; **to get** ~ zangar-se.

**anguish** ['æŋgwɪʃ] *n* (*physical*) dor *f*, sofrimento; (*mental*) angústia.

**angular** ['æŋgjulə*] *adj* (*shape*) angular; (*features*) anguloso.

**animal** ['ænɪml] *n* animal *m*; (*insect*) bicho // *adj* animal.

**animate** ['ænɪmeɪt] *vt* (*enliven*) animar; (*encourage*) encorajar; ~**d** *adj* animado.

**animosity** [ænɪ'mɒsɪtɪ] *n* animosidade *f*.

**aniseed** ['ænɪsiːd] *n* erva-doce *f*, anis *f*.

**ankle** ['æŋkl] *n* tornozelo.

**annex** ['æneks] *n* (*also*: **annexe**)

(*building*) anexo // *vt* [ə'neks] (*territory*) anexar; (*document*) ajuntar.

**annihilate** [ə'naɪəleɪt] *vt* aniquilar.

**anniversary** [ænɪ'vɔːsərɪ] *n* aniversário.

**annotate** ['ænəuteɪt] *vt* anotar.

**announce** [ə'nauns] *vt* anunciar; ~**ment** *n* anúncio; (*official*) comunicação *f*; **announcer** *n* (*RADIO, TV*) locutor(a) *m/f*.

**annoy** [ə'nɔɪ] *vt* aborrecer, irritar; **don't get** ~**ed!** não se aborreça; ~**ance** *n* aborrecimento; (*thing*) moléstia; ~**ing** *adj* aborrecido; (*person*) importuno.

**annual** ['ænjuəl] *adj* anual // *n* (*BOT*) anual *f*; (*book*) anuário *f*; ~**ly** *adv* anualmente, cada ano.

**annuity** [ə'njuːɪtɪ] *n* anuidade *f* or renda anual.

**annul** [ə'nʌl] *vt* anular, cancelar; (*law*) revogar; ~**ment** *n* anulação *f*, revogação *f*.

**annum** ['ænəm] *n* see **per**.

**anoint** [ə'nɔɪnt] *vt* ungir.

**anomaly** [ə'nɒməlɪ] *n* anomalia.

**anonymity** [ænə'nɪmɪtɪ] *n* anonimato; **anonymous** [ə'nɒnɪməs] *adj* anônimo.

**anorak** ['ænəræk] *n* anoraque *m*; (*Pt*) anorak *m*.

**anorexia** [ænə'reksɪə] *n* (*MED*) anorexia.

**another** [ə'nʌðə*] *adj*: ~ **book** (*one more*) outro livro; (*a different one*) um outro livro, um livro diferente // *pron* outro; see also **one**.

**answer** ['ɑːnsə*] *n* resposta; (*to problem*) solução *f* // *vi* responder, contestar // *vt* (*reply to*) responder a; (*problem*) resolver; **to** ~ **the phone** atender o telefone; **in** ~ **to your letter** em resposta or respondendo à sua carta; **to** ~ **the bell** or **the door** atender à porta; **to** ~ **back** *vi* replicar, retrucar; **to** ~ **for** *vt* *fus* responder por, responsabilizar-se por; **to** ~ **to** *vt* *fus* (*description*) corresponder a; (*needs*) satisfazer; **~able** *adj*: **~able to sb for sth** responsável perante alguém por algo.

**ant** [ænt] *n* formiga.

**antacid** [ænt'æsɪd] *adj* antiácido.

**antagonist** [æn'tægənɪst] *n* antagonista *m/f*, adversário/a; **~ic** [-'nɪstɪk] *adj* antagônico, hostil; (*opposed*) oposto, contrário; **antagonize** [-naɪz] *vt* contrariar, hostilizar.

**Antarctic** [ænt'ɑːktɪk] *n*: **the ~** o Antártico; **~a** n Antártica.

**antelope** ['æntɪləʊp] *n* antílope *m*.

**antenatal** ['æntɪ'neɪtl] *adj* pré-natal; **~ clinic** clínica pré-natal.

**antenna** [æn'tɛnə], *pl* **~e** [-niː] *n* antena.

**anthem** ['ænθəm] *n*: **national ~** hino nacional.

**anthology** [æn'θɒlədʒɪ] *n* antologia.

**anthropologist** [ænθrə'pɒlədʒɪst] *n* antropologista *m/f*, antropólogo/a; **anthropology** [-dʒɪ] *n* antropologia.

**anti...** [ænti] *pref* anti...; **~-aircraft** *adj* anti-aéreo.

**antibiotic** [æntɪbaɪ'ɒtɪk] *adj*, *n* antibiótico.

**anticipate** [æn'tɪsɪpeɪt] *vt* antecipar; (*foresee*) prever; (*expect*) esperar; (*forestall*) antecipar-se a; (*look forward to*) aguardar, esperar; **anticipation** [-'peɪʃən] *n* antecipação *f*; (*hope*) expectativa.

**anticlimax** [æntɪ'klaɪmæks] *n* desapontamento.

**anticlockwise** [æntɪ'klɒkwaɪz] *adv* em sentido anti-horário.

**antics** ['æntɪks] *npl* bobices *fpl*; (*of child*) travessuras.

**anticyclone** [æntɪ'saɪkləʊn] *n* anticiclone *m*.

**antidote** ['æntɪdəʊt] *n* antídoto, remédio.

**antifreeze** ['æntɪfriːz] *n* anticongelante *m*.

**antihistamine** [æntɪ'hɪstəmiːn] *n* antihistamínico.

**antiquated** ['æntɪkweɪtɪd] *adj* antiquado.

**antique** [æn'tiːk] *n* antiguidade *f*, antigualha // *adj* antigo; ~ **dealer** *n* antiquário; ~ **shop** *n* loja de antiguidades.

**antiquity** [æn'tɪkwɪtɪ] *n* antiguidade *f*.

**antiseptic** [æntɪ'sɛptɪk] *adj*, *n* antiséptico.

**antisocial** [æntɪ'səʊʃəl] *adj* antisocial.

**antlers** ['æntləz] *npl* esgalhos *mpl*, chifres *mpl*.

**anus** ['eɪnəs] *n* ânus *m*.

**anvil** ['ænvɪl] *n* bigorna.

**anxiety** [æŋ'zaɪətɪ] *n* (*worry*) inquietude *f*; (*eagerness*) ânsia; (*MED*) ansiedade *f*.

**anxious** ['æŋkʃəs] *adj* (*worried*) inquieto; (*keen*) desejoso; **~ly** *adv* ansiosamente.

**any** ['ɛnɪ] *adj* (*in negative and interrogative sentences = some*) algum/a; (*negative sense*) nenhum/a; (*no matter which*) qualquer; (*each and every*) todo; **I haven't ~ money/books** não tenho dinheiro/livros; **have you ~ butter/children?** tem manteiga/filhos?; **at ~ moment** a qualquer momento; **in ~ case** em todo o caso; **at ~ rate** de qualquer modo // *pron* algum, nenhum; (*anybody*) alguém; (*in negative and interrogative sentences*): **I haven't ~** não tenho nenhum; **have you got ~?** tem algum?; **can ~ of you sing?** algum de vocês sabe cantar? // *adv* (*in negative sentences*) nada; (*in interrogative and conditional constructions*) algo; **I can't hear him ~ more** não consigo mais ouvi-lo; **do you want ~ more** quer mais sopa?; **~body** *pron* qualquer um, qualquer pessoa; (*in interrogative sentences*) alguém; (*in negative sent-*

ences): **I don't see ~body** não vejo ninguém; **~how** adv de qualquer modo; (carelessly) descuidamente; **~one = ~body;** **~thing** pron algo, qualquer coisa; (in negative sentences) nada; (everything) tudo; **~time** adv (at any moment) a qualquer momento; (whenever) não importa quando; **~way** adv de qualquer modo; **~where** adv em qualquer parte; (negative sense) em parte nenhuma; (everywhere) em por toda a parte; **I don't see him ~where** não o vejo em parte nenhuma.

**apart** [ə'pɑːt] adv à parte, separado; **10 miles ~** separados por 10 milhas; **~ from** prep além de, à parte de.

**apartheid** [ə'pɑːteɪt] n apartheid m.

**apartment** [ə'pɑːtmənt] n (US) apartamento; (room) quarto; **~ house** (US) n quarteirão m.

**apathetic** [æpə'θetɪk] adj apático, indiferente; **apathy** ['æpəθɪ] n apatia, indiferença.

**ape** [eɪp] n macaco // vt macaquear, imitar.

**aperitif** [ə'perɪtɪv] n aperitivo.

**aperture** ['æpətʃjuə] n orifício, (PHOT) abertura.

**apex** ['eɪpeks] n ápice m; (fig) cume m.

**aphrodisiac** [æfrəʊ'dɪzɪæk] adj, n afrodisíaco.

**apiece** [ə'piːs] adv cada um, por cabeça.

**apologetic** [əpɒlə'dʒetɪk] adj (tone, letter) apologético, cheio de desculpas.

**apologize** [ə'pɒlədʒaɪz] vi: **to ~ (for sth to sb)** desculpar-se (de algo a alguém); **apology** [-dʒɪ] n desculpa, apologia.

**apostle** [ə'pɒsl] n apóstolo.

**apostrophe** [ə'pɒstrəfɪ] n apóstrofo.

**appal** [ə'pɔːl] vt horrorizar; **~ling** adj pavoroso; (awful) horrível.

**apparatus** [æpə'reɪtəs] n aparelho.

**apparent** [ə'pærənt] adj aparente; (obvious) claro; **~ly** adv aparentemente, pelo(s) visto(s).

**apparition** [æpə'rɪʃən] n aparição f; (ghost) fantasma m.

**appeal** [ə'piːl] vi (LAW) apelar // n (LAW) apelação f; (request) pedido; (plea) súplica; (charm) atração f (Pt: -cç-); **to ~ for** suplicar, solicitar; **to ~ to** (subj: person) suplicar a; (subj: thing) atrair, agradar; **to ~ to sb for mercy** pedir misericórdia a alguém; **it doesn't ~ to me** não me atrai; **~ing** adj (nice) atraente; (touching) comovedor(a), comovente.

**appear** [ə'pɪə*] vi aparecer; (LAW) apresentar-se, comparecer; (publication) ser publicado; (seem) parecer; **it would ~ that** pareceria que; **~ance** n aparência; (look, aspect) aspecto.

**appease** [ə'piːz] vt (pacify) apaziguar; (satisfy) satisfazer.

**appendicitis** [əpendɪ'saɪtɪs] n apendicite f.

**appendix** [ə'pendɪks], pl **-dices** [-dɪsiːz] n apêndice m.

**appetite** ['æpɪtaɪt] n apetite m; (fig) desejo, sede f.

**appetizing** ['æpɪtaɪzɪŋ] adj apetitoso.

**applaud** [ə'plɔːd] vt/i aplaudir; **applause** [-ɔːz] n aplausos mpl.

**apple** ['æpl] n maçã f; **~ tree** n macieira.

**appliance** [ə'plaɪəns] n (TEC) aparelho; **home ~s** eletrodomésticos (Pt: -ect-) mpl.

**applicable** [ə'plɪkəbl] adj aplicável; (relevant) apropriado.

**applicant** ['æplɪkənt] n candidato, concorrente m/f, requerente m/f.

**application** [æplɪ'keɪʃən] n aplicação f; (for a job, a grant etc) candidatura, requerimento; **~ form** n formulário.

**apply** [ə'plaɪ] vt: **to ~ (to)** aplicar (a) // vi: **to ~ to** apresentar-se a;

(*be suitable for*) ser aplicável a; (*be relevant to*) dizer respeito a; **to ~ for** (*permit, grant, job*) solicitar, pedir; **to ~ the brakes** frear, travar; **to ~ o.s.** to aplicar-se a, dedicar-se a.

**appoint** [əˈpɔɪnt] *vt* (*to post*) nomear; (*date, place*) marcar; **~ment** *n* (*engagement*) encontro, marcação *f*; (*date*) compromisso; (*act*) nomeação *f*; (*post*) cargo.

**apportion** [əˈpɔːʃən] *vt* repartir, distribuir; (*blame*) pôr.

**appraisal** [əˈpreɪzl] *n* avaliação *f*, estimatura.

**appreciable** [əˈpriːʃəbl] *adj* apreciável, notável.

**appreciate** [əˈpriːʃɪeɪt] *vt* (*like*) apreciar, estimar; (*be grateful for*) agradecer; (*assess*) avaliar, apreciar; (*be aware of*) compreender, perceber // *vi* (*COMM*) valorizar-se; **appreciation** [-ˈeɪʃən] *n* apreciação *f*, estima.

**appreciative** [əˈpriːʃɪətɪv] *adj* (*person*) agradecido; (*comment*) elogioso.

**apprehend** [æprɪˈhend] *vt* perceber, compreender; (*arrest*) prender.

**apprehension** [æprɪˈhenʃən] *n* compreensão *f*, apreensão *f*; (*fear*) receio; **apprehensive** [-ˈhensɪv] *adj* apreensivo, receoso.

**apprentice** [əˈprentɪs] *n* aprendiz *m/f*, **~ship** *n* aprendizagem *f*.

**approach** [əˈprəʊtʃ] *vi* aproximar-se // *vt* aproximar; (*be approximate*) aproximar-se a; (*ask, apply to*) dirigir-se a // *n* aproximação *f*; (*access*) acesso; (*proposal*) proposição *f*; **~able** *adj* (*person*) tratável; (*place*) acessível.

**appropriate** [əˈprəʊprɪeɪt] *vt* (*take*) apropriar-se de; (*allot*): **to ~ sth for** destinar algo a // *adj* [-rɪɪt] (*apt*) apropriado, próprio; (*relevant*) adequado.

**approval** [əˈpruːvəl] *n* aprovação *f*; **on ~** (*COMM*) à prova.

**approve** [əˈpruːv] *vt* aprovar; **~d school** *n* reformatório.

**approximate** [əˈprɒksɪmɪt] *adj* aproximado // *vt* [-meɪt] aproximar; **approximation** [-ˈmeɪʃən] *n* aproximação *f*.

**apricot** [ˈeɪprɪkɒt] *n* damasco, abricó.

**April** [ˈeɪprəl] *n* abril *m*; **~ Fool's Day** *n* Dia *m* da mentira; Primeiro-de-abril *m*.

**apron** [ˈeɪprən] *n* avental *m*.

**apt** [æpt] *adj* (*suitable*) adequado; (*appropriate*) apropriado; (*likely*): **~ to do** estar sujeito a fazer.

**aptitude** [ˈæptɪtjuːd] *n* aptidão *f*, talento.

**aqualung** [ˈækwəlʌŋ] *n* aparelho respiratório autônomo.

**aquarium** [əˈkwɛərɪəm] *n* aquário.

**Aquarius** [əˈkwɛərɪəs] *n* Aquário.

**aquatic** [əˈkwætɪk] *adj* aquático.

**aqueduct** [ˈækwɪdʌkt] *n* aqueduto.

**Arab** [ˈærəb] *n* árabe *m/f*.

**Arabia** [əˈreɪbɪə] *n* Arábia; **~n** *adj* árabe.

**Arabic** [ˈærəbɪk] *n* arábico.

**arable** [ˈærəbl] *adj* cultivável.

**arbitrary** [ˈɑːbɪtrərɪ] *adj* arbitrário.

**arbitrate** [ˈɑːbɪtreɪt] *vi* arbitrar; **arbitration** [-ˈtreɪʃən] *n* arbitragem *f*; **arbitrator** *n* árbitro.

**arc** [ɑːk] *n* arco.

**arcade** [ɑːˈkeɪd] *n* arcada; (*round a square*) arcos *mpl*; (*passage with shops*) galeria.

**arch** [ɑːtʃ] *n* arco; (*vault*) abóbada // *vt* arquear, curvar.

**archaeologist** [ɑːkɪˈɒlədʒɪst] *n* arqueólogo; **archaeology** [-dʒɪ] *n* arqueologia.

**archaic** [ɑːˈkeɪɪk] *adj* arcaico.

**archbishop** [ɑːtʃˈbɪʃəp] *n* arcebispo.

**arch-enemy** [ɑːtʃˈɛnɪmɪ] *n* arquiinimigo.

**archer** [ˈɑːtʃə*] *n* arqueiro, flecheiro; **~y** *n* tiro de arco.

**archetype** ['ɑːkɪtaɪp] n arquétipo.
**archipelago** [ɑːkɪ'pelɪgəʊ] n arquipélago.
**architect** ['ɑːkɪtekt] n arquiteto (Pt: -ct-); **~ural** [-'tektʃərəl] adj arquite(c)tónico; **~ure** n arquite(c)tura.
**archives** ['ɑːkaɪvz] npl arquivo sg.
**archway** ['ɑːtʃweɪ] n arco.
**Arctic** ['ɑːktɪk] adj ártico (Pt: -ct-) // n: the ~ o Ár(c)tico.
**ardent** ['ɑːdənt] adj (passionate) ardente, apaixonado; (fervent) fervoroso; **ardour; ardor** ['ɑːdə*] n ardor m; fervor m.
**arduous** ['ɑːdjuəs] adj (gen) árduo; (journey) difícil.
**are** [ɑː*] vb see be.
**area** ['ɛərɪə] n (gen) área; (MAT) superfície f, extensão f; (zone) zona, região f.
**arena** [ə'riːnə] n arena; (of circus) picadeiro; (Pt) pista; (for bullfight) arena; (Pt) praça.
**aren't** [ɑːnt] = **are not**.
**Argentina** [ɑːdʒən'tiːnə] n Argentina; **Argentinian** [-'tɪnɪən] adj, n argentino/a.
**argue** ['ɑːgjuː] vi (quarrel) discutir; (reason) argumentar; **to ~ that** sustentar que; **argument** n (reasons) argumento; (quarrel) discussão f; (debate) debate m; **argumentative** [-mentətɪv] adj discutidor(a).
**aria** ['ɑːrɪə] n (MUS) ária.
**arid** ['ærɪd] adj árido.
**Aries** ['ɛərɪz] n Áries m.
**arise** [ə'raɪz], pt **arose**, pp **arisen** [ə'rɪzn] vi (rise up) levantar-se, erguer-se; (emerge) surgir; **to ~ from** resultar de.
**aristocracy** [ærɪs'tɔkrəsɪ] n aristocracia; **aristocrat** ['ærɪstəkræt] n aristocrata m/f.
**arithmetic** [ə'rɪθmətɪk] n aritmética.
**ark** [ɑːk] n: Noah's A~ arca de Noé.
**arm** [ɑːm] n (ANAT) braço; (weapon)

arma // vt armar; **~s** pl (weapons) armas fpl; (HERALDRY) brasão m; **~s race** carreira armamentista; **~ in ~** de braço dado; **~band** n bracelete m; (Pt) braceleira; **~chair** n poltrona; **~ed** adj armado; **~ed robbery** n assalto à mão armada; **~ful** n braçada.
**armistice** ['ɑːmɪstɪs] n armistício.
**armour; armor** ['ɑːmə*] n armadura; **~ed car** n carro blindado; **~y** n arsenal m.
**armpit** ['ɑːmpɪt] n sovaco.
**army** ['ɑːmɪ] n exército.
**aroma** [ə'rəʊmə] n aroma; **~tic** [ærə'mætɪk] adj aromático.
**arose** [ə'rəʊz] pt of **arise**.
**around** [ə'raʊnd] adv em volta; (in the area) perto // prep em redor de, em volta de; (fig: about) cerca de.
**arouse** [ə'raʊz] vt despertar.
**arrange** [ə'reɪndʒ] vt arranjar; (programme) organizar; **~ment** n arranjo; (agreement) acordo; **~ments** npl (plans) planos mpl, medidas fpl; (preparations) preparativos mpl.
**arrears** [ə'rɪəz] npl atrasos mpl; **to be in ~ with one's rent** atrasar o aluguel.
**arrest** [ə'rest] vt prender, deter; (sb's attention) chamar, prender // n detenção f, prisão f; **under ~** preso.
**arrival** [ə'raɪvəl] n chegada; **new ~** recém-chegado.
**arrive** [ə'raɪv] vi chegar.
**arrogance** ['ærəgəns] n arrogância; **arrogant** [-gənt] adj arrogante.
**arrow** ['ærəʊ] n flecha, seta.
**arsenal** ['ɑːsɪnl] n arsenal m.
**arsenic** ['ɑːsnɪk] n arsênico.
**arson** ['ɑːsn] n incêndio premeditado.
**art** [ɑːt] n arte f; (craft) artes fpl; (skill) habilidade f, jeito; (technique) técnica; **A~s** npl (EDUC) Letras fpl; **~ gallery** n museu m de belas

artes; (*small and private*) galeria de arte.

**artery** ['ɑ:tərɪ] *n* (MED) artéria; (*fig*) estrada principal.

**arthritis** [ɑ:'θraɪtɪs] *n* artrite *f*.

**artichoke** ['ɑ:tɪtʃəʊk] *n* alcachofra; **Jerusalem ~** topinambo.

**article** ['ɑ:tɪkl] *n* artigo, objeto (*Pt: -ct-*); (*in newspaper*) artigo; (LAW: *training*): **~s** *npl* contrato de aprendizagem *sg*.

**articulate** [ɑ:'tɪkjʊlɪt] *adj* articulado // *vt* [-leɪt] articular, pronunciar; **~d lorry** *n* caminhão *m* articulado, jamanta.

**artificial** [ɑ:tɪ'fɪʃəl] *adj* artificial; (*teeth etc*) postiço, falso; **~ respiration** *n* respiração *f* artificial.

**artillery** [ɑ:'tɪlərɪ] *n* artilharia.

**artisan** [ɑ:'tɪzæn] *n* artesão/sã.

**artist** ['ɑ:tɪst] *n* artista *m/f*; (MUS) intérprete *m/f*; **~ic** [ɑ:'tɪstɪk] *adj* artístico; **~ry** *n* arte *f*, maestria.

**artless** ['ɑ:tlɪs] *adj* (*innocent*) natural, simples; (*clumsy*) desajeitado.

**as** [æz, əz] *conj* (*cause*) como, já que; (*time: moment*) quando; (*duration*) enquanto; (*manner*) como, conforme; (*in the capacity of*) como; **~ big ~** tão grande como; **twice ~ big ~** duas vezes maior que; **~ she said** como ela disse; **~ if** *or* **though** como se; **~ for** *or* **to** that quanto a isso; **~ or so long ~** *conj* desde que, contanto que; **~ much/many ~** tanto/s ... como; **~ soon ~** logo que, assim que; **~ such** *adv* como tal; **~ well** *adv* também; **~ well ~** *conj* assim como; *see also* **such.**

**asbestos** [æz'bɛstɒs] *n* asbesto, amianto.

**ascend** [ə'sɛnd] *vt* ascender, subir; **~ancy** *n* predomínio, ascendência.

**ascent** [ə'sɛnt] *n* subida; (*slope*) rampa; (*promotion*) ascensão *f*.

**ascertain** [æsə'teɪn] *vt* averiguar, verificar.

**ascetic** [ə'sɛtɪk] *adj* ascético.

**ascribe** [ə'skraɪb] *vt*: **to ~ sth to** atribuir algo a.

**ash** [æʃ] *n* cinza; (*tree*) freixo.

**ashamed** [ə'ʃeɪmd] *adj* envergonhado; **to be ~ of** ter vergonha de.

**ashen** ['æʃn] *adj* cinzento.

**ashore** [ə'ʃɔ:*] *adv* em terra.

**ashtray** ['æʃtreɪ] *n* cinzeiro.

**Asia** ['eɪʃə] *n* Ásia; **~n, ~tic** [eɪsɪ'ætɪk] *adj,* a asiático/a.

**aside** [ə'saɪd] *adv* de parte, de lado.

**ask** [ɑ:sk] *vt* (*question*) perguntar; (*demand*) exigir; (*invite*) convidar; **to ~ sb sth** perguntar algo a alguém; **to ~ sb to do sth** pedir a alguém para fazer algo; **to ~ sb about sth** perguntar a alguém sobre algo; **to ~ (sb) a question** fazer uma pergunta (a alguém); **to ~ sb out to dinner** convidar alguém para jantar; **to ~ for** *vt fus* pedir.

**askance** [ə'skɑ:ns] *adv*: **to look ~ at sb** olhar alguém de soslaio.

**askew** [ə'skju:] *adv* torto, de esguelha.

**asleep** [ə'sli:p] *adj* adormecido, dormindo; **to fall ~** adormecer.

**asparagus** [əs'pærəgəs] *n* aspargo (*Pt:* esp-).

**aspect** ['æspɛkt] *n* aspecto, aparência; (*direction in which a building etc faces*) orientação *f*.

**aspersions** [əs'pə:ʃənz] *npl*: **to cast ~ on** difamar, caluniar.

**asphalt** ['æsfælt] *n* asfalto; (*place*) pista asfaltada.

**asphyxiate** [æs'fɪksɪeɪt] *vt* asfixiar, sufocar // *vi* asfixiar-se, sufocar-se; **asphyxiation** [-'eɪʃən] *n* asfixia, sufocação *f*.

**aspiration** [æspə'reɪʃən] *n* (*fig*) aspiração *f*, ambição *f*.

**aspire** [əs'paɪə*] *vi*: **to ~ to** aspirar a.

**aspirin** ['æsprɪn] *n* aspirina.

**ass** [æs] *n* jumento, burro; (*col*) estúpido.

**assailant** [ə'seɪlənt] n assaltante m/f, atacante m/f.

**assassin** [ə'sæsɪn] n assassino; ~**ate** vt assassinar; ~**ation** [-'neɪʃən] n assassinato, assassínio.

**assault** [ə'sɔ:lt] n (gen: attack) assalto // vt assaltar, atacar; (sexually) agredir, violar.

**assemble** [ə'sɛmbl] vt reunir; (TECH) montar // vi reunir-se.

**assembly** [ə'sɛmblɪ] n (meeting) reunião f, assembleia; (people) congregação f; (construction) montagem f; ~ **line** n linha de produção.

**assent** [ə'sɛnt] n assentimento, aprovação f // vi consentir, assentir.

**assert** [ə'sə:t] vt afirmar; (claim etc) fazer valer; ~**ion** [ə'sə:ʃən] n afirmação f.

**assess** [ə'sɛs] vt avaliar; (tax, damages) fixar; (property etc: for tax) taxar; ~**ment** n avaliação f; ~**or** n avaliador(a) m/f; (of tax) avaliador(a) do fisco.

**asset** ['æsɛt] n bem m; (quality) vantagem f; ~**s** npl (funds) ativo (Pt: -ct-) sg, fundos mpl.

**assiduous** [ə'sɪdjuəs] adj assíduo.

**assign** [ə'saɪn] vt (date) fixar; (task) designar; (resources) destinar; (property) transmitir; ~**ment** n designação f; (task) tarefa.

**assimilate** [ə'sɪmɪleɪt] vt assimilar.

**assist** [ə'sɪst] vt ajudar; (progress etc) auxiliar; ~**ance** n ajuda, auxílio; (welfare) subsídio; ~**ant** n assistente m/f, auxiliar m/f; (also: **shop** ~ant) balconista m/f.

**assizes** [ə'saɪzɪz] npl sessão f de tribunal superior.

**associate** [ə'səʊʃɪɪt] adj associado // n colega m/f; (in crime) cúmplice m/f; (member) sócio // (vb: [-ʃɪeɪt]) vt associar // vi: **to** ~ **with sb** associar-se com alguém.

**association** [əsəʊsɪ'eɪʃən] n associação f; (COMM) sociedade f.

**assorted** [ə'sɔ:tɪd] adj sortido, variado.

**assortment** [ə'sɔ:tmənt] n sortimento.

**assume** [ə'sju:m] vt (suppose) supor, presumir; (responsibilities etc) assumir; (attitude, name) adotar (Pt: -pt-), tomar.

**assumption** [ə'sʌmpʃən] n (supposition) suposição f, presunção f; (act) assunção f.

**assurance** [ə'ʃuərəns] n garantia; (confidence) confiança; (certainty) certeza; (insurance) seguro.

**assure** [ə'ʃuə*] vt assegurar.

**asterisk** ['æstərɪsk] n asterisco.

**astern** [ə'stə:n] adv à popa; (direction) à ré.

**asteroid** ['æstərɔɪd] n asteróide m.

**asthma** ['æsmə] n asma; ~**tic** [æs'mætɪk] adj, n asmático/a.

**astonish** [ə'stɔnɪʃ] vt assombrar, espantar; ~**ment** n assombro, espanto.

**astound** [ə'staʊnd] vt assombrar, espantar.

**astray** [ə'streɪ] adv: **to go** ~ perder-se; **to lead** ~ desencaminhar.

**astride** [ə'straɪd] adv escarrapachado // prep a cavalo or montado sobre.

**astrologer** [əs'trɔlədʒə*] n astrólogo; **astrology** [-dʒɪ] n astrologia.

**astronaut** ['æstrənɔ:t] n astronauta m/f.

**astronomer** [əs'trɔnəmə*] n astrônomo; **astronomical** [æstrə'nɔmɪkəl] adj astronômico; (fig) enorme; **astronomy** [-mɪ] n astronomia.

**astute** [əs'tju:t] adj astuto, esperto.

**asylum** [ə'saɪləm] n (refuge) asilo, refúgio; (hospital) manicômio.

**at** [æt] prep em, a; ~ **the top** no cimo; ~ **4 o'clock** às quatro; ~ **a kilo** a uma libra o quilo; ~ **night** à noite; ~ **a stroke** de um golpe; **two**

~ **a time** de dois em dois; ~ **times** às vezes.

**ate** [eɪt] *pt of* **eat**.

**atheist** ['eɪθɪɪst] *n* ateu/ateia.

**Athens** ['æθɪnz] *n* Atenas *f*.

**athlete** ['æθliːt] *n* atleta *m/f*.

**athletic** [æθ'lɛtɪk] *adj* atlético; ~**s** *n* atletismo *sg*.

**Atlantic** [ət'læntɪk] *n*: **the** ~ **(Ocean)** o (Oceano) Atlântico.

**atlas** ['ætləs] *n* atlas *m*.

**atmosphere** ['ætməsfɪə*] *n* atmosfera; *(fig)* ambiente *m*.

**atom** ['ætəm] *n* átomo; ~**ic** [ə'tɔmɪk] *adj* atômico; ~**(ic) bomb** *n* bomba atômica; ~**izer** ['ætəmaɪzə*] *n* atomizador *m*, pulverizador *m*.

**atone** [ə'təun] *vi*: **to** ~ **for** expiar.

**atrocious** [ə'trəuʃəs] *adj (very bad)* atroz; *(fig)* horrível, detestável.

**atrocity** [ə'trɔsɪtɪ] *n* atrocidade *f*.

**attach** [ə'tætʃ] *vt (gen)* fixar; *(document, letter)* juntar; ~**ed** *adj (letter)* junto; **to be** ~**ed to sb/sth** *(to like)* ter afeição por alguém/algo.

**attaché** [ə'tæʃeɪ] *n* adido; ~ **case** *n* pasta.

**attachment** [ə'tætʃmənt] *n (tool)* acessório; *(love)*: ~ **(to)** afeição *f* (por).

**attack** [ə'tæk] *vt (MIL)* atacar; *(criminal)* agredir, assaltar; *(task etc)* empreender // *n* ataque *m*, assalto; **on sb's life** atentado; **heart** ~ ataque de coração or cardíaco; ~**er** *n* agressor(a) *m/f*, assaltante *m/f*.

**attain** [ə'teɪn] *vt (also*: ~ **to)** alcançar, atingir; *(achieve)* conseguir; ~**ments** *npl* dotes *mpl*, talento *sg*.

**attempt** [ə'tɛmpt] *n* tentativa; *(attack)* atentado // *vt* tentar, intentar.

**attend** [ə'tɛnd] *vt* assistir a; *(patient)* tratar; **to** ~ **to** *vt fus (needs, affairs etc)* ocupar-se de; *(speech etc)* prestar atenção a;

*(customer)* atender a; ~**ance** *n* comparecimento; *(people present)* assistência; ~**ant** *n* servidor(a) *m/f*; *(THEATRE)* arrumador(a) *m/f* // *adj* concomitante.

**attention** [ə'tɛnʃən] *n* atenção *f* // *excl (MIL)* sentido!; **for the** ~ **of...** *(ADMIN)* atenção...

**attentive** [ə'tɛntɪv] *adj* atento; *(polite)* cortês.

**attest** [ə'tɛst] *vi*: **to** ~ **to** atestar.

**attic** ['ætɪk] *n* sótão *m*, água-furtada.

**attitude** ['ætɪtjuːd] *n (gen)* atitude *f*; *(disposition)* disposição *f*.

**attorney** [ə'tɜːnɪ] *n (lawyer)* advogado; *(having proxy)* procurador *m*; **A**~ **General** *n (Brit)* procurador da coroa; *(US)* procurador geral.

**attract** [ə'trækt] *vt* atrair; *(attention)* chamar; **attraction** [ə'trækʃən] *n (gen pl)* encantos *mpl*; *(amusements)* diversões *fpl*; *(PHYSICS)* atração *(Pt*: -çç-) *f*; *(fig: towards sth)* atrativo *(Pt*: -ct-); ~**ive** *adj* atrativo; *(interesting)* atraente; *(pretty)* bonito.

**attribute** ['ætrɪbjuːt] *n* atributo // *vt* [ə'trɪbjuːt]: **to** ~ **sth to** atribuir or imputar algo a.

**aubergine** ['əubəʒiːn] *n* berinjela.

**auburn** ['ɔːbən] *adj* castanho-avermelhado.

**auction** ['ɔːkʃən] *n (also*: **sale by** ~**)** leilão *m* // *vt* leiloar; ~**eer** [-'nɪə*] *n* leiloeiro/a.

**audacious** [ɔː'deɪʃəs] *adj* audaz, atrevido; *(pej)* descarado; **audacity** [ɔː'dæsɪtɪ] *n* audácia, atrevimento; *(pej)* descaramento.

**audible** ['ɔːdɪbl] *adj* audível.

**audience** ['ɔːdɪəns] *n* auditório, público; *(interview)* entrevista.

**audio-visual** [ɔːdɪəu'vɪzjuəl] *adj* audiovisual.

**audit** ['ɔːdɪt] *vt* fiscalizar, examinar contas.

**audition** [ɔː'dɪʃən] *n* audição *f*.

**auditor** ['ɔːdɪtə*] n contador(a) m/f, auditor(a) m/f.

**auditorium** [ɔːdɪ'tɔːrɪəm] n auditório.

**augment** [ɔːg'ment] vt aumentar // vi aumentar-se.

**augur** ['ɔːgə*] vi: it ~s well é de bom augúrio.

**August** ['ɔːgəst] n agosto.

**aunt** [ɑːnt] n tia; ~ie, ~y n diminutive of **aunt**.

**au pair** ['əu'pɛə*] n (also: ~ girl) au pair f.

**aura** ['ɔːrə] n emanação f; (atmosphere) ambiente m.

**auspices** ['ɔːspɪsɪz] npl: under the ~ of sob os auspícios de.

**auspicious** [ɔːs'pɪʃəs] adj propício.

**austere** [ɔs'tɪə*] adj austero; (manner) severo; **austerity** [ɔ'sterɪtɪ] n austeridade f.

**Australia** [ɔs'treɪlɪə] n Austrália; ~n adj, n australiano/a.

**Austria** ['ɔstrɪə] n Áustria; ~n adj, n austríaco/a.

**authentic** [ɔː'θentɪk] adj autêntico.

**author** ['ɔːθə] n autor(a) m/f.

**authoritarian** [ɔːθɔrɪ'tɛərɪən] adj autoritário.

**authoritative** [ɔː'θɔrɪtətɪv] adj autorizado; (manner) autoritário.

**authority** [ɔː'θɔrɪtɪ] n autoridade f; **the authorities** npl as autoridades.

**authorize** ['ɔːθəraɪz] vt autorizar.

**auto** ['ɔːtəu] (US) n carro, automóvel m.

**autobiography** [ɔːtəbaɪ'ɔgrəfɪ] n autobiografia.

**autocratic** [ɔːtə'krætɪk] adj autocrático.

**autograph** ['ɔːtəgrɑːf] n autógrafo // vt (photo etc) autografar.

**automatic** [ɔːtə'mætɪk] adj automático // n (gun) pistola automática.

**automation** [ɔːtə'meɪʃən] n automação f.

**automaton** [ɔː'tɔmətən] pl **-mata** [-tə] n autómato.

**automobile** ['ɔːtəməbiːl] (US) n carro, automóvel m.

**autonomous** [ɔː'tɔnəməs] adj autônomo.

**autopsy** ['ɔːtɔpsɪ] n autópsia.

**autumn** ['ɔːtəm] n outono.

**auxiliary** [ɔːg'zɪlɪərɪ] adj, n m/f.

**Av.** abbr of **avenue**.

**avail** [ə'veɪl] vt: to ~ o.s. of aproveitar, valer-se de // n: to no ~ em vão, inutilmente.

**availability** [əveɪlə'bɪlɪtɪ] n disponibilidade f.

**available** [ə'veɪləbl] adj disponível; (usable) utilizável.

**avalanche** ['ævəlɑːnʃ] n avalanche, alude m.

**avant-garde** ['ævæŋ'gɑːd] adj de vanguarda.

**avaricious** [ævə'rɪʃəs] adj avarento, avaro.

**Ave.** abbr of **avenue**.

**avenge** [ə'vendʒ] vt vingar.

**avenue** ['ævənjuː] n avenida; (path) caminho.

**average** ['ævərɪdʒ] n média, termo médio // adj (mean) médio; (ordinary) vulgar, comum // vt calcular a média de; on ~ em média; to ~ out vt tirar a média // vi: to ~ out at resultar como média, ser por regra geral.

**averse** [ə'vɜːs] adj: to be ~ to sth/doing ser avesso or pouco disposto a algo/a fazer algo; **aversion** [ə'vɜːʃən] n aversão f, repugnância.

**avert** [ə'vɜːt] vt prevenir; (blow, one's eyes) desviar.

**aviary** ['eɪvɪərɪ] n aviário, viveiro de aves.

**aviation** [eɪvɪ'eɪʃən] n aviação f.

**avid** ['ævɪd] adj ávido.

**avocado** [ævə'kɑːdəu] n (also: ~ pear) abacate m.

**avoid** [ə'vɔɪd] vt evitar, iludir; ~able adj evitável; ~ance n evitação f.

**await** [əˈweɪt] vt esperar, aguardar.

**awake** [əˈweɪk] adj acordado // (vb: pt **awoke**, pp **awoken** or **awaked**) vt despertar, acordar // vi despertar, acordar; **~ning** n despertar m.

**aw[** [əˈwɔːd] n (prize) prêmio, ~oração f; (LAW) sentença; (act) concessão f // vt (prize) outorgar, conceder; (LAW: damages) adjudicar.

**aware** [əˈwɛə*] adj consciente; (informed) informado; **to become ~ of** reparar em, saber; **~ness** n consciência; (knowledge) conhecimento.

**awash** [əˈwɔʃ] adj inundado.

**away** [əˈweɪ] adv (gen: far ~) muito longe; **two kilometres ~ a** dois quilômetros de distância; **two hours ~ by car** a duas horas de carro; **the holiday was two weeks ~** faltavam duas semanas para as férias; **~ from** longe de; **he's ~ for a week** está ausente uma semana; **to take ~** vt levar; **to work/pedal ~** trabalhar/pedalar sem parar; **to fade ~** desvanecer-se; (sound) apagar-se; **~ match** n (SPORT) jogo de fora.

**awe** [ɔː] n temor m respeitoso; **~-inspiring**, **~some** adj imponente; **~-struck** adj pasmado.

**awful** [ˈɔːfəl] adj terrível, horrível; **~ly** adv (very) muito.

**awhile** [əˈwaɪl] adv por algum tempo, um pouco.

**awkward** [ˈɔːkwəd] adj (clumsy) desajeitado; (shape) incômodo; (problem) difícil; (embarrassing) embaraçoso, delicado.

**awning** [ˈɔːnɪŋ] n toldo.

**awoke** [əˈwəuk], **awoken** [-kən] pt, pp of **awake**.

**awry** [əˈraɪ] adv: **to be ~** estar de viés or de esguelha; **to go ~** sair mal.

**axe, ax** (US) [æks] n machado // vt

(employee) despedir; (project etc) parar; (jobs) reduzir.

**axiom** [ˈæksɪəm] n axioma m.

**axis** [ˈæksɪs], pl **axes** [-siːz] n eixo.

**axle** [ˈæksl] n eixo.

**ay(e)** [aɪ] excl (yes) sim; **the ayes** npl os que votam a favor.

**Aztec** [ˈæztɛk] adj, n asteca m/f.

# B

**B.A.** abbr of **Bachelor of Arts** Licenciado/Bacharel em Letras.

**babble** [ˈbæbl] vi balbuciar.

**baboon** [bəˈbuːn] n babuíno.

**baby** [ˈbeɪbɪ] n criança, bebê m/f; **~-carriage** n (US) carrinho de bebê; **~-ish** adj. infantil; **~-sit** vi tomar conta de crianças; **~-sitter** n pessoa que toma conta de crianças.

**bachelor** [ˈbætʃələ*] n solteiro; (EDUC) bacharel m.

**back** [bæk] n (of person) costas fpl; (of animal) lombo; (of hand) dorso; (of house, car, train) parte f de trás; (of chair) encosto; (of page) verso; (of coin) reverso; (FOOTBALL) zagueiro, beque m; (: Pt) defesa m // vt (also: ~ up) apoiar; (horse: at races) apostar em; (car) recuar or fazer marcha-à-ré (Pt: marcha atrás) // vi (car etc) recuar // adj (in compounds) de trás; **~seats/wheels** (AUT) assentos mpl/ rodas fpl de trás; **~ payments** pagamentos atrasados mpl; **~ rent** aluguel m atrasado // adv (not forward) para trás; (returned): **he's ~** ele voltou; **he ran ~** recuou correndo; (restitution): **throw the ball ~** devolva a bola; **can I have it ~?** pode devolvê-lo?; (again): **he called ~** chamou de novo; **to ~ down** vi desistir; **to ~ out (of)** vi (promise) não cumprir (com).

**back:** **~ache** n dor f nas costas;

**~bencher** n membro do parlamento sem liderança; **~biting** n difamação f; **~bone** n coluna vertebral; **~cloth** n pano de cortina; **~date** vt (letter) pôr data atrasada em; **~dated pay rise** aumento de vencimento com efeito retroativo; **~er** n partidário; (COMM) promotor m; **~fire** n (AUT) retorno de chama // vi (plans) falhar; **~gammon** n gamão m; **~ground** n fundo; (of events) antecedentes mpl; (basic knowledge) bases fpl; (experience) conhecimentos mpl, experiência; **family ~ground** origem f, antecedentes mpl; **~hand** n (TENNIS: also: **~hand stroke**) revés m; **~handed** adj (fig) ambíguo, insincero; **~hander** n (bribe) suborno; (Pt) peita; **~ing** n (fig) apoio; **~lash** n reação (Pt: -cç-) f; **~log** n: **~log of work** atrasos mpl; **~ number** n (of magazine etc) número atrasado; **~ pay** n pagamento atrasado; **~side** n (col) traseiro; **~stage** adv nos bastidores; **~stroke** n nado de costas; **~ward** adj (movement) para trás; (person, country) atrasado; (shy) tímido; **~wards** adv (move, go) para trás; (read a list) às avessas; (fall) de costas; **~water** n (fig) lugar m atrasado; **~yard** n quintal m.

**bacon** ['beɪkən] n toucinho.

**bacteria** [bæk'tɪərɪə] npl bactérias fpl.

**bad** [bæd] adj mau; (serious) grave; (meat, food) estragado; **to go ~** estragar-se.

**badge** [bædʒ] n emblema m; (of policeman) crachá m.

**badger** ['bædʒə*] n texugo.

**badly** ['bædlɪ] adv (work, dress etc) mal; **~ wounded** gravemente ferido; **he needs it ~** faz-lhe grande falta; **to be ~ off (for money)** estar com pouco dinheiro.

**badminton** ['bædmɪntən] n badminton m.

**bad-tempered** ['bæd'tɛmpəd] adj de mau humor; (temporary) mal humorado.

**baffle** ['bæfl] vt (puzzle) confundir.

**bag** [bæg] n saco, bolsa; (handbag) bolsa; (satchel) sacola; (case) mala; (of hunter) caça // vt (col: take) apanhar; **~ful** n saco cheio; **~gage** n bagagem f; **~gage checkroom** (US) n depósito da bagagem; **~gy** adj largo; **~pipes** npl gaita de foles.

**bail** [beɪl] n fiança // vt (prisoner: gen: give ~ to) libertar sob fiança; (boat: also: ~ out) esgotar a água de; **to ~ sb out** tirar alguém da prisão sob fiança; see also **bale**.

**bailiff** ['beɪlɪf] n oficial m de justiça; (Pt) oficial m de diligências.

**bait** [beɪt] n isca, engodo // vt iscar, cevar.

**bake** [beɪk] vt cozer ao forno // vi (cook) cozer-se; (be hot) fazer um calor terrível; **~d beans** npl feijão m cozido; **~r** n padeiro; **~ry** n (for bread) padaria; (for cakes) confeitaria; **baking** n (act) cozimento; (batch) fornada; **baking powder** n fermento em pó.

**balance** ['bæləns] n equilíbrio; (scales) balança; (COMM) balanço; (remainder) resto, saldo // vt equilibrar; (budget) nivelar; (account) fazer o balanço; (compensate) contrabalançar; **~ of trade/payments** balança do comércio/de pagamentos; **~d** adj (personality, diet) equilibrado; **~ sheet** n balanço geral.

**balcony** ['bælkənɪ] n (open) varanda; (closed) galeria.

**bald** [bɔːld] adj calvo; **~ness** n calvície f.

**bale** [beɪl] n (AGR) fardo; **to ~ out** (of a plane) atirar-se de pára-quedas; **to ~ sb out of a difficulty** ajudar alguém a sair dum problema.

**baleful** ['beɪlful] adj (look) triste; (sinister) funesto, sinistro.

**ball** [bɔːl] n (gen) bola; (dance) baile m.

**ballad** ['bæləd] n balada.

**ballast** ['bæləst] n lastro.

**ballerina** [bælə'riːnə] n bailarina.

**ballet** ['bæleɪ] n balé m, bailado; ~ **dancer** n bailarino/a.

**balloon** [bə'luːn] n balão m; bola de soprar; ~**ist** n aeronauta m/f.

**ballot** ['bælət] n votação f; ~ **box** n urna; ~ **paper** n cédula eleitoral.

**ball-point pen** ['bɔːlpɔɪnt-] n (caneta) esferográfica.

**ballroom** ['bɔːlrum] n salão m de baile.

**balmy** ['bɑːmɪ] adj (breeze, air) suave, fragrante; (col) = **barmy**.

**Baltic** ['bɔːltɪk] n: **the ~ (Sea)** o (Mar) Báltico.

**balustrade** ['bæləstreɪd] n balaustrada.

**bamboo** [bæm'buː] n bambu m.

**ban** [bæn] n proibição f, interdição f // vt proibir, interditar; (exclude) excluir.

**banal** [bə'nɑːl] adj banal, vulgar.

**banana** [bə'nɑːnə] n banana.

**band** [bænd] n (group) bando, banda; (gang) quadrilha, bando; (strip) faixa, cinta; (at a dance) orquestra; (MIL) banda; **to ~ together** vi juntar-se, associar-se.

**bandage** ['bændɪdʒ] n atadura; (Pt) ligadura // vt enfaixar.

**bandit** ['bændɪt] n bandido; one-armed ~ caça-níqueis m inv; (Pt) máquina de tragar.

**bandstand** ['bændstænd] n coreto.

**bandwagon** ['bændwægən] n: **to jump on the ~** (fig) seguir a corrente or a moda.

**bandy** ['bændɪ] vt (jokes, insults) trocar.

**bandy-legged** ['bændɪ'legd] adj cambaio, de perna torta, cambota.

**bang** [bæŋ] n estalo; (of door) estrondo; (blow) pancada // vt bater com força; (door) fechar com violência // vi produzir estrondo; **to**

~ **upon** bater com força em.

**banger** ['bæŋə*] n (car: gen: old ~) calhambeque m, carroça.

**bangle** ['bæŋgl] n bracelete m, pulseira.

**banish** ['bænɪʃ] vt desterrar, exilar; banir.

**banister(s)** ['bænɪstə(z)] n(pl) corrimão m.

**banjo** ['bændʒəu], pl ~**es** or ~**s** n banjo.

**bank** [bæŋk] n (COMM) banco; (of river, lake) borda, margem f; (of earth) rampa, ladeira // vi (AVIAT) ladear-se; **to ~ on** vt fus contar com; **to ~ with** ter a conta com; ~ **account** n conta bancária; ~**er** n banqueiro; **B~ holiday** n feriado nacional; ~**ing** n transações f pl bancárias; ~**note** n nota; ~ **rate** n (Br) taxa bancária.

**bankrupt** ['bæŋkrʌpt] n falido/a, quebrado/a // adj falido, quebrado; **to go ~** falir; **to be ~** estar falido/quebrado; ~**cy** n falência; (fraudulent) bancarrota.

**banner** ['bænə*] n bandeira; (in demonstration) estandarte m.

**banns** [bænz] npl proclamas f pl.

**banquet** ['bæŋkwɪt] n banquete m.

**baptism** ['bæptɪzəm] n batismo (Pt: -pt-).

**baptize** [bæp'taɪz] vt batizar (Pt: -pt-).

**bar** [bɑː*] n (gen, MUS) barra; (of window etc) tranca; (of soap) sabão m; (fig: hindrance) obstáculo; (prohibition) impedimento; (pub) bar m; (counter: in pub) balcão m // vt (road) obstruir; (window) trancar; (person) excluir; (activity) proibir; **behind ~s** na prisão; **the B~** (LAW) (profession) a advocacia; (people) o corpo de advogados; ~ **none** sem exceção (Pt: -pç-).

**barbaric** [bɑː'bærɪk] adj bárbaro.

**barbarous** ['bɑːbərəs] adj bárbaro.

**barbecue** ['bɑːbɪkjuː] n churrasco.

**barbed wire** ['bɑːbd-] n arame m farpado.

**barber** ['bɑːbə*] n barbeiro, cabeleireiro.

**barbiturate** [bɑː'bitjurit] n barbitúrico.

**bare** [beə*] adj nu; (head) descoberto // vt desnudar, descobrir; **to ~ one's teeth** mostrar os dentes; **~back** adv em pêlo, sem arreios; **~faced** adj descarado; **~foot** adj, adv descalço; **~ly** adv apenas, mal.

**bargain** ['bɑːgin] n contrato, negócio; (good buy) pechincha // vi negociar; (haggle) regatear; **into the ~** ainda por cima.

**barge** [bɑːdʒ] n barcaça; **to ~ in** vi entrar sem permissão; **to ~ into** vt fus (collide with) atropelar (interrupt) intrometer-se.

**baritone** ['bæritəun] n barítono.

**bark** [bɑːk] n (of tree) casca; (of dog) latido // vi ladrar, latir.

**barley** ['bɑːli] n cevada.

**barmaid** ['bɑːmeid] n garçonete f; (Pt) empregada (de bar).

**barman** ['bɑːmən] n garçom m; (Pt) empregado (de bar).

**barmy** ['bɑːmi] adj (col) maluco.

**barn** [bɑːn] n celeiro.

**barnacle** ['bɑːnəkl] n craca f.

**barometer** [bə'rɔmitə*] n barômetro.

**baron** ['bærən] n barão m; **~ess** n baronesa.

**barracks** ['bærəks] npl quartel m, caserna.

**barrage** ['bærɑːʒ] n (MIL) fogo de barragem; (dam) barragem f.

**barrel** ['bærəl] n barril m, barrica; (of gun) cano.

**barren** ['bærən] adj (sterile) estéril; (land) árido.

**barricade** [bæri'keid] n barricada // vt barricar.

**barrier** ['bæriə*] n barreira; (obstacle) obstáculo.

**barring** ['bɑːriŋ] prep exceto (Pt: -pt-), salvo.

**barrister** ['bæristə*] n advogado/a.

**barrow** ['bærəu] n (cart) carrinho (de mão).

**bartender** ['bɑːtendə*] n (US) garçom m, (Pt) empregado (de bar).

**barter** ['bɑːtə*] vt: **to ~ sth for sth** trocar algo por algo.

**base** [beis] n base f // vt: **to ~ sth on** basear or fundamentar algo em // adj baixo, inferior; **~ball** n beisebol m; **~ment** n porão m, subsolo.

**bash** [bæʃ] vt (col) sovar, dar uma surra a or bova.

**bashful** ['bæʃful] adj tímido, envergonhado.

**bashing** ['bæʃiŋ] n (col) sova, surra.

**basic** ['beisik] adj básico; **~ally** adv fundamentalmente, basicamente.

**basil** ['bæzl] n manjericão m.

**basin** ['beisn] n (vessel) bacia, tigela; (GEO) bacia; (also: **wash~**) pia.

**basis** ['beisis], pl **-ses** [-siːz] n base f.

**bask** [bɑːsk] vi: **to ~ in the sun** pegar sol; (Pt) tomar o sol.

**basket** ['bɑːskit] n cesto; (with handle) cesta; **~ball** n basquete(bol) m; **~work** n obra de verga, trabalho de vime.

**Basque** [bæsk] adj, n basco/a; **~ Country** País m Basco.

**bass** [beis] n (MUS) baixo; (fish) robalo, perca.

**bassoon** [bə'suːn] n fagote m.

**bastard** ['bɑːstəd] n bastardo/a.

**baste** [beist] vt (CULIN) untar.

**bastion** ['bæstiən] n baluarte m.

**bat** [bæt] n (ZOOL) morcego; (for ball games) bastão m; (for cricket, baseball) bastão m; (for table tennis) raquete f; **he didn't ~ an eyelid** ele nem pistanejou.

**batch** [bætʃ] n (of bread) fornada;

(*pile of papers*) monte *m*; (*lot*) remessa.

**bated** ['beitid] *adj*: with ~ **breath** contendo a respiração.

**bath** [bɑːθ, *pl* bɑːðz] *n* (~*tub*) banho, banheira; (*also*: ~**s** *pl*) banhos, piscina // *vt* banhar; **to have a** ~ tomar um banho; ~**chair** *n* cadeira de rodas.

**bathe** [beið] *vi* banhar-se // *vt* banhar, lavar; **bather** *n* banhista *m/f*.

**bathing** ['beiðiŋ] *n* banho; ~ **cap** *n* touca de banho; ~ **costume** *n* roupa de banho; (*Pt*) fato de banho; (*woman's*) maiô *m*; ~ **trunks** *npl* calção *msg* de banho, sunga.

**bath**: ~**mat** *n* tapete *m* de borracha; ~**room** *n* quarto de banho, banheiro; (*Pt*) casa de banho; ~**s** *npl* piscina *sg*; ~ **towel** *n* toalha de banho.

**baton** ['bætən] *n* (*MUS*) batuta.

**battalion** [bə'tæliən] *n* batalhão *m*.

**batter** ['bætə*] *vt* espancar, bater / *n* massa; ~**ed** *adj* (*hat, pan*) amassado, muito usado.

**battery** ['bætəri] *n* bateria; (*of torch*) pilha.

**battle** ['bætl] *n* batalha; (*fig*) luta // *vi* lutar; ~**field** *n* campo de batalha; ~**ments** *npl* ameias *fpl*; ~**ship** *n* couraçado.

**bawdy** ['bɔːdi] *adj* indecente; (*joke*) imoral.

**bawl** [bɔːl] *vi* gritar, berrar.

**bay** [bei] *n* (*GEO*) baía; (*BOT*) louro // *vi* ladrar; **to hold sb at** ~ manter alguém a distância.

**bayonet** ['beiənit] *n* baioneta.

**bay window** ['bei-] *n* janela saliente.

**bazaar** [bə'zɑː*] *n* bazar *m*.

**bazooka** [bə'zuːkə] *n* bazuca.

**b. & b., B. & B.** *abbr of* **bed and breakfast** cama e café da manhã; (*Pt*) cama e pequeno almoço.

**BBC** *n abbr of* **British Broad-**

**casting Corporation.**

**B.C.** *adv abbr of* **before Christ** antes de Cristo, a.c.

**be** [biː] *pt* **was, were,** *pp* **been** *vi* (*of permanent place/state*) ser; (*of temporary place/condition*) estar; **I am English** sou inglês; **I am tired** estou cansado; **how are you?** como está?; **who is it?** quem é?; **it is raining** está chovendo; **I am warm** estou com calor; **it is cold** está frio; **where is the bank?** onde é o banco?; **how much is it?** quanto é *or* custa?; **he is four** (*years old*) tem quatro anos; **2 and 2 are 4** dois e dois são quatro; **where have you been?** onde tem estado?, onde você estava?

**beach** [biːtʃ] *n* praia // *vt* puxar para a terra *or* praia, encalhar.

**beacon** ['biːkən] *n* (*lighthouse*) farol *m*; (*marker*) guia.

**bead** [biːd] *n* (*necklace*) conta; (*of sweat*) gota.

**beak** [biːk] *n* bico.

**beaker** ['biːkə*] *n* copo com bico.

**beam** [biːm] *n* (*ARCH*) viga; (*of light*) raio; (*NAUT*) través *m* // *vi* brilhar; (*smile*) sorrir; ~**ing** *adj* (*sun, smile*) radiante.

**bean** [biːn] *n* feijão *m*; **runner** ~ feijão *or* verde; **broad** ~ vagem *f*; (*Pt*) fava; **coffee** ~ grão *m* de café.

**bear** [bɛə*] *n* urso // (*vb*: *pt* **bore,** *pp* **borne**) *vt* (*weight etc*) levar; (*cost*) pagar; (*responsibility*) ter; (*endure*) suportar, agüentar; (*stand up to*) resistir a; (*children*) ter, dar à luz / *vi*: **to** ~ **right/left** virar à direita/à esquerda; ~**able** *adj* suportável, tolerável.

**beard** [biəd] *n* barba; ~**ed** *adj* barbado.

**bearing** ['bɛəriŋ] *n* porte *m*, comportamento; (*position*) posição *f*; (*connection*) relação *f*; (*ball*) ~ *n* rolamento de esferas; ~**s** *npl* orientação *f*; **to take a** ~ orientar-se; **to find one's** ~**s** encontrar o rumo.

**beast** [biːst] n besta, animal m; (col) bruto, selvagem m; **~ly** adj bestial; (awful) horrível.

**beat** [biːt] n batida; (MUS) ritmo, compasso; (of policeman) ronda // (vb: pt **beat**, pp **beaten**) vt (hit) golpear; (eggs) bater; (defeat) vencer, derrotar; (better) ultrapassar; (drum) tocar; (rhythm) marcar // vi (heart) bater; to ~ **about the bush** fazer rodeios; to ~ **it** ir embora; to ~ **off** vt repelir; to ~ **up** vt (col: person) dar uma sova em; ~**er** n (for eggs, cream) batedeira; ~**ing** n batida; (of person) sova, surra.

**beautiful** ['bjuːtiful] adj belo, lindo, formoso; ~**ly** adv maravilhosamente, lindamente; **beautify** [-faɪ] vt embelezar.

**beauty** ['bjuːti] n beleza, formosura; (person) beldade f, beleza; ~ **salon** n salão m de beleza; ~ **spot** n 'sinal' m (de beleza na pele); (TOURISM) lugar m de beleza excepcional.

**beaver** ['biːvəʳ] n castor m.

**becalmed** [bɪ'kɑːmd] adj parado devido a calmaria.

**became** [bɪ'keɪm] pt of **become**.

**because** [bɪ'kɔz] conj porque; ~ **of** prep por causa de.

**beck** [bɛk] n: to be at the ~ and **call of** estar às ordens de.

**beckon** ['bɛkən] vt (also: ~ **to**) chamar com sinais, acenar para.

**become** [bɪ'kʌm] (irr: like **come**) vi (suit) favorecer, ficar bem // vi (+ noun) fazer-se, tornar-se; (+ adj) tornar-se, ficar; to ~ **fat** engordar-se.

**becoming** [bɪ'kʌmɪŋ] adj (behaviour) decoroso; (clothes) favorecedor(a), elegante.

**bed** [bɛd] n cama; (of flowers) canteiro m; (of coal, clay) camada, base f; to **go to** ~ ir dormir; **single/double** ~ cama de solteiro/de casal; ~**clothes** npl

**bedlam** ['bɛdləm] n confusão f.

**bedraggled** [bɪ'dræɡld] adj molhado, ensopado; (dirty) enlameado.

**bed:** ~**ridden** adj acamado; ~**room** n quarto de dormir; ~**side** n: at sb's ~**side** à cabeceira de alguém; ~**sit(ter)** n kitinete f, kitchinete f; ~**spread** n colcha.

**bee** [biː] n abelha.

**beech** [biːtʃ] n faia.

**beef** [biːf] n carne f de vaca; **roast** ~ rosbife m.

**bee:** ~**hive** n colméia; ~**line** n: to **make a ~line** for ir direto a.

**been** [biːn] pp of **be**.

**beer** [biəʳ] n cerveja.

**beetle** ['biːtl] n besouro.

**beetroot** ['biːtruːt] n beterraba.

**before** [bɪ'fɔːʳ] prep (of time) antes de; (of space) diante de // conj antes que // adv (time) antes, anteriormente; (space) diante, adiante; **the week** ~ a semana anterior; **I've never seen it** ~ nunca vi isso antes.

**befriend** [bɪ'frɛnd] vt fazer amizade com; fazer-se amigo de.

**beg** [bɛg] vi pedir, rogar; (as beggar) pedir esmola // vt pedir, rogar por; (entreat) suplicar.

**began** [bɪ'ɡæn] pt of **begin**.

**beggar** ['bɛgəʳ] n mendigo.

**begin** [bɪ'ɡɪn] pt **began**, pp **begun** vt/i começar, principiar; ~**ner** n principiante m/f; ~**ning** n princípio, começo.

**begrudge** [bɪ'ɡrʌdʒ] vt: to ~ **sb sth** invejar algo de alguém.

**begun** [bɪ'ɡʌn] pp of **begin**.

**behalf** [bɪ'hɑːf] n: **on** ~ **of** em nome de, em favor de.

**behave** [bɪ'heɪv] vi (person) portar-se, comportar-se; (thing) funcionar; (well: also: ~ **o.s.**) comportar-se (bem); **behaviour, behavior** (US) n comportamento, conduta.

**behind** [bɪˈhaɪnd] prep atrás de // adv atrás, detrás, para trás // n traseiro; ~ **time** atrasado.

**behold** [bɪˈhəuld] (irr: like hold) vt contemplar.

**beige** [beɪʒ] adj bege.

**being** [ˈbiːɪŋ] n (state) existência; (entity) ser m; **to come into** ~ nascer, aparecer.

**belated** [bɪˈleɪtɪd] adj atrasado, tardio.

**belch** [beltʃ] vi arrotar // vt (gen: ~ **out**: smoke etc) vomitar.

**belfry** [ˈbelfrɪ] n campanário.

**Belgian** [ˈbeldʒən] adj, n belga m/f.

**Belgium** [ˈbeldʒəm] n Bélgica.

**belie** [bɪˈlaɪ] vt desmentir, contradizer.

**belief** [bɪˈliːf] n (opinion) opinião f; (trust, faith) fé f; (acceptance as true) crença, convicção f.

**believable** [bɪˈliːvəbl] adj crível, acreditável.

**believe** [bɪˈliːv] vt/i crer, acreditar; **believer** n crente m/f, fiel m/f, (POL) partidário m.

**belittle** [bɪˈlɪtl] vt diminuir, depreciar.

**bell** [bel] n sino; (small, door) campainha; (animal's, on toy) guizo, sininho.

**belligerent** [bɪˈlɪdʒərənt] adj (at war) beligerante; (fig) agressivo.

**bellow** [ˈbeləu] vi berrar, mugir; (person) bramar // vt (orders) gritar, berrar.

**bellows** [ˈbeləuz] npl fole m.

**belly** [ˈbelɪ] n barriga, ventre m.

**belong** [bɪˈlɒŋ] vi: **to** ~ **to** pertencer a; (club etc) ser sócio de; ~**ings** npl bens mpl.

**beloved** [bɪˈlʌvɪd] adj, n querido, amado.

**below** [bɪˈləu] prep abaixo de, debaixo de // adv em baixo; **see** ~ ver abaixo.

**belt** [belt] n cinto; (MED) faixa; (TECH) correia, cinta // vt (thrash) surrar; ~**way** n (US) via circular.

**bench** [bentʃ] n banco; **the B**~ (LAW) tribunal m; (people) magistratura.

**bend** [bend], pt, pp **bent** vt dobrar, curvar; (leg, arm) dobrar // vi dobrar-se, inclinar-se // n (in road) curva; (in pipe, river) ângulo, curva; **to** ~ **down** vi dobrar-se; **to** ~ **over** vi inclinar-se.

**beneath** [bɪˈniːθ] prep abaixo de, em baixo de, debaixo de (Pt); (unworthy of) indigno de // adv em baixo.

**benefactor** [ˈbenɪfæktə*] n benfeitor(a) m/f.

**beneficial** [benɪˈfɪʃəl] adj proveitoso, benéfico.

**benefit** [ˈbenɪfɪt] n benefício, proveito; (profit) bonificação f; (money) subsídio // vt beneficiar, aproveitar // vi: **he'll** ~ **from it** há-de beneficiar-se disso.

**Benelux** [ˈbenɪlʌks] n Benelux m.

**benevolent** [bɪˈnevələnt] adj benévolo.

**bent** [bent] pt, pp of bend // n inclinação f; **to have a** ~ **for** queda para // adj: **to be** ~ **on** estar empenhado em.

**bequeath** [bɪˈkwiːð] vt legar.

**bequest** [bɪˈkwest] n legado.

**bereaved** [bɪˈriːvd] n: **the** ~ os enlutados mpl; **bereavement** [-ˈriːvmənt] n privação f, luto.

**beret** [ˈbereɪ] n boina.

**berm** [bəːm] n (US) berma.

**berry** [ˈberɪ] n baga.

**berserk** [bəˈsəːk] adj: **to go** ~ perder as estribeiras.

**berth** [bəːθ] n (bed) cama; (cabin) beliche m; (for ship) ancoradouro // vi ancorar, prover com beliche.

**beseech** [bɪˈsiːtʃ], pt, pp **besought** [-ˈsɔːt] vt suplicar.

**beset** [bɪˈset], pt, pp **beset** vt assediar; (person) acossar.

**beside** [bɪˈsaɪd] prep junto de, ao lado de, ao pé de; **to be** ~ **o.s.** (with anger) estar fora de si.

**besides** [bɪ'saɪdz] *adv* além disso // *prep* (*as well as*) além de; (*except*) salvo, exceto (*Pt:* -pt-).

**besiege** [bɪ'si:dʒ] *vt* (*town*) sitiar, pôr cerco a; (*fig*) assediar.

**best** [bɛst] *adj* melhor // *adv* (o) melhor; **the ~ part of** (*quantity*) a maior parte de; **at ~** quando muito; **to make the ~ of sth** tirar o maior partido possível de algo; **to the ~ of my knowledge** que eu saiba; **to the ~ of my ability** o melhor que eu puder; **~ man** *n* padrinho de casamento.

**bestow** [bɪ'stəʊ] *vt* outorgar; (*affection*) dar, oferecer.

**bestseller** ['bɛst'sɛlə*] *n* sucesso de vendagem, best-seller *m*.

**bet** [bɛt] *n* aposta // *vt/i, pt, pp* **bet** or **betted** apostar, jogar.

**betray** [bɪ'treɪ] *vt* trair, atraiçoar; (*denounce*) delatar; **~al** *n* traição *f*.

**better** ['bɛtə*] *adj, adv* melhor // *vt* melhorar; (*go above*) superar // *n*: **to get the ~ of** levar vantagem sobre, levar a melhor; **you had ~ do it** é melhor você fazer isso; **he thought ~ of it** pensou melhor, mudou de opinião; **to get ~** melhorar(-se); (*MED*) recuperar-se; **~ off** *adj* em melhor situação.

**betting** ['bɛtɪŋ] *n* jogo, aposta; **~ shop** *n* agência de apostas.

**between** [bɪ'twi:n] *prep* no meio de, entre; **~ you and me** cá entre nós, aqui entre nós // *adv* no meio.

**beverage** ['bɛvərɪdʒ] *n* bebida.

**bevy** ['bɛvɪ] *n*: **a ~ of** um grupo/bando de.

**beware** [bɪ'wɛə*] *vi*: **to ~ (of)** precaver-se (de), ter cuidado (com) // *excl* cuidado!

**bewildered** [bɪ'wɪldəd] *adj* perturbado, perplexo.

**bewitching** [bɪ'wɪtʃɪŋ] *adj* feiticeiro, encantador(a), sedutor(a).

**beyond** [bɪ'jɔnd] *prep* (*in space*) além de; (*exceeding*) acima de, fora

de; (*above*) superior a; **~ doubt** fora de dúvida; **~ repair** irreparável; **~ reach** fora do alcance // *adv* além, mais longe.

**bias** ['baɪəs] *n* (*prejudice*) preconceito, prevenção *f*; (*preference*) inclinação *f*; **~(s)ed** *adj* (*against*) preconceituoso (contra); (*towards*) parcial.

**bib** [bɪb] *n* babadouro, babador *m*.

**Bible** ['baɪbl] *n* Bíblia.

**bibliography** [bɪblɪ'ɔgrəfɪ] *n* bibliografia.

**bicker** ['bɪkə*] *vi* discutir.

**bicycle** ['baɪsɪkl] *n* bicicleta.

**bid** [bɪd] *n* (*at auction*) oferta, lance *m*; (*attempt*) tentativa // *vb*: *pt* **bade** [bæd] *or* **bid**, *pp* **bidden** ['bɪdn] *or* **bid**) *vi* fazer uma oferta; (*COMM*) licitar, lançar // *vt* mandar, ordenar; **to ~ sb good day** desejar bom dia a alguém; **~der** *n* (*COMM*) licitante *m*; **the highest ~der** quem oferece mais; **~ding** *n* (*at auction*) lance *m*; (*COMM*) licitação *f*; (*order*) ordem *f*.

**bide** [baɪd] *vt*: **to ~ one's time** esperar o momento adequado.

**bidet** ['bi:deɪ] *n* bidé *m*.

**bier** [bɪə*] *n* féretro.

**big** [bɪg] *adj* grande; (*important*) importante; (*error*) grave.

**bigamy** ['bɪgəmɪ] *n* bigamia.

**bigheaded** ['bɪg'hɛdɪd] *adj* vaidoso.

**bigot** ['bɪgət] *n* fanático, intolerante *m/f*; **~ed** *adj* fanático, intolerante; **~ry** *n* fanatismo, intolerância.

**bike** [baɪk] *n* bicicleta.

**bikini** [bɪ'ki:nɪ] *n* biquíni *m*.

**bile** [baɪl] *n* bílis *f*.

**bilingual** [baɪ'lɪŋgwəl] *adj* bilíngüe.

**bill** [bɪl] *n* (*account*) conta; (*invoice*) fatura (*Pt:* -ct-); (*POL*) projeto (*Pt:* -ct-) de lei; (*US: banknote*) bilhete *m*, nota; (*of bird*) bico; **stick no ~s** é proibido afixar cartazes.

**billet** ['bɪlɪt] *n* alojamento.

**billfold** ['bɪlfəʊld] *n* (*US*) carteira para notas.

**billiards** ['bɪlɪədz] n bilhar m.

**billion** ['bɪlɪən] n (Brit:=1,000,000,000,000) trilhão m; (US:=1,000,000,000) bilhão m.

**billy goat** ['bɪlɪ-] n bode m.

**bin** [bɪn] n (gen) caixa; **bread/litter** ~ cesta de pão/lata de lixo.

**bind** [baɪnd] pt, pp **bound** vt atar, ligar; (wound) pôr atadura em, pensar; (book) encadernar; (oblige) obrigar; ~**ing** adj (contract) sujeitante.

**binge** [bɪndʒ] n bebedeira, farra.

**bingo** ['bɪŋɡəu] n bingo.

**binoculars** [bɪ'nɔkjuləz] n binóculo msg.

**bio...** [baɪə] pref: ~**chemistry** n bioquímica; ~**graphy** [baɪ'ɔɡrəfɪ] n biografia; ~**logical** adj biológico; ~**logy** [baɪ'ɔlədʒɪ] n biologia.

**birch** [bɜːtʃ] n bétula; (cane) vara de vidoeiro.

**bird** [bɜːd] n ave f, pássaro m; (col: girl) menina, moça; ~**cage** n gaiola; ~'**s eye view** n vista aérea or geral; ~ **watcher** n ornitófilo.

**birth** [bɜːθ] n nascimento m; (MED) parto; **to give** ~ **to** dar à luz; ~**certificate** n certidão m de nascimento; ~ **control** n controle m de natalidade; (methods) métodos mpl anticoncepcionais; ~**day** n aniversário; (Pt) dia m de anos; ~**place** n lugar m de nascimento; ~**rate** n índice m de natalidade.

**biscuit** ['bɪskɪt] n bolacha, biscoito.

**bisect** [baɪ'sɛkt] vt dividir ao meio.

**bishop** ['bɪʃəp] n bispo.

**bit** [bɪt] pt of **bite** // n pedaço, bocado; (of horse) freio; **a** ~ **of** um pouco de; **a** ~ **mad** um pouco doido; ~ **by** ~ pouco a pouco.

**bitch** [bɪtʃ] n (dog) cadela, cachorra.

**bite** [baɪt] pt **bit**, pp **bitten** vt/i morder; (insect etc) picar // n mordedura; (insect ~) picadura; (mouthful) bocado; **let's have a** ~ (**to eat**) vamos comer algo.

**biting** ['baɪtɪŋ] adj cortante; (wind) penetrante; (sharp) mordaz.

**bitten** ['bɪtn] pp of **bite**.

**bitter** ['bɪtə*] adj amargo; (wind, criticism) cortante, penetrante; (battle) encarniçado // n (beer) cerveja amarga; ~**ness** n amargor m; (anger) rancor m.

**bizarre** [bɪ'zɑː*] adj esquisito.

**blab** [blæb] vi chocalhar, dar à língua, dar/bater com a língua nos dentes // vt (also: ~ **out**) revelar, chocalhar.

**black** [blæk] adj (colour) negro, preto; (dark) escuro, sombrio // n negro, preto; (colour) cor f preta // vt (shoes) lustrar; (Pt) engraxar; (INDUSTRY) boicotar; **to give sb a** ~ **eye** dar um soco em alguém (no olho), (col) engraxar alguém; ~ **and blue** adj contuso, contundido; ~**berry** n amora preta; (Pt) amora silvestre; ~**bird** n melro; ~**board** n quadro(-negro); ~**currant** n groselha negra; ~**en** vt enegrecer; (fig) denegrir; ~ **jack** n (US) vinte-e-um m; ~ **leg** n fura-greve m; ~**list** n lista negra; ~**mail** n chantagem f // vt fazer chantagem a; ~**mailer** n chantagista m/f; ~ **market** n mercado or câmbio negro; ~**out** n blecaute m; (fainting) desmaio; ~**smith** n ferreiro.

**bladder** ['blædə*] n bexiga.

**blade** [bleɪd] n folha; (cutting edge) lâmina; **a** ~ **of grass** uma folha de relva.

**blame** [bleɪm] n culpa // vt: **to** ~ **sb for sth** culpar alguém por algo; **to be to** ~ ter a culpa; ~**less** adj (person) inocente.

**bland** [blænd] adj suave; (taste) brando.

**blank** [blæŋk] adj em branco; (shot) sem bala; (look) sem expressão // n lacuna, espaço em branco; (cartridge) cartucho sem bala; **a** ~ de festim.

**blanket** ['blæŋkɪt] n cobertor m,

manta // vt cobrir, tapar.

**blare** [blɛə*] vi (horn) buzinar.

**blasé** ['blɑːzeɪ] adj indiferente.

**blasphemy** ['blæsfɪmɪ] n blasfêmia.

**blast** [blɑːst] n (of wind) rajada; pé-de-vento m; (of whistle) toque m; (of explosive) explosão f; (force) choque m // vt (blow up) fazer voar; (blow open) abrir com uma carga explosiva; ~ **furnace** n alto forno; ~**-off** n (SPACE) lançamento.

**blatant** ['bleɪtənt] adj descarado.

**blaze** [bleɪz] n (fire) fogo; (flames) chamas fpl; (fig) explosão f // vi (fire) arder; (fig) resplandecer // vt: **to** ~ **a trail** (fig) abrir (um) caminho.

**blazer** ['bleɪzə*] n casaco esportivo, blazer m.

**bleach** [bliːtʃ] n (also: **household** ~) lixívia // vt (linen) branquear; ~**ed** adj (hair) oxigenado; (linen) alvejante.

**bleak** [bliːk] adj (countryside) desolado; (prospect) desanimador(a).

**bleary-eyed** ['blɪərɪ'aɪd] adj remelenta, de olhos cansados, (Br) olho-de-peixe-morto.

**bleat** [bliːt] vi balir.

**bleed** [bliːd], pt, pp **bled** [blɛd] vt/i sangrar.

**blemish** ['blemɪʃ] n mancha, falha.

**blend** [blɛnd] n mistura // vt misturar // vi (colours etc) combinar-se, misturar-se.

**bless** [blɛs], pt, pp **blessed** or **blest** [blɛst] vt abençoar; ~**ing** n bênção f; (advantage) benefício, vantagem f.

**blew** [bluː] pt of **blow**.

**blight** [blaɪt] vt (hopes etc) frustrar, gorar.

**blimey** ['blaɪmɪ] excl (col) meu Deus!

**blind** [blaɪnd] adj cego // n (for window) persiana f // vt cegar;

(dazzle) deslumbrar; ~ **alley** n beco-sem-saída m; ~ **corner** n canto oculto; ~**fold** n venda // adj, adv com os olhos vendados, às cegas // vt vendar os olhos a; ~**ly** adv às cegas, cegamente; ~**ness** n cegueira; ~ **spot** n ponto cego.

**blink** [blɪŋk] vi piscar; (light) cintilar, piscar; ~**ers** npl (AUT) luzes fpl intermitentes, farois mpl pisca-pisca, pisca-pisca m; (horse) antolhos mpl.

**blinking** ['blɪŋkɪŋ] adj (col): **this** ~... este danado..., este infame...

**bliss** [blɪs] n felicidade f; (fig) êxtase m.

**blister** ['blɪstə*] n (on skin) bolha, empola // vi (paint) empolar-se; ~**ing** adj (heat) causticante.

**blithe** [blaɪð] adj alegre.

**blithering** ['blɪðərɪŋ] adj (col): **this** ~ **idiot** esta besta quadrada.

**blitz** [blɪts] n bombardeio aéreo.

**blizzard** ['blɪzəd] n nevasca.

**bloated** ['bləʊtɪd] adj inchado.

**blob** [blɒb] n (drop) gota; (stain, spot) mancha.

**block** [blɒk] n bloco; (in pipes) entupimento; (of buildings) quarteirão m // vt (gen) obstruir, bloquear; (progress) impedir; ~**ade** [-'keɪd] n bloqueio // vt bloquear; ~**age** n estorvo, obstrução f; ~ **of flats** n prédio de apartamentos; ~ **letters** npl letras fpl maiúsculas.

**bloke** [bləʊk] n (col) cara m, tipo, sujeito; (Pt) gajo.

**blond(e)** [blɒnd] adj, n louro/a.

**blood** [blʌd] n sangue m; ~ **donor** n doador(a) m/f de sangue; ~ **group** n grupo sanguíneo; ~ **hound** n sabujo; ~ **pressure** n pressão f sanguínea; ~**shed** n matança; ~ **shot** adj injetado (Pt: -ct-); ~**stained** adj manchado de sangue; ~**stream** n corrente f sanguínea; ~**thirsty** adj sanguinário; ~ **transfusion** n transfusão f de sangue; ~**y** adj sangrento, miserável, desgraçado;

(col!): this ~y... esse maldito/infame..., esse puto de...; ~y strong/good (col!) terrìvelmente forte/bom; ~y-minded adj (col) mal-intencionado.

bloom [blu:m] n flor f; (fig) florescimento, viço // vi florescer; ~ing adj (col): this ~ing... esse maldito..., esse miserável....

blossom ['blɔsəm] n flor f // vi florescer; (fig) desabrochar-se.

blot [blɔt] n borrão m // vt secar; (ink) manchar; to ~ out vt (view) apagar, ocultar.

blotchy ['blɔtʃi] adj (complexion) cheio de manchas.

blotting paper ['blɔtiŋ-] n mata-borrão m.

blouse [blauz] n blusa.

blow [bləu] n golpe m // (vb: pt blew, pp blown [bləun]) vi soprar // vt (glass) soprar; (fuse) queimar; (instrument) tocar; to ~ one's nose assoar; to ~ away vt levar, arrancar; to ~ down vt derrubar; to ~ off vt levar; to ~ out vt apagar; to ~ over vi passar, ser esquecido; to ~ up vi explodir; (fig) perder a paciência // vt dinamitar; (tyre) encher; (PHOT) ampliar; ~lamp n maçarico; ~-out n (of tyre) furo, estouro.

blubber ['blʌbə*] n óleo de baleia // vi (pej) chorar.

blue [blu:] adj azul, campânula; ~ film/joke filme/anedota picante; to have the ~s sentir-se melancólico; ~bell n campainha (azul), campânula; ~bottle n varejeira azul; ~ jeans npl jeans mpl, calça 'lee'; ~print n anteprojeto (Pt: -ct-).

bluff [blʌf] vi enganar, mentir // n blefe m; (crag) penhasco.

blunder ['blʌndə*] n erro crasso, asneira, disparate m // vi cometer um erro crasso.

blunt [blʌnt] adj boto, embotado; ~erson) franco, direto (Pt: -ct-) //

vt embotar; ~ness n (of person) franqueza, rudeza.

blur [blə:*] n borrão m, nebulosidade f // vt borrar, nublar.

blurt [blə:t]: ~ out vt (say) deixar escapar, dizer impensadamente.

blush [blʌʃ] vi corar, ruborizar-se // n rubor m, vermelhidão f.

blustering ['blʌstəriŋ] adj (person) fanfarrão/rona.

blustery ['blʌstəri] adj (weather) borrascoso, tormentoso.

board [bɔ:d] n tábua; (on wall) quadro; (for chess etc) tabuleiro; (committee) junta, conselho; (in firm) diretoria (Pt: -ct-), conselho administrativo // vt (ship) embarcar; (train) embarcar em; full ~ pensão f completa; to go by the ~ (fig) ficar abandonado; to ~ up (door) guarnecer de tábuas; ~ and lodging n pensão f; ~er n hóspede m/f; (SCOL) interno; ~ing house n pensão m; ~ing pass n (US) cartão m de embarque; ~ing school n internato; ~ room n gabinete m da diretoria da administração.

boast [bəust] vi gabar-se, jactar-se // vt ostentar // n jactância, bazófia; ~ful adj vaidoso, jactancioso.

boat [bəut] n barco, bote m; (big) navio; ~er n (hat) chapéu m de palha; ~ing n (esporte) remo; ~man n barqueiro; ~swain ['bəusn] n contramestre m.

bob [bɔb] vi (boat, cork on water: also: ~ up and down) balouçar-se; to ~ up vi aparecer, surgir // n (col) = shilling.

bobbin ['bɔbin] n (of sewing machine) bobina, carretel m.

bobby ['bɔbi] n (col) polícia m/f; (Br) tira m/f.

bobsleigh ['bɔbslei] n bob m, trenó duplo.

bodice ['bɔdis] n corpete m.

bodily ['bɔdili] adj corpóreo,

corporal // adv (in person) em pessoa; (lift) em peso.

**body** ['bɔdɪ] n corpo; (corpse) cadáver m; (of car) carroçaria; (fig: society) conjunto; (fig: quantity) parte f principal; **in a** ~ todos juntos; ~**guard** n guarda-costas m inv; ~**work** n lanternagem f; (Pt) carroçaria.

**bog** [bɔg] n pântano, atoleiro // vt: **to get** ~**ged down** (fig) atolar-se.

**boggle** ['bɔgl] vi: **the mind** ~**s** que confusão!

**bogus** ['bougəs] adj falso; (person) fingido, farsante.

**boil** [bɔɪl] vt cozer; (eggs) cozinhar // vi ferver // n (MED) furúnculo; **to come to the** ~ começar a ferver; **to** ~ **down to** (fig) reduzir-se a; ~**er** n caldeira; ~**er suit** n macacão m; ~**ing point** n ponto de ebulição.

**boisterous** ['bɔɪstərəs] adj (noisy) barulhento; (excitable) agitado; (crowd) turbulento.

**bold** [bould] adj (brave) valente, audaz; (excessively) atrevido; (pej) descarado; (outline, colour) forte; ~**ness** n arrojo, coragem f; (cheek) audácia, descaramento.

**Bolivia** [bə'lɪvɪə] n Bolívia; ~**n** adj, n boliviano/a.

**bollard** ['bɔləd] n (AUT) poste m.

**bolster** ['boulstə*] n travesseiro; **to** ~ **up** vt reforçar; (fig) sustentar.

**bolt** [boult] n (lock) trinco, ferrolho; (with nut) parafuso, cavilha // vt (door) fechar a ferrolho, trancar; (food) engolir // vi fugir; (horse) disparar.

**bomb** [bɔm] n bomba // vt bombardear; ~**ard** ['bɑːd] vt bombardear; (fig) assediar; ~**ardment** [-'bɑːdmənt] n bombardeio.

**bombastic** [bɔm'bæstɪk] adj empolado; (person) pomposo.

**bomb**: ~ **disposal** n desmontagem f de explosivos; ~**er** n (AVIAT) bombardeiro; ~**shell** n granada de artilharia; (fig) bomba.

**bona fide** ['bounə'faɪdɪ] adj genuíno, autêntico.

**bond** [bɔnd] n (binding promise) título; (FINANCE) obrigação f; (link) vínculo, laço.

**bondage** [bɔndɪdʒ] n escravidão f.

**bone** [boun] n osso; (of fish) espinha // vt tirar as espinhas de, desossar; ~**dry** adj completamente seco; ~ **idle** adj preguiçoso.

**bonfire** ['bɔnfaɪə*] n fogueira.

**bonnet** ['bɔnɪt] n boina; (Brit: of car) capô f.

**bonus** ['bounəs] n bônus m, prêmio.

**bony** ['bounɪ] adj (arm, face, MED: tissue) ossudo; (meat) cheio de ossos; (fish) cheio de espinhas.

**boo** [buː] vt apupar, vaiar.

**booby trap** ['buːbɪ-] n armadilha com bomba.

**book** [buk] n livro; (notebook) caderno; (of stamps etc) livro; (COMM): ~**s** as contas // vt reservar; (driver) contratar; ~**case** n estante f para livros; ~**ing office** n (RAIL, THEATRE) bilheteria; (Pt) bilheteira; ~**keeping** n escrituração f, contabilidade f; ~**let** n livrinho, brochura; ~**maker** n agenciador m de apostas; ~**seller** n livreiro; ~**shop** n livraria; ~**stall** n banca de livros.

**boom** [buːm] n (noise) barulho, estrondo; (in prices etc) aumento rápido; (ECON) fase f or aumento de prosperidade.

**boomerang** ['buːməræŋ] n bumerangue m.

**boon** [buːn] n benefício.

**boost** [buːst] n estímulo // vt estimular; ~**er** n (MED) revacinação f.

**boot** [buːt] n bota; (Brit: of car) porta-bagagem m // vt dar pontapé em; **to** ~ (in addition) ainda por cima.

**booth** [buːð] n (at fair) barraca, tenda; (telephone ~, voting ~) cabine f.

**booty** ['buːtɪ] n despojos mpl, pilhagem f.

**booze** [buːz] (col) n bebedeira, bebida alcoólica // vi embebedar-se.

**border** ['bɔːdə*] n margem f, borda; (of a country) fronteira // adj fronteiriço; **to ~ on** vt fus limitar-se com; (fig) chegar às raias de; **~line** n (fig) fronteira.

**bore** [bɔː*] pt of **bear** // vt (hole) furar, perfurar; (person) maçar, aborrecer // n (person) chato, maçante; (of gun) calibre m; **what a ~!** que chateação!; (Pt) que maçada!; **~dom** n aborrecimento, tédio.

**boring** ['bɔːrɪŋ] adj aborrecido, maçante, chato.

**born** [bɔːn] adj: **to be ~** nascer; **I was ~ in 1960** nasci em 1960.

**borne** [bɔːn] pp of **bear**.

**borough** ['bʌrə] n município.

**borrow** ['bɔrəu] vt: **to ~ sth (from sb)** pedir algo emprestado a alguém.

**borstal** ['bɔːstl] n reformatório (de menores).

**bosom** ['buzəm] n peito; (fig) seio; **~ friend** n amigo do peito or íntimo.

**boss** [bɔs] n chefe m/f; (employer) patrão/troa m; (agriculture, industry etc) capataz m // vt dar ordens a, mandar; **~y** adj mandão/dona.

**bosun** ['bəusn] n contramestre m.

**botanist** ['bɔtənɪst] n botânico; **botany** [-nɪ] n botânica.

**botch** [bɔtʃ] vt (also: **~ up**) estropiar, atamancar.

**both** [bəuθ] adj, pron ambos, os dois; **~ of us went, we ~ went** nós dois fomos, ambos fomos // adv: **~ A and B** tanto A como B.

**bother** ['bɔðə*] vt (worry) preocupar; (disturb) incomodar, molestar // vi (gen: **~ o.s.**) preocupar-se; **to ~ doing** dar-se o trabalho de fazer; **to ~ about**

preocupar-se com // n: **what a ~!** que chateação! (Pt) que maçada!

**bottle** ['bɔtl] n garrafa; (small) frasco; (baby's) biberão m, (Br) mamadeira // vt engarrafar; **to ~ up** vt conter, refrear; **~neck** n (traffic) engarrafamento; (bottle) gargalo; **~-opener** n abridor m de garrafas; (Pt) abre-garrafas m inv.

**bottom** ['bɔtəm] n (of box, sea) fundo; (buttocks) traseiro; (col) bunda; (of page, list) pé m // adj (low) inferior, mais baixo; (last) último; **~less** adj sem fundo; (fig) insondável.

**bough** [bau] n ramo.

**bought** [bɔːt] pt, pp of **buy**.

**boulder** ['bəuldə*] n pedregulho, matacão m.

**bounce** [bauns] vi (ball) saltar, quicar; (cheque) ser devolvido // vt fazer saltar // n (rebound) salto.

**bound** [baund] pt, pp of **bind** // n (leap) pulo, salto; (gen pl: limit) limites mpl // vi (leap) pular, saltar // adj: **~ by** (limited by) limitado por; **to be ~ to do sth** (obliged) ter o dever de fazer algo; (likely) estar certo de fazer algo; **out of ~s** entrada proibida, fora dos limites; **~ for** com destino a.

**boundary** ['baundrɪ] n limite m, fronteira.

**boundless** ['baundlɪs] adj ilimitado.

**bouquet** ['bukeɪ] n (of flowers) ramalhete m; (of wine) aroma m.

**bout** [baut] n (of malaria etc) ataque m; (: outbreak) surto; (BOXING etc) combate m.

**bow** [bau] n (knot) laço; (weapon, MUS) arco // n [bau] (of the head) reverência; (NAUT) proa // vi [bau] curvar-se, fazer uma reverência; (yield): **to ~ to or before** ceder ante, submeter-se a.

**bowels** [bauəlz] npl intestinos mpl, tripas fpl.

**bowl** [bəul] n tigela, taça grande; (for washing) bacia; (ball) bola de madeira // vi (CRICKET) arremessar a bola; ~s n jogo de boliche.

**bow-legged** ['bəulgid] adj cambaio, cambota.

**bowler** ['bəulə*] n (CRICKET) lançador m (da bola); (also: ~ hat) chapéu-de-coco m.

**bowling** ['bəuliŋ] n (game) boliche m; ~ alley n pista de boliche; ~ green n gramado para boliches.

**bow tie** ['bəu-] n gravata borboleta.

**box** [bɔks] n (also: **cardboard** ~) caixa, caixote m; (for jewels) estojo; (for money) cofre m; (THEATRE) camarote m // vt encaixotar // vi (SPORT) boxear; ~er n (person) boxeador m, pugilista; (dog) boxer m; ~ing n (SPORT) boxe m, pugilismo; **B~ing Day** n Dia de Santo Estêvão, 26 de dezembro; ~ing gloves npl luvas fpl de boxe; ~ing ring n ringue m de boxe; ~ office n bilheteria, (Pt) bilheteira; ~room n quarto pequeno.

**boy** [bɔi] n (young) menino, garoto; (older) moço, rapaz m; (servant) criado.

**boycott** ['bɔikɔt] n boicote m, boicotagem f // vt boicotar.

**boyfriend** ['bɔifrend] n namorado.

**boyish** ['bɔiiʃ] adj de menino, pueril.

**B.R.** abbr of **British Rail**.

**bra** [brɑ:] n soutien m.

**brace** [breis] n reforço, braçadeira; (on teeth) aparelho; (tool) arco de pua // vt firmar, reforçar; ~s npl suspensórios mpl; **to ~ o.s.** (fig) recobrar ânimo.

**bracelet** ['breislit] n pulseira, bracelete m.

**bracing** ['breisiŋ] adj tonificante.

**bracken** ['brækən] n samambaia, (Pt) feto.

**bracket** ['brækit] n (TECH) suporte m; (group) classe f, grupo; (also: **brace** ~) suporte, braçadeira; (also: **round** ~) parêntese m; (gen: **square** ~) colchete m // vt (group) agrupar.

**brag** [bræg] vi gabar-se.

**braid** [breid] n (trimming) galão m; (of hair) trança.

**Braille** [breil] n braile m.

**brain** [brein] n cérebro; ~s npl inteligência, miolos mpl; ~child n idéia original; ~wash vt fazer uma lavagem cerebral a; ~wave n inspiração f, ideia maravilhosa; ~y adj inteligente or muito esperto.

**braise** [breiz] vt estufar.

**brake** [breik] n (on vehicle) freio, breque m; (Pt) travão m // vt/i frear; (Pt) travar; ~ **drum** n tambor m de freio; ~ **fluid** n óleo de freio.

**bramble** ['bræmbl] n amora-preta.

**branch** [brɑ:ntʃ] n ramo, galho; (fig) ramificação f, seção f (Pt: -çç-) f; (road) ramal m; (COMM) sucursal f, filial f // vi (also: ~ **out**) ramificar-se; (fig) desenvolver-se, ampliar-se.

**brand** [brænd] n marca; (iron) ferro de marcar // vt (cattle) marcar com ferro quente.

**brandish** ['brændiʃ] vt brandir.

**brand-new** ['brænd'nju:] adj novo em folha, completamente novo.

**brandy** ['brændi] n conhaque m.

**brash** [bræʃ] adj (rough) grosseiro; (cheeky) descarado.

**brass** [brɑ:s] n latão m; ~ **band** n banda de música, charanga.

**brassière** ['bræsiə*] n soutien m.

**brat** [bræt] n (pej) pirralho, fedelho.

**bravado** [brə'vɑ:dəu] n bravata.

**brave** [breiv] adj valente, corajoso // n guerreiro pele-vermelha // vt (challenge) desafiar; (resist) encarar; ~ry n coragem f, bravura.

**brawl** [brɔ:l] n briga, rixa // vi brigar.

**brawn** [brɔ:n] n força; (meat) patê m de carne; ~y adj musculoso, carnudo.

**bray** [brei] n zurro, ornejo // vi zurrar, ornejar.

**brazen** ['breizn] adj descarado //

vt: **to ~ it out** defender-se descaradamente.

**brazier** ['breiziə*] n braseiro.

**Brazil** [brə'zil] n Brasil m; **~ian** adj, n brasileiro/a.

**breach** [bri:tʃ] vt abrir brecha em // n (gap) brecha; (breaking): **~ of contract** inadimplência; (Pt) inadimplemento; **~ of the peace** perturbação f da ordem pública.

**bread** [bred] n pão m; **~ and butter** n pão com manteiga; (fig) ganha-pão m, sustento // adj comum e corrente; **~crumbs** npl migalhas fpl; (CULIN) farinha de rosca.

**breadth** [bretθ] n largura; (fig) amplitude f.

**breadwinner** ['bredwinə*] n arrimo de família.

**break** [breik] pt **broke**, pp **broken** vt (gen) quebrar, romper; (split) partir; (promise) quebrar; (word) faltar a; (fall) amortecer; (journey) interromper; (law) violar, transgredir; (record) bater; (news) revelar // vi quebrar-se, partir-se; (storm) estalar // n (gap) abertura; (crack) fenda;. (fracture) fratura (Pt: -ct-); (breakdown) ruptura, rompimento; (rest) descanso; (time) intervalo; (at school) recreio; (chance) oportunidade f; (escape) evasão f, fuga; **to ~ down** vt (figures, data) analisar; (undermine) acabar com // vi desarranjar-se; (TECH: parar) enguiçar; (MED) sofrer um colapso; (AUT) avariar-se; (person) desatar a chorar; **to ~ even** vi sair sem ganhar nem perder; **to ~ free or loose** vi escapar-se, libertar-se; **to ~ in** vt (horse etc) domar; (US: car) fazer a rodagem de // vi (burglar) forçar uma entrada; **to ~ into** vt fus (house) arrombar; **to ~ off** vi (speaker) parar-se, deter-se; (branch) partir; **to ~ open** vt (door etc) abrir com esforço, forçar; **to ~ out** vi estalar, rebentar; **to ~ out in**

**spots** aparecer coberto de manchas to **~ up** vi romper-se // vt romper; (intervene) intervir em; **~able** adj quebradiço, frágil; **~age** n quebradura; (COMM) quebra; **~down** n (AUT) avaria; (in communications) interrupção f; (machine) enguiço; (MED: also: **nervous ~down**) colapso, crise f nervosa; **~down lorry** (Brit) n guincho de guindaste; (Pt) pronto socorro; **~er** n onda grande.

**breakfast** ['brekfəst] n café m da manhã; (Pt) pequeno almoço.

**break: ~through** n ruptura; (fig) avanço, irrupção f; **~water** n quebra-mar m.

**breast** [brest] n (of woman) peito, seio; (chest) peito; **~-stroke** n nado de peito.

**breath** [breθ] n fôlego, hálito, respiração f; out of **~** ofegante, sem fôlego; **~alyser** n instrumento para medir o álcool pela respiração.

**breathe** [bri:ð] vt/i respirar; (noisily) ressonar; **breather** n respiro, pausa.

**breath: ~less** adj sem fôlego, ofegante; **~taking** adj pasmoso, empolgante.

**breed** [bri:d] pt, pp **bred** [bred] vt criar, gerar // vi reproduzir-se, procriar-se // n raça, casta; **~er** n (person) criador/a) m/f; **~ing** n (of person) educação f.

**breeze** [bri:z] n brisa, aragem f.

**breezy** ['bri:zi] adj ventoso; (person) despreocupado, animado.

**brevity** ['breviti] n brevidade f.

**brew** [bru:] vt (tea) fazer; (beer) fermentar // vi fazer-se, preparar-se; (fig) armar-se; **~er** n cervejeiro; **~ery** n cervejaria.

**bribe** [braib] n suborno // vt subornar, peitar; **~ry** n suborno, peita.

**brick** [brik] n tijolo; **~layer** n assentador m de tijolos, pedreiro; **~works** n fábrica de tijolos.

**bridal** ['braɪdl] adj nupcial.

**bride** [braɪd] n noiva; **~groom** n noivo; **bridesmaid** n dama de honra.

**bridge** [brɪdʒ] n ponte f; (NAUT) ponte de comando; (of nose) ponte f; (Pl) cavalete m; (CARDS) bridge m // vt (river) lançar uma ponte sobre; **~head** n cabeça-de-ponte f.

**bridle** ['braɪdl] n cabeçada, freio // vt enfrear; (fig) refrear, conter; **~ path** n senda.

**brief** [bri:f] adj breve, curto // n (LAW) causa // vt (inform) informar; (instruct) instruir; **~s** npl (for men) cueca sg; (for women) calcinha sg; **~case** n pasta; **~ing** n (PRESS) instruções fpl.

**brigade** [brɪ'geɪd] n (MIL) brigada.

**brigadier** [brɪgə'dɪə*] n general m de brigada, brigadeiro.

**bright** [braɪt] adj claro, brilhante; (weather) resplendecente; (person: clever) esperto, inteligente; (: lively) alegre, animado; (colour) vivo; **~en** (also: **~ up**) vt (room) tornar mais alegre // vi (weather) clarear; (person: gen: **~ up**) animar-se, alegrar-se.

**brilliance** ['brɪljəns] n brilho, claridade f; **brilliant** [-ənt] adj brilhante; (clever) inteligente, esperto.

**brim** [brɪm] n borda; (of hat) aba; **~ful** adj cheio até as bordas; (fig) repleto.

**brine** [braɪn] n (CULIN) salmoura.

**bring** [brɪŋ], pt, pp **brought** vt (thing) trazer; (person) conduzir; to **~ about** vt ocasionar, produzir; to **~ back** vt tornar a trazer; (return) devolver; to **~ down** vt baixar; (price) reduzir; to **~ forward** vt adiantar; to **~ in** vt (harvest) recolher; to **~ off** vt (task, plan) conseguir; to **~ out** vt (object) tirar; to **~ round** vt (unconscious person) fazer voltar a si; (convince) convencer, ganhar; to **~ up** vt (person) educar, criar; (carry up) subir; (question) introduzir.

**brink** [brɪŋk] n borda.

**brisk** [brɪsk] adj vigoroso; (speedy) rápido; (trade) ativo (Pt: -ct-).

**brisket** ['brɪskɪt] n carne f de vaca para assar.

**bristle** ['brɪsl] n cerda // vi eriçar-se; to **~ with** estar cheio de.

**Britain** ['brɪtən] n Grã-Bretanha.

**British** ['brɪtɪʃ] adj britânico; the **~** npl os Britânicos; the **~ Isles** npl as Ilhas Britânicas.

**Briton** ['brɪtən] n britânico.

**brittle** ['brɪtl] adj quebradiço, frágil.

**broach** [brəʊtʃ] vt (subject) abordar, trazer à baila.

**broad** [brɔːd] adj amplo, largo; (accent) carregado; **in ~ daylight** em pleno dia; **~cast** n transmissão f // (vb: pt, pp **~cast**) vt (RADIO, TV) transmitir // vi falar ou tocar pelo rádio; **~casting** n radiodifusão f, transmissão f; **~en** vt alargar // vi alargar-se, ampliar-se; **~ly** adv em geral; **~-minded** adj tolerante, liberal.

**brochure** ['brəʊʃjuə*] n folheto, brochura.

**broil** [brɔɪl] vt (US) grelhar.

**broke** [brəʊk] pt of **break** // adj (col) sem vintém, duro.

**broken** ['brəʊkən] pp of **break** // adj: **~ leg** perna quebrada; **in ~ English** num inglês mascavado; **~-hearted** com o coração partido or quebrado.

**broker** ['brəʊkə*] n corretor(a) m/f.

**bronchitis** [brɔŋ'kaɪtɪs] n bronquite f.

**bronze** [brɔnz] n bronze m.

**brooch** [brəʊtʃ] n broche m.

**brood** [bruːd] n ninhada; (children) filhos mpl; (pej) prole f // vi (hen) chocar; (obsessively) cismar, parafusar, matutar.

**brook** [brʊk] n arroio, ribeiro.

**broom** [brum] n vassoura; (BOT) giesta; **~stick** n cabo de vassoura.

**Bros.** abbr of **Brothers**.

**broth** [brɔθ] n caldo.

**brothel** ['brɔθl] n bordel m.

**brother** ['brʌðə*] n irmão m; ~-in-law n cunhado.

**brought** [brɔːt] pt, pp of **bring**.

**brow** [brau] n fronte f; (forehead) testa; (of hill) cimo, cume m.

**brown** [braun] adj castanho, marrom; (hair) castanho; (tanned) bronzeado, moreno // n (colour) cor f castanha // vt tostar; (tan) bronzear; (CULIN) dourar; ~**ie** n menina 'Girl Guide', fadinha de bandeirante.

**browse** [brauz] vi (among books) folhear livros.

**bruise** [bruːz] n hematoma m, contusão f // vt magoar, contundir.

**brunette** [bruːˈnɛt] n morena, trigueira.

**brunt** [brʌnt] n: **the ~ of** o ímpeto de; (greater part) a maior parte de.

**brush** [brʌʃ] n escova; (for painting, shaving etc) pincel m; (BOT) mato rasteiro; (quarrel) escaramuça // vt escovar; (gen: ~ past, ~ against) tocar ao passar, roçar; **to ~ aside** vt afastar, não fazer caso de; **to ~ up** vt (knowledge) retocar, revisar; ~**wood** n (bushes) mato; (sticks) lenha, gravetos mpl.

**brusque** [bruːsk] adj brusco, áspero.

**Brussels** ['brʌslz] n Bruxelas; ~ **sprout** n couve-de-bruxelas f.

**brutal** ['bruːtl] adj brutal; ~**ity** [-'tælɪtɪ] n brutalidade f.

**brute** [bruːt] n bruto; (person) animal m.

**B.Sc.** abbr of **Bachelor of Science** licenciado/a em ciências.

**bubble** ['bʌbl] n bolha, borbulha // vi borbulhar; ~ **gum** n chiclete m; (Pt) pastilha elástica.

**buck** [bʌk] n macho; (US: col) dólar m // vi corcovear; **to pass the ~** fazer o jogo do empurra; **to ~ up** vi (cheer up) animar-se, cobrar ânimo.

**bucket** ['bʌkɪt] n balde m, alcatruz m.

**buckle** ['bʌkl] n fivela // vt afivelar // vi torcer-se, cambar-se.

**bud** [bʌd] n broto, rebento; (of flower) botão m // vi brotar, desabrochar; (fig) florescer.

**Buddhism** ['budɪzm] n budismo.

**budding** ['bʌdɪŋ] adj em botão, nascente.

**buddy** ['bʌdɪ] n (US) camarada m, companheiro.

**budge** [bʌdʒ] vt mover; (fig) fazer ceder // vi mexer-se.

**budgerigar** ['bʌdʒərɪɡɑː*] n periquito.

**budget** ['bʌdʒɪt] n orçamento.

**budgie** ['bʌdʒɪ] n = **budgerigar**.

**buff** [bʌf] adj (colour) cor f de camurça // n (enthusiast) entusiasta m/f.

**buffalo** ['bʌfələu], pl ~ or ~**es** n búfalo.

**buffer** ['bʌfə*] n pára-choque m.

**buffet** ['bufeɪ] n (bar) bar m, cafeteria; (food) bufê m // vt ['bʌfɪt] (strike) esbofetear; (wind etc) fustigar; ~ **car** n vagão-restaurante m.

**buffoon** [bəˈfuːn] n bufão m.

**bug** [bʌg] n (insect) percevejo; (: gen) bicho; (fig: germ) micróbio; (spy device) microfone m oculto; (tap) escuta telefônica; (machine for tapping) aparelho de escuta; grampo // vt (fam) maçar, enfadar; (spy on) escutar, grampear.

**bugle** ['bjuːgl] n trompa, corneta.

**build** [bɪld] n (of person) talhe m, estatura // vt, pt, pp **built** construir, edificar; ~**er** n construtor m; (contractor) contratista m/f; empreiteiro/a m/f; ~**ing** n (act of) construção f; (habitation, offices) edifício, prédio; ~**ing society** n sociedade f imobiliária, financiadora; **to ~ up** vt (MED) fortalecer; (stress) acumular.

**built** [bɪlt] pt, pp of **build** // adj: ~-**in** (cupboard) embutido; (device) interior, incorporado, embutido:

**bulb** [bʌlb] n (BOT) bulbo; (ELEC) lâmpada.

**Bulgaria** [bʌlˈgɛərɪə] n Bulgária; **~n** adj, n búlgaro/a.

**bulge** [bʌldʒ] n bojo, saliência // vi inchar-se; (pocket etc) fazer bojo.

**bulk** [bʌlk] n (mass) massa, volume m; (major part) parte f principal, grosso; **in ~** (COMM) a granel; **the ~ of** a maior parte de; **~head** n anteparo; **~y** adj volumoso; (person) corpulento.

**bull** [bul] n touro; **~dog** n buldogue m.

**bulldozer** [ˈbuldəuzə*] n escavadora.

**bullet** [ˈbulɪt] n bala; **~proof** adj à prova de balas; **~ wound** n ferida de bala.

**bulletin** [ˈbulɪtɪn] n boletim m; **~ board** n (US) quadro de anúncios.

**bullfight** [ˈbulfaɪt] n tourada; **~er** n toureiro; **~ing** n os touros mpl; (art of ~ing) tauromaquia.

**bullion** [ˈbuljən] n ouro or prata em barras.

**bullock** [ˈbulək] n boi m, novilho.

**bull's-eye** [ˈbulzaɪ] n centro do alvo, (Br) mosca (do alvo).

**bully** [ˈbulɪ] n fanfarrão m, valentão m // vt intimidar, tiranizar.

**bum** [bʌm] n (col: backside) traseiro, bunda; (tramp) vagabundo, vadio.

**bumblebee** [ˈbʌmblbiː] n (ZOOL) mamangaba.

**bump** [bʌmp] n (blow) choque m, embate m, baque m; (jolt) sacudida; (on head) bossa, galo, inchaço; (sound) baque // vt (strike) bater contra, dar encontrão em // vi dar sacudidas; **to ~ into** vt fus chocar-se contra, colidir com; (person) dar com; **~er** n (Brit) pára-choque m // adj: **~er crop/harvest** abundante colheita.

**bumpy** [ˈbʌmpɪ] adj (road) cheio de altos e baixos; (journey) cheio de solavancos.

**bun** [bʌn] n pão m doce; (Pt) pãozinho; (of hair) coque m.

**bunch** [bʌntʃ] n (of flowers) ramo; (of keys) molho; (of bananas) cacho; (of people) grupo.

**bundle** [ˈbʌndl] n (gen) embrulho, pacote m; (of sticks) feixe m; (of papers) maço // vt (also: ~ up) embrulhar, atar; (put): **to ~ sth/sb into** meter algo/alguém às pressas em.

**bung** [bʌŋ] n tampão m, batoque m // vt abatocar; (throw: gen: ~ into) botar em.

**bungalow** [ˈbʌŋgələu] n bangalô m, chalé m.

**bungle** [ˈbʌŋgl] vt estropear, estragar, fazer mal feito.

**bunion** [ˈbʌnjən] n joanete m.

**bunk** [bʌŋk] n tolice f, disparate m; **~ beds** npl beliche msg.

**bunker** [ˈbʌŋkə*] n (coal store) carvoeira; (MIL) abrigo, casamata; (GOLF) obstáculo bunker m.

**bunny** [ˈbʌnɪ] n (also: ~ rabbit) coelhinho.

**bunting** [ˈbʌntɪŋ] n bandeiras fpl.

**buoy** [bɔɪ] n bóia; **to ~ up** vt fazer boiar; (fig) sustentar, animar; **~ant** adj flutuante; (person) alegre.

**burden** [ˈbəːdn] n carga; (fig) fardo // vt carregar.

**bureau** [bjuˈrəu], pl **~x** [-z] n (furniture) secretária, escrivaninha; (office) escritório, agência.

**bureaucracy** [bjuəˈrɔkrəsɪ] n burocracia; **bureaucrat** [ˈbjuərəkræt] n burocrata m/f.

**burglar** [ˈbəːglə*] n arrombador m, ladrão/ladrona m/f; **~ alarm** n alarme m contra ladrões; **~y** n roubo por arrombamento; **burgle** [ˈbəːgl] vt arrombar.

**burial** [ˈbɛrɪəl] n enterro; **~ ground** n cemitério.

**burlesque** [bəːˈlesk] n paródia.

**burly** [ˈbəːlɪ] adj robusto, forte.

**burn** [bəːn], *pt, pp* **burned** or **burnt** *vt* queimar; (*house*) incendiar // *vi* queimar-se, arder, incendiar-se; (*sting*) arder, picar // *n* queimadura; **to ~ down** *vt* incendiar; **~er** *n* (*gas*) bico de gás, fogo; **~ing** *adj* ardente.

**burp** [bəːp] (*col*) *n* arroto // *vi* arrotar.

**burrow** [ˈbʌrəu] *n* toca, lura // *vt* fazer uma toca, cavar.

**bursar** [ˈbəːsə*] *n* tesoureiro; (*student*) bolsista; (*Pt*) bolseiro; **~y** *n* (*grant*) bolsa.

**burst** [bəːst], *pt, pp* **burst** *vt* (*balloon, pipe*) rebentar; (*banks etc*) romper // *vi* rebentar-se, romper-se; (*tyre*) furar-se; (*bomb*) explodir // *n* (*gen*) estoiro *m*, rebentamento; (*explosion*) explosão *f*; (*shots*) rajada; **a ~ of energy** uma explosão de energia; **to ~ into flames** incendiar-se de repente; **to ~ into laughter** começar a rir; (*Pt*) desatar a rir; **to ~ into tears** começar a chorar; (*Pt*) desatar a chorar; **to be ~ing with** arrebentar-se de; (*Pt*) rebentar por; **to ~ into** *vt fus* (*room etc*) irromper em; **to ~ open** *vi* abrir-se de repente.

**bury** [ˈbɛri] *vt* enterrar; (*body*) enterrar, sepultar.

**bus** [bʌs] *n* ônibus *m*, (*Pt*) autocarro.

**bush** [buʃ] *n* arbusto; (*scrub land*) sertão *m*; **to beat about the ~** falar com rodeios; (*Pt*) fazer rodeios; **~y** *adj* (*thick*) espesso, denso.

**busily** [ˈbizili] *adv* atarefadamente.

**business** [ˈbiznis] *n* (*matter*) negócio; (*trading*) comércio, negócios *mpl*; (*firm*) empresa, casa; (*occupation*) profissão *f*; (*affair*) assunto; **it's my ~ to...** encarrego-me de...; **it's none of my ~** eu não tenho nada com isto; **that's my ~** isso é cá comigo; **he means ~** fala a sério; **~like** *adj* eficiente, metódico; **~man** *n* homem *m* de negócios, comerciante *m/f*.

**bus-stop** [ˈbʌsstɔp] *n* ponto de ônibus; (*Pt*) paragem *f* de autocarro.

**bust** [bʌst] *n* (*ANAT*) busto // *adj* (*broken*) partido, rasgado; **to go ~** falir.

**bustle** [ˈbʌsl] *n* animação *f*, movimento // *vi* apressar-se, andar azafamado; **bustling** *adj* (*town*) animado, movimentado.

**busy** [ˈbizi] *adj* ocupado, atarefado; (*shop, street*) animado, movimentado; (*TEL*) ocupado; (*Pt*) interrompido // *vt*: **to ~ o.s. with** ocupar-se em; **~ness** *n* intrometido.

**but** [bʌt] *conj* mas, porém // *prep* exceto (*Pt*: -pt-), menos; **nothing ~** só, somente; **~ for** sem, se não fosse; **all ~ finished** quase acabado, tudo menos acabado.

**butane** [ˈbjuːtein] *n* butano.

**butcher** [ˈbutʃə*] *n* açougueiro; (*Pt*) homem do talho // *vt* chacinar; (*cattle etc for meat*) abater e carnear; **~'s (shop)** *n* açougue *m*; (*Pt*) talho.

**butler** [ˈbʌtlə*] *n* mordomo.

**butt** [bʌt] *n* (*cask*) tonel *m*; (*for rain*) barril *m*; (*thick end*) cabo, extremidade *f*; (*of gun*) coronha; (*of cigarette*) toco; (*Pt*) ponta; (*fig: target*) alvo // *vt* dar cabeçadas contra, marrar.

**butter** [ˈbʌtə*] *n* manteiga // *vt* untar com manteiga; **~ bean** *n* fava; **~cup** *n* botão-de-ouro *m*, ranúnculo.

**butterfly** [ˈbʌtəflai] *n* borboleta.

**buttocks** [ˈbʌtəks] *npl* nádegas *fpl*.

**button** [ˈbʌtn] *n* botão *m* // *vt* abotoar; **~hole** *n* casa de botão, botoeira; (*flower*) flor *f* na lapela // *vt* obrigar a ouvir.

**buttress** [ˈbʌtris] *n* contraforte *m*; (*fig*) apoio, esteio.

**buxom** [ˈbʌksəm] *adj* (*baby*) saudável; (*woman*) rechonchudo.

**buy** [bai], *pt, pp* **bought** *vt* comprar // *n* compra; **to ~ sb sth/sth from sb** comprar algo para alguém/algo a alguém; ~**er** *n* comprador(a) *m/f*.

**buzz** [bʌz] *n* zumbido; (*col: phone call*) telefonema *m* // *vi* zumbir.

**buzzard** [ˈbʌzəd] *n* abutre *m*, urubu *m*.

**buzzer** [ˈbʌzə*] *n* sirene *f*; (*doorbell*) campaínha, cigarra.

**by** [bai] *prep* por; (*beside*) perto de, ao pé de, junto a; (*according to*) segundo, de acordo com; (*before*): ~ **4 o'clock** antes das quatro // *adv see* **pass, go** *etc*; ~ **bus/car** de ônibus/carro; **paid** ~ **the hour** pago por hora; ~ **night/day** de noite/dia; (**all**) ~ **oneself** (completamente) só, sozinho; ~ **the way** a propósito; ~ **and large** em geral; ~ **and** ~ logo, mais tarde.

**bye(-bye)** [ˈbai(ˈbai)] *excl* adeus, até logo.

**by(e)-law** [ˈbailɔː] *n* lei *f* de município.

**by-election** [ˈbailɛkʃən] *n* eleição *f* parcial.

**bygone** [ˈbaigɔn] *adj* passado, antigo // *n*: **let** ~**s be** ~**s** que passou passou, águas passadas não movem moinhos.

**bypass** [ˈbaipɑːs] *n* via secundária, desvio // *vt* evitar.

**by-product** [ˈbaiprɔdʌkt] *n* subproduto, produto derivado.

**bystander** [ˈbaistændə*] *n* circunstante *m/f*, observador(a) *m/f*, curioso.

**byword** [ˈbaiwəːd] *n*: **to be a** ~ **for** ser conhecido por.

## C

**C.** *abbr of* **centigrade**.

**C.A.** *abbr* *of* **chartered accountant**.

**cab** [kæb] *n* táxi *m*; (*of truck*) cabine *m*.

**cabaret** [ˈkæbərei] *n* cabaré *m*.

**cabbage** [ˈkæbidʒ] *n* couve *f*, repolho.

**cabin** [ˈkæbin] *n* cabana; (*on ship*) camarote *m*; ~ **cruiser** *n* lancha a motor com cabine.

**cabinet** [ˈkæbinit] *n* (*POL*.) conselho de ministros; (*furniture*) armário; (*also*: **display** ~) armário com vitrina; ~**-maker** *n* marceneiro.

**cable** [ˈkeibl] *n* cabo; (*telegram*) cabograma *m* // *vt* enviar cabograma; ~**-car** *n* trem *m* funicular.

**cackle** [ˈkækl] *vi* cacarejar.

**cactus** [ˈkæktəs], *pl* **-ti** [-tai] *n* cacto.

**caddie** [ˈkædi] *n* caddie *m*.

**cadet** [kəˈdɛt] *n* (*MIL*) cadete *m*.

**cadge** [kædʒ] *vt* filar; **cadger** *n* filante *m/f*.

**Caesarean (section)** [siːˈzɛəriən] *n* cesariana.

**café** [ˈkæfei] *n* café *m*; **cafeteria** [kæfiˈtiəriə] *n* café *m*.

**caffein(e)** [ˈkæfiːn] *n* cafeína.

**cage** [keidʒ] *n* gaiola, jaula // *vt* engaiolar, enjaular.

**cagey** [ˈkeidʒi] *adj* (*col*) cuidadoso, reservado.

**Cairo** [ˈkaiərəu] *n* Cairo.

**cajole** [kəˈdʒəul] *vt* lisonjear.

**cake** [keik] *n* (*large*) bolo; (*small*) bolinho, queque *m*; (*of soap*) sabonete *m*; ~**d with** empastado de.

**calamitous** [kəˈlæmitəs] *adj* calamitoso; **calamity** [-iti] *n* calamidade *f*.

**calcium** [ˈkælsiəm] *n* cálcio.

**calculate** [ˈkælkjuleit] *vt* calcular; **calculating** *adj* (*clever*) matreiro, calculista; (*devious*) esperto; **calculation** [-ˈleiʃən] *n* cálculo; **calculator** *n* calculador *m*.

**calculus** [ˈkælkjuləs] *n* cálculo.

**calendar** [ˈkæləndə*] *n* calendário; ~ **month/year** mês *m*/ano civil.

**calf** [kɑːf], *pl* **calves** *n* (*of cow*) bezerro, vitela; (*of other animals*) cria; (also: ~**skin**) pele f or couro de bezerro; (ANAT) barriga-da-perna.

**calibre, caliber** (US) ['kælıbə*] n calibre m.

**call** [kɔːl] vt/i chamar; (telephone) telefonar; (visit: also: ~ **in,** ~ **round**) fazer uma visita // n (shout) chamada; (TEL) telefonema m; (of bird) canto; (appeal) chamamento, apelo; **to ~ for** vt fus (demand) pedir, exigir; (fetch) ir buscar; **to ~ off** vt (cancel) cancelar; **to ~ on** vt fus (visit) visitar; (turn to) recorrer a; **to ~ out** vi gritar, bradar; **to ~ up** vt (MIL) chamar às fileiras; ~**box** n cabine f telefônica; ~**er** n visita m/f; (TEL) chamador m; ~ **girl** n prostituta; ~**ing** n vocação f, profissão f.

**callous** ['kæləs] adj insensível, cruel.

**calm** [kɑːm] n calma, tranquilidade f // vt acalmar, tranquilizar // adj (gen) tranquilo; (sea) calmo, sereno; ~**ly** adv tranquilamente, com calma; ~**ness** n tranquilidade f; **to ~ down** vi acalmar-se, tranquilizar-se // vt acalmar, tranquilizar.

**calorie** ['kælərı] n caloria.

**calve** [kɑːv] vi parir.

**calves** [kɑːvz] pl of **calf.**

**camber** ['kæmbə*] n (of road) curvatura, curva.

**Cambodia** [kæm'bəudjə] n Camboja.

**came** [keım] pt of **come.**

**camel** ['kæməl] n camelo.

**cameo** ['kæmıəu] n camafeu m.

**camera** ['kæmərə] n máquina fotográfica; (CINEMA, TV) câmara; **in ~** em câmara; ~**man** n cameraman m.

**camouflage** ['kæməflɑːʒ] n camuflagem f // vt camuflar.

**camp** [kæmp] n campo, acampamento // vi acampar // adj afetado (Pt: -ct-), afeminado.

**campaign** [kæm'peın] n (MIL, POL etc) campanha // vi fazer campanha.

**camp:** ~**bed** n cama de campanha; ~**er** n campista m/f; (vehicle) reboque m; ~**ing** n campismo, camping m; **to go** ~**ing** fazer campismo or camping; ~**site** n área de camping; (Pt) parque m de campismo.

**campus** ['kæmpəs] n cidade f universitária.

**can** [kæn] auxiliary vb (gen) poder; (know how to) saber; **I** ~ **swim** sei nadar // n (of oil, water) lata, caneco // vt enlatar; (preserve) conservar em latas.

**Canada** ['kænədə] n Canadá m; **Canadian** [kə'neıdıən] adj, n canadense m/f.

**canal** [kə'næl] n canal m.

**canary** [kə'nɛərı] n canário; **C~ Islands** npl (Ilhas) Canárias fpl.

**cancel** ['kænsəl] vt cancelar; (train) cancelar; (appointment) anular; (cross out) riscar, invalidar; ~**lation** [-'leıʃən] n cancelamento, anulação f.

**cancer** ['kænsə*] n câncer m, cancro; **C~** (ASTRO) Câncer.

**candid** ['kændıd] adj franco, sincero, cândido/a.

**candidate** ['kændıdeıt] n candidato.

**candle** ['kændl] n vela; (in church) círio; ~**stick** n (also: ~ **holder**) (single) castiçal m; (bigger, ornate) candelabro, lustre m.

**candour** ['kændə*] n franqueza.

**candy** ['kændı] n açúcar m cristalizado or cande; (US) doce m, confeito, bombom m.

**cane** [keın] n (BOT) cana; (stick) vara, bengala // vt (SCOL) castigar (com bengala).

**canine** ['kænaın] adj canino.

**canister** ['kænıstə*] n caixa, lata.

**cannabis** ['kænəbıs] n cânhamo, maconha.

**canned** [kænd] *adj* em lata, enlatado.

**cannibal** [ˈkænɪbəl] *n* canibal *m/f*; ~**ism** *n* canibalismo.

**cannon** [ˈkænən], *pl* ~ *or* ~**s** *n* canhão *m*; ~**ball** *n* bala (de canhão).

**cannot** [ˈkænɔt] = **can not.**

**canny** [ˈkænɪ] *adj* astuto.

**canoe** [kəˈnuː] *n* canoa; ~**ing** *n* (SPORT) remar uma canoa; ~**ist** *n* canoeiro.

**canon** [ˈkænən] *n* (*clergyman*) cónego; (*standard*) cânone *m*.

**canonize** [ˈkænənaɪz] *vt* canonizar.

**can opener** [ˈkænəupnə*] *n* abridor *m* de latas.

**canopy** [ˈkænəpɪ] *n* dossel *m*; (ARCH) baldaquino.

**can't** [kænt] = **can not.**

**cantankerous** [kænˈtæŋkərəs] *adj* rabujento, irritável.

**canteen** [kænˈtiːn] *n* cantina; (*bottle*) cantil *m*; (*of cutlery*) jogo (de talheres).

**canter** [ˈkæntə*] *n* meio galope // *vi* ir a meio galope.

**canvas** [ˈkænvəs] *n* (*gen*) lona; (*painting*) tela; (NAUT) velas *fpl*; **under** ~ (*camping*) em barracas.

**canvass** [ˈkænvəs] *vt* (POL) pedir votos de.

**canyon** [ˈkænjən] *n* canhão *m*, garganta, desfiladeiro.

**cap** [kæp] *n* gorro, barrete *m*; (*of pen*) tampa; (*of bottle*) tampa; (MED) diafragma *m* // *vt* rematar; (*outdo*) superar; (FOOTBALL) selecionar (Pt: -cc-) (para a equipe nacional).

**capability** [keɪpəˈbɪlɪtɪ] *n* capacidade *f*; **capable** [ˈkeɪpəbl] *adj* capaz.

**capacity** [kəˈpæsɪtɪ] *n* capacidade *f*; (*position*) posição *f*.

**cape** [keɪp] *n* capa; (GEO) cabo.

**caper** [ˈkeɪpə*] *n* (CULIN: *gen*: ~**s**) alcaparra; (*prank*) asneira, travessura.

**capital** [ˈkæpɪtl] *n* (*also*: ~ *city*)

capital *f*; (*money*) capital *m*; (*also*: ~ **letter**) maiúscula; ~**ism** *n* capitalismo; ~**ist** *adj, n* capitalista *m/f*, ~ **punishment** *n* pena de morte.

**capitulate** [kəˈpɪtjuleɪt] *vi* capitular, render-se; **capitulation** [-ˈleɪʃən] *n* capitulação *f*, rendição *f*.

**capricious** [kəˈprɪʃəs] *adj* caprichoso.

**Capricorn** [ˈkæprɪkɔːn] *n* Capricórnio.

**capsize** [kæpˈsaɪz] *vt* emborcar, soçobrar // *vi* emborcar-se, soçobrar.

**capstan** [ˈkæpstən] *n* cabrestante *m*.

**capsule** [ˈkæpsjuːl] *n* cápsula.

**captain** [ˈkæptɪn] *n* capitão *m* // *vt* capitanear, ser o capitão de.

**caption** [ˈkæpʃən] *n* (*heading*) título; (*to picture*) legenda.

**captivate** [ˈkæptɪveɪt] *vt* cativar, fascinar.

**captive** [ˈkæptɪv] *adj, n* cativo; **captivity** [-ˈtɪvɪtɪ] *n* cativeiro.

**capture** [ˈkæptʃə*] *vt* prender, aprisionar; (*place*) tomar; (*attention*) captar, chamar // *n* captura, tomada; (*thing taken*) presa.

**car** [kɑː*] *n* carro, automóvel *m*; (RAIL) vagão *m*.

**carafe** [kəˈræf] *n* garrafa de mesa.

**caramel** [ˈkærəmɪ] *n* caramelo.

**carat** [ˈkærət] *n* quilate *m*.

**caravan** [ˈkærəvæn] *n* reboque *m*, trailer *m*; (*of camels*) caravana.

**caraway** [ˈkærəweɪ] *n*: ~ **seed** alcaravia, cariz *m*.

**carbohydrate** [kɑːbəuˈhaɪdreɪt] *n* hidrato de carbónio; (*food*) carboidrato.

**carbon** [ˈkɑːbən] *n* carbono, carbónio; ~ **copy** *n* cópia de papel carbono; ~ **paper** *n* papel *m* carbono.

**carburettor**, (US) **carburetor** [kɑːbjuˈretə*] *n* carburador *m*.

**carcass** ['kɑːkəs] n cadáver m de animal, carcaça.

**card** [kɑːd] n carta, bilhete m; (visiting ~, post~ etc) cartão m, bilhete m; ~**board** n cartão, papelão m; ~ **game** n jogo de cartas.

**cardiac** ['kɑːdɪæk] adj cardíaco.

**cardigan** ['kɑːdɪgən] n casaco de lã, cardigã m.

**cardinal** ['kɑːdɪnl] adj cardeal; (MAT) cardinal // n (REL) cardeal m; (MAT) número cardinal.

**card index** n fichário.

**care** [kɛə*] n (gen) cuidado; (worry) preocupação f, ansiedade f; (charge) encargo, custódia // vi: to ~ **about** preocupar-se com, ter interesse em; in sb's ~ a cargo de alguém; to **take** ~ to cuidar-se or ter o cuidado de; to **take** ~ **of** vt cuidar de; to ~ **for** vt fus cuidar de; (like) gostar de; I **don't** ~ não me importa.

**career** [kə'rɪə*] n carreira // vi (also: ~ **along**) correr a toda velocidade.

**carefree** ['kɛəfriː] adj despreocupado.

**careful** ['kɛəful] adj cuidadoso; (cautious) cauteloso; (be) ~! tenha cuidado!; ~**ly** adv com cuidado, cuidadosamente.

**careless** ['kɛəlɪs] adj descuidado; (heedless) desatento; ~**ly** adv sem cuidado, sem preocupação; ~**ness** n descuido, falta de atenção.

**caress** [kə'rɛs] n carícia // vt acariciar.

**caretaker** ['kɛəteɪkə*] n curador(a) m/f, guarda m/f, zelador(a) m/f.

**car-ferry** ['kɑːfɛrɪ] n balsa para carros; (Pt) barco de passagem.

**cargo** ['kɑːgəu], pl ~**es** n carregamento, carga; (freight) frete m.

**Caribbean** [kærɪ'biːən] n: the ~

(Sea) Mar m das Antilhas, Mar das Caraíbas.

**caricature** ['kærɪkətjuə*] n caricatura.

**carnal** ['kɑːnl] adj carnal.

**carnation** [kɑː'neɪʃən] n cravo.

**carnival** ['kɑːnɪvəl] n carnaval m.

**carnivore** ['kɑːnɪvɔː*] n carnívoro.

**carol** ['kærəl] n: (Christmas) ~ cântico de Natal.

**carp** [kɑːp] n (fish) carpa; to ~ **at** vt fus queixar-se de.

**car park** n estacionamento.

**carpenter** ['kɑːpɪntə*] n carpinteiro; **carpentry** [-trɪ] n carpintaria.

**carpet** ['kɑːpɪt] n tapete m // vt atapetar; ~ **slippers** npl pantufas fpl.

**carriage** ['kærɪdʒ] n carruagem f; coche m; (RAIL) vagão m; (for goods) transporte m; (bearing) porte m; ~**way** n (part of road) pista; dual ~**way** pista-dupla.

**carrier** ['kærɪə*] n carregador(a) m/f, transportador(a) m/f; (company) empresa de transportes; ~ **bag** n saco, sacola.

**carrot** ['kærət] n cenoura.

**carry** ['kærɪ] vt (gen) levar; (transport) transportar; (a motion, bill) aprovar; (involve: responsibilities etc) implicar // vi (sound) transportar; to ~ **on** vi (continue) seguir, continuar; (fam: complain) queixar-se, protestar // vt prosseguir, continuar; to ~ **out** vt (orders) cumprir; (investigation) levar a cabo, realizar.

**cart** [kɑːt] n carroça, carreta; (US: for luggage) carrinho // vt transportar (em carroça).

**cartilage** ['kɑːtɪlɪdʒ] n cartilagem f.

**cartographer** [kɑː'tɔgrəfə*] n cartógrafo.

**carton** ['kɑːtən] n (box) caixa (de papelão); (of yogurt) pote m.

**cartoon** [kɑː'tuːn] n (PRESS) caricatura, cartum m; (comic strip) história em quadrinhos; (*Pt*) banda desenhada; (*film*) desenho animado; ~ist *n* caricaturista *m/f*, cartunista *m/f*.

**cartridge** ['ka:trɪdʒ] *n* cartucho.

**carve** [ka:v] *vt* (*meat*) trinchar; (*wood, stone*) cinzelar, esculpir; (*on tree*) gravar; **to ~ up** dividir, repartir; **carving** *n* (*in wood etc*) escultura, obra de talha or de entalhe; **carving knife** *n* trinchante *m*, faca-de-trinchar *f*.

**car wash** *n* lavagem *f* de carros.

**cascade** [kæs'keɪd] *n* cascata, queda d'água; (*fig*) cachoeira // *vi* cascatear, cair em cascata.

**case** [keɪs] *n* (*container*) caixa; (*MED*) caso; (*for jewels etc*) estojo; (*LAW*) causa judicial, processo; (*also*: suit~) mala; **in ~ of** em caso (de); **in any ~** em todo o caso; **just in ~** (*conj*) se por acaso; (*adv*) por via das dúvidas; **to make a good ~** ter bons argumentos.

**cash** [kæʃ] *n* dinheiro (em espécie) // *vt* cobrar, descontar; **to pay (in) ~** pagar em dinheiro; **to ~ on delivery** reembolsar contra entrega; ~**book** *n* livro-caixa *m*; ~**desk** *n* caixa.

**cashew** [kæ'ʃu:] *n* (*also*: ~ **nut**) caju *m*.

**cashier** [kæ'ʃɪə*] *n* caixa *m/f*.

**cashmere** [kæʃ'mɪə*] *n* caxemira, cachemira.

**cash register** *n* caixa-registadora.

**casing** ['keɪsɪŋ] *n* cobertura; (*of boiler etc*) revestimento.

**casino** [kə'si:nəu] *n* casino.

**cask** [ka:sk] *n* barril *m*, casco.

**casket** ['ka:skɪt] *n* cofre *m*, guarda-joias; (*US*: *coffin*) caixão *m*.

**casserole** ['kæsərəul] *n* panela de barro or de vidro de cozer; (*food*) guisado/ensopado no forno.

**cassette** [kæ'set] *n* cassete *m*; ~**player** *n* gravador *m*.

**cassock** ['kæsək] *n* sotaina, batina.

**cast** [ka:st], *pt, pp* **cast** *vt* (*throw*) lançar, atirar; (*skin*) mudar, perder; (*metal*) fundir; (*THEATRE*) dar o papel (de) // *vi* (*FISHING*) lançar // *n* (*THEATRE*) elenco; (*mould*) forma, molde *m*; (*also*: plaster ~) gesso; **to ~ away** *vt* desperdiçar; **to ~ down** *vt* abater, desalentar; **to ~ loose** soltar; **to ~ one's vote** votar; **to ~ off** *vi* (*NAUT*) soltar o cabo.

**castanets** [kæstə'nets] *npl* castanholas *fpl*.

**castaway** ['ka:stəwei] *n* náufrago.

**caste** [ka:st] *n* casta.

**casting vote** ['ka:stɪŋ-] *n* voto decisivo, voto de minerva.

**cast iron** *n* ferro fundido.

**castle** ['ka:sl] *n* castelo; (*CHESS*) torre *f*.

**castor** ['ka:stə*] *n* (*wheel*) rodízio; ~ **oil** *n* óleo de rícino; ~ **sugar** *n* açúcar *m* branco refinado.

**castrate** [kæs'treɪt] *vt* castrar.

**casual** ['kæʒjul] *adj* (*by chance*) fortuito; (*irregular*: work *etc*) eventual, incerto; (*unconcerned*) despreocupado; (*informal*: clothes) esportivo, sem cerimônia; ~**ly** *adv* casualmente, sem refletir.

**casualty** ['kæʒjultɪ] *n* vítima *f* ferido; (*dead*) morto; (*MIL*) baixa; **casualties** *npl* perdas *fpl*.

**cat** [kæt] *n* gato; ~**'s eye** *n* (*Brit*: AUTO) olho de gato.

**Catalan** ['kætələn] *adj, n* catalão/lã *m/f*.

**catalogue, catalog** (*US*) ['kætələg] *n* catálogo // *vt* catalogar.

**Catalonia** [kætə'ləunɪə] *n* Catalunha.

**catalyst** ['kætəlɪst] *n* catalisador *m*.

**catapult** ['kætəpʌlt] *n* catapulta.

**cataract** ['kætərækt] *n* (*also MED*) catarata.

**catarrh** [kə'ta:*] *n* catarro.

**catastrophe** [kə'tæstrəfɪ] *n* catástrofe *f*; **catastrophic** [kætə'strɔfɪk] *adj* catastrófico.

**catch** [kætʃ], *pt, pp* **caught** *vt*

(gen) apanhar; (arrest) deter; (grasp) agarrar; (breath) pegar; (person: by surprise) surpreender; (attract: attention) ganhar; (MED) apanhar; (also: ~ up) alcançar // vi (fire) pegar fogo; (in branches etc) prender-se // n (fish etc) pesca; (act of catching) captura; (trick) manha, armadilha; (of lock) fecho, fechadura; to ~ on vi (understand) perceber, pegar; (grow popular) popularizar-se; to ~ sight of ver; to ~ up vi (fig) pôr em dia.

**catch:** ~ing adj (MED) contagioso; ~ment area n zona de contágio; ~phrase n cliché m, slogan m; ~y adj (tune) atraente.

**catechism** ['kætɪkɪzəm] n (REL) catecismo.

**categoric(al)** [kætɪ'gɔrɪk(əl)] adj categórico, terminante.

**categorize** ['kætɪgəraɪz] vt classificar; **category** [-rɪ] n categoria, classe f.

**cater** ['keɪtə*] vi: to ~ for fornecer a; (needs) atender a; (consumers) prover de; ~er n fornecedor m, abastecedor m; ~ing n serviço de bufê; (trade) abastecimento.

**caterpillar** ['kætəpɪlə*] n lagarta; ~ track n esteira de (lagarta).

**cathedral** [kə'θiːdrəl] n catedral f.

**catholic** [kæθəlɪk] adj católico; **C~** adj, n (REL) católico/a.

**cattle** ['kætl] npl gado sg.

**catty** ['kætɪ] adj malicioso, rancoroso.

**Caucasus** ['kɔːkəsəs] n Cáucaso.

**caught** [kɔːt] pt, pp of **catch**.

**cauliflower** ['kɔlɪflauə*] n couve-flor f.

**cause** [kɔːz] n causa, motivo, razão f // vt causar; (provoke) provocar.

**causeway** ['kɔːzweɪ] n (road) calçada; (embankment) banqueta.

**caustic** ['kɔːstɪk] adj cáustico; (fig) mordaz.

**caution** ['kɔːʃən] n cautela,

prudência; (warning) aviso // vt acautelar, avisar.

**cautious** ['kɔːʃəs] adj cauteloso, prudente, precavido; ~ly adv com cautela; ~ness n cautela, prudência.

**cavalier** [kævə'lɪə*] adj arrogante, descortês.

**cavalry** ['kævəlrɪ] n cavalaria.

**cave** [keɪv] n caverna, gruta; to ~ in vi dar de si; (roof etc) ceder; ~man n troglodita m, homem m das cavernas; ~woman n troglodita f, mulher f das cavernas.

**cavern** ['kævən] n caverna.

**caviar(e)** ['kævɪɑː*] n caviar m.

**cavity** ['kævɪtɪ] n buraco, cavidade f.

**cavort** [kə'vɔːt] vi cabriolar.

**caw** [kɔː] vi grasnar.

**CBI** n abbr of **Confederation of British Industries.**

**cc** abbr of **cubic centimetres; carbon copy.**

**cease** [siːs] vt/i cessar; ~fire n cessar-fogo m; ~less adj contínuo, incessante; ~lessly adv sem parar, sem cessar.

**cedar** ['siːdə*] n cedro.

**cede** [siːd] vt ceder.

**ceiling** ['siːlɪŋ] n teto (PT: -ct-); (fig) limite m.

**Celsius** ['sɛlsɪəs] (US) adj = **centigrade.**

**celebrate** ['sɛlɪbreɪt] vt celebrar, // vi divertir-se; ~d adj célebre; **celebration** [-'breɪʃən] n festa; celebração f.

**celebrity** [sɪ'lɛbrɪtɪ] n celebridade f.

**celery** ['sɛlərɪ] n aipo.

**celestial** [sɪ'lɛstɪəl] adj (of sky) celeste; (divine) celestial.

**celibacy** ['sɛlɪbəsɪ] n celibato.

**cell** [sɛl] n cela; (BIOL) célula; (ELEC) pilha.

**cellar** ['sɛlə*] n porão m; (for wine) adega.

**'cello** ['tʃɛləu] n violoncelo.

**ellophane** ['sɛləfeɪn] *n* celofane *m*.

**ellular** ['sɛljulə*] *adj* celular.

**ellulose** ['sɛljuləus] *n* celulose *f*.

**'elt** [kɛlt, sɛlt] *adj, n* celta *m/f*; ~**ic** *adj* celta.

**'ement** [sə'mɛnt] *n* cimento // *vt* cimentar; (*fig*) cimentar, fortalecer.

**'emetery** ['sɛmɪtrɪ] *n* cemitério *m*.

**'enotaph** ['sɛnətɑːf] *n* cenotáfio.

**'ensor** ['sɛnsə*] *n* censor // *vt* (*cut*) cortar, expurgar; ~**ship** *n* censura.

**'ensure** ['sɛnʃə*] *vt* censurar.

**'ensus** ['sɛnsəs] *n* censo.

**'ent** [sɛnt] *n* (*US: coin*) centavo, cêntimo; *see also* **per.**

**'entenary** [sɛn'tiːnərɪ] *n* centenário.

**'enti...** [sɛntɪ] *pref:* ~**grade** *adj* centígrado; ~**litre** *n* centilitro; ~**metre** *n* centímetro; ~**pede** *n* centopéia.

**'entral** ['sɛntrəl] *adj* central; **C~** **American** *adj* centroamericano; ~**heating** *n* aquecimento central; ~**ize** *vt* centralizar.

**'entre** ['sɛntə*] *n* centro; ~**-forward** *n* (*SPORT*) centro-avante *m*, centro; ~**-half** *n* (*SPORT*) centromédio.

**'entury** ['sɛntjurɪ] *n* século; **20th** ~ século vinte.

**'eramic** [sɪ'ræmɪk] *adj* cerâmico; ~**s** *n* cerâmica *sg*.

**'ereal** ['siːrɪəl] *n* cereal *m*.

**'eremony** ['sɛrɪmənɪ] *n* cerimônia.

**'ertain** ['sɜːtən] *adj* (*gen*) certo; **for** ~ com certeza; ~**ly** *adv* certamente, com certeza; ~**ty** *n* certeza, segurança.

**'ertificate** [sə'tɪfɪkɪt] *n* certificado; **certified public accountant** (*US*) *n* = **chartered accountant.**

**'ertify** ['sɜːtɪfaɪ] *vt* certificar.

**'ervix** ['sɜːvɪks] *n* cerviz *f*.

**'essation** [sə'seɪʃən] *n* cessação *f*, suspensão *f*.

**'cf.** *abbr* = **compare** .

**chafe** [tʃeɪf] *vt* (*rub*) roçar; (*wear*) gastar; (*irritate*) irritar.

**chaffinch** ['tʃæfɪntʃ] *n* tentilhão *m*.

**chagrin** ['ʃægrɪn] *n* desgosto, mortificação *f*.

**chain** [tʃeɪn] *n* (*gen*) corrente *f*, cadeia // *vt* (*also:* ~ **up**) encadear; ~ **reaction** *n* reação (*Pt:* -cç-) *f* em cadeia; ~ **store** *n* grande armazem *f*.

**chair** [tʃɛə*] *n* cadeira; (*armchair*) cadeira de braços; (*of university*) cátedra // *vt* (*meeting*) presidir; ~**lift** *n* teleférico; ~**man** *n* presidente *m*.

**chalet** ['ʃæleɪ] *n* chalé *m*.

**chalice** ['tʃælɪs] *n* cálice *m*.

**chalk** [tʃɔːk] *n* (*GEO*) greda; (*for writing*) giz *m*.

**challenge** ['tʃælɪndʒ] *n* desafio, repto // *vt* desafiar, reptar; (*statement, right*) disputar, contestar; **to** ~ **sb to do sth** desafiar alguém para fazer algo; **challenger** *n* (*SPORT*) competidor(a) *m/f*; **challenging** *adj* desafiante; (*tone*) de desafio.

**chamber** ['tʃeɪmbə*] *n* sala, câmara; ~ **of commerce** câmara de comércio; ~**maid** *n* arrumadeira; (*Pt*) empregada; ~ **music** *n* música de câmara.

**chamois** ['ʃæmwɑː] *n* camurça.

**champagne** [ʃæm'peɪn] *n* champanha *m*, champanhe *m*.

**champion** ['tʃæmpɪən] *n* campeão/peã *m/f*; ~**ship** *n* campeonato.

**chance** [tʃɑːns] *n* (*luck*) sorte *f*, oportunidade *f*; (*fate*) azar *m*; (*opportunity*) oportunidade, ocasião *f*; (*likelihood*) possibilidade *f*; (*risk*) risco // *vt* arriscar // *adj* fortuito, casual; **to** ~ **it** aventurar-se, arriscar-se; **to take a** ~ arriscar-se; **by** ~ por acaso.

**chancel** ['tʃɑːnsəl] *n* coro, capela-mor *f*.

**chancellor** ['tʃɑːnsələ*] *n*

**chanceler** m; (Brit) **C~ of the Exchequer** n Ministro das Finanças.

**chandelier** [ʃændə'liə*] n candelabro.

**change** [tʃeɪndʒ] vt (gen) mudar, trocar; (replace) substituir; (gear, clothes, house) mudar de, trocar de; (exchange) trocar; (transform) transformar // vi (gen) trocar(-se), mudar(-se); (trains) mudar; **to ~ into** transformar-se em // n câmbio, modificação f, transformação f; (coins) dinheiro miúdo; (money returned) troco; **for a ~** para variar; **~able** adj (weather) variável, instável; **~less** adj imutável; **~over** n (to new system) mudança.

**changing** ['tʃeɪndʒɪŋ] adj variável; **~ room** n vestiário.

**channel** ['tʃænl] n (TV) canal m; (of river) leito; (of sea) braço (de mar), estreito; (groove) ranhura; (fig: medium) meio, via // vt canalizar; **the (English) C~** o Canal da Mancha; **the C~ Islands** Ilhas Anglo-Normandas fpl.

**chant** [tʃɑːnt] n cântico // vt cantar; (fig) entoar.

**chaos** ['keɪɒs] n caos m; **chaotic** [keɪ'ɒtɪk] adj caótico.

**chap** [tʃæp] n (col: man) tipo, sujeito, cara m // vi (skin) agretar-se.

**chapel** ['tʃæpəl] n capela.

**chaperon** ['ʃæpərəʊn] n mulher f acompanhante.

**chaplain** ['tʃæplɪn] n capelão m.

**chapter** ['tʃæptə*] n capítulo.

**char** [tʃɑː*] vt (burn) tostar, queimar // n = **charlady**.

**character** ['kærɪktə*] n caráter (Pt: -ct-) m, natureza, qualidade f; (in novel, film) personagem m; (role) papel m; **~istic** [-'rɪstɪk] adj característico // n característica; **~ize** vt caracterizar.

**charade** [ʃə'rɑːd] n charada.

**charcoal** ['tʃɑːkəʊl] n carvão m de lenha; (ART) carvão.

**charge** [tʃɑːdʒ] n carga; (LAW) encargo, acusação f; (cost) preço custo; (responsibility) encarg (task) incumbência // vt (LAW: with acusar de; (gun, battery, MIL: enemy atacar; (price) cobrar; (customer pedir; (sb with task) encarregar vi atacar, precipitar-se; (make pay cobrar; **~s** npl: **bank ~s** taxa cobradas pelo banco; **free of ~** grátis; **to reverse the ~s** (TE telefonar a cobrar; **to take ~ o** encarregar-se de; **to be in ~** estar a cargo de or encarregado do **how much do you ~?** quanto voc cobra?; **to ~ an expense (up) t** sb's account pôr a despesa na cont de alguém.

**charitable** ['tʃærɪtəbl] ad caritativo.

**charity** ['tʃærɪtɪ] n (gen) caridade (sympathy) compaixão f; (organ zation) organização f de caridade.

**charlady** ['tʃɑːleɪdɪ] n mulher f d limpezas, faxineira.

**charm** [tʃɑːm] n charme m encanto, atrativo (Pt: -ct-); (spell feitiço; (object) amuleto // v encantar, enfeitiçar; **~ing** ad encantador(a), simpático, char moso.

**chart** [tʃɑːt] n quadro; (graph gráfico; (map) mapa m // vt faze um gráfico de; (course) traçar.

**charter** ['tʃɑːtə*] vt (plane) fretar alugar; (ship) fretar // (document) carta, alvará m; **~ed accountant** n perito contador; **flight** n vôo m charter or fretado.

**charwoman** ['tʃɑːwʊmən] n = **charlady**.

**chase** [tʃeɪs] vt (follow) persegui (hunt) caçar, dar caça a // perseguição f, caça; **to ~ afte** correr atrás.

**chasm** ['kæzəm] n abismo.

**chassis** ['ʃæsɪ] n chassi m.

**chaste** [tʃeɪst] adj casto; **chastity** ['tʃæstɪtɪ] n castidade f.

**chat** [tʃæt] vi (also: **have a ~**) falar, conversar, bater papo // n conversa, bate-papo m.

**chatter** ['tʃætə*] vi (person) falar; (teeth) bater os dentes // n (of birds) chilro; (of people) tagarelice m; **~box** n tagarela m/f, falador(a) m/f.

**chatty** ['tʃætɪ] adj (style) familiar; (person) conversador(a).

**chauffeur** ['ʃəʊfə*] n chofer m, motorista m/f.

**cheap** [tʃiːp] adj barato; (trick) de mau gosto; (poor quality) barato, de pouca qualidade // adv barato; **~en** vt baixar o preço de, rebaixar; to **~en o.s.** rebaixar-se; **~ly** adv barato, por baixo preço.

**cheat** [tʃiːt] vi trapacear, colar; (Pt) trapacear, fazer batota // vt defraudar, enganar // n fraude f; (person) trapaceiro/a; **~ing** n trapaça.

**check** [tʃek] vt (examine) controlar; (facts) verificar; (count) contar; (halt) impedir, deter; (restrain) parar, refrear // n (inspection) controle m, inspeção (Pt: -çç-) f; (curb) freio; (bill) conta; (obstacle) impedimento, estorvo; (token) ficha, talão m; (pattern: gen pl) xadrez m; to **~ in** vi (in hotel) registrar-se; (in airport) apresentar-se // vt (luggage) entregar; to **~ out** vi (of hotel) pagar a conta e sair; to **~ up** vi: to **~ up on sth** verificar algo; to **~ up on sb** investigar alguém; **~ing account** (US) n conta corrente; **~mate** n xeque-mate m; **~out** n caixa; **~point** n (ponto de controle m; **~up** n (MED) revisão f geral; (of machine) revisão.

**cheek** [tʃiːk] n bochecha; (impudence) descaramento; **~bone** n maçã f do rosto; **~y** adj insolente, descarado.

**cheer** [tʃɪə*] vt dar vivas; aplaudir;

(gladden) alegrar, animar // vi aplaudir, gritar com entusiasmo // n grito (de aplauso); **~s** npl aplausos mpl; **~s!** saúde!; to **~ up** vi animar-se, alegrar-se // vt alegrar, animar; **~ful** adj alegre; **~fulness** n alegria.

**cheerio** excl até logo!, adeus!; **~less** adj triste, sombrio.

**cheese** [tʃiːz] n queijo.

**chef** [ʃef] n cozinheiro-chefe m/f.

**chemical** ['kemɪkəl] adj, n químico.

**chemist** ['kemɪst] n farmacêutico; (scientist) químico; **~ry** n química; **~'s (shop)** n farmácia.

**cheque** [tʃek] n cheque m; **~book** n talão m de cheques; (Pt) livro de cheques.

**chequered** ['tʃekəd] adj (fig) variado, acidentado.

**cherish** ['tʃerɪʃ] vt (love) querer, apreciar; (protect) cuidar; (hope etc) acalentar.

**cherry** ['tʃerɪ] n cereja.

**chess** [tʃes] n xadrez m; **~board** n tabuleiro de xadrez); **~man** n peça, pedra (de xadrez).

**chest** [tʃest] n (ANAT) peito; (box) caixa, cofre m; **~ of drawers** n cômoda.

**chestnut** ['tʃesnʌt] n castanha; **~ (tree)** n castanheiro.

**chew** [tʃuː] vt mastigar; **~ing gum** n chiclete m, chicle m.

**chic** [ʃiːk] adj elegante, chique.

**chick** [tʃɪk] n pinto, pintainho; (fam) moça.

**chicken** ['tʃɪkɪn] n galinha; (food) galinha, frango; **~pox** n varicela.

**chickpea** ['tʃɪkpiː] n grão-de-bico m.

**chicory** ['tʃɪkərɪ] n (for coffee) chicória; (salad) escarola.

**chief** [tʃiːf] n chefe m/f // adj principal; **~ly** adv principalmente.

**chiffon** ['ʃɪfɔn] n gaze f.

**chilblain** ['tʃɪlbleɪn] n frieira.

**child** [tʃaɪld], pl **~ren** ['tʃɪldrən] n criança; (offspring) filho; **~birth** n parto; **~hood** n infância, meninice f; **~ish** adj infantil, pueril; **~like** adj

Chile 48 chubby

próprio (de criança); ~ minder n
cuidadora de crianças.
Chile [tʃɪl] n Chile m; ~an adj, n
chileno/a.
chill [tʃɪl] n frio; (MED) resfriamento
// vt esfriar; (CULIN) semi-congelar;
~y adj frio.
chime [tʃaɪm] n (peal) repique m,
som m // vi repicar, soar.
chimney [tʃɪmnɪ] n chaminé f; ~
sweep n limpador m de chaminés.
chimpanzee [tʃɪmpæn'zi:] n
chimpanzé m.
chin [tʃɪn] n queixo.
china [tʃaɪnə] n porcelana; (gen)
louça fina.
China [tʃaɪnə] n China; Chinese
[tʃaɪ'niːz] adj chinês/esa; the Chinese
os Chineses // n (LING) chinês m.
chink [tʃɪŋk] n (opening) greta,
abertura; (noise) tinir.
chip [tʃɪp] n (gen pl: CULIN) batata
frita; (of wood) lasca; (of glass,
stone) lasca, pedaço; (at poker)
ficha // vt (cup, plate) lascar; to ~
in vi interromper; (contribute)
compartilhar as despesas.
chiropodist [kɪ'rɔpədɪst] n
pedicuro.
chirp [tʃəːp] vi chilrar, piar;
(cricket) chilrear.
chisel [tʃɪzl] n (for wood) formão
m; (for stone) cinzel m.
chit [tʃɪt] n talão m.
chitchat [tʃɪttʃæt] n palestra,
bisbilhotice f.
chivalrous [ʃɪvəlrəs] adj
cavalheiresco; chivalry [-rɪ] n
cavalaria.
chives [tʃaɪvz] npl cebolinha sg.
chlorine [klɔːriːn] n cloro.
chock [tʃɔk] ~-a-block, ~-full
adj abarrotado, apinhado.
chocolate [tʃɔklɪt] n chocolate m.
choice [tʃɔɪs] n seleção (Pt: -cç-) f,
escolha; (preference) preferência //
adj seleto (Pt: -ct-), escolhido.
choir [kwaɪə*] n coro; ~boy n
menino de coro.

choke [tʃəuk] vi sufocar-se; (on food)
engasgar-se // vt afogar, sufoca
(block) obstruir // n (AUT) afogado
m; (Pt) ar m; choker n (necklace
colar m curto.
cholera [kɔlərə] n cólera.
choose [tʃuːz], pt chose, p
chosen vt escolher; (team
selecionar (Pt: -cc-).
chop [tʃɔp] vt (wood) cortar, talhar
(CULIN. also: ~ up) cortar er
pedaços; (meat) picar // n golpe m
(CULIN) costeleta; ~s npl (jaws
boca sg, lábios mpl; ~py adj (sea
agitado; ~sticks npl pauzinhos mp
palitos mpl.
choral [kɔːrəl] adj coral.
chord [kɔːd] n (MUS) acorde m.
chore [tʃɔː*] n tarefa; (routine task
trabalho de rotina.
choreographer [kɔrɪ'ɔgrəfə*] r
coreógrafo/a.
chorister [kɔristə*] n corista m/f.
chortle [tʃɔːtl] vi rir, gargalhar.
chorus [kɔːrəs] n coro; (repeate
part of song) estribilho.
chose [tʃəuz], chosen [tʃəuzn] pt
pp of choose.
Christ [kraɪst] n Cristo.
christen [krɪsn] vt batizar (Pt
-pt-); ~ing n batismo (Pt: -pt-).
Christian [krɪstʃən] adj,
cristão/tã m/f; ~ity [-'ænɪtɪ] n
cristianismo; ~ name n nome m de
batismo (Pt: -pt-).
Christmas [krɪsməs] n Natal m
Merry ~! Feliz Natal!; ~ Eve n
véspera de Natal.
chrome [krəum], chromium
[krəumɪəm] n cromo.
chromosome [krəuməsəum] n
cromossomo.
chronic [krɔnɪk] adj crônico.
chronicle [krɔnɪkl] n crônica.
chronological [krɔnə'lɔdʒɪkəl] adj
cronológico.
chrysanthemum [krɪ'sæn-
θəməm] n crisântemo.
chubby [tʃʌbɪ] adj roliço.

**chuck** [tʃʌk] vt lançar, deitar; **to ~ out** vt jogar fora, expulsar; (Pt) deitar fora; **to ~ (up)** vt abandonar.

**chuckle** ['tʃʌkl] vi rir.

**chug** [tʃʌg] vi andar fazendo ruído da descarga; **to ~ along** vi (fig) ir manejando.

**chum** [tʃʌm] n camarada m, amigo.

**chunk** [tʃʌŋk] n pedaço, naco.

**church** [tʃɔːtʃ] n igreja; **~yard** n adro, cemitério.

**churlish** ['tʃɔːlɪʃ] adj grosseiro, rude.

**churn** [tʃɔːn] n (for butter) batedeira; (for milk) lata, vasilha // vt bater, agitar.

**chute** [ʃuːt] n (also: **rubbish ~**) despejador m; (children's slide) rampa, tobogã m.

**chutney** ['tʃʌtnɪ] n conserva picante.

**CID** n abbr of **Criminal Investigation Department** Brigada de Investigação Criminal.

**cider** ['saɪdə*] n sidra.

**cigar** [sɪ'gɑː*] n charuto.

**cigarette** [sɪgə'ret] n cigarro; **~ case** n cigarreira; **~ end** n ponta de cigarro; **~ holder** n piteira; (Pt) boquilha.

**Cinderella** [sɪndə'relə] n gata borralheira.

**cinders** ['sɪndəz] npl cinzas fpl.

**cine** [sɪnɪ]: **~-camera** n câmara cinematográfica; **~-film** n filme m cinematográfico.

**cinema** ['sɪnəmə] n cinema m.

**cinnamon** ['sɪnəmən] n canela.

**cipher** ['saɪfə*] n cifra.

**circle** ['səːkl] n círculo; (in cinema) balcão m // vi dar voltas // vt (surround) rodear, cercar; (move round) dar a volta.

**circuit** ['səːkɪt] n circuito; (tour) volta; (track) pista; (lap) volta; **~ous** [səː'kjuːtəs] adj tortuoso, indireto (Pt: -ct-).

**circular** ['səːkjulə*] adj circular // n circular f.

**circulate** ['səːkjuleɪt] vi circular // vt pôr em circulação, espalhar; **circulation** [-'leɪʃən] n circulação f; (of newspaper) tiragem f.

**circumcise** ['səːkəmsaɪz] vt circuncidar.

**circumference** [sə'kʌmfərəns] n circunferência.

**circumspect** ['səːkəmspekt] adj circunspeto (Pt: -ct-), prudente.

**circumstances** ['səːkəmstənsɪz] npl circunstâncias fpl; (financial condition) situação f econômica.

**circus** ['səːkəs] n circo; (round-about) rotunda, praça circular.

**cistern** ['sɪstən] n tanque m, reservatório; (in toilet) caixa d'água.

**cite** [saɪt] vt citar.

**citizen** ['sɪtɪzn] n (POL) cidadão/dã m/f; (resident) habitante m/f; **~ship** n cidadania.

**citrus fruit** ['sɪtrəs-] n citrinos mpl.

**city** ['sɪtɪ] n cidade f; **the C~** centro financeiro de Londres.

**civic** ['sɪvɪk] adj cívico, municipal.

**civil** ['sɪvɪl] adj civil; (polite) delicado, cortês; (defence) passivo; (well-bred) educado; **~ engineer** n engenheiro civil; **C~ Service** n administração f pública; **~ian** [sɪ'vɪlɪən] adj civil, paisano // n m/f, paisano/a.

**civilization** [sɪvɪlaɪ'zeɪʃən] n civilização f.

**civilized** ['sɪvɪlaɪzd] adj civilizado.

**claim** [kleɪm] vt exigir, reclamar; (rights etc) reivindicar; (assert) pretender // vi (for insurance) reclamar // n reclamação f; (LAW) direito; (pretension) pretensão f; **~ant** n (ADMIN, LAW) reclamante m/f.

**clairvoyant** [kleə'vɔɪənt] n clarividente m/f.

**clam** [klæm] n mexilhão m, sururu m.

**clamber** ['klæmbə*] vi trepar.

**clammy** ['klæmɪ] adj (cold) frio e

úmido; (sticky) pegajoso.
**clamp** [klæmp] n grampo // vt
segurar; **to ~ down on** vt fus
suprimir, proibir.
**clan** [klæn] n clã m.
**clang** [klæŋ] n retintim m, som
metálico // vi retinir.
**clap** [klæp] vi aplaudir // vt (hands)
bater palmas; (put) pôr // n (of
hands) palmada; (of thunder)
ribombar m do trovão; **~ping** n
aplausos mpl.
**claret** ['klærət] n clarete m.
**clarification** [klærɪfɪ'keɪʃən] n
esclarecimento; **clarify** ['klærɪfaɪ] vt
esclarecer, aclarar, clarificar.
**clarinet** [klærɪ'nɛt] n clarinete m,
clarineta f.
**clarity** ['klærɪtɪ] n claridade f.
**clash** [klæʃ] n colisão f; (fig) choque
m // vi (meet) encontrar-se;
(battle) chocar; (disagree) estar em
conflito.
**clasp** [klɑːsp] n fecho; (on jewels)
fivela // vt afivelar; (hand) apertar;
(embrace) abraçar.
**class** [klɑːs] n (gen) classe f // vt
de classe // vt classificar.
**classic** ['klæsɪk] adj clássico // n
(work) obra clássica; **~al** adj
clássico.
**classification** [klæsɪfɪ'keɪʃən] n
classificação f; **classify** ['klæsɪfaɪ] vt
classificar.
**class: ~mate** n colega m/f de aula;
**~room** n sala de aula.
**clatter** ['klætə*] n ruído, estrépito;
(of hooves) barulho de casco // vi
fazer barulho ou ruído.
**clause** [klɔːz] n cláusula; (LING)
oração f.
**claustrophobia** [klɔːstrə'fəubɪə] n
claustrofobia.
**claw** [klɔː] n (of cat) pata, unha; (of
bird of prey) garra; (of lobster)
pinça; (TECH) unha // vt: **to ~ at**
arranhar; (tear) rasgar.
**clay** [kleɪ] n argila.
**clean** [kliːn] adj limpo; (clear)

nítido, bem definido // vt limpar; **to
~ out** vt limpar; **to ~ up** vt limpar,
assear; **~~cut** adj (person) honesto;
(clear) nítido; **~er** n (person)
limpador(a) m/f, faxineiro/a; **~ing**
n (gen) limpeza; (clothes) lavagem
f; **~liness** ['klɛnlɪnɪs] n limpeza;
**~-shaven** adj sem barba, de cara
raspada.
**cleanse** [klɛnz] vt limpar; **cleanser**
n limpador m; (for face)
demaquilador m; **cleansing
department** n departamento de
limpeza.
**clear** [klɪə*] adj claro; (road, way)
limpo, livre; (complete) completo //
vt (space) despejar, limpar; (LAW:
suspect) absolver; (obstacle) salvar,
passar sobre; (debt) liquidar //
vi (gen) esclarecer-se, aclarar-se; (fog
etc) clarear-se // adv: **~ of** a salvo
de; **to ~ up** vt limpar; (mystery)
resolver, esclarecer; **~ance** n
(removal) despejo; (permission)
permissão f; **~~cut** adj bem
definido, nítido; **~ing** n (in wood)
clareira; **~ing bank** n câmara de
compensação; **~ly** adv claramente;
**~way** n (Brit) estrada onde não se
pode estacionar.
**cleaver** ['kliːvə] n cutelo (de
açougueiro).
**clef** [klɛf] n (MUS) clave f.
**clemency** ['klɛmənsɪ] n clemência.
**clench** [klɛntʃ] vt apertar, cerrar.
**clergy** ['klɜːdʒɪ] n clero; **~man** n
clérigo, pastor m.
**clerical** ['klɛrɪkəl] adj clerical.
**clerk** [klɑːk, (US) klɑːrk] n caixeiro,
empregado/a m/f.
**clever** ['klɛvə*] adj (mentally)
inteligente, esperto; (deft, crafty)
hábil; (device, arrangement)
engenhoso.
**cliché** ['kliːʃeɪ] n clichê m, frase f
feita.
**click** [klɪk] vt (tongue) dar estalido
com; (heels) bater.

**client** ['klaɪənt] *n* cliente *m/f*; **~ele** [kli:ɑːn'tel] *n* clientela.

**cliff** [klɪf] *n* penhasco.

**climate** ['klaɪmɪt] *n* clima *m*; *(fig)* ambiente *m*.

**climax** ['klaɪmæks] *n* clímax *m*, ponto culminante; *(sexual)* clímax.

**climb** [klaɪm] *vi* subir, trepar // *vt (stairs)* subir; *(tree)* trepar; *(hill)* escalar // *n* subida; **~er** *n* alpinista *m/f*; **~ing** *n* alpinismo.

**clinch** [klɪntʃ] *vt (deal)* fechar; *(argument)* decidir, resolver.

**cling** [klɪŋ], *pt, pp* **clung** [klʌŋ] *vi*: **to ~ to** pegar-se a, aderir a; *(of clothes)* agarrar-se a, ajustar-se a.

**clinic** ['klɪnɪk] *n* clínica; **~al** *adj* clínico.

**clink** [klɪŋk] *vi* tinir.

**clip** [klɪp] *n (for hair)* prendedor *m*, fivela; *(also:* **paper ~)** mola, clipe *m; (clamp)* fecho // *vt (cut)* cortar; *(shorten)* aparar; *(clamp)* grampear; **~pers** *npl (for gardening)* podadeira *sg; (for hair)* máquina *sg; (for nails)* tesoura *sg* para cortar unhas; **~ping** *n* recorte *m*.

**clique** [kliːk] *n* camarilha, panelinha.

**cloak** [kləuk] *n* capa, manto // *vt (fig)* encobrir; **~room** *n* vestiário; *(WC)* lavatórios *mpl*.

**clock** [klɔk] *n* relógio; *(in taxi)* taxímetro; *(fam)* cara; **~wise** *adv* em sentido horário; **~work** *n* mecanismo de relógio // *adj* de corda.

**clog** [klɔg] *n* tamanco, soco // *vt* entupir // *vi* entupir-se, emperrar.

**cloister** ['klɔɪstə*] *n* claustro.

**close** *adj, adv and derivatives* [kləus] *adj* próximo, reservado; *(print, weave)* denso, compacto; *(friend)* íntimo; *(connection)* estreito; *(examination)* detalhado, minucioso; *(weather)* abafado; *(atmosphere)* sufocante; *(room)* mal arejado // *adv* perto, próximo // *vb and*

**derivatives** [kləuz] *vt (shut)* fechar, encerrar; *(end)* acabar, concluir // *vi (shop etc)* fechar-se; *(end)* concluir-se, terminar-se // *n (end)* fim *m*, conclusão *f*, terminação *f*; **to ~ down** *vi* fechar-se definitivamente; **~d** *adj (shop etc)* fechado; **~d shop** *n* estabelecimento industrial só para empregados sindicalizados; **~ly** *adv (exactly)* fielmente; *(carefully)* rigorosamente.

**closet** ['klɔzɪt] *n (cupboard)* armário; *(WC)* retrete *m*, privada.

**close-up** ['kləusʌp] *n* primeiro plano.

**closure** ['kləuʒə*] *n (close-down)* encerramento, fechamento; *(end)* fim *m*.

**clot** [klɔt] *n (gen: blood ~)* coágulo, coalho; *(fam: idiot)* imbecil *m/f* // *vi (blood)* coagular-se, coalhar-se.

**cloth** [klɔθ] *n (material)* tecido, fazenda; *(rag)* pano, trapo.

**clothe** [kləuð] *vt* vestir; *(fig)* revestir; **~s** *npl* roupa *sg*; **~s brush** *n* escova (para a roupa); **~s line** *n* corda (para estender a roupa); **~s peg**, **~s pin** *n (US)* pregador *m*; **clothing** *n* = **clothes**.

**cloud** [klaud] *n* núvem *f*; **~burst** *n* aguaceiro; **~y** *adj* nublado; *(liquid)* turvo.

**clout** [klaut] *vt* dar uma bofetada em.

**clove** [kləuv] *n* cravo; **~ of garlic** dente *m* de alho.

**clover** ['kləuvə*] *n* trevo.

**clown** [klaun] *n* palhaço // *vi (also:* **~ about**, **~ around)** fazer palhaçadas.

**club** [klʌb] *n (society)* clube *m*; *(weapon)* cacete *m*; *(also:* **golf ~)** taco, clube // *vt* esbordoar // *vi:* **to ~ together** cotizar-se; **~s** *npl (CARDS)* paus *mpl*; **~ car** *(US)* *n* vagão-restaurante *m*; **~house** *n* sala de reunião.

**cluck** [klʌk] *vi* cacarejar.

**clue** [kluː] *n* sinal *m*; (*in crosswords*) indício, pista; **I haven't a ~** não faço ideia.

**clump** [klʌmp] *n* (*of trees*) grupo.

**clumsy** [ˈklʌmzɪ] *adj* (*person*) desajeitado; (*movement*) deselegante, mal-feito.

**cluster** [ˈklʌstə*] *n* grupo; (*BOT*) cacho, ramo // *vi* agrupar-se, apinhar-se.

**clutch** [klʌtʃ] *n* (*grip, grasp*) alcance *m*, garra; (*AUT*) embreagem *f*; (*Pt*: embraiagem); (*pedal*) pedal *m* de embreagem (*Pt*: embraiagem) // *vt* empunhar, pegar em.

**clutter** [ˈklʌtə*] *vt* abarrotar, encher desordenadamente.

**Co.** *abbr of* **county; company.**

**c/o** *abbr of* **care of** a/c, ao cuidado de.

**coach** [kəutʃ] *n* (*bus*) camioneta, ônibus *m*; (*horse-drawn*) carruagem *f*, coche *m*; (*of train*) vagão *m*; (*SPORT*) treinador *m*, instrutor *m* // *vt* (*SPORT*) treinar; (*student*) preparar, ensinar.

**coagulate** [kəuˈægjuleɪt] *vi* coagular-se.

**coal** [kəul] *n* carvão *m*; **~ face** *n* frente *f* de carvão; **~field** *n* região *f* carbonífera.

**coalition** [kəuəˈlɪʃən] *n* coalizão *f.*

**coal:** **~man**, **~ merchant** *n* carvoeiro; **~mine** *n* mina de carvão.

**coarse** [kɔːs] *adj* grosso, áspero; (*vulgar*) grosseiro, ordinário.

**coast** [kəust] *n* costa, litoral *m* // *vi* (*AUT*) ir em ponto morto; **~al** *adj* costeiro, litorâneo; **~er** *n* embarcação *f* costeira, barco de cabotagem; **~guard** *n* guarda costeira; **~line** *n* litoral *m.*

**coat** [kəut] *n* (*jacket*) casaco; (*overcoat*) sobretudo; (*of animal*) pelo, lã *f*; (*of paint*) demão *f*, camada // *vt* cobrir, revestir; **~ of arms** *n* brasão *m*; **~ hanger** *n* cabide *m*; **~ing** *n* camada, mão *f.*

**coax** [kəuks] *vt* persuadir com meiguice.

**cob** [kɔb] *n see* **corn.**

**cobbler** [ˈkɔblə] *n* sapateiro-remendão *m.*

**cobbles** [ˈkɔblz], **cobblestones** [ˈkɔblstəunz] *npl* pedras arredondadas *fpl.*

**cobra** [ˈkəubrə] *n* cobra.

**cobweb** [ˈkɔbweb] *n* teia de aranha.

**cocaine** [kəˈkeɪn] *n* cocaína.

**cock** [kɔk] *n* (*rooster*) galo; (*male bird*) macho // *vt* (*gun*) engatilhar; **~atoo** *n* cacatua; **~erel** *n* frango, galo pequeno.

**cockle** [ˈkɔkl] *n* berbigão *m.*

**cockpit** [ˈkɔkpɪt] *n* (*in aircraft*) cabina.

**cockroach** [ˈkɔkrəutʃ] *n* barata.

**cocktail** [ˈkɔkteɪl] *n* cocktail *m*, coquetel *m*; **~ cabinet** *n* móvel-bar *m*; **~ party** *n* coquetel *m*, cocktail *m.*

**cocoa** [ˈkəukəu] *n* cacau *m*; (*drink*) chocolate *m.*

**coconut** [ˈkəukənʌt] *n* coco.

**cocoon** [kəˈkuːn] *n* casulo.

**cod** [kɔd] *n* bacalhau *m.*

**code** [kəud] *n* código; (*cipher*) cifra; **codify** *vt* codificar.

**coerce** [kəuˈəːs] *vt* forçar, obrigar; **coercion** [-ˈəːʃən] *n* coerção *f.*

**coexistence** [ˈkəuɪgˈzɪstəns] *n* coexistência.

**coffee** [ˈkɔfɪ] *n* café *m*; **~ bean** *n* grão *m* de café; **~ grounds** *npl* borras *fpl* de café; **~pot** *n* cafeteira.

**coffin** [ˈkɔfɪn] *n* caixão *m.*

**cog** [kɔg] *n* dente *m*; **~wheel** *n* roda dentada.

**cognac** [ˈkɔnjæk] *n* conhaque *m.*

**coherent** [kəuˈhɪərənt] *adj* coerente.

**coil** [kɔɪl] *n* rolo; (*rope*) corda enrolada; (*ELEC*) bobina; (*contraceptive*) espiral *f*, D.I.U. *m* // *vi* enrolar-se, espiralar-se.

**coin** [kɔɪn] *n* moeda // *vt* cunhar, criar; **~age** *n* cunhagem *f*;

~**-box** n caixa de moedas, cofrinho.

**coincide** [kəun'saɪd] vi coincidir; (agree) estar de acordo; **coincidence** [kəu'ɪnsɪdəns] n coincidência.

**coke** [kəuk] n (coal) coque m; (drink) coca-cola f.

**colander** ['kɒləndə*] n coador m, passador m.

**cold** [kəuld] adj frio // n frio; (MED) resfriado, (Pt) constipação f; **it's** ~ está frio; **to be** ~ estar com frio; **to catch** ~ resfriar-se, (Pt) apanhar constipação; **to** ~**-shoulder** tratar com frieza; ~**ly** adv friamente; ~**sore** n herpes m labial.

**coleslaw** ['kəulslɔ:] n salada de repolho cru.

**colic** ['kɒlɪk] n cólica f.

**collaborate** [kə'læbəreɪt] vi colaborar; **collaboration** [-'reɪʃən] n colaboração f.

**collage** [kɒ'lɑ:ʒ] n colagem f.

**collapse** [kə'læps] vi (gen) cair, tombar; (MED) desmaiar // n (gen) queda, ruína; (MED) colapso; **collapsible** adj dobrável.

**collar** ['kɒlə*] n (of coat, shirt) colarinho, gola; ~**bone** n clavícula.

**collate** [kɒ'leɪt] vt cotejar.

**colleague** ['kɒli:g] n colega m/f.

**collect** [kə'lekt] vt reunir; (as a hobby) colecionar (Pt: -cc-); (call and pick up) recolher; (wages, debts) cobrar; (donations, subscriptions) colher // vi reunir-se, colecionar-se (Pt: -cc-); ~**ion** [kə'lekʃən] n coleção (Pt: -cç-) f; (of people) reunião f, grupo; (of donations) arrecadação f; (of post) coleta.

**collective** [kə'lektɪv] adj coletivo (Pt: -ct-).

**collector** [kə'lektə*] n colecionador (Pt: -cc-) m; (of taxes etc) cobrador m.

**college** ['kɒlɪdʒ] n colégio m; (faculty) faculdade f.

**collide** [kə'laɪd] vi chocar, colidir.

**collie** ['kɒli] n cão m pastor.

**collision** [kə'lɪʒən] n choque m.

**colloquial** [kə'ləukwɪəl] adj familiar, coloquial.

**colon** ['kəulən] n (sign) dois pontos; (MED) cólon m.

**colonel** ['kə:nl] n coronel m.

**colonial** [kə'ləunɪəl] adj colonial.

**colonize** ['kɒlənaɪz] vt colonizar.

**colony** ['kɒlənɪ] n colônia.

**colossal** [kə'lɒsl] adj colossal.

**colour, color** (US) ['kʌlə*] n cor f // vt colorir; (with crayons) colorir, pintar; (dye) tingir // vi (blush) corar-se; ~**s** npl (of party, club) cores fpl; ~**-blind** adj daltônico; ~**ed** adj colorido; (photo) colorido, (Pt) a cores; ~**s** npl gente f de cor; ~**film** n filme m colorido; (Pt) película a cores; ~**ful** adj colorido; (personality) vivo, animado; ~**ing** n colorido; ~**less** adj sem cor, pálido; ~**scheme** n combinação f de cores; ~**television** n televisão f a cores.

**colt** [kəult] n potro.

**column** ['kɒləm] n coluna; ~**ist** ['kɒləmnɪst] n cronista m/f.

**coma** ['kəumə] n coma m.

**comb** [kəum] n pente m; (ornamental) pente; (of cock) crista // vt (hair) pentear; (area) vasculhar.

**combat** ['kɒmbæt] n combate m // vt combater.

**combination** [kɒmbɪ'neɪʃən] n (gen) combinação f.

**combine** [kəm'baɪn] vt combinar; (qualities) reunir // vi combinar-se // n ['kɒmbaɪn] (ECON) associação f; (pej) monopólio; ~ (**harvester**) n ceifeiro.

**combustion** [kəm'bʌstʃən] n combustão f.

**come** [kʌm], pt **came**, pp **come** vi vir; **to** ~ **about** vi suceder, acontecer; **to** ~ **across** vt fus (person) topar; (thing) encontrar; **to** ~ **away** vi ir-se embora; **to** ~ **back** vi voltar; **to** ~ **by** vt fus (acquire) conseguir; **to ~ down** vi baixar; (plane) descer; (crash) desabar; (buildings) desmoronar-se; **to ~ forward** vi apresentar-se; **to ~ in** vi entrar; (train) chegar; (fashion) entrar na moda; **to ~ in for** vt fus (criticism etc) merecer; **to ~ into** vt fus (money) herdar; **to ~ off** vi (button) desprender-se, soltar-se; (attempt) realizar-se; **to ~ on** vi (pupil, undertaking) avançar, fazer progressos // vt (find) encontrar; **~ on!** vamos!, venha!; **to ~ out** vi sair, aparecer; (be revealed) revelar-se; **to ~ out for/against** declarar-se por/contra; **to ~ to** vi voltar a si; (total) somar; **to ~ up** vi subir; (sun) aparecer; (problem) surgir; **to ~ up against** vt fus (resistance, difficulties) tropeçar com; **to ~ up with** vt fus (idea) propor, sugerir; **to ~ upon** vt fus encontrar, achar; **~back** n (THEATRE) reaparição f.

**comedian** [kə'miːdɪən] n cômico; **comedienne** [-'ɛn] n cômica.

**comedown** ['kʌmdaun] n (fam) revés m, humiliação f.

**comedy** ['kɔmɪdɪ] n comédia.

**comet** ['kɔmɪt] n cometa m.

**comfort** ['kʌmfət] n comodidade f, conforto; (well-being) bem-estar m; (solace) consolo; (relief) alívio // vt confortar, aliviar; **~able** adj confortável; **~er** n (US) n edredon m.

**comic** ['kɔmɪk] adj (also: **~al**) cômico // n (magazine) humorístico; **~ strip** n história em quadrinhos; (Pt) banda desenhada.

**coming** ['kʌmɪŋ] n vinda, chegada // adj que vem, vindouro; **~(s) and going(s)** n(pl) vaivém m, azáfama.

**comma** ['kɔmə] n vírgula.

**command** [kə'mɑːnd] n ordem f, mandado; (MIL: authority) comando; (mastery) domínio // vt (troops) mandar; (give orders to) mandar, ordenar; (dispose of) dispor de; (deserve) merecer; **~eer** [kɔmən'dɪə*] vt requisitar; **~er** n (MIL)

comandante m/f, chefe m/f.

**commando** [kə'mɑːndəu] n comando.

**commemorate** [kə'mɛməreɪt] vt comemorar; **commemoration** [-'reɪʃən] n comemoração f; **commemorative** [-rətɪv] adj comemorativo.

**commence** [kə'mɛns] vt/i começar, iniciar.

**commend** [kə'mɛnd] vt (praise) elogiar, louvar; (recommend) recomendar; (entrust) encomendar; **~ation** [kɔmen'deɪʃən] n elogio, louvor m, recomendação f.

**commensurate** [kə'mɛnʃərɪt] adj igual (with a).

**comment** ['kɔmɛnt] n comentário // vi fazer comentários, comentar; **~ary** ['kɔməntərɪ] n comentário; **~ator** ['kɔmənteɪtə*] n comentarista m/f.

**commerce** ['kɔmɔːs] n comércio.

**commercial** [kə'mɔːʃəl] adj comercial // n (TV) anúncio (comercial); **~ break** n intervalo publicitário; **~ize** vt comercializar.

**commiserate** [kə'mɪzəreɪt] vi: **to ~ with** comiserar-se de, condoer-se de.

**commission** [kə'mɪʃən] n (fee) comissão f; (act) incumbência // vt (MIL) dar patente oficial; (work of art) encarregar; **out of ~** fora do serviço ativo (Pt: -ct-); **~aire** [kəmɪʃə'neə*] n porteiro; **~er** n comissário; (POLICE) chefe m, delegado/a m/f.

**commit** [kə'mɪt] vt (act) cometer; (to sb's care) entregar; **to ~ o.s. (to do)** comprometer-se (de fazer); **to ~ suicide** suicidar-se; **~ment** n compromisso.

**committee** [kə'mɪtɪ] n comitê m.

**commodity** [kə'mɔdɪtɪ] n mercadoria.

**common** ['kɔmən] adj (gen) comum; (pej) ordinário // n terrenos baldios mpl; **the C~s** a

Câmara dos Comuns; **in ~** em plebeu/béia *m/f*; **~ law** *n* lei *f* consuetudinária; **~ly** *adv* geralmente; **C~ Market** *n* Mercado Comum; **~place** *adj* vulgar, trivial // *n* lugar-comum *m*; **~room** *n* sala comum; **~sense** *n* bom senso; **the C~wealth** *n* Comunidade *f* Britânica.

**commotion** [kə'məʊʃən] *n* tumulto, confusão *f*.

**communal** ['kɔmjuːnl] *adj* comunal.

**commune** ['kɔmjuːn] *n* (*group*) comuna // *vi* [kə'mjuːn]: **to ~ with** comungar *or* conversar com.

**communicate** [kə'mjuːnɪkeɪt] *vt* comunicar // *vi*: **to ~ (with)** comunicar-se com.

**communication** [kɔmjuːnɪ'keɪʃən] *n* comunicação *f*; **~ cord** *n* som *m* de alarme.

**communion** [kə'mjuːnɪən] *n* (*also*: **Holy C~**) comunhão *f*.

**communiqué** [kə'mjuːnɪkeɪ] *n* comunicado.

**communism** ['kɔmjunɪzəm] *n* comunismo; **communist** *adj*, *n* comunista *m/f*.

**community** [kə'mjuːnɪtɪ] *n* comunidade *f*; (*large group*) multidão *f*; (*locals*) vizinhança; **~ centre** *n* centro social.

**commute** [kə'mjuːt] *vi* viajar diariamente // *vt* comutar; **commuter** *n* viajante *m/f* habitual.

**compact** [kəm'pækt] *adj* compacto, (*style*) sólido; (*packed*) apertado // *n* ['kɔmpækt] (*pact*) pacto; (*for powder*) estojo.

**companion** [kəm'pænɪən] *n* companheiro/a; **~ship** *n* companhia.

**company** ['kʌmpənɪ] *n* (*gen*) companhia, (*COMM*) sociedade *f*, companhia; **to keep sb ~** fazer companhia a alguém; **limited ~** sociedade *f* limitada.

**comparable** ['kɔmpərəbl] *adj* comparável.

**comparative** [kəm'pærətɪv] *adj* comparativo.

**compare** [kəm'peə*] *vt* comparar; (*set side by side*) cotejar // *vi*: **to ~ with** comparar-se com; **comparison** [-'pærɪsn] *n* comparação *f*; **in comparison with** em comparação com, comparado com.

**compartment** [kəm'pɑːtmənt] *n* (*also RAIL*) compartimento.

**compass** ['kʌmpəs] *n* bússola; **~es** *npl* compasso *sg*.

**compassion** [kəm'pæʃən] *n* compaixão *f*; **~ate** *adj* compassivo.

**compatible** [kəm'pætɪbl] *adj* compatível.

**compel** [kəm'pɛl] *vt* obrigar; **~ling** *adj* (*fig: argument*) convincente.

**compendium** [kəm'pɛndɪəm] *n* compêndio.

**compensate** ['kɔmpənseɪt] *vt* compensar // *vi*: **to ~ for** compensar; **compensation** [-'seɪʃən] *n* (*for loss*) indenização (*Pt*: -mn-) *f*.

**compère** ['kɔmpeə*] *n* apresentador(a) *m/f*.

**compete** [kəm'piːt] *vi* (*take part*) competir, concorrer; (*vie with*) competir (com), fazer competição (com).

**competence** ['kɔmpɪtəns] *n* competência, capacidade *f*; **competent** [-ənt] *adj* competente, capaz.

**competition** [kɔmpɪ'tɪʃən] *n* (*contest*) concurso; (*ECON*) concorrência; (*rivalry*) competição *f*.

**competitive** [kəm'petɪtɪv] *adj* (*ECON*) competitivo; (*spirit*) competidor(a), de rivalidade.

**competitor** [kəm'petɪtə*] *n* (*rival*) competidor(a) *m/f*; (*participant*) concorrente *m/f*.

**compile** [kəm'paɪl] *vt* compilar, compor.

**complacency** [kəm'pleɪsnsɪ] *n*

satisfação *f* consigo mesmo, complacência; **complacent** [-sənt] *adj* vaidoso.

**complain** [kəm'pleɪn] *vi* (*gen*) queixar-se; ~**t** *n* (*gen*) queixa; (*JUR*) querela; (*MED*) queixa, doença.

**complement** ['kɔmplɪmənt] *n* complemento; (*esp ship's crew*) tripulação *f*; ~**ary** [kɔmplɪ'mentəri] *adj* complementar.

**complete** [kəm'pli:t] *adj* (*full*) completo; (*finished*) acabado // *vt* (*fulfil*) completar; (*finish*) acabar; (*a form*) encher; ~**ly** *adv* completamente; **completion** *n* (*gen*) conclusão *f*, término; (*of contract etc*) realização *f*.

**complex** ['kɔmpleks] *adj* complexo // *n* (*gen*) complexo.

**complexion** [kəm'plekʃən] *n* (*of face*) cor *f*, tez *f*; (*fig*) aspecto.

**complexity** [kəm'pleksɪtɪ] *n* complexidade *f*.

**compliance** [kəm'plaɪəns] *n* (*submission*) submissão *f*; (*agreement*) conformidade *f*; **in** ~ **with** de acordo com; **compliant** [-ənt] *adj* complacente, submisso.

**complicate** ['kɔmplɪkeɪt] *vt* complicar; ~**d** *adj* complicado; **complication** [-'keɪʃən] *n* complicação *f*.

**compliment** *n* ['kɔmplɪmənt] (*formal*) cumprimento; (*lovers'*) galanteio; ~**s** *npl* cumprimentos *mpl*; **to pay sb a** ~ (*amorously*) galantear/cortejar alguém; ~**ary** [-'mentəri] *adj* lisonjeiro; (*free*) gratuito.

**comply** [kəm'plaɪ] *vi*: **to** ~ **with** cumprir com.

**component** [kəm'pəunənt] *adj* componente // *n* (*TECH*) peça.

**compose** [kəm'pəuz] *vt* compor; **to be** ~**d of** compor-se de; **to** ~ **o.s.** tranquilizar-se; ~**d** *adj* calmo; **composer** *n* (*MUS*) compositor(a) *m/f*.

**composite** ['kɔmpəzɪt] *adj* composto.

**composition** [kɔmpə'zɪʃən] *n* composição *f*.

**compost** ['kɔmpɔst] *n* adubo.

**composure** [kəm'pəuʒə*] *n* serenidade *f*, calma.

**compound** ['kɔmpaund] *n* (*CHEM, LING*) composto; (*enclosure*) recinto // *adj* (*gen*) composto; (*fracture*) complicado.

**comprehend** [kɔmprɪ'hend] *vt* compreender; **comprehension** [-'henʃən] *n* compreensão *f*.

**comprehensive** [kɔmprɪ'hensɪv] *adj* (*broad*) extenso; (*general*) abrangente; (*INSURANCE*) contra todo risco, global; ~ (**school**) *n* escola secundária de amplo programa.

**compress** [kəm'pres] *vt* comprimir // *n* ['kɔmpres] (*MED*) compressa; ~**ion** [-'preʃən] *n* compressão *f*.

**comprise** [kəm'praɪz] *vt* (*also: be* ~**d of**) compreender, constar de.

**compromise** ['kɔmprəmaɪz] *n* (*agreement*) compromisso, acordo; (*midpoint*) meio-termo // *vt* comprometer // *vi* transigir.

**compulsion** [kəm'pʌlʃən] *n* compulsão *f*.

**compulsive** [kəm'pʌlsɪv] *adj* maníaco; (*PSYCH*) compulsório.

**compulsory** [kəm'pʌlsərɪ] *adj* obrigatório.

**computer** [kəm'pju:tə*] *n* computador *m*, calculadora; ~**ize** *vt* computerizar; ~ **programmer** *n* programador(a) *m/f*; ~ **programming** *n* programação *f*; ~ **science** *n* ciência de computadores; **computing** *n* informática.

**comrade** ['kɔmrɪd] *n* camarada *m/f*; ~**ship** *n* camaradagem *f*.

**con** [kɔn] *vt* enganar // *n* vigarice *f*.

**concave** [kɔn'keɪv] *adj* côncavo.

**conceal** [kən'si:l] *vt* ocultar.

**concede** [kən'si:d] *vt* conceder // *vi* ceder, conceder.

**conceit** [kən'siːt] n presunção f; **~ed** adj presunçoso.

**conceivable** [kən'siːvəbl] adj concebível.

**conceive** [kən'siːv] vt/i conceber.

**concentrate** ['kɔnsəntreit] vi concentrar-se // vt concentrar.

**concentration** [kɔnsən'treiʃən] n concentração f; **~ camp** n campo de concentração.

**concept** ['kɔnsept] n conceito.

**conception** [kən'sepʃən] n (idea) conceito, ideia; (BIOL) concepção f.

**concern** [kən'səːn] n (matter) assunto; (COMM) empresa; (anxiety) preocupação f // vt dizer respeito a; **to be ~ed (about)** interessar-se (por); preocupar-se (com); **~ing** prep sobre, a respeito de, acerca de.

**concert** ['kɔnsət] n concerto; **~ hall** n sala de concertos; **~ master** (US) n primeiro violino de uma orquestra.

**concertina** [kɔnsə'tiːnə] n concertina.

**concerto** [kən'tʃəːtəu] n concerto.

**concession** [kən'seʃən] n concessão f; **tax ~** incentivo fiscal.

**conciliation** [kənsili'eiʃən] n conciliação f; **conciliatory** [-'siliətri] adj conciliador(a).

**concise** [kən'sais] adj conciso.

**conclude** [kən'kluːd] vt (finish) acabar, concluir; (treaty etc) firmar; (agreement) chegar a; (decide) chegar à conclusão de; **conclusion** [-'kluːʒən] n conclusão f; **conclusive** [-'kluːsiv] adj conclusivo, decisivo.

**concoct** [kən'kɔkt] vt (gen) confeccionar; (plot) fabricar, tramar.

**concrete** ['kɔnkriːt] n concreto, betão m // adj concreto.

**concur** [kən'kəː*] vi estar de acordo, concordar.

**concurrently** [kən'kʌrntli] adv ao mesmo tempo.

**concussion** [kən'kʌʃən] n concussão f cerebral.

**condemn** [kən'dem] vt condenar; **~ation** [kɔndem'neiʃən] n (gen) condenação f; (blame) censura.

**condensation** [kɔndən'seiʃən] n condensação f.

**condense** [kən'dens] vi condensar-se // vt condensar, abreviar; **~d milk** n leite m condensado.

**condescend** [kɔndi'send] vi condescender, dignar-se; **~ing** adj condescendente.

**condition** [kən'diʃən] n condição f // vt condicionar; **on ~ that** com a condição (de) que.

**condolences** [kən'dəulənsiz] npl pêsames mpl.

**condone** [kən'dəun] vt perdoar.

**conducive** [kən'djuːsiv] adj: **~ to** conducente para/a.

**conduct** ['kɔndʌkt] n conduta, comportamento // vt [kən'dʌkt] (lead) conduzir; (manage) levar, dirigir; (MUS) reger // vi (MUS) reger uma orquestra; **to ~ o.s.** comportar-se; **~or** n (of orchestra) regente m; (on bus) cobrador m; (RAIL) revisor m; (ELEC) condutor m; **~ress** n (on bus) cobradora.

**cone** [kəun] n cone m; (for ice-cream) casquinha.

**confectioner** [kən'fekʃənə*] n confeiteiro; (Pt) pasteleiro; **~'s (shop)** n confeitaria; (Pt) pastelaria; (sweet shop) confeitaria; **~y** n (cakes) bolos mpl; (sweets) doces mpl.

**confederation** [kənfedə'reiʃən] n confederação f.

**confer** [kən'fəː*] vt: **to ~ on** outorgar a // vi conferenciar.

**conference** ['kɔnfərns] n (meeting) congresso.

**confess** [kən'fes] vt confessar // vi confessar-se; **~ion** [-'feʃən] n confissão f; **~ional** [-'feʃənl] n confessionário; **~or** n confessor m.

**confetti** [kən'feti] n confete m.

**confide** [kən'faid] vi: **to ~ in** confiar em, fiar-se em.

**confidence** ['kɔnfɪdns] n (gen) confiança; (secret) confidência; ~ **trick** n conto do vigário; **confident** adj confiante, convicto; **confidential** [kɔnfɪ'denʃəl] adj confidencial; (secretary) de confiança.

**confine** [kən'faɪn] vt (limit) limitar; (shut up) encarcerar; ~**d** adj (space) reduzido, retido; ~**ment** n (prison) prisão f; (enclosure) reclusão f; (MED) parto; ~**s** ['kɔnfaɪnz] npl confins mpl.

**confirm** [kən'fɔ:m] vt confirmar; ~**ation** [kɔnfə'meɪʃən] n confirmação f; ~**ed** adj inveterado.

**confiscate** ['kɔnfɪskeɪt] vt confiscar; **confiscation** [-'keɪʃən] n confiscação f.

**conflict** ['kɔnflɪkt] n conflito // vi [kən'flɪkt] (opinions) opor-se, chocar; ~**ing** adj oposto, contraditório.

**conform** [kən'fɔ:m] vi conformar-se; **to** ~ **to** to ajustar-se a, acomodar-se a; ~**ist** n conformista m/f.

**confound** [kən'faʊnd] vt frustrar; ~**ed** adj maldito.

**confront** [kən'frʌnt] vt (problems) deparar-se com; (enemy, danger) defrontar-se com; ~**ation** [kɔn-frən'teɪʃən] n confrontação f.

**confuse** [kən'fju:z] vt (perplex) desconcertar; (mix up) confundir; ~**d** adj confuso; (person) perplexo; **confusing** adj confuso; **confusion** [-'fju:ʒən] n confusão f.

**congeal** [kən'dʒi:l] vi (freeze) congelar-se; (coagulate) coagular-se.

**congenial** [kən'dʒi:nɪəl] adj simpático, agradável.

**congenital** [kən'dʒenɪtl] adj congênito.

**congested** [kən'dʒestɪd] adj (gen) congestionado; **congestion** [-'dʒestʃən] n congestão f.

**conglomeration** [kənglɔmə-'reɪʃən] n conglomeração f, aglomeração f.

**congratulate** [kən'grætjuleɪt] vt felicitar; **congratulations** [-'leɪʃənz] npl parabéns mpl.

**congregate** ['kɔngrɪgeɪt] vi reunir-se; **congregation** [-'geɪʃən] n (in church) os fiéis mpl; (assembly) congregação f, reunião f.

**congress** ['kɔngres] n congresso; ~**man** n (US) deputado.

**conical** ['kɔnɪkl] adj cônico.

**conifer** ['kɔnɪfə*] n conífera; ~**ous** [kə'nɪfərəs] adj (forest) conífero.

**conjecture** [kən'dʒektʃə*] n conjetura (Pt: -ct-).

**conjugal** ['kɔndʒugl] adj conjugal.

**conjugate** ['kɔndʒugeɪt] vt conjugar.

**conjunction** [kən'dʒʌŋkʃən] n conjunção f.

**conjure** ['kʌndʒə*] vi adjurar; **to** ~ **up** vt (ghost, spirit) fazer aparecer, invocar; (memories) evocar; **conjurer** n prestidigitador(a) m/f; ilusionista m/f; **conjuring trick** n mágica.

**conk** [kɔŋk]: ~ **out** vi (col) enguiçar.

**con man** ['kɔn-] n vigarista m.

**connect** [kə'nekt] vt juntar, unir; (ELEC) ligar, conectar; (fig) relacionar, unir // vi: **to** ~ **with** (train) conectar com; ~**ion** [-ʃən] n ligação f, união f; (ELEC, RAIL) conexão f; (TEL) comunicação f; (fig) relação f.

**connive** [kə'naɪv] vi: **to** ~ **at** ser conivente em.

**connoisseur** [kɔnɪ'sə*] n conhecedor(a) m/f, apreciador(a) m/f.

**connotation** [kɔnə'teɪʃən] n conotação f.

**conquer** ['kɔŋkə*] vt (gen) conquistar; (enemy) vencer; (feelings) dominar; ~**or** n conquistador m.

**conquest** ['kɔŋkwest] n conquista f.

**cons** [kɔnz] npl see **pro.**

**conscience** ['kɔnʃəns] n consciência.

**conscientious** [kɔnʃɪˈenʃəs] *adj* conscienceioso; (*objection*) de consciência.

**conscious** [ˈkɔnʃəs] *adj* consciente; ~**ness** *n* consciência.

**conscript** [ˈkɔnskrɪpt] *n* recruta *m/f*; ~**ion** [kənˈskrɪpʃən] *n* serviço militar obrigatório.

**consecrate** [ˈkɔnsɪkreɪt] *vt* consagrar.

**consecutive** [kənˈsekjutɪv] *adj* sucessivo, seguido.

**consensus** [kənˈsensəs] *n* consenso.

**consent** [kənˈsent] *n* consentimento // *vi*: to ~ to consentir em.

**consequence** [ˈkɔnsɪkwəns] *n* conseqüência.

**consequently** [ˈkɔnsɪkwəntlɪ] *adv* por conseguinte.

**conservation** [kɔnsəˈveɪʃən] *n* conservação *f*.

**conservative** [kənˈsəːvətɪv] *adj* conservador; (*cautious*) moderado; **C**~ *adj*, *n* conservador(a) *m/f*.

**conservatory** [kənˈsəːvətrɪ] *n* conservatório; (*greenhouse*) estufa.

**conserve** [kənˈsəːv] *vt* conservar // *n* conserva.

**consider** [kənˈsɪdə*] *vt* (*gen*) considerar; (*take into account*) levar em consideração; (*study*) estudar, examinar; ~**able** *adj* considerável; (*sum*) importante.

**considerate** [kənˈsɪdərɪt] *adj* atencioso, delicado; **consideration** [-ˈreɪʃən] *n* consideração *f*; (*reward*) remuneração *f*.

**considering** [kənˈsɪdərɪŋ] *prep* em vista de.

**consign** [kənˈsaɪn] *vt* consignar; ~**ment** *n* consignação *f*.

**consist** [kənˈsɪst] *vi*: to ~ of consistir em.

**consistency** [kənˈsɪstənsɪ] *n* (*of person etc*) coerência, solidez *f*; (*thickness*) consistência.

**consistent** [kənˈsɪstənt] *adj*

(*person*) compatível, coerente; (*even*) constante.

**consolation** [kɔnsəˈleɪʃən] *n* consolação *f*, alívio.

**console** [kənˈsəʊl] *vt* consolar // [ˈkɔnsəʊl] *n* consolo.

**consolidate** [kənˈsɔlɪdeɪt] *vt* consolidar.

**consommé** [kənˈsɔmeɪ] *n* consomê *m*, caldo.

**consonant** [ˈkɔnsənənt] *n* consoante *f*.

**consortium** [kənˈsɔːtɪəm] *n* consórcio.

**conspicuous** [kənˈspɪkjuəs] *adj* (*visible*) visível; (*garish etc*) berrante; (*outstanding*) notável.

**conspiracy** [kənˈspɪrəsɪ] *n* conspiração *f*, trama.

**conspire** [kənˈspaɪə*] *vi* conspirar.

**constable** [ˈkʌnstəbl] *n* polícia *m/f*; **chief** ~ chefe *m* de polícia.

**constabulary** [kənˈstæbjulərɪ] *n* polícia (distrital).

**constant** [ˈkɔnstənt] *adj* (*gen*) constante; (*loyal*) leal, fiel.

**constellation** [kɔnstəˈleɪʃən] *n* constelação *f*.

**consternation** [kɔnstəˈneɪʃən] *n* consternação *f*.

**constipated** [ˈkɔnstɪpeɪtəd] *adj* com prisão de ventre.

**constituency** [kənˈstɪtjuənsɪ] *n* (*POL*) distrito eleitoral; **constituent** [-ənt] *n* (*POL*) eleitor(a) *m/f*; (*part*) componente *m*.

**constitute** [ˈkɔnstɪtjuːt] *vt* constituir.

**constitution** [kɔnstɪˈtjuːʃən] *n* constituição *f*, ~**al** *adj* constitucional.

**constrain** [kənˈstreɪn] *vt* obrigar; ~**ed** *adj*: to feel ~**ed** to... sentir-se compelido a...; ~**t** *n* (*force*) força, coação *f* (*Pt*: -çç-); (*confinement*) confinamento; (*shyness*) acanhamento.

**constrict** [kənˈstrɪkt] *vt* apertar, constringir.

**construct** [kən'strʌkt] vt construir; ~**ion** [-ʃən] n construção f; ~**ive** adj construtivo.

**construe** [kən'stru:] vt interpretar.

**consul** ['kɔnsl] n cônsul m/f; ~**ate** ['kɔnsjulit] n consulado.

**consult** [kən'sʌlt] vt/i consultar; ~**ant** n (MED) (médico) especialista m/f; (other specialist) assessor m; ~**ation** [kɔnsəl'teiʃən] n consulta; ~**ing room** n consultório.

**consume** [kən'sju:m] vt `(eat)` comer; (drink) beber; (fire etc, COMM) consumir; **consumer** n consumidor(a) m/f; **consumer goods** npl bens mpl de consumo; **consumer society** n sociedade f de consumo.

**consummate** ['kɔnsʌmeit] vt consumar.

**consumption** [kən'sʌmpʃən] n consumo.

**cont.** abbr of **continued.**

**contact** ['kɔntækt] n contato (Pt: -act-); (col) pistolão m / n entrar/pôr-se em conta(c)to com; **he has good** ~**s** tem boas relações; ~ **lenses** npl lentes fpl de conta(c)to.

**contagious** [kən'teidʒəs] adj contagioso.

**contain** [kən'tein] vt conter; **to** ~ **o.s.** conter-se; ~**er** n recipiente m; (for shipping etc) container m, cofre m de carga.

**contaminate** [kən'tæmineit] vt contaminar; **contamination** [-'nei-ʃən] n contaminação f.

**cont'd** abbr of **continued.**

**contemplate** ['kɔntəmpleit] vt (gen) contemplar; (expect) contar com; (intend) pretender, pensar; **contemplation** [-'pleiʃən] n contemplação f.

**contemporary** [kən'tempərəri] adj, n contemporâneo.

**contempt** [kən'tempt] n desprezo; ~**ible** adj desprezível; ~**uous** adj desdenhoso.

**contend** [kən'tend] vt (argue) afirmar // vi (struggle) lutar; ~**er** n contendor(a) m/f.

**content** [kən'tent] adj (happy) contente; (satisfied) satisfeito // vt contentar, satisfazer // n ['kɔntent] contentamento, satisfação f; ~**s** npl conteúdo sg; ~**ed** adj contente, satisfeito.

**contention** [kən'tenʃən] n contenda; (argument) argumento.

**contentment** [kən'tentmənt] n contentamento.

**contest** ['kɔntest] n contenda; (competition) concurso // vt [kən'test] (dispute) disputar; (legal case) defender; (POL) ser candidato a; ~**ant** [kən'testənt] n competidor(a) m/f; (in fight) adversário/a m/f.

**context** ['kɔntekst] n contexto.

**continent** ['kɔntinənt] n continente m; **the C**~ o continente europeu; ~**al** [-'nentl] adj continental.

**contingency** [kən'tindʒənsi] n contingência; **contingent** [-ənt] n contingente m.

**continual** [kən'tinjuəl] adj contínuo; ~**ly** adv constantemente.

**continuation** [kən'tinju'eiʃən] n prolongamento; (after interruption) continuação f.

**continue** [kən'tinju:] vi prosseguir, continuar // vt seguir, persistir em; (start again) recomeçar.

**continuity** [kɔnti'njuiti] n continuidade f.

**continuous** [kən'tinjuəs] adj contínuo.

**contort** [kən'tɔ:t] vt retorcer; ~**ion** [-'tɔ:ʃən] n contorção f; ~**ionist** [-'tɔ:ʃənist] n contorcionista m/f.

**contour** ['kɔntuə*] n contorno; (also: ~ **line**) curva de nível.

**contraband** ['kɔntrəbænd] n contrabando.

**contraception** [kɔntrə'sepʃən] n anticoncepção f; **contraceptive** [-'septiv] adj, n anticoncepcional f.

**contract** ['kɒntrækt] n contrato // (vb: [kən'trækt]) vi (COMM): to ~ to do sth comprometer-se por contrato para fazer algo; (become smaller) contrair-se, encolher-se // vt contrair; ~ion [-ʃən] n contração (Pt: -cç-) f; ~or n contratante m/f.

**contradict** [kɒntrə'dɪkt] vt (deny) desmentir; (be contrary to) contradizer; ~ion [-ʃən] n contradição f.

**contralto** [kən'træltəu] n contralto.

**contraption** [kən'træpʃən] n (pej) coisa sem valor.

**contrary** ['kɒntrərɪ] adj, n contrário.

**contrast** n ['kɒntrɑːst] n contraste m // vt [kən'trɑːst] contrastar, comparar; ~ing adj oposto.

**contravene** [kɒntrə'viːn] vt opor-se a; (law) infringir.

**contribute** [kən'trɪbjuːt] vi: to ~ to (gen) contribuir para; (newspaper) escrever para; **contribution** [kɒntrɪ'bjuːʃən] n (money) contribuição f; (to debate) intervenção f; (to journal) colaboração f; **contributor** n (to newspaper) colaborador(a) m/f.

**contrive** [kən'traɪv] vt (invent) idealizar; (carry out) efetuar (Pt: -ct-); (plot) tramar // vi: to ~ to do chegar a fazer.

**control** [kən'trəul] vt (gen) controlar; (traffic etc) dirigir; (machinery) regular; (temper) dominar // n (command) controle m, autoridade f; (of car) direção f; (Pt) condução f; (check) freio, controle; ~s npl mando sg; ~ panel n painel m de instrumentos; ~ room n sala de comando; ~ tower n (AVIAT) torre f de controle.

**controversial** [kɒntrə'vəːʃl] adj discutível; **controversy** ['kɒntrəvəːsɪ] n controvérsia.

**convalesce** [kɒnvə'les] vi convalescer; **convalescence** n

convalescença; **convalescent** adj, n convalescente m/f.

**convector** [kən'vektə*] n (heater) aquecedor m de convecção.

**convene** [kən'viːn] vt convocar // vi reunir-se.

**convenience** [kən'viːnɪəns] n (comfort) comodidade f; (advantage) vantagem f, conveniência; at your ~ quando lhe convier; **public** ~ banheiro público; (Pt) lavabos mpl; **convenient** [-ənt] adj cômodo; (useful) útil; (place) acessível; (time) oportuno, conveniente.

**convent** ['kɒnvənt] n convento; ~ **school** n colégio de freiras.

**convention** [kən'venʃən] n convenção f; (meeting) assembléia; ~**al** adj convencional.

**converge** [kən'vəːdʒ] vi convergir.

**conversant** [kən'vəːsnt] adj: to be ~ **with** estar familiarizado com.

**conversation** [kɒnvə'seɪʃən] n conversação f, conversa; ~**al** adj (familiar) familiar; (talkative) loquaz.

**converse** ['kɒnvəːs] n inverso // vi [kən'vəːs] conversar; ~**ly** [-'vəːslɪ] adv pelo contrário, inversamente.

**conversion** [kən'vəːʃən] n conversão f; ~ **table** n tábua de conversão.

**convert** [kən'vəːt] vt (REL, COMM) converter; (alter) transformar; // n ['kɒnvəːt] convertido; ~**ible** adj conversível // n conversível m.

**convex** ['kɒnveks] adj convexo.

**convey** [kən'veɪ] vt (gen) levar; (thanks) comunicar; (idea) exprimir; ~**or belt** n correia transportadora.

**convict** [kən'vɪkt] vt (gen) condenar; (sentence) declarar culpado // n ['kɒnvɪkt] presidiário; ~**ion** [-ʃən] n condenação f; (belief) fé f, convicção f.

**convince** [kən'vɪns] vt convencer; **convincing** adj convincente.

**convoy** ['kɔnvɔɪ] n escolta.
**convulse** [kən'vʌls] vt convulsionar; (laughter) fazer morrer de rir; **convulsion** [-'vʌlʃən] n convulsão f; (laughter) ataque m, acesso.
**coo** [ku:] vi arrulhar.
**cook** [kuk] vt (gen) cozinhar; (stew etc) guisar; (meal) preparar // vi cozer; (person) cozinhar // n cozinheiro/a; ~**er** n fogão m; ~**ery** n (dishes) cozinha; (art) arte f culinária; ~**ery book** n livro de receitas; ~**ie** n (US) bolacha, biscoito; ~**ing** n cozinha.
**cool** [ku:l] adj fresco; (not hot) tépido; (not afraid) calmo; (unfriendly) frio // vt esfriar // vi arrefecer-se; ~**ness** n frescura; (hostility) frieza; (indifference) indiferença.
**coop** [ku:p] n galinheiro, capoeira // vt: to ~ **up** (fig) confinar.
**co-op** ['kəuɔp] n abbr of **Cooperative (Society)**.
**cooperate** [kəu'ɔpəreɪt] vi cooperar, colaborar; **cooperation** [-'reɪʃən] n cooperação f, colaboração f; **cooperative** [-rətɪv] adj cooperativo // n cooperativa.
**coordinate** [kəu'ɔːdɪneɪt] vt coordenar; **coordination** [-'neɪʃən] n coordenação f.
**cop** [kɔp] n (col) polícia m.
**cope** [kəup] vi: to ~ **with** poder com; (problem) estar à altura de.
**co-pilot** ['kəu'paɪlət] n co-piloto.
**copious** ['kəupiəs] adj copioso, abundante.
**copper** ['kɔpə*] n (metal) cobre m; (col: policeman) polícia m; ~**s** npl moedas fpl de pouco valor.
**coppice** ['kɔpɪs], **copse** [kɔps] n bosquete m.
**copulate** ['kɔpjuleɪt] vi copular-se; **copulation** [-'leɪʃən] n cópula.
**copy** ['kɔpɪ] n cópia; (of book etc) exemplar m; (of writing) originais mpl // vt copiar; ~**right** n direitos

mpl de autor, direitos autorais mpl.
**coral** ['kɔrəl] n coral m; ~ **reef** recife m de coral.
**cord** [kɔːd] n corda; (ELEC) cordão m, cabo; (fabric) veludo cotelê.
**cordial** ['kɔːdɪəl] adj, n cordial m.
**cordon** ['kɔːdn] n cordão m; to ~ **off** vt isolar.
**corduroy** ['kɔːdərɔɪ] n veludo cotelê.
**core** [kɔ:*] n (gen) centro, núcleo; (of fruit) caroço // vt descaroçar.
**coriander** [kɔrɪ'ændə*] n coentro.
**cork** [kɔːk] n rolha; (tree) cortiça; ~**screw** n saca-rolhas m inv.
**cormorant** ['kɔːmərnt] n cormorão m, corvo marinho.
**corn** [kɔːn] n (wheat) trigo; (US: maize) milho; (cereals) grão m, cereal m; (on foot) calo; ~ **on the cob** (CULIN) espiga de milho.
**corned beef** [kɔːnd-] n carne f de boi enlatada.
**corner** ['kɔːnə*] n (gen) ângulo; (outside) esquina; (inside) canto; (in road) curva; (FOOTBALL) canto; corner m // vt (trap) apanhar; (COMM) monopolizar // vi (in car) dobrar a esquina; ~**stone** n pedra angular.
**cornet** ['kɔːnɪt] n (MUS) cornetim m; (of ice-cream) casquinha.
**cornflour, cornstarch** (US) n ['kɔːnflauə*, 'kɔːnstɑːtʃ] n farinha de milho.
**Cornwall** ['kɔːnwəl] n Cornualha.
**corny** ['kɔːnɪ] adj (col) velho, gasto.
**corollary** [kə'rɔlərɪ] n corolário.
**coronary** ['kɔrənərɪ] n: ~ (thrombosis) trombose f.
**coronation** [kɔrə'neɪʃən] n coroação f.
**coroner** ['kɔrənə*] n magistrado que investiga mortes suspeitas.
**coronet** ['kɔrənɪt] n coroa aberta, diadema.
**corporal** ['kɔːpərl] n cabo // adj corpóreo.

**corporate** [ˈkɔːpərɪt] *adj* corporativo.

**corporation** [kɔːpəˈreɪʃən] *n* (*of town*) junta; (*COMM*) corporação *f*.

**corps** [kɔː*], *pl* **corps** [kɔːz] *n* corpo.

**corpse** [kɔːps] *n* cadáver *m*.

**corpuscle** [ˈkɔːpʌsl] *n* corpúsculo.

**corral** [kəˈrɑːl] *n* curral *m*.

**correct** [kəˈrɛkt] *adj* (*accurate*) justo, exato (*Pt*: -ct-); (*proper*) correto (*Pt*: -ct-) // *vt* corrigir; ~**ion** [-ʃən] *n* correção (*Pt*: -cç-) *f*, retificação (*Pt*: -ct-); (*erasure*) emenda.

**correlate** [ˈkɔrɪleɪt] *vt* correlacionar.

**correspond** [kɔrɪsˈpɔnd] *vi* (*write*) escrever-se; (*be equal to*) corresponder; ~**ence** *n* correspondência; ~**ence course** *n* curso por correspondência; ~**ent** *n* correspondente *m/f*; ~**ing** *adj* correspondente.

**corridor** [ˈkɔrɪdɔː*] *n* corredor *m*, passagem *f*.

**corroborate** [kəˈrɔbəreɪt] *vt* corroborar.

**corrode** [kəˈrəud] *vt* corroer // *vi* corroer-se; **corrosion** [-ˈrəuʒən] *n* corrosão *f*.

**corrugated** [ˈkɔrəgeɪtɪd] *adj* ondulado; ~ **iron** *n* chapa ondulada *or* corrugada.

**corrupt** [kəˈrʌpt] *adj* corrompido; (*person*) venal, corrupto // *vt* corromper; (*bribe*) subornar; ~**ion** [-ʃən] *n* corrupção *f*.

**corset** [ˈkɔːsɪt] *n* espartilho.

**Corsica** [ˈkɔːsɪkə] *n* Córsega.

**cortège** [kɔːˈtɛːʒ] *n* séquito, cortejo.

**cortisone** [ˈkɔːtɪzəun] *n* cortisona.

**cosh** [kɔʃ] *n* cassete *m*.

**cosiness** [ˈkəuzɪnɪs] *n* conforto; (*atmosphere*) aconchego, conforto.

**cos lettuce** [kɔs–] *n* alface *m* (cos).

**cosmic** [ˈkɔzmɪk] *adj* cósmico.

**cosmonaut** [ˈkɔzmənɔːt] *n* cosmonauta *m/f*.

**cosmopolitan** [kɔzməˈpɔlɪtn] *adj* cosmopolita.

**cosmos** [ˈkɔzmɔs] *n* cosmo.

**cost** [kɔst] *n* (*gen*) custo, despesa; (*price*) preço; ~**s** *npl* custas *fpl* // *vi*, *pt*, *pp* **cost** custar, valer // *vt* custar; **at the** ~ **of** à custa de; **how much does it** ~? quanto custa?

**co-star** [ˈkəustɑː*] *n* co-estrela *m/f*.

**Costa Rican** [ˈkɔstəˈriːkən] *adj* costarriquenho.

**costly** [ˈkɔstlɪ] *adj* (*expensive*) caro, custoso; (*valuable*) suntuoso.

**cost price** *n* preço de custo.

**costume** [ˈkɔstjuːm] *n* traje *m*; (*also*: **swimming** ~) (*woman's*) maiô *m*; (*man's*) calção *m* de banho; (*Pt*) fato de banho.

**cosy** [ˈkəuzɪ] *adj* cômodo; (*atmosphere*) agasalhado, aconchegante; (*life*) folgado, confortável.

**cot** [kɔt] *n* (*child's*) cama (de criança), berço.

**cottage** [ˈkɔtɪdʒ] *n* casa de campo; (*rustic*) cabana; ~ **cheese** *n* ricota.

**cotton** [ˈkɔtn] *n* algodão *m*; (*thread*) fio, linha; **to** ~ **on to** *vt* (*col*) perceber; ~ **wool** *n*, ~ **batting** (*US*) *n* algodão (hidrófilo).

**couch** [kautʃ] *n* sofá *m*.

**cough** [kɔf] *vi* tossir // *n* tosse *f*; **to** ~ **up** *vt* expelir; ~ **drop** *n* pastilha para a tosse.

**could** [kud] *pt of* **can**; ~**n't** = **could not**.

**council** [ˈkaunsl] *n* conselho; **city** *or* **town** ~ câmara municipal; ~ **estate** *n* conjunto residencial subvencionado pelo governo; ~ **house** *n* moradia subvencionada; ~**lor** *n* vereador(a) *m/f*.

**counsel** [ˈkaunsl] *n* (*advice*) conselho; (*lawyer*) advogado // *vt* aconselhar; ~**lor** *n* (*US*) conselheiro.

**count** [kaunt] *vt* (*gen*) contar; (*include*) incluir // *vi* contar // *n* (gen) conta; (of votes) contagem f; (nobleman) conde m; (sum) total m, soma; **to ~ on** vt fus contar com; **that doesn't ~!** isso não vale!; **~down** n contagem f regressiva.

**counter** ['kauntə*] n (in shop) balcão m; (in games) ficha, pedra // vt contrariar; (blow) parar; (attack) contra-atacar // adv: **to ~** ao contrário a; **~act** vt opor-se a, neutralizar; **~act** n contra-ataque m // vi contra-atacar; **~balance** n contrapeso; **~espionage** n contra-espionagem f.

**counterfeit** ['kauntəfɪt] n falsificação f // vt falsificar // adj falso, falsificado.

**counterfoil** ['kauntəfɔɪl] n canhoto; (Pt) talão m.

**counterpart** ['kauntəpɑːt] n contrapartida; (of person) sósia m/f.

**counter-revolution** [kauntərevə-'luːʃən] n contra-revolução f.

**countersign** ['kauntəsaɪn] vt referendar.

**countess** ['kauntɪs] n condessa.

**countless** ['kauntlɪs] adj inumerável.

**country** ['kʌntrɪ] n país m; (native land) pátria; (as opposed to town) campo; (region) região f, terra; **~ dancing** n dança regional; **~ house** n casa de campo; **~side** n campo, paisagem f.

**county** ['kauntɪ] n condado, distrito; **~ town** n capital f do condado.

**coup** [kuː] n, pl **~s** [-z] n golpe m; **~ d'état/de grâce** golpe de estado/de graça.

**coupé** ['kuːpeɪ] n cupê m.

**couple** ['kʌpl] n (of things, people) par m; (married ~) casal m // vt (ideas, names) unir, juntar; (machinery) ligar, juntar; **a ~ of** um par de.

**coupling** ['kʌplɪŋ] n (RAIL) engate m.

**coupon** ['kuːpɔn] n cupão m, cupom m; (pools ~) talão m.

**courage** ['kʌrɪdʒ] n valentia, coragem f; **~ous** [kə'reɪdʒəs] adj corajoso, valente.

**courier** ['kurɪə*] n correio, (diplomatic) mala; (for tourists) guia m/f, agente m/f de turismo.

**course** [kɔːs] n (direction) direção (Pt: -çç-) f, caminho; (of river, ESCOL) curso; (of ship) rumo; (of bullet) trajetória (Pt: -ect-); (fig) procedimento; (GOLF) campo; (part of meal) prato; **of ~** adv claro, naturalmente; **of ~!** claro!, evidentemente!; (Pt) na devida altura.

**court** [kɔːt] n (royal) corte f; (LAW) tribunal m, sessão f de tribunal; (TENNIS) quadra de tênis // vt (woman) cortejar, namorar; (danger etc) procurar; **to take to ~** demandar, levar ao tribunal.

**courteous** ['kɔːtɪəs] adj cortês/esa.

**courtesan** [kɔːtɪ'zæn] n cortesã f.

**courtesy** ['kɔːtəsɪ] n cortesia; **by ~ of** com permissão de.

**court-house** ['kɔːthaus] n (US) palácio de justiça.

**courtier** ['kɔːtɪə*] n cortesão m.

**court:** **~-martial**, pl **~s-martial** n conselho de guerra // vt submeter a conselho de guerra; **~room** n sala de tribunal; **~yard** n pátio.

**cousin** ['kʌzn] n primo/a m/f; **first ~** primo/a carnal, primo irmão.

**cove** [kəuv] n angra, enseada.

**covenant** ['kʌvənənt] n convênio.

**cover** ['kʌvə*] vt (gen) cobrir; (with lid) tapar; (chairs etc) revestir; (distance) percorrer; (include) abranger; (protect) abrigar; (journalist) investigar; (issues) tratar // n (gen) coberta; (lid) tampa; (for chair etc) capa; (for bed) cobertor m; (envelope) envelope m; (for book) capa, forro; (of magazine) capa; (shelter) abrigo; (insurance) cobertura; **under ~** encoberto; **under ~** (indoors) abrigado; **under ~ of** sob o abrigo de; (fig) sob capa de; **to ~ up for sb** encobrir a alguém; **~age** n alcance m; **~ charge** n couvert m; **~ing** n cobertura, invólucro; **~ing letter** n carta de cobertura.

**covet** ['kʌvit] vt cobiçar.

**cow** [kau] n vaca // vt intimidar.

**coward** ['kauǝd] n covarde m/f; **~ice** [-ıs] n covardia; **~ly** adj covarde.

**cowboy** ['kauboɪ] n vaqueiro.

**cower** ['kauǝ*] vi encolher-se (de medo).

**cowshed** ['kauʃed] n estábulo.

**coxswain** ['kɔksn] n (abbr: **cox**) timoneiro/a m/f.

**coy** [kɔɪ] adj tímido.

**coyote** [kɔɪ'ǝutɪ] n coiote m.

**cozy** ['kǝuzɪ] (US) adj = **cosy**.

**crab** [kræb] n caranguejo; **~ apple** n maçã ácida.

**crack** [kræk] n greta; (noise) estalido; (of whip) estalo; (fam) pancada // vt estalar, quebrar; (nut) partir, descascar; (safe) forçar; (whip etc) estalar; (knuckles) estalar, partir; (joke) contar // adj (expert) excelente; **to ~ up** vi (MED) sofrer um colapso nervoso; **~er** n (biscuit) biscoito; (Christmas ~) busca-pé-surpresa m.

**crackle** ['krækl] vi crepitar; **crackling** n (of fire) crepitação f; (of leaves etc) estalidos mpl; (of pork) torresmo.

**cradle** ['kreɪdl] n berço.

**craft** [krɑːft] n (skill) arte f; (trade) ofício; (cunning) astúcia; (boat) barco.

**craftsman** ['krɑːftsmǝn] n artífice m, artesão m; **~ship** n artesanato.

**crafty** ['krɑːftɪ] adj astuto.

**crag** [kræg] n penhasco; **~gy** adj escarpado.

**cram** [kræm] vt (fill) encher, abarrotar; **~med** adj abarrotado.

**cramp** [kræmp] n (MED) cãibra; (TECH) grampo // vt (limit)

restringir; (annoy) estorvar; **~ed** adj apertado, confinado.

**crampon** ['kræmpǝn] n gato m de ferro.

**crane** [kreɪn] n (TECH) guindaste m; (bird) grou m.

**crank** [kræŋk] n manivela; (person) maníaco; **~shaft** n eixo de manivelas.

**cranky** ['kræŋkɪ] adj (eccentric) maníaco; (bad-tempered) irritadiço.

**cranny** ['krænɪ] n see **nook**.

**crash** [kræʃ] n (noise) estrondo; (of cars etc) choque m, batida; (of plane) acidente m de avião; (COMM) falência, quebra // vt (plane) espatifar // vi (plane) chocar-se; (two cars) chocar, bater; (fall noisily) cair (com estrondo); **~ course** n curso acelerado; **~ helmet** n capacete m protetor (Pt: -ect); **~ landing** n aterrissagem f forçada.

**crate** [kreɪt] n cesto grande de vime; (fam) cesta; (of beer) engradado.

**crater** ['kreɪtǝ*] n cratera.

**cravat(e)** [krǝ'væt] n gravata.

**crave** [kreɪv] vt: **to ~ for** ansiar por; **craving** n (of pregnant woman) desejo, ânsia.

**crawl** [krɔːl] vi (gen) arrastar-se; (child) engatinhar; (vehicle) arrastar-se a passo de tartaruga // n rastejo; (SWIMMING) crawl m.

**crayfish** ['kreɪfɪʃ] n, pl inv lagostim m.

**crayon** ['kreɪǝn] n lápis m de pastel, crayon m.

**craze** [kreɪz] n mania; (fashion) moda.

**crazy** ['kreɪzɪ] adj (person) louco, maluco, doido; (idea) disparatado.

**creak** [kriːk] vi chiar, ranger; (door etc) ranger.

**cream** [kriːm] n (of milk) nata; (gen) creme m; (fig) a fina flor // adj (colour) creme; **~ cake** n bolo de creme; **~ cheese** n queijo de nata; **~y** adj cremoso.

**crease** [kri:s] n (fold) ruga; (in trousers) vinco; (wrinkle) ruga // vt (fold) dobrar, vincar; (wrinkle) enrugar // vi (wrinkle up) enrugar-se.

**create** [kri:'eit] vt criar; creation [-ʃən] n criação f; **creative** adj criativo; **creator** n criador(a) m/f.

**creature** ['kri:tʃə*] n (animal) animal m, bicho; (living thing) criatura.

**crèche, creche** [krɛʃ] n creche f.

**credentials** [kri'dɛnʃlz] npl credenciais fpl.

**credibility** [krɛdɪ'bɪlɪtɪ] n credibilidade f.

**credible** ['krɛdɪbl] adj crível.

**credit** ['krɛdɪt] n (gen) crédito; (merit) mérito, honra // vt (believe) acreditar // adj creditício; ~s npl (CINEMA) fichas técnicas fpl; ~able adj louvável; ~ **card** n cartão m de crédito; ~**or** n credor(a) m/f.

**credulity** [krɪ'dju:lɪtɪ] n credulidade f.

**creed** [kri:d] n credo.

**creek** [kri:k] n ria, enseada; (US) arroio.

**creep** [kri:p] pt, pp **crept** vi (animal) rastejar; (gen) arrastar-se; (plant) trepar; ~**er** n trepadeira; ~**y** adj (frightening) horripilante.

**cremate** [krɪ'meɪt] vt cremar; **cremation** [-ʃən] n cremação f.

**crematorium** [krɛmə'tɔ:rɪəm], pl **-ria** [-rɪə] n crematório.

**creosote** ['krɪəsəut] n creosoto.

**crêpe** [kreɪp] n (fabric) crepe m; (paper) papel crepom m; ~ **bandage** n atadura de crepe.

**crept** [krɛpt] pt, pp of **creep**.

**crescent** ['krɛsnt] n meia-lua; (street) rua semicircular.

**cress** [krɛs] n agrião m.

**crest** [krɛst] n (of bird) crista; (of hill) cimo, topo; (of helmet) cimeira; (of coat of arms) timbre m; ~**fallen** adj abatido.

**Crete** [kri:t] n Creta.

**crevasse** [krɪ'væs] n fenda.

**crevice** ['krɛvɪs] n fenda, greta.

**crew** [kru:] n (of ship etc) tripulação f; (gang) bando, quadrilha; (MIL) guarnição f; ~-**cut** n corte m à escovinha; ~-**neck** n gola arredondada.

**crib** [krɪb] n manjedoira, presépio; (US: cot) berço // vt (col) plagiar, colar.

**crick** [krɪk] n (in neck) cãibra.

**cricket** ['krɪkɪt] n (insect) grilo; (game) críquete m, cricket m.

**crime** [kraɪm] n crime m; (less serious) delito; **criminal** ['krɪmɪnl] n criminoso // adj criminal; (law) penal; **the Criminal Investigation Department (CID)** Brigada de Investigação Criminal.

**crimson** ['krɪmzn] adj inv carmesim.

**cringe** [krɪndʒ] vi agachar-se, encolher-se.

**crinkle** ['krɪŋkl] vt enrugar.

**cripple** ['krɪpl] n coxo, aleijado // vt aleijar, inutilizar.

**crisis** ['kraɪsɪs], pl **-ses** [-si:z] n crise f.

**crisp** [krɪsp] adj fresco; (cooked) torrado; (hair) crespo; (manner) seco; ~s npl frita f batatinha.

**criss-cross** ['krɪskrɔs] adj cruzado.

**criterion** [kraɪ'tɪərɪən], pl **-ria** [-rɪə] n critério.

**critic** ['krɪtɪk] n (gen) crítico/a m/f; (paper) crítico; ~**al** adj (gen) crítico; (illness) grave; ~**ally** adv (ill) gravemente; ~**ism** ['krɪtɪsɪzm] n crítica; ~**ize** ['krɪtɪsaɪz] vt criticar.

**croak** [krəuk] vi (frog) coaxar; (raven) crocitar // n grasnido.

**crochet** ['krəuʃeɪ] n crochê m.

**crockery** ['krɔkərɪ] n louça.

**crocodile** ['krɔkədaɪl] n crocodilo.

**crocus** ['krəukəs] n açafrão-da-primavera m.

**croft** [krɔft] n pequena chácara; ~**er** n arrendatário.

**croissant** ['krwasã] n croissant m, meia-lua.

**crone** [krəun] n velha encarquilhada, bruxa.

**crony** ['krəunɪ] n camarada m/f, compadre m.

**crook** [kruk] n (fam) vigarista m/f; (of shepherd) cajado; (of arm) curva; ~ed ['krukɪd] adj torto; (path) tortuoso; (action) desonesto.

**crop** [krɔp] n (species) colheita; (quantity) safra // vt cortar, ceifar; to ~ up vi aparecer, vir à baila.

**croquet** ['krəukeɪ] n croquet m, croqué m.

**croquette** [krə'kɛt] n croquete m.

**cross** [krɔs] n cruz f // vt (street etc) cruzar, atravessar // adj zangado, mal-humorado; to ~ o.s. persignar-se; to ~ out vt riscar; to ~ over vi atravessar-se; ~bar n travessa; (SPORT) barra transversal; ~country (race) n corrida pelo campo; ~examination n interrogatório; ~examine vt interrogar; ~eyed adj vesgo; ~ing n (road) cruzamento; (rail) passagem f de nível; (sea-passage) travessia; (also: pedestrian ~ing) passagem para pedestres; ~ purposes npl: to be at ~ purposes não entender-se; ~reference n referência remissiva; ~roads n encruzilhada; ~ section n corte m transversal; (of population) grupo representativo; ~walk (US) n passagem f para pedestres; ~wind n vento costal; ~word n palavras cruzadas fpl.

**crotch** [krɔtʃ] n (of garment) forqueta.

**crotchet** ['krɔtʃɪt] n (MUS) semínima.

**crotchety** ['krɔtʃɪtɪ] adj (person) extravagante.

**crouch** [krautʃ] vi agachar-se.

**croupier** ['kru:pɪə] n crupiê m/f.

**crow** [krəu] n (bird) corvo; (of cock) canto, cocoricó m // vi (cock) cantar, cocoricar.

**crowbar** ['krəuba:*] n alavanca, pé-de-cabra m.

**crowd** [kraud] n multidão f; (SPORT) público; (unruly) tropel m; (common herd) turba, vulgo // vt (gather) amontoar; (fill) encher // vi (gather) reunir-se; (pile up) amontoar-se; ~ed adj (full) cheio; (well-attended) concorrido.

**crown** [kraun] n (of head) topo, alta; (of hat) copa; (of hill) cume m // vt coroar; ~ jewels npl jóias fpl reais; ~ prince n príncipe m herdeiro.

**crucial** ['kru:ʃl] adj decisivo.

**crucifix** ['kru:sɪfɪks] n crucifixo; ~ion [-'fɪkʃən] n crucificação f; **crucify** ['kru:sɪfaɪ] vt crucificar.

**crude** [kru:d] adj (materials) bruto; (fig: basic) tosco; (: vulgar) ordinário; ~ (oil) n óleo cru.

**cruel** ['kruəl] adj cruel; ~ty n crueldade f.

**cruet** ['kru:ɪt] n galheta.

**cruise** [kru:z] n cruzeiro, viagem f marítima // vi (ship) fazer um cruzeiro; (car) circular lentamente; **cruiser** n cruzador m.

**crumb** [krʌm] n migalha.

**crumble** ['krʌmbl] vt esmigalhar // vi (gen) desintegrar-se; (building) desmoronar-se; **crumbly** adj friável.

**crumpet** ['krʌmpɪt] n bolo leve.

**crumple** ['krʌmpl] vt (paper) enrugar; (material) amarrotar.

**crunch** [krʌntʃ] vt (food etc) mastigar; (underfoot) fazer ranger // n (fig) crise f; ~y adj mastigado, ruidoso.

**crusade** [kru:'seɪd] n cruzada.

**crush** [krʌʃ] n (people) esmagamento; (crowd) aglomeração f; (drink): **lemon** ~ limonada // vt (gen) esmagar; (paper) amassar; (cloth) enrugar; (fruit) espremer; ~ing adj (burden) esmagador(a).

**crust** [krʌst] n côdea; (MED) crosta.

**crutch** [krʌtʃ] n muleta.

**crux** [krʌks] n ponto crucial.

**cry** [kraɪ] vi chorar; (shout) gritar // n grito.

**crypt** [krɪpt] n cripta.

**cryptic** [ˈkrɪptɪk] adj enigmático, secreto.

**crystal** [ˈkrɪstl] n cristal m; ~**clear** adj cristalino, claro; **crystallize** vt cristalizar // vi cristalizar-se.

**cub** [kʌb] n filhote m.

**Cuba** [ˈkjuːbə] n Cuba; ~**n** adj, n cubano/a.

**cubbyhole** [ˈkʌbɪhəʊl] n esconderijo.

**cube** [kjuːb] n cubo // vt (MATH) elevar ao cubo; ~ **root** n raiz f cúbica; **cubic** adj cúbico.

**cubicle** [ˈkjuːbɪkl] n cubículo.

**cuckoo** [ˈkuku:] n cuco; ~ **clock** n relógio de cuco.

**cucumber** [ˈkjuːkʌmbə*] n pepino.

**cuddle** [ˈkʌdl] vt embalar // vi abraçar-se; **cuddly** adj mimoso.

**cue** [kjuː] n (snooker) taco; (THEATRE etc) deixa.

**cuff** [kʌf] n (of shirt, coat etc) punho; (blow) bofetada; **off the** ~ adv improvisado; ~**links** npl abotoaduras fpl.

**cuisine** [kwɪˈziːn] n cozinha.

**cul-de-sac** [ˈkʌldəsæk] n beco sem saída.

**culinary** [ˈkʌlɪnərɪ] adj culinário.

**cull** [kʌl] vt (flowers) escolher; (select) selecionar (Pt: -cc-); (kill) matar seletivamente.

**culminate** [ˈkʌlmɪneɪt] vi: **to** ~ **in** terminar em; **culmination** [-ˈneɪʃən] n culminação f, auge m.

**culpable** [ˈkʌlpəbl] adj culpável.

**culprit** [ˈkʌlprɪt] n culpado/a m/f, acusado/a m/f.

**cult** [kʌlt] n culto.

**cultivate** [ˈkʌltɪveɪt] vt (also fig) cultivar; **cultivation** [-ˈveɪʃən] n cultivo; (fig) cultura.

**cultural** [ˈkʌltʃərəl] adj cultural.

**culture** [ˈkʌltʃə*] n (also fig) cultura; ~**d** adj culto.

**cumbersome** [ˈkʌmbəsəm] adj pesado, incômodo.

**cumulative** [ˈkjuːmjulətɪv] adj cumulativo.

**cunning** [ˈkʌnɪŋ] n astúcia // adj astuto.

**cup** [kʌp] n xícara; (Pt) chávena; (prize, event) taça.

**cupboard** [ˈkʌbəd] n armário; (for crockery) guarda-louça.

**Cupid** [ˈkjuːpɪd] n Cupido.

**cupola** [ˈkjuːpələ] n cúpula.

**cup-tie** [ˈkʌptaɪ] n jogo eliminatório.

**cur** [kəː] n cão m vadio, vira-latas m inv; (person) patife m/f.

**curable** [ˈkjuərəbl] adj curável.

**curate** [ˈkjuərɪt] n coadjutor m.

**curator** [kjuəˈreɪtə*] n diretor (Pt: -ct-) m, curador m.

**curb** [kəːb] vt refrear // n meio-fio.

**curdle** [ˈkəːdl] vi coalhar.

**curds** [kəːdz] npl coalho.

**cure** [kjuə*] vt curar // n tratamento, cura.

**curfew** [ˈkəːfjuː] n hora de recolher.

**curio** [ˈkjuərɪəu] n antiguidade f.

**curiosity** [kjuərɪˈɒsɪtɪ] n curiosidade f, **curious** [ˈkjuərɪəs] adj curioso.

**curl** [kəːl] n anel m, caracol m // vt (hair) frisar, encrespar; (paper) enrolar; (lip) torcer // vi: **to** ~ **up** frisar-se, enrolar-se; (person) encaracolar-se; (fam) rir até morrer; ~**er** n rolo, bobe m; ~**y** adj frisado, crespo.

**currant** [ˈkʌrnt] n passa de corinto; (black, red) groselha.

**currency** [ˈkʌrnsɪ] n dinheiro, moeda.

**current** [ˈkʌrnt] n corrente f // adj corrente, atual (Pt: -ct-); ~ **account** n conta corrente; ~ **affairs** npl atualidades (Pt: -ct-) fpl; ~**ly** adv a(c)tualmente.

**curriculum** [kəˈrɪkjuləm], pl ~**s** or **-la** [-lə] n programa m de estudos; ~ **vitae** n curriculum vitae m.

**curry** [ˈkʌrɪ] n caril m // vt: **to ~ favour with** captar simpatia; ~ **powder** n pós mpl de caril, curry m.

**curse** [kəːs] vi praguejar // vt maldizer, amaldiçoar // n maldição f; (swearword) palavrão m, baixo calão m.

**cursory** [ˈkəːsərɪ] adj rápido, superficial.

**curt** [kəːt] adj seco, brusco.

**curtail** [kəːˈteɪl] vt (visit etc) abreviar, encurtar; (expenses etc) reduzir.

**curtain** [ˈkəːtn] n cortina; (THEATRE) pano; ~ **ring** n argola.

**curts(e)y** [ˈkəːtsɪ] n mesura, reverência // vi fazer reverência.

**curve** [kəːv] n curva // vt encurvar, torcer // vi encurvar-se, torcer-se; (road) fazer (uma) curva.

**cushion** [ˈkuʃən] n almofada; (SNOOKER) tabela // vt (seat) escorar com almofada; (shock) amortecer.

**custard** [ˈkʌstəd] n (for pouring) nata, creme m.

**custodian** [kʌsˈtəudiən] n guarda m/f.

**custody** [ˈkʌstədɪ] n custódia; **to take into ~** deter.

**custom** [ˈkʌstəm] n costume m; (COMM) clientela; ~**ary** adj costumeiro.

**customer** [ˈkʌstəmə*] n cliente m/f.

**custom-made** [ˈkʌstəmˈmeɪd] adj (US) feito à medida or sob encomenda.

**customs** [ˈkʌstəmz] npl alfândega sg; ~ **duty** n imposto alfandegário; ~ **officer** n empregado da alfândega.

**cut** [kʌt], pt, pp **cut** vt cortar; (price) baixar; (record) gravar; (reduce) reduzir // vi cortar; (intersect) interceptar-se // n (gen) corte m; (in skin) corte, golpe m; (with sword) corte; (of knife) incisão f; (in salary etc) redução f; (of meat) fatia, corte; (power) ~ corte; **to ~ a tooth** sair/nascer um dente; **to ~ down** vt (tree) derrubar; (reduce) abater; **to ~ off** vt (gen) cortar; (retreat) impedir; (troops) cercar; **to ~ out** vt (shape) recortar; (delete) suprimir; **to ~ through** vi abrir caminho; ~**back** n redução f.

**cute** [kjuːt] adj bonito, engraçado; (shrewd) astuto.

**cuticle** [ˈkjuːtɪkl] n cutícula.

**cutlery** [ˈkʌtlərɪ] n cutelaria, talheres mpl.

**cutlet** [ˈkʌtlɪt] n costeleta.

**cut:** ~**out** n figura para recortar; ~**price** adj, (US) ~**rate** adj a preço reduzido; ~**throat** n assassino // adj impiedoso, feroz.

**cutting** [ˈkʌtɪŋ] adj (gen) cortante; (remark) mordaz // n (PRESS) recorte m; (RAIL) corte m.

**cwt** abbr of **hundredweight.**

**cyanide** [ˈsaɪənaɪd] n cianeto.

**cyclamen** [ˈsɪkləmən] n cíclame m.

**cycle** [ˈsaɪkl] n ciclo; (bicycle) bicicleta // vi andar de bicicleta; **cycling** n ciclismo; **cyclist** n ciclista m/f.

**cyclone** [ˈsaɪkləun] n ciclone m.

**cygnet** [ˈsɪgnɪt] n cisne novo.

**cylinder** [ˈsɪlɪndə*] n cilindro; ~ **block** n bloco de cilindros; ~ **capacity** n capacidade f cilíndrica; ~ **head** n cilíndrico; ~**head gasket** n culatra.

**cymbals** [ˈsɪmblz] npl pratos mpl.

**cynic** [ˈsɪnɪk] n cínico/a; ~**al** adj cínico, sarcástico; ~**ism** [ˈsɪnɪsɪzm] n cepticismo, sarcasmo.

**cypress** [ˈsaɪprɪs] n cipreste m.

**Cypriot** [ˈsɪprɪət] adj, n cipriota m/f.

**Cyprus** [ˈsaɪprəs] n Chipre f.

**cyst** [sɪst] n cisto; ~**itis** n cistite f.

**czar** [zaː*] n czar m.

**Czech** [tʃek] adj, n tcheco/a.

**Czechoslovakia** [tʃekəslə'vækıə] *n*
Tchecoslováquia.

# D

**dab** [dæb] *vt* (*eyes, wound*) tocar
(ligeiramente); (*paint, cream*)
pintar de leve // *n* (*of paint*)
pincelada; (*of liquid*) gota; (*amount*)
pequena quantidade *f*.
**dabble** ['dæbl] *vi*: **to ~ in**
interessar-se por.
**dad** [dæd], **daddy** ['dædı] *n* papai
*m*; **daddy-long-legs** *n* pernilongo.
**daffodil** ['dæfədıl] *n* narciso-dos-
prados *m*.
**daft** [dɑːft] *adj* estúpido, maluco.
**dagger** ['dægə*] *n* punhal *m*, adaga;
**to look ~s at sb** lançar olhares
furiosos a alguém.
**daily** ['deılı] *adj* diário, cotidiano // *n* (*paper*) diário, (*domestic help*)
diarista; (Pt) mulher *f* a dias // *adv*
diariamente, cada dia.
**dainty** ['deıntı] *adj* delicado,
(*tasteful*) elegante, gracioso.
**dairy** ['dɛərı] *n* (*shop*) leiteria; (*on
farm*) vacaria // *adj* de laticínios; **~
farm** *n* fazenda de gado leiteiro; **~
produce** *n* produtos *mpl* lácteos.
**daisy** ['deızı] *n* margarida.
**dale** [deıl] *n* vale *m*.
**dam** [dæm] *n* represa, barragem *f* // *vt* represar.
**damage** ['dæmıdʒ] *n* dano, prejuízo;
(*to machine*) avaria // *vt* danificar,
prejudicar; **~s** *npl* (LAW)
indenização *f* por danos.
**damn** [dæm] *vt* condenar; (*curse*)
maldizer // *n* (*col*): **I don't give a ~**
não me importa, pouco se me dá // *adj* (*col*) (que) droga; **~ (it)!** (que)
porcaria!; **~ing** *adj* (*evidence*)
grave, sério.
**damp** [dæmp] *adj* úmido, molhado
// *n* umidade *f* // *vt* (*also:* **~en**)

(*cloth, rag*) molhar; (*enthusiasm
etc*) jogar água fria em; **~ness** *n*
umidade *f*.
**damson** ['dæmzən] *n* ameixa
pequena.
**dance** [dɑːns] *n* dança, baile *m* // *vi*
bailar, dançar; **~ hall** *n* salão *m* de
baile; **dancer** *n* bailarino/a; (*professional*) bailarino/a; **dancing**
*n* dança, baile *m*.
**dandelion** ['dændılaıən] *n* dente-de-
leão *m*.
**dandruff** ['dændrəf] *n* caspa.
**Dane** [deın] *n* dinamarquês/esa *m/f.*
**danger** ['deındʒə*] *n* perigo; (*risk*)
risco; **~!** (*on sign*) perigo!; **to be in ~ of** correr o risco de; **~ous** *adj*
perigoso; **~ously** *adv* perigosa-
mente.
**dangle** ['dæŋgl] *vt/i* pender
balançando.
**Danish** ['deınıʃ] *adj*, *n*
dinamarquês/esa *m/f.*
**dare** [dɛə*] *vt*: **to ~ sb to do sth**
desafiar alguém a fazer algo // *vi*:
**to ~ (to) do sth** atrever-se a fazer
algo; **~devil** *n* intrépido, atrevido;
**daring** *adj* atrevido, ousado // *n*
atrevimento, audácia.
**dark** [dɑːk] *adj* (*gen*) escuro;
(*complexion*) moreno; (*hair*) escuro;
(*cheerless*) triste, sombrio; (*fig*)
secreto, escondido // *n* (*gen*)
escuridão *f*; (*night*) trevas *fpl*; **to be
left in the ~ about** (*fig*) ser deixado
sem saber de nada sobre, ser
deixado no escuro sobre; **after ~**
depois de escurecer; **~en** *vt*
escurecer; (*colour*) fazer mais
escuro // *vi* escurecer-se; (*sky*)
anuviar-se; **~ glasses** *npl* óculos
*mpl* escuros; **~ness** *n* escuridão *f*,
trevas *fpl*; **~ room** *n* câmara
escura.
**darling** ['dɑːlıŋ] *adj*, *n* querido/a.
**darn** [dɑːn] *vt* remendar, cerzir.
**dart** [dɑːt] *n* (*gen*) dardo; (*in game*)
flecha, dardo // *vi* precipitar-se; **to ~
away/along** ir-se, seguir

precipidamente; ~**board** n alvo; ~**s** n jogo de dardos.

**dash** [dæʃ] n (*sign*) hífen m; (:*long*) travessão m; (*rush*) correria // vt (*throw*) arremessar; (*hopes*) frustrar // vi precipitar-se, ir depressa; **to ~ away** or **off** vi ir-se com pressa; ~**board** n painel m de instrumentos; ~**ing** adj arrojado.

**data** ['deɪtə] npl dados mpl; ~ **processing** n processamento de dados.

**date** [deɪt] n (*day*) data; (*with friend*) encontro; (*fruit*) tâmara; (*tree*) tamareira // vt datar; **to ~** adv até agora; **out of ~** desatualizado; **up to ~** moderno, em dia, ~**d** adj antiquado.

**daub** [dɔːb] vt borrar.

**daughter** ['dɔːtə*] n filha; ~**in-law** n nora.

**daunting** ['dɔːntɪŋ] adj desalentador(a).

**dawdle** ['dɔːdl] vi (*waste time*) perder o tempo; (*go slow*) andar devagar.

**dawn** [dɔːn] n madrugada, amanhecer m // vi (*day*) amanhecer; (*fig*): **it ~ed on him that...** começou a perceber que....

**day** [deɪ] n dia m; (*working ~*) jornada, dia útil; **the ~ before** véspera; **the following ~** o dia seguinte; **by ~** de dia; ~**break** n amanhecer m; ~**dream** n fantasia, devaneio // vi devanear; ~**light** n luz f (de dia); ~**time** n dia // adj de dia, diurno.

**daze** [deɪz] vt (*stun*) aturdir // n: **in a ~** aturdido.

**dazzle** ['dæzl] vt deslumbrar; **dazzling** adj deslumbrante.

**dead** [dɛd] adj (*gen*) morto; (*deceased*) falecido; (*telephone*) cortado; (*ELEC*) sem corrente // adv (*gen*) totalmente; (*exactly*) absolutamente; ~ **tired** morto de cansaço; **to stop ~** estacar; **the ~** os mortos mpl // vt (*blow, sound*)

amortecer; (*make numb*) anestesiar; ~ **end** n beco sem saída; ~ **heat** n (*SPORT*) empate m; ~**line** n prazo final; ~**lock** n impasse m, beco sem saída; ~**ly** adj mortal, fatal; ~**pan** adj sem expressão.

**deaf** [dɛf] adj surdo; ~**aid** n aparelho para a surdez; ~**en** vt ensurdecer; ~**ening** adj ensurdecedor(a); ~**ness** n surdez f; ~**mute** n surdo-mudo.

**deal** [diːl] n (*agreement*) acordo; (*business*) transação (Pt: -cç-) f, negócio; (*CARDS*) mão f // vt, pp, pp **dealt** [dɛlt] (*gen*) dar; **a great ~ (of)** bastante, muito; **to ~ in** tratar com; **to ~ with** vt (*people*) tratar com; (*problem*) ocupar-se de; (*subject*) tratar de; (*COMM*) negociar com; (*punish*) castigar; ~**er** n negociante m/f; (*CARDS*) carteador m, banqueiro; ~**ings** npl transações (Pt: -cç-) fpl; (*relations*) relações fpl.

**dear** [dɪə*] adj querido; (*expensive*) caro // n: **my ~** meu querido/ minha querida // excl: ~ **me!** Meu Deus!; **D~ Sir/Madam** (*in letter*) Ilmo. Senhor/Exma. Senhora; (*Pt*) Exmo. Senhor/Exma. Senhora; ~**ly** adv (*love*) ternamente; (*pay*) caro.

**death** [dɛθ] n morte f; ~**bed** n leito de morte; ~ **certificate** n certidão f de óbito; ~ **duties** npl (*Brit*) impostos mpl sobre inventário; ~**ly** adj mortal; (*silence*) profundo; ~ **penalty** n pena de morte; ~ **rate** n (índice f de) mortalidade.

**debar** [dɪˈbɑː*] vt (*exclude*) excluir.

**debase** [dɪˈbeɪs] vt degradar.

**debate** [dɪˈbeɪt] n debate m // vt debater.

**debauchery** [dɪˈbɔːtʃərɪ] n libertinagem f.

**debit** ['dɛbɪt] n débito // vt: **to ~ a sum to sb** or **to sb's account** lançar uma quantia ao débito de alguém ou à conta de alguém.

**debris** ['dɛbriː] n escombros mpl.

**debt** [dɛt] n dívida; **to be in ~** ter

dívidas; ~**or** n devedor(a) m/f.

**début** ['deɪbjuː] n estréia.

**decade** ['dɛkeɪd] n década.

**decadence** ['dɛkədəns] n decadência.

**decay** [dɪ'keɪ] n decadência; (*of building*) ruína; (*fig*) deterioração f; (*rotting*) podridão f; (*of tooth*) cárie f // vi (*rot*) apodrecer-se; (*fig*) decair.

**deceased** [dɪ'siːst] adj defunto, falecido.

**deceit** [dɪ'siːt] n engano; ~**ful** adj enganador(a).

**deceive** [dɪ'siːv] vt enganar.

**decelerate** [diː'sɛləreɪt] vt moderar a marcha de, desacelerar // vi diminuir a velocidade.

**December** [dɪ'sɛmbə*] n dezembro.

**decency** ['diːsənsɪ] n decência.

**decent** ['diːsənt] adj (*proper*) decente; (*person*) honesto, amável.

**decentralize** [diː'sɛntrəlaɪz] vt descentralizar.

**deception** [dɪ'sɛpʃən] n engano, decepção f; **deceptive** [-tɪv] adj enganoso.

**decibel** ['dɛsɪbɛl] n decibel m.

**decide** [dɪ'saɪd] vt (*person*) decidir; (*question, argument*) resolver // vi decidir; **to** ~ **on sth** decidir-se por algo; ~**d** adj (*resolute*) claro, definido; (*clear, definite*) claro, definido; ~**dly** [-dɪdlɪ] adv decididamente.

**deciduous** [dɪ'sɪdjuəs] adj decíduo, caduco.

**decimal** ['dɛsɪməl] adj decimal // n decimal m; ~ **point** n vírgula de decimais.

**decimate** ['dɛsɪmeɪt] vt dizimar.

**decipher** [dɪ'saɪfə*] vt decifrar.

**decision** [dɪ'sɪʒən] n decisão f.

**decisive** [dɪ'saɪsɪv] adj decisivo; (*conclusive*) terminante; (*manner*) categórico.

**deck** [dɛk] n (NAUT) coberta; (*of bus*) andar m; (*of cards*) baralho; ~**chair** n cadeira de lona.

**declaration** [dɛklə'reɪʃən] n declaração f; **declare** [dɪ'klɛə*] vt (*gen*) declarar.

**decline** [dɪ'klaɪn] n declínio, decadência; (*lessening*) diminuição f, baixa // vt recusar // vi decair, diminuir; (*fall*) baixar.

**declutch** ['diː'klʌtʃ] vi debrear.

**decode** ['diː'kəud] vt decifrar.

**decompose** [diːkəm'pəuz] vi decompor-se; **decomposition** [diːkɔmpə'zɪʃən] n decomposição f.

**decontaminate** [diːkən'tæmɪneɪt] vt descontaminar.

**décor** ['deɪkɔː*] n decoração f; (THEATRE) cenário.

**decorate** ['dɛkəreɪt] vt ornamentar, decorar; (*paint*) pintar; (*paper*) decorar com papel; **decoration** [-'reɪʃən] n adorno, decoração f; (*act*) decoração f; (*medal*) condecoração f; **decorator** n (*painter*) pintor m.

**decoy** ['diːkɔɪ] n engodo.

**decrease** ['diːkriːs] n diminuição f // (*vb*: [diː'kriːs]) vt diminuir, reduzir // vi reduzir-se.

**decree** [dɪ'kriː] n decreto; ~ **nisi** n ordem f provisória de divórcio.

**decrepit** [dɪ'krɛpɪt] adj decrépito.

**dedicate** ['dɛdɪkeɪt] vt dedicar; **dedication** [-'keɪʃən] n (*devotion*) dedicação f; (*in book*) dedicatória.

**deduce** [dɪ'djuːs] vt deduzir.

**deduct** [dɪ'dʌkt] vt deduzir; (*from wage etc*) descontar; ~**ion** [dɪ'dʌkʃən] n redução f, dedução f; (*conclusion*) conclusão f, dedução f.

**deed** [diːd] n feito, ato (PT: -ct-); (*feat*) façanha; (LAW) escritura, título.

**deem** [diːm] vt julgar.

**deep** [diːp] adj (*gen*) profundo; (*voice*) baixo, grave; (*breath*) profundo, com pulmão cheio; (*person*) insondável // adv: **the spectators stood** 20 ~ os espectadores formaram-se em 20 fileiras; **to be 4 metres** ~ ter 4 metros de profundidade; **~en** vt aprofundar // vi (darkness) escurecer-se; **~freeze** n congelador m; **~fry** vt fritar em recipiente fundo; **~sea diving** n pesca submarina; **~seated** adj (beliefs) arraigado; **~set** adj (eyes) fundo.

**deer** [dɪə*] n, pl inv veado, cervo; **~skin** n camurça, pele f de cervo.

**deface** [dɪˈfeɪs] vt desfigurar, deformar.

**defamation** [dɛfəˈmeɪʃən] n difamação f.

**default** [dɪˈfɔːlt] vi não pagar; (SPORT) não comparecer // n: **by ~** (LAW) à revelia; (SPORT) por ausência; **in ~ of** (in debt) devedor(a) m/f insolvente.

**defeat** [dɪˈfiːt] n derrota // vt derrotar, vencer; (fig: efforts) frustrar; **~ist** adj, n derrotista m/f.

**defect** ['diːfɛkt] n defeito // vi [dɪˈfɛkt] desertar; **~ive** [dɪˈfɛktɪv] adj (gen) defeituoso; (person) retardado mental.

**defence** [dɪˈfɛns] n defesa; **~less** adj indefeso.

**defend** [dɪˈfɛnd] vt defender; **~ant** n acusado/a; (in civil case) réu/ré m/f; **~er** n defensor(a) m/f.

**defensive** [dɪˈfɛnsɪv] adj defensivo; **on the ~** na defensiva.

**defer** [dɪˈfəː*] vt (postpone) adiar; **to ~** to submeter-se a; **~ence** ['dɛfərəns] n deferência, respeito.

**defiance** [dɪˈfaɪəns] n desafio; **in ~ of** sem respeito por; indiferente a; **defiant** [-ənt] adj (insolent) desafiante, insolente; (challenging) desafiador(a).

**deficiency** [dɪˈfɪʃənsɪ] n (lack) falta; (defect) defeito; **deficient** [-ənt] adj (lacking) deficiente; (incomplete) incompleto; (defective) imperfeito; (mentally) anormal; **deficient in** falto de, carente de.

**deficit** ['dɛfɪsɪt] n déficit m.

**defile** [dɪˈfaɪl] vt sujar, profanar.

**define** [dɪˈfaɪn] vt definir.

**definite** ['dɛfɪnɪt] adj (fixed) definitivo; (clear, obvious) claro, categórico; **he was ~ about it** ele foi categórico; **~ly** adv claramente.

**definition** [dɛfɪˈnɪʃən] n definição f.

**definitive** [dɪˈfɪnɪtɪv] adj definitivo.

**deflate** [diːˈfleɪt] vt (gen) esvasiar; (person) fazer perder o rebolado.

**deflect** [dɪˈflɛkt] vt desviar.

**deform** [dɪˈfɔːm] vt deformar; **~ed** adj deformado; **~ity** n deformidade f.

**defraud** [dɪˈfrɔːd] vt defraudar; **to ~ sb of sth** defraudar alguém de algo.

**defrost** [diːˈfrɒst] vt (fridge) descongelar; **~er** n (US) desembaçante m de pára-brisa.

**deft** [dɛft] adj destro, hábil.

**defunct** [dɪˈfʌŋkt] adj extinto, morto.

**defuse** [diːˈfjuːz] vt tirar o estopim or a espoleta a.

**defy** [dɪˈfaɪ] vt (resist) opor-se a; (challenge) desafiar; (order) desobedecer.

**degenerate** vi [dɪˈdʒɛnəreɪt] degenerar // adj [dɪˈdʒɛnərɪt] degenerado.

**degradation** [dɛgrəˈdeɪʃən] n degradação f; **degrading** [dɪˈgreɪdɪŋ] adj degradante.

**degree** [dɪˈgriː] n grau m; (SCOL) diploma m, título; **~ in maths** grau em matemática.

**dehydrated** [diːhaɪˈdreɪtɪd] adj desidratado; (milk) em pó.

**de-ice** [diːˈaɪs] vt (windscreen) descongelar.

**deign** [deɪn] vi: **to ~ to do** dignar-se a fazer.

**deity** ['diːɪtɪ] n divindade f, deidade f.

**dejected** [dɪˈdʒɛktɪd] adj abatido, desanimado; (face) triste; **dejection** [-ʃən] n desânimo.

**delay** [dɪˈleɪ] vt demorar, atrasar; (trains) atrasar // vi retardar-se //

*n* demora, atraso; **without** ~ sem demora, sem atraso.

**delegate** ['dɛligit] *n* delegado/a // *vt* ['dɛligeit] delegar; **delegation** [-'geiʃən] *n* delegação *f*.

**delete** [di'li:t] *vt* eliminar, riscar.

**deliberate** [di'libərit] *adj* (*intentional*) intencional; (*slow*) pausado, lento // *vi* [di'libəreit] deliberar; ~**ly** *adv* (*on purpose*) de propósito; (*slowly*) lentamente.

**delicacy** ['dɛlikəsi] *n* delicadeza; (*choice food*) iguaria.

**delicate** ['dɛlikit] *adj* (*gen*) delicado; (*fragile*) frágil; (*skilled*) fino.

**delicatessen** [dɛlikə'tɛsn] *n* loja especializada em comida exótica.

**delicious** [di'liʃəs] *adj* delicioso, saboroso.

**delight** [di'lait] *n* (*feeling*) prazer *m*, deleite *m*; (*object*) encanto, delícia // *vt* encantar, deleitar; **to take** ~ **in** deleitar-se com; ~**ful** *adj* encantador(a), delicioso.

**delinquency** [di'liŋkwənsi] *n* delinqüência; **delinquent** [-ənt] *adj*, *n* delinqüente *m/f*.

**delirious** [di'liriəs] *adj* delirante; **delirium** [-iəm] *n* delírio.

**deliver** [di'livə*] *vt* (*distribute*) distribuir; (*hand over*) entregar; (*message*) comunicar; (*speech*) proferir; (*blow*) dar, desfechar; (*MED*): **to be** ~**ed** dar à luz; ~**y** *n* entrega; (*distribution*) distribuição *f*; (*of speaker*) enunciação *f*; (*MED*) parto; (*saving*) libertação *f*; **to take** ~**y of** receber.

**delta** ['dɛltə] *n* delta *m*.

**delude** [di'lu:d] *vt* enganar.

**deluge** ['dɛlju:dʒ] *n* dilúvio // *vt* inundar.

**delusion** [di'lu:ʒən] *n* ilusão *f*, erro.

**de luxe** [di'lʌks] *adj* de luxo.

**delve** [dɛlv] *vi*: **to** ~ **into** investigar, pesquisar.

**demand** [di'mɑ:nd] *vt* (*gen*) exigir, pedir; (*rights*) reclamar // *n* (*gen*)

exigência, pedido; (*claim*) reclamação *f*; (*ECON*) procura; **to be in** ~ ser muito solicitado; **on** ~ à vista; ~**ing** *adj* (*boss*) exigente; (*work*) absorvente.

**demarcation** [di:mɑ:'keiʃən] *n* demarcação *f*.

**demean** [di'mi:n] *vt*: **to** ~ **o.s.** rebaixar-se.

**demeanour** [di'mi:nə*] *n* conduta, comportamento.

**demented** [di'mentid] *adj* demente, doido.

**demister** [di:'mistə*] *n* (*AUT*) desembaçante *m* de pára-brisa.

**democracy** [di'mɔkrəsi] *n* democracia; **democrat** ['dɛməkræt] *n* democrata *m/f*; **democratic** [dɛmə'krætik] *adj* democrático.

**demolish** [di'mɔliʃ] *vt* demolir, derrubar; **demolition** [dɛmə'liʃən] *n* demolição *f*, destruição *f*.

**demonstrate** ['dɛmənstreit] *vt* demonstrar // *vi* manifestar-se; **demonstration** [-'streiʃən] *n* (*POL*) manifestação *f*; (*proof*) prova, demonstração *f*; **demonstrator** *n* (*POL*) manifestante *m/f*.

**demoralize** [di'mɔrəlaiz] *vt* desmoralizar.

**demote** [di'məut] *vt* rebaixar de posto.

**demure** [di'mjuə*] *adj* recatado.

**den** [dɛn] *n* (*of animal*) covil *m*, (*study*) aposento privado, cantinho.

**denial** [di'naiəl] *n* (*refusal*) negativa; (*of report etc*) desmentido; **self**~ *n* abnegação *f*.

**denim** ['dɛnim] *n* ganga *f*; ~**s** *npl* brim *m*, zuarte *m*.

**Denmark** ['dɛnmɑ:k] *n* Dinamarca.

**denomination** [dinɔmi'neiʃən] *n* valor *m*, denominação *f*; (*REL*) seita.

**denominator** [di'nɔmineitə*] *n* denominador *m*.

**denote** [di'nəut] *vt* indicar, significar.

**denounce** [di'nauns] *vt* denunciar.

**dense** [dɛns] *adj* (*thick*) denso,

espesso; (: *foliage etc*) denso; (*stupid*) estúpido, bronco; ~**ly** *adv*: ~**ly populated** com grande densidade de população.

**density** ['dɛnsɪtɪ] *n* densidade *f*.

**dent** [dɛnt] *n* amolgadura, depressão *f* // *vt* (*also:* **make a ~ in**) amolgar, dentar.

**dental** ['dɛntl] *adj* dental; ~ **surgeon** *n* odontólogo.

**dentist** ['dɛntɪst] *n* dentista *m/f*; ~**ry** *n* odontologia.

**dentures** ['dɛntʃəz] *npl* dentadura *sg*.

**deny** [dɪ'naɪ] *vt* (*gen*) negar; (*report*) desmentir.

**deodorant** [diː'əudərənt] *n* desodorante *m*; (*Pt*) desodorizante *m*.

**depart** [dɪ'pɑːt] *vi* ir-se, partir; (*train*) sair; **to ~ from** (*fig: differ from*) afastar-se de.

**department** [dɪ'pɑːtmənt] *n* departamento; (*COMM*) seção (*Pt*: -cç-) *f*; (*POL*) ministério, repartição *f*; ~ **store** *n* magazine *m*, grande armazém *m*, shopping *m*.

**departure** [dɪ'pɑːtʃə*] *n* partida, ida; (*of train*) saída; **a new ~** nova orientação; ~**s board, board** (*US*) *n* horário de saídas.

**depend** [dɪ'pɛnd] *vi*: **to ~ on** depender de; (*rely on*) contar com; **it ~s** depende; ~**able** *adj* (*person*) de confiança, seguro; ~**ence** *n* dependência; ~**ant, ~ent** *n* dependente *m/f*.

**depict** [dɪ'pɪkt] *vt* (*in picture*) pintar; (*describe*) representar.

**depleted** [dɪ'pliːtɪd] *adj* depauperado.

**deplorable** [dɪ'plɔːrəbl] *adj* deplorável, lamentável; **deplore** [dɪ'plɔː*] *vt* deplorar, lamentar.

**deploy** [dɪ'plɔɪ] *vt* dispor.

**depopulation** ['diːpɔpju'leɪʃən] *n* despovoamento.

**deport** [dɪ'pɔːt] *vt* deportar; ~**ation**

[-'teɪʃən] *n* deportação *f*; ~**ment** *n* comportamento.

**depose** [dɪ'pəuz] *vt* depor.

**deposit** [dɪ'pɔzɪt] *n* (*gen*) depósito; (*CHEM*) sedimento; (*of ore, oil*) depósito // *vt* (*gen*) depositar; ~ **account** *n* conta de depósito a prazo; ~**or** *n* depositante *m/f*.

**depot** ['dɛpəu] *n* (*storehouse*) armazém *m*; (*for vehicles*) garagem *f*, parque *m*.

**depraved** [dɪ'preɪvd] *adj* depravado, viciado; **depravity** [-'prævɪtɪ] *n* depravação *f*, vício.

**depreciate** [dɪ'priːʃɪeɪt] *vi* depreciar-se, desvalorizar-se; **depreciation** [-'eɪʃən] *n* depreciação *f*.

**depress** [dɪ'prɛs] *vt* deprimir; (*press down*) apertar; ~**ed** *adj* deprimido; ~**ing** *adj* triste, desanimador(a); ~**ion** [dɪ'prɛʃən] *n* depressão *f*.

**deprivation** [dɛprɪ'veɪʃən] *n* privação *f*; (*loss*) perda.

**deprive** [dɪ'praɪv] *vt*: **to ~ sb of** privar alguém de; ~**d** *adj* pobre.

**depth** [dɛpθ] *n* (*gen*) profundidade *f*; (*of room etc*) comprimento; **in the ~s of** nas profundezas de.

**deputation** [dɛpju'teɪʃən] *n* delegação *f*.

**deputize** ['dɛpjutaɪz] *vi*: **to ~ for sb** substituir alguém.

**deputy** ['dɛpjutɪ] *adj*: ~ **head** diretor(a) (*Pt*: -ct-) adjunto/a *m/f* // *n* substituto/a, suplente *m/f*; (*POL*) deputado/a; (*agent*) representante *m/f*.

**derail** [dɪ'reɪl] *vt*: **to be ~ed** descarrilhar-se; ~**ment** *n* descarrilhamento.

**deranged** [dɪ'reɪndʒd] *adj* (*person*) louco, transtornado.

**derelict** ['dɛrɪlɪkt] *adj* abandonado.

**deride** [dɪ'raɪd] *vt* ridicularizar, zombar de; **derision** [-'rɪʒən] *n* irrisão *f*, escárnio.

**derivative** [dɪ'rɪvətɪv] *n* derivado

// adj derivado; (*work*) pouco original.

**derive** [dɪ'raɪv] vt derivar // vi: **to ~ from** derivar-se de.

**dermatitis** [dɜ:mə'taɪtɪs] n dermatite f; **dermatology** [-'tɔlədʒɪ] n dermatologia.

**derogatory** [dɪ'rɔgətərɪ] adj pejorativo.

**derrick** ['derɪk] n guindaste m, torre f de perfurar.

**descend** [dɪ'send] vt/i descer, baixar; **to ~ from** descer de; **~ant** n descendente m/f.

**descent** [dɪ'sent] n descida; (GEO) declive m, ladeira; (*origin*) descendência.

**describe** [dɪs'kraɪb] vt descrever; **description** [-'krɪpʃən] n descrição f; (*sort*) classe f, espécie f; **descriptive** [-'krɪptɪv] adj descritivo.

**desecrate** ['desɪkreɪt] vt profanar.

**desert** ['dezət] n deserto // (vb: [dɪ'zɜ:t]) vt abandonar // vi (MIL) desertar; **~er** n desertor m; **~ion** [dɪ'zɜ:ʃən] n deserção f.

**deserve** [dɪ'zɜ:v] vt merecer; **deserving** adj (*person*) digno; (*action, cause*) meritório.

**design** [dɪ'zaɪn] n (*sketch*) desenho, esboço; (*layout, shape*) plano, modelo; (*pattern*) projeto (Pt: -ct-); (*intention*) propósito, intenção f // vt (gen) desenhar; (*plan*) projetar (Pt: -ct-).

**designate** ['dezɪgneɪt] vt (*point to*) apontar; (*appoint*) nomear; (*destine*) designar // adj ['dezɪgnɪt] designado; **designation** [-'neɪʃən] n (*appointment*) nomeação f; (*name*) designação f.

**designer** [dɪ'zaɪnə*] n (ART) artista m/f gráfico/a; (TECH) desenhista m/f, projetista m/f; (*fashion ~*) modista m/f.

**desirable** [dɪ'zaɪərəbl] adj (*proper*) desejável; (*attractive*) atraente.

**desire** [dɪ'zaɪə*] n desejo // vt desejar.

**desk** [desk] n (*in office*) secretária; (*for pupil*) carteira f; (*in hotel, at airport*) recepção f.

**desolate** ['desəlɪt] adj (*place*) deserto; (*person*) desolado; **desolation** [-'leɪʃən] n (*of place*) desolação f; (*of person*) aflição f.

**despair** [dɪs'peə*] n desespero // vi: **to ~ of** desesperar-se de.

**despatch** [dɪs'pætʃ] n, vt = **dispatch**.

**desperate** ['despərɪt] adj desesperado; **~ly** adv desesperadamente; (*very*) terrivelmente, gravemente.

**desperation** [despə'reɪʃən] n desespero, desesperança; **in ~** desesperado.

**despicable** [dɪs'pɪkəbl] adj desprezível.

**despise** [dɪs'paɪz] vt desprezar.

**despite** [dɪs'paɪt] prep apesar de, a despeito de.

**despondent** [dɪs'pɔndənt] adj abatido, desanimado.

**dessert** [dɪ'zɜ:t] n sobremesa; **~spoon** n colher f de sobremesa.

**destination** [destɪ'neɪʃən] n destino.

**destiny** ['destɪnɪ] n destino.

**destitute** ['destɪtju:t] adj indigente, necessitado.

**destroy** [dɪs'trɔɪ] vt (gen) destruir; (*finish*) acabar com; **~er** n (NAUT) contratorpedeiro.

**destruction** [dɪs'trʌkʃən] n destruição f; (*fig*) ruína; **destructive** [-tɪv] adj destrutivo, destruidor(a).

**detach** [dɪ'tætʃ] vt separar; (*unstick*) desprender; **~able** adj separável; (TECH) desmontável; **~ed** (*attitude*) imparcial, objetivo (Pt: -ct-); (*house*) independente, isolado; **~ment** n (gen) separação f; (MIL) destacamento; (*fig*) obje(c)tividade f, imparcialidade f.

**detail** ['di:teɪl] n detalhe m // vt (gen) detalhar; (MIL) destacar; **in ~**

pormenorizado, em detalhe; **~ed**
adj detalhado.

**etain** [dɪ'teɪn] vt deter; (in
captivity) prender.

**etect** [dɪ'tekt] vt (gen) descobrir;
(MED, POLICE) identificar; (MIL,
RADAR, TECH) detectar; **~ion**
[dɪ'tekʃən] n descobrimento,
identificação f; **~ive** n detetive (Pt:
-ect-) m; **~ive story** n romance m
policial; **~or** n detetor (Pt: -tect-) m.

**étente** [deɪ'tɑːnt] n distensão f de
relações.

**etention** [dɪ'tenʃən] n detenção f,
prisão f.

**eter** [dɪ'tɜː*] vt (discourage)
desanimar; (dissuade) dissuadir;
(prevent) impedir.

**etergent** [dɪ'tɜːdʒənt] n
detergente m.

**eteriorate** [dɪ'tɪərɪəreɪt] vi
deteriorar-se; **deterioration** [-'reɪʃən]
n deterioração f.

**etermination** [dɪtɜːmɪ'neɪʃən] n
(gen) determinação f; (resolve)
resolução f.

**etermine** [dɪ'tɜːmɪn] vt (gen)
determinar; (limits etc) definir;
(dispute) resolver; **~d** adj (person)
resoluto, decidido.

**eterrent** [dɪ'terənt] n dissuasivo.

**etest** [dɪ'test] vt detestar; **~able**
adj detestável.

**etonate** [detəneɪt] vi explodir,
estalar // vt detonar; **detonator** n
detonador m.

**etour** [dɪ:tuə*] n desvio.

**etract** [dɪ'trækt] vt: to **~ from**
tirar prazer de, depreciar.

**etriment** [detrɪmənt] n: to the **~
of** em detrimento de; **~al**
[detrɪ'mentl] adj (to) prejudicial a.

**evaluation** [dɪvælju'eɪʃən] n
desvalorização f; **devalue** [-'vælju:]
vt desvalorizar.

**evastate** [devəsteɪt] vt devastar;
he was **~d** by the news as notícias
deixaram-no desolado; **devastating**
adj devastador(a); (fig) assolador(a).

**develop** [dɪ'veləp] vt (gen)
desenvolver; (PHOT) revelar;
(disease) contrair; (engine trouble)
começar a ter // vi desenvolver-se;
(advance) progredir; (appear)
aparecer; **~ing country** país m em
desenvolvimento; **~ment** n
desenvolvimento; (advance)
progresso; (of affair, case)
desenvolvimento, progresso; (of
land) urbanização f.

**deviate** [dɪ'vɪeɪt] vi desviar-se;
**deviation** [-'eɪʃən] n desvio.

**device** [dɪ'vaɪs] n (scheme)
estratagema m, plano; (apparatus)
aparelho, mecanismo.

**devil** ['devl] n diabo, demônio; **~ish**
adj diabólico.

**devious** [dɪ'vɪəs] adj intricado,
indireto (Pt: -ct-); (person)
indire(c)to.

**devise** [dɪ'vaɪz] vt idear, inventar.

**devoid** [dɪ'vɔɪd] adj: **~ of** destituído
de.

**devote** [dɪ'vəut] vt: to **~ sth to**
dedicar algo a; **~d** adj (loyal) leal,
fiel; **the book is ~d to politics** o
livro trata de política; **devotee**
[devəu'tiː] n adepto/a, entusiasta
m/f.

**devotion** [dɪ'vəuʃən] n dedicação f;
(REL) devoção f.

**devour** [dɪ'vauə*] vt devorar.

**devout** [dɪ'vaut] adj devoto.

**dew** [djuː] n orvalho.

**dexterity** [deks'terɪtɪ] n destreza.

**diabetes** [daɪə'biːtiːz] n diabete f;
**diabetic** [-'betɪk] adj, n diabético.

**diagnose** [daɪəg'nəuz] vt
diagnosticar; **diagnosis** [-'nəusɪs], pl
**-ses** [-'nəusiːz] n diagnóstico.

**diagonal** [daɪ'ægənl] adj diagonal
// n diagonal f.

**diagram** ['daɪəgræm] n diagrama
m, esquema m.

**dial** ['daɪəl] n quadrante m, disco //
vt (number) discar; **~ling code**, **~
code** (US) n código; **~ling tone**, **~
tone** (US) n ruído de discar.

**dialect** ['daɪəlekt] n dialeto (Pt: -ct-).

**dialogue** ['daɪəlɔg] n diálogo.

**diameter** [daɪ'æmɪtə*] n diâmetro.

**diamond** ['daɪəmənd] n diamante m; ~s npl (CARDS) ouros mpl.

**diaper** ['daɪəpə*] n (US) fralda.

**diaphragm** ['daɪəfræm] n diafragma m.

**diarrhoea, diarrhea** (US) [daɪə'riːə] n diarréia.

**diary** ['daɪərɪ] n (daily account) diário; (book) agenda.

**dice** [daɪs] n, pl inv dados mpl // vt (CULIN) cortar em cubos.

**dictate** [dɪk'teɪt] vt ditar; ~s ['dɪkteɪts] npl ditames mpl; **dictation** [-'teɪʃən] n ditado.

**dictator** [dɪk'teɪtə*] n ditador m; ~ship n ditadura.

**diction** ['dɪkʃən] n dicção f.

**dictionary** ['dɪkʃənrɪ] n dicionário.

**did** [dɪd] pt of **do**.

**die** [daɪ] vi morrer; **to** ~ **away** vi (sound, light) extinguir-se lentamente; **to** ~ **down** vi (gen) apagar-se; (wind) abrandar; **to** ~ **out** vi desaparecer, apagar-se.

**diesel** ['diːzəl]: ~ **engine** n motor m Diesel; ~ **(oil)** n óleo diesel.

**diet** ['daɪət] n dieta; (restricted food) regime m // vi (also: **be on a** ~) estar de dieta, fazer regime.

**differ** ['dɪfə*] vi (be different) ser diferente de, diferenciar-se de; (disagree) discordar; ~**ence** n diferença; (quarrel) desacordo; ~**ent** adj diferente; ~**entiate** [-'renʃɪeɪt] vt distinguir // vi diferenciar-se; **to** ~**entiate between** distinguir entre; ~**ently** adv de outro modo, de forma diferente.

**difficult** ['dɪfɪkəlt] adj difícil; ~y n dificuldade f.

**diffidence** ['dɪfɪdəns] n timidez f; **diffident** [-ənt] adj tímido.

**diffuse** adj [dɪ'fjuːs] adj difuso // vt [dɪ'fjuːz] difundir.

**dig** [dɪg] pt, pp **dug** vt (hole) cavar; (garden) cultivar; (coal) escava (nails etc) cravar // n (pro pontada; (archaeological) escava ção f; (remark) indireta (Pt: -ct-); ~ **in** vi cavar trincheiras; **to** ~ **in** vt (savings) consumir; **to** ~ **out** (hole) escavar; (fig) estudar co afinco; **to** ~ **up** vt desenterra (plant) arrancar.

**digest** [daɪ'dʒest] vt (food) digeri (facts) assimilar // n ['daɪdʒes sumário; ~**ion** [dɪ'dʒestʃən] digestão f.

**digital** ['dɪdʒɪtəl] adj digital.

**dignified** ['dɪgnɪfaɪd] adj grave sério; (action) honrado.

**dignity** ['dɪgnɪtɪ] n dignidade f.

**digress** [daɪ'gres] vi: **to** ~ **fro** afastar-se de; ~**ion** [daɪ'greʃən] digressão f.

**digs** [dɪgz] npl (Brit: col) pensão alojamento.

**dilapidated** [dɪ'læpɪdeɪtɪd] a arruinado, estragado.

**dilate** [daɪ'leɪt] vt dilatar // dilatar-se.

**dilemma** [daɪ'lemə] n dilema m.

**diligent** ['dɪlɪdʒənt] adj diligente.

**dilute** [daɪ'luːt] vt diluir // a diluído.

**dim** [dɪm] adj (light) fraco; (sigh turvo; (outline) indistinto; (stupi de poucas luzes; (room) escuro // (light) abaixar; (US: AUT) baixar faróis.

**dime** [daɪm] n (US) moeda de de centavos.

**dimension** [dɪ'menʃən] n dimensã f.

**diminish** [dɪ'mɪnɪʃ] vi diminuir/se

**diminutive** [dɪ'mɪnjutɪv] a diminuto // n (LING) diminutivo.

**dimly** ['dɪmlɪ] adv fracamente; (n clearly) indistintamente.

**dimple** ['dɪmpl] n covinha.

**din** [dɪn] n ruído, barulho.

**dine** [daɪn] vi jantar; **diner** (person) comensal m/f; (RAIL) dining car.

**dinghy** ['dɪŋgɪ] n dingue m, caiaque m, bote m; **rubber** ~ bote m de borracha.

**dingy** ['dɪndʒɪ] adj (room) escuro; (dirty) sujo; (dull) descolorido.

**dining** ['daɪnɪŋ]: ~ **car** n carro-restaurante m; ~ **room** n sala de jantar.

**dinner** ['dɪnə*] n (evening meal) jantar m; (lunch) comida, almoço; (public) jantar m, banquete m; ~ **jacket** n smoking m; ~ **party** n jantar; ~ **time** n hora de jantar or comer.

**diocese** ['daɪəsɪs] n diocese f.

**dip** [dɪp] n (slope) inclinação f; (in sea) banho m // vt (in water) mulhar; (ladle etc) meter; (AUT: lights) baixar, pôr à meia luz // vi mergulhar-se.

**diphtheria** [dɪf'θɪərɪə] n difteria.

**diploma** [dɪ'pləumə] n diploma m.

**diplomacy** [dɪ'pləuməsɪ] n diplomacia; **diplomat** ['dɪpləmæt] n diplomata m/f; **diplomatic** [dɪplə'mætɪk] adj diplomático.

**dipstick** ['dɪpstɪk] n (AUT) vara de metal graduada para indicar o nível de óleo.

**dire** [daɪə*] adj terrível, extremo.

**direct** [daɪ'rɛkt] adj (gen) direto (Pt: -ct-) // vt dirigir; **can you** ~ **me to...?** pode indicar-me onde fica...?

**direction** [dɪ'rɛkʃən] n direção (Pt: -çç) f; ~**s** npl (advice) ordens fpl, instruções fpl; ~**s for use** modo de emprego.

**directly** [dɪ'rɛktlɪ] adv (in straight line) diretamente (Pt: -ect-); (at once) imediatamente.

**director** [dɪ'rɛktə*] n diretor (Pt: -ct-) m; **managing** ~ **dire(c)tor** gerente.

**directory** [dɪ'rɛktərɪ] n (TEL) lista (telefónica).

**dirt** [də:t] n sujeira; ~**cheap** adj baratíssimo; ~**y** adj sujo; (joke) indecente // vt sujar; (stain)

manchar; ~**y trick** n golpe m baixo, sujeira.

**disability** [dɪsə'bɪlɪtɪ] n incapacidade f; **disabled** [dɪs'eɪbld] adj incapacitado, mutilado.

**disadvantage** [dɪsəd'vɑ:ntɪdʒ] n desvantagem f, inconveniente m.

**disagree** [dɪsə'gri:] vi (differ) discordar; (be against, think otherwise) **to** ~ (**with**) não estar de acordo (com); ~**able** adj desagradável; ~**ment** n (gen) desacordo; (quarrel) briga.

**disallow** ['dɪsə'lau] vt (goal) anular.

**disappear** [dɪsə'pɪə*] vi desaparecer; ~**ance** n desaparição f.

**disappoint** [dɪsə'pɔɪnt] vt desapontar; (hopes) frustrar; ~**ing** adj frustrante; ~**ment** n decepção f, desapontamento.

**disapproval** [dɪsə'pru:vəl] n desaprovação f.

**disapprove** [dɪsə'pru:v] vi: **to** ~ **of** desaprovar.

**disarm** [dɪs'ɑ:m] vt desarmar; ~**ament** n desarmamento; ~**ing** adj encantador(a).

**disaster** [dɪ'zɑ:stə*] n desastre m; **disastrous** adj desastroso.

**disband** [dɪs'bænd] vt dissolver // vi debandar.

**disbelief** [dɪsbə'li:f] n incredulidade f.

**disc, disk** (US) [dɪsk] n disco.

**discard** [dɪs'kɑ:d] vt (old things) desfazer-se de; (fig) descartar.

**discern** [dɪ'sə:n] vt perceber; ~**ing** adj perspicaz.

**discharge** [dɪs'tʃɑ:dʒ] vt (duties) cumprir, desempenhar; (patient) dar alta a; (employee) despedir; (soldier) licenciar; (defendant) pôr em liberdade // n ['dɪstʃɑ:dʒ] (ELEC) descarga; (dismissal) despedida; (of duty) desempenho; (of debt) pagamento, resgate m.

**disciple** [dɪ'saɪpl] n discípulo/a.

**discipline** ['dɪsɪplɪn] n disciplina // vt disciplinar.

**disclaim** [dɪs'kleɪm] vt negar.

**disclose** [dɪs'kləuz] vt revelar; **disclosure** [-'kləuʒə*] n revelação f.

**disco** ['dɪskəu] n abbr of **discothèque**.

**discoloured** [dɪs'kʌləd] adj descorado, desbotado.

**discomfort** [dɪs'kʌmfət] n desconforto; (unease) inquietação f; (physical) mal-estar m.

**disconcert** [dɪskən'sɜːt] vt desconcertar.

**disconnect** [dɪskə'nekt] vt (gen) separar; (ELEC etc) desligar.

**discontent** [dɪskən'tent] n descontentamento; ~**ed** adj descontente.

**discontinue** [dɪskən'tɪnjuː] vt interromper; (payments) suspender.

**discord** ['dɪskɔːd] n discórdia; (MUS) dissonância; ~**ant** [dɪs'kɔːdənt] adj dissonante.

**discothèque** ['dɪskəutek] n discoteca.

**discount** ['dɪskaunt] n desconto // vt [dɪs'kaunt] descontar.

**discourage** [dɪs'kʌrɪdʒ] vt desanimar; (oppose) desencorajar; **discouraging** adj desanimador(a).

**discourteous** [dɪs'kɜːtɪəs] adj descortês.

**discover** [dɪs'kʌvə*] vt descobrir; ~**y** n descobrimento, descoberta.

**discredit** [dɪs'kredɪt] vt desacreditar.

**discreet** [dɪ'skriːt] adj (tactful) discreto; (careful) circunspecto (Pt: -ct-); prudente; ~**ly** adv discretamente.

**discrepancy** [dɪ'skrepənsɪ] n (difference) diferença; (disagreement) discrepância.

**discretion** [dɪ'skreʃən] n (tact) discrição f; (care) prudência, circunspeção (Pt: -çç-) f.

**discriminate** [dɪ'skrɪmɪneɪt] vi: to ~ **between** fazer distinção entre; to

~ **against** discriminar contr **discriminating** adj acurado; **dis crimination** [-'neɪʃən] n (di cernment) discernimento; (bias discriminação f.

**discuss** [dɪs'kʌs] vt (gen) discuti (a theme) tratar de; ~**ion** [dɪ'skʌʃər n discussão f.

**disdain** [dɪs'deɪn] n desdém m // v desdenhar.

**disease** [dɪ'ziːz] n doença enfermidade f.

**disembark** [dɪsɪm'bɑːk] vt, v desembarcar.

**disengage** [dɪsɪn'geɪdʒ] vt solta (clutch) desprender.

**disentangle** [dɪsɪn'tæŋgl] v desenredar.

**disfigure** [dɪs'fɪgə*] vt disfigurar.

**disgrace** [dɪs'greɪs] n ignomínia (downfall) queda; (shame vergonha, desonra // (behaviour escandaloso.

**disgruntled** [dɪs'grʌntld] ac descontente, mal-humorado.

**disguise** [dɪs'gaɪz] n disfarce m // vt disfarçar; **in** ~ disfarçado.

**disgust** [dɪs'gʌst] n repugnância f vt repugnar a, dar nojo em; ~**in** adj repugnante, nojento.

**dish** [dɪʃ] n (gen) prato; **to do o wash the** ~**es** lavar os pratos; to ~ **up** vt servir; **to** ~ **out** vt servi repartir; ~**cloth** n pano de prato o de louça.

**dishearten** [dɪs'hɑːtn] v desalentar.

**dishevelled** [dɪ'ʃevəld] ac despenteado, desgrenhado.

**dishonest** [dɪs'ɒnɪst] adj (person desonesto, desleal; (means fraudulento; ~**y** n desonestidade f.

**dishonour** [dɪs'ɒnə*] n desonra ~**able** adj desonroso.

**dish towel** [dɪʃ'tauəl] n (US) pan de prato.

**dishwasher** ['dɪʃwɔʃə*] n máquina de lavar louça/pratos.

**disillusion** [dɪsɪ'luːʒən] *vt* desiludir.

**disinfect** [dɪsɪn'fɛkt] *vt* desinfetar (*Pt*: -ct-); ~**ant** *n* desinfe(c)tante *m*.

**disintegrate** [dɪs'ɪntɪɡreɪt] *vi* desagregar-se, desintegrar-se.

**disinterested** [dɪs'ɪntrəstɪd] *adj* desinteressado.

**disjointed** [dɪs'dʒɔɪntɪd] *adj* desconexo.

**disk** [dɪsk] *n* (*US*) = **disc**.

**dislike** [dɪs'laɪk] *n* antipatia, aversão *f* // *vt* antipatizar com, não gostar de.

**dislocate** [ˈdɪslǝkeɪt] *vt* deslocar.

**dislodge** [dɪs'lɒdʒ] *vt* desentocar; (*enemy*) desalojar.

**disloyal** [dɪs'lɔɪǝl] *adj* desleal.

**dismal** [ˈdɪzml] *adj* (*dark*) sombrio; (*depressing*) deprimente; (*depressed*) deprimido; (*very bad*) horrível.

**dismantle** [dɪs'mæntl] *vt* desmontar, desmantelar.

**dismay** [dɪs'meɪ] *n* consternação *f* // *vt* consternar.

**dismiss** [dɪs'mɪs] *vt* (*worker*) despedir; (*official*) demitir; (*idea*) descartar; (*LAW*) liberar; (*possibility*) rejeitar // *vi* (*MIL*) mandar fora de forma; ~**al** *n* despedida, demissão *f*.

**dismount** [dɪs'maunt] *vi* desmontar.

**disobedience** [dɪsǝ'biːdɪǝns] *n* desobediência; **disobedient** [-ǝnt] *adj* desobediente.

**disobey** [dɪsǝ'beɪ] *vt* desobedecer.

**disorder** [dɪs'ɔːdǝ*] *n* desordem *f*; (*rioting*) tumulto; (*MED*) indisposição *f*; (*disease*) doença; ~**ly** *adj* (*untidy*) desordenado; (*meeting*) tumultuado; (*conduct*) escandaloso.

**disorganized** [dɪs'ɔːɡǝnaɪzd] *adj* desorganizado.

**disorientated** [dɪs'ɔːrɪenteɪtǝd] *adj* desorientado.

**disown** [dɪs'ǝun] *vt* repudiar.

**disparaging** [dɪs'pærɪdʒɪŋ] *adj* depreciativo.

**disparity** [dɪs'pærɪtɪ] *n* desigualdade *f*.

**dispatch** [dɪs'pætʃ] *vt* despachar; (*kill*) liquidar, matar // *n* (*sending*) remessa; (*speed*) rapidez *f*, urgência; (*PRESS*) comunicado; (*MIL*) parte *f*.

**dispel** [dɪs'pel] *vt* dispersar.

**dispensary** [dɪs'pensǝrɪ] *n* dispensário, farmácia.

**dispense** [dɪs'pens] *vt* dispensar; **to** ~ **with** *vt fus* prescindir de; **dispenser** *n* (*container*) distribuidor *m* automático; **dispensing chemist** *n* farmacêutico/a.

**dispersal** [dɪs'pǝːsl] *n* dispersão *f*; **disperse** [-'pǝːs] *vt* dispersar // *vi* dispersar-se.

**displace** [dɪs'pleɪs] *vt* (*shift*) deslocar; ~**d person** *n* (*POL*) destituído; ~**ment** *n* deslocamento.

**display** [dɪs'pleɪ] *n* (*exhibition*) exposição *f*; (*MIL*) parada; (*of feeling*) manifestação *f*; (*pej*) ostentação *f*, espetáculo (*Pt*: -ct-) // *vt* expor, manifestar; (*ostentatiously*) ostentar.

**displease** [dɪs'pliːz] *vt* (*offend*) ofender; (*annoy*) desagradar; (*be unpleasant to*) desgostar; ~**d with** descontente com; **displeasure** [-'pleʒǝ*] *n* desgosto.

**disposable** [dɪs'pǝuzǝbl] *adj* descartável.

**disposal** [dɪs'pǝuzl] *n* (*sale*) venda; (*arrangement*) disposição *f*; (*of rubbish*) destruição *f*; **at one's** ~ **à** disposição de alguém.

**dispose** [dɪs'pǝuz] *vt*: **to** ~ **of** (*time, money*) dispor de; (*unwanted goods*) desfazer-se de; (*throw away*) jogar fora; (*Pt*) tirar fora; ~**d** *adj*: ~**d to do** disposto a fazer; **disposition** [-'zɪʃǝn] *n* disposição *f*.

**disproportionate** [dɪsprǝ-'pɔːʃǝnǝt] *adj* desproporcionado.

**disprove** [dɪs'pruːv] *vt* refutar.

**dispute** [dɪs'pjuːt] *n* disputa; (*verbal*) discussão *f*; (*also*:

**industrial** ~) contenda, disputa // vt (*argue*) discutir; (*question*) questionar.

**disqualification** [dɪskwɔlɪfɪˈkeɪʃən] n inabilitação f, incapacitação f; (*SPORT, from driving*) desqualificação f.

**disqualify** [dɪsˈkwɔlɪfaɪ] vt (*SPORT*) desqualificar; **to ~ sb for sth/from doing sth** desqualificar alguém para algo/de fazer algo.

**disregard** [dɪsrɪˈgɑːd] vt desconsiderar; (*ignore*) não fazer caso de.

**disrepair** [dɪsrɪˈpɛə*] n: **to fall into ~** ficar em mau estado de conservação.

**disreputable** [dɪsˈrɛpjutəbl] adj (*person*) de má fama; (*behaviour*) vergonhoso.

**disrespectful** [dɪsrɪˈspɛktful] adj desrespeitoso.

**disrupt** [dɪsˈrʌpt] vt (*plans*) desfazer; (*conversation*) interromper; **~ion** [-ˈrʌpʃən] n transtorno, interrupção f.

**dissatisfaction** [dɪssætɪsˈfækʃən] n descontentamento; **dissatisfied** [-ˈsætɪsfaɪd] adj descontente.

**dissect** [dɪˈsɛkt] vt dissecar.

**dissent** [dɪˈsɛnt] n desacordo.

**disservice** [dɪsˈsəːvɪs] n: **to do sb a ~** prejudicar alguém.

**dissident** [ˈdɪsɪdnt] adj, n dissidente m/f.

**dissipate** [ˈdɪsɪpeɪt] vt dispersar; (*waste*) dissipar, desperdiçar.

**dissociate** [dɪˈsəuʃɪeɪt] vt dissociar, separar.

**dissolute** [ˈdɪsəluːt] adj dissoluto.

**dissolve** [dɪˈzɔlv] vt dissolver // vi dissolver-se.

**dissuade** [dɪˈsweɪd] vt: **to ~ sb (from)** dissuadir alguém (de).

**distance** [ˈdɪstns] n distância; **in the ~** ao longe.

**distant** [ˈdɪstnt] adj distante; (*manner*) afastado, reservado.

**distaste** [dɪsˈteɪst] n repugnância;

~**ful** adj repugnante, desagradável.

**distil** [dɪsˈtɪl] vt destilar; ~**lery** n destilaria.

**distinct** [dɪsˈtɪŋkt] adj (*different*) distinto; (*clear*) claro; (*unmistakeable*) nítido; **as ~ from** diferente de fazendo distinção de; ~**ion** [dɪsˈtɪŋkʃən] n distinção f; ~**ive** adj distintivo; ~**ly** adv claramente.

**distinguish** [dɪsˈtɪŋgwɪʃ] v distinguir; ~**ed** adj (*eminent*) eminente, distinto; ~**ing** adj (*feature*) distinto.

**distort** [dɪsˈtɔːt] vt alterar; ~**ion** [dɪsˈtɔːʃən] n deformação f; (*of sound*) deturpação f.

**distract** [dɪsˈtrækt] vt distrair (*attention*) desviar; (*bewilder*) aturdir; ~**ed** adj distraído; ~**ion** [dɪsˈtrækʃən] n distração f; (*confusion*) aturdimento, perplexidade f; (*amusement*) diverti mento.

**distraught** [dɪsˈtrɔːt] adj desesperado, louco.

**distress** [dɪsˈtrɛs] n (*anguish*) angústia; (*misfortune*) desgraça (*want*) miséria; (*pain*) dor f (*danger*) perigo // vt (*cause anguish*) afligir; (*pain*) doer; ~**ing** adj aflitivo, angustioso; ~ **signal** r sinal m de socorro.

**distribute** [dɪsˈtrɪbjuːt] vt (*gen*) distribuir; (*share out*) repartir **distribution** [-ˈbjuːʃən] n distribuição f; **distributor** n (*AUT*) distribuidor m; (*COMM*) distribuidor(a).

**district** [ˈdɪstrɪkt] n (*of country, ADMIN*) distrito; (*of town*) bairro; ~ **attorney** n (*US*) promotor m público; ~ **nurse** n (*Brit*) enfermeira do distrito.

**distrust** [dɪsˈtrʌst] n desconfiança // vt desconfiar de.

**disturb** [dɪsˈtəːb] vt (*gen*) perturbar; (*bother*) incomodar (*interrupt*) interromper; (*upset*) transtornar; (*disorganize*) atrapalhar; ~**ance** n (*gen*) perturbação f; (political etc) distúrbio; (violence) agitação f; (of mind) transtorno; ~ing adj perturbador(a), inquietante.

**disuse** [dɪs'juːs] n: **to fall into ~** cair em desuso.

**disused** [dɪs'juːzd] adj desusado, abandonado.

**ditch** [dɪtʃ] n fosso; (irrigation ~) rego // vt (col) desfazer-se de.

**dither** ['dɪðə*] vi hesitar.

**ditto** ['dɪtəu] adv idem, o mesmo.

**divan** [dɪ'væn] n divã m.

**dive** [daɪv] n (from board) salto; (underwater, of submarine) mergulho; (AVIAT) picada f // vi saltar; mergulhar; picar; **diver** n (SPORT) saltador(a) m/f; (underwater) mergulhador(a) m/f.

**diverge** [daɪ'vɜːdʒ] vi divergir.

**diverse** [daɪ'vɜːs] adj diversos/as, vários/as.

**diversify** [daɪ'vɜːsɪfaɪ] vt diversificar.

**diversion** [daɪ'vɜːʃən] n (AUT) desvio; (distraction, MIL) diversão f.

**diversity** [daɪ'vɜːsɪti] n diversidade f.

**divert** [daɪ'vɜːt] vt (turn aside) desviar; (amuse) divertir.

**divest** [daɪ'vɛst] vt: **to ~ sb of sth** privar alguém de algo.

**divide** [dɪ'vaɪd] vt dividir; (separate) separar // vi dividir-se; (road) bifurcar-se; **~d highway** (US) n pista-dupla.

**dividend** ['dɪvɪdɛnd] n dividendo m; (fig) lucro.

**divine** [dɪ'vaɪn] adj divino.

**diving** ['daɪvɪŋ] n (SPORT) salto; (underwater) mergulho; **~ board** n trampolim m; **~ suit** n escafandro.

**divinity** [dɪ'vɪnɪti] n divindade f; (SCOL) teologia.

**division** [dɪ'vɪʒən] n divisão f; (sharing out) repartição f; (disagreement) discórdia; (POL) votação f.

**divorce** [dɪ'vɔːs] n divórcio // vt

divorciar-se de; **~d** adj divorciado/a.

**divorcee** [dɪvɔː'siː] n divorciado/a.

**divulge** [daɪ'vʌldʒ] vt divulgar, revelar.

**D.I.Y.** adj, n abbr of **do-it-yourself.**

**dizziness** ['dɪzɪnɪs] n vertigem f, tontura.

**dizzy** ['dɪzɪ] adj (person) tonto; (height) vertiginoso; **to feel ~** sentir-se tonto, sentir-se atordoado.

**DJ** n abbr of **disc jockey.**

**do** [duː] pt **did,** pp **done** vt/i (gen) fazer; (speed) ir a; (THEATRE) representar // n (col) festa; **he didn't laugh** ele não riu; **she swims better than I ~** ela nada melhor do que eu; **he laughed, didn't he?** ele riu, não foi?; **that will ~!** basta!, chega!; **to make ~ with** contentar-se com; **~ you agree?** concorda?; **to ~ one's hair** (comb) pentear-se; **will it ~?** dá?, chega?, serve?; **to ~ well** prosperar, ter êxito; **to ~ without** sth prescindir de algo; **to ~ away with** vt fus (kill) exterminar; (suppress) suprimir; **to ~ up** vt (laces) atar; (room) arrumar, renovar.

**docile** ['dəusaɪl] adj dócil.

**dock** [dɔk] n (NAUT) doca, estaleiro; (LAW) banco (dos réus); **~s** npl estaleiros mpl, porto // vi (arrive) chegar; (enter ~) entrar no estaleiro; (pay etc) deduzir; **~er** n estaleiro, trabalhador m portuário, estivador m; **~yard** n estaleiro.

**doctor** ['dɔktə*] n médico; (Ph.D. etc) doutor(a) m/f // vt (fig) tratar, falsificar; (drink etc) adulterar; **~'s office** n (US) consultório.

**doctrine** ['dɔktrɪn] n doutrina.

**document** ['dɔkjumənt] n documento; **~ary** [-'mɛntəri] adj documental // n documentário; **~ation** [-'teɪʃən] n documentação f.

**dodge** [dɔdʒ] n (of body) evasiva; (fig) trapaça // vt (gen) esquivar-se de, evitar; (*blow*) furtar-se a.

**dodgems** ['dodʒəmz] *npl* carros *mpl* de choque.

**dodgy** ['dodʒɪ] *adj* arriscado.

**dog** [dog] *n* cachorro, cão *m* // *vt* seguir os passos de; ~ **biscuits** *npl* biscoitos *mpl* de cachorro; ~ **collar** *n* coleira de cachorro; (*fig*) gola de padre.

**dogged** ['dogɪd] *adj* tenaz, persistente.

**dogma** ['dogmə] *n* dogma *m*; ~**tic** [-'mætɪk] *adj* dogmático.

**doings** ['duɪŋz] *npl* (*events*) acontecimentos *mpl*; (*acts*) atos (*Pt*: -ct-) *mpl*.

**do-it-yourself** [du:ɪtjɔː'sɛlf] *adj* que é feito por amadores.

**doldrums** ['doldrəmz] *npl*: **to be in the** ~ (*person*) estar abatido; (*business*) estar parado *or* estagnado.

**dole** [dəul] *n* (*Brit*) (*payment*) subsídio de desemprego; **on the** ~ desempregado; **to** ~ **out** *vt* repartir.

**doleful** ['dəulful] *adj* triste, lúgubre.

**doll** [dol] *n* boneca; **to** ~ **o.s. up** embonecar-se; (*Pt*) ataviar-se.

**dollar** ['dolə*] *n* dólar *m*.

**dolphin** ['dolfɪn] *n* golfinho.

**domain** [də'meɪn] *n* território, propriedade *f*; (*empire*) domínio.

**dome** [dəum] *n* (*ARCH*) cúpula; (*shape*) abóbada.

**domestic** [də'mɛstɪk] *adj* (*gen*) doméstico; (*national*) nacional; (*home-loving*) caseiro; (*internal*: *trade*) doméstico; (: *strife*) interno; ~**ated** *adj* domesticado; (*home-loving*) caseiro.

**dominant** ['domɪnənt] *adj* dominante.

**dominate** ['domɪneɪt] *vt* dominar; **domination** [-'neɪʃən] *n* dominação *f*.

**domineering** [domɪ'nɪərɪŋ] *adj* dominante, mandão/dona.

**dominion** [də'mɪnɪən] *n* domínio.

**domino** ['domɪnəu], *pl* ~**es** *n* peça

de dominó; ~**es** *n* (*game*) dominó *msg*.

**donate** [də'neɪt] *vt* doar; **donation** [də'neɪʃən] *n* doação *f*.

**done** [dʌn] *pp* of **do**.

**donkey** ['dɔŋkɪ] *n* burro.

**donor** ['dəunə*] *n* doador(a) *m/f*.

**don't** [dəunt] = **do not**.

**doom** [du:m] *n* (*fate*) sorte *f*; (*death*) morte *f* // *vt*: **to be** ~**ed to failure** estar destinado ao fracasso.

**door** [dɔː*] *n* porta; (*entry*) entrada **next** ~ na casa do lado; ~**bell** *n* campainha; ~ **handle** *n* maçaneta (*Pt*) puxador *m*; (*of car*) maçaneta ~ **knocker** *n* aldrava; ~**man** *n* (*in hotel*) porteiro; ~**mat** *n* capacho ~**step** *n* degrau *m* da porta.

**dope** [dəup] *n* (*col*: *person*) imbecil *m/f* // *vt* (*horse etc*) dopar.

**dopey** ['dəupɪ] *adj* (*dizzy*) tonto.

**dormant** ['dɔːmənt] *adj* inativo (*Pt* -ct-); (*latent*) latente.

**dormitory** ['dɔːmɪtrɪ] *n* dormitório.

**dormouse** ['dɔːmaus], *pl* -**mice** [-maɪs] *n* rato (de campo).

**dosage** ['dəusɪdʒ] *n* dose *f*.

**dose** [dəus] *n* dose *f* // *vt*: **to** ~ **o.s.** medicar-se.

**doss house** ['dos-] *n* pensão barata, casa de cômodos; (*Pt*) pensão *f* de malta.

**dot** [dot] *n* ponto; ~**ted with** salpicado de; **on the** ~ em ponto.

**dote** [dəut]: **to** ~ **on** *vt fus* adorar idolatrar.

**double** ['dʌbl] *adj* duplo // *adv* (*twice*): **to cost** ~ custar o dobro // *n* (*gen*) dobro // *vt* dobrar; (*efforts*) duplicar // *vi* duplicar-se; **at the** ~ em passo acelerado; ~**s** *n* (*TENNIS*) duplas *fpl*; ~ **bass** *n* contrabaixo; ~ **bed** *n* cama de casal; ~ **bend** *n* curva dupla; ~-**breasted** *adj* trespassado; ~**cross** *vt* (*trick*) enganar; (*betray*) atraiçoar; ~-**decker** *n* ônibus *m* de dois andares; (*Pt*) autocarro de dois andares; ~ **room** *n* quarto de casal;

**doubly** adv duplamente.

**doubt** [daut] n dúvida // vt duvidar; (suspect) desconfiar de; **to ~ that** duvidar que; **there is no ~ that** não há dúvida que; **~ful** adj duvidoso; (person) desconfiado; **~less** adv sem dúvida;

**dough** [dəu] n massa; **~nut** n sonho; (Pt) bola de Berlim.

**dove** [dʌv] n pomba; **~tail** vi (fig) encaixar-se.

**dowdy** ['daudi] adj desalinhada; (inelegant) deselegante, pouco elegante.

**down** [daun] n (fluff) lanugem f; (feathers) penugem f // adv abaixo; (~wards) para baixo; (on the ground) por terra // prep por, abaixo // vt (col: drink) beber; (: food) devorar; **~ with X!** abaixo X!; **~-at-heel** adj descuidado, desmazelado; (appearance) deselegante; **~cast** adj abatido; **~fall** n queda, ruína; **~hearted** adj desanimado; **~hill** adv: **to go ~hill** ir morro abaixo; **~ payment** n depósito, sinal m; **~pour** n aguaceiro; **~right** adj (clear) categórico; (out-and-out) completo, definitivo; **~stairs** adv (below) (lá) em baixo; (~wards) para baixo; **~stream** adv água ou rio abaixo; **~-to-earth** adj prático, realista; **~town** adv no centro da cidade; **~ward** adj, adv, **~wards** adv para baixo.

**dowry** ['dauri] n dote m.

**doz.** abbr of dozen.

**doze** [dəuz] vi dormitar; **to ~ off** vi cochilar.

**dozen** ['dʌzn] n dúzia.

**Dr.** abbr for doctor; drive.

**drab** [dræb] adj monótono, desinteressante.

**draft** [drɑ:ft] n (first copy) rascunho; (COMM) saque m, letra; (US: call-up) recrutamento // vt (plan) redigir; (conscript) recrutar; (write roughly) esboçar; (US) = **draught**.

**drag** [dræg] vt arrastar; (river) dragar // vi arrastar-se pelo chão // n (col) estorvo, maçada; **to ~ on** vi arrastar-se.

**dragonfly** ['drægənflai] n libélula.

**drain** [drein] n cano (de esgoto); (in street) sarjeta; (source of loss) escoamento; (loss) perda; (on resources) sorvedouro // vt (land, marshes) escoar; (MED) drenar; (reservoir) esvaziar; (fig) esgotar // vi escorrer; **~age** n (act) drenagem f; (MED, AGR) dreno; (sewage) esgoto; **~ing board**, **~board** (US) n escorredor m; **~pipe** n cano de esgoto.

**dram** [dræm] n (drink) trago.

**drama** ['drɑ:mə] n (art) teatro; (play) drama m; **~tic** [drə'mætik] adj dramático; **~tist** ['dræmətist] n dramaturgo.

**drank** [dræŋk] pt of **drink**.

**drape** [dreip] vt ornar, enroupar; **~s** npl (US) cortinas fpl; **draper** n negociante m de fazendas, fanqueiro.

**drastic** ['dræstik] adj (measure) severo; (change) drástico; (forceful) enérgico.

**draught** [drɑ:ft] n (of air) corrente f; (drink) trago; (NAUT) calado; (beer) chope m; **~s** n jogo de damas; **on ~** (beer) de barril; **~board** n tabuleiro de damas.

**draughtsman** ['drɑ:ftsmən] n desenhista m, projetista (Pt: -ect-) m.

**draw** [drɔ:], pt **drew**, pp **drawn** vt (pull) puxar, tirar; (take out) retirar; (attract) atrair; (picture) desenhar; (money) tirar, receber // vi (SPORT) empatar // n (SPORT) empate m; (lottery) sorteio; (attraction) atração (Pt: -cç-) f; **to ~ near** vi aproximar-se, **to ~ out** vi (lengthen) esticar, alargar; **to ~ up** vi (stop) parar(-se) // vt (document) redigir; **~back** n inconveniente m, desvantagem f; **~bridge** n ponte f levadiça.

**drawer** [drɔ:*] n gaveta.

**drawing** ['drɔ:ɪŋ] n desenho; **~board** n tábua (do desenhista), prancheta; **~ pin** n tachinha, percevejo; (Pt) pionés m; **~ room** n sala de visitas.

**drawl** [drɔ:l] n fala arrastada.

**drawn** [drɔ:n] pp of **draw**.

**dread** [drɛd] n medo, temor m // vt temer, recear, ter medo de; **~ful** adj terrível.

**dream** [dri:m] n sonho // vt/i, pt, pp **dreamed** or **dreamt** [drɛmt] sonhar; **~er** n sonhador(a) m/f; **~y** adj (distracted) sonhador(a), distraído; (music) sentimental.

**dreary** ['drɪərɪ] adj monótono, maçante.

**dredge** [drɛdʒ] vt dragar; **dredger** n (ship) draga; (also: **sugar dredger**) polvilhador m.

**dregs** [drɛgz] npl fezes fpl.

**drench** [drɛntʃ] vt encharcar; **to get ~ed** molhar-se, encharcar-se.

**dress** [drɛs] n vestido; (clothing) roupa // vt vestir; (wound) pensar; (CULIN) preparar, temperar // vi vestir-se; **to ~ up** vi vestir-se com elegância; (in fancy dress) fantasiar-se; **~ circle** n balcão m nobre; **~er** n (furniture) aparador m; (: US) cómoda de espelho; **~ing** n (MED) penso; (CULIN) molho; **~ing gown** n roupão m; **~ing room** n (THEATRE) camarim m; (SPORT) vestiário; **~ing table** n penteadeira; (Pt) toucador m; **~maker** n costureira, modista; **~making** n (arte f da) costura; **~ rehearsal** n ensaio geral; **~ shirt** n camisa social.

**drew** [dru:] pt of **draw**.

**dribble** ['drɪbl] vi gotejar, pingar; (baby) babar-se // vt (ball) driblar.

**dried** [draɪd] adj (gen) seco; (milk) em pó.

**drift** [drɪft] n (of current etc)

velocidade f; (of sand etc) monte m; (distance off course) deriva; (meaning) intenção f // vi (boat) derivar; (sand, snow) amontoar-se; **~wood** n madeira flutuante.

**drill** [drɪl] n furador m; (bit, of dentist) broca; (for mining etc) broca, furador m; (MIL) exercícios militares // vt furar, brocar // vi (for oil) perfurar; **~ing rig** n torre f de perfurar.

**drink** [drɪŋk] n bebida // vt/i, pt drank, pp drunk beber; **to have a ~** tomar uma bebida; **~er** n bebedor(a) m/f; **~ing water** n água potável.

**drip** [drɪp] n (act) gotejar m; (one ~) gota, pingo; (MED) gota a gota m // vi gotejar, pingar; **~dry** adj (shirt) de lavar e vestir; **~ping** n gordura; **~ping wet** adj encharcado.

**drive** [draɪv] n passeio (de automóvel); (journey) viagem f; (also: **~way**) entrada; (energy) energia, vigor m; (PSYCH) impulso; (SPORT) tiro, golpe m // vb: pt drove, pp driven ['drɪvn] vt conduzir; (car) dirigir; (Pt) guiar; (urge) fazer trabalhar; (by power) impelir; (nail) cravar; (push) empurrar; (TECH. motor) acionar (Pt: -cc-) // vi (AUT. al controls) conduzir; (: travel) passear de automóvel; **left/right-hand** n direção f à esquerda/direita.

**driver** ['draɪvə*] n motorista m/f; (of taxi, bus) chofer m, motorista; **~'s license** n (US) carteira de motorista; (Pt) carta de condução.

**driving** ['draɪvɪŋ] n automobilismo; **~ instructor** n instrutor(a) m/f de auto-escola (Pt: de condução); **~ lesson** n aula de direção (Pt: de condução); **~ licence** n (Brit) carteira de motorista; (Pt) carta de condução; **~ mirror** n retrovisor m; **~ school** n auto-escola f; **~ test** n exame m de motorista.

**drizzle** ['drɪzl] n chuvisco // vi chuviscar.

**drone** [drəun] n zumbido; (male bee) zangão m.

**drool** [dru:l] vi babar(-se); **to ~ over** sth adorar algo.

**droop** [dru:p] vi pender; (fig) decair, esmorecer.

**drop** [drɔp] n (of water) gota; (lessening) quebrada, baixa; (fall) queda; (of cliff) escarpa, declive m // vt (allow to fall) deixar cair; (voice, eyes, price) baixar; (set down from car) deixar (saltar/descer); (omit) omitir // vi cair; (price, temperature) baixar; (wind) parar; **to ~ off** vi (sleep) adormecer // (passenger) deixar (saltar); **to ~ out** vi (withdraw) retirar-se; **~out** n pessoa que abandona o trabalho/os estudos, etc; **~per** n conta-gotas m inv; **~pings** npl fezes fpl (de animal).

**drought** [draut] n seca.

**drove** [drəuv] pt of **drive**.

**drown** [draun] vt afogar // vi afogar-se.

**drowsy** ['drauzɪ] adj sonolento; **to be ~** ter sono.

**drudgery** ['drʌdʒərɪ] n trabalho monótono e árduo.

**drug** [drʌg] n medicamento; (narcotic) droga // vt drogar; **~ addict** n drogado/a; **~gist** n (US) farmacêutico/a; **~store** n (US) drogaria.

**drum** [drʌm] n tambor m; (large) bombo; (for oil, petrol) tambor, barril m; **~s** npl bateria sg // vi tocar tambor; (with fingers) tamborilar; **~mer** n baterista m; **~stick** n (MUS) baqueta; (of chicken) perna.

**drunk** [drʌŋk] pp of **drink** // adj bêbado // n (also: **~ard**) bêbado/a; **~en** adj bêbado; **~enness** n embriaguez f.

**dry** [draɪ] adj seco; (day) sem chuva; (climate) árido, seco // vt secar;

(tears) limpar // vi secar-se; **to ~ up** vi secar-se completamente; (in speech) calar-se; **~-cleaner's** n lavanderia; **~-cleaning** n lavagem f a seco; **~er** n secador m; **~ness** n secura; **~ rot** n putrefação f fungosa.

**dual** ['djuəl] adj dual, duplo; **~-control** adj duplo comando; **~ nationality** n dupla nacionalidade f; **~-purpose** adj de duplo uso.

**dubbed** [dʌbd] adj (CINEMA) dublado.

**dubious** ['dju:bɪəs] adj duvidoso; (reputation, company) suspeitoso.

**duchess** ['dʌtʃɪs] n duquesa.

**duck** [dʌk] n pato // vi mergulhar-se, abaixar-se repentinamente; **~ling** n patinho.

**duct** [dʌkt] n conduto, canal m.

**dud** [dʌd] n (shell) bomba falhada; (object, tool): **it's a ~** não presta // adj: **~ cheque** cheque m sem cobertura.

**due** [dju:] adj (proper) devido; (expected) esperado; (fitting) conveniente, oportuno // n dívida; (desert) aquilo que foi merecido // adv: **~ north** exatamente (Pt: -act-) ao norte; **~s** npl (for club, union) jóia sg; (in harbour) direitos mpl; **in ~ course** no devido tempo; **~ to** devido a.

**duel** ['djuəl] n duelo.

**duet** [dju:'et] n dueto.

**dug** [dʌg] pt, pp of **dig**.

**duke** [dju:k] n duque m.

**dull** [dʌl] adj (light) sombrio; (slow) lento; (boring) enfadonho; (sound, pain) surdo; (weather, day) escuro // vt (pain, grief) aliviar; (mind, senses) entorpecer.

**duly** ['dju:lɪ] adv devidamente; (on time) no devido tempo.

**dumb** [dʌm] adj mudo; (stupid) estúpido; **~founded** [dʌm'faundɪd] adj pasmado.

**dummy** ['dʌmɪ] n (tailor's model)

manequim m; (for baby) chupeta // adj falso, postiço.

**dump** [dʌmp] n (heap) montão m; (place) despejadouro; (col) lugar m desorganizado; (MIL) depósito // vt (put down) depositar, descarregar; (get rid of) desfazer-se de; (goods) inundar o mercado com; ~ing m (ECON) dumping m; (of rubbish): '**no ~ing**' 'proibido jogar lixo'; (Pt) 'proibido deitar lixo'.

**dumpling** ['dʌmplɪŋ] n bolinho cozido.

**dunce** [dʌns] n burro, ignorante.

**dune** [djuːn] n duna.

**dung** [dʌŋ] n estrume m.

**dungarees** [dʌŋgə'riːz] npl macacão msg.

**dungeon** ['dʌndʒən] n calabouço.

**dupe** [djuːp] n (victim) otário/a, trouxa m/f // vt enganar.

**duplicate** ['djuːplɪkət] n duplicado // vt ['djuːplɪkeɪt] duplicar; (on machine) reproduzir; **in ~** em duplicata; **duplicator** n duplicador m.

**durable** ['djuərəbl] adj durável.

**duration** [djuə'reɪʃən] n duração f.

**duress** [djuə'rɛs] n: **under ~** sob coação.

**during** ['djuərɪŋ] prep durante.

**dusk** [dʌsk] n crepúsculo, anoitecer m.

**dust** [dʌst] n pó m // vt (furniture) limpar o pó de; (cake etc): **to ~ with** polvilhar com; ~**bin** n (Brit) lata de lixo; ~**er** n espanador m de pó, pano de pó; ~ **jacket** n sobrecapa; ~**man** n (Brit) lixeiro; ~**y** adj poeirento.

**Dutch** [dʌtʃ] adj holandês/esa // (LING) holandês m; ~**man/woman** n holandês/esa m/f.

**duty** ['djuːtɪ] n dever m; (tax) taxa; (customs) direitos mpl alfandegários; **on ~** de serviço; (at night etc) de plantão, de guarda; **off ~** de folga; ~-**free** adj isento de taxas aduaneiras.

**dwarf** [dwɔːf], pl **dwarves** [dwɔːvz] n anão/anã m/f // vt diminuir-se.

**dwell** [dwɛl], pt, pp **dwelt** [dwɛlt] vi morar; **to ~ on** vt fus estender-se sobre; ~**ing** n residência.

**dwindle** ['dwɪndl] vi minguar, diminuir.

**dye** [daɪ] n tinta // vt tingir.

**dying** ['daɪɪŋ] adj moribundo, agonizante; (moments) final; (words) último.

**dynamic** [daɪ'næmɪk] adj dinâmico; ~**s** n, npl dinâmica sg.

**dynamite** ['daɪnəmaɪt] n dinamite f.

**dynamo** ['daɪnəməu] n dínamo m.

**dynasty** ['dɪnəstɪ] n dinastia f.

# E

**each** [iːtʃ] det cada inv // pron cada um; ~ **other** um ao outro; **they hate ~ other** (eles) se odeiam; **they have 2 books ~** eles têm 2 livros cada um.

**eager** ['iːgə*] adj (gen) ávido; (hopeful) desejoso; (ambitious) ambicioso; **to be ~ to do sth** ansiar por fazer algo; **to be ~ for** ansiar por.

**eagle** ['iːgl] n águia.

**ear** [ɪə*] n orelha; (MUS) ouvido; (of corn) espiga; ~**ache** n dor f de ouvidos; ~**drum** n tímpano.

**earl** [əːl] n conde m.

**early** ['əːlɪ] adv (gen) cedo; (before time) a tempo, com antecedência // adj (gen) prematuro; (reply) pronto; (first) primeiro; (work) juvenil; **have an ~ night** vá para cama cedo; **in the ~ or ~ in the spring/19th century** no princípio da primavera/do século dezenove; **as ~ as possible** o mais cedo possível.

**earmark** ['ɪəmɑːk] vt (keep) reservar (for para); (intend) destinar (for para); (mark) assinalar.

**earn** [əːn] vt (gen) ganhar; (salary) receber; (interest) ganhar; (praise) merecer.

**earnest** [ˈəːnɪst] adj sério; in ~ adv a sério.

**earnings** [ˈəːnɪŋz] npl (personal) vencimentos mpl, salário sg, ordenado sg; (company) lucro sg.

**ear:** ~phones npl fones mpl de ouvido; ~ring n brinco; ~shot n: within ~shot ao alcance do ouvido or da voz.

**earth** [əːθ] n (gen) terra; (ELEC) fio terra; what on ~! que diabo! // vt (ELEC) ligar à terra; ~enware n louça de barro; ~quake n terremoto; ~y adj (fig: vulgar) grosseiro; (: sensual) sensual.

**earwig** [ˈɪəwɪg] n lacrainha.

**ease** [iːz] n (gen) facilidade f; (relief) alívio; (calm) tranqüilidade f; (relaxed state) comodidade f // vt facilitar; (loosen) soltar; (relieve: pressure) afrouxar; (weight) aliviar; (help pass): to ~ sth in/out meter/tirar algo com cuidado; at ~! (MIL) descansar!; to be at ~ estar à vontade; to ~ off or up vi (gen) acalmar-se; (at work) deixar de trabalhar tanto; (wind) baixar; (rain) moderar-se.

**easel** [ˈiːzl] n cavalete m.

**east** [iːst] n leste m, este m // adj oriental, do leste // adv de leste; the E~ o Oriente.

**Easter** [ˈiːstə*] n Páscoa.

**easterly** [ˈiːstəlɪ] adj (to the east) para o leste; (from the east) do leste.

**eastern** [ˈiːstən] adj do leste, oriental.

**East Germany** n Alemanha Oriental.

**eastward(s)** [ˈiːstwəd(z)] adv ao leste.

**easy** [ˈiːzɪ] adj (gen) fácil; (simple) simples; (slow) lento, pacato; (comfortable) folgado, cômodo;

(relaxed) natural, complacente // adv: to take it or things ~ (not worry) levar as coisas com calma; (go slowly) ir devagar; (rest) descansar; ~ chair n espreguiçadeira, poltrona; ~going adj pacato, bonachão/ona.

**eat** [iːt], pt ate, pp eaten [ˈiːtn] vt (gen) comer; (supper) cear; to ~ into, to ~ away at vt fus corroer; ~able adj comestível.

**eau de Cologne** [əʊdəkəˈləʊn] n (água de) Colônia.

**eaves** [iːvz] npl beira sg, beiral msg.

**eavesdrop** [ˈiːvzdrɒp] vi escutar às escondidas (on sb a alguém).

**ebb** [eb] n maré f // vi baixar; (fig: also: ~ away) declinar; ~ tide n baixa-mar, maré f vazante.

**ebony** [ˈebənɪ] n ébano.

**eccentric** [ɪkˈsentrɪk] adj, n excêntrico.

**ecclesiastical** [ɪkliːzɪˈæstɪkəl] adj eclesiástico.

**echo** [ˈekəʊ], pl ~es n eco // vt (sound) ecoar, repetir // vi ressoar, repetir.

**eclipse** [ɪˈklɪps] n eclipse m // vt eclipsar.

**ecology** [ɪˈkɔlədʒɪ] n ecologia.

**economic** [iːkəˈnɔmɪk] adj econômico; (business etc) rentável; ~al adj econômico; ~s n economia; **economist** [ɪˈkɔnəmɪst] n economista m/f.

**economize** [ɪˈkɔnəmaɪz] vi economizar, poupar.

**economy** [ɪˈkɔnəmɪ] n economia.

**ecstasy** [ˈekstəsɪ] n êxtase m; **ecstatic** [-ˈtætɪk] adj extasiado.

**ecumenical** [iːkjuˈmenɪkl] adj ecumênico.

**eczema** [ˈeksɪmə] n eczema m.

**edge** [edʒ] n (of knife etc) fio; (of object) borda; (of lake etc) margem f // vt (SEWING) embainhar; on ~ (fig) = edgy; to ~ away from afastar-se pouco a pouco de; ~ways adv: he couldn't get a word in

**~ways** não pôde entrar na conversa; (SEWING) orla, fímbria; (of path) borda.

**edgy** ['edʒɪ] adj nervoso, inquieto.

**edible** ['edɪbl] adj comestível.

**edict** ['i:dɪkt] n édito.

**edifice** ['edɪfɪs] n edifício.

**edit** ['edɪt] vt (be the editor of) dirigir; (cut) cortar, modificar com cortes; **~ion** [ɪ'dɪʃən] n (gen) edição f; (number printed) tiragem f; **~or** n redator(a) (Pt: -ct-) m/f; (of newspaper) diretor (Pt: -ct-) m; (of book) organizador(a) m/f da edição; **~orial** ['i-'tɔ:rɪəl] adj editorial // n editorial m.

**educate** ['edjukeɪt] vt (gen) educar; (instruct) instruir.

**education** [edju'keɪʃən] n educação f; (schooling) ensino m; (SCOL) pedagogia; **~al** (policy etc) educacional; (teaching) docente; (instructive) educativo.

**EEC** n abbr of **European Economic Community** Comunidade f Econômica Européia.

**eel** [i:l] n enguia.

**eerie** ['ɪərɪ] adj (strange) estranho; (mysterious) misterioso.

**effect** [ɪ'fekt] n efeito // vt efetuar (Pt: -ct-), levar a cabo; **~s** npl bens mpl; to take **~** (drug) fazer efeito; **in ~** na realidade; **~ive** adj (gen) eficaz; (striking) impressionante; (real) efetivo (Pt: -ct-); **to become ~ive** entrar em vigor; **~iveness** n eficácia.

**effeminate** [ɪ'femɪnɪt] adj efeminado.

**effervescent** [efə'vesnt] adj efervescente.

**efficiency** [ɪ'fɪʃənsɪ] n (gen) eficiência; (of machine) rendimento.

**efficient** [ɪ'fɪʃənt] adj eficiente.

**effigy** ['efɪdʒɪ] n efígie f.

**effort** ['efət] n esforço f; **to make an ~** esforçar-se por; **~less** adj sem esforço (algum).

**effrontery** [ɪ'frʌntərɪ] n descaramento.

**effusive** [ɪ'fju:sɪv] adj efusivo.

**e.g.** adv abbr of **exempli gratia** por exemplo.

**egg** [eg] n ovo; **hard-boiled ~** ovo cozido; (Pt) ovo duro; **soft-boiled ~** ovo quente; **poached ~** ovo escalfado or pochê; **fried ~** ovo estrelado or frito; **scrambled ~s** ovos mexidos; **to ~ on** vt incitar; **~cup** n oveiro, taça para ovos quentes; **~ plant** n (US) beringela; **~shell** n casca de ovo.

**ego** ['i:gəu] n ego; **~ism** n egoísmo; **~ist** n egoísta m/f.

**Egypt** ['i:dʒɪpt] n Egito (Pt: -pt-); **~ian** [ɪ'dʒɪpʃən] adj, n egípcio/a.

**eiderdown** ['aɪdədaun] n edredão m, edredom m.

**eight** [eɪt] num oito; **eighteen** num dezoito; **eighth** adj, n oitavo; **~y** num oitenta.

**Eire** ['ɛərə] n Eire m.

**either** ['aɪðə*] det (each) cada; (any) qualquer; (both) ambos, um ou outro; **on ~ side** de ambos os lados // pron: **~ (of them)** cada um/qualquer/ambos (deles); **I don't like ~** não gosto nem de um nem do outro // adv tampouco, também não; **no, I don't ~** eu tampouco, eu também não // conj: **~ yes or no** ou sim ou não.

**eject** [ɪ'dʒekt] vt expelir; (tenant) despejar; **~or seat** n assento ejetor (Pt: -ct-).

**eke** [i:k]: **to ~ out** vt (make last) fazer durar; (add to) suprir as deficiências de.

**elaborate** [ɪ'læbərɪt] adj complicado; (decorated) rebuscado // (vb: [ɪ'læbəreɪt]) vt elaborar // vi explicar minuciosamente.

**elapse** [ɪ'læps] vi decorrer.

**elastic** [ɪ'læstɪk] adj, n elástico; **~ band** n tira de borracha, elástico.

**elated** [ɪ'leɪtɪd] adj: **to be ~**

rejubilar-se; **elation** [ɪ'leɪʃən] *n* exaltação *f*.

**elbow** ['elbəu] *n* cotovelo.

**elder** ['eldə*] *adj* mais velho // *n* (*tree*) sabugueiro; (*person*) o mais velho; (*of tribe*) ancião; (*of church*) presbítero; ~**ly** *adj* idoso, de idade madura // *n*: **the** ~**ly** as pessoas de idade, os idosos.

**eldest** ['eldɪst] *adj* mais velho // *n* o mais velho.

**elect** [ɪ'lekt] *vt* eleger; **to** ~ **to do** optar por fazer // *adj*: **the president** ~ o presidente eleito; ~**ion** [ɪ'lekʃən] *n* eleição *f*; ~**ioneering** [ɪlekʃə'nɪərɪŋ] *n* campanha eleitoral; ~**or** *n* eleitor(a) *m/f*; ~**oral** *adj* eleitoral; ~**orate** *n* eleitorado.

**electric** [ɪ'lektrɪk] *adj* elétrico (*Pt*: -ct-); ~**al** *adj* elé(c)trico; ~**blanket** *n* cobertor *m* elé(c)trico; ~**chair** *n* cadeira elé(c)trica; ~**cooker** *n* fogão *m* elé(c)trico; ~**fire** *n* aquecimento elé(c)trico.

**electrician** [ɪlek'trɪʃən] *n* eletricista (*Pt*: -ct-) *m/f*.

**electricity** [ɪlek'trɪsɪtɪ] *n* eletricidade (*Pt*: -ct-) *f*.

**electrify** [ɪ'lektrɪfaɪ] *vt* (*RAIL*) eletrificar (*Pt*: -ct-); (*audience*) eletrizar (*Pt*: -ct-).

**electro...** [ɪlektrəu] *pref*: ~**cute** [-kjuːt] *vt* eletrocutar (*Pt*: -ctr-); ~**de** [ɪlek'trəud] *n* eletródio (*Pt*: -ct-), eletrodo; ~**magnetic** *adj* eletromagnético (*Pt*: -ctr-).

**electron** [ɪ'lektrɔn] *n* elétron (*Pt*: -ct-) *m*.

**electronic** [ɪlek'trɔnɪk] *adj* eletrônico (*Pt*: -ct-); ~**s** *n* eletrônica (*Pt*: -ct-).

**elegance** ['elɪgəns] *n* elegância; **elegant** [-gənt] *adj* elegante.

**element** ['elɪmənt] *n* (*gen*) elemento; **to brave the** ~**s** enfrentar intempérie; ~**ary** [-'mentərɪ] *adj* (*gen*) elementar; (*primitive*) rudimentar; (*school, education*) primário.

**elephant** ['elɪfənt] *n* elefante *m*.

**elevate** ['elɪveɪt] *vt* (*gen*) elevar; (*in rank*) subir.

**elevation** [elɪ'veɪʃən] *n* elevação *f*; (*land*) eminência; (*height*) altura.

**elevator** ['elɪveɪtə*] *n* (*US*) elevador *m*, ascensor *m*.

**eleven** [ɪ'lɛvn] *num* onze; ~**ses** *npl* refeição *f* leve da manhã; ~**th** *adj* décimo-primeiro.

**elf** [elf], *pl* **elves** [ɛlvz] *n* elfo, duende *m*.

**elicit** [ɪ'lɪsɪt] *vt*: **to** ~ (**from**) arrancar (de), eliciar (de).

**eligible** ['elɪdʒəbl] *adj* elegível, apto; **to be** ~ **for** sth ter qualificações para algo.

**eliminate** [ɪ'lɪmɪneɪt] *vt* eliminar; (*strike out*) suprimir; (*suspect*) eliminar, excluir; **elimination** [-'neɪʃən] *n* eliminação *f*, exclusão *f*.

**élite** [eɪ'liːt] *n* elite *f*.

**elm** [elm] *n* olmo.

**elocution** [elə'kjuːʃən] *n* elocução *f*.

**elongated** ['iːlɔŋgeɪtɪd] *adj* alongado.

**elope** [ɪ'ləup] *vi* fugir de (casa) com namorado; ~**ment** *n* fuga de lar paterno.

**eloquence** ['elɔkwəns] *n* eloqüência; **eloquent** [-wənt] *adj* eloqüente.

**else** [els] *adv* outro, mais; **something** ~ outra coisa; **somewhere** ~ em outro lugar, alhures; **everywhere** ~ por todo o lado (menos aqui); **where** ~? onde mais? **what** ~ **can we do?** que mais podemos fazer? ~ *or* senão; **there was little** ~ **to do** não havia outra coisa a fazer; **nobody** ~ ninguém mais falou; ~**where** *adv* (*be*) em outro lugar; (*go*) para outro lugar.

**elucidate** [ɪ'luːsɪdeɪt] *vt* esclarecer, elucidar.

**elude** [ɪ'luːd] *vt* (*gen*) iludir; (*blow*) esquivar; (*pursuer*) escapar de, safar-se de.

**elusive** [ɪ'luːsɪv] adj esquivo; (answer) evasivo.

**emaciated** [ɪ'meɪsɪeɪtɪd] adj emaciado, macilento.

**emanate** ['eməneɪt] vi emanar, provir.

**emancipate** [ɪ'mænsɪpeɪt] vt emancipar; ~**d** adj emancipado; **emancipation** [-'peɪʃən] n emancipação f, liberação f.

**embalm** [ɪm'baːm] vt embalsamar.

**embankment** [ɪm'bæŋkmənt] n aterro; (riverside) dique m.

**embargo** [ɪm'baːgəu], pl ~**es** n embargo, proibição f.

**embark** [ɪm'baːk] vi embarcar // vi embarcar; **to** ~ **on** (fig) empreender, começar; ~**ation** [embaː'keɪʃən] n (people, goods) embarque m.

**embarrass** [ɪm'bærəs] vt embaraçar, atrapalhar; (financially etc) impedir, dificultar; ~**ing** adj embaraçoso; ~**ment** n embaraço; (financial) dificuldades fpl.

**embassy** ['embəsɪ] n embaixada f.

**embed** [ɪm'bed] vt (gen) embutir; (teeth etc) cravar.

**embellish** [ɪm'belɪʃ] vt embelezar; (fig) adornar.

**embers** ['embəz] npl brasa sg, borralho sg, cinzas fpl.

**embezzle** [ɪm'bezl] vt desviar; ~**ment** n desvio.

**embitter** [ɪm'bɪtə*] vt amargar; (fig) azedar, acirrar; ~**ed** adj amargurado.

**emblem** ['embləm] n emblema m.

**embody** [ɪm'bɒdɪ] vt (features) incorporar; (ideas) incluir.

**embossed** [ɪm'bɒst] adj realçado; ~ **with** ornado com relevos de.

**embrace** [ɪm'breɪs] vt abraçar, dar um abraço em; (include) abarcar, abranger; (adopt: idea) adotar (Pt: -pt-) // vi abraçar-se // n abraço.

**embroider** [ɪm'brɔɪdə*] vt bordar; (fig: story) melhorar, amplificar; ~**y** n bordado.

**embryo** ['embrɪəu] n (also fig) embrião m.

**emerald** ['emərəld] n esmeralda.

**emerge** [ɪ'məːdʒ] vi (gen) sair, aparecer; (arise) surgir; **emergence** n surgimento, aparecimento.

**emergency** [ɪ'məːdʒənsɪ] n (event) emergência; (crisis) crise f; (need) necessidade f urgente; **in an** ~ em caso de urgência; **state of** ~ estado de emergência; ~ **exit** n saída de emergência; ~ **landing** n aterrissagem f forçada; (Pt) aterragem f forçosa; ~ **meeting** n reunião f extraordinária.

**emery** ['eməri]: ~ **board** n lixa de unhas; ~ **paper** n lixa or papel m de esmeril.

**emetic** [ɪ'metɪk] n emético.

**emigrant** ['emɪgrənt] n emigrante m/f.

**emigrate** ['emɪgreɪt] vi emigrar; **emigration** [-'greɪʃən] n emigração f.

**eminence** ['emɪnəns] n eminência; **eminent** [-ənt] adj eminente.

**emission** [ɪ'mɪʃən] n emissão f.

**emit** [ɪ'mɪt] vt (gen) emitir; (smoke) deitar, soltar; (smell) exalar; (sound) produzir.

**emotion** [ɪ'məuʃən] n emoção f; ~**al** adj (person) sentimental; (scene) comovente; ~**ally** adv com emoção.

**emotive** [ɪ'məutɪv] adj emotivo.

**emperor** ['empərə*] n imperador m.

**emphasis** ['emfəsɪs], pl ~**ses** [-siːz] n ênfase f.

**emphasize** ['emfəsaɪz] vt (word, point) enfatizar, acentuar; (feature) salientar.

**emphatic** [em'fætɪk] adj (strong) enérgico; (unambiguous, clear) enfático; ~**ally** adv com ênfase.

**empire** ['empaɪə*] n império.

**empirical** [em'pɪrɪkl] adj empírico.

**employ** [ɪm'plɔɪ] vt empregar; ~**ee** [-iː] n empregado/a; ~**er** n empregador/a m/f, patrão/troa *m/f*; ~**ment** *n* (*gen*) emprego; (*work*) trabalho; ~**ment agency** *n* agência de empregos; ~**ment exchange** *n* bolsa de trabalho.

**empower** [ɪm'pauə*] *vt*: to ~ **sb** to do sth autorizar alguém para fazer algo.

**empress** ['emprɪs] *n* imperatriz *f*.

**emptiness** ['emptɪnɪs] *n* (*gen*) vazio, vácuo; (*of life etc*) vacuidade *f*, solidão *f*.

**empty** ['emptɪ] *adj* vazio; (*place*) deserto; (*house*) desocupado; (*threat*) vão/vã // *n* (*bottle*) vazio // *vt* esvaziar; (*place*) evacuar // *vi* esvaziar-se; (*house*) ficar desocupado; (*place*) ficar deserto; ~**handed** *adj* de mãos vazias.

**emulate** ['emjuleɪt] *vt* emular.

**emulsion** [ɪ'mʌlʃən] *n* emulsão *f*.

**enable** [ɪ'neɪbl] *vt*: to ~ **sb** to do sth (*allow*) permitir que alguém faça algo; (*prepare*) capacitar alguém para fazer algo.

**enact** [ɪn'ækt] *vt* (*law*) pôr em vigor, aprovar; (*play*) representar; (*role*) fazer.

**enamel** [ɪ'næməl] *n* esmalte *m*.

**enamoured** [ɪ'næməd] *adj*: to be ~ **of** (*person*) estar apaixonado por; (*activity etc*) ser louco por; (*idea*) encantar-se com.

**encased** [ɪn'keɪst] *adj*: ~ **in** (*enclosed*) encaixado em; (*covered*) coberto de.

**enchant** [ɪn'tʃɑːnt] *vt* encantar; ~**ing** *adj* encantador(a).

**encircle** [ɪn'sɜːkl] *vt* (*gen*) cercar, circundar; (*waist*) rodear.

**encl.** *abbr* (*of* **enclosed**) anexo, junto.

**enclose** [ɪn'kləuz] *vt* (*land*) cercar; (*with letter etc*) anexar, mandar em anexo; (*Pt*) enviar junto, juntar; (*in receptacle*) incluir; **please find** ~**d** anexamos; (*Pt*) junto enviamos.

**enclosure** [ɪn'kləuʒə*] *n* cercado, (*COMM*) anexo.

**encore** [ɔŋ'kɔː*] *excl* bis!, outra! // *n* bis *m*.

**encounter** [ɪn'kauntə*] *n* encontro // *vt* encontrar, topar com; (*difficulty*) enfrentar.

**encourage** [ɪn'kʌrɪdʒ] *vt* encorajar, animar; (*growth*) estimular; ~**ment** *n* estímulo; (*of industry*) fomento.

**encroach** [ɪn'krəutʃ] *vi*: to ~ (**up)on** (*gen*) invadir; (*time*) ocupar.

**encrusted** [ɪn'krʌstəd] *adj*: ~ **with** incrustado de.

**encumber** [ɪn'kʌmbə*] *vt*: to be ~**ed with** (*carry*) estar carregado de; (*debts*) estar sobrecarregado de.

**encyclop(a)edia** [ensaɪkləu-'piːdɪə] *n* enciclopédia.

**end** [end] *n* (*gen, also aim*) fim *m*; (*of table*) extremo; (*of street*) final *m*; (*SPORT*) ponta // *vt* acabar, terminar; (*also*: **bring to an** ~, **put an** ~ **to**) acabar com, pôr fim a // *vi* terminar, acabar; **in the** ~ ao fim, por fim, finalmente; **on** ~ (*object*) na ponta; **to stand on** ~ (*hair*) arrepiar-se; **for hours on** ~ durante horas seguidas; **to** ~ **up** *vi*: **to** ~ **up in** terminar em; (*place*) ir parar em.

**endanger** [ɪn'deɪndʒə*] *vt* pôr em perigo.

**endear** [ɪn'dɪə*] *vt*: to ~ **o.s. to sb** conquistar a afeição de alguém, cativar alguém; ~**ing** *adj* simpático, atrativo (*Pt*: -ct-); ~**ment** *n* carinho, meiguice *f*.

**endeavour** [ɪn'devə*] *n* esforço; (*attempt*) tentativa; (*striving*) empenho // *vi*: **to** ~ **to do** esforçar-se em fazer; (*try*) tentar fazer.

**ending** ['endɪŋ] *n* fim, conclusão *f*; (*of book*) desenlace *m*; (*LING*) terminação *f*.

**endless** ['endlɪs] *adj* interminável, infinito.

**endorse** [ɪn'dɔːs] *vt* (*cheque*) endossar; (*approve*) aprovar; ~**ment** *n* (*on driving licence*) descrição *f* das multas.

**endow** [ɪn'dau] *vt* (*provide with*

*money*) dotar; (: *institution*) fundar;
**to be ~ed with** ser dotado de.

**endurance** [ɪnˈdjʊərəns] *n*
resistência; **endure** *vt* (*bear*)
aguentar, suportar; (*resist*) resistir
// *vi* (*last*) durar; (*resist*) resistir.

**enemy** [ˈenəmɪ] *adj, n* inimigo.

**energetic** [enəˈdʒetɪk] *adj*
energético.

**energy** [ˈenədʒɪ] *n* energia.

**enforce** [ɪnˈfɔːs] *vt* (*LAW*) fazer
cumprir; **~d** *adj* forçoso.

**engage** [ɪnˈgeɪdʒ] *vt* (*attention*)
chamar; (*in conversation*) travar;
(*worker*) contratar; (*taxi*) chamar;
(*clutch*) engrenar // *vi* (*TECH*)
engrenar com; **to ~ in** dedicar-se a,
ocupar-se com; **~d** *adj* (*busy, in use*)
ocupado; (*betrothed*) noivo; **to get
~d** ficar noivo; **he is ~d in
research** dedica-se à pesquisa; **~d
tone** n sinal m de ocupado; **~ment** n
(*appointment*) encontro; (*battle*)
combate m; (*to marry, period*)
noivado; **~ment ring** n aliança de
noivado.

**engaging** [ɪnˈgeɪdʒɪŋ] *adj* atraente,
simpático.

**engender** [ɪnˈdʒendə*] *vt*
engendrar, gerar.

**engine** [ˈendʒɪn] *n* (*AUT*) máquina;
(*RAIL*) locomotiva; **~ driver** n
maquinista m.

**engineer** [endʒɪˈnɪə*] *n*
engenheiro; (*US: RAIL*) maquinista
m; **~ing** n engenharia.

**England** [ˈɪŋɡlənd] n Inglaterra.

**English** [ˈɪŋɡlɪʃ] *adj* inglês/esa // *n*
(*LING*) inglês *m*; **the ~** os ingleses;
**~man/woman** n inglês/esa m/f.

**engrave** [ɪnˈgreɪv] *vt* gravar;
**engraving** n gravura, gravação f.

**engulf** [ɪnˈɡʌlf] *vt* engolfar, tragar.

**enhance** [ɪnˈhɑːns] *vt* (*gen*)
aumentar; (*beauty*) realçar.

**enigma** [ɪˈnɪɡmə] *n* enigma *m*;
**~tic** [enɪɡˈmætɪk] *adj* enigmático.

**enjoy** [ɪnˈdʒɔɪ] *vt* (*possess*) possuir;
(*like*) gostar de; (*have: health,*

*fortune*) desfrutar de; (*food*) comer
com gosto; **to ~ o.s.** divertir-se;
**~able** *adj* (*pleasant*) agradável;
(*amusing*) divertido; **~ment** n (*use*)
prazer m; (*joy*) gozo, satisfação f.

**enlarge** [ɪnˈlɑːdʒ] *vt* aumentar;
(*broaden*) estender, alargar; (*PHOT*)
ampliar // *vi*: **to ~ on** (*subject*)
desenvolver, estender-se sobre;
**~ment** n (*PHOT*) ampliação f.

**enlighten** [ɪnˈlaɪtn] *vt* (*inform*)
informar, instruir; **~ed** *adj*
(*cultured*) culto; (*knowledgeable*)
bem informado; (*tolerant*)
compreensivo; **~ment** n
esclarecimento; (*HISTORY*): **the
E~ment** o Século das Luzes.

**enlist** [ɪnˈlɪst] *vt* alistar; (*support*)
conseguir, aliciar // *vi* alistar-se.

**enmity** [ˈenmɪtɪ] *n* inimizade f.

**enormity** [ɪˈnɔːmɪtɪ] *n* enormidade
f; **enormous** [-məs] *adj* enorme.

**enough** [ɪˈnʌf] *adj*: **~ time/books**
bastante tempo/bastantes livros // 
*n*: **have you got ~?** você tem
bastante? // *adv*: **big ~**
suficientemente grande; **he has not
worked ~** não tem trabalhado
bastante; **~! basta!, chega!; that's
~, thanks** chega, obrigado; **I've had
~ of him** estou farto dele; **... which,
funnily ~ ...** o que, por estranho
que pareça ...

**enquire** [ɪnˈkwaɪə*] *vt/i* =
**inquire**.

**enrage** [ɪnˈreɪdʒ] *vt* enfurecer,
enraivecer.

**enrich** [ɪnˈrɪtʃ] *vt* enriquecer.

**enrol** [ɪnˈrəʊl] *vt* inscrever; (*SCOL*)
matricular // *vi* inscrever-se,
matricular-se; **~ment** n inscrição f;
matrícula.

**en route** [ɔnˈruːt] *adv* (*on the way*)
no caminho; **~ to** a caminho de.

**ensign** [ˈensaɪn] *n* (*flag*) bandeira;
(*MIL*) insígnia; (*US: NAUT*) guarda-
marinha m.

**enslave** [ɪnˈsleɪv] *vt* escravizar.

**ensue** [ɪnˈsjuː] *vi* seguir-se; (*result*

resultar; (happen) acontecer.

**ensure** [ɪn'ʃuə*] vt assegurar.

**entail** [ɪn'teɪl] vt (imply) supor; (result in) acarretar.

**entangle** [ɪn'tæŋgl] vt enredar, emaranhar; ~**ment** n emaranhado.

**enter** ['entə*] vt (room) entrar em; (club) ficar or fazer-se sócio de; (army) alistar-se em; (sb for a competition) inscrever; (write down) anotar, apontar // vi entrar; **to ~ for** vt fus apresentar-se para; **to ~ into** vt fus (relations) estabelecer; (plans) fazer parte de; (debate) tomar parte em; (agreement) chegar a, firmar; **to ~ (up)on** vt fus (career) entrar para.

**enteritis** [entə'raɪtɪs] n enterite f.

**enterprise** ['entəpraɪz] n empresa; (spirit) iniciativa; **free ~** livre iniciativa; **private ~** iniciativa privada; **enterprising** adj empreendedor(a).

**entertain** [entə'teɪn] vt (amuse) divertir, entreter; (receive: guest) receber (em casa); (idea) acolher; (plan) estudar; ~**er** n artista m/f; ~**ing** adj divertido; ~**ment** n (amusement) diversão f; (show) espetáculo (Pt: -ct-); (party) festa.

**enthralled** [ɪn'θrɔ:ld] adj encantado, cativado.

**enthusiasm** [ɪn'θu:zɪæzəm] n entusiasmo.

**enthusiast** [ɪn'θu:zɪæst] n entusiasta m/f; ~**ic** [-'æstɪk] adj entusiástico; **to be ~ic about** entusiasmar-se por.

**entice** [ɪn'taɪs] vt atrair, tentar; (seduce) seduzir; **enticing** adj sedutor(a), tentador(a).

**entire** [ɪn'taɪə*] adj inteiro, completo, total; total, todo; ~**ly** adv totalmente; ~**ty** [ɪn'taɪərətɪ] n: **in its ~ty** na sua totalidade.

**entitle** [ɪn'taɪtl] vt: **to ~ sb to sth** dar a alguém direito a algo; ~**d** adj (book) intitulado; **to be ~d to do** ter direito de fazer.

**entourage** [ɔntu'rɑ:ʒ] n séquito.

**entrails** ['entreɪlz] npl entranhas fpl.

**entrance** ['entrəns] n entrada // [ɪn'trɑ:ns] encantar, fascinar; **to gain ~ to** (university etc) ser admitido em; ~ **examination** n exame m de admissão; (university) exame vestibular; ~ **fee** n matrícula; (Pt) propina, jóia.

**entrant** ['entrənt] n participante m/f.

**entreat** [en'tri:t] vt rogar, suplicar; ~**y** n rogo, súplica.

**entrée** ['ɔntreɪ] n (CULIN) entrada.

**entrenched** [en'trentʃd] adj entrincheirado.

**entrepreneur** [ɔntrəprə'nɔ:] n empresário; (of works) empreiteiro.

**entrust** [ɪn'trʌst] vt: **to ~ sth to sb** confiar algo a alguém.

**entry** ['entrɪ] n entrada; (permission to enter) acesso; (in register) registro, assentamento; (in account) lançamento; (dictionary) verbete m; ~ **form** n boletim m/formulário de inscrição; **no ~** entrada proibida; (AUT) contramão f, mão f única.

**enumerate** [ɪ'nju:məreɪt] vt enumerar.

**enunciate** [ɪ'nʌnsɪeɪt] vt pronunciar; (principle etc) enunciar.

**envelop** [ɪn'veləp] vt envolver.

**envelope** ['envələup] n envelope m.

**envious** ['envɪəs] adj invejoso; (look) de inveja.

**environment** [ɪn'vaɪərnmənt] n meio ambiente m; ~**al** [-'mentl] adj ambiental.

**envisage** [ɪn'vɪzɪdʒ] vt (foresee) prever; (imagine) conceber, imaginar.

**envoy** ['envɔɪ] n emissário.

**envy** ['envɪ] n inveja // vt ter inveja de; **to ~ sb sth** invejar alguém por algo, cobiçar algo de alguém.

**enzyme** ['enzaɪm] n enzima.

**ephemeral** [ɪ'femərəl] adj efêmero.

**epic** ['epɪk] n epopéia // adj épico.

**epidemic** [ɛpɪ'dɛmɪk] n epidemia.
**epilepsy** [ˈɛpɪlɛpsɪ] n epilepsia;
**epileptic** [-ˈlɛptɪk] adj, n epiléptico/a
(Pt: -pt-).
**episode** [ˈɛpɪsəud] n episódio.
**epistle** [ɪˈpɪsl] n epístola.
**epitaph** [ˈɛpɪtɑːf] n epitáfio.
**epitome** [ɪˈpɪtəmɪ] n epítome m;
**epitomize** vt epitomar, resumir.
**epoch** [ˈiːpɔk] n época.
**equable** [ˈɛkwəbl] adj uniforme,
igual; (character) tranqüilo, calmo.
**equal** [ˈiːkwl] adj (gen) igual;
(treatment) equitativo, equivalente
// n igual m/f // vt ser igual a; **to be
~ to** (task) estar à altura de; **~ity**
[iːˈkwɔlɪtɪ] n igualdade f; **~ize** vt/i
igualar; (sport) empatar; **~izer** n
empate m; **~ly** adv igualmente;
(share etc) por igual.
**equanimity** [ɛkwəˈnɪmɪtɪ] n
equanimidade f.
**equate** [ɪˈkweit] vt: **to ~ sth with**
equiparar algo com; **equation**
[ɪˈkweiʒən] n (MATH) equação f.
**equator** [ɪˈkweitə*] n equador m;
**~ial** [ɛkwəˈtɔːrɪəl] adj equatorial.
**equilibrium** [iːkwɪˈlɪbrɪəm] n
equilíbrio.
**equinox** [ˈiːkwɪnɔks] n equinócio.
**equip** [ɪˈkwɪp] vt (gen) equipar;
(person) prover, munir; **to be well
~ped** estar bem preparado or
equipado; **~ment** n equipamento;
(tools) aprestos mpl, apetrechos
mpl.
**equitable** [ˈɛkwɪtəbl] adj
equitativo.
**equivalent** [ɪˈkwɪvələnt] adj
equivalente; **to be ~ to** ser
equivalente a // n equivalente m.
**equivocal** [ɪˈkwɪvəkl] adj equívoco;
(open to suspicion) ambíguo.
**era** [ˈɪərə] n era, época.
**eradicate** [ɪˈrædɪkeit] vt erradicar,
extirpar.
**erase** [ɪˈreiz] vt apagar, raspar;
**eraser** n borracha (de apagar).
**erect** [ɪˈrɛkt] adj erguido, ereto (Pt:

-ct-) // vt erigir, levantar;
(assemble) montar.
**erection** [ɪˈrɛkʃən] n construção f;
(assembly) montagem f; (structure)
edifício, (MED) ereção (Pt: -çç-) f.
**ermine** [ˈəːmɪn] n arminho.
**erode** [ɪˈrəud] vt (GEO) causar
erosão; (metal) corroer; **erosion**
[ɪˈrəuʒən] n erosão f, desgaste m.
**erotic** [ɪˈrɔtɪk] adj erótico; **~ism**
[ɪˈrɔtɪsɪzm] n erotismo.
**err** [əː*] vi errar, enganar-se; (REL)
pecar.
**errand** [ˈɛrnd] n recado, missão f;
**~ boy** n mensageiro; (Pt) moço de
recados.
**erratic** [ɪˈrætɪk] adj errático;
(uneven) irregular.
**erroneous** [ɪˈrəunɪəs] adj errôneo.
**error** [ˈɛrə*] n engano, erro.
**erupt** [ɪˈrʌpt] vi entrar em erupção;
(MED) causar erupção; (fig)
explodir; **~ion** [ɪˈrʌpʃən] n erupção
f; (fig) explosão f.
**escalate** [ˈɛskəleit] vi estender-se,
intensificar-se; **escalation** [-ˈleiʃən] n
escalada, intensificação f.
**escalator** [ˈɛskəleitə*] n escada
rolante.
**escapade** [ɛskəˈpeid] n travessura.
**escape** [ɪˈskeip] n (gen) fuga; (from
duties) escapatória; (from chase)
fuga, evasão f // vi (gen) escapar;
(flee) fugir, evadir-se; (leak) vazar,
escapar // vt evitar, fugir de;
(consequences) fugir de; **to ~ from**
(place) escapar de; (person)
escapulir de; (clutches) livrar-se de;
**escapism** n escapismo, fuga à
realidade.
**escort** [ˈɛskɔːt] n acompanhante
m/f, (MIL, NAUT) escolta // vt [ɪˈskɔːt]
acompanhar; (MIL, NAUT) escoltar.
**Eskimo** [ˈɛskɪməu] n esquimó m/f.
**especially** [ɪˈspɛʃlɪ] adv (gen)
especialmente; (above all) sobre
tudo; (particularly) em particular.
**espionage** [ˈɛspɪɔnɑːʒ] n
espionagem f.

**esplanade** [ɛsplə'neɪd] n (by sea) avenida beira-mar, esplanada.

**espouse** [ɪ'spauz] vt casar com, desposar; (cause) abraçar.

**Esquire** [ɪ'skwaɪə] n (abbr **Esq.**): **J. Brown**, ~ Sr. J. Brown.

**essay** ['eseɪ] n (SCOL) ensaio.

**essence** ['esns] n essência.

**essential** [ɪ'senʃl] adj (necessary) indispensável; (basic) essencial; **~ly** adv essencialmente.

**establish** [ɪ'stæblɪʃ] vt estabelecer; (facts) verificar; (proof) demonstrar; (relations) fundar; ~**ed** adj (business) com boa reputação; (staff) fixo; ~**ment** n estabelecimento; **the E~ment** a classe dirigente.

**estate** [ɪ'steɪt] n (land) fazenda, (Pt) propriedade f, (property) propriedade; (inheritance) herança; (POL) estado; **housing** ~ urbanização f; **industrial** ~ zona industrial; ~ **agent** n agente m/f imobiliário; ~ **car** n (Brit) furgão m.

**esteem** [ɪ'stiːm] n: **to hold sb in high** ~ estimar muito alguém // vt estimar.

**estimate** ['estɪmət] n estimativa; (assessment) avaliação f, cálculo; (COMM) orçamento // vt [-meɪt] estimar, avaliar, calcular; **estimation** [-'meɪʃən] n estimação f, opinião f; (esteem) apreço.

**estrange** [ɪ'streɪndʒ] vt alienar.

**estuary** ['estjuərɪ] n estuário.

**etching** ['etʃɪŋ] n água-forte f.

**eternal** [ɪ'tɜːnl] adj eterno.

**eternity** [ɪ'tɜːnɪtɪ] n eternidade f.

**ether** ['iːθə] n éter m.

**ethical** ['eθɪkl] adj ético; (honest) honrado; **ethics** ['eθɪks] n ética // npl moral f.

**ethnic** ['eθnɪk] adj étnico.

**etiquette** ['etɪkɛt] n etiqueta.

**eucalyptus** [juːkə'lɪptəs] n eucalipto.

**euphemism** ['juːfəmɪzm] n eufemismo.

**euphoria** [juː'fɔːrɪə] n euforia.

**Europe** ['juərəp] n Europa; **European** [-'pɪən] adj, n europeu/péia.

**euthanasia** [juːθə'neɪzɪə] n eutanásia.

**evacuate** [ɪ'vækjueɪt] vt evacuar; **evacuation** [-'eɪʃən] n evacuação f.

**evade** [ɪ'veɪd] vt evadir, evitar.

**evaluate** [ɪ'væljueɪt] vt avaliar; (value) determinar o valor de; (evidence) interpretar.

**evangelist** [ɪ'vændʒəlɪst] n evangelista [-'lɪst] m/f, (preacher) evangelizador(a) m/f.

**evaporate** [ɪ'væpəreɪt] vi evaporar-se // vt evaporar; ~**d milk** n leite m evaporado; **evaporation** [-'reɪʃən] n evaporação f.

**evasion** [ɪ'veɪʒən] n evasão f, fuga; (fig) evasiva; **evasive** [-sɪv] adj evasivo.

**eve** [iːv] n: **on the** ~ **of** na véspera de.

**even** ['iːvn] adj (level) plano; (smooth) liso; (speed, temperature) uniforme; (number) par; (nature) equilibrado; (SPORT) igual // adv até, mesmo, ainda; ~ **more** ainda mais; **so** mesmo assim; **never** ~ nem sequer; **not** ~ nem mesmo; ~ **he was there** até ele esteve ali; ~ **if** ainda que; ~ **on Sundays** até nos domingos; **to** ~ **out** vi nivelar-se; **to get** ~ **with sb** ficar quite com alguém.

**evening** ['iːvnɪŋ] n tarde f; (dusk) anoitecer m; (night) noite f; (event) noitada; **in the** ~ à tarde; ~ **class** n aula noturna (Pt: -ct-); ~ **dress** n traje m de rigor; (Pt) traje de cerimônia; (woman's) vestido de noite.

**event** [ɪ'vent] n acontecimento; (SPORT) prova; **in the** ~ **of** no caso de (que); ~**ful** adj notável; (game etc) cheio de emoção, memorável.

**eventual** [ɪ'ventjuəl] adj (last) final; (resulting) definitivo; ~**ity** [-'ælɪtɪ] n

eventualidade f; ~**ly** adv (finally)
finalmente; (in time) por fim.

**ever** ['ɛvə*] adv já, alguma vez; (in
negative) nunca, jamais; (at all
times) alguma vez; **the best** ~ o
melhor que já se viu; **have you** ~
**seen it?** você alguma vez já viu
isto?; **better than** ~ melhor que
nunca; ~ **since** adv desde então //
conj depois que; ~**green** n sempre-
verde f; ~**lasting** adj eterno,
perpétuo.

**every** ['ɛvrɪ] det (each) cada; (all)
todo; ~ **day** todo dia; ~ **other car**
carro sim, carro não; ~ **now and
then** de vez em quando; ~ **3 weeks**
de 3 em 3 semanas; ~**body** pron
todos mpl, toda a gente, todo o
mundo; ~**day** adj (daily) diário;
(usual) corrente; (common) comum;
(Pt) vulgar; (routine) rotineiro;
~**one** = ~**body**; ~**thing** pron tudo;
~**where** adv (be) em toda a parte;
(go) a or por toda a parte.

**evict** [ɪ'vɪkt] vt expulsar; ~**ion**
[ɪ'vɪkʃən] n expulsão f, despejo.

**evidence** ['ɛvɪdns] n (proof)
prova(s); (of witness) testemunho,
depoimento; (facts) dados mpl,
evidência; **to give** ~ testemunhar,
prestar depoimento.

**evident** ['ɛvɪdənt] adj evidente; ~**ly**
adv naturalmente, evidentemente.

**evil** ['iːvl] adj mau/má; (influence)
funesto; (smell) horrível // n mal m,
maldade f; ~**doer** n malfeitor(a)
m/f.

**evocative** [ɪ'vɔkətɪv] adj evocativo,
sugestivo.

**evoke** [ɪ'vəuk] vt evocar.

**evolution** [iːvə'luːʃən] n evolução f,
desenvolvimento.

**evolve** [ɪ'vɔlv] vt desenvolver // vi
desenvolver-se.

**ewe** [juː] n ovelha.

**ex-...** [ɛks] pref ex....

**exact** [ɪg'zækt] adj exato (Pt: -ct-) //
vt: **to** ~ **sth (from)** exigir algo (de);
~**ing** adj exigente; (conditions)

difícil; ~**itude** n exatidão (Pt: -ct-) f,
~**ly** adv exatamente (Pt: -act-);
(time) em ponto.

**exaggerate** [ɪg'zædʒəreɪt] vt//
exagerar; **exaggeration** [-'reɪʃən] n
exagero.

**exalted** [ɪg'zɔːltɪd] adj exaltado,
elevado.

**exam** [ɪg'zæm] n abbr of
**examination.**

**examination** [ɪgzæmɪ'neɪʃən] n
(gen) exame m; (LAW) inquirição f;
(inquiry) investigação f.

**examine** [ɪg'zæmɪn] vt (gen)
examinar; (inspect) inspecionar (Pt:
-cc-); (SCOL, LAW: person) interrogar;
(at customs: luggage) revistar;
**examiner** n inspetor(a) (Pt: -ct-)
m/f, examinador(a) m/f.

**example** [ɪg'zɑːmpl] n exemplo;
(copy) exemplar m; **for** ~ por
exemplo.

**exasperate** [ɪg'zɑːspəreɪt] vt
exasperar, irritar; **exasperating** adj
irritante.

**excavate** ['ɛkskəveɪt] vt escavar;
**excavation** [-'veɪʃən] n escavação f.

**exceed** [ɪk'siːd] vt exceder;
(number) ser superior a; (speed
limit) ultrapassar; (limits) suplantar;
(powers) exceder-se em; (hopes)
superar; ~**ingly** adv extremamente,
muitíssimo.

**excel** [ɪk'sɛl] vi sobressair,
distinguir-se.

**excellence** ['ɛksələns] n
excelência.

**Excellency** ['ɛksələnsɪ] n: **His** ~
Sua Excelência.

**excellent** ['ɛksələnt] adj excelente.

**except** [ɪk'sɛpt] prep (also: ~ **for,**
~**ing**) exceto (Pt: -pt-), salvo,
menos // vt excetuar (Pt: -pt-),
excluir; ~ **if/when** exce(p)to
se/quando; ~ **that** salvo que; ~**ion**
[ɪk'sɛpʃən] n exeção (Pt: -pç-) f; **to
take** ~**ion to** ressentir-se de;
~**ional** [ɪk'sɛpʃənl] adj excepcional.

**excerpt** ['ɛksəːpt] n extrato (Pt: -cto), excerto.

**excess** [ɪk'sɛs] n excesso; (COMM) excedente m; ~ **baggage** n excesso de bagagem; ~ **fare** n sobretaxa de excesso; ~**ive** adj excessivo.

**exchange** [ɪks'tʃeɪndʒ] n permuta, câmbio; (of goods, of ideas) troca; (also: **telephone** ~) centro telefônico // vt trocar, permutar.

**exchequer** [ɪks'tʃɛkə*] n Ministério da Fazenda.

**excise** ['ɛksaɪz] n imposto de consumo // vt [ɛk'saɪz] cortar (fora).

**excite** [ɪk'saɪt] vt (stimulate) excitar; (awaken desire) excitar, entusiasmar; **to get** ~**d** entusiasmar-se; ~**ment** n excitação f; (anticipation) ilusão f; (agitation) agitação f; **exciting** adj excitante, emocionante.

**exclaim** [ɪk'skleɪm] vi exclamar; **exclamation** [ɛksklə'meɪʃən] n exclamação f; **exclamation mark** n ponto de exclamação.

**exclude** [ɪk'skluːd] vt excluir; (except) excetuar (Pt: -pt-); **exclusion** [ɪk'skluːʒən] n exclusão f.

**exclusive** [ɪk'skluːsɪv] adj exclusivo; (club, district) privativo; ~ **of tax** sem se incluir os impostos; ~**ly** adv unicamente.

**excommunicate** [ɛkskə'mjuːnɪkeɪt] vt excomungar.

**excrement** ['ɛkskrəmənt] n excremento.

**excrete** [ɪk'skriːt] vi excretar.

**excruciating** [ɪk'skruːʃɪeɪtɪŋ] adj (ex)cruciante, torturante.

**excursion** [ɪk'skəːʃən] n excursão f.

**excusable** [ɪk'skjuːzəbl] adj perdoável, excusável.

**excuse** [ɪk'skjuːs] n desculpa, escusa; (evasion) pretexto // vt [ɪk'skjuːz] desculpar, perdoar; **to** ~ **sb from doing sth** dispensar alguém de fazer algo; ~ **me!** desculpe!, perdão!, (com) licença; **if you will** ~ **me** com a sua licença.

**execute** ['ɛksɪkjuːt] vt (plan) realizar; (order) cumprir; (person) executar; **execution** n realização f; execução f; **executioner** n verdugo, carrasco.

**executive** [ɪg'zɛkjutɪv] n (COMM, POL) executivo // adj executivo.

**executor** [ɪg'zɛkjutə*] n executor m; (JUR) testamenteiro.

**exemplary** [ɪg'zɛmplərɪ] adj exemplar.

**exemplify** [ɪg'zɛmplɪfaɪ] vt exemplificar.

**exempt** [ɪg'zɛmpt] adj: ~ **from** isento de // vt: **to** ~ **sb from** dispensar or isentar alguém de; ~**ion** [ɪg'zɛmpfən] n isenção f; dispensa; (immunity) imunidade f.

**exercise** ['ɛksəsaɪz] n exercício m; (right) valer-se de; (dog) levar para passear // vi fazer exercício; ~ **book** n caderno.

**exert** [ɪg'zəːt] vt exercer; **to** ~ **o.s.** esforçar-se, empenhar-se; (overdo things) trabalhar demasiado; ~**ion** n esforço.

**exhaust** [ɪg'zɔːst] n (pipe) escape m, exaustor m; (fumes) escapamento (de gás) // vt esgotar; ~**ion** [ɪg'zɔːstʃən] n exaustão f; **nervous** ~ esgotamento nervoso; ~**ive** adj exaustivo.

**exhibit** [ɪg'zɪbɪt] n (ART) obra exposta; (LAW) objeto (Pt: -ct-) exposto // vt (show) manifestar; (emotion) demonstrar, acusar; (film) apresentar; (paintings) expor; ~**ion** [ɛksɪ'bɪʃən] n exposição f; ~**ionist** [ɛksɪ'bɪʃənɪst] n exibicionista m/f.

**exhilarating** [ɪg'zɪləreɪtɪŋ] adj estimulante, tônico.

**exhort** [ɪg'zɔːt] vt exortar.

**exile** ['ɛksaɪl] n exílio; (person) exilado // vt desterrar, exilar.

**exist** [ɪg'zɪst] vi existir; (live) viver; ~**ence** n existência; (life) vida; ~**ing** adj existente, atual (Pt: -ct-).

**exit** ['ɛksɪt] n saída.

**exonerate** [ɪg'zɒnəreɪt] vt: to ~ from exonerar de.

**exorcize** ['ɛksɔːsaɪz] vt exorcizar.

**exotic** [ɪg'zɒtɪk] adj exótico.

**expand** [ɪk'spænd] vt (widen) ampliar; (number) aumentar // vi (trade, gas, etc) expandir-se; (metal) dilatar-se.

**expanse** [ɪk'spæns] n extensão f; (of wings) envergadura.

**expansion** [ɪk'spænʃən] n (of town) desenvolvimento; (of trade) expansão f.

**expatriate** [ɛks'pætrɪət] n expatriado.

**expect** [ɪk'spɛkt] vt (anticipate) esperar; (count on) contar com; (suppose) supor // vi: to be ~ing estar grávida; ~ant mother n (mulher f) grávida; ~ation [ɛkspɛk'teɪʃən] n esperança, expectativa.

**expedience** [ɛk'spiːdɪəns], **expediency** [ɛk'spiːdɪənsɪ] n conveniência; **expedient** adj conveniente, oportuno // n expediente m, recurso.

**expedition** [ɛkspə'dɪʃən] n expedição f.

**expel** [ɪk'spɛl] vt expelir; (SCOL) expulsar.

**expend** [ɪk'spɛnd] vt gastar; (use up) consumir; ~able adj prescindível; ~iture n gasto, despesa.

**expense** [ɪk'spɛns] n gasto, despesa; (high cost) custo; ~s npl (COMM) gastos mpl; at the ~ of à custa de; ~ account n relatório de despesas.

**expensive** [ɪk'spɛnsɪv] adj caro, custoso.

**experience** [ɪk'spɪərɪəns] n experiência // vt experimentar; (suffer) sofrer; ~d adj experimentado, experiente.

**experiment** [ɪk'spɛrɪmənt] n experimento // vi fazer experimentos; ~al [-'mɛntl] adj experimental.

**expert** ['ɛkspɜːt] adj hábil, perito // n perito; (specialist) especialista m/f; ~ise [-'tiːz] n perícia.

**expire** [ɪk'spaɪə*] vi (gen) expirar; (end) terminar; (run out) acabar; **expiry** n expiração f; termo, acabamento.

**explain** [ɪk'spleɪn] vt explicar; (clarify) esclarecer; (demonstrate) expor; **explanation** [ɛksplə'neɪʃən] n explicação f; **explanatory** [ɪk'splænətrɪ] adj explicativo.

**explicit** [ɪk'splɪsɪt] adj explícito.

**explode** [ɪk'spləud] vi estourar, explodir; (with anger) rebentar // vt detonar, fazer explodir.

**exploit** ['ɛksplɔɪt] n façanha // vt [ɪk'splɔɪt] explorar; ~ation [-'teɪʃən] n exploração f.

**exploration** [ɛksplɔ'reɪʃən] n exploração f; **exploratory** [ɪk'splɔrətrɪ] adj (fig: talks) exploratório, de pesquisa.

**explore** [ɪk'splɔː*] vt explorar; (fig) examinar, pesquisar; **explorer** n explorador(a) m/f.

**explosion** [ɪk'spləuʒən] n explosão f; **explosive** [-sɪv] adj, n explosivo.

**exponent** [ɪk'spəunənt] n representante m/f, expoente m/f.

**export** [ɛk'spɔːt] vt exportar // n ['ɛkspɔːt] exportação f // cmp de exportação; ~ation [-'teɪʃən] n exportação f; ~er n exportador(a) m/f.

**expose** [ɪk'spəuz] vt expor; (unmask) revelar; ~d adj exposto; (position) desabrigado.

**exposure** [ɪk'spəuʒə*] n exposição f; (PHOT) revelação f; (: shot) fotografia; **to die from** ~ (MED) morrer de frio; ~ **meter** n fotômetro.

**expound** [ɪk'spaund] vt expor, explicar.

**express** [ɪk'sprɛs] adj (definite) expresso, explícito; (letter etc) urgente // n (train) rápido // adv (send) por via urgente or expressa // vt exprimir; (squeeze) espremer;

~sion [ɪk'spreʃən] n expressão f; ~ive adj expressivo; ~ly adv expressamente; ~way n auto-estrada.

expulsion [ɪk'spʌlʃən] n expulsão f.

exquisite [ɛk'skwɪzɪt] adj (dress) bonito, refinado.

extend [ɪk'stɛnd] vt (visit, street) prolongar; (building) aumentar; (offer) oferecer // vi (land) estender-se.

extension [ɪk'stɛnʃən] n extensão f; (building) acréscimo, expansão f; (TEL: line) linha derivada; (: telephone) extensão f; (of deadline) prolongamento, prorrogação f.

extensive [ɪk'stɛnsɪv] adj (gen) extenso; (broad) vasto, amplo; (frequent) geral, comum; he's travelled ~ly tem viajado por muitos países.

extent [ɪk'stɛnt] n (breadth) extensão f; (scope) alcance m; to some ~ até certo ponto; to the ~ of... a ponto de...; to such an ~ that... a tal ponto que...; to what ~? até que ponto?

exterior [ɛk'stɪərɪə*] adj exterior, externo // n exterior m; (appearance) aspecto.

exterminate [ɪk'stɜːmɪneɪt] vt exterminar; extermination [-'neɪʃən] n extermínio.

external [ɪk'stɜːnl] adj externo, exterior; ~ly adv por fora.

extinct [ɪk'stɪŋkt] adj extinto; ~ion [ɪk'stɪŋkʃən] n extinção f.

extinguish [ɪk'stɪŋgwɪʃ] vt extinguir; ~er n extintor m.

extort [ɪk'stɔːt] vt arrancar à força, extorquir; ~ion [ɪk'stɔːʃən] n extorsão f; ~ionate [ɪk'stɔːʃnət] adj extorsivo, excessivo.

extra ['ɛkstrə] adj adicional; (excessive) de mais, extra; (bonus: payment) extraordinário // adv (in addition) adicionalmente // n (addition) extra m, suplemento;

(THEATRE) extra m/f; (newspaper) edição f extra.

extra... ['ɛkstrə] pref extra...

extract [ɪk'strækt] vt tirar, extrair; (confession) arrancar, obter // n ['ɛkstrækt] extrato (Pt: -ct-).

extradite ['ɛkstrədaɪt] vt (from country) conceder a extradição de; (to country) obter a extradição de; extradition [-'dɪʃən] n extradição f.

extramarital [ɛkstrə'mærɪtl] adj extramatrimonial.

extramural [ɛkstrə'mjuərl] adj externo; (course) de extensão universitária.

extraordinary [ɪk'strɔːdnrɪ] adj extraordinário; (odd) raro.

extravagant [ɪk'strævəgənt] adj (lavish) pródigo, (wasteful) gastador(a), esbanjador(a); (price) exorbitante; (praise) excessivo; (odd) extravagante.

extreme [ɪk'striːm] adj (poverty etc) extremo; (case) excessivo // n extremidade f; ~ly adv muito, extremamente; extremist adj, n extremista m/f.

extremity [ɪk'strɛmətɪ] n extremidade f, ponta; (need) apuro, necessidade f.

extricate ['ɛkstrɪkeɪt] vt livrar.

extrovert ['ɛkstrəvəːt] n extrovertido.

exuberant [ɪg'zjuːbərnt] adj (person) eufórico; (style) exuberante.

exude [ɪg'zjuːd] vt ressumar.

exult [ɪg'zʌlt] vi regozijar-se.

eye [aɪ] n olho // vt olhar, observar; to keep an ~ on vigiar, ficar de olho em; ~ball n globo ocular; ~bath n recipiente m para lavar o olho; ~brow n sobrancelha; ~brow pencil n lápis m de sobrancelha; ~catching adj de chamar a atenção; ~drops npl gotas fpl para os olhos; ~glasses npl (US) óculos mpl; ~lash n cílio; ~lid n pálpebra; ~-opener n revelação f, grande surpresa; ~**shadow** n sombra de olhos; ~**sight** n vista, visão f; ~**sore** n monstruosidade f; ~**wash** n (fig) disparates mpl, maluquices fpl; ~**witness** n testemunha f ocular.

**eyrie** ['ɪərɪ] n ninho de ave de rapina.

# F

**F.** abbr of **Fahrenheit.**

**fable** ['feɪbl] n fábula.

**fabric** ['fæbrɪk] n tecido, pano.

**fabrication** [fæbrɪ'keɪʃən] n maquinação f.

**fabulous** ['fæbjuləs] adj fabuloso.

**façade** [fə'sɑːd] n fachada.

**face** [feɪs] n (ANAT) cara, rosto; (of clock) mostrador m; (side, surface) superfície f // vt (person) encarar; (building) dar para, ter frente para; **to lose** ~ perder o prestígio; **in the** ~ **of** it a julgar pelas aparências, à primeira vista; ~ **to** ~ cara a cara; **to** ~ **up to** vt fus enfrentar; ~ **cloth** n toalha de rosto; ~ **cream** n creme m facial; ~ **lift** n operação f plástica; ~ **powder** n pó m de arroz; ~**saving** adj para salvar as aparências.

**facet** ['fæsɪt] n faceta.

**facetious** [fə'siːʃəs] adj engraçado, faceto.

**face value** ['feɪs'væljuː] n (of stamp) valor m nominal; **to take sth at** ~ (fig) aceitar as aparências de algo.

**facial** ['feɪʃəl] adj facial.

**facile** ['fæsaɪl] adj fácil, fluente.

**facilitate** [fə'sɪlɪteɪt] vt facilitar.

**facilities** [fə'sɪlɪtɪz] npl facilidades fpl, instalações fpl.

**facing** ['feɪsɪŋ] prep em face de // adj em frente, defronte.

**fact** [fækt] n fato (Pt: -ct-); **in** ~ realmente, na verdade.

**faction** ['fækʃən] n facção f.

**factor** ['fæktə*] n fator (Pt: -ct-) m.

**factory** ['fæktərɪ] n fábrica.

**factual** ['fæktjuəl] adj real, fatual (Pt: -ct-).

**faculty** ['fækəltɪ] n faculdade f; (US: teaching staff) corpo docente.

**fade** [feɪd] vi desbotar; (sound, hope) desvanecer-se; (light) apagar-se; (flower) murchar.

**fag** [fæg] n (col: cigarette) cigarro; ~ **end** n ponta de cigarro, guimba; ~ **ged out** adj (col) estafado.

**fail** [feɪl] vt (candidate) faltar a; (exam) não passar, ser reprovado // vi acabar-se; (engine) falhar; (voice) falhar; (patient) enfraquecer-se; **to** ~ **to do sth** (neglect) deixar de fazer algo; (be unable) não poder fazer algo; **without** ~ sem falta; ~**ing** n defeito // prep na/à falta de; ~**ure** ['feɪljə*] n fracasso; (person) fracassado; (mechanical etc) falha.

**faint** [feɪnt] adj fraco, débil; (recollection) vago; (mark) indistinto // n desmaio // vi desmaiar; **to feel** ~ sentir que vai desmaiar; ~**-hearted** adj pusilânime; ~**ly** adv debilmente, vagamente; ~**ness** n debilidade f.

**fair** [fɛə*] adj justo; (colour) louro, claro; (weather) bom; (good enough) suficiente; (sizeable) considerável // adv (play) limpo // n feira; (funfair) parque m de diversões; ~**ly** adv (justly) com justiça; (equally) com imparcialidade; (quite) bastante; ~**ness** n justiça; (impartiality) imparcialidade f.

**fairy** ['fɛərɪ] n fada; ~ **tale** n conto de fadas.

**faith** [feɪθ] n fé f; (trust) confiança; (sect) religião f; ~**ful** adj fiel; ~**fully** adv fielmente; **yours** ~**fully** De V. Sa, atenciosamente.

**fake** [feɪk] n (painting etc) falsificação f; (person) impostor(a) *m/f* // *adj* falso // *vt* fingir; (*painting etc*) falsificar; **his illness is a** ~ sua doença é fingimento *or* um embuste.

**falcon** ['fɔːlkən] *n* falcão *m*.

**fall** [fɔːl] *n* queda; (*US: autumn*) outono // *vi, pt* **fell**, *pp* **fallen** ['fɔːlən] cair; (*price*) baixar; ~**s** *npl* (*waterfall*) cascata, queda d'água; **to** ~ **flat** *vi* (*on one's face*) cair de cara no chão; (*plan*) falhar; **to** ~ **back** *vi* retroceder; **to** ~ **back on** *vt fus* (*remedy etc*) recorrer a; **to** ~ **backwards** *vi* cair de costas; **to** ~ **behind** *vi* ficar para trás; **to** ~ **down** *vi* (*person*); (*building*) desabar; (*hopes*) cair por terra; **to** ~ **for** *vt fus* (*trick*) deixar-se enganar por; (*person*) enamorar-se por; **to** ~ **in** *vi* (*roof*) ruir; (*MIL*) alinhar-se; **to** ~ **off** *vi* cair; (*diminish*) declinar, diminuir; **to** ~ **out** *vi* (*friends etc*) brigar; (*MIL*) sair da fila; **to** ~ **through** *vi* (*plan, project*) falhar, fracassar.

**fallacy** ['fæləsɪ] *n* (*error*) erro; (*lie*) mentira, falácia.

**fallible** ['fæləbl] *adj* falível.

**fallout** ['fɔːlaut] *n* chuva radioativa (*Pt:* -ct-); ~ **shelter** *n* refúgio contra chuva radioa(c)tiva.

**false** [fɔːls] *adj* (*gen*) falso; (*hair, teeth etc*) postiço; (*disloyal*) desleal, traidor(a); (*faiseness*) falsidade *f*; ~**hood** *n* (*lie*) mentira; (*faiseness*) falsidade *f*; ~**ly** *adv* (*accuse*) com falsidade; ~ **teeth** *npl* dentadura postiça *sg*.

**falter** ['fɔːltə*] *vi* vacilar.

**fame** [feɪm] *n* fama.

**familiar** [fə'mɪlɪə*] *adj* familiar; (*well-known*) conhecido; (*tone*) íntimo; **to be** ~ **with** (*subject*) estar familiarizado com; ~**ity** [fəmɪlɪ'ærɪtɪ] *n* familiaridade *f*; ~**ize** [fə'mɪlɪəraɪz] *vr:* **to** ~**ize o.s. with** familiarizar-se.

**family** ['fæmɪlɪ] *n* família; ~ **business** *n* negócio familiar; ~ **doctor** *n* médico da família.

**famine** ['fæmɪn] *n* fome *f*.

**famished** ['fæmɪʃt] *adj* faminto.

**famous** ['feɪməs] *adj* famoso, célebre; ~**ly** *adv* (*get on*) maravilhosamente.

**fan** [fæn] *n* leque *m*, (*Pt*) abano; (*ELEC*) ventilador *m*; (*person*) fã *m/f* // *vt* abanar; (*fire, quarrel*) atiçar; **to** ~ **out** *vi* espalhar-se.

**fanatic** [fə'nætɪk] *n* fanático/a; ~**al** *adj* fanático.

**fan belt** ['fænbelt] *n* corrente *f* de ventilador.

**fanciful** ['fænsɪful] *adj* (*gen*) fantástico; (*imaginary*) imaginário.

**fancy** ['fænsɪ] *n* (*whim*) capricho; (*taste*) inclinação *f*, gosto; (*imagination*) imaginação *f* // *adj* (*decorative*) ornamental; (*luxury*) luxuoso; (*as decoration*) como decoração // *vt* (*feel like, want*) desejar, querer; (*imagine*) imaginar; (*think*) crer; **to take a** ~ **to** tomar gosto por; **it took** *or* **caught my** ~ gostei disso; **to** ~ **that...** imaginar que...; **he fancies her** ele gosta dela; ~ **dress** *n* fantasia; ~**-dress ball** *n* baile *m* à fantasia.

**fang** [fæŋ] *n* presa, dente *m* canino.

**fantastic** [fæn'tæstɪk] *adj* fantástico.

**fantasy** ['fæntəzɪ] *n* fantasia.

**far** [fɑː*] *adj* (*distant*) distante, longe // *adv* (*also* ~ **away,** ~ **off**) longe; ~ **better** muito melhor; ~ **from** longe de; **by** ~ de longe; **go as** ~ **as the farm** vá até a fazenda; **as** ~ **as I know** que eu saiba; **how** ~? até onde?; (*fig*) até que ponto?; **the F** ~ **East** O Extremo Oriente; ~**away** *adj* remoto, distante.

**farce** [fɑːs] *n* farsa; **farcical** *adj* farsante.

**fare** [fɛə*] *n* (*on trains, buses*) preço (da passagem); (*in taxi: cost*) tarifa; (*: passenger*) passageiro; (*food*) comida.

**farewell** [fɛə'wel] *excl, n* adeus *m*.

**farm** [fɑːm] *n* fazenda, (*Pt*) quinta // *vt* cultivar; ~**er** *n* fazendeiro, agricultor *m*; ~**hand** *n* lavrador *m*, trabalhador *m* rural; ~**house** *n* casa da fazenda; ~**ing** *n* (*gen*) agricultura; (*tilling*) cultura; ~**land** *n* terra de cultivo; ~**worker** *n* = ~**hand**; ~**yard** *n* curral *m*.

**far-sighted** ['fɑ:'saitid] *adj* hipermetrope, perspicaz.

**fart** [fɑ:t] (*col!*) *n* peido *m* // *vi* soltar um peido.

**farther** ['fɑ:ðə*] *adv* mais distante, mais afastado.

**farthest** ['fɑ:ðist] *superlative of* **far**.

**fascinate** ['fæsineit] *vt* fascinar; **fascination** [-'neiʃən] *n* fascinação *f*.

**fascism** ['fæʃizəm] *n* fascismo; **fascist** [-ist] *adj*, *n* fascista *m/f*.

**fashion** ['fæʃən] *n* moda; (*manner*) maneira // *vt* amoldar; **in** ~ na moda; **out of** ~ fora da moda; ~**able** *adj* na moda, elegante; ~**show** *n* desfile *m* de modas.

**fast** [fɑ:st] *adj* rápido; (*dye*, *colour*) firme, permanente; (*clock*): **to be** ~ estar adiantado; ~ **asleep** profundamente adormecido // *adv* rapidamente, depressa; (*stuck*, *held*) firmemente // *n* jejum *m* // *vi* jejuar.

**fasten** ['fɑ:sn] *vt* segurar, sujeitar; (*coat*, *belt*) apertar, atar // *vi* amarrar, fixar-se; ~**er**, ~**ing** *n* (*gen*) presilha, fecho; (*of door etc*) fechadura; **zip** ~**er** *n* zíper *m*; fecho ecler.

**fastidious** [fæs'tidiəs] *adj* (*fussy*) delicado; (*demanding*) exigente.

**fat** [fæt] *adj* gordo; (*meat*) com muita gordura; (*greasy*) gorduroso // *n* (*on person*) gordura; (*lard*) banha, gordura.

**fatal** ['feitl] *adj* (*gen*) fatal; (*injury*) mortal; (*consequence*) funesto; ~**ism** *n* fatalismo; ~**ity** [fə'tæliti] *n* (*road death etc*) vítima *m/f*; ~**ly** *adv*: ~**ly injured** mortalmente ferido.

**fate** [feit] *n* destino; (*of person*) sorte *f*; ~**ful** *adj* fatídico.

**father** ['fɑ:ðə*] *n* pai *m*; ~**hood** *n* paternidade *f*; ~**-in-law** *n* sogro; ~**ly** *adj* paternal.

**fathom** ['fæðəm] *n* braça // *vt* (*NAUT*) sondar; (*unravel*) penetrar, deslindar; (*understand*) compreender.

**fatigue** [fə'ti:g] *n* fatiga, cansaço.

**fatten** ['fætn] *vt/i* engordar.

**fatty** ['fæti] *adj* (*food*) gorduroso // *n* (*fam*) gorducho/a.

**faucet** ['fɔ:sit] *n* (*US*) torneira.

**fault** [fɔ:lt] *n* (*error*) erro, falta; (*blame*) culpa; (*defect*: *in character*) defeito; (*in manufacture*) imperfeição *f*; (*GEO*) falha // *vt* criticar; **it's my** ~ é minha culpa; **to find** ~ **with** criticar, queixar-se de; **at** ~ culpado; ~**less** *adj* (*action*) impecável; (*person*) irrepreensível; ~**y** *adj* imperfeito, defeituoso.

**fauna** ['fɔ:nə] *n* fauna.

**faux pas** ['fəu'pɑ:] *n* passo em falso; (*gaffe*) gafe *f*.

**favour, favor** (*US*) ['feivə*] *n* favor *m*; (*support*) apoio; (*approval*) aprovação *f* // *vt* (*proposition*) favorecer, aprovar; (*person etc*) favorecer; (*assist*) auxiliar; **to ask a** ~ **of** pedir um favor a; **to do sb a** ~ fazer favor a alguém; **to find** ~ **with** cair nas boas graças de; **in** ~ **of** em favor de; ~**able** *adj* favorável; ~**ite** [-rit] *adj*, *n* favorito; ~**itism** *n* favoritismo.

**fawn** [fɔ:n] *n* cervo novo, cervato // *adj* (*also*: ~**-coloured**) castanho-claro.

**fear** [fiə*] *n* medo, temor *m* // *vt* ter medo de, temer; **for** ~ **of** com medo de; ~**ful** *adj* medonho, temível; (*cowardly*) medroso; (*awful*) terrível; ~**less** *adj* sem medo, intrépido; (*bold*) audaz.

**feasible** ['fi:zəbl] *adj* praticável, factível.

**feast** [fi:st] *n* banquete *m*; (*REL*: *also*:

~ **day** festa // vt/i banquetear-se.

**feat** [fi:t] n façanha, feito.

**feather** ['feðə*] n pena; ~**-weight** n (BOXING) peso-pena m.

**feature** ['fi:tʃə*] n (gen) característica; (ANAT) feição, traço; (article) artigo // vt (subj: film) apresentar // vi figurar; ~**s** npl (of face) feições fpl; ~ **film** n filme m principal.

**February** ['februəri] n fevereiro.

**fed** [fed] pt, pp of **feed.**

**federal** ['fedərəl] adj federal; **federation** [-'reiʃən] n federação f.

**fed-up** ['fed∧p] adj: **to be** ~ estar farto or de saco cheio.

**fee** [fi:] n taxa; (Pt) propina; (school) matrícula; (of club) jóia, quota.

**feeble** ['fi:bl] adj fraco, débil; ~**-minded** adj imbecil.

**feed** [fi:d] n (gen) comida; (of baby) alimento infantil; (of animal) ração f // vt, pp **fed** (gen) alimentar; (baby: breastfeed) amamentar; (animal) dar de comer a; (data, information): **to** ~ **into** suprir, subministrar; **to** ~ **on** vt fus alimentar-se de; ~**ing bottle** n mamadeira.

**feel** [fi:l] n (sensation) sensação f; (sense of touch) tato (Pt: -ct-) // vt, pp **felt** tocar, apalpar; (cold, pain etc) sentir; (think, believe) crer, acreditar; **to** ~ **hungry/cold** ter fome/frio, estar com fome/frio; **to** ~ **lonely/better** sentir-se só/melhor; **it** ~**s soft** é macio; **to** ~ **like** (want) querer; **to** ~ **about** or **around** apalpar, tatear (Pt: -ct-); ~**er** n (of insect) antena; **to put out** ~**ers** (fig) sondar opiniões; ~**ing** n (gen) sensação f; (foreboding) pressentimento; (opinion) opinião f; (emotion) sentimento.

**feet** [fi:t] pl of **foot.**

**feign** [fein] vt fingir.

**feline** ['fi:lain] adj felino.

**fell** [fel] pt of **fall** // vt (tree) lançar por terra, derrubar.

**fellow** ['feləu] n (gen) camarada m/f, (fam) cara; (Pt) tipo; (of learned society) sócio/a; ~ **students** colegas m/fpl de curso; ~ **citizen** n concidadão/dã m/f; ~ **countryman** n compatriota m/f; ~ **men** npl semelhantes mpl; ~**-ship** n amizade f; (grant) bolsa de estudo.

**felony** ['feləni] n crime m.

**felt** [felt] pt, pp of **feel** // n feltro; ~**-tip pen** n hidrocor m.

**female** ['fi:meil] n (woman) mulher f; (ZOOL) fêmea // adj feminino.

**feminine** ['feminin] adj feminino.

**feminist** ['feminist] n feminista.

**fence** [fens] n cerca // vt (also: ~ **in**) cercar // vi esgrimir; **fencing** n (sport) esgrima.

**fend** [fend] vi: **to** ~ **for o.s.** defender-se sozinho.

**fender** ['fendə*] n guarda-fogo m; (US: AUT) pára-choque m; (: RAIL) limpa-trilhos m inv.

**ferment** [fə'ment] vi fermentar // n ['fə:ment] (fig) agitação f; ~**ation** [-'teiʃən] n fermentação f.

**fern** [fə:n] n samambaia; (Pt) feto.

**ferocious** [fə'rəuʃəs] adj feroz; **ferocity** [-'rɔsiti] n ferocidade f.

**ferret** ['ferit] n furão m // vt: **to** ~ **out** descobrir, desentocar.

**ferry** ['feri] n (small) barco de travessia), balsa // vt transportar em barco.

**fertile** ['fə:tail] adj fértil; (BIOL) fecundo; **fertility** [fə'tiliti] n fertilidade f, fecundidade f; **fertilize** ['fə:tilaiz] vt fertilizar, fecundar; (AGR) adubar; **fertilizer** n adubo.

**fervent** ['fə:vənt] adj ardente, apaixonado.

**fester** ['festə*] vi inflamar-se.

**festival** ['festivəl] n (REL) festa; (ART, MUS) festival m.

**festive** ['festiv] adj festivo; **the** ~ **season** (Christmas) a época do Natal.

**festivities** [fes'tivitiz] npl festas fpl, festividades fpl.

**fetch** [fɛtʃ] vt ir buscar, trazer; (sell for) atingir.

**fetching** ['fɛtʃɪŋ] adj atraente.

**fête** [feit] n festa.

**fetish** ['fɛtɪʃ] n fetiche m.

**fetters** ['fɛtəz] npl grilhões mpl.

**feud** [fju:d] n (hostility) inimizade f; (quarrel) disputa, rixa.

**feudal** ['fju:dl] adj feudal; ~ism n feudalismo.

**fever** ['fi:və*] n febre f; ~ish adj febril.

**few** [fju:] adj (not many) poucos; (some) alguns; **a** ~ adj uns poucos // pron alguns; ~er adj menos; ~est adj os/as menos.

**fiancé** [fɪ'ɑːŋseɪ] n noivo; ~e n noiva.

**fiasco** [fɪ'æskəu] n fiasco.

**fibre, fiber** (US) ['faɪbə*] n fibra; ~-glass n fibra de vidro.

**fickle** ['fɪkl] adj inconstante.

**fiction** ['fɪkʃən] n (gen) ficção f; ~al adj de ficção; **fictitious** [fɪk'tɪʃəs] adj fictício.

**fiddle** ['fɪdl] n (MUS) violino; (cheating) fraude f, embuste m; (swindle) trapaça // vt (accounts) falsificar; **to ~ with** vt fus brincar com; **fiddler** n violinista m/f.

**fidelity** [fɪ'dɛlɪtɪ] n fidelidade f.

**fidget** ['fɪdʒɪt] vi estar irrequieto; ~y adj inquieto, nervoso.

**field** [fiːld] n (gen, ELEC) campo; (fig) esfera, especialidade f; (competitors) competidores mpl; (entrants) concorrentes mpl; ~ **glasses** npl binóculo msg; ~ **marshal** n marechal-de-campo m; ~work n trabalho de campo.

**fiend** [fiːnd] n demônio; ~ish adj diabólico.

**fierce** [fɪəs] adj feroz; (wind, attack) violento; (heat) intenso; (fighting, enemy) feroz, violento.

**fiery** ['faɪərɪ] adj (burning) ardente; (temperament) apaixonado.

**fifteen** [fɪf'tiːn] num quinze.

**fifth** [fɪfθ] adj, n quinto.

**fiftieth** ['fɪftɪɪθ] adj quinquagésimo.

**fifty** ['fɪftɪ] num cinqüenta.

**fig** [fɪg] n figo.

**fight** [faɪt] n (gen) briga; (MIL) combate m; (struggle) luta // (vb: pt, pp fought) vt lutar contra; (cancer, alcoholism) combater // vi brigar, lutar; ~er n combatente m/f; (fig) lutador(a) m/f; (plane) caça; ~ing n (gen) a luta; (battle) batalha.

**figment** ['fɪgmənt] n: **a ~ of the imagination** um produto da imaginação.

**figurative** ['fɪgjurətɪv] adj figurado.

**figure** ['fɪgə*] n (DRAWING, MATH) figura, desenho; (number, cipher) número, cifra; (body, outline) talhe m, forma; (of woman) corpo // vt (esp US) imaginar // vi (appear) figurar; **to ~ out** vt (understand) compreender; ~head n (NAUT) carranca de proa; (fig) chefe m nominal; ~ **skating** n movimentos mpl de patinação.

**file** [faɪl] n (tool) lixa; (dossier) fichário, arquivo; (folder) pasta de papéis; (row) fila, coluna // vt lixar; (papers) arquivar; (LAW: claim) apresentar, dar entrada em; (store) arquivar; **to ~ in/out** vi entrar/sair em fila; **to ~ past** vt fus desfilar em frente de/ante; **filing** n arquivamento; **filing cabinet** n fichário, arquivo.

**fill** [fɪl] vt encher // n: **to eat one's** ~ encher-se, fartar-se de comer; **to** ~ **in** vt preencher; **to** ~ **up** vt encher (até a borda) // vi (AUT) abastecer.

**fillet** ['fɪlɪt] n filete m, filé m.

**filling** ['fɪlɪŋ] n (CULIN) recheio; (for tooth) obturação f, chumbo; ~ **station** n posto de gasolina.

**film** [fɪlm] n filme m, película // vt (scene) rodar // vi filmar; ~ **star** n astro, estrela de cinema.

**filter** ['fɪltə*] n filtro // vt filtrar; ~ **tip** n piteira // adj com filtro.

**filth** [fɪlθ] n sujeira; ~**y** adj sujo; (language) indecente, obsceno.

**fin** [fɪn] n (gen) barbatana.

**final** ['faɪnl] adj (last) final, último; (definitive) definitivo // n (SPORT) final f; ~**s** npl (SCOL) exames mpl finais.

**finale** [fɪ'nɑːlɪ] n final m.

**final:** ~**ist** n (SPORT) finalista m/f; ~**ize** vt concluir, completar; ~**ly** adv (lastly) finalmente, por fim; (eventually) por fim; (irrevocably) definitivamente.

**finance** [faɪ'næns] n (money) fundos mpl; ~**s** npl finanças fpl // vt financiar; **financial** [-'nænʃəl] adj financeiro; (economic) econômico; **financier** n (gen) financista m/f; (investor) investidor/a) m/f.

**find** [faɪnd], pt, pp **found** vt (gen) encontrar, achar; (come upon) descobrir // n achado, descoberta; **to** ~ **sb guilty** (LAW) declarar alguém culpado; **to** ~ **out** vt verificar; (truth, secret) descobrir; ~**ings** npl (LAW) veredito sg, decisão fsg; (of report) recomendações fpl.

**fine** [faɪn] adj (delicate) fino; (good) bom/boa; (small, thin) delgado; (beautiful) bonito // adv (well) bem // n (LAW) multa // vt (LAW) multar; **to be** ~ (weather) fazer bom tempo; ~ **arts** npl belas artes fpl.

**finery** ['faɪnərɪ] n enfeites mpl.

**finesse** [fɪ'nɛs] n sutileza (Pt: -bt-).

**finger** ['fɪŋgə*] n dedo // vt (touch) manusear; (MUS) dedilhar; **little/index** ~ dedo mínimo/ indicador; ~**nail** n unha; ~**print** n impressão f digital; ~**tip** n ponta do dedo.

**finicky** ['fɪnɪkɪ] adj (fussy) afetado (Pt: -ct-), meticuloso.

**finish** ['fɪnɪʃ] n (end) fim m; (goal) remate m; (polish etc) polimento // vt/i terminar, concluir; ~ **off** vt acabar; (kill) liquidar; **to** ~ **third** chegar no terceiro lugar; ~**ing line** n linha de chegada, meta.

**finite** ['faɪnaɪt] adj finito.

**Finland** ['fɪnlənd] n Finlândia.

**Finn** [fɪn] n finlandês/esa m/f; ~**ish** adj finlandês/esa // n (LING) finlandês m.

**fiord** [fjɔːd] n fiorde m.

**fir** [fɜː*] n abeto.

**fire** ['faɪə*] n (gen) fogo; (accidental) incêndio // vt (gun) disparar; (set fire to) incendiar; (excite) exaltar; (interest) despertar; (dismiss) despedir // vi incendiar-se; **on** ~ em chamas; ~ **alarm** n alarme m de incêndio; ~**arm** n arma de fogo; ~ **brigade** n (corpo de) bombeiros mpl; ~ **engine** n carro de bombeiro; ~ **escape** n escada de incêndio; ~ **extinguisher** n extintor m de incêndio; ~**man** n bombeiro; ~**place** n lareira; ~**proof** adj à prova de fogo; ~**side** n lugar m junto à lareira; ~ **station** n quartel m do corpo de bombeiros; ~**wood** n lenha; ~**works** npl fogos mpl de artifício.

**firing** ['faɪərɪŋ] n (MIL) tiros mpl, tiroteio; ~ **squad** n pelotão m de fuzilamento.

**firm** [fɜːm] adj firme // n firma; ~**ly** adv firmemente; ~**ness** n firmeza.

**first** [fɜːst] adj primeiro // adv (before others) primeiro; (when listing reasons etc) em primeiro lugar // n (person: in race) primeiro/a; (AUT) primeira; **at** ~ a/no princípio; ~ **of all** antes de tudo, antes de mais nada; ~-**aid kit** n estojo de pronto socorro; ~-**class** adj de primeira classe; ~-**hand** adj de primeira mão; ~**ly** adv primeiramente, em primeiro lugar; ~ **name** n primeiro nome m; ~-**rate** adj de primeira categoria.

**fir tree** n abeto.

**fiscal** ['fɪskəl] adj fiscal.

**fish** [fɪʃ] n, pl inv peixe m // vt/i pescar; **to go** ~**ing** ir pescar; ~**erman** n pescador m; ~**ery** n pescaria; ~ **fingers** npl filés mpl de peixe; ~**ing boat** n barco de pesca; ~**ing line** n linha de pesca; ~**ing rod** n vara (de pesca); ~**ing tackle** n apetrecho (de pesca); ~ **market** n mercado de peixe; ~**monger** n peixeiro; ~**monger's (shop)** n peixaria; ~**y** adj (fig) suspeito.

**fission** ['fɪʃən] n fissão f.

**fissure** ['fɪʃə*] n fenda, fissura.

**fist** [fɪst] n punho.

**fit** [fɪt] adj (MED, SPORT) em (boa) forma; (proper) adequado, apropriado // vt (clothes) ficar bem a, assentar a; (try on: clothes) experimentar, provar; (facts) enquadrar-se or condizer com; (accommodate) ajustar, adaptar; (correspond exactly) encaixar em // vi (clothes) servir; (in space, gap) caber; (correspond) encaixar-se // n (MED) ataque m; ~ **to** bom para; ~ **for** adequado para; **this dress is a good** ~ este vestido fica-me bem; **to** ~ **in** vi (gen) encaixar-se; (fig: person) dar-se bem (com todos); **to** ~ **out** (also: ~ **up**) vt equipar; ~**ful** adj espasmódico, intermitente; ~**ment** n móvel m; ~**ness** n (MED) saúde f, boa forma; (of remark) conveniência; ~**ter** n ajustador m, montador m; ~**ting** adj próprio, apropriado // n (of dress) prova; ~**tings** npl instalações fpl, acessórios mpl.

**five** [faɪv] num cinco; **fiver** n (Brit: col) nota de cinco libras.

**fix** [fɪks] vt (secure) fixar, colocar; (arrange) arranjar; (mend) consertar // n: **to be in a** ~ estar em apuros; ~**ed** [fɪkst] adj (prices etc) fixo; ~**ture** ['fɪkstʃə*] n coisa fixa; (furniture) móvel m fixo; (SPORT) desafio, encontro.

**fizz** [fɪz] vi efervescer.

**fizzle** [ˈfɪzl] ~ **out** vi concluir fracamente.

**fizzy** ['fɪzɪ] adj (drink) gasoso; (gen) efervescente.

**fjord** [fjɔːd] = **fiord**.

**flabbergasted** ['flæbəgɑːstɪd] adj pasmado.

**flabby** ['flæbɪ] adj frouxo; (fat) flácido.

**flag** [flæg] n bandeira; (stone) laje f // vi acabar-se, descair; **to** ~ **sb down** fazer sinais a alguém para que pare; ~**pole** n mastro de bandeira.

**flagrant** ['fleɪgrənt] adj flagrante.

**flair** [flɛə*] n aptidão f, inclinação f especial.

**flake** [fleɪk] n (of rust, paint) lasca; (of snow, soap powder) floco // vi (also: ~ **off**) lascar, descamar-se.

**flamboyant** [flæm'bɔɪənt] adj (dress) espalhafatoso; (person) extravagante.

**flame** [fleɪm] n chama.

**flamingo** [fləˈmɪŋgəu] n flamingo.

**flammable** ['flæməbl] adj inflamável.

**flan** [flæn] n torta.

**flank** [flæŋk] n flanco; (of person) lado // vt ladear.

**flannel** ['flænl] n (also: **face** ~) pano; (fabric) flanela; (col) disparate m; ~**s** npl calças fpl de flanela.

**flap** [flæp] n (of pocket) aba, portinhola, lapela; (of envelope) dobra; (of table) aba; (wing movement) o bater das asas // vt (wings) bater // vi (sail, flag) ondular.

**flare** [flɛə*] n fogacho, chama; (MIL) sinal m luminoso; (in skirt etc) folga; **to** ~ **up** vi chamejar; (fig: person) encolerizar-se; (: revolt) irromper.

**flash** [flæʃ] n relâmpago; (also: **news** ~) notícias fpl de última hora; (PHOT) flash m // vt (light, headlights) piscar; (torch) acender // vi brilhar, relampejar; **in a** ~ num instante; **he** ~**ed by** or **past** passou como um raio; ~**back** n flashback m; ~ **bulb** n lâmpada de ash; ~er n (AUT) pisca-pisca, intermitente m.

ashy ['ʃæʃɪ] adj (pej) espalhafatoso.

ask [flɑːsk] n frasco; (also: vacuum ~) garrafa térmica.

at [flæt] adj chato, plano; (smooth) liso; (tyre) vazio; (beer) choco; (MUS) desafinado // n (apartment) apartamento m; (MUS) bemol m; (AUT) pneu m murcho; ~ly adv terminantemente; ~ness n (of land) chateza, lisura; ~ten vt (also: ~ten out) aplanar; (smooth out) alisar; (demolish) derrubar; (col) esmagar.

atter ['flætə*] vt adular, lisonjear; ~er n adulador(a) m/f; ~ing adj sonjeiro; ~y n bajulação f.

atulence ['flætjuləns] n flatulência f.

aunt [flɔːnt] vt ostentar, pavonear.

avour, flavor (US) ['fleɪvə*] n sabor m, gosto // vt condimentar, aromatizar; ~ed with com sabor e; ~ing n condimento.

aw [flɔː] n defeito; ~less adj impecável.

ax [flæks] n linho; ~en adj de cor e linho.

ea [fliː] n pulga; ~pit n (cinema) pulgueiro.

ee [fliː] pt, pp fled [fled] vt fugir e, abandonar // vi desaparecer, fugir.

eece [fliːs] n velo; (wool) lã f // vt (col) pelar, depenar.

eet [fliːt] n (gen, of lorries etc) frota; (of ships) esquadra.

eeting ['fliːtɪŋ] adj fugaz.

emish ['flemɪʃ] adj flamengo.

esh [fleʃ] n carne f; (of fruit) polpa; ~ and blood de carne e osso.

ew [fluː] pt of fly.

ex [fleks] n fio // (of muscles) obrar; ~ibility [-'bɪlɪtɪ] n flexibilidade f; ~ible adj flexível.

ick [flɪk] n pancada leve; (with finger) piparote m; (with whip)

chicotada // vt dar pancada leve em; to ~ through vt fus folhear.

flicker ['flɪkə*] vi (light) tremeluzir; (flame) tremular // n tremulação f.

flier ['flaɪə*] n voador(a) m/f.

flight [flaɪt] n vôo m; (escape) fuga; (also: ~ of steps) lance m; to take ~ fugir, pôr-se em fuga; to put to ~ pôr em fuga; ~ deck n (AVIAT) cabine f do piloto.

flimsy ['flɪmzɪ] adj (thin) delgado, franzino; (weak) débil.

flinch [flɪntʃ] vi acovardar-se.

fling [flɪŋ] pt, pp flung vt lançar.

flint [flɪnt] n pederneira; (in lighter) pedra.

flip [flɪp] vt dar a volta em; (coin) tirar cara ou coroa.

flippant ['flɪpənt] adj petulante, pouco sério.

flirt [flɜːt] vi flertar // n namorador(a) m/f, paquerador(a) m/f; ~ation [-'teɪʃən] n namoro, paquera.

flit [flɪt] vi esvoaçar.

float [fləut] n bóia; (in procession) carro alegórico // vi flutuar; (swimmer) boiar // vt (gen) fazer flutuar; (company) lançar.

flock [flɒk] n (of sheep) rebanho; (of birds) bando; (of people) multidão f.

flog [flɒg] vt açoitar; (col) vender.

flood [flʌd] n cheia, inundação f; (of words, tears etc) torrente m // vt inundar; ~ing n inundação f; ~light n refletor (Pt: -ct-) m, holofote m.

floor [flɔː*] n chão m; (storey) andar m; (of sea) fundo; (dance ~) pista de dança // vt (fig) confundir, pasmar; ground ~ (Brit), first ~ (US) andar térreo; (Pt) rés-do-chão m; first ~ (Brit), second ~ (US) primeiro andar; ~board n tábua de assoalho.

flop [flɒp] n fracasso // vi (fail) fracassar.

floppy ['flɒpɪ] adj frouxo.

**flora** ['flɔ:rə] n flora; **floral** ['flɔ:rl] adj floral.

**florid** ['flɔrɪd] adj (style) florido.

**florist** ['flɔrɪst] n florista m/f; ~'s (shop) n floresta, floricultura.

**flounce** [flauns] n babado, debrum m; to ~ out vi sair indignada.

**flounder** ['flaundə*] vi atrapalhar-se.

**flour** ['flauə*] n farinha.

**flourish** ['flʌrɪʃ] vi florescer; ~ing adj próspero.

**flout** [flaut] vt zombar de.

**flow** [fləu] n (movement) fluxo; circulação f; (direction) curso; (tide) corrente f // vi correr, fluir; (blood) circular.

**flower** ['flauə*] n flor f // vi florescer, florir; ~ bed n canteiro; ~pot n vaso; ~y adj florido.

**flown** [fləun] pp of **fly**.

**flu** [flu:] n gripe f.

**fluctuate** ['flʌktjueɪt] vi flutuar; **fluctuation** n flutuação f.

**fluent** ['flu:ənt] adj (speech) fluente; **he speaks ~ French, he's ~ in French** ele fala francês fluentemente; ~ly adv fluentemente.

**fluff** [flʌf] n felpa, penugem f; ~y adj macio, fofo.

**fluid** ['flu:ɪd] adj, n fluido.

**fluke** [flu:k] n (col) bambúrrio, fortuna inesperada.

**flung** [flʌŋ] pt, pp of **fling**.

**fluorescent** [fluə'resnt] adj fluorescente.

**fluoride** ['fluəraɪd] n fluoreto.

**flurry** ['flʌrɪ] n (of snow) lufada; (haste) agitação f; ~ of activity muita atividade (Pt: -ct-).

**flush** [flʌʃ] n (on face) rubor m; (plenty) abundância // vt lavar com água // vi ruborizar-se // adj: ~ with no mesmo nível de; to ~ the toilet dar descarga; ~ed adj ruborizado, corado.

**flustered** ['flʌstəd] adj atrapalhado.

**flute** [flu:t] n flauta.

**flutter** ['flʌtə*] n agitação f; (of

wings) bater m de asas; (fam: bet) aposta // vi agitar-se, esvoaçar.

**flux** [flʌks] n fluxo; **in a state of ~** mudando continuamente.

**fly** [flaɪ] n (insect) mosca; (trousers: also: **flies**) braguilha (vb: pt **flew**, pp **flown**) vt (gen) fazer voar; (plane) pilotar; (cargo) transportar (de avião); (distances) percorrer // vi voar; (passengers) subir no avião; (escape) fugir; (flag) hastear; to let ~ descarregar, desafogar; ~ing n (activity) voar m // adj: ~ing visit visita de médico; with ~ing colours brilhantemente; ~ing saucer n disco voador; ~over n (Brit: bridge) estrada em desnível or superior; ~past n desfile aéreo; ~sheet n (for tent) duplo teto (Pt: -ct-).

**foal** [fəul] n potro.

**foam** [fəum] n espuma // vi espumar; ~ rubber n espuma borracha.

**fob** [fɔb] vt: to ~ sb off oferecer falso como verdadeiro a alguém.

**focal** ['fəukəl] adj focal.

**focus** ['fəukəs], pl ~es n foco // (field glasses etc) enfocar; to ~ enfocar, focalizar; **in/out of** ~ enfocado/desenfocado or em foco fora de foco.

**fodder** ['fɔdə*] n forragem f.

**foe** [fəu] n inimigo.

**foetus** ['fi:təs] n feto.

**fog** [fɔg] n nevoeiro; ~gy adj: **it's ~gy** está nevoento, está brumoso.

**foil** [fɔɪl] n vt frustrar // n folha metálica; (also: **kitchen** ~) folha papel m de alumínio; (FENCING) florete m.

**fold** [fəuld] n (bend, crease) vinco, prega; (of skin) ruga; (AGR) redil curral m // vt dobrar; to ~ up (map etc) dobrar; (business) abrir falência // vt (map etc) dobrar; ~er n (for papers) pasta; (brochure) folheto; ~ing adj (chair, bed) dobrável.

**foliage** ['fəʊlɪɪdʒ] n folhagem f.

**folk** [fəʊk] npl gente f // adj popular, folclórico; **~s** npl (family) família sg, parentes mpl; (people) a gente; **~lore** ['fəʊkləʊ*] n folclore m; **~song** n canção f popular or folclórica.

**follow** ['fɔləʊ] vt seguir // vi seguir; (result) resultar; **he ~ed suit** ele fez o mesmo; **to ~ up** vt (letter, offer) responder a, acompanhar; (case) investigar; **~er** n seguidor(a) m/f; (POL) partidário/a; **~ing** adj seguinte // n séquito, adeptos mpl.

**folly** ['fɔlɪ] n loucura.

**fond** [fɔnd] adj (loving) amoroso, carinhoso; **to be ~ of** gostar de.

**fondle** ['fɔndl] vt acariciar.

**fondness** ['fɔndnɪs] n (for things) gosto, afeição f; (for people) carinho.

**font** [fɔnt] n pia batismal (Pt: -p-).

**food** [fu:d] n comida; **~ mixer** n batedeira; **~ poisoning** n envenenamento por alimento; **~stuffs** npl comestíveis mpl.

**fool** [fu:l] n tolo; (CULIN) purê m de frutas com creme // vt enganar // vi (gen: **~ around**) brincar; (waste time) perder tempo; **~hardy** adj temerário; **~ish** adj bobo; (stupid) burro; (careless) imprudente; **~proof** adj (plan etc) infalível.

**foot** [fut], pl **feet** n pé m; (measure) pé (= 304 mm); (of animal) pata // vt (bill) pagar; **on ~** a pé; **~ball** n bola; (game) futebol m; **~baller** n futebolista m; **~brake** n freio de pé; (Pt) travão de pé; **~bridge** n passarela; **~hills** npl contraforte msg; **~hold** n apoio para pés; **~ing** n (fig) posição f; **to lose one's ~ing** escorregar; **on an equal ~ing** em pé de igualdade; **~lights** npl ribalta sg; **~man** n lacaio; **~note** n nota de rodapé or ao pé duma página; **~path** n senda, vereda, caminho; (pavement) calçada; **~sore** adj com

os pés doloridos; **~step** n passo; **~wear** n calçado.

**for** [fɔ:*] prep (gen) para; (as, in exchange for, because of) por; (during) durante; (in spite of) apesar de (and) pois, porque; **it was sold ~ 100 pesetas** foi vendido por 100 pesetas; **what ~?** para quê?; **what's it ~?** para que serve?; **he was away ~ 2 years** esteve fora 2 anos; **he went ~ the paper** foi pegar o jornal; **~ sale** vende-se.

**forage** ['fɔrɪdʒ] n forragem f.

**foray** ['fɔreɪ] n incursão f.

**forbid** [fə'bɪd], pt **forbad(e)** [fə'bæd], pp **forbidden** [fə'bɪdn] vt proibir; **~ding** adj (gloomy) lúgubre; (severe) severo.

**force** [fɔ:s] n força // vt forçar; **to ~ o.s.** to forçar-se a; **the F~s** npl Forças Armadas; **in ~** em vigor; **~d** [fɔ:st] adj forçado; **~ful** adj forçoso.

**forceps** ['fɔ:sɛps] npl fórceps m inv.

**forcibly** ['fɔ:səblɪ] adv à força.

**ford** [fɔ:d] n vau m // vt vadear.

**forearm** ['fɔ:rɑ:m] n antebraço.

**foreboding** [fɔ:'bəʊdɪŋ] n presságio.

**forecast** ['fɔ:kɑ:st] n prognóstico // vt (irr: like **cast**) prognosticar.

**forefathers** ['fɔ:fɑ:ðəz] npl antepassados mpl.

**forefinger** ['fɔ:fɪŋgə*] n (dedo) indicador m.

**forego** = **forgo**.

**foregone** ['fɔ:gɒn] adj: **it's a ~ conclusion** é uma conclusão inevitável.

**foreground** ['fɔ:graund] n primeiro plano.

**forehead** ['fɔrɪd] n testa.

**foreign** ['fɔrɪn] adj estrangeiro; (trade) exterior; **~er** n estrangeiro; **~ exchange** n câmbio (de moeda estrangeira); **F~ Minister** n Ministro das Relações Exteriores; **F~ Office** n Ministério das Relações Exteriores.

**foreleg** ['fɔːlɛg] n perna dianteira.

**foreman** ['fɔːmən] n capataz m; (in construction) contramestre m.

**foremost** ['fɔːməust] adj principal.

**forensic** [fə'rɛnsɪk] adj forense.

**forerunner** ['fɔːrʌnə*] n precursor(a) m/f.

**foresee** [fɔː'siː] (irr: like see) vt prever; **~able** adj previsível.

**foresight** ['fɔːsaɪt] n previsão f.

**forest** ['fɔrɪst] n floresta.

**forestall** [fɔː'stɔːl] vt prevenir.

**forestry** ['fɔrɪstrɪ] n silvicultura.

**foretaste** ['fɔːteɪst] n (gen) antegosto, antegozo; (sample) amostra.

**foretell** [fɔː'tɛl] (irr: like tell) vt predizer, profetizar.

**forever** [fə'rɛvə*] adv para sempre.

**foreword** ['fɔːwəːd] n prefácio.

**forfeit** ['fɔːfɪt] n prenda, perda; (fine) multa // vt perder (direito a).

**forgave** [fə'geɪv] pt de **forgive**.

**forge** [fɔːdʒ] n forja; (smithy) ferraria // vt (signature, money) falsificar; (metal) forjar; **to ~ ahead** vi avançar constantemente; **forger** n falsificador(a) m/f; **~ry** n falsificação f.

**forget** [fə'gɛt], pt **forgot**, pp **forgotten** vt esquecer // vi esquecer-se (de); **~ful** adj esquecido; **~fulness** n (gen) esquecimento; (thoughtlessness) descuido; (oblivion) falta de memória.

**forgive** [fə'gɪv], pt **forgave**, pp **forgiven** vt perdoar; **to ~ sb for sth** perdoar algo a alguém; **~ness** n perdão m.

**forgo** [fɔː'gəu] (irr: like **go**) vt (give up) renunciar a; (go without) abster-se de.

**forgot** [fə'gɔt] pt de **forget**.

**forgotten** [fə'gɔtn] pp de **forget**.

**fork** [fɔːk] n (for eating) garfo; (for gardening) forquilha; (of roads) bifurcação f // vi (road) bifurcar-se; **to ~ out** vt (col: pay) desembolsar;

**~ed** [fɔːkt] adj (lightning) em zigzag; **~-lift truck** n empilhadeira.

**form** [fɔːm] n forma; (SCOL) série f; (questionnaire) formulário // vt formar; **in top ~** em plena forma.

**formal** ['fɔːməl] adj (offer, receipt) oficial; (person etc) cerimonioso; (occasion, dinner) formal; (dress) a rigor; **~ity** [-'mælɪtɪ] n cerimônia; **~ities** npl formalidades fpl; **~ly** adv oficialmente, formalmente.

**format** ['fɔːmæt] n formato.

**formation** [fɔː'meɪʃən] n formação f.

**formative** ['fɔːmətɪv] adj (years) formativo.

**former** ['fɔːmə*] adj anterior, (earlier) antigo; (ex) ex; **the ~** ... **the latter** ... aquele ... este ...; **~ly** adv antigamente.

**formidable** ['fɔːmɪdəbl] adj terrível, temível.

**formula** ['fɔːmjulə] n fórmula.

**formulate** ['fɔːmjuleɪt] vt formular.

**forsake** [fə'seɪk], pt **forsook** [fə'suk], pp **forsaken** [fə'seɪkn] vt (gen) abandonar; (plan) renunciar a.

**fort** [fɔːt] n forte m.

**forte** ['fɔːtɪ] n forte m.

**forth** [fɔːθ] adv para adiante; **back and ~** de cá para lá; **and so ~** e assim por diante; **~coming** adj próximo, que está para aparecer; (character) comunicativo; (book) no prelo; **~right** adj franco.

**fortieth** ['fɔːtɪɪθ] adj quadragésimo.

**fortification** [fɔːtɪfɪ'keɪʃən] n fortificação f; **fortify** ['fɔːtɪfaɪ] vt fortalecer.

**fortitude** ['fɔːtɪtjuːd] n fortaleza.

**fortnight** ['fɔːtnaɪt] n quinzena; **~ly** adj quinzenal // adv quinzenalmente.

**fortress** ['fɔːtrɪs] n fortaleza.

**fortuitous** [fɔː'tjuːɪtəs] adj fortuito.

**fortunate** ['fɔːtʃənɪt] adj: **to be ~** ter sorte; **it is ~ that...** é uma sorte que...; **~ly** adv afortunadamente, felizmente.

**fortune** ['fɔ:tʃən] n sorte f; (wealth) fortuna; **~-teller** n adivinho/a.

**forty** ['fɔ:tɪ] num quarenta.

**forum** ['fɔ:rəm] n foro.

**forward** ['fɔ:wəd] adj (movement, position) avançado; (front) dianteiro; (not shy) atrevido // n (SPORT) atacante m // vt (letter) remeter a novo endereço; (career) progredir; **to move ~** avançar; **~(s)** adv (para) adiante.

**fossil** ['fɔsl] n fóssil m.

**foster** ['fɔstə*] vt fomentar; **~ brother** n irmão m de criação; **~ child** n filho adotivo (Pt: -pt-); **~ mother** n mãe f ado(p)tiva.

**fought** [fɔ:t] pt, pp of **fight**.

**foul** [faul] adj (gen) sujo, porco; (weather) horrível; (smell etc) nojento // n (FOOTBALL) falta // vt (dirty) sujar; (block) entupir; (football player) cometer uma falta contra; **~ play** n (SPORT) jogada suja; (LAW) crime m violento.

**found** [faund] pt, pp of **find** // vt (establish) fundar; **~ation** [-'deɪʃən] n (act) fundação f; (basis) base f; (also: **~ation cream**) creme m base; **~ations** npl (of building) alicerces mpl.

**founder** ['faundə*] n fundador(a) m/f // vi afundar-se.

**foundry** ['faundrɪ] n fundição f.

**fountain** ['fauntɪn] n fonte f; **~ pen** n caneta-tinteiro.

**four** [fɔ:*] num quatro; **on all ~s** de quatro; **~-poster** n cama com colunas; **~some** ['fɔ:səm] n grupo de quatro pessoas; **~teen** num catorze; **~teenth** adj décimo-quarto; **~th** adj quarto.

**fowl** [faul] n ave f (doméstica).

**fox** [fɔks] n raposo // vt confundir, enganar; **~trot** n foxtrote m.

**foyer** ['fɔɪeɪ] n vestíbulo.

**fracas** ['fræka:] n desordem f, rixa.

**fraction** ['frækʃən] n fração (Pt: -cç-) f.

**fracture** ['fræktʃə*] n fratura (Pt: -ct-) // vt fraturar (Pt: -ct-).

**fragile** ['frædʒaɪl] adj frágil.

**fragment** ['frægmənt] n fragmento; **~ary** adj fragmentário.

**fragrance** ['freɪgrəns] n fragrância; **fragrant** [-ənt] adj fragrante, perfumado.

**frail** [freɪl] adj (fragile) frágil, quebradiço; (weak) delicado.

**frame** [freɪm] n (gen) estrutura; (body) talhe m; (TECH) armação f; (of picture, door) moldura; (of spectacles: also: **~s**) armação f // vt encaixilhar; (reply) formular; (fam) incriminar; **~ of mind** n estado de espírito; **~-work** n armação f.

**France** [fra:ns] n França.

**franchise** ['fræntʃaɪz] n (POL) direito de voto, privilégio.

**frank** [fræŋk] adj franco // vt (letter) franquear; **~ly** adv francamente; **~ness** n franqueza.

**frantic** ['fræntɪk] adj frenético.

**fraternal** [frə'tə:nl] adj fraterno; **fraternity** [-nɪtɪ] n (club) fraternidade f; (US) clube m de estudantes; (guild) confraria; **fraternize** ['frætənaɪz] vi confraternizar.

**fraud** [frɔ:d] n fraude m; (person) impostor(a) m/f; **~ulent** adj fraudulento.

**fraught** [frɔ:t] adj: **~ with** repleto de.

**fray** [freɪ] n combate m, luta // vi esfiapar-se; **tempers were ~ed** estavam com os nervos em frangalhos.

**freak** [fri:k] n (person) anormal m/f; (event) anomalia; (thing) aberração f.

**freckle** ['frekl] n sarda.

**free** [fri:] adj (gen) livre; (not fixed) solto; (gratis) gratuito; (unoccupied) livre; (liberal) generoso // vt (prisoner etc) pôr em liberdade; (jammed object) soltar; ~ (of charge) adv grátis; ~**dom** ['fri:dəm] n liberdade f; ~**for-all** n quebra-quebra m; ~ **kick** n (tiro) livre m; ~**lancer** n colaborador(a) m/f independente, franco-atirador m; ~**ly** adv livremente; ~**mason** n maçom m; ~ **trade** n mercado livre; ~**way** n (US) auto-estrada; ~**wheel** vi ir em ponto morto; ~**will** n livre arbítrio; **of one's own** ~ will por sua própria vontade.

**freeze** [fri:z], pt **froze**, pp **frozen** vi gelar-se, congelar-se // vt gelar; (prices, food, salaries) congelar // n geada, congelamento; **freezer** n congelador m.

**freezing** ['fri:zɪŋ] adj gelado; ~ **point** n ponto de congelamento; **3 degrees below** ~ 3 graus abaixo de zero.

**freight** [freit] n (goods) carga; (money charged) frete m; ~ **car** n (US) vagão m de carga.

**French** [frentʃ] adj francês/esa // n (LING) francês m; **the** ~ os franceses; ~ **fried (potatoes)** npl batatas fpl fritas; ~**man/woman** n francês m/f; ~ **window** n porta-janela, janela de batente.

**frenzy** ['frenzɪ] n frenesi m.

**frequency** ['fri:kwənsɪ] n freqüência; **frequent** [-ənt] adj freqüente // vt [fri'kwent] freqüentar; **frequently** [-əntlɪ] adv freqüentemente, a miúdo.

**fresco** ['freskəu] n fresco m.

**fresh** [freʃ] adj (gen) fresco; (new) novo; (water) doce; ~**en** vi (wind, air) tornar-se mais forte; to ~**en up** vi (person) lavar-se, refrescar-se; ~**ly** adv (newly) novamente, (recently) recentemente; ~**ness** n frescura.

**fret** [fret] vi afligir-se.

**friar** ['fraɪə*] n frade m; (before name) frei m.

**friction** ['frɪkʃən] n fricção f.

**Friday** ['fraɪdɪ] n sexta-feira f.

**fridge** [frɪdʒ] n geladeira, (Pt frigorífico.

**friend** [frend] n amigo; ~**liness** simpatia; ~**ly** adj simpático; ~**ship** n amizade f.

**frieze** [fri:z] n friso.

**frigate** ['frɪgɪt] n fragata.

**fright** [fraɪt] n susto; **to take** ~ assustar-se; ~**en** vt assustar ~**ening** adj assustador(a); ~**ful** adj assustador(a), horrível; ~**fully** adv terrivelmente.

**frigid** ['frɪdʒɪd] adj (MED) frígido frio; ~**ity** [frɪ'dʒɪdɪtɪ] n frialdade f (MED) frigidez f.

**frill** [frɪl] n babado.

**fringe** [frɪndʒ] n franja; (edge: of forest etc) orla, margem f; ~ **benefits** npl vantagens fp suplementares.

**frisky** ['frɪskɪ] adj alegre brincalhão/lhona.

**fritter** ['frɪtə*] n filhó m, doce empanada; **to** ~ **away** vt desperdiçar.

**frivolous** ['frɪvələs] adj frívolo.

**frizzy** ['frɪzɪ] adj frisado.

**fro** [frəu] see **to**.

**frock** [frɔk] n vestido.

**frog** [frɔg] n rã f; ~**man** n homem-rã m.

**frolic** ['frɔlɪk] vi brincar.

**from** [frɔm] prep de; ~ **January** (**on**) a partir de janeiro; ~ **what** he says pelo que ele diz.

**front** [frʌnt] n (foremost part) parte f dianteira; (of house) fachada; (promenade: also: **sea** ~) orla marítima; (MIL. POL. METEOROLOGY) frente f; (fig: appearances) aparências fpl // adj dianteiro, da frente; **in** ~ (**of**) em frente (de); ~**al** adj frontal; ~ **door** n porta principal; ~**ier** ['frʌntɪə*] n fronteira; ~ **page** n primeira página; ~ **room** n (Brit) salão m, sala de estar; ~**wheel drive** n tração (Pt: -cç-) f dianteira.

**frost** [frɔst] n (gen) geada; (visible) gelo; ~**bite** n enregelamento; ~**ed** adj (glass) fosco; ~**y** adj (window) coberto de geada; (welcome) glacial.

**froth** [frɔθ] n espuma.

**frown** [fraun] n olhar m carrancudo, franzimento do cenho or da testa // vi franzir o cenho or a testa.

**froze** [frəuz] pt of **freeze**.

**frozen** ['frəuzn] pp of **freeze**.

**frugal** ['fru:gəl] adj frugal.

**fruit** [fru:t] n, pl inv fruto; (to eat) fruta; ~**erer** n fruteiro, quitandeiro; ~**erer's (shop)** n frutaria; ~**ful** adj proveitoso; ~**ion** [fru:'ɪʃən] n: **to come to** ~**ion** realizar-se; ~ **machine** n caça-níqueis m inv.

**frustrate** [frʌs'treɪt] vt frustrar; ~**d** adj frustrado; **frustration** [-'treɪʃən] n frustração f.

**fry** [fraɪ], pt, pp **fried** vt fritar; **small** ~ gente f insignificante; ~**ing pan** n frigideira.

**ft.** abbr of **foot**, **feet**.

**fuchsia** ['fju:ʃə] n fúcsia.

**fuel** [fjuəl] n (for heating) combustível m; (coal) carvão m; (wood) lenha; (for propelling) carburante m; ~ **oil** n óleo combustível; ~ **tank** n depósito de combustível.

**fugitive** ['fju:dʒɪtɪv] n fugitivo.

**fulfil** [ful'fɪl] vt (function) cumprir com; (condition) satisfazer; (wish, desire) realizar; ~**ment** n satisfação f; realização f.

**full** [ful] adj cheio; (fig) completo, pleno; (complete) completo; (information) detalhado // adv: ~ **well** perfeitamente; **I'm** ~ estou cheio; ~ **employment** n pleno emprego; ~ **fare** passagem f completa; **a** ~ **two hours** duas horas completas; **at** ~ **speed** a toda a velocidade; **in** ~ (reproduce, quote) integralmente; ~**length** adj (portrait) de corpo inteiro; ~ **moon**

n lua cheia; ~**sized** adj (portrait etc) em tamanho natural; ~ **stop** n ponto (final); ~**time** adj (work) de tempo completo or integral // n (SPORT) final m; ~**y** adv completamente; ~**y-fledged** adj (teacher, barrister) diplomado.

**fumble** ['fʌmbl]: **to** ~ **with** vt fus atrapalhar-se com.

**fume** [fju:m] vi fumegar, soltar fumo; ~**s** npl fumaça sg, gases mpl.

**fumigate** ['fju:mɪgeɪt] vt fumigar.

**fun** [fʌn] n (amusement) divertimento; (joy) alegria; **to have** ~ divertir-se; **for** ~ de brincadeira; **to make** ~ **of** vt fus fazer troça de, zombar de.

**function** ['fʌŋkʃən] n função f // vi funcionar; ~**al** adj funcional.

**fund** [fʌnd] n provisão f, fundos mpl; (source, store) fonte f; ~**s** npl fundos mpl.

**fundamental** [fʌndə'mentl] adj fundamental.

**funeral** ['fju:nərəl] n (burial) enterro; (ceremony) exéquias fpl; ~ **service** n missa fúnebre.

**funfair** ['fʌnfɛə*] n parque m de diversões.

**fungus** ['fʌŋgəs], pl -**gi** [-gaɪ] n fungo.

**funnel** ['fʌnl] n funil m; (of ship) chaminé m.

**funnily** ['fʌnɪlɪ] adv divertidamente.

**funny** ['fʌnɪ] adj engraçado, divertido; (strange) esquisito, raro.

**fur** [fə:*] n pele f; (in kettle etc) sarburra, crosta; ~ **coat** n casaco de peles.

**furious** ['fjuərɪəs] adj furioso; (effort) violento; ~**ly** adv com fúria.

**furlong** ['fə:lɔŋ] n oitava parte de uma milha.

**furlough** ['fə:ləu] n (US) licença.

**furnace** ['fə:nɪs] n forno.

**furnish** ['fə:nɪʃ] vt mobilar, mobiliar; (supply) fornecer; ~**ings** npl mobília, equipamento.

**furniture** ['fə:nɪtʃə*] n mobília,

móveis *mpl*; **piece of** ~ móvel *m*; ~ **polish** *n* cera de lustrar móveis.

**furrier** ['fʌrɪə*] *n* peleiro.

**furrow** ['fʌrəu] *n* sulco.

**furry** ['fɜːrɪ] *adj* peludo.

**further** ['fɜːðə*] *adj* (*new*) novo, adicional; (*place*) mais longe // *adv* mais adiante; (*more*) mais; (*moreover*) além disso // *vt* promover, adiantar; ~ **education** *n* educação *f* superior; ~**more** [fɜːðə'mɔː*] *adv* além disso.

**furthest** ['fɜːðɪst] *superlative of* **far**.

**furtive** ['fɜːtɪv] *adj* furtivo.

**fury** ['fjʊərɪ] *n* fúria.

**fuse, fuze** (*US*) [fjuːz] *n* fusível *m*; (*for bomb etc*) mecha // *vt* (*metal*) fundir; (*fig*) unir // *vi* fundir-se; unir-se; (*ELEC*): **to** ~ **the lights** queimar as luzes; ~ **box** *n* caixa de fusíveis.

**fuselage** ['fjuːzəlɑːʒ] *n* fuselagem *f*.

**fusion** ['fjuːʒən] *n* fusão *f*.

**fuss** [fʌs] *n* (*noise*) rebuliço; (*dispute*) espalhafato; (*complaining*) protesto; (*ceremony*) cerimônias *fpl*; **to make a** ~ criar caso; ~**y** *adj* (*person*) exigente, meticuloso.

**futile** ['fjuːtaɪl] *adj* fútil, inútil; **futility** [-'tɪlɪtɪ] *n* inutilidade *f*.

**future** ['fjuːtʃə*] *adj* (*gen*) futuro; (*coming*) vindouro // *n* futuro; **futuristic** [-'rɪstɪk] *adj* futurístico.

**fuzzy** ['fʌzɪ] *adj* (*PHOT*) indistinto; (*hair*) frisado, encrespado.

# G

**gabble** ['gæbl] *vi* tagarelar; (*gossip*) fazer fofoca.

**gable** ['geɪbl] *n* cumeeira.

**gadget** ['gædʒɪt] *n* aparelho; (*in kitchen*) pequeno utensílio.

**Gaelic** ['geɪlɪk] *n* (*LING*) gaélico.

**gag** [gæg] *n* (*joke*) mordaça // *vt* amordaçar.

**gaiety** ['geɪtɪ] *n* alegria.

**gaily** ['geɪlɪ] *adv* alegremente.

**gain** [geɪn] *n* lucro, ganho // *vt* ganhar // *vi* (*watch*) adiantar-se; **to** ~ **by sth** tirar proveito de algo; **to** ~ **on sb** aproximar-se de alguém.

**gait** [geɪt] *n* o modo de andar.

**gala** ['gɑːlə] *n* festa, gala.

**galaxy** ['gæləksɪ] *n* galáxia.

**gale** [geɪl] *n* (*wind*) ventania.

**gallant** ['gælənt] *adj* valente; (*towards ladies*) galante; ~**ry** *n* valentia; (*courtesy*) galanteria.

**gall-bladder** ['gɔːlblædə*] *n* vesícula biliar.

**gallery** ['gælərɪ] *n* galeria; (*also*: **art** ~) galeria de arte.

**galley** ['gælɪ] *n* (*ship's kitchen*) cozinha; (*ship*) galé *f*.

**gallon** ['gæln] *n* galão *m* (4.543 *litros*).

**gallop** ['gæləp] *n* galope *m* // *vi* galopar.

**gallows** ['gæləuz] *n* forca *sg*.

**gallstone** ['gɔːlstəun] *n* cálculo biliar.

**gamble** ['gæmbl] *n* (*risk*) risco; (*bet*) aposta // *vt*: **to** ~ **on** apostar em; (*fig*) confiar em // *vi* jogar, arriscar; (*COMM*) especular; **gambler** *n* jogador/a *m/f*; **gambling** *n* jogo.

**game** [geɪm] *n* (*gen*) jogo; (*match*) encontro; (*of cards, of football*) partida; (*HUNTING*) caça // *adj* valente; (*ready*): **to be** ~ **for anything** estar pronto para qualquer coisa; ~ **bird** *n* ave *f* de caça; ~**keeper** *n* guarda-caça *m*.

**gammon** ['gæmən] *n* (*bacon*) toucinho (*defumado*); (*ham*) presunto.

**gang** [gæŋ] *n* gangue *f*, grupo; (*of workmen*) turma // *vi*: **to** ~ **up on sb** conspirar contra alguém.

**gangrene** ['gæŋgriːn] *n* gangrena.

**gangster** ['gæŋstə*] *n* gângster *m*.

**gangway** ['gæŋweɪ] *n* (*in theatre etc*) passagem *f*, coxia; (*on ship*) passadiço; (*on dock*) portaló *m*.

**gaol** [dʒeɪl] = **jail.**

**gap** [gæp] n brecha, fenda; (in trees, traffic) abertura; (in time) intervalo.

**gape** [geɪp] vi estar or ficar boquiaberto; **gaping** adj (hole) muito aberto.

**garage** ['gærɑ:ʒ] n garagem f.

**garbage** ['gɑ:bɪdʒ] n lixo; ~ **can** n (US) lata de lixo.

**garbled** ['gɑ:bld] adj (distorted) falsificado, deturpado.

**garden** ['gɑ:dn] n jardim m; ~**er** n jardineiro; ~**ing** n jardinagem f.

**gargle** ['gɑ:gl] vi gargarejar.

**gargoyle** ['gɑ:gɔɪl] n gárgula.

**garish** ['gɛərɪʃ] adj espalhafatoso.

**garland** ['gɑ:lənd] n guirlanda.

**garlic** ['gɑ:lɪk] n alho.

**garment** ['gɑ:mənt] n peça de roupa.

**garnish** ['gɑ:nɪʃ] vt adornar; (CULIN) enfeitar.

**garrison** ['gærɪsn] n guarnição f // vt guarnecer.

**garrulous** ['gærjuləs] adj tagarela.

**garter** ['gɑ:tə*] n liga; ~ **belt** n cinta-liga.

**gas** [gæs] n gás m; (US: gasoline) gasolina // vt asfixiar com gás; ~ **cooker** n fogão m a gás; ~ **cylinder** n bujão m de gás; ~ **fire** n aquecedor m a gás.

**gash** [gæʃ] n talho; (on face) corte m // vt (gen) talhar; (with knife) cortar.

**gasket** ['gæskɪt] n (AUT) junta, gaxeta.

**gas: ~mask** n máscara antigás; ~**meter** n medidor m de gás.

**gasoline** ['gæsəli:n] n (US) gasolina.

**gasp** [gɑ:sp] n arfada // vi arfar; (pant) esforçar-se para respirar; to ~ **out** vt (say) dizer com voz entrecortada.

**gas: ~ring** n tampa; ~ **station** n (US) posto de gasolina; ~ **stove** n fogão m a gás; ~**sy** adj gasoso; ~ **tap** n torneira do gás.

**gastric** ['gæstrɪk] adj gástrico; ~ **ulcer** n úlcera gástrica.

**gate** [geɪt] n portão m; (RAIL) barreira; ~**crash** vt entrar de penetra; ~**way** n portão m, passagem f.

**gather** ['gæðə*] vt (flowers, fruit) colher; (assemble) reunir; (pick up) colher; (SEWING) franzir; (understand) compreender // vi (assemble) reunir-se; ~**ing** n reunião f, assembleia.

**gauche** [gəʊʃ] adj desajeitado.

**gaudy** ['gɔ:dɪ] adj ostentoso, de mau gosto.

**gauge** [geɪdʒ] n padrão m, medida, medidor m; (RAIL) bitola; (instrument) indicador m // vt medir.

**gaunt** [gɔ:nt] adj descarnado; (grim, desolate) desolado.

**gauntlet** ['gɔ:ntlɪt] n (fig): to run the ~ expor-se (à crítica); to throw down the ~ desafiar.

**gauze** [gɔ:z] n gaze f.

**gave** [geɪv] pt of give.

**gay** [geɪ] adj (person) alegre; (colour) vistoso, vivo; (homosexual) homossexual.

**gaze** [geɪz] n olhar fixo; to ~ **at** sth fitar algo.

**gazelle** [gə'zɛl] n gazela.

**gazetteer** [gæzə'tɪə*] n dicionário geográfico.

**G.B.** abbr of **Great Britain.**

**gear** [gɪə*] n equipamento; (TECH) engrenagem f; (AUT) mudança, marcha; **top/low** ~ quarta/primeira (marcha); **in** ~ engrenado; ~ **box** n caixa de mudança; ~ **lever**, ~ **shift** (US) n alavanca de mudança; ~ **wheel** n roda dentada.

**geese** [gi:s] pl of goose.

**gelatin(e)** ['dʒɛləti:n] n gelatina.

**gelignite** ['dʒɛlɪgnaɪt] n gelignite f.

**gem** [dʒɛm] n jóia, gema.

**Gemini** ['dʒɛmɪnaɪ] n Gêmeis m, Gêmeos mpl.

**gender** ['dʒendə*] n gênero.

**general** ['dʒenərl] n general m // adj geral; in ~ em geral; ~ **election** n eleições fpl gerais; ~**ization** [-ar'zeiʃən] n generalização f; ~**ize** vi generalizar; ~**ly** adv geralmente; ~ **practitioner (G.P.)** n clínico-geral m.

**generate** ['dʒenəreit] vt (ELEC) gerar; (fig) produzir.

**generation** [dʒenə'reiʃən] n geração f.

**generator** ['dʒenəreitə*] n gerador m.

**generosity** [dʒenə'rɔsiti] n generosidade f; **generous** ['dʒenərəs] adj generoso; (helping etc) abundante.

**genetics** [dʒi'netiks] n genética.

**Geneva** [dʒi'ni:və] n Genebra.

**genial** ['dʒi:niəl] adj jovial, simpático.

**genitals** ['dʒenitlz] npl órgãos mpl genitais.

**genius** ['dʒi:niəs] n gênio.

**genocide** ['dʒenəusaid] n genocídio.

**gent** [dʒent] n abbr of **gentleman.**

**genteel** [dʒen'ti:l] adj fino, elegante.

**gentle** ['dʒentl] adj (sweet) amável, doce; (touch etc) leve, suave; (animal) manso.

**gentleman** ['dʒentlmən] n senhor m; (well-bred man) cavalheiro.

**gentleness** ['dʒentlnis] n doçura, meiguice f; (of touch) suavidade f; (of animal) brandura.

**gently** ['dʒentli] adv devagar, suavemente.

**gentry** ['dʒentri] n gente f de nobreza.

**gents** [dʒents] n (lavabos de) cavalheiros mpl.

**genuine** ['dʒenjuin] adj autêntico; (person) sincero.

**geographic(al)** [dʒiə'græfik(l)] adj geográfico; **geography** [dʒi'ɔgrəfi] n geografia.

**geological** [dʒiə'lɔdʒikl] adj geológico; **geologist** [dʒi'ɔlədʒist] n

geólogo/a; **geology** [dʒi'ɔlədʒi] n geologia.

**geometric(al)** [dʒiə'metrik(l)] adj geométrico; **geometry** [dʒi'ɔmətri] n geometria.

**geranium** [dʒi'reinjəm] n gerânio.

**germ** [dʒəːm] n (gen) micróbio, bacilo; (BIO, fig) germe m.

**German** ['dʒəːmən] adj alemão/mã // n alemão/mã m/f; (LING) alemão m; ~ **measles** n rubéola.

**Germany** ['dʒəːməni] n Alemanha.

**germination** [dʒəːmi'neiʃən] n germinação f.

**gesticulate** [dʒɛs'tikjuleit] vi gesticular.

**gesture** ['dʒɛstjə*] n gesto.

**get** [get], pt, pp **got**, pp **gotten** (US) vt (obtain) obter; (receive) receber; (achieve) conseguir; (find) encontrar; (catch) apanhar; (fetch) ir buscar; (understand) compreender // vi (become) fazer-se, chegar a; to ~ **old** envelhecer; to ~ to (place) chegar a; **he got under the fence** passou por baixo da cerca; to ~ **ready** preparar-se; to ~ **washed** lavar-se; to ~ **sb to do sth** convencer alguém a fazer algo; to ~ **sth out of sth** conseguir algo de algo; to ~ **about** vi sair muito, viajar muito; (news) divulgar-se; to ~ **along** vi (agree) entender-se; (depart) pôr-se a andar, ir embora; (manage) — to get by; to ~ **at** vt fus (attack) atacar; (reach) chegar a; (the truth) descobrir; to ~ **away** vi partir; (on holiday) ir-se de férias; (escape) escapar; to ~ **away with** vt fus fazer impunemente; to ~ **back** vi (return) regressar // vt voltar; to ~ **by** vi (pass) passar; (manage) arranjar-se; to ~ **down** vi baixar-se // vt (object) baixar; (depress) deprimir; to ~ **down to** vt fus (work) pôr-se a (fazer); to ~ **in** vi (train) chegar; (arrive home) voltar para casa // vt fus (car etc) subir a; to ~ **off** vi (from train etc)

descer, saltar; (depart: person, car)
sair // vt fus (train, bus) sair de,
saltar de; to ~ on vi (at exam etc)
ter sucesso; (agree) entender-se //
vt (train etc) subir a; to ~ out vi
sair; (of vehicle) sair; (news) saber
// vt (take out) tirar; to ~ out of vt
fus sair de; (duty etc) escapar de; to
~ over vt (illness) restabelecer-se
de; (put across) fazer compreender;
to ~ round vt fus rodear; (fig:
person) convencer; to ~ through vt
fus (TEL) comunicar-se com; to ~
together vi reunir-se; to ~ up vi
(rise) levantar-se // vt fus levantar;
to ~ up to vt fus (reach) chegar a;
(prank etc) fazer; ~away n fuga,
escape m.

**geyser** ['gi:zə*] n esquentador m de
água; (GEO) gêiser m.

**Ghana** ['gɑːnə] n Ghana.

**ghastly** ['gɑːstlɪ] adj horrível; (pale)
pálido.

**gherkin** ['gəːkɪn] n pepino em
vinagre.

**ghetto** ['gɛtəu] n gueto.

**ghost** [gəust] n fantasma m; ~ly
adj fantasmal.

**giant** ['dʒaɪənt] n gigante m // adj
gigantesco, gigante.

**gibberish** ['dʒɪbərɪʃ] n engrimanço.

**gibe** [dʒaɪb] n zombaria.

**giblets** ['dʒɪblɪts] npl miúdos mpl.

**giddiness** ['gɪdɪnɪs] n vertigem f;
**giddy** adj (dizzy) tonto; (speed)
vertiginoso; (frivolous) frívolo; **it
makes me giddy** me dá vertigem.

**gift** [gɪft] n (gen) presente m;
(offering) oferta; (ability) talento;
~ed adj dotado.

**gigantic** [dʒaɪˈgæntɪk] adj
gigantesco.

**giggle** ['gɪgl] vi rir-se tolamente // n
risadinha tola.

**gill** [dʒɪl] n (measure) = 0.14 l // n
[gɪl] (of fish) guelra, brânquia.

**gilt** [gɪlt] adj, n dourado; ~-edged
adj (COMM) do Estado.

**gimmick** ['gɪmɪk] n truque m
(publicitário).

**gin** [dʒɪn] n (liquor) gim m, genebra.

**ginger** ['dʒɪndʒə*] n gengibre m; ~
ale n cerveja de gengibre; ~bread
n pão m de gengibre; ~-haired adj
ruivo.

**gingerly** ['dʒɪndʒəlɪ] adv
cuidadosamente.

**gipsy** ['dʒɪpsɪ] n cigano.

**giraffe** [dʒɪˈrɑːf] n girafa.

**girder** ['gəːdə*] n viga, trave f.

**girdle** ['gəːdl] n (corset) cinta // vt
cintar.

**girl** [gəːl] n (small) menina; (Pt)
rapariga; (young woman) jovem f,
moça; **an English** ~ uma moça
inglesa; ~**friend** n (of girl) amiga;
(of boy) namorada; ~**ish** adj
ameninado, de menina.

**girth** [gəːθ] n circunferência;
(stoutness) gordura.

**gist** [dʒɪst] n o essencial m.

**give** [gɪv], pt gave, pp given vt
(gen) dar; (deliver) entregar; (as
gift) oferecer // vi (break) dar
folga; (stretch: fabric) dar de si; to
~ sb sth, ~ sth to sb dar algo a
alguém; to ~ away vt (give free)
dar de graça; (betray) traiçoar;
(disclose) revelar; to ~ back vt
devolver; to ~ in vi ceder // vt
entregar; to ~ off vt despedir; to ~
out vt distribuir; to ~ up vi
renunciar, dar-se por vencido // vt
renunciar a; to ~ up smoking
deixar de fumar; to ~ way vi ceder;
(AUT) deixar passar.

**glacier** ['glæsɪə*] n glaciar m,
geleira.

**glad** [glæd] adj contente; ~den vt
alegrar.

**gladioli** [glædɪˈəulaɪ] npl gladíolos
mpl.

**gladly** ['glædlɪ] adv com muito
prazer.

**glamorous** ['glæmərəs] adj
encantador(a), glamoroso; **glamour**
n encanto, glamour m,

**glance** [glɑːns] n relance m, vista // vi: to ~ at olhar (de relance); to ~ off (bullet) resvalar; **glancing** adj (blow) oblíquo.

**gland** [glænd] n glândula.

**glare** [glɛə*] n luz f, brilho // vi deslumbrar; to ~ at olhar furiosamente para; **glaring** adj (mistake) notório.

**glass** [glɑːs] n vidro, cristal m; (for drinking) copo; (:with stem) cálice m; (also: **looking ~**) espelho; ~es npl óculos mpl; ~**house** n estufa; ~**ware** n objetos de cristal; ~y adj (eyes) vidrado.

**glaze** [gleɪz] vt (door) envidraçar; (pottery) vitrificar // n verniz m; ~d adj (eye) vidrado; (pottery) vitrificado.

**glazier** ['gleɪzɪə*] n vidraceiro.

**gleam** [gliːm] n vislumbre m // vi brilhar; ~**ing** adj brilhante.

**glee** [gliː] n alegria, regozijo.

**glen** [glɛn] n vale m.

**glib** [glɪb] adj loquaz, tagarela; ~**ness** n verbosidade f.

**glide** [glaɪd] vi deslizar; (AVIAT, birds) planar // n deslizamento; (AVIAT) vôo planado; **glider** n (AVIAT) planador m; **gliding** n (AVIAT) vôo sem motor.

**glimmer** ['glɪmə*] n luz f trêmula.

**glimpse** [glɪmps] n olhar m de relance, vislumbre m // vt vislumbrar, ver de relance.

**glint** [glɪnt] n brilho; (in the eye) cintilação f // vi cintilar.

**glisten** ['glɪsn] vi cintilar, resplandecer.

**glitter** ['glɪtə*] vi reluzir, brilhar // n brilho.

**gloat** [gləut] vi: to ~ (over) exultar (com).

**global** ['gləubl] adj mundial; (sum) global.

**globe** [gləub] n globo, esfera.

**gloom** [gluːm] n escuridão f; (sadness) tristeza; ~y adj (dark)

escuro; (sad) triste; (pessimistic) pessimista.

**glorify** ['glɔːrɪfaɪ] vt glorificar; (praise) adorar.

**glorious** ['glɔːrɪəs] adj glorioso; **glory** n glória.

**gloss** [glɔs] n (shine) brilho; (paint) pintura brilhante, esmalte m; to ~ over vt fus encobrir.

**glossary** ['glɔsərɪ] n glossário.

**glossy** ['glɔsɪ] adj lustroso.

**glove** [glʌv] n luva; ~ **compartment** n (AUT) porta-luvas m inv.

**glow** [gləu] vi (shine) brilhar; (fire) arder // n brilho.

**glower** ['glauə*] vi: to ~ at olhar de modo ameaçador.

**glucose** ['gluːkəus] n glicose f.

**glue** [gluː] n cola // vt colar.

**glum** [glʌm] adj (mood) abatido; (person, tone) triste.

**glut** [glʌt] n abundância, fartura.

**glutton** ['glʌtn] n glutão/ona m/f; a ~ for work um trabalhador incansável; ~y n gula.

**glycerin(e)** ['glɪsəriːn] n glicerina.

**gnarled** [nɑːld] adj nodoso.

**gnat** [næt] n mosquito.

**gnaw** [nɔː] vt roer.

**gnome** [nəum] n gnomo.

**go** [gəu], pt **went**, pp **gone** vi ir; (travel) viajar; (depart) partir, ir-se; (work) funcionar, trabalhar; (be sold) vender; (time) passar; (become) ficar; (break etc) romper-se; (fit, suit): to ~ **with** acompanhar, combinar com // n, pl ~**es**: **to have a ~** at tentar sorte com; **to be on the ~** mexer-se, estar a trabalhar; **whose ~ is it?** de quem é a vez?; **he's going to do it** ele vai fazê-lo; **to ~ for a walk** ir passear; **to ~ dancing** ir dançar; **how did it ~?** como foi? or que tal saiu isso?; **to ~ about** vi (rumour) propagar-se // vt fus: **how do I ~ about this?** como é que eu faço isso?; **to ~ ahead** vi (make progress) avançar; (get going) continuar; **to ~ along** vi assistir // vt fus ladear; **to ~ along with** acompanhar; **to ~ away** vi ir-se, ir embora; **to ~ back** vi voltar; (fall back) retroceder; **to ~ back on** vt fus (promise) faltar com; **to ~ by** vi (years, time) passar // vt fus guiar-se por; **to ~ down** vi descer, baixar; (ship) afundar; (sun) pôr-se // vt fus baixar por; **to ~ for** vt fus (fetch) ir buscar; (like) gostar de; (attack) atacar; **to ~ in** vi entrar; **to ~ in for** vt fus (competition) apresentar-se em; **to ~ into** vt fus entrar em; (investigate) investigar; (embark on) embarcar em; **to ~ off** vi ir-se, andar; (food) passar, apodrecer; (explode) explodir; (event) realizar-se // vt fus deixar de gostar de; **to ~ on** vi seguir, continuar; (happen) acontecer, ocorrer; **to ~ on doing sth** continuar a fazer algo; **to ~ out** vi sair; (fire, light) apagar-se; **to ~ over** vi (ship) soçobrar // vt fus (check) revisar; **to ~ through** vt fus (town etc) atravessar; **to ~ up** vi subir; **to ~ without** vt fus passar sem.

**goad** [gəud] vt aguilhoar.

**go-ahead** ['gəuəhɛd] adj empreendedor(a) // n luz f verde, permissão f para prosseguir.

**goal** [gəul] n meta, alvo; (score) gol m; **~keeper** n goleiro; (Pt) guarda-redes m; **~post** n meta, trave f.

**goat** [gəut] n cabra; (masculino) bode m.

**gobble** ['gɔbl] vt (also: ~ **down**, ~ **up**) engolir rapidamente, devorar.

**goblet** ['gɔblɪt] n cálice m.

**goblin** ['gɔblɪn] n duende m.

**go-cart** ['gəukɑːt] n andadeira, andador m.

**god** [gɔd] n deus m; **G~** n Deus m; **~child** n afilhado; **~dess** n deusa; **~father** n padrinho; **~forsaken** adj miserável, abandonado; **~send** n dádiva do céu; **~son** n afilhado.

**goggles** ['gɔglz] npl óculos mpl de proteção (Pt: -cç-).

**going** ['gəuɪŋ] adj: **the ~ rate** tarifa corrente or em vigor.

**gold** [gəuld] n ouro // adj de ouro; **~en** adj (made of ~) de ouro, dourado; (~ in colour) dourado; **~fish** n peixe-dourado m; **~mine** n mina de ouro.

**golf** [gɔlf] n golfe m; **~ club** n clube m de golfe; (stick) taco; **~ course** n campo de golfe; **~er** n jogador(a) m/f de golfe.

**gondola** ['gɔndələ] n gôndola.

**gone** [gɔn] pp of **go.**

**gong** [gɔŋ] n gongo.

**gonorrhea** [gɔnə'rɪə] n gonorréia.

**good** [gud] adj (gen) bom/boa; (kind) bom, bondoso; (well-behaved) educado; (useful) útil // n bem m, proveito; **~s** npl bens mpl; (COMM) mercadorias fpl; **to be ~** at ser bom em; **to be ~ for** servir para; **it's ~ for you** faz-lhe bem; **would you be ~ enough to...?** podia fazer-me o favor de...?, poderia me fazer a gentileza de...?; **a ~ deal (of)** muito; **a ~ many** muitos; **to make ~** vi reparar; **for ~** para sempre, definitivamente; **~ morning/afternoon!** bom dia/boa tarde!; **~ evening!** boa tarde!, boa noite!; **~ night!** boa noite!; **~-bye!** adeus!; **to say ~-bye** despedir-se; **G~ Friday** n Sexta-Feira Santa; **~-looking** adj de boa aparência; **~ness** n (of person) bondade f; **for ~ness sake!** pelo amor de Deus!; **~ness gracious!** meu Deus!; **~will** n boa vontade f.

**goose** [guːs], pl **geese** n ganso.

**gooseberry** ['guzbərɪ] n groselha.

**gooseflesh** ['guːsflɛʃ] n, **goose pimples** npl pele f arrepiada.

**gore** [gɔː*] vt escornar // n sangue m.

**gorge** [gɔːdʒ] n desfiladeiro // vr: **to ~ o.s. (on)** empanturrar-se de.

**gorgeous** ['gɔːdʒəs] adj magnífico, maravilhoso.

**gorilla** [gə'rilə] n gorila m.

**gorse** [gɔːs] n tojo.

**gory** ['gɔːri] adj sangrento.

**go-slow** ['gəu'sləu] n greve f de trabalho lento, operação f tartaruga.

**gospel** ['gɔspl] n evangelho.

**gossip** ['gɔsip] n (scandal) escândalo; (chat) fofoca, bisbilhotice f; (scandalmonger) fofoqueiro/a; (talker) bisbilhoteiro/a m/f // vi tagarelar, bisbilhotar.

**got** [gɔt] pt, pp of get; ~**ten** (US) pp of get.

**gout** [gaut] n gota.

**govern** ['gʌvən] vt (gen) governar; (dominate) dominar.

**governess** ['gʌvənis] n governanta.

**government** ['gʌvnmənt] n governo; ~**al** [-'mentl] adj governamental.

**governor** ['gʌvənə*] n governador m; (of jail) diretor/a (Pt: -ct-) m/f.

**gown** [gaun] n vestido; (of teacher, judge) toga.

**G.P.** n abbr of general practitioner.

**GPO** n abbr of General Post Office.

**grab** [græb] vt agarrar, apanhar.

**grace** [greis] n (REL) graça; (gracefulness) elegância, fineza // vt (favour) honrar; (adorn) adornar; **5 days'** ~ um prazo de 5 dias; **to say** ~ dar graças (antes de comer); ~**ful** adj elegante, gracioso; **gracious** ['greiʃəs] adj gracioso, afável.

**grade** [greid] n (quality) classe f, qualidade f; (degree) grau m; (US: SCOL) classe; ~ **crossing** n (US) passagem f de nível // vt classificar.

**gradient** ['greidiənt] n declive m.

**gradual** ['grædjuəl] adj gradual, suave; ~**ly** adv gradualmente.

**graduate** ['grædjuit] n graduado, licenciado // vi ['grædjueit] formar-se, licenciar-se; **graduation** [-'eiʃən] n graduação f.

**graft** [grɑːft] n (AGR, MED) enxerto; (bribery) suborno; (col) bola // vt enxertar.

**grain** [grein] n grão m; (corn) grãos mpl, cereais mpl; (in wood) veio, fibra.

**gram** [græm] n grama m.

**grammar** ['græmə*] n gramática; **grammatical** [grə'mætikl] adj gramatical.

**gramme** [græm] n = **gram**.

**gramophone** ['græməfəun] n gramofone m, toca-discos m inv; (Pt) giradiscos m inv.

**granary** ['grænəri] n celeiro.

**grand** [grænd] adj grande, magnífico; ~**children** npl netos mpl; ~**dad** n vovô m; ~**daughter** n neta; ~**eur** ['grændjə*] n grandeza, magnificência; ~**father** n avô m; ~**iose** ['grændiəuz] adj grandioso; (pej) pomposo; ~**ma** n vóvó f; ~**mother** n avó f; ~**pa** n = ~**dad**; ~ **piano** n piano de cauda; ~**son** n neto; ~**stand** n (SPORT) tribuna principal.

**granite** ['grænit] n granito.

**granny** ['græni] n avó f, vóvó f.

**grant** [grɑːnt] vt (concede) conceder; (admit) admitir // n (SCOL) bolsa; **to take sth for** ~**ed** dar algo por certo.

**granulated sugar** ['grænjuleitid-] n açúcar m granulado.

**granule** ['grænjuːl] n grânulo.

**grape** [greip] n uva; **sour** ~**s** (fig) inveja.

**grapefruit** ['greipfruːt] n toranja.

**graph** [grɑːf] n gráfico; ~**ic** adj gráfico.

**grapple** ['græpl] vi: **to** ~ **with sth** esforçar-se por resolver algo.

**grasp** [grɑːsp] vt agarrar, segurar; (understand) compreender, entender // n (grip) ato (Pt: -ct-) de agarrar; (reach) alcance m; (understanding) compreensão f; ~**ing** adj avaro.

**grass** [grɑːs] n grama; (lawn) relva;

~**hopper** n gafanhoto; ~**land** n
pradaria; ~**roots** adj popular; ~
**snake** n serpente f; ~**y** adj coberto
de grama.

**grate** [greit] n (fireplace) lareira;
(of iron) grelha // vi ranger // vt
(CULIN) ralar.

**grateful** ['greitful] adj agradecido.

**grater** ['greitəʳ] n ralador m, ralo.

**gratify** ['grætifai] vt gratificar,
(whim) satisfazer; ~**ing** adj grato,
gratificante.

**grating** ['greitiŋ] n (iron bars) n
grade f // adj (noise) áspero.

**gratitude** ['grætitju:d] n
agradecimento.

**gratuity** [grə'tju:iti] n gratificação
f, gorjeta.

**grave** [greiv] n túmulo // adj sério,
grave; ~**digger** n coveiro.

**gravel** ['grævl] n cascalho.

**grave:** ~**stone** n lápide f; ~**yard** n
cemitério.

**gravity** ['græviti] n gravidade f;
(seriousness) seriedade f.

**gravy** ['greivi] n molho.

**gray** [grei] adj = **grey.**

**graze** [greiz] vi pastar // vt (touch
lightly) roçar; (scrape) raspar // n
(MED) esfoladura, arranhadura.

**grease** [gri:s] n (fat) gordura;
(lubricant) lubrificante m // vt
engordurar; ~**proof** adj à prova de
gordura; (paper) papel m de cera
(vegetal); **greasy** adj gorduroso.

**great** [greit] adj grande; (col)
magnífico, estupendo; **G~ Britain** n
Grã-Bretanha; ~**grandfather** n
bisavô m; ~**grandmother** n bisavó
f; ~**ly** adv imensamente, muito;
~**ness** n grandeza.

**Greece** [gri:s] n Grécia.

**greed** [gri:d] n (also: ~**iness**)
avidez f, cobiça; (for food) gula;
~**ily** adv com avidez; ~**y** adj
avarento; (for food) guloso.

**Greek** [gri:k] adj grego // n
grego/a; (LING) grego.

**green** [gri:n] adj verde; (in-

experienced) inexperiente // n
verde m; (stretch of grass) relvado,
relva; ~**s** npl verduras fpl; ~**gage** n
rainha-cláudia; ~**grocer** n
verdureiro; ~**house** n estufa; ~**ish**
adj esverdeado.

**Greenland** ['gri:nlənd] n
Groenlândia.

**greet** [gri:t] vt saudar; (welcome)
dar as boas vindas a; ~**ing** n (greet)
cumprimento; (welcome) acolhimento.

**gregarious** [grə'gɛərɪəs] adj
gregário.

**grenade** [grə'neid] n granada.

**grew** [gru:] pt of **grow.**

**grey** [grei] adj cinzento; ~**-haired**
adj grisalho; ~**hound** n galgo.

**grid** [grid] n grade f; (ELEC) rede f.

**grief** [gri:f] n dor f, pena.

**grievance** ['gri:vəns] n motivo de
queixas, agravo.

**grieve** [gri:v] vi afligir-se, sofrer //
vt dar pena a; **to ~ for** chorar por.

**grievous** ['gri:vəs] adj penoso.

**grill** [gril] n (on cooker) grelha // vt
grelhar; (question) interrogar
cerradamente.

**grille** [gril] n grade f.

**grim** [grim] adj sinistro; (fam)
horrível.

**grimace** [gri'meis] n careta // vi
fazer caretas.

**grime** [graim] n sujeira; **grimy** adj
sujo.

**grin** [grin] n sorriso largo // vi
sorrir abertamente.

**grind** [graind], pt, pp **ground** vt
(coffee, pepper etc) moer; (make
sharp) afiar // n (work) trabalho
pesado e aborrecido; **to ~ one's
teeth** ranger os dentes.

**grip** [grip] n (hands) aperto;
(handle) punho; (of racquet etc)
cabo; (holdall) valise f;
(understanding) compreensão f // vt
agarrar; **to come to ~s with** atacar
algo de frente; ~**ping** adj
absorvente.

**grisly** ['grɪzlɪ] *adj* horrendo, medonho.

**gristle** ['grɪsl] *n* cartilagem *f*.

**grit** [grɪt] *n* areia, grão *m* de areia; (*courage*) coragem *f* // *vt* (*road*) pôr areia em; **to ~ one's teeth** ranger os dentes.

**groan** [grəun] *n* gemido // *vi* gemer.

**grocer** ['grəusə*] *n* dono de mercearia; **~ies** *npl* comestíveis *mpl*; **~'s (shop)** *n* mercearia.

**groggy** ['grɔgɪ] *adj* cambaleante; (*BOXING*) grogue.

**groin** [grɔɪn] *n* virilha.

**groom** [gruːm] *n* cavalariço; (*also:* **bride~**) noivo *m* // *vt* (*horse*) tratar; **well~ed** bem-posto.

**groove** [gruːv] *n* ranhura, entalhe *m*.

**grope** [grəup] *vi* andar às apalpadelas; **to ~ for** *vt fus* procurar às apalpadelas.

**gross** [grəus] *adj* grosso; (*COMM*) bruto; **~ly** *adv* (*greatly*) enormemente, gritantemente.

**grotesque** [grə'tɛsk] *adj* grotesco.

**grotto** ['grɔtəu] *n* gruta.

**ground** [graund] *pt, pp of* **grind** // *n* terreno, chão *m*; (*SPORT*) campo, terreno; (*reason: gen pl*) causa, razão *f* // *vt* (*plane*) manter em terra; (*US: ELEC*) ligar à terra // *vi* (*ship*) encalhar; **~s** *npl* (*of coffee etc*) borra; (*gardens etc*) jardins *mpl*, parque *m*; **on the ~** no chão; **to the ~** por terra; **~ floor** *n* andar *m* térreo; (*Pt*) rés-do-chão *m*; **~ing** *n* (*in education*) conhecimentos *mpl* básicos; **~less** *adj* infundado; **~sheet** *n* capa impermeável; **~ staff** *n* pessoal *m* de terra; **~work** *n* base *f*, preparação *f*.

**group** [gruːp] *n* grupo; (*musical*) conjunto // *vb: also:* **~ together**) *vt* agrupar // *vi* agrupar-se.

**grouse** [graus] *n, pl inv* (*bird*) tetraz *m*, galo-silvestre *m* // *vi* (*complain*) queixar-se.

**grove** [grəuv] *n* arvoredo.

**grovel** ['grɔvl] *vi* (*fig*) humilhar-se.

**grow** [grəu], *pt* **grew**, *pp* **grown** *vi* (*gen*) crescer; (*plants*) cultivar; (*increase*) aumentar; (*spread*) espalhar-se, estender-se; (*become*) tornar-se; **to ~ rich/weak** enriquecer-se/enfraquecer-se // *vt* cultivar, deixar crescer; **to ~ up** *vi* crescer, fazer-se homem/mulher; **~er** *n* cultivador(a) *m/f*, produtor(a) *m/f*; **~ing** *adj* crescente.

**growl** [graul] *vi* rosnar.

**grown** [grəun] *pp of* **grow**; **~-up** *n* adulto, pessoa mais velha.

**growth** [grəuθ] *n* crescimento, desenvolvimento; (*what has grown*) aumento; (*MED*) abcesso, tumor *m*.

**grub** [grʌb] *n* larva, lagarta; (*col: food*) bóia.

**grubby** ['grʌbɪ] *adj* sujo, porco.

**grudge** [grʌdʒ] *n* motivo de rancor // *vt*: **to ~ sb sth** dar algo a alguém de má vontade, invejar algo a alguém; **to bear sb a ~** guardar rancor a alguém por algo; **he ~s (giving) the money** ele dá dinheiro de má vontade.

**gruelling** ['gruəlɪŋ] *adj* duro, árduo.

**gruesome** ['gruːsəm] *adj* horrível.

**gruff** [grʌf] *adj* (*voice*) rouca; (*manner*) brusco.

**grumble** ['grʌmbl] *vi* resmungar, queixar-se.

**grumpy** ['grʌmpɪ] *adj* rabugento.

**grunt** [grʌnt] *vi* grunhir // *n* grunhido.

**guarantee** [gærən'tiː] *n* garantia // *vt* garantir.

**guarantor** [gærən'tɔː*] *n* fiador(a) *m/f*.

**guard** [gɑːd] *n* guarda; (*RAIL*) condutor *m* de trem (*Pt: de comboio*) // *vt* guardar; (*fig*) cauteloso; **~ian** *n* protetor (*-ct-*) *m/f*; (*of minor*) tutor(a) *m/f*.

**guerrilla** [gə'rɪlə] *n* guerrilheiro(a) *m/f*; **~ warfare** *n* guerrilha.

**guess** [gɛs] *vt, vi* (*gen*) adivinhar;

*(suppose)* supor // n suposição f, conjetura *(Pt: -ct-)*; **to take** *or* **have a ~** adivinhar; **~work** n conjeturas *(Pt: -ct-)* fpl.

**guest** [gɛst] n convidado; *(in hotel)* hóspede m/f; **~-house** n casa de hóspedes, pensão f; **~ room** n quarto de hóspedes.

**guffaw** [gʌˈfɔ:] n gargalhada // vi rir-se às gargalhadas.

**guidance** ['gaɪdns] n *(gen)* orientação f; *(advice)* conselhos mpl.

**guide** [gaɪd] n *(person)* guia m/f; *(fig)* guia m // vt guiar; **(girl) ~** n escoteira; **~book** n guia m; **~ dog** n cão-guia m; **~ lines** npl *(fig)* princípios mpl gerais, diretrizes fpl.

**guild** [gɪld] n grêmio; **~hall** n *(Brit)* sede f da prefeitura.

**guile** [gaɪl] n astúcia; **~less** adj ingênuo, cândido.

**guillotine** ['gɪləti:n] n guilhotina.

**guilt** [gɪlt] n culpa; **~y** adj culpado.

**guinea pig** ['gɪnɪpɪg] n porquinho-da-Índia m, cobaia.

**guise** [gaɪz] n: **in** *or* **under the ~ of** sob a aparência de.

**guitar** [gɪˈtɑː*] n violão m; **~ist** n violonista m/f.

**gulf** [gʌlf] n golfo; *(abyss)* abismo.

**gull** [gʌl] n gaivota.

**gullet** ['gʌlɪt] n esôfago; *(fam)* garganta.

**gullible** ['gʌlɪbl] adj crédulo.

**gully** ['gʌlɪ] n barranco.

**gulp** [gʌlp] vi engolir saliva // vt *(also: ~ down)* engolir // n: **at one ~** de um gole.

**gum** [gʌm] n *(ANAT)* gengiva; *(glue)* goma; *(sweet)* chiclete m; *(Pt)* pastilha elástica // vt colar; **~boots** npl botas fpl de borracha, galochas fpl.

**gun** [gʌn] n *(gen)* arma de fogo; *(small)* pistola; *(shotgun)* espingarda de caça; *(rifle)* espingarda; *(cannon)* canhão m; **~boat** n canhoneira; **~fire** n fogo, tiroteio;

**~man** n pistoleiro; **~ner** n artilheiro; **at ~point** sob a ameaça de uma arma; **~powder** n pólvora; **~shot** n tiro de arma de fogo; **~smith** n armeiro.

**gurgle** ['gɜːgl] vi gorgolejar.

**gush** [gʌʃ] vi jorrar; *(fig)* alvoroçar-se.

**gusset** ['gʌsɪt] n nesga.

**gust** [gʌst] n *(of wind)* rajada.

**gusto** ['gʌstəʊ] n entusiasmo.

**gut** [gʌt] n intestino, tripa; *(MUS etc)* corda de tripa; **~s** npl *(courage)* coragem f.

**gutter** ['gʌtə*] n *(of roof)* calha; *(in street)* sarjeta.

**guttural** ['gʌtərl] adj gutural.

**guy** [gaɪ] n *(also: ~rope)* corda; *(col: man)* tipo, sujeito.

**guzzle** ['gʌzl] vi comer *or* beber com gula // vt engolir.

**gym** [dʒɪm] n *(also: gymnasium)* ginásio; *(also: gymnastics)* ginástica; **~nast** n ginasta m/f; **~nastics** n ginástica; **~ shoes** npl sapatos mpl de ginástica; **~ slip** n túnica de ginástica.

**gynaecologist, gynecologist** *(US)* [gaɪnɪˈkɒlədʒɪst] n ginecologista m/f; **gynaecology, gynecology** *(US)* [-nəˈkɒlədʒɪ] n ginecologia.

**gypsy** ['dʒɪpsɪ] n = **gipsy**.

**gyrate** [dʒaɪˈreɪt] vi girar.

# H

**haberdashery** ['hæbəˈdæʃərɪ] n armarinho.

**habit** ['hæbɪt] n hábito, uso, costume m; *(costume)* hábito.

**habitable** ['hæbɪtəbl] adj habitável.

**habitual** [həˈbɪtjuəl] adj habitual, costumeiro; *(drinker, liar)* invete-rado; **~ly** adv habitualmente.

**hack** [hæk] vt *(cut)* cortar; *(slice)*

talhar // n corte m; (axe blow) talho.

**hackneyed** ['hæknɪd] adj corriqueiro, batido.

**had** [hæd] pt, pp of **have**.

**haddock** ['hædək] n pl or ~s n hadoque m.

**hadn't** ['hædnt] = **had not**.

**haemorrhage, hemorrhage** (US) ['hemərɪdʒ] n hemorragia.

**haemorrhoids, hemorrhoids** (US) ['hemərɔɪdz] npl hemorróidas fpl.

**haggard** ['hægəd] adj emaciado, macilento.

**haggle** ['hægl] vi (argue) discutir; (bargain) pechinchar, regatear.

**Hague** [heɪg] n: **The ~** a Haia.

**hail** [heɪl] n (weather) granizo // vt cumprimentar, saudar; (call) chamar // vi chover granizo; **~stone** n pedra de granizo.

**hair** [hɛə*] n (gen) cabelo, pêlo; (one ~) fio de cabelo, pêlo; (head of ~) cabeleira; (on legs) pêlo; **grey ~** cabelo grisalho; **~brush** n escova de cabelo; **~cut** n corte m de cabelo; **~do** n penteado; **~dresser** n cabeleireiro/a; **~dresser's** n cabeleireiro; **~drier** n secador m de cabelo; **~net** n rede f de cabelo; **~ piece** n trança postiça; **~pin** n grampo, pinça; **~pin bend** n curva fechada; **~raising** adj horripilante, de arrepiar os cabelos; **~ remover** n depilador m; (cream) creme m depilatório; **~ spray** n spray m para o cabelo; **~style** n penteado; **~y** adj cabeludo, peludo.

**half** [hɑːf], pl **halves** n metade f // adj meio // adv ao meio, pela metade; **~-an-hour** meia hora; **two and a ~** dois e meio; **~ a pound** meia libra; **to cut sth in ~** cortar algo ao meio; **~ asleep** meio adormecido; **~-price** pela metade do preço; **~-back** n (SPORT) meio-campo; **~-breed, ~-caste** n mestiço; **~-hearted** adj irresoluto,

indiferente; **~-hour** n meia hora; **~-time** n meio tempo; **~ way** adv a meio caminho.

**halibut** ['hælɪbət] n, pl inv hipoglosso.

**hall** [hɔːl] n (for concerts) sala; (entrance way) hall m, vestíbulo; **town ~** prefeitura; **~ of residence** n residência universitária.

**hallmark** ['hɔːlmɑːk] n (mark) marca; (seal) selo.

**hallo** ['hʌləʊ] excl = **hello**.

**hallucination** [həluːsɪ'neɪʃən] n alucinação f.

**halo** ['heɪləʊ] n (of saint) auréola.

**halt** [hɔːlt] n (stop) alto, parada; (Pt) paragem f; (RAIL) pequena parada // vi parar // vt deter; (process) interromper.

**halve** [hɑːv] vt dividir ao meio.

**halves** [hɑːvz] pl of **half**.

**ham** [hæm] n presunto, pernil m; (actor) ator m (Pt: -ct-) exagerado.

**hamburger** ['hæmbəːgə*] n hambúrguer m.

**hamlet** ['hæmlɪt] n aldeola, lugarejo.

**hammer** ['hæmə*] n martelo // vt martelar // vi (on door) bater insistentemente.

**hammock** ['hæmɔk] n rede f.

**hamper** ['hæmpə*] vt dificultar, atrapalhar // n cesto.

**hand** [hænd] n mão f; (of clock) ponteiro; (writing) letra; (applause) aplauso; (worker) trabalhador m; (measure) palmo // vt (give) dar, transmitir; (deliver) entregar; **to give sb a ~** dar uma mão a alguém, ajudar alguém; **at ~** à mão, disponível; **in ~** sob controle; (COMM) em caixa, à disposição; **on the one ~ ..., on the other ~ ..** por um lado .., por outro (lado) ..; **to ~ in** vt entregar; **to ~ out** vt distribuir; **to ~ over** vt (deliver) entregar; (surrender) ceder; **~bag** n bolsa; **~basin** n pia; **~book** n manual m; **~brake** n freio de mão; (Pt) travão *m* de mão; **~cuffs** *npl* algemas *fpl*; **~ful** *n* punhado.

**handicap** [ˈhændɪkæp] *n* handicap *m*, desvantagem *f* // *vt* pôr obstáculos; **mentally/physically ~ped** deficiente mental/físico.

**handicraft** [ˈhændɪkrɑːft] *n* artesanato, trabalho manual.

**handkerchief** [ˈhæŋkətʃɪf] *n* lenço.

**handle** [ˈhændl] *n* (*of door etc*) maçaneta, puxador *m*; (*of cup etc*) asa; (*of knife etc*) cabo; (*for winding*) manivela; (*fam: name*) título // *vt* (*touch*) tocar; (*deal with*) tratar de; (*treat: people*) lidar com; **'~ with care'** 'cuidado – frágil'; **to fly off the ~** perder as estribeiras; **~bar(s)** *n*(*pl*) guidão *m*.

**hand-luggage** [ˈhændlʌgɪdʒ] *n* bagagem *f* de mão.

**handmade** [ˈhændmeɪd] *adj* feito à mão.

**handout** [ˈhændaʊt] *n* (*distribution*) distribuição *f*; (*charity*) doação *f*, esmola; (*leaflet*) folheto; (*university*) apostila.

**handshake** [ˈhændʃeɪk] *n* aperto de mão.

**handsome** [ˈhænsəm] *adj* bonito.

**handwriting** [ˈhændraɪtɪŋ] *n* caligrafia.

**handy** [ˈhændɪ] *adj* (*close at hand*) à mão; (*convenient*) prático (*Pt*: -ct-); (*skilful*) habilidoso, hábil; **~man** *n* biscateiro.

**hang** [hæŋ], *pt*, *pp* **hung** *vt* pendurar; (*criminal*: *pt*, *pp* **hanged**) enforcar; (*head*) baixar // *vi* pendurar-se; **to ~ about** *vi* rondar, ficar perto; **to ~ on** *vi* (*wait*) esperar; **to ~ up** *vi* (*TEL*) desligar.

**hangar** [ˈhæŋə*] *n* hangar *m*.

**hanger** [ˈhæŋə*] *n* cabide *m*; **~-on** *n* parasita *m/f*, filão/filona *m/f*.

**hangover** [ˈhæŋəʊvə*] *n* (*after drinking*) ressaca.

**hang-up** [ˈhæŋʌp] *n* mania, grilo.

**hanker** [ˈhæŋkə*] *vi*: **to ~ after**

(*miss*) sentir saudade de; (*long for*) desejar ardentemente.

**hankie, hanky** [ˈhæŋkɪ] *n* abbr of **handkerchief.**

**haphazard** [hæpˈhæzəd] *adj* fortuito, acidental.

**happen** [ˈhæpən] *vi* ocorrer, suceder; (*take place*) acontecer, realizar-se; **to ~ upon** encontrar por acaso; **~ing** *n* acontecimento, ocorrência.

**happily** [ˈhæpɪlɪ] *adv* (*luckily*) felizmente; (*cheerfully*) alegremente.

**happiness** [ˈhæpɪnɪs] *n* (*gen*) felicidade *f*; (*joy*) alegria.

**happy** [ˈhæpɪ] *adj* feliz, contente; **to be ~ (with)** estar contente (com); **to be ~** ser feliz.

**harass** [ˈhærəs] *vt* atormentar, hostilizar; **~ment** *n* perseguição *f*; (*worry*) preocupação *f*.

**harbour, harbor** (*US*) [ˈhɑːbə*] *n* porto; (*fig*) refúgio // *vt* (*hope etc*) abrigar; (*hide*) esconder.

**hard** [hɑːd] *adj* (*gen*) duro; (*difficult*) difícil; (*work*) árduo; (*person*) severo, cruel // *adv* (*work*) muito, diligentemente; (*think*, *try*) seriamente; **to look ~ (at)** olhar firme or fixamente (para); **no ~ feelings!** sem ressentimentos!; **to be ~ of hearing** ser surdo; **to be done by** ser tratado injustamente; **~back** *n* livro de capa dura; **~board** *n* madeira compensada; **~en** *vt* endurecer; (*fig*) tornar insensível // *vi* endurecer-se; **~-headed** *adj* prático (*Pt*: -ct-), pouco sentimental; **~ labour** *n* trabalhos *mpl* forçados.

**hardly** [ˈhɑːdlɪ] *adv* (*scarcely*) apenas, mal; **that can ~ be true** dificilmente pode ser verdade; **~ ever** quase nunca.

**hardness** [ˈhɑːdnɪs] *n* dureza.

**hardship** [ˈhɑːdʃɪp] *n* (*troubles*) sofrimento; (*financial*) privação *f*.

**hard-up** [ˌhɑːdˈʌp] *adj* (*col*) liso, duro.

**hardware** [ˈhɑːdwɛə*] *n* ferragens *fpl*, maquinaria; (*COMPUTERS*) material *m*; ~ **shop** *n* loja de ferragens.

**hard-wearing** [hɑːdˈwɛərɪŋ] *adj* resistente, duradouro.

**hard-working** [hɑːdˈwɜːkɪŋ] *adj* trabalhador(a).

**hardy** [ˈhɑːdɪ] *adj* forte; (*plant*) resistente.

**hare** [hɛə*] *n* lebre *f*; ~-**brained** *adj* estonteado, desatinado.

**harem** [hɑːˈriːm] *n* harém *m*.

**harm** [hɑːm] *n* dano, mal *m* // *vt* (*person*) causar dano, prejudicar; (*thing*) danificar; **out of** ~'s **way** a salvo; ~**ful** *adj* prejudicial; (*pest*) daninho; ~**less** *adj* inofensivo.

**harmonica** [hɑːˈmɒnɪkə] *n* gaita de boca, harmônica.

**harmonious** [hɑːˈməʊnɪəs] *adj* harmonioso; **harmonize** [ˈhɑːmənaɪz] *vt/i* harmonizar; **harmony** [ˈhɑːmənɪ] *n* harmonia.

**harness** [ˈhɑːnɪs] *n* arreios *mpl* // *vt* (*horse*) arrear, pôr arreios em; (*resources*) aproveitar.

**harp** [hɑːp] *n* harpa // *vi*: **to** ~ **on about** bater sempre na mesma tecla sobre; ~**ist** *n* harpista *m/f*.

**harpoon** [hɑːˈpuːn] *n* arpão *m*.

**harrowing** [ˈhærəʊɪŋ] *adj* doloroso, pungente.

**harsh** [hɑːʃ] *adj* (*hard*) duro, cruel; (*severe*) severo; (*unpleasant*) desagradável; (*: colour*) dissonante; (*contrast*) violento; ~**ness** *n* dureza.

**harvest** [ˈhɑːvɪst] *n* colheita; (*of grapes*) vindima // *vt/i* colher; ~**er** *n* (*machine*) segadeira.

**has** [hæz] *vb see* **have**.

**hash** [hæʃ] *n* (*CULIN*) picadinho; (*fig: mess*) confusão *f*, bagunça.

**hashish** [ˈhæʃɪʃ] *n* haxixe *m*.

**hasn't** [ˈhæznt] = **has not**.

**hassle** [ˈhæsl] *n* briga, dificuldade *f* // *vt* molestar, chatear.

**haste** [heɪst] *n* pressa; **hasten** [ˈheɪsn] *vt* acelerar // *vi* apressar-se; **hastily** *adv* depressa; **hasty** *adj* apressado.

**hat** [hæt] *n* chapéu *m*.

**hatch** [hætʃ] *n* (*NAUT: also*: ~**way**) escotilha // *vi* sair do ovo, chocar // *vt* incubar; (*plot*) tramar, maquinar.

**hatchback** [ˈhætʃbæk] *n* (*AUT*) carro com porta traseira.

**hatchet** [ˈhætʃɪt] *n* machadinha.

**hate** [heɪt] *vt* odiar, detestar // *n* ódio; ~**ful** *adj* odioso; **hatred** *n* ódio.

**hat trick** [ˈhættrɪk] *n* (*SPORT, also fig*) três triunfos seguidos.

**haughty** [ˈhɔːtɪ] *adj* soberbo, arrogante.

**haul** [hɔːl] *vt* puxar; (*by lorry*) carregar, fretar // *n* (*of fish*) redada; (*of stolen goods etc*) pilhagem *f*, presa; ~**age** *n* transporte *m*; (*costs*) gasto com transporte; ~**ier** *n* contratador *m* de frete, fretador *m*.

**haunch** [hɔːntʃ] *n* anca, quadril *m*; (*of meat*) quarto traseiro.

**haunt** [hɔːnt] *vt* (*subj: ghost*) assombrar; (*frequent*) freqüentar; (*obsess*) obcecar // *n* lugar *m* freqüentado; ~**ed house** casa mal-assombrada.

**have** [hæv], *pt, pp* **had** *vt* (*gen*) ter; (*possess*) possuir; (*shower*) tomar; (*meal*) comer; **to** ~ **sth done** mandar fazer algo; **she has to do it** ela tem que fazê-lo; **I had better leave** é melhor que eu vá embora; **I won't** ~ **it** não vou agüentar isso; **he has gone** foi embora; **to** ~ **it out with sb** ajustar as contas com alguém; **to** ~ **a baby** dar à luz, ter um nenê.

**haven** [ˈheɪvn] *n* porto; (*fig*) abrigo, refúgio.

**haven't** [ˈhævnt] = **have not**.

**haversack** [ˈhævəsæk] *n* mochila.

**havoc** [ˈhævək] *n* destruição *f*.

**hawk** [hɔːk] *n* falcão *m*.

**hay** [heɪ] *n* feno; ~ **fever** *n* febre *f*

do feno; **~stack** n palheiro.

**haywire** ['heɪwaɪə*] adj (col): **to go ~** (person) ficar maluco; (plan) desorganizar-se, degringolar.

**hazard** ['hæzəd] n risco, acaso // vt aventurar; **~ous** adj (dangerous) perigoso; (risky) arriscado.

**haze** [heɪz] n névoa, neblina.

**hazelnut** ['heɪzlnʌt] n avelã f.

**hazy** ['heɪzɪ] adj nublado; (idea) confuso.

**he** [hi:] pron ele; **~ who...** ele que ..., aquele que ...; **~-man** n macho.

**head** [hɛd] n cabeça; (leader) chefe m/f, líder m/f // vt (list) encabeçar; (group) liderar; **~s (or tails)** cara (ou coroa); **~ first** de cabeça; **~ over heels** de pernas para o ar; **to ~ the ball** cabecear a bola; **to ~ for** vt fus dirigir-se a; **~ache** n dor f de cabeça; **~ing** n título, cabeçalho; **~lamp** n farol m (de veículo); **~land** n promontório; **~light** n ~lamp; **~line** n manchete f, título; **~long** adv (fall) de cabeça; (rush) precipitadamente; **~master** n diretor (Pt: -ct-) m (de escola); **~mistress** n diretora (Pt: -ct-) f (de escola); **~ office** n matriz f; **~-on** adj (collision) de frente; **~phones** npl fones mpl de ouvido; **~quarters (HQ)** npl sede f geral; (MIL) quartel m general; **~rest** n apoio para a cabeça; **~room** n (in car) espaço (para a cabeça); (under bridge) vão m livre; **~scarf** n lenço de cabeça; **~stone** n lápide f de ponta cabeça; **~strong** adj voluntarioso, teimoso; **~ waiter** n maitre m, garçom m chefe; **~way** n progresso; **to make ~way** avançar; **~wind** n vento contrário.

**heal** [hi:l] vt curar // vi cicatrizar.

**health** [hɛlθ] n saúde f; **good ~!** saúde!; **~ food** n comida natural or saudável; **H~ Service** n Previdência Social; **~y** adj (gen) são/sã, sadio.

**heap** [hi:p] n pilha, montão m // vt

amontoar, empilhar; (plate) encher.

**hear** [hɪə*], pt, pp **heard** [hə:d] vt ouvir; (listen to) escutar; (lecture) assistir // vi ouvir; **to ~ about** ouvir falar de; **to ~ from sb** ter notícias de alguém; **~ing** n (sense) audição f, ouvido; (LAW) audiência; **~ing aid** n aparelho para a surdez; **~say** n boato, ouvir-dizer m.

**hearse** [hə:s] n carro fúnebre.

**heart** [ha:t] n coração m; **~s** npl (CARDS) copas fpl; **at ~** no fundo; **by ~** (learn, know) de cor; **~ attack** n ataque m de coração; **~beat** n batida do coração; **~breaking** adj desolador(a); **to be ~broken** estar desolado; **~burn** n azia; **~ failure** n parada cardíaca; **~felt** adj (cordial) cordial; (deeply felt) sincero.

**hearth** [ha:θ] n (gen) lar m; (fireplace) lareira.

**heartily** ['ha:tɪlɪ] adv sinceramente, cordialmente; (laugh) a gargalhadas, com vontade; (eat) apetitosamente.

**heartless** [hɑ:s] adj cruel.

**hearty** ['ha:tɪ] adj cordial, sincero.

**heat** [hi:t] n (gen) calor m; (ardour) ardor m; (SPORT: also: qualifying ~) prova eliminatória // vt esquentar; (fig) acalorar; **to ~ up** vi (gen) aquecer-se; **~ed** adj quente; (fig) acalorado; **~er** n aquecedor m.

**heath** [hi:θ] n (Brit) charneca.

**heathen** ['hi:ðn] n pagão/pagã m/f.

**heather** ['hɛðə*] n urze f.

**heating** ['hi:tɪŋ] n aquecimento.

**heatstroke** ['hi:tstrəʊk] n insolação f.

**heatwave** ['hi:tweɪv] n onda de calor.

**heave** [hi:v] vt (pull) puxar; (push) empurrar (com esforço); (lift) levantar (com esforço) // vi (water) agitar-se // n puxão m; empurrão m; (effort) esforço; (throw) arremesso.

**heaven** ['hɛvn] n céu m; (REL) paraíso; ~**ly** adj celestial; (REL) divino.

**heavily** ['hɛvɪlɪ] adv pesadamente; (drink, smoke) excessivamente; (sleep, sigh) profundamente.

**heavy** ['hɛvɪ] adj pesado; (work) duro; (sea) violento; (rain, meal) forte; (drinker, smoker) grande; (eater) comilão/lona; ~**weight** n (SPORT) peso-pesado.

**Hebrew** ['hiːbruː] adj hebreu/ hebréia; (LING) hebraico.

**heckle** ['hɛkl] vt interromper.

**hectic** ['hɛktɪk] adj febril, agitado.

**he'd** [hiːd] = he would; he had.

**hedge** [hɛdʒ] n cerca-viva, sebe f // vt cercar (com uma sebe) // vi dar evasivas; **to ~ one's bets** (fig) resguardar-se.

**hedgehog** ['hɛdʒhɔg] n ouriço.

**heed** [hiːd] vt (also: take ~ of) (attend to) prestar atenção a; (bear in mind) levar em consideração; ~**less** adj desatento, negligente.

**heel** [hiːl] n salto, calcanhar m // vt (shoe) pôr salto em.

**hefty** ['hɛftɪ] adj (person) robusto; (piece) grande; (price) alto.

**heifer** ['hɛfə*] n novilha, bezerra.

**height** [haɪt] n (of person) estatura; (of building) altura; (high ground) monte m; (altitude) altitude f; ~**en** vt elevar; (fig) aumentar.

**heir** [ɛə*] n herdeiro; ~**ess** n herdeira; ~**loom** n relíquia de família.

**held** [hɛld] pt, pp of **hold**.

**helicopter** ['hɛlɪkɔptə*] n helicóptero.

**hell** [hɛl] n inferno; ~**!** diabos!

**he'll** [hiːl] = he will; he shall.

**hellish** ['hɛlɪʃ] adj infernal; (fam) terrível.

**hello** [hə'ləu] excl oi!, olá!, alô!; (surprise) caramba!

**helm** [hɛlm] n (NAUT) timão m, leme m.

**helmet** ['hɛlmɪt] n elmo, capacete m.

**help** [hɛlp] n ajuda; (charwoman) empregada doméstica, faxineira; (assistant etc) auxiliar m/f // vt ajudar; ~**!** socorro!; ~ **yourself** sirva-se; **he can't** ~ **it** não tem culpa; ~**er** n ajudante m/f; ~**ful** adj útil, benéfico; ~**ing** n porção f; ~**less** adj (incapable) incapaz; (defenceless) indefeso.

**hem** [hɛm] n bainha; **to ~ in** vt cercar, encurralar.

**hemisphere** ['hɛmɪsfɪə*] n hemisfério.

**hen** [hɛn] n galinha.

**hence** [hɛns] adv (therefore) daí, portanto; **2 years** ~ daqui a 2 anos; ~**forth** adv de agora em diante, doravante.

**henchman** ['hɛntʃmən] n partidário, jagunço.

**henpecked** ['hɛnpɛkt] adj dominado pela esposa.

**her** [həː*] pron (direct) a; (indirect) lhe; (stressed, after prep) ela // adj seu/sua or dela; ~ **name** o nome dela.

**herald** ['hɛrəld] n (forerunner) precursor(a) m/f // vt anunciar.

**heraldry** ['hɛrəldrɪ] n heráldica.

**herb** [həːb] n erva.

**herd** [həːd] n rebanho.

**here** [hɪə*] adv aqui; ~**!** (present) presente!; ~ **she is** aqui está ela; ~**after** adv daqui por diante // n: **the** ~**after** a vida de além-túmulo; ~**by** adv (in letter) por este meio.

**hereditary** [hɪ'rɛdɪtrɪ] adj hereditário; **heredity** [-tɪ] n hereditariedade f, herança.

**heresy** ['hɛrəsɪ] n heresia.

**heretic** ['hɛrətɪk] n herege m/f; ~**al** [hɪ'rɛtɪkl] adj herético.

**heritage** ['hɛrɪtɪdʒ] n (gen) herança; (fig) patrimônio.

**hermit** ['həːmɪt] n eremita.

**hernia** ['həːnɪə] n hérnia.

**hero** ['hɪərəu], pl ~**es** n herói m;

(*in book, film*) protagonista *m*; ~**ic**
[hɪ'rəuɪk] *adj* heróico.

**heroin** ['hεrəuɪn] *n* heroína.

**heroine** ['hεrəuɪn] *n* heroína; (*in
book, film*) protagonista.

**heroism** ['hεrəuɪzm] *n* heroísmo.

**heron** ['hεrən] *n* garça.

**herring** ['hεrɪŋ] *n* arenque *m*.

**hers** [həːz] *pron* (o) seu/(a) sua,
(o/a) dela.

**herself** [həː'sεlf] *pron* (*reflexive*) se;
(*emphatic*) ela mesma; (*after prep*)
si (mesma).

**he's** [hiːz] = **he is; he has.**

**hesitant** ['hεzɪtənt] *adj* hesitante,
indeciso.

**hesitate** ['hεzɪteɪt] *vi* hesitar,
duvidar; **hesitation** [-'teɪʃən] *n*
hesitação *f*, indecisão *f*.

**hew** [hjuː] *vt* cortar (com machado).

**hexagon** ['hεksəgən] *n* hexágono;
~**al** [-'sægənl] *adj* hexagonal.

**hi** [haɪ] *excl* oi!, olá!, ei!

**hibernate** ['haɪbəneɪt] *vi* hibernar.

**hiccough, hiccup** ['hɪkʌp] *vi*
estar com soluço; ~**s** *npl* soluço *sg*.

**hid** [hɪd] *pt of* **hide.**

**hidden** ['hɪdn] *pp of* **hide.**

**hide** [haɪd] *n* (*skin*) pele *f* // (*vb: pt
hid, pp hidden*) *vt* esconder, ocultar
// vi: **to** ~ (**from sb**) esconder-se *or*
ocultar-se (de alguém); ~**and-seek**
*n* esconde-esconde *m*; ~**away** *n*
refúgio, esconderijo.

**hideous** ['hɪdɪəs] *adj* horrível.

**hiding** ['haɪdɪŋ] *n* (*beating*) surra; **to
be in** ~ (*concealed*) estar
escondido; ~ **place** *n* esconderijo.

**hierarchy** ['haɪərɑːkɪ] *n*
hierarquia.

**high** [haɪ] *adj* (*gen, speed*) alto; (*number*) grande; (*price*) alto,
elevado; (*wind*) forte; (*voice*) agudo
// *adv*: **it is 20
m** ~ tem 20 m de altura; ~ **in the
air** nas alturas; ~**brow** *adj* culto,
metido a intelectual; ~**chair** *n*
cadeira alta (para criança); ~**handed** *adj* despótico; ~**heeled**

*adj* de salto alto; ~**jack** = **hijack**; ~
**jump** *n* (SPORT) salto em altura;
~**light** *n* (fig: of event) ponto alto //
*vt* realçar; ~**ly** *adv* altamente; ~**ly
strung** *adj* tenso, irritadiço; **H~
Mass** *n* missa cantada; ~**ness** *n*
altura; **Her H~ness** Sua Alteza;
~**pitched** *adj* agudo; ~**rise block**
*n* edifício alto, espigão *m*; ~ **school**
*n* escola secundária; ~ **street** *n* rua
principal; ~**way** *n* estrada, rodovia.

**hijack** ['haɪdʒæk] *vt* seqüestrar;
~**er** *n* seqüestrador/a *m/f*.

**hike** [haɪk] *vi* (go walking)
caminhar; (*tramp*) vagar // *n*
caminhada; **hiker** *n* caminhante
*m/f*, andarilho.

**hilarious** [hɪ'lεərɪəs] *adj*
(*behaviour, event*) hilariante,
alegre.

**hill** [hɪl] *n* colina; (*high*) montanha;
(*slope*) ladeira, rampa; ~**side** *n*
vertente *f*; ~**y** *adj* montanhoso;
(*uneven*) acidentado.

**hilt** [hɪlt] *n* (of sword) punho,
guarda; **to the** ~ plenamente.

**him** [hɪm] *pron* (*direct*) o; (*indirect*)
lhe; (*stressed, after prep*) ele; ~**self**
*pron* (*reflexive*) se; (*emphatic*) ele
mesmo; (*after prep*) si (mesmo).

**hind** [haɪnd] *adj* traseiro // *n* corça.

**hinder** ['hɪndə*] *vt* impedir,
estorvar; **hindrance** ['hɪndrəns] *n*
impedimento, estorvo.

**Hindu** ['hɪnduː] *n* hindu *m/f*.

**hinge** [hɪndʒ] *n* dobradiça, gonzo //
vi (fig): **to** ~ **on** depender de.

**hint** [hɪnt] *n* insinuação *f*; (*advice*)
palpite *m*, dica // vt: **to** ~ **that**
insinuar que // *vi* dar indiretas (Pt:
~**s**); **to** ~ **at** fazer alusão a.

**hip** [hɪp] *n* quadril *m*; ~ **pocket** *n*
bolso traseiro.

**hippopotamus** [hɪpə'pɒtəməs], *pl*
~**es** *or* ~**mi** [-maɪ] *n* hipopótamo.

**hire** ['haɪə*] *vt* (car, equipment)
alugar; (*worker*) contratar // *n*
aluguel *m*; (of person) salário; **for** ~
aluga-se; (*taxi*) livre; ~ **purchase**

**(H.P.)** n compra a prazo.

**his** [hɪz] pron (o) seu/(a) sua, (o/a) dele // adj seu/sua or dele; ~ **name** o nome dele.

**Hispanic** [hɪsˈpænɪk] adj hispânico.

**hiss** [hɪs] vi silvar, vaiar // n silvo, vaia.

**historian** [hɪˈstɔːrɪən] n historiador(a) m/f.

**historic(al)** [hɪˈstɔrɪk(l)] adj histórico.

**history** [ˈhɪstərɪ] n história.

**hit** [hɪt], pt, pp **hit** vt (strike) bater em, golpear; (reach: target) acertar, alcançar; (collide with: car) bater em, colidir com // n golpe m, colisão f; (success) sucesso, grande êxito; to ~ **it off with sb** dar-se bem com alguém.

**hitch** [hɪtʃ] vt (fasten) atar, amarrar; (also: ~ **up**) levantar // n (difficulty) dificuldade f; to ~ **a lift** pedir carona.

**hitch-hike** [ˈhɪtʃhaɪk] vi pedir carona; (Pt) andar à boléia; **hitch-hiker** n carona m/f.

**hive** [haɪv] n colméia.

**hoard** [hɔːd] n provisão f // vt acumular; ~**ing** n acumulação f; (for posters) tapume m.

**hoarfrost** [ˈhɔːfrɔst] n geada.

**hoarse** [hɔːs] adj rouco, roufenho.

**hoax** [həʊks] n peça, logro.

**hobble** [ˈhɔbl] vi coxear // vt (horse) pear, estar peado.

**hobby** [ˈhɔbɪ] n hobby m, passatempo predileto (Pt: -ct-); ~**horse** n (fig) tema m favorito.

**hobo** [ˈhəʊbəʊ] n (US) vagabundo.

**hockey** [ˈhɔkɪ] n hóquei m.

**hoe** [həʊ] n enxada // vt trabalhar com enxada, capinar.

**hog** [hɔg] n porco; (person) glutão m // vt (fig) monopolizar; **to go the whole** ~ ir até o fim.

**hoist** [hɔɪst] n (lift) guincho; (crane) guindaste m.

**hold** [həʊld], pt, pp **held** vt ter; (contain) conter; (keep back) reter;

(believe) sustentar; (take ~ of) segurar; (take weight) agüentar; (meeting) realizar // vi (withstand pressure) ser válido; (stick) colar-se // n (handle) apoio (para a mão); (fig: grasp) influência, domínio; (NAUT) porão m de navio; **to ~ the line!** (TEL) não desligue!; **to ~ one's own** (fig) sair-se bem; **to catch or get (a)** ~ of agarrar-se a; **to ~ back** vt conter-se; (secret) manter, guardar; **to ~ down** vt (person) oprimir; (job) manter; **to ~ off** vt (enemy) afastar, repelir; **to ~ on** vi agarrar-se; (wait) esperar; ~ **on!** (TEL) não desligue!; **to ~ on to** vt fus agarrar-se a; (keep) guardar; **to ~ out** vt estender // vi (resist) resistir; **to ~ up** vt (raise) levantar; (support) apoiar; (delay) atrasar; (rob) assaltar; ~**all** n frasqueira; ~**er** n (of ticket, record) possuidor(a) m/f; (of office, title etc) titular m/f; ~**ing** n (share) títulos, ações fpl; ~**up** n (robbery) assalto; (delay) demora; (in traffic) engarrafamento.

**hole** [həʊl] n buraco // vt esburacar.

**holiday** [ˈhɔlɪdɪ] n férias fpl; (day off) feriado; ~**-maker** n pessoa (que está) de férias; ~ **resort** n local m de férias.

**holiness** [ˈhəʊlɪnɪs] n santidade f.

**Holland** [ˈhɔlənd] n Holanda.

**hollow** [ˈhɔləʊ] adj oco, vazio; (eyes) fundo; (sound) surdo; (doctrine) falso // n (gen) buraco; (in ground) cavidade f, depressão f // vt: **to ~ out** escavar.

**holly** [ˈhɔlɪ] n azevinho; ~**hock** n malva-rosa.

**holster** [ˈhəʊlstə*] n coldre m.

**holy** [ˈhəʊlɪ] adj (gen) santo, sagrado; (water) bento; **H~ Ghost** or **Spirit** n Espírito Santo.

**homage** [ˈhɔmɪdʒ] n homenagem f; **to pay** ~ **to** prestar homenagem a.

**home** [həʊm] n casa, lar m; (country) pátria; (institution) asilo

// adj (domestic) caseiro, doméstico; (ECON, POL) nacional, interno // adv (direction) para casa; **at ~** em casa; **to go/come ~** ir/vir para casa; **make yourself at ~** fique à vontade; **~ address** n endereço residencial; **~land** n terra natal; **~less** adj sem casa, sem teto (Pt: -ct-); **~ly** adj (domestic) caseiro; (simple) simples; **~-made** adj caseiro; **~ rule** n autonomia; **H~ Secretary** n (Brit) Ministro do Interior; **~sick** adj: **to be ~sick** estar com saudade or saudoso (do lar); **~ town** n cidade f natal; **~ward** ['həumwəd] adj (journey) para casa, para a terra natal; **~work** n dever m de casa.

**homicide** ['hɔmisaid] n (US) homicídio.

**homosexual** [hɔməu'sɛksjuəl] adj, n homossexual m.

**honest** ['ɔnist] adj honesto; (sincere) sincero, franco; **~ly** adv honestamente, francamente; **~y** n honestidade f, sinceridade f.

**honey** ['hʌni] n mel m; **~comb** n favo de mel; (pattern) em forma de favo; **~moon** n lua-de-mel f; (trip) viagem f de lua-de-mel.

**honk** [hɔŋk] vi (AUT) buzinar.

**honorary** ['ɔnərəri] adj não remunerado; (duty, title) honorário.

**honour, honor** (US) ['ɔnə*] vt honrar // n honra, fama; **~able** adj honrado; **~s degree** n (SCOL) diploma m com distinção.

**hood** [hud] n capuz m, touca; (Brit: AUT) capota; (US: AUT) capô m.

**hoodlum** ['hu:dləm] n arruaceiro.

**hoof** [hu:f], pl **hooves** n casco, pata.

**hook** [huk] n gancho; (on dress) colchete m; (for fishing) anzol m // vt enganchar, fisgar.

**hooligan** ['hu:ligən] n desordeiro, baguncero.

**hoop** [hu:p] n arco.

**hoot** [hu:t] vi (AUT) buzinar; (siren)

tocar a sirena // n buzinada, toque m de sirena; **to ~ with laughter** morrer de rir; **~er** n (AUT) buzina; (NAUT) sirena.

**hooves** [hu:vz] pl of **hoof.**

**hop** [hɔp] vi saltar, pular; (on one foot) pular num pé só // n salto, pulo.

**hope** [həup] vi esperar, ter esperança de, confiar (em) // n esperança; **I ~ so/not** espero que sim/não; **~ful** adj (person) otimista (Pt: -pt-), esperançoso; (situation) promissor(a); **~fully** adv esperançosamente, o(p)otimisticamente; **~less** adj desesperado, irremediável.

**hops** [hɔps] npl lúpulo sg.

**horde** [hɔ:d] n horda, bando.

**horizon** [hə'raizn] n horizonte m; **~tal** [hɔri'zɔntl] adj horizontal.

**hormone** ['hɔ:məun] n hormônio.

**horn** [hɔ:n] n corno, chifre m; (MUS) trompa; (AUT) buzina; **~ed** adj (animal) com chifres, chifrudo.

**hornet** ['hɔ:nit] n vespão m.

**horn-rimmed** ['hɔ:n-rimd] adj com aro de chifre or de tartaruga.

**horny** ['hɔ:ni] adj (material) córneo; (hands) calejado.

**horoscope** ['hɔrəskəup] n horóscopo.

**horrible** ['hɔribl] adj horrível.

**horrid** ['hɔrid] adj hórrido, horrível.

**horrify** ['hɔrifai] vt horrorizar.

**horror** ['hɔrə*] n horror m; **~ film** n filme m de terror.

**hors d'œuvre** [ɔ:'də:vrə] n antepasto, entrada.

**horse** [hɔ:s] n cavalo; **on ~back** a cavalo; **~man** n cavaleiro or ginete m; **~woman** n amazona; **~power (h.p.)** n cavalo-vapor m; **~-racing** n corrida de cavalo; **~radish** n rábano-bastardo; **~shoe** n ferradura.

**horticulture** ['hɔ:tikʌltfə*] n horticultura.

**hose** [həuz] n (also: ~pipe) mangueira.

**hosiery** ['həuzıərı] n loja de meias e lingerie.

**hospitable** ['hɔspɪtəbl] adj hospitaleiro.

**hospital** ['hɔspɪtl] n hospital m.

**hospitality** [hɔspɪ'tælɪtɪ] n hospitalidade f.

**host** [həust] n anfitrião m; (in hotel etc) hospedeiro; (REL) hóstia; (large number): **a ~ of** uma multidão de.

**hostage** ['hɔstɪdʒ] n refém m.

**hostel** ['hɔstl] n hospedaria; **youth ~** n albergue m para jovens.

**hostess** ['həustɪs] n anfitriã f; (air ~) aeromoça; (in night-club) recepcionista.

**hostile** ['hɔstaɪl] adj hostil; **hostility** [-'stɪlɪtɪ] n hostilidade f.

**hot** [hɔt] adj quente; (as opposed to only warm) muito quente, ardente; (spicy) picante; (fig) ardente, veemente; ~ **dog** n cachorro-quente m.

**hotel** [həu'tɛl] n hotel m; ~**ier** n hoteleiro/a.

**hot:** ~**headed** adj impetuoso, fogoso; ~**house** n estufa; ~**ly** adv ardentemente, apaixonadamente; ~**water bottle** n bolsa de água quente.

**hound** [haund] vt acossar, perseguir // n cão m de caça, sabujo.

**hour** ['auə*] n hora; ~**ly** adv de hora em hora.

**house** [haus, pl: 'hauz'z] n (also: firm) casa; (POL) câmara; (THEATRE) assistência, platéia // vt [hauz] (person) alojar; **on the ~** (fig) por conta da casa; ~ **arrest** n prisão f domiciliar; ~**boat** n casa flutuante; ~**breaking** n arrombamento de domicílio; ~**coat** n roupão m; ~**hold** n pessoas fpl da casa, família; ~**keeper** n governanta; ~**keeping** n (work) trabalhos mpl domésticos; ~**keeping** (money) economia doméstica; ~ **trailer** n

(US) reboque m; ~-**warming party** n festa de inauguração de uma casa; ~**wife** n dona de casa; ~**work** n trabalhos mpl domésticos.

**housing** ['hauzɪŋ] n (act) alojamento; (houses) residências fpl; ~ **estate** n urbanização f, conjunto residencial.

**hovel** ['hɔvl] n choupana, casebre m.

**hover** ['hɔvə*] vi pairar; ~**craft** n aerobarco.

**how** [hau] adv como; ~ **are you?** como vai?, como tem passado?; ~ **long have you been here?** quanto tempo faz que você está aqui?; ~ **lovely!** que lindo!; ~ **many/much?** quantos/quanto?; ~ **old are you?** quantos anos você tem?; ~**ever** adv de qualquer modo; (+ adjective) por mais ... que; (in questions) como // conj no entanto, contudo, todavia.

**howl** [haul] n uivo // vi uivar.

**h.p., H.P.** abbr of **hire purchase; horse power.**

**HQ** abbr of **headquarters.**

**hub** [hʌb] n (of wheel) centro.

**hubbub** ['hʌbʌb] n algazarra, vozerio.

**hubcap** ['hʌbkæp] n calota.

**huddle** ['hʌdl] vi: **to ~ together** aconchegar-se.

**hue** [hju:] n cor f, matiz m; ~ **and cry** n alarme m, gritaria.

**huff** [hʌf] n: **in a ~** com raiva.

**hug** [hʌg] vt abraçar // n abraço.

**huge** [hju:dʒ] adj enorme, imenso.

**hulk** [hʌlk] n (wreck) navio velho; (hull) casco, carcaça.

**hull** [hʌl] n (of ship) casco.

**hullo** [hə'ləu] excl = **hello.**

**hum** [hʌm] vt cantarolar, trautear // vi fazer 'hum'; (insect) zumbir // n zumbido.

**human** ['hju:mən] adj, n humano.

**humane** [hju:'meɪn] adj humano, humanitário.

**humanity** [hju:'mænɪtɪ] n humanidade f.

**humble** ['hʌmbl] adj humilde // vt

humilhar; **humbly** adv humilde-
mente.
**humbug** ['hʌmbʌg] n fraude f,
embuste m; (sweet) bala de hortelã.
**humdrum** ['hʌmdrʌm] adj (boring)
monótono, enfadonho; (routine)
rotineiro.
**humid** ['hju:mɪd] adj úmido; ~**ity**
['-ˈmɪdɪtɪ] n umidade f.
**humiliate** [hju:'mɪlɪeɪt] vt
humilhar; **humiliation** [-'eɪʃən] n
humilhação f.
**humility** [hju:'mɪlɪtɪ] n humildade f.
**humorist** ['hju:mərɪst] n humorista
m/f.
**humorous** ['hju:mərəs] adj
engraçado, divertido.
**humour, humor** (US) ['hju:mə*] n
humorismo, senso de humor;
(mood) humor m // vt (person)
condescender.
**hump** [hʌmp] n (in ground)
elevação f; (camel's) corcova, giba.
**hunch** [hʌntʃ] n (premonition)
pressentimento; ~**back** n corcunda;
~**ed** adj corcunda.
**hundred** ['hʌndrəd] num cento;
(collective) centena; (short form)
cem; ~**weight** n (Brit) = 50.8 kg;
112 lb; (US) = 45.3 kg; 100 lb.
**hung** [hʌŋ] pt, pp of **hang**.
**Hungarian** [hʌŋ'gɛərɪən] adj, n
húngaro/a.
**Hungary** ['hʌŋgərɪ] n Hungria.
**hunger** ['hʌŋgə*] n fome f // vi: to
~ **for** (gen) ter fome de; (desire)
desejar ardentemente; ~ **strike** n
greve f de fome; **hungrily** [-grəlɪ]
adv avidamente, com fome; **hungry**
[-grɪ] adj faminto, esfomeado; to be
**hungry** estar com fome.
**hunt** [hʌnt] vt (seek) buscar,
perseguir; (SPORT) caçar // vi caçar
// n caça, caçada; ~**er** n caçador
m; ~**ing** n caça.
**hurdle** ['hə:dl] n (SPORT) barreira;
(fig) obstáculo.
**hurl** [hə:l] vt arremessar, lançar.

**hurrah** [hu'rɑ:], **hurray** [hu'reɪ] n
viva!, hurra!
**hurricane** ['hʌrɪkən] n furacão m.
**hurried** ['hʌrɪd] adj (fast)
apressado; (rushed) feito às pressas;
~**ly** adv depressa, apressadamente.
**hurry** ['hʌrɪ] n pressa // vi apressar-
se // vt (person) apressar; (also:
~ **up**) acelerar; **to be in a** ~ estar com
pressa.
**hurt** [hə:t], pt, pp **hurt** vt
machucar, ferir; (pain) doer; (fig)
magoar // vi doer // adj
machucado, ferido; ~**ful** adj (pain)
danoso; (remark) doloroso, que
magoa.
**hurtle** ['hə:tl] vi: to ~ **past** passar
como um raio; to ~ **down** cair com
violência.
**husband** ['hʌzbənd] n marido,
esposo.
**hush** [hʌʃ] n silêncio, quietude f //
vt fazer calar; (cover up) abafar,
encobrir; ~! silêncio!
**husk** [hʌsk] n (of wheat) casca.
**husky** ['hʌskɪ] adj rouco; (burly)
robusto // n cão m esquimó.
**hustle** ['hʌsl] vt (push) empurrar;
(hurry) apressar // n agitação f,
atividade (Pt: -ct-) f febril; ~ **and**
**bustle** n vaivém m.
**hut** [hʌt] n choupana, barraca;
(shed) alpendre m.
**hutch** [hʌtʃ] n coelheira.
**hyacinth** ['haɪəsɪnθ] n jacinto.
**hybrid** ['haɪbrɪd] adj, n híbrido.
**hydrant** ['haɪdrənt] n (also: fire ~)
hidrante m.
**hydraulic** [haɪ'drɔ:lɪk] adj
hidráulico.
**hydroelectric** [haɪdrəuɪ'lɛktrɪk]
adj hidroelétrico (Pt: -ct-).
**hydrogen** ['haɪdrədʒən] n
hidrogênio.
**hyena** [haɪ'i:nə] n hiena.
**hygiene** ['haɪdʒi:n] n higiene f;
**hygienic** [-'dʒi:nɪk] adj higiênico.
**hymn** [hɪm] n hino.
**hyphen** ['haɪfən] n hífen m.

**hypnosis** [hɪp'nəusɪs] n hipnose f;
**hypnotic** [-'nɔtɪk] adj hipnótico;
**hypnotism** ['hɪpnətɪzm] n
hipnotismo; **hypnotist** ['hɪpnətɪst] n
hipnotizador(a) m/f; **hypnotize**
['hɪpnətaɪz] vt hipnotizar.

**hypocrisy** [hɪ'pɔkrɪsɪ] n hipocrisia;
**hypocrite** ['hɪpəkrɪt] n hipócrita
m/f; **hypocritical** [hɪpə'krɪtɪkl] adj
hipócrita.

**hypothesis** [haɪ'pɔθɪsɪs], pl **-ses**
[-si:z] n hipótese f; **hypothetic(al)**
[-pəu'θεtɪk(l)] adj hipotético.

**hysteria** [hɪ'stɪərɪə] n histeria;
**hysterical** [-'stεrɪkl] adj histérico.
**hysterics** [-'stεrɪks] npl histeria sg,
histerismo sg.

# I

**I** [aɪ] pron eu.

**ice** [aɪs] n gelo // vt (cake) cobrir
com glacê; (drink) gelar // vi (also:
~ **over**, ~ **up**) gelar; ~ **age** n era
glacial; ~ **axe** n picareta para o
gelo; ~**berg** n iceberg m; ~**box** n
(US) geladeira; ~-**cold** adj gelado;
~ **cream** n sorvete m; (Pt) gelado;
~ **cube** n cubo or pedra de gelo; ~
**hockey** n hóquei m sobre o gelo.

**Iceland** ['aɪslənd] n Islândia; ~**er** n
islandês/esa m/f; ~**ic** [-'lændɪk] adj
islandês/esa.

**ice:** ~ **rink** n pista de gelo; ~
**skating** n patinação f no gelo.

**icicle** ['aɪsɪkl] n pingente m de gelo.

**icing** ['aɪsɪŋ] n (CULIN) glacê m;
(AVIAT etc) formação f de gelo; ~
**sugar** n açúcar m glacê.

**icon** ['aɪkɔn] n ícone m.

**icy** ['aɪsɪ] adj (road) gelado; (fig)
glacial, indiferente.

**I'd** [aɪd] = **I would; I had**.

**idea** [aɪ'dɪə] n idéia.

**ideal** [aɪ'dɪəl] n ideal m // adj ideal;
~**ist** n idealista m/f.

**identical** [aɪ'dεntɪkl] adj idêntico.

**identification** [aɪdεntɪfɪ'keɪʃən] n
identificação f; **means of** ~
documentos mpl pessoais.

**identify** [aɪ'dεntɪfaɪ] vt identificar.

**identikit picture** [aɪ'dεntɪkɪt-] n
retrato falado.

**identity** [aɪ'dεntɪtɪ] n identidade f.

**ideological** [aɪdɪə'lɔdʒɪkəl] adj
ideológico; **ideology** [-dɪ'ɔlɔdʒɪ] n
ideologia.

**idiocy** ['ɪdɪəsɪ] n idiotice f; (stupid
act) estupidez f.

**idiom** ['ɪdɪəm] n expressão f
idiomática; (style of speaking)
idioma m, linguagem f.

**idiosyncrasy** [ɪdɪəu'sɪŋkrəsɪ] n
idiossincrasia; (col) mania.

**idiot** ['ɪdɪət] n (gen) idiota m/f;
(fool) tolo, imbecil; ~**ic** [-'ɔtɪk] adj
idiota, néscio.

**idle** ['aɪdl] adj (gen) indolente, vadio;
(lazy) preguiçoso; (unemployed)
desocupado; (pointless) inútil,
vão/vã // vi (machine) funcionar
com a transmissão desligada // vt:
**to** ~ **away the time** perder or
desperdiçar tempo; ~**ness** n
ociosidade f; preguiça; inutilidade f.

**idol** ['aɪdl] n ídolo; ~**ize** vt idolatrar.

**if** [ɪf] conj se.

**igloo** ['ɪglu:] n iglu m.

**ignite** [ɪg'naɪt] vt acender; (set fire
to) incendiar // vi acender.

**ignition** [ɪg'nɪʃən] n (AUT) ignição f;
**to switch on/off the** ~
ligar/desligar o motor; ~ **key** n
(AUT) chave f de ignição.

**ignorance** ['ɪgnərəns] n
ignorância; **ignorant** [-ənt] adj
ignorante; **to be ignorant of** ignorar.

**ignore** [ɪg'nɔː*] vt (person) não
fazer caso de; (fact) não levar em
consideração, ignorar.

**I'll** [aɪl] = **I will, I shall**.

**ill** [ɪl] adj doente, indisposto; (bad)
mau/má // n (fig) desgraça
// adv mal; **to take** or **be taken** ~
ficar doente; ~-**advised** adj pouco

recomendado; *(misled)* mal aconselhado; ~-at-ease *adj* constrangido, pouco à vontade.

**illegal** [ɪˈliːgl] *adj* ilegal, ilegítimo.

**illegible** [ɪˈledʒɪbl] *adj* ilegível.

**illegitimate** [ɪlɪˈdʒɪtɪmət] *adj* ilegítimo.

**ill:** ~-fated *adj* malfadado, azarento; ~ feeling *n* má vontade *f*, rancor *m*.

**illicit** [ɪˈlɪsɪt] *adj* ilícito.

**illiterate** [ɪˈlɪtərət] *adj* analfabeto.

**ill-mannered** [ɪlˈmænəd] *adj* mal-educado, grosseiro.

**illness** [ˈɪlnɪs] *n* doença.

**illogical** [ɪˈlɒdʒɪkl] *adj* ilógico.

**ill-treat** [ɪlˈtriːt] *vt* maltratar.

**illuminate** [ɪˈluːmɪneɪt] *vt* *(room, street)* iluminar, clarear; *(subject)* esclarecer; **illumination** [-ˈneɪʃən] *n* iluminação *f*; **illuminations** *npl* luminárias *fpl.*

**illusion** [ɪˈluːʒən] *n* ilusão *f*; to be under the ~ that... estar com a ilusão de que...; **illusory** [-sərɪ] *adj* ilusório.

**illustrate** [ˈɪləstreɪt] *vt* *(gen)* ilustrar; *(subject)* esclarecer; *(point)* exemplificar; **illustration** [-ˈstreɪʃən] *n* *(example)* exemplo; *(explanation)* esclarecimento; *(in book)* gravura, ilustração *f.*

**illustrious** [ɪˈlʌstrɪəs] *adj* ilustre.

**ill will** [ɪlˈwɪl] *n* animosidade *f*, má vontade *f.*

**I'm** [aɪm] = **I am.**

**image** [ˈɪmɪdʒ] *n* imagem *f.*

**imaginary** [ɪˈmædʒɪnərɪ] *adj* imaginário; **imagination** [-ˈneɪʃən] *n* imaginação *f*; *(inventiveness)* inventividade *f*; *(illusion)* fantasia; **imaginative** [-nətɪv] *adj* imaginativo; **imagine** *vt* imaginar; *(delude o.s.)* fantasiar.

**imbalance** [ɪmˈbæləns] *n* *(gen)* desequilíbrio; *(inequality)* desigualdade.

**imbecile** [ˈɪmbəsiːl] *n* imbecil *m/f.*

**imbue** [ɪmˈbjuː] *vt*: to ~ sth with imbuir *or* impregnar algo de.

**imitate** [ˈɪmɪteɪt] *vt* imitar; **imitation** [-ˈteɪʃən] *n* imitação *f*; *(copy)* cópia; *(mimicry)* mímica.

**immaculate** [ɪˈmækjulət] *adj* impecável; *(REL)* imaculado.

**immaterial** [ɪməˈtɪərɪəl] *adj* imaterial; it is ~ whether... é indiferente se...

**immature** [ɪməˈtjuə*] *adj* *(person)* imaturo; *(of one's youth)* juvenil.

**immediate** [ɪˈmiːdɪət] *adj* imediato; *(pressing)* urgente, premente; ~ly *adv* *(at once)* imediatamente; ~ly next to bem junto a.

**immense** [ɪˈmens] *adj* imenso, enorme.

**immerse** [ɪˈməːs] *vt* *(submerge)* submergir; *(sink)* afundar, mergulhar; to be ~d in *(fig)* estar absorto em.

**immersion heater** [ɪˈməːʃn/ *n* aquecedor *m* de imersão.

**immigrant** [ˈɪmɪgrənt] *n* imigrante *m/f*; **immigrate** [-greɪt] *vi* imigrar; **immigration** [-ˈgreɪʃən] *n* imigração *f.*

**imminent** [ˈɪmɪnənt] *adj* iminente.

**immobile** [ɪˈməubaɪl] *adj* imóvel; **immobilize** [-bɪlaɪz] *vt* imobilizar

**immoral** [ɪˈmɒrl] *adj* imoral; ~ity [-ˈrælɪtɪ] *n* imoralidade *f.*

**immortal** [ɪˈmɔːtl] *adj* imortal; ~ize *vt* imortalizar.

**immune** [ɪˈmjuːn] *adj*: ~ to imune a, imunizado contra; **immunity** *n* *(MED)* imunidade *f*; *(COMM)* isenção *f.*

**immunization** [ɪmjunaɪˈzeɪʃən] *n* imunização *f*; **immunize** [ˈɪmjunaɪz] *vt* imunizar.

**imp** [ɪmp] *n* diabinho, criança levada.

**impact** [ˈɪmpækt] *n* *(gen)* impacto.

**impair** [ɪmˈpeə*] *vt* prejudicar.

**impale** [ɪmˈpeɪl] *vt* perfurar, empalar.

**impart** [ɪmˈpɑːt] *vt* dar, comunicar.

**impartial** [ɪmˈpɑːʃl] *adj* imparcial.

~**ity** [impɑːʃiˈælɪtɪ] *n* imparcialidade
f.

**impassable** [imˈpɑːsəbl] *adj* (*barrier, river*) intransponível; (*road*)
intransitável.

**impatience** [imˈpeɪʃəns] *n*
impaciência; **impatient** [-ənt] *adj*
impaciente; **to get** *or* **grow**
**impatient** impacientar-se.

**impeccable** [imˈpekəbl] *adj*
impecável.

**impede** [imˈpiːd] *vt* impedir,
estorvar.

**impediment** [imˈpedɪmənt] *n*
obstáculo, impedimento; (*also*:
**speech** ~) defeito (de fala).

**impending** [imˈpendɪŋ] *adj* (*near*)
iminente, próximo.

**impenetrable** [imˈpenɪtrəbl] *adj*
(*gen*) impenetrável; (*unfathomable*)
incompreensível.

**imperative** [imˈperətɪv] *adj* (*tone*)
imperioso, obrigatório; (*necessary*)
indispensável; (*pressing*) premente
// *n* (LING) imperativo.

**imperceptible** [impəˈseptɪbl] *adj*
imperceptível.

**imperfect** [imˈpɜːfɪkt] *adj*
imperfeito; (*goods etc*) defeituoso;
~**ion** [-ˈfekʃən] *n* (*blemish*) defeito;
(*state*) imperfeição f.

**imperial** [imˈpɪərɪəl] *adj* imperial;
~**ism** *n* imperialismo.

**imperil** [imˈperɪl] *vt* pôr em perigo,
arriscar.

**impersonal** [imˈpɜːsənl] *adj*
impessoal.

**impersonate** [imˈpɜːsəneɪt] *vt*
fazer-se passar por, personificar;
(*THEATRE*) representar o papel de.

**impertinent** [imˈpɜːtɪnənt] *adj*
impertinente, insolente.

**impervious** [imˈpɜːvɪəs] *adj*
impenetrável; (*fig*): ~ **to** insensível
a.

**impetuous** [imˈpetjʊəs] *adj*
impetuoso, precipitado.

**impetus** [ˈimpətəs] *n* ímpeto; (*fig*)
impulso.

**impinge** [imˈpɪndʒ]: **to** ~ **on** *vt fus*
impressionar, impingir em; (*affect*)
afetar (*Pt*: -ct-).

**implausible** [imˈplɔːzɪbl] *adj*
inverossímil.

**implement** [ˈimplɪmənt] *n*
instrumento, ferramenta // *vt*
[ˈimplɪment] efetivar (*Pt*: -ct-);
(*carry out*) realizar, executar.

**implicate** [ˈimplɪkeɪt] *vt* (*compromise*) comprometer; (*involve*)
implicar, envolver; **implication**
[-ˈkeɪʃən] *n* implicação f,
consequência.

**implicit** [imˈplɪsɪt] *adj* (*gen*)
implícito; (*complete*) absoluto.

**implore** [imˈplɔː*] *vt* (*person*)
implorar, suplicar.

**imply** [imˈplaɪ] *vt* (*involve*)
implicar; (*mean*) significar; (*hint*)
dar a entender que; **it is implied** se
subentende.

**impolite** [impəˈlaɪt] *adj* indelicado.

**import** [imˈpɔːt] *vt* importar // *n*
[ˈimpɔːt] (*COMM*) importação f;
(: *article*) mercadoria importada;
(*meaning*) significado, sentido.

**importance** [imˈpɔːtəns] *n*
importância; importante [-ənt] *adj*
importante; **it's not important** não
tem importância.

**importer** [imˈpɔːtə*] *n*
importador(a) *m/f*.

**impose** [imˈpəʊz] *vt* impor // *vi*: **to**
~ **on sb** abusar de alguém;
**imposing** *adj* imponente.

**impossible** [imˈpɔsɪbl] *adj*
impossível; (*person*) insuportável.

**impostor** [imˈpɔstə*] *n* impostor(a)
*m/f*.

**impotence** [ˈimpətəns] *n*
impotência; **impotent** [-ənt] *adj*
impotente.

**impound** [imˈpaʊnd] *vt* confiscar.

**impoverished** [imˈpɔvərɪʃt] *adj*
empobrecido; (*land*) esgotado.

**impracticable** [imˈpræktɪkəbl]
*adj* impraticável, inexequível.

**impractical** [ɪm'præktɪkl] *adj* (*person*) pouco prático.

**imprecise** [ɪmprɪ'saɪs] *adj* impreciso, vago.

**impregnable** [ɪm'prɛgnəbl] *adj* invulnerável; it vi causar boa impressão; **to ~ sth on sb** inculcar algo em alguém; **it ~ed itself on me** fiquei com isso gravado (na memória).

**impregnate** ['ɪmprɛgneɪt] *vt* (*gen*) impregnar; (*soak*) embeber; (*fertilize*) fecundar.

**impresario** [ɪmprɪ'sɑːrɪəʊ] *n* gerente *m* de companhia lírica ou de concertos.

**impress** [ɪm'prɛs] *vt* impressionar; (*mark*) imprimir // vi causar boa impressão; **to ~ sth on sb** inculcar algo em alguém; **it ~ed itself on me** fiquei com isso gravado (na memória).

**impression** [ɪm'prɛʃən] *n* impressão *f*; (*footprint etc*) marca; (*print run*) edição *f*; **to be under the ~** that estar com a impressão de que; **~able** *adj* impressionável; (*sensitive*) sensível; **~ist** *n* impressionista *m/f*.

**impressive** [ɪm'prɛsɪv] *adj* impressionante, imponente.

**imprint** ['ɪmprɪnt] *n* impressão *f*; marca.

**imprison** [ɪm'prɪzn] *vt* encarcerar; **~ment** *n* encarceramento.

**improbable** [ɪm'prɒbəbl] *adj* improvável, duvidoso.

**impromptu** [ɪm'prɒmptjuː] *adj* improvisado // *adv* de improviso.

**improper** [ɪm'prɒpə*] *adj* (*incorrect*) impróprio; (*unseemly*) indecoroso; (*indecent*) indecente.

**impropriety** [ɪmprə'praɪətɪ] *n* falta de decoro, inconveniência; (*indecency*) indecência; (*of language*) impropriedade *f*.

**improve** [ɪm'pruːv] *vt* melhorar // vi (*become perfect*) aperfeiçoar-se; (*pupils*) progredir; **~ment** *n* melhoria; aperfeiçoamento, progresso.

**improvise** [ɪmprəvaɪz] *vt/i* improvisar.

**imprudent** [ɪm'pruːdnt] *adj* imprudente.

**impudent** ['ɪmpjudnt] *adj* insolente, impudente.

**impulse** ['ɪmpʌls] *n* impulso, ímpeto; **to act on ~** agir sem pensar; **impulsive** [-'pʌlsɪv] *adj* impulsivo.

**impunity** [ɪm'pjuːnɪtɪ] *n*: **with ~** impunemente.

**impure** [ɪm'pjuə*] *adj* (*adulterated*) adulterado; (*not pure*) impuro; **impurity** *n* (*gen*) impureza.

**in** [ɪn] *prep* em; (*within*) dentro de; (*with time: during, within*): **~ 2 days** em or dentro de 2 dias; (*: after*): **~ 2 weeks** dentro de 2 semanas; (*with town, country*): **it's ~ France** está na França; (*Pt*) fica na França // *adv* dentro, para dentro; (*fashionable*) na moda; **is he ~?** ele está em casa/no escritório?; **~ the country** no campo; **the distance** ao longe; **~ town** no centro (da cidade); **the sun ~** ao/sob o sol; **the rain ~** na chuva; **~ French** em francês; **1 ~ 10** 1 em 10, 1 em cada 10; **~ hundreds** às centenas; **the best pupil ~ the class** o melhor aluno da classe; **written ~ pencil** escrito a lápis; **~ saying this** ao dizer isto; **their party is ~** seu partido chegou ao poder; **to ask sb ~** convidar alguém para entrar; **to run/limp ~** entrar correndo/mancando; **the ~s and outs** os cantos e recantos, os pormenores *mpl*.

**in., ins** *abbr of* **inch(es).**

**inability** [ɪnə'bɪlɪtɪ] *n* incapacidade *f*.

**inaccessible** [ɪnək'sɛsɪbl] *adj* inacessível.

**inaccuracy** [ɪn'ækjʊrəsɪ] *n* inexatidão (*Pt*: -ct-), imprecisão *f*; **inaccurate** [-rət] *adj* inexato (*Pt*: -ct-).

**inactivity** [ɪnæk'tɪvɪtɪ] *n* inatividade (*Pt*: -ct-) *f*.

**inadequate** [ɪnˈædɪkwət] *adj* (*insufficient*) insuficiente; (*unsuitable*) inadequado; (*person*) impróprio.

**inadvertently** [ɪnədˈvəːtntlɪ] *adv* inadvertidamente, sem querer.

**inadvisable** [ɪnədˈvaɪzəbl] *adj* não aconselhável, inoportuno.

**inane** [ɪˈneɪn] *adj* tolo; (*fatuous*) vazio.

**inanimate** [ɪnˈænɪmət] *adj* inanimado.

**inapplicable** [ɪnˈæplɪkəbl] *adj* inaplicável.

**inappropriate** [ɪnəˈprəuprɪət] *adj* inadequado, inconveniente; (*word, expression*) impróprio.

**inapt** [ɪnˈæpt] *adj* inapto; **~itude** *n* incapacidade f, inaptidão f.

**inarticulate** [ɪnɑːˈtɪkjulət] *adj* (*person*) incapaz de expressar-se (bem); (*speech*) inarticulado.

**inasmuch as** [ɪnəzˈmʌtʃæz] *adv* (*given that*) visto que; (*since*) desde que, já que.

**inattentive** [ɪnəˈtɛntɪv] *adj* desatento.

**inaudible** [ɪnˈɔːdɪbl] *adj* inaudível.

**inaugural** [ɪˈnɔːgjurəl] *adj* (*speech*) inaugural, de posse; **inaugurate** [-reɪt] *vt* inaugurar; **inauguration** [-ˈreɪʃən] *n* inauguração f.

**in-between** [ɪnbɪˈtwiːn] *adj* intermediário, entre dois extremos.

**inborn** [ɪnˈbɔːn] *adj* (*feeling*) inato.

**inbred** [ɪnˈbrɛd] *adj* inato; (*family*) de procriação consanguínea.

**incalculable** [ɪnˈkælkjuləbl] *adj* incalculável.

**incapable** [ɪnˈkeɪpəbl] *adj* incapaz.

**incapacitate** [ɪnkəˈpæsɪteɪt] *vt*: to ~ **sb** incapacitar alguém.

**incapacity** [ɪnkəˈpæsɪtɪ] *n* (*inability*) incapacidade f.

**incarcerate** [ɪnˈkɑːsəreɪt] *vt* encarcerar.

**incarnate** [ɪnˈkɑːnɪt] *adj* encarnado, personificado // *vt* [ˈɪnkɑːneɪt] encarnar; **incarnation** [-ˈneɪʃən] *n* encarnação f.

**incendiary** [ɪnˈsɛndɪərɪ] *adj* incendiário.

**incense** [ˈɪnsɛns] *n* incenso // *vt* [ɪnˈsɛns] (*anger*) exasperar, enraivecer.

**incentive** [ɪnˈsɛntɪv] *n* incentivo, estímulo.

**incessant** [ɪnˈsɛsnt] *adj* incessante, contínuo; **~ly** *adv* constantemente.

**incest** [ˈɪnsɛst] *n* incesto.

**inch** [ɪntʃ] *n* polegada; **to be within an ~** of estar a um passo de; **he didn't give an ~** ele não cedeu nem um milímetro; **to ~ forward** avançar palmo a palmo.

**incidence** [ˈɪnsɪdns] *n* (*of crime, disease*) incidência.

**incident** [ˈɪnsɪdnt] *n* incidente *m*, evento; (*in book*) episódio.

**incidental** [ɪnsɪˈdɛntl] *adj* acessório, não essencial; (*unplanned*) acidental, casual; **~ly** [-ˈdɛntlɪ] *adv* (*by the way*) a propósito.

**incinerator** [ɪnˈsɪnəreɪtə*] *n* incinerador *m*.

**incipient** [ɪnˈsɪpɪənt] *adj* incipiente.

**incision** [ɪnˈsɪʒən] *n* incisão f.

**incisive** [ɪnˈsaɪsɪv] *adj* (*mind*) penetrante, perspicaz; (*tone*) mordaz, sarcástico; (*remark etc*) incisivo.

**incite** [ɪnˈsaɪt] *vt* incitar, provocar.

**inclination** [ɪnklɪˈneɪʃən] *n* (*tendency*) tendência, inclinação f.

**incline** [ˈɪnklaɪn] *n* inclinação f, ladeira // (*vb*: [ɪnˈklaɪn]) *vt* (*slope*) inclinar; (*head*) curvar, inclinar // *vi* inclinar-se; **to be ~d to** (*tend*) tender, estar propenso a; (*be willing*) estar disposto a.

**include** [ɪnˈkluːd] *vt* incluir, conter; (*in letter*) anexar; **including** *prep* inclusive, inclusivo.

**inclusion** [ɪnˈkluːʒən] *n* inclusão f; **inclusive** [-sɪv] *adj* inclusivo, incluso // *adv* inclusive.

**incognito** [ɪnkɔgˈniːtəu] *adv* incógnito.

**incoherent** [ɪnkəʊˈhɪərənt] adj incoerente.

**income** [ˈɪŋkʌm] n (personal) rendimentos mpl; (from property etc) renda; (profit) lucro; ~ **tax** n imposto de renda; ~ **tax inspector** n fiscal m/f do imposto de renda; ~ **tax return** n declaração f do imposto de renda.

**incoming** [ˈɪnkʌmɪŋ] adj: ~ **flight** vôo que chega.

**incomparable** [ɪnˈkɒmpərəbl] adj incomparável.

**incompatible** [ɪnkəmˈpætɪbl] adj incompatível.

**incompetence** [ɪnˈkɒmpɪtəns] n incompetência; **incompetent** [-ənt] adj incompetente.

**incomplete** [ɪnkəmˈpliːt] adj incompleto; (unfinished) por terminar.

**incomprehensible** [ɪnkɒmprɪˈhɛnsɪbl] adj incompreensível.

**inconceivable** [ɪnkənˈsiːvəbl] adj inconcebível.

**inconclusive** [ɪnkənˈkluːsɪv] adj inconclusivo; (argument) pouco convincente.

**incongruous** [ɪnˈkɒŋgrʊəs] adj (foolish) ridículo, absurdo; (remark, act) incongruente, ilógico.

**inconsiderate** [ɪnkənˈsɪdərət] adj sem consideração; **how** ~ **of him!** que falta de consideração (de sua parte)!

**inconsistent** [ɪnkənˈsɪstnt] adj inconsistente, incompatível; ~ **with** (que) não está de acordo com.

**inconspicuous** [ɪnkənˈspɪkjuəs] adj insignificante, modesto; **to make o.s.** ~ não chamar a atenção.

**inconstant** [ɪnˈkɒnstnt] adj inconstante.

**incontinent** [ɪnˈkɒntɪnənt] adj incontinente.

**inconvenience** [ɪnkənˈviːnjəns] n (gen) inconvenientes mpl, inconveniência; (trouble) incômodo, transtorno // vt incomodar;

**inconvenient** [-ənt] adj inconveniente, incômodo; (time, place) inoportuno.

**incorporate** [ɪnˈkɔːpəreɪt] vt incorporar; (contain) compreender; (add) incluir; ~**d** adj: ~**d company** (US: abbr **Inc.**) Sociedade f Anônima.

**incorrect** [ɪnkəˈrɛkt] adj incorreto (Pt: -ct-).

**incorruptible** [ɪnkəˈrʌptɪbl] adj (gen) incorruptível; (not open to bribes) insubornável.

**increase** [ˈɪnkriːs] n aumento // vi [ɪnˈkriːs] aumentar; (grow) crescer; (price) subir; **increasing** adj (number) crescente, em aumento; **increasingly** adv cada vez mais, mais e mais.

**incredible** [ɪnˈkrɛdɪbl] adj incrível.

**incredulous** [ɪnˈkrɛdjuləs] adj incrédulo, cético (Pt: -ct-).

**increment** [ˈɪnkrɪmənt] n aumento, incremento.

**incriminate** [ɪnˈkrɪmɪneɪt] vt incriminar.

**incubation** [ɪnkjuˈbeɪʃən] n incubação f; **incubator** [ˈɪnkjubeɪtə*] n incubadora, chocadeira.

**incumbent** [ɪnˈkʌmbənt] n titular m/f // adj: **it is** ~ **on him to...** cabe a ele...

**incur** [ɪnˈkɜː*] vt (gen) incorrer em; (expenses) contrair.

**incurable** [ɪnˈkjuərəbl] adj incurável; (fig) irremediável.

**incursion** [ɪnˈkɜːʃən] n incursão f.

**indebted** [ɪnˈdɛtɪd] adj: **to be** ~ **to sb** estar em dívida, dever obrigação a alguém.

**indecent** [ɪnˈdiːsnt] adj indecente; ~ **assault** n atentado contra o pudor; ~ **exposure** n exibição f obscena.

**indecisive** [ɪndɪˈsaɪsɪv] adj indeciso; (discussion) inconcludente, sem resultados.

**indeed** [ɪnˈdiːd] adv de fato (Pt: -ct-), realmente; **yes** ~! claro que sim!

**indefinite** [ɪn'defɪnɪt] *adj* indefinido; (*uncertain*) impreciso; **~ly** *adv* (*wait*) indefinidamente.

**indelible** [ɪn'delɪbl] *adj* indelével.

**indemnify** [ɪn'demnɪfaɪ] *vt* indenizar (*Pt*: -emn-), compensar.

**indentation** [ɪnden'teɪʃən] *n* entalhe *m*, recorte *m*; (*TYP*) parágrafo, recuo.

**independence** [ɪndɪ'pendns] *n* independência; **independent** [-ənt] *adj* independente; **to become independent** tornar-se independente.

**index** ['ɪndeks] *n* (*pl*: **~es**: *in book*) índice *m*; (: *in library etc*) catálogo; (*pl*: **indices** ['ɪndɪsi:z]: *ratio, sign*) expoente *m*; **~ card** *n* ficha de arquivo; **~ finger** *n* dedo indicador; **~-linked** *adj* vinculado ao índice (do custo de vida).

**India** ['ɪndɪə] *n* Índia; **~n** *adj, n* indiano/a; **Red ~n** *n* pele vermelha *m/f*.

**indicate** ['ɪndɪkeɪt] *vt* indicar; **indication** [-'keɪʃən] *n* indício, sinal *m*; **indicator** *n* (*gen*) indicador *m*.

**indices** ['ɪndɪsi:z] *pl of* **index**.

**indict** [ɪn'daɪt] *vt* acusar; **~ment** *n* acusação *f*, denúncia.

**indifference** [ɪn'dɪfrəns] *n* indiferença; **indifferent** [-ənt] *adj* indiferente; (*poor*) regular, medíocre.

**indigenous** [ɪn'dɪdʒɪnəs] *adj* indígena *m/f*, nativo.

**indigestion** [ɪndɪ'dʒestʃən] *n* indigestão *f*.

**indignant** [ɪn'dɪgnənt] *adj*: **to be ~ about sth** estar indignado com algo, indignar-se de algo; **indignation** [-'neɪʃən] *n* indignação *f*.

**indignity** [ɪn'dɪgnɪtɪ] *n* indignidade *f*; (*insult*) ultraje *m*, afronta.

**indigo** ['ɪndɪgəu] *adj* cor de anil // *n* anil *m*.

**indirect** [ɪndɪ'rekt] *adj* indireto (*Pt*: -ct-); **~ly** *adv* indire(c)tamente.

**indiscreet** [ɪndɪ'skri:t] *adj* indiscreto; (*rash*) imprudente;

**indiscretion** [-'skreʃən] *n* indiscrição *f*; imprudência.

**indiscriminate** [ɪndɪ'skrɪmɪnət] *adj* indiscriminado.

**indispensable** [ɪndɪ'spensəbl] *adj* indispensável, imprescindível.

**indisposed** [ɪndɪ'spəuzd] *adj* (*unwell*) indisposto.

**indisputable** [ɪndɪ'spju:təbl] *adj* incontestável.

**indistinct** [ɪndɪ'stɪŋkt] *adj* indistinto; (*memory, noise*) confuso, vago.

**individual** [ɪndɪ'vɪdjuəl] *n* indivíduo, pessoa // *adj* individual; (*personal*) pessoal; (*for/of one only*) particular; **~ist** *n* individualista *m/f*; **~ity** [-'ælɪtɪ] *n* individualidade *f*; **~ly** *adv* individualmente, particularmente.

**indoctrinate** [ɪn'dɒktrɪneɪt] *vt* doutrinar; **indoctrination** [-'neɪʃən] *n* doutrinação *f*.

**indolent** ['ɪndələnt] *adj* indolente, preguiçoso.

**indoor** ['ɪndɔ:*] *adj* (*inner*) interior; (*household*) de casa; (*inside*) da porta para dentro; (*swimming-pool*) coberto; (*games, sport*) de salão; **~s** [ɪn'dɔ:z] *adv* dentro; (*at home*) em casa.

**induce** [ɪn'dju:s] *vt* induzir; (*bring about*) causar, produzir; (*provoke*) provocar; **~ment** *n* (*incentive*) incentivo, estímulo.

**induction** [ɪn'dʌkʃən] *n* (*MED: of birth*) indução *f*; **~ course** *n* curso de indução.

**indulge** [ɪn'dʌldʒ] *vt* (*desire*) satisfazer; (*whim*) condescender com; (*person*) comprazer; (*child*) fazer a vontade de // *vi*: **to ~ in** entregar-se a, satisfazer-se com; **indulgence** *n* (*of desire*) satisfação *f*; (*leniency*) indulgência, tolerância; **indulgent** *adj* indulgente.

**industrial** [ɪn'dʌstrɪəl] *adj* industrial; **~ action** *n* greve *f*; **~ estate** *n* zona industrial; **~ist** *n* industrial *m/f;* ~ize *vt* industrializar.

industrious [ɪnˈdʌstrɪəs] *adj* (gen) trabalhador(a); (*student*) aplicado.

industry [ˈɪndəstrɪ] *n* indústria; (*diligence*) aplicação *f*, diligência.

inebriated [ɪˈniːbrɪeɪtd] *adj* embriagado, bêbado.

inedible [ɪnˈedɪbl] *adj* não-comestível.

ineffective [ɪnɪˈfektɪv] *adj* ineficaz, inútil.

inefficiency [ɪnɪˈfɪʃənsɪ] *n* ineficácia; inefficient [-ənt] *adj* ineficaz, ineficiente.

ineligible [ɪnˈelɪdʒɪbl] *adj* (*candidate*) inelegível; to be ~ for sth não estar qualificado para algo.

inept [ɪˈnept] *adj* inepto.

inequality [ɪnɪˈkwɒlɪtɪ] *n* desigualdade *f*.

inert [ɪˈnəːt] *adj* inerte; (*immobile*) imóvel; ~ia [ɪˈnəːʃə] *n* inércia; (*laziness*) lerdeza.

inescapable [ɪnɪˈskeɪpəbl] *adj* inevitável.

inestimable [ɪnˈestɪməbl] *adj* inestimável, incalculável.

inevitable [ɪnˈevɪtəbl] *adj* inevitável; (*necessary*) forçoso, necessário.

inexcusable [ɪnɪksˈkjuːzəbl] *adj* imperdoável, indesculpável.

inexhaustible [ɪnɪgˈzɔːstɪbl] *adj* inesgotável, inexaurível.

inexorable [ɪnˈeksərəbl] *adj* inexorável.

inexpensive [ɪnɪkˈspensɪv] *adj* barato, econômico.

inexperience [ɪnɪkˈspɪərɪəns] *n* inexperiência, falta de experiência; ~d *adj* inexperiente.

inexplicable [ɪnɪksˈplɪkəbl] *adj* inexplicável.

inextricable [ɪnɪksˈtrɪkəbl] *adj* inextricável.

infallible [ɪnˈfælɪbl] *adj* infalível.

infamous [ˈɪnfəməs] *adj* infame, abominável; infamy [-mɪ] *n* infâmia.

infancy [ˈɪnfənsɪ] *n* infância.

infant [ˈɪnfənt] *n* (*baby*) bebê *m;* (*young child*) criança; ~ile *adj* infantil; (*pej*) acriançado; ~ school *n* escola primária.

infantry [ˈɪnfəntrɪ] *n* infantaria; ~man *n* soldado de infantaria.

infatuated [ɪnˈfætjueɪtɪd] *adj:* ~ with (gen) gamado por; (*in love*) apaixonado por; infatuation [-ˈeɪʃən] *n* gamação *f*, paixão *f* louca.

infect [ɪnˈfekt] *vt* (*wound*) infeccionar; (*person*) contagiar; (*fig: pej*) corromper, contaminar; ~ed with (*illness*) contagiado por; ~ion [ɪnˈfekʃən] *n* infecção *f;* (*fig*) contágio; ~ious [ɪnˈfekʃəs] *adj* contagioso; (*also: fig*) infeccioso.

infer [ɪnˈfəː*] *vt* deduzir, inferir; ~ence [ˈɪnfərəns] *n* dedução *f*, inferência.

inferior [ɪnˈfɪərɪə*] *adj, n* inferior *m/f;* ~ity [-ɪˈɔrətɪ] *n* inferioridade *f;* ~ity complex *n* complexo de inferioridade.

infernal [ɪnˈfəːnl] *adj* infernal.

inferno [ɪnˈfəːnəu] *n* inferno; (*fig*) inferno de chamas.

infertile [ɪnˈfəːtaɪl] *adj* infértil, estéril; infertility [-ˈtɪlɪtɪ] *n* infertilidade *f*, esterilidade *f*.

infested [ɪnˈfestɪd] *adj:* ~ (with) infestado (de), assolado (por).

infidelity [ɪnfɪˈdelɪtɪ] *n* infidelidade *f*.

in-fighting [ˈɪnfaɪtɪŋ] *n* (*fig*) lutas *fpl* internas, conflitos *mpl* internos.

infiltrate [ˈɪnfɪltreɪt] *vt* (*troops etc*) infiltrar-se em // *vi* infiltrar-se.

infinite [ˈɪnfɪnɪt] *adj* infinito.

infinitive [ɪnˈfɪnɪtɪv] *n* infinitivo.

infinity [ɪnˈfɪnɪtɪ] *n* (*also MATH*) infinito; (*an* ~) infinidade *f*.

infirm [ɪnˈfəːm] *adj* enfermo, fraco; ~ary *n* enfermaria, hospital *m;* ~ity *n* fraqueza; (*illness*) enfermidade *f*, achaque *m*.

inflame [ɪnˈfleɪm] *vt* inflamar.

inflammable [ɪnˈflæməbl] *adj*

inflamável; (*explosive*) explosivo.

**inflammation** [ɪnfləˈmeɪʃən] *n* inflamação *f*.

**inflate** [ɪnˈfleɪt] *vt* (*tyre, balloon*) inflar, encher; (*fig*) inchar; **~d** *adj* (*style*) empolado, pomposo; (*value*) excessivo; **inflation** [ɪnˈfleɪʃən] *n* (ECON) inflação *f*; **inflationary** [ɪnˈfleɪʃnərɪ] *adj* inflacionário.

**inflexible** [ɪnˈflɛksɪbl] *adj* inflexível.

**inflict** [ɪnˈflɪkt] *vt*: **to ~ on** infligir em; (*tax etc*) impor; **~ion** [ɪnˈflɪkʃən] *n* imposição *f*, inflição *f*.

**inflow** [ˈɪnfləu] *n* afluência.

**influence** [ˈɪnfluəns] *n* influência // *vt* influir sobre, influenciar; (*persuade*) persuadir; **under the ~ of alcohol** em estado de embriaguez; **influential** [-ˈɛnfl] *adj* influente.

**influenza** [ɪnfluˈɛnzə] *n* gripe *f*.

**influx** [ˈɪnflʌks] *n* afluxo, influxo.

**inform** [ɪnˈfɔːm] *vt*: **to ~ sb of sth** informar alguém de algo; (*warn*) avisar alguém de algo; (*communicate*) comunicar algo a alguém // *vi* denunciar; **to ~ on sb** delatar alguém.

**informal** [ɪnˈfɔːml] *adj* (*person, manner*) sem formalidade; (*tone*) informal; (*visit, discussion*) extra-oficial; (*intimate*) familiar; **~ity** [-ˈmælɪtɪ] *n* falta de cerimônia; (*intimacy*) intimidade *f*; (*familiarity*) familiaridade *f*; (*ease*) informalidade *f*.

**information** [ɪnfəˈmeɪʃən] *n* informação *f*, informações *fpl*; (*news*) notícias *fpl*; (*knowledge*) conhecimento *f*; (LAW) denúncia; **a piece of ~** um dado, uma informação.

**informative** [ɪnˈfɔːmətɪv] *adj* informativo.

**informer** [ɪnˈfɔːmə*] *n* delator(a) *m/f*; (*also*: **police ~**) informante *m/f*, dedo-duro *m/f*.

**infra-red** [ɪnfrəˈrɛd] *adj* infravermelho.

**infrequent** [ɪnˈfriːkwənt] *adj* infreqüente.

**infringe** [ɪnˈfrɪndʒ] *vt* infringir, transgredir // *vi*: **to ~ on** invadir, violar; **~ment** *n* transgressão *f*; (*of rights*) violação *f*; (SPORT) infração (*Pt*: -cç-) *f*.

**infuriate** [ɪnˈfjuərɪeɪt] *vt* enfurecer, enraivecer; **infuriating** *adj* de dar raiva, enfurecedor(a).

**ingenious** [ɪnˈdʒiːnjəs] *adj* engenhoso; **ingenuity** [-dʒɪˈnjuːɪtɪ] *n* engenho, habilidade *f*.

**ingenuous** [ɪnˈdʒɛnjuəs] *adj* ingênuo.

**ingot** [ˈɪŋgət] *n* lingote *m*, barra.

**ingrained** [ɪnˈgreɪnd] *adj* arraigado, enraizado.

**ingratiate** [ɪnˈgreɪʃɪeɪt] *vt*: **to ~ o.s.** with cair nas (boas) graças de.

**ingratitude** [ɪnˈgrætɪtjuːd] *n* ingratidão *f*.

**ingredient** [ɪnˈgriːdɪənt] *n* ingrediente *m*.

**inhabit** [ɪnˈhæbɪt] *vt* habitar, viver em; (*occupy*) ocupar; **~ant** *n* habitante *m/f*.

**inhale** [ɪnˈheɪl] *vt* inalar // *vi* (*in smoking*) aspirar.

**inherent** [ɪnˈhɪərənt] *adj*: **~ in** *or* **to** inerente a.

**inherit** [ɪnˈhɛrɪt] *vt* herdar; **~ance** *n* herança; (*fig*) patrimônio.

**inhibit** [ɪnˈhɪbɪt] *vt* inibir, reprimir; **to ~ sb from doing sth** impedir alguém de fazer algo; **~ion** [-ˈbɪʃən] *n* inibição *f*.

**inhospitable** [ɪnhɔsˈpɪtəbl] *adj* (*person*) inospitaleiro; (*place*) inóspito.

**inhuman** [ɪnˈhjuːmən] *adj* inumano, desumano.

**inimitable** [ɪˈnɪmɪtəbl] *adj* inimitável.

**iniquity** [ɪˈnɪkwɪtɪ] *n* iniqüidade *f*, (*injustice*) injustiça.

**initial** [ɪˈnɪʃl] *adj* inicial; (*first*)

primeiro // n inicial f // vt marcar com iniciais; ~**s** npl iniciais fpl; (abbreviation) abreviatura, siglas fpl; ~**ly** adv inicialmente, em primeiro lugar.

**initiate** [ɪ'nɪʃɪeɪt] vt (liquid) iniciar, começar; **to ~ sb into a secret** revelar um segredo a alguém; **to ~ proceedings against sb** (LAW) abrir um processo contra alguém; **initiation** [-'eɪʃən] n (into secret etc) iniciação f; (beginning) começo.

**initiative** [ɪ'nɪʃɪətɪv] n iniciativa.

**inject** [ɪn'dʒɛkt] vt (liquid) injetar (Pt: -ct-); (fig) introduzir; ~**ion** [ɪn'dʒɛkʃən] n injeção (Pt: -cç-) f.

**injunction** [ɪn'dʒʌŋkʃən] n injunção f, ordem f.

**injure** [ˈɪndʒə*] vt ferir, lesar; (fig) prejudicar; (offend) ofender, magoar; **injury** n ferida, lesão f; (wrong) dano, prejuízo; **injury time** n (SPORT) desconto.

**injustice** [ɪn'dʒʌstɪs] n injustiça.

**ink** [ɪŋk] n tinta.

**inkling** [ˈɪŋklɪŋ] n suspeita, insinuação f; (idea) ideia vaga.

**inlaid** [ˈɪnleɪd] adj embutido, marchetado.

**inland** [ˈɪnlənd] adj interior, interno // adv [ɪnˈlænd] para o interior; **I~ Revenue** n (Brit) receita federal, fisco.

**in-laws** [ˈɪnlɔːz] npl parentes mpl por afinidade.

**inlet** [ˈɪnlɛt] n (GEO) enseada, angra; (TECH) entrada.

**inmate** [ˈɪnmeɪt] n (in prison) presidiário/a; (in asylum) internado/a.

**inn** [ɪn] n hospedaria, taberna.

**innate** [ɪ'neɪt] adj inato.

**inner** [ˈɪnə*] adj interno, interior; ~ **city** n centro da cidade; ~ **tube** n (of tyre) câmara.

**innocence** [ˈɪnəsns] n inocência; **innocent** [-nt] adj inocente.

**innocuous** [ɪ'nɔkjuəs] adj inócuo.

**innovation** [ɪnəu'veɪʃən] n inovação f, novidade f.

**innuendo** [ɪnjuˈɛndəu] pl ~**es** n insinuação f, indireta (Pt: -ct-).

**innumerable** [ɪ'njuːmrəbl] adj inumerável.

**inoculation** [ɪnɔkjuˈleɪʃən] n inoculação f, vacinação f.

**inopportune** [ɪnˈɔpətjuːn] adj inoportuno.

**inordinately** [ɪ'nɔːdɪnɪtlɪ] adv desmedidamente, excessivamente.

**inorganic** [ɪnɔːˈgænɪk] adj inorgânico.

**in-patient** [ˈɪnpeɪʃənt] n paciente m/f interno.

**input** [ˈɪnput] n (ELEC) insumo, entrada; (COMM) investimento.

**inquest** [ˈɪnkwɛst] n inquérito policial; (coroner's) inquérito judicial.

**inquire** [ɪn'kwaɪə*] vi pedir informação // vt (ask) perguntar; (seek information about) pedir informação sobre; **to ~ about** vt fus (person) perguntar por; (fact) informar-se sobre; **to ~ into** vt fus investigar, indagar; **inquiring** adj (mind) inquiridor(a); (look) interrogativo; **inquiry** n pergunta; (LAW) investigação f, pesquisa; (commission) comissão f de inquérito; **inquiry office** n guichê m de informações.

**inquisitive** [ɪn'kwɪzɪtɪv] adj (curious) curioso, perguntador(a); (prying) indiscreto, intrometido.

**inroad** [ˈɪnrəud] n incursão f; (fig) invasão f.

**insane** [ɪn'seɪn] adj louco, doido; (MED) demente, insano.

**insanitary** [ɪn'sænɪtərɪ] adj insalubre.

**insanity** [ɪn'sænɪtɪ] n insanidade f, demência.

**insatiable** [ɪn'seɪʃəbl] adj insaciável.

**inscribe** [ɪn'skraɪb] vt inscrever;

(*book etc*): **to ~ (to sb)** dedicar (a alguém).

**inscription** [ɪnˈskrɪpʃən] n (*gen*) inscrição f; (*in book etc*) dedicatória.

**inscrutable** [ɪnˈskruːtəbl] adj inescrutável, impenetrável.

**insect** [ˈɪnsɛkt] n inseto (*Pt*: -ct-); **~icide** [ɪnˈsɛktɪsaɪd] n inse(c)ticida m.

**insecure** [ɪnsɪˈkjuə*] adj inseguro; **insecurity** n insegurança.

**insensible** [ɪnˈsɛnsɪbl] adj impassível, insensível; (*unconscious*) inconsciente.

**insensitive** [ɪnˈsɛnsɪtɪv] adj insensível.

**inseparable** [ɪnˈsɛprəbl] adj inseparável; **they were ~ friends** eles eram amigos inseparáveis.

**insert** [ɪnˈsɜːt] vt (*between things*) intercalar; (*into sth*) introduzir, inserir; (*in paper*) publicar; (: *advert*) pôr // n [ˈɪnsɜːt] folha solta; **~ion** [ɪnˈsɜːʃən] n inserção f; (*publication*) publicação f; (*of pages*) matéria inserida.

**inshore** [ɪnˈʃɔː*] adj perto da costa, costeiro // adv (*be*) perto da costa; (*move*) em direção à costa.

**inside** [ˈɪnˈsaɪd] n interior m; (*lining*) forro // adj interior, interno; (*secret*) secreto // adv (*within*) (por) dentro; (*with movement*) para dentro; (*fam: in prison*) na prisão // prep dentro de; (*of time*): **~ 10 minutes** em menos de 10 minutos; **~s** npl (*col*) entranhas fpl; **~ forward** n (*SPORT*) centro avante; **~ lane** n (*AUT*: in Britain) pista da direita; **~ out** adv (*turn*) às avessas, ao revés; (*know*) perfeitamente, a fundo.

**insidious** [ɪnˈsɪdɪəs] adj insidioso; (*underground*) clandestino.

**insight** [ˈɪnsaɪt] n idéia luminosa, estalo.

**insignificant** [ɪnsɪgˈnɪfɪknt] adj insignificante.

**insincere** [ɪnsɪnˈsɪə*] adj insincero;

**insincerity** [-ˈsɛrɪtɪ] n insinceridade f.

**insinuate** [ɪnˈsɪnjueɪt] vt insinuar, sugerir; **insinuation** [-ˈeɪʃən] n insinuação f; (*hint*) indireta (*Pt*: -ct-).

**insipid** [ɪnˈsɪpɪd] adj insípido, sem graça.

**insist** [ɪnˈsɪst] vi insistir; **to ~ on doing** teimar em fazer; **to ~ that** insistir em que; (*claim*) exigir que; **~ence** n insistência; (*stubbornness*) tenacidade f; **~ent** adj insistente, pertinaz.

**insole** [ˈɪnsəul] n palmilha.

**insolence** [ˈɪnsələns] n insolência, atrevimento; **insolent** [-ənt] adj insolente, atrevido.

**insoluble** [ɪnˈsɔljubl] adj insolúvel.

**insolvent** [ɪnˈsɔlvənt] adj insolvente.

**insomnia** [ɪnˈsɔmnɪə] n insônia.

**inspect** [ɪnˈspɛkt] vt inspecionar (*Pt*: -cc-), examinar; (*troops*) passar revista em; **~ion** [ɪnˈspɛkʃən] n inspeção (*Pt*: -cç-) f, exame m; **~or** n inspetor(a) m/f; (*RAIL*) fiscal m.

**inspiration** [ɪnspəˈreɪʃən] n inspiração f; **inspire** [ɪnˈspaɪə*] vt inspirar.

**instability** [ɪnstəˈbɪlɪtɪ] n instabilidade f.

**install** [ɪnˈstɔːl] vt instalar; **~ation** [ɪnstəˈleɪʃən] n instalação f.

**instalment, installment** (*US*) [ɪnˈstɔːlmənt] n prestação f; (*of story*) fascículo; (*of TV serial etc*) capítulo.

**instance** [ˈɪnstəns] n exemplo, caso; **for ~** por exemplo; **in the first ~** em primeiro lugar.

**instant** [ˈɪnstənt] n instante m, momento // adj instantâneo, imediato; (*coffee*) instantâneo; **~ly** adv imediatamente.

**instead** [ɪnˈstɛd] adv em vez disso; **~ of** em vez de, em lugar de.

**instep** [ˈɪnstɛp] n peito do pé.

**instigation** [ɪnstɪˈɡeɪʃən] n instigação f.

**instil** [ɪnˈstɪl] vt: to ~ into infundir em, incutir em.

**instinct** [ˈɪnstɪŋkt] n instinto; ~ive [ˈstɪŋktɪv] adj instintivo; ~ively [ˈstɪŋktɪvlɪ] adv por instinto, instintivamente.

**institute** [ˈɪnstɪtjuːt] n instituto; (professional body) associação f // vt (inquiry) começar, iniciar; (proceedings) instituir, estabelecer.

**institution** [ɪnstɪˈtjuːʃən] n (gen) instituição f; (beginning) início; (organization) instituto; (MED: home) asilo; (asylum) manicômio; (custom) costume m.

**instruct** [ɪnˈstrʌkt] vt: to ~ sb in sth instruir alguém em or sobre algo; to ~ sb to do sth dar instruções a alguém para fazer algo; ~ion [ɪnˈstrʌkʃən] n (teaching) instrução f; ~ions fpl ordens fpl; ~ions (for use) modo sg de usar; ~ive adj instrutivo; ~or n instrutor(a) m/f.

**instrument** [ˈɪnstrəmənt] n instrumento; ~al [ˈmentl] adj (MUS) instrumental; to be ~al in contribuir para; ~ panel n painel m de instrumentos.

**insubordinate** [ɪnsəˈbɔːdənɪt] adj insubordinado; **insubordination** [ˈneɪʃən] n insubordinação f; (disobedience) desobediência f.

**insufferable** [ɪnˈsʌfrəbl] adj insuportável.

**insufficient** [ɪnsəˈfɪʃənt] adj insuficiente.

**insular** [ˈɪnsjulə*] adj insular; (outlook) de mente limitada.

**insulate** [ˈɪnsjuleɪt] vt isolar; **insulating tape** n fita isolante; **insulation** [ˈleɪʃən] n isolamento, vedação f.

**insulin** [ˈɪnsjulɪn] n insulina.

**insult** [ˈɪnsʌlt] n insulto; (offence) ofensa // vt [ɪnˈsʌlt] insultar,

ofender; ~ing adj insultante, ofensivo.

**insuperable** [ɪnˈsjuːprəbl] adj insuperável.

**insurance** [ɪnˈʃuərəns] n seguro; **fire** ~ seguro contra incêndio; **life** ~ seguro de vida; ~ **agent** n agente m/f de seguros; ~ **policy** n apólice f de seguro.

**insure** [ɪnˈʃuə*] vt assegurar, pôr no seguro.

**insurrection** [ɪnsəˈrekʃən] n insurreição f.

**intact** [ɪnˈtækt] adj intacto, íntegro; (unharmed) ileso, são e salvo.

**intake** [ˈɪnteɪk] n (TEC) entrada, tomada; (: pipe) tubo de entrada; (of food) quantidade f ingerida; (SCOL): **an** ~ **of 200 a year** 200 matriculados por ano.

**intangible** [ɪnˈtændʒɪbl] adj intangível.

**integral** [ˈɪntɪɡrəl] adj (whole) integral, total; (part) integrante.

**integrate** [ˈɪntɪɡreɪt] vt integrar // vi integrar-se.

**integrity** [ɪnˈteɡrɪtɪ] n integridade f, honestidade f, retidão (Pt: -ct-) f.

**intellect** [ˈɪntəlekt] n intelecto; ~**ual** [ˈlektjuəl] adj, n intelectual m/f.

**intelligence** [ɪnˈtelɪdʒəns] n inteligência; (MIL etc) informações fpl; **I~ Service** n Serviço de Inteligência; **intelligent** [ˈənt] adj inteligente.

**intelligible** [ɪnˈtelɪdʒɪbl] adj inteligível, compreensível.

**intend** [ɪnˈtend] vt (gift etc): to ~ sth for destinar algo a; to ~ to do sth tencionar or pretender fazer algo; ~**ed** adj (effect) desejado // n noivo/a.

**intense** [ɪnˈtens] adj intenso; (person) muito emotivo // adv intensamente; (very) extremamente.

**intensify** [ɪnˈtensɪfaɪ] vt intensificar; (increase) aumentar.

**intensity** [ɪn'tɛnsɪtɪ] n intensidade f; (strength) força, veemência.

**intensive** [ɪn'tɛnsɪv] adj intensivo; ~ **care unit** n unidade f de tratamento intensivo.

**intent** [ɪn'tɛnt] n intenção f // adj (absorbed) absorto; (attentive) atento; **to all** ~**s and purposes** para todos os efeitos; **to be** ~ **on doing sth** estar resolvido a fazer algo.

**intention** [ɪn'tɛnʃən] n intenção f, propósito; (plan) projeto (PT: -ct-); ~**al** adj intencional, premeditado; ~**ally** adv de propósito.

**intently** [ɪn'tɛntlɪ] adv atentamente, decididamente.

**inter** [ɪn'tɜ:*] vt enterrar.

**interact** [ɪntər'ækt] vi interagir; ~**ion** [-'ækʃən] n interação (PT: -cç-) f, ação (PT: -cç-) f recíproca.

**intercede** [ɪntə'si:d] vi: **to** ~ (**with**) interceder (junto a).

**intercept** [ɪntə'sɛpt] vt interceptar; (stop) deter; ~**ion** [-'sɛpʃən] n interceptação f; detenção f.

**interchange** ['ɪntətʃeɪndʒ] n intercâmbio; (exchange) troca, permuta; (on motorway) trevo // [ɪntə'tʃeɪndʒ] vt intercambiar, trocar; ~**able** adj permutável.

**intercom** ['ɪntəkɔm] n interfone m.

**interconnect** [ɪntəkə'nɛkt] vi (rooms) interconectar-se, interligar.

**intercourse** ['ɪntəkɔ:s] n (sexual) intercurso, coito, relações fpl; (social) trato.

**interest** ['ɪntrɪst] n (also COMM) juros mpl, interesse m; (profit) lucro, benefício // vt interessar; **to be** ~**ed in** estar interessado em; ~**ing** adj interessante, curioso.

**interfere** [ɪntə'fɪə*] vi: **to** ~ **in** (quarrel, other people's business) interferir or intrometer-se em; **to** ~ **with** (hinder) impedir; (damage) danificar; (radio) interferir com.

**interference** [ɪntə'fɪərəns] n (gen) intromissão f, (RADIO, TV) interferência.

**interim** ['ɪntərɪm] n: **in the** ~ neste ínterim, nesse meio tempo.

**interior** [ɪn'tɪərɪə*] n interior m // adj interior.

**interject** [ɪntə'dʒɛkt] vt inserir, interpor; ~**ion** [-'dʒɛkʃən] n interjeição f, exclamação f.

**interlock** [ɪntə'lɔk] vi entrelaçar-se; (wheels etc) engatar-se, engrenar-se.

**interloper** ['ɪntələupə*] n intruso/a.

**interlude** ['ɪntəlu:d] n interlúdio; (rest) descanso; (THEATRE) intervalo.

**intermarry** [ɪntə'mærɪ] vi ligar-se por casamento.

**intermediary** [ɪntə'mi:dɪərɪ] n intermediário.

**intermediate** [ɪntə'mi:dɪət] adj intermédio, intermediário.

**intermission** [ɪntə'mɪʃən] n (THEATRE) intervalo.

**intermittent** [ɪntə'mɪtnt] adj intermitente.

**intern** [ɪn'tɜ:n] vt internar; (enclose) encerrar // n ['ɪntɜ:n] (US) médico-interno.

**internal** [ɪn'tɜ:nl] adj interno, interior; ~**ly** adv interiormente; **'not to be taken** ~**ly'** 'uso externo'; ~ **revenue** n (US) receita federal.

**international** [ɪntə'næʃənl] adj internacional; ~ **game** jogo internacional; ~ **player** jogador(a) m/f internacional.

**interplay** ['ɪntəpleɪ] n interação (PT: -cç-) f.

**interpret** [ɪn'tɜ:prɪt] vt interpretar; (translate) traduzir; (understand) compreender // vi interpretar; ~**ation** [-'teɪʃən] n interpretação f; tradução f; entendimento; ~**er** n intérprete m/f, tradutor(a) m/f.

**interrelated** [ɪntərɪ'leɪtɪd] adj inter-relacionado.

**interrogate** [ɪn'tɛrəugeɪt] vt interrogar; **interrogation** [-'geɪʃən] n interrogatório; **interrogative** [ɪntə-

'rɔgətiv] adj interrogativo.

**interrupt** [intə'rʌpt] vt/i interromper; **~ion** [-'rʌpʃən] n interrupção f.

**intersect** [intə'sɛkt] vt cruzar // vi (roads) cruzar-se; **~ion** [-'sɛkʃən] n intersecção f; (of roads) cruzamento.

**intersperse** [intə'spəːs] vt intercalar, entremear.

**intertwine** [intə'twain] vt entrelaçar // vi entrelaçar-se.

**interval** ['intəvl] n pausa; (SCOL) recreio, intervalo; (THEATRE, SPORT) intervalo; **at ~s** de vez em quando, de tempos em tempos.

**intervene** [intə'viːn] vi (gen) intervir, interceder; (take part) participar; (occur) ocorrer; **intervention** [-'vɛnʃən] n intervenção f.

**interview** ['intəvjuː] n (RADIO, TV etc) entrevista // vt entrevistar; **~ee** [-'iː] n entrevistado/a; **~er** n entrevistador/a m/f.

**intestine** [in'tɛstin] n: **large/small** ~ intestino grosso/delgado.

**intimacy** ['intiməsi] n intimidade f; (relations) relações fpl sexuais.

**intimate** ['intimət] adj íntimo; (friendship, knowledge) profundo // vt ['intimeit] (announce) insinuar, sugerir.

**intimidate** [in'timideit] vt intimidar, amedrontar; **intimidation** [-'deiʃən] n intimidação f.

**into** ['intu] prep (gen) em; (towards) para; (inside) para dentro de; **~ 3 pieces/French** em 3 pedaços/francês.

**intolerable** [in'tɔlərəbl] adj intolerável, insuportável; **intolerance** [-rəns] n intolerância; **intolerant** [-rənt] adj: **intolerant of** intolerante com or para com.

**intonation** [intəu'neiʃən] n entonação f, inflexão f.

**intoxicate** [in'tɔksikeit] vt embriagar; **~d** adj embriagado;

**intoxication** [-'keiʃən] n intoxicação f, embriaguez f.

**intractable** [in'træktəbl] adj (child) intratável; (material) difícil de trabalhar; (problem) espinhoso.

**intransigent** [in'trænsidʒənt] adj intransigente.

**intransitive** [in'trænsitiv] adj intransitivo.

**intravenous** [intrə'viːnəs] adj intravenoso.

**intrepid** [in'trepid] adj intrépido.

**intricate** ['intrikət] adj intricado; (complex) complexo, complicado.

**intrigue** [in'triːg] n intriga // vt interessar, deixar intrigado // vi fazer intriga; **intriguing** adj intrigante.

**intrinsic** [in'trinsik] adj intrínseco.

**introduce** [intrə'djuːs] vt introduzir, inserir; **to ~ sb** (to sb) apresentar alguém (a outrem); **to ~ sb to** (pastime, technique) iniciar or introduzir alguém em; **introduction** [-'dʌkʃən] n introdução f; (of person) apresentação f; **introductory** [-'dʌktəri] adj introdutório, preliminar.

**introspective** [intrəu'spɛktiv] adj introspectivo.

**introvert** ['intrəuvəːt] adj, n introvertido/a.

**intrude** [in'truːd] vi (person) intrometer-se; **to ~ on** or **into** importunar; **intruder** n intruso/a m/f; **intrusion** [-ʒən] n intromissão f; **intrusive** [-siv] adj intruso.

**intuition** [intjuː'iʃən] n intuição f; **intuitive** [-'tjuːitiv] adj intuitivo.

**inundate** ['inʌndeit] vt: **to ~ with** inundar de.

**invade** [in'veid] vt invadir; **invader** n invasor/a m/f.

**invalid** n ['invəlid] n inválido/a // adj [in'vælid] (not valid) inválido, nulo; **~ate** [in'vælideit] vt invalidar, anular.

**invaluable** [in'væljuəbl] adj inestimável, impagável.

**invariable** [in'vɛəriəbl] adj invariável.

**invasion** [in'veiʒən] n invasão f.

**invent** [in'vɛnt] vt inventar; ~ion [in'vɛnʃən] n invenção f; (inventiveness) engenho; (lie) ficção f, mentira; ~ive adj engenhoso; ~iveness n engenhosidade f, inventiva; ~or n inventor m/f.

**inventory** ['invəntri] n inventário, relação f.

**inverse** [in'və:s] adj, n inverso; ~ly adv inversamente.

**invert** [in'və:t] vt inverter, transpor; ~ed commas npl aspas fpl.

**invertebrate** [in'və:tibrət] n invertebrado.

**invest** [in'vɛst] vt/i investir.

**investigate** [in'vɛstigeit] vt investigar; (study) estudar, examinar; **investigation** [-'geiʃən] n investigação f, pesquisa; **investigator** n investigador(a) m/f, investidor(a) m/f.

**investiture** [in'vɛstitʃə*] n investidura.

**investment** [in'vɛstmənt] n investimento.

**investor** [in'vɛstə*] n inversionista m/f, investidor(a) m/f.

**inveterate** [in'vɛtərət] adj inveterado.

**invigorating** [in'vigəreitiŋ] adj revigorante.

**invincible** [in'vinsibl] adj invencível.

**inviolate** [in'vaiələt] adj inviolado.

**invisible** [in'vizibl] adj invisível; ~ **ink** n tinta invisível.

**invitation** [invi'teiʃən] n convite m.

**invite** [in'vait] vt (gen, drink, food) convidar; (opinions etc) solicitar, pedir; (trouble) provocar; **inviting** adj tentador(a), atraente; (look) convidativa, sedutor(a); (food) apetitoso.

**invoice** ['invɔis] n fatura (Pt: -ct-) // vt fa(c)turar.

**invoke** [in'vəuk] vt invocar; (aid) implorar; (law) apelar para.

**involuntary** [in'vɔləntri] adj involuntário.

**involve** [in'vɔlv] vt (entail) implicar; to ~ **sb** (in) envolver alguém (em); ~d adj envolvido; (emotionally) comprometido; ~**ment** n (gen) envolvimento; (obligation) compromisso; (difficulty) apuro.

**invulnerable** [in'vʌlnərəbl] adj invulnerável.

**inward** ['inwəd] adj (movement) interior, interno; (thought, feeling) íntimo; ~**ly** adv (feel, think etc) para si, para dentro; ~(**s**) adv para dentro.

**iodine** ['aiəudi:n] n iodo.

**iota** [ai'əutə] n (fig) pouquinho, tiquinho.

**IOU** n abbr of I owe you vale m.

**IQ** n abbr of **intelligence quotient** quociente m intelectual or de inteligência.

**Iran** [i'ra:n] n Irã m; ~**ian** [i'reiniən] adj, n iraniano/a m/f.

**Iraq** [i'ra:k] n Iraque m; ~i adj, n iraquiano/a m/f.

**irascible** [i'ræsibl] adj irascível.

**irate** [ai'reit] adj irado, enfurecido.

**Ireland** ['aiələnd] n Irlanda.

**iris** ['airis], pl ~ **es** n íris f.

**Irish** ['airiʃ] adj irlandês/esa // npl: **the** ~ os irlandeses; ~**man** n irlandês m; ~**woman** n irlandesa.

**irk** [ə:k] vt aborrecer; ~**some** adj aborrecido.

**iron** ['aiən] n ferro; (for clothes) ferro de passar roupa // adj de ferro // vt (clothes) passar; ~**s** npl (chains) grilhões mpl; **to** ~ **out** vt (crease) tirar; (fig) resolver.

**ironic(al)** [ai'rɔnik(l)] adj irônico.

**ironing** ['aiəniŋ] n (ironed clothes) roupa passada; (to be ironed) roupa a ser passada; ~ **board** n tábua de passar roupa.

**ironmonger** ['aɪənmʌŋgə*] n ferreiro; ~**'s (shop)** n loja de ferragens.

**iron ore** ['aɪənɔ:*] n minério de ferro.

**irony** ['aɪrəni] n ironia; **the ~ of it is that...** o irônico é que...

**irrational** [ɪ'ræʃənl] adj irracional.

**irreconcilable** [ɪrekən'saɪləbl] adj irreconciliável, incompatível.

**irrefutable** [ɪrɪ'fju:təbl] adj irrefutável.

**irregular** [ɪ'regjulə*] adj irregular; (surface) desigual; (illegal) ilegal; ~**ity** [-'lærɪtɪ] n irregularidade f, desigualdade f.

**irrelevant** [ɪ'reləvənt] adj irrelevante, descabido.

**irreparable** [ɪ'repərəbl] adj irreparável.

**irreplaceable** [ɪrɪ'pleɪsəbl] adj insubstituível.

**irrepressible** [ɪrɪ'presəbl] adj irreprimível, irrefreável.

**irreproachable** [ɪrɪ'prəutʃəbl] adj irrepreensível.

**irresistible** [ɪrɪ'zɪstɪbl] adj irresistível.

**irresolute** [ɪ'rezəlu:t] adj irresoluto.

**irrespective** [ɪrɪ'spektɪv]: ~ **of** prep independente de, sem considerar.

**irresponsible** [ɪrɪ'spɔnsɪbl] adj (act, person) irresponsável.

**irreverent** [ɪ'revərnt] adj irreverente, desrespeitoso.

**irrevocable** [ɪ'revəkəbl] adj irrevogável.

**irrigate** ['ɪrɪgeɪt] vt irrigar; **irrigation** [-'geɪʃən] n irrigação f.

**irritable** ['ɪrɪtəbl] adj irritável; (mood) de mal humor, nervoso.

**irritate** ['ɪrɪteɪt] vt irritar; (MED) coçar; **irritation** [-'teɪʃən] n irritação f, chateação f; (MED) coceira.

**is** [ɪz] vb see **be**.

**Islam** ['ɪzlɑ:m] n islamismo.

**island** ['aɪlənd] n ilha; (also: **traffic** ~) abrigo; ~**er** n ilhéu/ilhoa m/f.

**isle** [aɪl] n ilhota, ilha.

**isn't** ['ɪznt] = **is not**.

**isolate** ['aɪsəleɪt] vt isolar; ~**d** adj isolado; **isolation** [-'leɪʃən] n isolamento.

**isotope** ['aɪsəutəup] n isótopo.

**Israel** ['ɪzreɪl] n (Estado de) Israel m; ~**i** [ɪz'reɪlɪ] adj, n israelense m/f.

**issue** ['ɪsju:] n questão f, tema m; (outcome) emissão f; (of banknotes etc) número; (of newspaper etc) número; (offspring) sucessão f, descendência // vt (rations, equipment) distribuir; (orders) dar; (certificate) emitir; (decree) promulgar; (book) publicar; (cheques, banknotes, stamps) emitir.

**isthmus** ['ɪsməs] n istmo.

**it** [ɪt] pron (subject) ele/ela; (direct object) o/a; (indirect object) lhe; (impersonal) isto, isso; (after prep) ele, ela; ~**'s raining** está chovendo; (Pt) está a chover; **where is ~?** onde está?; **he's proud of** ~ ele orgulha-se disso; **he agreed to** ~ ele está de acordo com isso.

**Italian** [ɪ'tæljən] adj italiano // n italiano/a; (LING) italiano.

**italic** [ɪ'tælɪk] adj itálico, cursivo; ~**s** npl itálico sg.

**Italy** ['ɪtəlɪ] n Itália.

**itch** [ɪtʃ] n comichão f; (fig) desejo ardente // vi (person) sentir or estar com comichão; (part of body) comichar, coçar; **I'm ~ing to do sth** estou louco para fazer algo; ~**ing** n comichão f; ~**y** adj: **to be ~y** sentir comichão.

**it'd** ['ɪtd] = **it would; it had**.

**item** ['aɪtəm] n (gen) item m; (detail) detalhe m; (on agenda) assunto; (in programme) número; (also: **news** ~) notícia; ~**ize** vt detalhar, especificar.

**itinerant** [ɪ'tɪnərənt] adj itinerante.

**itinerary** [aɪ'tɪnərərɪ] n itinerário f.

**it'll** ['ɪtl] = **it will, it shall**.

**its** [ɪts] *adj* seu/sua // *pron* (o) seu/(a) sua.

**it's** [ɪts] = **it is; it has.**

**itself** [ɪt'sɛlf] *pron* (*reflexive*) si mesmo/a; (*emphatic*) ele mesmo/ela mesma.

**ITV** *n abbr of* **Independent Television.**

**I.U.D.** *n abbr of* **intra-uterine device.**

**I've** [aɪv] = **I have.**

**ivory** ['aɪvərɪ] *n* marfim *m*; ~ **tower** *n* (*fig*) torre *f* de marfim.

**ivy** ['aɪvɪ] *n* hera.

# J

**jab** [dʒæb] *vt* (*elbow*) acotovelar; (*punch*) esmurrar, socar; **to** ~ **sth into sth** cravar algo em algo // *n* cotovelada, murro; (*MED: col*) picada.

**jabber** ['dʒæbə*] *vt/i* tagarelar.

**jack** [dʒæk] *n* (*AUT*) macaco; (*BOWLS*) boliche *m*; (*CARDS*) valete *m*; **to** ~ **up** *vt* (*AUT*) levantar com macaco.

**jackdaw** ['dʒækdɔ:] *n* gralha.

**jacket** ['dʒækɪt] *n* jaqueta, casaco curto; (*of boiler etc*) capa, forro; (*of book*) sobrecapa; **potatoes in their** ~**s** batatas com casca.

**jack-knife** ['dʒæknaɪf] *n* canivete *m*.

**jackpot** ['dʒækpɔt] *n* bolada, sorte *f* grande.

**jade** [dʒeɪd] *n* (*stone*) jade *m*.

**jaded** ['dʒeɪdɪd] *adj* (*tired*) cansado; (*fed-up*) aborrecido, amolado.

**jagged** ['dʒægɪd] *adj* dentado, denteado.

**jail** [dʒeɪl] *n* prisão *f*, cadeia; ~**break** *n* fuga da prisão; ~**er** *n* carcereiro.

**jam** [dʒæm] *n* geléia; (*also*: **traffic** ~) engarrafamento; (*difficulty*)

**apuro** // *vt* (*passage etc*) obstruir, fechar; (*mechanism, drawer etc*) emperrar; (*RADIO*) interferir // *vi* comprimir, abarrotar; **to** ~ **sth into sth** enfiar algo à força dentro de algo.

**Jamaica** [dʒə'meɪkə] *n* Jamaica.

**jangle** ['dʒæŋgl] *vi* soar estridentemente, desafinar.

**janitor** ['dʒænɪtə*] *n* (*caretaker*) zelador *m*, porteiro.

**January** ['dʒænjuərɪ] *n* janeiro.

**Japan** [dʒə'pæn] *n* Japão *m*; ~**ese** [dʒæpə'ni:z] *adj* japonês/esa // *n, pl inv* japonês/esa *m/f*; (*LING*) japonês *m*.

**jar** [dʒɑ:*] *n* (*glass: large*) jarro; (: *small*) pote *m* // *vi* (*sound*) ranger, chiar; (*colours*) destoar.

**jargon** ['dʒɑ:gən] *n* jargão *m*, gíria.

**jasmin(e)** ['dʒæzmɪn] *n* jasmim *m*.

**jaundice** ['dʒɔ:ndɪs] *n* icterícia; ~**d** *adj* (*fig*: *embittered*) amargurado, despeitado; (: *disillusioned*) desiludido.

**jaunt** [dʒɔ:nt] *n* excursão *f*; ~**y** *adj* alegre, jovial.

**javelin** ['dʒævlɪn] *n* dardo de arremesso.

**jaw** [dʒɔ:] *n* mandíbula, maxilar *m*.

**jaywalker** ['dʒeɪwɔ:kə*] *n* pedestre *m/f* imprudente.

**jazz** [dʒæz] *n* jazz *m*; **to** ~ **up** *vt* (*liven up*) animar, avivar; ~**y** *adj* de cor berrante.

**jealous** ['dʒɛləs] *adj* (*gen*) ciumento; (*envious*) invejoso; **to be** ~ **estar com ciúmes**; ~**y** *n* ciúmes *mpl*; (*envy*) inveja.

**jeans** [dʒi:nz] *npl* jeans *mpl*, calça Lee.

**jeep** [dʒi:p] *n* jipe *m*.

**jeer** [dʒɪə*] *vi*: **to** ~ **(at)** (*boo*) vaiar; (*mock*) zombar (de).

**jelly** ['dʒɛlɪ] *n* geléia, gelatina; ~**fish** *n* água-viva.

**jeopardize** ['dʒɛpədaɪz] *vt* arriscar, pôr em perigo; **jeopardy** [-dɪ] *n*: **to**

**be in jeopardy** estar em perigo or correndo risco.

**jerk** [dʒɜːk] n (jolt) sacudida; (wrench) puxão m // vt sacudir, empurrar // vi (vehicle) mover-se aos solavancos.

**jerkin** ['dʒɜːkɪn] n jaqueta.

**jerky** ['dʒɜːkɪ] adj espasmódico, aos arrancos.

**jersey** ['dʒɜːzɪ] n suéter m/f.

**jest** [dʒɛst] n gracejo, brincadeira.

**jet** [dʒɛt] n (of gas, liquid) jato (Pt: -ct-), forro; (AVIAT) avião m a ja(c)to; **~-black** adj da cor do azeviche; **~ engine** n motor m a ja(c)to.

**jettison** ['dʒɛtɪsn] vt espasmar carga.

**jetty** ['dʒɛtɪ] n quebra-mar m, cais m.

**Jew** [dʒuː] n judeu; **~ess** n judia.

**jewel** ['dʒuːəl] n jóia, rubi m; **~ler** n joalheiro; **~ler's (shop)** n joalheria; **~lery** n jóias fpl, pedrarias fpl.

**Jewish** ['dʒuːɪʃ] adj judeu/judia.

**jibe** [dʒaɪb] n zombaria.

**jiffy** ['dʒɪfɪ] n (col): **in a ~** num instante.

**jig** [dʒɪg] n jiga.

**jigsaw** ['dʒɪgsɔː] n (also: **~ puzzle**) quebra-cabeça m.

**jilt** [dʒɪlt] vt dar o fora em.

**jingle** ['dʒɪŋgl] n (advert) música de propaganda // vi tilintar, retinir.

**jinx** [dʒɪŋks] n (col) caipora, pé m frio.

**jitters** ['dʒɪtəz] npl (col): **to get the ~** ficar muito nervoso.

**job** [dʒɔb] n (gen) trabalho; (task) tarefa; (duty) dever m; (post) emprego; (fam: difficulty) dificuldade f; **it's a good ~ that...** ainda bem que...; **just the ~!** isto é o que queria!; **~less** adj desempregado.

**jockey** ['dʒɔkɪ] n jóquei m // vi: **to ~ for position** manobrar or trapacear para conseguir uma posição.

**jocular** ['dʒɔkjulə*] adj (humorous)

jocoso, divertido; (merry) alegre.

**jog** [dʒɔg] vt empurrar, sacudir // vi (run) fazer jogging or cooper; **to ~ along** ir levando; **to ~ sb's memory** refrescar a memória de alguém; **~ging** n jogging m.

**join** [dʒɔɪn] vt (things) juntar, unir; (become member of) associar-se a, afiliar-se a; (meet: people) reunir-se or encontrar-se com // vi (roads, rivers) confluir // n junção f; **to ~ up** vi (MIL) alistar-se.

**joiner** ['dʒɔɪnə*] n carpinteiro, marceneiro; **~y** n carpintaria.

**joint** [dʒɔɪnt] n (TEC) junta, união f; (wood) encaixe m; (ANAT) articulação f; (CULIN) quarto; (col: place) espelunca // adj (common) comum; (combined) combinado; (committee) misto; **by ~ agreement** por comum acordo; **~ly** adv (gen) junto, em comum; (collectively) coletivamente (Pt: -ect-); (together) conjuntamente.

**joke** [dʒəʊk] n piada; (also: **practical ~**) brincadeira // vi brincar; **to play a ~ on** pregar uma peça em; **joker** n piadista m/f, brincalhão/lhona m/f; (CARDS) coringa m.

**jolly** ['dʒɔlɪ] adj (merry) alegre; (enjoyable) divertido // adv (col) muito, extremamente.

**jolt** [dʒəʊlt] n (shake) sacudida, solavanco; (blow) golpe m; (shock) susto // vt sacudir.

**Jordan** ['dʒɔːdən] n Jordânia.

**jostle** ['dʒɔsl] vt acotovelar, empurrar.

**jot** [dʒɔt] n: **not one ~** nem um pouquinho; **to ~ down** vt anotar, apontar; **~ter** n bloco (de anotações); (SCOL) caderno.

**journal** ['dʒɜːnl] n (paper) jornal m; (magazine) revista; (diary) diário; **~ese** [-'liːz] n (pej) linguagem f jornalística; **~ism** n jornalismo; **~ist** n jornalista m/f.

**journey** ['dʒɜːnɪ] n viagem f;

(distance covered) trajeto (Pt: -ct-) // vi viajar; **return** ~ viagem de volta.

**joy** [dʒɔɪ] n alegria; **~ful, ~ous** adj alegre; **~ ride** n passeio de carro; (illegal) (col) pega.

**J.P.** n abbr of **Justice of the Peace.**

**Jr, Jun., Junr** abbr of **junior.**

**jubilant** ['dʒuːbɪlnt] adj jubilante; **jubilation** [-'leɪʃən] n júbilo, regozijo.

**jubilee** ['dʒuːbɪliː] n jubileu m.

**judge** [dʒʌdʒ] n juiz m, árbitro // vt (gen) julgar; (estimate) considerar; **judg(e)ment** n juízo; (punishment) decisão f, sentença.

**judicial** [dʒuːˈdɪʃl] adj judicial.

**judicious** [dʒuːˈdɪʃəs] adj judicioso.

**judo** ['dʒuːdəʊ] n judô m.

**jug** [dʒʌg] n jarro, moringa.

**juggernaut** ['dʒʌgənɔːt] n (huge truck) jamanta.

**juggle** ['dʒʌgl] vi fazer malabarismos; **juggler** n malabarista m/f.

**Jugoslav** ['juːgəʊˈslaːv] adj, n = **Yugoslav.**

**juice** [dʒuːs] n suco; (Pt) sumo; **juicy** adj suculento.

**jukebox** ['dʒuːkbɒks] n máquina toca-músicas automática, juke-box m.

**July** [dʒuːˈlaɪ] n julho.

**jumble** ['dʒʌmbl] n confusão f, mixórdia // vt (also: **~ up**: mix up) misturar confusamente; (: disarrange) desorganizar; **~ sale** n (Brit) venda de objetos usados, bazar m.

**jumbo (jet)** ['dʒʌmbəʊ] n avião m jumbo.

**jump** [dʒʌmp] vi saltar, pular; (start) sobressaltar-se; (increase) aumentar // vt pular, saltar // n pulo, salto; (increase) alta; **to ~ the queue** furar fila.

**jumper** ['dʒʌmpə*] n suéter m/f, pulôver m.

**jumpy** ['dʒʌmpɪ] adj nervoso.

**junction** ['dʒʌŋkʃən] n (of roads) cruzamento, trevo; (RAIL) entroncamento.

**juncture** ['dʒʌŋktʃə*] n: **at this ~** neste momento, nesta conjuntura.

**June** [dʒuːn] n junho.

**jungle** ['dʒʌŋgl] n selva, mato.

**junior** ['dʒuːnɪə*] adj (in age) mais novo or moço; (competition) juvenil; (position) subalterno // n jovem m/f; **~ school** n escola primária.

**junk** [dʒʌŋk] n (cheap goods) tranqueira, velharias fpl; (lumber) traste m; (rubbish) lixo; (ship) junco; **~shop** n loja de objetos usados.

**jurisdiction** [dʒuərɪsˈdɪkʃən] n jurisdição f.

**jurisprudence** [dʒuərɪsˈpruːdəns] n jurisprudência.

**jury** ['dʒuərɪ] n júri m, jurados mpl.

**just** [dʒʌst] adj justo // adv (exactly) exatamente (Pt: -ct-); (only) apenas, somente; **he's ~ done it/left** ele acaba de fazê-lo/ir; **~ right** perfeito; **~ two o'clock** duas (horas) em ponto; **~ as well that...** ainda bem que...; **~ as he was leaving** no momento em que ele saía; **~ before/enough** justo antes/o suficiente; **~ here** bem aqui; **he ~ missed** falhou por pouco; **~ listen** escute aqui!

**justice** ['dʒʌstɪs] n justiça; **J~ of the Peace (J.P.)** n juiz m de paz.

**justifiable** [dʒʌstɪˈfaɪəbl] adj justificável; **justifiably** adv justificadamente.

**justification** [dʒʌstɪfɪˈkeɪʃən] n justificativa, justificação f; **justify** ['dʒʌstɪfaɪ] vt justificar.

**justly** ['dʒʌstlɪ] adv (gen) justamente; (with reason) com razão.

**justness** ['dʒʌstnɪs] n justiça, justeza.

**jut** [dʒʌt] vi (also: **~ out**) sobressair.

**juvenile** ['dʒuːvənaɪl] adj juvenil; (court) de menores; (books) juvenil

// n jovem m/f, menor m/f de idade.

**juxtapose** ['dʒʌkstəpəuz] vt justapor.

# K

**kaleidoscope** [kə'laɪdəskəup] n calidoscópio, caleidoscópio.

**kangaroo** [kæŋgə'ru:] n canguru m.

**keel** [ki:l] n quilha; **on an even ~** (fig) em equilíbrio.

**keen** [ki:n] adj (interest, desire) grande, vivo; (eye, intelligence) penetrante; (competition) intenso; (edge) afiado; (eager) entusiasmado; **to be ~ to do** or **on doing sth** sentir muita vontade de fazer algo; **to be ~ on sth/sb** gostar de algo/alguém; **~ness** n (eagerness) entusiasmo, interesse m.

**keep** [ki:p], pt, pp **kept** vt (retain, preserve) reter; (hold back) guardar, ficar com; (shop, diary) ter; (feed: family etc) manter; (promise) cumprir; (chickens, bees etc) criar // vi (food) conservar-se; (remain) continuar // n (of castle) torre f de menagem; **to ~ doing sth** continuar fazendo algo; **to ~ sb from doing sth** impedir alguém de fazer algo; **to ~ sth from happening** impedir que algo aconteça; **to ~ sb happy** fazer alguém feliz; **to ~ a place tidy** manter um lugar limpo; **to ~ sth to o.s.** guardar algo para si mesmo; **to ~ sth (back) from sb** ocultar algo de alguém; **to ~ time** (clock) marcar a hora exata (Pt: -ct-); **to ~ on** vi persistir, continuar; **to ~ out** vi (stay out) permanecer fora; **"~ out"** "entrada proibida"; **to ~ up** vi manter // vi não atrasar-se, acompanhar; **to ~ up with** (pace) acompanhar; (level) manter-se ao nível de; **~er** n guarda m, guardião/diã m/f; **~ing** n (care)

cuidado; **in ~ing with** de acordo com; **~sake** n lembrança.

**keg** [kɛg] n barrilete m, barril m pequeno.

**kennel** ['kɛnl] n casa de cachorro; **~s** npl canil msg.

**Kenya** ['kɛnjə] n Quênia.

**kept** [kɛpt] pt, pp of **keep.**

**kerb** [kə:b] n meio-fio.

**kernel** ['kə:nl] n amêndoa.

**kerosene** ['kɛrəsi:n] n querosene m.

**ketchup** ['kɛtʃəp] n molho de tomate, ketchup m.

**kettle** ['kɛtl] n chaleira.

**key** [ki:] n (gen) chave f; (MUS) clave f; (of piano, typewriter) tecla; **~board** n teclado; **~hole** n buraco da fechadura; **~note** n (MUS) tônica; **~ring** n chaveiro; **~stone** n pedra angular.

**khaki** ['kɑ:kɪ] adj cáqui.

**kick** [kɪk] vt (person) dar um pontapé em; (ball) chutar // vi (horse) dar coices // n pontapé m, chute m; (of rifle) recuo; (thrill): **he does it for ~s** faz isso para divertir-se; **to ~ off** vi (SPORT) dar o pontapé inicial; **~-off** n (SPORT) pontapé m inicial.

**kid** [kɪd] n (child) criança; (animal) cabrito; (leather) pelica // vi (col) caçoar, brincar.

**kidnap** ['kɪdnæp] vt seqüestrar; **~per** n seqüestrador(a) m/f; **~ping** n seqüestro.

**kidney** ['kɪdnɪ] n rim m.

**kill** [kɪl] vt (gen) matar; (murder) assassinar; (destroy) destruir; (finish off) acabar com, aniquilar // n ato de matar; (Pt: -ct-) **~er** n assassino/a; **~ing** n (one) assassinato; (several) matança // adj (funny) divertido, engraçado.

**kiln** [kɪln] n forno.

**kilo** ['ki:ləu] n quilo; **~gram(me)** ['kɪləugræm] n quilograma m; **~metre, ~meter** (US) ['kɪləmi:tə*] *n* quilômetro; ~**watt** [ˈkɪləuwɔt] *n* quilowatt *m*.

**kilt** [kɪlt] *n* saiote *m* escocês.

**kimono** [kɪˈməunəu] *n* quimono.

**kin** [kɪn] *n* parentela.

**kind** [kaɪnd] *adj* (*generous*) generoso; (*good*) bom, bondoso, amável // *n* espécie *f*, classe *f*; (*species*) gênero; **in** ~ (*comm*) em espécie; **a** ~ **of** uma espécie de; **two of a** ~ dois da mesma espécie.

**kindergarten** [ˈkɪndəgɑːtn] *n* jardim *m* de infância.

**kind-hearted** [kaɪndˈhɑːtɪd] *adj* de bom coração.

**kindle** [ˈkɪndl] *vt* acender.

**kindly** [ˈkaɪndlɪ] *adj* (*gen*) bondoso; (*good*) bom/boa; (*gentle*) gentil, carinhoso // *adv* bondosamente, amavelmente; **will you** ~... você pode fazer o favor de...

**kindness** [ˈkaɪndnɪs] *n* bondade *f*, amabilidade *f*.

**kindred** [ˈkɪndrɪd] *n* parentela, parentesco // *adj*: ~ **spirit** com os mesmos gostos.

**king** [kɪŋ] *n* rei *m*; ~**dom** *n* reino; ~**fisher** *n* martim-pescador *m*; ~**-size** *adj* tamanho grande.

**kink** [kɪŋk] *n* (*of rope*) dobra, coca.

**kinky** [ˈkɪŋkɪ] *adj* (*odd*) excêntrico, esquisito; (*pej*) pervertido.

**kiosk** [ˈkiːɔsk] *n* banca de jornais; (*TEL*) cabine *f*.

**kipper** [ˈkɪpə*] *n* tipo de arenque *m* defumado.

**kiss** [kɪs] *n*, *vt* beijar; **to** ~ (**each other**) beijar-se.

**kit** [kɪt] *n* (*gen*) apetrechos *mpl*; (*equipment*) equipamento; (*set of tools etc*) caixa de ferramentas; (*for assembly*) kit *m* para montar.

**kitchen** [ˈkɪtʃɪn] *n* cozinha; ~ **garden** *n* horta; ~ **sink** *n* pia (de cozinha); ~**ware** *n* bateria de cozinha.

**kite** [kaɪt] *n* (*toy*) papagaio, pipa.

**kitten** [ˈkɪtn] *n* gatinho.

**kitty** [ˈkɪtɪ] *n* (*pool of money*) fundo

comum, vaquinha; (*CARDS*) bolo (esportivo).

**kleptomaniac** [klɛptəuˈmeɪnɪæk] *n* cleptomaníaco/a.

**knack** [næk] *n*: **to have the** ~ **of doing sth** ter um jeito or queda para fazer algo.

**knapsack** [ˈnæpsæk] *n* mochila.

**knead** [niːd] *vt* amassar.

**knee** [niː] *n* joelho; ~**cap** *n* rótula.

**kneel** [niːl] *pt, pp* **knelt** *vi* ajoelhar-se.

**knell** [nɛl] *n* dobre *m* de finados.

**knelt** [nɛlt] *pt, pp of* **kneel.**

**knew** [njuː] *pt of* **know.**

**knickers** [ˈnɪkəz] *npl* calcinha *fsg*; (*Pt*) cuecas *fpl*.

**knife** [naɪf], *pl* **knives** *n* faca // *vt* esfaquear.

**knight** [naɪt] *n* cavaleiro; (*CHESS*) cavalo; ~**hood** *n* cavalaria; (*title*): **to get a** ~**hood** receber o título de sir.

**knit** [nɪt] *vt* tricotar; (*Pt*) fazer de malha; (*brows*) franzir // *vi* tricotar; (*bones*) consolidar-se; **to** ~ **together** (*fig*) unir, juntar; ~**ting** *n* trabalho de tricô; (*Pt*) malha; ~**ting machine** *n* máquina de tricotar; ~**ting needle** *n* agulha de tricô; ~**wear** *n* malha.

**knives** [naɪvz] *pl of* **knife.**

**knob** [nɔb] *n* (*of door*) maçaneta *or* puxador *m* redondo; (*of stick*) castão *m*; (*lump*) calombo; (*fig*): **a** ~ **of butter** uma porção de manteiga.

**knock** [nɔk] *vt* (*strike*) bater; (*bump into*) colidir com; (*fig: col*) criticar, malhar // *n* pancada, golpe *m*; (*on door*) batida; **to** ~ **at** *or* **on the door** bater à porta; **to** ~ **down** *vt* derrubar; **to** ~ **off** *vi* (*col: finish*) parar // *vt* (*col: steal*) roubar; **to** ~ **out** *vt* derrotar; (*remove*) remover; (*BOXING*) nocautear; ~**er** *n* (*on door*) aldrava; ~**kneed** *adj* cambaio; ~**out** *n* (*BOXING*) nocaute *m*.

**knot** [nɔt] *n* (*gen*) nó *m* // *vt* dar nó

em; ~**ty** adj (fig) complicado.

**know** [nəu], pt **knew**, pp **known**
vt (gen) saber; (person, author,
place) conhecer; **to ~ that...** saber
que...; **to ~ how to swim** saber
nadar; ~**all** n sabichão/chona m/f;
~**how** n know-how m, experiência;
~**ing** adj (look: of complicity) de
cumplicidade; (: spiteful) malicioso;
~**ingly** adv (purposely) de
propósito; (spitefully) maliciosamente.

**knowledge** ['nɔlɪdʒ] n (gen)
conhecimento; (range of learning)
saber m, conhecimentos mpl;
(learning) erudição f, ciência;
~**able** adj entendido, versado.

**known** [nəun] pp of **know**.

**knuckle** ['nʌkl] n nó m.

**K.O.** n abbr of **knockout**.

**Koran** [kɔ'rɑːn] n Alcorão m.

# L

**l.** abbr of **litre**.

**lab** [læb] n abbr of **laboratory**.

**label** ['leɪbl] n etiqueta, rótulo;
(brand: of record) marca // vt
etiquetar, rotular.

**laboratory** [lə'bɔrətərɪ] n
laboratório.

**laborious** [lə'bɔːrɪəs] adj laborioso.

**labour, labor** (US) ['leɪbə*] n
(task) trabalho; (~ force) mão-de-
obra f; (workers) trabalhadores
mpl; (MED) (costela de) parto // vi:
**to ~ (at)** trabalhar (em) // vt
insistir em; **in ~** (MED) na hora
de parto; **L~**, **the L~ party** o
partido trabalhista; **hard ~**
trabalhos mpl forçados; ~**ed** adj
(movement) forçado; (style)
elaborado; ~**er** n operário; (on
farm) trabalhador m rural, peão m;
(day ~er) diarista m.

**labyrinth** ['læbɪrɪnθ] n labirinto.

**lace** [leɪs] n renda; (of shoe etc)
cordão m // vt (shoe) amarrar.

**lack** [læk] n (absence) falta;
(scarcity) escassez f // vt carecer
de; **through** or **for ~ of** por falta de;
**to be ~ing** faltar.

**lackadaisical** [lækə'deɪzɪkl] adj
(careless) descuidado; (indifferent)
apático, aéreo.

**laconic** [lə'kɔnɪk] adj lacônico.

**lacquer** ['lækə*] n laca, verniz m.

**lad** [læd] n menino, rapaz m, moço;
(in stable etc) empregado.

**ladder** ['lædə*] n escada-de-mão f;
(in tights) defeito (em forma de
escada) // vt (tights) desfiar.

**laden** ['leɪdn] adj: ~ **(with)**
carregado (de).

**ladle** ['leɪdl] n concha (de sopa).

**lady** ['leɪdɪ] n senhora;
(distinguished, noble) dama; **young
~** senhorita; **'ladies' (toilets)**
'senhoras'; ~**bird**, ~**bug** (US)
n joaninha; ~**in-waiting** n dama de
companhia; ~**like** adj elegante,
refinado.

**lag** [læg] vi (also: ~ **behind**) atrasar-
se, ficar atrás // vt (pipes) revestir
com isolante térmico.

**lager** ['lɑːgə*] n cerveja leve e clara.

**lagging** ['lægɪŋ] n revestimento.

**lagoon** [lə'guːn] n lagoa.

**laid** [leɪd] pt, pp of **lay**.

**lain** [leɪn] pp of **lie**.

**lair** [lɛə*] n covil m, toca.

**lake** [leɪk] n lago.

**lamb** [læm] n cordeiro; (meat)
carne f de cordeiro; ~ **chop** n
costeleta de cordeiro; **lambswool** n
lã f de cordeiro.

**lame** [leɪm] adj coxo, manco;
(weak) pouco convincente, fraco.

**lament** [lə'mɛnt] n lamento, queixa
// vt lamentar-se de; ~**able**
['læməntəbl] adj lamentável.

**laminated** ['læmɪneɪtɪd] adj
laminado.

**lamp** [læmp] n lâmpada.

**lampoon** [læm'puːn] vt satirizar.

**lamp:** ~**post** n poste m; ~**shade** n abajur m, quebra-luz m.

**lance** [lɑːns] n lança //  vt (MED) lancetar; ~ **corporal** n cabo.

**lancet** [ˈlɑːnsɪt] n lanceta.

**land** [lænd] n (gen) terra; (country) país m; (piece of ~) terreno; (estate) terras fpl, propriedades fpl; (AGR) solo // vi (from ship) desembarcar; (AVIAT) aterrissar; (fig: fall) cair, terminar // vt (obtain) conseguir; (passengers, goods) desembarcar; **to ~ up in/at** ir parar em; ~**ing** n desembarque m, aterrissagem f; (of staircase) patamar m; ~**ing craft** n navio para desembarque; ~**ing gear** n trem m de aterrissagem; ~**ing stage** n cais m de desembarque; ~**ing strip** n pista de aterrissagem; ~**lady** n (of boarding house) senhoria; (owner) proprietária; ~**locked** adj cercado de terra; ~**lord** n senhorio, locador m; (of pub etc) dono, proprietário; ~**lubber** n pessoa desacostumada ao mar; ~**mark** n lugar m conhecido; (fig) marco; **to be a ~mark** (fig) marcar uma época; ~**owner** n latifundiário/a m/f.

**landscape** [ˈlænskeɪp] n paisagem f; ~**d** adj projetado paisagisticamente, urbanizado.

**landslide** [ˈlændslaɪd] n (GEO) desmoronamento, desabamento; (fig: POL) vitória esmagadora.

**lane** [leɪn] n (in country) azinhaga; (in town) rua estreita; (AUT) pista; (in race) raia; (for air or sea traffic) rota.

**language** [ˈlæŋgwɪdʒ] n linguagem f; (national tongue) idioma m, língua; **bad ~** linguagem indecente or grosseira.

**languid** [ˈlæŋgwɪd] adj lânguido.

**languish** [ˈlæŋgwɪʃ] vi elanguescer, debilitar-se.

**lank** [læŋk] adj (hair) liso.

**lanky** [ˈlæŋkɪ] adj magricela.

**lantern** [ˈlæntn] n lanterna.

**lap** [læp] n (of track) volta; (of body): **to sit on sb's ~** sentar-se no colo de alguém // vt (also: ~ **up**) lamber // vi (waves) marulhar; ~**dog** n cãozinho de estimação.

**lapel** [ləˈpɛl] n lapela.

**Lapland** [ˈlæplænd] n Lapônia; **Lapp** [læp] adj, n lapão/ona m/f.

**lapse** [læps] n lapso, engano; (moral) decadência // vi (expire) caducar; (LAW) prescrever; (morally) decair; (time) passar, transcorrer; **to ~ into bad habits** degenerar; ~ **of time** lapso, intervalo.

**larceny** [ˈlɑːsənɪ] n furto; **petty ~** delito leve.

**lard** [lɑːd] n banha de porco.

**larder** [ˈlɑːdə*] n despensa.

**large** [lɑːdʒ] adj (gen) grande; (fat) gordo; **at ~** (free) em liberdade; (generally) em geral; ~**ly** adv em grande parte; ~**-scale** adj (map) em grande escala; (fig) importante.

**lark** [lɑːk] n (bird) cotovia; (joke) brincadeira, peça; **to ~ about** vi divertir-se, brincar.

**larva** [ˈlɑːvə], pl ~**vae** [-viː] n larva.

**laryngitis** [lærɪnˈdʒaɪtɪs] n laringite f.

**larynx** [ˈlærɪŋks] n laringe f.

**lascivious** [ləˈsɪvɪəs] adj lascivo.

**laser** [ˈleɪzə*] n laser m.

**lash** [læʃ] n chicote m, açoite m; (punishment) chicotada; (gen: eyelash) pestana, cílio // vt chicotear, açoitar; (tie) atar; **to ~ out** vi ~ **to ~ out at or against sb** atacar alguém violentamente; **to ~ out** (col: spend) esbanjar.

**lass** [læs] n moça.

**lasso** [læˈsuː] n laço // vt laçar.

**last** [lɑːst] adj (gen) último; (final) derradeiro // adv em último lugar // vi (endure) durar; (continue) continuar; ~ **week** na semana passada; ~ **night** ontem à noite; **at ~** afinal; ~ **but one** penúltimo;

~ing *adj* durável, duradouro; ~minute *adj* de última hora.

**latch** [lætʃ] *n* trinco, fecho, tranca; ~**key** *n* chave *f* de trinco.

**late** [leit] *adj* (*not on time*) atrasado, tarde; (*far on in day etc*) tardio; (*hour*) avançado; (*recent*) recente; (*former*) antigo, ex-, anterior; (*dead*) falecido // *adv* tarde; (*behind time, schedule*) atrasado; **of** ~ recentemente; **in** ~ **May** no final de maio; **the** ~ **Mr X** o falecido Sr. X; ~**comer** *n* retardatário/a; ~**ly** *adv* ultimamente; ~**ness** *n* (*of person*) atraso; (*of event*) demora.

**latent** [ˈleitnt] *adj* latente.

**later** [ˈleitə*] *adj* (*date etc*) posterior; (*version etc*) mais recente // *adv* mais tarde, depois.

**lateral** [ˈlætərl] *adj* lateral.

**latest** [ˈleitist] *adj* último; **at the** ~ no mais tardar.

**lathe** [leið] *n* torno.

**lather** [ˈlɑːðə*] *n* espuma (de sabão) // *vt* ensaboar // *vi* fazer espuma.

**Latin** [ˈlætin] *n* latim *m* // *adj* latino; ~ **America** *n* América Latina; ~**American** *adj*, *n* latino-americano/a.

**latitude** [ˈlætitjuːd] *n* latitude *f*.

**latrine** [ləˈtriːn] *n* latrina.

**latter** [ˈlætə*] *adj* último; (*of two*) segundo // *n*: **the** ~ o último, este; ~**ly** *adv* ultimamente.

**lattice** [ˈlætis] *n* treliça; (*on window*) gelosia, rótula.

**laudable** [ˈlɔːdəbl] *adj* louvável.

**laugh** [lɑːf] *n* riso, risada; (*loud*) gargalhada // *vi* rir, dar risada or gargalhada; **to** ~ **at** *vt fus* rir de; ridicularizar; **to** ~ **off** *vt* disfarçar sorrindo; ~**able** *adj* risível, ridículo; **to be the** ~**ing stock of** ser o alvo de chacota; ~**ter** *n* riso, ri[...]

**launch** [lɔːntʃ] [...] also ~ing [...] lançar; lança[...]

~(**ing**) **pad** *n* plataforma de lançamento.

**launder** [ˈlɔːndə*] *vt* lavar e passar.

**launderette** [lɔːnˈdrɛt] *n* lavanderia automática.

**laundry** [ˈlɔːndri] *n* lavanderia; (*clothes*) roupa para lavar; **to do the** ~ lavar a roupa.

**laureate** [ˈlɔːriət] *adj see* **poet.**

**laurel** [ˈlɔrl] *n* louro; (BOT) loureiro.

**lava** [ˈlɑːvə] *n* lava.

**lavatory** [ˈlævətəri] *n* privada; (Pt) casa de banho; **lavatories** *npl* banheiro, toalete *m*.

**lavender** [ˈlævəndə*] *n* lavanda.

**lavish** [ˈlæviʃ] *adj* profuso, perdulário; (*giving freely*): ~ **with** pródigo em or generoso com // *vt*: **to** ~ **sth on sb** encher or cobrir alguém de algo.

**law** [lɔː] *n* lei *f*; (*study*) direito; (*of game*) regra; ~**abiding** *adj* obediente à lei; ~ **and order** *n* ordem *f* pública; ~**breaker** *n* infrator(a) (Pt: -ct-) *m/f* (da lei); ~**court** *n* tribunal *m* de justiça; ~**ful** *adj* legal, lícito; ~**fully** *adv* legalmente; ~**less** *adj* (*act*) ilegal; (*person*) rebelde; (*country*) sem lei, desordenado.

**lawn** [lɔːn] *n* gramado; ~ **mower** *n* cortador *m* de grama; ~ **tennis** [ˈtɛnis] *n* tênis *m* de gramado.

**law:** ~ **school** *n* faculdade *f* de direito; ~ **student** *n* estudante *m/f* de direito.

**lawsuit** [ˈlɔːsuːt] *n* ação [...] judicial, processo [...]

**law**[...] [ˈlɔːjə*] *n* adv[...]ião/li[...] sales, wills e[...]idado; (*negligent*) [...] [ˈlæksitv] *n* laxante *m*. ~ [ˈlæksiti] *n* frouxidão *f;* complacência; ~[...] (*negligence*) [...]; (Pt: -ct-) *adj* leigo; (*n*[...] [lei] *pt* of **lie** // *adj* leigo; (*n*[...] *expert*) profano // *vt*, *pt*, *pp* p[...]

*(place)* colocar; *(eggs, table)* pôr; *(trap)* armar; **to ~ aside or by** vt pôr de lado; **to ~ down** vt *(pen etc)* baixar, repousar; *(~ flat)* deitar-se; *(arms)* depor; *(policy)* estabelecer; **to ~ down the law** impor a lei; **to ~ off** vt *(workers)* demitir, cessar; **to ~ on** vt *(water, gas)* instalar; *(provide)* prover; **to ~ out** vt *(design)* planejar; *(display)* dispor; *(spend)* esbanjar; **to ~ up** vt *(store)* armazenar; *(ship)* pôr fora de serviço; *(subj: illness)* guardar o leito; **~about** n vadio, preguiçoso; **~by** n acostamento.

**layer** ['leɪə*] n camada.

**layette** [leɪ'ɛt] n enxoval m de bebê.

**layman** ['leɪmən] n pessoa não entendida or não especializada; *(REL)* leigo.

**layout** ['leɪaʊt] n *(design)* leiaute m, esquema m; *(disposition)* disposição f; *(PRESS)* composição f.

**laze** [leɪz] vi viver na ociosidade; *(pej)* vadiar, malandrar; **laziness** n preguiça; **lazy** adj preguiçoso, indolente.

**lb.** abbr of **pound** *(weight)*.

**lead** [liːd] n *(front position)* dianteira; *(SPORT)* liderança; *(distance, time ahead)* vantagem f; *(clue)* pista; *(ELEC)* cabo; *(for dog)* correia; *(THEATRE)* papel m principal // n [lɛd] chumbo; *(in pencil)* grafite f // *(vb: pt, pp* **led**) vt conduzir; *(induce)* levar, induzir; *(be leader of)* dirigir; *(SPORT)* liderar // vi encabeçar; **to ~ to** levar a, conduzir a; **to ~ astray** vt desviar; **to ~ away** vt levar; **to ~ on** vt enganar; **to ~ on to** *(cause)* provocar; **to ~ up to** conduzir a; **leader** ['liːdə*] n chefe m/f; *(of union)* líder m/f; *(of gang)* cabeça f; *(of newspaper)* guia m/f; **~ship** n liderança; fundo;

*(Pt:* -çç-) f; *(quality)* poder m de liderança.

**leading** ['liːdɪŋ] adj *(main)* principal; *(outstanding)* destacado, notável; *(first)* primeiro; *(front)* dianteiro; **~ lady** n *(THEATRE)* primeira atriz f; **~ light** n *(person)* figura principal.

**leaf** [liːf], pl **leaves** n folha // vi: **to ~ through** folhear; **to turn over a new ~** começar vida nova.

**leaflet** ['liːflɪt] n folheto.

**league** [liːg] n associação f; *(FOOTBALL)* liga; **to be in ~ with** estar de comum acordo com.

**leak** [liːk] n *(of liquid, gas)* escape m, vazamento; *(hole)* buraco, rombo; *(in roof)* goteira; *(of money)* desfalque m // vi *(ship)* fazer água; *(shoe)* entrar água; *(pipe)* vazar; *(roof)* gotejar; *(container)* sair; *(gas)* escapar; *(fig: news)* transpirar // vt *(gen)* deixar escapar; *(exude)* escoar; **the information was ~ed to the enemy** as informações foram passadas para o inimigo; **the news ~ed out** a notícia veio a público.

**lean** [liːn] adj magro // *(vb: pt, pp* **leaned** or **leant** [lɛnt]) vt: **to ~ sth on** apoiar algo em // vi *(slope)* inclinar-se; *(rest)*: **to ~ against** apoiar-se contra; **to ~ on** apoiar-se em; *(fig: rely on)* contar com (o apoio de); **to ~ back/forward** vi inclinar-se para trás/frente; **to ~ over** vt/i inclinar-se (sobre); **~ing** adj inclinação f, tendência // n: **~ing (towards)** inclinação f (para); **~-to** n alpendre m.

**leap** [liːp] n salto, pulo // vi, pt, pp **leaped** or **leapt** [lɛpt] saltar; **~frog** n carniça; **~ year** n ano bissexto.

**learn** [ləːn] pt, pp **learned** or **learnt** vt *(gen)* aprender; *(come to know of)* informar-se de, ficar sabendo // vi aprender; **to ~ how to** [de]aprender a fazer algo; **~ed** [...] adj erudito; **~er** n [...]; **~ing** n [...]

aprendizagem f, erudição f.

**lease** [li:s] n arrendamento, locação f // vt arrendar, alugar.

**leash** [li:ʃ] n trela, correia.

**least** [li:st] adj menor; (smallest amount of) mínimo // adv o menos // n: **the** ~ o mínimo; **the** ~ **possible effort** o menor esforço possível; **at** ~ pelo menos; **not in the** ~ de maneira nenhuma.

**leather** ['leðə*] n couro.

**leave** [li:v] pt, pp **left** vt deixar; (go away from) abandonar // vi ir-se; (train) sair // n permissão f, licença; **to be left** sobrar; **there's some milk left over** sobrou um pouco de leite; **on** ~ de licença; **to take one's** ~ of despedir-se de; **to** ~ **out** vt omitir, excluir.

**leaves** [li:vz] pl of **leaf**.

**Lebanon** ['lebənən] n Líbano m.

**lecherous** ['letʃərəs] adj lascivo.

**lecture** ['lektʃə*] n conferência; (SCOL) aula // vi dar uma aula // vt (scold) passar um sermão; **to give a** ~ **on** dar uma conferência sobre; **lecturer** n conferencista m/f; (at university) professor(a) m/f.

**led** [led] pt, pp of **lead**.

**ledge** [ledʒ] n (of window, on wall) saliência, borda; (of mountain) proeminência.

**ledger** ['ledʒə*] n livro-razão m.

**lee** [li:] n sotavento.

**leek** [li:k] n alho-poró m.

**leer** [lɪə*] vi: **to** ~ **at sb** olhar maliciosamente para alguém.

**leeway** ['li:weɪ] n (fig): **to have some** ~ ter certa liberdade de ação (Pt: -cç-).

**left** [left] pt, pp of **leave** // adj esquerdo; (POL) de esquerda // n esquerda // adv à esquerda; **the L**~ (POL) a Esquerda; ~**-handed** adj canhoto; **the** ~**-hand side** n a esquerda; ~ **luggage (office)** n depósito de bagagem; ~**overs** npl sobras fpl; ~**-wing** adj (POL) de extrema esquerda, esquerdista.

**leg** [leg] n perna; (of animal) pata; (of chair) pé m; (CULIN: of meat) perna; (of journey) etapa; **lst/2nd** ~ (SPORT) partida de ida/de volta; **to pull sb's** ~ brincar or mexer com alguém.

**legacy** ['legəsɪ] n legado.

**legal** ['li:gl] adj (gen) lícito; (of law) legal; (enquiry etc) jurídico; ~**ize** vt legalizar; ~**ly** adv legalmente; ~ **tender** n moeda corrente.

**legend** ['ledʒənd] n legenda; ~**ary** adj legendário.

**legible** ['ledʒəbl] adj legível.

**legion** ['li:dʒən] n legião f.

**legislate** ['ledʒɪsleɪt] vi legislar; **legislation** [-'leɪʃən] n legislação f; **legislative** ['-lətɪv] adj legislativo; **legislature** [-lətʃə*] n legislatura.

**legitimacy** [lɪ'dʒɪtɪməsɪ] n legitimidade f; **legitimate** [-mət] adj legítimo.

**leg-room** ['legru:m] n espaço para as pernas.

**leisure** ['leʒə*] n lazer m, ócio; **at** ~ desocupado, livre; ~ **centre** n centro de lazer; ~**ly** adj calmo, vagaroso.

**lemon** ['lemən] n limão m; ~**ade** [-'neɪd] n (fruit juice) limonada; (fizzy) refresco de limão.

**lend** [lend], pt, pp **lent** vt: **to** ~ **sth to sb** emprestar algo a alguém; ~**er** n emprestador m/f; ~**ing library** n biblioteca volante.

**length** [leŋθ] n comprimento, extensão f; (section: of road, pipe etc) trecho; **at** ~ (at last) finalmente, afinal; (lengthily) por extenso; ~**en** vt encompridar // vi encompridar-se; ~**ways** adv longitudinalmente; ~**y** adj comprido, prolixo; (meeting) prolongado.

**leniency** ['li:nɪənsɪ] n indulgência; **lenient** [-ənt] adj indulgente, clemente.

**lens** [lenz] n (of spectacles) lente f; (of camera) objetiva (Pt: -ct-).

**lent** [lɛnt] *pt, pp of* **lend.**

**Lent** [lɛnt] *n* Quaresma.

**lentil** [ˈlɛntl] *n* lentilha.

**Leo** [ˈliːəu] *n* Leão *m.*

**leopard** [ˈlɛpəd] *n* leopardo.

**leotard** [ˈliːətɑːd] *n* collant *m.*

**leper** [ˈlɛpə*] *n* leproso/a; **leprosy** [-prəsɪ] *n* lepra.

**lesbian** [ˈlɛzbɪən] *n* lésbica.

**less** [lɛs] *det adj (in size, degree etc)* menor; *(in quantity)* menos // *pron, adv* menos; ~ **than half** menos da metade; ~ **and** ~ cada vez menos; **the** ~ **he works...** quanto menos trabalha...

**lessen** [ˈlɛsn] *vi* diminuir, minguar // *vt* diminuir, reduzir.

**lesson** [ˈlɛsn] *n* lição *f*; **a maths** ~ uma aula *or* uma lição de matemática.

**lest** [lɛst] *conj:* ~ **it happen** para que não aconteça.

**let** [lɛt], *pt, pp* **let** *vt (allow)* deixar, permitir; *(lease)* alugar; ~**'s go** vamos!; ~ **him come** deixa ele vir!; **"to** ~ **"** "aluga-se"; **to** ~ **down** *vt (lower)* abaixar; *(dress)* encumprідar; *(tyre)* esvaziar; *(hair)* soltar; *(disappoint)* desapontar; **to** ~ **go** *vt/i* soltar; **to** ~ **in** *vt* deixar entrar; *(visitor etc)* fazer entrar; **to** ~ **off** *vt* deixar livre; *(firework etc)* disparar; **to** ~ **on** *vt (col)* divulgar *(that que)*; **to** ~ **out** *vt* deixar sair; *(dress)* alargar; **to** ~ **up** *vi* cessar, afrouxar.

**lethal** [ˈliːθl] *adj* letal; *(wound)* mortal.

**lethargic** [lɛˈθɑːdʒɪk] *adj* letárgico; **lethargy** [ˈlɛθədʒɪ] *n* letargia.

**letter** [ˈlɛtə*] *n (of alphabet)* letra; *(correspondence)* carta; ~ **bomb** *n* carta com bomba; ~**box** *n* caixa do correio; ~**ing** *n* letras *fpl.*

**lettuce** [ˈlɛtɪs] *n* alface *f.*

**let-up** [ˈlɛtʌp] *n* pausa, trégua.

**leukaemia, leukemia** *(US)* [luːˈkiːmɪə] *n* leucemia.

**level** [ˈlɛvl] *adj (flat)* plano;

*(flattened)* nivelado; *(uniform)* uniforme // *adv* no mesmo nível // *n* nível *m*; *(flat place)* plano // *vt* nivelar, aplanar; **to be** ~ **with** estar no mesmo nível que; **on the** ~ *(fig: honest)* a sério, sincero; **to** ~ **off** *or* **out** *vi (prices etc)* estabilizar-se; ~ **crossing** *n* passagem *f* de nível; ~**-headed** *adj* sensato.

**lever** [ˈliːvə*] *n* alavanca // *vt:* **to** ~ **up** levantar com alavanca; ~**age** *n (fig: influence)* influência.

**levity** [ˈlɛvɪtɪ] *n* leviandade *f*, frivolidade *f.*

**levy** [ˈlɛvɪ] *n* arrecadação *f*, tributo // *vt* arrecadar, exigir.

**lewd** [luːd] *adj* obsceno, lascivo.

**liability** [laɪəˈbɪlɪtɪ] *n* responsabilidade *f*; *(handicap)* desvantagem *f*; *(risk)* risco; **liabilities** *npl* obrigações *fpl*; *(COMM)* dívidas *fpl*, passivo *sg.*

**liable** [ˈlaɪəbl] *adj (subject):* ~ **to** sujeito a; **to be** ~ **for** ser responsável por; **to be** ~ **to** *(likely)* ter uma tendência para.

**liaison** [liːˈeɪzɔn] *n (coordination)* ligação *f*; *(affair)* relação *f* amorosa.

**liar** [ˈlaɪə*] *n* mentiroso/a.

**libel** [ˈlaɪbl] *n* libelo, calúnia // *vt* caluniar, difamar.

**liberal** [ˈlɪbərl] *adj (gen)* liberal; *(generous):* ~ **with** generoso com.

**liberate** [ˈlɪbəreɪt] *vt* liberar; **liberation** [-ˈreɪʃən] *n* liberação *f.*

**liberty** [ˈlɪbətɪ] *n* liberdade *f*; **to be at** ~ **to** ter permissão para; **to take the** ~ **of doing sth** tomar a liberdade de fazer algo.

**Libra** [ˈliːbrə] *n* Libra.

**librarian** [laɪˈbrɛərɪən] *n* bibliotecário/a; **library** [ˈlaɪbrərɪ] *n* biblioteca.

**libretto** [lɪˈbrɛtəu] *n* libreto.

**Libya** [ˈlɪbɪə] *n* Líbia; ~**n** *adj, n* líbio/a.

**lice** [laɪs] *pl of* **louse.**

**licence, license** *(US)* [ˈlaɪsns] *n (gen)* licença; *(permit)* permissão *f*;

*(also:* **driving** ~) carteira de motorista; *(Pt)* carta de condução; *(excessive freedom)* libertinagem *f*; ~ **number** *n* número da placa; ~ **plate** *n* placa (do carro).

**license** ['laɪsns] *n (US)* = **licence** // *vt* autorizar, licenciar; ~**d** *adj (for alcohol)* autorizado para vender bebida alcoólica.

**licensee** [laɪsənˈsiː] *n (in a pub)* dono/a *m/f.*

**licentious** [laɪˈsɛnʃəs] *adj* licencioso.

**lichen** ['laɪkən] *n* líquem *m.*

**lick** [lɪk] *vt* lamber // *n* lambida; **a** ~ **of paint** uma mão de pintura.

**licorice** ['lɪkərɪs] *n* = **liquorice.**

**lid** [lɪd] *n (of box, case, of pan)* tampa.

**lido** ['laɪdəu] *n* piscina pública ao ar livre.

**lie** [laɪ] *n* mentira // *vi* mentir // *vi, pt* **lay**, *pp* **lain** *(act)* deitar; *(state)* estar deitado; *(of object: be situated)* estar, encontrar-se; to ~ **low** *(fig)* esconder-se; to ~ **about** *vi (things)* estar espalhado; *(people)* vadiar; to **have a** ~-**down** descansar, tirar uma soneca; to **have a** ~-**in** dormir até tarde or até estourar.

**lieu** [luː]: **in** ~ **of** *prep* em vez de.

**lieutenant** [lɛfˈtɛnənt] *n* lugar-tenente *m*; *(MIL)* tenente *m.*

**life** [laɪf], *pl* **lives** *n (gen)* vida; *(way of* ~) modo de viver; *(of licence etc)* vigência; ~ **assurance** *n* seguro de vida; ~-**belt** *n* cinto salva-vidas; ~-**boat** *n* barco salva-vidas; ~-**guard** *n* guarda *m* salva-vidas; ~ **jacket** *n* colete *m* salva-vidas; ~**less** *adj* sem vida; *(dull)* sem graça; ~**like** *adj* natural; ~-**line** *n* corda salva-vidas; ~ **long** *adj* vitalício, perpétuo; ~ **preserver** *n (US)* colete *m* salva-vidas; ~-**saver** *n* guarda *m* salva-vidas; ~ **sentence** *n* prisão *f* perpétua; ~-**sized** *adj* de tamanho natural; ~ **span** *n* vida, duração *f*; ~ **support system** *n*

*(MED)* sistema *m* de respiração artificial; ~**time** *n*: **in his** ~**time** durante a sua vida; **once in a** ~**time** uma vez na vida.

**lift** [lɪft] *vt* levantar; *(steal)* roubar // *vi (fog)* dispersar-se, dissipar-se // *n (elevator)* elevador *m*; **to give sb a** ~ dar uma carona para alguém; ~-**off** *n* decolagem *f.*

**ligament** ['lɪgəmənt] *n* ligamento.

**light** [laɪt] *n (gen)* luz *f*; *(flame)* chama, lume *m*; *(lamp)* luz, lâmpada; *(daylight)* luz do dia; *(headlight)* farol *m*; *(rear* ~) luz traseira; *(for cigarette etc)*: **have you got a** ~? *(você)* tem fogo? // *vt, pt, pp* **lighted** *or* **lit** *(candle, cigarette, fire)* acender; *(room)* iluminar // *adj (colour)* claro; *(not heavy, also fig)* leve; *(room)* iluminado; **to** ~ **up** *vi (smoke)* acender um cigarro; *(face)* iluminar-se // *vt (illuminate)* iluminar, acender; ~ **bulb** *n* lâmpada; ~**en** *vi (grow* ~) clarear // *vt (give light to)* iluminar; *(make lighter)* clarear; *(make less heavy)* tornar mais leve; ~**er** *n (also: cigarette* ~**er**) isqueiro, acendedor *m*; ~-**headed** *adj (dizzy)* aturdido, tonto; *(excited)* exaltado; *(by nature)* estouvado; ~-**hearted** *adj* alegre, despreocupado; ~-**house** *n* farol *m*; ~**ing** *n (act, system)* iluminação *f*; ~**ly** *adv (touch)* ligeiramente; *(thoughtlessly)* despreocupadamente; *(slightly)* levemente; *(not seriously)* levianamente; **to get off** ~**ly** não ser castigado o suficiente; ~ **meter** *n (PHOT)* fotômetro; ~**ness** *n* claridade *f*; *(in weight)* leveza.

**lightning** ['laɪtnɪŋ] *n* relâmpago, raio; ~ **conductor** *n* pára-raios *m inv.*

**light:** ~**weight** *adj (suit)* leve // *n (BOXING)* peso-leve *m*; ~ **year** *n* ano-luz *m.*

**like** [laɪk] *vt (person)* gostar de,

simpatizar-se com; (things) gostar de // prep como // adj parecido, semelhante // n: **the ~ coisas parecidas;** his **~s and dislikes** seus gostos e aversões; **I would ~, I'd ~** (eu) gostaria de; **would you ~ a coffee?** você quer um café?; **to be or look ~ sb/sth** assemelhar-se a or parecer-se com alguém/algo; **that's just ~ him** é típico dele; **it is nothing ~ ...** não se parece nada com ...; **~able** adj simpático, agradável.

**likelihood** ['laiklihud] n probabilidade f; **likely** [-lɪ] adj provável; **he's likely to leave** é provável que ele se vá.

**like-minded** [laik'maindid] adj da mesma opinião.

**liken** ['laikən] vt: **to ~ sth to sth** comparar algo com algo.

**likewise** ['laikwaiz] adv igualmente.

**liking** ['laikiŋ] n: **to his ~** ao seu gosto.

**lilac** ['lailək] n lilás m // adj (colour) de cor lilás.

**lily** ['lɪlɪ] n lírio, açucena; **~ of the valley** n lírio-do-vale m.

**limb** [lim] n membro.

**limber** ['limbə*]: **to ~ up** vi (fig) tornar-se flexível; (SPORT) fazer aquecimento.

**limbo** ['limbəu] n: **to be in ~** (fig) cair no ostracismo.

**lime** [laim] n (tree) limeira; (fruit) lima; (GEO) cal f.

**limelight** ['laimlait] n: **to be in the ~** (fig) ser o centro das atenções.

**limerick** ['limərik] n quintilha humorística.

**limestone** ['laimstəun] n pedra calcária.

**limit** ['limit] n limite m // vt limitar; **~ation** [-'teiʃən] n limitação f; **~ed** adj limitado; **to be ~ed** to limitar-se a; **~ed (liability) company (Ltd)** n sociedade f anônima; **~less** adj ilimitado.

**limousine** ['liməzi:n] n limusine f.

**limp** [limp] n: **to have a ~** mancar, ser coxo // vi coxear // adj frouxo.

**limpet** ['limpit] n lapa.

**limpid** ['limpid] adj límpido, cristalino.

**line** [lain] n (gen) linha; (straight ~) traço; (rope) corda; (for fishing) linha; (US: queue) fila; (Pt) bicha; (wire) arame m; (row, series) fila, fileira; (of writing) verso, linha; (on face) ruga; (speciality) ramo (de negócio) // vt (SEWING) forrar (with de); **to ~ the streets** ocupar as ruas; **in ~ with** de acordo com; **to ~ up** vi fazer fila // vt alinhar, pôr em fila; **~d** adj (face) enrugado; (paper) pautado.

**linear** ['liniə*] adj linear.

**linen** ['linin] n roupa branca or de cama; (cloth) linho.

**liner** ['lainə*] n navio de linha regular.

**linesman** ['lainzmən] n (SPORT) juiz m de linha.

**line-up** ['lainʌp] n formação f em linha, alinhamento; (players) escalação f.

**linger** ['liŋgə*] vi demorar-se, retardar-se; (smell, tradition) persistir.

**lingerie** ['lænʒəri:] n lingerie f, roupa de baixo (de mulher).

**lingering** ['liŋgəriŋ] adj persistente; (death) lento, vagaroso.

**lingo** ['liŋgəu], pl **~es** n (pej) linguagem f (de minorias), gíria.

**linguist** ['liŋgwist] n lingüista m/f; **~ic** adj lingüístico; **~ics** nsg lingüística.

**lining** ['lainiŋ] n forro.

**link** [liŋk] n (of a chain) elo; (connection) conexão f; (bond) vínculo, laço // vt vincular, unir; **~s** npl campo sg de golfe; **to ~ up** vt acoplar // vi unir-se; **~-up** n (gen) união f; (in space) acoplamento.

**lino** ['lainəu], **linoleum** [li'nəuliəm] n linóleo.

**lintel** ['lɪntl] n verga.

**lion** ['laɪən] n leão m; **~ess** n leoa.

**lip** [lɪp] n lábio; (of jug) bico; (of cup etc) borda; **~read** vi ler os lábios; **~ service** n: **to pay ~ service to sth** devotar-se a or elogiar algo falsamente; **~stick** n batom m.

**liquefy** ['lɪkwɪfaɪ] vt liquefazer.

**liqueur** [lɪ'kjuə*] n licor m.

**liquid** ['lɪkwɪd] adj, n líquido.

**liquidate** ['lɪkwɪdeɪt] vt liquidar; **liquidation** [-'deɪʃən] n liquidação f; **liquidator** n liquidador(a) m/f.

**liquidize** ['lɪkwɪdaɪz] vt (CULIN) liquidificar, passar no liquidificador.

**liquor** ['lɪkə*] n licor m, bebida alcoólica.

**liquorice** ['lɪkərɪs] n alcaçuz m.

**lisp** [lɪsp] n ceceio // vi cecear, falar com a língua presa.

**list** [lɪst] n lista; (of ship) inclinação f // vt (write down) fazer uma lista or relação de; (enumerate) enumerar // vi (ship) inclinar-se.

**listen** ['lɪsn] vi escutar, ouvir; (pay attention) prestar atenção; **~er** n ouvinte m/f.

**listless** ['lɪstlɪs] adj apático, indiferente.

**lit** [lɪt] pt, pp of **light**.

**litany** ['lɪtənɪ] n ladainha, litania.

**literacy** ['lɪtərəsɪ] n capacidade f de ler e escrever; **~ campaign** campanha de alfabetização.

**literal** ['lɪtərl] adj literal; **~ly** adv literalmente.

**literary** ['lɪtərərɪ] adj literário.

**literate** ['lɪtərət] adj alfabetizado, instruído; (fig) culto, letrado.

**literature** ['lɪtərɪtʃə*] n literatura; (brochures etc) folhetos mpl.

**lithe** [laɪð] adj ágil, flexível.

**litigation** [lɪtɪ'ɡeɪʃən] n litígio.

**litre, liter** (US) ['liːtə*] n litro.

**litter** ['lɪtə*] n (rubbish) lixo; (paper) papel m jogado; (young animals) ninhada; (stretcher) maca, padiola; **~ bin** n lata de lixo; **~ed** adj: **~ed with** (scattered) semeado

de; (covered with) coberto de.

**little** ['lɪtl] adj (small) pequeno; (not much) pouco; often translated by suffix: eg **~ house** casinha // adv pouco; **a ~** um pouco (de); **~ by ~** pouco a pouco.

**liturgy** ['lɪtədʒɪ] n liturgia.

**live** [lɪv] vi viver // (a life) levar; (experience) viver // adj [laɪv] (animal) vivo; (wire) eletrizado (PT: -ct-); (broadcast) ao vivo; (shell) carregado; **to ~ down** vt fazer esquecer; **to ~ on** vt fus (food) viver de, alimentar-se de; **to ~ up to** vt fus (fulfil) cumprir; (justify) justificar.

**livelihood** ['laɪvlɪhud] n meio de vida, subsistência.

**lively** ['laɪvlɪ] adj (gen) vivo; (talk) animado; (pace) rápido; (party, tune) alegre.

**liver** ['lɪvə*] n (ANAT) fígado; **~ish** adj (fig) rabugento, mal-humorado.

**lives** [laɪvz] npl of **life**.

**livestock** ['laɪvstɔk] n gado.

**livid** ['lɪvɪd] adj lívido; (furious) furioso.

**living** ['lɪvɪŋ] adj (alive) vivo // n: **to earn** or **make a ~** ganhar a vida; **~ conditions** npl condições fpl de vida; **~ room** n sala de estar; **~ standards** npl padrão m or nível m de vida; **~ wage** n salário de subsistência.

**lizard** ['lɪzəd] n lagarto, lagartixa.

**llama** ['lɑːmə] n lhama.

**load** [ləud] n (gen) carga; (weight) peso // vt: **to ~ (with)** carregar (de); (fig) cumular (de), encher (de); **a ~ of, ~s of** (fig) (grande) quantidade de, um montão de; **~ed** adj (dice) viciado; (question, word) intencionado; (col: rich) cheio da nota; (: drunk) chumbado, de porre.

**loaf** [ləuf], pl **loaves** (bisnaga de) pão m // vi (also: **~ about, ~ around**) vadiar, vagabundar.

**loan** [ləun] n (gen, COMM) empréstimo // vt emprestar; **on ~** emprestado.

**loath** [ləυθ] *adj*: to be ~ to do sth estar pouco inclinado a fazer algo.

**loathe** [ləυð] *vt* aborrecer; (*person*) odiar; **loathing** *n* aversão *f*; ódio; **it fills me with loathing** me dá (um) ódio.

**loaves** [ləυvz] *pl of* **loaf**.

**lobby** [ˈlɔbɪ] *n* vestíbulo, saguão *m*; (POL: *pressure group*) grupo de pressão // *vt* pressionar.

**lobe** [ləυb] *n* lóbulo.

**lobster** [ˈlɔbstə*] *n* lagostim *m*; (*large*) lagosta.

**local** [ˈləυkl] *adj* local // *n* (*pub*) bar *m* (local); **the** ~**s** *npl* os moradores *mpl* locais; ~**ity** [-ˈkælɪtɪ] *n* localidade *f*; ~**ly** [-kəlɪ] *adv* nos arredores, na vizinhança.

**locate** [ləυˈkeɪt] *vt* (*find*) localizar, situar; (*situate*) colocar.

**location** [ləυˈkeɪʃən] *n* posição *f*; on ~ (CINEMA) no local, externas.

**loch** [lɔx] *n* lago.

**lock** [lɔk] *n* (*of door, box*) fechadura; (*of canal*) eclusa, comporta; (*stop*) tranca; (*of hair*) anel *m*, mecha // *vt* (*with key*) fechar à chave; (*immobilize*) imobilizar // *vi* (*door etc*) fechar-se à chave; (*wheels*) travar-se.

**locker** [ˈlɔkə*] *n* compartimento com chave.

**locket** [ˈlɔkɪt] *n* medalhão *m*.

**lockout** [ˈlɔkaυt] *n* greve *f* de patrões.

**locomotive** [ləυkəˈməυtɪv] *n* locomotiva.

**locum** [ˈləυkəm] *n* (MED) (médico) interino.

**locust** [ˈləυkəst] *n* gafanhoto.

**lodge** [lɔdʒ] *n* casa do guarda; (*porter's*) portaria; (FREEMASONRY) loja // *vi* (*person*): to ~ (*with*) alojar-se (na casa de) // *vt* (*complaint*) apresentar; **lodger** *n* inquilino/a *m/f*, hóspede *m/f*.

**lodgings** [ˈlɔdʒɪŋz] *npl* alojamento *sg*; (*house*) casa *sg* de hóspedes.

**loft** [lɔft] *n* sótão *m*.

**lofty** [ˈlɔftɪ] *adj* alto; (*fig*) sublime; (*haughty*) altivo, arrogante.

**log** [lɔg] *n* (*of wood*) tronco, lenho; (*book*) = **logbook**.

**logarithm** [ˈlɔgərɪðəm] *n* logaritmo.

**logbook** [ˈlɔgbuk] *n* (NAUT) diário de bordo; (AVIAT) diário de vôo; (*of car*) documentação *f* (do carro).

**loggerheads** [ˈlɔgəhedz] *npl*: at ~ (with) em desacordo (com).

**logic** [ˈlɔdʒɪk] *n* lógica; ~**al** *adj* lógico.

**logistics** [lɔˈdʒɪstɪks] *n* logística.

**loin** [lɔɪn] *n* (CULIN) (carne de) lombo; ~**s** *npl* lombo *sg*, dorso *sg*; ~ **cloth** *n* tanga.

**loiter** [ˈlɔɪtə*] *vi* perder tempo; (*pej*) vadiar, vagabundar.

**loll** [lɔl] *vi* (*also*: ~ **about**) refestelar-se, reclinar-se.

**lollipop** [ˈlɔlɪpɔp] *n* pirulito; (*iced*) picolé *m*; ~ **man/lady** *n* pessoa que ajuda as crianças a atravessarem a rua.

**London** [ˈlʌndən] *n* Londres; ~**er** *n* londrino/a.

**lone** [ləυn] *adj* solitário; (*deserted*) ermo.

**loneliness** [ˈləυnlɪnɪs] *n* solidão *f*, isolamento; **lonely** [-lɪ] *adj* solitário, isolado.

**loner** [ˈləυnə*] *n* solitário.

**long** [lɔŋ] *adj* longo, comprido // *adv* muito tempo, longamente // *vi*: to ~ **for sth** ansiar or suspirar por algo; **in the** ~ **run** no final das contas; **so or as** ~ **as** contanto que; **don't be** ~! não demore!, volte logo!; **how** ~ **is the street?** qual é a extensão da rua?; **how** ~ **is the lesson?** quanto dura a lição?; **6 metres** ~ de 6 metros de extensão, que mede 6 metros; **6 months** ~ de 6 meses de duração, que dura 6 meses; **all night** ~ a noite inteira; ~ **before** muito antes; **before** ~ (+ *future*) dentro de pouco; (+ *past*) pouco tempo depois; **at** ~ **last** por fim, no final; ~-**distance** adj (race) de longa distância; (call) interurbano; ~-**haired** adj cabeludo; ~**hand** n escrita usual; ~-**ing** n desejo, anseio; (nostalgia) saudade f // adj saudoso.

**longitude** ['lɒŋgitjuːd] n longitude f.

**long:** ~ **jump** n salto em distância; ~-**lost** adj perdido há muito (tempo); ~-**playing record** (L.P.) n elepê m; ~-**range** adj de longo alcance; ~-**sighted** adj (fig) previdente; ~-**standing** adj de muito tempo; ~-**suffering** adj paciente, resignado; ~-**term** adj a longo prazo; ~ **wave** adj de onda longa; ~-**winded** adj prolixo, cansativo.

**loo** [luː] n (col) banheiro; (Pt) casa de banho.

**loofah** ['luːfə] n tipo de esponja.

**look** [luk] vi olhar; (seem) parecer; (building etc) to ~ **south/on to** the sea dar para o sul/o mar // n olhar m; (glance) olhadela, vista de olhos; (appearance) aparência, aspecto; ~**s** npl físico, aparência; to ~ **like** sb parecer-se com alguém; to ~ **after** vt fus cuidar de; to ~ **at** vt fus olhar (para); (consider) considerar; to ~ **back** vi recordar, rever o passado; to ~ **down on** vt fus (fig) desdenhar, desprezar; to ~ **for** vt fus procurar; to ~ **forward to** vt fus aguardar com prazer, ansiar por; to ~ **into** vt investigar; to ~ **on** vi assistir; to ~ **out** vi (beware): to ~ **out (for)** tomar cuidado (com); to ~ **out for** vt fus (seek) procurar; (await) esperar; to ~ **round** vi virar a cabeça; to ~ **to** vt fus cuidar de; (rely on) contar com; to ~ **up** vi levantar os olhos; (improve) melhorar // vt (word) procurar; (friend) visitar; to ~ **up to** vt fus admirar, respeitar; ~-**out** n (tower etc) posto de observação, guarita; (person) vigia m; to **be on the**

~-**out for sth** estar na expectativa de algo.

**loom** [luːm] n tear m // vi assomar-se; (threaten) ameaçar.

**loony** ['luːni] n (col) lunático/a; ~ **bin** n (col) hospício, manicômio.

**loop** [luːp] n laço; (bend) volta, curva; (contraceptive) D.I.U. m; ~**hole** n escapatória.

**loose** [luːs] adj (gen) solto; (not tight) frouxo; (wobbly etc) bambo; (clothes) folgado; (morals, discipline) relaxado; **to be at a ~ end** não ter o que fazer; ~**ly** adv livremente, folgadamente; **loosen** vt (free) soltar; (untie) desatar; (slacken) afrouxar.

**loot** [luːt] n saque m, despojo// vt saquear, pilhar; ~**ing** n pilhagem f.

**lop** [lɒp]: to ~ **off** vt cortar; (branches) podar.

**lop-sided** ['lɒp'saidid] adj desequilibrado, torto.

**lord** [lɔːd] n senhor m; L~ Smith Lord Smith; **the** L~ o Senhor; the (**House of**) L~**s** a Câmara dos Lordes; ~**ly** adj senhorial; (arrogant) arrogante; ~**ship** n: **your** L~**ship** Vossa senhoria.

**lore** [lɔː*] n sabedoria popular, tradições fpl.

**lorry** ['lɒri] n caminhão m; (Pt) camião m; ~ **driver** n caminhoneiro; (Pt) camioneiro.

**lose** [luːz] pt, pp **lost** vt perder // vi perder, ser vencido; to ~ (**time**) (clock) atrasar-se; **loser** n perdedor/a m/f.

**loss** [lɒs] n perda; **to be at a ~** estar perplexo; **to be a dead ~** ser totalmente inútil.

**lost** [lɒst] pt, pp of **lose** // adj perdido; ~ **property** n objetos (Pt: -ct-) mpl perdidos e achados.

**lot** [lɒt] n (at auctions) lote m; (destiny) destino, sorte f; **the** ~ o todo, todos/as; **a** ~ muito, bastante; **a** ~ **of**, ~**s of** muito(s) (pl); **to draw**

~s tirar à sorte; **I read a** ~ leio bastante.

**lotion** ['ləʊʃən] n loção f.

**lottery** ['lɒtərɪ] n loteria.

**loud** [laud] adj (voice) alto; (shout) forte; (noisy) barulhento; (gaudy) berrante // adv (speak etc) em voz alta; ~**hailer** n megafone m; ~**ly** adv (noisily) ruidosamente; (aloud) em voz alta; ~**speaker** n autofalante m.

**lounge** [laundʒ] n sala de estar f, salão m // vi recostar-se, espreguiçar-se; ~ **suit** n terno; (Pt) fato.

**louse** [laus], pl **lice** n piolho.

**lousy** ['lauzɪ] adj (fig) desprezível, vil.

**lout** [laut] n rústico, grosseiro.

**lovable** ['lʌvəbl] adj adorável, simpático.

**love** [lʌv] n amor m // vt amar, adorar; **to** ~ **to do** gostar muito de fazer; **to be in** ~ **with** estar apaixonado por; **to make** ~ fazer amor; **for the** ~ **of** pelo amor de; **'15** ~' (TENNIS) 15 a zero; **I** ~ **coffee** adoro o café; **'with** ~' com carinho; ~ **affair** n aventura (amorosa, caso (de amor); ~ **letter** n carta de amor; ~ **life** n vida sentimental.

**lovely** ['lʌvlɪ] adj (delightful) encantador(a), delicioso; (beautiful) lindo, belo.

**lover** ['lʌvə*] n amante m/f; (amateur): **a** ~ **of** um apreciador de or um amante de.

**lovesong** ['lʌvsɒŋ] n canção f de amor.

**loving** ['lʌvɪŋ] adj carinhoso, afetuoso (Pt: -ct-).

**low** [ləʊ] adj, adv baixo // n (METEOROLOGY) área de baixa pressão // vi (cow) mugir; **to feel** ~ sentir-se deprimido; **to turn (down)** ~ vt baixar, diminuir; ~**cut** adj (dress) decotado.

**lower** ['ləʊə*] vt abaixar; (reduce)

reduzir, diminuir // vr: **to** ~ **o.s. to** (fig) rebaixar-se a.

**low:** ~**grade** adj de baixa qualidade; ~**ly** adj humilde; ~**lying** adj de abaixo nível.

**loyal** ['lɔɪəl] adj leal; ~**ty** n lealdade f.

**lozenge** ['lɒzɪndʒ] n (MED) pastilha.

**L.P.** n abbr of **long-playing record**.

**L-plates** ['elpleɪts] npl placa de aprendiz de motorista.

**Ltd** abbr of **limited company**.

**lubricant** ['lu:brɪkənt] n lubrificante m; **lubricate** ['lu:brɪkeɪt] vt lubrificar.

**lucid** ['lu:sɪd] adj lúcido; ~**ity** [-'sɪdɪtɪ] n lucidez f.

**luck** [lʌk] n sorte f; **bad** ~ má sorte; **good** ~! boa sorte!; ~**ily** adv por sorte, felizmente; ~**y** adj feliz, felizardo.

**lucrative** ['lu:krətɪv] adj lucrativo.

**ludicrous** ['lu:dɪkrəs] adj ridículo.

**ludo** ['lu:dəʊ] n ludo m.

**lug** [lʌg] vt (drag) arrastar; (pull) puxar.

**luggage** ['lʌgɪdʒ] n bagagem f; ~ **rack** n (in train) rede f para bagagem; (on car) porta-bagagem m, bagageira.

**lukewarm** ['lu:kwɔ:m] adj morno, tépido; (fig) indiferente.

**lull** [lʌl] n trégua, calmaria // vt (child) embalar, acalentar; (person, fear) acalmar.

**lullaby** ['lʌləbaɪ] n canção f de ninar.

**lumbago** [lʌm'beɪgəʊ] n lumbago.

**lumber** ['lʌmbə*] n (junk) trastes velhos mpl; (wood) madeira serrada, tábua; ~**jack** n madeireiro, lenhador m.

**luminous** ['lu:mɪnəs] adj luminoso.

**lump** [lʌmp] n torrão m; (fragment) pedaço; (in sauce) caroço, pelota; (in throat) nó m; (swelling) inchaço, protuberância // adj (also: ~ **together**) amontoar; **a** ~ **sum** soma global, montante *m*; ~y *adj* (*sauce*) empelotado.

**lunacy** ['lu:nəsɪ] *n* loucura.

**lunar** ['lu:nə*] *adj* lunar.

**lunatic** ['lu:nətɪk] *adj*, *n* louco/a; ~ **asylum** *n* manicômio, hospício.

**lunch** [lʌntʃ] *n* almoço, comida // *vi* almoçar; ~ **time** *n* hora do almoço *or* da comida.

**luncheon** ['lʌntʃən] *n* almoço formal; ~ **meat** *n* bolo de carne.

**lung** [lʌŋ] *n* pulmão *m*; ~ **cancer** *n* câncer *m* de pulmão.

**lunge** [lʌndʒ] *vi* (*also*: ~ **forward**) dar estocada *or* bote; **to** ~ **at** arremeter-se contra.

**lurch** [lɜ:tʃ] *vi* guinar // *n* sacudida, solavanco; **to leave sb in the** ~ deixar alguém em dificuldades.

**lure** [luə*] *n* (*bait*) isca; (*decoy*) chamariz *m*, engodo // *vt* atrair, seduzir.

**lurid** ['luərɪd] *adj* (*light*) avermelhado; (*dress*) berrante; (*account*) sensacional; (*detail*) horrível.

**lurk** [lɜ:k] *vi* (*hide*) esconder-se; (*wait*) estar à espreita.

**luscious** ['lʌʃəs] *adj* delicioso.

**lush** [lʌʃ] *adj* exuberante.

**lust** [lʌst] *n* luxúria; (*greed*) cobiça; **to** ~ **after** *vt fus* cobiçar; ~**ful** *adj* lascivo, sensual.

**lustre, luster** (*US*) ['lʌstə*] *n* lustre *m*, brilho.

**lusty** ['lʌstɪ] *adj* robusto, forte.

**lute** [lu:t] *n* alaúde *m*.

**Luxembourg** ['lʌksəmbə:g] *n* Luxemburgo.

**luxuriant** [lʌg'zjuərɪənt] *adj* luxuriante, exuberante.

**luxurious** [lʌg'zjuərɪəs] *adj* luxuoso; (*person*) amante do luxo.

**luxury** ['lʌkʃərɪ] *n* luxo // *cmp* de luxo.

**lying** ['laɪŋ] *n* mentiras *fpl* // *adj* mentiroso, falso.

**lynch** [lɪntʃ] *vt* linchar; ~**ing** *n* linchamento.

**lynx** [lɪŋks] *n* lince *m*.

**lyre** ['laɪə*] *n* lira.

**lyric** ['lɪrɪk] *adj* lírico; ~**s** *npl* (*of song*) letra *sg*; ~**al** *adj* lírico.

# M

**m.** *abbr of* **metre; mile; million.**

**M.A.** *abbr of* **Master of Arts** licenciado/a em letras.

**mac** [mæk] *n* capa impermeável.

**macaroni** [mækə'rəunɪ] *n* macarrão *m*.

**mace** [meɪs] *n* (*BOT*) macis *m*.

**machine** [mə'ʃi:n] *n* máquina // *vt* (*dress etc*) trabalhar *or* coser à máquina; ~ **gun** *n* metralhadora; ~**ry** *n* maquinaria; (*fig*) mecanismo; **machinist** *n* operário (de máquina); (*RAIL*) maquinista *m*.

**mackerel** ['mækrl] *n*, *pl inv* cavala.

**mackintosh** ['mækɪntɔʃ] *n* capa impermeável.

**mad** [mæd] *adj* (*gen*) louco; (*crazed*) demente; (*angry*) furioso.

**madam** ['mædəm] *n* senhora, madame *f*.

**madden** ['mædn] *vt* enlouquecer; (*irritate*) irritar.

**made** [meɪd] *pt*, *pp of* **make**; ~**-to-measure** *adj* feito sob medida.

**madly** ['mædlɪ] *adv* loucamente.

**madman** ['mædmən] *n* louco.

**madness** ['mædnɪs] *n* loucura, demência.

**magazine** [mægə'zi:n] *n* revista; (*MIL*: *store*) depósito; (*of firearm*) câmara.

**maggot** ['mægət] *n* larva de inseto (*Pt*: -ct-).

**magic** ['mædʒɪk] *n* magia // *adj* mágico; ~**al** *adj* mágico; ~**ian** [mə'dʒɪʃən] *n* mago, mágico; (*conjurer*) prestidigitador *m*.

**magistrate** ['mædʒɪstreɪt] *n* magistrado, juiz/juíza *m/f*.

**magnanimous** [mæg'nænɪməs] *adj* magnânimo.

**magnate** ['mægneɪt] *n* magnata *m*.

**magnet** ['mægnɪt] *n* ímã *m*; **~ic** [-'netɪk] *adj* magnético; **~ism** *n* magnetismo.

**magnification** [mægnɪfɪ'keɪʃən] *n* aumento.

**magnificence** [mæg'nɪfɪsns] *n* magnificência; **magnificent** [-nt] *adj* magnífico.

**magnify** ['mægnɪfaɪ] *vt* aumentar; (*fig*) exagerar; **~ing glass** *n* lupa, lente *f* de aumento.

**magnitude** ['mægnɪtjuːd] *n* magnitude *f*.

**magnolia** [mæg'nəʊlɪə] *n* magnólia.

**magpie** ['mægpaɪ] *n* pega.

**mahogany** [mə'hɒgənɪ] *n* mogno // *cmp* de mogno.

**maid** [meɪd] *n* empregada; **old ~** (*pej*) solteirona.

**maiden** ['meɪdn] *n* moça, donzela // *adj* (*aunt etc*) solteirona; (*speech, voyage*) inaugural; **~ name** *n* nome *m* de solteira.

**mail** [meɪl] *n* correio; (*letters*) cartas *fpl* // *vt* (*post*) pôr no correio; (*send*) mandar pelo correio; **~box** *n* (*US*) caixa do correio; **~order** *n* pedido por reembolso postal; (*business*) venda por correspondência.

**maim** [meɪm] *vt* mutilar, aleijar.

**main** [meɪn] *adj* principal // *n* (*pipe*) cano *m* ou esgoto principal; **the ~s** (*ELEC*) a rede elétrica (*Pt*: -ct-); **in the ~** na maior parte; **~land** *n* continente *m*; **~stay** *n* (*fig*) suporte *m*, esteio; **~stream** *n* corrente *f* principal.

**maintain** [meɪn'teɪn] *vt* manter; (*keep up*) conservar (em bom estado); (*affirm*) afirmar; **maintenance** ['meɪntənəns] *n* manutenção *f*.

**maize** [meɪz] *n* milho.

**majestic** [mə'dʒestɪk] *adj*

majestoso; **majesty** ['mædʒɪstɪ] *n* majestade *f*.

**major** ['meɪdʒə*] *n* (*MIL*) major *m* // *adj* principal; (*MUS*) maior.

**Majorca** [mə'jɔːkə] *n* Maiorca.

**majority** [mə'dʒɒrɪtɪ] *n* maioria.

**make** [meɪk], *pt*, *pp* **made** *n* marca // *vt* fazer; (*manufacture*) fabricar, produzir; (*cause to be*): **to ~ sb sad** entristecer alguém ou fazer alguém ficar triste; (*force*): **to ~ sb do sth** fazer com que alguém faça algo; (*equal*): **2 and 2 ~ 4** dois e dois são quatro; **to ~ do with** contentar-se com; **to ~ for** *vt fus* (*place*) dirigir-se a; **to ~ out** *vt* (*decipher*) decifrar; (*understand*) compreender; (*see*) divisar, avistar; **to ~ up** *vt* (*invent*) inventar; (*parcel*) embrulhar // *vi* reconciliar-se; (*with cosmetics*) maquilar-se; **to ~ up for** *vt fus* compensar; **~believe** *adj* fingido, simulado; **maker** *n* fabricante *m/f*; **~shift** *adj* provisório; **~up** *n* maquilagem *f*.

**making** ['meɪkɪŋ] *n* (*fig*): **in the ~** em vias de formação.

**malaise** [mæ'leɪz] *n* mal-estar *m*, indisposição *f*.

**malaria** [mə'leərɪə] *n* malária.

**Malay** [mə'leɪ] *adj*, *n* malaio/a.

**Malaysia** [mə'leɪzɪə] *n* Malásia.

**male** [meɪl] *n* (*BIOL*, *ELEC*) macho // *adj* (*sex*, *attitude*) masculino; (*child etc*) menino.

**malevolent** [mə'levələnt] *adj* malévolo.

**malfunction** [mæl'fʌŋkʃən] *n* funcionamento defeituoso.

**malice** ['mælɪs] *n* (*ill will*) malícia; (*rancour*) rancor *m*; **malicious** [mə'lɪʃəs] *adj* malicioso, mal-intencionado.

**malign** [mə'laɪn] *vt* caluniar, difamar // *adj* maligno.

**malignant** [mə'lɪgnənt] *adj* (*MED*) maligno.

**malingerer** [mə'lɪŋgərə*] *n* doente *m* fingido.

**malleable** ['mælɪəbl] adj maleável.

**mallet** ['mælɪt] n maço, marreta.

**malnutrition** [mælnjuː'trɪʃən] n desnutrição f.

**malpractice** [mæl'præktɪs] n falta profissional.

**malt** [mɔːlt] n malte m; ~ **whisky** uísque m de malte.

**Malta** ['mɔːltə] n Malta; **Maltese** [-'tiːz] adj, n, pl inv maltês/esa m/f.

**maltreat** [mæl'triːt] vt maltratar.

**mammal** ['mæml] n mamífero.

**mammoth** ['mæməθ] n mamute m // adj gigantesco, imenso.

**man** [mæn], pl **men** n homem m; (CHESS) peça // vt (NAUT) tripular; (MIL) guarnecer; **an old** ~ um velho; ~ **and wife** marido e mulher; **a young** ~ um jovem.

**manacle** ['mænəkl] n algema; ~**s** npl grilhões mpl.

**manage** ['mænɪdʒ] vi arranjar-se // vt (be in charge of) dirigir, administrar; (person etc) influenciar, saber lidar com; ~**able** adj manejável; ~**ment** n direção (Pt: -cç-) f, gerência; **manager/ess** n diretor(a) (Pt: -ct-) m/f; (SPORT) treinador(a) m/f; **managerial** [-ə'dʒɪərɪəl] adj administrativo; **managing director** n dire(c)tor m geral, dire(c)tor-gerente m.

**mandarin** ['mændərɪn] n (also: ~ **orange**) tangerina; (person) mandarim m.

**mandate** ['mændeɪt] n mandato.

**mandatory** ['mændətərɪ] adj obrigatório.

**mandolin(e)** ['mændəlɪn] n bandolim m.

**mane** [meɪn] n (of horse) crina; (of lion) juba.

**manfully** ['mænfəlɪ] adv virilmente.

**mangle** ['mæŋgl] vt mutilar, estropiar // n calandra.

**mango** ['mæŋgəʊ], pl ~**es** n manga.

**mangy** ['meɪndʒɪ] adj sarnento, esfarrapado.

**manhandle** ['mænhændl] vt maltratar.

**manhole** ['mænhəʊl] n poço de inspeção (Pt: -cç-).

**manhood** ['mænhʊd] n idade f adulta, virilidade f.

**man-hour** ['mæn'aʊə*] n hora-homem f.

**manhunt** ['mænhʌnt] n caça ao homem.

**mania** ['meɪnɪə] n mania; **maniac** ['meɪnɪæk] n maníaco/a; (fig) louco/a.

**manicure** ['mænɪkjʊə*] n manicure f // vt (person) fazer as unhas a; ~ **set** n estojo de manicure.

**manifest** ['mænɪfest] vt manifestar, mostrar // adj manifesto, evidente; ~**ation** [-'teɪʃən] n manifestação f.

**manifesto** [mænɪ'festəʊ] n manifesto.

**manipulate** [mə'nɪpjʊleɪt] vt manipular, manejar.

**mankind** [mæn'kaɪnd] n humanidade f, raça humana.

**manly** ['mænlɪ] adj másculo, viril.

**man-made** ['mæn'meɪd] adj sintético, artificial.

**manner** ['mænə*] n modo, maneira; (behaviour) conduta, comportamento; (type) espécie f, gênero; ~**s** npl modos mpl, educação f; **bad** ~**s** falta de educação; ~**ism** n maneirismo, hábito.

**manoeuvre, maneuver** (US) [mə'nuːvə*] vt/i manobrar // n manobra.

**manor** ['mænə*] n (also: ~ **house**) casa senhorial, solar m.

**manpower** ['mænpaʊə*] n potencial m humano, mão-de-obra f.

**mansion** ['mænʃən] n mansão f, palacete m.

**manslaughter** ['mænslɔːtə*] n homicídio involuntário.

**mantelpiece** ['mæntlpi:s] *n* consolo da lareira.

**mantle** ['mæntl] *n* manto; (*fig*) camada.

**manual** ['mænjuəl] *adj* manual // *n* manual *m*; (*MUS*) teclado.

**manufacture** [mænju'fæktʃə*] *vt* manufaturar (*Pt:* -ct-), fabricar // *n* fabricação *f*; **manufacturer** *n* fabricante *m/f*.

**manure** [mə'njuə*] *n* estrume *m*, adubo.

**manuscript** ['mænjuskript] *n* manuscrito.

**many** ['meni] *det* muitos/as // *pron* muitos/as; **a great** ~ muitíssimos; ~ **a time** muitas vezes.

**map** [mæp] *n* mapa *m* // *vt* fazer o mapa de; **to** ~ **out** *vt* planejar cuidadosamente.

**maple** ['meipl] *n* bordo.

**mar** [ma:*] *vt* estragar.

**marathon** ['mærəθən] *n* maratona.

**marauder** [mə'rɔ:də*] *n* saqueador *m*; (*intruder*) intruso.

**marble** ['ma:bl] *n* mármore *m*; (*toy*) bola de gude.

**March** [ma:tʃ] *n* março.

**march** [ma:tʃ] *vi* (*MIL*) marchar // *n* marcha; (*fig*) curso; (*demonstration*) manifestação *f*, (*procession*) passeata; ~**past** *n* desfile *m*.

**mare** [mɛə*] *n* égua.

**margarine** [ma:dʒə'ri:n] *n* margarina.

**margin** ['ma:dʒin] *n* margem *f*, ~**al** *adj* marginal.

**marigold** ['mærigəuld] *n* malmequer *m*.

**marijuana** [mæri'wɑ:nə] *n* maconha.

**marina** [mə'ri:nə] *n* marina.

**marine** [mə'ri:n] *adj* marinho, marítimo // *n* fuzileiro naval.

**marital** ['mæritl] *adj* matrimonial, marital; ~ **status** estado civil.

**maritime** ['mæritaim] *adj* marítimo.

**marjoram** ['ma:dʒərəm] *n* manjerona.

**mark** [ma:k] *n* marca, sinal *m*; (*imprint*) impressão *f*; (*stain*) mancha; (*SCOL*) nota; (*currency*) marco; **to hit the** ~ acertar no alvo // *vt* marcar; (*stain*) manchar; (*SCOL*) dar nota em; **to** ~ **time** marcar passo; **to** ~ **out** *vt* traçar; ~**ed** *adj* marcado; ~**er** *n* (*sign*) marcador *m*, marca; (*bookmark*) marcador.

**market** ['ma:kit] *n* mercado // *vt* (*COMM*) vender; **black** ~ mercado negro or paralelo; **Common M**~ Mercado Comum; ~ **day** *n* dia *m* de mercado; ~ **garden** *n* (*Brit*) horta; ~**ing** *n* compra e venda, marketing *m*; ~**place** *n* mercado; ~ **research** *n* pesquisa de mercado.

**marksman** ['ma:ksmən] *n* bom atirador *m*; ~**ship** *n* boa pontaria.

**marmalade** ['ma:məleid] *n* geléia de laranja.

**maroon** [mə'ru:n] *vt*: **to be** ~**ed** ficar abandonado (numa ilha) // *adj* de cor castanho-avermelhado.

**marquee** [ma:'ki:] *n* toldo, tenda.

**marquess, marquis** ['ma:kwis] *n* marquês *m*.

**marriage** ['mæridʒ] *n* (*state*) matrimônio; (*wedding*) núpcias *fpl*, boda; (*act*) casamento; ~ **bureau** *n* agência matrimonial; ~ **certificate** *n* certidão *f* de casamento.

**married** ['mærid] *adj* casado; (*life, love*) conjugal; **to get** ~ casar-se.

**marrow** ['mærəu] *n* medula; (*vegetable*) abobrinha.

**marry** ['mæri] *vt* casar-se com; (*subj: father, priest etc*) casar, unir // *vi* (*also:* **get married**) casar-se.

**marsh** [ma:ʃ] *n* pântano; (*salt* ~) marisma.

**marshal** ['ma:ʃl] *n* (*MIL*) marechal *m*; (*at sports meeting etc*) oficial *m* // *vt* (*facts*) dispor, ordenar; (*soldiers*) formar.

**marshmallow** [ma:ʃ'mæləu] *n*

*espécie de doce de malvavisco.*

**marshy** ['mɑːʃɪ] *adj* pantanoso.

**martial** ['mɑːʃl] *adj* marcial; ~ **law** *n* lei *f* marcial.

**martyr** ['mɑːtə*] *n* mártir *m/f* // *vt* martirizar; ~**dom** *n* martírio.

**marvel** ['mɑːvl] *n* maravilha, prodígio // *vi*: **to ~ (at)** maravilhar-se (de/com); ~**lous**, ~**ous** (*US*) *adj* maravilhoso, incrível.

**Marxism** ['mɑːksɪzəm] *n* marxismo; **Marxist** [-sɪst] *adj*, *n* marxista *m/f*.

**marzipan** ['mɑːzɪpæn] *n* maçapão *m*.

**mascara** [mæs'kɑːrə] *n* rímel *m*.

**mascot** ['mæskət] *n* mascote *m*.

**masculine** ['mæskjulɪn] *adj* masculino; **masculinity** [-'lɪnɪtɪ] *n* masculinidade *f*.

**mash** [mæʃ] *n* (*mix*) mistura; (*pulp*) pasta, papa; ~**ed potatoes** purê *m* de batatas.

**mask** [mɑːsk] *n* máscara // *vt* mascarar.

**masochist** ['mæsəukɪst] *n* masoquista *m/f*.

**mason** ['meɪsn] *n* (*also:* **stone~**) pedreiro; (*also:* **free~**) maçom *m*; ~**ic** [mə'sɔnɪk] *adj* maçônico; ~**ry** *n* maçonaria; (*building*) alvenaria.

**masquerade** [mæskə'reɪd] *n* baile *m* de máscaras; (*fig*) farsa, embuste *m* // *vi*: **to ~ as** disfarçar-se de, fazer-se passar por.

**mass** [mæs] *n* (*people*) multidão *f*; (*PHYSICS*) massa; (*REL*) missa; (*great quantity*) montão *m* // *vi* reunir-se; (*MIL*) concentrar-se; **the ~es** as massas.

**massacre** ['mæsəkə*] *n* massacre *m*, carnificina // *vt* massacrar.

**massage** ['mæsɑːʒ] *n* massagem *f* // *vt* fazer massagem em, massagear.

**masseur** [mæ'sɔ:*] *n* massagista *m*; **masseuse** [-'sɔ:z] *n* massagista *f*.

**massive** ['mæsɪv] *adj* (*solid*) sólido,

(*head etc*) enorme; (*support, intervention*) massivo.

**mass media** ['mæs'miːdɪə] *npl* meios *mpl* de comunicação de massa.

**mass-production** ['mæsprə'dʌkʃən] *n* produção *f* em massa or em série.

**mast** [mɑːst] *n* (*NAUT*) mastro; (*RADIO etc*) antena.

**master** ['mɑːstə*] *n* mestre *m*; (*landowner*) senhor *m*, dono; (*in secondary school*) professor *m*; (*title for boys*): **M~ X** o menino X // *vt* dominar; (*learn*) conhecer a fundo; ~ **key** *n* chave *f* mestra; ~**ly** *adj* magistral; ~**mind** *n* (*fig*) cabeça // *vt* dirigir, planejar; **M~ of Arts** *n* Licenciado *m* em Letras; ~**piece** *n* obra-prima; ~ **plan** *n* plano piloto; ~ **stroke** *n* golpe *m* de mestre; ~**y** *n* domínio.

**masturbate** ['mæstəbeɪt] *vi* masturbar-se; **masturbation** [-'beɪʃən] *n* masturbação *f*.

**mat** [mæt] *n* esteira; (*also:* **door~**) capacho // *adj* = **matt**.

**match** [mætʃ] *n* fósforo; (*game*) jogo, partida; (*fig*) igual *m/f* // *vt* casar, emparelhar; (*go well with*) combinar com; (*equal*) igualar // *vi* casar-se, combinar; **to be a good ~** formar um bom casal; (*colours*) combinar; ~**box** *n* caixa de fósforo; ~**ing** *adj* que combina (com); ~**less** *adj* sem igual, incomparável.

**mate** [meɪt] *n* companheiro/a; (*assistant*) ajudante *m/f*; (*CHESS*) mate *m*; (*in merchant navy*) imediato // *vi* acasalar-se // *vt* acasalar.

**material** [mə'tɪərɪəl] *n* (*substance*) matéria; (*equipment*) material *m*; (*cloth*) pano, tecido; (*data*) dados *mpl* // *adj* material; (*important*) importante; ~**s** *npl* materiais *mpl*; ~**istic** [-'lɪstɪk] *adj* materialista; ~**ize** *vi* materializar-se, concretizar-se.

**maternal** [mə'tə:nl] adj maternal.

**maternity** [mə'tə:niti] n maternidade f; ~ **dress** n vestido de gestante; ~ **hospital** n maternidade f.

**mathematical** [mæθə'mætikl] adj matemático; **mathematician** [-mə'tiʃn] n matemático/a; **mathematics** [-tiks], **maths** [mæθs] n matemática sg.

**matinée** ['mætinei] n matinê f.

**mating** ['meitiŋ] n acasalamento; ~ **call** n chamado do macho; ~ **season** n época de cio.

**matriarchal** [meitri'ɑ:kl] adj matriarcal.

**matrices** ['meitrisi:z] pl of **matrix**.

**matriculation** [mətrikju'leiʃən] n matrícula.

**matrimonial** [mætri'məuniəl] adj matrimonial.

**matrimony** ['mætriməni] n matrimônio, casamento.

**matrix** ['meitriks], pl **matrices** n matriz f.

**matron** ['meitrən] n (in hospital) enfermeira-chefe; (in school) inspetora (Pt: -ct-); ~**ly** adj matronal; (fig: figure) corpulento.

**matt** [mæt] adj fosco, sem brilho.

**matted** ['mætid] adj emaranhado.

**matter** ['mætə*] n questão f, assunto; (PHYSICS) matéria, substância; (content) conteúdo; (MED: pus) pus m // vi importar; **it doesn't** ~ não importa; **what's the** ~? o que (é que) há?, qual o problema?; **no** ~ **what** aconteça o que acontecer; **as a** ~ **of course** o que se é de esperar; (routine) por rotina; **as a** ~ **of fact** na realidade, de fato (Pt: -ct-); ~**-of-fact** adj prosaico, prático.

**mattress** ['mætris] n colchão m.

**mature** [mə'tjuə*] adj maduro // vi amadurecer; **maturity** n maturidade f.

**maudlin** ['mɔ:dlin] adj piegas inv

**maul** [mɔ:l] vt machucar, maltratar.

**mausoleum** [mɔ:sə'liəm] n mausoléu m.

**mauve** [məuv] adj cor de malva.

**maxim** ['mæksim] n máxima.

**maxima** ['mæksimə] pl of **maximum**.

**maximum** ['mæksiməm] adj máximo // n, pl **maxima** máximo.

**May** [mei] n maio.

**may** [mei] vi (conditional: **might**) (indicating possibility): **he** ~ **come** pode ser que ele venha; (be allowed to): ~ **I smoke?** posso fumar? (wishes): ~ **God bless you!** que Deus lhe abençoe.

**maybe** ['meibi:] adv talvez.

**mayday** ['meidei] n S.O.S. m (chamada de socorro internacional).

**mayhem** ['meihɛm] n lesão corporal dolosa.

**mayonnaise** [meiə'neiz] n maionese f.

**mayor** [mɛə*] n prefeito; ~**ess** n prefeita.

**maypole** ['meipəul] n mastro usado no dia primeiro de maio.

**maze** [meiz] n labirinto.

**M.D.** abbr of **Doctor of Medicine**.

**me** [mi:] pron me; (stressed, after prep) mim; **with** ~ comigo; **it's** ~ sou eu.

**meadow** ['mɛdəu] n prado, campina.

**meagre, meager** (US) ['mi:gə*] adj escasso, pobre.

**meal** [mi:l] n refeição f; (flour) farinha; ~**time** n hora da refeição.

**mean** [mi:n] adj (with money) avarento, pão-duro; (unkind) mesquinho; (shabby) surrado, miserável; (of poor quality) inferior; (average) médio // vt, pt, pp **mean** (signify) significar, querer dizer; (intend): **to** ~ **to do sth** pretender ou tencionar fazer algo // n meio, meio termo; ~s npl meio sg, método sg; (resource) recursos mpl, meios mpl; by ~s of por meio de, mediante; by all ~s! claro que sim!, evidentemente!; do you ~ it? você está falando sério?; what do you ~? o que você quer dizer?

**meander** [mɪ'ændə*] vi (river) serpentear; (person) vadiar, perambular.

**meaning** ['mi:nɪŋ] n sentido, significado; ~ful adj significativo; ~less adj sem sentido.

**meanness** ['mi:nnɪs] n (with money) avareza, sovinice f; (shabbiness) vileza, baixeza; (unkindness) maldade f, mesquinharia.

**meant** [mɛnt] pt, pp of **mean.**

**meantime** ['mi:ntaɪm], **meanwhile** ['mi:nwaɪl] adv (also: in the ~) entrementes, enquanto isso.

**measles** ['mi:zlz] n sarampo sg; **German ~** rubéola.

**measly** ['mi:zlɪ] adj (col) miserável.

**measure** ['mɛʒə*] vt medir; (for clothes etc) tirar as medidas de; (consider) avaliar, ponderar // vi medir // n medida; (ruler) régua; (tone) ponderado; ~d adj medido, calculado; ~ments npl medidas fpl.

**meat** [mi:t] n carne f; **cold ~** frios mpl; ~ball n almôndega; ~ pie n bolo de carne; ~y adj carnudo; (fig) substancial.

**mechanic** [mɪ'kænɪk] n mecânico; ~s n mecânica sg // npl mecanismo sg; ~al adj mecânico.

**mechanism** ['mɛkənɪzm] n mecanismo.

**mechanization** [mɛkənaɪ'zeɪʃən] n mecanização f.

**medal** ['mɛdl] n medalha, condecoração f; ~lion [mɪ'dælɪən] n medalhão m; ~list, ~ist (US) n (SPORT) ganhador(a) m/f.

**meddle** ['mɛdl] vi: to ~ in meter-se em, intrometer-se em; **to ~ with**

sth mexer em algo; ~**some** adj intrometido.

**media** ['mi:dɪə] npl meios mpl de comunicação.

**mediaeval** [mɛdɪ'i:vl] adj = **medieval.**

**mediate** ['mi:dɪeɪt] vi mediar; **mediation** [-'eɪʃən] n mediação f; **mediator** n mediador(a) m/f, árbitro.

**medical** ['mɛdɪkl] adj médico // n exame m médico.

**medicated** ['mɛdɪkeɪtɪd] adj medicinal, higienizado.

**medicinal** [mɛ'dɪsɪnl] adj medicinal.

**medicine** ['mɛdsɪn] n medicina; (drug) remédio, medicamento; ~ **chest** n armário de remédios.

**medieval** [mɛdɪ'i:vl] adj medieval.

**mediocre** [mi:dɪ'əukə*] adj medíocre; **mediocrity** [-'ɔkrɪtɪ] n mediocridade f.

**meditate** ['mɛdɪteɪt] vi meditar; **meditation** [-'teɪʃən] n meditação f.

**Mediterranean** [mɛdɪtə'reɪnɪən] adj mediterrâneo; **the ~ (Sea)** o (mar) Mediterrâneo.

**medium** ['mi:dɪəm] adj médio, regular // n (pl media: means) meio; (pl mediums: person) médium m/f.

**medley** ['mɛdlɪ] n mistura; (MUS) pot-pourri m.

**meek** [mi:k] adj manso, dócil.

**meet** [mi:t] pt, pp **met** vt (gen) encontrar; (accidentally) topar com, dar com; (by arrangement) reunir-se com, ir ao encontro de; (for the first time) conhecer; (go and fetch) ir buscar; (opponent) enfrentar; (obligations) cumprir // vi (in session) reunir-se; (join: objects) unir-se; (get to know) conhecer-se; **to ~ with** vt fus reunir-se com; (face: difficulty) tropeçar em; ~**ing** n encontro; (session: of club etc) reunião f; (interview) entrevista;

(COMM) junta, sessão f; (POL) assembléia.

**megalomaniac** [megələʊ'meiniæk] adj, n megalomaníaco/a.

**megaphone** ['megəfəʊn] n megafone m.

**melancholy** ['melənkəli] n melancolia // adj melancólico.

**melee** ['melei] n briga, refrega.

**mellow** ['meləʊ] adj (sound) melodioso, suave; (colour) suave; (fruit) maduro // vi (person) amadurecer.

**melodious** [mi'ləʊdiəs] adj melodioso.

**melodrama** ['melə(ʊ)drɑːmə] n melodrama m.

**melody** ['melədi] n melodia.

**melon** ['melən] n melão m.

**melt** [melt] vi (metal) fundir-se; (snow) derreter; (fig) desvanecer-se // vt (also: ~ **down**) fundir; **to ~ away** vi desaparecer; **~ing point** n ponto de fusão; **~ing pot** n (fig) cadinho, mistura de raças.

**member** ['membə*] n (gen) membro; (of club) sócio; **M~ of Parliament (M.P.)** n deputado; **~ship** n (members) número de sócios; **to seek ~ship of** candidatar-se a sócio de; **~ship card** n carteira de sócio.

**membrane** ['membrein] n membrana.

**memento** [mə'mentəʊ] n lembrança.

**memo** ['meməʊ] n memorando, nota.

**memoirs** ['memwɑːz] npl memórias fpl.

**memorable** ['memərəbl] adj memorável.

**memorandum** [memə'rændəm], pl -**da** [-də] n memorando, lembrete m; (POL) memorando.

**memorial** [mi'mɔːriəl] n memorial m, monumento comemorativo // adj comemorativo.

**memorize** ['meməraiz] vt decorar, aprender de cor.

**memory** ['meməri] n memória; (recollection) lembrança.

**men** [men] pl of **man**.

**menace** ['menəs] n ameaça // vt ameaçar; **menacing** adj ameaçador(a).

**mend** [mend] vt consertar, reparar; (darn) remendar; **to ~ one's ways** corrigir-se // vi restabelecer-se // n (gen) remendo; **to be on the ~** estar melhorando; **~ing** n reparação f; (clothes) roupas fpl por consertar.

**menial** ['miːniəl] adj doméstico; (pej) baixo // n empregado/a.

**meningitis** [menin'dʒaitis] n meningite f.

**menopause** ['menəʊpɔːz] n menopausa.

**menstruate** ['menstrueit] vi menstruar; **menstruation** [-'eiʃən] n menstruação f.

**mental** ['mentl] adj mental; **~ity** [-'tæliti] n mentalidade f.

**mention** ['menʃən] n menção f // vt mencionar; (speak of) falar de; **don't ~ it!** não tem de quê!, de nada!

**menu** ['menjuː] n (set ~) menu m; (printed) cardápio; (Pt) ementa.

**mercenary** ['mɔːsinəri] adj, n mercenário.

**merchandise** ['mɔːtʃəndaiz] n mercadorias fpl.

**merchant** ['mɔːtʃənt] n comerciante m/f; ~ **bank** n banco mercantil; ~ **navy** n marinha mercante.

**merciful** ['mɔːsiful] adj piedoso, misericordioso; (fortunate) afortunado.

**merciless** ['mɔːsilis] adj desapiedado, impiedoso.

**mercury** ['mɔːkjuri] n mercúrio.

**mercy** ['mɔːsi] n piedade f; (REL) misericórdia; **at the ~ of** à mercê de.

**mere** [miə*] adj mero, simples; ~**ly** adv simplesmente, somente, apenas.

**merge** [mɔːdʒ] vt (join) unir; (mix)

misturar; (*fuse*) fundir // *vi* unir-se; (*COMM*) fundir-se; **merger** *n* (*COMM*) fusão *f*.

**meridian** [mə'rɪdɪən] *n* meridiano.

**meringue** [mə'ræŋ] *n* suspiro, merengue *m*.

**merit** ['mɛrɪt] *n* mérito // *vt* merecer.

**mermaid** ['mɜːmeɪd] *n* sereia.

**merriment** ['mɛrɪmənt] *n* alegria.

**merry** ['mɛrɪ] *adj* alegre; **M~ Christmas!** Feliz Natal; **~-go-round** *n* carrossel.

**mesh** [mɛʃ] *n* malha; (*TECH*) engrenagem *f* // *vi* (*gears*) engrenar.

**mesmerize** ['mɛzməraɪz] *vt* hipnotizar.

**mess** [mɛs] *n* (*gen*) confusão *f*; (*of objects*) desordem *f*; (*tangle*) bagunça; (*MIL*) rancho; **to ~ about** *vi* (*col*) perder tempo; (*pass the time*) vadiar; **to ~ about with** *vt fus* (*col*) (*play with*) divertir-se com; (*handle*) manusear; **to ~ up** *vt* (*disarrange*) desarrumar; (*spoil*) estragar; (*dirty*) sujar.

**message** ['mɛsɪdʒ] *n* recado, mensagem *f*.

**messenger** ['mɛsɪndʒə*] *n* mensageiro/a.

**messy** ['mɛsɪ] *adj* (*dirty*) sujo; (*untidy*) desarrumado.

**met** [mɛt] *pt, pp of* **meet**.

**metabolism** [mɛ'tæbəlɪzəm] *n* metabolismo.

**metal** ['mɛtl] *n* metal *m*; **~lic** [-'tælɪk] *adj* metálico; **~lurgy** [-'tælədʒɪ] *n* metalurgia.

**metamorphosis** [mɛtə'mɔːfəsɪs], *pl* **-ses** [-siːz] *n* metamorfose *f*.

**metaphor** ['mɛtəfə*] *n* metáfora.

**metaphysics** [mɛtə'fɪzɪks] *n* metafísica *sg*.

**mete** [miːt]: **to ~ out** *vt fus* (*gen*) distribuir; (*punishment*) infligir.

**meteor** ['miːtɪə*] *n* meteoro.

**meteorological** [miːtɪərə'lɔdʒɪkl] *adj* meteorológico; **meteorology**

[-'rɔlədʒɪ] *n* meteorologia.

**meter** ['miːtə*] *n* (*instrument*) medidor *m*; (*US*) = **metre**.

**method** ['mɛθəd] *n* método; **~ical** [mɪ'θɔdɪkl] *adj* metódico.

**Methodist** ['mɛθədɪst] *n* metodista *m/f*.

**meths** [mɛθs], **methylated spirits** ['mɛθɪleɪtɪd-] *n* álcool *m* metílico or desnaturado.

**meticulous** [mɛ'tɪkjuləs] *adj* meticuloso.

**metre, meter** (*US*) ['miːtə*] *n* metro.

**metric** ['mɛtrɪk] *adj* métrico.

**metronome** ['mɛtrənəum] *n* metrônomo.

**metropolis** [mɪ'trɔpəlɪs] *n* metrópole *f*.

**mettle** ['mɛtl] *n* (*spirit*) caráter (*Pt*: -ct-) *m*, têmpera; (*tone*) índole *f*.

**mew** [mjuː] *vi* (*cat*) miar.

**Mexican** ['mɛksɪkən] *adj, n* mexicano/a.

**Mexico** ['mɛksɪkəu] *n* México *m*.

**mezzanine** ['mɛtsəniːn] *n* sobreloja, mezanino.

**miaow** [miː'au] *vi* miar.

**mice** [maɪs] *pl of* **mouse**.

**microbe** ['maɪkrəub] *n* micróbio.

**micro...** [maɪkrəu] *pref* micro...; **~film** *n* microfilme *m*; **~phone** *n* microfone *m*; **~processor** *n* microprocessador *m*; **~scope** *n* microscópio; **~scopic** [-'skɔpɪk] *adj* microscópico; **~wave** *n* microonda.

**mid** [mɪd] *adj*: **in ~ May** em meados de maio; **in ~ afternoon** no meio da tarde; **in ~ air** em pleno ar; **~day** *n* meio-dia *m*.

**middle** ['mɪdl] *n* meio, centro; (*half*) meado *f*; (*waist*) cintura // *adj* meio; (*quantity, size*) médio, mediano; **~-aged** *adj* de meia idade; **M~ Ages** *npl* Idade Média *sg*; **~-class** *adj* de classe média; **M~ East** *n* Oriente *m* Médio; **~man** *n* intermediário; (*COMM*) atravessador m; ~ **name** n segundo nome.

**middling** ['mɪdlɪŋ] adj mediano.

**midge** [mɪdʒ] n mosquito.

**midget** ['mɪdʒɪt] n anão/anã m/f // adj minúsculo, miniatura.

**midnight** ['mɪdnaɪt] n meia-noite f.

**midriff** ['mɪdrɪf] n diafragma m.

**midst** [mɪdst] n: **in the ~ of** no meio de, entre.

**midsummer** [mɪd'sʌmə*] n: **a ~ day** um dia em pleno verão.

**midway** [mɪd'weɪ] adj, adv: ~ **(between)** no meio do caminho (entre).

**midweek** [mɪd'wiːk] adv no meio da semana.

**midwife** ['mɪdwaɪf], pl **-wives** [-waɪvz] n parteira; ~**ry** [-wɪfərɪ] n trabalho de parteira.

**midwinter** [mɪd'wɪntə*] n: **in ~** em pleno inverno.

**might** [maɪt] vb: **he ~ be there** pode ser que ele esteja ali; **I ~ as well go** mais vale que eu vá; **you ~ like to try** você poderia tentar // n poder m, força; ~**y** adj poderoso, forte.

**migraine** ['miːgreɪn] n enxaqueca.

**migrant** ['maɪɡrənt] n (bird) ave f de arribação; (person) emigrante m/f; (fig) nômade m/f // adj migratório; (worker) emigrante.

**migrate** [maɪ'ɡreɪt] vi emigrar; **migration** [-'ɡreɪʃən] n emigração f.

**mike** [maɪk] n abbr of **microphone** microfone m.

**mild** [maɪld] adj (character) pacífico; (climate) temperado; (slight) ligeiro; (taste) suave; (illness) leve, benigno.

**mildew** ['mɪldjuː] n mofo; (BOT) míldio.

**mildness** ['maɪldnɪs] n (softness) suavidade f; (gentleness) doçura; (quiet character) brandura.

**mile** [maɪl] n milha (1609 metros); ~**age** n número de milhas; (AUT) quilometragem f; **mileometer** n conta-quilômetros m inv; ~**stone** n

marco miliário; (event) fato que marca época.

**milieu** ['miːljəː] n meio, meio social.

**militant** ['mɪlɪtənt] adj, n militante m/f.

**military** ['mɪlɪtərɪ] adj militar.

**militate** ['mɪlɪteɪt] vi: **to ~ against** militar contra.

**militia** [mɪ'lɪʃə] n milícia.

**milk** [mɪlk] n leite m // vt (cow) ordenhar; (fig) explorar, chupar; ~**man** n leiteiro; ~ **shake** n leite batido com sorvete; ~**y** adj leitoso; **M~y Way** n Via Láctea.

**mill** [mɪl] n (windmill etc) moinho; (coffee ~) moedor m de café; (factory) moinho, engenho; (spinning ~) fábrica de tecelagem // vt moer // vi (also: ~ **about**) aglomerar-se, mover-se em círculos.

**millennium** [mɪ'lenɪəm], pl ~**s** or **-ia** [-nɪə] n milênio, milenário.

**miller** ['mɪlə*] n moleiro.

**millet** ['mɪlɪt] n milhete m.

**milli...** ['mɪlɪ] pref: ~**gram(me)** n miligrama m; ~**litre**, ~**liter** (US) n mililitro; ~**metre**, ~**meter** (US) n milímetro.

**milliner** ['mɪlɪnə*] n chapeleiro/a de senhoras; ~**y** n chapelaria de senhoras.

**million** ['mɪljən] n milhão m; **a ~ times** um milhão de vezes; ~**aire** n milionário.

**millstone** ['mɪlstəʊn] n mó f, pedra (de moinho).

**milometer** [maɪ'lɒmɪtə*] n marcador m de quilômetros.

**mime** [maɪm] n mimo; (actor) mímico, comediante m/f // vt imitar // vi fazer mímica.

**mimic** ['mɪmɪk] n mímico, imitador(a) m/f // adj mímico, simulado // vt imitar, parodiar; ~**ry** n imitação f.

**min.** abbr of **minute(s)**; **minimum**.

**minaret** [mɪnə'rɛt] n minarete m.

**mince** [mɪns] vt moer // vi (in

*walking)* andar com afetação (*Pt:* -ct-) // *n* (*CULIN*) carne *f* moída; ~**meat** *n* recheio de sebo e frutas picadas; ~ **pie** *n* pastel *m* com recheio de sebo e frutas picadas; **mincer** *n* moedor *m* de carne.

**mind** [maind] *n* (*gen*) mente *f*; (*intellect*) inteligência; (*contrasted with matter*) espírito // *vt* (*attend to, look after*) tomar conta de, cuidar de; (*be careful of*) ter cuidado com; (*object to*): **I don't** ~ **the noise** não me importa o ruído; **it is on my** ~ não me sai da cabeça; **to my** ~ a meu ver; **to be out of one's** ~ estar fora de si; **never** ~! não faz mal!, não importa!; (*don't worry*) não se preocupe!; **to bear sth in** ~ levar algo em consideração, não esquecer-se de algo; **to change one's** ~ mudar de opinião; **to make up one's** ~ decidir-se; '~ **the step**' 'cuidado com o degrau'; ~**ful** *adj* ~**ful of** consciente de; ~**less** *adj* estúpido, insensato.

**mine** [main] *pron* (o) meu/(a) minha *etc* // *adj*: **this book is** ~ este livro é meu // *n* mina // *vt* (*coal*) extrair, explorar; (*ship, beach*) minar; ~**field** *n* campo minado; **miner** *n* mineiro.

**mineral** ['minərəl] *adj* mineral // *n* mineral *m*; ~**s** *npl* (*soft drinks*) águas *fpl* minerais *or* gasificadas.

**minesweeper** ['mainswi:pə*] *n* caça-minas *m inv.*

**mingle** ['mingl] *vi:* **to** ~ **with** misturar-se com.

**mingy** ['mindʒi] *adj* (*col*) pão-duro.

**miniature** ['minətʃə*] *adj* em miniatura // *n* miniatura.

**minibus** ['minibʌs] *n* micro-ônibus *m.*

**minicab** ['minikæb] *n* mini-táxi *m.*

**minim** ['minim] *n* (*MUS*) mínima.

**minimal** ['miniml] *adj* mínimo.

**minimize** ['minimaiz] *vt* minimizar.

**minimum** ['miniməm] *n, pl*

**minima** ['minimə] *mínimo // adj* mínimo.

**mining** ['mainiŋ] *n* exploração *f* de minas // *adj* mineiro.

**miniskirt** ['miniskə:t] *n* minissaia.

**minister** ['ministə*] *n* (*POL*) ministro; (*REL*) pastor *m* // *vi* prestar assistência; ~**ial** [-'tiəriəl] *adj* (*POL*) ministerial.

**ministry** ['ministri] *n* ministério.

**mink** [miŋk] *n* marta; ~ **coat** *n* casaco de marta.

**minnow** ['minəu] *n* peixinho (de água doce).

**minor** ['mainə*] *adj* menor; (*unimportant*) de pouca importância; (*inferior*) inferior; (*MUS*) menor // *n* (*LAW*) menor *m/f* de idade.

**minority** [mai'nɔriti] *n* minoria; (*age*) menoridade *f.*

**minster** ['minstə*] *n* catedral *f.*

**minstrel** ['minstrəl] *n* menestrel *m.*

**mint** [mint] *n* (*plant*) hortelã *f*; (*sweet*) bala de hortelã // *vt* (*coins*) cunhar; **the (Royal) M**~ a Real Casa da Moeda; **in** ~ **condition** em perfeito estado.

**minuet** [minju'et] *n* minueto.

**minus** ['mainəs] *n* (*also:* ~ **sign**) sinal *m* de subtração (*Pt:* -cç-) // *prep* menos; (*without*) sem.

**minute** ['minit] *n* minuto; (*fig*) momento, instante *m*; ~**s** *npl* atas *fpl* // *adj* [mai'nju:t] miúdo, diminuto; (*search*) minucioso; **at the last** ~ no último momento.

**miracle** ['mirəkl] *n* milagre *m*; **miraculous** [mi'rækjuləs] *adj* milagroso.

**mirage** ['mira:ʒ] *n* miragem *f.*

**mirror** ['mirə*] *n* espelho; (*in car*) retrovisor *m* // *vt* refletir (*Pt:* -ct-).

**mirth** [mə:θ] *n* alegria; (*laughter*) risada.

**misadventure** [misəd'ventʃə*] *n* desgraça, infortúnio.

**misanthropist** [mi'zænθrəpist] *n* misantropo.

**misapprehension** ['mɪsæprɪ'henʃən] n mal-entendido, engano.

**misbehave** [mɪsbɪ'heɪv] vi comportar-se mal; **misbehaviour** n mau comportamento.

**miscalculate** [mɪs'kælkjuleɪt] vt calcular mal; **miscalculation** [-'leɪʃən] n erro de cálculo.

**miscarriage** ['mɪskærɪdʒ] n (MED) aborto; (failure) fracasso; ~ of **justice** erro judicial.

**miscellaneous** [mɪsɪ'leɪnɪəs] adj variado, diverso.

**mischance** [mɪs'tʃɑːns] n fatalidade f, azar m.

**mischief** ['mɪstʃɪf] n (naughtiness) travessura; (harm) dano, prejuízo; (maliciousness) malícia; **mischievous** [-ʃɪvəs] adj malicioso; (playful) travesso.

**misconception** ['mɪskən'sepʃən] n concepção f errada, conceito errado.

**misconduct** [mɪs'kɔndʌkt] n comportamento impróprio; **professional** ~ má conduta profissional.

**miscount** [mɪs'kaunt] vt/i contar mal.

**misdeed** [mɪs'diːd] n delito, ofensa.

**misdemeanour**, **misde-meanor** (US) [mɪsdɪ'miːnə*] n má ação (Pt: -cç-) f.

**misdirect** [mɪsdɪ'rekt] vt (person) orientar or informar mal; (letter) endereçar mal.

**miser** ['maɪzə*] n avaro/a m/f, sovina m/f.

**miserable** ['mɪzərəbl] adj (unhappy) triste, sorumbático; (wretched) miserável; (despicable) desprezível.

**miserly** ['maɪzəlɪ] adj avarento, mesquinho.

**misery** ['mɪzərɪ] n (unhappiness) tristeza, angústia; (wretchedness) miséria, penúria.

**misfire** [mɪs'faɪə*] vi falhar.

**misfit** ['mɪsfɪt] n (person)

inadaptado/a, deslocado/a.

**misfortune** [mɪs'fɔːtʃən] n desgraça, infortúnio.

**misgiving(s)** [mɪs'gɪvɪŋ(z)] n(pl) (mistrust) desconfiança, receio; (apprehension) mau pressentimento.

**misguided** [mɪs'gaɪdɪd] adj enganado.

**mishandle** [mɪs'hændl] vt (treat roughly) maltratar; (mismanage) manejar mal.

**mishap** ['mɪshæp] n desgraça, contratempo.

**mishear** [mɪs'hɪə*] (irr: like hear) vt ouvir mal.

**misinform** [mɪsɪn'fɔːm] vt informar mal.

**misinterpret** [mɪsɪn'tɜːprɪt] vt interpretar mal.

**misjudge** [mɪs'dʒʌdʒ] vt fazer um juízo errado de, julgar mal.

**mislay** [mɪs'leɪ] (irr: like lay) vt extraviar, perder.

**mislead** [mɪs'liːd] (irr: like lead) vt induzir em erro, enganar; ~**ing** adj enganoso, errôneo.

**mismanage** [mɪs'mænɪdʒ] vt administrar mal; ~**ment** n má administração f.

**misnomer** [mɪs'nəumə*] n termo impróprio or errado.

**misogynist** [mɪ'sɔdʒɪnɪst] n misógino.

**misplace** [mɪs'pleɪs] vt (lose) extraviar, perder; (wrongly) colocar em lugar errado.

**misprint** ['mɪsprɪnt] n erro tipográfico.

**mispronounce** [mɪsprə'nauns] vt pronunciar mal.

**misread** [mɪs'riːd] (irr: like read) vt interpretar or ler mal.

**misrepresent** [mɪsreprɪ'zent] vt desvirtuar, deturpar.

**miss** [mɪs] vt (train etc) perder; (fail to hit) errar, não acertar em; (regret the absence of): I ~ him sinto a falta dele or sinto a sua falta

// *vi* falhar // *n* (*shot*) tiro perdido *or* errado; (*fig*): **that was a near ~** (*near accident*) por pouco não batemos; **to ~ out** *vt* omitir.

**Miss** [mɪs] *n* senhorita.

**missal** ['mɪsl] *n* missal *m*.

**misshapen** [mɪs'ʃeɪpən] *adj* disforme.

**missile** ['mɪsaɪl] *n* (AVIAT) míssil *m*; (*object thrown*) projétil (*Pt*: -ct-) *m*.

**missing** ['mɪsɪŋ] *adj* (*pupil*) ausente; (*thing*) perdido; (MIL) desaparecido; **to go ~** desaparecer.

**mission** ['mɪʃən] *n* missão *f*; **~ary** *n* missionário/a.

**misspent** ['mɪs'spent] *adj*: **my ~ youth** sua juventude desperdiçada.

**mist** [mɪst] *n* (*light*) neblina; (*heavy*) névoa; (*at sea*) bruma // *vi* (*also*: **~ over, ~ up**) embaçar.

**mistake** [mɪs'teɪk] *n* erro // *vt* (*irr*: *like* **take**) entender *or* interpretar mal; **to ~ A for B** confundir A com B; **mistaken** *adj* (*idea etc*) errado; **to be mistaken** enganar-se, equivocar-se.

**mister** ['mɪstə*] *n* (*col*) senhor *m*; *see* **Mr.**

**mistletoe** ['mɪsltəu] *n* visco.

**mistook** [mɪs'tuk] *pt of* **mistake.**

**mistreat** [mɪs'triːt] *vt* maltratar; **~ment** *n* mau trato.

**mistress** ['mɪstrɪs] *n* (*lover*) amante *f*; (*of house*) dona (da casa); (*school*) professora, mestra; *see* **Mrs.**

**mistrust** [mɪs'trʌst] *vt* desconfiar de, duvidar de.

**misty** ['mɪstɪ] *adj* enevoado, nebuloso; (*day*) nublado; (*glasses*) embaciado.

**misunderstand** [mɪsʌndə'stænd] (*irr*: *like* **understand**) *vt/i* entender *or* interpretar mal; **~ing** *n* mal-entendido.

**misuse** [mɪs'juːs] *n* mau uso; (*of power*) abuso // *vt* [mɪs'juːz] abusar de; (*funds*) desviar.

**mitigate** ['mɪtɪgeɪt] *vt* mitigar, atenuar.

**mitre, miter** (US) ['maɪtə*] *n* mitro; (CARPENTRY) meia-esquadria.

**mitt(en)** ['mɪt(n)] *n* mitene *f*.

**mix** [mɪks] *vt* (*gen*) misturar; (*combine*) combinar // *vi* misturar-se; (*people*) entrosar-se // *n* mistura; **to ~ up** *vt* misturar; (*confuse*) confundir; **~ed** *adj* (*assorted*) sortido, variado; (*school etc*) misto; **~ed-up** *adj* (*confused*) confuso; **~er** *n* (*for food*) batedeira; (*person*) pessoa sociável; **~ture** *n* mistura; **~-up** *n* trapalhada, confusão *f*.

**moan** [məun] *n* gemido, lamento // *vi* gemer; (*col*: *complain*): **to ~** (*about*) queixar-se (de).

**moat** [məut] *n* fosso.

**mob** [mɔb] *n* multidão *f*; (*pej*): **the ~** chusma, povinho // *vt* atacar, cercar.

**mobile** ['məubaɪl] *adj* móvel // *n* móvel *m*; **~ home** *n* trailer *m*, casa móvel.

**mobility** [məu'bɪlɪtɪ] *n* mobilidade *f*.

**mobilize** ['məubɪlaɪz] *vt* mobilizar.

**moccasin** ['mɔkəsɪn] *n* mocassim *m*.

**mock** [mɔk] *vt* (*make ridiculous*) ridicularizar; (*laugh at*) zombar de // *adj* falso, fingido; **~ery** *n* zombaria; **~ing** *adj* zombeteiro; **~-up** *n* maqueta *f*.

**mode** [məud] *n* modo; (*fashion*) moda.

**model** ['mɔdl] *n* (*gen*) modelo; (ARCH) maqueta; (*person: for fashion, ART*) modelo *m/f* // *adj* modelar // *vt* modelar // *vi* servir de modelo; **~ railway** trenzinho de brinquedo; **to ~ clothes** desfilar apresentando modelos.

**moderate** ['mɔdərət] *adj*, *n* moderado/a // (*vb*: [-reɪt]) *vi* moderar-se, acalmar-se // *vt* moderar; **moderation** [-'reɪʃən] *n* moderação *f*.

**modern** ['mɔdən] *adj* moderno; ~**ize** *vt* modernizar, atualizar (Pt: -ct-).

**modest** ['mɔdɪst] *adj* modesto; ~**y** *n* modéstia.

**modicum** ['mɔdɪkəm] *n*: **a** ~ **of** um mínimo de.

**modification** [mɔdɪfɪ'keɪʃən] *n* modificação *f*; **modify** ['mɔdɪfaɪ] *vt* modificar.

**modulation** [mɔdju'leɪʃən] *n* modulação *f*.

**mohair** ['məuhɛə*] *n* angorá *m*.

**moist** [mɔɪst] *adj* úmido (Pt: hú-), molhado; ~**en** ['mɔɪsn] *vt* (h)umedecer; ~**ure** ['mɔɪstʃə*] *n* (h)umidade *f*; ~**urizer** ['mɔɪstʃəraɪzə*] *n* creme *m* hidratante.

**molar** ['məulə*] *n* molar *m*.

**molasses** [məu'læsɪz] *n* melaço *sg*, melado *sg*.

**mole** [məul] *n* (*animal*) toupeira; (*spot*) sinal *m*, lunar *m*.

**molecule** ['mɔlɪkjuːl] *n* molécula.

**molehill** ['məulhɪl] *n* montículo (feito por uma toupeira).

**molest** [məu'lɛst] *vt* molestar, importunar.

**mollusc** ['mɔləsk] *n* molusco.

**mollycoddle** ['mɔlɪkɔdl] *vt* mimar.

**molten** ['məultən] *adj* fundido; (*lava*) liquefeito.

**moment** ['məumənt] *n* momento; ~**ary** *adj* momentâneo; ~**ous** [-'mɛntəs] *adj* importantíssimo.

**momentum** [məu'mɛntəm] *n* momento; (*fig*) ímpeto; **to gather** ~ ganhar ímpeto.

**monarch** ['mɔnək] *n* monarca *m/f*; ~**y** *n* monarquia.

**monastery** ['mɔnəstərɪ] *n* mosteiro, convento.

**monastic** [mə'næstɪk] *adj* monástico.

**Monday** ['mʌndɪ] *n* segunda-feira *f*.

**monetary** ['mʌnɪtərɪ] *adj* monetário.

**money** ['mʌnɪ] *n* dinheiro; **to make** ~ ganhar dinheiro; ~**lender** *n*

agiota *m/f*; ~ **order** *n* vale (postal) *m*.

**mongol** ['mɔŋgɔl] *adj*, *n* (MED) mongoloide *m/f*.

**mongrel** ['mʌŋgrəl] *n* (*dog*) cão cruzado, vira-lata *m*.

**monitor** ['mɔnɪtə*] *n* (SCOL) monitor *m*; (*also:* **television** ~) visor *m* // *vt* controlar.

**monk** [mʌŋk] *n* monge *m*.

**monkey** ['mʌŋkɪ] *n* macaco; ~ **nut** *n* amendoim *m*; ~ **wrench** *n* chave *f* inglesa.

**mono...** [mɔnəu] *pref*: ~**chrome** *adj* monocromático.

**monocle** ['mɔnəkl] *n* monóculo.

**monogram** ['mɔnəgræm] *n* monograma *m*.

**monologue** ['mɔnɔlɔg] *n* monólogo.

**monopoly** [mə'nɔpəlɪ] *n* monopólio.

**monorail** ['mɔnəureɪl] *n* monotrilho.

**monosyllabic** [mɔnəusɪ'læbɪk] *adj* monossilábico.

**monotone** ['mɔnətəun] *n* monotonia; **to speak in a** ~ falar num tom monótono.

**monotonous** [mə'nɔtənəs] *adj* monótono; **monotony** [-nɪ] *n* monotonia.

**monsoon** [mɔn'suːn] *n* monção *f*.

**monster** ['mɔnstə*] *n* monstro.

**monstrosity** [mɔns'trɔsɪtɪ] *n* monstruosidade *f*.

**monstrous** ['mɔnstrəs] *adj* (*huge*) descomunal; (*atrocious*) monstruoso.

**montage** [mɔn'tɑːʒ] *n* montagem *f*.

**month** [mʌnθ] *n* mês *m*; ~**ly** *adj* mensal // *adv* mensalmente // *n* (*magazine*) revista mensal.

**monument** ['mɔnjumənt] *n* monumento; ~**al** [-'mɛntl] *adj* monumental.

**moo** [muː] *vi* mugir.

**mood** [muːd] *n* humor *m*; **to be in a good/bad** ~ estar de bom/mal humor; ~**y** *adj* (*variable*) caprichoso, de veneta; (sullen) melancólico.

**moon** [mu:n] n lua; ~**beam** n raio de lua; ~**light** n luar m; ~**lit** adj: **a** ~**lit night** uma noite de lua.

**moor** [muə*] n charneca // vt (ship) amarrar // vi fundear, atracar.

**Moor** [muə*] n mouro/a.

**moorings** ['muəriŋz] npl (chains) amarras fpl; (place) ancoradouro sg.

**Moorish** ['muəriʃ] adj mouro; (architecture) mourisco.

**moorland** ['muələnd] n charneca.

**moose** [mu:s] n, pl inv alce m.

**mop** [mɔp] n esfregão m; (of hair) grenha // vt esfregar; **to** ~ **up** vt limpar.

**mope** [məup] vi estar or andar deprimido or desanimado.

**moped** ['məupɛd] n (Brit) bicicleta motorizada.

**moral** ['mɔrl] adj moral // n moral f; ~**s** npl moralidade f, costumes mpl.

**morale** [mɔ'ra:l] n moral f, estado de espírito.

**morality** [mɔ'ræliti] n moralidade f.

**morass** [mɔ'ræs] n pântano, brejo.

**morbid** ['mɔ:bid] adj (depressed) doentio; (MED) mórbido; **don't be** ~! não seja mórbido!

**more** [mɔ:*] det, adv mais; **once** ~ outra vez; **I want** ~ quero mais; ~ **dangerous than** mais perigoso que; ~ **or less** mais ou menos; ~ **than ever** mais do que nunca.

**moreover** [mɔ:'rəuvə*] adv além do mais, além disso.

**morgue** [mɔ:g] n necrotério.

**moribund** ['mɔribʌnd] adj moribundo, agonizante.

**Mormon** ['mɔ:mən] n mórmon m/f.

**morning** ['mɔ:niŋ] n (gen) manhã f; (early ~) madrugada; **good** ~ bom dia; **in the** ~ de manhã; **7 o'clock in the** ~ (as) 7 da manhã; **tomorrow** ~ amanhã de manhã.

**Moroccan** [mɔ'rɔkən] adj, n marroquino/a.

**Morocco** [mɔ'rɔkəu] n Marrocos msg.

**moron** ['mɔ:rɔn] n débil mental m/f, idiota m/f; ~**ic** [mɔ'rɔnik] adj mentecapto.

**morose** [mɔ'rəus] adj taciturno, rabugento.

**morphine** ['mɔ:fi:n] n morfina.

**Morse** [mɔ:s] n (also: ~ **code**) código Morse.

**morsel** ['mɔ:sl] n (of food) bocado.

**mortal** ['mɔ:tl] adj, n mortal m/f; ~**ity** [-'tæliti] n mortalidade f.

**mortar** ['mɔ:tə*] n argamassa; (dish) pilão m, almofariz m.

**mortgage** ['mɔ:gidʒ] n hipoteca // vt hipotecar.

**mortify** ['mɔ:tifai] vt humilhar, mortificar.

**mortuary** ['mɔ:tjuəri] n necrotério.

**mosaic** [məu'zeiik] n mosaico.

**Moscow** ['mɔskəu] n Moscou m.

**Moslem** ['mɔzləm] adj, n = **Muslim**.

**mosque** [mɔsk] n mesquita.

**mosquito** [mɔs'ki:təu], pl ~**es** n mosquito.

**moss** [mɔs] n musgo.

**most** [məust] det a maior parte de, a maioria de // pron a maior parte, a maioria // adv o mais; (very) muito; **the** ~ (also: + adjective) mais; ~ **of them** a maioria deles; **I saw the** ~ vi mais; **at the (very)** ~ quando muito, no máximo; **to make the** ~ **of** aproveitar ao máximo; ~**ly** adv principalmente, na maior parte; **a** ~ **interesting book** um livro interessantíssimo.

**motel** [məu'tɛl] n motel m.

**moth** [mɔθ] n mariposa; (clothes ~) traça; ~**ball** n bola de naftalina; ~-**eaten** adj roído pelas traças.

**mother** ['mʌðə*] n mãe f, mamãe f // adj materno // vt (care for) cuidar (como uma mãe); ~**hood** n maternidade f; ~-**in-law** n sogra;

~**ly** adj maternal; ~**-of-pearl** n madrepérola; ~**-to-be** n futura mamãe; ~ **tongue** n língua materna or pátria.

**motif** ['mou'ti:f] n motivo; (theme) tema m.

**motion** ['mouʃən] n movimento; (gesture) gesto, sinal m; (at meeting) moção f // vt/i: to ~ (to) **sb to do sth** fazer sinal a alguém para que faça algo; ~**less** adj imóvel; ~ **picture** n filme m (cinematográfico).

**motivated** ['mouttiveittd] adj motivado; **motivation** [-'veiʃən] n motivação f.

**motive** ['moutiv] n motivo // adj motor/motriz.

**motley** ['mɒtli] adj variado, heterogêneo.

**motor** ['mouto*] n motor m; (col: vehicle) carro, automóvel m // adj motor/motriz; ~**bike** n motocicleta; ~**boat** n barco a motor; ~**car** n carro, automóvel m; ~**cycle** n motocicleta; ~**cyclist** n motociclista m/f; ~**ing** n automobilismo; ~**ist** n automobilista m/f, motorista m/f; ~**oil** n óleo de motor; ~**racing** n corrida de carros, automobilismo; ~**scooter** n moto f, Lambretta; ~**vehicle** n automóvel m; ~**way** n (Brit) auto-estrada.

**mottled** ['mɒtld] adj mosqueado, em furta-cores.

**motto** ['mɒtəu], pl ~**es** n lema m; (watchword) senha.

**mould, mold** (US) [mould] n molde m; (mildew) mofo, bolor m // vt moldar; (fig) modelar, plasmar; ~**er** vi (decay) desfazer-se; ~**ing** n moldura; ~**y** adj mofado.

**moult, molt** (US) [moult] vi mudar (de penas etc).

**mound** [maund] n montão m, montículo.

**mount** [maunt] n monte m; (horse) montaria; (for jewel etc) engaste m;

(for picture) moldura // vt montar em, subir a // vi (also: ~ up) subir, aumentar.

**mountain** ['mauntin] n montanha // cmp de montanha; ~**eer** [-'nɪə*] n alpinista m/f, montanhista m/f; ~**eering** [-'nɪərɪŋ] n alpinismo; to go ~**eering** praticar o alpinismo; ~**ous** adj montanhoso; ~**side** n lado da montanha.

**mourn** [mɔ:n] vt chorar, lamentar // vi: to ~ **for** chorar ou lamentar a morte de; ~**er** n parente/a m/f or amigo/a do defunto; ~**ful** adj desolado, triste; ~**ing** n luto // cmp (dress) de luto; (to be) in ~**ing** (estar) de luto.

**mouse** [maus], pl **mice** n camundongo; (Pt) rato; ~**trap** n ratoeira.

**moustache** [məs'ta:ʃ] n bigode m.

**mousy** ['mausi] adj (person) tímido; (hair) pardacento.

**mouth** [mauθ], pl ~**s** [-ðz] n boca; (of river) desembocadura; ~**ful** n bocado; ~**organ** n gaita; ~**piece** n (of musical instrument) bocal m; (spokesman) porta-voz m; ~**wash** n líquido para limpeza bucal; ~**watering** adj que dá água na boca.

**movable** ['mu:vəbl] adj móvel.

**move** [mu:v] n (movement) movimento; (in game) jogada; (: turn to play) turno, vez f; (change of house) mudança // vt mover; (emotionally) comover; (POL: resolution etc) propor // vi (gen) mover-se, mexer-se; (traffic) circular; (also: ~ **house**) mudar-se; to ~ **sb to do sth** convencer alguém a fazer algo; to **get a** ~ **on** apressar-se; to ~ **about** vi ir de um lado para o outro; (travel) viajar; to ~ **along** vi avançar; to ~ **away** vi afastar-se; to ~ **back** vi recuar; to ~ **forward** vi avançar // vt adiantar; to ~ **in** vi (to a house) instalar-se (numa casa); to ~ **on** vi ir andando; to ~ **out** vi (of house) abandonar (uma casa); to

~ **up** vi subir; (employee) ser promovido.

**movement** ['muːvmənt] n movimento; (TECH) mecanismo.

**movie** ['muːvɪ] n filme m; **to go to the ~s** ir ao cinema; ~ **camera** n câmara cinematográfica.

**moving** ['muːvɪŋ] adj (emotional) comovente; (that moves) móvel.

**mow** [məu], pt **mowed**, pp **mowed** or **mown** vt (grass) cortar; (corn: also: ~ **down**) ceifar; ~**er** n ceifeira; (for lawn) cortador m de grama.

**M.P.** (Brit) n abbr of **Member of Parliament.**

**m.p.h.** abbr of **miles per hour.**

**Mr** ['mɪstə*] n: ~ **Smith** (o) Sr. Smith.

**Mrs** ['mɪsɪz] n: ~ **Smith** (a) Sra. Smith.

**Ms** [mɪz] n = **Miss** or **Mrs**: ~ **X** (a) Sa X.

**M.Sc.** (Brit) abbr of **Master of Science.**

**much** [mʌtʃ] det, adv, pron muito // n muito, grande parte; **how ~ is it?** quanto é?, quanto custa?; **too ~** demais, demasiado; **it's not ~** não é muito; **as ~ as** tanto como; **however ~ he tries** por mais que tente.

**muck** [mʌk] n (dirt) sujeira; (manure) estrume m; (fig) porcaria; **to ~ about** vi (col) perder o tempo; (enjoy o.s.) divertir-se; **to ~ up** vt (col: ruin) estragar; ~**y** adj (dirty) sujo.

**mucus** ['mjuːkəs] n muco.

**mud** [mʌd] n lama, lodo.

**muddle** ['mʌdl] n confusão f, desordem f; (mix-up) trapalhada f // vt (also: ~ **up**) confundir, misturar; **to ~ through** vi sair-se bem.

**mud:** ~**dy** adj enlameado; ~**guard** n pára-lama m; ~**pack** n máscara (de beleza); ~**-slinging** n difamação f, injúria.

**muff** [mʌf] n regalo // vt (chance)

desperdiçar, perder; (lines) estropiar.

**muffle** ['mʌfl] vt (sound) abafar; (against cold) agasalhar; ~**d** adj abafado, surdo; ~**r** (US) n abafador m; (Pt) panela de escape.

**mufti** ['mʌftɪ] n: **in ~** vestido à paisana.

**mug** [mʌg] n (cup) caneca; (: for beer) caneco, canecão m; (: col: face) careta; (: fool) bobo // vt (assault) assaltar; ~**ging** n assalto.

**muggy** ['mʌgɪ] adj abafado.

**mule** [mjuːl] n mula.

**mull** [mʌl]: **to ~ over** vt meditar sobre.

**mulled** [mʌld] adj: ~ **wine** vinho quente com canela etc.

**multi...** ['mʌltɪ] pref multi...; ~**coloured**, ~**colored** (US) adj multicor.

**multifarious** [mʌltɪˈfɛərɪəs] adj variado.

**multiple** ['mʌltɪpl] adj, n múltiplo; ~ **sclerosis** n esclerose f múltipla; ~ **store** n cadeia de lojas.

**multiplication** [mʌltɪplɪˈkeɪʃən] n multiplicação f; **multiply** ['mʌltɪplaɪ] vt multiplicar // vi multiplicar-se.

**multitude** ['mʌltɪtjuːd] n multidão f.

**mum** [mʌm] n mamãe f // adj: **to keep ~** ficar calado.

**mumble** ['mʌmbl] vt/i resmungar, murmurar.

**mummy** ['mʌmɪ] n (mother) mamãe f; (embalmed) múmia.

**mumps** [mʌmps] n papeira sg, caxumba sg.

**munch** [mʌntʃ] vt/i mascar.

**mundane** [mʌnˈdeɪn] adj mundano.

**municipal** [mjuːˈnɪsɪpl] adj municipal; ~**ity** [-ˈpælɪtɪ] n municipalidade f.

**munitions** [mjuːˈnɪʃənz] npl munições fpl.

**mural** ['mjuərl] n mural m.

**murder** ['mɜːdə*] n assassinato; (in law) homicídio // vt assassinar;

(*spoil*) estragar; ~**er** n assassino; ~**ess** n assassina; ~**ous** adj homicida.

**murky** ['mɜːki] adj escuro; (*fig*) sombrio.

**murmur** ['mɜːmə*] n murmúrio n // vt/i murmurar.

**muscle** ['mʌsl] n músculo; (*fig: strength*) força (muscular); **to ~ in** vi abrir caminho à força; **muscular** ['mʌskjulə*] adj (*person*) musculoso.

**muse** [mjuːz] vi meditar // n musa.

**museum** [mjuːˈzɪəm] n museu m.

**mushroom** ['mʌʃrum] n (*gen*) cogumelo, fungo; (*food*) cogumelo // vi (*fig*) crescer da noite para o dia.

**mushy** ['mʌʃi] adj mole; (*pej*) piegas inv.

**music** ['mjuːzɪk] n música; ~**al** adj melodioso; (*person*) musical // n (*show*) musical m; ~**al instrument** n instrumento musical; ~**al hall** n teatro de variedades; ~**ian** [-'zɪʃən] n músico/a.

**musket** ['mʌskɪt] n mosquete m.

**Muslim** ['mʌzlɪm] adj, n muçulmano/a m/f.

**muslin** ['mʌzlɪn] n musselina.

**mussel** ['mʌsl] n mexilhão m, sururu m.

**must** [mʌst] auxiliary vb (*obligation*): **I ~ do it** tenho que or devo fazer isso; (*probability*): **he ~ be there by now** ele já deve estar lá agora // n (*wine*) mosto; (*necessity*): **it's a ~** é imprescindível.

**mustard** ['mʌstəd] n mostarda.

**muster** ['mʌstə*] vt reunir, juntar.

**mustn't** ['mʌsnt] = **must not.**

**musty** ['mʌsti] adj mofado, com cheiro de bolor.

**mute** [mjuːt] adj, n mudo/a.

**muted** ['mjuːtɪd] adj calado; (*MUS*) abafado.

**mutilate** ['mjuːtɪleɪt] vt mutilar; **mutilation** [-'leɪʃən] n mutilação f.

**mutinous** ['mjuːtɪnəs] adj (*troops*) amotinado; (*attitude*) rebelde.

**mutiny** ['mjuːtɪnɪ] n motim m, rebelião f // vi amotinar-se.

**mutter** ['mʌtə*] vt/i resmungar, murmurar.

**mutton** ['mʌtn] n carne f de carneiro.

**mutual** ['mjuːtʃuəl] adj mútuo; (*gen: shared*) comum; ~**ly** adv reciprocamente.

**muzzle** ['mʌzl] n focinho; (*protective device*) focinheira; (*of gun*) boca // vt amordaçar; (*dog*) pôr focinheira em.

**my** [maɪ] adj meu/minha // interj: ~! meu Deus!

**mynah bird** ['maɪnə-] n mainá m.

**myopic** [maɪˈɒpɪk] adj míope.

**myself** [maɪˈsɛlf] pron (*reflexive*) me; (*emphatic*) eu mesmo; (*after prep*) mim mesmo, mim próprio.

**mysterious** [mɪsˈtɪərɪəs] adj misterioso; **mystery** ['mɪstərɪ] n mistério.

**mystic** ['mɪstɪk] adj, n místico/a; ~**al** adj místico.

**mystify** ['mɪstɪfaɪ] vt (*perplex*) mistificar, confundir; (*disconcert*) desconcertar.

**myth** [mɪθ] n mito; ~**ical** adj mítico; ~**ological** [mɪθə'lɒdʒɪkl] adj mitológico; ~**ology** [mɪ'θɒlədʒɪ] n mitologia.

# N

**nab** [næb] vt (*col: grab*) pegar, prender; (: *catch out*) pegar (em flagrante).

**nag** [næg] n (*pej: horse*) rocim m // vt (*scold*) ralhar; (*annoy*) aborrecer; ~**ging** adj (*doubt*) persistente; (*pain*) contínuo // n queixas fpl, censuras fpl.

**nail** [neɪl] n (*human*) unha; (*metal*)

prego // vt pregar, cravar; (fig: catch) agarrar, pegar; **to ~ sb down to doing sth** comprometer alguém para que faça algo; **~brush** n escova de unhas; **~file** n lixa de unhas; **~ polish** n esmalte m de unhas; **~ scissors** npl tesourinha de unhas; **~ varnish** n = **~ polish**.

**naïve** [naɪ'iːv] adj ingênuo; (simple) simples.

**naked** ['neɪkɪd] adj (nude) nu/nua; (fig) desprotegido; (flame) exposto ao ar; **with the ~ eye** a olho nu; **~ness** n nudez f.

**name** [neɪm] n (gen) nome m; (surname) sobrenome m; (reputation) reputação f, fama f // vt (child) pôr nome em; (criminal) dar o nome de; (appoint) nomear; **by ~** de nome; **in the ~ of** em nome de; **what's your ~?** como (você) se chama?; **to give one's ~ and address** dar o nome e o endereço; **~less** adj sem nome, anônimo; **~ly** adv a saber, isto é; **~sake** n xará m/f, tocaio/a.

**nanny** ['nænɪ] n babá f; **~ goat** n cabra.

**nap** [næp] n (sleep) soneca, soninho; (cloth) felpa.

**napalm** ['neɪpɑːm] n napalm m.

**nape** [neɪp] n: **the ~ of the neck** nuca, cangote m.

**napkin** ['næpkɪn] n (also: **table ~**) guardanapo; (Brit: for baby) fralda.

**nappy** ['næpɪ] n fralda; **~ liner** n gaze f; **~ rash** n assadura.

**narcissus** [nɑː'sɪsəs], pl **-si** [-saɪ] n narciso.

**narcotic** [nɑː'kɔtɪk] adj, n narcótico.

**narrate** [nə'reɪt] vt narrar, contar; **narrative** ['nærətɪv] n narrativa // adj narrativo; **narrator** n narrador(a) m/f.

**narrow** ['nærəu] adj estreito; (shoe) apertado; (fig) intolerante, limitado // vi estreitar-se; (diminish) diminuir-se; **to ~ down** the

**possibilities to** restringir as possibilidades a; **~ly** adv (miss) por pouco; **~-minded** adj de visão limitada, bitolado.

**nasal** ['neɪzl] adj nasal.

**nastiness** ['nɑːstɪnɪs] n' (malice) maldade f; (rudeness) grosseria.

**nasty** ['nɑːstɪ] adj (unpleasant: remark) desagradável; (: person) mau, ruim; (malicious) maldoso; (rude) grosseiro, obsceno; (revolting: taste, smell) repugnante, asqueroso; (wound, disease etc) grave, sério.

**nation** ['neɪʃən] n nação f.

**national** ['næʃənl] adj, n nacional m/f; **~ism** n nacionalismo; **~ist** adj, n nacionalista m/f; **~ity** [-'nælɪtɪ] n nacionalidade f; **~ization** [-aɪ'zeɪʃən] n nacionalização f; **~ize** vt nacionalizar; **~ly** adv (nationwide) de âmbito nacional; (as a nation) nacionalmente, como nação.

**nationwide** ['neɪʃənwaɪd] adj de âmbito or a nível nacional.

**native** ['neɪtɪv] n (local inhabitant) natural m/f, nativo/a; (in colonies) indígena m/f; nativo/a // adj (indigenous) indígena; (of one's birth) natal; (innate) inato, natural.

**NATO** ['neɪtəu] n abbr of **North Atlantic Treaty Organization** OTAN, Organização do Tratado do Atlântico Norte.

**natter** ['nætə*] vi conversar fiado.

**natural** ['nætʃrəl] adj natural; (unaffected: manner) sem afetação (Pt: -ct-); **~ist** n naturalista m/f; **~ize** vt: **to become ~ized** (person) naturalizar-se; (plant) aclimatar-se; **~ly** adv naturalmente; (of course) claro, evidentemente; (instinctively) por instinto, espontaneamente; **~ness** n naturalidade f.

**nature** ['neɪtʃə*] n natureza; (group, sort) tipo, espécie f; (character) caráter (Pt: -ct-) m, índole f; **by ~** por natureza.

**naughty** ['nɔːtɪ] *adj* (*child*) travesso, peralta; (*story, film*) picante.

**nausea** ['nɔːsɪə] *n* náusea; **nauseate** [-sɪeɪt] *vt* dar náuseas a; (*fig*) repugnar; **nauseating** [-sɪeɪtɪŋ] *adj* nauseabundo, enjoativo; (*fig*) nojento, repugnante.

**nautical** ['nɔːtɪkl] *adj* náutico; (*mile*) marítimo.

**naval** ['neɪvl] *adj* naval; **~ officer** *n* oficial *m* de marinha.

**nave** [neɪv] *n* nave *f*.

**navel** ['neɪvl] *n* umbigo.

**navigable** ['nævɪgəbl] *adj* navegável.

**navigate** ['nævɪgeɪt] *vt* (*guide*) pilotar; (*sail along*) navegar; (*fig*) dirigir // *vi* navegar; **navigation** [-'geɪʃən] *n* (*action*) navegação *f*; (*science*) náutica; **navigator** *n* navegante *m/f*, navegador(a) *m/f*.

**navvy** ['nævɪ] *n* trabalhador *m* braçal, cavouqueiro.

**navy** ['neɪvɪ] *n* marinha de guerra; (*ships*) armada, frota; **~(-blue)** *adj* azul-marinho.

**Nazi** ['nɑːtsɪ] *n* nazista *m/f*; **Nazism** *n* nazismo.

**neap tide** [niːp-] *n* maré *f*.

**near** [nɪə*] *adj* (*place*) perto, vizinho; (*time*) próximo, perto; (*relation*) íntimo // *adv* perto // *prep* (*also:* **~ to**) (*space*) perto de, junto de; (*time*) perto de, quase // *vt* aproximar-se de, abeirar-se de; **~by** [nɪə'baɪ] *adj* próximo, vizinho // *adv* à mão, perto; **N~ East** *n* Oriente *m* Próximo; **~ly** *adv* quase, por pouco; **I ~ly fell** quase que caí; **~ miss** *n* tiro que passou de raspão; **~ness** *n* proximidade *f*; (*relationship*) intimidade *f*, familiaridade *f*; **~side** *n* (*AUT, Brit*) lado esquerdo; (*: Br, Pt*) lado direito; **~sighted** *adj* míope.

**neat** [niːt] *adj* (*place*) arrumado, em ordem; (*person*) asseado, arrumado; (*skilful*) hábil; (*: plan*) engenhoso,

bem bolado; (*spirits*) puro.

**nebulous** ['nebjuləs] *adj* nebuloso; (*fig*) vago, confuso.

**necessarily** ['nesɪsrɪlɪ] *adv* necessariamente.

**necessary** ['nesɪsrɪ] *adj* necessário; **he did all that was ~** fez tudo o que foi necessário.

**necessitate** [nɪ'sesɪteɪt] *vt* exigir, tornar necessário.

**necessity** [nɪ'sesɪtɪ] *n* (*thing needed*) necessidade *f*, requisito; (*compelling circumstances*) a necessidade; **necessities** *npl* artigos *mpl* de primeira necessidade.

**neck** [nek] *n* (*ANAT*) pescoço, colo; (*of animal*) pescoço // *vi* ficar com agarramento, tirar um sarro; **~ and ~** emparelhados; **to stick one's ~ out** arriscar-se.

**necklace** ['neklɪs] *n* colar *m*.

**neckline** ['neklaɪn] *n* decote *m*.

**necktie** ['nektaɪ] *n* gravata.

**née** [neɪ] *adj*: **~ Scott** em solteira Scott.

**need** [niːd] *n* (*lack*) falta, carência; (*necessity*) necessidade *f*; (*thing needed*) requisito, necessidade // *vt* (*require*) necessitar; **I ~ to do it** tenho que or devo fazê-lo; **you don't ~ to go** você não precisa ir.

**needle** ['niːdl] *n* agulha // *vt* (*fig: fam*) provocar, picar, alfinetar.

**needless** ['niːdlɪs] *adj* inútil, desnecessário; **~ to say** é escusado dizer que.

**needlework** ['niːdlwɜːk] *n* (*activity*) trabalho *m* de agulha, costura.

**needy** ['niːdɪ] *adj* necessitado.

**negation** [nɪ'geɪʃən] *n* negação *f*.

**negative** ['negətɪv] *n* (*PHOT*) negativo; (*answer*) negativa // *adj* negativo.

**neglect** [nɪ'glekt] *vt* (*one's duty*) negligenciar, não cumprir com; (*child*) descuidar, esquecer-se de // *n* (*gen*) descuido, desatenção *f*;

(*personal*) desleixo; (*of duty*) negligência.

**negligee** ['neglɪʒeɪ] *n* (*nightdress*) négligé *m*, camisola fina; (*housecoat*) roupão *m*.

**negligence** ['neglɪdʒəns] *n* negligência, descuido; **negligent** [-ənt] *adj* (*careless*) negligente, desleixado; (*forgetful*) esquecido.

**negligible** ['neglɪdʒɪbl] *adj* insignificante, desprezível, ínfimo.

**negotiable** [nɪ'gəuʃɪəbl] *adj* (*cheque*) negociável; (*road*) transitável.

**negotiate** [nɪ'gəuʃɪeɪt] *vi* negociar // *vt* (*treaty*) negociar; (*transaction*) efetuar (*Pt*: -ct-), fazer; (*obstacle*) transpor, vencer; **negotiation** [-'eɪʃən] *n* negociação *f*, transação *f*; **negotiator** *n* negociador(a) *m/f*.

**Negress** ['niːgrɪs] *n* negra.

**Negro** ['niːgrəu] *adj*, *n* negro/a.

**neigh** [neɪ] *n* relincho // *vi* relinchar.

**neighbour, neighbor** (*US*) ['neɪbə*] *n* vizinho/a; ~**hood** *n* (*place*) vizinhança, bairro; (*people*) vizinhos *mpl*; ~**ing** *adj* vizinho; ~**ly** *adj* amistoso, prestativo.

**neither** ['naɪðə*] *adj* nem // *conj*: I didn't move and — did he não me movi nem ele // *pron* nenhum (dos dois), nem um nem outro // *adj*: — **good nor bad** nem bom nem mau.

**neo...** [niːəu] *pref* neo-.

**neon** ['niːɒn] *n* neônio, néon *m*; ~ **light** *n* luz *f* de neônio.

**nephew** ['nevjuː] *n* sobrinho.

**nerve** [nɜːv] *n* (*ANAT*) nervo; (*courage*) coragem *f*; (*impudence*) descaramento, atrevimento; ~**racking** *adj* exasperante, enervante; ~**s** *npl* (*fig*: *anxiety*) nervosismo.

**nervous** ['nɜːvəs] *adj* (*anxious*, *ANAT*) nervoso; (*timid*) tímido, acanhado; ~ **breakdown** *n* esgotamento nervoso; ~**ly** *adv* nervosamente, timidamente; ~**ness**

*n* nervosismo; (*timidity*) timidez *f*.

**nest** [nest] *n* (*of bird*) ninho; (*of wasp*) vespeiro // *vi* aninhar-se.

**nestle** ['nesl] *vi*: **to** ~ **up to sb** aconchegar-se a alguém.

**net** [net] *n* (*gen*) rede *f*; (*fig*) armadilha // *adj* (*COMM*) líquido // *vt* pegar ou cobrir com rede; (*SPORT*) atirar na rede; ~**ball** *n* (espécie de) basquetebol *m*.

**Netherlands** ['neðələndz] *npl*: **the** ~ os Países Baixos.

**nett** [net] *adj* = **net**.

**netting** ['netɪŋ] *n* rede *f*, redes *fpl*.

**nettle** ['netl] *n* urtiga.

**network** ['netwɜːk] *n* rede *f*, cadeia.

**neurosis** [njuə'rəusɪs], *pl* **-ses** [-siːz] *n* neurose *f*; **neurotic** [-'rɔtɪk] *adj*, *n* neurótico/a.

**neuter** ['njuːtə*] *adj* (*sexless*) assexuado, castrado; (*LING*) neutro // *vt* castrar, capar.

**neutral** ['njuːtrəl] *adj* neutro // *n* (*AUT*) ponto morto; ~**ity** [-'trælɪtɪ] *n* neutralidade *f*.

**neutron** ['njuːtrɒn] *n* nêutron *m*; ~ **bomb** *n* bomba de nêutrons.

**never** ['nevə*] *adv* nunca; **I** ~ **went** nunca fui; ~ **in my life** nunca na minha vida; ~**-ending** *adj* sem fim, interminável; ~**theless** [nevəðə'les] *adv* todavia, contudo.

**new** [njuː] *adj* (*brand* ~) novo (em folha); (*recent*) recente; (*different*) diferente; (*inexperienced*) inexperiente, principiante; ~ **born** *adj* recém-nascido; ~**comer** ['njuː-kʌmə*] *n* recém-chegado; ~**ly** *adv* recém, novamente; ~ **moon** *n* lua nova; ~**ness** *n* novidade *f*; (*fig*) inexperiência.

**news** [njuːz] *n* notícias *fpl*; **a piece of** ~ uma notícia; **the** ~ (*RADIO*, *TV*) as notícias *fpl*, o noticiário; ~ **agency** *n* agência de notícias; ~**agent**, ~**dealer** (*US*) *n* jornaleiro/a *m/f*; ~**caster** *n* locutor(a) *m/f* de notícias; ~ **flash** *n* notícia de última hora; ~ **letter** *n* boletim *m* informativo; ~**paper** n jornal m; (material) papel m de jornal; ~**reel** n jornal m cinematográfico; ~**stand** n banca de jornais.

**New Year** ['njuː'jɪə*] n ano novo; ~**'s Day** n dia m de ano novo; ~**'s Eve** n véspera de ano novo.

**New York** ['njuː'jɔːk] n Nova Iorque.

**New Zealand** [njuː'ziːlənd] n Nova Zelândia.

**next** [nɛkst] adj (in space) próximo, vizinho; (in time) seguinte, próximo // adj (place) depois; (time) depois, logo; ~ **time** na próxima vez; ~ **year** (n)o ano que vem, (n)o próximo ano; ~ **door** adv na casa do lado // adj vizinho, seguinte; ~**of-kin** n parentes mpl mais próximos; ~ **to** prep junto a, ao lado de.

**N.H.S.** (Brit) n abbr of **National Health Service.**

**nib** [nɪb] n ponta or bico da pena.

**nibble** ['nɪbl] vt mordiscar, beliscar; (ZOOL) roer.

**nice** [naɪs] adj (likeable) simpático; (kind) amável, atencioso; (pleasant) agradável; (attractive) atraente, bonito; (subtle) sutil, fino; ~**-looking** adj bonitão/tona, bem-apessoado; ~**ly** adv agradavelmente, bem.

**niche** [niːʃ] n nicho.

**nick** [nɪk] n (wound) corte m, arranhão m; (cut, indentation) entalhe m, incisão f // vt (col) furtar; **in the** ~ **of time** na hora H, no momento exato (Pt: -ct-).

**nickel** ['nɪkl] n níquel m.

**nickname** ['nɪkneɪm] n apelido, alcunha // vt apelidar de.

**nicotine** ['nɪkətiːn] n nicotina.

**niece** [niːs] n sobrinha.

**Nigeria** [naɪ'dʒɪərɪə] n Nigéria; ~**n** adj, n nigeriano/a.

**niggardly** ['nɪgədlɪ] adj (person) avarento, sovina; (amount) miserável.

**niggling** ['nɪglɪŋ] adj (trifling)

insignificante, mesquinho; (annoying) irritante.

**night** [naɪt] n (gen) noite f; (evening) noitinha, anoitecer m; **last** ~ ontem à noite; **the** ~ **before last** anteontem à noite; **good** ~! boa noite!; **at** or **by** ~ à or de noite; ~**cap** n (drink) bebida tomada antes de dormir; ~ **club** n boate f, cabaré m; ~**dress** n camisola; ~**fall** n cair da noite, anoitecer m; ~**gown** n, ~**ie** ['naɪtɪ] n camisola.

**nightingale** ['naɪtɪŋgeɪl] n rouxinol m.

**nightly** ['naɪtlɪ] adj noturno (Pt: -ct-), de noite // adv todas as noites, cada noite.

**night**: ~**mare** n pesadelo; ~**school** n escola no(c)turna; ~**shift** n turno no(c)turno or da noite; ~**-time** n noite f; ~**watchman** n vigia m, guarda-no(c)turno.

**nil** [nɪl] n nada, zero.

**nimble** ['nɪmbl] adj (agile) ágil, ligeiro; (skilful) hábil, esperto.

**nine** [naɪn] num nove; ~**teen** num dezenove; (Pt) dezanove; ~**ty** num noventa.

**ninth** [naɪnθ] adj nono.

**nip** [nɪp] vt (pinch) beliscar; (bite) morder // n (drink) gole m, trago.

**nipple** ['nɪpl] n (ANAT) bico do seio, mamilo; (of bottle) bocal m, bico; (TECH) bocal (roscado).

**nippy** ['nɪpɪ] adj (person) rápido, ágil; (taste) picante; (cold) frio.

**nitrate** ['naɪtreɪt] n nitrato.

**nitrogen** ['naɪtrədʒən] n nitrogênio.

**no** [nəu] adv não // adj nenhum, não ... algum; **I have** ~ **money** não tenho dinheiro algum // n não m, negativa.

**nobility** [nəu'bɪlɪtɪ] n nobreza.

**noble** ['nəubl] adj (person) nobre; (title) de nobreza; (generous) magnânimo; ~**man** n nobre m, fidalgo.

**nobody** ['nəubədɪ] pron ninguém.

**nod** [nɔd] vi cumprimentar com a

cabeça; (*in agreement*) acenar (que sim) com a cabeça; (*doze*) dormitar, cochilar dando cabeçada // *vt* inclinar (a cabeça) // *n* inclinação *f*; **to ~ off** *vi* cochilar.

**noise** [nɔiz] *n* ruído, barulho; (*din*) algazarra, gritaria; **noisily** *adv* ruidosamente; **noisy** *adj* (*gen*) ruidoso; (*child*) barulhento.

**nomad** [ˈnəuməd] *n* nômade *m/f*; **~ic** [-ˈmædik] *adj* nômade.

**nominal** [ˈnɔminl] *adj* nominal.

**nominate** [ˈnɔmineit] *vt* (*propose*) propor; (*appoint*) nomear; **nomination** [-ˈneiʃən] *n* nomeação *f*; (*proposal*) proposta.

**nominee** [nɔmiˈniː] *n* candidato/a, pessoa nomeada.

**non...** [nɔn] *pref* não-, des..., in..., anti-...; **~alcoholic** *adj* não-alcoólico; **~aligned** *adj* não-alinhado; **~chalant** *adj* des-preocupado; **~committal** [ˈnɔn-kəˈmitl] *adj* (*reserved*) reservado; (*uncommitted*) evasivo; **~conformist** *adj* não-conformista, dissidente; **~descript** [ˈnɔndiskript] *adj* indeterminado; (*pej*) medíocre.

**none** [nʌn] *pron* (*person*) ninguém; (*thing*) nenhum, nada // *adv* de modo algum.

**nonentity** [nɔˈnentiti] *n* nulidade *f*, zero à esquerda *m*; (*person*) João Ninguém.

**nonetheless** [nʌnðəˈles] *adv* no entanto, apesar disso, contudo.

**non:** **~-fiction** *n* literatura de não-ficção; **~plussed** *adj* perplexo, pasmado.

**nonsense** [ˈnɔnsəns] *n* disparate *m*, asneira, ninharia.

**non-stop** [ˈnɔnˈstɔp] *adj* ininterrupto (*RAIL*) direto (*Pt*: -ct-); (*AER*) sem escala // *adv* sem parar.

**noodles** [ˈnuːdlz] *npl* talharim *msg*.

**nook** [nuk] *n* canto, recanto; **~s and crannies** escondeirijos *mpl*.

**noon** [nuːn] *n* meio-dia *m*.

**no-one** [ˈnəuwʌn] *pron* = **nobody**.

**noose** [nuːs] *n* laço corrediço; (*hangman's*) corda da forca.

**nor** [nɔː*] *conj* = **neither** // *adv* see **neither**.

**norm** [nɔːm] *n* norma, regra.

**normal** [ˈnɔːml] *adj* (*usual*) normal; (*ordinary*) comum, regular; **~ly** *adv* normalmente.

**north** [nɔːθ] *n* norte *m* // *adj* do norte, setentrional // *adv* ao ou para o norte; **N~ America** *n* América do Norte; **~east** *n* nordeste *m*; **~ern** [ˈnɔːðən] *adj* do norte, setentrional; **N~ern Ireland** *n* Irlanda do Norte; **N~ Pole** *n* Polo Norte; **N~ Sea** *n* Mar *m* do Norte; **~ward(s)** [ˈnɔːθwəd(z)] *adv* em direção ao norte; **~west** *n* noroeste *m*.

**Norway** [ˈnɔːwei] *n* Noruega; **Norwegian** [-ˈwiːdʒən] *adj*, *n* norueguês/esa.

**nose** [nəuz] *n* (*ANAT*) nariz *m*; (*ZOOL*) focinho; (*sense of smell*) olfato; **to turn up one's ~** at desdenhar // *vt* **to ~ about** bisbilhotar; **~bleed** *n* hemorragia nasal; **~dive** *n* (*deliberate*) vôo picado; (*involuntary*) parafuso; **~y** *adj* intro-metido, abelhudo.

**nostalgia** [nɔsˈtældʒiə] *n* nostalgia, saudades *fpl*; **nostalgic** *adj* nostálgico, saudoso.

**nostril** [ˈnɔstril] *n* narina; **~s** *npl* focinho, fuça.

**nosy** [ˈnəuzi] *adj* = **nosey**.

**not** [nɔt] *adv* não; **~ at all** não ... de modo nenhum; **~ that he knows** não é que ele o saiba; **~ yet** ainda não; **~ now** agora não; **why ~?** porque não?

**notable** [ˈnəutəbl] *adj* notável.

**notary** [ˈnəutəri] *n* tabelião *m*.

**notch** [nɔtʃ] *n* entalhe *m*, corte *m*.

**note** [nəut] *n* (*MUS*, *bank*~) nota; (*letter*) nota, bilhete *m*; (*record*) nota, anotação *f*; (*fame*) fama, reputação *f*; (*tone*) tom *m* // *vt* (*observe*) observar, reparar em; (*write down*) anotar, tomar nota de;

~**book** n caderno (de notas), agenda; ~**case** n carteira; ~**d** ['nəutɪd] adj célebre, conhecido; ~**paper** n papel m de carta.

**nothing** ['nʌθɪŋ] n nada; (zero) zero; **for** ~ (free) grátis; (in vain) em vão, por nada.

**notice** ['nəutɪs] n (announcement) notícia, anúncio; (attention) atenção f, interesse m; (warning) aviso; (dismissal) destituição f; (resignation) demissão f; (period of time) prazo // vt (observe) observar, notar; **to take** ~ of prestar atenção a, fazer caso de; **at short** ~ a curto prazo, com pouca antecipação; **until further** ~ até nova ordem; ~**able** adj evidente, óbvio; ~**board** n (Brit) quadro de avisos.

**notification** [nəutɪfɪ'keɪʃən] n aviso, notificação f; **notify** ['nəutɪfaɪ] vt avisar, notificar.

**notion** ['nəuʃən] n noção f, idéia; (opinion) opinião f; ~**s** npl (US) miudezas fpl.

**notorious** [nəu'tɔːrɪəs] adj célebre, notório.

**notwithstanding** [nɔtwɪθ'stændɪŋ] adv no entanto, não obstante; ~ **this** apesar disto.

**nougat** ['nuːgɑː] n nogado, nugá m.

**nought** [nɔːt] n zero, nada m.

**noun** [naun] n substantivo, nome m.

**nourish** ['nʌrɪʃ] vt nutrir, alimentar; (fig) fomentar, alentar; ~**ing** adj nutritivo, alimentício; ~**ment** n alimento, nutrimento.

**novel** ['nɔvl] n romance m; (short) novela // adj (new) novo, recente; (unexpected) insólito; ~**ist** n romancista m/f, novelista m/f; ~**ty** n novidade f.

**November** [nəu'vɛmbə*] n novembro.

**novice** ['nɔvɪs] n principiante m/f, novato/a; (REL) noviço/a.

**now** [nau] adv (at the present time) agora; (these days) atualmente (Pt:

act-), hoje em dia; **right** ~ agora mesmo; ~ **and then**, ~ **and again** de vez em quando; **from** ~ **on** de agora em diante; ~**adays** ['nauədeɪz] adv a(c)tualmente, hoje em dia.

**nowhere** ['nəuwɛə*] adv (direction) a lugar nenhum; (location) em parte alguma.

**nozzle** ['nɔzl] n (gen) bico, bocal m; (TECH) tubeira; (: hose) agulheta.

**nuance** ['njuːɑːns] n nuança, matiz m.

**nuclear** ['njuːklɪə*] adj nuclear.

**nucleus** ['njuːklɪəs], pl -**lei** [-lɪaɪ] n núcleo.

**nude** [njuːd] adj, n nu/nua; **in the** ~ nu, despido.

**nudge** [nʌdʒ] vt acotovelar.

**nudist** ['njuːdɪst] n nudista m/f.

**nudity** ['njuːdɪtɪ] n nudez f.

**nuisance** ['njuːsns] n amolação f, aborrecimento; (person) chato; **what a** ~! que amolação!; (Pt) que chatice!

**null** [nʌl] adj: ~ **and void** írrito e nulo; ~**ify** ['nʌlɪfaɪ] vt anular, invalidar.

**numb** [nʌm] adj dormente, entorpecido; (fig) insensível // vt adormecer, entorpecer.

**number** ['nʌmbə*] n número; (numeral) algarismo // vt (pages etc) numerar; (amount to) atribuir um número a; **to be** ~**ed among** achar-se entre; **a** ~ **of** vários, muitos; **they were ten in** ~ eram em número de dez; ~ **plate** n placa (do carro).

**numbness** ['nʌmnɪs] n torpor m, dormência; (fig) insensibilidade f.

**numeral** ['njuːmərəl] n numeral m, algarismo.

**numerical** [njuː'mɛrɪkl] adj numérico.

**numerous** ['njuːmərəs] adj numeroso.

**nun** [nʌn] n freira, monja.

**nurse** [nəːs] n enfermeiro/a;

*(nanny)* ama-seca, babá *f //* *vt (patient)* cuidar, tratar; *(baby)* criar, amamentar; *(fig)* alimentar; **wet ~** ama de leite.

**nursery** [ˈnəːsəri] *n (institution)* creche *f; (room)* quarto das crianças; *(for plants)* viveiro; **~ rhyme** *n* poesia infantil; **~ school** *n* (escola) maternal; **~ slope** *n (SKI)* rampa para principiantes.

**nursing** [ˈnəːsiŋ] *n (profession)* enfermagem *f; (care)* cuidado, assistência; **~ home** *n* sanatório, clínica de repouso.

**nut** [nʌt] *n (TECH)* porca; *(BOT)* noz *f;* **~s** *adj (col)* maluco, biruta; **~case** *n (col)* doido, biruta *m/f;* **~crackers** *npl* quebra-nozes *m inv;* **~meg** [ˈnʌtmeg] *n* noz-moscada.

**nutrient** [ˈnjuːtriənt] *n* nutrimento.

**nutrition** [njuˈtriʃən] *n* nutrição *f,* alimentação *f;* **nutritious** [-ʃəs] *adj* nutritivo.

**nutshell** [ˈnʌtʃel] *n* casca de noz; **in a ~** em poucas palavras.

**nylon** [ˈnailɔn] *n* nylon *m //* adj de nylon; **~s** *npl* meias *fpl* (de nylon).

**nymph** [nimf] *n* ninfa.

# O

**oaf** [əuf] *n* imbecil *m/f.*

**oak** [əuk] *n* carvalho *//* adj de carvalho.

**O.A.P.** *abbr of* **old-age pensioner.**

**oar** [ɔː*] *n* remo; **oarsman** *n* remador *m.*

**oasis** [əuˈeisis] *, pl* **~ses** [-siːz] *n* oásis *m.*

**oath** [əuθ] *n* juramento; *(swear word)* palavrão *f; (curse)* praga; **on ~** sob juramento; **to take an ~** prestar juramento.

**oatmeal** [ˈəutmiːl] *n* farinha *or* mingau *m* de aveia.

**oats** [əuts] *n* aveia *sg.*

**obedience** [əˈbiːdiəns] *n* obediência; **in ~ to** em conformidade *f com;* **obedient** [-ənt] *adj* obediente.

**obesity** [əuˈbiːsiti] *n* obesidade *f.*

**obey** [əˈbei] *vt* obedecer; *(instructions, regulations)* cumprir.

**obituary** [əˈbitjuəri] *n* necrológio.

**object** [ˈɔbdʒikt] *n (gen, LING)* objeto (*Pt:* -ct-); *(purpose)* obje(c)tivo *// vi* [əbˈdʒekt]: **to ~ to** *(attitude)* desaprovar, objetar a; *(proposal)* opor-se a; **I ~!** protesto!; **~ion** [əbˈdʒekʃən] *n* objeção (*Pt:* -çç-) *f,* **I have no ~ion to...** não tenho nada contra...; **~ionable** [əbˈdʒekʃənəbl] *adj (gen)* desagradável; *(conduct)* censurável; **~ive** *adj,* *n* obje(c)tivo; **~ivity** [ɔbdʒikˈtiviti] *n* obje(c)tividade *f;* **~or** *n* o opositor(a) *m/f.*

**obligation** [ɔbliˈgeiʃən] *n* obrigação *f; (debt)* dever *m;* **without ~** sem compromisso.

**obligatory** [əˈbligətəri] *adj* obrigatório.

**oblige** [əˈblaidʒ] *vt (force):* **to ~ sb to do sth** obrigar *or* forçar alguém a fazer algo; *(do a favour for)* obsequiar, fazer um favor a; **I should be ~d if...** agradeceria muito se...; **obliging** *adj* amável, prestativo.

**oblique** [əˈbliːk] *adj* oblíquo; *(allusion)* indireto *(Pt:* -ct-).

**obliterate** [əˈblitəreit] *vt (erase)* apagar; *(destroy)* destruir.

**oblivion** [əˈbliviən] *n* esquecimento; **oblivious** [-iəs] *adj:* **oblivious of** inconsciente de, esquecido de.

**oblong** [ˈɔblɔŋ] *adj* oblongo, retangular *(Pt:* -ct-) *//* *n* re(c)tângulo.

**obnoxious** [əbˈnɔkʃəs] *adj* odioso, detestável; *(smell)* enjoativo.

**oboe** [ˈəubəu] *n* oboé *m.*

**obscene** [əbˈsiːn] *adj* obsceno; **obscenity** [-ˈseniti] *n* obscenidade *f.*

**obscure** [əbˈskjuə*] *adj* obscuro,

pouco claro // vt escurecer; (hide: sun) esconder; **obscurity** n obscuridade f, escuridão f.

**obsequious** [ɔb'siːkwɪəs] adj obsequioso, servil.

**observance** [əb'zəːvns] n observância, cumprimento; (ritual) prática, hábito.

**observant** [əb'zəːvnt] adj observador(a).

**observation** [ɔbzə'veɪʃən] n observação f; (by police etc) vigilância; (MED) exame m.

**observatory** [əb'zəːvətri] n observatório.

**observe** [əb'zəːv] vt (gen) observar; (rule) cumprir; **observer** n observador(a) m/f.

**obsess** [əb'sɛs] vt obsedar, obcecar; ~**ion** [əb'sɛʃən] n obsessão f, idéia fixa; ~**ive** adj obsessivo.

**obsolescence** [ɔbsə'lɛsns] n obsolescência; **obsolete** ['ɔbsəliːt] adj obsoleto; **to become** ~ cair em desuso.

**obstacle** ['ɔbstəkl] n obstáculo; (nuisance) estorvo, impedimento; ~ **race** n corrida de obstáculos.

**obstetrician** [ɔbstə'trɪʃən] n obstetra m/f; **obstetrics** [-'stɛtrɪks] n obstetrícia sg.

**obstinate** ['ɔbstɪnɪt] adj teimoso, obstinado; (determined) pertinaz.

**obstruct** [əb'strʌkt] vt obstruir; (block) entupir; (hinder) estorvar; ~**ion** [əb'strʌkʃən] n obstrução f; (hindrance) estorvo, obstáculo.

**obtain** [əb'teɪn] vt (get) obter; (achieve) conseguir; ~**able** adj alcançável.

**obtrusive** [əb'truːsɪv] adj (person) intrometido, intruso; (building etc) que dá muito na vista.

**obvious** ['ɔbvɪəs] adj (clear) óbvio, evidente; (unsubtle) nada sutil; ~**ly** adv evidentemente.

**occasion** [ə'keɪʒən] n (gen) ocasião f; (chance) oportunidade f, ensejo; (reason) motivo; (time) momento,

vez f; (event) acontecimento // vt ocasionar, causar; ~**ally** adv de vez em quando.

**occult** [ɔ'kʌlt] adj (gen) oculto.

**occupant** ['ɔkjupənt] n (of house) inquilino/a; (of car) ocupante m/f.

**occupation** [ɔkju'peɪʃən] n (of house) posse f; (job) emprego; (: calling) ofício; **unfit for** ~ (house) inabitável; ~**al hazard** n risco profissional.

**occupier** ['ɔkjupaɪə*] n inquilino/a.

**occupy** ['ɔkjupaɪ] vt (gen) ocupar; (house) morar em; (time) encher, tomar; (attention) entreter; **to o.s. with** or **by doing** (as job) dedicar-se a fazer; (to pass time) preencher o tempo fazendo.

**occur** [ə'kəː*] vi ocorrer, acontecer; **to** ~ **to** vir à mente; **it** ~**s to me that...** ocorre-me que...; ~**rence** n (event) acontecimento; (existence) existência.

**ocean** ['əuʃən] n oceano; ~**-going** adj de longo curso; ~ **liner** n transatlântico.

**o'clock** [ə'klɔk] adv: **it is 5** ~ são cinco horas.

**octagonal** [ɔk'tægənl] adj octogonal.

**octane** ['ɔktein] n octano.

**octave** ['ɔktɪv] n oitava f.

**October** [ɔk'təubə*] n outubro m.

**octopus** ['ɔktəpəs] n polvo.

**odd** [ɔd] adj (strange) estranho, esquisito; (number) ímpar; (left over) avulso, de sobra; **60-**~ 60 e tantos; **at** ~ **times** às vezes, quando calha; **to be the** ~ **one out** ficar sobrando, servir de vela; ~**ity** n coisa estranha, esquisitice f; (person) excêntrico; ~**job man** n faz-tudo m; ~ **jobs** npl biscates mpl, bicos; ~**ly** adv curiosamente; ~**ments** npl (COMM) retalhos mpl; ~**s** npl (in betting) pontos mpl de vantagem; **it makes no** ~**s** dá no mesmo; **at** ~**s** brigados/as, de mal.

**ode** [əud] n ode f.

**odious** [ˈəudɪəs] adj odioso.

**odometer** [əuˈdɔmɪtə*] n (US) conta-quilômetros m m.

**odour, odor** (US) [ˈəudə*] n odor m; (perfume) fragrância, perfume m; ~**less** adj inodoro.

**of** [ɔv, əv] prep de; **a friend ~ ours** um amigo nosso; **3 ~ them** 3 deles; **the 5th ~ July** o 5 de julho; **a boy ~ 10** um menino de 10 anos; **made ~ wood** feito de madeira.

**off** [ɔf] adj, adv (engine) desligado; (light) apagado; (tap) fechado; (food: bad) passado; (milk) talhado; (cancelled) anulado // prep de; **to be ~ (to leave)** ir(-se) embora; **to be 5 km ~** estar a 5 km de distância; **a day ~** um dia de folga or livre; **today I had an ~ day** hoje não foi o meu dia; **he had his coat ~** ele havia tirado o casaco; **10% ~** (COMM) 10% de abatimento or desconto; **5 km ~ (the road)** a 5 km (da estrada); **~ the coast** em frente à costa; **on the ~ chance** por acaso.

**offal** [ˈɔfl] n (CULIN) sobras fpl, restos mpl.

**off-colour** [ˈɔfˈkʌlə*] adj (ill) indisposto.

**offence, offense** (US) [əˈfɛns] n (crime) delito; (insult) insulto, ofensa; **to take ~** at ofender-se com, melindrar-se com.

**offend** [əˈfɛnd] vt (person) ofender; ~**er** n delinquente m/f; (against regulations) infrator(a) (Pt: -ct-).

**offensive** [əˈfɛnsɪv] adj ofensivo, chocante; (smell etc) repugnante // n (MIL) ofensiva.

**offer** [ˈɔfə*] n (gen) oferta; (proposal) proposta // vt oferecer; (opportunity) proporcionar; **'on ~'** (COMM) 'em oferta'; ~**ing** n oferenda; ~**tory** n (REL) ofertório.

**offhand** [ɔfˈhænd] adj informal // adv de improviso.

**office** [ˈɔfɪs] n (place) escritório; (room) gabinete m; (position) cargo, função f; **to take ~** tomar posse; ~

**block** n conjunto de escritórios; ~ **boy** n mensageiro, contínuo; ~ **officer** n (MIL etc) oficial m; (of organization) diretor (Pt: -ct-) m; (also: **police officer**) agente m/f policial or de polícia; ~ **worker** n empregado/a or funcionário/a de escritório.

**official** [əˈfɪʃl] adj (authorized) autorizado, oficial // n funcionário/a (público/a); ~**dom** n burocracia.

**officious** [əˈfɪʃəs] adj intrometido.

**offing** [ˈɔfɪŋ] n: **in the ~** (fig) em perspectiva.

**off:** ~**-licence** n (Brit: shop) loja de bebidas alcoólicas; ~**-peak** adj de temporada de pouco consumo or pouca atividade (Pt: act-); ~**-putting** adj desconcertante; ~**-season** adj, adv fora de estação or temporada.

**offset** [ˈɔfsɛt] (irr: like set) vt (counteract) compensar, contrabalançar // n (also: ~ **printing**) ofsete m.

**offshore** [ˈɔfʃɔ:*] adv a pouca distância da costa.

**offside** [ˈɔfˈsaɪd] adj (SPORT) impedido.

**offspring** [ˈɔfsprɪŋ] n descendência, prole f.

**off:** ~**stage** adv nos bastidores; ~**-the-peg** adv pronto; ~**-white** adj quase branco.

**often** [ˈɔfn] adv muitas vezes, frequentemente.

**ogle** [ˈəugl] vt comer com os olhos.

**oil** [ɔɪl] n óleo; (petroleum) petróleo; (CULIN) azeite m // vt (machine) lubrificar; ~**can** n almotolia; ~**field** n campo petrolífero; ~**-fired** adj que usa óleo combustível; ~ **painting** n pintura a óleo; ~ **refinery** n refinaria de petróleo; ~ **rig** n torre f de perfuração; ~**skins** npl capa sg de oleado; ~ **tanker** n petroleiro; ~ **well** n poço petrolífero; ~**y** adj oleoso; (food) gorduroso.

**ointment** ['ɔɪntmənt] n ungüento.

**O.K., okay** ['əu'keɪ] excl O.K., tudo bem!, está legal!; (Pt) está bem, óptimo // adj certo, correto (Pt: -ct-) // vt aprovar.

**old** [əuld] adj velho; (former) antigo, anterior; **how ~ are you?** quantos anos você tem?; **he's 10 years ~** ele tem 10 anos; **~er brother** irmão m mais velho; **~ age** n velhice f; **~age pensioner (O.A.P.)** n aposentado/a; (Pt) reformado/a; **~fashioned** adj antiquado, fora de moda.

**olive** ['ɔlɪv] n (fruit) azeitona; (tree) oliveira // adj (also: **~green**) verde-oliva; **~ oil** n azeite m de oliva.

**Olympic** [əu'lɪmpɪk] adj olímpico; **the ~ Games, the ~s** os Jogos Olímpicos, as Olimpíadas.

**omelet(te)** ['ɔmlɪt] n omelete f.

**omen** ['əumən] n presságio, agouro.

**ominous** ['ɔmɪnəs] adj ameaçador(a), de mau agouro.

**omission** [əu'mɪʃən] n omissão f; (error) descuido, negligência.

**omit** [əu'mɪt] vt omitir; (by mistake) esquecer.

**on** [ɔn] prep sobre, em (cima de) // adv (machine) em funcionamento; (light) aceso; (radio) ligado; (tap) aberto; **is the meeting still ~?** ainda vai haver reunião?; **when is this film ~?** quando vão passar este filme?; **~ the wall** (pendurado) na parede; **~ television** na televisão; **~ horseback** a cavalo; **~ seeing this** ao ver isto; **~ arrival** ao chegar; **~ the left** à esquerda; **~ Friday** na sexta-feira; **a week ~ Friday** daqui a uma semana a partir de sexta-feira; **to have one's coat ~** estar vestido de um casaco; **to go ~** continuar (em frente); **it's not ~!** isso não se faz!

**once** [wʌns] adv uma vez; (formerly) outrora // conj uma vez que; **at ~** imediatamente; (simultaneously) ao mesmo tempo; **~ a week** uma vez por semana; **~ more** mais uma vez; **~ and for all** definitivamente; **~ upon a time** era uma vez.

**oncoming** ['ɔnkʌmɪŋ] adj (traffic) que vem de frente.

**one** [wʌn] det, num um/uma // pron um/uma; (impersonal) a gente; (+ verb : impersonal) se // adj (sole) único; (same) mesmo; **this ~** este/esta; **that ~** esse/essa, aquele/aquela; **~ by ~** um por um; **~ never knows** nunca se sabe; **~ another** um ao outro; **~ day excursion** n (US) bilhete m de ida e volta; **~man** adj (business) individual; **~man band** n um homem-orquestra; **~self** pron se; (mesmo/a); **~way** adj (street) (mesmo/a); **~way'** 'mão única'.

**ongoing** ['ɔngəuɪŋ] adj contínuo, em andamento.

**onion** ['ʌnjən] n cebola.

**onlooker** ['ɔnlukə*] n espectador(a) m/f.

**only** ['əunlɪ] adv somente, apenas // adj único, só // conj só que, porém; **an ~ child** um filho único; **not ~ ... but also...** não só ... mas também...

**onset** ['ɔnset] n (beginning) começo; (attack) ataque m.

**onslaught** ['ɔnslɔːt] n ataque m violento, arremetida.

**onto** ['ɔntu] prep = **on to**.

**onus** ['əunəs] n responsabilidade f.

**onward(s)** ['ɔnwəd(z)] adv (move) para diante, para a frente; **from this time ~** de (ag)ora em diante.

**onyx** ['ɔnɪks] n ônix m.

**ooze** [uːz] vi ressumar, filtrar-se.

**opal** ['əupl] n opala.

**opaque** [əu'peɪk] adj opaco, fosco.

**open** ['əupn] adj (gen) aberto; (road) livre; (meeting) público; (admiration) declarado // vt abrir // vi (flower, eyes, door, debate) abrir-se; (book etc: commence) começar; **to ~ on to** vt fus (subj: room, door) dar para, ter vista para; **to ~ up** vt abrir; (blocked road) desobstruir // vi abrir-se, começar; in the ~ (air) ao ar livre; ~ing n abertura; (start) início; (opportunity) oportunidade f; (job) vaga; ~ly adv abertamente; ~-minded adj aberto, imparcial; ~-necked adj aberto no colo.

opera ['ɔpərə] n ópera; ~ glasses npl binóculo sg de teatro; ~ house n teatro lírico or de ópera.

operate ['ɔpəreit] vt (machine) fazer funcionar, pôr em funcionamento; (company) dirigir // vi funcionar; (drug) fazer efeito; to ~ on sb (MED) operar alguém.

operatic [ɔpə'rætik] adj lírico, operístico.

operating ['ɔpəreitiŋ]: ~ table n mesa de operações; ~ theatre n sala de operações.

operation [ɔpə'reiʃən] n (gen) operação f; (of machine) funcionamento; to be in ~ estar em vigor or funcionando; ~al adj operacional.

operative ['ɔpərətiv] adj (measure) em vigor.

operator ['ɔpəreitə*] n (of machine) operador(a) m/f, manipulador(a) m/f; (TEL) telefonista m/f.

operetta [ɔpə'rɛtə] n opereta.

ophthalmic [ɔf'θælmik] adj oftálmico.

opinion [ə'piniən] n (gen) opinião f; (point of view) parecer m, juízo; in my ~ a meu ver; ~ated adj teimoso, opinioso; ~ poll n pesquisa.

opium ['əupiəm] n ópio.

opponent [ə'pəunənt] n adversário/a, oponente m/f.

opportune ['ɔpətjuːn] adj oportuno; opportunist [-'tjuːnist] n oportunista m/f.

opportunity [ɔpə'tjuːniti] n oportunidade f.

oppose [ə'pəuz] vt opor-se a; to be ~d to sth opor-se a algo, estar

contra algo; opposing adj (side) oposto, contrário.

opposite ['ɔpəzit] adj oposto; (house etc) de em frente // adv (lá) em frente // prep em frente de, defronte de // n o oposto, o contrário.

opposition [ɔpə'ziʃən] n oposição f.

oppress [ə'prɛs] vt oprimir; ~ion [ə'prɛʃən] n opressão f; ~ive adj opressivo.

opt [ɔpt] vi: to ~ for escolher; to ~ to do optar por fazer; to ~ out of doing sth optar por não fazer algo.

optical ['ɔptikl] adj ótico (Pt: -pt-).

optician [ɔp'tiʃən] n oculista m/f.

optimism ['ɔptimizəm] n otimismo (Pt: -pt-).

optimist ['ɔptimist] n o(p)timista m/f; ~ic [-'mistik] adj o(p)timista.

optimum ['ɔptiməm] adj ó(p)timo.

option ['ɔpʃən] n opção f; to keep one's ~s open (fig) manter as opções em aberto; ~al adj opcional, facultativo.

opulent ['ɔpjulənt] adj opulento.

or [ɔː*] conj ou; (with negative): he hasn't seen ~ heard anything ele não viu nem ouviu nada; ~ else senão.

oracle ['ɔrəkl] n oráculo.

oral ['ɔːrəl] adj oral // n exame m oral.

orange ['ɔrindʒ] n (fruit) laranja // adj cor de laranja, alaranjado.

oration [ɔː'reiʃən] n oração f; orator ['ɔrətə*] n orador(a) m/f.

orbit ['ɔːbit] n órbita // vt/i orbitar.

orchard ['ɔːtʃəd] n pomar m.

orchestra ['ɔːkistrə] n orquestra; orchestral [ɔː'kɛstrəl] adj orquestral.

orchid ['ɔːkid] n orquídea.

ordain [ɔː'dein] vt (REL) ordenar, decretar; (decide) decidir, mandar.

ordeal [ɔː'diːl] n experiência penosa, provação f.

order ['ɔːdə*] n (gen) ordem f; (type, kind) tipo; (state) estado; (COMM) pedido, encomenda // vt (*also*: **put in ~**) pôr em ordem, arrumar; (*COMM*) encomendar, pedir; (*command*) mandar, ordenar; **in ~** (*of document*) em ordem; **in ~ to do** a fim de fazer; **to ~ sb to do sth** mandar alguém fazer algo; **~ly** *n* (*MIL*) ordenança *m*; (*MED*) servente *m/f* // *adj* (*room*) arrumado, ordenado; (*person*) metódico.

**ordinary** ['ɔːdnrɪ] *adj* comum, usual; (*pej*) ordinário, medíocre; **out of the ~** fora do comum.

**ordnance** ['ɔːdnəns] *n* (*MIL*: *unit*) artilharia; **O~ Survey** (*Brit*) *n* serviço oficial de topografia e cartografia.

**ore** [ɔː*] *n* minério.

**organ** ['ɔːgən] *n* (*gen*) órgão *m*; **~ic** [ɔː'gænɪk] *adj* orgânico.

**organism** ['ɔːgənɪzəm] *n* organismo.

**organist** ['ɔːgənɪst] *n* organista *m/f*.

**organization** [ɔːgənaɪ'zeɪʃən] *n* organização *f*; **organize** ['ɔːgənaɪz] *vt* organizar; **organizer** ['ɔːgənaɪzə*] *n* organizador(a) *m/f*.

**orgasm** ['ɔːgæzəm] *n* orgasmo.

**orgy** ['ɔːdʒɪ] *n* orgia.

**Orient** ['ɔːrɪənt] *n* Oriente *m*; **oriental** ['ɛntl] *adj* oriental.

**orientate** ['ɔːrɪənteɪt] *vt* orientar.

**origin** ['ɔrɪdʒɪn] *n* origem *f*; (*point of departure*) procedência.

**original** [ə'rɪdʒɪnl] *adj* original; (*first*) primeiro; (*earlier*) primitivo // *n* original *m*; **~ity** [-'nælɪtɪ] *n* originalidade *f*; **~ly** *adv* (*at first*) originalmente; (*with originality*) com originalidade.

**originate** [ə'rɪdʒɪneɪt] *vi*: **to ~ from** *or* **in** originar-se de, surgir de.

**ornament** ['ɔːnəmənt] *n* ornamento; (*trinket*) quinquilharia; **~al** [-'mɛntl] *adj* decorativo, ornamental.

**ornate** [ɔː'neɪt] *adj* paramentado, vistoso.

**ornithologist** [ɔːnɪ'θɔlədʒɪst] *n*

**ornitólogo**; **ornithology** [-dʒɪ] *n* ornitologia.

**orphan** ['ɔːfn] *n* órfão/órfã // *vt*: **to be ~ed** ficar órfão; **~age** *n* orfanato.

**orthodox** ['ɔːθədɔks] *adj* ortodoxo; **~y** *n* ortodoxia.

**orthopaedic, orthopedic** (*US*) [ɔːθə'piːdɪk] *adj* ortopédico; **~s** *n* ortopedia *sg*.

**oscillate** ['ɔsɪleɪt] *vi* oscilar; (*person*) vacilar, hesitar.

**ostensibly** [ɔs'tɛnsɪblɪ] *adv* aparentemente.

**ostentatious** [ɔstɛn'teɪʃəs] *adj* aparatoso, pomposo; (*person*) ostentoso.

**osteopath** ['ɔstɪəpæθ] *n* osteopata *m/f*.

**ostracize** ['ɔstrəsaɪz] *vt* condenar ao ostracismo.

**ostrich** ['ɔstrɪtʃ] *n* avestruz *m/f*.

**other** ['ʌðə*] *adj* outro; **~ than** (*in another way*) de outro modo que; (*apart from*) senão; **~wise** *adv*, *conj* de outra maneira; (*if not*) senão.

**otter** ['ɔtə*] *n* lontra.

**ought** [ɔːt] *pt* **ought** *auxiliary vb*: **I ~ to do it** eu deveria fazê-lo; **this ~ to have been corrected** isto deveria ter sido corrigido; **he ~ to win** (*probability*) ele deve ganhar.

**ounce** [auns] *n* onça (*28.35g*).

**our** ['auə*] *adj* nosso; **~s** *pron* (o) nosso(/a) nossa etc; **~selves** *pron pl* (*reflexive, after prep*) nós; (*emphatic*) nós mesmos/as.

**oust** [aust] *vt* desalojar, expulsar.

**out** [aut] *adv* fora; (*not at home*) fora (de casa); (*light, fire*) apagado; **~ there** lá, lá fora; **he's ~** (*absent*) não está, está fora; **get ~!** fora!; **to be ~ in one's calculations** enganar-se nos cálculos; **to run ~** sair correndo; **~ loud** em voz alta; **~ of** (*outside*) fora de; (*because of*: *anger etc*) por; **~ of petrol** sem gasolina; **"~ of order"** "não funciona", "avariado"; **~-of-the-way** (*fig*) fora do comum; (place) remoto.

**outback** ['autbæk] n interior m.

**outboard** ['autbɔ:d] adj: ~ **motor** motor m de popa.

**outbreak** ['autbreɪk] n (of war) deflagração f; (of disease) surto epidêmico; (of violence etc) eclosão f, estopim m.

**outburst** ['autbɜ:st] n explosão f.

**outcast** ['autkɑ:st] n pária m/f.

**outcome** ['autkʌm] n resultado m.

**outcry** ['autkraɪ] n manifestação f de protesto, gritaria.

**outdated** [aut'deɪtɪd] adj antiquado, fora da moda.

**outdo** [aut'du:] (irr: like **do**) vt ultrapassar, exceder.

**outdoor** [aut'dɔ:*] adj, ~**s** adv ao ar livre.

**outer** ['autə*] adj exterior, externo; ~ **space** n o espaço (exterior).

**outfit** ['autfɪt] n equipamento; (clothes) roupa, traje m; ~**ter's** n fornecedor m de roupas.

**outgoing** ['autgəuɪŋ] adj (character) extrovertido; sociável; ~**s** npl despesas fpl.

**outgrow** [aut'grəu] (irr: like **grow**) vt: he has ~n his clothes a roupa ficou pequena para ele.

**outing** ['autɪŋ] n excursão f; passeio.

**outlandish** [aut'lændɪʃ] adj estrambótico, exótico.

**outlast** [aut'lɑ:st] vt sobreviver a.

**outlaw** ['autlɔ:] n foragido, proscrito // vt (person) declarar fora da lei; (practice) declarar ilegal.

**outlay** ['autleɪ] n despesa.

**outlet** ['autlet] n saída; (of pipe) desagüe m, escoadouro; (for emotion) desabafo; (US: ELEC) tomada; (also: retail ~) posto de venda.

**outline** ['autlaɪn] n (shape) contorno, perfil m; (of plan) traçado; (sketch) esboço, linhas fpl gerais.

**outlive** [aut'lɪv] vt sobreviver a.

**outlook** ['autluk] n perspectiva;

(opinion) ponto de vista.

**outlying** ['autlaɪɪŋ] adj afastado, remoto.

**outmoded** [aut'məudɪd] adj antiquado, fora de moda, obsoleto.

**outnumber** [aut'nʌmbə*] vt exceder em número.

**outpatient** ['autpeɪʃənt] n paciente m/f externo/a or de ambulatório.

**outpost** ['autpəust] n posto avançado.

**output** ['autput] n (volume m de) produção f, (TEC) rendimento.

**outrage** ['autreɪdʒ] n (scandal) escândalo; (atrocity) atrocidade f // vt ultrajar; ~**ous** [-'reɪdʒəs] adj ultrajante, escandaloso.

**outright** [aut'raɪt] adv completamente // adj ['autraɪt] completo.

**outset** ['autset] n início, princípio.

**outside** [aut'saɪd] n exterior m; (surface) superfície f; (aspect) aspecto (exterior) // adj exterior, externo // adv (lá) fora // prep fora de; (beyond) além (dos limites) de; **at the** ~ (fig) no máximo; ~ **lane** n (AUT: Brit) pista da direita; ~-**left** n (FOOTBALL) ponta esquerda; (player) ponta m esquerda; **outsider** n (stranger) estranho, forasteiro.

**outsize** ['autsaɪz] adj (clothes) de tamanho extra-grande.

**outskirts** ['autskɜ:ts] npl arredores mpl, subúrbios mpl.

**outspoken** [aut'spəukən] adj franco, sem rodeios.

**outstanding** [aut'stændɪŋ] adj excepcional, saliente; (unfinished) pendente.

**outstay** [aut'steɪ] vt: **to** ~ **one's welcome** abusar da hospitalidade (demorando mais tempo).

**outstretched** [aut'stretʃt] adj (hand) estendido, esticado.

**outward** ['autwəd] adj (sign, appearances) externo; (journey) de ida; ~**ly** adv aparentemente, para fora.

**outweigh** [aut'weɪ] *vt* pesar mais que.

**outwit** [aut'wɪt] *vt* superar, ser mais esperto que.

**oval** ['əuvl] *adj* ovalado // *n* oval *m*.

**ovary** ['əuvərɪ] *n* ovário.

**ovation** [əu'veɪʃən] *n* ovação *f*.

**oven** ['ʌvn] *n* forno; ~**proof** *adj* refratário (*Pt*: -ct-).

**over** ['əuvə*] *adj* (*or adv*) (*finished*) acabado // *prep* por cima de; (*above*) sobre; (*on the other side of*) do outro lado de; (*more than*) mais de; (*during*) durante; ~ **here** por aqui, cá; ~ **there** por ali, lá; **all** ~ (*everywhere*) por todos os lados; (*finished*) acabado; ~ **and** ~ (*again*) repetidamente; ~ **and above** além de; **to ask sb** ~ convidar alguém; **to bend** ~ inclinar-se (sobre).

**over...** ['əuvə*] *pref* sobre..., super...; ~**abundant** *adj* superabundante.

**overall** ['əuvərɔːl] *adj* (*length*) total; (*study*) global // *adv* ['əuvər'ɔːl] globalmente; ~**s** *npl* macacão *msg or* guarda-pó *msg*.

**overbalance** [əuvə'bæləns] *vi* perder o equilíbrio, desequilibrar-se.

**overbearing** [əuvə'bɛərɪŋ] *adj* autoritário, dominador(a); (*arrogant*) arrogante.

**overboard** [əuvə'bɔːd] *adv* (*NAUT*) ar mar; **man** ~**!** homem ao mar!

**overcast** ['əuvəka:st] *adj* nublado.

**overcharge** [əuvə'tʃɑːdʒ] *vt*: **to** ~ **sb** cobrar alguém em excesso.

**overcoat** ['əuvəkəut] *n* sobretudo, casaco.

**overcome** [əuvə'kʌm] (*irr*: *like* **come**) *vt* (*gen*) vencer, dominar; (*difficulty*) superar.

**overcrowded** [əuvə'kraudɪd] *adj* superlotado, apinhado de gente; (*country*) superpovoado.

**overdo** [əuvə'duː] *vt* (*irr*: *like* **do**) *vt* exagerar, exceder; (*overcook*) cozinhar demais.

**overdose** ['əuvədəus] *n* dose *f* excessiva.

**overdraft** ['əuvədra:ft] *n* saldo negativo.

**overdrawn** [əuvə'drɔːn] *adj* (*account*) sem fundos, a descoberto.

**overdue** [əuvə'djuː] *adj* atrasado; (*COMM*) vencido; (*recognition*) tardio.

**overestimate** [əuvər'ɛstɪmeɪt] *vt* sobrestimar.

**overexcited** [əuvərɪk'saɪtɪd] *adj* superexcitado.

**overexpose** [əuvərɪk'spəuz] *vt* (*PHOT*) expor demasiado (à luz).

**overflow** [əuvə'fləu] *vi* transbordar // *n* ['əuvəfləu] (*excess*) excesso; (*of river*) inundação *f*; (*also*: ~ **pipe**) tubo de descarga, ladrão *m*.

**overgrown** [əuvə'grəun] *adj* (*garden*) coberto de vegetação.

**overhaul** [əuvə'hɔːl] *vt* examinar, revisar // *n* ['əuvəhɔːl] revisão *f*.

**overhead** [əuvə'hed] *adv* por cima, em cima // *adj* ['əuvəhed] aéreo, elevado; (*railway*) suspenso // *n* ~ (*US*), ~**s** *npl* despesas *fpl* gerais.

**overhear** [əuvə'hɪə*] (*irr*: *like* **hear**) *vt* ouvir por acaso.

**overjoyed** [əuvə'dʒɔɪd] *adj* maravilhado, cheio de alegria.

**overland** ['əuvəlænd] *adj, adv* por terra.

**overlap** [əuvə'læp] *vi* coincidir *or* sobrepor-se em parte // *n* ['əuvəlæp] sobreposição *f*.

**overleaf** [əuvə'liːf] *adv* no verso.

**overload** [əuvə'ləud] *vt* sobrecarregar.

**overlook** [əuvə'luk] *vt* (*have view on*) dar para; (*miss*: *by mistake*) deixar passar; (*: deliberately*) fazer vista grossa a; (*forgive*) perdoar.

**overnight** [əuvə'naɪt] *adv* durante a noite; (*fig*) da noite para o dia // *adj* noturno (*Pt*: -ct-); **to stay** ~ passar a noite, pernoitar.

**overpass** ['əuvəpɑːs] *n* passagem *f* elevada.

**overpower** [əuvə'pauə*] vt
dominar, subjugar; ~ing adj (heat,
stench) sufocante.

**overrate** [əuvə'reit] vt sobrestimar,
supervalorizar; (cost) cotar acima
do preço.

**override** (irr: like ride)
vt (order, objection) não fazer caso
de, ignorar; **overriding** adj
primordial.

**overrule** [əuvə'ru:l] vt (decision)
anular; (claim) indeferir.

**overseas** [əuvə'si:z] adv ultra-mar;
(abroad) no estrangeiro, no exterior
// adj (trade) exterior; (visitor)
estrangeiro.

**overseer** ['əuvəsiə*] n (in factory)
superintendente m/f; (foreman)
capataz m.

**overshadow** [əuvə'ʃædəu] vt (fig)
eclipsar, ofuscar.

**overshoot** [əuvə'ʃu:t] (irr: like
shoot) vt exceder.

**oversight** ['əuvəsait] n descuido.

**oversleep** [əuvə'sli:p] (irr: like
sleep) vi dormir além da hora.

**overspend** [əuvə'spɛnd] (irr: like
spend) vi gastar demais.

**overspill** ['əuvəspil] n excesso (de
população).

**overstate** [əuvə'steit] vt exagerar;
~ment n afirmação f exagerada.

**overt** [əu'və:t] adj aberto,
indissimulado.

**overtake** [əuvə'teik] (irr: like take)
vt superar, exceder; (AUT)
ultrapassar; **overtaking** n (AUT)
ultrapassagem m.

**overthrow** [əuvə'θrəu] (irr: like
throw) vt (government) derrubar.

**overtime** ['əuvətaim] n horas fpl
extras.

**overtone** ['əuvətəun] n (fig)
insinuação f, alusão f.

**overture** ['əuvətʃuə*] n (MUS)
abertura; (fig) proposta, oferta.

**overturn** [əuvə'tə:n] vt/i virar;
(AUT) capotar.

**overweight** [əuvə'weit] adj gordo

demais, com excesso de peso.

**overwhelm** [əuvə'wɛlm] vt
esmagar; ~ing adj (victory, defeat)
esmagador(a); (desire) irresistível.

**overwork** [əuvə'wə:k] n excesso de
trabalho // vt sobrecarregar de
trabalho // vi trabalhar demais.

**overwrought** [əuvə'rɔ:t] adj
extenuado, superexcitado.

**owe** [əu] vt dever; to ~ sb sth, to ~
sth to sb dever algo a alguém;
**owing to** prep devido a, por causa
de.

**owl** [aul] n coruja, mocho.

**own** [əun] vt possuir, ter // adj
próprio; **a room of my ~** meu
próprio quarto; **to get one's ~ back**
ir à forra; **on one's ~** sozinho;
(unaided) sem auxílio; **to ~ up** vi
confessar; ~**er** n dono,
proprietário/a; (possessor)
possuidor(a) m/f; ~**ership** n posse f.

**ox** [ɔks], pl ~**en** ['ɔksn] n boi m.

**oxide** ['ɔksaid] n óxido.

**oxtail** ['ɔksteil] n: ~ **soup** rabada.

**oxygen** ['ɔksidʒən] n oxigênio; ~
**mask/tent** máscara/tenda de
oxigênio.

**oyster** ['ɔistə*] n ostra.

**oz.** abbr of **ounce(s)**.

**ozone** ['əuzəun] n ozônio.

# P

**p** [pi:] abbr of **penny, pence**.

**p.a.** abbr of **per annum**.

**pa** [pɑ:] n (col) papai m, paizinho.

**pace** [peis] n (step) passo; (rhythm)
ritmo // vi: **to ~ up and down**
andar de um lado para o outro; **to
keep ~ with** acompanhar o passo
de; (events) manter-se inteirado de
or atualizado em; ~**maker** n (MED)
regulador m cardíaco, marca-passo
m.

**pacific** [pə'sifik] adj pacífico // n:

the P~ **(Ocean)** o (Oceano) Pacífico.

**pacifier** ['pæsɪfaɪə*] n (US) chupeta.

**pacifist** ['pæsɪfɪst] n pacifista m/f.

**pacify** ['pæsɪfaɪ] vt (soothe) acalmar, serenar; (country) pacificar.

**pack** [pæk] n (gen) pacote m, embrulho; (US: packet) maço; (of hounds) matilha; (of thieves etc) bando, quadrilha; (of cards) baralho; (bundle) fardo; (back ~) mochila // vi fazer as malas // vt (wrap) empacotar, embrulhar; (fill) encher; (in suitcase etc) arrumar, acondicionar (na mala); (cram) apinhar, entulhar; (fig: meeting etc) encher de partidários; **to ~ sb off** despachar alguém; ~ **it in!** (col) pára com isso!; **to ~ one's cases** fazer as malas.

**package** ['pækɪdʒ] n pacote m; (bulky) embrulho, fardo; (also: ~ **deal**) pacote de acordo; ~ **tour** n excursão f organizada.

**packet** ['pækɪt] n pacote m, maço; (NAUT) paquete m.

**packing** ['pækɪŋ] n embalagem f; (external) envoltório; (internal) enchimento; ~ **case** n caixa de embalagem.

**pact** [pækt] n pacto; (COMM) convênio.

**pad** [pæd] n (of paper) bloco; (cushion) almofada; (launching ~) plataforma (de lançamento); (foot) pata; (col: flat) casa // vi caminhar sem ruído; ~**ding** n enchimento, recheio; (fig) palavreado inútil.

**paddle** ['pædl] n (oar) remo curto // vt remar // vi (with feet) patinhar; ~ **steamer** n vapor m movido a rodas; **paddling pool** n lago de recreação.

**paddock** ['pædək] n cercado, paddock m.

**paddy field** ['pædɪ-] n arrozal m.

**padlock** ['pædlɔk] n cadeado // vt fechar com cadeado.

**padre** ['pɑːdrɪ] n capelão m, padre m.

**paediatrics, pediatrics** (US) [piːdɪ'ætrɪks] n pediatria sg.

**pagan** ['peɪɡən] adj, n pagão/pagã m/f.

**page** [peɪdʒ] n página; (also: ~ **boy**) mensageiro // vt (in hotel etc) mandar chamar.

**pageant** ['pædʒənt] n (procession) cortejo suntuoso; (show) desfile alegórico; ~**ry** n pompa, fausto.

**pagoda** [pə'ɡəudə] n pagode m.

**paid** [peɪd] pt, pp of **pay** // adj (work) remunerado; (official) assalariado; **to put ~ to** acabar com).

**pail** [peɪl] n balde m.

**pain** [peɪn] n dor f; **to be in ~** sofrer, sentir dor; **on ~ of death** sob pena de morte; **to take ~s to do sth** dar-se ao trabalho de fazer algo; ~**ed** adj (expression) magoado, aflito; ~**ful** adj doloroso; (difficult) penoso; (disagreeable) desagradável; ~**fully** adv (fig: very) terrivelmente; ~**killer** n analgésico, calmante m; ~**less** adj sem dor, indolor; **painstaking** ['peɪnzteɪkɪŋ] adj (person) esmerado, meticuloso.

**paint** [peɪnt] n pintura // vt pintar; **to ~ one's face** pintar-se, maquilar; **to ~ the town red** (fig) cair na farra; **to ~ the door blue** pintar a porta de azul; ~**brush** n (artist's) pincel m; (decorator's) broxa; ~**er** n pintor(a) m/f; ~**ing** n pintura.

**pair** [pɛə*] n (of shoes, gloves etc) par m; (of people) casal m; **a ~ of scissors** uma tesoura; **a ~ of trousers** uma calça.

**pajamas** [pɪ'dʒɑːməz] npl (US) pijama msg.

**Pakistan** [pɑːkɪ'stɑːn] n Paquistão m; ~**i** adj, n paquistanês/esa m/f.

**pal** [pæl] n (col) camarada m/f, companheiro/a.

**palace** ['pæləs] n palácio.

**palatable** ['pælɪtəbl] adj saboroso, apetitoso; (acceptable) aceitável.

**palate** ['pælɪt] n paladar m.

**palaver** [pə'lɑ:və*] n (fuss) barulho; (hindrances) incômodo.

**pale** [peɪl] adj (gen) pálido; (colour) claro; **to grow ~** empalidecer; **to be beyond the ~** passar dos limites; **~ness** n palidez f.

**Palestine** ['pælɪstaɪn] n Palestina; **Palestinian** [-'tɪnɪən] adj, n palestino/a.

**palette** ['pælɪt] n palheta.

**paling** ['peɪlɪŋ] n (stake) estaca; (fence) cerca.

**palisade** [pælɪ'seɪd] n paliçada.

**pall** [pɔ:l] n (of smoke) manto // vi tornar-se insípido, (fig) perder a graça.

**pallid** ['pælɪd] adj pálido, descorado.

**palm** [pɑ:m] n (hand) palma; (also: **~ tree**) palmeira // vt: **to ~ sth off on sb** (col) impingir algo a alguém; **~ist** n quiromante m/f; **P~ Sunday** n Domingo de Ramos.

**palpable** ['pælpəbl] adj palpável.

**palpitation** [pælpɪ'teɪʃən] n palpitação f; **to have ~s** sentir palpitações.

**paltry** ['pɔ:ltrɪ] adj (insignificant) insignificante, fútil; (miserable) vil, reles inv.

**pamper** ['pæmpə*] vt mimar.

**pamphlet** ['pæmflət] n panfleto.

**pan** [pæn] n (also: **sauce~**) panela, caçarola; (also: **frying ~**) frigideira; (of lavatory) pia // vi (CINEMA) tomar uma panorâmica.

**panacea** [pænə'sɪə] n panacéia.

**Panama** ['pænəmɑ:] n Panamá m.

**pancake** ['pænkeɪk] n panqueca.

**panda** ['pændə] n panda m/f; **~ car** n patrulhinha.

**pandemonium** [pændɪ'məʊnɪəm] n (noise) pandemônio; (mess) caos m.

**pander** ['pændə*] vi: **to ~ to** favorecer.

**pane** [peɪn] n vidraça, vidro.

**panel** ['pænl] n (of wood) painel m; (of cloth) pano; (RADIO, TV) júri m; **~ling, ~ing** (US) n painéis mpl.

**pang** [pæŋ] n: **~s of conscience** dor f de consciência; **~s of hunger** torturas fpl da fome.

**panic** ['pænɪk] n pânico // vi entrar em pânico; **~ky** adj (person) assustadiço, apavorado; **~-stricken** adj tomado de pânico.

**pannier** ['pænɪə*] n (on bicycle) cesta; (on mule etc) cesto, alcofa.

**panorama** [pænə'rɑ:mə] n panorama m.

**pansy** ['pænzɪ] n (BOT) amor-perfeito; (col) bicha.

**pant** [pænt] vi arquejar, ofegar.

**panther** ['pænθə*] n pantera.

**panties** ['pæntɪz] (Brit) npl calcinha sg.

**pantomime** ['pæntəmaɪm] n pantomima, revista musical representada no Natal, baseada em contos de fada.

**pantry** ['pæntrɪ] n despensa.

**pants** [pænts] n (woman's) calcinhas fpl; (: Pt) cuecas fpl; (man's) cuecas fpl; (US: trousers) calça sg; **panty hose** (US) n meias-calça fpl.

**papal** ['peɪpəl] adj papal.

**paper** ['peɪpə*] n papel m; (also: **news~**) jornal m, diário; (study, article) artigo, dissertação f; (exam) exame m, prova // adj de papel // vt empapelar; (identity) **~s** npl documentos mpl; **~back** n livro de capa mole; **~ bag** n saco de papel; **~ clip** n clipe m; **~ hankie** n lenço de papel; **~ money** n papel-moeda m; **~weight** n pesa-papéis m inv; **~work** n trabalho burocrático; (pej) papelada.

**papier-mâché** ['pæpɪeɪ'mæʃeɪ] n papel m machê.

**paprika** ['pæprɪkə] n páprica, pimentão-doce m.

**par** [pɑ:*] n par m; (GOLF) média f; **to be on a ~ with** estar em igualdade de condições com.

**parable** ['pærəbl] n parábola.

**parachute** ['pærəʃu:t] n pára-quedas m inv // vi saltar de pára-quedas; **~ jump** n salto de pára-quedas.

**parade** [pə'reɪd] n desfile m // vt (gen) desfilar; (show off) exibir // vi desfilar; (MIL) passar revista.

**paradise** ['pærədaɪs] n paraíso.

**paradox** ['pærədɔks] n paradoxo; **~ical** [-'dɔksɪkl] adj paradoxal.

**paraffin** ['pærəfɪn] n: ~ (oil) petróleo.

**paragraph** ['pærəgrɑ:f] n parágrafo.

**parallel** ['pærəlɛl] adj paralelo; (fig) correspondente // n (line) paralela; (fig, Geo) paralelo.

**paralysis** [pə'rælɪsɪs] n paralisia; **paralyze** ['pærəlaɪz] vt paralisar.

**paramount** ['pærəmaunt] adj: **of ~ importance** de suma importância, primordial.

**paranoia** [pærə'nɔɪə] n paranóia; **paranoiac** adj paranóico.

**paraphernalia** [pærəfə'neɪlɪə] n (gear) acessórios mpl, equipamento.

**paraplegic** [pærə'pli:dʒɪk] n paraplégico/a.

**parasite** ['pærəsaɪt] n parasito/a.

**parasol** ['pærəsɔl] n guarda-sol m, sombrinha.

**paratrooper** ['pærətru:pə*] n pára-quedista m/f.

**parcel** ['pɑ:sl] n pacote m // vt (also: ~ up) embrulhar, empacotar.

**parch** [pɑ:tʃ] vt secar, ressecar; **~ed** adj (person) morto de sede.

**parchment** ['pɑ:tʃmənt] n pergaminho.

**pardon** ['pɑ:dn] n perdão m; (LAW) indulto // vt perdoar; (LAW) indultar; **~!** desculpe!; ~ **me!, I beg your ~!**

desculpe-me; **(I beg your) ~?** como?, como disse?

**parent** ['pɛərənt] n pai m/mãe f; **~s** npl pais mpl; **~al** [pə'rɛntl] adj paternal/maternal, dos pais.

**parenthesis** [pə'rɛnθɪsɪs], pl **-theses** [-θɪsi:z] n parêntese m.

**Paris** ['pærɪs] n Paris m.

**parish** ['pærɪʃ] n paróquia, freguesia; **~ioner** [pə'rɪʃənə*] n paroquiano/a.

**Parisian** [pə'rɪzɪən] adj, n parisiense m/f.

**parity** ['pærɪtɪ] n paridade f, igualdade f.

**park** [pɑ:k] n parque m // vi estacionar; ~ **ing** n estacionamento; **'no ~ing'** 'estacionamento proibido'; **~ing lot** n (US) (parque do estacionamento); **~ing meter** n parquímetro.

**parliament** ['pɑ:ləmənt] n parlamento, assembléia; **~ary** [-'mɛntərɪ] adj parlamentar.

**parlour, parlor** (US) ['pɑ:lə*] n sala de visitas, salão m, saleta.

**parochial** [pə'rəukɪəl] adj paroquial; (pej) provinciano.

**parody** ['pærədɪ] n paródia // vt parodiar.

**parole** [pə'rəul] n: **on ~** em liberdade condicional, sob promessa.

**parquet** ['pɑ:keɪ] n: **~ floor(ing)** parquete m, assoalho de tacos.

**parrot** ['pærət] n louro, papagaio; **~ fashion** adv mecanicamente.

**parry** ['pærɪ] vt aparar, desviar.

**parsimonious** [pɑ:sɪ'məunɪəs] adj parco.

**parsley** ['pɑ:slɪ] n salsa.

**parsnip** ['pɑ:snɪp] n cherivia, pastinaga.

**parson** ['pɑ:sn] n (parish) pároco, (gen) padre m, clérigo.

**part** [pɑ:t] n (gen, MUS) parte f; (bit) pedaço; (of machine) peça; (THEATRE etc) papel m; (of serial) episódio; (US: in hair) risca, repartido // adv = **partly** // vt dividir; (break) partir // vi (people) separar-se; (roads) bifurcar-se; (crowd) dispersar-se; (break) partir-se; **to take ~** in participar de, tomar parte em; **to take sth in good** ~ não se ofender com algo; **to take sb's** ~ defender alguém; **for my** ~ de minha parte; **for the most** ~ na maior parte; **to** ~ **with** vt fus ceder, entregar; (money) pagar; (get rid of) desfazer-se de; **in** ~ **exchange** como parte do pagamento; **spare** ~ peça sobressalente.

**partial** ['pɑːʃl] adj parcial; **to be** ~ **to** gostar de, ser apreciador de; ~**ly** adv parcialmente.

**participant** [pɑːˈtɪsɪpənt] n (in competition) participante m/f; **participate** [-peɪt] vi: **to participate in** participar de; **participation** [-ˈpeɪʃən] n participação f.

**participle** ['pɑːtɪsɪpl] n particípio.

**particle** ['pɑːtɪkl] n partícula; (of dust) grão m; (fig) bocadinho.

**particular** [pəˈtɪkjulə*] adj (special) particular; (concrete) concreto; (given) determinado; (detailed) detalhado, minucioso; (fussy) exigente, minucioso; ~**s** npl (information) dados mpl, detalhes mpl; (details) pormenores mpl; ~**ly** adv em particular, especialmente.

**parting** ['pɑːtɪŋ] n (act of separation) separação f; (farewell) despedida; (in hair) risca, repartido // adj de despedida.

**partisan** [pɑːtɪˈzæn] adj, n partidário/a.

**partition** [pɑːˈtɪʃən] n (POL) divisão f; (wall) tabique m, divisória // vt separar com tabique; (fig) dividir.

**partly** ['pɑːtlɪ] adv em parte.

**partner** ['pɑːtnə*] n (COMM) sócio/a; (SPORT) parceiro/a; (at dance) par m; (spouse) cônjuge m/f; (friend etc) companheiro/a // vt acompanhar; ~**ship** n (gen) associação f; (COMM) sociedade f.

**partridge** ['pɑːtrɪdʒ] n perdiz f.

**part-time** ['pɑːt'taɪm] adj, adv de meio expediente, de meio dia.

**party** ['pɑːtɪ] n (POL) partido; (celebration) festa; (group) grupo; (LAW) parte f interessada, litigante m/f // adj (POL) do partido; (dress etc) de gala, de luxo.

**pass** [pɑːs] vt (time, object, exam) passar; (place) passar por; (overtake, surpass) ultrapassar; (approve) aprovar // vi (SCOL) ser aprovado, passar // n (permit) passe m; (membership card) carteira; (in mountains) garganta, desfiladeiro; (SPORT) passe m; (SCOL: also: ~ **mark**): **to get a** ~ in ser aprovado em; **to** ~ **sth through sth** passar algo por algo; **to** ~ **away** vi falecer; **to** ~ **by** vi passar // vt (ignore) passar por cima de; **to** ~ **for** ser tomado por; **to** ~ **out** vi desmaiar; **to** ~ **up** vt rejeitar; ~**able** adj (road) transitável; (work) aceitável.

**passage** ['pæsɪdʒ] n (also: ~**way**) corredor m; (act of passing) trânsito; (fare, in book) passagem f; (by boat) travessia; (MECH, MED) conduto.

**passenger** ['pæsɪndʒə*] n passageiro/a, viajante m/f.

**passer-by** [pɑːsəˈbaɪ] n transeunte m/f.

**passing** ['pɑːsɪŋ] adj (fleeting) passageiro, fugaz; **in** ~ de passagem.

**passion** ['pæʃən] n paixão f; (anger) cólera; ~**ate** adj apaixonado, irado.

**passive** ['pæsɪv] adj (also LING) passivo.

**Passover** ['pɑːsəuvə*] n Páscoa (dos judeus).

**passport** ['pɑːspɔːt] n passaporte m.

**password** ['pɑːswɜːd] n senha, contra-senha.

**past** [pɑːst] prep (further than) além de; (later than) depois de // adj passado; (president etc) ex-, anterior // n o passado; (antecedents) antecedentes mpl; he's ~ forty ele tem mais de quarenta anos; **for the ~ few days** nos últimos dias; **to run ~** passar correndo por.

**pasta** ['pæstə] n macarrão m, massa.

**paste** [peɪst] n (gen) pasta; (glue) grude m, cola // vt (stick) grudar; (glue) colar.

**pastel** [pæstl] adj pastel; (painting) a pastel.

**pasteurized** ['pæstəraɪzd] adj pasteurizado.

**pastille** ['pæstl] n pastilha.

**pastime** ['pɑːstaɪm] n passatempo.

**pastor** ['pɑːstə*] n pastor m.

**pastoral** ['pɑːstərl] adj pastoral.

**pastry** ['peɪstrɪ] n massa; (cakes) bolos mpl.

**pasture** ['pɑːstʃə*] n (grass) pasto; (land) pastagem f, pasto.

**pasty** ['pæstɪ] n empadão m de carne // adj ['peɪstɪ] pastoso; (complexion) pálido.

**pat** [pæt] vt dar palmadinhas em; (dog etc) afagar // n (of butter) porção f; **to give sb a ~ on the back** dar animar alguém.

**patch** [pætʃ] n (of material) retalho; (piece) pedaço; (mend) remendo; (of land) lote m, terreno // vt (clothes) remendar; **to ~ up** vt (mend temporarily) consertar provisoriamente; (quarrel) resolver; **~work** n (feito de retalhos; **~y** adj desigual.

**pâté** ['pæteɪ] n patê m.

**patent** ['peɪtnt] n patente f // vt patentear // adj patente, evidente; **~ leather** n verniz m.

**paternal** [pə'tɜːnl] adj paternal; (relation) paterno; **paternity** [-nɪtɪ] n paternidade f.

**path** [pɑːθ] n caminho; (trail, track) trilha, pista; (of missile) trajetória (Pt: -ct-).

**pathetic** [pə'θetɪk] adj (pitiful)

patético, digno de pena; (very bad) péssimo; (moving) comovente.

**pathologist** [pə'θɔlədʒɪst] n patologista m/f; **pathology** [-dʒɪ] n patologia.

**pathos** ['peɪθɔs] n patos msg, patético.

**pathway** ['pɑːθweɪ] n caminho, trilha.

**patience** ['peɪʃns] n paciência.

**patient** ['peɪʃnt] n paciente m/f // adj paciente, resignado.

**patio** ['pætɪəu] n pátio.

**patriot** ['peɪtrɪət] n patriota m/f; **~ic** [pætrɪ'ɔtɪk] adj patriótico.

**patrol** [pə'trəul] n patrulha // vt patrulhar; **~ car** n carro de patrulha, radiopatrulha f; **~man** n (US) guarda m, polícia m.

**patron** ['peɪtrən] n (in shop) cliente m/f; (of charity) benfeitor(a) m/f; **~ of the arts** mecenas msg; **~age** ['pætrənɪdʒ] n patrocínio m; **~ize** ['pætrənaɪz] vt (shop) ser cliente de; (business) patrocinar; (look down on) tratar com ar de superioridade; **~ saint** n (santo) padroeiro.

**patter** ['pætə*] n tamborilada; (of feet) passos miúdos mpl; (sales talk) jargão m profissional // vi correr dando passinhos; (rain) tamborilar.

**pattern** ['pætən] n modelo, padrão m; (SEWING) molde m; (design) desenho; (sample) amostra.

**paunch** [pɔːntʃ] n pança, barriga.

**pauper** ['pɔːpə*] n pobre m/f.

**pause** [pɔːz] n pausa; (interval) intervalo // vi fazer uma pausa.

**pave** [peɪv] vt pavimentar; **to ~ the way for** preparar o terreno para.

**pavement** ['peɪvmənt] n (Brit) calçada, passeio.

**pavilion** [pə'vɪlɪən] n pavilhão m; (for band etc) coreto; (SPORT) barraca.

**paving** ['peɪvɪŋ] n pavimento, calçamento; **~ stone** n laje f, paralelepípedo.

**paw** [pɔː] n pata; (of cat) garra // vt

passar a pata; (*touch*) manusear; (*amorously*) apalpar.

**pawn** [pɔ:n] *n* (CHESS) peão *m*; (*fig*) títere *m* // *vt* empenhar; ~**broker** *n* agiota *m/f*; ~**shop** *n* loja de penhores.

**pay** [peɪ] *n* paga, pagamento; (*wage etc*) salário // (*vb*: *pt, pp* **paid**) *vt* pagar; (*debt*) liquidar, saldar; (*visit*) fazer; (*respect*) apresentar // *vi* pagar; (*be profitable*) valer a pena, render; **to ~ attention (to)** prestar atenção (a); **to ~ back** *vt* (*money*) devolver; (*person*) pagar; **to ~ for** *vt* pagar; **to ~ in** *vt* depositar; **to ~ off** *vt* saldar; **to ~ up** *vt* pagar, liquidar; ~**able** *adj* pagável; ~ **day** *n* dia *m* do pagamento; ~**ee** *n* pessoa a quem se paga; ~**ing** *adj* remunerador(a); ~**ment** *n* pagamento; **advance** ~**ment** pagamento adiantado; **monthly** ~**ment** mensalidade *f*; ~ **packet** *n* envelope *m* com o pagamento; ~**roll** *n* folha de pagamento; ~ **slip** *n* contracheque *m*.

**p.c.** *abbr of* **per cent.**

**pea** [pi:] *n* ervilha; **sweet** ~ ervilha-de-cheiro *f*.

**peace** [pi:s] *n* paz *f*; (*calm*) tranqüilidade *f*, quietude *f*; ~**able** *adj* pacato; ~**ful** *adj* (*gentle*) pacífico; (*calm*) tranqüilo, sossegado; ~**keeping** *n* pacificação *f*; ~ **offering** *n* proposta de paz.

**peach** [pi:tʃ] *n* pêssego *m*.

**peacock** ['pi:kɔk] *n* pavão *m*.

**peak** [pi:k] *n* (*of mountain: top*) cume *m*; (: *point*) pico; (*of cap*) pala, viseira; (*fig*) apogeu *m*, máximo; ~ **hours** *npl* horas *fpl* do 'rush'; (*Pt*) horas *fpl* de ponta.

**peal** [pi:l] *n* (*of bells*) repique *m*, toque *m* de sinos; ~ **of laughter** gargalhada.

**peanut** ['pi:nʌt] *n* amendoim *m*; ~ **butter** *n* manteiga de amendoim.

**pear** [pɛə*] *n* pêra; ~ **tree** *n* pereira.

**pearl** [pɔ:l] *n* pérola.

**peasant** ['pɛznt] *n* camponês/esa *m/f*.

**peat** [pi:t] *n* turfa.

**pebble** ['pɛbl] *n* seixo, calhau *m*.

**peck** [pɛk] *vt* (*also*: ~ **at**) bicar, dar bicadas em; (*food*) beliscar // *n* bicada; (*kiss*) beijoca; ~**ing order** *n* ordem *f* de hierarquia; ~**ish** *adj* (*col*) faminto.

**peculiar** [pɪ'kju:lɪə*] *adj* (*odd*) estranho, esquisito; (*typical*) próprio, característico; (*marked*) especial; ~ **to próprio de**; ~**ity** [pɪkju:lɪ'ærɪtɪ] *n* peculiaridade *f*; (*feature*) característica; (*oddity*) excentricidade *f*, singularidade *f*.

**pedal** ['pɛdl] *n* pedal *m* // *vi* pedalar.

**pedantic** [pɪ'dæntɪk] *adj* pedante.

**peddle** ['pɛdl] *vt* vender nas ruas, mascatear; **peddler** *n* mascate *m/f*, camelô *m*.

**pedestal** ['pɛdəstl] *n* pedestal *m*.

**pedestrian** [pɪ'dɛstrɪən] *n* pedestre *m/f* // *adj* pedestre; ~ **crossing** *n* faixa para pedestres; (*Pt*) passadeira.

**pedigree** ['pɛdɪgri:] *n* genealogia; (*of animal*) raça // *cmp* (*animal*) de raça.

**peek** [pi:k] *vi* espiar, espreitar.

**peel** [pi:l] *n* pele *f*; (*of orange, lemon*) casca // *vt* descascar // *vi* (*paint etc*) descascar; (*wallpaper*) desprender-se.

**peep** [pi:p] *n* (*look*) espiadela; (*sound*) pio // *vi* (*look*) espreitar; (*sound*) piar; **to ~ out** *vi* mostrar-se, surgir; ~**hole** *n* vigia.

**peer** [pɪə*] *vi* **to ~ at** perscrutar, fitar // *n* (*noble*) par *m*; (*equal*) igual *m*; ~**age** *n* nobreza; ~**less** *adj* sem igual.

**peeved** [pi:vd] *adj* irritado.

**peevish** ['pi:vɪʃ] *adj* rabugento.

**peg** [pɛg] *n* cavilha; (*for coat etc*) cabide *m*; (*also*: **clothes** ~) pregador *m*; (*tent* ~) estaca // *vt* (prices) fixar; **off the** ~ adv pronto.

**pejorative** [pɪˈdʒɔrətɪv] adj pejorativo.

**pekingese** [piːkɪˈniːz] n pequinês/esa m/f.

**pelican** [ˈpɛlɪkən] n pelicano.

**pellet** [ˈpɛlɪt] n bolinha; (bullet) pelota de chumbo.

**pelmet** [ˈpɛlmɪt] n sanefa.

**pelt** [pɛlt] vt: **to ~ sb with sth** atirar algo em alguém // vi (rain) chover a cântaros // n pele f (não curtida).

**pelvis** [ˈpɛlvɪs] n pelvis f, bacia.

**pen** [pɛn] n caneta; (for sheep) redil m, cercado; ~ **pal** (US) n amigo/a por correspondência, correspondente m/f; ~ **name** n pseudônimo.

**penal** [ˈpiːnl] adj penal; ~**ize** vt impor penalidade; (SPORT) penalizar.

**penalty** [ˈpɛnltɪ] n (gen) pena, penalidade f; (fine) multa; (SPORT) punição f; ~ (**kick**) n (FOOTBALL) pênalti m.

**penance** [ˈpɛnəns] n penitência.

**pence** [pɛns] pl of **penny**.

**pencil** [ˈpɛnsl] n lápis m; (for eyebrows) lápis de sobrancelha; ~ **propelling** ~ n lapiseira; ~ **sharpener** n apontador m.

**pendant** [ˈpɛndnt] n pingente m.

**pending** [ˈpɛndɪŋ] prep (during) durante; (until) até // adj pendente.

**pendulum** [ˈpɛndjuləm] n pêndulo.

**penetrate** [ˈpɛnɪtreɪt] vt penetrar; **penetrating** adj penetrante; **penetration** [-ˈtreɪʃən] n penetração f.

**penfriend** [ˈpɛnfrɛnd] n amigo/a por correspondência, correspondente m/f.

**penguin** [ˈpɛŋgwɪn] n pingüim m.

**penicillin** [pɛnɪˈsɪlɪn] n penicilina.

**peninsula** [pəˈnɪnsjulə] n península.

**penis** [ˈpiːnɪs] n pênis m.

**penitence** [ˈpɛnɪtəns] n penitência.

**penitent** [-nt] adj (gen) arrependido; (REL) penitente.

**penitentiary** [pɛnɪˈtɛnʃərɪ] n (US) penitenciária, presídio.

**penknife** [ˈpɛnnaɪf] n canivete m.

**pennant** [ˈpɛnənt] n flâmula.

**penniless** [ˈpɛnɪlɪs] adj sem dinheiro; (col) sem um tostão.

**penny** [ˈpɛnɪ], pl **pennies** [ˈpɛnɪz] or **pence** [pɛns] n pêni m.

**pension** [ˈpɛnʃən] n (gen) pensão f; (old-age) aposentadoria f; (MIL) reserva; ~**er** n pensionista m/f; ~ **fund** n fundo da aposentadoria.

**pensive** [ˈpɛnsɪv] adj pensativo; (withdrawn) absorto.

**pentagon** [ˈpɛntəgən] n pentágono.

**Pentecost** [ˈpɛntɪkɔst] n Pentecostes m.

**penthouse** [ˈpɛnthaus] n cobertura.

**pent-up** [ˈpɛntʌp] adj (feelings) reprimido.

**penultimate** [pɛˈnʌltɪmət] adj penúltimo.

**people** [ˈpiːpl] npl gente f, pessoas fpl; (citizens) povo sg, cidadãos mpl // n (nation, race) nação f, raça // vt povoar; **several** ~ **came** vieram várias pessoas; ~ **say that...** dizem que...

**pep** [pɛp] n (col) energia, dinamismo; **to ~ up** vt animar.

**pepper** [ˈpɛpə*] n pimenta; (vegetable) pimentão m // vt (fig) salpicar; ~**mint** n hortelã-pimenta; (sweet) bala de hortelã.

**peptalk** [ˈpɛptɔːk] n (col) conversa para levantar o espírito.

**per** [pə:*] prep por; ~ **day/person** por dia/pessoa; ~ **cent** por cento; ~ **annum** por ano.

**perceive** [pəˈsiːv] vt perceber; (realize) compreender.

**percentage** [pəˈsɛntɪdʒ] n percentagem f.

**perception** [pəˈsɛpʃən] n percepção f; (insight) perspicácia; **perceptive** [-ˈsɛptɪv] adj perceptivo.

**perch** [pə:tʃ] n (fish) perca; (for bird) poleiro // vi empoleirar-se, pousar.

**percolator** [ˈpəːkəleitə*] n cafeteira de filtro.

**percussion** [pəˈkʌʃən] n percussão f.

**peremptory** [pəˈremptəri] adj peremptório, decisivo; (person: imperious) autoritário.

**perennial** [pəˈreniəl] adj perene.

**perfect** [ˈpəːfikt] adj perfeito // n (also: ~ tense) perfeito // vt [pəˈfekt] aperfeiçoar; ~ion n [-ˈfekʃən] perfeição f; ~ionist n perfeccionista m/f.

**perforate** [ˈpəːfəreit] vt perfurar; ~d adj (stamp) picotado; **perforation** [-ˈreiʃən] n perfuração f.

**perform** [pəˈfɔːm] vt (carry out) realizar, fazer; (concert etc) executar; (piece of music) interpretar // vi (animal) fazer truques de amestramento; (THEATRE) representar; (TECH) funcionar; ~ance n (of task) cumprimento, realização f; (of an artist, of player etc) atuação (Pt: -ct-) f; (of car, engine) funcionamento; (of function) desempenho; ~er n (actor) artista m/f, ator/atriz (Pt: -ct-) m/f; (MUS) intérprete m/f; ~ing adj (animal) amestrado, adestrada.

**perfume** [ˈpəːfjuːm] n perfume m // vt perfumar.

**perhaps** [pəˈhæps] adv talvez.

**peril** [ˈperil] n perigo, risco.

**perimeter** [pəˈrimitə*] n perímetro.

**period** [ˈpiəriəd] n período; (HISTORY) época, era; (time limit) prazo; (SCOL) aula; (full stop) ponto final; (MED) menstruação f, regra // adj (costume, furniture) da época; ~ic [-ˈɔdik] adj periódico; ~ical [-ˈɔdikl] n periódico; ~ically [-ˈɔdikli] adv periodicamente, de vez em quando.

**peripheral** [pəˈrifərəl] adj, n periférico; **periphery** [-ri] n periferia.

**periscope** [ˈperiskəup] n periscópio.

**perish** [ˈperiʃ] vi perecer; (decay) deteriorar-se, estragar; ~able adj perecível, deteriorável; ~ing (col: cold) gelado, glacial.

**perjure** [ˈpəːdʒə*] vt: to ~ o.s. prestar falso testemunho; **perjury** n (LAW) perjúrio.

**perk** [pəːk] n pagamento além do salário; to ~ up vi (cheer up) animar-se; (in health) recuperar-se; ~y adj (cheerful) animado, alegre.

**perm** [pəːm] n permanente f.

**permanent** [ˈpəːmənənt] adj permanente.

**permissible** [pəˈmisibl] adj permissível, lícito.

**permission** [pəˈmiʃən] n permissão f; (authorization) autorização f.

**permissive** [pəˈmisiv] adj permissivo.

**permit** [ˈpəːmit] n permissão f, licença // vt [pəˈmit] permitir; (authorize) autorizar; (accept) consentir em.

**permutation** [pəːmjuˈteiʃən] n permutação f.

**pernicious** [pəːˈniʃəs] adj nocivo; (MED) pernicioso, maligno.

**perpendicular** [pəːpənˈdikjulə*] adj perpendicular.

**perpetrate** [ˈpəːpitreit] vt cometer.

**perpetual** [pəˈpetjuəl] adj perpétuo.

**perpetuate** [pəˈpetjueit] vt perpetuar.

**perplex** [pəˈpleks] vt deixar perplexo.

**persecute** [ˈpəːsikjuːt] vt (pursue) perseguir; (harass) importunar; **persecution** [-ˈkjuːʃən] n perseguição f.

**persevere** [pəːsiˈviə*] vi perseverar.

**Persian** [ˈpəːʃən] adj, n persa m/f.

**persist** [pəˈsist] vi: to ~ (in doing sth) persistir (em fazer algo); ~ence n persistência; (of disease) insistência; ~ent adj persistente;

*(determined)* teimoso; *(disease)* insistente, persistente.

**person** ['pɜːsn] n pessoa; ~**able** adj atraente, bem apessoado; ~**al** adj pessoal; *(private)* particular; *(visit)* em pessoa, pessoal; *(TEL)* particular, pessoa a pessoa; *(column)* de anúncios pessoais; ~**ality** [-'nælɪtɪ] n personalidade f; ~**ally** adv pessoalmente; ~**ify** [-'sɔnɪfaɪ] vt personificar.

**personnel** [pɜːsə'nɛl] n pessoal m.

**perspective** [pə'spɛktɪv] n perspectiva.

**perspiration** [pɜːspɪ'reɪʃən] n transpiração f, suor m; **perspire** [-'spaɪə*] vi transpirar, suar.

**persuade** [pə'sweɪd] vt persuadir; **persuasion** [-'sweɪʒən] n persuasão f; *(persuasiveness)* poder m de persuasão; *(creed)* convicção f, crença; **persuasive** [-'sweɪsɪv] adj persuasivo.

**pert** [pɜːt] adj atrevido, descarado.

**pertaining** [pə'teɪnɪŋ]: ~ **to** prep relativo a, próprio de.

**pertinent** ['pɜːtɪnənt] adj pertinente, a propósito.

**perturb** [pə'tɜːb] vt perturbar.

**Peru** [pə'ruː] n Peru m.

**peruse** [pə'ruːz] vt ler com atenção, examinar.

**Peruvian** [pə'ruːvjən] adj, n peruano/a.

**pervade** [pə'veɪd] vt impregnar, penetrar em.

**perverse** [pə'vɜːs] adj perverso; *(stubborn)* teimoso; *(wayward)* caprichoso; **perversion** [-'vɜːʃən] n perversão f.

**pervert** ['pɜːvɜːt] n pervertido/a // vt [pə'vɜːt] perverter, corromper.

**pessary** ['pɛsərɪ] n pessário.

**pessimism** ['pɛsɪmɪzəm] n pessimismo m; **pessimist** [-mɪst] n pessimista m/f; **pessimistic** [-'mɪstɪk] adj pessimista.

**pest** [pɛst] n peste f, praga; *(insect)*

inseto *(Pt: -ct-)* nocivo; *(fig)* peste f, chato.

**pester** ['pɛstə*] vt incomodar.

**pesticide** ['pɛstɪsaɪd] n pesticida m.

**pet** [pɛt] n animal m de estimação; *(favourite)* preferido/a // vt acariciar // vi *(col)* acariciar-se, emburrar.

**petal** ['pɛtl] n pétala.

**peter** ['piːtə*]: **to** ~ **out** vi esgotar-se, acabar-se.

**petite** [pə'tiːt] adj delicado, frágil.

**petition** [pə'tɪʃən] n petição f.

**petrified** ['pɛtrɪfaɪd] adj *(fig)* petrificado, paralisado; **petrify** vt paralisar; *(frighten)* petrificar.

**petrol** ['pɛtrəl] n *(Brit)* gasolina; *(for lighter)* fluido.

**petroleum** [pə'trəʊlɪəm] n petróleo.

**petrol**: ~ **pump** n bomba da gasolina; ~ **station** n posto de gasolina; ~ **tank** n tanque m de gasolina.

**petticoat** ['pɛtɪkəʊt] n anágua; *(slip)* combinação f.

**pettiness** ['pɛtɪnɪs] n mesquinharia f.

**petty** ['pɛtɪ] adj *(mean)* mesquinho; *(unimportant)* insignificante; ~ **cash** n fundo para despesas miúdas; ~ **officer** n suboficial m da marinha.

**petulant** ['pɛtjʊlənt] adj petulante, rabugento.

**pew** [pjuː] n banco de igreja.

**pewter** ['pjuːtə*] n peltre m.

**phallic** ['fælɪk] adj fálico.

**phantom** ['fæntəm] n fantasma m.

**Pharaoh** ['fɛərəʊ] n faraó m.

**pharmacist** ['fɑːməsɪst] n farmacêutico/a; **pharmacy** [-sɪ] n farmácia.

**phase** [feɪz] n fase f // vt: **to** ~ **sth in/out** introduzir/retirar algo por etapas.

**Ph.D.** abbr of **Doctor of Philosophy.**

**pheasant** ['fɛznt] n faisão m.

**phenomenon** [fə'nɔmɪnən] pl
-**mena** [-mɪnə] n fenômeno.

**phial** ['faɪəl] n frasco.

**philanthropist** [fɪ'lænθrəpɪst] n
filantropo/a.

**philately** [fɪ'lætəlɪ] n filatelia.

**Philippines** ['fɪlɪpi:nz] npl (also:
**Philippine Islands**) Filipinas fpl.

**philosopher** [fɪ'lɔsəfə*] n
filósofo/a; **philosophical** [fɪlə'sɔfɪkl]
adj filosófico; **philosophy** [-fɪ] n
filosofia.

**phlegm** [flɛm] n fleuma; ~**atic**
[flɛg'mætɪk] adj fleumático.

**phobia** ['fəubjə] n fobia.

**phone** [fəun] n telefone m // vt
telefonar; **to be on the** ~ **ter**
telefone; (be calling) estar
telefonando; **to** ~ **back** vt/i ligar de
volta.

**phonetics** [fə'nɛtɪks] n fonética sg.

**phoney** ['fəunɪ] adj falso; (person)
fingido // n (person) impostor(a)
m/f.

**phosphate** ['fɔsfeɪt] n fosfato.

**phosphorus** ['fɔsfərəs] n fósforo.

**photo** ['fəutəu] n foto f.

**photo...** ['fəutəu] pref: ~**copier** n
fotocopiadora f; ~**copy** n fotocópia
// vt fotocopiar; ~**genic** [-'dʒɛnɪk]
adj fotogênico; ~**graph** n fotografia
// vt fotografar; ~**grapher**
[fə'tɔgrəfə*] n fotógrafo/a; ~**graphic**
[-'græfɪk] adj fotográfico; ~**graphy**
[fə'tɔgrəfɪ] n fotografia; ~**stat**
['fəutəustæt] n cópia fotostática.

**phrase** [freɪz] n frase f, expressão f
// vt exprimir; ~**book** n livro de
expressões idiomáticas.

**physical** ['fɪzɪkl] adj físico.

**physician** [fɪ'zɪʃən] n médico/a.

**physicist** ['fɪzɪsɪst] n físico/a.

**physics** ['fɪzɪks] n física sg.

**physiology** [fɪzɪ'ɔlədʒɪ] n fisiologia.

**physiotherapy** [fɪzɪəu'θerəpɪ] n
fisioterapia.

**physique** [fɪ'zi:k] n físico.

**pianist** ['pi:ənɪst] n pianista m/f.

**piano** [pɪ'ænəu] n piano; **grand** ~
piano de cauda.

**pick** [pɪk] n (tool: also: ~**axe**)
picareta, picão m // vt (select)
escolher, selecionar (Pt: -cc-);
(gather) colher; (lock) forçar; **take
your** ~ escolha o que quiser; **the** ~
**of** o melhor de; **to** ~ **one's teeth**
palitar os dentes; **to** ~ **pockets**
roubar or bater carteira; **to** ~ **off** vt
(kill) matar de um tiro; **to** ~ **on** vt
fus (person) azucrinar, apoquentar;
**to** ~ **out** vt escolher; (distinguish)
distinguir; **to** ~ **up** vi (improve)
melhorar // vt (from floor)
apanhar; (telephone) atender, tirar
do gancho; (buy) comprar; (find)
encontrar; (learn) aprender com
facilidade; **to** ~ **up speed** acelerar;
**to** ~ **o.s. up** levantar-se.

**picket** ['pɪkɪt] n (in strike) piquete
m // vt formar piquete; ~ **line** n
fileira de grevistas, piquete m.

**pickle** ['pɪkl] n (also: ~**s**: as
condiment) picles mpl; (fig: mess)
apuro // vt (in vinegar) conservar
em vinagre.

**pickpocket** ['pɪkpɔkɪt] n
batedor(a) m/f de carteira; (Pt)
carteirista m/f.

**pickup** ['pɪkʌp] n (on record player)
pick-up m; (small truck) camioneta.

**picnic** ['pɪknɪk] n piquenique m //
vi fazer um piquenique.

**pictorial** [pɪk'tɔːrɪəl] adj pictórico;
(magazine etc) ilustrado.

**picture** ['pɪktʃə*] n (painting)
quadro; (painting) pintura;
(photograph) fotografia; (film) filme
m // vt pintar; **the** ~**s** o cinema; ~
**book** n livro de figuras.

**picturesque** [pɪktʃə'resk] adj
pitoresco.

**pidgin** ['pɪdʒɪn] adj: ~ **English**
forma achinesada do inglês usada
entre comerciantes.

**pie** [paɪ] n (meat) pastelão m; (open)
torta; (of meat) empadão m.

**piebald** ['paɪbɔːld] adj malhado.

**piece** [piːs] n pedaço, parte f; (of land) lote m; (of cake) porção f; (item): **a ~ of furniture/advice** um móvel/um conselho // vt: **to ~ together** unir, juntar; (TECH) montar; **to take to ~s** desmontar; **~meal** adv pouco a pouco; **~work** n trabalho por empreitada.

**pier** [piə*] n cais m; (jetty) embarcadouro, molhe m.

**pierce** [piəs] vt penetrar, romper; (puncture) furar, perfurar.

**piercing** [ˈpiəsɪŋ] adj (cry) penetrante, agudo.

**piety** [ˈpaiəti] n piedade f.

**pig** [pɪg] n porco; (fig) porcalhão/lhona m/f.

**pigeon** [ˈpɪdʒən] n pombo/a; **~hole** n escaninho.

**piggy bank** [ˈpɪgibæŋk] n cofre m em forma de porquinho.

**pigheaded** [ˈpɪgˈhedɪd] adj teimoso, cabeçudo.

**pigment** [ˈpɪgmənt] n pigmento; **~ation** [-ˈteiʃən] n pigmentação f.

**pigmy** [ˈpɪgmɪ] n = **pygmy**.

**pigsty** [ˈpɪgstai] n chiqueiro.

**pigtail** [ˈpɪgteil] n (girl's) trança; (Chinese) rabicho, rabo-de-cavalo.

**pike** [paik] n (spear) lança, pique m; (fish) lúcio.

**pilchard** [ˈpɪltʃəd] n sardinha.

**pile** [pail] n (heap) pilha, monte m; (of carpet) pêlo; (of cloth) lado felpudo // vb: also: **~ up**) vt amontoar; (fig) acumular // vi amontoar-se.

**piles** [pailz] npl (MED) hemorróidas fpl.

**pile-up** [ˈpailʌp] n (AUT) acidente m com vários carros.

**pilfer** [ˈpɪlfə*] vt furtar, afanar; **~ing** n furto.

**pilgrim** [ˈpɪlgrɪm] n peregrino/a; **~age** n peregrinação f, romaria.

**pill** [pɪl] n pílula; **the ~** a pílula.

**pillage** [ˈpɪlɪdʒ] n pilhagem f, saque m.

**pillar** [ˈpɪlə*] n (gen) pilar m;

(concrete) coluna; **~ box** n (Brit) caixa coletora (do correio); (Pt) marco do correio.

**pillion** [ˈpɪljən] n (of motor cycle) assento traseiro.

**pillory** [ˈpɪlərɪ] vt expor ao ridículo.

**pillow** [ˈpɪləu] n travesseiro, almofada; **~case** n fronha.

**pilot** [ˈpailət] n piloto // adj (scheme etc) piloto // vt pilotar; (fig) guiar; **~ light** n piloto.

**pimp** [pɪmp] n proxeneta m, cáften m.

**pimple** [ˈpɪmpl] n espinha.

**pin** [pɪn] n alfinete m; (TECH) cavilha; (wooden) pino // vt alfinetar; **~s and needles** comichão f sg, sensação f de formigamento; **rolling ~** rolo de cozinha; **safety ~** alfinete de segurança; **to ~ sb down** (fig) conseguir que alguém assuma uma posição; **to ~ sth on sb** (fig) culpar alguém de algo.

**pinafore** [ˈpɪnəfɔː*] n avental m; **~ dress** n saia inteiriça.

**pinball** [ˈpɪnbɔːl] n fliper m, fliperama m.

**pincers** [ˈpɪnsəz] npl alicate msg, pinça sg, tenaz fsg.

**pinch** [pɪntʃ] n beliscão m; (of salt etc) pitada // vt beliscar; (col: steal) furtar; (: arrest) deter, dar uma batida em // vi (shoe) apertar; **to feel the ~** passar por um aperto.

**pincushion** [ˈpɪnkuʃən] n alfineteira.

**pine** [pain] n (also: **~ tree**) pinho // vi: **to ~ for** ansiar por; **to ~ away** consumir-se, estar definhando.

**pineapple** [ˈpainæpl] n abacaxi m; (Pt) ananás m.

**ping** [pɪŋ] n (noise) silvo, sibilo; (of bullet through air) zumbido; **~pong** n pingue-pongue m.

**pink** [pɪŋk] adj rosa, cor de rosa // n (colour) cor m de rosa; (BOT) cravo, cravina.

**pinnacle** [ˈpɪnəkl] n cume m; (fig) auge m.

**pinpoint** ['pɪnpɔɪnt] vt localizar com precisão.

**pint** [paɪnt] n pinta (0.57 litros), quartilho; **to go for a ~** ir tomar uma cerveja.

**pin-up** ['pɪnʌp] n pin-up f, retrato de mulher atraente.

**pioneer** [paɪə'nɪə*] n pioneiro.

**pious** ['paɪəs] adj piedoso, devoto.

**pip** [pɪp] n (seed) caroço, semente f; (time signal on radio) sinal m.

**pipe** [paɪp] n cano, tubo; (for smoking) cachimbo // vt canalizar, encanar; **~s** npl (gen) canalização fsg; (also: **bag~s**) gaita fsg de foles; **to ~ down** vi (col) calar o bico, meter a viola no saco; **~ dream** n sonho impossível, castelo no ar; **~line** n encanamento; (for oil) oleoduto; (for gas) gasoduto; **piper** n (gen) flautista m/f; (with bagpipes) gaiteiro.

**piping** ['paɪpɪŋ] adv: **~ hot** chiando de quente.

**piquant** ['pi:kənt] adj picante.

**pique** [pi:k] n ressentimento, melindre m.

**pirate** ['paɪərət] n pirata m; **~ radio** n rádio pirata or ilegal.

**pirouette** [pɪru'ɛt] n pirueta // vi fazer piruetas.

**Pisces** ['paɪsi:z] n Pisces m, peixes mpl.

**piss** [pɪs] vi (col) mijar; **~ed** adj (col: drunk) bêbado, de porre.

**pistol** ['pɪstl] n pistola.

**piston** ['pɪstən] n pistão m, êmbolo.

**pit** [pɪt] n cova, fossa; (also: **coal ~**) mina de carvão; (in garage) poço de inspeção (Pt: -ct-); (also: **orchestra ~**) fosso; (quarry) canteira, pedreira // vt: **to ~ A against B** opor A a B; **~s** npl (AUT) box m.

**pitch** [pɪtʃ] n (throw) arremesso, lance m; (MUS) tom m; (SPORT) campo; (tar) piche m, breu m; (in market etc) barraca // vt arremessar, lançar // vi (fall) tombar, cair; (NAUT) jogar, arfar; **to**

**~ a tent** armar uma tenda; **~-black** adj escuro como o breu; **~ed battle** n batalha campal.

**pitcher** ['pɪtʃə*] n jarro, cântaro; (US: baseball) arremessador m.

**pitchfork** ['pɪtʃfɔ:k] n forcado.

**piteous** ['pɪtɪəs] adj lastimável.

**pitfall** ['pɪtfɔ:l] n perigo (imprevisto), armadilha.

**pith** [pɪθ] n (of orange) casca interna e branca; (fig) essência, parte f essencial.

**pithy** ['pɪθɪ] adj substancial, rico.

**pitiable** ['pɪtɪəbl] adj deplorável.

**pitiful** ['pɪtɪful] adj (touching) comovente, tocante; (contemptible) desprezível, lamentável.

**pitiless** ['pɪtɪlɪs] adj impiedoso.

**pittance** ['pɪtns] n ninharia, miséria.

**pity** ['pɪtɪ] n (compassion) compaixão f, piedade f; (shame) pena // vt ter pena de, compadecer-se de; **what a ~!** que pena!

**pivot** ['pɪvət] n pino, eixo; (fig) pivô m // vi: **to ~ on** girar sobre; (fig) depender de.

**pixie** ['pɪksɪ] n duende m.

**placard** ['plækɑ:d] n (sign) placar m; (in march etc) cartaz m.

**placate** [plə'keɪt] vt apaziguar, aplacar.

**place** [pleɪs] n lugar m, (Pt) sítio; (rank) posição f; (seat) assento, lugar m; (post) posto; (home): **at/to his ~** em/para a casa dele // vt (object) pôr, colocar, botar; (identify) identificar, situar; (find a post for) colocar; **to take ~** realizar-se, ocorrer; **to be ~d** (in race, exam) classificar-se; **out of ~** (not suitable) fora de lugar; **in the first ~** em primeiro lugar; **to change ~s with sb** trocar de lugar com alguém.

**placid** ['plæsɪd] adj plácido, sereno.

**plagiarism** ['pleɪdʒərɪzm] n plágio.

**plague** [pleɪg] n praga; (MED)

peste *f* // *vt* (*fig*) atormentar, importunar; **to ~ sb** amofinar alguém.

**plaice** [pleɪs] *n, pl inv* solha.

**plaid** [plæd] *n* (*material*) tecido enxadrezado; (*pattern*) xadrez *m* escocês.

**plain** [pleɪn] *adj* (*clear*) claro, evidente; (*simple*) simples, despretensioso; (*frank*) franco, sem rodeios; (*not handsome*) sem atrativos (Pt: -tti-); (*pure*) puro, natural // *adv* claramente, com franqueza // *n* planície *f*, campina; **in ~ clothes** (*police*) à paisana; **~ly** *adv* claramente, obviamente; (*frankly*) francamente; **~ness** *n* clareza; simplicidade *f*; franqueza.

**plaintiff** [ˈpleɪntɪf] *n* querelante *m/f*, queixoso/a.

**plait** [plæt] *n* trança, dobra // *vt* trançar.

**plan** [plæn] *n* (*drawing*) plano; (*scheme*) esquema *m*, projeto (Pt: -ct-); (*schedule*) programa *m* // *vt* (*think in advance*) idear, proje(c)tar; (*prepare*) planejar, programar // *vi* fazer planos; **to ~ to do** tencionar fazer, propor-se fazer.

**plane** [pleɪn] *n* (AVIAT) avião *m*; (*tree*) plátano; (*tool*) plaina; (MATH) plano.

**planet** [ˈplænɪt] *n* planeta *m*; **~arium** [-ˈtɛərɪəm] *n* planetário.

**plank** [plæŋk] *n* tábua; (POL) item *m* da plataforma política.

**planner** [ˈplænə*] *n* projetista (Pt: -ect-) *m/f*.

**planning** [ˈplænɪŋ] *n* planejamento; **family ~** planejamento familiar.

**plant** [plɑːnt] *n* planta; (*machinery*) maquinaria; (*factory*) fábrica // *vt* plantar; (*field*) semear; (*bomb*) colocar, pôr; (*fam*) pôr às escondidas.

**plantation** [plænˈteɪʃən] *n* plantação *f*, roça; (*estate*) fazenda.

**plaque** [plæk] *n* placa, insígnia.

**plasma** [ˈplæzmə] *n* plasma *m*.

**plaster** [ˈplɑːstə*] *n* (*for walls*) reboco; (*also:* **sticking ~**) esparadrapo, band-aid *m*; **~ of Paris** gesso // *vt* rebocar; (*cover*): **to ~ with** encher *or* cobrir de; **~ed** *adj* (*col*) bêbado, de porre; **~er** *n* rebocador *m*, caiador *m*.

**plastic** [ˈplæstɪk] *n* plástico // *adj* de plástico.

**plasticine** [ˈplæstɪsiːn] *n* plasticina.

**plastic surgery** [ˈplæstɪkˈsəːdʒərɪ] *n* cirurgia *or* operação *f* plástica.

**plate** [pleɪt] *n* (*dish*) prato; (*metal*) placa, chapa; (PHOT) chapa; (*dental*) dentadura.

**plateau** [ˈplætəu], *pl* **~s** *or* **~x** [-z] *n* planalto, platô *m*.

**plateful** [ˈpleɪtful] *n* pratada.

**plate glass** [pleɪtˈɡlɑːs] *n* vidro laminado.

**platform** [ˈplætfɔːm] *n* (RAIL) plataforma; (Pt) cais *m*; (*stage*) estrado; (*at meeting*) tribuna; (POL) programa *m* partidário; **~ ticket** *n* bilhete *m* de plataforma.

**platinum** [ˈplætɪnəm] *n* platina.

**platitude** [ˈplætɪtjuːd] *n* lugar *m* comum, chavão *m*.

**platoon** [pləˈtuːn] *n* pelotão *m*.

**platter** [ˈplætə*] *n* travessa.

**plausible** [ˈplɔːzɪbl] *adj* plausível, aceitável; (*person*) convincente.

**play** [pleɪ] *n* (*gen*) jogo; (*also:* **~time**) recreio; (THEATRE) obra, peça // *vt* (*game*) jogar; (*instrument*) tocar; (THEATRE) representar; (: *part*) fazer o papel de; (*fig*) desempenhar // *vi* jogar; (*amuse o.s.*) divertir-se; (*frolic*) brincar; **to ~ down** *vt* não ligar para; **to ~ up** *vt* (*cause trouble to*) importunar, incomodar; **~acting** *n* teatro; **~er** *n* jogador(a) *m/f*; (THEATRE) ator/atriz (Pt: -ct-) *m/f*; (MUS) músico/a; **~ful** *adj* brincalhão/lhona; **~ground** *n* pátio de recreio; **~group** *n* espécie de jardim de infância; **~ing card** *n* carta de baralho; ~**ing field** n campo de esportes; (*Pt*) campo de jogos; ~**mate** n companheiro de brincadeira; ~**off** n (*SPORT*) partida de desempate; ~**pen** n cercado para crianças; ~**thing** n brinquedo; ~**wright** n dramaturgo/a.

**plea** [pliː] n (*request*) apelo, petição f; (*excuse*) justificativa, pretexto; (*LAW: defence*) defesa.

**plead** [pliːd] vt (*LAW*) defender, advogar; (*give as excuse*) alegar, argumentar // vi (*LAW*) declarar-se; (*beg*): **to ~ with sb** suplicar ou rogar a alguém; **to ~ guilty** confessar-se culpado; **to ~ not guilty** negar a acusação.

**pleasant** ['plɛznt] adj agradável; (*surprise*) grato; (*person*) simpático; ~**ness** n (*of person*) amabilidade f, simpatia; (*of place*) encanto; ~**ries** npl (*polite remarks*) amenidades fpl (na conversa).

**please** [pliːz] vt (*give pleasure to*) agradar, dar prazer a; (*get on well with*) dar-se bem com // vi (*think fit*): **do as you ~** faça o que quiser ou o que lhe der na telha; ~! por favor!; ~ **yourself!** como queira!; ~**d** (*happy*) satisfeito, contente; ~**d** (*with*) satisfeito com; **pleasing** adj (*gen*) agradável; (*surprise*) grato; (*flattering*) lisonjeiro.

**pleasure** ['plɛʒə*] n prazer m; (*delight*) deleite m; (*will*) vontade f // cmp de recreio; ~ **trip** n viagem f de recreio; **'it's a ~'** o prazer é (todo) meu; **it's a ~ to see him** é um prazer vê-lo.

**pleat** [pliːt] n prega.

**plebs** [plɛbz] npl (*pej*) plebe fsg.

**plectrum** ['plɛktrəm] n plectro.

**pledge** [plɛdʒ] n (*object*) garantia, penhor m; (*promise*) promessa, voto m; (*pawn*) empenhar, pôr no prego; (*promise*) prometer.

**plentiful** ['plɛntɪful] adj abundante, profuso.

**plenty** ['plɛntɪ] n abundância; ~ **of**

(*enough*) bastante; (*many*) muitos/as.

**pleurisy** ['pluərɪsɪ] n pleurisia.

**pliable** ['plaɪəbl] adj flexível; (*fig*) adaptável, influenciável.

**pliers** ['plaɪəz] npl alicate msg.

**plight** [plaɪt] n situação f difícil, apuro.

**plimsolls** ['plɪmsəlz] npl tênis mpl, calçado sg de lona.

**plod** [plɔd] vi caminhar pesadamente, (*fig*) trabalhar laboriosamente; ~**der** n (*col*) cu-de-ferro, cê-dê-efe m/f; ~**ding** adj caminhador(a); (*in work*) mourejador(a).

**plonk** [plɔŋk] (*col*) n (*wine*) vinho de segunda (categoria) // vt: **to ~ sth down** deixar cair algo (pesadamente).

**plot** [plɔt] n (*scheme*) trama, conspiração f, complô m; (*of story, play*) enredo; (*of land*) lote m // vt (*mark out*) traçar; (*conspire*) tramar, planejar // vi conspirar; ~**ter** n conspirador(a) m/f.

**plough, plow** (*US*) [plau] n arado // vt (*earth*) arar; **to ~ back** vt (*COMM*) reinvestir; **to ~ through** vt fus (*crowd*) abrir caminho por.

**ploy** [plɔɪ] n estratagema m.

**pluck** [plʌk] vt (*fruit*) colher; (*musical instrument*) dedilhar; (*bird*) depenar // n coragem f, puxão m; **to ~ up courage** reunir coragem; ~**y** adj corajoso, valente.

**plug** [plʌg] n tampão m; (*ELEC*) pino, tomada; (: *Pt*) ficha; (*AUT: also: sparking* ~) vela (de ignição) // vt (*hole*) tapar; (*col: advertise*) fazer (insistente) propaganda de; **to ~ in** (*ELEC*) ligar.

**plum** [plʌm] n (*fruit*) ameixa // adj (*col: job*) vantajoso.

**plumage** ['pluːmɪdʒ] n plumagem f.

**plumb** [plʌm] adv (*exactly*) exatamente (*Pt: -act-*) // vt

**plumber** ['plʌmə*] n bombeiro, encanador m; (*Pt*) canalizador m;

**plumbing** [-mɪŋ] n (trade) ofício de encanador; (piping) encanamento.

**plume** [pluːm] n (gen) pluma; (on helmet) penacho.

**plummet** ['plʌmɪt] vi: **to ~ (down)** cair verticalmente.

**plump** [plʌmp] adj roliço, rechonchudo // vt: **to ~ sth (down)** on deixar cair algo em; **to ~ for** (col: choose) optar por.

**plunder** ['plʌndə*] n saque m, pilhagem f; (loot) despojo // vt pilhar, espoliar; (tomb) saquear.

**plunge** [plʌndʒ] n (dive) salto; (submersion) mergulho; (bath) imersão f, banho // vt mergulhar, afundar // vi (fall) cair; (dive) mergulhar; (person) lançar-se; (sink) afundar-se; **to take the ~** decidir-se; **plunger** n êmbolo; **plunging** adj (neckline) decotado.

**pluperfect** [pluː'pəːfɪkt] n mais-que-perfeito.

**plural** ['pluərl] n plural m.

**plus** [plʌs] n (also: **~ sign**) sinal m de adição // prep mais, e; **ten/twenty ~** dez/vinte e tantos.

**plush** [plʌʃ] adj de pelúcia.

**ply** [plaɪ] vt (a trade) exercer // vi (ship) ir e vir; (for hire) oferecer-se para alugar; **three ~** (wool) de três fios; **to ~ sb with drink** insistir para que alguém beba; **to ~ sb with questions** bombardear alguém com perguntas; **~wood** n madeira compensada.

**P.M.** abbr of **Prime Minister**.

**p.m.** adv abbr of **post meridiem** da tarde, da noite.

**pneumatic** [njuː'mætɪk] adj pneumático.

**pneumonia** [njuː'məunɪə] n pneumonia.

**poach** [pəutʃ] vt (cook) escaldar, escalfar; (eggs) fazer (ovo) pochê; (steal) furtar // vi caçar/pescar em propriedade alheia; **~ed** adj (egg) escalfado, pochê; **~er** n caçador m furtivo; **~ing** n caça furtiva.

**pocket** ['pɔkɪt] n bolso; (of air, GEO, fig) bolsa; (BILLIARDS) caçapa, ventanilha // vt embolsar, meter no bolso; (steal) apropriar-se de; (BILLIARDS) encaçapar; **to be out of ~** perder, ter prejuízo; **~book** n (US: wallet) carteira, capanga; **~ knife** n canivete m; **~ money** n dinheiro para despesas miúdas.

**pod** [pɔd] n vagem f.

**podgy** ['pɔdʒɪ] adj nédio, mole.

**podiatrist** (US) n pedicuro.

**poem** ['pəuɪm] n poema m.

**poet** ['pəuɪt] n poeta m/f; **~ess** n poetisa; **~ic** [-'ɛtɪk] adj poético; **~ laureate** n poeta laureado; **~ry** n poesia.

**poignant** ['pɔɪnjənt] adj comovente; (sharp) agudo.

**point** [pɔɪnt] n (gen) ponto; (tip) ponta; (purpose) finalidade f, objetivo (Pt: -ct-); (use) utilidade f; (significant part) relevância; (characteristic) característica; (also: **decimal ~): 2 ~ 3 (2.3)** dois ponto três; **to the ~** pertinente // vt (show) mostrar, indicar; (gun etc): **to ~ sth at sb** apontar algo para alguém // vi indicar com o dedo; **~s** n pl (AUT) platinado, contato (Pt: -ct-) sg; (RAIL) agulhas fpl; **to make a ~ of** fazer questão de, insistir em; **to get the ~** compreender; **to come to the ~** ir ao que interessa, falar sem rodeios; **there's no ~ (in doing)** não adianta nada (fazer); **to ~ out** vt mostrar, realçar; **to ~** indicar com o dedo; (fig) indicar; **~-blank** adv (also: **at ~-blank range**) à queima-roupa; **~ed** adj (shape) pontudo, agudo; (remark) mordaz, intencional; **~edly** adv mordazmente; **~er** n (stick) indicador m, ponteiro n; (needle) agulha; **~less** adj (useless) inútil; (senseless) sem sentido; (motiveless) sem razão; **~ of view** n ponto de vista.

**poise** [pɔɪz] n (balance) equilíbrio;

(of head, body) porte m; (calmness) serenidade f.

**poison** ['pɔɪzn] n veneno // vt envenenar; ~**ing** n envenenamento; ~**ous** adj venenoso; (fumes etc) tóxico; (fig) pernicioso.

**poke** [pəuk] vt (fire) atiçar; (jab with finger, stick etc) cutucar; (put) : **to ~ sth in(to)** meter algo em // n (to fire) remexida; (push) empurrão m; (with elbow) cotovelada; **to ~ about** vi escarafunchar, espionar; **to ~ one's nose into** meter o nariz em.

**poker** ['pəukə*] n atiçador m; (CARDS) pôquer m; ~**-faced** adj com rosto impassível.

**poky** ['pəukɪ] adj acanhado, apertado.

**Poland** ['pəuländ] n Polônia.

**polar** ['pəulə*] adj polar; ~ **bear** n urso polar.

**polarize** ['pəuləraɪz] vt polarizar.

**pole** [pəul] n vara; (GEO) pólo; (TEL) poste m; (flag~) mastro; (tent ~) estaca.

**Pole** [pəul] n polonês/esa m/f.

**pole vault** ['pəulvɔ:lt] n salto com vara.

**police** [pə'li:s] n polícia // vt policiar; ~ **car** n rádio-patrulha f; ~**man** n polícia m, guarda m; ~ **state** n estado policial; ~ **station** n delegacia (de polícia); (Pt) esquadra; ~**woman** n policial f (feminina).

**policy** ['pɔlɪsɪ] n política; (also: **insurance** ~) apólice f.

**polio** ['pəulɪəu] n poliomielite f, polio f.

**Polish** ['pəulɪʃ] adj, n polonês/esa m/f.

**polish** ['pɔlɪʃ] n (for shoes) graxa; (for floor) cera (para encerar); (for nails) esmalte m; (shine) verniz m, polimento; (fig: refinement) refinamento, cultura // vt (shoes) engraxar; (make shiny) lustrar, dar brilho a; (fig: improve) refinar, polir; **to ~ off** vt (work) dar os

arremates a; (food) raspar; ~**ed** adj (fig: person) culto; (: manners) refinado.

**polite** [pə'laɪt] adj gentil, bem educado; (formal) cortês; ~**ness** n gentileza, cortesia.

**politic** ['pɔlɪtɪk] adj prudente; ~**al** [pə'lɪtɪkl] adj político; ~**ian** [-'tɪʃən] n político; ~**s** npl política sg.

**polka** ['pɔlkə] n polca; ~ **dot** n pinta.

**poll** [pəul] n (votes) votação f; (also: **opinion** ~) pesquisa, sondagem f // vt (votes) receber, obter.

**pollen** ['pɔlən] n pólen m.

**pollination** [pɔlɪ'neɪʃən] n polinização f.

**polling** ['pəulɪŋ]: ~ **booth** n cabine f de votar; ~ **day** n dia m de eleição; ~ **station** n centro eleitoral.

**pollute** [pə'lu:t] vt poluir; **pollution** [-'lu:ʃən] n poluição f, contaminação f.

**polo** ['pəuləu] n (sport) pólo; ~**-neck** adj de gola rolê.

**polyester** [pɔlɪ'ɛstə*] n poliéster m.

**polygamy** [pɔ'lɪgəmɪ] n poligamia.

**polytechnic** [pɔlɪ'tɛknɪk] n politécnico, escola politécnica.

**polythene, polyethylene** (US) ['pɔlɪθi:n, pɔlɪ'ɛθɪli:n] n politeno.

**pomegranate** ['pɔmɪgrænɪt] n (fruit) romã f.

**pommel** ['pɔml] n botão m; (saddle) maçaneta // vt esmurrar.

**pomp** [pɔmp] n pompa.

**pompous** ['pɔmpəs] adj pomposo.

**pond** [pɔnd] n (natural) lago pequeno; (artificial) tanque m.

**ponder** ['pɔndə*] vt ponderar, meditar sobre; ~**ous** adj pesado.

**pontiff** ['pɔntɪf] n pontífice m.

**pontificate** [pɔn'tɪfɪkeɪt] vi (fig): **to ~ (about)** pontificar (sobre).

**pontoon** [pɔn'tu:n] n pontão m; (card game) vinte-e-um m.

**pony** ['pəunɪ] n pônei m; ~**tail** n

rabo-de-cavalo; ~ **trekking** n
excursão f em pônei.

**poodle** ['pu:dl] n cão-d'água m.

**pool** [pu:l] n (of rain) poça, charco;
(pond) lago; (also: **swimming** ~)
piscina; (billiards) sinuca // vt
reunir; (football) ~**s** loteria
esportiva; (Pt) totobola.

**poor** [puə*] adj pobre; (bad) inferior,
mau // npl: **the** ~ os pobres mpl;
~**ly** adj adoentado, indisposto.

**pop** [pɔp] n bum!; (sound) ruído seco,
estouro; (MUS) pop m; (US: col:
father) paizinho; (lemonade) bebida
gasosa // vt (put) pôr // vi estourar;
(cork) saltar; **to** ~ **in** vi entrar de
repente; (visit) dar um pulo; **to** ~
**out** vi sair de repente; **to** ~ **up** vi
aparecer inesperadamente; ~
**concert** n concerto pop; ~**corn**
n pipoca.

**pope** [pəup] n Papa m.

**poplar** ['pɔplə*] n álamo, choupo.

**poplin** ['pɔplin] n popeline f.

**poppy** ['pɔpi] n papoula.

**populace** ['pɔpjuləs] n populaça,
povão m.

**popular** ['pɔpjulə*] adj popular;
(fashionable) na moda; ~**ity**
[-'læriti] n popularidade f; ~**ize** vt
popularizar; (disseminate) vulgari-
zar.

**populate** ['pɔpjuleit] vt povoar;
**population** [-'leiʃən] n população f.

**populous** ['pɔpjuləs] adj populoso.

**porcelain** ['pɔ:slin] n porcelana.

**porch** [pɔ:tʃ] n pórtico m; (US)
varanda.

**porcupine** ['pɔ:kjupain] n porco-
espinho.

**pore** [pɔ:*] n poro // vi: **to** ~ **over**
examinar com atenção.

**pork** [pɔ:k] n carne f de porco.

**pornographic** [pɔ:nə'græfik] adj
pornográfico; **pornography** [-'nɔ-
grəfi] n pornografia.

**porous** ['pɔ:rəs] adj poroso.

**porpoise** ['pɔ:pəs] n golfinho, boto.

**porridge** ['pɔridʒ] n mingau m (de
aveia).

**port** [pɔ:t] n (harbour) porto; (NAUT:
left side) bombordo; (wine) vinho do
Porto.

**portable** ['pɔ:təbl] adj portátil.

**portend** [pɔ:'tend] vt pressagiar;
**portent** ['pɔ:tent] n presságio,
portento.

**porter** ['pɔ:tə*] n (for luggage)
carregador; (doorkeeper) porteiro.

**porthole** ['pɔ:thəul] n vigia.

**portion** ['pɔ:ʃən] n porção f, quinhão
m; (helping) ração f.

**portly** ['pɔ:tli] adj corpulento.

**portrait** ['pɔ:treit] n retrato.

**portray** [pɔ:'trei] vt retratar; (in
writing) descrever; ~**al** n
representação f.

**Portugal** ['pɔ:tjugl] n Portugal m.

**Portuguese** [pɔ:tju'gi:z] adj portu-
guês/esa // n, pl inv português/esa
m/f; (LING) português m.

**pose** [pəuz] n postura, pose f; (pej)
pose, afetação (Pt: -ct-) f // vi
(pretend): **to** ~ **as** fazer-se passar
por // vt (question) colocar.

**posh** [pɔʃ] adj (col) fino, elegante.

**position** [pə'ziʃən] n posição f; (job)
cargo // vt colocar, situar.

**positive** ['pɔzitiv] adj positivo;
(certain) certo; (definite) definitivo.

**posse** ['pɔsi] n (US) pelotão m de
civis armados.

**possess** [pə'zes] vt possuir; ~**ion**
[pə'zeʃən] n posse f, possessão f;
~**ive** adj possessivo.

**possibility** [pɔsi'biliti] n
possibilidade f; **possible** ['pɔsibl] adj
possível; **as big as possible** o maior
possível; **possibly** ['pɔsibli] adv
(perhaps) possivelmente, talvez; **I
cannot possibly come** estou
impossibilitado de vir.

**post** [pəust] n (letters, delivery)
correio; (job, situation) posto,
cargo; (pole) poste m // vt (send by post) pôr no
correio; (MIL) nomear; (bills) afixar,
pregar; (appoint): **to** ~ **to** destinar

a; ~age *n* porte *m*, franquia; ~al *adj* postal; ~al order *n* vale *m* postal; ~box *n* caixa do correio; ~card *n* cartão *m* postal.

**postdate** [pəust'deit] *vt* (*cheque*) pós-datar.

**poster** ['pəustə*] *n* cartaz *m*.

**posterior** [pɔs'tiəriə*] *n* (*col*) traseiro, nádegas *fpl*; (*col*) bunda.

**posterity** [pɔs'tɛriti] *n* posteridade *f*.

**postgraduate** ['pəust'grædjuət] *n* pós-graduado/a.

**posthumous** ['pɔstjuməs] *adj* póstumo.

**post:** ~man *n* carteiro; ~mark *n* carimbo do correio; ~master *n* agente *m/f* do correio; (*Pt*) chefe *m/f* do correio.

**post-mortem** [pəust'mɔːtəm] *n* autópsia.

**post office** ['pəustɔfis] *n* (*building*) agência do correio, correio; (*organization*) Departamento dos Correios e Telégrafos; (*Pt*) C.T.T. (Correios, Telégrafos e Telefones); ~box (P.O. box) *n* caixa postal.

**postpone** [pəs'pəun] *vt* adiar; ~ment *n* adiamento.

**postscript** ['pəustskript] *n* pós-escrito.

**postulate** ['pɔstjuleit] *vt* postular.

**posture** ['pɔstʃə*] *n* postura, atitude *f*.

**postwar** [pəust'wɔː*] *adj* de após-guerra.

**posy** ['pəuzi] *n* ramalhete *m*.

**pot** [pɔt] *n* (*for cooking*) panela; (*for flowers*) vaso; (*for jam*) pote *m*; (*col: marijuana*) maconha // *vt* (*plant*) plantar em vaso; (*conserve*) pôr em conserva.

**potato** [pə'teitəu] *pl* ~es *n* batata.

**potent** ['pəutnt] *adj* potente, poderoso; (*drink*) forte.

**potential** [pə'tɛnʃl] *adj* potencial, latente // *n* potencial *m*.

**pothole** ['pɔthəul] *n* (*in road*) buraco; (*underground*) caldeirão *m*,

cova; **potholer** *n* espeleologista *m/f*; **potholing** *n*: to go potholing dedicar-se à espeleologia.

**potion** ['pəuʃən] *n* poção *f*.

**potluck** [pɔt'lʌk] *n*: to take ~ contentar-se com o que houver.

**potshot** ['pɔtʃɔt] *n*: to take a ~ at sth atirar em algo a esmo.

**potted** ['pɔtid] *adj* (*food*) em conserva; (*plant*) de vaso.

**potter** ['pɔtə*] *n* (*artistic*) ceramista *m/f*; (*artisan*) oleiro // *vi*: to ~ around, ~ about desperdiçar tempo com ninharias; ~y *n* cerâmica, olaria.

**potty** ['pɔti] *adj* (*col: mad*) maluco, doido // *n* urinol *m* (de criança).

**pouch** [pautʃ] *n* (*zool*) bolsa; (*for tobacco*) tabaqueira.

**pouf(fe)** [puːf] *n* pufe *m*.

**poultice** ['pəultis] *n* cataplasma.

**poultry** ['pəultri] *n* aves *fpl* domésticas; ~ farm *n* granja avícola.

**pounce** [pauns] *vi*: to ~ on lançar-se sobre // *n* salto, arremetida.

**pound** [paund] *n* (*gen*) libra; (*for dogs*) canil *m*; (*for cars*) depósito // *vt* (*beat*) socar, esmurrar; (*crush*) triturar // *vi* (*beat*) dar pancadas; ~ sterling *n* libra esterlina.

**pour** [pɔː*] *vt* despejar; (*tea*) servir // *vi* fluir, correr; (*rain*) chover a cântaros; to ~ away or off *vt* esvaziar, decantar; to ~ in *vi* (*people*) entrar em torrente; to ~ out *vi* (*people*) sair aos borbotões; *vt* (*drink*) servir; ~ing *adj*: ~ing rain chuva torrencial.

**pout** [paut] *vi* fazer beicinho.

**poverty** ['pɔvəti] *n* pobreza; (*fig*) falta, escassez *f*; ~stricken *adj* indigente, necessitado.

**powder** ['paudə*] *n* pó *m*; (*face* ~) pó-de-arroz *m*; (*gun*~) pólvora // *vt* pulverizar; (*face*) empoar, passar pó em; ~ compact *n* estojo (de pó-de-arroz); ~ room *n* toucador *m*; ~y *adj* poeirento.

**power** ['pauə*] n (gen) poder m; (strength) força; (nation) potência; (ability, POL: of party, leader) poder, poderio; (drive) propulsão f; (TECH) potência; (ELEC) força, energia // vt (ELEC) alimentar; ~ **cut** n corte m de energia; ~**ed** adj: ~**ed by** com propulsão a; ~**ful** adj poderoso; (engine) potente; (build) vigoroso; (emotion) intenso; ~**less** adj impotente; ~ **line** n fio de alta tensão; ~ **point** n tomada; ~ **station** n central f elétrica (Pt: -ct-).

**practicable** ['præktikəbl] adj (scheme) praticável, viável.

**practical** ['præktikl] adj prático; ~ **joke** n brincadeira pesada, peça; ~**ly** adv (almost) praticamente.

**practice** ['præktis] n (habit) costume m, hábito; (exercise) prática, exercício; (training) treinamento; (MED) clientela // vt/i (US) = **practise**; **in** ~ (in reality) na prática; **out of** ~ destreinado.

**practise**, **practice** (US) ['præktis] vt (carry out) praticar; (be in the habit of) ter por costume; (profession) exercer; (train at) fazer exercícios de // vi exercer (profissão); (train) treinar, exercitar-se; **practising** adj (Christian etc) praticante; (lawyer) que exerce.

**practitioner** [præk'tifənə*] n praticante m/f; (MED) médico/a.

**pragmatic** [præg'mætik] adj pragmático.

**prairie** ['preəri] n campina, pradaria.

**praise** [preiz] n louvor m, elogio; ~**worthy** adj louvável, digno de elogio.

**pram** [præm] n carrinho de bebê.

**prance** [pra:ns] vi (horse) curvetear, fazer cabriolas.

**prank** [præŋk] n travessura, peça.

**prattle** ['prætl] vi tagarelar; (child) balbuciar.

**prawn** [prɔːn] n pitu m; (small) camarão m.

**pray** [prei] vi rezar; ~**er** n oração f, prece f; (entreaty) súplica, rogo; ~**er book** n missal m, livro de orações.

**preach** [priːtʃ] vi pregar; ~**er** n pregador(a) m/f; (US) pastor m.

**preamble** [pri'æmbl] n preâmbulo.

**prearranged** [priːə'reindʒd] adj combinado de antemão.

**precarious** [pri'keəriəs] adj precário.

**precaution** [pri'kɔːʃən] n precaução f.

**precede** [pri'siːd] vt/i preceder.

**precedence** ['presidəns] n precedência; (priority) prioridade f.

**precedent** [-ənt] n precedente m.

**preceding** [pri'siːdiŋ] adj precedente.

**precept** ['priːsept] n preceito.

**precinct** ['priːsiŋkt] n recinto; ~**s** npl arredores mpl; **pedestrian** ~ área de pedestres; **shopping** ~ zona comercial.

**precious** ['preʃəs] adj precioso; (stylized) afetado (Pt: -ct-).

**precipice** ['presipis] n precipício.

**precipitate** [pri'sipitit] adj (hasty) precipitado, apressado // vt [pri'sipiteit] (hasten) precipitar, acelerar; (bring about) causar; **precipitation** [-'teiʃən] n precipitação f.

**precipitous** [pri'sipitəs] adj (steep) íngreme, escarpado.

**precise** [pri'sais] adj exato (Pt: -ct-), preciso; (person) escrupuloso, meticuloso; ~**ly** adv exa(c)tamente; **precision** [-'siʒən] n precisão f.

**preclude** [pri'kluːd] vt excluir.

**precocious** [pri'kəuʃəs] adj precoce.

**preconceived** [priːkən'siːvd] adj (idea) preconcebido.

**precursor** [priː'kɜːsə*] n precursor(a) m/f.

**predator** ['predətə*] n predador m;

~y adj predatório, rapace.

**predecessor** [ˈpriːdɪsesəˀ] n predecessor(a) m/f, antepassado/a.

**predestination** [priːdestɪˈneɪʃən] n predestinação f, destino.

**predetermine** [priːdɪˈtəːmɪn] vt predeterminar, predispor.

**predicament** [prɪˈdɪkəmənt] n predicamento, apuro.

**predict** [prɪˈdɪkt] vt predizer, prognosticar; ~**ion** [-ˈdɪkʃən] n prognóstico.

**predominant** [prɪˈdɒmɪnənt] adj predominante, preponderante; **predominate** [-neɪt] vi predominar.

**pre-eminent** [priːˈemɪnənt] adj preeminente.

**pre-empt** [priːˈemt] vt adquirir por preempção or de antemão.

**preen** [priːn] vt: **to ~ itself** (bird) limpar e alisar as penas (com o bico); **to ~ o.s.** enfeitar-se, envaidecer-se.

**prefab** [ˈpriːfæb] n casa pré-fabricada.

**prefabricated** [priːˈfæbɾɪkeɪtɪd] adj pré-fabricado.

**preface** [ˈprefəs] n prefácio.

**prefect** [ˈpriːfekt] n (Brit: in school) monitor m, tutor m.

**prefer** [prɪˈfəːˀ] vt preferir; ~**able** [ˈprefɾəbl] adj preferível; ~**ably** [ˈprefɾəbli] adv de preferência; ~**ence** [ˈprefɾəns] n preferência, prioridade f; ~**ential** [prefəˈrenʃəl] adj preferencial.

**prefix** [ˈpriːfɪks] n prefixo.

**pregnancy** [ˈpregnənsɪ] n gravidez f; **pregnant** [-ənt] adj grávida; **to be pregnant** estar grávida; **pregnant with** rico de, cheio de.

**prehistoric** [ˈpriːhɪsˈtɒrɪk] adj pré-histórico.

**prejudge** [priːˈdʒʌdʒ] vt fazer um juízo antecipado de, prejulgar.

**prejudice** [ˈpredʒudɪs] n (bias) preconceito; (harm) prejuízo // vt (predispose) predispor; (harm) prejudicar; ~**d** adj (person)

predisposto, preconceituoso; (view) parcial, preconcebido.

**prelate** [ˈprelət] n prelado.

**preliminary** [prɪˈlɪmɪnərɪ] adj preliminar, prévio.

**prelude** [ˈpreljuːd] n prelúdio.

**premarital** [ˈpriːˈmærɪtl] adj pré-nupcial.

**premature** [ˈprɛmətʃuəˀ] adj prematuro, precoce.

**premeditated** [priːˈmedɪteɪtɪd] adj premeditado.

**premier** [ˈpremɪəˀ] adj primeiro, principal // n (POL) primeiro-ministro.

**première** [ˈpremɪɛəˀ] n estréia.

**premise** [ˈpremɪs] n premissa; ~**s** npl local msg; (house) casa sg; (shop) loja sg; **on the ~s** no local.

**premium** [ˈpriːmɪəm] n prêmio, recompensa; (COMM) prêmio; **to be at a ~** ser difícil de obter.

**premonition** [prɛməˈnɪʃən] n presságio, pressentimento.

**preoccupation** [priːɔkjuˈpeɪʃən] n preocupação f; **preoccupied** [-ˈɔkjupaɪd] adj (worried) preocupado, apreensivo; (absorbed) absorto.

**prep** [prep] n (SCOL: study) deveres mpl; ~ **school** n = **preparatory school**.

**prepaid** [priːˈpeɪd] adj com porte pago.

**preparation** [prepəˈreɪʃən] n preparação f; ~**s** npl preparativos mpl.

**preparatory** [prɪˈpærətərɪ] adj preparatório, introdutório; ~ **to** antes de; ~ **school** n escola preparatória.

**prepare** [prɪˈpɛəˀ] vt preparar, aprontar // vi: **to ~ for** preparar-se or aprontar-se para; (make preparations) fazer preparativos para; ~**d to** preparado or pronto para.

**preponderance** [prɪˈpɒndərns] n preponderância, predomínio.

**preposition** [prɛpə'zɪʃən] *n* preposição *f*.

**preposterous** [prɪ'pɒstərəs] *adj* absurdo, disparatado.

**prerequisite** [pri:'rɛkwɪzɪt] *n* pré-requisito, condição *f* prévia.

**prerogative** [prɪ'rɒgətɪv] *n* prerrogativa, privilégio.

**presbyterian** [prɛzbɪ'tɪərɪən] *adj*, *n* presbiteriano/a.

**preschool** ['pri:'sku:l] *adj* pré-escolar.

**prescribe** [prɪ'skraɪb] *vt* prescrever; (MED) receitar.

**prescription** [prɪ'skrɪpʃən] *n* prescrição *f*, ordem *f*; (MED) receita.

**presence** ['prɛzns] *n* presença; (*attendance*) assistência; ~ **of mind** *n* presença de espírito.

**present** ['prɛznt] *adj* (*in attendance*) presente; (*current*) atual (Pt: -ct-) // *n* (*gift*) presente *m*; (*actuality*) a(c)tualidade *f*, momento; **for the** ~ por enquanto // *vt* [prɪ'zɛnt] (*introduce*) apresentar; (*expound*) expor; (*give*) presentear, oferecer; (THEATRE) representar; **at** ~ no momento, agora; ~**able** [prɪ'zɛntəbl] *adj* apresentável; ~**ation** [-'teɪʃən] *n* apresentação *f*; (*gift*) presente; (*of case*) −exposição *f*; (THEATRE) representação *f*; ~**-day** *adj* atual (Pt: -ct-); ~**ly** *adv* (*soon*) logo, em breve.

**preservation** [prɛzə'veɪʃən] *n* conservação *f*, preservação *f*.

**preservative** [prɪ'zɜːvətɪv] *n* preservativo.

**preserve** [prɪ'zɜːv] *vt* (*keep safe*) preservar, proteger; (*maintain*) conservar, manter; (*food*) pôr em conserva; (*in salt*) conservar em sal, salgar // *n* (*for game*) reserva de caça, coutada; (*often pl*: *jam*) compota, conserva.

**preside** [prɪ'zaɪd] *vi* presidir.

**presidency** ['prɛzɪdənsɪ] *n* presidência; **president** [-ənt] *n*

presidente/a *m/f*; **presidential** [-'dɛnʃl] *adj* presidencial.

**press** [prɛs] *n* (*tool, machine, newspapers*) prensa; (*printer's*) imprensa, prelo; (*crowd*) turba, apinhamento; (*of hand*) apertão *m* // *vt* (*push*) empurrar; (*squeeze*) apertar, espremer; (*clothes: iron*) passar; (TECH) prensar; (*harry*) assediar; **to** ~ **down** (*button*) carregar em; (*insist*): **to** ~ **sth on sb** insistir para que alguém aceite algo // *vi* (*squeeze*) apertar; (*pressurize*) pressionar; **we are** ~**ed for time** estamos com pouco tempo; **to** ~ **on** *vi* avançar; (*hurry*) apertar o passo; ~ **agency** *n* agência (de imprensa); ~ **conference** *n* entrevista coletiva (para a imprensa); ~ **cutting** *n* recorte *m* de jornal; ~**ing** *adj* urgente; ~ **stud** *n* botão *m* de pressão.

**pressure** ['prɛʃə*] *n* pressão *f*; (*urgency*) premência, urgência; (*influence*) coação (Pt: -çç-) *f*; (MED) pressão *f* sanguínea; ~ **cooker** *n* panela de pressão; ~ **gauge** *n* manômetro; ~ **group** *n* grupo de pressão; **pressurized** *adj* pressurizado.

**prestige** [prɛs'tiːʒ] *n* prestígio; **prestigious** [-'tɪdʒəs] *adj* de prestígio.

**presumably** [prɪ'zjuːməblɪ] *adv* presumivelmente, provavelmente.

**presume** [prɪ'zjuːm] *vt* presumir, supor; **to** ~ **to do** (*dare*) ousar, atrever-se a; (*set out to*) pretender.

**presumption** [prɪ'zʌmpʃən] *n* suposição *f*; (*pretension*) presunção *f*; (*boldness*) atrevimento, audácia.

**presuppose** [priːsə'pəuz] *vt* pressupor, implicar.

**pretence, pretense** (US) [prɪ'tɛns] *n* (*claim*) pretensão *f*; (*display*) ostentação *f*; (*pretext*) pretexto; (*make-believe*) fingimento; **on the** ~ **of** sob o pretexto de.

**pretend** [prɪ'tend] *vt* (*feign*) fingir; // *vi* (*feign*) fingir; (*claim*): **to ~ to sth** aspirar a *or* pretender a algo.

**pretension** [pr'tenʃən] *n* (*presumption*) presunção *f*; (*claim*) pretensão *f*.

**pretentious** [prɪ'tenʃəs] *adj* pretensioso, presunçoso; (*ostentatious*) exibicionista, ostentativo.

**pretext** ['priːtekst] *n* pretexto.

**pretty** ['prɪti] *adj* (*gen*) lindo; (*person*) bonito; (*dress*) lindo; (*sum*) considerável // *adv* (*quite*) bastante; (*nearly*) quase.

**prevail** [prɪ'veɪl] *vi* (*win*) triunfar; (*be current*) imperar; (*be in fashion*) estar na moda; (*be usual*) prevalecer, vigorar; (*persuade*): **to ~ (up)on sb to do sth** persuadir alguém a fazer algo; **~ing** *adj* (*dominant*) reinante; (*usual*) corrente.

**prevalent** ['prevələnt] *adj* (*dominant*) predominante; (*usual*) corrente; (*fashionable*) dominante, da moda; (*present-day*) atual (*Pt*: -ct-).

**prevent** [prɪ'vent] *vt*: **to ~ (sb) from doing sth** impedir (alguém) de fazer algo; **~able** *adj* evitável; **~ative** *adj* preventivo; **~ion** [-'venʃən] *n* prevenção *f*, impedimento; **~ive** *adj* preventivo.

**preview** ['priːvjuː] *n* (*of film*) pré-estréia; (*fig*) antecipação *f*.

**previous** ['priːvɪəs] *adj* prévio, anterior; (*hasty*) apressado; **~ly** *adv* previamente, antecipadamente; (*in earlier times*) antes, anteriormente.

**prewar** [priː'wɔː*] *adj* anterior à guerra.

**prey** [preɪ] *n* presa *f*; // *vi*: **to ~ on** viver às custas de; (*feed on*) alimentar-se de; (*plunder*) saquear, pilhar; **it was ~ing on his mind** preocupava-o, atormentava-o.

**price** [praɪs] *n* preço // *vt* (*goods*) fixar o preço de; **~less** *adj* inestimável.

**prick** [prɪk] *n* picada; (*with pin*) alfinetada; (*sting*) ferroada // *vt* picar, furar; **to ~ up one's ears** aguçar os ouvidos.

**prickle** ['prɪkl] *n* (*sensation*) comichão, ardência; (*bot*) espinho; (*zool*) acúleo; **prickly** *adj* espinhoso; (*fig: person*) irritadiço; (: *touchy*) susceptível, melindroso.

**pride** [praɪd] *n* orgulho; (*pej*) soberba // *vt*: **to ~ o.s. on** orgulhar-se de, vangloriar-se de.

**priest** [priːst] *n* sacerdote *m*, padre *m*; **~ess** *n* sacerdotisa; **~hood** *n* (*practice*) sacerdócio; (*priests*) clero.

**prig** [prɪg] *n* pedante *m/f*.

**prim** [prɪm] *adj* (*formal*) empertigado; (*affected*) afetado (*Pt*: -ct-); (*prudish*) que afe(c)ta recato.

**primarily** ['praɪmərɪlɪ] *adv* (*above all*) fundamentalmente, antes de nada; (*firstly*) em primeiro lugar.

**primary** ['praɪmərɪ] *adj* primário; (*first in importance*) principal; **~ school** *n* escola primária.

**primate** ['praɪmɪt] *n* (*rel*) primaz *m* // *n* ['praɪmeɪt] (*zool*) primata *m*.

**prime** [praɪm] *adj* primeiro, principal; (*basic*) fundamental, primário; (*excellent*) superior // (*gun*, *pump*) escorvar; (*fig*) aprontar, preparar; **in the ~ of life** na primavera da vida; **~ minister** *n* primeiro-ministro; **~r** *n* (*book*) livro de leitura; (*paint*) pintura de base.

**primitive** ['prɪmɪtɪv] *adj* primitivo; (*crude*) rudimentar; (*uncivilized*) grosseiro, inculto.

**primrose** ['prɪmrəuz] *n* prímula, primavera.

**primus (stove)** ['praɪməs] *n* fogão *m* portátil a petróleo.

**prince** [prɪns] *n* príncipe *m*.

**princess** [prɪn'ses] *n* princesa.

**principal** ['prɪnsɪpl] *adj* principal, fundamental // *n* diretor(a) (*Pt*: -ct-) *m/f*.

**principality** [prɪnsɪ'pælɪtɪ] *n* principado.

**principle** ['prɪnsɪpl] *n* princípio.

**print** [prɪnt] *n* (*impression*) impressão *f*, marca; (*letters*) letra de forma; (*fabric*) estampado; (*ART*) estampa, gravura; (*PHOT*) cópia // *vt* (*gen*) imprimir; (*on mind*) gravar; (*write in capitals*) escrever em letra de imprensa; **out of ~** esgotado; **~ed matter** *n* impressos *mpl*; **~er** *n* impressor(a) *m/f*; **~ing** *n* (*art*) imprensa; (*act*) impressão *f*; (*quantity*) tiragem *f*; **~ing press** *n* prelo, máquina impressora.

**prior** ['praɪə*] *adj* anterior, prévio // *n* prior *m*; **~ to doing** antes de *or* até fazer.

**priority** [praɪ'ɔrɪtɪ] *n* prioridade *f*.

**prise** [praɪz] *vt*: **to ~ open** abrir com alavanca, arrombar.

**prism** ['prɪzəm] *n* prisma *m*.

**prison** ['prɪzn] *n* prisão *f*, cárcere *m* // *adj* carcerário; **~er** *n* (*in prison*) preso, prisioneiro; (*under arrest*) detido; (*in dock*) acusado, réu *m*.

**privacy** ['prɪvəsɪ] *n* (*seclusion*) isolamento, solidão *f*; (*intimacy*) intimidade *f*, privacidade *f*.

**private** ['praɪvɪt] *adj* (*personal*) particular; (*confidential*) confidencial, reservado; (*intimate*) privado, íntimo; (*sitting etc*) a portas fechadas // *n* soldado raso; '**~**' (*on envelope*) 'confidencial'; (*on door*) 'particular'; **in ~** em particular; **~ enterprise** *n* a iniciativa privada; **~ eye** *n* detetive (*Pt*: *-ct-*) *m* particular; **~ly** *adv* em particular; (*in o.s.*) no fundo.

**privet** ['prɪvɪt] *n* alfena.

**privilege** ['prɪvɪlɪdʒ] *n* privilégio; (*prerogative*) prerrogativa; **~d** *adj* privilegiado.

**privy** ['prɪvɪ] *adj*: **to be ~ to** estar inteirado de; **P~ Council** *n* Conselho Privado.

**prize** [praɪz] *n* prêmio // *adj* premiado; (*first class*) de primeira

classe // *vt* estimar, apreciar; **~-giving** *n* distribuição *f* dos prêmios; **~winner** *n* premiado/a.

**pro** [prəu] *n* (*SPORT*) profissional *m/f*; **the ~s and cons** os prós e os contras.

**probability** [prɔbə'bɪlɪtɪ] *n* probabilidade *f*; **probable** ['prɔbəbl] *adj* provável; (*plausible*) verossímil; **probably** ['prɔbəblɪ] *adv* provavelmente.

**probation** [prə'beɪʃən] *n*: **on ~** (*employee*) em estágio probatório; (*LAW*) em liberdade condicional.

**probe** [prəub] *n* (*MED, SPACE*) sonda; (*enquiry*) pesquisa // *vt* sondar; (*investigate*) investigar, esquadrinhar.

**problem** ['prɔbləm] *n* problema *m*; **~atic** [-'mætɪk] *adj* problemático.

**procedure** [prə'si:dʒə*] *n* (*ADMIN, LAW*) procedimento; (*method*) método, processo; (*bureaucratic*) protocolo.

**proceed** [prə'si:d] *vi* proceder; (*continue*): **to ~ (with)** continuar *or* prosseguir (com); **~ings** *npl* ato (*Pt*: *-ct-*) *sg*, procedimento *sg*; (*LAW*) processo *sg*; (*meeting*) reunião *fsg*; (*records*) atas (*Pt*: *-ct-*) *fpl*; **~s** ['prəusi:dz] *npl* produto *sg*.

**process** ['prəuses] *n* processo; (*method*) método, sistema *m*; (*proceeding*) procedimento // *vt* processar, elaborar; **in ~** em andamento; **~ing** *n* processamento.

**procession** [prə'seʃən] *n* procissão *f*; *funeral* ~ cortejo fúnebre.

**proclaim** [prə'kleɪm] *vt* proclamar; (*announce*) anunciar; **proclamation** [prɔklə'meɪʃən] *n* proclamação *f*; (*written*) promulgação *f*.

**procreation** [prəukrɪ'eɪʃən] *n* procriação *f*.

**procure** [prə'kjuə*] *vt* obter.

**prod** [prɔd] *vt* (*push*) empurrar; (*with elbow*) cutucar, acotovelar; (*jab*) espetar // *n* empurrão *m*; cotovelada; espetada.

**prodigal** ['prɒdɪgl] adj pródigo.

**prodigious** [prə'dɪdʒəs] adj prodigioso, extraordinário.

**prodigy** ['prɒdɪdʒɪ] n prodígio.

**produce** ['prɒdju:s] n (AGR) produtos mpl agrícolas // vt [prə'dju:s] (gen) produzir; (profit) render; (show) apresentar, exibir; (THEATRE) pôr em cena or em cartaz; (offspring) dar a luz; **producer** n (THEATRE) diretor(a) (Pt: -ct-) m/f; (AGR, CINEMA) produtor(a) m/f.

**product** ['prɒdʌkt] n (thing) produto; (result) fruto, resultado.

**production** [prə'dʌkʃən] n (act) produção f; (thing) produto; (THEATRE) representação f, encenação f; ~ **line** n linha de produção or de montagem.

**productive** [prə'dʌktɪv] adj produtivo; **productivity** [prɒdʌk-'tɪvɪtɪ] n produtividade f.

**profane** [prə'feɪn] adj profano; (language etc) irreverente, sacrílego.

**profess** [prə'fes] vt professar; (regret) manifestar.

**profession** [prə'feʃən] n profissão f; ~**al** n profissional m/f; (expert) experto, versado // adj perito; (by profession) de carreira, por profissão.

**professor** [prə'fesə*] n catedrático/a.

**proficiency** [prə'fɪʃənsɪ] n proficiência, capacidade f; **proficient** [-ənt] adj proficiente, capaz.

**profile** ['prəufaɪl] n perfil m.

**profit** ['prɒfɪt] n (COMM) lucro; (fig) vantagem f // vi: **to** ~ **by** or **from** aproveitar-se de, tirar proveito de; ~**ability** [-ə'bɪlɪtɪ] n rentabilidade f; ~**able** adj (ECON) lucrativo, rendoso; (useful) proveitoso; ~**eering** [-'tɪərɪŋ] n (pej) lucros mpl excessivos.

**profound** [prə'faund] adj profundo.

**profuse** [prə'fju:s] adj profuso, pródigo; ~**ly** adv abundantemente; **profusion** [-'fju:ʒən] n profusão f, abundância.

**progeny** ['prɒdʒɪnɪ] n prole f, progênie f.

**programme, program** (US) ['prəugræm] n programa m // vt programar; **programming, programing** (US) n programação f.

**progress** ['prəugres] n progresso; (development) desenvolvimento // vi [prə'gres] progredir, avançar; **in** ~ em andamento; ~**ion** [-'greʃən] n progressão f, avanço; ~**ive** [-'gresɪv] adj progressivo // n (person) progressista m/f.

**prohibit** [prə'hɪbɪt] vt proibir; **to** ~ **sb from doing sth** proibir alguém de fazer algo; ~**ion** [prəuɪ'bɪʃən] n (US) lei f seca; ~**ive** adj (price etc) proibitivo, excessivo.

**project** ['prɒdʒekt] n projeto (Pt: -ct-) // (vb: [prə'dʒekt]) vt proje(c)tar // vi (stick out) ressaltar, sobressair.

**projectile** [prə'dʒektaɪl] n projétil (Pt: -ct-) m.

**projection** [prə'dʒekʃən] n projeção (Pt: -cç-) f; (overhang) saliência.

**projector** [prə'dʒektə*] n projetor (Pt: -ct-) m.

**proletarian** [prəulɪ'tɛərɪən] adj, n proletário/a; **proletariat** [-rɪət] n proletariado.

**proliferate** [prə'lɪfəreɪt] vi proliferar, multiplicar-se; **proliferation** [-'reɪʃən] n proliferação f.

**prolific** [prə'lɪfɪk] adj prolífico.

**prologue** ['prəulɒg] n prólogo.

**prolong** [prə'lɒŋ] vt prolongar, estender.

**promenade** [prɒmə'nɑːd] n (by sea) passeio (à orla marítima).

**prominence** ['prɒmɪnəns] n (fig) eminência, importância; **prominent** [-ənt] adj (standing out) proeminente; (*important*) eminente, notório.

**promiscuous** [prə'mɪskjuəs] *adj* (*sexually*) promíscuo, libertino.

**promise** ['prɒmɪs] *n* promessa // *vt/i* prometer; **promising** *adj* prometedor(a).

**promontory** ['prɒməntrɪ] *n* promontório.

**promote** [prə'məut] *vt* (*gen*) promover; (*new product*) fazer propaganda de; (*MIL*) promover; **promoter** *n* (*of sporting event*) patrocinador(a) *m/f*; **promotion** [-'məuʃən] *n* (*gen*) promoção *f*, fomento; (*MIL*) promoção *f*.

**prompt** [prɒmpt] *adj* pronto, rápido // *adv* (*punctually*) pontualmente // *vt* (*urge*) incitar, impelir; (*THEATRE*) servir de ponto a; **to ~ sb to do sth** induzir alguém a fazer algo; **~er** *n* (*THEATRE*) ponto; **~ly** *adv* (*punctually*) pontualmente; (*rapidly*) rapidamente; **~ness** *n* pontualidade *f*; rapidez *f*.

**prone** [prəun] *adj* (*lying*) inclinado, de bruços; **~ to** propenso a, predisposto a.

**prong** [prɒŋ] *n* dente *m*, ponta.

**pronoun** ['prəunaun] *n* pronome *m*.

**pronounce** [prə'nauns] *vt* pronunciar; (*declare*) declarar, afirmar // *vi*: **to ~ (up)on** pronunciar-se sobre; **~d** *adj* (*marked*) marcado, nítido; **~ment** *n* pronunciamento.

**pronunciation** [prənʌnsɪ'eɪʃən] *n* pronúncia.

**proof** [pruːf] *n* prova; (*of alcohol*) teor *m* alcoólico // *adj*: **~ against** à prova de; **~reader** *n* revisor(a) *m/f* de provas.

**prop** [prɒp] *n* suporte *m*, escora; (*fig*) amparo, apoio // *vt* (*also*: **~ up**) apoiar, escorar; (*lean*): **to ~ sth against** apoiar algo contra.

**propaganda** [prɒpə'gændə] *n* propaganda.

**propagate** ['prɒpəgeɪt] *vt* propagar.

**propel** [prə'pɛl] *vt* propelir, propulsionar; **~ler** *n* hélice *f*; **~ling pencil** *n* lapiseira.

**proper** ['prɒpə*] *adj* (*suited, right*) próprio; (*exact*) preciso; (*apt*) apropriado, conveniente; (*timely*) oportuno; (*seemly*) decente, respeitável; (*authentic*) genuíno; (*col: real*) autêntico; **~ly** *adv* corre(c)tamente; (*well*) bem.

**property** ['prɒpətɪ] *n* (*gen*) propriedade *f*; (*goods*) posses *fpl*, bens *mpl*; (*estate*) propriedade *f*, fazenda; **it's their ~** é seu, pertence a eles.

**prophecy** ['prɒfɪsɪ] *n* profecia; **prophesy** [-saɪ] *vt* profetizar; (*fig*) predizer.

**prophet** ['prɒfɪt] *n* profeta *m/f*; **~ic** [prə'fɛtɪk] *adj* profético.

**proportion** [prə'pɔːʃən] *n* proporção *f*; (*share*) parte *f*, porção *f*; **~al** *adj* proporcional; **~ate** *adj* proporcionado.

**proposal** [prə'pəuzl] *n* proposta; (*offer*) oferta; (*plan*) plano; (*of marriage*) pedido; (*suggestion*) sugestão *f*.

**propose** [prə'pəuz] *vt* propor; (*offer*) oferecer // *vi* declarar-se; **to ~ to do** propor-se fazer.

**proposition** [prɒpə'zɪʃən] *n* proposta, proposição *f*.

**proprietor** [prə'praɪətə*] *n* proprietário/a, dono/a.

**propulsion** [prə'pʌlʃən] *n* propulsão *f*.

**pro rata** [prəu'rɑːtə] *adv* pro rata, proporcionalmente.

**prosaic** [prəu'zeɪɪk] *adj* prosaico.

**prose** [prəuz] *n* prosa.

**prosecute** ['prɒsɪkjuːt] *vt* (*LAW*) processar, acionar (*Pt:* -cc-); **prosecution** [-kjuːʃən] *n* acusação *f*; (*accusing side*) autor *m* da demanda; **prosecutor** *n* promotor(a) *m/f*; (*also*: **public prosecutor**) promotor(a) m/f público/a.

**prospect** ['prɔspekt] n (view) vista; (chance) probabilidade f; (outlook) perspectiva; (hope) esperança // (vb: [prə'spekt]) vt explorar // vi procurar; ~s npl (for work etc) probabilidades fpl; ~ing n prospecção f; ~ive adj (possible) provável, esperado; (certain) futuro; (heir) presumível; (legislation) em perspectiva; ~or n explorador(a) m/f.

**prospectus** [prə'spektəs] n prospecto, programa m.

**prosper** ['prɔspə*] vi prosperar; ~ity [-'speriti] n prosperidade f; ~ous adj próspero, bem sucedido.

**prostitute** ['prɔstitjuːt] n prostituta.

**prostrate** ['prɔstreit] adj prostrado; (fig) abatido, aniquilado.

**protagonist** [prə'tægənist] n protagonista m/f.

**protect** [prə'tekt] vt proteger; ~ion n proteção f (Pt: -cç-) f; ~ive adj protec(t)or(a); ~or n prote(c)tor(a) m/f.

**protégé** ['prəuteʒei] n protegido/a.

**protein** ['prəutiːn] n proteína.

**protest** ['prəutest] n protesto // (vb: [prə'test]) vi protestar // vt (affirm) afirmar, declarar; ~er n manifestante m/f.

**Protestant** ['prɔtistənt] adj, n protestante m/f.

**protocol** ['prəutəkɔl] n protocolo.

**prototype** ['prəutətaip] n protótipo.

**protracted** [prə'træktid] adj prolongado, demorado.

**protrude** [prə'truːd] vi projetar-se (Pt: -ct-), sobressair, ressaltar.

**proud** [praud] adj orgulhoso; (pej) vaidoso, soberbo; (imposing) imponente, magnífico.

**prove** [pruːv] vt provar; (verify) comprovar; (show) demonstrar // vi: to ~ correct vir a ser ou mostrar estar correto (Pt: -ct-); to ~ o.s. pôr-se à prova.

**proverb** ['prɔvəːb] n provérbio;

~ial [prə'vəːbiəl] adj proverbial.

**provide** [prə'vaid] vt proporcionar, providenciar; to ~ sb with sth munir alguém de algo; to ~ for vt (person) prover à subsistência; (emergency) prevenir; ~d (that) conj contanto que, sob condição de (que).

**providing** [prə'vaidiŋ] conj contanto que, desde que.

**province** ['prɔvins] n província; (fig) esfera; **provincial** [prə'vinʃəl] adj provincial; (pej) provinciano.

**provision** [prə'viʒən] n (gen) provisão f; (supply) fornecimento; (supplying) abastecimento; ~s npl (food) mantimentos mpl; ~al adj provisório; (temporary) interino, temporário.

**proviso** [prə'vaizəu] n condição f, disposição f, cláusula.

**provocation** [prəvə'keiʃən] n provocação f, estímulo.

**provocative** [prə'vɔkətiv] adj provocante; (stimulating) sugestivo.

**provoke** [prə'vəuk] vt (arouse) provocar; (cause) causar, motivar; (anger) irritar, exasperar.

**prow** [prau] n proa.

**prowess** ['prauis] n (skill) destreza, perícia; (courage) coragem f; (deed) proeza.

**prowl** [praul] vi (also: ~ about, ~ around) rondar, andar à espreita // n: on the ~ de ronda, rondando; ~er n o que faz a ronda; (thief) gatuno/a m/f.

**proximity** [prɔk'simiti] n proximidade f.

**proxy** ['prɔksi] n procuração f; (person) procurador(a) m/f; by ~ por procuração.

**prudence** ['pruːdns] n prudência, cautela; **prudent** [-ənt] adj prudente.

**prudish** ['pruːdiʃ] adj melindroso, puritano.

**prune** [pruːn] n ameixa seca // vt podar, aparar.

**pry** [praɪ] *vi*: **to ~ into** (intro)meter-se em.

**psalm** [sɑːm] *n* salmo.

**pseudo-** [sjuːdəʊ] *pref* pseudo-; **~nym** *n* pseudônimo.

**psychiatric** [saɪkɪ'ætrɪk] *adj* psiquiátrico; **psychiatrist** [-'kaɪə-trɪst] *n* psiquiatra *m/f*; **psychiatry** [-'kaɪətrɪ] *n* psiquiatria.

**psychic** ['saɪkɪk] *adj* (*also*: **~al**) paranormal // *n* médium *m/f*.

**psychoanalyse** [saɪkəʊ'ænəlaɪz] *vt* psicanalisar; **psychoanalysis** [-kəʊə'nælɪsɪs] *n* psicanálise *f*; **psychoanalyst** [-'ænəlɪst] *n* psicanalista *m/f*.

**psychological** [saɪkə'lɒdʒɪkl] *adj* psicológico.

**psychologist** [saɪ'kɒlədʒɪst] *n* psicólogo/a; **psychology** [-dʒɪ] *n* psicologia.

**psychopath** ['saɪkəʊpæθ] *n* psicopata *m/f*.

**psychosomatic** ['saɪkəʊsə'mætɪk] *adj* psicossomático.

**psychotic** [saɪ'kɒtɪk] *adj*, *n* psicótico/a.

**pub** [pʌb] *n abbr of* **public house** bar *m*, botequim *m*.

**puberty** ['pjuːbətɪ] *n* puberdade *f*.

**public** ['pʌblɪk] *adj*, *n* público.

**publican** ['pʌblɪkən] *n* taberneiro.

**publication** [pʌblɪ'keɪʃən] *n* publicação *f*.

**public:** **~ convenience** *n* banheiro público; **~ house** *n* bar *m*, taberna.

**publicity** [pʌb'lɪsɪtɪ] *n* publicidade *f*.

**publicly** ['pʌblɪklɪ] *adv* publicamente, abertamente.

**public:** **~ opinion** *n* opinião *f* pública; **~ relations** *n* relações *fpl* públicas; **~ school** *n* (*Brit*) escola particular; **~-spirited** *adj* zeloso pelo bem-estar público.

**publish** ['pʌblɪʃ] *vt* publicar; **~er** *n* editor(a) *m/f*; **~ing** *n* (*industry*) a indústria editorial.

**puce** [pjuːs] *adj* marrom arroxeado.

**pucker** ['pʌkə*] *vt* (*pleat*) enrugar, preguear; (*brow etc*) franzir.

**pudding** ['pʊdɪŋ] *n* sobremesa; (*sweet*) pudim *m*, doce *m*; **black ~** morcela.

**puddle** ['pʌdl] *n* poça.

**puff** [pʌf] *n* sopro; (*from mouth*) baforada; (*gust*) rajada, lufada; (*sound*) sopro; (*also*: **powder ~**) pompom *m* // *vt*: **to ~ one's pipe** tirar baforadas do cachimbo // *vi* (*gen*) soprar; (*pant*) arquejar; **to ~ out smoke** lançar uma baforada; **to ~ up** *vt* inflar; **~ed** *adj* (*col*: *out of breath*) sem fôlego.

**puffin** ['pʌfɪn] *n* papagaio-do-mar *m*.

**puffy** ['pʌfɪ] *adj* inchado, entumecido.

**pull** [pʊl] *n* (*fig*: *advantage*) vantagem *f*, (*: influence*) influência, pistolão *m*; (*tug*) to give sth a ~ dar um puxão em algo // *vt* puxar; (*tug*) rebocar; (*muscle*) distender; (*haul*) puxar, arrastar // *vi* puxar, dar um puxão; **to ~ a face** fazer caretas; **to ~ to pieces** picar em pedacinhos; **to ~ one's punches** não usar toda a força; **to ~ one's weight** fazer a sua parte; **to ~ o.s. together** recompor-se; **to ~ sb's leg** fazer hora com alguém, caçoar de alguém; **to ~ apart** *vt* (*break*) romper; **to ~ down** *vt* (*house*) demolir; **to ~ in** *vi* (*AUT*: *at the kerb*) parar (junto ao meio-fio); (*RAIL*) chegar (na plataforma); **to ~ off** *vt* (*deal etc*) concluir or realizar com sucesso; **to ~ out** *vi* ir(-se) embora, partir; (*AUT*: *from kerb*) afastar-se // *vt* tirar, arrancar; **to ~ through** *vi* sair-se bem (de um aperto); (*MED*) restabelecer-se; **to ~ up** *vi* (*stop*) deter-se, parar // *vt* (*uproot*) desarraigar, arrancar; (*stop*) parar.

**pulley** ['pʊlɪ] *n* roldana.

**pullover** ['pʊləʊvə*] *n* pulôver *m*.

**pulp** [pʌlp] *n* (*of fruit*) polpa; (*for paper*) pasta, massa.

**pulpit** ['pulpit] n púlpito.

**pulsate** [pʌl'seit] vi pulsar, palpitar.

**pulse** [pʌls] n (ANAT) pulso; (of music, engine) cadência f; (BOT) legumes mpl.

**pulverize** ['pʌlvəraiz] vt pulverizar; (fig) esmagar, aniquilar.

**puma** ['pju:mə] n puma, onça-parda.

**pummel** ['pʌml] vt esmurrar, socar.

**pump** [pʌmp] n bomba; (shoe) sapatilha (de dança) // vt bombear; (fig: col) sondar; **to ~ up** vt encher (pneu).

**pumpkin** ['pʌmpkin] n abóbora.

**pun** [pʌn] n jogo de palavras.

**punch** [pʌntʃ] n (blow) soco, murro; (tool) punção m; (for tickets) furador m; (drink) ponche m // vt (hit): **to ~ sb/sth** esmurrar or socar alguém/algo; (make a hole in) perfurar, picotar; ~ **a card** cartão m perfurado; ~**-up** n (col) briga.

**punctual** ['pʌŋktjuəl] adj pontual; ~**ity** [-'æliti] n pontualidade f.

**punctuate** ['pʌŋktjueit] vt pontuar; (interrupt) interromper; **punctuation** [-'eiʃən] n pontuação f.

**puncture** ['pʌŋktʃə*] n picada, furo // vt picar, furar.

**pundit** ['pʌndit] n erudito, sábio.

**pungent** ['pʌndʒənt] adj pungente, acre.

**punish** ['pʌniʃ] vt punir, castigar; ~**ment** n castigo, punição f.

**punt** [pʌnt] n (boat) chalana.

**punter** ['pʌntə*] n (gambler) jogador(a) m/f.

**puny** ['pju:ni] adj débil, fraco.

**pup** [pʌp] n filhote m de cachorro; (Pt) cachorro.

**pupil** ['pju:pl] n aluno/a.

**puppet** ['pʌpit] n marionete f.

**puppy** ['pʌpi] n filhote m de cachorro, cachorrinho; (Pt) cachorro.

**purchase** ['pə:tʃis] n compra; (grip) ponto de apoio // vt comprar; **purchaser** n comprador(a) m/f.

**pure** [pjuə*] adj puro.

**purée** ['pjuərei] n purê m.

**purge** [pə:dʒ] n (MED) purgante m; (POL) expurgo m // vt purgar; (POL) expurgar.

**purification** [pjuərifi'keiʃən] n purificação f, depuração f; **purify** ['pjuərifai] vt purificar, depurar.

**purist** ['pjuərist] n purista m/f.

**puritan** ['pjuəritən] n puritano/a; ~**ical** [-'tænikl] adj puritano.

**purity** ['pjuəriti] n pureza, limpeza.

**purl** [pə:l] n ponto reverso.

**purple** ['pə:pl] adj roxo, purpúreo.

**purport** [pə:'pɔ:t] vi: **to ~ to be/do** dar a entender que é/faz.

**purpose** ['pə:pəs] n propósito; **on ~** de propósito, adrede; ~**ful** adj intencional, resoluto.

**purr** [pə:*] n ronrom m // vi ronronar.

**purse** [pə:s] n carteira; (bag) bolsa // vt enrugar, franzir.

**purser** ['pə:sə*] n (NAUT) comissário de bordo.

**pursue** [pə'sju:] vt perseguir, seguir; (profession) exercer; **pursuer** n perseguidor(a) m/f.

**pursuit** [pə'sju:t] n (chase) caça; (persecution) perseguição f; (occupation) ocupação f, atividade f; (Pt: -ct- f; (pastime) passatempo.

**purveyor** [pə'veiə*] n fornecedor(a) m/f.

**pus** [pʌs] n pus m.

**push** [puʃ] n (gen) empurrão m; (shove) impulso; (attack) ataque m, arremetida; (advance) avanço // vt empurrar; (button) apertar; (promote) promover; (thrust): **to ~ sth (into)** introduzir algo à força (em) // vi empurrar; (fig) esforçar-se; **to ~ aside** vt afastar com a mão; **to ~ off** vi (col) ir embora; **to ~ on** vi (continue) prosseguir; **to ~ through** vt (measure) forçar a aceitação de; **to ~ up** vt (total, prices) forçar a alta de; ~**chair** n carrinho; ~**ing** adj empre-

endedor(a); ~ **over** n (col): **it's a
~over** está de bandeja or de graça;
~**y** adj (pej) intrometido, agressivo.
**puss** [pus], **pussy(-cat)**
['pusɪ(kæt)] n gatinho.
**put** [put], pt, pp **put** vt (place) pôr,
colocar; (~ into) meter; (say) dizer,
expressar; (a question) fazer;
(estimate) avaliar, calcular; **to ~
about** vi (NAUT) mudar de rumo //
vt (rumour) espalhar; **to ~ across**
vt (ideas etc) expressar, comunicar;
**to ~ away** vt (store) guardar; **to ~
back** vt (replace) repor; (postpone)
adiar; **to ~ by** vt (money) poupar,
pôr de lado; **to ~ down** vt (on
ground) pôr no chão; (animal)
sacrificar; (in writing) anotar,
inscrever; (suppress: revolt etc)
sufocar; (attribute) atribuir; **to ~
forward** vt (ideas) apresentar,
propor; (date) adiantar; **to ~ in** vt
(application, complaint) apresentar;
**to ~ off** vt (postpone) adiar,
protelar; (discourage) desencorajar;
**to ~ on** vt (clothes, lipstick etc) pôr;
(light etc) acender; (play etc)
encenar; (weight gain) ganhar; (brake)
aplicar; (attitude) fingir, simular; **to
~ out** vt (fire, light) apagar; (one's
hand) estender; (news, rumour)
publicar, editar; (tongue etc)
mostrar; (person: inconvenience)
incomodar; **to ~ right** consertar; **to
~ up** vt (raise) levantar, erguer;
(hang) alçar, içar; (build) construir,
edificar; (increase) aumentar;
(accommodate) hospedar; **to ~ up
with** vt fus suportar, agüentar.
**putrid** ['pju:trɪd] adj pútrido, podre.
**putt** [pʌt] vt (golf) dar uma tacada
de leve // n tacada leve; **~er** n
(GOLF) taco; **~ing green** n campo
de golfe em miniatura.
**putty** ['pʌtɪ] n massa de vidraceiro,
betume m.
**puzzle** ['pʌzl] n (riddle) charada;
(jigsaw) quebra-cabeça m;
(crossword) palavras cruzadas fpl;

(mystery) enigma m // vt
desconcertar, confundir // vi estar
perplexo; **puzzling** adj enigmático,
misterioso.
**pygmy** ['pɪgmɪ] n pigmeu m.
**pyjamas** [pɪ'dʒɑːməz] npl pijama
msg.
**pylon** ['paɪlən] n pilono, poste m,
torre f.
**pyramid** ['pɪrəmɪd] n pirâmide f.
**python** ['paɪθən] n pitão m.

# Q

**quack** [kwæk] n (of duck) grasnido; (pej: doctor) curandeiro,
charlatão/tã m/f // vi grasnar.
**quad** [kwɒd] abbr of **quadrangle;
quadruplet.**
**quadrangle** ['kwɒdræŋgl] n
(courtyard: abbr: **quad**) pátio
quadrangular.
**quadruple** ['kwɒdrupl] adj
quádruplo // n quádruplo // vt/i
quadruplicar.
**quadruplets** [kwɔ:'dru:plɪts] npl
quadrigêmeos mpl, quádruplos mpl.
**quagmire** ['kwægmaɪə*] n lamaçal
m, atoleiro.
**quail** [kweɪl] n (bird) codorniz f;
(Br) codorna // vi acovardar-se.
**quaint** [kweɪnt] adj curioso,
esquisito; (picturesque) pitoresco.
**quake** [kweɪk] vi tremer,
estremecer // n abbr of **earthquake.**
**Quaker** ['kweɪkə*] n quacre m/f.
**qualification** [kwɔlɪfɪ'keɪʃən] n
(reservation) restrição f; (modification) modificação f; (act) qualificação f; (degree) título; **qualified**
['kwɔlɪfaɪd] adj (trained) habilitado,
qualificado; (fit) apto, capaz;
(limited) limitado; (professionally)
diplomado.
**qualify** ['kwɔlɪfaɪ] vt qualificar;
(capacitate) capacitar; (modify)

modificar; (*limit*) restringir, limitar; **to ~ (as)** classificar (como) // vi (*SPORT*) classificar-se; **to ~ (as)** formar-se (em); **to ~ (for)** reunir os requisitos (para).

**quality** ['kwɔlɪtɪ] *n* qualidade *f*; (*moral*) valor *m*.

**qualm** [kwɑːm] *n* escrúpulo.

**quandary** ['kwɔndrɪ] *n*: **to be in a ~** estar num dilema.

**quantity** ['kwɔntɪtɪ] *n* quantidade *f*, **unknown ~** (*MATH*) incógnita.

**quarantine** ['kwɔrəntiːn] *n* quarentena.

**quarrel** ['kwɔrl] *n* (*argument*) discussão *f*, querela; (*fight*) briga // vi brigar, discutir; **~some** adj brigão/gona.

**quarry** ['kwɔrɪ] *n* (*for stone*) pedreira; (*animal*) presa, caça.

**quart** [kwɔːt] *n* quarto de galão = 1.136 litros.

**quarter** ['kwɔːtə*] *n* quarto, quarta parte *f*; (*of year*) trimestre *m*; (*district*) bairro // vt dividir em quatro; (*MIL: lodge*) aquartelar; **~s** *npl* (*barracks*) quartel *msg*; (*living ~s*) alojamento *sg*; **a ~ of an hour** um quarto de hora; **~ final** a quarta de final; **~ly** adj trimestral // adv trimestralmente; **~master** *n* (*MIL*) quartel-mestre *m*; (*NAUT*) contra-mestre *m*.

**quartet(te)** [kwɔː'tɛt] *n* quarteto.

**quartz** [kwɔːts] *n* quartzo.

**quash** [kwɔʃ] *vt* (*verdict*) anular.

**quasi-** ['kweɪzaɪ] *pref* quase-, semi-.

**quaver** ['kweɪvə*] *n* (*MUS*) colcheia // vi tremer; (*trill*) trinar, gorjear.

**quay** [kiː] *n* (*also: ~side*) cais *m*.

**queasy** ['kwiːzɪ] adj (*sickly*) enjoado.

**queen** [kwiːn] *n* (*gen*) rainha; (*CARDS etc*) dama; **~ mother** *n* rainha-mãe *f*.

**queer** [kwɪə*] adj (*odd*) esquisito, estranho; (*suspect*) suspeito, duvidoso // *n* (*col*) bicha *m*, veado.

**quell** [kwɛl] *vt* abrandar, acalmar; (*put down*) sufocar.

**quench** [kwɛntʃ] *vt* apagar; (*thirst*) saciar.

**query** ['kwɪərɪ] *n* (*question*) pergunta; (*doubt*) dúvida; (*fig*) incerteza // *vt* perguntar, questionar.

**quest** [kwɛst] *n* busca; (*journey*) expedição *f*.

**question** ['kwɛstʃən] *n* pergunta; (*matter*) questão *f*, assunto, problema *m* // *vt* (*gen*) perguntar; (*doubt*) duvidar, questionar; (*interrogate*) interrogar, inquirir; **it is a ~ of** é questão de; **beyond ~** sem dúvida; **out of the ~** fora de cogitação, impossível; **~able** adj discutível, questionável; (*doubtful*) duvidoso; **~ mark** *n* ponto de interrogação; **~naire** [-'nɛə*] *n* questionário.

**queue** [kjuː] *n* fila; (*Pt*) bicha // vi fazer fila; (*Pt*) fazer bicha.

**quibble** ['kwɪbl] vi usar de evasivas, tergiversar.

**quick** [kwɪk] adj rápido; (*temper*) vivo; (*agile*) ágil; (*mind*) sagaz, despachado; (*ear*) agudo; (*eye*) apurado; **be ~!** ande depressa! (*Pt*) mexa-se!; **~en** *vt* apressar // vi apressar-se, acelerar; **~ly** adv rapidamente, depressa; **~ness** *n* rapidez *f*; (*agility*) agilidade *f*; (*liveliness*) vivacidade *f*; **~sand** *n* areia movediça; **~tempered** adj irascível; **~witted** adj perspicaz, vivo.

**quid** [kwɪd] *n, pl inv* (*Brit: col*) libra.

**quiet** ['kwaɪət] adj (*tranquil*) tranqüilo, calmo; (*still*) quieto; (*silent*) silencioso; (*: person*) calado; (*ceremony*) discreto // *n* sossego, quietude *f*; **keep ~!** cale-se!, fique quieto!; **~en** (*also: ~en down*) vi (*grow calm*) acalmar-se; (*grow silent*) calar-se // *vt* tranqüilizar, fazer calar; **~ly** adv (*gen*) tranqüilamente; (*silently*) silenci-

osamente; ~**ness** n (silence)
quietude f; (calm) tranquilidade f.

**quilt** [kwɪlt] n acolchoado, colcha;
(continental) ~ n edredão m.

**quin** [kwɪn] abbr of **quintuplet.**

**quince** [kwɪns] n (fruit) marmelo.

**quinine** [kwɪˈniːn] n quinina.

**quintet(te)** [kwɪnˈtet] n quinteto.

**quintuplets** [kwɪnˈtjuːplɪts] npl
quíntuplos mpl.

**quip** [kwɪp] n escárnio, dito
espirituoso.

**quirk** [kwɜːk] n peculiaridade f.

**quit** [kwɪt], pt, pp **quit** or **quitted**
vt deixar, desistir de; (premises)
abandonar // vi parar; (give up)
desistir; (go away) ir(-se) embora;
(resign) renunciar, demitir-se; (stop
work) deixar o emprego; **to be ~ of**
ficar livre de.

**quite** [kwaɪt] adv (rather) bastante;
(entirely) totalmente; ~ **a few of**
**them** um bom número deles; ~
(so)! exatamente! (Pt: -ct-), isso
mesmo!, perfeitamente!

**quits** [kwɪts] adj: ~ (with) quite
(com).

**quiver** [ˈkwɪvə*] vi estremecer // n
(for arrows) carcás m, aljava.

**quiz** [kwɪz] n (game) concurso (de
cultura geral); (questioning)
questionário, teste m // vt
interrogar; ~**zical** adj zombeteiro.

**quoits** [kwɔɪts] npl jogo de malha.

**quorum** [ˈkwɔːrəm] n quorum m.

**quota** [ˈkwəutə] n cota, quota.

**quotation** [kwəuˈteɪʃən] n citação f;
(estimate) orçamento, cotação f; ~
**marks** npl aspas fpl.

**quote** [kwəut] n citação f; (COMM)
cotação f // vt (sentence) citar;
(price) cotar, fixar // vi: **to ~ from**
citar de, transcrever de.

**quotient** [ˈkwəuʃənt] n quociente m.

# R

**rabbi** [ˈræbaɪ] n rabino.

**rabbit** [ˈræbɪt] n coelho; ~ **hole** n
toca, lura; ~ **hutch** n coelheira.

**rabble** [ˈræbl] n (pej) plebe f,
povinho, ralé f.

**rabies** [ˈreɪbiːz] n raiva, hidrofobia.

**RAC** n abbr of **Royal**
**Automobile Club.**

**raccoon** [rəˈkuːn] n espécie de mão-
pelada ou guaxinim.

**race** [reɪs] n (gen) corrida; (species)
raça, espécie f // vt (horse) fazer
correr; (engine) acelerar // vi
(compete) competir; (run) correr;
(pulse) bater rapidamente;
~**course** n hipódromo; ~**horse** n
cavalo de corridas; ~**track** n pista
de corridas; (for cars) autódromo.

**racial** [ˈreɪʃl] adj racial; ~**ism** n
racismo; ~**ist** adj, n racista m/f.

**racing** [ˈreɪsɪŋ] n corrida; ~ **car** n
carro de corrida; ~ **driver** n piloto
de corrida.

**racist** [ˈreɪsɪst] adj, n (pej) racista
m/f.

**rack** [ræk] n (also: **luggage** ~)
bagageiro; (shelf) estante f; (also:
**roof** ~) xalmas fpl, porta-bagagem
m; (clothes ~) cabide m // vt
(cause pain to) atormentar.

**racket** [ˈrækɪt] n (for tennis)
raqueta; (noise) barulheira, folia;
(swindle) negócio ilegal, fraude f.

**racoon** [rəˈkuːn] n = **raccoon.**

**racquet** [ˈrækɪt] n raqueta.

**racy** [ˈreɪsɪ] adj vivo, espirituoso,
picante.

**radar** [ˈreɪdɑː*] n radar m.

**radiance** [ˈreɪdɪəns] n brilho,
esplendor m; **radiant** [-ənt] adj
radiante, brilhante.

**radiate** [ˈreɪdɪeɪt] vt (heat) irradiar;
(emit) emitir // vi (lines) difundir-
se, estender-se.

**radiation** [reɪdɪˈeɪʃən] n radiação f.

**radiator** ['reɪdɪeɪtə*] n radiador m; ~ **cap** n tampa do radiador.

**radical** ['rædɪkl] adj radical.

**radio** ['reɪdɪəu] n rádio; **on the** ~ no rádio; ~ **station** n emissora, estação f de rádio.

**radio...** [reɪdɪəu] pref: ~**active** adj radioativo (Pt: -ct-); ~**activity** n radioatividade (Pt: -ct-) f; ~**-controlled** adj controlado por rádio; ~**graphy** [-'ɔgrəfɪ] n radiografia; ~**logy** [-'ɔlədʒɪ] n radiologia; ~**telephone** n radiotelefone m; ~**therapy** n radioterapia.

**radish** ['rædɪʃ] n rabanete m.

**radius** ['reɪdɪəs], pl **radii** [-ɪaɪ] n raio.

**raffia** ['ræfɪə] n ráfia.

**raffle** ['ræfl] n rifa, sorteio // vt rifar, sortear.

**raft** [rɑ:ft] n (also: **life** ~) balsa.

**rafter** ['rɑ:ftə*] n viga, caibro.

**rag** [ræg] n (piece of cloth) trapo; (torn cloth) farrapo; (pej: newspaper) jornaleco; (for charity) atividades estudantis beneficentes // vt encarnar em, zombar de; ~**s** npl trapos mpl, farrapos mpl; ~**-and-bone man** n negociante m/f de trastes; ~ **doll** n boneca de trapo.

**rage** [reɪdʒ] n (fury) raiva, furor m; (fashion) voga, moda // vi (person) estar furioso; (storm) bramar; **to fly into a** ~ enfurecer-se.

**ragged** ['rægɪd] adj (edge) irregular, desigual; (cuff) puído, gasto; (appearance) esfarrapado, andrajoso; (coastline) acidentado.

**raid** [reɪd] n (MIL) incursão f; (criminal) assalto; (attack) ataque m; (by police) batida // vt invadir, atacar, assaltar; ~**er** n atacante m/f; (criminal) assaltante m/f.

**rail** [reɪl] n (on stair) corrimão m; (on bridge, balcony) parapeito, anteparo; (of ship) amurada; (for train) trilho; (Pt) carril m; ~**s** npl: **off the** ~**s** descarrilado; **by** ~ de

trem, por estrada de ferro; (Pt) por caminho de ferro; ~ **ing(s)** n(pl) grade fsg, balaustrada sg; ~**road** (US), ~**way** n estrada de ferro; (Pt) ferroviário; ~**wayman** n ferroviário; ~**way station** n estação f de estrada de ferro; (Pt) estação f de caminho de ferro.

**rain** [reɪn] n chuva // vi chover; **in the** ~ na chuva; **it's** ~**ing** está chovendo; (Pt) está a chover; ~**bow** n arco-íris m inv; ~**coat** n impermeável m, capa de chuva; ~**drop** n gota de chuva; ~**fall** n chuva, pluviosidade f; ~**y** adj chuvoso.

**raise** [reɪz] n aumento // vt (lift) levantar; (build) erguer, edificar; (increase) aumentar; (doubts) suscitar, despertar; (a question) fazer, expor; (cattle, family) criar; (crop) cultivar, plantar; (army) recrutar, alistar; (funds) angariar; (loan) levantar, obter; **to** ~ **one's voice** levantar a voz.

**raisin** ['reɪzn] n passa, uva seca.

**rake** [reɪk] n (tool) ancinho; (person) libertino // vt (garden) revolver or limpar com o ancinho; (fire) remover as cinzas; (with machine gun) varrer.

**rakish** ['reɪkɪʃ] adj (suave) elegante; **at a** ~ **angle** de banda, inclinado.

**rally** ['rælɪ] n (POL etc) reunião f, comício; (AUT) rally m, rali m; (TENNIS) rebatida // vt reunir; (encourage) animar, encorajar // vi reorganizar-se; (sick person, Stock Exchange) recuperar-se; **to** ~ **round** vt fus (fig) dar apoio a.

**ram** [ræm] n carneiro; (TECH) êmbolo, aríete m // vt (crash into) introduzir à força, cravar; (tread down) pisar, calcar.

**ramble** ['ræmbl] n caminhada, excursão f a pé // vi (pej: also: ~ **on**) divagar; **rambler** n caminhante m/f; (BOT) trepadeira; **rambling** adj (speech) desconexo, incoerente // n excursionismo.

**ramp** [ræmp] n rampa.

**rampage** [ræm'peɪdʒ] n: **to be on the ~** alvoroçar-se // vi: **they went rampaging through the town** correram feito loucos pela cidade.

**rampant** ['ræmpənt] adj (disease etc) violento, implacável.

**rampart** ['ræmpɑːt] n baluarte m; (wall) muralha.

**ramshackle** ['ræmʃækl] adj prestes a desmoronar, em ruínas.

**ran** [ræn] pt of **run**.

**ranch** [rɑːntʃ] n rancho, fazenda, estância; **~er** n rancheiro, fazendeiro.

**rancid** ['rænsɪd] adj rançoso, râncio.

**rancour, rancor** (US) ['ræŋkə*] n rancor m, ódio.

**random** ['rændəm] adj ao acaso, casual, fortuito // n: **at ~** a esmo, aleatoriamente.

**randy** ['rændɪ] adj (col) excitado, luxurioso.

**rang** [ræŋ] pt of **ring**.

**range** [reɪndʒ] n (of mountains) cadeia, cordilheira; (of missile) alcance m; (of voice) extensão f; (series) série f; (of products) sortimento; (also: **shooting ~**) campo de alcance; (also: **kitchen ~**) fogão m // vt (place) colocar; (arrange) arrumar, ordenar // vi: **to ~ over** (wander) percorrer; (extend) estender-se por; **to ~ from ... to...** variar de a ..., oscilar entre ... e ...; **ranger** n guarda-florestal m.

**rank** [ræŋk] n (row) fila, fileira; (MIL) posto, graduação f; (status) categoria, posição f; (also: **taxi ~**) ponto de táxi // vi: **to ~ among** figurar entre // adj (stinking) fétido, malcheiroso; **the ~ and file** (fig) a gente f comum.

**rankle** ['ræŋkl] vi (insult) doer, magoar.

**ransack** ['rænsæk] vt (search) revistar; (plunder) saquear, pilhar.

**ransom** ['rænsəm] n resgate m; **to hold sb to ~** (fig) encostar alguém contra a parede.

**rant** [rænt] vi falar em tom declamatório; **~ing** n palavreado oco.

**rap** [ræp] n batida breve e seca // vt bater de leve.

**rape** [reɪp] n violação f, estupro // vt violentar, estuprar.

**rapid** ['ræpɪd] adj rápido; **~s** npl (GEO) cachoeira sg; **~ity** [rə'pɪdɪtɪ] n rapidez f.

**rapist** ['reɪpɪst] n estuprador m.

**rapport** [ræ'pɔː*] n harmonia, afinidade f.

**rapture** ['ræptʃə*] n êxtase m, arrebatamento; **rapturous** adj extático; (applause) entusiasta.

**rare** [rɛə*] adj raro, fora do comum; (CULIN: steak) mal passado.

**rarely** ['rɛəlɪ] adv raramente.

**rarity** ['rɛərɪtɪ] n raridade f.

**rascal** ['rɑːskl] n maroto, malandro.

**rash** [ræʃ] adj impetuoso, precipitado // n (MED) exantema m, erupção f cutânea.

**rasher** ['ræʃə*] n fatia fina.

**rashness** ['ræʃnɪs] n impetuosidade f.

**rasp** [rɑːsp] n (tool) lima, raspadeira.

**raspberry** ['rɑːzbərɪ] n framboesa; **~ bush** n framboeseira.

**rasping** ['rɑːspɪŋ] adj: **a ~ noise** ruído áspero e irritante.

**rat** [ræt] n rato, ratazana.

**ratchet** ['rætʃɪt] n (TECH) roquete m, catraca.

**rate** [reɪt] n (ratio) razão f; (percentage) percentagem f, proporção f; (price) preço, taxa; (: of hotel) diária; (of interest) taxa; (speed) velocidade f // vt (value) taxar; (estimate) avaliar; **at any ~** de qualquer modo; **~ of exchange** taxa de câmbio; **to ~ as** ser considerado como; ~s *npl* (*Brit*) imposto *sg* municipal; (*fees*) taxa *sg*; ~**able value** *n* valor *m* tributável; ~**payer** *n* contribuinte *m/f*.

**rather** ['rɑːðə*] *adv* antes, preferivelmente; (*in speech*) melhor dito; **it's** ~ **expensive** é um pouco caro; (*too much*) é caro demais; **there's** ~ **a lot** há bastante *or* muito; **I would** *or* **I'd** ~ **go** preferiria ir.

**ratify** ['rætɪfaɪ] *vt* ratificar.

**rating** ['reɪtɪŋ] *n* (*valuation*) avaliação *f*; (*value*) valor *m*; (*standing*) posição *f*; (*NAUT. category*) posto; (*: sailor*) marinheiro.

**ratio** ['reɪʃɪəu] *n* razão *f*, proporção *f*; **in the** ~ **of 100 to 1** na proporção de 100 para 1.

**ration** ['ræʃən] *n* ração *f*; ~**s** *npl* mantimentos *mpl*, víveres *mpl* // *vt* racionar.

**rational** ['ræʃənl] *adj* racional; (*solution, reasoning*) lógico; (*person*) sensato, razoável; **rationale** [-'nɑːl] *n* razão *f* fundamental; ~**ize** *vt* racionalizar, organizar logicamente; ~**ly** *adv* racionalmente; (*logically*) logicamente.

**rationing** ['ræʃnɪŋ] *n* racionamento.

**rattle** ['rætl] *n* batida, rufar *m*; (*of train etc*) chocalhada; (*of hail*) saraivada; (*object: of baby*) chocalho; (*: of sports fan*) matraca; (*of snake*) guizo // *vi* chocalhar; (*small objects*) tamborilar // *vt* sacudir, fazer bater; (*person*) desconcertar; ~**snake** *n* cascavel *f*.

**raucous** ['rɔːkəs] *adj* áspero, rouco.

**ravage** ['rævɪdʒ] *vt* devastar, estragar; ~**s** *npl* estragos *mpl*.

**rave** [reɪv] *vi* (*in anger*) encolerizar-se; (*with enthusiasm*) falar com entusiasmo; (*MED*) delirar, desvairar.

**raven** ['reɪvən] *n* corvo.

**ravenous** ['rævənəs] *adj* faminto, esfaimado, voraz.

**ravine** [rə'viːn] *n* ravina, barranco.

**raving** ['reɪvɪŋ] *adj*: ~ **lunatic** doido *or* varrido(a).

**ravioli** [rævɪ'əulɪ] *n* ravióli *m*.

**ravish** ['rævɪʃ] *vt* arrebatar; (*delight*) encantar; ~**ing** *adj* encantador(a).

**raw** [rɔː] *adj* (*uncooked*) cru; (*not processed*) bruto; (*sore*) vivo; (*inexperienced*) inexperiente, novato; ~ **material** *n* matéria-prima.

**ray** [reɪ] *n* raio; ~ **of hope** raio de esperança.

**rayon** ['reɪɒn] *n* raiom *m*.

**raze** [reɪz] *vt* arrasar, aniquilar.

**razor** ['reɪzə*] *n* (*open*) navalha; (*safety* ~) aparelho de barbear; ~ **blade** *n* gilete *m*, lâmina.

**Rd** *abbr of* **road**.

**re** [riː] *prep* referente a.

**reach** [riːtʃ] *n* alcance *m*; (*BOXING*) campo de ação; (*of river etc*) braço do rio entre duas voltas // *vt* alcançar, atingir; (*achieve*) conseguir; (*stretch out*) estender, esticar // *vi* alcançar; (*stretch*) estender-se; **within** ~ (*object*) ao alcance (da mão); **out of** ~ fora de alcance; **to** ~ **out for sth** estender *or* esticar a mão para pegar (em) algo.

**react** [riː'ækt] *vi* reagir; ~**ion** [-'ækʃən] *n* reação (*Pt*: -cç-) *f*; ~**ionary** [-'ækʃənri] *adj*, *n* reacionário/a (*Pt*: -cc-).

**reactor** [riː'æktə*] *n* reator (*Pt*: -ct-) *m*.

**read** [riːd], *pt*, *pp* **read** [red] *vi* ler // *vt* ler; (*understand*) compreender; (*study*) estudar; **to** ~ **out** *vt* ler em voz alta; ~**able** *adj* (*writing*) legível; (*book*) que merece ser lido; ~**er** *n* leitor/a *m/f*; (*book*) livro de leituras; (*at university*) professor/a adjunto/a *m/f*; ~**ership** *n* (*of paper etc*) número de leitores.

**readily** ['redɪlɪ] *adv* (*willingly*) de boa vontade; (*easily*) facilmente;

(*quickly*) sem demora, prontamente.

**readiness** ['redɪnɪs] *n* boa vontade *f*, prontidão *f*; (*preparedness*) preparação *f*; **in ~** (*prepared*) preparado, pronto.

**reading** ['riːdɪŋ] *n* leitura; (*understanding*) compreensão *f*; (*on instrument*) indicação *f*.

**readjust** [riːə'dʒʌst] *vt* reajustar // *vi* (*person*): **to ~ to** reorientar-se para.

**ready** ['redɪ] *adj* pronto, preparado; (*willing*) disposto; (*available*) disponível; **to get ~** preparar-se // *adv:* **~-cooked** pronto para comer // *n*: **at the ~** (*MIL*) pronto para atirar; **~-made** *adj* (já) feito; (*clothes*) pronto; **~ reckoner** *n* tabela de cálculos feitos.

**reaffirm** [riːə'fəːm] *vt* reafirmar.

**real** [rɪəl] *adj* verdadeiro, autêntico; **in ~ terms** em termos reais; **~ estate** *n* bens *mpl* imobiliários or de raiz; **~ism** *n* (*also ART*) realismo; **~ist** *n* realista *m/f*; **~istic** [-'lɪstɪk] *adj* realista.

**reality** [riː'ælɪtɪ] *n* realidade *f*; **in ~** na verdade.

**realization** [rɪəlaɪ'zeɪʃən] *n* realização *f*; (*understanding*) compreensão *f*; (*COMM*) conversão *f* em dinheiro, realização.

**realize** ['rɪəlaɪz] *vt* (*understand*) perceber, compreender; (*a project*, *COMM: asset*) realizar.

**really** ['rɪəlɪ] *adv* realmente, na verdade; **~?** é mesmo?, deveras?

**realm** [relm] *n* reino; (*fig*).

**realtor** ['rɪəltə] *n* (*US*) imobiliária.

**reap** [riːp] *vt* segar, ceifar; colher; **~er** *n* segador/a *m/f*, ceifeiro/a.

**reappear** [riːə'pɪə*] *vi* reaparecer; **~ance** *n* reaparição *f*.

**reapply** [riːə'plaɪ] *vi:* **to ~ for** aplicar de novo.

**rear** [rɪə*] *adj* traseiro, posterior // *n* traseira, retaguarda // *vt* (*cattle*,

*family*) criar // *vi* (*also*: **~ up**) (*animal*) empinar-se; **~-engined** *adj* (*AUT*) com motor traseiro; **~guard** *n* retaguarda.

**rearm** [riː'ɑːm] *vt/i* rearmar; **~ament** *n* rearmamento *m*.

**rearrange** [riːə'reɪndʒ] *vt* arrumar de novo, reorganizar.

**rear-view** ['rɪəvjuː] *adj:* **~ mirror** (*AUT*) espelho retrovisor.

**reason** ['riːzn] *n* (*gen*) razão *f*; (*cause*) motivo, causa; (*sense*) sensatez *f* // *vi:* **to ~ with sb** argumentar com alguém, persuadir alguém; **it stands to ~ that** é razoável or lógico que; **~able** *adj* razoável; (*sensible*) sensato; **~ably** *adv* razoavelmente; **~ed** *adj* (*argument*) fundamentado; **~ing** *n* raciocínio, argumentação *f*.

**reassemble** [riːə'sembl] *vt* (*machine*) montar de novo // *vi* reunir-se de novo.

**reassert** [riːə'səːt] *vt* reafirmar.

**reassure** [riːə'ʃuə*] *vt* tranqüilizar, animar; **to ~ sb of** reafirmar a confiança de alguém acerca de; **reassuring** *adj* animador(a).

**rebate** ['riːbeɪt] *n* (*on product*) abatimento *m*; (*on tax etc*) desconto, devolução *f*.

**rebel** ['rebl] *n* rebelde *m/f* // *vi* [rɪ'bel] rebelar-se, sublevar-se; **~lion** *n* rebelião *f*, revolta; **~lious** *adj* insurreto (*Pt:* -ct-); (*child*) rebelde.

**rebirth** [riː'bəːθ] *n* renascimento.

**rebound** [rɪ'baund] *vi* (*ball*) quicar // *n* ['riːbaund] quicado, ricochete *m*.

**rebuff** [rɪ'bʌf] *n* repulsa, recusa // *vt* repelir.

**rebuild** [riː'bɪld] (*irr: like build*) *vt* reconstruir.

**rebuke** [rɪ'bjuːk] *n* reprimenda, censura // *vt* repreender.

**recalcitrant** [rɪ'kælsɪtrənt] *adj* recalcitrante, teimoso.

**recall** [rɪ'kɔːl] *vt* (*remember*)

recordar, lembrar; (*ambassador etc*) mandar voltar // *n* chamada (de volta); (*memory*) recordação *f*.

**ecant** [rɪ'kænt] *vi* retratar-se (*Pt: -act-*).

**ecap** ['ri:kæp] *vt/i* recapitular.

**ecapture** [ri:'kæptʃə*] *vt* (*town*) retomar, recobrar; (*atmosphere*) recriar.

**ecede** [rɪ'si:d] *vi* retroceder; **receding** *adj* (*forehead, chin*) metido/puxado para dentro.

**eceipt** [rɪ'si:t] *n* (*document*) recibo; (*act of receiving*) recepção *f*; **~s** *npl* (*COMM*) rendimentos *mpl*; **on ~ of** ao receber.

**eceive** [rɪ'si:v] *vt* receber; (*guest*) acolher; (*wound*) sofrer; **receiver** *n* (*TEL*) receptor *m*, fone *m*; (*rádio*) receptor *m*; (*of stolen goods*) receptador(a) *m/f*; (*COMM*) curador(a) *m/f* or síndico/a de massa falida.

**ecent** ['ri:snt] *adj* recente; **~ly** *adv* recentemente, ultimamente.

**eceptacle** [rɪ'sɛptɪkl] *n* receptáculo, recipiente *m*.

**eception** [rɪ'sɛpʃən] *n* (*gen*) recepção *f*; (*welcome*) acolhida; **~ desk** *n* mesa de recepção; **~ist** *n* recepcionista *m/f*.

**eceptive** [rɪ'sɛptɪv] *adj* receptivo.

**ecess** [rɪ'sɛs] *n* (*in room*) recesso, vão *m*; (*for bed*) nicho; (*secret place*) esconderijo; (*POL etc: holiday*) férias *fpl*; **~ion** *n* recessão *f*.

**echarge** [ri:'tʃɑ:dʒ] *vt* (*battery*) recarregar.

**ecipe** ['rɛsɪp] *n* receita.

**ecipient** [rɪ'sɪpɪənt] *n* recipiente *m/f*, recebedor(a) *m/f*; (*of letter*) destinatário/a.

**eciprocal** [rɪ'sɪprəkl] *adj* recíproco.

**ecital** [rɪ'saɪtl] *n* recital *m*.

**ecite** [rɪ'saɪt] *vt* (*poem*) recitar; (*complaints etc*) enumerar.

**eckless** ['rɛkləs] *adj* temerário, estouvado; (*speed*) imprudente;

excessivo; **~ly** *adv* temerariamente, sem prudência.

**reckon** ['rɛkən] *vt* (*count*) calcular, contar; (*consider*) considerar, crer; (*think*) **I ~ that...** acho que ..., suponho que ...; **~ing** *n* (*calculation*) cálculo; **the day of ~ing** o dia do Juízo Final.

**reclaim** [rɪ'kleɪm] *vt* recuperar; (*land*) desbravar; (*: from sea*) aterrar; (*demand back*) reivindicar; **reclamation** [rɛklə'meɪʃən] *n* recuperação *f*.

**recline** [rɪ'klaɪn] *vi* reclinar-se; (*lean*) apoiar-se, recostar-se; **reclining** *adj* (*seat*) reclinável.

**recluse** [rɪ'klu:s] *n* recluso/a.

**recognition** [rɛkəg'nɪʃən] *n* reconhecimento; **transformed beyond ~** tão transformado que está irreconhecível.

**recognizable** ['rɛkəgnaɪzəbl] *adj* reconhecível.

**recognize** ['rɛkəgnaɪz] *vt* reconhecer; (*accept*) aceitar; **to ~ by/as** reconhecer por/como.

**recoil** [rɪ'kɔɪl] *vi* (*gun*) retroceder, recuar, dar coice; (*person*): **to ~ from doing sth** recusar-se a fazer algo.

**recollect** [rɛkə'lɛkt] *vt* lembrar, recordar; **~ion** [-'lɛkʃən] *n* recordação *f*, lembrança.

**recommend** [rɛkə'mɛnd] *vt* recomendar, aconselhar; **~ation** [-'deɪʃən] *n* recomendação *f*.

**recompense** ['rɛkəmpɛns] *vt* recompensar // *n* recompensa.

**reconcile** ['rɛkənsaɪl] *vt* (*two people*) reconciliar; (*two facts*) conciliar, harmonizar; **to ~ o.s. to sth** resignar-se a *or* conformar-se com algo; **reconciliation** [-sɪlɪ'eɪʃən] *n* reconciliação *f*.

**reconnaissance** [rɪ'kɔnɪsns] *n* (*MIL*) reconhecimento.

**reconnoitre, reconnoiter** (*US*) [rɛkə'nɔɪtə*] *vt* (*MIL*) reconhecer.

**reconsider** [ri:kən'sɪdə*] vt reconsiderar.

**reconstitute** [ri:'kɒnstɪtjuːt] vt reconstituir.

**reconstruct** [ri:kən'strʌkt] vt reconstruir; ~ion [-kʃən] n reconstrução f.

**record** ['rekɔːd] n (MUS) disco; (of meeting etc) ata (Pt: -ct-), minuta; (register) registro; (Pt) registo; (file) arquivo; (also: police ~) antecedentes mpl; (written) história; (SPORT) recorde m // ir ['rekɔːd] (set down) assentar, registrar (Pt: registar); (relate) relatar, referir; (MUS: song etc) gravar; **in ~ time** num tempo recorde; **off the ~** adj confidencial // adv confidencialmente; ~ **card** n (in file) ficha; ~**er** n (MUS) flauta; (TECH) indicador m mecânico; (official) escrivão m; ~ **holder** n (SPORT) detentor(a) m/f de recorde; ~**ing** n (MUS) gravação f; ~ **player** n toca-discos m inv; (Pt) gira-discos m inv.

**recount** [rɪ'kaunt] vt relatar.

**re-count** ['riːkaunt] n (POL: of votes) nova contagem f, recontagem f // vt [riː'kaunt] recontar.

**recoup** [rɪ'kuːp] vt: **to ~ one's losses** ser indenizado (Pt: -mn-) pelas perdas.

**recourse** [rɪ'kɔːs] n recurso; **to have ~ to** recorrer a.

**recover** [rɪ'kʌvə*] vt recuperar, reconquistar; (rescue) resgatar // vi (from illness) restabelecer-se; (from shock) refazer-se; ~**y** n recuperação f, restabelecimento; (MED) melhora.

**recreate** [riːkrɪ'eɪt] vt recriar.

**recreation** [rekrɪ'eɪʃən] n recreação f; (play) recreio; ~**al** adj recreativo.

**recrimination** [rɪkrɪmɪ'neɪʃən] n recriminação f.

**recruit** [rɪ'kruːt] n recruta m/f // vt

recrutar; ~**ment** n recrutamento.

**rectangle** ['rektæŋgl] n retângulo (Pt: -ct-); **rectangular** [-'tæŋgjulə adj retangular (Pt: -ct-).

**rectify** ['rektɪfaɪ] vt retificar (F -ct-).

**rector** ['rektə*] n (REL) pároco (SCOL) reitor(a) m/f; ~**y** n residência paroquial.

**recuperate** [rɪ'kuːpəreɪt] vi restabelecer-se, recuperar-se.

**recur** [rɪ'kəː*] vi repetir-se, ocorre outra vez; (opportunity) surgir de novo; ~**rence** n repetição f; ~**ren** adj repetido, periódico.

**red** [red] n vermelho // a vermelho; **to be in the ~** estar em situação deficitária; **R~ Cross** Cruz f Vermelha; ~**currant** n groselha; ~**den** vt avermelhar // corar, ruborizar-se; ~**dish** adj (hai avermelhado.

**redecorate** [riː'dekəreɪt] decorar de novo, redecorar; **redeco ration** [-'reɪʃən] n remodelação f.

**redeem** [rɪ'diːm] vt (gen) redimi (sth in pawn) tirar do prego; (fi also REL) resgatar; ~**ing** adj: ~**in feature** lado bom or que salva.

**redeploy** [riːdɪ'plɔɪ] vt (resource troops) redistribuir.

**red:** ~-**haired** adj ruivo; ~-**hande** adj: **to be caught** ~-**handed se** apanhado em flagrante; ~-**head** ruivo/a; ~-**hot** adj incandescente.

**redirect** [riːdaɪ'rekt] vt (mail endereçar de novo.

**redness** ['rednɪs] n rubor n avermelhado; (of hair) vermelhidã f.

**redo** [riː'duː] (irr: like **do**) vt refazer

**redouble** [riː'dʌbl] vt: **to ~ one' efforts** redobrar os esforços.

**redress** [rɪ'dres] n reparação f // retificar (Pt: -ct-), remediar.

**red tape** n (fig) formalidades fp papelada, rotina burocrática.

**reduce** [rɪ'djuːs] vt reduzir; (lower rebaixar; **'~ speed now'** (AU' 'diminua a velocidade agora'; **at a ~d price** (of goods) a preço remarcado; **reduction** [rɪ'dʌkʃən] n redução f; (of price) abatimento m; (discount) desconto.

**edundancy** [rɪ'dʌndənsɪ] n desemprego; (unemployment) redundância f.

**edundant** [rɪ'dʌndnt] adj (worker) desempregado; (detail, object) redundante, supérfluo; **to be made** ~ ficar sem trabalho or desempregado.

**eed** [ri:d] n (BOT) junco; (MUS. of clarinet etc) palheta.

**eef** [ri:f] n (at sea) recife m.

**eek** [ri:k] vi: **to ~ (of)** cheirar (a), feder (a).

**eel** [ri:l] n (gen) carretel m, bobina; (of film) rolo, filme m // vt (TECH) bobinar, enrolar // vi (sway) cambalear, oscilar.

**e-election** [ri:ɪ'lekʃən] n reeleição f.

**e-enter** [ri:'entə*] vt reentrar; **re-entry** n reentrada.

**ef** [ref] n (col) abbr of **referee**.

**efectory** [rɪ'fektərɪ] n refeitório.

**efer** [rɪ'fə:*] vt (send) remeter, encaminhar; (ascribe) referir, atribuir // vi: **to ~ to** (allude to) referir-se a, aludir a; (apply to) aplicar-se a; (consult) recorrer a.

**eferee** [refə'ri:] n árbitro; (for job application) pessoa que dá referência // vt arbitrar.

**eference** ['refrəns] n (mention) referência, menção f; (sending) envio, indicação f; (relevance) relação f; (for job application: letter) referência, carta de recomendação; **with ~ to** com relação a; (COMM. in letter) com referência a; **~ book** n livro de consulta.

**eferendum** [refə'rendəm], pl **-da** [-də] n referendum m, plebiscito.

**efill** [ri:'fɪl] vt reencher, reabastecer // n ['ri:fɪl] peça sobressalente, carga nova.

**refine** [rɪ'faɪn] vt (sugar, oil) refinar; **~d** adj (person, taste) refinado, culto; **~ment** n (of person) cultura, refinamento, requinte m; **~ry** n refinaria.

**reflect** [rɪ'flekt] vt (light, image) refletir (Pt: -ct-) // vi (think) refle(c)tir, meditar; **it ~s badly/ well on him** prejudica-o/lhe dá crédito; **~ion** [-'flekʃən] n (act) reflexão f; (image) reflexo; **on ~** depois de refle(c)tir bem; **~or** n (also AUT) refle(c)tor m; **~ stud** n (US: AUT) olho de gato.

**reflex** ['ri:fleks] adj, n reflexo; **~ive** [rɪ'fleksɪv] adj (LING) reflexivo.

**reform** [rɪ'fɔ:m] n reforma // vt reformar; **the R~ation** [refə-'meɪʃən] n a Reforma; **~er** n reformador(a) m/f; **~ist** n reformista m/f.

**refrain** [rɪ'freɪn] vi: **to ~ from doing** abster-se de fazer // n estribilho, refrão m.

**refresh** [rɪ'freʃ] vt refrescar; **~er course** n curso de atualização (Pt: -ct-); **refreshing** adj refrescante; **~ments** npl (drinks) refrescos mpl.

**refrigeration** [rɪfrɪdʒə'reɪʃən] n refrigeração f; **refrigerator** [-'frɪdʒəreɪtə*] n refrigerador m, geladeira.

**refuel** [ri:'fjuəl] vi reabastecer (de combustível).

**refuge** ['refju:dʒ] n refúgio, asilo; **to take ~ in** refugiar-se em.

**refugee** [refju'dʒi:] n refugiado/a.

**refund** ['ri:fʌnd] n reembolso // vt [rɪ'fʌnd] devolver, reembolsar.

**refurbish** [ri:'fə:bɪʃ] vt renovar.

**refusal** [rɪ'fju:zəl] n recusa, negativa; **first ~** primeira opção f.

**refuse** ['refju:s] n refugo, lixo // (vb: [rɪ'fju:z]) vt (reject) rejeitar; (say no to) negar-se a, recusar // vi negar-se; (horse) recusar; **~ bin** n lata de lixo; **~ tip** n depósito.

**refute** [rɪ'fju:t] vt refutar, contradizer.

**regain** [rɪ'geɪn] vt recuperar, recobrar, readquirir.

**regal** [ri:gl] adj real, régio.

**regalia** [rɪ'geɪlɪə] n, npl insígnias fpl reais.

**regard** [rɪ'gɑ:d] n (gaze) olhar m; (aspect) respeito; (attention) atenção f; (esteem) estima, consideração f // vt (consider) considerar; (look at) olhar; 'with kindest ~s' 'atenciosamente'; ~ing, as ~s, with ~ to com relação a, com respeito a, quanto a; ~less adv sem considerar as consequências; ~less of apesar de.

**regatta** [rɪ'gætə] n regata.

**regent** [ri:dʒənt] n regente m/f.

**régime** [reɪ'ʒi:m] n regime m.

**regiment** [redʒɪmənt] n regimento // vt regulamentar; ~al [-'mentl] adj regimental; ~ation [-'teɪʃən] n organização f.

**region** [ri:dʒən] n região f; in the ~ of (fig) por volta de, ao redor de; ~al adj regional.

**register** [redʒɪstə*] n (gen) registro (Pt: registo); (list) lista // vt registrar (Pt: registar); (subj: instrument) marcar, indicar // vi (at hotel) registrar-se (Pt: registar-se); (sign on) inscrever-se; (make impression) causar impressão; ~ed adj (design, letter) registrado (Pt: registado).

**registrar** [redʒɪstrɑ:*] n oficial m de registro (Pt: registo), escrivão/vã m/f.

**registration** [redʒɪs'treɪʃən] n (act) registro (Pt: registo), inscrição f; (AUT: also: ~ number) número da placa.

**registry** [redʒɪstrɪ] n registro (Pt: registo), arquivo; ~ office n regist(r)o civil, cartório; to get married in a ~ office casar-se no civil.

**regret** [rɪ'gret] n desgosto, pesar m; (remorse) remorso // vt sentir, lamentar; (repent of) arrepender-se de; ~fully adv com pesar,

pesarosamente; ~table adj deplorável; (loss) lamentável.

**regroup** [ri:'gru:p] vt reagrupar // vi reagrupar-se.

**regular** [regjulə*] adj (gen) regular; (usual) normal, habitual; (soldier) de linha; (intensive) verdadeiro, completo // n (client etc) cliente m/f, habitual m/f; ~ity [-'lærɪtɪ] n regularidade f; ~ly adv regularmente.

**regulate** [regjuleɪt] vt regular; (TECH) ajustar; **regulation** [-'leɪʃən] n (rule) regra, regulamento; (adjustment) ajuste m.

**rehabilitation** [ri:həbɪlɪ'teɪʃən] n reabilitação f.

**rehearsal** [rɪ'hə:səl] n ensaio; **rehearse** vt ensaiar.

**reign** [reɪn] n reinado; (fig) domínio // vi reinar; (fig) imperar; ~ing adj (monarch) reinante atual (Pt: -ct-); (predominant) imperante, predominante.

**reimburse** [ri:ɪm'bə:s] vt reembolsar; ~ment n reembolso.

**rein** [reɪn] n (for horse) rédea; to give ~ to dar rédeas a, dar rédea larga a.

**reincarnation** [ri:ɪnkɑ:'neɪʃən] n reencarnação f.

**reindeer** [reɪndɪə*] n, pl inv rena.

**reinforce** [ri:ɪn'fɔ:s] vt reforçar; ~d adj (concrete) armado; ~ment n (action) reforço; ~ments npl (MIL) reforços mpl.

**reinstate** [ri:ɪn'steɪt] vt (worker) reintegrar ao seu posto, reempossar.

**reiterate** [ri:'ɪtəreɪt] vt reiterar, repetir.

**reject** [ri:dʒekt] n (COMM) artigo defeituoso // vt [rɪ'dʒekt] rejeitar; (plan) recusar; (solution) descartar; ~ion n [rɪ'dʒekʃən] n rejeição f.

**rejoice** [rɪ'dʒɔɪs] vi: to ~ at or over regozijar-se or alegrar-se de.

**rejuvenate** [rɪ'dʒu:vəneɪt] vt rejuvenescer.

**ekindle** [ri:'kɪndl] vt reacender; (fig) despertar, reanimar.

**elapse** [ri'læps] n (MED) recaída; (into crime) reincidência.

**elate** [ri'leɪt] vt (tell) contar, relatar; (connect) relacionar // vi relacionar-se; ~d adj afim, ligado; (person) aparentado; ~d to com referência a; **relating to** prep relativo a, acerca de.

**elation** [ri'leɪʃən] n (person) parente m/f; (link) relação f, conexão f; ~ship n relacionamento; (personal ties) relações fpl; (also: **family** ~ship) parentesco.

**elative** ['rɛlətɪv] n parente/a m/f, familiar m/f // adj relativo.

**elax** [ri'læks] vi descansar; (person: unwind) descontrair-se // vt relaxar; (mind, person) descansar; ~ation [ri:læk'seɪʃən] n (rest) descanso; (ease) relaxamento, relax m; (amusement) passatempo; (entertainment) diversão f; ~ing adj relaxado; (tranquil) tranqüilo; ~ing adj calmante, relaxante.

**elay** ['ri:leɪ] n (race) corrida de revezamento // vt (message) retransmitir.

**elease** [ri'li:s] n (from prison) libertação f; (from obligation) liberação f; (of shot) disparo; (of gas etc) escape m; (of film etc) estréia // vt (prisoner) pôr em liberdade; (book, film) lançar, estrear; (report, news) lançar; (gas etc) escapar; (free: from wreckage etc) soltar; (TECH: catch, spring etc) desengatar; (let go) soltar, afrouxar.

**elegate** ['rɛləgeɪt] vt relegar, afastar; (SPORT): to be ~d descer.

**elent** [ri'lɛnt] vi abrandar-se; (yield) ceder; ~less adj implacável.

**elevance** ['rɛləvəns] n relevância, pertinência; **relevant** [-ənt] adj (fact) relevante, pertinente; (apt) apropriado.

**eliable** [ri'laɪəbl] adj (person, firm) digno de confiança; (method,

*machine*) seguro; (news) fidedigno; **reliably** adv: **to be reliably informed that...** saber de fonte segura que... .

**reliance** [ri'laɪəns] n: ~ (on) confiança (em), esperança (em).

**relic** ['rɛlɪk] n (REL) relíquia; (of the past) vestígio.

**relief** [ri'li:f] n (from pain, anxiety) alívio; (help, supplies) ajuda, socorro; (ART, GEO) relevo.

**relieve** [ri'li:v] vt (pain, patient) aliviar; (bring help to) ajudar, socorrer; (burden) abrandar, mitigar; (take over from: gen) substituir, revezar; (: guard) render; to ~ sb of sth tirar algo de alguém; to ~ o.s. fazer as necessidades.

**religion** [ri'lɪdʒən] n religião f; **religious** adj religioso.

**relinquish** [ri'lɪŋkwɪʃ] vt abandonar; (plan, habit) renunciar a.

**relish** ['rɛlɪʃ] n (CULIN) condimento, tempero; (enjoyment) entusiasmo; (flavour) sabor m, gosto // vt (food etc) saborear; to ~ doing gostar de fazer.

**reload** [ri:'ləud] vt recarregar.

**reluctance** [ri'lʌktəns] n relutância; **reluctant** [-ənt] adj relutante; **reluctantly** [-əntli] adv relutantemente, de má vontade.

**rely** [ri'laɪ]: to ~ on vt fus confiar em, contar com; (be dependent on) depender de.

**remain** [ri'meɪn] vi (survive) ficar; (be left) sobrar; (continue) continuar, manter-se; ~der n resto, restante m; ~ing adj restante; ~s npl (mortal) restos mortais; (leftovers) sobras fpl.

**remand** [ri'mɑ:nd] n: on ~ sob prisão preventiva // vt: to ~ in custody recolocar em prisão preventiva, manter sob custódia; ~ home n instituição f do juizado de menores.

**remark** [ri'mɑ:k] n observação f //

*vt* comentar, reparar; *(notice)* observar; **~able** *adj* notável; *(outstanding)* extraordinário.

**remarry** [ri:'mæri] *vi* casar-se de novo, contrair segundas núpcias.

**remedial** [ri'mi:diəl] *adj* *(tuition, classes)* de reforço.

**remedy** ['rɛmədi] *n* remédio, cura // *vt* remediar, curar.

**remember** [ri'mɛmbə*] *vt* lembrar-se de, recordar-se de; *(bear in mind)* ter presente; **remembrance** *n* *(memory)* memória; *(souvenir)* lembrança, recordação *f*.

**remind** [ri'maind] *vt*: to ~ sb to do sth lembrar a alguém que tem de fazer algo; to ~ sb of sth lembrar algo a alguém; **she ~s me of her mother** ela me lembra a mãe dela; **~er** *n* aviso, lembrete *m*; *(souvenir)* lembrança.

**reminisce** [rɛmi'nis] *vi* relembrar velhas histórias; **reminiscent** *adj*: to be reminiscent of sth lembrar algo.

**remiss** [ri'mis] *adj* remisso, desleixado; **it was ~ of him** foi um descuido seu.

**remission** [ri'miʃən] *n* remissão *f*; *(of debt, sentence)* perdão *m*.

**remit** [ri'mit] *vt* *(send: money)* remeter, enviar, mandar; **~tance** *n* remessa, envio.

**remnant** ['rɛmnənt] *n* resto; *(of cloth)* retalho.

**remorse** [ri'mɔ:s] *n* remorso; **~ful** *adj* arrependido; **~less** *adj* *(fig)* desapiedado, implacável.

**remote** [ri'məut] *adj* *(distant)* remoto, distante; *(person)* reservado, afastado; **~ control** *n* controle *m* remoto; **~ly** *adv* remotamente; *(slightly)* levemente; **~ness** *n* afastamento, isolamento.

**remould** [ri:'məuld] *vt* *(tyre)* recauchutar.

**removable** [ri'mu:vəbl] *adj* *(detachable)* removível, desmontável.

**removal** [ri'mu:vəl] *n* *(taking away)* remoção *f*; *(from house)* mudança; *(from office: sacking)* afastamento, demissão *f*; *(MED)* extração *(Pt: -cç-)* *f*; **~ van** *n* caminhão *(Pt: camião)* *m* de mudanças.

**remove** [ri'mu:v] *vt* tirar; *(employee)* afastar, demitir; *(name: from list)* eliminar, remover; *(doubt, abuse)* eliminar, remover; *(TECH)* retirar, separar; *(MED)* extrair, extirpar; **removers** *npl* *(company)* companhia de mudanças.

**remuneration** [rimju:nə'reiʃən] *n* remuneração *f*.

**rend** [rɛnd], *pt, pp* **rent** *vt* rasgar, despedaçar.

**render** ['rɛndə*] *vt* *(give)* dar, prestar; *(hand over)* entregar; *(reproduce)* reproduzir; *(make)* fazer, tornar; *(return)* devolver; *(translate)* traduzir; **~ing** *n* *(MUS etc)* interpretação *f*.

**rendez-vous** ['rɔndivu:] *n* encontro; *(place)* ponto de encontro.

**renegade** ['rɛnigeid] *n* renegado.

**renew** [ri'nju:] *vt* renovar; *(resume)* retomar, recomeçar; *(loan etc)* prorrogar; *(negotiations, acquaintance)* reatar; **renewable** *adj* renovável; **~al** *n* renovação *f*; *(loan)* prorrogação *f*.

**renounce** [ri'nauns] *vt* renunciar a; *(disown)* repudiar, rejeitar.

**renovate** ['rɛnəveit] *vt* renovar; **renovation** [-'veiʃən] *n* renovação *f*.

**renown** [ri'naun] *n* renome *m*; **~ed** *adj* renomado, famoso.

**rent** [rɛnt] *pt, pp of* **rend** // *n* aluguel *m* // *vt* alugar; **~al** *n* *(for television, car)* aluguel *m*.

**renunciation** [rinʌnsi'eiʃən] *n* renúncia.

**reorganize** [ri:'ɔ:gənaiz] *vt* reorganizar.

**rep** [rɛp] *n* *abbr of* **representative; repertory.**

**repair** [ri'pɛə*] *n* reparação *f*, conserto; *(patch)* remendo // *vt* reparar, remediar; (*shoes*) consertar; **in good/bad** ~ em bom/mau estado; ~ **kit** *n* (*tool box*) caixa de ferramentas.

**repartee** [repɑː'tiː] *n* resposta arguta e engenhosa; (*skill*) presteza em replicar.

**repay** [riː'peɪ] (*irr: like* **pay**) *vt* (*money*) reembolsar, restituir; (*person*) pagar de volta; (*debt*) saldar, liquidar; (*sb's efforts*) corresponder, retribuir; ~**ment** *n* reembolso, retribuição *f*; (*of debt*) pagamento.

**repeal** [riː'piːl] *n* (*of law*) revogação *f*; (*of sentence*) anulação *f* // *vt* revogar, anular.

**repeat** [riː'piːt] *n* (*RADIO, TV*) repetição *f* // *vt* repetir // *vi* repetir-se; ~**edly** *adv* repetidamente.

**repel** [riː'pel] *vt* (*lit, fig*) repelir, repugnar; ~**lent** *adj* repelente, repugnante // *n*: **insect** ~ repelente *m* de insetos (*Pt*: -ct-).

**repent** [riː'pent] *vi*: to ~ (of) arrepender-se (de); ~**ance** *n* arrependimento.

**repercussion** [riːpə'kʌʃən] *n* (*consequence*) repercussão *f*; **to have** ~**s** repercutir.

**repertoire** ['repətwɑː*] *n* repertório.

**repertory** ['repətəri] *n* (*also*: ~ **theatre**) teatro de repertório.

**repetition** [repi'tɪʃən] *n* repetição *f*.

**repetitive** [riː'petɪtɪv] *adj* (*movement, work*) repetitivo, reiterativo; (*speech*) prolixo, redundante.

**replace** [riː'pleɪs] *vt* (*put back*) repor, devolver; (*take the place of*) substituir, ocupar o lugar de; ~**ment** *n* (*gen*) substituição *f*; (*act*) reposição *f*; (*person*) substituto/a.

**replenish** [riː'plenɪʃ] *vt* (*glass*) reencher; (*stock etc*) completar, prover; (*with fuel*) reabastecer.

**replete** [riː'pliːt] *adj* repleto; (*well-fed*) cheio, empanturrado.

**replica** ['replɪkə] *n* réplica, cópia, reprodução *f*.

**reply** [riː'plaɪ] *n* resposta, réplica // *vi* responder, replicar.

**report** [riː'pɔːt] *n* relatório; (*PRESS etc*) reportagem *f*; (*also*: **school** ~) boletim *m* escolar; (*of gun*) estampido, detonação *f*; (*weather* ~) boletim *m* meteorológico // *vt* informar sobre; (*PRESS etc*) fazer uma reportagem sobre; (*bring to notice*: *occurrence*) comunicar, anunciar // *vi* (*make a report*) apresentar um relatório; (*present o.s.*): to ~ (to sb) apresentar-se (a), comparecer; ~**er** *n* jornalista *m/f*, repórter *m/f*.

**reprehensible** [repri'hensɪbl] *adj* repreensível, censurável, condenável.

**represent** [repri'zent] *vt* representar; (*fig*) falar em nome de; (*COMM*) ser representante de; ~**ation** [-'teɪʃən] *n* representação *f*; (*petition*) petição *f*; ~**ations** *npl* (*protest*) reclamação *fsg*, protesto *sg*; ~**ative** *n* representante *m/f* // *adj* representativo.

**repress** [riː'pres] *vt* reprimir, subjugar; ~**ion** [-'preʃən] *n* repressão *f*; ~**ive** *adj* repressivo.

**reprieve** [riː'priːv] *n* (*LAW*) suspensão *f* temporária; (*fig*) alívio // *vt* suspender temporariamente, aliviar.

**reprimand** ['reprimɑːnd] *n* reprimenda // *vt* repreender, censurar.

**reprint** ['riːprint] *n* reimpressão *f* // *vt* [riː'print] reimprimir, reeditar.

**reprisal** [riː'praɪzl] *n* represália.

**reproach** [riː'prəʊtʃ] *n* repreensão *f*, censura // *vt*: to ~ sb with sth repreender alguém por algo; **beyond** ~ irrepreensível, impecável; ~**ful** *adj* repreensivo, acusatório.

**reproduce** [riːprə'djuːs] *vt* reproduzir // *vi* reproduzir-se;

**reproduction** [-'dʌkʃən] n reprodução f; **reproductive** [-'dʌktɪv] adj reprodutivo.

**reprove** [rɪ'pruːv] vt: **to ~ sb for sth** repreender alguém por algo.

**reptile** ['reptaɪl] n réptil m.

**republic** [rɪ'pʌblɪk] n república; **~an** adj, n republicano/a.

**repudiate** [rɪ'pjuːdɪeɪt] vt (accusation) rejeitar, negar; (friend) repudiar; (obligation) desconhecer.

**repugnant** [rɪ'pʌgnənt] adj repugnante, repulsivo.

**repulse** [rɪ'pʌls] vt rejeitar, repelir; **repulsive** adj repulsivo.

**reputable** ['repjutəbl] adj (make etc) bem conceituado, de confiança; (person) honrado, respeitável.

**reputation** [repju'teɪʃən] n reputação f.

**repute** [rɪ'pjuːt] n reputação f, renome m; **~d** adj suposto, pretenso; **~dly** adv segundo se diz, supostamente.

**request** [rɪ'kwest] n pedido; (formal) petição f; **on ~** a pedido // vt: **to ~ sth of** or **from sb** pedir algo a alguém; (formally) solicitar algo a alguém.

**requiem** ['rekwɪəm] n réquiem m.

**require** [rɪ'kwaɪə*] vt (need: subj: person) precisar de, necessitar; (: thing, situation) requerer, exigir; (want) pedir; (order) mandar, ordenar; **~ment** n requisito; (need) necessidade f.

**requisite** ['rekwɪzɪt] n requisito // adj necessário, indispensável; **toilet ~s** artigos mpl de toalete pessoal.

**requisition** [rekwɪ'zɪʃən] n: **~ (for)** requerimento (para) // vt (MIL) requisitar, confiscar.

**reroute** [riː'ruːt] vt (train etc) desviar.

**resale** [riː'seɪl] n revenda.

**rescue** ['reskjuː] n salvamento, resgate m // vt salvar, livrar; **to ~ from** livrar de; **~ party** n grupo or expedição f de salvamento; **rescuer**

n salvador(a) m/f, libertador(a) m/f.

**research** [rɪ'səːtʃ] n pesquisa, investigação f // vt pesquisar; **~er** n pesquisador(a) m/f; **~ work** n trabalho de pesquisa.

**resell** [riː'sel] vt revender.

**resemblance** [rɪ'zembləns] n parecença, semelhança; **to bear a ~ to** assemelhar-se a; **resemble** vt parecer-se com.

**resent** [rɪ'zent] vt ressentir-se de; **~ful** adj ressentido; **~ment** n ressentimento.

**reservation** [rezə'veɪʃən] n (gen) reserva; (on road: also: **central ~**) canteiro central.

**reserve** [rɪ'zəːv] n (gen) reserva; (SPORT) suplente m/f // vt (seats etc) reservar; **~s** npl (MIL) (tropas da) reserva sg; **in ~** de reserva; **~d** adj reservado.

**reservoir** ['rezəvwɑː*] n (large) represa; (small) depósito.

**reshape** [riː'ʃeɪp] vt (policy) reformar, remodelar.

**reshuffle** [riː'ʃʌfl] n: **Cabinet ~** (POL) reformulação f do Ministério.

**reside** [rɪ'zaɪd] vi residir, viver.

**residence** ['rezɪdəns] n residência; (formal: home) domicílio; (length of stay) permanência, estadia; **resident** [-ənt] n residente m/f, (in hotel) hóspede m/f // adj (population) permanente; (doctor) interno, residente; **residential** [-'denʃəl] adj residencial.

**residue** ['rezɪdjuː] n resíduo, resto; (COMM) montante m líquido.

**resign** [rɪ'zaɪn] vt (one's post) renunciar a // vi demitir-se; **to ~ o.s. to** (endure) resignar-se a; **~ation** [rezɪg'neɪʃən] n renúncia; (state of mind) resignação f, submissão f; **~ed** adj resignado.

**resilience** [rɪ'zɪlɪəns] n (of material) elasticidade f; (of person) resistência; **resilient** [-ənt] adj (person) resistente.

**resin** ['rezɪn] n resina.

**resist** [rɪˈzɪst] vt resistir; ~**ance** n resistência.

**resolute** [ˈrezəluːt] adj resoluto, firme.

**resolution** [rezəˈluːʃən] n (gen) resolução f; (purpose) propósito.

**resolve** [rɪˈzɔlv] n resolução f; (purpose) intenção f // vt resolver // vi resolver-se; **to** ~ **to do** resolver-se a fazer; ~**d** adj decidido.

**resonant** [ˈrezənənt] adj ressonante.

**resort** [rɪˈzɔːt] n (town) local m turístico, estação f de veraneio; (recourse) recurso // vi: **to** ~ **to** recorrer a, fazer uso de; **in the last** ~ em último caso, em última instância.

**resound** [rɪˈzaund] vi ressoar, retumbar; **the room** ~**ed with shouts** os gritos ressoaram no quarto; ~**ing** adj retumbante; (fig) clamoroso.

**resource** [rɪˈsɔːs] n recurso; ~**s** npl recursos mpl, meios mpl; ~**ful** adj desembaraçado, engenhoso, expedito.

**respect** [rɪsˈpekt] n (consideration) respeito, consideração f; (relation) respeito; ~**s** npl saudações fpl, cumprimentos mpl // vt respeitar; **with** ~ **to** com respeito a; **in this** ~ a este respeito; ~**ability** [-əˈbɪlɪtɪ] n respeitabilidade f; ~**able** adj respeitável; (large) considerável; (passable) aceitável; ~**ful** adj atencioso, respeitador(a).

**respective** [rɪsˈpektɪv] adj respectivo; ~**ly** adv respectivamente.

**respiration** [respɪˈreɪʃən] n respiração f.

**respiratory** [rɪsˈpɪrətərɪ] adj respiratório.

**respite** [ˈrespaɪt] n pausa, folga; (LAW) adiamento, suspensão f.

**resplendent** [rɪsˈplendənt] adj resplandecente, brilhante.

**respond** [rɪsˈpɔnd] vi responder;

(react) reagir; **response** [-ˈpɔns] n resposta, reação (Pt: -cç-) f.

**responsibility** [rɪspɔnsɪˈbɪlɪtɪ] n responsabilidade f.

**responsible** [rɪsˈpɔnsɪbl] adj (liable): ~ **(for)** responsável por; (character) sério, respeitável; (job) de responsabilidade.

**responsive** [rɪsˈpɔnsɪv] adj sensível.

**rest** [rest] n descanso, repouso; (MUS) pausa; (break) intervalo; (support) apoio; (remainder) resto // vi descansar; (be supported): **to** ~ **on** apoiar-se em // vt (lean): **to** ~ **sth on/against** apoiar algo em or sobre/apoiar algo contra.

**restart** [riːˈstɑːt] vt (engine) arrancar de novo; (work) reiniciar, recomeçar.

**restaurant** [ˈrestərɔŋ] n restaurante m; ~ **car** n vagão-restaurante m.

**restful** [ˈrestful] adj sossegado, tranqüilo, repousante.

**rest home** n asilo, casa de repouso.

**restitution** [restɪˈtjuːʃən] n: **to make** ~ **to sb for sth** restituir or indenizar (Pt: -mn-) alguém de algo.

**restive** [ˈrestɪv] adj inquieto, impaciente; (horse) rebelde, teimoso.

**restless** [ˈrestlɪs] adj desassossegado, irrequieto; ~**ly** adv inquietamente.

**restoration** [restəˈreɪʃən] n restauração f; **restore** [rɪsˈtɔː*] vt (building) restaurar; (sth stolen) restituir, repor; (health) restabelecer.

**restrain** [rɪsˈtreɪn] vt (feeling) reprimir, refrear; (person): **to** ~ **(from doing)** impedir (de fazer); ~**ed** adj (style) moderado, comedido; ~**t** n (restriction) limitação f, coibição f; (moderation) moderação f, comedimento; (of style) sobriedade f.

**restrict** [rɪsˈtrɪkt] vt restringir, limitar; ~**ion** [-kʃən] n restrição f, limitação f; ~**ive** adj restritivo.

**rest room** (US) n banheiro; (Pt) lavabo.

**result** [rɪˈzʌlt] n resultado // vi: to ~ in resultar em; as a ~ of como consequência de.

**resume** [rɪˈzjuːm] vt (work, journey) retomar, recomeçar.

**résumé** [ˈreɪzjuːmeɪ] n resumo.

**resumption** [rɪˈzʌmpʃən] n reatamento, recomeço.

**resurgence** [rɪˈsəːdʒəns] n ressurgimento.

**resurrection** [rezəˈrekʃən] n ressureição f.

**resuscitate** [rɪˈsʌsɪteɪt] vt (MED) ressuscitar, reanimar; **resuscitation** [-ˈteɪʃn] n ressuscitação f.

**retail** [ˈriːteɪl] n varejo; (Pt) venda a retalho // cmp a varejo; (Pt) a retalho // vt vender a varejo; (Pt) vender a retalho; ~**er** n varejista m/f; (Pt) retalhista m/f.

**retain** [rɪˈteɪn] vt (keep) reter, conservar; (employ) contratar; ~**er** n (servant) empregado; (fee) sinal m, partido; (: Pt) honorários mpl.

**retaliate** [rɪˈtælɪeɪt] vi: to ~ (against) fazer represália (contra); **retaliation** [-ˈeɪʃən] n represália, vingança.

**retarded** [rɪˈtɑːdɪd] adj retardado.

**retch** [retʃ] vi fazer esforço para vomitar.

**retentive** [rɪˈtentɪv] adj (memory) retentivo, fiel.

**reticent** [ˈretɪsnt] adj reservado.

**retina** [ˈretɪnə] n retina.

**retinue** [ˈretɪnjuː] n séquito, comitiva; (escort) escolta.

**retire** [rɪˈtaɪə*] vi (give up work) aposentar-se; (withdraw) retirar-se; (go to bed) deitar-se; ~**d** adj (person) aposentado; (Pt) reformado; **retiree** (US) n aposentado/a; (Pt) reformado/a; ~**ment** n (state, act) aposentadoria; **retiring** adj

(leaving) de saída; (shy) acanhado, retraído.

**retort** [rɪˈtɔːt] n (reply) réplica // vi replicar, retorquir.

**retrace** [riːˈtreɪs] vt: to ~ one's steps voltar sobre (os) seus passos, refazer o mesmo caminho.

**retract** [rɪˈtrækt] vt (statement) retirar, retratar (Pt: -act-); (claws) encolher; (undercarriage, aerial) recolher // vi retratar-se (Pt: -act-); ~**able** adj retrátil (Pt: -áct-); revogável.

**retrain** [riːˈtreɪn] vt reeducar, retreinar; ~**ing** n readaptação f profissional.

**retreat** [rɪˈtriːt] n (place) retiro; (act) retraimento; (MIL) retirada // vi retirar-se; (flood) retroceder.

**retribution** [retrɪˈbjuːʃən] n desforra, revide m, vingança.

**retrieve** [rɪˈtriːv] vt (gen) reaver, recuperar; (situation, honour) salvar; (error, loss) reparar; **retriever** n cão m de busca, perdigueiro.

**retrospect** [ˈretrəspekt] n: in ~ retrospectivamente, em retrospecto; ~**ive** [-ˈspektɪv] adj (law) retrospectivo, retroativo (Pt: -act-).

**return** [rɪˈtəːn] n (going or coming back) regresso, volta; (of sth stolen etc) devolução f; (recompense) recompensa; (FINANCE: from land, shares) rendimento, lucro; (report) relatório // cmp (journey) de regresso, de volta; (ticket) de ida e volta; (match) de revanche // vi (person etc: come or go back) voltar, regressar; (symptoms etc) voltar // vt devolver; (favour, love etc) retribuir; (verdict) proferir, anunciar; (POL: candidate) eleger; ~**s** npl (COMM) receita sg; in ~ em troca; **many happy** ~**s (of the day)!** parabéns! mpl.

**reunion** [riːˈjuːnɪən] n reunião f.

**reunite** [riːjuːˈnaɪt] vt reunir; (reconcile) reconciliar.

**rev** [rɛv] n abbr of **revolution** (AUT) // (vb: also: ~ **up**) vt aumentar a velocidade (do motor) // vi acelerar.

**reveal** [rɪˈviːl] vt (make known) revelar; ~**ing** adj revelador(a).

**reveille** [rɪˈvælɪ] n (MIL) toque m de alvorada.

**revel** [ˈrɛvl] vi: **to ~ in sth/in doing sth** deleitar-se com algo/em fazer algo.

**revelation** [rɛvəˈleɪʃən] n revelação f.

**reveller** [ˈrɛvlə*] n farrista m/f, folião/liã m/f; **revelry** [-rɪ] n festança, folia.

**revenge** [rɪˈvɛndʒ] n vingança, desforra; (in sport) revanche f; **to take ~ on** vingar-se de.

**revenue** [ˈrɛvənjuː] n receita, renda; (on investment) rendimento; (profit) lucro.

**reverberate** [rɪˈvɑːbəreɪt] vi (sound) ressoar, repercutir, ecoar; **reverberation** [-ˈreɪʃən] n reverberação f, repercussão f.

**revere** [rɪˈvɪə*] vt reverenciar, venerar; **reverence** [ˈrɛvərəns] n reverência; **reverent** [ˈrɛvərənt] adj reverente.

**reverie** [ˈrɛvərɪ] n devaneio, sonho.

**reversal** [rɪˈvɛːsl] n (of order) reversão f; (of direction) mudança em sentido contrário; (of decision) revogação f.

**reverse** [rɪˈvɛːs] n (opposite) contrário; (back: of cloth) avesso; (: of coin) reverso; (: of paper) dorso; (AUT: also: ~ **gear**) marcha à ré; (Pt) marcha atrás // adj (order) inverso, oposto; (direction) contrário // vt (turn over) virar do lado do avesso; (invert) inverter; (change) mudar (totalmente) de // vi (AUT) dar marcha à ré; (Pt) fazer marcha atrás; **reversible** adj reversível.

**revert** [rɪˈvɛːt] vi: **to ~ to** voltar a.

**review** [rɪˈvjuː] n (magazine, MIL) revista; (of book, film) crítica, resenha; (examination) recapitulação f, exame m // vt rever, examinar; (MIL) passar em revista; (book, film) fazer a crítica or resenha de; ~**er** n crítico/a.

**revile** [rɪˈvaɪl] vt ultrajar, injuriar, vilipendiar.

**revise** [rɪˈvaɪz] vt (manuscript) corrigir; (opinion) alterar, modificar; (study: subject) recapitular; (look over) revisar, rever; **revision** [rɪˈvɪʒən] n correção f (Pt: -cç-) f, modificação f, revisão f.

**revitalize** [riːˈvaɪtəlaɪz] vt revitalizar, revivificar.

**revival** [rɪˈvaɪvəl] n (recovery) restabelecimento, (of interest) renascença, renascimento; (THEATRE) reestréia; (of faith) despertar m.

**revive** [rɪˈvaɪv] vt (gen) ressuscitar; (custom) restabelecer, restaurar; (hope, courage) despertar, reanimar; (play) reapresentar // vi (person) voltar a si; (from faint) recuperar os sentidos; (activity) renascer.

**revoke** [rɪˈvəʊk] vt revogar.

**revolt** [rɪˈvəʊlt] n revolta, rebelião f; insurreição f // vi revoltar-se // vt causar aversão, repugnar; ~**ing** adj revoltante, repulsivo.

**revolution** [rɛvəˈluːʃən] n revolução f; ~**ary** adj, n revolucionário/a; ~**ize** vt revolucionar.

**revolve** [rɪˈvɒlv] vi revolver, girar.

**revolver** [rɪˈvɒlvə*] n revólver m.

**revolving** [rɪˈvɒlvɪŋ] adj (chair etc) giratório; ~ **door** n porta giratória.

**revue** [rɪˈvjuː] n (THEATRE) revista.

**revulsion** [rɪˈvʌlʃən] n aversão f, repugnância.

**reward** [rɪˈwɔːd] n prêmio, recompensa // vt: **to ~ (for)** recompensar or premiar (por);

**~ing** *adj* (*fig*) gratificante, compensador(a) *m/f.*

**rewire** [ri:'waɪə*] *vt* (*house*) renovar a instalação elétrica (*Pt: -ct-*) de.

**reword** [ri:'wə:d] *vt* reformular, exprimir em outras palavras.

**rewrite** [ri:'raɪt] (*irr: like* write) *vt* reescrever, escrever de novo.

**rhapsody** ['ræpsədɪ] *n* (*MUS*) rapsódia; (*fig*) elocução *f* exagerada *or* empolada.

**rhetoric** ['rɛtərɪk] *n* retórica; **~al** [rɪ'tɒrɪkl] *adj* retórico.

**rheumatic** [ru:'mætɪk] *adj* reumático; **rheumatism** ['ru:mə-tɪzəm] *n* reumatismo.

**Rhine** [raɪn] *n*: **the ~** o (rio) Reno.

**rhinoceros** [raɪ'nɔsərəs] *n* rinoceronte *m.*

**rhododendron** [rəudə'dɛndrn] *n* rododendro.

**Rhone** [rəun] *n*: **the ~** o (rio) Ródano.

**rhubarb** ['ru:bɑ:b] *n* ruibarbo.

**rhyme** [raɪm] *n* rima; (*verse*) verso(s) rimado(s), poesia.

**rhythm** ['rɪðm] *n* ritmo, cadência; **~ method** método anticoncepcional por tabelinha; **~ic(al)** [*adj*] rítmico, compassado.

**rib** [rɪb] *n* (*ANAT*) costela // *vt* (*mock*) zombar de, encarnar em.

**ribald** ['rɪbəld] *adj* vulgarmente engraçado, irreverente.

**ribbon** ['rɪbən] *n* fita; (*strip*) faixa, tira; **in ~s** (*torn*) em tirinhas, esfarrapado.

**rice** [raɪs] *n* arroz *m*; **~field** *n* arrozal *m*; **~ pudding** *n* arroz doce.

**rich** [rɪtʃ] *adj* rico; (*banquet*) suntuoso, opulento; (*soil*) fértil; (*food*) suculento, forte; (: *sweet*) rico; **the ~** os ricos; **~es** *npl* riquezas *fpl*, bens *mpl*; **~ness** *n* riqueza, opulência; (*soil, etc*) fertilidade *f.*

**rickets** ['rɪkɪts] *n* raquitismo.

**rickety** ['rɪkɪtɪ] *adj* raquítico;

(*shaky*) sem firmeza, vacilante.

**rickshaw** ['rɪkʃɔ:] *n* jinriquixá *m.*

**ricochet** ['rɪkəʃeɪ] *n* ricochete *m* // *vi* ricochetear.

**rid** [rɪd], *pt, pp* **rid** *vt*: **to ~ sb of sth** livrar alguém de algo; **to get ~ of** livrar-se *or* desembaraçar-se de.

**ridden** ['rɪdn] *pp* of **ride.**

**riddle** ['rɪdl] *n* (*conundrum*) adivinhação *f*; (*mystery*) enigma *m*, charada; (*sieve*) crivo, peneira // *vt*: **to be ~d** with estar cheio *or* crivado de.

**ride** [raɪd] *n* (*gen*) passeio; (*on horse*) passeio a cavalo; (*distance covered*) percurso, trajeto (*Pt: -ct-*) // (*vb: pt* **rode**, *pp* **ridden**) *vi* (*as sport*) cavalgar, montar; (*go somewhere: on horse, bicycle*) passear *or* andar (a cavalo, de bicicleta); (*journey: on bicycle, motor cycle, bus*) viajar // *vt* (*a horse*) montar a; (*distance*) viajar; **to ~ a bicycle** andar de bicicleta; **to ~ at anchor** (*NAUT*) estar ancorado; **to take sb for a ~** (*fig*) enganar alguém; **rider** *n* (*on horse: male*) cavaleiro; (: *female*) amazona; (*on bicycle*) ciclista *m/f*; (*on motorcycle*) motociclista *m/f.*

**ridge** [rɪdʒ] *n* (*of hill*) cume *m*, topo; (*of roof*) cumeeira; (*wrinkle*) ruga.

**ridicule** ['rɪdɪkju:l] *n* escárnio, zombaria, mofa // *vt* ridicularizar, zombar de; **ridiculous** [-'dɪkjuləs] *adj* ridículo, absurdo.

**riding** ['raɪdɪŋ] *n* equitação *f*, passeio a cavalo; **~ school** *n* escola de equitação.

**rife** [raɪf] *adj*: **to be ~** ser comum; **to be ~ with** estar repleto de, abundar em.

**riffraff** ['rɪfræf] *n* plebe *f*, ralé *f*, povinho.

**rifle** ['raɪfl] *n* rifle *m*, fuzil *m* // *vt* saquear; **~ range** *n* campo de tiro; (*at fair*) tiro ao alvo.

**rift** [rɪft] *n* (*fig: disagreement: between friends*) desentendimento;

(: *in party*) rompimento, divergência.
**rig** [rɪg] *n* (*also*: **oil** ~) torre *f* de
perfuração // *vt* (*election etc*)
adulterar *or* falsificar os resultados;
**to** ~ **out** *vt* ataviar, vestir; **to** ~ **up**
*vt* instalar, montar, improvisar;
~**ging** *n* (NAUT) cordame *m*.
**right** [raɪt] *adj* (*true, correct*) certo,
correto; (*suitable*) adequado,
conveniente; (*proper*) apropriado,
próprio; (*just*) justo; (*morally good*)
honrado, bom; (*not left*) direito; **it
serves you** ~! bem feito! // *n* (*right,
claim*) direito; (*not left*) direita //
*adv* (*correctly*) bem, corretamente
(*Pt*: -ct-); (*straight*) diretamente (*Pt*:
-ct-), direto (*Pt*: -ct-); (*not on the left*)
à direita; (*to the* ~) para a direita //
*vt* endireitar // *excl* muito bem!,
certo!, bom!; **to be** ~ (*person*) ter
razão; **all** ~! tudo bem!, está bem;
(*enough*) chega!, basta!; ~ **now**
agora mesmo; ~ **in the middle** bem
no meio; ~ **away** imediatamente,
logo, já; **by** ~**s** por direito; **on the** ~
à direita; ~ **angle** *n* ângulo reto (*Pt*:
-ct-); ~**eous** ['raɪtʃəs] *adj* justo,
honrado; (*anger*) justificado;
~**eousness** ['raɪtʃəsnɪs] *n* justiça;
~**ful** *adj* (*heir*) legítimo; ~**handed**
*adj* à direita; ~**handed** *adj* (*person*)
destro; ~**ly** *adv* corre(c)tamente,
devidamente; (*with reason*) com
razão; ~**wing** *adj* (POL) de direita.
**rigid** ['rɪdʒɪd] *adj* rígido; (*principle*)
inflexível; ~**ity** [-'dʒɪdɪtɪ] *n* rigidez
*f*, inflexibilidade *f*.
**rigorous** ['rɪgərəs] *adj* rigoroso.
**rigour, rigor** (US) ['rɪgə*] *n* rigor
*m*, severidade *f*.
**rig-out** ['rɪgaut] *n* (col) roupa, traje
*m*.
**rile** [raɪl] *vt* irritar, aborrecer.
**rim** [rɪm] *n* borda, beira, orla; (*of
spectacles, wheel*) aro.
**rind** [raɪnd] *n* (*of bacon*) couro, pele
*f*; (*of lemon etc*) casca; (*of cheese*)
crosta, casca.

**ring** [rɪŋ] *n* (*of metal*) aro; (*on
finger*) anel *m*; (*of people, objects*)
círculo, grupo; (*of spies*) grupo; (*for
boxing*) ringue *m*; (*of circus*) pista,
picadeiro; (*bull*~) picadeiro, arena;
(*sound of bell*) toque *m*, badalada;
(*telephone call*) chamada
(telefônica), telefonema *m* // *vb*: *pt*
**rang**, *pp* **rung** *vi* (*on telephone*)
telefonar; (*large bell*) tocar, badalar;
(*also*: ~ **out**: *voice, words*) soar;
(*ears*) zumbir // *vt* (TEL: *also*: ~ **up**)
telefonar; (*bell etc*) badalar;
(*doorbell*) tocar; **to** ~ **back** *vi* (*t*
(TEL) telefonar de volta; **to** ~ **off** *vi*
(TEL) desligar; ~**ing** *n* (*of large
bell*) repicar *m*; (*in ears*) zumbido;
~**leader** *n* (*of gang*) cabeça *m/f*,
cérebro.
**ringlets** ['rɪŋlɪts] *npl* caracóis *mpl*,
argolinhas *fpl*.
**ring road** *n* estrada periférica *or*
perimetral.
**rink** [rɪŋk] *n* (*also*: **ice** ~) pista de
patinação, ringue *m*.
**rinse** [rɪns] *n* (*of dishes*) limpeza,
enxágue *m*; (*of hair*) rinsagem *f* //
*vt* enxaguar, fazer uma rinsagem.
**riot** ['raɪət] *n* distúrbio, motim *m*,
desordem *f* // *vi* provocar
distúrbios, amotinar-se; **to run** ~
desenfrear-se; ~**er** *n* desordeiro,
amotinado(a) *m/f*; ~**ous** *adj* (gen)
desordeiro; (*party*) tumultuado,
barulhento; (*uncontrolled*) desenfreado.
**rip** [rɪp] *n* rasgão *m*; (*opening*)
abertura // *vt* rasgar, romper // *vi*
correr; ~**cord** *n* corda de abertura
(de pára-quedas); ~ **off** *n*: **this is a**
~ **off** isto custa os olhos da cara.
**ripe** [raɪp] *adj* (*fruit*) maduro;
(*ready*) pronto; ~**n** *vt*/*i*
amadurecer; ~**ness** *n* maturidade *f*,
amadurecimento.
**ripple** ['rɪpl] *n* ondulação *f*,
encrespação *f*; (*sound*) murmúrio //
*vi* encrespar-se // *vt* ondular.
**rise** [raɪz] *n* (*slope*) elevação *f*,

ladeira; *(hill)* colina, rampa; *(increase: in wages)* aumento; (: *in prices, temperature)* subida; *(fig: to power etc)* ascensão *f* // *vi, pt* **rose**, *pp* **risen** ['rɪzn] *(gen)* levantar-se, erguer-se; *(prices, waters)* subir; *(river)* encher; *(sun)* nascer; *(person: from bed etc)* levantar-se; *(also:* ~ **up**: *rebel)* sublevar-se; *(in rank)* ascender, subir; **to give** ~ **to** ocasionar, dar origem a; **to** ~ **to the occasion** mostrar-se à altura da situação.

**risk** [rɪsk] *n* risco, perigo // *vt (gen)* arriscar; *(dare)* atrever-se a; **to take** *or* **run the** ~ **of doing** correr o risco de fazer; **at** ~ em perigo; **at one's own** ~ por sua própria conta e risco; ~**y** *adj* arriscado, perigoso.

**risqué** ['riːskeɪ] *adj (joke)* malicioso, picante, indecente.

**rissole** ['rɪsəʊl] *n* rissole *m*.

**rite** [raɪt] *n* rito; *funeral* ~**s** exéquias *fpl*, cerimônia fúnebre.

**ritual** ['rɪtjʊəl] *adj* ritual // *n* ritual *m*, rito, cerimonial *m*.

**rival** ['raɪvl] *n* rival *m/f*; *(in business)* concorrente *m/f* // *adj* rival, adversário, competidor(a) // *vt* rivalizar, competir com; ~**ry** *n* rivalidade *f*, concorrência.

**river** ['rɪvə*] *n* rio; **up/down** ~ rio acima/abaixo; ~**bank** *n* margem *f* (do rio); ~**bed** *n* leito (do rio); ~**side** *n* beira, beira do (do rio) // *cmp (port, traffic)* do rio, fluvial.

**rivet** ['rɪvɪt] *n* rebite *m*, cravo // *vt* rebitar; *(fig)* cravar.

**Riviera** [rɪvɪ'ɛərə] *n*: **the** (**the French**) ~ a Costa Azul (francesa), a Riviera francesa.

**road** [rəʊd] *n (gen)* caminho, via; *(motorway etc)* estrada (de rodagem); *(in town)* rua; ~**block** *n* barricada; ~**hog** *n* dono da estrada; ~ **map** *n* mapa *m* rodoviário; ~**side** *n* beira da estrada // *cmp* ao lado da estrada; ~**sign** *n* sinal *m* (da estrada), placa de sinalização; ~

**user** *n* usuário da via pública; ~**way** *n* pista, estrada; ~**worthy** *adj (car)* pronto para ser usado *or* dirigido.

**roam** [rəʊm] *vi* vagar, perambular, errar // *vt* vagar por, vadiar por.

**roar** [rɔː*] *n (of animal)* rugido, urro; *(of crowd)* bramido; *(of vehicle, storm)* estrondo; *(of laughter)* barulho // *vi* rugir, bramar, bradar; *(with laughter* rir ruidosamente *or* espalhafatosamente; **to do a** ~**ing trade** fazer um bom negócio.

**roast** [rəʊst] *n* carne *f* assada, assado // *vt (meat)* assar; *(coffee)* torrar.

**rob** [rɔb] *vt* roubar; **to** ~ **sb of sth** roubar algo de alguém; *(fig: deprive)* despojar alguém de algo; ~**ber** *n* ladrão/ladra *m/f*; ~**bery** *n* roubo.

**robe** [rəʊb] *n (for ceremony etc)* toga, beca; *(also:* bath ~) roupão *m* (de banho).

**robin** ['rɔbɪn] *n* pisco-de-peito-ruivo, *(Pt)* pintarroxo.

**robot** ['rəʊbɔt] *n* robô *m*, autômato.

**robust** [rəʊ'bʌst] *adj* robusto, forte.

**rock** [rɔk] *n (gen)* rocha, rochedo; *(boulder)* penhasco, recife *m*; *(sweet)* pirulito // *vt (swing gently: cradle)* balançar, oscilar; (: *child)* embalar, acalentar; *(shake)* sacudir // *vi* balançar-se; *(child)* embalar-se; *(shake)* sacudir-se; **on the** ~**s** *(drink)* com gelo; *(marriage etc)* arruinado, em dificuldades; **to** ~ **the boat** *(fig)* criar confusão; ~ **and roll** *n* rock-and-roll *m*; ~**bottom** *adj (fig)* mínimo, ínfimo; ~**ery** *n* jardim *m* de plantas rasteiras entre pedras.

**rocket** ['rɔkɪt] *n* foguete *m*.

**rocking** ['rɔkɪŋ]: ~ **chair** *n* cadeira de balanço; ~ **horse** *n* cavalo de balanço.

**rocky** ['rɔkɪ] *adj (gen)* rochoso, pedregoso; *(unsteady: table)* bamba, sem firmeza.

**rod** [rɔd] *n* vara, varinha; *(TECH)*

haste *f*; (*also*: **fishing** ~) vara de pescar.

**rode** [rəud] *pt of* **ride**.

**rodent** ['rəudnt] *n* roedor *m*.

**rodeo** ['rəudɪəu] *n* rodeio.

**roe** [rəu] *n* (*species*: *also*: ~ **deer**) corça, cerva; (*of fish*): **hard/soft** ~ ova/esperma *m* de peixe.

**rogue** [rəug] *n* velhaco, maroto; . **roguish** *adj* brincalhão/lhona.

**role** [rəul] *n* rol *m*, parte *f*, função *f*.

**roll** [rəul] *n* rolo; (*of banknotes*) maço; (*also*: **bread** ~) pãozinho; (*register*) rol *m*, lista; (*sound* *of drums etc*) rufar *m*; (*movement* *of ship*) jogo // *vt* rolar; (*also*: ~ **up**: *string*) enrolar; (: *sleeves*) arregaçar; (*cigarettes*) enrolar; (*also*: ~ **out**: *pastry*) esticar, alisar // *vi* (*gen*) rolar, rodar; (*drum*) rufar; (*in walking*) gingar; (*ship*) balançar, jogar; **to** ~ **by** *vi* (*time*) passar; **to** ~ **in** *vi* (*mail*, *cash*) chegar em grande quantidade; **to** ~ **over** *vi* dar uma volta; **to** ~ **up** *vi* (*col*: *arrive*) chegar, aparecer // *vt* (*carpet*) enrolar; ~**call** *n* chamada, toque *m* de chamada; ~**er** *n* rolo; (*wheel*) roda, roldana; ~**er skates** *npl* patins *mpl* de roda.

**rollicking** ['rɔlɪkɪŋ] *adj* alegre, brincalhão/lhona, divertido.

**rolling** ['rəulɪŋ] *adj* (*landscape*) ondulado; ~ **pin** *n* rolo de pastel; ~ **stock** *n* (*RAIL*) material *m* rodante.

**Roman** ['rəumən] *adj*, *n* romano/a; ~ **Catholic** *adj*, *n* católico(romano).

**romance** [rə'mæns] *n* (*love affair*) aventura amorosa, romance *m*; (*charm*) romantismo.

**Romanesque** [rəumə'nɛsk] *adj* românico, romanesco.

**Romania** [rəu'meɪnɪə] *n* = **Rumania**.

**romantic** [rə'mæntɪk] *adj* romântico; **romanticism** [-tɪsɪzəm] *n* romantismo.

**romp** [rɔmp] *n* brincadeira,

travessura // *vi* (*also*: ~ **about**) brincar, jogar.

**rompers** ['rɔmpəz] *npl* roupa de bebê.

**roof** [ruːf], *pl* ~ **s** *n* (*gen*) teto; (*Pt*) tecto; (*of house*) teto(e)/cto, telhado; (*of car*) capota, teto // *vt* telhar, cobrir com telhas; **the** ~ **of the mouth** o céu da boca; ~**ing** *n* cobertura; ~**rack** *n* (*AUT*) porta-bagagem *m inv*, xalmas *fpl*.

**rook** [ruk] *n* (*bird*) gralha; (*CHESS*) torre *f*.

**room** [ruːm] *n* (*in house*) quarto, sala, aposento; (*also*: **bed**~) dormitório, quarto; (*in school etc*) sala; (*space*) espaço, lugar *m*; ~**s** *npl* (*lodging*) alojamento *sg*; '~**s to let**' 'alugam-se quartos *or* apartamentos'; **single** ~ quarto individual; **double** ~ quarto duplo/de casal/para duas pessoas; ~**mate** *n* companheiro/a de quarto; ~ **service** *n* serviço de quarto; ~**y** *adj* espaçoso.

**roost** [ruːst] *n* poleiro // *vi* empoleirar-se, pernoitar.

**rooster** ['ruːstə*] *n* galo.

**root** [ruːt] *n* (*BOT*, *MATH*) raiz *f* // *vi* (*plant*, *belief*) enraizar, arraigar; **to** ~ **about** *vi* (*fig*) revirar ao buscar; **to** ~ **for** *vt fus* torcer para; **to** ~ **out** *vt* desarraigar, extirpar.

**rope** [rəup] *n* corda; (*NAUT*) cabo // *vt* (*box*) atar *or* amarrar com uma corda; (*climbers*: *also*: ~ **together**) ligar-se (uns aos outros) com cordas; **to** ~ **sb in** (*fig*) persuadir alguém a tomar parte de; **to know the** ~**s** (*fig*) estar por dentro (do assunto); ~ **ladder** *n* escada de corda.

**rosary** ['rəuzərɪ] *n* rosário.

**rose** [rəuz] *pt of* **rise** // *n* rosa; (*also*: ~**bush**) roseira; (*on watering can*) crivo // *adj* rosado, cor de rosa.

**rosé** ['rəuzeɪ] *n* rosado, rosé *m*.

**rose**: ~**bed** *n* roseiral *m*; ~**bud** *n* botão de rosa; ~**bush** *n* roseira.

**rosemary** ['rəuzmərɪ] *n* alecrim *m*.

**rosette** [rəuˈzɛt] n rosácea, roseta.

**roster** [ˈrɔstəʳ] n: **duty** ~ lista de tarefas, escala de serviço.

**rostrum** [ˈrɔstrəm] n tribuna.

**rosy** [ˈrəuzɪ] adj rosado, rosáceo; **a** ~ **future** um futuro promissor.

**rot** [rɔt] n (decay) putrefação (Pt: -cç-) f, podridão f; (fig: pej) decadência f // vt/i apodrecer.

**rota** [ˈrəutə] n rodízio.

**rotary** [ˈrəutərɪ] adj rotativo.

**rotate** [rəuˈteɪt] vt (revolve) fazer girar, dar voltas em; (change round: crops) alternar; (: jobs) alternar, revezar // vi (revolve) girar, dar voltas; **rotating** adj (movement) rotativo; **rotation** [-ˈteɪʃən] n rotação f; **in rotation** por turnos.

**rotor** [ˈrəutəʳ] n rotor m.

**rotten** [ˈrɔtn] adj (decayed) podre; (wood) carcomido, (fig) corrupto; (col: bad) detestável, miserável; **to feel** ~ (ill) sentir-se péssimo.

**rotting** [ˈrɔtɪŋ] adj podre.

**rotund** [rəuˈtʌnd] adj rotundo.

**rouble, ruble** (US) [ˈruːbl] n rublo.

**rouge** [ruːʒ] n rouge m, blush m, carmim m.

**rough** [rʌf] adj (skin, surface) áspero; (terrain) acidentado; (road) desigual; (voice) áspero, rouco; (person, manner: coarse) grosseiro, grosso; (weather) tempestuoso; (treatment) brutal, mau; (sea) agitado; (cloth) grosseiro; (plan) preliminar; (guess) aproximado; (violent) violento // n (person) grosseirão m; (GOLF): **in the** ~ na grama crescida; **to** ~ **it** passar aperto; **to sleep** ~ dormir na rua; ~**-and-ready** adj improvisado, feito às pressas; ~**en** vt (surface) tornar áspero; ~**ly** adv (handle) bruscamente; (make) toscamente; (approximately) aproximadamente; ~**ness** n aspereza; (rudeness) grosseria; (suddenness) brusquidão f.

**roulette** [ruːˈlɛt] n roleta.

**round** [raund] adj redondo // n círculo; (of toast) rodela; (of policeman) ronda; (of milkman) trajeto (Pt: -ct-); (of doctor) visitas fpl; (game: of cards, in competition) partida; (of ammunition) cartucho; (BOXING) rounde m, assalto; (of talks) ciclo // vt (corner) virar // prep ao/em redor de, em/à volta de // adv: **all** ~ por todos os lados; **the long way** ~ o caminho mais comprido; **all the year** ~ durante todo o ano; **it's just** ~ **the corner** (fig) está logo depois de virar a esquina; **to go** ~ **to sb's (house)** dar um pulinho na casa de alguém; **to go** ~ **the back** passar por detrás; **to go** ~ **a house** visitar uma casa; **to go the** ~**s** (story) divulgar-se; **to** ~ **off** vt (speech etc) terminar, completar; **to** ~ **up** vt (cattle) encurralar; (people) reunir; (prices) arredondar; ~**about** n (AUT) cruzamento circular, balão m; (at fair) carrossel m // adj (route, means) indireto (Pt: -ct-); **a** ~ **of applause** uma salva de palmas; **a** ~ **of drinks** uma rodada de bebidas; ~**ed** adj arredondado; (style) expressivo; ~**ly** adv (fig) energicamente, totalmente; ~**shouldered** adj encurvado; ~ **trip** n viagem f de ida e volta; ~**up** n rodeio; (of criminals) batida.

**rouse** [rauz] vt (wake up) despertar, acordar; (stir up) suscitar; **rousing** adj emocionante, vibrante.

**rout** [raut] n (MIL) derrota; (flight) fuga, debandada // vt derrotar.

**route** [ruːt] n caminho, rota; (of bus) trajeto; (of shipping) rumo, rota; ~ **map** n (for journey) mapa m rodoviário.

**routine** [ruːˈtiːn] adj (work) rotineiro // n rotina; (THEATRE) número.

**roving** [ˈrəuvɪŋ] adj (wandering)

errante; (*salesman*) ambulante.
**row** [rəu] *n* (*line*) fila, fileira; (*KNITTING*) carreira, fileira; ~ **boat** (*US*) *n* barco a remo // *n* [rau] (*noise*) barulho, ruído; (*racket*) escândalo; (*dispute*) discussão *f*, rixa; (*fuss*) confusão *f*, bagunça; (*scolding*) repreensão *f* // *vi* (*in boat*) remar // *vt* [rau] brigar // *vt* (*boat*) remar.

**rowdy** ['raudɪ] *adj* (*person: noisy*) barulhento; (: *quarrelsome*) brigão; (*occasion*) tumultuado // *n* encrenqueiro, criador *m* de caso.

**rowing** ['rəuɪŋ] *n* remo; ~ **boat** *n* barco a remo.

**royal** ['rɔɪəl] *adj* real; ~**ist** *adj*, *n* monárquico; ~**ty** *n* (~ *persons*) família real, realeza; (*payment to author*) direitos *mpl* autorais.

**R.S.V.P.** *abbr of répondez s'il vous plait* Q.R.P.G., Queira Responder Por Gentileza.

**rub** [rʌb] *vt* (*gen*) esfregar; (*hard*) friccionar; (*polish*) polir, lustrar // *n* (*gen*) esfregadela, fricção *f*; (*touch*) roçar *m*; **to ~ sb up the wrong way** irritar alguém; **to ~ off** *vi* tirar esfregando; **to ~ off on** transmitir-se para, influir sobre; **to ~ out** *vt* apagar.

**rubber** ['rʌbə*] *n* borracha; (*Brit: eraser*) borracha; ~ **band** *n* elástico, fita elástica; ~ **plant** *n* (*tree*) seringueira; (*plant*) figueira; ~**y** *adj* elástico.

**rubbish** ['rʌbɪʃ] *n* (*from household*) lixo; (*waste*) rebotalho, resto; (*fig: pej*) disparates *mpl*, asneiras *fpl*; (*trash*) refugo; ~ **bin** *n* lata do lixo; ~ **dump** *n* (*in town*) depósito (de lixo).

**rubble** ['rʌbl] *n* escombros *mpl*.

**ruby** ['ru:bɪ] *n* rubi *m*.

**rucksack** ['rʌksæk] *n* mochila.

**ructions** ['rʌkʃənz] *npl* confusão *fsg*, tumulto *sg*.

**rudder** ['rʌdə*] *n* leme *m*.

**ruddy** ['rʌdɪ] *adj* (*face*) corado,

avermelhado; (*col: damned*) maldito, desgraçado.

**rude** [ru:d] *adj* (*impolite: person*) grosso, mal-educado; (: *word, manners*) grosseiro; (*sudden*) brusco; (*shocking*) obsceno, chocante; ~**ly** *adv* rudemente, bruscamente; ~**ness** *n* grosseria, descortesia.

**rudiment** ['ru:dɪmənt] *n* rudimento; ~**s** *npl* primeiras noções *fpl*; ~**ary** [-'mentərɪ] *adj* rudimentar.

**rue** [ru:] *vt* arrepender-se de; ~**ful** *adj* arrependido.

**ruffian** ['rʌfɪən] *n* brigão *m*, desordeiro.

**ruffle** ['rʌfl] *vt* (*hair*) despentear, desmanchar; (*clothes*) enrugar, amarrotar; (*fig: person*) perturbar, irritar.

**rug** [rʌg] *n* tapete *m*; (*for knees*) manta (de viagem).

**rugby** ['rʌgbɪ] *n* (*also*: ~ **football**) rúgbi *m*.

**rugged** ['rʌgɪd] *adj* (*landscape*) acidentado, irregular; (*features*) marcado; (*character*) severo, austero.

**rugger** ['rʌgə*] *n* (*col*) rúgbi *m*.

**ruin** ['ru:ɪn] *n* ruína // *vt* arruinar; (*spoil*) estragar; ~**s** *npl* escombros *mpl*, destroços *mpl*; ~**ous** *adj* desastroso.

**rule** [ru:l] *n* (*norm*) norma, regulamento; (*regulation*) regra; (*government*) governo, domínio; (*ruler*) régua // *vt* (*country, person*) governar; (*decide*) decidir; (*draw: lines*) traçar // *vi* reger; (*LAW*) decretar; **to ~ out** excluir; **as a ~** via de regra; ~**d** *adj* (*paper*) pautado; ~**r** (*sovereign*) soberano/a; (*for measuring*) régua; **ruling** *adj* (*party*) dominante; (*class*) dirigente // *n* (*LAW*) parecer *m*, decisão *f*.

**rum** [rʌm] *n* rum *m*.

**Rumania** [ru:'meɪnɪə] *n* Romênia; ~**n** *adj*, *n* romeno/a.

**rumble** ['rʌmbl] *n* ruído surdo,

barulho; (of thunder) estrondo, ribombo // vi ribombar, troar; (stomach, pipe) fazer barulho, ressoar.

**rummage** ['rʌmɪdʒ] vi esquadrinhar, remexer, revistar.

**rumour, rumor** (US) ['ruːmə*] n rumor m, boato // vt: **it is ~ed that...** corre o boato de que ...

**rump** [rʌmp] n (of animal) anca, garupa; **~steak** n alcatra.

**rumpus** ['rʌmpəs] n (col) barulho, confusão f, zorra; (quarrel) rixa, discussão f.

**run** [rʌn] n corrida; (outing) passeio, excursão f; (distance travelled) trajeto (Pt: -ct-), percurso; (series) série f; (THEATRE) temporada; (SKI) pista // (vb: pt **ran**, pp **run**) vt (operate: business) dirigir; (: competition, course) organizar; (: hotel, house) administrar; (to pass: hand) passar; (water, bath) deixar correr // vi (gen) correr; (work: machine) funcionar; (bus, train: operate) circular, fazer o percurso; (: travel) ir; (continue: play) continuar; (: contract) ser válido; (flow: river, bath) fluir, correr; (colours, washing) desbotar; (in election) candidatar-se; **there was a ~ on** (meat, tickets) houve muita procura de; **in the long ~** no final de contas, mais cedo ou mais tarde; **I'll ~ you to the station** vou lhe dar uma carona até a estação; (Pt) dou-lhe uma boléia até à estação; **to ~ a risk** correr um risco; **to ~ about** vi (children) correr por todos os lados; **to ~ across** vt fus (find) encontrar por acaso, topar com, cruzar com; **to ~ away** vi fugir; **to ~ down** vi (clock) parar // vt (AUT) atropelar; (criticize) falar mal de, criticar; **to be ~ down** estar enfraquecido or exausto; **to ~ off** vt (water) deixar correr // vi partir correndo; **to ~ out** vi (person) sair correndo;

(liquid) escorrer, esgotar-se; (lease) caducar, vencer; (money) acabar; **to ~ out of** vt fus ficar sem; **to ~ over** vt sep (AUT) atropelar // vt fus (revise) recapitular; **to ~ through** vt fus (instructions) examinar, recapitular; **to ~ up** vt (debt) acumular; **to ~ up against** (difficulties) tropeçar em; **~away** adj (horse) desembestado; (truck) sem freios; (person) fugitivo.

**rung** [rʌŋ] pp of **ring** // n (of ladder) degrau m.

**runner** ['rʌnə*] n (in race: person) corredor(a) m/f; (: horse) cavalo de corrida; (on sledge) patim m, lâmina; (on curtain) anel m; (wheel) roldana, roda; **~ bean** n (BOT) feijão m verde; **~-up** n segundo/a colocado/a m/f.

**running** ['rʌnɪŋ] n (sport, race) corrida // adj (water) corrente; (commentary) contínuo, seguido; **6 days ~** 6 dias seguidos; **~ board** n estribo.

**runny** ['rʌnɪ] adj derretido, gotejante.

**run-of-the-mill** ['rʌnɔvðə'mɪl] adj comum, normal.

**runt** [rʌnt] n (also: pej) nanico, anão/anã m/f.

**runway** ['rʌnweɪ] n (AVIAT) pista de decolagem.

**rupee** [ruː'piː] n rupia.

**rupture** ['rʌptʃə*] n (MED) hérnia // vt: **to ~ o.s.** provocar-se uma hérnia.

**rural** ['ruərl] adj rural, campestre.

**ruse** [ruːz] n ardil m, manha.

**rush** [rʌʃ] n ímpeto, investida; (hurry) pressa; (COMM) grande procura or demanda; (BOT) junco; (current) corrente f forte, torrente f // vt apressar; (work) fazer depressa; (attack: town etc) assaltar // vi apressar-se, precipitar-se; **~ hour** n hora do rush; (Pt) hora ponta.

**rusk** [rʌsk] n rosca, biscoito.

**Russia** ['rʌʃə] n Rússia; ~**n** adj, n russo/a.

**rust** [rʌst] n ferrugem f; (BOT) mofo, bolor m // vi enferrujar.

**rustic** ['rʌstɪk] adj rústico, camponês/esa.

**rustle** ['rʌsl] vi sussurrar // vt (paper) farfalhar; (US: cattle) roubar, afanar.

**rustproof** ['rʌstpruːf] adj inoxidável, à prova de ferrugem.

**rusty** ['rʌstɪ] adj enferrujado.

**rut** [rʌt] n sulco, trilho; (ZOOL) cio; to be in a ~ ser escravo da rotina.

**ruthless** ['ruːθlɪs] adj desapiedado, cruel; ~**ness** n crueldade f, desumanidade f, insensibilidade f.

**rye** [raɪ] n centeio; ~ **bread** n pão m de centeio.

# S

**sabbath** ['sæbəθ] n domingo; (Jewish) sábado.

**sabbatical** [sə'bætɪkl] adj: ~ **year** ano sabático or de licença.

**sabotage** ['sæbətɑːʒ] n sabotagem f // vt sabotar.

**saccharin(e)** ['sækərɪn] n sacarina, adoçante m.

**sack** [sæk] n (bag) saco, saca // vt (dismiss) despedir; (plunder) saquear; to get the ~ ser demitido; ~**ing** n (dismissal) demissão f; (material) aniagem f.

**sacrament** ['sækrəmənt] n sacramento.

**sacred** ['seɪkrɪd] adj sagrado.

**sacrifice** ['sækrɪfaɪs] n sacrifício // vt sacrificar, renunciar.

**sacrilege** ['sækrɪlɪdʒ] n sacrilégio.

**sacrosanct** ['sækrəʊsæŋkt] adj sacrossanto.

**sad** [sæd] adj (unhappy) triste; (deplorable) deplorável; ~**den** vt entristecer.

**saddle** ['sædl] n sela; (of cycle) selim m // vt (horse) selar; to be ~**d with sth** (col) estar sobrecarregado com algo; ~**bag** n alforje m.

**sadism** ['seɪdɪzm] n sadismo; **sadist** n sadista m/f; **sadistic** [sə'dɪstɪk] adj sádico.

**sadly** ['sædlɪ] adv tristemente; ~ **lacking (in)** muito carente de).

**sadness** ['sædnɪs] n tristeza.

**safari** [sə'fɑːrɪ] n safári m.

**safe** [seɪf] adj (out of danger) fora de perigo; (not dangerous) seguro; (unharmed) ileso, incólume; (trustworthy) digno de confiança // n cofre m, caixa-forte f; ~ **and sound** são e salvo; (just) to be on the ~ **side** como precaução; ~**guard** n salvaguarda, proteção (Pt: -cç-) f // vt proteger, defender; ~**keeping** n custódia, prote(c)ção; ~**ly** adv com segurança, a salvo; (without mishap) sem perigo.

**safety** ['seɪftɪ] n segurança // adj de segurança; ~ **first!** cuidado!; ~ **belt** n cinto de segurança; ~ **pin** n alfinete m de segurança.

**saffron** ['sæfrən] n açafrão m.

**sag** [sæg] vi afrouxar.

**sage** [seɪdʒ] n (herb) salva; (man) sábio.

**Sagittarius** [sædʒɪ'tɛərɪəs] n Sagitário.

**sago** ['seɪgəʊ] n sagu m.

**said** [sɛd] pt, pp of **say**.

**sail** [seɪl] n (on boat) vela; (trip): to go for a ~ ir dar um passeio de barco a vela // vt (boat) governar // vi (travel: ship) navegar, velejar; (: passenger) passear de barco; (set off) zarpar; **to** ~ **through** vt/i fus (fig) fazer com facilidade; ~**boat** n (US) veleiro, barco a vela; ~**ing** n (SPORT) navegação f a vela, vela; to go ~**ing** ir velejar; ~**ing ship** n veleiro; ~**or** n marinheiro, marujo.

**saint** [seɪnt] n santo/a; S~ **John** São João; ~**ly** adj santo, santificado.

**sake** [seɪk] n: **for the ~ of** por (causa de), em consideração a; **for my ~** por mim.

**salad** ['sæləd] n salada; **~ bowl** n saladeira; **~ cream** n maionese m; **~ dressing** n tempero ou molho da salada; **~ oil** n azeite m de mesa.

**salami** [sə'lɑːmɪ] n salame m.

**salary** ['sælərɪ] n salário.

**sale** [seɪl] n venda; (at reduced prices) liquidação f, saldo; **"grand ~"** "grande liquidação"; **"for ~"** "à venda", "vende-se"; **on ~** à venda; **~room** n sala de vendas; **salesman/woman** n vendedor(a) m/f; (in shop) balconista m/f; (representative) vendedor(a) m/f viajante; **salesmanship** n arte f de vender.

**saliva** [sə'laɪvə] n saliva.

**sallow** ['sæləʊ] adj amarelado.

**salmon** ['sæmən] n, pl inv salmão m.

**saloon** [sə'luːn] n (US) bar m, botequim m; (AUT) carro espaçoso; (ship's lounge) salão m.

**salt** [sɒlt] n sal m // vt salgar; (put ~ on) pôr sal em; **~ cellar** n saleiro; **~water** adj de água salgada; **~y** adj salgado.

**salutary** ['sæljʊtərɪ] adj salutar.

**salute** [sə'luːt] n saudação f; (of guns) salva; (MIL) continência // vt saudar; (guns) dar salvas; (MIL) fazer continência a.

**salvage** ['sælvɪdʒ] n (saving) salvamento, recuperação f; (things saved) salvados mpl // vt salvar.

**salvation** [sæl'veɪʃən] n salvação f; **S~ Army** n Exército da Salvação.

**salve** [sælv] n (cream etc) unglento, pomada.

**salver** ['sælvə*] n bandeja, salva.

**same** [seɪm] adj mesmo // adv do mesmo modo, igualmente // pron: **the ~** o mesmo a mesma; **the ~ book as** o mesmo livro que; **all or just the ~** apesar de tudo, mesmo assim; **it's all the ~** dá no mesmo,

tanto faz; **to do the ~ (as sb)** fazer o mesmo (que alguém); **the ~ to you!** igualmente!

**sample** ['sɑːmpl] n amostra // vt (food, wine) provar, experimentar.

**sanatorium** [sænə'tɔːrɪəm], pl **-ria** [-rɪə] n sanatório.

**sanctify** ['sæŋktɪfaɪ] vt santificar.

**sanctimonious** [sæŋktɪ'məʊnɪəs] adj santarrão/rona, sacripanta.

**sanction** ['sæŋkʃən] n sanção f, pena // vt sancionar, ratificar.

**sanctity** ['sæŋktɪtɪ] n (gen) santidade f; divindade f; (inviolability) inviolabilidade f.

**sanctuary** ['sæŋktjʊərɪ] n (gen) santuário; (refuge) refúgio, asilo.

**sand** [sænd] n areia; (beach) praia // vt arear, jogar areia em.

**sandal** ['sændl] n sandália; (wood) sândalo.

**sand: ~bag** n saco de areia; **~bank** n banco de areia; **~castle** n castelo de areia; **~dune** n duna (de areia); **~paper** n lixa; **~pit** n (for children) caixa de areia; **~stone** n arenito, grés m.

**sandwich** ['sændwɪtʃ] n sanduíche m // vt (also: **~ in**) intercalar; **~ed between** encaixado entre; **cheese/ham ~** sanduíche de queijo/presunto; **~ board** n cartaz m ambulante; **~ course** n curso de teoria e prática alternadas.

**sandy** ['sændɪ] adj arenoso; (colour) vermelho amarelado.

**sane** [seɪn] adj são/sã do juízo; (sensible) ajuizado, sensato.

**sang** [sæŋ] pt of **sing**.

**sanitarium** [sænɪ'tɛərɪəm] (US) = **sanatorium**.

**sanitary** ['sænɪtərɪ] adj (system, arrangements) sanitário; (clean) higiênico; **~ towel**, **~ napkin** (US) n toalha higiênica or absorvente.

**sanitation** [sænɪ'teɪʃən] n (in house) higiene f; (in town) saneamento.

**sanity** ['sænɪtɪ] n sanidade f,

equilíbrio mental; (*common sense*) juízo, sensatez f.

**sank** [sæŋk] *pt of* **sink**.

**Santa Claus** [sæntə'klɔ:z] *n* Papai Noel *m*.

**sap** [sæp] *n* (*of plants*) seiva // *vt* (*strength*) esgotar, minar.

**sapling** ['sæplɪŋ] *n* árvore *f* nova.

**sapphire** ['sæfaɪə*] *n* safira.

**sarcasm** ['sɑ:kæzm] *n* sarcasmo; **sarcastic** [-'kæstɪk] *adj* sarcástico.

**sardine** [sɑ:'di:n] *n* sardinha.

**Sardinia** [sɑ:'dɪnɪə] *n* Sardenha.

**sari** ['sɑːrɪ] *n* sári *m*.

**sash** [sæʃ] *n* faixa, banda; (*belt*) cinto.

**sat** [sæt] *pt, pp of* **sit**.

**Satan** ['seɪtn] *n* Satanás *m*, Satã *m*.

**satchel** ['sætʃl] *n* bolsa; (*child's*) sacola escolar a tiracolo.

**satellite** ['sætəlaɪt] *n* satélite *m*.

**satin** ['sætɪn] *n* cetim *m* // *adj* acetinado.

**satire** ['sætaɪə*] *n* sátira; **satirical** [sə'tɪrɪkl] *adj* satírico; **satirize** ['sætɪraɪz] *vt* satirizar.

**satisfaction** [sætɪs'fækʃən] *n* satisfação *f*; (*of debt*) liquidação *f*, pagamento; **satisfactory** [-'fæktərɪ] *adj* satisfatório.

**satisfy** ['sætɪsfaɪ] *vt* satisfazer; (*pay*) liquidar, saldar; (*convince*) convencer, persuadir; **~ing** *adj* satisfatório.

**saturate** ['sætʃəreɪt] *vt*: **to ~ (with)** saturar *or* embeber (de); **saturation** [-'reɪʃən] *n* saturação *f*.

**Saturday** ['sætədɪ] *n* sábado.

**sauce** [sɔ:s] *n* molho; (*sweet*) creme *m*, calda; (*fig: cheek*) atrevimento; **~pan** *n* panela, caçarola.

**saucer** ['sɔ:sə*] *n* pires *msg*.

**saucy** ['sɔ:sɪ] *adj* atrevido, descarado; (*flirtatious*) flertivo, provocante.

**sauna** ['sɔ:nə] *n* sauna.

**saunter** ['sɔ:ntə*] *vi* caminhar devagar, perambular.

**sausage** ['sɔsɪdʒ] *n* salsicha,

lingüiça; (*cold meat*) frios *mpl*; **~roll** *n* folheado de salsicha.

**sauté** ['səuteɪ] *adj* sauté, frito rapidamente.

**savage** ['sævɪdʒ] *adj* (*cruel, fierce*) cruel, feroz; (*primitive*) selvagem // *n* selvagem *m/f* // *vt* (*attack*) atacar ferozmente; **~ry** *n* selvageria, ferocidade *f*.

**save** [seɪv] *vt* (*rescue*) salvar, resgatar; (*money, time*) poupar, economizar; (*put by*) guardar; (*SPORT*) impedir; (*avoid: trouble*) evitar // *vi* (*also*: **~ up**) poupar // *n* (*SPORT*) salvamento // *prep* salvo, exceto (*Pt*: -pt-).

**saving** ['seɪvɪŋ] *n* (*on price etc*) economia // *adj*: **the ~ grace of** o único mérito de; **~s** *npl* economias *fpl*; **~s bank** *n* caixa econômica, caderneta de poupança.

**saviour** ['seɪvjə*] *n* salvador(a) *m/f*.

**savour, savor** (*US*) ['seɪvə*] *n* sabor *m* // *vt* saborear; **~y** *adj* saboroso; (*dish: not sweet*) não doce; (: *salted*) salgado.

**saw** [sɔ:] *pt of* see // *n* (*tool*) serra // *vt, pt* sawed, *pp* sawed *or* sawn serrar; **~dust** *n* serragem *f*, pó *m* de serra; **~mill** *n* serraria.

**saxophone** ['sæksəfəun] *n* saxofone *m*.

**say** [seɪ] *n*: **to have one's ~** exprimir sua opinião; **to have a** *or* **some ~ in sth** opinar sobre algo, ter que ver com algo // *vt, pt, pp* **said** dizer; **to ~ yes/no** dizer (que) sim/não; **that is to ~** ou seja; **that goes without ~ing** é óbvio, nem é preciso dizer; **~ing** *n* ditado, provérbio.

**scab** [skæb] *n* casca, crosta (de ferida); (*pej*) canalha *m/f*, furagreves *m/f inv*; **~by** *adj* cheio de casca *or* cicatrizes.

**scaffold** ['skæfəuld] *n* (*for execution*) cadafalso, patíbulo; **~ing** *n* andaime *m*.

**scald** [skɔ:ld] *n* escaldadura // *vt*

escaldar, queimar; ~**ing** adj (hot) escaldante.

**scale** [skeɪl] n (gen, MUS) escala; (of fish) escama; (of salaries, fees etc) tabela; (of map, also size, extent) escala // vi (mountain) escalar; (tree) trepar, subir; ~ **s** npl balança sg; **on a large** ~ em grande escala; ~ **of charges** tarifa, lista de preços; **social** ~ escala social; ~ **drawing** n desenho em escala; ~ **model** n maquete m em escala.

**scallop** ['skɔləp] n (ZOOL) vieira, venera; (SEWING) barra, arremate m.

**scalp** [skælp] n escalpo, couro cabeludo // vt escalpar.

**scalpel** ['skælpl] n escalpelo, bisturi m.

**scamp** [skæmp] n moleque m, malandro, patife m.

**scamper** ['skæmpə*] vi: **to** ~ **away**, ~ **off** sair correndo, fugir precipitadamente.

**scan** [skæn] vt (examine) esquadrinhar, perscrutar; (glance at quickly) passar uma vista de olhos por; (TV, RADAR) explorar.

**scandal** ['skændl] n escândalo; (gossip) mexerico; ~**ize** vt escandalizar; ~**ous** adj escandaloso; (libellous) difamatório, calunioso.

**Scandinavia** [skændɪ'neɪvɪə] n Escandinávia; ~**n** adj, n escandinavo/a.

**scant** [skænt] adj escasso, insuficiente; ~**y** adj escasso.

**scapegoat** ['skeɪpgəut] n bode m expiatório.

**scar** [skɑ:] n cicatriz f // vt marcar (com uma cicatriz) // vi cicatrizar.

**scarce** [skɛəs] adj escasso, raro; ~**ly** adv mal, quase não; **scarcity** n escassez f; (shortage) falta, carência.

**scare** [skɛə*] n susto, espanto; (panic) pânico // vt assustar, espantar; **to** ~ **sb stiff** deixar alguém morrendo de medo; **bomb** ~ ameaça de bomba; ~**crow** n espantalho; ~**d** adj: **to be** ~**d** estar assustado or apavorado.

**scarf** [skɑ:f], pl **scarves** n (long) cachecol m; (square) lenço (de cabeça).

**scarlet** ['skɑ:lɪt] adj escarlate; ~ **fever** n escarlatina.

**scarves** [skɑ:vz] pl of **scarf.**

**scary** ['skɛərɪ] adj (col) assustador(a), medroso.

**scathing** ['skeɪðɪŋ] adj mordaz, severo.

**scatter** ['skætə*] vt (spread) espalhar; (put to flight) dispersar // vi espalhar-se, debandar; ~**brained** adj desmiolado, avoado; (forgetful) esquecido.

**scavenger** ['skævəndʒə*] n (refuse collector) varredor m de rua, gari m; (ZOOL) animal m/ave f que se alimenta de carniça.

**scene** [si:n] n (THEATRE, fig etc) cena; (of crime, accident) cenário; (sight, view) vista, panorama m; (fuss) escândalo; ~**ry** n (THEATRE) cenário; (landscape) paisagem f; **scenic** adj (picturesque) pitoresco.

**scent** [sɛnt] n perfume m; (smell) aroma; (fig: track) pista, rastro; (sense of smell) olfato m // vt perfumar; (smell) cheirar; (sniff out) farejar; (suspect) suspeitar, pressentir.

**sceptic, skeptic** (US) ['skɛptɪk] n cético/a (Pt: -pt-); ~**al** adj cético (Pt: -pt-); ~**ism** ['skɛptɪsɪzm] n ceticismo (Pt: -pt-).

**sceptre, scepter** (US) ['sɛptə*] n cetro; (fig) autoridade f real.

**schedule** ['ʃɛdju:l] n (of trains) horário; (of events) programa m; (plan) plano; (list) lista // vt (timetable) planejar, estabelecer; (list) catalogar, fazer lista de; (visit) marcar (a hora de); **on** ~ na hora, sem atraso; **to be ahead of/behind** ~ estar adiantado/atrasado.

**scheme** [ski:m] n (plan) plano,

**schism** ['skɪzəm] n cisma m.

**schizophrenia** [skɪtsəʊ'friːnɪə] n esquizofrenia; **schizophrenic** [-sə-'frenɪk] adj esquizofrênico.

**scholar** ['skɒlə*] n (pupil) aluno/a, estudante m/f; (learned person) sábio/a, erudito/a; ~ly adj erudito, douto; ~ship n erudição f; (grant) bolsa de estudo.

**school** [skuːl] n (gen) escola, colégio; (in university) faculdade f // vt (animal) adestrar, treinar; ~age n idade f escolar; ~book n livro de textos or escolar; ~boy n aluno; ~days npl anos mpl escolares; ~girl n aluna; ~ing n educação f, ensino; ~master/mistress n (primary, secondary) professor(a) m/f; ~room n sala de aula; ~teacher n professor(a) m/f.

**schooner** ['skuːnə*] n (ship) escuna; (glass) caneca, canecão m.

**sciatica** [saɪ'ætɪkə] n ciática.

**science** ['saɪəns] n ciência; ~ fiction n ficção f científica; scientific [-'tɪfɪk] adj científico; scientist n cientista m/f.

**scimitar** ['sɪmɪtə*] n cimitarra.

**scintillating** ['sɪntɪleɪtɪŋ] adj cintilante, brilhante.

**scissors** ['sɪzəz] npl tesoura; a pair of ~ uma tesoura.

**scoff** [skɒf] vt (col: eat) engolir // vi: to ~ (at) (mock) zombar (de).

**scold** [skəʊld] vt ralhar, xingar.

**scone** [skɒn] n bolinho.

**scoop** [skuːp] n colherona; (for flour etc) pá f; (PRESS) furo (jornalístico); to ~ out vt escavar; to ~ up vt juntar.

**scooter** ['skuːtə*] n (motor cycle) moto f, lambreta; (toy) patinete m.

**scope** [skəʊp] n (of plan, under-

taking) âmbito; (reach) alcance m; (of person) alçada, esfera de ação (PT: -çç-); (opportunity) oportunidade f.

**scorch** [skɔːtʃ] vt (clothes) chamuscar; (earth, grass) secar, queimar; ~er n (col: hot day) dia m quente or abafado; ~ing adj ardente.

**score** [skɔː*] n (points etc) escore m, contagem f; (MUS) partitura; (reckoning) conta; (twenty) jogo de vinte, vintena f // vt (goal, point) fazer; (mark) marcar, entalhar // vi ganhar; (FOOTBALL) marcar or fazer um gol; (keep score) marcar o escore; **on that** ~ a esse respeito, por esse motivo; **to** ~ **6 out of 10** conseguir um escore de 6 num total de 10; ~**board** n marcador m; ~**card** n (SPORT) cartão m de marcação; **scorer** n marcador m.

**scorn** [skɔːn] n desprezo // vt desprezar, rejeitar; ~**ful** adj desdenhoso, zombador(a).

**Scorpio** ['skɔːpɪəʊ] n Escorpião m.

**scorpion** ['skɔːpɪən] n escorpião m.

**Scot** [skɒt] n escocês/esa m/f.

**scotch** [skɒtʃ] vt (rumour) desmentir; (plan) estragar; **S~** n uísque m escocês; **S~ tape** n ® sellotape.

**Scotland** ['skɒtlənd] n Escócia; **Scotsman/woman** n escocês/esa m/f; **Scottish** ['skɒtɪʃ] adj escocês/esa.

**scoundrel** ['skaundrl] n canalha m/f, patife m.

**scour** ['skauə*] vt (clean) limpar, esfregar; (search) percorrer, procurar; ~**er** n esponja de aço.

**scourge** [skɔːdʒ] n açoite m, flagelo.

**scout** [skaut] n (also: **boy** ~) escoteiro; (MIL) explorador m, batedor m; **to** ~ **around** explorar, fazer reconhecimento.

**scowl** [skaul] vi franzir a testa; **to** ~

**at sb** olhar alguém carrancudamente.

**scraggy** ['skrægɪ] *adj* magricela, descarnado.

**scram** [skræm] *vi* (*col*) dar o fora, safar-se.

**scramble** ['skræmbl] *n* (*climb*) escalada (difícil); (*struggle*) luta // *vi*: **to ~ out/through** conseguir sair com dificuldade; **to ~ for** lutar por; **~d eggs** *npl* ovos *mpl* mexidos.

**scrap** [skræp] *n* (*bit*) pedacinho; (*fig*) pouquinho; (*fight*) rixa, luta; (*also*: **~ iron**) ferro velho, sucata // *vt* reduzir a ferro velho, jogar no ferro velho; (*discard*) desfazer-se de, descartar // *vi* brigar, armar uma briga; **~s** *npl* (*waste*) sobras *fpl*, restos *mpl*; **~book** *n* álbum *m* de recortes.

**scrape** [skreɪp] *n* (*fig*) aperto, enrascada // *vt* raspar; (*skin etc*) arranhar; (**~ against**) roçar // *vi*: **to ~ together** juntar com dificuldade; **scraper** *n* raspador *m*.

**scrap**: **~ heap** *n* (*fig*): **on the ~ heap** rejeitado, jogado fora; **~ merchant** *n* sucateiro; **~ paper** *n* papel *m* de rascunho; **~py** *adj* (*poor*) pobre; (*speech*) incoerente, desconexo; (*bitty*) fragmentário.

**scratch** [skrætʃ] *n* arranhão *m*; (*from claw*) arranhadura // *adj*: **~ team** time *m* improvisado, escrete *m* // *vt* (*record*) marcar, riscar; (*with claw, nail*) arranhar, unhar // *vi* coçar(-se); **to start from ~** começar do princípio, partir do zero; **to be up to ~** estar à altura (das circunstâncias).

**scrawl** [skrɔːl] *n* garrancho, garatujas *fpl* // *vi* garatujar, rabiscar.

**scream** [skriːm] *n* grito // *vi* gritar.

**screech** [skriːtʃ] *vi* guinchar.

**screen** [skriːn] *n* (*CINEMA, TV*) tela; (*Pt*) écran *m*; (*movable*) biombo; (*wall*) tabume *m*; (*also*: **wind~**) pára-brisa *m*; (*fig*) cortina // *vt*

(*conceal*) esconder, tapar; (*from the wind etc*) proteger; (*film*) projetar (*Pt*: -ct-); (*candidates etc*) examinar, checar; **~ing** *n* (*MED*) exame *m* médico; **~ test** *n* teste *m* cinematográfico.

**screw** [skruː] *n* parafuso; (*propeller*) hélice *f* // *vt* aparafusar; (*also*: **~ in**) apertar, atarraxar; **~driver** *n* chave *f* de fenda *or* de parafuso; **~y** *adj* (*col*) maluco, estranho.

**scribble** ['skrɪbl] *n* garrancho // *vt* escrevinhar, rabiscar.

**script** [skrɪpt] *n* (*CINEMA etc*) roteiro, script *m*; (*writing*) escrita, caligrafia.

**Scripture** ['skrɪptʃə*] *n* Sagrada Escritura.

**scriptwriter** ['skrɪptraɪtə*] *n* roteirista *m/f*.

**scroll** [skrəʊl] *n* rolo de pergaminho.

**scrounge** [skraʊndʒ] *vt* (*col*): **to ~ sth off** *or* **from sb** filar algo de alguém // *vi*: **to ~ on sb** viver às custas de alguém; **scrounger** *n* filão/lona *m/f*.

**scrub** [skrʌb] *n* (*clean*) esfregação *f*, limpeza; (*land*) mato, cerrado // *vt* esfregar; (*reject*) cancelar, eliminar.

**scruff** [skrʌf] *n*: **by the ~ of the neck** pelo cangote.

**scruffy** ['skrʌfɪ] *adj* sujo, desmazelado.

**scruple** ['skruːpl] *n* escrúpulo; **scrupulous** *adj* escrupuloso.

**scrutinize** ['skruːtɪnaɪz] *vt* examinar minuciosamente; (*votes*) escrutinar; **scrutiny** [-nɪ] *n* escrutínio, exame *m* cuidadoso.

**scuff** [skʌf] *vt* desgastar.

**scuffle** ['skʌfl] *n* luta confusa.

**scullery** ['skʌlərɪ] *n* copa.

**sculptor** ['skʌlptə*] *n* escultor *m*; **sculptress** [-trɪs] *n* escultora; **sculpture** [-tʃə*] *n* escultura.

**scum** [skʌm] *n* (*on liquid*) espuma;

*(pej: people)* ralé *f*, gentinha; *(fig)* escória.

**scurry** ['skʌrɪ] *vi:* **to ~ off** sair correndo, dar no pé.

**scurvy** ['skɜːvɪ] *n* escorbuto.

**scuttle** ['skʌtl] *n (also:* **coal ~)** balde *m* para carvão // *vt (ship)* afundar voluntariamente, fazer ir a pique // *vi (scamper):* **to ~ away, ~ off** sair em disparada.

**scythe** [saɪð] *n* segadeira, foice *f* grande.

**sea** [siː] *n* mar *m*; **on the ~ (boat)** no mar; *(town)* junto ao mar; **to be all at ~** *(fig)* estar confuso or desorientado; **out to** or **at ~** em alto mar; **~ bird** *n* ave *f* marinha; **~board** *n* costa, litoral *m*; **~ breeze** *n* brisa marítima, viração *f*; **~farer** *n* marinheiro, homem *m* do mar; **~food** *n* marisco; **~ front** *n (beach)* praia; *(prom)* passeio or avenida à beira-mar; **~going** *adj (ship)* de longo curso; **~gull** *n* gaivota.

**seal** [siːl] *n (animal)* foca; *(stamp)* selo // *vt (close)* fechar; (: *with ~)* selar; **to ~ off** vedar, lacrar; **it ~ed his fate** decidiu seu destino.

**sea level** ['siːlevl] *n* nível *m* do mar.

**sealing wax** ['siːlɪŋwæks] *n* lacre *m*.

**sea lion** ['siːlaɪən] *n* leão-marinho *m*.

**seam** [siːm] *n* costura; *(of metal)* junta, junção *f*; *(of coal)* veio, filão *m*.

**seaman** ['siːmən] *n* marinheiro.

**seamless** ['siːmlɪs] *adj* sem costura.

**seamstress** ['sɛmstrɪs] *n* costureira.

**seance** ['seɪɒns] *n* sessão *f* espírita.

**sea:** **~plane** *n* hidroavião *m*; **~port** *n* porto de mar.

**search** [sɜːtʃ] *n (for person, thing)* busca, procura; *(of drawer, pockets)* revista; *(inspection)* exame *m*, investigação *f* // *vt (look in)* procurar em; *(examine)* examinar,

*(person, place)* revistar // *vi:* **to ~ through** *vt fus* dar busca em; **in ~ of** à procura de; **~ing** *adj* penetrante, perscrutador(a); **~light** *n* holofote *m*; **~ party** *n* equipe *f* de salvamento; **~ warrant** *n* mandado de busca.

**sea:** **~shore** *n* praia, beira-mar *f*, litoral *m*; **~sick** *adj* enjoado, mareado; **~side** *n* costa, litoral *m*; **~side resort** *n* balneário.

**season** ['siːzn] *n (gen)* época, período; *(of year)* estação *f*; *(sporting etc)* temporada // *vt (food)* temperar; **~al** *adj* sazona, periódico; **~ing** *n* condimento, tempero; **~ ticket** *n* entrada or ticket *m* de assinatura.

**seat** [siːt] *n (in bus, train: place)* assento; *(chair)* cadeira; *(POL)* lugar *m*, cadeira; *(bicycle)* selim *m*; *(buttocks)* traseiro, nádegas *fpl*; *(of government)* sede *f* // *vt* sentar; *(have room for)* ter capacidade para; **to be ~ed** estar sentado; **~ belt** *n* cinto de segurança.

**sea:** **~ water** *n* água do mar; **~weed** *n* alga marinha; **~worthy** *adj* em condições de navegar, resistente.

**sec.** *abbr of* **second(s).**

**secede** [sɪˈsiːd] *vi* separar-se.

**secluded** [sɪˈkluːdɪd] *adj* retirado; *(place)* afastado; **seclusion** [-ˈkluːʒən] *n* reclusão *f*, isolamento.

**second** ['sɛkənd] *adj* segundo // *adv (in race etc)* em segundo lugar // *n (gen)* segundo; *(AUT: also:* **~ gear)** segunda; *(COMM)* artigo defeituoso // *vt (motion)* apoiar, secundar; **~ary** *adj* secundário; **~ary school** *n* escola secundária; **~-class** *adj* de segunda classe; **~hand** *adj* de (Pt: em) segunda mão, usado; **~ hand** *n (on clock)* ponteiro de segundos; **~ly** *adv* em segundo lugar; **~ment** [sɪˈkɒndmənt] *n* substituição temporária; ~-**rate** adj de segunda categoria.

**secrecy** ['si:krəsɪ] n segredo, discrição f; **secret** [-krɪt] adj, n secreto.

**secretarial** [sɛkrɪ'tɛərɪəl] adj de secretário/a, secretarial.

**secretariat** [sɛkrɪ'tɛərɪət] n secretaria, secretariado.

**secretary** ['sɛkrətərɪ] n secretário/a; **S~ of State** (Brit: POL) Ministro de Estado.

**secretive** ['si:krɪtɪv] adj sigiloso, reservado, secretório.

**sect** [sɛkt] n seita; ~**arian** [-'tɛərɪən] adj sectário.

**section** ['sɛkʃən] n seção (Pt: -cç-) f; (part) parte f, porção f; (of document) parágrafo, artigo; (of opinion) setor (Pt: -ct-) m; ~**al** adj (drawing) transversal, secional (Pt: -cc-).

**sector** ['sɛktə*] n setor (Pt: -ct-) m.

**secular** ['sɛkjulə*] adj secular, leigo.

**secure** [sɪ'kjuə*] adj (free from anxiety) seguro; (firmly fixed) firme, rígido // (fix) assegurar, garantir; (get) conseguir, obter.

**security** [sɪ'kjuərɪtɪ] n segurança; (for loan) fiança, garantia; (: object) penhor m.

**sedan** [sɪ'dæn] n (US) sedã m.

**sedate** [sɪ'deɪt] adj (calm) sossegado, tranqüilo; (formal) sério, ponderado // vt sedar, tratar com calmantes.

**sedation** [sɪ'deɪʃən] n (MED) sedação f; **sedative** ['sɛdɪtɪv] n calmante m, sedativo.

**sedentary** ['sɛdntrɪ] adj sedentário.

**sediment** ['sɛdɪmənt] n sedimento.

**seduce** [sɪ'dju:s] vt (gen) seduzir; **seduction** [-'dʌkʃən] n sedução f; **seductive** [-'dʌktɪv] adj sedutor(a).

**see** [si:] n (irr: pt **saw**, pp **seen**) vt (gen) ver; (understand) compreender, entender; (look at) olhar (para); (accompany): **to ~ sb to the door**

acompanhar or levar alguém até a porta // vi ver // n sé f, sede f; **to ~ that** (ensure) assegurar que; **to ~ about** vt tratar de, encarregar-se de; **to ~ off** vt despedir-se de; **to ~ through** vt enxergar através de // vt fus realizar, terminar; (help) ajudar em momento difícil; **to ~ to** vt fus providenciar.

**seed** [si:d] n semente f; (in fruit) caroço; (sperm) sêmen m, esperma; (fig) germe m; (TENNIS) pré-selecionado/a (Pt: -cc-); ~**ling** n planta brotada da semente, muda; ~**y** adj (shabby) gasto, surrado; (person) maltrapilho.

**seeing** ['si:ɪŋ] conj: ~ (**that**) visto (que), considerando (que).

**seek** [si:k], pt, pp **sought** vt (gen) procurar, buscar; (post) solicitar.

**seem** [si:m] vi parecer; ~**ingly** adv aparentemente, pelo que aparenta.

**seen** [si:n] pp of **see**.

**seep** [si:p] vi filtrar-se, penetrar.

**seesaw** ['si:sɔ:] n gangorra, balanço.

**seethe** [si:ð] vi ferver; **to ~ with anger** estar fulo de raiva; (Br) ficar uma arara.

**segment** ['sɛgmənt] n segmento.

**segregate** ['sɛgrɪgeɪt] vt segregar; **segregation** [-'geɪʃən] n segregação f.

**seismic** ['saɪzmɪk] adj sísmico.

**seize** [si:z] vt (grasp) agarrar, pegar; (take possession of) apoderar-se de, confiscar; (: territory) tomar posse de; (opportunity) aproveitar; **to ~ (up)on** vt fus valer-se de; **to ~ up** vi (TECH) gripar.

**seizure** ['si:ʒə*] n (MED) ataque m, acesso; (LAW) confisco, embargo.

**seldom** ['sɛldəm] adv raramente.

**select** [sɪ'lɛkt] adj seleto (Pt: -ct-), escolhido // vt escolher, selecionar (Pt: -cc-); (SPORT) selecionar; ~**ion** [-'lɛkʃən] n seleção (Pt: -cç-) f, escolha; (COMM) sortimento; ~**ive** adj seletivo (Pt: -ct-); ~**or** n (*person*) sele(c)cionador(a) *m/f*, sele(c)tor(a) *m/f*.

**self** [sɛlf], *pl* **selves** *pron see* **myself, yourself, himself, herself, itself, oneself, ourselves, themselves** // *n:* **the** ~ o eu.

**self...** *pref* auto...; ~**appointed** *adj* auto-nomeado; ~**assured** *adj* seguro de si; ~**catering** *adj* sem pensão; ~**centred** *adj* egocêntrico; ~**coloured** *adj* de cor natural; (*of one colour*) de uma só cor; ~**confidence** *n* auto-confiança, confiança em si; ~**conscious** *adj* inibido, constrangido; ~**contained** *adj* (*gen*) independente; (*flat*) completo, autônomo; ~**control** *n* autocontrole *m*, autodomínio; ~**defence** *n* legítima defesa, autodefesa; ~**discipline** *n* autodisciplina; ~**employed** *adj* autônomo; ~**evident** *adj* patente; ~**governing** *adj* autônomo; ~**important** *adj* presunçoso, que se dá muita importância; ~**indulgent** *adj* que se permite excessos; ~**interest** *n* egoísmo; ~**ish** *adj* egoísta; ~**ishness** *n* egoísmo; ~**lessly** *adv* desinteressadamente; ~**pity** *n* pena de si mesmo; ~**portrait** *n* auto-retrato; ~**possessed** *adj* calmo, senhor de si; ~**preservation** *n* auto-preservação *f*; ~**reliant** *adj* seguro de si, independente; ~**respect** *n* amor m próprio; ~**righteous** *adj* farisaico, santarrão/rona; ~**sacrifice** *n* abnegação *f*, altruísmo; ~**satisfied** *adj* satisfeito consigo mesmo; ~**service** *adj* de auto-serviço; ~**sufficient** *adj* auto-suficiente; ~**taught** *adj* autodidata (*Pt:* -acta).

**sell** [sɛl], *pt*, *pp* **sold** *vt* vender // *vi* vender-se; **to** ~ **at** or **for £10** vender a *or* por 10 libras; **to** ~ **off** *vt* liquidar; **to** ~ **out** *vi* vender todo o estoque; ~**er** *n* vendedor(a) *m/f*; ~**ing price** *n* preço de venda.

**sellotape** ['sɛləuteɪp] *n* fita adesiva, (fita) durex.

**sellout** ['sɛlaut] *n* traição *f*; (*of tickets*): **it was a** ~ foi um sucesso de bilheteria (*Pt:* -teira).

**selves** [sɛlvz] *pl of* **self.**

**semaphore** ['sɛməfɔ:*] *n* semáforo.

**semen** ['si:mən] *n* sêmen *m*.

**semi...** [sɛmɪ] *pref* semi..., meio...; ~**circle** *n* semicírculo; ~**colon** *n* ponto e vírgula; ~**conscious** *adj* semiconsciente; ~**detached (house)** *n* (*casa*) geminada; ~**final** *n* semifinal *f*.

**seminar** ['sɛmɪnɑ:*] *n* seminário.

**semitone** ['sɛmɪtəun] *n* (*MUS*) semitom *m*.

**semolina** [sɛmə'li:nə] *n* sêmola, semolina.

**senate** ['sɛnɪt] *n* senado; **senator** *n* senador(a) *m/f*.

**send** [sɛnd], *pt*, *pp* **sent** *vt* mandar, enviar; (*dispatch*) expedir, remeter; (*telegram*) passar; **to** ~ **away** *vt* (*letter, goods*) expedir, mandar; **to** ~ **away for** *vt fus* encomendar; **to** ~ **back** *vt* devolver; **to** ~ **for** *vt fus* mandar buscar; **to** ~ **off** *vt* (*goods*) despachar, expedir; (*SPORT: player*) expulsar; **to** ~ **out** *vt* (*invitation*) distribuir; (*signal*) emitir; **to** ~ **up** *vt* (*person, price*) fazer subir; (*parody*) parodiar; ~**er** *n* remetente *m/f*; ~**off** *n*: **a good** ~**off** uma boa despedida.

**senile** ['si:naɪl] *adj* senil; **senility** [sɪ'nɪlɪtɪ] *n* senilidade *f*.

**senior** ['si:nɪə*] *adj* (*older*) mais velho *or* idoso; (: *on staff*) mais antigo; (*of higher rank*) superior // *n* sênior *m/f*; ~**ity** [-'ɔrɪtɪ] *n* antiguidade *f*.

**sensation** [sɛn'seɪʃən] *n* sensação *f*; ~**al** *adj* sensacional; ~**alism** *n* sensacionalismo.

**sense** [sɛns] *n* sentido; (*feeling*) sensação *f*; (*good* ~) bom senso; (*sentiment*) opinião *f* // *vt* sentir, perceber; **it makes** ~ faz sentido;

~less adj insensato, estúpido; (unconscious) sem sentidos, inconsciente.

sensibility [sɛnsɪ'bɪlɪtɪ] n sensibilidade f; sensibilities npl suscetibilidade (Pt: -pt-) fsg.

sensible ['sɛnsɪbl] adj sensato, de bom senso; (cautious) cauteloso, prudente; (reasonable) lógico, razoável; (perceptible) sensível, ponderado.

sensitive ['sɛnsɪtɪv] adj sensível, impressionável; (touchy) suscetível (Pt: -pt-); sensitivity [-'tɪvɪtɪ] n sensibilidade f; susce(p)tibilidade f.

sensual ['sɛnsjuəl] adj sensual.

sensuous ['sɛnsjuəs] adj sensual.

sent [sɛnt] pt, pp of send.

sentence ['sɛntns] n (LING) frase f, oração f; (LAW) sentença, decisão f // vt: to ~ sb to death/to 5 years condenar alguém à morte/a 5 anos de prisão.

sentiment ['sɛntɪmənt] n sentimento; (opinion) opinião f; ~al [-'mɛntl] adj sentimental; ~ality [-'tælɪtɪ] n sentimentalismo.

sentry ['sɛntrɪ] n sentinela f.

separate ['sɛprɪt] adj separado; (distinct) diferente // (vb: ['sɛpəreɪt]) vt separar; (part) dividir // vi separar-se; ~ly adv separadamente; ~s npl (clothes) roupas que fazem jogo; separation [-'reɪʃən] n separação f.

September [sɛp'tɛmbə*] n setembro.

septic ['sɛptɪk] adj sético (Pt: -pt-).

sequel ['siːkwl] n consequência, resultado; (of story) continuação f.

sequence ['siːkwəns] n série f, sequência; (CINEMA) série f.

sequin ['siːkwɪn] n lantejoula.

serenade [sɛrə'neɪd] n serenata // vt fazer serenata para.

serene [sɪ'riːn] adj sereno, tranquilo; serenity [sə'rɛnɪtɪ] n serenidade f, tranquilidade f.

sergeant ['saːdʒənt] n sargento.

serial ['sɪərɪəl] n seriado, história em folhetim; ~ize vt publicar em folhetim; ~ number n número de série.

series ['sɪəriːs] n série f.

serious ['sɪərɪəs] adj sério; (grave) grave; ~ly adv a sério, com seriedade; (gravely) gravemente; ~ness n seriedade f; gravidade f.

sermon ['səːmən] n sermão m.

serrated [sɪ'reɪtɪd] adj serrado, dentado.

serum ['sɪərəm] n soro.

servant ['səːvənt] n (gen) servidor(a) m/f; (house ~) empregado/a m/f; civil ~ funcionário (público).

serve [səːv] vt (gen) servir; (in shop: goods) vender, servir; (: customer) atender; (subj: train) passar por; (treat) tratar; (apprenticeship) fazer; (prison term) cumprir // vi (also TENNIS) sacar; (be useful): to ~ as/for/to do servir como/para/para fazer // n (TENNIS) saque m; to ~ out, ~ up vt (food) servir.

service ['səːvɪs] n (gen) serviço; (REL) cerimônia religiosa, culto; (AUT) manutenção f; (of dishes) baixela, jogo // vt (car, washing machine) fazer a manutenção de; (: repair) consertar; the S~s as Forças Armadas; to be of ~ to sb ser útil a alguém; ~able adj aproveitável, prático, durável; ~ area n (on motorway) posto de gasolina com bar, restaurante etc; ~man n militar m; ~ station n posto de gasolina, manutenção etc; (Pt) estação f de serviço.

serviette [səːvɪ'ɛt] n guardanapo.

servile ['səːvaɪl] adj servil.

session ['sɛʃən] n (sitting) sessão f; to be in ~ estar celebrando uma sessão.

set [sɛt] n jogo, coleção (Pt: -çç-) f; (RADIO) (aparelho de) rádio; (TV) televisão f; (of utensils) bateria de cozinha; (of cutlery) talher m; (of *books*) cole(c)ção; (*group of people*) grupo; (TENNIS, CINEMA) set *m*; (THEATRE) cenário; (HAIRDRESSING) penteado // *adj* (*fixed*) marcado, fixo; (*ready*) pronto; (*resolved*) decidido, estabelecido // (*vb*: *pt*, *pp* **set**) *vt* (*place*) pôr, colocar, botar; (*fix*) fixar; (: *a time*) marcar; (*adjust*) ajustar, consertar; (*decide*: *rules etc*) estabelecer, decidir // (*sun*) pôr-se; (*jam*, *jelly*, *concrete*) endurecer, solidificar-se; **to be ~ on doing sth** estar decidido a fazer algo; **to ~ to music** musicar, pôr música em; **to ~ on fire** botar fogo em, incendiar; **to ~ free** libertar; **to ~ sth going** botar algo para funcionar, pôr algo em movimento; **to ~ sail** zarpar, alçar velas; **to ~ about** *vt fus* (*task*) começar a; **to ~ aside** *vt* pôr à parte, deixar de lado; **to ~ back** *vt* (*in time*) atrasar (por); **to ~ off** *vi* partir, ir indo // *vt* (*bomb*) fazer explodir; (*cause to start*) colocar em funcionamento; (*show up well*) ressaltar; **to ~ out** *vi*: **to ~ out to do sth** começar or pôr-se a fazer algo // *vt* (*arrange*) colocar em ordem, arrumar, providenciar; (*state*) expor, explicar; **to ~ up** *vt* (*organization*, *record*) estabelecer; **to ~ up shop** (*fig*) estabelecer-se; **~back** *n* (*hitch*) revés *m*, contratempo.

**settee** [sɛˈtiː] *n* sofá *m*.

**setting** [ˈsɛtɪŋ] *n* (*frame*) moldura; (*placing*) colocação *f*; (*of sun*) pôr(-do-sol) *m*; (*of jewel*) engaste *m*; (*location*) cenário.

**settle** [ˈsɛtl] *vt* (*argument*, *matter*) resolver, esclarecer; (*accounts*) ajustar, liquidar; (*land*) colonizar; (MED.: *calm*) acalmar, tranqüilizar-se // *vi* (*dust etc*) depositar-se; (*weather*) firmar, melhorar; (*also*: **~ down**) instalar-se, estabilizar-se; **to ~ for sth** concordar em aceitar algo; **to ~ in** *vi* instalar-se; **to ~ on sth** decidir

algo; **to ~ up with sb** ajustar as contas com alguém; **~ment** *n* (*payment*) liquidação *f*; (*agreement*) acordo, convênio; (*village etc*) povoado, povoação *f*; **settler** *n* colono/a, colonizador(a) *m/f*.

**setup** [ˈsɛtʌp] *n* (*arrangement*) sistema *m*, organização *f*; (*situation*) situação *f*.

**seven** [ˈsɛvn] *num* sete; **~teen** *num* dezessete; (*Pt*) dezassete; **~th** *adj* sétimo; **~ty** *num* setenta.

**sever** [ˈsɛvə*] *vt* cortar, separar; (*relations*) romper.

**several** [ˈsɛvərl] *adj*, *pron* vários *mpl*, diversos *mpl*; **~ of us** vários de nós.

**severance** [ˈsɛvərəns] *n* (*of relations*) rompimento; **~ pay** *n* indenização *f* pela demissão.

**severe** [sɪˈvɪə*] *adj* severo; (*serious*) austero, grave; (*hard*) duro; (*pain*) intenso; **severity** [sɪˈvɛrɪtɪ] *n* severidade *f*, austeridade *f*; intensidade *f*.

**sew** [səu], *pt* **sewed**, *pp* **sewn** *vt/i* coser, costurar; **to ~ up** *vt* coser, cerzir.

**sewage** [ˈsuːɪdʒ] *n* (*effluence*) detritos *mpl*; (*system*) esgoto.

**sewer** [ˈsuːə*] *n* (*cano do*) esgoto, bueiro.

**sewing** [ˈsəuɪŋ] *n* costura; **~ machine** *n* máquina de costura.

**sewn** [səun] *pp of* **sew**.

**sex** [sɛks] *n* sexo; **to have ~ with sb** fazer sexo com alguém; **~ act** *n* ato (*Pt*: -ct-) sexual.

**sextet** [sɛksˈtɛt] *n* sexteto.

**sexual** [ˈsɛksjuəl] *adj* sexual.

**sexy** [ˈsɛksɪ] *adj* sexy.

**shabby** [ˈʃæbɪ] *adj* (*person*) esfarrapado, maltrapilho; (*clothes*) usado, surrado.

**shack** [ʃæk] *n* choupana, barraco.

**shackles** [ˈʃæklz] *npl* algemas *fpl*, grilhões *mpl*.

**shade** [ʃeɪd] *n* sombra; (*for lamp*) quebra-luz *m*; (*for eyes*) viseira; (*of* *colour*) tom *m*, tonalidade *f*; (*window*) estore *m* // *vt* sombrear, dar sombra a; **in the ~** à sombra.

**shadow** ['ʃædəu] *n* sombra // *vt* (*follow*) seguir de perto (sem ser visto); **~ cabinet** *n* (POL) gabinete *m* paralelo formado pelo partido da oposição; **~y** *adj* escuro; (*dim*) vago, indistinto.

**shady** ['ʃeidi] *adj* sombreado, à sombra; (*fig: dishonest*) suspeito, duvidoso; (: *deal*) desonesto.

**shaft** [ʃɑːft] *n* (*of arrow, spear*) haste *f*; (*column*) fuste *m*; (AUT, TECH) eixo, manivela; (*of mine, of lift*) poço; (*of light*) raio.

**shaggy** ['ʃægi] *adj* peludo, felpudo.

**shake** [ʃeik], *pt* **shook**, *pp* **shaken** *vt* sacudir; (*building*) fazer tremer; (*perturb*) perturbar, inquietar; (*weaken*) enfraquecer; (*surprise*) surpreender // *vi* estremecer(-se); (*tremble*) tremer // *n* (*movement*) sacudidela; (*violent*) safanão *m*; **to ~ hands with sb** apertar a mão de alguém; **to ~ off** *vt* sacudir; (*fig*) livrar-se de; **to ~ up** *vt* reorganizar; **shaky** *adj* (*hand, voice*) trêmulo, inseguro; (*building*) pardieiro.

**shall** [ʃæl] *auxiliary vb*: **I ~ go** irei.

**shallot** [ʃə'lɒt] *n* cebolinha.

**shallow** ['ʃæləu] *adj* raso; (*fig*) superficial, leviano.

**sham** [ʃæm] *n* fraude *f*, fingimento // *adj* falso, simulado // *vt* fingir, simular.

**shambles** ['ʃæmblz] *n* confusão *fsg*.

**shame** [ʃeim] *n* vergonha; (*pity*) pena // *vt* envergonhar; **it is a ~ that/to do é** (uma) pena que/fazer; **what a ~!** que pena!; **~-faced** *adj* envergonhado; **~ful** *adj* indecente, vergonhoso; **~less** *adj* sem vergonha, descarado; (*immodest*) cínico, impudico.

**shampoo** [ʃæm'puː] *n* xampu *m*; (*Pt*) champô *m* // *vt* lavar o cabelo (com xampu).

**shamrock** ['ʃæmrɔk] *n* trevo.

**shandy** ['ʃændi] *n* mistura de cerveja com refresco gaseificado.

**shan't** [ʃɑːnt] = **shall not.**

**shanty town** ['ʃænti-] *n* favela.

**shape** [ʃeip] *n* forma // *vt* formar, modelar; (*sb's ideas*) moldar; (*sb's life*) determinar // *vi* (*also: ~ up*) (*events*) desenrolar-se; (*person*) amadurecer, tomar jeito; **to take ~** tomar forma; **-shaped** *suff*: **heart-shaped** em forma de coração; **~less** *adj* informe, sem forma definida; **~ly** *adj* bem proporcionado *or* talhado, escultural.

**share** [ʃɛə*] *n* (*part*) parte *f*, porção *f*; (*contribution*) cota; (COMM) ação (*Pt*: -cç-) *f* // *vt* dividir; (*have in common*) compartilhar; **to ~ out** (*among or between*) distribuir (*entre*); **~holder** *n* acionista (*Pt*: -cc-) *m/f*.

**shark** [ʃɑːk] *n* tubarão *m*.

**sharp** [ʃɑːp] *adj* (*razor, knife*) afiado; (*point*) pontiagudo; (*outline*) definido, bem marcado; (*pain*) agudo; (MUS) desafinado; (*contrast*) marcado; (*voice*) agudo; (*person*: *quick-witted*) perspicaz; (*dishonest*) desonesto // *n* (MUS) sustenido // *adv*: **at 2 o'clock** às 2 (horas) em ponto; **~en** *vt* afiar; (*pencil*) apontar, fazer a ponta de; (*fig*) aguçar; **~ener** *n* (*also:* **pencil ~ener**) apontador *m*; **~-eyed** *adj* de vista aguda; **~-witted** *adj* perspicaz, observador(a).

**shatter** ['ʃætə*] *vt* despedaçar, esmigalhar; (*fig: ruin*) destruir, acabar // *vi* despedaçar-se; **I feel ~ed** estou morto de cansaço.

**shave** [ʃeiv] *vt* barbear, fazer a barba // *vi* barbear-se // *n*: **to have a ~** barbear-se; **shaver** *n* aparelho de barbear, barbeador *m*; **electric shaver** barbeador *m* elétrico.

**shaving** ['ʃeiviŋ] *n*: **~ brush** *n* pincel *m* de barba; **~ cream** *n* creme *m* de barbear; ~s *npl* (*of wood etc*) aparas *fpl*.

**shawl** [ʃɔ:l] *n* xale *m*.

**she** [ʃi:] *pron* ela; ~**cat** *n* gata.

**sheaf** [ʃi:f], *pl* **sheaves** *n* (*of corn*) gavela; (*of arrows*) feixe *m*; (*of papers*) maço.

**shear** [ʃiə*], *pt* **sheared**, *pp* **sheared** or **shorn** *vt* (*sheep*) tosquiar, tosar; **to ~ off** *vt* cercear; ~s *npl* (*for hedge*) tesoura *sg* de jardim.

**sheath** [ʃi:θ] *n* bainha; (*contraceptive*) camisa-de-vênus *f*, camisinha.

**sheaves** [ʃi:vz] *pl of* **sheaf**.

**shed** [ʃed] *n* alpendre *m*, galpão *m* // *vt, pt, pp* **shed** (*gen*) desprender-se de; (*skin*) mudar; (*tears*) derramar.

**she'd** [ʃi:d] = **she had; she would**.

**sheep** [ʃi:p] *n, pl inv* ovelha; ~**dog** *n* cão *m* pastor; ~**ish** *adj* tímido, acanhado; ~**skin** *n* pele *f* de carneiro, pelego.

**sheer** [ʃiə*] *adj* (*utter*) puro, completo; (*steep*) íngreme, empinado; (*almost transparent*) fino, translúcido // *adv* a pique.

**sheet** [ʃi:t] *n* (*on bed*) lençol *m*; (*of paper*) folha; (*of glass, metal*) lâmina, chapa.

**sheik(h)** [ʃeik] *n* xeque *m*.

**shelf** [ʃelf], *pl* **shelves** *n* estante *f*, prateleira.

**shell** [ʃel] *n* (*on beach*) concha; (*of egg, nut etc*) casca; (*explosive*) obus *m*, granada; (*of building*) armação *f*, esqueleto // *vt* (*peas*) descascar; (*MIL*) bombardear.

**she'll** [ʃi:l] = **she will; she shall**.

**shellfish** [ʃelfiʃ] *n, pl inv* crustáceo, molusco; (*pl: as food*) frutos *mpl* do mar, marisco.

**shelter** [ʃeltə*] *n* abrigo, refúgio // *vt* (*aid*) amparar, proteger; (*give lodging to*) abrigar; (*hide*) esconder // *vi* abrigar-se, refugiar-se; ~**ed** *adj* (*life*) protegido; (*spot*) abrigado, protegido.

**shelve** [ʃelv] *vt* (*fig*) pôr de lado, engavetar; ~s *pl of* **shelf**.

**shepherd** [ʃepəd] *n* pastor *m* // *vt* (*guide*) guiar, conduzir; ~**ess** *n* pastora; ~'s **pie** *n* empadão *m* de carne e batata.

**sheriff** [ʃerif] *n* xerife *m*.

**sherry** [ʃeri] *n* (vinho de) Xerez *m*.

**she's** [ʃi:z] = **she is; she has**.

**shield** [ʃi:ld] *n* escudo; (*TECH*) blindagem *f* // *vt*: **to ~ (from)** proteger contra.

**shift** [ʃift] *n* (*change*) mudança; (*of place*) transferência; (*of workers*) turno // *vt* transferir; (*remove*) tirar // *vi* mudar; (*change place*) mudar de lugar; ~**work** *n* trabalho por turno; ~**y** *adj* esperto, trapaceiro; (*eyes*) velhaco, maroto.

**shilling** [ʃiliŋ] *n* xelim *m*.

**shimmer** [ʃimə*] *n* reflexo trêmulo // *vi* cintilar, tremeluzir.

**shin** [ʃin] *n* canela (da perna).

**shine** [ʃain] *n* brilho, lustre *m* // (*vb: pt, pp* **shone**) *vi* brilhar, reluzir // *vt* (*shoes*) lustrar; **to ~ a torch on sth** apontar uma lanterna para algo.

**shingle** [ʃiŋgl] *n* (*on beach*) pedrinhas *fpl*, seixinhos *mpl*; ~s *n* (*MED*) herpes *mpl*.

**shiny** [ʃaini] *adj* brilhante, lustroso.

**ship** [ʃip] *n* navio, barco // *vt* (*goods*) embarcar; (*oars*) desarmar, guardar; (*send*) transportar or mandar (*por via marítima*); ~**building** *n* construção *f* naval; ~**ment** *n* (*act*) embarque *m*; (*goods*) carregamento; ~**per** *n* exportador(a) *m/f*; ~**ping** *n* (*act*) embarque *m*; (*traffic*) transporte *m*; ~**shape** *adj* em ordem; ~**wreck** *n* naufrágio; ~**yard** *n* estaleiro.

**shire** [ʃaiə*] *n* condado.

**shirk** [ʃə:k] *vt* eludir, esquivar-se; (*obligations*) não cumprir, faltar a.

**shirt** [ʃəːt] *n* camisa, blusa; **in ~ sleeves** em manga de camisa.

**shiver** [ˈʃivəʳ] *n* tremor *m*, arrepio // *vi* tremer, estremecer, tiritar.

**shoal** [ʃəul] *n* (*of fish*) cardume *m*.

**shock** [ʃɔk] *n* (*impact*) choque *m*; (*ELEC*) descarga; (*emotional*) comoção *f*, abalo; (*start*) susto, sobressalto; (*MED*) trauma *m* // *vt* dar um susto em, chocar; (*offend*) escandalizar; ~ **absorber** *n* amortecedor *m*; ~**ing** *adj* (*awful*) chocante, lamentável; (*improper*) escandaloso; ~**proof** *adj* à prova de choque.

**shod** [ʃɔd] *pt, pp* of **shoe** // *adj* calçado.

**shoddy** [ˈʃɔdi] *adj* ordinário, de má qualidade.

**shoe** [ʃuː] *n* sapato; (*for horse*) ferradura; (*brake ~*) sapata // *vt, pt, pp* **shod** (*horse*) ferrar; ~**brush** *n* escova de sapato; ~**horn** *n* calçadeira; ~**lace** *n* cadarço, cordão *m* (de sapato); ~**maker** *n* sapateiro; ~ **polish** *n* graxa de sapato; ~**shop** *n* sapataria.

**shone** [ʃɔn] *pt, pp* of **shine**.

**shook** [ʃuk] *pt* of **shake**.

**shoot** [ʃuːt] *n* (*on branch, seedling*) rebento, broto // (*vb: pt, pp* **shot**) *vt* disparar; (*kill*) matar a bala; (*wound*) ferir a bala; (*execute*) fuzilar; (*film*) filmar, rodar // *vi* (*with gun, bow*): **to ~ (at)** atirar (em); (*FOOTBALL*) chutar; **to ~ down** *vt* derrubar, abater; **to ~ in/out** *vi* entrar correndo/sair em disparada; **to ~ up** *vi* (*fig*) subir vertiginosamente; ~**ing** *n* (*shots*) tiros *mpl*, tiroteio; (*HUNTING*) caçada (com espingarda); ~**ing star** *n* estrela cadente.

**shop** [ʃɔp] *n* loja; (*workshop*) oficina // *vi* (*also:* **go ~ping**) ir fazer compras; ~ **assistant** *n* vendedor/a *m/f*, empregado/a; ~ **floor** *adj* (*fig*) que veio de baixo; ~**keeper** *n* lojista *m/f*; ~**lifter** *n*

larápio de loja; ~**lifting** *n* furto (em lojas); ~**per** *n* comprador/a *m/f*; ~**ping** *n* (*goods*) compras *fpl*; ~**ping bag** *n* bolsa (de compras); ~**ping centre**, ~**ping center** (*US*) *n* shopping centre *m*; ~**soiled** *adj* manuseado; ~ **steward** *n* (*INDUSTRY*) representante *m/f* sindical; ~ **window** *n* vitrina; (*Pt*) montra; ~**worn** *adj* (*US*) = ~**soiled**.

**shore** [ʃɔːʳ] *n* (*of sea*) costa, praia; (*lake*) margem *f* // *vt*: **to ~ (up)** reforçar, escorar.

**shorn** [ʃɔːn] *pp* of **shear**.

**short** [ʃɔːt] *adj* (*not long*) curto; (*in time*) breve, de curta duração; (*person*) baixo; (*curt*) seco, brusco; (*insufficient*) insuficiente, em falta // *vi* (*ELEC*) dar um curto-circuito // *n* (*also:* ~**film**) curta-metragem *m*; (**a pair of**) ~**s** (um) short *m*; **to be ~ of sth** estar em falta de algo; **in ~** em resumo; **it is ~ for** é a abreviação de; **to cut ~** (*speech, visit*) encurtar, interromper; **to fall ~** ser deficiente; **to stop ~** parar de repente; **to stop ~ of** chegar a beira de; ~**age** *n* escassez *f*, falta; ~**circuit** *n* curto-circuito // *vt* provocar um curto-circuito // *vi* entrar em curto-circuito; ~**coming** *n* defeito, imperfeição *f*, falha; ~**(crust) pastry** *n* massa amanteigada; ~**cut** *n* atalho; ~**en** *vt* encurtar, reduzir; (*visit*) abreviar, interromper; ~**hand** *n* taquigrafia; ~**hand typist** *n* estenodatilógrafa (*Pt*: -act-); ~ **list** *n* (*for job*) lista dos candidatos escolhidos; ~**lived** *adj* efêmero, fugaz; ~**ly** *adv* em breve, dentro em pouco; ~**ness** *n* (*of distance*) curteza; (*of time*) brevidade *f*; (*manner*) maneira brusca, secura; ~**sighted** *adj* míope; (*fig*) imprevidente; ~ **story** *n* conto; ~**tempered** *adj* irritadiço, de pavio curto; ~**term** *adj* (*effect*) a curto prazo; ~**wave** n (RADIO) onda curta.

**shot** [ʃɔt] pt, pp of **shoot** // n (sound) tiro, disparo; (cannon) bala; (person) atirador(a) m/f; (try) tentativa; (injection) injeção (Pt: -cç-) f; (PHOT) fotografia; ~**gun** n espingarda.

**should** [ʃud] auxiliary vb: **I** ~ **go now** devo ir embora agora; **he** ~ **be there now** ele já deve ter chegado; **I** ~ **go if I were you** se eu fosse você eu iria; **I** ~ **like to** eu gostaria de.

**shoulder** [ˈʃəuldə*] n ombro; (of road): **hard** ~ acostamento; (Pt) berma // vt (fig) arcar com; ~**blade** n omoplata m.

**shouldn't** [ˈʃudnt] = **should not**.

**shout** [ʃaut] n grito // vt gritar // vi gritar, berrar; **to** ~ **down** vt fazer calar com gritos; ~**ing** n gritaria, berreiro.

**shove** [ʃʌv] n empurrão m // vt empurrar; (col: put): **to** ~ **sth in** fazer algo entrar à força; **to** ~ **off** vi (NAUT) zarpar, partir; (fig: col) dar o fora; (Pt) cavar.

**shovel** [ˈʃʌvl] n pá f; (mechanical) escavadeira // vt cavar com pá.

**show** [ʃəu] n (of emotion) demonstração f; (semblance) aparência; (exhibition) exibição f; (THEATRE) espetáculo, (Pt: -ct-), representação f // (vb: pt **showed**, pp **shown**) vt mostrar; (courage etc) demonstrar, dar prova de; (exhibit) exibir, expor; (film) passar // vi mostrar-se; (appear) aparecer; **to** ~ **sb in** mandar alguém entrar; **to** ~ **off** vi (pej) mostrar-se, exibir-se // vt (display) exibir, mostrar; (pej) fazer ostentação de; **to** ~ **sb out** acompanhar alguém à porta; **to** ~ **up** vi (stand out) destacar-se; (col: turn up) aparecer // vt descobrir; (unmask) desmascarar; ~ **business** n o mundo do espetáculo (Pt: -ct-); ~**down** n hora de botar as pingos nos ii.

**shower** [ˈʃauə*] n (rain) pancada de chuva; (of stones etc) chuva, enxurrada; (also: ~**bath**) banho de chuveiro // vi chover // vt: **to** ~ **sb with sth** cumular alguém de algo; ~**proof** adj impermeável; ~**y** adj (weather) chuvoso.

**showing** [ˈʃəuɪŋ] n (of film) projeção (Pt: -cç-) f, exibição f.

**show jumping** [ˈʃəuʤʌmpɪŋ] n exibição f de hipismo.

**shown** [ʃəun] pp of **show**.

**show-**: ~**off** n (col: person) exibicionista m/f, faroleiro; ~**piece** n (of exhibition etc) obra mais importante; ~**room** n sala de exposição.

**shrank** [ʃræŋk] pt of **shrink**.

**shrapnel** [ˈʃræpnl] n estilhaços mpl.

**shred** [ʃrɛd] n (gen pl) tira, pedaço // vt rasgar em tiras, retalhar; (CULIN) desfiar, picar.

**shrewd** [ʃru:d] adj astuto, perspicaz, sutil; ~**ness** n astúcia.

**shriek** [ʃri:k] n guincho, grito // vt/i guinchar, berrar.

**shrill** [ʃril] adj agudo, estridente.

**shrimp** [ʃrimp] n camarão m.

**shrine** [ʃrain] n santuário, relicário.

**shrink** [ʃriŋk], pt **shrank**, pp **shrunk** vi encolher; (be reduced) reduzir-se // vt fazer encolher; **to** ~ **from doing sth** não se atrever a fazer algo; ~**age** n o encolhimento, redução f.

**shrivel** [ˈʃrivl] (also: ~ **up**) vt (dry) secar; (crease) enrugar // vi secar-se, enrugar-se, murchar.

**shroud** [ʃraud] n mortalha // vt: ~**ed in mystery** envolto em mistério.

**Shrove Tuesday** [ˈʃrəuv'tju:zdi] n terça-feira gorda.

**shrub** [ʃrʌb] n arbusto; ~**bery** n arbustos mpl.

**shrug** [ʃrʌg] n encolhimento dos ombros // vt/i: **to** ~ **(one's shoulders)** encolher os ombros; **to** ~ **off** vt negar a importância de.

**shrunk** [ʃrʌŋk] *pp of* **shrink.**

**shudder** [ʃʌdə*] *n* estremecimento, tremor *m* // *vi* estremecer, tremer de medo.

**shuffle** [ʃʌfl] *vt* (*cards*) embaralhar; **to ~** (*one's feet*) arrastar os pés.

**shun** [ʃʌn] *vt* evitar, afastar-se de.

**shunt** [ʃʌnt] *vt* (*RAIL*) manobrar, desviar // *vi*: **to ~ to and fro** mandar daqui para lá.

**shut** [ʃʌt], *pt, pp* **shut** *vt* fechar // *vi* fechar-se; **to ~ down** *vt/i* fechar, encerrar; **to ~ off** *vt* (*supply etc*) cortar, interromper; **to ~ up** *vi* (*col: keep quiet*) calar-se, calar a boca // *vt* (*close*) fechar; (*silence*) calar; **~ter** *n* veneziana; (*PHOT*) obturador *m*.

**shuttle** [ʃʌtl] *n* lançadeira; (*also: ~ service*) (*plane*) ponte *f* aérea.

**shuttlecock** [ʃʌtlkɔk] *n* peteca.

**shy** [ʃaɪ] *adj* tímido; (*reserved*) reservado, esquivo; (*unsociable*) insociável; **~ness** *n* timidez *f*; acanhamento.

**Siamese** [saɪə'miːz] *adj*: **~ cat** gato siamês.

**Sicily** [sɪsɪlɪ] *n* Sicília.

**sick** [sɪk] *adj* (*ill*) doente; (*nauseated*) enjoado, indisposto; (*humour*) negro; (*vomiting*): **to be ~** vomitar; **to feel ~** estar enjoado; **to be ~ of** (*fig*) estar cheio or farto de; **~ bay** *n* enfermaria; **~en** *vt* dar náuseas // *vi* adoecer; **~ening** *adj* (*fig*) repugnante.

**sickle** [sɪkl] *n* foice *f*.

**sick:** **~ leave** *n* licença por doença; **~ly** *adj* doentio; (*causing nausea*) nauseante; **~ness** *n* doença, indisposição *f*; (*vomiting*) náusea, enjôo; **~ pay** *n* auxílio-doença *m*.

**side** [saɪd] *n* (*gen*) lado; (*of body*) flanco; (*of lake*) margem *f*; (*aspect*) aspeto; (*team*) time *m*, equipe *f*; (*of hill*) declive *m* // *adj* (*door, entrance*) lateral // *vi*: **to ~ with sb** tomar o partido de alguém; **by the**

**~ of** ao lado de; **~ by ~** lado a lado, juntos; **from all ~s** de todos os lados; **to take ~s with** pôr-se ao lado de; **~board** *n* aparador *m*; **~boards**, **~burns** *npl* suíças *fpl*, costeletas *fpl*; **~ effect** *n* efeito colateral; **~light** *n* (*AUT*) luz *f* lateral; **~line** *n* (*SPORT*) linha lateral; (*fig*) linha adicional de produtos; (: *job*) emprego suplementar; **~long** *adj* de soslaio; **~ road** *n* rua lateral; (*street*) rua de silhão; **~ show** *n* (*stall*) barraca; (*fig*) exibição *f* suplementar; **~step** *vt* (*fig*) evitar, esquivar-se de; **~track** *vt* (*fig*) desviar (do seu propósito); **~walk** *n* (*US*) calçada; **~ways** *adv* de lado.

**siding** [saɪdɪŋ] *n* (*RAIL*) desvio, ramal *m*.

**sidle** [saɪdl] *vi*: **to ~ up (to)** aproximar-se furtivamente (de).

**siege** [siːdʒ] *n* sítio, assédio, cerco.

**sieve** [sɪv] *n* peneira // *vt* peneirar.

**sift** [sɪft] *vt* peneirar; (*fig: information*) esquadrinhar, analisar minuciosamente.

**sigh** [saɪ] *n* suspiro // *vi* suspirar.

**sight** [saɪt] *n* (*faculty*) vista, visão *f*; (*spectacle*) espetáculo (*Pt*: -ct-); (*on gun*) alça, mira // *vt* avistar, mirar; **in ~** à vista; **out of ~** longe dos olhos; **~seeing** *n* turismo; **to go ~seeing** visitar lugares turísticos.

**sign** [saɪn] *n* (*with hand*) sinal *m*, aceno; (*indication*) indício; (*trace*) rastro, vestígio; (*notice*) letreiro, tabuleta; (*written*) signo // *vt* assinar; **to ~ over** *vt* **to sb** assinar a transferência de algo para alguém; **to ~ up** *vi* (*MIL*) alistar-se // *vt* (*contract*) firmar contrato com.

**signal** [sɪgnl] *n* sinal *m*, aviso; (*US: TEL*) ruído discal // *vi* (*AUT*) sinalizar // *vt* (*person*) fazer sinais para; (*message*) transmitir.

**signature** [sɪgnətʃə*] *n* assinatura.

**signet ring** [sɪgnətrɪŋ] *n* anel *m*

com o sinete *or* a chancela.

**significance** [sɪg'nɪfɪkəns] *n* significado; (*importance*) importância; **significant** [-ənt] *adj* significativo, importante.

**signify** ['sɪgnɪfaɪ] *vt* significar.

**sign:** ~ **language** *n* mímica, linguagem *f* através de sinais; ~**post** *n* indicador *m*; (*traffic*) placa de sinalização.

**silence** ['saɪlns] *n* silêncio // *vt* silenciar, impor silêncio a; (*guns*) silenciar; **silencer** *n* (*on gun*) silenciador *m*; (*AUT*) silencioso.

**silent** ['saɪlnt] *adj* (*gen*) silencioso; (*not speaking*) calado; (*film*) mudo; **to remain** ~ manter-se em silêncio.

**silhouette** [sɪlu:'et] *n* silhueta; ~**d against** em silhueta contra.

**silicon chip** ['sɪlɪkən'tʃɪp] *n* placa *or* chip *m* de silicone.

**silk** [sɪlk] *n* seda // *adj* de seda; ~**y** *adj* sedoso.

**silly** ['sɪlɪ] *adj* (*person*) bobo, idiota, imbecil; (*idea*) absurdo, ridículo.

**silt** [sɪlt] *n* sedimento, aluvião *m*.

**silver** ['sɪlvə*] *n* prata; (*money*) moedas *fpl* // *adj* de prata; ~ **paper** *n* papel *m* de prata; ~**-plated** *adj* prateado, banhado a prata; ~**smith** *n* ourives *m* de prata; ~**y** *adj* prateado.

**similar** ['sɪmɪlə*] *adj*: ~ **to** parecido com, semelhante a; ~**ity** [-'lærɪt] *n* semelhança, similitude *f*; ~**ly** *adv* da mesma maneira.

**simmer** ['sɪmə*] *vi* cozer em fogo lento, ferver lentamente.

**simpering** ['sɪmpərɪŋ] *adj* afetado (*Pt*: -ct-); (*foolish*) bobo, idiota, bobalhão/lhona *m/f*.

**simple** ['sɪmpl] *adj* (*easy*) fácil; (*mere*, *COMM*) simples *inv*; (*foolish*) ingênuo, humilde; ~**ton** *n* simplório, pateta *m/f*; **simplicity** [-'plɪsɪtɪ] *n* simplicidade *f*; (*foolishness*) ingenuidade *f*; **simplify** ['sɪmplɪfaɪ] *vt* simplificar.

**simulate** ['sɪmjuleɪt] *vt* simular;

**simulation** [-'leɪʃən] *n* simulação *f*.

**simultaneous** [sɪməl'teɪnɪəs] *adj* simultâneo; ~**ly** *adv* simultaneamente.

**sin** [sɪn] *n* pecado // *vi* pecar.

**since** [sɪns] *adv* desde então, depois // *prep* desde // *conj* (*time*) desde que; (*because*) porque, visto que, já que; ~ **then** desde então.

**sincere** [sɪn'sɪə*] *adj* sincero; **yours** ~**ly** atenciosamente; **sincerity** [-'sɛrɪtɪ] *n* sinceridade *f*.

**sinful** ['sɪnful] *adj* (*thought*) pecaminoso; (*person*) pecador(a).

**sing** [sɪŋ], *pt* **sang**, *pp* **sung** *vt* cantar // *vi* (*gen*) cantar; (*bird*) gorjear; (*ears*) zumbir.

**singe** [sɪndʒ] *vt* chamuscar.

**singer** ['sɪŋə*] *n* cantor(a) *m/f*.

**singing** ['sɪŋɪŋ] *n* (*gen*) canto; (*songs*) canções *fpl*; (*in the ears*) zumbido.

**single** ['sɪŋgl] *adj* único, só; (*unmarried*) solteiro; (*not double*) simples *inv*; (*bed*, *room*) individual // *n* (*also*: ~ **ticket**) passagem *f* de ida; (*record*) compacto; ~**s** *npl* (*TENNIS*) individual *fsg*; **to** ~ **out** *vt* (*choose*) escolher; (*point out*) distinguir, preferir; ~ **bed** *n* cama de solteiro; **in** ~ **file** em fila indiana; ~**-handed** *adv* sem ajuda, sozinho; ~**-minded** *adj* determinado; ~ **room** *n* quarto individual.

**singular** ['sɪŋgjulə*] *adj* (*odd*) esquisito, peculiar; (*LING*) singular // *n* (*LING*) singular *m*.

**sinister** ['sɪnɪstə*] *adj* sinistro.

**sink** [sɪŋk] *n* pia // (*vb*: *pt* **sank**, *pp* **sunk**) *vt* (*ship*) afundar; (*foundations*) escavar; (*piles etc*): **to** ~ **sth** enterrar algo // *vi* (*gen*) afundar-se, ir a pique; **to** ~ **in** *vi* (*fig*) penetrar, entranhar-se; **a** ~**ing feeling** um vazio no estômago.

**sinner** ['sɪnə*] *n* pecador(a) *m/f*.

**sinus** ['saɪnəs] *n* (*ANAT*) seio (nasal).

**sip** [sɪp] *n* gole *m* // *vt* tomar um

golinho de, sorver, bebericar.
**siphon** ['saɪfən] n sifão m; **to ~ off**
vt extrair com sifão.
**sir** [sə*] n senhor m; **S~ John Smith**
Sir John Smith; **yes ~** sim, senhor.
**siren** ['saɪərn] n sirena; (mermaid)
sereia.
**sirloin** ['sə:lɔɪn] n lombo de vaca.
**sister** ['sɪstə*] n irmã f; (nurse)
enfermeira-chefe f; (nun) freira;
**~-in-law** n cunhada.
**sit** [sɪt], pt, pp **sat** vi sentar-se; (be
sitting) estar sentado; (assembly)
reunir-se // vt (exam) prestar; **to ~
down** vi sentar-se; **to ~ in on**
assistir a; **to ~ up** vi endireitar-se;
(not go to bed) aguardar acordado,
velar.
**site** [saɪt] n local m, sítio m; (also:
**building ~**) lote m (de terreno) //
vt situar, localizar.
**sit-in** ['sɪtɪn] n (demonstration)
ocupação f de um local como forma
de protesto, manifestação f pacífica.
**sitting** ['sɪtɪŋ] n (of assembly etc)
sessão f; (in canteen) turno; **~ room**
n sala de estar.
**situated** ['sɪtjueɪtɪd] adj situado.
**situation** [sɪtju'eɪʃən] n situação f.
**six** [sɪks] num seis; **~teen** num
dezesseis (Pt: -ass-); **~th** adj sexto;
**~ty** num sessenta.
**size** [saɪz] n (gen) tamanho; (extent)
dimensão f, proporção f; (of
clothing) tamanho, medida; (of
shoes) número; (glue) goma; **to ~
up** vt avaliar, formar uma opinião
sobre; **~able** adj considerável,
importante.
**sizzle** ['sɪzl] vi chiar.
**skate** [skeɪt] n patim m; (fish: pl
inv) arraia // vi patinar; **~board** n
skate m, patim-tábua m; **skater** n
patinador(a) m/f; **skating** n
patinação f; **skating rink** n ringue m
de patinação.
**skeleton** ['skelɪtn] n esqueleto;
(TECH) armação f, (outline)
esquema m, esboço; **~ key** n chave

f mestra; **~ staff** n pessoal m
reduzido (ao mínimo).
**sketch** [sketʃ] n (drawing) desenho;
(outline) esboço, croqui m;
(THEATRE) pequena peça teatral,
esquete m // vt desenhar, esboçar;
**~ book** n caderno de rascunho; **~
pad** n bloco de desenho; **~y** adj
incompleto, esboçado.
**skewer** ['skjuːə*] n espetinho.
**ski** [skiː] n esqui m // vi esquiar; **~
boot** n bota de esquiar.
**skid** [skɪd] n derrapagem f // vi
derrapar, deslizar; **~mark** n marca
da derrapagem.
**ski:** **~er** n esquiador(a) m/f; **~ing** n
esqui m; **~ jump** n pista para saltos
de esqui.
**skilful** ['skɪlful] adj habilidoso,
jeitoso.
**ski lift** n ski lift m.
**skill** [skɪl] n habilidade f, perícia;
**~ed** adj hábil, perito; (worker)
especializado, qualificado.
**skim** [skɪm] vt (milk) desnatar;
(glide over) roçar // vi: **to ~
through** (book) folhear.
**skimp** [skɪmp] vt (work)
atamancar; (cloth etc) economizar,
regatear; **~y** adj (meagre) escasso,
insuficiente; (skirt) sumário.
**skin** [skɪn] n (gen) pele f;
(complexion) cútis f // vt (fruit etc)
pelar, descascar; (animal) tirar a
pele a; **~-deep** adj superficial; **~-
diving** n caça-submarina; **~ny** adj
magro, descarnado; **~tight** adj
(dress etc) justo, grudado (no
corpo).
**skip** [skɪp] n salto, pulo; (container)
balde m // vi saltar; (with rope)
pular (corda) // vt (pass over)
omitir, saltar.
**ski pants** npl calça sg de esquiar.
**skipper** ['skɪpə*] n (NAUT, SPORT)
capitão m.
**skipping rope** ['skɪpɪŋ-] n corda
(de pular).
**skirmish** ['skə:mɪʃ] n escaramuça.

**skirt** [skə:t] *n* saia // *vt* (*surround*) rodear; (*go round*) orlar, circundar; ~**ing board** *n* rodapé *m*.

**skit** [skit] *n* paródia, sátira.

**skittle** ['skitl] *n* pau *m*; ~**s** *n* (*game*) espécie de boliche *m*.

**skive** [skaiv] *vi* (*Brit: col*) evitar trabalhar.

**skull** [skʌl] *n* caveira; (*ANAT*) crânio.

**skunk** [skʌŋk] *n* gambá *m*; (*fig: person*) cafajeste *m/f*, pessoa vil.

**sky** [skai] *n* céu *m*; ~**-blue** *adj* azul celeste; ~**light** *n* clarabóia, escotilha; ~**scraper** *n* arranha-céu *m*.

**slab** [slæb] *n* (*stone*) bloco; (*flat*) laje *f*; (*of cake*) fatia grossa.

**slack** [slæk] *adj* (*loose*) frouxo, bambo; (*slow*) lerdo; (*careless*) descuidoso, desmazelado; ~**s** *npl* calça *sg* comprida; ~**en** (*also*: ~**en off**) *vi* afrouxar-se // *vt* afrouxar; (*speed*) diminuir.

**slag** [slæg] *n* escória, escombros *mpl*; ~ **heap** *n* monte *m* de escória or de escombros.

**slalom** ['slɑ:ləm] *n* slalom *m*.

**slam** [slæm] *vt* (*door*) bater or fechar (com violência); (*throw*) atirar violentamente; (*criticize*) malhar, criticar // *vi* fechar-se (com violência).

**slander** ['slɑ:ndə*] *n* calúnia, difamação *f* // *vt* caluniar, difamar; ~**ous** *adj* calunioso, difamatório.

**slang** [slæŋ] *n* gíria; (*jargon*) jargão *m*.

**slant** [slɑ:nt] *n* declive *m*, inclinação *f*; (*fig*) ponto de vista; ~**ed**, ~**ing** *adj* inclinado, de esguelha.

**slap** [slæp] *n* palmada, tapa *m*; (*in face*) bofetada; (*fig*) repulsa, fora // *vt* dar um tapa or uma bofetada em // *adv* (*directly*) diretamente (*Pt*: -ct-), exatamente (*Pt*: -ct-); ~**dash** *adj* impetuoso, descuidado; ~**stick** *n* (*comedy*) palhaçada vulgar.

**slash** [slæʃ] *vt* cortar, talhar; (*fig: prices*) cortar.

**slate** [sleit] *n* lousa, ardósia // *vt* (*fig: criticize*) criticar duramente, arrasar.

**slaughter** ['slɔ:tə*] *n* (*of animals*) matança; (*of people*) carnificina // *vt* matar; ~**house** *n* matadouro.

**Slav** [slɑ:v] *adj, m/f* eslavo/a.

**slave** [sleiv] *n* escravo // *vi* (*also*: ~ *away*) trabalhar como escravo; ~**ry** *n* escravidão *f*; **slavish** *adj* servil.

**Slavonic** [slə'vɔnik] *adj* eslavo.

**slay** [slei] *vt* matar.

**sleazy** ['sli:zi] *adj* (*fig: place*) abandonado, maltratado.

**sledge** [slɛdʒ], **sled** (*US*) *n* trenó *m*; ~**hammer** *n* marreta, malho.

**sleek** [sli:k] *adj* (*gen*) macio, lustroso; (*neat*) limpo.

**sleep** [sli:p] *n* sono // *vi, pt, pp* **slept** dormir; **to go to** ~ dormir, adormecer; **to** ~ **in** *vi* (*oversleep*) dormir demais; ~**er** *n* (*person*) dorminhoco/a *m/f*; (*RAIL: on track*) dormente; (: *train*) carro-dormitório; ~**ily** *adv* sonolentamente; ~**ing bag** *n* saco de dormir; ~**ing car** *n* carro-dormitório; ~**ing pill** *n* pílula para dormir; ~**lessness** *n* insônia; ~**walker** *n* sonâmbulo; ~**y** *adj* sonolento.

**sleet** [sli:t] *n* chuva com neve or granizo.

**sleeve** [sli:v] *n* manga; (*TECH*) camisa de cilindro; ~**less** *adj* (*garment*) sem manga.

**sleigh** [slei] *n* trenó *m*.

**sleight** [slait] *n*: ~ **of hand** prestidigitação *f*.

**slender** ['slendə*] *adj* magro, delgado; (*means*) escasso, insuficiente.

**slept** [slept] *pt, pp* of **sleep**.

**slice** [slais] *n* (*of meat*) fatia; (*of bread*) pedaço; (*of lemon*) rodela; (*of fish*) posta; (*utensil*) pá *f* or espátula de bolo // *vt* cortar em fatias, partir.

**slick** [slik] *adj* (*skilful*) jeitoso, ágil,

engenhoso; (quick) rápido; (astute) astuto // n (also: oil ~) mancha de óleo.

**slid** [slɪd] pt, pp of **slide**.

**slide** [slaɪd] n (in playground) escorregador m; (PHOT) slide m; (also: hair ~) passador m // (vb: pt, pp **slid**) vt deslizar, patinar // vi (slip) escorregar; (glide) deslizar; **sliding** adj (door) corrediço.

**slight** [slaɪt] adj (slim) fraco, franzino; (frail) delicado; (pain etc) leve; (trifling) insignificante; (small) pequeno // n desfeita, desconsideração f // vt (offend) desdenhar, menosprezar; **not in the ~est** em absoluto, de maneira alguma; **~ly** adv ligeiramente, um pouco.

**slim** [slɪm] adj magro, esbelto // vi emagrecer, tornar-se esbelto.

**slime** [slaɪm] n lodo, limo, lama; **slimy** adj viscoso, pegajoso.

**slimming** ['slɪmɪŋ] n emagrecimento; **a ~ diet** um regime ou uma dieta para emagrecer.

**sling** [slɪŋ] n (MED) tipóia; (weapon) estilingue m, funda // vt, pt, pp **slung** atirar, arremessar, lançar.

**slip** [slɪp] n (slide) tropeço m; (fall) escorregão m; (mistake) erro, lapso; (underskirt) combinação f; (of paper) tira // vt (slide) deslizar // vi (slide) escorregar; (stumble) tropeçar; (decline) decair; **to give sb the ~** esgueirar-se ou escapar de alguém; **to ~ away** vi escapulir; **to ~ in** vt meter // vi meter-se; **to ~ out** vi (go out) sair (um momento).

**slipper** ['slɪpə*] n chinelo.

**slippery** ['slɪpərɪ] adj escorregadio.

**slip:** **~shod** adj descuidoso, desmazelado; **~up** n (error) equívoco, mancada; (by neglect) descuido; **~way** n carreira.

**slit** [slɪt] n fenda; (cut) corte m // vt, pt, pp **slit** rachar, cortar, fender.

**slither** ['slɪðə*] vi escorregar, deslizar.

**slob** [slɔb] n (col) desmazelado, lambão m.

**slog** [slɔg] vi mourejar; **it was a ~** deu um trabalho louco.

**slogan** ['sləugən] n lema m, slogan m.

**slop** [slɔp] vi (also: ~ over) transbordar, derramar // vt transbordar, entornar.

**slope** [sləup] n (up) ladeira, rampa; (down) declive m; (side of mountain) encosta, vertente f // vi: **to ~ down** estar em declive; **to ~ up** inclinar-se; **sloping** adj inclinado, em declive.

**sloppy** ['slɔpɪ] adj (work) descuidado; (appearance) relaxado.

**slot** [slɔt] n ranhura, abertura; **~ machine** n máquina caça-níqueis.

**slouch** [slautʃ] vi: **to ~ about** (laze) vadiar, viver na ociosidade.

**slovenly** ['slʌvənlɪ] adj (dirty) desalinhado, sujo; (careless) desmazelado.

**slow** [sləu] adj lento, vagaroso; (watch): **to be ~** atrasar-se // adv lentamente, devagar // vt/i (also: ~ down, ~ up) retardar; **'~'** (road sign) 'devagar'; **~down** n (US) go-slow; **~ly** adv lentamente, devagar; **in ~ motion** em câmara lenta; **~ness** n lentidão f.

**sludge** [slʌdʒ] n lama, lodo.

**slug** [slʌg] n lesma; (bullet) bala, metralha; **~gish** adj (slow) lerdo; (lazy) preguiçoso.

**sluice** [slu:s] n (gate) comporta, eclusa; (channel) canal m.

**slum** [slʌm] n (area) favela; (house) cortiço, barraco.

**slumber** ['slʌmbə*] n sono, soneca.

**slump** [slʌmp] n (economic) depressão f // vi baixar repentinamente.

**slung** [slʌŋ] pt, pp of **sling**.

**slur** [slə:*] n calúnia // vt difamar,

caluniar; (word) pronunciar indistintamente.

**slush** [slʌʃ] n neve f meio derretida; **~y** adj (snow) meio derretido; (street) lamacento; (fig) sentimentalóide.

**slut** [slʌt] n mulher f desmazelada; (whore) prostituta.

**sly** [slaɪ] adj (clever) astuto; (nasty) malicioso, velhaco.

**smack** [smæk] n (slap) palmada; (blow) tabefe m; (kiss) beijoca // vt dar uma palmada or um tabefe em // vi: **to ~ of** cheirar a, saber a.

**small** [smɔːl] adj pequeno; **~holder** n pequeno proprietário; **~ish** adj de pequeno porte; **~pox** n varíola; **~ talk** n conversa fiada.

**smart** [smɑːt] adj elegante; (clever) inteligente, astuto; (quick) vivo, esperto // vi arder, coçar; **to ~en up** vi arrumar-se, melhorar // vt arrumar.

**smash** [smæʃ] n (also: **~-up**) colisão f, choque m // vt (break) escangalhar, despedaçar; (car etc) chocar-se com; (SPORT: record) quebrar // vi (collide) colidir; (against wall etc) espatifar-se; **~ing** adj (col) genial, excelente.

**smattering** ['smætərɪŋ] n: **a ~ of** conhecimento superficial de.

**smear** [smɪə*] n mancha, nódoa; (MED) esfregação // vt untar, lambuzar; (fig) caluniar, difamar.

**smell** [smel] n cheiro; (sense) olfato // (vb: pt, pp smelt or smelled) vt // vi cheirar; **it ~s good/of garlic** cheira bem/a alho; **~y** adj fedorento, malcheiroso.

**smile** [smaɪl] n sorriso // vi sorrir; **smiling** adj sorridente, risonho.

**smirk** [smə:k] n sorriso falso or afetado (Pt: -ct-).

**smith** [smɪθ] n ferreiro; **~y** ['smɪðɪ] n forja, oficina de ferreiro.

**smock** [smɔk] n guarda-pó m; (children's) avental m.

**smoke** [sməuk] n fumaça, fumo //

vi fumar; (chimney) fumegar // vt (cigarettes) fumar; **~d** adj (bacon) defumado; (glass) fumeê; **smoker** n (person) fumante m/f; (RAIL) vagão m para fumantes; **~ screen** n cortina de fumaça; **~ shop** n (US) tabacaria; **smoking** n: **'no smoking'** (sign) 'proibido fumar'; **smoky** adj (gen) fumegante; (room) cheio de fumaça.

**smooth** [smu:ð] adj (gen) liso, macio; (sea) tranqüilo, calmo; (flat) plano; (flavour, movement) suave; (person) culto, refinado; (: pej) meloso // vt alisar; (also: **~ out**) (difficulties) acalmar, aplainar.

**smother** ['smʌðə*] vt sufocar, suprimir; (repress) reprimir.

**smoulder** ['sməuldə*] vi arder sem chamas, estar latente.

**smudge** [smʌdʒ] n mancha // vt manchar, sujar.

**smug** [smʌg] adj metido, convencido.

**smuggle** ['smʌgl] vt contrabandear; **smuggler** n contrabandista m/f; **smuggling** n contrabando.

**smutty** ['smʌtɪ] adj (fig) obsceno, indecente, manchado.

**snack** [snæk] n merenda, lanche m; **~ bar** n lanchonete f.

**snag** [snæg] n dificuldade f, obstáculo.

**snail** [sneɪl] n caramujo, lesma.

**snake** [sneɪk] n (gen) serpente f, cobra, víbora.

**snap** [snæp] n (sound) estalo; (of whip) estalido; (click) clique m; (photograph) foto f // adj repentino // vt (fingers, whip) estalar; (break) quebrar; (photograph) tirar uma foto de // vi (break) despedaçar-se; (fig: person) retrucar asperamente; (sound) fazer um clique; **to ~ shut** fechar ruidosamente; **to ~ at** vt fus (subj: dog) tentar morder; **to ~** vi (break) partir-se; **to ~ up** vt arrebatar, comprar rapidamente;

~**shot** *n* foto *f* (instantânea).

**snare** [snɛə*] *n* armadilha, laço // *vt* apanhar no laço *or* na armadilha; (*fig*) enganar.

**snarl** [snɑ:l] *n* grunhido // *vi* grunhir.

**snatch** [snætʃ] *n* (*fig*) roubo; (*small amount*): ~**es of** pedacinhos *mpl* de // *vt* (~ *away*) arrebatar; (*grasp*) agarrar, tirar à força.

**sneak** [sni:k] *vi*: **to** ~ **in/out** entrar/sair furtivamente // *n* (*fam*) pessoa covarde *or* vil; ~**y** *adj* sorrateiro.

**sneer** [snɪə*] *n* sorriso de desprezo // *vi* rir-se com desdém; (*mock*) zombar de, escarnecer de.

**sneeze** [sni:z] *n* espirro // *vi* espirrar.

**sniff** [snɪf] *n* (*of dog*) farejada; (*of person*) fungadela // *vi* fungar // *vt* fungar, farejar.

**snigger** ['snɪɡə*] *n* riso dissimulado // *vi* rir-se com dissimulação.

**snip** [snɪp] *n* tesourada; (*piece*) pedaço, retalho; (*bargain*) pechincha // *vt* cortar com tesoura.

**sniper** ['snaɪpə*] *n* franco-atirador(a) *m/f*.

**snippet** ['snɪpɪt] *n* pedacinho.

**snivelling** ['snɪvlɪŋ] *adj* (*whimpering*) chorão/rona, lamuriento.

**snob** [snɔb] *n* esnobe *m/f*; ~**bery** *n* esnobismo; ~**bish** *adj* esnobe.

**snooker** ['snu:kə*] *n* sinuca.

**snoop** [snu:p] *vi*: **to** ~ **about** bisbilhotar; ~**er** *n* bisbilhoteiro/a *m/f*.

**snooty** ['snu:tɪ] *adj* arrogante.

**snooze** [snu:z] *n* soneca, sesta // *vi* tirar uma soneca, dormitar.

**snore** [snɔ:*] *vi* roncar, ressonar // *n* ronco.

**snorkel** ['snɔ:kl] *n* tubo snorkel.

**snort** [snɔ:t] *n* bufo, bufido // *vi* bufar.

**snout** [snaut] *n* focinho, nariz *m*.

**snow** [snəu] *n* neve *f* // *vi* nevar; ~**ball** *n* bola de neve // *vi*

acumular-se; ~**bound** *adj* bloqueado pela neve; ~**drift** *n* monte *m* de neve (formado pelo vento); ~**drop** *n* campainha branca; ~**fall** *n* nevada; ~**flake** *n* floco de neve; ~**man** *n* boneco de neve; ~**plough**, ~**plow** (*US*) *n* máquina limpa-neve; ~**storm** *n* nevasca, tempestade *f* de neve; **S**~ **White** *n* Branca de Neve.

**snub** [snʌb] *vt* desdenhar, menosprezar // *n* desdém *m*, repulsa.

**snuff** [snʌf] *n* rapé *m*.

**snug** [snʌg] *adj* (*sheltered*) abrigado, protegido; (*fitted*) justo, cômodo.

**snuggle** ['snʌgl] *vi*: **to** ~ **up to sb** aconchegar-se *or* aninhar-se a alguém.

**so** [səu] *adv* (*degree*) tão; (*manner*: *thus*) assim, deste modo // *conj* consequentemente, portanto; ~ **that** (*purpose*) para que, a fim de que; (*result*) de modo que; ~ **do I** eu também; **if** ~ se for assim, se assim é; **I hope** ~ espero que sim; **10 or** ~ 10 mais ou menos; ~ **far** até aqui; ~ **long!** tchau!; ~ **many** tantos; ~ **much** *adv, det* tanto; ~ **and** ~ *n* fulano/a.

**soak** [səuk] *vt* (*drench*) embeber, ensopar; (*put in water*) pôr de molho // *vi* estar de molho, impregnar-se; **to** ~ **in** *vi* infiltrar; **to** ~ **up** *vt* absorver.

**soap** [səup] *n* sabão *m*; ~**flakes** *npl* flocos *mpl* de sabão; ~**powder** *n* sabão em pó; ~**y** *adj* ensaboado.

**soar** [sɔ:*] *vi* (*on wings*) elevar-se em vôo; (*building etc*) levantar-se.

**sob** [sɔb] *n* soluço // *vi* soluçar.

**sober** ['səubə*] *adj* (*serious*) sério; (*sensible*) sensato; (*moderate*) moderado; (*not drunk*) sóbrio; (*colour, style*) discreto; **to** ~ **up** *vi* tornar-se sóbrio.

**Soc.** *abbr of* **society**.

**so-called** ['səu'kɔ:ld] *adj* chamado.

**soccer** ['sɔkə*] *n* futebol *m*.

**sociable** ['səʊʃəbl] *adj* sociável.

**social** ['səʊʃl] *adj* (*gen*) social; (*sociable*) sociável // *n* reunião *f* social; ~ **climber** *n* arrivista *m/f*; ~ **club** *n* clube *m*; ~**ism** *n* socialismo; ~**ist** *adj, n* socialista *m/f*; ~**ly** *adv* socialmente; ~ **science** *n* ciências *fpl* sociais; ~ **security** *n* previdência social; ~ **work** *n* assistência social, serviço social; ~ **worker** *n* assistente *m/f* social.

**society** [sə'saɪətɪ] *n* sociedade *f*; (*club*) associação *f*; (*also*: **high** ~) alta sociedade.

**sociologist** [səʊsɪ'ɒlədʒɪst] *n* sociólogo/a; **sociology** [-dʒə] *n* sociologia.

**sock** [sɒk] *n* meia (curta); (*Pt*) peúga.

**socket** ['sɒkɪt] *n* (*ELEC*) tomada.

**sod** [sɒd] *n* (*of earth*) gramado, torrão *m*; (*col!*) droga!; (*person*) idiota *m/f*.

**soda** ['səʊdə] *n* (*CHEM*) soda; (*also*: ~ **water**) água com gás.

**sodden** ['sɒdn] *adj* encharcado.

**sodium** ['səʊdɪəm] *n* sódio.

**sofa** ['səʊfə] *n* sofá *m*.

**soft** [sɒft] *adj* (*gen*) macio; (*gentle, not loud*) suave; (*kind*) meigo, bondoso; (*weak*) fraco; (*stupid*) idiota; ~ **drink** *n* refrigerante *m*; ~**en** ['sɒfn] *vt* amolecer, amaciar, enternecer // *vi* abrandar-se, enternecer-se, suavizar-se; ~**hearted** *adj* bondoso, caridoso; ~**ly** *adv* suavemente; (*gently*) delicadamente, devagarinho; ~**ness** *n* suavidade *f*, afabilidade *f*; (*sweetness*) doçura; (*tenderness*) ternura.

**soggy** ['sɒgɪ] *adj* ensopado, encharcado.

**soil** [sɔɪl] *n* (*earth*) terra, solo // *vt* sujar, manchar; ~**ed** *adj* sujo.

**solace** ['sɒlɪs] *n* consolo.

**solar** ['səʊlə*] *adj* solar.

**sold** [səʊld] *pt, pp* of **sell**; ~ **out** (*COMM*) esgotado.

**solder** ['səʊldə*] *vt* soldar // *n* solda.

**soldier** ['səʊldʒə*] *n* (*gen*) soldado; (*army man*) militar *m*.

**sole** [səʊl] *n* (*of foot, of shoe*) sola; (*fish: pl inv*) solha, linguado // *adj* único; ~**ly** *adv* somente, unicamente.

**solemn** ['sɒləm] *adj* solene.

**solicitor** [sə'lɪsɪtə*] *n* (*for wills etc*) tabelião *m*; (*in court*) advogado em causas simples.

**solid** ['sɒlɪd] *adj* (*not hollow*) sólido; (*gold etc*) maciço; (*person*) sério // *n* sólido.

**solidarity** [sɒlɪ'dærɪtɪ] *n* solidariedade *f*.

**solidify** [sə'lɪdɪfaɪ] *vi* solidificar-se.

**solitaire** [sɒlɪ'tɛə*] *n* (*gem*) solitário; (*game*) solitário, jogo de paciência.

**solitary** ['sɒlɪtrɪ] *adj* solitário, só; (*isolated*) isolado, retirado; (*only*) único; ~ **confinement** *n* prisão *f* solitária.

**solitude** ['sɒlɪtjuːd] *n* solidão *f*.

**solo** ['səʊləʊ] *n* solo; ~**ist** *n* solista *m/f*.

**soluble** ['sɒljubl] *adj* solúvel.

**solution** [sə'luːʃən] *n* solução *f*.

**solve** [sɒlv] *vt* resolver, solucionar.

**solvent** ['sɒlvənt] *adj* (*COMM*) solvente // *n* (*CHEM*) solvente *m*.

**sombre, somber** (*US*) ['sɒmbə*] *adj* sombrio, escuro, lúgubre.

**some** [sʌm] *det* (*a few*) alguns/algumas; (*certain*) algum(a); (*a certain number or amount*) see phrases below; (*unspecified*) um pouco de // *pron* alguns/algumas; (*a bit*) um pouco // *adv*: ~ **10 people** umas 10 pessoas; ~ **children came** algumas crianças vieram; **have** ~ **tea** tome um pouco de chá; **there's** ~ **milk in the fridge** há leite na geladeira; ~ **was left** ficou um pouco; **I've got** ~ (*books etc*) tenho alguns; (*milk, money etc*) tenho um pouco de; ~**body** *pron* alguém; ~**day** *adv* algum dia; ~**how** *adv* de alguma maneira; (*for some reason*) por uma razão ou outra; ~**one** *pron* = ~**body**.

**somersault** ['sʌməsɔːlt] *n* (*deliberate*) salto mortal; (*accidental*) cambalhota // *vi* dar um salto mortal *or* uma cambalhota.

**something** ['sʌmθɪŋ] *pron* algo; (*Pt*) alguma coisa.

**sometime** ['sʌmtaɪm] *adv* (*in future*) algum dia, em outra oportunidade; (*in past*): ~ **last month** durante o mês passado.

**sometimes** ['sʌmtaɪmz] *adv* às vezes, de vez em quando.

**somewhat** ['sʌmwɔt] *adv* um tanto.

**somewhere** ['sʌmwɛə*] *adv* (*be*) em algum lugar; (*go*) para algum lugar; ~ **else** (*be*) em outro lugar; (*go*) para outro lugar.

**son** [sʌn] *n* filho.

**song** [sɔŋ] *n* canção *f*; ~**writer** *n* compositor(a) *m/f* de canções.

**sonic** ['sɔnɪk] *adj* (*boom*) sônico.

**son-in-law** ['sʌnɪnlɔː] *n* genro.

**sonnet** ['sɔnɪt] *n* soneto.

**soon** [suːn] *adv* logo, brevemente; (*early*) cedo; ~ **afterwards** pouco depois; *see also* **as**; ~**er** *adv* (*time*) antes, mais cedo; (*preference*): **I would** ~**er do that** preferiria fazer isso; ~**er or later** mais cedo ou mais tarde.

**soot** [sut] *n* fuligem *f*.

**soothe** [suːð] *vt* acalmar, sossegar; (*pain*) aliviar, suavizar.

**sophisticated** [səˈfɪstɪkeɪtɪd] *adj* sofisticado, cosmopolita.

**soporific** [sɔpəˈrɪfɪk] *adj* soporífico.

**sopping** ['sɔpɪŋ] *adj*: ~ **wet** totalmente encharcado *or* molhado.

**soppy** ['sɔpɪ] *adj* (*pej*) sentimentalóide.

**soprano** [səˈprɑːnəu] *n* soprano *m/f*.

**sorcerer** ['sɔːsərə*] *n* feiticeiro.

**sordid** ['sɔːdɪd] *adj* (*dirty*) imundo, sórdido; (*wretched*) miserável.

**sore** [sɔː*] *adj* (*painful*) doloroso, doído; (*offended*) magoado, ofendido // *n* chaga, ferida; ~**ly** *adv*: **I am** ~**ly tempted** estou muito tentado.

**sorrow** ['sɔrəu] *n* tristeza, mágoa, dor *f*; ~**ful** *adj* triste, aflito, magoado.

**sorry** ['sɔrɪ] *adj* (*regretful*) arrependido; (*condition*, *excuse*) lamentável; ~**! desculpe!, perdão!, sinto muito!; to feel** ~ **for sb** sentir pena de alguém; **I feel** ~ **for him** estou com pena dele.

**sort** [sɔːt] *n* espécie *f*, gênero, tipo // *vt* (*also*: ~ **out**: *papers*) classificar; (: *problems*) solucionar, resolver; ~**ing office** *n* departamento de distribuição.

**so-so** ['səusəu] *adv*. mais ou menos, regular.

**soufflé** [suːˈfleɪ] *n* suflê *m*.

**sought** [sɔːt] *pt*, *pp* of **seek**.

**soul** [səul] *n* alma; ~**destroying** *adj* embrutecedor(a); ~**ful** *adj* emocional, sentimental; ~**less** *adj* desalmado.

**sound** [saund] *adj* (*healthy*) saudável, sadio; (*safe, not damaged*) sólido, completo; (*secure*) seguro; (*reliable, not superficial*) digno de confiança; (*sensible*) sensato // *adv*: ~ **asleep** dormindo profundamente // *n* (*noise*) som *m*, ruído, barulho; (*GEO*) estreito, braço (de mar) // *vt* (*alarm*) soar; (*also*: ~ **out**: *opinions*) sondar // *vi* soar, tocar; (*fig*: *seem*) parecer; **to** ~ **like** soar como; ~ **barrier** *n* barreira do som; ~ **effects** *npl* efeitos *mpl* sonoros; ~**ing** *n* (*NAUT etc*) sondagem *f*; ~**ly** *adv* (*sleep*) profundamente; (*beat*) completamente; ~**proof** *adj* à prova de som; ~**track** *n* (*of film*) trilha sonora.

**soup** [suːp] *n* (*thick*) sopa; (*thin*) caldo; **in the** ~ (*fig*) numa encrenca; ~**spoon** *n* colher *f* de sopa.

**sour** ['sauə*] *adj* azedo, ácido; (*milk*) talhado; (*fig*) mal-humorado, rabugento.

**source** [sɔːs] *n* fonte *f.*

**south** [sauθ] *n* sul *m* // *adj* do sul, meridional // *adv* ao or para o sul; **S~ Africa** *n* África do Sul; **S~ African** *adj*, *n* sul-africano/a; **S~ America** *n* América do Sul; **S~ American** *adj*, *n* sul-americano/a; **~east** *n* sudeste *m*; **~erly** [ˈsʌðəli] *adj* meridional; (*from the* ~) do sul; **~ern** [ˈsʌðən] *adj* do sul, sulista; **S~ Pole** *n* Pólo Sul; **~ward(s)** *adv* para o sul; **~west** *n* sudoeste *m.*

**souvenir** [suːvəˈnɪə*] *n* lembrança.

**sovereign** [ˈsɔvrɪn] *adj*, *n* soberano/a; **~ty** *n* soberania.

**soviet** [ˈsəuvɪət] *adj* soviético; **the S~ Union** a União Soviética.

**sow** [sau] *n* porca // *vt* [sau], *pp* **sowed**, *pp* **sown** [səun] (*gen*) semear; (*spread*) disseminar, espalhar.

**soy** [sɔɪ] *n*: **~ sauce** molho de soja.

**soya bean** [ˈsɔɪəbiːn] *n* semente *f* de soja.

**spa** [spɑː] *n* (*spring*) fonte *f* de água mineral; (*town*) estância hidro-mineral.

**space** [speɪs] *n* (*gen*) espaço; (*room*) lugar *m* // *vt* (*also*: ~ **out**) espaçar; **~craft** *n* nave *f* espacial; **~man/woman** *n* astronauta *m/f*, cosmonauta *m/f*; **spacing** *n* espaçamento, espaçamento.

**spacious** [ˈspeɪʃəs] *adj* espaçoso.

**spade** [speɪd] *n* (*tool*) pá *f*; **~s** *npl* (*CARDS*) espadas *fpl.*

**spaghetti** [spəˈgɛti] *n* espaguete *m.*

**Spain** [speɪn] *n* Espanha.

**span** [spæn] *n* (*of bird, plane*) envergadura; (*of hand*) palma; (*of arch*) vão *m*; (*in time*) lapso, espaço // *vt* estender-se sobre, atravessar; (*fig*) abarcar.

**Spaniard** [ˈspænjəd] *n* espanhol(a) *m/f.*

**spaniel** [ˈspænjəl] *n* spaniel *m.*

**Spanish** [ˈspænɪʃ] *adj* espanhol(a) // *n* (*LING*) espanhol *m*, castelhano.

**spank** [spæŋk] *vt* bater, dar palmadas.

**spanner** [ˈspænə*] *n* chave *f* inglesa.

**spar** [spɑː*] *n* mastro, verga // *vi* (*BOXING*) boxear.

**spare** [spɛə*] *adj* (*free*) vago, desocupado; (*surplus*) de sobra, a mais; (*available*) disponível, de reserva // *n* (*part*) peça sobressalente // *vt* (*do without*) dispensar, passar sem; (*afford to give*) dispor de, ter de sobra; (*refrain from hurting*) perdoar, poupar; (*be grudging with*) dar frugalmente; **~ part** *n* peça sobressalente; **~ time** *n* tempo livre.

**sparing** [ˈspɛərɪŋ] *adj*: **to be ~ with** ser econômico com; **~ly** *adv* escassamente.

**spark** [spɑːk] *n* chispa, faísca; (*fig*) centelha; **~(ing) plug** *n* vela de ignição.

**sparkle** [ˈspɑːkl] *n* cintilação *f*, brilho // *vi* cintilar; (*shine*) brilhar, faiscar; **sparkling** *adj* cintilante; (*wine*) espumante.

**sparrow** [ˈspærəu] *n* pardal *m.*

**sparse** [spɑːs] *adj* escasso; (*hair*) ralo.

**spasm** [ˈspæzəm] *n* (*MED*) espasmo; (*fig*) acesso, ataque *m*; **~odic** [-ˈmɔdɪk] *adj* espasmódico.

**spastic** [ˈspæstɪk] *n* espástico/a.

**spat** [spæt] *pt*, *pp* of **spit**.

**spate** [speɪt] *n* (*fig*) jorro, fluxo; **in ~** (*river*) em cheia.

**spatter** [ˈspætə*] *vt* borrifar, salpicar.

**spatula** [ˈspætjulə] *n* espátula.

**spawn** [spɔːn] *vi* desovar, procriar // *n* ovas *fpl.*

**speak** [spiːk], *pt* **spoke**, *pp* **spoken** (*language*) falar; (*truth*) dizer // *vi* falar; (*make a speech*) discursar; **to ~ to sb/of or about sth** falar com alguém/de or sobre algo; **~ up!** fale alto!; **~er** *n* (*in public*) orador(a) *m/f*; (*also:* **loud~er**) alto-falante *m*; (POL): **the S~er** o Presidente da Câmara.

**spear** [spɪə*] *n* lança, (*for fishing*) arpão *m // vt* lancear, arpoar; **~head** *n* ponta-de-lança.

**special** ['spɛʃl] *adj* especial; (*edition etc*) extra; (*delivery*) rápida; **take ~ care** tome muito cuidado; **~ist** *n* especialista *m/f*; **~ity** [spɛʃɪˈælɪtɪ] *n* especialidade *f*; **~ize** *vi*: **to ~ize (in)** especializar-se (em); **~ly** *adv* sobretudo, especialmente.

**species** ['spiːʃɪːz] *n* espécie *f*.

**specific** [spəˈsɪfɪk] *adj* específico; **~ally** *adv* especificamente.

**specification** [spɛsɪfɪˈkeɪʃən] *n* especificação *f*; **~s** *npl* detalhes *mpl*, características *fpl*; **specify** ['spɛsɪfaɪ] *vt/i* especificar, pormenorizar.

**specimen** ['spɛsɪmən] *n* espécime *m*, amostra; (*fig*) exemplar *m*.

**speck** [spɛk] *n* mancha, ponta.

**speckled** ['spɛkld] *adj* manchado.

**specs** [spɛks] *npl* (*col*) óculos *mpl*.

**spectacle** ['spɛktəkl] *n* espetáculo (*Pt:* -ct-); **~s** *npl* óculos *mpl*; **spectacular** [-ˈtækjulə*] *adj* espetacular (*Pt:* -ct-); (*success*) impressionante, tremendo.

**spectator** [spɛkˈteɪtə*] *n* espectador(a) *m/f*.

**spectre, specter** (*US*) ['spɛktə*] *n* espectro *m*, aparição *f*.

**spectrum** ['spɛktrəm], *pl* **-tra** [-trə] *n* espectro.

**speculate** ['spɛkjuleɪt] *vi* especular; (*try to guess*): **to ~ about** especular sobre; **speculation** [-ˈleɪʃən] *n* especulação *f*.

**speech** [spiːtʃ] *n* (*faculty*) fala, palavra; (*formal talk*) discurso; (*talk*) conversa; (*language*) idioma *m*, linguagem *f*; **~less** *adj* estupefato (*Pt:* -cto), emudecido.

**speed** [spiːd] *n* velocidade *f*, rapidez *f*; (*haste*) pressa; (*promptness*) prontidão *f*; **at full** *or* **top ~** a toda

velocidade; **to ~ up** *vi* acelerar // *vt* acelerar; **~boat** *n* lancha; **~ily** *adv* depressa, rapidamente; **~ing** *n* (AUT) excesso de velocidade; **~ limit** *n* limite *m* de velocidade, velocidade *f* máxima; **~ometer** [spɪˈdɒmɪtə*] *n* velocímetro; **~way** *n* (SPORT) pista de corrida, rodovia de alta velocidade; **~y** *adj* (*fast*) veloz, rápido; (*prompt*) pronto, imediato.

**spell** [spɛl] *n* (*also:* **magic ~**) encanto, feitiço; (*period of time*) período breve, intervalo; (*turn*) turno, temporada // *vt, pt, pp* **spelt** *or* **spelled** (*also:* **~ out**) soletrar; (*fig*) pressagiar, ser sinal de; **to cast a ~ on sb** enfeitiçar alguém; **he can't ~** não sabe escrever bem, comete erros de ortografia; **~bound** *adj* enfeitiçado, fascinado; **~ing** *n* ortografia.

**spend** [spɛnd], *pt, pp* **spent** [spɛnt] *vt* (*money*) gastar; (*time*) desperdiçar; (*life*) passar, dedicar; **~thrift** *n* esbanjador(a) *m/f*, perdulário/a.

**sperm** [spəːm] *n* esperma; **~ whale** *n* cachalote *m*.

**spew** [spjuː] *vt* vomitar, lançar.

**sphere** [sfɪə*] *n* esfera; **spherical** ['sfɛrɪkl] *adj* esférico.

**sphinx** [sfɪŋks] *n* esfinge *f*.

**spice** [spaɪs] *n* especiaria // *vt* condimentar; **spicy** *adj* condimentado; (*fig*) picante.

**spider** ['spaɪdə*] *n* aranha.

**spike** [spaɪk] *n* (*point*) ponta, espigão *m*; (BOT) espiga.

**spill** [spɪl], *pt, pp* **spilt** *or* **spilled** *vt* entornar, derramar // *vi* derramar-se; **to ~ over** transbordar-se.

**spin** [spɪn] *n* (*revolution of wheel*) volta, rotação *f*; (AVIAT) parafuso; (*trip in car*) volta *or* passeio de carro // (*vb: pt, pp* **spun**) *vt* (*wool etc*) fiar, tecer; (*wheel*) girar // *vi* girar, rodar; **to ~ out** *vt* prolongar, alargar.

**spinach** ['spinitʃ] *n* espinafre *m*.

**spinal** ['spainl] *adj* espinhal; ~ **cord** *n* coluna vertebral, espinha dorsal.

**spindly** ['spindli] *adj* alto e magro, espigado.

**spin-drier** ['spin'draiə*] *n* máquina de secar centrífuga.

**spine** [spain] *n* espinha dorsal; (*thorn*) espinho; ~**less** *adj* (*fig*) fraco, covarde.

**spinning** ['spiniŋ] *n* (*of thread, art*) fiação *f*; ~ **top** *n* pião *m*; ~ **wheel** *n* roca de fiar.

**spinster** ['spinstə*] *n* solteira; (*pej*) solteirona.

**spiral** ['spaiərl] *n* espiral *f* // *adj* em espiral, helicoidal; ~ **staircase** *n* escada em caracol.

**spire** ['spaiə*] *n* flecha, agulha.

**spirit** ['spirit] *n* (*gen*) espírito; (*soul*) alma; (*ghost*) fantasma *m*; (*humour*) humor *m*; (*courage*) coragem *f*, ânimo; ~**s** *npl* (*drink*) álcool *msg*, bebida alcoólica *sg*; **in good** ~**s** alegre, de bom humor; ~**ed** *adj* animado, espirituoso; ~**level** *n* nível *m* de bolha.

**spiritual** ['spiritjuəl] *adj* espiritual // *n* (*also*: **Negro** ~) canto religioso dos negros; ~**ism** *n* espiritualismo.

**spit** [spit] *n* (*for roasting*) espeto; (*NAUT*) restinga // *vi, pt, pp* **spat** cuspir; (*sound*) escarrar.

**spite** [spait] *n* rancor *m*, ressentimento // *vt* mortificar, contrariar; **in** ~ **of** apesar de, a despeito de; ~**ful** *adj* rancoroso, malévolo.

**spittle** ['spitl] *n* saliva, cuspe *m*.

**splash** [splæʃ] *n* (*sound*) borrifo, respingo; (*of colour*) mancha *f* // *vt* salpicar (*with* de) // *vi* (*also*: ~ **about**) borrifar, respingar.

**spleen** [spli:n] *n* (*ANAT*) baço.

**splendid** ['splendid] *adj* esplêndido; **splendour, splendor** (*US*) ['-də*] *n* esplendor *m*; (*of achievement*) pompa, glória.

**splint** [splint] *n* tala, lasca.

**splinter** ['splintə*] *n* (*of wood*) lasca; (*in finger*) farpa // *vi* lascar-se, estilhaçar-se, despedaçar-se.

**split** [split] *n* fenda, brecha; (*fig*) rompimento; (*POL*) divisão *f* // (*vb*: *pt, pp* **split**) *vt* partir, fender; (*party*) dividir; (*work, profits*) rachar, repartir // *vi* (*divide*) dividir-se, repartir-se; **to** ~ **up** *vi* (*couple*) separar-se, romper; (*meeting*) terminar.

**splutter** ['splʌtə*] *vi* crepitar; (*person*) balbuciar, gaguejar.

**spoil** [spɔil], *pt, pp* **spoilt** *or* **spoiled** *vt* (*damage*) danificar; (*mar*) estragar, arruinar; (*child*) mimar, estragar; ~**s** *npl* despojo *sg*, saque *m*; ~**sport** *n* desmancha-prazeres *m/f inv*.

**spoke** [spəuk] *pt of* **speak** // *n* (*of wheel*) raio.

**spoken** ['spəukn] *pp of* **speak**.

**spokesman** ['spəuksmən] *n* porta-voz *m/f*.

**sponge** [spʌndʒ] *n* esponja; (*cake*) pão-de-ló *m* // *vt* (*wash*) lavar com esponja // *vi*: **to** ~ **on sb** viver às custas de alguém; ~ **bag** *n* esponjeira, porta-esponja; ~ **cake** *n* pão-de-ló *m*; **spongy** *adj* esponjoso, absorvente.

**sponsor** ['sponsə*] *n* (*RADIO, TV*) patrocinador(a) *m/f*; (*for membership*) padrinho *m*, madrinha *f*; (*COMM*) fiador(a) *m/f*, financiador *m* // *vt* patrocinar; apadrinhar; fiar; (*idea etc*) promover; ~**ship** *n* patrocínio.

**spontaneous** [spɔn'teiniəs] *adj* espontâneo.

**spool** [spu:l] *n* carretel *m*; (*of sewing machine*) bobina, novelo.

**spoon** [spu:n] *n* colher *f*; ~-**feed** *vt* dar de comer com colher; (*fig*) mimar, dar de mão beijada; ~**ful** *n* colherada.

**sporadic** [spə'rædik] *adj* esporádico.

**sport** [spɔ:t] *n* esporte *m*; (*Pt*)

desporto; (person) bom perdedor(a) m/f; ~ing adj esportivo; (Pt) desportivo; ~s car n carro esporte; ~(s) jacket n casaco (d)esportivo; sportsman n (d)esportista m/f; sportsmanship n espírito (d)esportivo; sportswear n roupa (d)esportiva or esporte; sportswoman n (d)esportista; ~y adj de espírito esportivo

spot [spɔt] n lugar m, local m; (dot: on pattern) mancha, ponto; (pimple) espinha; (freckle) sarda, pinta; (small amount): a ~ of um pouquinho de // vt (notice) localizar, notar; on the ~ no ato (Pt: -ct-), ali mesmo; (in difficulty) em apuros; ~ check n fiscalização f de surpresa; ~less adj sem mancha, imaculado; ~light n holofote m, refletor (Pt: -ct-) m; ~ted adj (pattern) com bolinhas; ~ty adj (face) manchado.

spouse [spauz] n cônjuge m/f.

spout [spaut] n (of jug) bico; (pipe) cano // vi jorrar.

sprain [sprein] n distensão f, torcedura // vt: to ~ one's ankle torcer o tornozelo.

sprang [spræŋ] pt of spring.

sprawl [sprɔːl] vi esparramar-se.

spray [sprei] n spray m, borrifador m; (of sea) borrifo; (container) atomizador m; (of paint) pistola borrifadora; (of flowers) ramalhete m // vt pulverizar; (crops) borrifar, regar.

spread [sprɛd] n extensão f; (distribution) expansão f, difusão f; (col: food) mesa coberta de comida, banquete m // (vb: pt, pp spread) vt espalhar; (butter) untar, passar; (wings, sails) abrir, desdobrar; (scatter) disseminar // vi espalhar-se, alastrar-se, difundir-se.

spree [spri:] n: to go on a ~ fazer uma farra.

sprightly ['spraitli] adj vivo, esperto, desembaraçado.

spring [spriŋ] n (leap) salto, pulo; (coiled metal) mola; (season) primavera; (of water) fonte f, nascente f // vi, pt sprang, pp sprung (arise) brotar, nascer; (leap) pular, saltar; to ~ up vi nascer or aparecer de repente; ~board n trampolim m; ~clean n (also: ~cleaning) limpeza total, faxina (geral); ~time n primavera; ~y adj elástico, flexível; (grass) macio.

sprinkle ['spriŋkl] vt (pour) salpicar, borrifar; to ~ water on, ~ with water borrifar or salpicar de água; ~d with (fig) salpicado or polvilhado de.

sprint [sprint] n corrida de pequena distância // vi (gen) correr a toda velocidade; ~er n corredor(a) m/f; (horse) sprinter m.

sprite [sprait] n duende m, elfo.

sprout [spraut] vi brotar, germinar; (Brussels) ~s npl couve-de-Bruxelas fsg.

spruce [spruːs] n (BOT) abeto // adj arrumado, limpo, elegante.

sprung [sprʌŋ] pp of spring.

spry [sprai] adj vivo, ativo, ágil.

spun [spʌn] pt, pp of spin.

spur [spə:*] n espora; (fig) estímulo // vt (also: ~ on) incitar, estimular; on the ~ of the moment de improviso, de repente.

spurn [spə:n] vt desdenhar, desprezar.

spurt [spə:t] n esforço supremo; (of energy) acesso, acometida; (water) jorro // vi fazer um esforço supremo; (water) jorrar.

spy [spai] n espião/espiã m/f // vi: to ~ on espiar, espionar // vt (see) enxergar, avistar; ~ing n espionagem f.

sq. abbr of square.

squabble ['skwɔbl] n briga, bate-boca m // vi brigar, altercar, discutir.

squad [skwɔd] n (MIL, POLICE) pelotão m, esquadra.

**squadron** ['skwɔdrn] *n* (MIL) esquadrão *m*; (AVIAT) esquadrilha; (NAUT) esquadra.

**squalid** ['skwɔlɪd] *adj* esquálido, sórdido.

**squall** [skwɔːl] *n* (storm) tempestade *f*; (wind) pé *m* (de vento), rajada.

**squalor** ['skwɔlə*] *n* sordidez *f*.

**squander** ['skwɔndə*] *vt* (money) esbanjar, dissipar; (chances) desperdiçar.

**square** [skwɛə*] *n* quadrado, (in town) praça; (MATH: instrument) esquadro // *adj* quadrado; (col: ideas, tastes) quadrado, antiquado // *vt* (arrange) ajustar, acertar; (MATH) elevar ao quadrado; **all** ~ igual, quite; **a** ~ **meal** uma refeição substancial; **2 metres** ~ um quadrado de dois metros de lado; **1** ~ **metre** um metro quadrado; ~**ly** *adv* em forma quadrada; (fully) em cheio.

**squash** [skwɔʃ] *n* (drink): **lemon/orange** ~ suco *or* (Pt) sumo de limão/laranja; (SPORT) squash *m*, jogo de raquetes // *vt* esmagar; **to** ~ **together** apinhar.

**squat** [skwɔt] *adj* agachado; (short) atarracado // *vi* agachar-se, acocorar-se; ~**ter** *n* posseiro/a.

**squawk** [skwɔːk] *vi* grasnar.

**squeak** [skwiːk] *vi* grunhido, chiado; (of shoe) rangido; (of mouse) guincho // *vi* grunhir, chiar; ranger; guinchar.

**squeal** [skwiːl] *vi* guinchar, gritar agudamente; (tell on) delatar.

**squeamish** ['skwiːmɪʃ] *adj* melindroso, delicado.

**squeeze** [skwiːz] *n* (gen) aperto, compressão *f*; (of hand) apertão *m*; (in bus etc) apinhamento // *vt* comprimir, socar; (hand, arm) apertar; **to** ~ **out** *vt* espremer; (fig) extorquir; **to** ~ **through** abrir caminho.

**squelch** [skwɛltʃ] *vt* esmagar // *vi*

fazer ruído de passos na lama.

**squid** [skwɪd] *n* lula.

**squint** [skwɪnt] *vi* olhar *or* ser vesgo // *n* (MED) estrabismo; **to** ~ **at sth** olhar algo de soslaio *or* de esguelha.

**squirm** [skwəːm] *vi* retorcer-se, mexer-se, contorcer-se.

**squirrel** ['skwɪrəl] *n* esquilo.

**squirt** [skwəːt] *vi* jorrar, esguichar.

**Sr** *abbr of* **senior**.

**St** *abbr of* **saint; street**.

**stab** [stæb] *n* (with knife etc) punhalada; (of pain) pontada; (col: try): **to have a** ~ **at (doing) sth** tentar (fazer) algo // *vt* apunhalar.

**stability** [stəˈbɪlɪtɪ] *n* estabilidade *f*; **stabilize** ['steɪbəlaɪz] *vt* estabilizar // *vi* estabilizar-se; **stable** ['steɪbl] *adj* estável // *n* estábulo, cavalariça.

**stack** [stæk] *n* montão *m*, pilha // *vt* amontoar, empilhar.

**stadium** ['steɪdɪəm] *n* estádio.

**staff** [stɑːf] *n* (work force) pessoal *m*, corpo administrativo; (stick) cajado, bastão *m* // *vt* prover de pessoal.

**stag** [stæg] *n* veado, cervo.

**stage** [steɪdʒ] *n* cena, cenário; (profession): **the** ~ palco, teatro; (point) etapa, fase *f*; (platform) plataforma, estrado // *vt* (play) pôr em cena, representar; (demonstration) montar, organizar; (fig: perform): **recovery etc** realizar; ~**coach** *n* diligência; ~ **door** *n* entrada dos artistas; ~ **manager** *n* diretor(a) (Pt: -ct-) *m/f* de cena.

**stagger** ['stægə*] *vi* cambalear // *vt* (amaze) surpreender, chocar; (hours, holidays) escalonar; ~**ing** *adj* (amazing) surpreendente, chocante.

**stagnant** ['stægnənt] *adj* estagnado; **stagnate** [-'neɪt] *vi* estagnar-se.

**stag party** *n* festa só para homens.

**staid** [steɪd] *adj* sério, sóbrio.

**stain** [steɪn] *n* mancha; (colouring) tinta, tintura // *vt* manchar; (wood) tingir; ~**ed glass window** *n* janela com vitral; ~**less** adj (steel) inoxidável.

**stair** [stɛəʳ] n (step) degrau m; ~**s** npl escada sg; ~**case**, ~**way** n escadaria, escada.

**stake** [steik] n estaca, poste m; (BETTING) aposta // vt apostar; **to be at** ~ estar em jogo or em perigo.

**stalactite** ['stæləktait] n estalactite f.

**stalagmite** ['stæləgmait] n estalagmite f.

**stale** [steil] adj (bread) amanhecido; (food) passado, estragado.

**stalemate** ['steilmeit] n empate m; (fig) impasse m, beco sem saída.

**stalk** [stɔːk] n caule m, talo, haste f // vt caçar de tocaia; **to** ~ **off** andar com arrogância.

**stall** [stɔːl] n (in market) barraca; (in stable) baia // vt (AUT) parar // vi (AUT) parar, atolar-se; (fig) esquivar-se, ganhar tempo; ~**s** npl (in cinema, theatre) platéia sg.

**stallion** ['stæliən] n garanhão m.

**stalwart** ['stɔːlwət] n (in build) robusto, rijo; (in spirit) valente, leal.

**stamina** ['stæminə] n resistência.

**stammer** ['stæməʳ] n gagueira // vi gaguejar, balbuciar.

**stamp** [stæmp] n selo, estampilha; (mark, also fig) marca, impressão f; (on document) timbre m, sinete m // vi pisar, esmagar // vt bater com o pé; (letter) dispatch sapatear; (letter) selar; (with rubber ~) carimbar; ~ **album** n álbum m de selos; ~ **collecting** n filatelia.

**stampede** [stæm'piːd] n debandada, estouro (da boiada).

**stance** [stæns] n postura, posição f.

**stand** [stænd] n (position) posição f, postura; (for taxis) ponto; (hall ~) pedestal m; (music ~) estante f; (SPORT) tribuna, palanque m; (news ~) banca de jornais // vi: pt, pp **stood** vi (be) estar, encontrar-se; (be on foot) estar em pé; (rise) levantar-se; (remain) ficar em pé //

vt (place) pôr, colocar; (tolerate, withstand) aguentar, suportar; (cost) pagar; (invite) convidar; **to make a** ~ resistir; (fig) ater-se a um princípio; **to** ~ **for parliament** apresentar-se como candidato ao parlamento; **to** ~ **by** vi (be ready) estar a postos // vt fus (opinion) aferrar-se a; **to** ~ **for** vt fus (defend) apoiar; (signify) significar; (tolerate) tolerar, permitir; **to** ~ **in for** vt fus substituir; **to** ~ **out** vi (be prominent) destacar-se; **to** ~ **up** vi (rise) levantar-se; **to** ~ **up for** vt fus defender; **to** ~ **up to** vt fus enfrentar.

**standard** ['stændəd] n padrão m, critério; (flag) estandarte m; (degree) grau m // adj (size etc) padronizado, regular, normal; ~**s** npl (morals) valores mpl morais; ~**ize** vt padronizar, uniformizar; ~ **lamp** n abajur m de pé; ~ **of living** n padrão de vida.

**stand-by** ['stændbai] n (alert) alerta, aviso; **to be on** ~ estar de sobreaviso; ~ **ticket** n (AVIAT) passagem f stand-by or de lista de espera.

**stand-in** ['stændin] n suplente m/f; (CINEMA) double m/f.

**standing** ['stændiŋ] adj (upright) ereto (PT: -ct-), vertical; (on foot) em pé // n posição f, reputação f; **of many years'** ~ que leva muito tempo; ~ **order** n (at bank) instrução f permanente; ~ **orders** npl (MIL) regulamento sg geral; ~ **room** n lugar m em pé.

**stand:** ~**offish** adj incomunicável, reservado; ~**point** n ponto de vista; ~**still** n: **at a** ~**still** paralisado, parado; **to come to a** ~**still** ficar or estar paralisado.

**stank** [stæŋk] pt of **stink**.

**staple** ['steipl] n (for papers) grampo // adj (food etc) básico // vt grampear; **stapler** n grampeador m.

**star** [stɑːʳ] n estrela; (celebrity)

astro, estrela // *vi:* to ~ **in** ser a estrela em.

**starboard** ['stɑːbəd] *n* estibordo.

**starch** [stɑːtʃ] *n* amido, fécula, goma; ~**ed** *adj* (*collar*) engomado; ~**y** *adj* amiláceo.

**stardom** ['stɑːdəm] *n* estrelato, qualidade *f* de estrela.

**stare** [stɛə*] *n* olhar *m* fixo // *vt:* to ~ **at** olhar fixamente, fitar.

**starfish** ['stɑːfɪʃ] *n* estrela-do-mar *f.*

**stark** [stɑːk] *adj* (*bleak*) severo, áspero // *adv:* ~ **naked** completamente nu, em pêlo.

**starlight** ['stɑːlaɪt] *n:* **by** ~ à luz das estrelas.

**starling** ['stɑːlɪŋ] *n* estorninho.

**starry** ['stɑːrɪ] *adj* estrelado; ~**eyed** *adj* (*innocent*) deslumbrado.

**start** [stɑːt] *n* (*beginning*) princípio, começo; (*departure*) partida; (*sudden movement*) sobressalto, ímpeto; (*advantage*) vantagem *f* // *vt* começar, iniciar; (*cause*) causar; (*found*) fundar; (*engine*) ligar // *vi* (*begin*) começar, iniciar; (*with fright*) sobressaltar-se, assustar-se; (*train etc*) sair; to ~ **off** *vi* começar, principiar; (*leave*) sair, pôr-se a caminho; to ~ **up** *vi* começar; (*car: motor*) pegar, pôr-se em marcha // *vt* começar; (*car*) pôr em marcha; ~**er** *n* (*AUT*) arranque *m*; (*SPORT: official*) juiz(a) *m/f* da partida; (*: runner*) corredor(a) *m/f;* (*CULIN*) entrada; ~**ing point** *n* ponto de partida.

**startle** ['stɑːtl] *vt* assustar, aterrar; **startling** *adj* surpreendente.

**starvation** [stɑːˈveɪʃən] *n* fome *f*; (*MED*) inanição *f*; **starve** *vi* passar fome; (*to death*) morrer de fome // *vt* fazer passar fome; (*fig*) privar (*of* de); **I'm starving** estou morrendo de fome, estou com fome.

**state** [steɪt] *n* estado // *vt* (*say, declare*) afirmar, declarar; (*a case*) expor, apresentar; **the S**~**s** os

Estados Unidos; **to be in a** ~ estar agitado; ~**ly** *adj* majestoso, imponente; ~**ment** *n* afirmação *f*; (*LAW*) declaração *f*, balanço; **statesman** *n* estadista *m.*

**static** ['stætɪk] *n* (*RADIO*) interferência // *adj* estático; ~ **electricity** *n* eletricidade *f* estática.

**station** ['steɪʃən] *n* (*gen*) estação *f*; (*place*) posto, lugar *m*; (*RADIO*) emissora; (*rank*) posição *f* social // *vt* colocar, botar; (*MIL*) designar para um posto.

**stationary** ['steɪʃnərɪ] *adj* estacionário.

**stationer's (shop)** ['steɪʃənəz] *n* papelaria; **stationery** [-nərɪ] *n* artigos *mpl* de papelaria *or* para escrever.

**station master** *n* (*RAIL*) chefe *m* da estação.

**station wagon** *n* (*US*) camioneta, perua.

**statistic** [stəˈtɪstɪk] *n* estatística; ~**s** *npl* (*science*) estatística *sg*; ~**al** *adj* estatístico.

**statue** ['stætjuː] *n* estátua.

**stature** ['stætʃə*] *n* estatura, altura; (*fig*) tamanho.

**status** ['steɪtəs] *n* posição *f*, categoria; (*reputation*) reputação *f*, status *m*; (*the* ~ **quo** o status quo; ~ **symbol** *n* símbolo de prestígio.

**statute** ['stætjuːt] *n* estatuto, lei *f*; **statutory** *adj* estatutário.

**staunch** [stɔːntʃ] *adj* firme, constante.

**stave** [steɪv] *vt:* to ~ **off** (*attack*) repelir; (*threat*) evitar, protelar.

**stay** [steɪ] *n* (*period of time*) estadia, estada // *vi* (*remain*) ficar; (*as guest*) hospedar-se; (*spend some time*) demorar-se; to ~ **put** não se mexer; to ~ **the night** pernoitar; to ~ **behind** *vi* ficar atrás; to ~ **in** *vi* (*at home*) ficar em casa; to ~ **on** *vi* ficar; to ~ **out** *vi* (*of house*) ficar fora de casa; to ~ **up** *vi* (*at night*) velar, ficar acordado; ~**ing power** n resistência, "raça".

**steadfast** ['stɛdfɑːst] adj firme, estável, resoluto.

**steadily** ['stɛdɪlɪ] adv (firmly) firmemente; (unceasingly) sem parar; (fixedly) fixamente; (walk) normalmente; (drive) a uma velocidade constante.

**steady** ['stɛdɪ] adj (constant) constante, fixo; (unswerving) firme; (regular) regular; (person, character) sensato, equilibrado; (diligent) trabalhador(a); (calm) calmo, sereno // vt (hold) manter firme; (stabilize) estabilizar; (nerves) acalmar; **to ~ o.s.** on or against sth firmar-se em algo.

**steak** [steɪk] n (gen) filé m; (beef) bife m.

**steal** [stiːl], pt **stole**, pp **stolen** vt/i roubar.

**stealth** [stɛlθ] n: **by ~** furtivamente, às escondidas; ~**y** adj furtivo, secreto.

**steam** [stiːm] n vapor m; (mist) névoa // vt condensar umidade; (CULIN) cozer a vapor // vi exalar vapor; (ship): **to ~ along** avançar or mover-se (a vapor); ~ **engine** n máquina a vapor; ~**er** n vapor m, navio (a vapor); ~**roller** n rolo compressor (a vapor); ~**y** adj vaporoso; (room) cheio de vapor, úmido (Pt: hú-); (window) embaçado.

**steel** [stiːl] n aço // adj de aço; ~**works** n siderurgia.

**steep** [stiːp] adj íngreme, escarpado; (stair) empinado; (price) exorbitante // vt ensopar, embeber, impregnar.

**steeple** ['stiːpl] n campanário, torre f; ~**chase** n corrida de obstáculos; ~**jack** n consertador m de torres or de chaminés altas.

**steer** [stɪə*] vt guiar, dirigir, pilotar // vi conduzir; ~**ing** n (AUT) direção (Pt: -cç-) f; ~**ing wheel** n volante m.

**stellar** ['stɛlə*] adj estelar.

**stem** [stɛm] n (of plant) caule m, haste f; (of glass) pé m; (of pipe) tubo // vt deter, reter; (blood) estancar; **to ~ from** vt fus originar-se de.

**stench** [stɛntʃ] n fedor m.

**stencil** ['stɛnsl] n (typed) estêncil m; (lettering) gabarito de letra // vt imprimir com estêncil.

**stenographer** [stɛ'nɔgrəfə*] n (US) estenodatilógrafa, estenógrafa.

**step** [stɛp] n passo; (sound) passada, pisada; (stair) degrau m // vi: **to ~ forward** avançar, dar um passo em frente; ~**s** npl = **~ladder**; **to ~ down** vi (fig) retirar-se; **to ~ off** vt fus descer de; **to ~ on** vt fus pisar, calcar; **to ~ over** vt fus passar por cima de; **to ~ up** vt (increase) aumentar; ~**brother** n meio-irmão m; ~**daughter** n enteada; ~**father** n padrasto; ~**ladder** n escada portátil or de abrir; ~**mother** n madrasta; ~**ping stone** n pedra utilizada em passarelas; (fig) trampolim m; ~**sister** n meia-irmã f; ~**son** n enteado.

**stereo** ['stɛrɪəʊ] n estéreo // adj (also: ~**phonic**) estereofônico.

**stereotype** ['stɪərɪətaɪp] n estereótipo // vt estereotipar.

**sterile** ['stɛraɪl] adj estéril; **sterility** ['rɪlɪtɪ] n esterilidade f; **sterilization** [-'zeɪʃən] n esterilização f; **sterilize** ['stɛrɪlaɪz] vt esterilizar.

**sterling** ['stɜːlɪŋ] adj esterlino; (silver) de lei; (fig) genuíno, puro.

**stern** [stɜːn] adj severo, austero // n (NAUT) popa, ré f.

**stethoscope** ['stɛθəskəʊp] n estetoscópio.

**stew** [stjuː] n guisado, ensopado; (fig: mess) apuro, confusão f // vt/i guisar, ensopar; (fruit) cozinhar.

**steward** ['stjuəd] n (AVIAT) comissário de bordo; ~**ess** n aeromoça.

**stick** [stɪk] n pau m; (as weapon)

cacete *m*; (*walking* ~) bengala, cajado // (*vb*: *pt*, *pp* stuck) *vt* (*glue*) colar; (*thrust*): to ~ sth into cravar *or* enfiar algo em; (*col: put*) meter; (*col: tolerate*) agüentar, suportar, aturar // *vi* colar-se, aderir-se; (*come to a stop*) ficar parado; (*in mind etc*) gravar-se; (*pin etc*) pregar-se; to ~ out, ~ up *vi* estar saliente, projetar-se (*Pt*: -ct-); to ~ up for *vt* *fus* defender; ~er *n* etiqueta adesiva, adesivo.

**stickler** ['stiklə\*] *n*: to be a ~ for ser um defensor ferrenho de.

**stick-up** ['stikʌp] *n* assalto armado.

**sticky** ['stiki] *adj* pegajoso; (*label*) adesivo; (*fig*) difícil.

**stiff** [stif] *adj* rígido, forte; (*hard*) duro; (*difficult*) difícil; (*person*) inflexível, obstinado; (*price*) exorbitante; ~en *vt* endurecer; (*limb*) entumecer // *vi* enrijecer-se; (*grow stronger*) fortalecer-se; ~ness *n* rigidez *f*, inflexibilidade *f*; (*character*) indiferença.

**stifle** ['staifl] *vt* sufocar-se, abafar-se; **stifling** *adj* (*heat*) sufocante, abafado.

**stigma** ['stigmə], *pl* (*BOT, MED, REL*) ~ta [-tə], (*fig*) ~s *n* estigma *m*.

**stile** [stail] *n* degraus para passar por sobre uma cerca ou muro.

**stiletto** [sti'letəu] *n* estilete *m*; (*also*: ~ **heel**) salto (de sapato) fino.

**still** [stil] *adj* imóvel, quieto // *adv* (*up to this time*) até agora; (*even*) ainda; (*nonetheless*) entretanto, contudo; ~**born** *adj* nascido morto, natimorto; ~ **life** *n* natureza morta.

**stilt** [stilt] *n* perna de pau; (*pile*) estaca, suporte *m*.

**stilted** ['stiltid] *adj* afetado (*Pt*: -ct-).

**stimulant** ['stimjulənt] *n* estimulante *m*.

**stimulate** ['stimjuleit] *vt* estimular; **stimulating** *adj* estimulante; **stimulation** [-'leiʃən] *n* estímulo.

**stimulus** ['stimjuləs], *pl* -**li** [-lai] *n* estímulo, incentivo.

**sting** [stiŋ] *n* (*wound*) picada; (*pain*) ferroada, dor *f* forte; (*of insect*) ferrão *m* // (*vb*: *pt*, *pp* stung) *vt* picar // *vi* arder, doer.

**stingy** ['stindʒi] *adj* pão-duro, sovina.

**stink** [stiŋk] *n* fedor *m*, catinga // *vi*, *pt* stank, *pp* stunk feder, cheirar mal; ~**ing** *adj* fedorento, fétido.

**stint** [stint] *n* tarefa, parte *f*; to do one's ~ fazer a sua parte // *vi*: to ~ on restringir.

**stipend** ['staipend] *n* (*of vicar etc*) estipêndio, remuneração *f*.

**stipulate** ['stipjuleit] *vt* estipular, estabelecer; **stipulation** [-'leiʃən] *n* estipulação *f*, cláusula.

**stir** [stə:\*] *n* (*fig: agitation*) comoção *f*, rebuliço // *vt* (*tea etc*) mexer; (*fire*) atiçar; (*move*) mover; (*fig: emotions*) comover // *vi* mover-se, remexer-se; to ~ up *vt* excitar; (*trouble*) provocar; ~**ring** *adj* comovedor(a).

**stirrup** ['stirəp] *n* estribo.

**stitch** [stitʃ] *n* (*SEWING, KNITTING, MED*) ponto; (*pain*) pontada // *vt* costurar; (*MED*) dar pontos.

**stoat** [stəut] *n* arminho.

**stock** [stɔk] *n* (*COMM: reserves*) estoque *m*, provisão *f*; (: *selection*) sortimento; (*AGR*) gado; (*CULIN*) caldo; (*fig: lineage*) estirpe *f*, linhagem *f*; (*FINANCE*) fundo, capital *m*; (: *shares*) ações (*Pt*: -cç-) *fpl*; ~**s** *npl* tronco *sg*, canga *sg*; ~**s and shares** ações (*Pt*: -cç-) e valores // *adj* (*fig: reply etc*) trivial, comum // *vt* (*have in* ~) ter em estoque, estocar; (*supply*) prover, sortir; to take ~ of (*fig*) fazer um balanço, examinar; to ~ up with *vt* abastecer-se de.

**stockade** [stɔ'keid] *n* estacada.

**stockbroker** ['stɔkbrəukə\*] *n* corretor(a) (*Pt*: -ct-) *m/f* de valores *or* da Bolsa.

**stock exchange** *n* Bolsa de Valores.

**stock holder** n (US) acionista (Pt: -cc-) m/f.

**stocking** ['stɔkɪŋ] n meia.

**stock market** n Bolsa de Valores.

**stockpile** ['stɔkpaɪl] n reserva // vt acumular reservas, estocar.

**stocktaking** ['stɔkteɪkɪŋ] n (COMM) inventário, balanço.

**stocky** ['stɔkɪ] adj (strong) robusto; (short) atarracado.

**stodgy** ['stɔdʒɪ] adj maçante, enfadonho.

**stoical** ['stəʊɪkəl] adj estóico.

**stoke** [stəʊk] vt atiçar, alimentar.

**stole** [stəʊl] pt of **steal** // n estola.

**stolen** ['stəʊln] pp of **steal**.

**stomach** ['stʌmək] n (ANAT) estômago; (belly) barriga, ventre m; (appetite) apetite m // vt suportar, tolerar; ~ **ache** n dor f de estômago.

**stone** [stəʊn] n pedra; (in fruit) caroço; (weight) medida de peso (6.348kg) // adj de pedra, pétreo // vt apedrejar; ~**cold** adj gelado; ~**deaf** adj totalmente surdo; ~**work** n (art) cantaria; (stones) pedras fpl; **stony** adj pedregoso; (glance) glacial.

**stood** [stʊd] pt, pp of **stand**.

**stool** [stu:l] n tamborete m, banco.

**stoop** [stu:p] vi (also: **have a** ~) ser corcunda; (bend) debruçar-se, curvar-se.

**stop** [stɔp] n parada, interrupção f; (de ônibus etc) parada, ponto; (: Pt) paragem f; (in punctuation) ponto // vt parar, deter; (break off) paralisar, cessar; (block) tapar, obstruir; (also: **put a** ~ **to**) terminar, pôr fim a // vi parar-se, deter-se; (end) acabar-se; **to** ~ **doing sth** deixar de fazer algo; **to** ~ **dead** vi parar de repente; **to** ~ **off** vi fazer pausa; **to** ~ **up** vt (hole) tapar, obstruir; ~**gap** n substituto provisório; ~**lights** npl (AUT) luz f do sinal or da sinaleira; ~**over** n escala.

**stoppage** ['stɔpɪdʒ] n (strike) greve

f; (temporary stop) paralisação f; (of pay) suspensão f; (blockage) obstrução f.

**stopper** ['stɔpə*] n tampa, rolha.

**stopwatch** ['stɔpwɔtʃ] n cronômetro.

**storage** ['stɔːrɪdʒ] n armazenagem f.

**store** [stɔː*] n (stock) suprimento; (depot, large shop) armazém m; (reserve) estoque m; ~**s** npl víveres mpl, provisões fpl // vt armazenar; (keep) guardar; **to** ~ **up** vt acumular; ~**room** n depósito, almoxarifado.

**storey, story** (US) ['stɔːrɪ] n andar m.

**stork** [stɔːk] n cegonha.

**storm** [stɔːm] n tempestade f; (wind) borrasca, vendaval m; (fig) tumulto // vi (fig) enfurecer-se // vt tomar de assalto, assaltar; ~**cloud** n nuvem f de tempestade; ~**y** adj tempestuoso.

**story** ['stɔːrɪ] n história, estória; (LIT) narrativa; (joke) anedota, piada; (plot) enredo; (lie) mentira, conto; (US) = **storey**; ~**book** n livro de contos; ~**teller** n contador(a) m/f de estórias; (: liar) mentiroso/a.

**stout** [staʊt] adj (strong) sólido, forte; (fat) gordo, corpulento // n cerveja preta.

**stove** [stəʊv] n (for cooking) fogão m; (for heating) estufa, fogareiro.

**stow** [stəʊ] vt guardar, meter; (NAUT) estivar; ~**away** vi viajar como clandestino.

**straddle** ['strædl] vi escarranchar-se // vt cavalgar.

**straggle** ['strægl] vi (wander) vagar, perambular; (lag behind) ficar atrás, extraviar-se; **straggler** n pessoa extraviada; **straggling, straggly** adj (hair) rebelde, emaranhado.

**straight** [streɪt] adj reto (Pt: -ct-), correto (Pt: -ct-); (honest) honrado; (frank) franco, direto (Pt: -ct-);

(*simple*) simples *inv*; (*in order*) em ordem // *adv* direito, diretamente (*Pt*: -ct-); (*drink*) puro; **to put or get sth ~** falar com toda franqueza; **~ away, ~ off** (*at once*) imediatamente; **~en** *vt* (*also*: **~en out**) endireitar, pôr em ordem; **~-faced** *adj* inexpressivo, solene; **~forward** *adj* (*simple*) simples, direto (*Pt*: -ct-); (*honest*) honesto, franco.

**strain** [streɪn] *n* (*gen*) tensão *f*; (*TECH*) esforço; (*MED*) distensão *f*, luxação *f*; (*breed*) raça, estirpe *f* // *vt* (*back etc*) forçar, torcer, distender; (*tire*) extenuar; (*stretch*) puxar, estirar; (*filter*) filtrar // *vi* esforçar-se; **~s** *npl* (*MUS*) sons *mpl* musicais; **~ed** *adj* (*muscle*) distendido; (*laugh*) forçado; (*relations*) tenso; **~er** *n* coador *m*, peneira.

**strait** [streɪt] *n* (*GEO*) estreito; **~-jacket** *n* camisa-de-força; **~-laced** *adj* puritano, austero.

**strand** [strænd] *n* (*of thread*) fio; (*of hair*) madeixa; (*of rope*) cordão *m*; (*shore*) praia; **~ed** *adj* abandonado (sem recursos), desamparado.

**strange** [streɪndʒ] *adj* (*not known*) desconhecido; (*odd*) estranho, esquisito; **stranger** *n* desconhecido; (*from another area*) forasteiro/a.

**strangle** [ˈstræŋgl] *vt* estrangular; (*sobs etc*) sufocar; **~hold** *n* (*fig*) domínio total; **strangulation** [-ˈleɪʃən] *n* estrangulação *f*.

**strap** [stræp] *n* correia; (*of slip, dress*) alça // *vt* prender com correia, apertar; (*punish*) açoitar.

**strapping** [ˈstræpɪŋ] *adj* corpulento, robusto, forte.

**strata** [ˈstrɑːtə] *pl of* **stratum.**

**stratagem** [ˈstrætɪdʒəm] *n* estratagema *m*.

**strategic** [strəˈtiːdʒɪk] *adj* estratégico.

**strategy** [ˈstrætɪdʒɪ] *n* estratégia.

**stratum** [ˈstrɑːtəm], *pl* **-ta** *n* estrato, camada.

**straw** [strɔː] *n* palha; (*drinking ~*) canudo.

**strawberry** [ˈstrɔːbərɪ] *n* morango; (*plant*) morangueiro.

**stray** [streɪ] *adj* (*animal*) extraviado; (*bullet*) perdido; (*scattered*) disperso // *vi* extraviar-se, perder-se.

**streak** [striːk] *n* listra, traço; (*fig: of madness etc*) sinal *m* // *vt* listrar // *vi*: **~ past** passar como um raio; **~y** *adj* listrado.

**stream** [striːm] *n* riacho, córrego; (*jet*) jato (*Pt*: -cto-); (*current*) fluxo, corrente *f*; (*of people*) fluxo // *vt* (*SCOL*) classificar // *vi* correr, fluir; **to ~ in/out** (*people*) entrar/sair aos montões.

**streamer** [ˈstriːmə*] *n* serpentina; (*pennant*) flâmula.

**streamlined** [ˈstriːmlaɪnd] *adj* aerodinâmico.

**street** [striːt] *n* rua // *adj* da rua; **~car** (*US*) *n* bonde *m*; (*Pt*) eléctrico; **~ lamp** *n* poste *m*.

**strength** [streŋθ] *n* força; (*of girder, knot etc*) firmeza, resistência; **~en** *vt* fortalecer, intensificar.

**strenuous** [ˈstrɛnjuəs] *adj* (*tough*) árduo, estrênuo; (*energetic*) enérgico; (*determined*) tenaz.

**stress** [strɛs] *n* (*force, pressure*) pressão *f*; (*mental strain*) tensão *f*; (*accent*) ênfase *f*, acento; (*TECH*) tensão // *vt* realçar, dar ênfase a.

**stretch** [strɛtʃ] *n* (*of sand etc*) trecho // *vi* esticar-se; (*extend*) **to ~ to or as far as** estender-se até (a) // *vt* estirar, esticar; (*make demands of*) exigir o máximo de; **to ~ out** *vi* deitar-se // *vt* (*arm etc*) esticar; (*spread*) estirar.

**stretcher** [ˈstrɛtʃə*] *n* maca, padiola.

**strewn** [struːn] *adj*: **~ with** coberto or cheio de.

**stricken** ['strɪkən] adj (wounded) ferido; (ill) doente.

**strict** [strɪkt] adj (person) severo, rigoroso; (precise) exato (Pt: -ct-), preciso; ~**ly** adv (exactly) estritamente; (totally) terminantemente; (severely) rigorosamente; ~**ness** n exatidão (Pt: -ct-) f; rigor m, severidade f.

**stride** [straɪd] n passo largo // vi, pt **strode**, pp **stridden** ['strɪdn] andar a passos largos.

**strident** ['straɪdnt] adj estridente; (colour) berrante.

**strife** [straɪf] n luta, conflito.

**strike** [straɪk] n greve f; (of oil etc) descoberta; (attack) ataque m; (SPORT) golpe m // vb: pt, pp **struck** vt bater, golpear; (oil etc) descobrir; (obstacle) chocar-se com // vi entrar em greve; (attack) atacar; (clock) bater, dar (as horas); **to ~ a match** acender um fósforo; **to ~ out** vt cancelar, rasurar; **to ~ up** vt (MUS) começar a tocar; (conversation, friendship) travar; ~**breaker** n fura-greve m/f inv; **striker** n grevista m/f; (SPORT) atacante m/f; **striking** adj impressionante; (nasty) chocante; (colour) chamativo.

**string** [strɪŋ] n (gen) fio, corda; (row) série f, fileira // vt, pt, pp **strung**: **to ~ together** enfiar // vi: **to ~ out** estender-se; **the ~s** npl (MUS) os instrumentos de corda; **to pull ~s** (fig) usar pistolão; ~ **bean** n vagem f; ~(**ed**) **instrument** n (MUS) instrumento de corda.

**stringent** ['strɪndʒənt] adj severo, estrito.

**strip** [strɪp] n tira; (of land) faixa; (of metal) lâmina, tira // vt despir; (also: ~ **down**: machine) desmontar // vi despir-se; ~ **cartoon** n história em quadrinhos.

**stripe** [straɪp] n listra, faixa; (MIL) galão m; ~**d** adj listrado, com listras.

**stripper** ['strɪpə*] n artista m/f de striptease.

**striptease** ['strɪptiːz] n striptease m.

**strive** [straɪv], pt **strove**, pp **striven** ['strɪvn] vi: **to ~ to do sth** esforçar-se por or batalhar para fazer algo.

**strode** [strəud] pt of **stride**.

**stroke** [strəuk] n (blow) pancada, golpe m; (MED) ataque m apoplético (Pt: -pt-); (caress) carícia; (of pen) traço // vt acariciar, afagar; **at a ~** de repente, de golpe.

**stroll** [strəul] n volta, passeio // vi passear, dar uma volta; **stroller** n (US) carrinho.

**strong** [strɒŋ] adj forte; **they are 50 ~** são 50; ~**box** n cofre-forte f; ~**hold** n fortaleza; (fig) baluarte m; ~**ly** adv fortemente, vigorosamente; (believe) firmemente; ~**room** n caixa-forte f.

**strove** [strəuv] pt, pp of **strive**.

**struck** [strʌk] pt, pp of **strike**.

**structural** ['strʌktʃərəl] adj estrutural; **structure** n estrutura; (building) construção f.

**struggle** ['strʌgl] n luta, contenda // vi lutar, brigar.

**strum** [strʌm] vt (guitar) dedilhar.

**strung** [strʌŋ] pt, pp of **string**.

**strut** [strʌt] n escora, suporte m // vi pavonear-se, empertigar-se.

**stub** [stʌb] n (of ticket etc) canhoto; (of cigarette) toco, ponta; **to ~ out** vt apagar; **to ~ one's toe** tropeçar, dar topada.

**stubble** ['stʌbl] n restolho; (on chin) barba por fazer.

**stubborn** ['stʌbən] adj teimoso, cabeçudo, obstinado.

**stuck** [stʌk] pt, pp of **stick** // adj (jammed) engarrafado; ~**-up** adj convencido, metido, esnobe.

**stud** [stʌd] n (shirt ~) botão m; (of boot) cravo; (of horses) haras msg; (also: ~ **horse**) garanhão m // vt (fig): ~**ded with** salpicado de.

**student** ['stju:dənt] n estudante m/f // adj estudantil; ~**driver** n (US) principiante m/f.

**studio** ['stju:dɪəu] n estúdio m; (sculptor's) ateliê m.

**studious** ['stju:dɪəs] adj estudioso, aplicado; (studied) calculado; ~**ly** adv (carefully) com esmero.

**study** ['stʌdɪ] n (gen) estudo m // vt estudar; (examine) examinar, investigar // vi estudar.

**stuff** [stʌf] n matéria; (cloth) tecido; (substance) material m, substância // vt encher; (CULIN) rechear; (animals) empalhar; ~**ing** n recheio; ~**y** adj (room) abafado, mal ventilado; (person) rabugento, melindroso.

**stumble** ['stʌmbl] vi tropeçar, dar topada; **to** ~ **across** (fig) topar com; **stumbling block** n obstáculo, impedimento.

**stump** [stʌmp] n (of tree) toco; (of limb) coto // vt: **to be** ~**ed** ficar perplexo.

**stun** [stʌn] vt aturdir, pasmar.

**stung** [stʌŋ] pt, pp of **sting**.

**stunk** [stʌŋk] pp of **stink**.

**stunning** ['stʌnɪŋ] adj (fig) atordoante.

**stunt** [stʌnt] n façanha sensacional; (AVIAT) vôo acrobático; (publicity ~) truque m publicitário; ~**ed** adj atrofiado, retardado; ~**man** n dublê m.

**stupefy** ['stju:pɪfaɪ] vt deixar estupefato (Pt: -ct-).

**stupendous** [stju:'pɛndəs] adj assombroso, prodigioso, monumental.

**stupid** ['stju:pɪd] adj estúpido, idiota; ~**ity** [-'pɪdɪtɪ] n estupidez f; ~**ly** adv estupidamente.

**stupor** ['stju:pə*] n estupor m.

**sturdy** ['stə:dɪ] adj robusto, (firm) resoluto.

**stutter** ['stʌtə*] n gagueira, gaguez f // vi gaguejar.

**sty** [staɪ] n (for pigs) chiqueiro.

**stye** [staɪ] n (MED) terçol m.

**style** [staɪl] n estilo; **stylish** adj elegante, da moda.

**stylus** ['staɪləs] n (of record player) agulha.

**suave** [swɑ:v] adj suave, melífluo.

**sub...** [sʌb] pref sub...; ~**conscious** adj do subconsciente // n subconsciente m; ~**divide** vt subdividir; ~**division** n subdivisão f.

**subdue** [səb'dju:] vt subjugar; (passions) dominar; ~**d** adj (light) tênue; (person) submisso, subjugado.

**subject** ['sʌbdʒɪkt] n súdito (Pt: -bd-); (SCOL) assunto, tópico // vt [səb'dʒɛkt]: **to** ~ **sb to sth** submeter alguém a algo; **to be** ~ **to** (law) estar sujeito a; (person) ser propenso a; ~**ion** [-'dʒɛkʃən] n submissão f, dependência; ~**ive** adj subjetivo (Pt: -ct-); ~ **matter** n assunto; (content) conteúdo.

**subjugate** ['sʌbdʒugeɪt] vt subjugar, submeter.

**sublet** [sʌb'lɛt] vt sublocar.

**sublime** [sə'blaɪm] adj sublime.

**submachine gun** ['sʌbmə'ʃi:n] n metralhadora de mão.

**submarine** [sʌbmə'ri:n] n submarino.

**submerge** [səb'mə:dʒ] vt submergir; (flood) inundar // vi submergir-se.

**submission** [səb'mɪʃən] n submissão f; **submissive** [-'mɪsɪv] adj submisso.

**submit** [səb'mɪt] vt submeter // vi submeter-se.

**subnormal** [sʌb'nɔ:məl] adj anormal, subnormal; (backward) atrasado.

**subordinate** [sə'bɔ:dɪnət] adj, n subordinado/a.

**subpoena** [səb'pi:nə] (LAW) n intimação f judicial // vt intimar a comparecer judicialmente.

**subscribe** [səb'skraɪb] vi subscrever; **to** ~ **to** (opinion) concordar com; (fund) contribuir para; (newspaper) assinar;

**subscriber** n (to periodical, telephone) assinante m/f.

**subscription** [səb'skrɪpʃən] n subscrição (Pt: -pç-) f, assinatura.

**subsequent** ['sʌbsikwənt] adj subseqüente, posterior; ~ly adv mais tarde, depois.

**subside** [səb'saɪd] vi baixar; (flood) descer; (wind) acalmar-se; **subsidence** [-'saɪdns] n baixa.

**subsidiary** [səb'sɪdɪərɪ] n subsidiário, sucursal f.

**subsidize** [sʌb'sɪdaɪz] vt subsidiar; **subsidy** [-dɪ] n subsídio.

**subsistence** [səb'sɪstəns] n subsistência; (allowance) subsídio, ajuda de custo.

**substance** ['sʌbstəns] n substância; (fig) essência.

**substandard** [sʌb'stændəd] adj inferior ao padrão.

**substantial** [səb'stænʃl] adj substancial, essencial; (fig) importante; ~ly adv substancialmente.

**substantiate** [səb'stænʃieit] vt comprovar, justificar.

**substitute** [sʌb'stɪtju:t] n substituto; (person) suplente m/f // vt: to ~ A for B substituir B por A; **substitution** [-'tju:ʃən] n substituição f, troca.

**subterfuge** ['sʌbtəfju:dʒ] n subterfúgio.

**subterranean** [sʌbtə'reɪnɪən] adj subterrâneo.

**subtitle** ['sʌbtaɪtl] n subtítulo.

**subtle** ['sʌtl] adj sutil; ~ty n sutileza.

**subtract** [səb'trækt] vt subtrair, deduzir; ~ion [-'trækʃən] n subtração (Pt: -cç-) f, dedução f.

**suburb** ['sʌbə:b] n subúrbio, arrabalde m; ~an [sə'bə:bən] adj suburbano; (train etc) de subúrbio.

**subversive** [səb'və:sɪv] adj subversivo.

**subway** ['sʌbweɪ] n (Brit)

passagem f subterrânea; (US) metrô (Pt: -o) m.

**succeed** [sək'si:d] vi (person) ser bem sucedido, ter êxito; (plan) sair bem // vt suceder a; **to ~ in doing** conseguir fazer; ~ing adj (following) sucessivo, posterior.

**success** [sək'ses] n sucesso, êxito; (gain) triunfo; ~ful adj (venture) bem sucedido; **to be ~ful (in doing)** conseguir (fazer); ~fully adv com sucesso, com êxito.

**succession** [sək'seʃən] n (series) sucessão f, série f; (descendants) descendência; **successive** ['-sɛsɪv] adj sucessivo, consecutivo; **successor** [-'sɛsə*] n sucessor(a) m/f.

**succinct** [sək'sɪŋkt] adj sucinto.

**succulent** ['sʌkjulənt] adj suculento.

**succumb** [sə'kʌm] vi sucumbir.

**such** [sʌtʃ] adj, det tal, semelhante; (of that kind): ~ **a book** um livro parecido; ~ **books** tais livros; (so much): ~ **courage** tanta coragem; ~ **a long trip** uma viagem tão longa; ~ **a lot of** tanto; ~ **as** (like) tal como; **a noise** ~ **as** to um ruído tal que; **as** ~ adv como tal // pron os/as que; ~**-and**~ det tal e qual; **until** ~ **time as** até que.

**suck** [sʌk] vt chupar; (bottle) tragar, tomar; (breast) mamar; ~**er** n (BOT) rebento; (ZOOL) ventosa; (col) trouxa m/f, otário.

**suckle** ['sʌkl] vt amamentar.

**suction** ['sʌkʃən] n sucção f.

**sudden** ['sʌdn] adj (rapid) repentino, súbito; (unexpected) imprevisto; **all of a** ~, ~**ly** adv de repente; (unexpectedly) inesperadamente.

**suds** [sʌdz] npl água de sabão, espuma.

**sue** [su:] vt processar.

**suede** [sweɪd] n camurça.

**suet** ['suɪt] n sebo.

**suffer** ['sʌfə*] vt sofrer, padecer;

(*bear*) agüentar; (*allow*) permitir // *vi* sofrer, padecer; **~er** *n* sofredor(a) *m/f*; (*MED*) doente *m/f*, paciente *m/f*; **~ing** *n* sofrimento, padecimento; (*pain*) dor *f*.

**suffice** [səˈfaɪs] *vi* bastar, ser suficiente.

**sufficient** [səˈfɪʃənt] *adj* suficiente, bastante.

**suffix** [ˈsʌfɪks] *n* sufixo.

**suffocate** [ˈsʌfəkeɪt] *vi* sufocar-se, asfixiar-se; **suffocation** [-ˈkeɪʃən] *n* sufocação *f*, asfixia.

**suffrage** [ˈsʌfrədʒ] *n* sufrágio; (*vote*) direito de voto.

**sugar** [ˈʃugəˀ] *n* açúcar *m* // *vt* pôr açúcar em; **~ beet** *n* beterraba; **~ cane** *n* cana-de-açúcar *f*; **~y** *adj* açucarado.

**suggest** [səˈdʒest] *vt* sugerir; (*advise*) aconselhar; **~ion** [-ˈdʒestʃən] *n* insinuação *f*; (*hypnotic*) sugestão *f*; **~ive** *adj* sugestivo, (*pej*) indecente.

**suicidal** [suɪˈsaɪdl] *adj* suicida; **suicide** [ˈsuɪsaɪd] *n* suicídio; (*person*) suicida *m/f*.

**suit** [suːt] *n* (*man's*) terno; (*woman's*) conjunto; (*CARDS*) naipe *m* // *vt* (*gen*) convir a; (*clothes*) ficar bem a; (*adapt*): to **~ sth to** adaptar *or* acomodar algo a; **~able** *adj* conveniente, (*apt*) apropriado; **~ably** *adv* convenientemente, apropriadamente.

**suitcase** [ˈsuːtkeɪs] *n* mala, maleta.

**suite** [swiːt] *n* (*of rooms*) conjunto de salas; (*MUS*) suite *f*; (*furniture*): **bedroom/dining room ~** conjunto de quarto/de sala de jantar.

**suitor** [ˈsuːtəˀ] *n* pretendente *m*.

**sulk** [sʌlk] *vi* estar de mau humor; **~y** *adj* amuado, emburrado.

**sullen** [ˈsʌlən] *adj* rabujento, teimoso.

**sulphur, sulfur** (*US*) [ˈsʌlfəˀ] *n* enxofre *m*.

**sultan** [ˈsʌltən] *n* sultão *m*.

**sultana** [sʌlˈtɑːnə] *n* (*fruit*) passa.

**sultry** [ˈsʌltrɪ] *adj* (*weather*) abafado, mormacento; (*seductive*) sedutor(a).

**sum** [sʌm] *n* (*gen*) soma; (*total*) total *m*; to **~ up** *vt* sumariar, fazer um resumo; // *vi* resumir.

**summarize** [ˈsʌmərɑɪz] *vt* resumir.

**summary** [ˈsʌmərɪ] *n* resumo, sumário // *adj* (*justice*) sumário.

**summer** [ˈsʌməˀ] *n* verão *m* // *adj* estival; **~house** *n* (*in garden*) estufa; **~time** *n* (*season*) verão *m*; **~ time** *n* (*by clock*) horário de verão.

**summit** [ˈsʌmɪt] *n* topo, cume *m*; (*fig*) apogeu *m*; **~ (conference)** *n* (conferência de) cúpula.

**summon** [ˈsʌmən] *vt* (*person*) mandar chamar; (*meeting*) convocar; (*LAW*) citar; to **~ up** *vt* (*forces*) concentrar; (*courage*) armar-se de; **~s** *n* citação *f*, intimação *f* // *vt* citar, intimar.

**sump** [sʌmp] *n* (*AUT*) cárter *m*.

**sumptuous** [ˈsʌmptjuəs] *adj* suntuoso, magnífico, esplêndido.

**sun** [sʌn] *n* sol *m*; **~bathe** *vi* tomar banho de sol; **~burn** *n* (*painful*) queimadura; (*tan*) bronzeado; **~burnt** *adj* (*tanned*) bronzeado; (*painfully*) queimado.

**Sunday** [ˈsʌndɪ] *n* domingo.

**sundial** [ˈsʌndaɪəl] *n* relógio de sol.

**sundry** [ˈsʌndrɪ] *adj* vários, diversos; **all and ~** todos; **sundries** *npl* gêneros *mpl* diversos.

**sunflower** [ˈsʌnflauəˀ] *n* girassol *m*.

**sung** [sʌŋ] *pp of* **sing**.

**sunglasses** [ˈsʌnɡlɑːsɪz] *npl* óculos *mpl* de sol.

**sunk** [sʌŋk] *pp of* **sink**.

**sun**: **~light** *n* luz *f* do sol; **~lit** *adj* iluminado pelo sol; **~ny** *adj* cheio de sol; (*day*) ensolarado; (*fig*) alegre; **~rise** *n* nascer *m* do sol; **~set** *n* pôr *m* do sol; **~shade** *n* (*over table*) pára-sol *m*; **~shine** *n* luz f do sol; ~spot n mancha solar; ~stroke n insolação f; ~tan n bronzeado; ~tan oil n óleo de bronzear, bronzeador m.

super ['suːpə*] adj (col) bacana; (: Pt) muito giro.

superannuation [suːpərænjuˈeiʃən] n aposentadoria, pensão f.

superb [suːˈpəːb] adj soberbo, magnífico, excelente.

supercilious [suːpəˈsiliəs] adj (disdainful) arrogante, desdenhoso; (haughty) altivo.

superficial [suːpəˈfiʃl] adj superficial.

superfluous [suˈpəːfluəs] adj supérfluo, desnecessário.

superhuman [suːpəˈhjuːmən] adj sobre-humano.

superimpose ['suːpərimˈpəuz] vt sobrepor.

superintendent [suːpərinˈtendənt] n superintendente m/f; (POLICE) chefe m de polícia.

superior [suˈpiəriə*] adj superior; (smug) desdenhoso // n superior m; ~ity [-ˈɔriti] n superioridade f; desdém m.

superlative [suˈpəːlətiv] adj, n superlativo.

superman ['suːpəmæn] n super-homem m.

supermarket ['suːpəmɑːkit] n supermercado.

supernatural [suːpəˈnætʃərəl] adj sobrenatural.

superpower ['suːpəpauə*] n (POL) superpotência.

supersede [suːpəˈsiːd] vt suplantar.

supersonic [suːpəˈsɔnik] adj supersônico.

superstition [suːpəˈstiʃən] n superstição f; superstitious [-ʃəs] adj supersticioso.

supertanker ['suːpətæŋkə*] n superpetroleiro.

supervise ['suːpəvaiz] vt supervisar, supervisionar; supervision [-ˈviʒən] n supervisão f;

supervisor n supervisor(a) m/f; (academic) orientador(a) m/f.

supper ['sʌpə*] n jantar m, ceia; to have ~ jantar.

supple ['sʌpl] adj flexível.

supplement ['sʌplimənt] n suplemento // vt [sʌpliˈment] suprir; ~ary [-ˈmentəri] adj suplementar.

supplier [səˈplaiə*] n abastecedor(a) m/f, fornecedor(a) m/f; (COMM) distribuidor(a) m/f.

supply [səˈplai] vt (provide) abastecer, fornecer; (equip): to ~ (with) suprir de // n fornecimento, provisão f; (supplying) abastecimento f (teacher etc) suplente; supplies npl (food) víveres mpl, (MIL) apetrechos mpl; ~ and demand oferta e procura.

support [səˈpɔːt] n (moral, financial etc) apoio; (TECH) suporte m // vt apoiar; (financially) manter; (uphold) sustentar; ~er n (POL etc) partidário; (SPORT) torcedor(a) m/f.

suppose [səˈpəuz] vt/i (gen) supor; (imagine) imaginar; to be ~d to do sth dever fazer algo; ~dly [səˈpəuzidli] adv supostamente, pretensamente; supposing conj se, supondo-se que; supposition [sʌpəˈziʃən] n suposição f.

suppository [səˈpɔzitər*] n supositório.

suppress [səˈpres] vt suprimir, reprimir; (yawn) conter; ~ion [səˈpreʃən] n repressão f.

supremacy [suˈpreməsi] n supremacia f; supreme [-ˈpriːm] adj supremo.

surcharge ['səːtʃɑːdʒ] n sobrecarga; (extra tax) sobretaxa.

sure [ʃuə*] adj (gen) seguro; (definite, convinced) certo, firme; (aim) certeiro; ~! (of course) claro que sim!; ~-footed adj de andar seguro; ~ly adv (certainly) certamente.

surety ['ʃuərəti] n garantia, fiança; (person) fiador(a) m/f.

**surf** [sə:f] n surfe m.

**surface** ['sə:fis] n superfície f // vt (road) revestir // vi vir à superfície or à tona.

**surfboard** ['sə:fbɔ:d] n prancha de surfe.

**surfeit** ['sə:fit] n: **a ~ of** um excesso de.

**surfing** ['sə:fiŋ] n surfe m.

**surge** [sə:dʒ] n onda, vaga // vi encapelar-se, crescer de repente; **to ~ forward** avançar em tropel.

**surgeon** ['sə:dʒən] n cirurgião m; **dental ~** cirurgião-dentista m.

**surgery** ['sə:dʒəri] n cirurgia; (room) consultório; **to undergo ~** operar-se; **~ hours** npl horas fpl de consulta.

**surgical** ['sə:dʒikl] adj cirúrgico; **~ spirit** n álcool m.

**surly** ['sə:li] adj malcriado, rude.

**surmount** [sə:'maunt] vt superar, sobrepujar, vencer.

**surname** ['sə:neim] n sobrenome m.

**surpass** [sə:'pɑ:s] vt superar, exceder, ultrapassar.

**surplus** ['sə:pləs] n (gen) excedente m; (COMM) superávit m // adj excedente, de sobra.

**surprise** [sə'praiz] n (gen) surpresa; (astonishment) assombro // vt surpreender, assombrar; **surprising** adj surpreendente, inesperado.

**surrealist** [sə'riəlist] adj, n surrealista m/f.

**surrender** [sə'rendə*] n rendição f, entrega // vi render-se, entregar-se.

**surreptitious** [sʌrəp'tiʃəs] adj clandestino, furtivo.

**surround** [sə'raund] vt circundar, rodear; (MIL etc) cercar; **~ing** adj circundante, adjacente; **~ings** npl arredores mpl, cercanias fpl.

**surveillance** [sə:'veiləns] n vigilância.

**survey** ['sə:vei] n inspeção (Pt: -cç-) f, vistoria; (inquiry) pesquisa,

levantamento // vt [sə:'vei] (gen) inspecionar (Pt: -cc-), vistoriar; (look at) observar, contemplar; (make inquiries about) pesquisar, fazer um levantamento de; **~or** n agrimensor m.

**survival** [sə'vaivl] n sobrevivência; **survive** vi sobreviver; (custom etc) perdurar // vt sobreviver a; **survivor** n sobrevivente m/f.

**susceptible** [sə'septibl] adj: **~ (to)** suscetível (Pt: -pt-) or sensível a.

**suspect** ['sʌspekt] adj, n suspeito/a // vt [səs'pekt] suspeitar, desconfiar.

**suspend** [səs'pend] vt suspender; **~er belt** n cinta-liga; **~ers** npl ligas fpl; (US) suspensórios mpl.

**suspense** [səs'pens] n incerteza, ansiedade f; (in film etc) suspense m.

**suspension** [səs'penʃən] n (gen) suspensão f; **~ bridge** n ponte f pênsil.

**suspicion** [səs'piʃən] n (gen) suspeita; (distrust) receio; (trace) traço, vestígio; **suspicious** [-ʃəs] adj (suspecting) suspeitoso; (causing ~) suspeito.

**sustain** [səs'tein] vt sustentar, manter; (suffer) sofrer, agüentar; **~ed** adj (effort) contínuo.

**sustenance** ['sʌstinəns] n sustento.

**swab** [swɔb] n (MED) mecha de algodão.

**swagger** ['swægə*] vi andar com arrogância.

**swallow** ['swɔləu] n (bird) andorinha; (of food etc) bocado, trago // vt engolir, tragar; **to ~ up** vt (savings etc) consumir.

**swam** [swæm] pt of **swim**.

**swamp** [swɔmp] n pântano, brejo // vt atolar, inundar, sobrecarregar; **~y** adj pantanoso.

**swan** [swɔn] n cisne m.

**swap** [swɔp] n troca, permuta // vt: **to ~ (for)** trocar (por).

**swarm** [swɔ:m] n (of bees) enxame

m; (gen) multidão f // vi formigar, aglomerar-se.

**swarthy** ['swɔːðɪ] adj moreno.

**swastika** ['swɒstɪkə] n suástica.

**swat** [swɒt] vt esmagar, bater.

**sway** [sweɪ] vi balançar-se, oscilar, inclinar-se // vt (influence) influenciar, ter influência sobre.

**swear** [sweə*], pt **swore**, pp **sworn** vi jurar, xingar; **to ~ to sth** afirmar algo sob juramento; **~word** n palavrão m.

**sweat** [swet] n suor m // vi suar.

**sweater** ['swetə*] n suéter m/f.

**sweaty** ['swetɪ] adj suado.

**swede** [swiːd] n tipo de nabo.

**Swede** [swiːd] n sueco/a; **Sweden** n Suécia; **Swedish** adj sueco // n (LING) sueco.

**sweep** [swiːp] n (act) varredura (de arm) movimento circular; (range) extensão f, alcance m; (also: **chimney ~**) limpador m de chaminés // (vb: pt, pp **swept**) vt/i varrer; **to ~ away** vt varrer; (rub out) apagar; **to ~ past** vi passar rapidamente; (brush by) roçar; **to ~ up** vi recolher o lixo; **~ing** adj (gesture) abarcador(a); (victory) arrasador(a); (generalized) generalizado.

**sweet** [swiːt] n (candy) doce m, bombom m; (pudding) sobremesa // adj doce; (sugary) açucarado; (fresh) fresco; (fig) meigo, agradável; **~corn** n milho; **~en** vt adoçar; (add sugar to) pôr açúcar em; **~heart** n namorado/a; (in speech) amor m; **~ly** adv docemente; (gently) suavemente; **~ness** n (gen) doçura; (amount of sugar) o doce; **~pea** n ervilha-de-cheiro f.

**swell** [swel] n (of sea) vaga, onda // adj (col: excellent) excelente, elegante // (vb: pt **swelled**, pp **swollen** or **swelled**) vt inchar, inflar // vi inchar-se, dilatar-se; **~ing** n (MED) inchação f.

**sweltering** ['sweltərɪŋ] adj sufocante, mormacento; (burning) abrasador(a).

**swept** [swept] pt, pp of **sweep**.

**swerve** [swəːv] vi desviar-se bruscamente, dar uma guinada.

**swift** [swɪft] n (bird) andorinhão m // adj rápido, veloz; **~ness** n rapidez f, ligeireza.

**swig** [swɪg] n (col: drink) trago, gole m.

**swill** [swɪl] n água de lavagem // vt (also: **~ out**, **~ down**) lavar, limpar com água.

**swim** [swɪm] n: **to go for a ~** ir nadar // (vb: pt **swam**, pp **swum**) vi nadar; (head, room) sentir-se tonto // vt atravessar a nado; **~mer** n nadador(a) m/f; **~ming** n natação f; **~ming baths** npl piscina sg; **~ming cap** n touca de natação; **~ming costume** n (woman) maiô m; (man) sunga (de praia), calção m de banho; **~ming pool** n piscina; **~suit** n maiô m, calção m de banho.

**swindle** ['swɪndl] n fraude f // vt defraudar; **swindler** n vigarista m/f.

**swine** [swaɪn] n, pl inv porcos mpl; (col!) canalha sg, calhorda sg.

**swing** [swɪŋ] n (in playground) balanço; (movement) balanceio, oscilação f; (change of direction) virada; (rhythm) ritmo // (vb: pt, pp **swung**) vt fazer girar; (on a ~) balançar; (also: **~ round**) girar, rodar // vi balançar-se, mover-se; (also: **~ round**) voltar-se bruscamente; **to be in full ~** estar em plena atividade (Pt: -ct-); **~ bridge** n ponte f giratória; **~ door** n porta giratória.

**swipe** [swaɪp] n pancada violenta // vt (hit) bater com violência; (col: steal) afanar, roubar.

**swirl** [swəːl] vi redemoinhar.

**Swiss** [swɪs] adj, n, pl inv suíço/a.

**switch** [swɪtʃ] n (for light, radio etc) interruptor m; (change) mudança; (of hair) trança postiça // vt (*change*) mudar de; **to ~ off** *vt* apagar; (*engine*) desligar; **to ~ on** *vt* acender; (*engine, machine*) ligar; **~board** *n* (*TEL*) mesa telefônica.

**Switzerland** ['switsələnd] *n* Suíça.

**swivel** ['swivl] *vi* (*also:* **~ round**) girar (sobre um eixo), fazer pião.

**swollen** ['swəulən] *pp* of **swell**.

**swoon** [swu:n] *vi* desmaiar, desfalecer, ter uma síncope.

**swoop** [swu:p] *n* (*by police etc*) batida // *vi* (*also:* **~ down**) precipitar-se, cair.

**swop** [swɔp] = **swap**.

**sword** [sɔ:d] *n* espada; **~fish** *n* peixe-espada *m*.

**swore** [swɔ:*] *pt* of **swear**.

**sworn** [swɔ:n] *pp* of **swear**.

**swot** [swɔt] *vt, vi* trabalhar *or* estudar arduamente.

**swum** [swʌm] *pp* of **swim**.

**swung** [swʌŋ] *pt, pp* of **swing**.

**sycamore** ['sikəmɔ:*] *n* sicômoro.

**syllable** ['siləbl] *n* sílaba.

**syllabus** ['siləbəs] *n* programa *m* de estudos.

**symbol** ['simbl] *n* símbolo; **~ic(al)** [-'bɔlik(l)] *adj* simbólico; **~ism** *n* simbolismo; **~ize** *vt* simbolizar.

**symmetrical** [si'mɛtrikl] *adj* simétrico; **symmetry** ['simitri] *n* simetria.

**sympathetic** [simpə'θɛtik] *adj* solidário; (*pleasant*) simpático; **~ally** *adv* solidariamente.

**sympathize** ['simpəθaiz] *vi*: **to ~ with sb** compadecer-se de alguém; **sympathizer** *n* (*POL*) simpatizante *m/f*.

**sympathy** ['simpəθi] *n* (*pity*) compaixão *f*; (*liking*) simpatia; **with our deepest ~** com nossos mais profundos pêsames; **~ strike** *n* greve *f* de solidariedade.

**symphony**-['simfəni] *n* sinfonia; **~ orchestra** *n* orquestra sinfônica.

**symposium** [sim'pəuziəm] *n* simpósio.

**symptom** ['simptəm] *n* sintoma *m*;

(*sign*) indício; **~atic** [-'mætik] *adj* sintomático.

**synagogue** ['sinəgɔg] *n* sinagoga.

**synchronize** ['siŋkrənaiz] *vt* sincronizar // *vi*: **to ~ with** sincronizar-se com.

**syndicate** ['sindikit] *n* (*gen*) sindicato; (*of newspapers*) cadeia.

**syndrome** ['sindrəum] *n* síndrome *f*.

**synonym** ['sinənim] *n* sinônimo; **~ous** [si'nɔniməs] *adj*: **~ous (with)** sinônimo (de).

**synopsis** [si'nɔpsis], *pl* **-ses** [-si:z] *n* sinopse *f*.

**syntax** ['sintæks] *n* sintaxe *f*.

**synthesis** ['sinθəsis], *pl* **-ses** [-si:z] *n* síntese *f*.

**synthetic** [sin'θɛtik] *adj* sintético.

**syphilis** ['sifilis] *n* sífilis *f*.

**syphon** ['saifən] = **siphon**.

**Syria** ['siriə] *n* Síria; **~n** *adj, n* sírio/a.

**syringe** [si'rindʒ] *n* seringa.

**syrup** ['sirəp] *n* xarope *m*, melado, melaço.

**system** ['sistəm] *n* (*gen*) sistema *m*; (*method*) método; (*ANAT*) organismo; **~atic** [-'mætik] *adj* sistemático; **~s analyst** *n* analista *m/f* de sistemas.

# T

**ta** [ta:] *excl* (*Brit: col*) obrigado/a.

**tab** [tæb] *n* (*gen*) lingüeta, aba; (*label*) etiqueta; **to keep ~s on** (*fig*) vigiar.

**tabby** ['tæbi] *n* (*also:* **~ cat**) gato malhado *or* listrado.

**table** ['teibl] *n* mesa; (*of statistics etc*) quadro, tabela // *vt* (*motion etc*) apresentar; **to lay** *or* **set the ~** pôr a mesa; **~cloth** *n* toalha de mesa; **~ d'hôte** [ta:bl'dəut] *n* refeição *f* comercial; **~mat** *n* toalha individual; ~**spoon** n colher f de sopa; (also: ~**spoonful**: as measurement) colherada.

**tablet** ['tæblɪt] n (MED) tablete m, comprimido; (for writing) bloco; (of stone) lápide f.

**table**: ~ **tennis** n pingue-pongue m, tênis m de mesa; ~ **wine** n vinho de mesa.

**taboo** [tə'buː] n tabu m // adj tabu.

**tacit** ['tæsɪt] adj tácito, implícito.

**taciturn** ['tæsɪtəːn] adj taciturno.

**tack** [tæk] n (nail) tachinha, percevejo; (stitch) alinhavo; (NAUT) amura // vt (nail) prender com tachinha; (stitch) alinhavar // vi virar de bordo.

**tackle** ['tækl] n (gear) equipamento; (also: fishing ~) petrechos mpl; (for lifting) guincho ~ (RUGBY) ato de agarrar o adversário // vt (difficulty) enfrentar; (grapple with) atracar-se com; (RUGBY) agarrar.

**tacky** ['tækɪ] adj pegajoso, grudento.

**tact** [tækt] n tato (Pt: -ct-), diplomacia; ~**ful** adj com ta(c)to, diplomático; ~**fully** adv discretamente, com tato.

**tactical** ['tæktɪkl] adj tático (Pt: -ct-); **tactics** [-tɪks] n, npl tá(c)tica sg.

**tactless** ['tæktlɪs] adj sem ta(c)to, sem diplomacia; ~**ly** adv indiscretamente.

**tadpole** ['tædpəʊl] n girino.

**tag** [tæg] n (label) etiqueta; (loose end) rabo, penduricalho; to ~ **along with sb** acompanhar alguém.

**tail** [teɪl] n (gen) rabo; (of bird, comet etc) cauda; (of shirt, coat) aba // vt (follow) seguir bem de perto; to ~ **away**, ~ **off** (in size, quality etc) diminuir gradualmente; ~ **coat** n fraque m; ~ **end** n cauda, parte f final; ~**gate** n tampa traseira.

**tailor** ['teɪlə*] n alfaiate m; ~**ing** n (cut) feitio; (craft) ofício de alfaiate;

~-**made** adj feito sob medida; (fig) especial.

**tailwind** ['teɪlwɪnd] n vento de popa or de cauda.

**tainted** ['teɪntɪd] adj (food) estragado, passado; (water, air) poluído; (fig) manchado.

**take** [teɪk], pt **took**, pp **taken** vt (gen) tomar; (grab) pegar (em); (gain: prize) ganhar; (require: effort, courage) requerer, exigir; (tolerate) agüentar; (hold: passengers etc): **it ~s 50 people** cabem 50 pessoas; (accompany, bring, carry) levar; (exam) prestar; **to ~ sth from** (drawer etc) tirar algo de; (person) pegar algo de; **I ~ it that...** suponho que...; to ~ **after** vt fus parecer-se com; to ~ **apart** vt desmontar; to ~ **away** vt (remove) tirar; (carry off) levar; to ~ **back** vt (return) devolver; (one's words) retratar-se; (Pt: -act-); to ~ **down** vt (building) demolir; (letter etc) tomar por escrito; to ~ **in** vt (deceive) enganar; (understand) compreender; (include) abranger; (lodger) acolher, receber; to ~ **off** vi (AVIAT) decolar // vt (remove) tirar; (imitate) imitar; to ~ **on** vt (work) empreender; (employee) empregar; (opponent) desafiar; to ~ **out** vt tirar; (remove) extrair; to ~ **over** vt (business) tomar posse de // vi: to ~ **over from sb** suceder a alguém; to ~ **to** vt fus (person) simpatizar com; (activity) devotar-se a, viciar-se em; to ~ **up** vt (a dress) encurtar; (occupy: time, space) ocupar; (engage in: hobby etc) dedicar-se a; ~**away** adj (food) para levar; ~-**home pay** n salário líquido; ~**off** n (AVIAT) decolagem f; ~**over** n (COMM) absorção f, fusão f; ~**over bid** n oferta de compra.

**takings** ['teɪkɪŋz] npl (COMM) receita, renda.

**talc** [tælk] n (also: ~**um powder**) talco.

**tale** [teɪl] *n* (*story*) conto; (*account*) narrativa; **to tell ~s** (*fig*: *lie*) dizer mentiras.

**talent** ['tælnt] *n* talento, gênio; **~ed** *adj* talentoso.

**talk** [tɔːk] *n* (*gen*) conversa, fala; (*gossip*) mexerico, fofoca; (*conversation*) conversa, conversação *f* // *vi* (*speak*) falar; (*chatter*) bater papo, conversar; **to ~ about** falar sobre; **to ~ sb into doing sth** persuadir alguém de que deve fazer algo; **to ~ sb out of doing sth** dissuadir alguém de fazer algo; **to ~ shop** falar de assuntos profissionais; **to ~ over** *vt* discutir; **~ative** *adj* loquaz, tagarela.

**tall** [tɔːl] *adj* (*gen*) alto; (*tree*) grande; **to be 6 feet ~** medir 6 pés, ter 6 pés de altura; **~boy** *n* cômoda alta; **~ness** *n* altura; **~ story** *n* estória inverossímil.

**tally** ['tælɪ] *n* conta // *vi*: **to ~ (with)** conferir (com).

**talon** ['tælən] *n* garra.

**tambourine** [tæmbəˈriːn] *n* tamborim *m*, pandeiro.

**tame** [teɪm] *adj* (*mild*) manso; (*tamed*) domesticado; (*fig*: *story*, *style*) sem graça, insípido.

**tamper** ['tæmpə*] *vi*: **to ~ with** intrometer-se em.

**tampon** ['tæmpɔn] *n* tampão *m*.

**tan** [tæn] *n* (*also*: **sun~**) bronzeado // *vt* bronzear // *vi* bronzear-se // *adj* (*colour*) bronzeado, marrom claro.

**tandem** ['tændəm] *n* tandem *m*.

**tang** [tæŋ] *n* sabor *m* forte.

**tangerine** [tændʒəˈriːn] *n* tangerina, mexerica.

**tangible** ['tændʒəbl] *adj* tangível.

**tangle** ['tæŋgl] *n* emaranhado; **to get in(to) a ~** meter-se num rolo.

**tango** ['tæŋgəu] *n* tango.

**tank** [tæŋk] *n* (*water ~*) depósito, tanque *m*; (*for fish*) aquário; (*MIL*) tanque *m*.

**tanker** ['tæŋkə*] *n* (*ship*) navio-

tanque *m*; (*truck*) caminhão-tanque *m*.

**tanned** [tænd] *adj* (*skin*) moreno, bronzeado.

**tantalizing** ['tæntəlaɪzɪŋ] *adj* tentador(a).

**tantamount** ['tæntəmaunt] *adj*: **~ to** equivalente a.

**tantrum** ['tæntrəm] *n* chilique *m*, birra.

**tap** [tæp] *n* (*on sink etc*) torneira; (*gentle blow*) palmadinha; (*gas ~*) chave *f* // *vt* dar palmadinha em, bater de leve; (*resources*) utilizar, explorar; **~-dancing** *n* sapateado.

**tape** [teɪp] *n* fita; (*also*: **magnetic ~**) fita magnética; (*sticky ~*) fita adesiva // *vt* (*record*) gravar (em fita); **~ measure** *n* fita métrica, trena.

**taper** ['teɪpə*] *n* círio // *vi* afilar-se, estreitar-se.

**tape recorder** ['teɪprɪkɔːdə*] *n* gravador *m*.

**tapered** ['teɪpəd], **tapering** ['teɪpərɪŋ] *adj* afilado.

**tapestry** ['tæpɪstrɪ] *n* (*object*) tapete *m* de parede; (*art*) tapeçaria.

**tapioca** [tæpɪˈəukə] *n* tapioca.

**tar** [tɑː] *n* alcatrão *m*, piche *m*.

**tarantula** [təˈræntjulə] *n* tarântula.

**target** ['tɑːgɪt] *n* (*gen*) alvo, mira; **~ practice** tiro ao alvo.

**tariff** ['tærɪf] *n* tarifa.

**tarmac** ['tɑːmæk] *n* (*on road*) macadame *m* betuminoso; (*AVIAT*) pista de aterrissagem.

**tarnish** ['tɑːnɪʃ] *vt* perder o brilho.

**tarpaulin** [tɑːˈpɔːlɪn] *n* lona encerada or alcatroada.

**tarragon** ['tærəgən] *n* estragão *m*.

**tart** [tɑːt] *n* (*CULIN*) torta; (*col*: *pej*: *woman*) prostituta // *adj* (*flavour*) ácido, azedo.

**tartan** ['tɑːtn] *n* pano escocês axadrezado, tartan *m* // *adj* axadrezado.

**tartar** ['tɑːtə*] *n* (*on teeth*) tártaro; **~(e) sauce** *n* molho tártaro.

**task** [tɑ:sk] *n* tarefa, dever *m*; **to take to** ~ repreender; ~ **force** *n* (*MIL. POLICE*) força-tarefa.

**tassel** ['tæsl] *n* borla, pendão *m*.

**taste** [teist] *n* sabor *m*, gosto; (*also:* **after**~) gosto residual; (*sip*) golinho; (*fig: glimpse, idea*) amostra, idéia // *vt* provar // *vi:* **to** ~ **of** or **like** (*fish etc*) ter gosto de, saber a; **you can** ~ **the garlic (in it)** sente-se o gosto de alho; **can I have a** ~ **of this wine?** posso provar o vinho?; **to have a** ~ **for** sentir predileção por; **in good/bad** ~ **de bom/mau gosto; ~ful** *adj* de bom gosto; ~**fully** *adv* com bom gosto; ~**less** *adj* (*food*) insípido, insosso; (*remark*) de mau gosto; **tasty** *adj* saboroso, delicioso.

**tattered** ['tætəd] *adj* see **tatters**.

**tatters** ['tætəz] *npl:* **in** ~ (*also:* **tattered**) esfarrapado.

**tattoo** [tə'tu:] *n* tatuagem *f*; (*spectacle*) espetáculo (*Pt:* -ct-) militar // *vt* tatuar.

**tatty** ['tæti] *adj* (*col: worn*) surrado; (*: dirty*) enxovalhado.

**taught** [tɔ:t] *pt, pp of* **teach**.

**taunt** [tɔ:nt] *n* zombaria, escárnio // *vt* zombar de, mofar de.

**Taurus** ['tɔ:rəs] *n* Touro.

**taut** [tɔ:t] *adj* esticado, retesado.

**tawdry** ['tɔ:dri] *adj* de mau gosto, espalhafatoso, berrante.

**tawny** ['tɔ:ni] *adj* moreno, trigueiro.

**tax** [tæks] *n* imposto // *vt* lançar imposto sobre, tributar; (*fig: test*) sobrecarregar; (*: patience*) esgotar; **direct** ~ contribuição *f* direta (*Pt:* -ct-); ~**ation** [-'seiʃən] *n* impostos *mpl;* ~ **collector** *n* cobrador(a) *m/f* de impostos; ~**free** *adj* isento de imposto.

**taxi** ['tæksi] *n* táxi *m* // *vi* (*AVIAT*) taxiar.

**taxidermist** ['tæksidə:mist] *n* taxidermista *m/f*.

**taxi:** ~ **driver** *n* motorista *m/f* de táxi; ~ **rank,** ~ **stand** *n* ponto de táxi.

**tax:** ~ **payer** *n* contribuinte *m/f;* ~ **return** *n* declaração *f* de rendimentos.

**TB** *abbr of* **tuberculosis.**

**tea** [ti:] *n* chá *m;* (*snack*) lanche *m;* **high** ~ jantar-lanche *m;* ~ **bag** *n* saquinho de chá; ~ **break** *n* pausa para o chá; ~**cake** *n* bolo para o chá.

**teach** [ti:tʃ], *pt, pp* **taught** *vt:* **to** ~ **sb sth,** ~ **sth to sb** ensinar algo a alguém // *vi* ensinar; (*be a teacher*) lecionar (*Pt:* -cc-); ~**er** *n* professor(a) *m/f;* ~**ing** *n* ensino.

**tea:** ~ **cosy** *n* coberta do bule, abafador *m;* ~**cup** *n* xícara de chá.

**teak** [ti:k] *n* (madeira) de teca.

**tea leaves** *npl* folhas *fpl* de chá.

**team** [ti:m] *n* equipe *f*, time *m;* (*of animals*) parelha; ~**work** *n* trabalho de equipe.

**teapot** ['ti:pɔt] *n* bule *m* de chá.

**tear** [tɛə*] *n* rasgão *m*, ruptura // [tiə*] *n* lágrima // (*vb: pt* **tore,** *pp* **torn**) *vt* rasgar // *vi* rasgar-se, despedaçar-se; **in** ~**s** chorando, em lágrimas; **to burst into** ~**s** romper em lágrimas; **to** ~ **along** *vi* (*rush*) precipitar-se; ~**ful** *adj* choroso; ~**gas** *n* gás *m* lacrimogênio.

**tearoom** ['ti:ru:m] *n* salão *m* de chá.

**tease** [ti:z] *n* gozador(a) *m/f* // *vt* gozar (de).

**tea:** ~**spoon** *n* colher *f* de chá; (*also:* ~**spoonful:** *as measurement*) (conteúdo de) colher de chá.

**teat** [ti:t] *n* (*of bottle*) bico (de mamadeira).

**tea:** ~**time** *n* hora do chá; ~ **towel** *n* pano de prato.

**technical** ['tɛknikl] *adj* técnico; ~**ity** [-'kæliti] *n* detalhe *m* técnico; ~**ly** *adv* tecnicamente.

**technician** [tɛk'niʃn] *n* técnico/a.

**technique** [tɛk'ni:k] *n* técnica.

**technological** [tɛknə'lɔdʒikl] *adj* tecnológico; **technology** [-'nɔlədʒi] *n* tecnologia.

**teddy (bear)** ['tedɪ] n ursinho de pelúcia.

**tedious** ['ti:dɪəs] adj maçante, chato.

**tee** [ti:] n (GOLF) montículo.

**teem** [ti:m] vi abundar, pulular; to ~ with abundar em; it is ~ing (with rain) está chovendo a cântaros.

**teenage** ['ti:neɪdʒ] adj (fashions etc) de or para adolescentes; **teenager** n jovem m/f or adolescente m/f (entre 13 e 19 anos); (col) brotinho, broto.

**teens** [ti:nz] npl: to be in one's ~ estar entre os 13 e 19 anos or na adolescência.

**tee-shirt** ['ti:ʃə:t] n = **T-shirt**.

**teeter** ['ti:tə*] vi balançar-se.

**teeth** [ti:θ] pl of **tooth**.

**teethe** [ti:ð] vi nascer dentes.

**teething** ['ti:ðɪŋ] ~ **ring** n mastigador m para dentição; ~ **troubles** npl (fig) dificuldades fpl iniciais.

**teetotal** ['ti:'təutl] adj (person) abstêmio.

**telecommunications** ['telɪkəmju:nɪ'keɪʃənz] n telecomunicações fpl.

**telegram** ['telɪgræm] n telegrama m.

**telegraph** ['telɪgrɑ:f] n telégrafo; ~**ic** [-'græfɪk] adj telegráfico; ~ **pole** n poste m de telégrafos.

**telepathic** ['telɪ'pæθɪk] adj telepático; **telepathy** [tə'lepəθɪ] n telepatia.

**telephone** ['telɪfəun] n telefone m // vt (person) telefonar para, chamar ao telefone; (message) telefonar; ~ **booth**, ~ **box** n cabine f telefônica; ~ **call** n telefonema; ~ **directory** n guia telefônica; (Pt) lista telefónica; ~ **exchange** n centro telefônico; ~ **number** n número de telefone; **telephonist** [tə'lefənɪst] n telefonista m/f.

**telephoto** ['telɪ'fəutəu] adj: ~ **lens** teleobjetivo (Pt: -ct-).

**teleprinter** ['telɪprɪntə*] n teletipo.

**telescope** ['telɪskəup] n telescópio; **telescopic** [-'skɔpɪk] adj telescópico.

**televise** ['telɪvaɪz] vt televisar.

**television** ['telɪvɪʒən] n televisão f; ~ **set** n (aparelho de) televisão f, televisor m.

**telex** ['teleks] n telex m.

**tell** [tel], pt, pp **told** vt dizer; (relate: story) contar; (distinguish): to ~ **sth from** distinguir algo de // vi (have effect) produzir efeito; to ~ **sb to do** sth mandar alguém fazer algo; to ~ **sb off** repreender or dar bronca em alguém; ~**er** n (in bank) caixa m/f; ~**ing** adj (impressive) impressionante; (remark, detail) revelador(a); ~**tale** adj (sign) denunciador(a), revelador(a).

**telly** ['telɪ] n (col) abbr of **television**.

**temerity** [tə'merɪtɪ] n temeridade f.

**temper** ['tempə*] n (nature) temperamento; (mood) humor m; (bad ~) mau gênio; (fit of anger) cólera; (of child) birra // vt (moderate) moderar; **to be in a** ~ estar de mau humor; **to lose one's** ~ perder a paciência or a calma.

**temperament** ['tempərəmənt] n (nature) temperamento; ~**al** [-'mentl] adj temperamental.

**temperance** ['tempərns] n moderação f; (in drinking) sobriedade f.

**temperate** ['temprət] adj moderado; (climate) temperado.

**temperature** ['temprətʃə*] n temperatura; **to have** or **run a** ~ ter febre.

**tempered** ['tempəd] adj (steel) temperado.

**tempest** ['tempɪst] n tempestade f.

**temple** ['templ] n (building) templo; (ANAT) têmpora.

**tempo** ['tempəu], pl ~**s** or **tempi** [-pi:] n tempo; (fig: of life etc) ritmo.

**temporal** ['tempərl] *adj* temporal.

**temporarily** ['tempərərɪlɪ] *adv* temporariamente.

**temporary** ['tempərərɪ] *adj* temporário, efêmero; *(passing)* transitório; *(worker)* provisório.

**tempt** [tempt] *vt* tentar; **to ~ sb into doing sth** tentar *or* induzir alguém a fazer algo; **~ation** [-'teɪʃən] *n* tentação *f*; **~ing** *adj* tentador(a).

**ten** [ten] *num* dez.

**tenable** ['tenəbl] *adj* sustentável.

**tenacious** [tə'neɪʃəs] *adj* tenaz; **tenacity** [-'næsɪtɪ] *n* tenacidade *f*.

**tenancy** ['tenənsɪ] *n* aluguel *m*; *(of house)* locação *f*; **tenant** *n* *(rent-payer)* inquilino/a, locatário/a; *(occupant)* ocupante *m/f*.

**tend** [tend] *vt* tender // *vi*: **to ~ to do sth** tender a fazer algo.

**tendency** ['tendənsɪ] *n* tendência.

**tender** ['tendə*] *adj* macio, tenro; *(delicate)* delicado, meigo; *(gentle)* terno; *(sore)* sensível, dolorido; *(affectionate)* carinhoso, afetuoso *(Pt:* -ct-*); (meat)* tenro // *n (COMM: offer)* oferta, proposta; *(money)*: **legal ~** moeda corrente *or* legal // *vt* oferecer; **~ize** *vt (CULIN)* amaciar; **~ness** *n* ternura; *(of meat)* maciez *f*.

**tendon** ['tendən] *n* tendão *m*.

**tenement** ['tenəmənt] *n* conjunto habitacional.

**tennis** ['tenɪs] *n* tênis *m*; **~ ball** *n* bola de tênis; **~ court** *n* quadra de tênis; **~ racket** *n* raquete *f* de tênis.

**tenor** ['tenə*] *n (MUS)* tenor *m*.

**tenpin bowling** ['tenpɪn-] *n* boliche *m* com 10 paus.

**tense** [tens] *adj* tenso; *(stretched)* estirado, esticado; *(stiff)* rígido, teso // *n (LING)* tempo; **~ness** *n* tensão *f*.

**tension** ['tenʃən] *n* tensão *f*.

**tent** [tent] *n* tenda, barraca.

**tentacle** ['tentəkl] *n* tentáculo.

**tentative** ['tentətɪv] *adj* *(conclusion)* provisório, tentativo.

**tenterhooks** ['tentəhuks] *npl*: **on ~** em suspense.

**tenth** [tenθ] *adj* décimo.

**tent**: **~ peg** *n* estaca; **~ pole** *n* pau *m*.

**tenuous** ['tenjuəs] *adj* tênue.

**tenure** ['tenjuə*] *n* posse *f*; *(time)* ocupação *f*.

**tepid** ['tepɪd] *adj* tépido, morno.

**term** [təːm] *n (limit)* limite *m*; *(COMM)* prazo; *(word)* termo; *(period)* período; *(SCOL)* trimestre *m* // *vt* denominar; **~s** *npl (conditions)* condições *fpl*; *(COMM)* cláusulas *fpl*, termos *mpl*; **in the short/long ~** a curto/longo prazo; **to be on good ~s with sb** dar-se bem com alguém; **to come to ~s with** *(person)* chegar a um acordo com; *(problem)* adaptar-se a.

**terminal** ['təːmɪnl] *adj* terminal; *(disease)* mortal, letal // *n (ELEC)* borne *m*; *(also:* **air ~**) terminal *m*; *(also:* **coach ~**) estação *f* terminal.

**terminate** ['təːmɪneɪt] *vt* terminar, pôr fim a // *vi*: **to ~ in** acabar em; **termination** [-'neɪʃən] *n* término; *(of contract)* conclusão *f*.

**terminology** [təːmɪ'nɔlədʒɪ] *n* terminologia, nomenclatura.

**terminus** ['təːmɪnəs], *pl* **-mini** [-mɪnaɪ] *n* término, terminal *m*.

**termite** ['təːmaɪt] *n* cupim *m*.

**terrace** ['terəs] *n* terraço; *(row of houses)* renque *m* de casas; **the ~s** *(SPORT)* a geral; **~ed** *adj* de duas águas; *(garden)* em terraços.

**terrain** [te'reɪn] *n* terreno.

**terrible** ['terɪbl] *adj* terrível, horroroso; *(fam)* travesso; **terribly** *adv* terrivelmente; *(very badly)* pessimamente.

**terrier** ['terɪə*] *n* terrier *m*.

**terrific** [tə'rɪfɪk] *adj* terrível, magnífico; *(wonderful)* maravilhoso.

**terrify** ['terɪfaɪ] *vt* aterrorizar.

**territorial** [terɪ'təːrɪəl] *adj* territorial.

**territory** ['terɪtərɪ] *n* território.

**terror** [ˈtɛrə*] n terror m; ~**ism** n terrorismo; ~**ist** n terrorista m/f; ~**ize** vt aterrorizar.

**terse** [təːs] adj (style) conciso, sucinto; (reply) brusco.

**test** [tɛst] n (trial, check) prova, ensaio; (: of goods in factory) controle m; (of courage etc, CHEM) prova; (MED) exame m; (exam) teste m, prova; (also: driving ~) exame de motorista // vt testar, pôr à prova.

**testament** [ˈtɛstəmənt] n testamento; **the Old/New T~** o Velho/Novo Testamento.

**testicle** [ˈtɛstɪkl] n testículo.

**testify** [ˈtɛstɪfaɪ] vi (LAW) prestar declaração, testemunhar; **to ~ to sth** afirmar ou asseverar algo.

**testimonial** [tɛstɪˈməunɪəl] n (reference) carta de recomendação; (gift) obséquio, tributo.

**testimony** [ˈtɛstɪmənɪ] n (LAW) testemunho, depoimento.

**test:** ~ **match** n (CRICKET, RUGBY) jogo internacional; ~ **pilot** n piloto de prova; ~ **tube** n proveta, tubo de ensaio.

**testy** [ˈtɛstɪ] adj rabugento, irritável.

**tetanus** [ˈtɛtənəs] n tétano.

**tether** [ˈtɛðə*] vt prender com corda // n: **at the end of one's** ~ a ponto de perder a paciência ou as estribeiras.

**text** [tɛkst] n texto; ~**book** n livro didático (Pt: -ct-), compêndio.

**textiles** [ˈtɛkstaɪlz] npl têxteis mpl, tecidos mpl.

**texture** [ˈtɛkstʃə*] n textura.

**Thai** [taɪ] adj, n tailandês/esa m/f; ~**land** n Tailândia.

**Thames** [tɛmz] n: **the** ~ o Tâmisa m.

**than** [ðæn, ðən] conj do que; (with numerals): **more** ~ **10**/once mais de 10/uma vez; **I have more/less** ~ **you** tenho mais/menos (do) que você.

**thank** [θæŋk] vt agradecer; ~ **you**

(very much) muito obrigado/a; ~**s** npl agradecimento, graças fpl; ~**s to prep** graças a; ~**ful** adj: ~**ful (for)** agradecido (por); ~**less** adj ingrato; **Thanksgiving (Day)** n dia m de ação (Pt: -cç-) de graças.

**that** [ðæt, ðət] conj que // det esse/essa; (more remote) aquele/aquela // pron esse/essa, aquele/aquela; (neuter) isso, aquilo; (relative) que, quem, o qual/a qual etc; (with time): **on the day** ~ **he came** no dia em que ele veio // adv: ~ **high** dessa altura, até essa altura; **it's about** ~ **high** é mais ou menos dessa altura; **what's** ~? o que é isso?; **who's** ~? quem é?; **is** ~ **you?** é você?; (formal) é o/a senhor(a)?; ~'s **what he said** foi isso o que ele disse; **all** ~ tudo isso; **I can't work** ~ much não posso trabalhar tanto.

**thatched** [θætʃt] adj (roof) de sapê, colmado; ~ **cottage** n chalé m com telhado de sapê ou de colmo.

**thaw** [θɔː] n degelo // vi (ice) derreter-se; (food) descongelar-se // vt (food) descongelar.

**the** [ðiː, ðə] def art o/a; (pl) os/as; ~ **sooner** ~ **better** quanto mais cedo, melhor.

**theatre, theater** (US) [ˈθɪətə*] n teatro; ~**-goer** n freqüentador(a) m/f de teatro.

**theatrical** [θɪˈætrɪkl] adj teatral.

**theft** [θɛft] n roubo.

**their** [ðɛə*] adj seu/sua; ~**s** pron (o) seu/(a) sua; **a friend of** ~**s** um amigo seu/deles.

**them** [ðɛm, ðəm] pron (direct) os/as; (indirect) lhes; (stressed, after prep) a eles/a elas; **I see** ~ eu os vejo; **give** ~ **the book** dê o livro a eles.

**theme** [θiːm] n tema m; ~ **song** n tema musical.

**themselves** [ðəmˈsɛlvz] pl pron (subject) eles mesmos/elas mesmas; (*complement*) se; (*after prep*) si (mesmos/as).

**then** [ðɛn] *adv* (*at that time*) então; (*next*) em seguida; (*later*) logo, depois; (*and also*) além disso // *conj* (*therefore*) então, nesse caso, portanto // *adj*: the ~ president o então presidente; **from** ~ **on** a partir de então.

**theological** [θɪəˈlɔdʒɪkl] *adj* teológico; **theology** [θɪˈɔlədʒɪ] *n* teologia.

**theorem** [ˈθɪərəm] *n* teorema *m*.

**theoretical** [θɪəˈrɛtɪkl] *adj* teórico; **theorize** [ˈθɪəraɪz] *vi* teorizar, elaborar uma teoria; **theory** [ˈθɪərɪ] *n* teoria.

**therapeutic(al)** [θɛrəˈpjuːtɪk(l)] *adj* terapêutico.

**therapist** [ˈθɛrəpɪst] *n* terapeuta *m/f*; **therapy** *n* terapia.

**there** [ðɛəˈ] *adv* aí, ali, lá; ~, ~! calma!; **it's** ~ está aí; ~ **is**, ~ **are** há; ~ **he is** lá está ele; **on/in** ~ lá or aí encima/dentro; ~**abouts** *adv* por aí; ~**after** *adv* depois disso; ~**fore** *adv* portanto; ~**'s** = ~ **is**; ~ **has**.

**thermal** [ˈθəːml] *adj* termal, térmico.

**thermometer** [θəˈmɔmɪtə*] *n* termômetro.

**Thermos** [ˈθəːmɔs] *n* garrafa térmica.

**thermostat** [ˈθəːməustæt] *n* termostato.

**thesaurus** [θɪˈsɔːrəs] *n* tesouro.

**these** [ðiːz] *pl det, pron* estes/estas.

**thesis** [ˈθiːsɪs], *pl* **-ses** [-siːz] *n* tese *f*.

**they** [ðeɪ] *pl pron* eles/elas; (*stressed*) eles (mesmos)/elas (mesmas); ~ **say that...** (*it is said that*) diz-se que..., dizem que...; ~**'d** = they had; they would; ~**'ll** = they shall, they will; ~**'re** = they are; ~**'ve** = they have.

**thick** [θɪk] *adj* espesso, grosso; (*fat*) gordo; (*dense*) denso, compacto; (*stupid*) estúpido, bronco // *n*: **in the** ~ **of the battle** em plena batalha; **it's 20 cm** ~ tem 20 cm de espessura; ~**en** *vi* espessar-se // *vt* (*sauce etc*) engrossar; ~**ness** *n* espessura, grossura; ~**set** *adj* troncudo; ~**skinned** *adj* (*fig*) insensível, indiferente.

**thief** [θiːf], *pl* **thieves** [θiːvz] *n* ladrão/ladra *m/f*.

**thieving** [ˈθiːvɪŋ] *n* roubo, furto.

**thigh** [θaɪ] *n* coxa.

**thimble** [ˈθɪmbl] *n* dedal *m*.

**thin** [θɪn] *adj* (*gen*) magro; (*watery*) aguado; (*light*) tênue; (*hair, crowd*) escasso, ralo; (*fog*) pouco denso // *vt*: **to** ~ (**down**) (*sauce, paint*) diluir.

**thing** [θɪŋ] *n* (*gen*) coisa; (*object*) objeto (*Pt*: -ct-), artigo; (*matter*) assunto, negócio; (*mania*) mania; ~**s** *npl* (*belongings*) pertences *mpl*; **the best** ~ **would be to...** o melhor seria...; **how are** ~**s?** como vai?, tudo bem?

**think** [θɪŋk], *pt, pp* **thought** [θɔːt] *vi* pensar // *vt* pensar, achar, supor; (*imagine*) imaginar; **what did you** ~ **of them?** o que você achou deles?; **to** ~ **about sth/sb** pensar em algo/alguém; **I'll** ~ **about it** vou pensar sobre isso; **to** ~ **of doing sth** pensar em fazer algo; **I** ~ **so/not** acho que sim/não; **to** ~ **well of sb** fazer bom juízo de alguém; **to** ~ **over** *vt* refletir (*Pt*: -ct-) sobre, meditar sobre; **to** ~ **up** *vt* engendrar; ~**ing** *adj* pensativo.

**thinly** [ˈθɪnlɪ] *adv* (*cut*) em fatias finas; (*spread*) numa camada fina.

**thinness** [ˈθɪnnɪs] *n* magreza.

**third** [θəːd] *adj* terceiro // *n* terceiro/a; (*fraction*) terço; (*scol: degree*) terceira categoria; ~**ly** *adv* em terceiro lugar; ~ **party insurance** *n* seguro contra terceiros; ~**rate** *adj* ordinário, reles *inv*; **the T~ World** *n* o Terceiro Mundo.

**thirst** [θəːst] *n* sede *f*; ~**y** *adj*

(*person*) sedento, com sede; **to be ~y** estar com sede.

**thirteen** [ˈθəːˈtiːn] *num* treze.

**thirty** [ˈθəːtɪ] *num* trinta.

**this** [ðɪs] *det* este/esta // *pron* este/esta; (*neuter*) isto; **~ is what he said** foi isto o que ele disse; **~ high** dessa altura.

**thistle** [ˈθɪsl] *n* cardo.

**thong** [θɒŋ] *n* correia, tira de couro.

**thorn** [θɔːn] *n* espinho; **~y** *adj* espinhoso.

**thorough** [ˈθʌrə] *adj* (*search*) minucioso; (*knowledge*, *research*) profundo; **~bred** *adj* (*horse*) de puro sangue; **~fare** *n* via, passagem *f*; **"no ~fare"** "passagem proibida"; **~ly** *adv* minuciosamente, profundamente, a fundo.

**those** [ðəuz] *pl pron, det* esses/essas; (*more remote*) aqueles/aquelas.

**though** [ðəu] *conj* embora, se bem que // *adv* no entanto.

**thought** [θɔːt] *pt, pp* of **think** // *n* pensamento; (*opinion*) opinião *f*; (*intention*) intenção *f*; **~ful** *adj* pensativo; (*considerate*) atencioso; **~less** *adj* descuidado, desatento.

**thousand** [ˈθauzənd] *num* mil; **two ~** dois mil; **~s (of)** milhares *mpl* (de); **~th** *adj* milésimo.

**thrash** [θræʃ] *vt* surrar, malhar; (*defeat*) derrotar; **to ~ about** *vi* debater-se; **to ~ out** *vt* discutir exaustivamente.

**thread** [θrɛd] *n* fio, linha; (*of screw*) rosca // *vt* (*needle*) enfiar; **~bare** *adj* surrado, puído.

**threat** [θrɛt] *n* ameaça; **~en** *vi* ameaçar // *vt*: **to ~en sb with sth/to do** ameaçar alguém com algo/de fazer.

**three** [θriː] *num* três; **~-dimensional** *adj* tridimensional, em três dimensões; **~fold** *adv*: **to increase ~fold** triplicar; **~-piece suit** *n* terno (3 peças); (*Pt*) fato de 3 peças; **~-piece suite** *n* conjunto de sofá e duas poltronas; **~-ply** *adj* (*wool*)

triple, com três fios; **~-wheeler** *n* (*car*) carro de três rodas.

**thresh** [θrɛʃ] *vt* (*AGR*) debulhar.

**threshold** [ˈθrɛʃhəuld] *n* limiar *m*.

**threw** [θruː] *pt* of **throw**.

**thrift** [θrɪft] *n* economia, poupança; **~y** *adj* econômico, frugal.

**thrill** [θrɪl] *n* (*excitement*) emoção *f*; (*shudder*) estremecimento // *vt* emocionar, vibrar; **to be ~ed** (*with gift etc*) estar emocionado; **~er** *n* novela/filme *m* de suspense.

**throat** [θrəut] *n* garganta; **to have a sore ~** estar com dor de garganta.

**throb** [θrɒb] *n* (*of heart*) batida; (*of engine*) vibração *f* // *vi* bater, palpitar; (*pain*) dar pontadas.

**throes** [θrəuz] *npl*: **in the ~ of** no meio de.

**thrombosis** [θrɒmˈbəusɪs] *n* trombose *f*.

**throne** [θrəun] *n* trono.

**throttle** [ˈθrɒtl] *n* (*AUT*) acelerador *m* // *vt* estrangular.

**through** [θruː] *prep* por, através de; (*time*) durante; (*by means of*) por meio de, por intermédio de; (*owing to*) devido a // *adj* (*ticket, train*) direto (*Pt*: -ct-) // *adv* completamente, do começo ao fim; **to put sb ~ to sb** (*TEL*) ligar alguém com alguém; **to be ~** (*TEL*) estar na linha; (*have finished*) acabar; **"no ~ way"** "rua sem saída"; **~out** *prep* (*place*) por todas as partes; (*time*) durante todo, todo // *adj* por or em todas as partes.

**throw** [θrəu] *n* arremesso, tiro; (*SPORT*) lançamento // *vt, pt* **threw**, *pp* **thrown** jogar, atirar; (*SPORT*) lançar; (*rider*) derrubar; (*fig*) desconcertar; **to ~ a party** dar uma festa; **to ~ away** *vt* desperdiçar; **to ~ in** *vt* (*SPORT*) pôr em jogo; **to ~**

**off** *vt* desfazer-se de; **to ~ out** *vt* expulsar; **to ~ up** *vi* vomitar; **~away** *adj* descartável, para jogar fora.

**thru** [θru:] *(US)* = **through**.

**thrush** [θrʌʃ] *n* tordo; *(MED)* sapinhos *mpl*, sapinho.

**thrust** [θrʌst] *n* impulso; *(TECH)* empuxo // *vt*, *pt*, *pp* **thrust** empurrar; *(push in)* enfiar, meter.

**thud** [θʌd] *n* baque *m*, som *m* surdo.

**thug** [θʌg] *n (criminal)* criminoso/a *m/f*; *(pej)* facínora *m/f*.

**thumb** [θʌm] *n (ANAT)* polegar *m*; *(col)* dedão *m* // *vt (book)* folhear; **to ~ a lift** pedir carona; *(Pt)* fazer boléia; **~tack** *n (US)* percevejo.

**thump** [θʌmp] *n* murro, pancada; *(sound)* baque *m* // *vt* dar um murro em, golpear.

**thunder** [ˈθʌndə*] *n (gen)* trovão *m*; *(sudden noise)* trovoada; *(of applause etc)* estrondo // *vi* trovejar; *(train etc)*: **to ~ past** passar como um raio; **~bolt** *n* raio; **~clap** *n* estampido do trovão; **~storm** *n* tempestade *f* com trovoada, temporal *m*; **~struck** *adj* estupefato *(Pt:* -ct-); **~y** *adj* tempestuoso.

**Thursday** [ˈθəːzdɪ] *n* quinta-feira.

**thus** [ðʌs] *adv* assim, desta maneira.

**thwart** [θwɔːt] *vt* frustrar.

**thyme** [taɪm] *n* tomilho.

**thyroid** [ˈθaɪrɔɪd] *n* tireóide *f*.

**tiara** [tɪˈɑːrə] *n* tiara, diadema *m*.

**tic** [tɪk] *n* tic *m*.

**tick** [tɪk] *n (sound: of clock)* tiquetaque *m*; *(mark)* traço *m*, marca; *(ZOOL)* carrapato; *(col)*: **in a ~** num instante // *vi* fazer tique-taque // *vt* marcar; **to ~ off** *vt* assinalar; *(person)* censurar.

**ticket** [ˈtɪkɪt] *n* passagem *f*, bilhete *m*; *(for cinema)* entrada; *(in shop: on goods)* etiqueta; *(for library)* cartão *m*; **~ collector** *n* revisor *m*; **~ office** *n* bilheteria; *(Pt)* bilheteira.

**tickle** [ˈtɪkl] *n* cócegas *fpl* // *vt* fazer

cócegas; **ticklish** *adj* coceguento.

**tidal** [ˈtaɪdl] *adj* de maré; **~ wave** *n* macaréu *m*, onda gigantesca.

**tiddlywinks** [ˈtɪdlɪwɪŋks] *n* jogo de fichas.

**tide** [taɪd] *n* maré *f*; *(fig: of events)* marcha, curso.

**tidiness** [ˈtaɪdɪnɪs] *n (good order)* ordem *f*; *(neatness)* asseio, limpeza.

**tidy** [ˈtaɪdɪ] *adj (room)* arrumado; *(dress, work)* limpo; *(person)* bem arrumado // *vt (also:* **~ up**) pôr em ordem, arrumar.

**tie** [taɪ] *n (string etc)* fita, corda; *(also:* **neck~**) gravata; *(fig: link)* vínculo, laço; *(SPORT: draw)* empate *m* // *vt (gen)* amarrar, atar // *vi (SPORT)* empatar; **to ~ in a bow** dar um laço; **to ~ a knot in sth** dar um nó em algo; **to ~ down** *vt* amarrar; *(fig)*: **to ~ sb down** to obrigar alguém a; **to ~ up** *vt (parcel)* embrulhar; *(dog)* prender; *(boat)* amarrar; *(arrangements)* concluir; **to be ~d up** *(busy)* estar ocupado; **~-up** *n (US)* engarrafamento.

**tier** [tɪə*] *n* fileira; *(of cake)* camada.

**tiger** [ˈtaɪgə*] *n* tigre *m*.

**tight** [taɪt] *adj (rope)* esticado, firme; *(money)* escasso; *(clothes)* justo; *(budget, programme)* apertado; *(col: drunk)* bêbado // *adv (squeeze)* bem forte; *(shut)* hermeticamente; **~s** *npl* meia-calça *sg*; *(for gym)* malha *sg*; **~en** *vt (rope)* esticar; *(screw)* apertar // *vi* apertar-se, esticar-se; **~-fisted** *adj* pão-duro; **~ly** *adv (grasp)* firmemente; **~-rope** *n* corda esticada para acrobacias.

**tile** [taɪl] *n (on roof)* telha; *(on floor)* ladrilho; *(on wall)* azulejo, ladrilho; **~d** *adj* ladrilhado.

**till** [tɪl] *n* caixa (registradora) // *vt (land)* cultivar // *prep, conj =* **until**.

**tiller** [ˈtɪlə*] *n (NAUT)* cana do leme.

**tilt** [tɪlt] *vt* inclinar // *vi* inclinar-se.

**timber** [ˈtɪmbə*] *n (material)*

madeira; (*trees*) mata, floresta.
**time** [taɪm] *n* tempo; (*epoch: often pl*) época; (*by clock*) hora; (*moment*) momento; (*occasion*) vez *f*; (*MUS*) compasso // *vt* (*gen*) calcular *or* medir o tempo de; (*race*) cronometrar; (*remark etc*) escolher o momento para; **a long ~** muito tempo; **for the ~ being** por enquanto; **from ~ to ~** de vez em quando; **in ~** (*soon enough*) a tempo; (*after some time*) com o tempo; (*MUS*) no compasso; **in a week's ~** dentro de uma semana; **on ~** na hora; **5 ~ 5 is 25** 5 vezes 5 são 25; **what ~ is it?** que horas são?; **to have a good ~** divertir-se, distrair-se; **~ bomb** *n* bomba de ação retardada; **~keeper** *n* (*SPORT*) cronometrista *m/f*; **~less** *adj* eterno; **~ limit** *n* (*gen*) limite *m* de tempo; (*COMM*) prazo; **~ly** *adj* oportuno; **~ off** *n* tempo livre; **timer** *n* (*in kitchen*) relógio programador; **~ switch** *n* interruptor *m*; **~table** *n* horário; **~ zone** *n* fuso horário.
**timid** ['tɪmɪd] *adj* tímido.
**timing** ['taɪmɪŋ] *n* (*SPORT*) cronometragem *f*; (*gen*) escolha do momento; **the ~ of his resignation** o momento que escolheu para se demitir.
**timpani** ['tɪmpənɪ] *npl* tímbalos *mpl*.
**tin** [tɪn] *n* estanho; (*also: ~ plate*) folha-de-flandres *f*; (*can*) lata; **~ foil** *n* papel *m* de estanho.
**tinge** [tɪndʒ] *n* matiz *m*, toque *m* // *vt*: **~d with** tingido de.
**tingle** ['tɪŋgl] *n* comichão *f* // *vi* sentir comichão.
**tinker** ['tɪŋkə*] *n* funileiro; (*gipsy*) cigano; **to ~ with** *vt* mexer com.
**tinkle** ['tɪŋkl] *vi* tilintar, tinir // *n* (*col*): **to give sb a ~** bater um fio para alguém.
**tinned** [tɪnd] *adj* (*food*) em lata, em conserva.

**tin opener** ['tɪnəʊpnə*] *n* abridor *m* de latas.
**tinsel** ['tɪnsl] *n* ouropel *m*.
**tint** [tɪnt] *n* matiz *m*; (*for hair*) tonalidade *f*, tom *m*.
**tiny** ['taɪnɪ] *adj* pequenino, diminuto.
**tip** [tɪp] *n* (*end*) ponta; (*gratuity*) gorjeta; (*for rubbish*) depósito; (*advice*) dica // *vt* (*waiter*) dar uma gorjeta a; (*tilt*) inclinar; (*overturn: also: ~ over*) virar, emborcar; (*empty: also: ~ out*) esvaziar, entornar; **~-off** *n* (*hint*) aviso; **~ped** *adj* (*cigarette*) com filtro.
**tipsy** ['tɪpsɪ] *adj* embriagado, tocado, alto, alegre.
**tiptoe** ['tɪptəʊ] *n*: **on ~** na ponta dos pés.
**tiptop** ['tɪp'tɔp] *adj*: **in ~ condition** em perfeitas condições.
**tire** ['taɪə*] *n* (*US*) = **tyre** // *vt* cansar // *vi* (*gen*) cansar-se; (*become bored*) chatear-se; **~d** *adj* cansado; **to be ~d of sth** estar farto *or* cheio de algo; **tiredness** *n* cansaço; **~less** *adj* incansável; **~some** *adj* enfadonho, chato; **tiring** *adj* cansativo.
**tissue** ['tɪʃuː] *n* tecido; (*paper handkerchief*) lenço de papel; **~ paper** *n* papel *m* de seda.
**tit** [tɪt] *n* (*bird*) passarinho; **to give ~ for tat** pagar na mesma moeda.
**titbit** ['tɪtbɪt] *n* (*food*) guloseima; (*news*) boato, rumor *m*.
**titillate** ['tɪtɪleɪt] *vt* titilar, excitar.
**titivate** ['tɪtɪveɪt] *vt* arrumar.
**title** ['taɪtl] *n* título; **~ deed** *n* (*LAW*) título de propriedade; **~ role** *n* papel *m* principal.
**titter** ['tɪtə*] *vi* rir-se com riso sufocado.
**titular** ['tɪtjʊlə*] *adj* (*in name only*) nominal, titular.
**to** [tuː, tə] *prep* a, para; (*towards*) para; (*of time*) até; (*of*) de; **give it ~ me** dê-mo para mim; **the key ~ the front door** a chave da porta da frente; **the main thing is ~...** o principal é...; **to**

**go** ~ **France/school** ir à França/ao colégio; **a quarter** ~ **5** quinze para as 5; (*Pt*) 5 menos um quarto; **pull/push**   **the**   **door** ~ puxar/empurrar a porta; **to go** ~ **and fro** ir de um lado para outro.

**toad** [təud] *n* sapo; ~**stool** *n* chapéu-de-cobra *m*, cogumelo venenoso.

**toast** [təust] *n* (*CULIN: also: piece of* ~) torrada; (*drink, speech*) brinde *m* // *vt* (*CULIN*) torrar; (*drink to*) brindar; ~**er** *n* torradeira.

**tobacco** [tə'bækəu] *n* tabaco, fumo; ~**nist** *n* vendedor(a) *m/f* de tabaco; ~**nist's** (**shop**) *n* charutaria; (*Pt*) tabacaria.

**toboggan** [tə'bɔgən] *n* tobogã *m*.

**today** [tə'dei] *adv*, *n* (*also fig*) hoje *m*.

**toddler** ['tɔdlə*] *n* criança que começa a andar.

**toddy** ['tɔdi] *n* ponche *m* quente.

**toe** [təu] *n* dedo do pé; (*of shoe*) bico; **to** ~ **the line** (*fig*) conformar-se, cumprir as obrigações; ~**nail** *n* unha do pé.

**toffee** ['tɔfi] *n* puxa-puxa *m*, bala "tofee"; ~ **apple** *n* maçã *f* do amor.

**toga** ['təugə] *n* toga.

**together** [tə'gɛðə*] *adv* juntos; (*at same time*) ao mesmo tempo; ~ **with** *prep* junto com; ~**ness** *n* companheirismo, camaradagem *f*.

**toil** [tɔil] *n* faina, labuta // *vi* labutar, trabalhar arduamente.

**toilet** ['tɔilət] *n* (*lavatory*) banheiro, W.C. *m*; (*Pt*) casa de banho // *cmp* (*bag, soap etc*) de toalete; ~ **bowl** *n* vaso sanitário; ~ **paper** *n* papel *m* higiênico; ~**ries** *npl* artigos *mpl* de toalete; (*make-up etc*) artigos de toucador; ~ **roll** *n* rolo de papel higiênico; ~ **water** *n* perfume *m* suave.

**token** ['təukən] *n* (*sign*) sinal *m*, símbolo, prova; (*souvenir*) lembrança; (*voucher*) cupom *m*; **book/record** ~ vale *m* para comprar livros/discos.

**told** [təuld] *pt, pp of* tell.

**tolerable** ['tɔlərəbl] *adj* (*bearable*) suportável; (*fairly good*) passável.

**tolerance** ['tɔlərns] *n* (*also: TECH*) tolerância; **tolerant** *adj*: **tolerant of** tolerante com.

**tolerate** ['tɔləreit] *vt* tolerar; **toleration** [-'reiʃən] *n* tolerância.

**toll** [təul] *n* (*of casualties*) número de baixas; (*tax, charge*) pedágio; (*Pt*) portagem *f* // *vi* (*bell*) dobrar, tanger; ~**bridge** *n* ponte *f* de pedágio; (*Pt*) ponte de portagem.

**tomato** [tə'ma:təu], *pl* ~**es** *n* tomate *m*.

**tomb** [tu:m] *n* tumba.

**tombola** [tɔm'bəulə] *n* tômbola.

**tomboy** ['tɔmbɔi] *n* menina-moleque *f*.

**tombstone** ['tu:mstəun] *n* lápide *f*.

**tomcat** ['tɔmkæt] *n* gato.

**tomorrow** [tə'mɔrəu] *adv*, *n* (*also fig*) amanhã; **the day after** ~ depois de amanhã; ~ **morning** amanhã de manhã.

**ton** [tʌn] *n* tonelada; ~**s of** (*col*) um monte de, carradas de.

**tone** [təun] *n* tom *m* // *vi* dar o tom, harmonizar; **to** ~ **down** *vt* (*colour, criticism*) suavizar; (*sound*) baixar; (*MUS*) entoar; **to** ~ **up** *vt* (*muscles*) fortalecer; ~**deaf** *adj* que não tem ouvido.

**tongs** [tɔŋz] *npl* (*for coal*) tenaz *fsg*; (*for hair*) pinças *fpl*.

**tongue** [tʌŋ] *n* língua; ~ **in cheek** *adv* ironicamente; ~**-tied** *adj* (*fig*) calado; ~**-twister** *n* expressão *f* difícil de pronunciar.

**tonic** ['tɔnik] *n* (*MED*) tônico; (*MUS*) tônica; (*also:* ~ **water**) (água) tônica.

**tonight** [tə'nait] *adv*, *n* esta noite, hoje à noite.

**tonnage** ['tʌnidʒ] *n* (*NAUT*) tonelagem *f*.

**tonsil** ['tɔnsl] *n* amígdala, amídala; ~**litis** [-'laitis] *n* amigdalite *f*, amidalite *f*.

**too** [tu:] *adv* (*excessively*) demasiado, demais; (*very*) muito; (*also*) também; ~ **much** *adv* demais; ~ **many** *det* demasiados/as; ~ **good** demasiado bom, bom demais.

**took** [tuk] *pt of* **take**.

**tool** [tu:l] *n* ferramenta; ~ **box** *n* caixa de ferramentas.

**toot** [tu:t] *n* (*of horn*) buzinada; (*of whistle*) apito // *vi* (*with car-horn*) buzinar, tocar a buzina.

**tooth** [tu:θ], *pl* **teeth** *n* (ANAT, TECH) dente *m*; (*molar*) molar *m*; ~dor *f* de dente; ~**brush** *n* escova de dente; ~**paste** *n* pasta de dente; ~**pick** *n* palito.

**top** [tɔp] *n* (*of mountain*) cume *m*, cimo; (*of head*) cocuruto; (*of ladder*) o alto; (*of cupboard, table*) superfície *f*, topo; (*lid: of box, jar, bottle*) tampa; (*of list etc*) cabeça *m*; (*toy*) pião *m* // *adj* mais alto, máximo; (*in rank*) principal, superior; (*best*) melhor // *vt* (*exceed*) exceder; (*be first in*) estar à cabeça de; **on** ~ **of** sobre, em cima de; **from** ~ **to toe** da cabeça aos pés; **to** ~ **up** *vt* encher; ~**coat** *n* sobretudo; ~ **hat** *n* cartola; ~**heavy** *adj* (*object*) desequilibrado.

**topic** ['tɔpɪk] *n* tópico, assunto; ~**al** *adj* atual (Pt: -ct-).

**top:** ~**less** *adj* (*bather etc*) topless, sem a parte superior do biquíni; ~**level** *adj* (*talks*) de alto nível; ~**most** *adj* supremo, o mais alto.

**topple** ['tɔpl] *vt* derrubar, desabar // *vi* cair para frente, ruir.

**topsy-turvy** ['tɔps 'tɜ:vɪ] *adj, adv* de pernas para o ar, confuso, às avessas.

**torch** [tɔ:tʃ] *n* tocha, archote *m*; (*electric*) lanterna.

**tore** [tɔ:*] *pt of* **tear**.

**torment** ['tɔ:ment] *n* tormento, suplício // *vt* [tɔ:'ment] atormentar; (*fig: annoy*) chatear, aborrecer.

**torn** [tɔ:n] *pp of* **tear**.

**tornado** [tɔ:'neɪdəu], *pl* ~**es** *n* tornado.

**torpedo** [tɔ:'pi:dəu], *pl* ~**es** *n* torpedo.

**torrent** ['tɔrnt] *n* torrente *f*, corrente *f*; ~**ial** [-'rɛnʃl] *adj* torrencial.

**torso** ['tɔ:səu] *n* torso.

**tortoise** ['tɔ:təs] *n* tartaruga; ~**shell** ['tɔ:təʃl] *adj* de tartaruga.

**tortuous** ['tɔ:tjuəs] *adj* tortuoso.

**torture** ['tɔ:tʃə*] *n* tortura // *vt* torturar; (*fig*) atormentar.

**Tory** ['tɔ:rɪ] *adj, n* conservador(a) *m/f*.

**toss** [tɔs] *vt* atirar, arremessar; (*head*) sacudir, lançar para trás; **to** ~ **a coin** tirar cara ou coroa; **to** ~ **up for sth** jogar cara ou coroa por algo; **to** ~ **and turn in bed** virar de um lado para o outro na cama.

**tot** [tɔt] *n* (*drink*) copinho, golinho; (*child*) criancinha *f*.

**total** ['təutl] *adj* total, inteiro // *n* total *m*, soma // *vt* (*add up*) somar; (*amount to*) montar a.

**totalitarian** [təutælɪ'tɛərɪən] *adj* totalitário.

**totem pole** ['təutəm-] *n* mastro totêmico.

**totter** ['tɔtə*] *vi* cambalear-se.

**touch** [tʌtʃ] *n* (*gen*) toque *m*, tato (Pt: -ct-); (*contact*) contato (Pt: -ct-); (FOOTBALL): **in** ~ fora do campo // *vt* (*gen*) tocar, apalpar; (*emotionally*) comover; **a** ~ **of** (*fig*) uma pitada de, um pouquinho de; **to get in** ~ **with sb** entrar em conta(c)to com alguém; **to lose** ~ (*friends*) perder o conta(c)to; **to** ~ **on** *vt fus* (*topic*) aludir a, fazer menção de; **to** ~ **up** *vt* (*paint*) retocar; ~**-and-go** *adj* arriscado; ~**down** *n* aterrissagem *f*; (*on sea*) amerissagem *f*; ~**ed** *adj* comovido; (*col*) tocado, muito louco; ~**ing** *adj* comovedor(a); ~**line** *n* (SPORT) linha de fundo; ~**y** *adj* (*person*) suscetível, melindroso.

**tough** [tʌf] *adj* (*gen*) duro, forte; (*difficult*) difícil; (*resistant*) resistente; (*person*) tenaz, obstinado; (: *pej*) rude // *n* (*gangster etc*) bandido, capanga *m*; ~**en** *vt* endurecer; ~**ness** *n* dureza, dificuldade *f*; resistência, tenacidade *f*.

**toupee** ['tu:peɪ] *n* peruca.

**tour** ['tuə*] *n* viagem *f*, excursão *f*; (*also*: **package** ~) excursão organizada; (*of town, museum*) visita // *vt* excursionar por; ~**ing** *n* viagens *fpl* turísticas, turismo.

**tourism** ['tuərɪzm] *n* turismo.

**tourist** ['tuərɪst] *n* turista *m/f* // *cmp* turístico; ~ **office** *n* agência de turismo.

**tournament** ['tuənəmənt] *n* torneio.

**tousled** ['tauzld] *adj* (*hair*) despenteado.

**tout** [taut] *vi*: **to** ~ **for** angariar clientes para // *n*: **ticket** ~ cambista *m/f*.

**tow** [təu] *vt* rebocar; '**on** ~' (*AUT*) rebocado.

**toward(s)** [tə'wɔ:d(z)] *prep* para; (*of attitude*) com respeito a, para com; (*of purpose*) para.

**towel** ['tauəl] *n* toalha; ~**ling** *n* (*fabric*) tecido para toalhas; ~ **rail** *n* toalheiro.

**tower** ['tauə*] *n* torre *f*; ~ **block** *n* arranha-céu *m*; ~**ing** *adj* elevado, eminente.

**town** [taun] *n* cidade *f*; **to go to** ~ ir à cidade; (*fig*) fazer com entusiasmo; ~ **clerk** *n* administrador(a) *m/f* municipal; ~ **council** *n* câmara municipal; ~ **hall** *n* prefeitura; (*Pt*) concelho; ~ **planning** *n* urbanismo.

**towrope** ['təurəup] *n* cabo de reboque; **tow truck** *n* = **breakdown lorry**.

**toxic** ['tɔksɪk] *adj* tóxico.

**toy** [tɔɪ] *n* brinquedo; **to** ~ **with** *vt fus* jogar com; (*idea*) andar com;

~**shop** *n* loja de brinquedos.

**trace** [treɪs] *n* traço, rasto // *vt* (*draw*) traçar, esboçar; (*follow*) seguir a pista de; (*locate*) encontrar.

**track** [træk] *n* (*mark*) pegada, vestígio; (*path*: *gen*) caminho, vereda; (: *of bullet etc*) trajetória (*Pt*: -ct-); (: *of suspect, animal*) pista, rasto; (*RAIL*) via, trilhos; (*on tape*) trilha; (*SPORT*) pista // *vt* seguir a pista de; **to keep** ~ **of** não perder de vista, manter-se informado sobre; **to** ~ **down** *vt* (*prey*) seguir a pista de; (*sth lost*) procurar e encontrar; ~ **suit** *n* roupa de jogging.

**tract** [trækt] *n* (*GEO*) região *f*; (*pamphlet*) folheto.

**tractor** ['træktə*] *n* trator (*Pt*: -ct-) *m*.

**trade** [treɪd] *n* comércio, negócio; (*skill, job*) ofício, emprego // *vi* negociar, comerciar; **to** ~ **in** *vt* (*old car etc*) dar como parte do pagamento; ~-**in price** *n* valor de um objeto usado que se desconta do preço do outro novo; ~**mark** *n* marca de indústria *or* comércio; ~ **name** *n* nome *m* comercial; **trader** *n* comerciante *m/f*; **tradesman** *n* (*shopkeeper*) lojista *m*; ~ **union** *n* sindicato; ~ **unionism** *n* sindicalismo; **trading** *n* comércio; **trading estate** *n* zona comercial.

**tradition** [trə'dɪʃən] *n* tradição *f*; ~**al** *adj* tradicional.

**traffic** ['træfɪk] *n* (*gen*, *AUT*) trânsito, tráfico; (*air* ~ *etc*) tráfego // *vi*: **to** ~ **in** (*pej*: *liquor, drugs*) traficar com, fazer tráfico com; ~ **circle** *n* (*US*) cruzamento circular, balão *m*; ~ **jam** *n* engarrafamento, congestionamento; ~ **lights** *npl* sinal *msg* luminoso; ~ **warden** *n* guarda *m/f* de trânsito.

**tragedy** ['trædʒədɪ] *n* tragédia.

**tragic** ['trædʒɪk] *adj* trágico.

**trail** [treɪl] *n* (*tracks*) rasto, pista; (*path*) caminho, trilha; (*wake*) esteira // *vt* (*drag*) arrastar;

*(follow)* seguir a pista de; *(follow closely)* vigiar // *vi* arrastar-se; **to ~ behind** *vi* atrasar-se; **~er** *n (AUT)* trailer *m*; *(US)* carro-reboque *m*; *(CINEMA)* trailer.

**train** [treɪn] *n* trem *m*; *(Pt)* comboio; *(of dress)* cauda; *(series)* sequência, série *f*; *(retinue)* séquito, comitiva // *vt (educate)* ensinar; *(teach skills to)* instruir, treinar; *(sportsman)* treinar; *(dog)* adestrar, amestrar; *(point: gun etc)*: **to ~ on** apontar para // *vi (SPORT)* ser treinado; *(be educated)* ser instruído; **~ed** *(worker)* instruído; *(teacher)* formado; *(animal)* adestrado; **~ee** [treɪ'niː] *n* aluno; *(in trade)* aprendiz *m*; **~er** *n (SPORT)* adestrador *m/f*; *(of animals)* treinador(a) *m/f*; **~ing** *n* instrução *f*, preparo; **in ~ing** *(SPORT)* em treinamento; **~ing college** *n (for teachers)* escola normal.

**traipse** [treɪps] *vi* arrastar os pés.

**trait** [treɪt] *n* traço.

**traitor** ['treɪtə*] *n* traidor(a) *m/f*.

**tram** [træm] *n (also: ~car)* bonde *m*; *(Pt)* eléctrico.

**tramp** [træmp] *n (person)* vagabundo/a // *vi* caminhar pesadamente.

**trample** ['træmpl] *vt:* **to ~ (underfoot)** calcar aos pés.

**trampoline** ['træmpəliːn] *n* trampolim *m*.

**trance** [trɑːns] *n* estupor *m*; *(MED)* transe *m* hipnótico.

**tranquil** ['træŋkwɪl] *adj* tranquilo; **~lity** *n* tranquilidade *f*; **~lizer** *n (MED)* tranquilizante *m*.

**transact** [træn'zækt] *vt (business)* negociar; **~ion** [-'zækʃən] *n* transação *(Pt*: -cç-) *f*, negócio.

**transatlantic** [trænzət'læntɪk] *adj* transatlântico.

**transcend** [træn'sɛnd] *vt* transcender, exceder.

**transcript** ['trænskrɪpt] *n* cópia,

traslado; **~ion** [-'skrɪpʃən] *n* transcrição *f*.

**transept** ['trænsɛpt] *n* transepto.

**transfer** ['trænsfə*] *n (gen)* transferência; *(picture, design)* decalcomania // *vt* [træns'fəː*] transferir, trasladar; **to ~ the charges** *(TEL)* ligar a cobrar; **~able** [-'fəːrəbl] *adj* transferível; **not ~able** intransferível.

**transform** [træns'fɔːm] *vt* transformar; **~ation** [-'meɪʃən] *n* transformação *f*; **~er** *n (ELEC)* transformador *m*.

**transfusion** [træns'fjuːʒən] *n* transfusão *f*.

**transient** ['trænzɪənt] *adj* transitório.

**transistor** [træn'zɪstə*] *n (ELEC)* transistor *m*; **~ radio** *n* rádio transistor.

**transit** ['trænzɪt] *n:* **in ~** em trânsito, de passagem.

**transition** [træn'zɪʃən] *n* transição *f*; **~al** *adj* transitório.

**transitive** ['trænzɪtɪv] *adj (LING)* transitivo.

**transitory** ['trænzɪtərɪ] *adj* transitório.

**translate** [trænz'leɪt] *vt* traduzir; **translation** [-'leɪʃən] *n* tradução *f*; **translator** *n* tradutor(a) *m/f*.

**transmission** [trænz'mɪʃən] *n* transmissão *f*.

**transmit** [trænz'mɪt] *vt* transmitir; **~ter** *n* transmissor *m*; *(station)* emissora.

**transparency** [træns'pɛərnsɪ] *n (PHOT)* transparência, diapositivo.

**transparent** [træns'pærnt] *adj* transparente.

**transplant** [træns'plɑːnt] *vt* transplantar // *n* ['trænsplɑːnt] *(MED)* transplante *m*.

**transport** [træns'pɔːt] *n (gen)* transporte *m*; *(also: road/rail ~)* transporte rodoviário/ferroviário // *vt* [-'pɔːt] transportar; *(carry)* acarretar; **~ation** [-'teɪʃən] *n* transporte m; ~ **café** n bar m de estrada.

**transverse** ['trænzvə:s] adj transversal.

**transvestite** [trænz'vestart] n travesti m/f.

**trap** [træp] n (snare, trick) armadilha, cilada; (carriage) aranha, charrete f // vt pegar em armadilha; (immobilize) bloquear; (jam) emperrar; ~ **door** n alçapão m.

**trapeze** [trə'pi:z] n trapézio.

**trappings** ['træpɪŋz] npl adornos mpl, enfeites mpl.

**trash** [træʃ] n (pej: goods) refugo, escória; (: nonsense) besteira; ~ **can** n (US) lata de lixo.

**trauma** ['trɔ:mə] n trauma m; ~**tic** [-'mætɪk] adj traumático.

**travel** ['trævl] n viagem f // vi viajar // vt (distance) percorrer; ~ **agency** n agência de viagens; ~**ler**, ~**er** (US) n viajante m/f; ~**ler's cheque** n cheque m de viagem; ~**ling**, ~**ing** (US) n as viagens fpl, viajar m; ~ **sickness** n enjôo.

**traverse** ['trævəs] vt atravessar.

**travesty** ['trævəstɪ] n paródia.

**trawler** ['trɔ:lə*] n traineira.

**tray** [treɪ] n bandeja.

**treacherous** ['tretʃərəs] adj traiçoeiro; **treachery** n traição f.

**treacle** ['tri:kl] n melaço, melado.

**tread** [trɛd] n (step) passo, pisada; (sound) passada; (of tyre) banda de rodagem // vi, pt **trod**, pp **trodden** pisar, esmagar com os pés; **to ~ on** vt fus pisar sobre.

**treason** ['tri:zn] n traição f.

**treasure** ['treʒə*] n tesouro // vt (value) apreciar, estimar; ~ **hunt** n caça ao tesouro.

**treasurer** ['treʒərə*] n tesoureiro.

**treasury** ['treʒərɪ] n: **the T**~ (POL) Ministério da Fazenda.

**treat** [tri:t] n (present) regalo, deleite m; (pleasure) prazer m // vt

tratar; **to ~ sb to sth** convidar alguém para algo.

**treatise** ['tri:tɪz] n tratado.

**treatment** ['tri:tmənt] n tratamento, trato.

**treaty** ['tri:tɪ] n tratado, acordo.

**treble** ['trebl] adj tríplice // n (MUS) soprano // vt triplicar // vi triplicar-se.

**tree** [tri:] n árvore f; ~ **trunk** n tronco de árvore.

**trek** [trɛk] n (long journey) viagem penosa e comprida; (tiring walk) caminhada; (as holiday) excursão f.

**trellis** ['trelɪs] n grade f de ripas, latada.

**tremble** ['trembl] vi tremer; **trembling** n tremor m // adj trêmulo, trepidante.

**tremendous** [trɪ'mendəs] adj tremendo; (enormous) enorme; (excellent) formidável, fantástico.

**tremor** ['tremə*] n tremor m; (also: **earth ~**) tremor de terra.

**trench** [trentʃ] n trincheira.

**trend** [trend] n (tendency) inclinação f, (of events) curso; (fashion) tendência; ~**y** adj (idea) de acordo com a tendência atual (Pt: -ct-); (clothes) da última moda.

**trepidation** [trepɪ'deɪʃən] n trepidação f; (fear) apreensão f.

**trespass** ['trespəs] vi: **to ~ on** invadir; **"no ~ing"** "passagem proibida".

**tress** [tres] n trança.

**trestle** ['tresl] n cavalete m; ~ **table** n mesa de cavaletes.

**trial** ['traɪəl] n (LAW) julgamento, processo; (test: of machine etc) prova, teste m; (hardship) provação f; **by ~ and error** por ensaio e erro.

**triangle** ['traɪæŋgl] n (MATH, MUS) triângulo; **triangular** [-'æŋgjulə*] adj triangular.

**tribal** ['traɪbəl] adj tribal.

**tribe** [traɪb] n tribo f; **tribesman** n membro da tribo.

**tribulation** [tribjuˈleiʃən] *n* tribulação *f*, aflição *f*.

**tribunal** [traiˈbjuːnl] *n* tribunal *m*.

**tributary** [ˈtribjutəri] *n* (*river*) afluente *m*.

**tribute** [ˈtribjuːt] *n* homenagem *f*; (*payment*) tributo; **to pay ~ to** prestar homenagem a.

**trice** [trais] *n*: **in a ~** num instante.

**trick** [trik] *n* truque *m*; (*deceit*) fraude *f*, trapaça; (*joke*) brincadeira; (*CARDS*) vaza // *vt* enganar; **to play a ~ on sb** pregar uma peça em alguém; **~ery** *n* trapaça.

**trickle** [ˈtrikl] *n* (*of water etc*) fio de água // *vi* gotejar, pingar.

**tricky** [ˈtriki] *adj* difícil, complicado.

**tricycle** [ˈtraisikl] *n* triciclo.

**trifle** [ˈtraifl] *n* bagatela; (*CULIN*) *tipo de bolo com fruta e creme* // *adv*: **a ~ long** um pouquinho longo; **trifling** *adj* insignificante.

**trigger** [ˈtrigə*] *n* (*of gun*) gatilho; **to ~ off** *vt* desencadear.

**trigonometry** [trigəˈnɔmətri] *n* trigonometria.

**trill** [tril] *n* (*of bird*) trinado, trilo.

**trim** [trim] *adj* (*elegant*) elegante; (*house*) arrumado; (*garden*) bem cuidado; (*figure*) bem vestido, esbelto // *n* (*haircut etc*) aparada; (*on car*) estofamento // *vt* arrumar; (*cut*) aparar, cortar; (*decorate*) enfeitar; (*NAUT*: **a sail**) ajustar; **~mings** *npl* decoração *fsg*; (*cuttings*) aparas *fpl*.

**Trinity** [ˈtriniti] *n*: **the ~** a Trindade.

**trinket** [ˈtriŋkit] *n* bugiganga; (*piece of jewellery*) berloque *m*, bijuteria.

**trio** [ˈtriːəu] *n* trio, terceto.

**trip** [trip] *n* viagem *f*; (*excursion*) excursão *f*; (*stumble*) tropeço *m* // *vi* (*also*: **~ up**) tropeçar; (*go lightly*) andar com passos ligeiros // *vt* fazer tropeçar.

**tripe** [traip] *n* (*CULIN*) bucho, tripa; (*pej*: *rubbish*) bobagem *f*.

**triple** [ˈtripl] *adj* triplo, tríplice.

**triplets** [ˈtriplits] *npl* trigêmeos/as.

**triplicate** [ˈtriplikət] *n*: **in ~** em triplicata.

**tripod** [ˈtraipɔd] *n* tripé *m*.

**trite** [trait] *adj* vulgar, gasto.

**triumph** [ˈtraiʌmf] *n* triunfo // *vi*: **to ~ (over)** triunfar (sobre); **~ant** [ˈʌmfənt] *adj* triunfante.

**trivia** [ˈtriviə] *npl* trivialidades *fpl*.

**trivial** [ˈtriviəl] *adj* insignificante; (*commonplace*) trivial; **~ity** [-ˈælɪti] *n* trivialidade *f*.

**trod** [trɔd], **trodden** [ˈtrɔdn] *pt*, *pp* of **tread**.

**trolley** [ˈtrɔli] *n* carrinho; **~ bus** *n* ônibus *m* elétrico, trolley *m*.

**trombone** [trɔmˈbəun] *n* trombone *m*.

**troop** [truːp] *n* bando, grupo; **~s** *npl* (*MIL*) tropa *fsg*; **to ~ in/out** *vi* entrar/sair em bando; **~er** *n* (*MIL*) soldado de cavalaria.

**trophy** [ˈtrəufi] *n* troféu *m*.

**tropic** [ˈtrɔpik] *n* trópico; **~al** *adj* tropical.

**trot** [trɔt] *n* trote *m* // *vi* trotar; **on the ~** (*fig*: *col*) atarefado.

**trouble** [ˈtrʌbl] *n* problema *m*, dificuldade *f*; (*worry*) preocupação *f*; (*bother, effort*) incômodo, esforço; (*unrest*) inquietude *f*; (*MED*): **stomach ~** problemas *mpl* gástricos // *vt* perturbar; (*worry*) preocupar, incomodar // *vi*: **to ~ to do sth** incomodar-se or preocupar-se de fazer algo; **~s** *npl* (*POL etc*) distúrbios *mpl*; **to be in ~** estar num aperto; **to go to the ~ of doing sth** dar-se ao trabalho de fazer algo; **what's the ~?** qual é o problema?; **~d** *adj* (*person*) preocupado; (*epoch, life*) agitado; **~maker** *n* criador-de-casos *m*; (*child*) encrenqueiro; **~shooter** *n* (*in conflict*) conciliador *m*; **~some** *adj* incômodo, importuno.

**trough** [trɔf] n (also: drinking ~) bebedouro, cocho; (also: feeding ~) gamela; (channel) canal m.

**troupe** [truːp] n companhia teatral.

**trousers** ['trauzəz] npl calça.

**trousseau** ['truːsəu], pl ~x or ~s [-z] n enxoval m.

**trout** [traut] n, pl inv truta.

**trowel** ['trauəl] n colher f de jardineiro or de pedreiro.

**truant** ['truənt] n: to play ~ fazer gazeta, matar aula.

**truce** [truːs] n trégua, armistício.

**truck** [trʌk] n caminhão m; (Pt) camião m; (RAIL) vagão m; ~ driver n motorista m/f de caminhão; ~ farm n (US) horta; ~ stop n (US) bar m de estrada.

**truculent** ['trʌkjulənt] adj agressivo.

**trudge** [trʌdʒ] vi andar com dificuldade, arrastar-se.

**true** [truː] adj verdadeiro; (accurate) exato (Pt: -ct-); (genuine) autêntico; (faithful) fiel, leal.

**truffle** ['trʌfl] n trufa.

**truly** ['truːlɪ] adv exatamente (Pt: -act-); (truthfully) verdadeiramente; (faithfully) fielmente; yours ~ (in letter) atenciosamente.

**trump** [trʌmp] n trunfo; ~ed-up adj inventado, forjado.

**trumpet** ['trʌmpɪt] n trombeta.

**truncheon** ['trʌntʃən] n cassetete m.

**trundle** ['trʌndl] vt/i: to ~ along rolar or rodar fazendo ruído.

**trunk** [trʌŋk] n (of tree, person) tronco; (of elephant) tromba; (case) baú m, mala grande; (US: AUT), porta-mala; ~s npl calção de banho, sunga de praia; ~ call n (TEL) ligação f interurbana.

**truss** [trʌs] n (MED) funda; to ~ (up) vt atar, amarrar.

**trust** [trʌst] n confiança; (COMM) truste m, monopólio; (obligation) responsabilidade f; (LAW)

fideicomisso // vt (rely on) confiar em; (entrust): to ~ sth to sb confiar algo a alguém; ~ed adj de confiança; ~ee [trʌs'tiː] n (LAW) fideicomissário, depositário; (of school etc) administrador(a) m/f; ~ful, ~ing adj confiante; ~worthy adj digno de confiança; ~y adj fidedigno, fiel.

**truth** [truːθ], pl ~s [truːðz] n verdade f; ~ful adj (person) sincero, honesto; ~fully adv sinceramente; ~fulness n veracidade f.

**try** [traɪ] n tentativa, experimento; (RUGBY) ensaio // vt (LAW) julgar; (test: sth new) provar, pôr à prova; (attempt) tentar; (strain) cansar // vi provar; to ~ to do sth tentar fazer algo; to ~ on vt (clothes) experimentar, provar; to ~ out vt experimentar; ~ing adj penoso, árduo.

**tsar** [zɑː*] n czar m.

**T-shirt** ['tiːʃəːt] n camiseta.

**tub** [tʌb] n balde m; (bath) tina, banheira.

**tuba** ['tjuːbə] n tuba.

**tubby** ['tʌbɪ] adj gorducho.

**tube** [tjuːb] n tubo, cano; (underground) metrô m; (Pt) metro (-politano); (for tyre) câmara-de-ar f; ~less adj sem câmara.

**tuberculosis** [tjubəːkju'ləusɪs] n tuberculose f.

**tube station** n estação f do metrô.

**tubing** ['tjuːbɪŋ] n tubulação f, encanamento; a piece of ~ um pedaço de tubo.

**tubular** ['tjuːbjulə*] adj tubular; (furniture) tubiforme.

**TUC** n abbr of Trades Union Congress.

**tuck** [tʌk] n (SEWING) prega, dobra // vt (put) enfiar, meter; to ~ away vt esconder; to ~ in vt enfiar a beirada de; (child) cobrir bem // vi (eat) comer com apetite; to ~ up vt (*child*) cobrir bem; ~ **shop** *n* loja de guloseimas.

**Tuesday** ['tju:zdɪ] *n* terça-feira.

**tuft** [tʌft] *n* penacho; (*of grass etc*) tufo.

**tug** [tʌg] *n* (*ship*) rebocador *m* // *vt* rebocar; ~**-of-war** *n* cabo-de-guerra *m*; (*fig*) disputa.

**tuition** [tju:'ɪʃən] *n* ensino; (*private* ~) aulas *fpl* particulares.

**tulip** ['tju:lɪp] *n* tulipa.

**tumble** ['tʌmbl] *n* (*fall*) queda // *vi* cair, tropeçar // *vt* tombar, desabar; ~**down** *adj* em ruínas *fpl*; ~ **dryer** *n* máquina de secar roupa.

**tumbler** ['tʌmblə*] *n* copo.

**tummy** ['tʌmɪ] *n* (*col: belly*) barriga; (: *stomach*) estômago.

**tumour** ['tju:mə*] *n* tumor *m*.

**tumult** ['tju:mʌlt] *n* tumulto; ~**uous** ['-mʌltjuəs] *adj* tumultuado.

**tuna** ['tju:nə] *n, pl inv* (*also:* ~ **fish**) atum *m*.

**tune** [tju:n] *n* (*melody*) melodia // *vt* (*MUS*) afinar; (*RADIO, TV*) sintonizar; (*AUT*) ajustar; **to be in/out of** ~ (*instrument*) estar afinado/ desafinado; (*singer*) cantar bem/mal; **to be in/out of** ~ **with** (*fig*) harmonizar-se com/desentoar de; **to** ~ **up** *vi* (*musician*) afinar (seu instrumento); ~**ful** *adj* melodioso; **tuner** *n* (*radio set*) sintonizador *m*; **piano tuner** afinador *m* de pianos.

**tunic** ['tju:nɪk] *n* túnica.

**tuning** ['tju:nɪŋ] *n* sintonização *f*; (*MUS*) afinação *f*; ~ **fork** *n* diapasão *m*.

**Tunisia** [tju:'nɪzɪə] *n* Tunísia.

**tunnel** ['tʌnl] *n* túnel *m*; (*in mine*) galeria // *vi* abrir um túnel/uma galeria.

**tunny** ['tʌnɪ] *n* atum *m*.

**turban** ['tɔ:bən] *n* turbante *m*.

**turbine** ['tɔ:baɪn] *n* turbina.

**turbulence** ['tɔ:bjuləns] *n* (*AVIAT*) turbulência; **turbulent** *adj* turbulento.

**tureen** [tə'ri:n] *n* terrina.

**turf** [tɔ:f] *n* torrão *m*, turfa; (*clod*) gramado // *vt* relvar, gramar; **to** ~ **out** *vt* (*col*) pôr no olho da rua.

**turgid** ['tɔ:dʒɪd] *adj* (*speech*) pomposo.

**Turk** [tɔ:k] *n* turco/a.

**turkey** ['tɔ:kɪ] *n* peru/perua *m/f*.

**Turkey** ['tɔ:kɪ] *n* Turquia; **Turkish** *adj, n* turco/a; **Turkish bath** *n* banho turco.

**turmoil** ['tɔ:mɔɪl] *n* tumulto, distúrbio, agitação *f*.

**turn** [tɔ:n] *n* volta, turno; (*in road*) curva; (*go*) vez *f*, turno; (*tendency: of mind, events*) propensão *f*, tendência; (*THEATRE*) número; (*MED*) choque *m* // *vt* dar volta a, fazer girar; (*collar*) virar; (*steak*) virar; (*change*): **to** ~ **sth into** converter algo em // *vi* voltar; (*person: look back*) voltar-se; (*reverse direction*) mudar de direção (Pt: -cç-); (*milk*) azedar; (*change*) mudar; (*become*) converter-se em; **a good** ~ um favor; **it gave me quite a** ~ me deu um susto enorme; **'no left** ~' (*AUT*) 'proibido dobrar à esquerda'; **it's your** ~ é a sua vez; **in** ~ por sua vez; **to take** ~**s** revezar; **to** ~ **about** *vi* dar uma volta completa; **to** ~ **away** *vi* virar a cabeça; **to** ~ **back** *vi* voltar atrás; **to** ~ **down** *vt* (*refuse*) recusar; (*reduce*) baixar; (*fold*) dobrar, virar para baixo; **to** ~ **in** *vi* (*col: go to bed*) ir dormir // *vt* (*fold*) dobrar para dentro; **to** ~ **off** *vi* (*from road*) desviar-se // *vt* (*light, radio etc*) apagar; (*engine*) desligar; **to** ~ **on** *vt* (*light, radio etc*) acender; (*engine*) ligar; **to** ~ **out** *vt* (*light, gas*) apagar // *vi* ~ **to be** revelar-se (ser)..., resultar (ser)...; **to** ~ **up** *vi* (*person*) chegar, apresentar-se; (*lost object*) aparecer // *vt* (*gen*) subir; ~**ing** *n* (*in road*) volta, curva; ~**ing point** *n* (*fig*) momento decisivo, virada.

**turnip** ['tə:nɪp] n nabo.

**turnout** ['tə:naut] n assistência.

**turnover** ['tə:nəuvə\*] n (COMM: amount of money) volume m de negócios; (: of goods) movimento.

**turnpike** ['tə:npaɪk] n (US) estrada or rodovia com pedágio (Pt: com portagem).

**turnstile** ['tə:nstaɪl] n roleta.

**turntable** ['tə:nteɪbl] n (on record player) prato.

**turn-up** ['tə:nʌp] n (on trousers) volta, dobra.

**turpentine** ['tə:pəntaɪn] n (also: turps) terebentina, aguarrás f.

**turquoise** ['tə:kwɔɪz] n (stone) turquesa // adj cor turquesa.

**turret** ['tʌrɪt] n torre f pequena.

**turtle** ['tə:tl] n tartaruga, cágado.

**tusk** [tʌsk] n presa, colmilho.

**tussle** ['tʌsl] n (fight) luta; (scuffle) contenda, rixa.

**tutor** ['tju:tə\*] n (gen) professor(a) m/f; ~**ial** [-'tɔ:rɪəl] n (SCOL) seminário.

**T.V.** [ti:'vi:] n abbr of **television**.

**twaddle** ['twɔdl] n bobagens fpl, disparates mpl.

**twang** [twæŋ] n (of instrument) dedilhado; (of voice) timbre m nasal or fanhoso // vi vibrar // vt (guitar) dedilhar.

**tweed** [twi:d] n tweed m, pano grosso de lã.

**tweezers** ['twi:zəz] npl pinça (pequena).

**twelfth** [twelfθ] adj décimo-segundo; **T~ Night** n noite f de Reis, Epifania.

**twelve** [twelv] num doze.

**twentieth** ['twentiθ] adj vigésimo.

**twenty** ['twenti] num vinte.

**twerp** [twə:p] n (col) imbecil m/f.

**twice** [twais] adv duas vezes; ~ **as much** duas vezes mais.

**twig** [twig] n graveto, varinha // vi (col) perceber.

**twilight** ['twaɪlaɪt] n crepúsculo, meia-luz f.

**twin** [twin] adj, n gêmeo/a // vt irmanar-se, emparelhar.

**twine** [twain] n barbante m // vi (plant) enroscar-se, enrolar-se.

**twinge** [twindʒ] n (of pain) pontada; (of conscience) remorso.

**twinkle** ['twɪŋkl] n cintilação f // vi cintilar; (eyes) pestanejar.

**twirl** [twə:l] n giro, volta // vt fazer girar // vi girar rapidamente.

**twist** [twist] n (action) torção f; (in road, coil) curva; (in wire, flex) virada; (in story) mudança imprevista // vt torcer, retorcer; (weave) entrelaçar; (roll around) enrolar; (fig) deformar // vi serpentear.

**twit** [twit] n (col) idiota, bobo.

**twitch** [twitʃ] n puxão m; (nervous) tique m nervoso // vi contrair-se, puxar bruscamente, contorcer-se.

**two** [tu:] num dois; **to put** ~ **and** ~ **together** (fig) concluir pela evidência dos fatos (Pt: -ct-); ~**-door** adj (AUT) de duas portas; ~**-faced** adj (pej: person) falso; ~**fold** adv: **to increase** ~**fold** duplicar; ~**-piece** (suit) n traje m de duas peças; ~**-piece** (swimsuit) n maiô m de duas peças, biquíni m; ~**-seater** (plane) avião m de dois lugares; (car) carro de dois lugares; ~**some** n (people) casal m; ~**-way** adj: ~**-way traffic** trânsito em mão dupla.

**tycoon** [taɪ'ku:n] n: (**business**) ~ magnata m, ricaço.

**type** [taip] n (category) tipo, espécie f; (model) modelo; (TYP) tipo, letra // vt (letter etc) datilografar (Pt: -ct-); ~**script** n texto da(c)tilografado; ~**writer** n máquina de escrever; ~**written** adj da(c)tilografado.

**typhoid** ['taifɔɪd] n febre f tifóide.

**typhoon** [tai'fu:n] n tufão m.

**typhus** ['taɪfəs] n tifo.

**typical** ['tɪpɪkl] adj típico; **typify** [-fai] vt tipificar, simbolizar.

**typing** ['taɪpɪŋ] n datilografia (Pt: -ct-); **typist** n datilógrafo/a (Pt: -ct-) m/f.

**tyranny** ['tɪrənɪ] n tirania.

**tyrant** ['taɪərnt] n tirano/a.

**tyre, tire** (US) ['taɪə*] n pneu m, pneumático.

**tzar** [zɑː*] n = **tsar.**

# U

**U-bend** ['juːbɛnd] n (in pipe) curva em U.

**ubiquitous** [juːˈbɪkwɪtəs] adj ubíquo, onipresente (Pt: -mn-).

**udder** ['ʌdə*] n ubre f.

**UFO** ['juːfəʊ] n abbr of **unidentified flying object** O.V.N.I. m (objeto voador não identificado).

**ugliness** ['ʌglɪnɪs] n feiúra; **ugly** adj feio; (dangerous) perigoso.

**U.K.** n abbr of **United Kingdom** Reino Unido.

**ulcer** ['ʌlsə*] n úlcera.

**Ulster** ['ʌlstə*] n Ulster m, Irlanda do Norte.

**ulterior** [ʌlˈtɪərɪə*] adj ulterior; ~ **motive** motivo oculto.

**ultimate** ['ʌltɪmɪt] adj último, final; (authority) máximo; ~**ly** adv (in the end) no final, por último; (fundamentally) no fundo.

**ultimatum** [ʌltɪˈmeɪtəm] n ultimato.

**ultraviolet** ['ʌltrəˈvaɪəlɪt] adj ultravioleta.

**umbilical cord** [ʌmbɪˈlaɪkl-] n cordão m umbilical.

**umbrella** [ʌmˈbrɛlə] n guarda-chuva m.

**umpire** ['ʌmpaɪə*] n árbitro // vt arbitrar.

**umpteen** [ʌmpˈtiːn] adj inúmeros; **for the** ~**th time** pela enegésima vez.

**UN, UNO** abbr of **United Nations**

**(Organization)** O.N.U. f (Organização f das) Nações Unidas fpl.

**unable** [ʌnˈeɪbl] adj: **to be** ~ **to do sth** ser incapaz de or não poder fazer algo.

**unabridged** [ʌnəˈbrɪdʒd] adj integral.

**unaccompanied** [ʌnəˈkʌmpənɪd] adj desacompanhado.

**unaccountably** [ʌnəˈkauntəblɪ] adv inexplicavelmente.

**unaccustomed** [ʌnəˈkʌstəmd] adj: **to be** ~ **to** não estar acostumado a.

**unaided** [ʌnˈeɪdɪd] adj sem ajuda, por si só.

**unanimous** [juːˈnænɪməs] adj unânime; ~**ly** adv unanimamente.

**unarmed** [ʌnˈɑːmd] adj (without a weapon) desarmado; (defenceless) indefeso.

**unassuming** [ʌnəˈsjuːmɪŋ] adj modesto, despretencioso.

**unattached** [ʌnəˈtætʃt] adj (person) livre; (part etc) solto, separado.

**unattended** [ʌnəˈtɛndɪd] adj (car, luggage) sem vigilância, abandonado.

**unattractive** [ʌnəˈtræktɪv] adj sem atrativos (Pt: -ct-), pouco atraente.

**unauthorized** [ʌnˈɔːθəraɪzd] adj não autorizado, proibido.

**unavoidable** [ʌnəˈvɔɪdəbl] adj inevitável.

**unaware** [ʌnəˈwɛə*] adj: **to be** ~ **of** ignorar, não perceber; ~**s** adv improvisamente, de surpresa.

**unbalanced** [ʌnˈbælənst] adj desequilibrado; (mentally) desajustado.

**unbearable** [ʌnˈbɛərəbl] adj insuportável.

**unbeatable** [ʌnˈbiːtəbl] adj (team) invencível; (price) sem igual.

**unbeaten** [ʌnˈbiːtn] adj invicto.

**unbeknown(st)** [ʌnbɪˈnəʊn(st)] adv: ~ **to me** desconhecido por mim.

**unbelievable** [ʌnbɪ'liːvəbl] adj inacreditável, incrível.

**unbend** [ʌn'bend] (irr: like bend) vi relaxar-se // vt (wire) desentortar.

**unblock** [ʌn'blɔk] vt (pipe) desentupir.

**unborn** [ʌn'bɔːn] adj por nascer, futuro.

**unbounded** [ʌn'baundɪd] adj ilimitado, infinito, imenso.

**unbreakable** [ʌn'breɪkəbl] adj inquebrável.

**unbridled** [ʌn'braɪdld] adj (fig) desenfreado.

**unbroken** [ʌn'brəukən] adj (seal) intacto; (series) ininterrupto; (record) mantido; (spirit) indômito.

**unburden** [ʌn'bɔːdn] vr: **to ~ o.s.** desabafar.

**unbutton** [ʌn'bʌtn] vt desabotoar.

**uncalled-for** [ʌn'kɔːldfɔː*] adj desnecessário, gratuito.

**uncanny** [ʌn'kænɪ] adj (strange) estranho; (mysterious) sobrenatural.

**unceasing** [ʌn'siːsɪŋ] adj ininterrupto.

**uncertain** [ʌn'sɔːtn] adj incerto; (character) indeciso; **~ty** n incerteza.

**unchanged** [ʌn'tʃeɪndʒd] adj sem mudar, inalterado.

**uncharitable** [ʌn'tʃærɪtəbl] adj sem caridade.

**uncharted** [ʌn'tʃɑːtɪd] adj inexplorado.

**unchecked** [ʌn'tʃekt] adj desenfreado, livre.

**uncivil** [ʌn'sɪvɪl] adj grosseiro, rude.

**uncle** ['ʌŋkl] n tio.

**uncomfortable** [ʌn'kʌmfətəbl] adj incômodo; (uneasy) pouco à vontade.

**uncommon** [ʌn'kɔmən] adj raro, incomum, excepcional.

**unconcerned** [ʌnkən'sɔːnd] adj indiferente, despreocupado.

**unconditional** [ʌnkən'dɪʃənl] adj incondicional.

**unconscious** [ʌn'kɔnʃəs] adj sem

sentidos, desacordado; (unaware) inconsciente // n: **the ~** o inconsciente; **~ly** adv inconscientemente.

**uncontrollable** [ʌnkən'trəuləbl] adj (temper) ingovernável; (laughter) incontrolável.

**uncouth** [ʌn'kuːθ] adj rude, grosseiro, inculto.

**uncover** [ʌn'kʌvə*] vt (gen) descobrir; (take lid off) destapar, destampar.

**undecided** [ʌndɪ'saɪdɪd] adj (character) indeciso; (question) não respondido, pendente.

**undeniable** [ʌndɪ'naɪəbl] adj inegável.

**under** ['ʌndə*] prep debaixo de; (fig) sob; (less than) menos de, inferior a; (according to) segundo, de acordo com; **~ there** ali embaixo; **~ repair** em conserto // adv embaixo.

**under...** ['ʌndə*] pref sub-; **~age** adj menor de idade; **~carriage** n trem m de aterrissagem; **~clothes** npl roupa sg de baixo; **~coat** n (paint) primeira mão f; **~cover** adj secreto, furtivo; **~current** n corrente f submarina; (fig) tendência oculta; **~cut** vt irr rebaixar o preço para competir com; **~developed** adj subdesenvolvido; **~dog** n injustiçado; **~done** adj (CULIN) mal passado; **~estimate** vt subestimar; **~exposed** adj (PHOT) sem exposição suficiente; **~fed** adj subnutrido; **~foot** adv sob os pés; **~go** vt irr sofrer; (treatment) receber; **~graduate** n estudante m/f universitário/a; **~ground** n (RAILWAY) metrô m; (Pt) metro (-politano); (POL) organização f clandestina // adj subterrâneo; **~growth** n vegetação f rasteira; **~hand(ed)** adj (fig) desleal; **~lie** vt irr estar debaixo de; (fig) ser a base de; **~line** vt sublinhar, frisar; **~ling** ['ʌndəlɪŋ] n (pej) subalterno/a;

~**mine** vt minar, solapar; ~**neath** [ʌndə'niːθ] adv debaixo, embaixo, por baixo // prep debaixo de, sob; ~**paid** adj mal pago; ~**pants** npl (Brit) cueca(s) f(pl); ~**pass** n passagem f inferior; ~**price** vt vender abaixo do preço; ~**privileged** adj menos favorecido; ~**rate** vt depreciar, subestimar; ~**side** n parte f inferior; ~**skirt** n anágua.

**understand** [ʌndə'stænd] (irr: like stand) vt/i entender, compreender; (assume) subentender; ~**able** adj compreensível; ~**ing** adj compreensivo // n compreensão f, entendimento; (agreement) acordo.

**understatement** [ʌndə'steitmənt] n descrição f atenuada; (quality) modéstia (excessiva).

**understood** [ʌndə'stud] pt, pp of **understand** // adj entendido; (implied) subentendido, implícito.

**understudy** ['ʌndəstʌdi] n ator (Pt: -ct-) m substituto.

**undertake** [ʌndə'teik] (irr: like take) vt empreender; **to ~ to do sth** comprometer-se a fazer algo.

**undertaker** ['ʌndəteikə*] n agente m funerário; (col) papa-defuntos m inv.

**undertaking** [ʌndə'teikiŋ] n empreendimento; (promise) promessa.

**underwater** [ʌndə'wɔːtə*] adv sob a água // adj subaquático.

**underwear** ['ʌndəweə*] n roupa de baixo, roupa íntima.

**underweight** [ʌndə'weit] adj de peso inferior ao normal; (person) magro.

**underworld** ['ʌndəwəːld] n (of crime) submundo.

**underwriter** ['ʌndəraitə*] n (INSURANCE) subscritor(a) m/f (que faz resseguro).

**undesirable** [ʌndi'zaiərəbl] adj indesejável.

**undies** ['ʌndiz] npl (col) roupa de baixo.

**undignified** [ʌn'dignifaid] adj sem dignidade, indecoroso.

**undisputed** [ʌndi'spjuːtid] adj incontestável, evidente.

**undo** [ʌn'duː] (irr: like do) vt desfazer; ~**ing** n ruína, desgraça.

**undoubted** [ʌn'dautid] adj indubitável; ~**ly** adv sem dúvida, indubitavelmente.

**undress** [ʌn'dres] vi despir-se.

**undue** [ʌn'djuː] adj indevido, excessivo.

**undulating** ['ʌndjuleitiŋ] adj ondulante.

**unduly** [ʌn'djuːli] adv indevidamente, impropriamente.

**unearth** [ʌn'əːθ] vt desenterrar.

**unearthly** [ʌn'əːθli] adj: **at an ~ hour of the night** na calada da noite.

**uneasy** [ʌn'iːzi] adj inquieto, desassossegado; (worried) preocupado.

**uneconomic(al)** ['ʌniːkə'nɔmik(l)] adj antieconômico.

**uneducated** [ʌn'edjukeitid] adj inculto, sem instrução, não escolarizado.

**unemployed** [ʌnim'plɔid] adj desempregado // n: **the ~** os desempregados; **unemployment** [-'plɔimənt] n desemprego.

**unending** [ʌn'endiŋ] adj interminável.

**unenthusiastic** [ʌninθuːzi'æstik] adj sem entusiasmo.

**unerring** [ʌn'əːriŋ] adj infalível.

**uneven** [ʌn'iːvn] adj desigual; (road etc) irregular, acidentado.

**unexpected** [ʌnik'spektid] adj inesperado.

**unfair** [ʌn'feə*] adj: ~ **(to)** injusto (com); ~**ly** adv injustamente.

**unfaithful** [ʌn'feiθful] adj infiel.

**unfamiliar** [ʌnfə'miliə*] adj pouco familiar, desconhecido.

**unfashionable** [ʌnˈfæʃnəbl] adj fora da moda.

**unfasten** [ʌnˈfɑːsn] vt desatar.

**unfavourable, unfavorable** (US) [ʌnˈfeɪvərəbl] adj desfavorável.

**unfeeling** [ʌnˈfiːlɪŋ] adj insensível.

**unfinished** [ʌnˈfɪnɪʃt] adj incompleto, inacabado.

**unfit** [ʌnˈfɪt] adj sem preparo físico or mental; (incompetent) incompetente, incapaz; ~ **for work** inapto para trabalhar.

**unflagging** [ʌnˈflægɪŋ] adj incansável.

**unfold** [ʌnˈfəʊld] vt desdobrar; (fig) revelar // vi abrir-se, desdobrar-se.

**unforeseen** [ˈʌnfɔːˈsiːn] adj imprevisto.

**unforgettable** [ʌnfəˈgɛtəbl] adj inesquecível.

**unforgivable** [ʌnfəˈgɪvəbl] adj imperdoável.

**unfortunate** [ʌnˈfɔːtʃnət] adj infeliz; (event, remark) inoportuno; ~**ly** adv infelizmente.

**unfounded** [ʌnˈfaʊndɪd] adj infundado.

**unfriendly** [ʌnˈfrɛndlɪ] adj hostil, antipático.

**unfurnished** [ʌnˈfɜːnɪʃt] adj desmobiliado, sem mobília.

**ungainly** [ʌnˈgeɪnlɪ] adj desalinhado.

**unhappiness** [ʌnˈhæpɪnɪs] n tristeza; **unhappy** adj (sad) triste; (unfortunate) desventurado; (childhood) infeliz; **unhappy with** (arrangements etc) descontente com, insatisfeito com.

**unharmed** [ʌnˈhɑːmd] adj ileso; (col) são e salvo.

**unhealthy** [ʌnˈhɛlθɪ] adj (gen) insalubre; (person) doentio, doente.

**unheard-of** [ʌnˈhɜːdɒv] adj (extraordinary) inaudito, insólito; (unknown) desconhecido.

**unhook** [ʌnˈhuk] vt desenganchar; (from wall) despendurar; (dress) abrir, soltar.

**unhurt** [ʌnˈhɜːt] adj ileso.

**unidentified** [ʌnaɪˈdɛntɪfaɪd] adj não-identificado.

**uniform** [ˈjuːnɪfɔːm] n uniforme m // adj uniforme; ~**ity** [-ˈfɔːmɪtɪ] n uniformidade f.

**unify** [ˈjuːnɪfaɪ] vt unificar, unir.

**unilateral** [juːnɪˈlætərəl] adj unilateral.

**unintentional** [ʌnɪnˈtɛnʃənəl] adj involuntário, não intencional.

**union** [ˈjuːnjən] n união f; (also: **trade** ~) sindicato (de trabalhadores) // adj sindical; **U~ Jack** n bandeira britânica.

**unique** [juːˈniːk] adj único, igual.

**unison** [ˈjuːnɪsn] n: **in** ~ em harmonia, em uníssono.

**unit** [ˈjuːnɪt] n unidade f; (team, squad) grupo; **kitchen** ~ móvel m de cozinha.

**unite** [juːˈnaɪt] vt unir // vi unir-se; ~**d** adj unido; **U~d Kingdom (U.K.)** n (o) Reino Unido; **U~d Nations (Organization)** (UN, UNO) n (Organização f das) Nações Unidas fpl (O.N.U.); **U~d States (of America) (US, USA)** n (os) Estados Unidos mpl (da América) (E.U.A.).

**unity** [ˈjuːnɪtɪ] n unidade f.

**universal** [juːnɪˈvɜːsl] adj universal.

**universe** [ˈjuːnɪvɜːs] n universo.

**university** [juːnɪˈvɜːsɪtɪ] n universidade f.

**unjust** [ʌnˈdʒʌst] adj injusto.

**unkempt** [ʌnˈkɛmpt] adj desleixado, descuidado; (hair) despenteado.

**unkind** [ʌnˈkaɪnd] adj descortês, indelicado; (comment etc) cruel.

**unknown** [ʌnˈnəʊn] adj desconhecido.

**unladen** [ʌnˈleɪdn] adj (ship, weight) sem carga.

**unleash** [ʌnˈliːʃ] vt soltar; (fig) desencadear.

**unless** [ʌnˈlɛs] conj a menos que, a não ser que; ~ **he comes** a menos que ele venha; ~ otherwise stated salvo indicação contrária.

**unlike** [ʌnˈlaɪk] adj diferente // prep diferentemente de, ao contrário de.

**unlikely** [ʌnˈlaɪklɪ] adj improvável, inverossímil.

**unlimited** [ʌnˈlɪmɪtɪd] adj ilimitado.

**unload** [ʌnˈləud] vt descarregar.

**unlock** [ʌnˈlɔk] vt destrancar.

**unlucky** [ʌnˈlʌkɪ] adj infeliz; (object, number) de mau agouro; **to be ~** ser azarado.

**unmarried** [ʌnˈmærɪd] adj solteiro.

**unmask** [ʌnˈmɑːsk] vt desmascarar.

**unmistakable** [ʌnmɪsˈteɪkəbl] adj inconfundível.

**unmitigated** [ʌnˈmɪtɪgeɪtɪd] adj não mitigado, absoluto.

**unnatural** [ʌnˈnætʃrəl] adj (gen) antinatural, artificial; (manner) afetado (Pt: -ct-); (habit) depravado.

**unnecessary** [ʌnˈnɛsəsərɪ] adj desnecessário, inútil.

**unnoticed** [ʌnˈnəutɪst] adj: **to go ~** passar despercebido.

**unobtainable** [ʌnəbˈteɪnəbl] adj inalcançável.

**unoccupied** [ʌnˈɔkjupaɪd] adj (seat etc) desocupado, livre.

**unofficial** [ʌnəˈfɪʃl] adj não-oficial, informal; (strike) desautorizado.

**unorthodox** [ʌnˈɔːθədɔks] adj pouco ortodoxo, heterodoxo.

**unpack** [ʌnˈpæk] vi desfazer as malas, desembrulhar.

**unpalatable** [ʌnˈpælətəbl] adj não apetecível; (truth) desagradável.

**unparalleled** [ʌnˈpærəleld] adj (unequalled) sem paralelo; (unique) único, incomparável.

**unpleasant** [ʌnˈplɛznt] adj (disagreeable) desagradável; (person, manner) antipático.

**unplug** [ʌnˈplʌg] vt desligar.

**unpopular** [ʌnˈpɔpjulə*] adj impopular.

**unprecedented** [ʌnˈprɛsɪdəntɪd] adj sem precedentes.

**unpredictable** [ʌnprɪˈdɪktəbl] adj imprevisível.

**unproductive** [ʌnprəˈdʌktɪv] adj improdutivo.

**unqualified** [ʌnˈkwɔlɪfaɪd] adj leigo; (teacher) não qualificado, inabilitado; (success) irrestrito, absoluto.

**unravel** [ʌnˈrævl] vt desemaranhar.

**unreal** [ʌnˈrɪəl] adj irreal, ilusório.

**unrealistic** [ʌnrɪəˈlɪstɪk] adj pouco realista.

**unreasonable** [ʌnˈriːznəbl] adj despropositado; (demand) absurdo, injusto.

**unrelated** [ʌnrɪˈleɪtɪd] adj sem relação; (family) sem parentesco.

**unrelenting** [ʌnrɪˈlɛntɪŋ] adj implacável.

**unreliable** [ʌnrɪˈlaɪəbl] adj (person) indigno de confiança; (machine) incerto, perigoso.

**unrelieved** [ʌnrɪˈliːvd] adj (monotony) monótono.

**unrepeatable** [ʌnrɪˈpiːtəbl] adj (offer) irrepetível.

**unrepresentative** [ʌnrɛprɪˈzɛntətɪv] adj pouco representativo or característico.

**unrest** [ʌnˈrɛst] n inquietação f, desassossego; (POL) distúrbios mpl.

**unroll** [ʌnˈrəul] vt desenrolar.

**unruly** [ʌnˈruːlɪ] adj indisciplinado.

**unsafe** [ʌnˈseɪf] adj (journey) perigoso; (car etc) inseguro.

**unsaid** [ʌnˈsɛd] adj: **to leave sth ~** deixar algo sem dizer.

**unsatisfactory** [ˈʌnsætɪsˈfæktərɪ] adj insatisfatório.

**unsavoury, unsavory** (US) [ʌnˈseɪvərɪ] adj (fig) repugnante, vil.

**unscathed** [ʌnˈskeɪðd] adj ileso.

**unscrew** [ʌnˈskruː] vt desparafusar.

**unscrupulous** [ʌnˈskruːpjuləs] adj inescrupuloso, imoral.

**unsettled** [ʌnˈsɛtld] adj incerto,

duvidoso; (weather) variável, instável.

**unshaven** [ʌn'ʃeɪvn] adj sem barbear.

**unsightly** [ʌn'saɪtlɪ] adj feio, disforme.

**unskilled** [ʌn'skɪld] adj: ~ **worker** operário não-especializado.

**unspeakable** [ʌn'spi:kəbl] adj indizível; (bad) inqualificável.

**unsteady** [ʌn'stɛdɪ] adj instável.

**unstuck** [ʌn'stʌk] adj: **to come** ~ despregar-se; (fig) fracassar.

**unsuccessful** [ʌnsək'sɛsful] adj (attempt) frustrado, vão/vã; (writer, proposal) sem êxito; **to be** ~ (in attempting sth) ser mal sucedido; ~**ly** adv em vão, debalde.

**unsuitable** [ʌn'su:təbl] adj inadequado, inconveniente.

**unsure** [ʌn'ʃuə*] adj inseguro, incerto.

**unsuspecting** [ʌnsə'spɛktɪŋ] adj confiante, insuspeitado.

**unswerving** [ʌn'swɜ:vɪŋ] adj inabalável, firme, resoluto.

**untangle** [ʌn'tæŋgl] vt desemaranhar, desenredar.

**untapped** [ʌn'tæpt] adj (resources) inexplorado.

**unthinkable** [ʌn'θɪŋkəbl] adj impensável, inconcebível, incalculável.

**untidy** [ʌn'taɪdɪ] adj (room) desarrumado, desleixado; (appearance) desmazelado, desalinhado.

**untie** [ʌn'taɪ] vt desatar, desfazer.

**until** [ən'tɪl] prep até (a) // conj até que; ~ **he comes** até que ele venha; ~ **then** até então.

**untimely** [ʌn'taɪmlɪ] adj inoportuno, intempestivo; (death) prematuro.

**untold** [ʌn'təʊld] adj (story) inédito; (suffering) incalculável; (wealth) inestimável.

**untoward** [ʌntə'wɔ:d] adj desfavorável, inconveniente.

**unused** [ʌn'ju:zd] adj novo, sem uso.

**unusual** [ʌn'ju:ʒuəl] adj incomum, extraordinário, insólito.

**unveil** [ʌn'veɪl] vt (statue) desvelar, descobrir.

**unwavering** [ʌn'weɪvərɪŋ] adj firme, inabalável.

**unwelcome** [ʌn'wɛlkəm] adj (at a bad time) inoportuno, indesejável; (unpleasant) desagradável.

**unwell** [ʌn'wɛl] adj: **to feel** ~ estar indisposto; **to be** ~ estar adoentado.

**unwieldy** [ʌn'wiːldɪ] adj difícil de manejar, pesado.

**unwilling** [ʌn'wɪlɪŋ] adj: **to be** ~ **to do sth** estar relutante em fazer algo; ~**ly** adv de má vontade.

**unwind** [ʌn'waɪnd] (irr: like wind) vt desenrolar // vi (relax) relaxar-se.

**unwitting** [ʌn'wɪtɪŋ] adj inconsciente, involuntário.

**unworthy** [ʌn'wɜ:ðɪ] adj indigno.

**unwrap** [ʌn'ræp] vt desembrulhar.

**up** [ʌp] prep: **to go/be** ~ **sth** subir algo/estar em cima de algo // adv em cima, para cima; ~ **there** lá em cima; ~ **above** em cima; **to be** ~ (out of bed) estar levantado; **it is** ~ **to you** você é quem sabe, você decide; **what is he** ~ **to?** o que ele está querendo?, o que ele está tramando?; **he is not** ~ **to it** ele não é capaz de fazê-lo; ~-**and-coming** adj promedor(a); ~**s and downs** npl (fig) altos e baixos mpl.

**upbringing** ['ʌpbrɪŋɪŋ] n educação f, criação f.

**update** [ʌp'deɪt] vt atualizar (Pt: -ct-), pôr em dia; (contract etc) a(c)tualizar.

**upgrade** [ʌp'greɪd] vt elevar o nível de; (job) promover.

**upheaval** [ʌp'hi:vl] n transtorno; (unrest) convulsão f.

**uphill** [ʌp'hɪl] adj ladeira acima; (fig: task) trabalhoso, árduo // adv: **to go** ~ ir morro acima.

**uphold** [ʌp'həʊld] (irr: like hold) vt suster, sustentar.

**upholstery** [ʌpˈhəulstəri] n estofamento, tapeçaria.

**upkeep** [ˈʌpkiːp] n manutenção f.

**upon** [əˈpɔn] prep sobre.

**upper** [ˈʌpə*] adj superior, de cima // n (of shoe) gáspea, parte f superior; ~-**class** adj da classe alta; ~**most** adj o mais elevado; **what was ~most in my mind** o que me preocupava mais.

**upright** [ˈʌpraɪt] adj vertical; (fig) honrado, honesto.

**uprising** [ˈʌpraɪzɪŋ] n sublevação f, levante m.

**uproar** [ˈʌprɔː*] n tumulto, algazarra, fuzuê m.

**uproot** [ʌpˈruːt] vt desarraigar, arrancar.

**upset** [ˈʌpset] n (to plan etc) revés m, reviravolta; (MED) indisposição f // vt [ʌpˈset] (irr: like set) (glass etc) virar; (spill) derramar; (plan) perturbar; (person) aborrecer, perturbar // adj [ʌpˈset] aborrecido, contrariado; (stomach) indisposto.

**upshot** [ˈʌpʃɔt] n resultado.

**upside-down** [ʌpsaɪddaun] adv de cabeça para baixo.

**upstairs** [ʌpˈstɛəz] adv em cima, lá em cima // adj (room) de cima // n andar m de cima.

**upstart** [ˈʌpstɑːt] n novo-rico, pessoa sem classe.

**upstream** [ʌpˈstriːm] adv rio acima.

**uptake** [ˈʌpteɪk] n: **he is quick on the** ~ ele vê longe; **he is slow on the** ~ ele tem raciocínio lento.

**up-to-date** [ˈʌptəˈdeɪt] adj moderno, atualizado.

**upturn** [ˈʌptəːn] n (in luck) virada.

**upward** [ˈʌpwəd] adj ascendente, para cima; ~**(s)** adv para cima.

**uranium** [juəˈreɪnɪəm] n urânio.

**urban** [ˈəːbən] adj urbano, da cidade.

**urbane** [əːˈbeɪn] adj gentil, urbano.

**urchin** [ˈəːtʃɪn] n moleque m, criança maltrapilho.

**urge** [əːdʒ] n (force) impulso,

(desire) desejo // vt: **to** ~ **sb to do sth** incitar alguém a fazer algo.

**urgency** [ˈəːdʒənsɪ] n urgência; (of tone) insistência; **urgent** adj urgente.

**urinal** [juəˈraɪnl] n urinol m, mictório.

**urinate** [juəˈraɪneɪt] vi urinar; **urine** n urina.

**us** [ʌs] pron nos; (after prep) nós.

**US, USA** n abbr of **United States (of America)** E.U.A., Estados Unidos (da América) mpl.

**usage** [ˈjuːzɪdʒ] n uso, costume m.

**use** [juːs] n uso, emprego; (usefulness) utilidade f // vt [juːz] usar, empregar; **she** ~**d to do it** (ela) costumava fazê-lo; **in** ~ em uso; **out of** ~ fora de uso, antiquado; **to be of** ~ servir; **it's no** ~ (pointless) é inútil; (not useful) não serve; **to be** ~**d to** estar acostumado a; **to** ~ **up** vt esgotar, consumir; ~**d** adj (car) usado; ~**ful** adj útil; **to be** ~**ful** servir, ser útil; ~**less** adj inútil; **user** n usuário.

**usher** [ˈʌʃə*] n porteiro; (LAW) oficial m de justiça; ~**ette** [-ˈrɛt] n (in cinema) lanterninha m/f, vaga-lume m/f.

**USSR** n: **the** ~ **(a)** U.R.S.S.

**usual** [ˈjuːʒuəl] adj usual, habitual; ~**ly** adv normalmente.

**usurp** [juːˈzəːp] vt usurpar.

**utensil** [juːˈtɛnsl] n utensílio; **kitchen** ~**s** utensílios de cozinha.

**uterus** [ˈjuːtərəs] n útero.

**utilitarian** [juːtɪlɪˈtɛərɪən] adj utilitário.

**utility** [juːˈtɪlɪtɪ] n utilidade f; ~ **room** n copa.

**utilize** [ˈjuːtɪlaɪz] vt utilizar.

**utmost** [ˈʌtməust] adj maior // n: **to do one's** ~ fazer todo o possível.

**utter** [ˈʌtə*] adj completo, total // vt proferir, pronunciar; ~**ance** n declaração f; ~**ly** adv completamente, totalmente.

**U-turn** [ˈjuːtəːn] n curva em U.

# V

**v.** abbr of **verse**; **versus**; **volt**.

**vacancy** ['veɪkənsɪ] n (job) vaga; (room) quarto livre; **vacant** adj desocupado, livre; (expression) distraído; **vacate** [-'neɪfən] vt (house) desocupar; (job) deixar; (throne) renunciar a.

**vacation** [və'keɪʃən] n férias fpl; ~er n (US) pessoa de férias.

**vaccinate** ['væksɪneɪt] vt vacinar; **vaccination** [-'neɪʃən] n vacinação f.

**vaccine** ['væksiːn] n vacina.

**vacuum** ['vækjum] n vácuo m; ~-cleaner n aspirador m de pó; ~-flask n garrafa térmica.

**vagabond** ['vægəbɒnd] n vagabundo/a.

**vagina** [və'dʒaɪnə] n vagina.

**vagrant** ['veɪgrnt] n vagabundo/a.

**vague** [veɪg] adj vago; (blurred: memory) fraco; (uncertain) incerto, impreciso; (person: que divaga); ~ly adv vagamente.

**vain** [veɪn] adj (conceited) vaidoso; (useless) vão/vã, inútil; **in** ~ em vão.

**vale** [veɪl] n vale m.

**valentine** ['væləntaɪn] n: **V~'s Day** dia m dos namorados.

**valid** ['vælɪd] adj válido; (ticket, law) vigente; ~**ity** [-'lɪdɪtɪ] n validade f; vigência.

**valley** ['vælɪ] n vale m.

**valour, valor** (US) ['vælə*] n valor m, valentia.

**valuable** ['væljuəbl] adj (jewel) de valor; (time) valioso; ~s npl objetos (Pt: -ct-) mpl de valor.

**valuation** [vælju'eɪʃən] n avaliação f, estimativa.

**value** ['væljuː] n valor m; (importance) importância // vt (fix price of) avaliar, calcular; (esteem) estimar; (cherish) apreciar; ~ **added tax** (**VAT**) n imposto sobre

circulação de mercadorias (ICM); ~d adj (appreciated) apreciado, estimado.

**valve** [vælv] n (gen) válvula.

**vampire** ['væmpaɪə*] n vampiro/a m/f.

**van** [væn] n (AUT) camioneta, camionete f; (RAIL) vagão m da bagagem.

**vandal** ['vændl] n vândalo; ~**ism** n vandalismo; ~**ize** vt destruir, depredar.

**vanilla** [və'nɪlə] n baunilha.

**vanish** ['vænɪʃ] vi desaparecer, sumir.

**vanity** ['vænɪtɪ] n vaidade f; ~ **case** n bolsa de maquilagem.

**vantage point** ['vɑːntɪdʒ-] n posição f estratégica.

**vapour, vapor** (US) ['veɪpə*] n vapor m; (steam) exalação f.

**variable** ['vɛərɪəbl] adj variável.

**variance** ['vɛərɪəns] n: **to be at** ~ (**with**) estar em desacordo (com).

**variation** [vɛərɪ'eɪʃən] n variação f, variante f; (in opinion) variedade f.

**varicose** ['værɪkəus] adj: ~ **veins** varizes fpl.

**varied** ['vɛərɪd] adj variado.

**variety** [və'raɪətɪ] n variedade f, diversidade f; (quantity) sortimento; ~ **show** n espetáculo de variedades.

**various** ['vɛərɪəs] adj vários/as, diversos/as.

**varnish** ['vɑːnɪʃ] n (gen) verniz m; (nail) esmalte m // vt (gen) envernizar; (nails) pintar (com esmalte).

**vary** ['vɛərɪ] vt variar; (change) mudar // vi (disagree) divergir, discrepar; (deviate) desviar-se; ~**ing** adj variado.

**vase** [vɑːz] n vaso.

**vaseline** ['væsɪliːn] n vaselina.

**vast** [vɑːst] adj vasto, enorme; (success) imenso; ~**ness** n imensidão f.

**vat** [væt] n tina, cuba.

**VAT** [væt] n abbr of **Value Added Tax.**

**Vatican** ['vætɪkən] n: **the** ~ o Vaticano.

**vault** [vɔːlt] n (of roof) abóbada; (tomb) sepulcro; (in bank) caixa-forte // vt (also: ~ **over**) saltar (por cima de).

**veal** [viːl] n carne f de vitela.

**veer** [vɪə*] vi virar, mudar de direção (Pt: -cç-).

**vegetable** ['vedʒtəbl] n (BOT) vegetal m; (edible plant) legume m, hortaliça; ~**s** npl (cooked) verduras fpl // adj vegetal; ~ **garden** n horta.

**vegetarian** [vedʒɪ'tɛərɪən] adj, n vegetariano.

**vegetate** ['vedʒɪteɪt] vi vegetar.

**vegetation** [vedʒɪ'teɪʃən] n vegetação f.

**vehement** ['viːmənt] adj veemente; (impassioned) apaixonado.

**vehicle** ['viːɪkl] n veículo.

**veil** [veɪl] n véu m // vt velar.

**vein** [veɪn] n veia; (of ore etc) filão m.

**velocity** [vɪ'lɒsɪtɪ] n velocidade f.

**velvet** ['velvɪt] n veludo // adj aveludado.

**vendetta** [ven'detə] n vendeta.

**vending machine** ['vendɪŋ-] n vendedor m automático.

**vendor** ['vendə*] n vendedor(a) m/f.

**veneer** [və'nɪə*] n capa exterior, folheado; (wood) compensado; (fig) verniz m, aparência.

**venereal** [vɪ'nɪərɪəl] adj: ~ **disease** (VD) doença venérea.

**Venetian blind** [vɪ'niːʃən-] n persiana, veneziana.

**Venezuela** [vene'zweɪlə] n Venezuela; ~**n** adj, n venezuelano/a.

**vengeance** ['vendʒəns] n vingança; **with a** ~ (fig) com fúria, com violência.

**venison** ['venɪsn] n carne f de veado.

**venom** ['venəm] n veneno; ~**ous** adj venenoso.

**vent** [vent] n (opening) abertura; (air-hole) respiradouro; (in wall) abertura para ventilação // vt (fig: feelings) desabafar, descarregar.

**ventilate** ['ventɪleɪt] vt ventilar; **ventilation** n ventilação f; **ventilator** n ventilador m.

**ventriloquist** [ven'trɪləkwɪst] n ventríloquo.

**venture** ['ventʃə*] n empreendimento // vt aventurar; (opinion) arriscar // vi arriscar-se, ousar.

**venue** ['venjuː] n local m; (meeting place) ponto de encontro.

**veranda(h)** [və'rændə] n varanda; (with glass) jardim m de inverno.

**verb** [vəːb] n verbo; ~**al** adj verbal.

**verbatim** [vəː'beɪtɪm] adj, adv palavra por palavra, literalmente.

**verbose** [vəː'bəus] adj prolixo.

**verdict** ['vəːdɪkt] n veredicto, decisão f; (fig) opinião f, parecer m.

**verge** [vəːdʒ] n limite m, margem f; **to be on the** ~ **of doing sth** estar a ponto de fazer algo; **to** ~ **on** vt fus beirar em.

**verify** ['verɪfaɪ] vt verificar.

**vermin** ['vəːmɪn] npl (animals) bichos mpl; (insects, fig) insetos (Pt: -ct-) mpl nocivos; (fig) canalha, gente f vil.

**vermouth** ['vəːməθ] n vermute m.

**vernacular** [və'nækjulə*] n vernáculo, língua materna.

**versatile** ['vəːsətaɪl] adj (person) versátil; (machine, tool etc) polivalente; (mind) ágil, flexível.

**verse** [vəːs] n verso, poesia; (stanza) estrofe f; (in bible) versículo.

**versed** [vəːst] adj: (**well-**)~ **in** versado em, especialista em.

**version** ['vəːʃən] n versão f.

**versus** ['vəːsəs] prep contra, versus.

**vertebra** ['vəːtɪbrə], pl ~**e** [-briː] n

vértebra; **vertebrate** [-brɪt] *n* vertebrado.

**vertical** ['vɔːtɪkl] *adj* vertical.

**vertigo** ['vɔːtɪgəu] *n* vertigem *f.*

**very** ['vɛrɪ] *adv* muito // *adj:* the ~ book which o mesmo livro que; the ~ last o último (de todos), bem o último; at the ~ least no mínimo; ~ much muitíssimo.

**vespers** ['vɛspəz] *npl* vésperas *fpl.*

**vessel** ['vɛsl] *n* (*ANAT*) vaso; (*NAUT*) navio, barco; (*container*) vaso, vasilha.

**vest** [vɛst] *n* camiseta; (*US: waistcoat*) colete *m;* ~ed interests *npl* (*COMM*) interesses *mpl* ocultos.

**vestibule** ['vɛstɪbjuːl] *n* vestíbulo.

**vestige** ['vɛstɪdʒ] *n* vestígio, rasto.

**vestry** ['vɛstrɪ] *n* sacristia.

**vet** [vɛt] *n abbr of* **veterinary surgeon** // *vt* examinar.

**veteran** ['vɛtərn] *n* veterano/a; ~ **car** *n* carro antigo.

**veterinary** ['vɛtrɪnərɪ] *adj* veterinário; ~ **surgeon** *n* veterinário/a.

**veto** ['viːtəu], *pl* ~**es** *n* veto // *vt* vetar, proibir.

**vex** [vɛks] *vt* (*irritate*) irritar, apoquentar; (*make impatient*) impacientar; ~**ed** *adj* (*question*) controvertido, discutido.

**via** ['vaɪə] *prep* por, por via de.

**viable** ['vaɪəbl] *adj* viável.

**viaduct** ['vaɪədʌkt] *n* viaduto.

**vibrate** [vaɪ'breɪt] *vi* vibrar; **vibration** [-'breɪʃən] *n* vibração *f.*

**vicar** ['vɪkə*] *n* vigário; ~**age** *n* vicariato.

**vice** [vaɪs] *n* (*evil*) vício; (*TECH*) torno mecânico.

**vice-** ['vaɪs] *pref* vice-; ~ **chairman** *n* vice-presidente *m/f.*

**vice versa** ['vaɪsɪ'vɔːsə] *adv* vice-versa.

**vicinity** [vɪ'sɪnɪtɪ] *n* (*area*) vizinhança; (*nearness*) proximidade *f.*

**vicious** ['vɪʃəs] *adj* (*violent*)

violento; (*depraved*) depravado, vicioso; (*cruel*) cruel; (*bitter*) rancoroso; ~**ness** *n* violência; depravação *f;* crueldade *f;* rancor *m.*

**victim** ['vɪktɪm] *n* vítima *f;* ~**ization** [-'zeɪʃən] *n* (*gen*) perseguição *f;* (*in strike*) represálias *fpl;* ~**ize** *vt* (*strikers etc*) fazer represália contra.

**victor** ['vɪktə*] *n* vencedor(a) *m/f.*

**Victorian** [vɪk'tɔːrɪən] *adj* vitoriano.

**victorious** [vɪk'tɔːrɪəs] *adj* vitorioso.

**victory** ['vɪktərɪ] *n* vitória.

**video** ['vɪdɪəu] *cmp* vídeo; ~(-**tape**) **recorder** *n* gravador *m* de videoteipe, vídeo-cassete *m.*

**vie** [vaɪ] *vi:* **to** ~ **with** competir com.

**Vienna** [vɪ'ɛnə] *n* Viena.

**view** [vjuː] *n* vista, perspectiva; (*landscape*) paisagem *f;* (*opinion*) opinião *f,* parecer *m* // *vt* (*look at*) olhar; (*examine*) examinar; **on** ~ (*in museum etc*) em exposição; **in full** ~ (**of**) à plena vista (de); **in** ~ **of the fact that** em vista do fato (*Pt:* -ct-) de que; ~**er** *n* (*small projector*) visor *m;* (*TV*) telespectador(a) *m/f;* ~**finder** *n* visor *m;* ~**point** *n* ponto de vista.

**vigil** ['vɪdʒɪl] *n* vigília; **to keep** ~ velar; ~**ance** *n* vigilância; ~**ant** *adj* vigilante.

**vigorous** ['vɪgərəs] *adj* enérgico, vigoroso; **vigour**, **vigor** (*US*) *n* energia, vigor *m.*

**vile** [vaɪl] *adj* (*action*) vil, infame; (*smell*) repugnante, repulsivo.

**vilify** ['vɪlɪfaɪ] *vt* vilipendiar.

**villa** ['vɪlə] *n* (*country house*) casa de campo; (*suburban house*) vila, quinta.

**village** ['vɪlɪdʒ] *n* aldeia, povoado; **villager** *n* aldeão/aldeã *m/f.*

**villain** ['vɪlən] *n* (*scoundrel*)

velhaco, patife *m*; *(criminal)* meliante *m/f*.

**vindicate** ['vɪndɪkeɪt] *vt* vingar, desagravar.

**vindictive** [vɪn'dɪktɪv] *adj* vingativo.

**vine** [vaɪn] *n* vinha, videira.

**vinegar** ['vɪnɪgə*] *n* vinagre *m*.

**vineyard** ['vɪnjɑːd] *n* vinha, vinhedo.

**vintage** ['vɪntɪdʒ] *n* vindima; *(year)* safra, colheita; **~ wine** *n* vinho velho.

**vinyl** ['vaɪnl] *n* vinil *m*.

**violate** ['vaɪəleɪt] *vt* violar; **violation** [-'leɪʃən] *n* violação *f*.

**violence** ['vaɪələns] *n* violência; **violent** *adj* (*gen*) violento; (*intense*) intenso.

**violet** ['vaɪələt] *adj* violeta // *n* (*plant*) violeta.

**violin** [vaɪə'lɪn] *n* violino; **~ist** *n* violinista *m/f*.

**viper** ['vaɪpə*] *n* víbora.

**virgin** ['vəːdʒɪn] *n* virgem *m/f* // *adj* virgem; **the Blessed V~** a Virgem Santíssima; **~ity** [-'dʒɪnɪtɪ] *n* virgindade *f*.

**Virgo** ['vəːgəu] *n* Virgem *f*.

**virile** ['vɪraɪl] *adj* viril; **virility** [vɪ'rɪlɪtɪ] *n* virilidade *f*, (*fig*) machismo.

**virtually** ['vəːtjuəlɪ] *adv* (*almost*) virtualmente.

**virtue** ['vəːtjuː] *n* virtude *f*; **by ~ of** em virtude de.

**virtuoso** [vəːtju'əuzəu] *n* virtuoso/a.

**virtuous** ['vəːtjuəs] *adj* virtuoso.

**virulent** ['vɪrulənt] *adj* virulento.

**virus** ['vaɪərəs] *n* vírus *m*.

**visa** ['viːzə] *n* visto.

**vis-à-vis** [viːzə'viː] *prep* com relação a.

**visibility** [vɪzɪ'bɪlɪtɪ] *n* visibilidade *f*.

**visible** ['vɪzəbl] *adj* visível; **visibly** *adv* visivelmente.

**vision** ['vɪʒən] *n* (*sight*) vista, visão

*f*; (*foresight, in dream*) visão *f*; **~ary** *n* visionário/a.

**visit** ['vɪzɪt] *n* visita // *vt* (*person*) visitar, fazer uma visita a; (*place*) ir a, ir conhecer; **~or** *n* (*gen*) visitante *m/f*; (*to one's house*) visita; (*tourist*) turista *m/f*; (*tripper*) excursionista *m/f*; **~ors' book** *n* livro de visitas.

**visor** ['vaɪzə*] *n* viseira.

**vista** ['vɪstə] *n* vista, perspectiva.

**visual** ['vɪzjuəl] *adj* visual; **~ize** *vt* visualizar; (*foresee*) prever.

**vital** ['vaɪtl] *adj* (*essential*) essencial, indispensável; (*important*) de importância vital; (*crucial*) crucial; (*person*) vivo, animado; (*of life*) vital; **~ity** [-'tælɪtɪ] *n* energia, vitalidade *f*; **~ly** *adv*: **~ly important** de importância vital.

**vitamin** ['vɪtəmɪn] *n* vitamina.

**vivacious** [vɪ'veɪʃəs] *adj* vivaz, espirituoso.

**vivid** ['vɪvɪd] *adj* (*account*) vívido; (*light*) claro, brilhante; (*imagination*) vivo.

**vivisection** [vɪvɪ'sɛkʃən] *n* vivissecção *f*.

**V-neck** ['viːnɛk] *n* gola em V.

**vocabulary** [vəu'kæbjulərɪ] *n* vocabulário.

**vocal** ['vəukl] *adj* vocal; (*noisy*) clamoroso; **~ chords** *npl* cordas *fpl* vocais; **~ist** *n* vocalista *m/f*, cantor(a) *m/f*.

**vocation** [vəu'keɪʃən] *n* vocação *f*; **~al** *adj* vocacional.

**vociferous** [və'sɪfərəs] *adj* vociferante.

**vodka** ['vɔdkə] *n* vodca.

**vogue** [vəug] *n* voga, moda.

**voice** [vɔɪs] *n* voz *f*; **in a low/loud ~** em voz baixa/alta // *vt* (*opinion*) expressar.

**void** [vɔɪd] *n* vazio; (*hole*) oco // *adj* (*gen*) vazio; (*vacant*) vago; (*null*) nulo, inútil.

**volatile** ['vɔlətaɪl] *adj* volátil.

**volcanic** [vɔl'kænɪk] *adj* vulcânico;

**volcano** [-'keɪnəʊ], pl -es n vulcão m.

**volley** ['vɔlɪ] n (of gunfire) descarga, salva; (of stones etc) chuva; (TENNIS etc) voleio; ~**ball** n voleibol m.

**volt** [vəʊlt] n volt m; ~**age** n voltagem f.

**voluble** ['vɔljʊbl] adj tagarela, loquaz.

**volume** ['vɔljuːm] n (gen) volume m.

**voluntarily** ['vɔləntrɪlɪ] adv livremente, voluntariamente.

**voluntary** ['vɔləntərɪ] adj voluntário, intencional; (unpaid) (a título) gratuito.

**volunteer** [vɔlən'tɪə*] n voluntário/a m/f // vi oferecer-se voluntariamente.

**voluptuous** [və'lʌptjʊəs] adj voluptuoso.

**vomit** ['vɔmɪt] n vômito // vt/i vomitar.

**vote** [vəʊt] n voto; (votes cast) votação f; (right to ~) direito de votar; (franchise) título de eleitor // vt (chairman) eleger // vi votar; **voter** n votante m/f, eleitor(a) m/f; **voting** n votação f.

**vouch** [vaʊtʃ]: **to ~ for** vt garantir, responder por.

**voucher** ['vaʊtʃə*] n (for meal, petrol) vale m.

**vow** [vaʊ] n voto // vi fazer votos.

**vowel** ['vaʊəl] n vogal f.

**voyage** ['vɔɪdʒ] n (journey) viagem f; (crossing) travessia.

**vulgar** ['vʌlgə*] adj (rude) grosseiro, ordinário; (in bad taste) vulgar, baixo; ~**ity** ['gærɪtɪ] n grosseria, vulgaridade f.

**vulnerable** ['vʌlnərəbl] adj vulnerável.

**vulture** ['vʌltʃə*] n abutre m.

# W

**wad** [wɔd] n (of cotton wool) chumaço; (of paper) bola; (of banknotes etc) maço.

**waddle** ['wɔdl] vi gingar, bambolear.

**wade** [weɪd] vi: **to ~ through** vadear; (fig: a book) ler com dificuldade; (river) atravessar (a vau).

**wafer** ['weɪfə*] n (biscuit) bolacha; (REL) hóstia.

**waffle** ['wɔfl] vi encher lingüiça.

**waft** [wɔft] vt levar // vi flutuar.

**wag** [wæg] vt sacudir, menear // vi acenar, abanar.

**wage** [weɪdʒ] n (also: ~s) salário, ordenado // vt: **to ~ war** empreender guerra; ~ **claim** n pedido de aumento salarial; ~ **earner** n assalariado/a; ~ **freeze** n congelamento de salários.

**wager** ['weɪdʒə*] n aposta, parada // vi apostar.

**waggle** ['wægl] vt sacudir, agitar.

**wag(g)on** ['wægən] n (horse-drawn) carroça; (truck) caminhão m; (: Pt) camião m; (RAIL) vagão m.

**wail** [weɪl] n lamento, gemido // vi lamentar-se, gemer.

**waist** [weɪst] n cintura; ~**coat** n colete m; ~**line** n cintura.

**wait** [weɪt] n espera; (interval) pausa // vi esperar; **to lie in ~ for** aguardar em emboscada; **I can't ~ to** (fig) mal posso esperar para; **to ~ for** esperar, aguardar; **to ~ on** vt fus servir; "**no ~ing**" (AUT) "proibido estacionar"; ~**er** n garção m; ~**ing list** n lista de espera; ~**ing room** n sala de espera; ~**ress** n garçonete f.

**waive** [weɪv] vt renunciar a.

**wake** [weɪk], pt **woke** or **waked**, pp **woken** or **waked** vt (also: ~ **up**) acordar, despertar // vi (also:

~ **up**) despertar-se // n (for dead person) velório; (NAUT) esteira; **waken** vt/i = **wake**.

**Wales** [weilz] n País m de Gales.

**walk** [wɔːk] n passeio; (hike) excursão f a pé, caminhada; (gait) passo, modo de andar; (in park etc) alameda, passeio // vi andar; (for pleasure, exercise) passear // vt (distance) percorrer a pé, andar; (dog) levar para passear; **it's 10 minutes'** ~ **from here** daqui são 10 minutos a pé; **people from all** ~**s of life** pessoas de todos os níveis; ~**er** n (person) caminhante m/f; ~**ie-talkie** [wɔːkɪ'tɔːkɪ] n transmissor-receptor portátil m, walkie-talkie m; ~**ing** n o andar m; ~**ing shoes** npl sapatos para andar; ~**ing stick** n bengala; ~**out** n (of workers) greve f branca; ~**over** n (col) barbada; ~**way** n passeio.

**wall** [wɔːl] n parede f; (exterior) muro; (city ~ etc) muralha; ~**ed** adj (city) cercado por muralhas; (garden) murado, cercado.

**wallet** [wɔlit] n carteira.

**wallflower** [wɔːlflauə*] n goivo-amarelo; **to be a** ~ (fig) tomar chá de cadeira.

**wallop** [wɔləp] vt (col) surrar, espancar.

**wallow** [wɔləu] vi chafurdar.

**wallpaper** [wɔːlpeipə*] n papel m de parede.

**walnut** [wɔːlnʌt] n noz f; (tree) nogueira.

**walrus** [wɔːlrəs], pl ~ or ~**es** n morsa, vaca marinha.

**waltz** [wɔːlts] n valsa // vi valsar.

**wand** [wɔnd] n (also: **magic** ~) varinha de condão.

**wander** [wɔndə*] vi (person) vagar, perambular; (thoughts) divagar; (get lost) extraviar-se // vt percorrer; ~**er** n vagabundo; ~**ing** adj errante; (thoughts) distraído.

**wane** [wein] vi diminuir; (moon) minguar.

**wangle** [wæŋgl] vt (col): **to** ~ **sth** conseguir algo através de pistolão.

**want** [wɔnt] vt (wish for) querer, desejar; (demand) exigir; (need) precisar (de), necessitar; (lack) carecer de // n: **for** ~ **of** por falta de; ~**s** npl (needs) necessidades fpl; **to** ~ **to do** querer fazer; **to** ~ **sb to do sth** querer que alguém faça algo; ~**ing** adj falto, deficiente; **to be found** ~**ing** não estar à altura da situação.

**wanton** [wɔntn] adj (playful) brincalhão/lhona; (licentious) libertino, lascivo.

**war** [wɔː*] n guerra; **to make** ~ fazer guerra.

**ward** [wɔːd] n (in hospital) ala, enfermaria; (POL) distrito eleitoral; (LAW: child) tutelado, pupilo; **to** ~ **off** vt desviar, aparar; (attack) repelir.

**warden** [wɔːdn] n (of institution) diretor(a) (Pt: -ct-) m/f; (of park, game reserve) administrador m; (also: **traffic** ~) guarda m/f.

**warder** [wɔːdə*] n carcereiro.

**wardrobe** [wɔːdrəub] n (cupboard) armário; (clothes) guarda-roupa.

**warehouse** [wɛəhaus] n armazém m, depósito.

**wares** [wɛəz] npl artigos mpl, mercadorias fpl.

**war:** ~**fare** n guerra, combate m; ~**head** n ogiva (de combate).

**warily** [wɛərɪlɪ] adv cautelosamente, com precaução.

**warlike** [wɔːlaɪk] adj guerreiro, bélico.

**warm** [wɔːm] adj quente, morno, cálido; (thanks, welcome) cordial; (clothes, day) quente; **it's** ~ está quente; **I'm** ~ estou com calor; **to** ~ **up** vi (person, room) aquecer, esquentar; (athlete) fazer aquecimento; (discussion) esquentar-se // vt esquentar; ~**-hearted** adj afetuoso (Pt: -ct-); ~**ly** adv calorosamente, afetuosamente (*Pt*: -ct-); **~th** *n* calor *m*.

**warn** [wɔːn] *vt* prevenir, avisar; **~ing** *n* advertência, aviso; **~ing light** *n* luz *f* de advertência.

**warp** [wɔːp] *vt* deformar // *vi* empenar, deformar-se.

**warrant** ['wɔrnt] *n* (*guarantee*) garantia, fiança; (*LAW*) ordem *f* judicial.

**warranty** ['wɔrənti] *n* garantia.

**warren** ['wɔrən] *n* (*of rabbits*) lura; (*house*) coelheira.

**warrior** ['wɔriə*] *n* guerreiro.

**warship** ['wɔːʃip] *n* navio de guerra.

**wart** [wɔːt] *n* verruga.

**wartime** ['wɔːtaim] *n*: **in ~** em , tempo de guerra.

**wary** ['wɛəri] *adj* cauteloso, precavido.

**was** [wɔz] *pt of* **be**.

**wash** [wɔʃ] *vt* lavar // *vi* lavar-se // *n* (*clothes etc*) lavagem *f*; (*bath*) banho; (*of ship*) esteira; **to have a ~** lavar-se; **to ~ away** *vt* (*stain*) tirar ao lavar; (*subj: river etc*) levar, arrastar; (*fig*) purificar; **to ~ off** *vt* tirar lavando; **to ~ up** *vi* lavar a louça; (*US*) lavar-se; **~able** *adj* lavável; **~basin** *n*, **~bowl** (*US*) *n* pia, bacia; **~er** *n* (*TECH*) arruela, anilha; **~ing** *n* (*dirty*) roupa suja; (*clean*) roupa lavada; **~ing machine** *n* máquina de lavar; **~ing powder** *n* sabão *m* em pó; **~ing-up** *n* lavagem *f* da louça; **~out** *n* (*col*) fracasso, fiasco; **~room** *n* banheiro; (*Pt*) casa de banho.

**wasn't** ['wɔznt] = **was not**.

**wasp** [wɔsp] *n* vespa.

**wastage** ['weistidʒ] *n* desgaste *m*, desperdício; (*loss*) perda; **natural ~** desgaste natural.

**waste** [weist] *n* desperdício, esbanjamento; (*wastage*) desperdício; (*of time*) perda; (*food*) sobras *fpl*; (*rubbish*) lixo // *adj* (*material*) de refugo; (*left over*) de sobra; (*land*) baldio // *vt* (*squander*) esbanjar, dissipar; (*time*) perder;

(*opportunity*) desperdiçar; (*use up*) consumir; **to ~ away** *vi* consumir-se; **~bin** *n* lata de lixo; **~ disposal unit** *n* triturador *m* de lixo; **~ful** *adj* esbanjador(a); (*process*) anti-econômico; **~ ground** *n* terreno baldio; **~paper basket** *n* cesta de papel; **~ pipe** *n* cano de esgoto.

**watch** [wɔtʃ] *n* relógio; (*act of watching*) vigia; (*vigilance*) vigilância; (*guard*: *MIL*) sentinela *f*; (*NAUT*: *spell of duty*) quarto // *vt* (*look at*) observar, olhar; (*programme*) ver; (*go and see*) assistir a; (*spy on, guard*) vigiar; (*be careful of*) tomar cuidado com // *vi* ver, olhar; (*keep guard*) montar guarda; **to ~ out** *vi* cuidar-se, ter cuidado; **~dog** *n* cão m de guarda; **~ful** *adj* vigilante, atento; **~maker** *n* relojoeiro; **~man** *n* vigia *m*; (*also*: **night ~man**) guarda *m* noturno; (*in factory*) vigia *m* noturno; **~ strap** *n* pulseira (do relógio); **~word** *n* lema *m*, divisa.

**water** ['wɔːtə*] *n* água // *vt* (*plant*) regar; **to ~ down** *vt* (*milk*) aguar; **~colour** *n* aquarela; **~cress** *n* agrião *m*; **~fall** *n* cascata, cachoeira; **~ hole** *n* bebedouro, poço; **~ing can** *n* regador *m*; **~ level** *n* nível *m* d'água; **~ lily** *n* nenúfar *m*; **~ line** *n* (*NAUT*) linha d'água; **~logged** *adj* alagado; **~ main** *n* adutora; **~mark** *n* (*on paper*) filigrana; **~melon** *n* melancia; **~ polo** *n* polo-aquático; **~proof** *adj* impermeável; (*watch*) à prova d'água; **~shed** *n* (*fig*) momento crítico; **~-skiing** *n* esqui *m* aquático; **~ tank** *n* depósito d'água; **~tight** *adj* hermético, à prova d'água; **~works** *npl* sistema hidráulico; **~y** *adj* (*colour*) pálido; (*coffee*) aguado; (*eyes*) úmido.

**watt** [wɔt] *n* vátio, watt *m*.

**wave** [weiv] *n* onda; (*of hand*) aceno, sinal *m*; (*RADIO*) onda, vaga; (*in hair*) onda, ondulação *f*; (*fig*:

*series*) série *f* // *vi* acenar com a mão; (*flag*) tremular, flutuar // *vt* (*handkerchief*) acenar com; (*weapon*) brandir; (*hair*) ondular; ~**length** *n* comprimento de onda.

**waver** ['weɪvə*] *vi* vacilar; (*person*) hesitar.

**wavy** ['weɪvɪ] *adj* ondulado, ondulante.

**wax** [wæks] *n* cera // *vt* encerar // *vi* (*moon*) crescer; ~**works** *npl* museu *msg* de cera.

**way** [weɪ] *n* (*gen*) caminho; (*distance*) percurso; (*direction*) direção (*Pt*: -çç-) *f*, sentido; (*manner*) maneira, modo; (*habit*) costume *m*; (*condition*) estado; **which** ~? em qual dire(c)ção?, qual é o caminho?; **to be on one's** ~ estar a caminho; **to be in the** ~ estorvar; **to go out of one's** ~ **to do** sth dar-se ao trabalho de fazer algo; **to lose one's** ~ perder-se; **in a** ~ de certo modo, até certo ponto; **by the** ~ a propósito; "~ **out**" "saída"; **the** ~ **back** o caminho de volta; "**give** ~" (*AUT*) "via preferencial".

**waylay** [weɪ'leɪ] (*irr: like* lay) *vt* armar uma cilada para.

**wayward** ['weɪwəd] *adj* (*wilful*) voluntarioso, teimoso; (*capricious*) caprichoso; (*naughty*) travesso.

**W.C.** ['dʌblju:'si:] *n* W.C. *m*, banheiro; (*Pt*) casa de banho.

**we** [wi:] *pl pron* nós.

**weak** [wi:k] *adj* (*gen*) fraco, débil; (*tea*) aguado, ralo; ~**en** *vi* enfraquecer-se; (*give way*) ceder // *vt* atenuar; (*lessen*) diminuir; ~**ling** *n* pessoa fraca or delicada; ~**ness** *n* fraqueza; (*fault*) ponto fraco.

**wealth** [welθ] *n* (*money, resources*) riqueza; (*of details*) abundância; ~**y** *adj* rico, abastado.

**wean** [wi:n] *vt* desmamar.

**weapon** ['wɛpən] *n* arma.

**wear** [wɛə*] *n* (*use*) uso; (*deterioration through use*) desgaste *m*; (*clothing*): **sports/baby** ~ roupa

de esporte/infantil // (*vb*: *pt* wore, *pp* worn) *vt* (*clothes*) usar; (*shoes*) usar, calçar; (*put on*) vestir; (*damage: through use*) desgastar // *vi* (*last*) durar; (*rub through etc*) gastar-se; ~ **and tear** *n* desgaste *m* natural; **to** ~ **away** *vt* gastar // *vi* desgastar-se; **to** ~ **down** *vt* gastar; (*strength*) esgotar; **to** ~ **off** *vi* (*pain etc*) passar; **to** ~ **out** *vt* desgastar; (*person, strength*) esgotar.

**weariness** ['wɪərɪnɪs] *n* cansaço, fadiga; (*boredom*) aborrecimento.

**weary** ['wɪərɪ] *adj* (*tired*) cansado; (*dispirited*) deprimido // *vt* aborrecer // *vi*: **to** ~ **of** cansar-se de.

**weasel** ['wi:zl] *n* (*ZOOL*) doninha.

**weather** ['wɛðə*] *n* tempo // *vt* (*storm, crisis*) resistir a; ~**-beaten** *adj* curtido; ~ **cock** *n* cata-vento; ~ **forecast** *n* boletim *m* meteorológico; ~ **vane** *n see* ~ **cock.**

**weave** [wi:v] *pt* wove, *pp* woven *vt* (*cloth*) tecer; (*fig*) compor, criar; **weaver** *n* tecelão/loa *m/f*; **weaving** *n* tecelagem *f*.

**web** [wɛb] *n* (*of spider*) teia; (*on foot*) membrana; (*network*) rede *f*; ~**bed** *adj* (*foot*) palmípede; ~**bing** *n* (*on chair*) tira de tecido forte.

**wed** [wɛd] *pt*, *pp* **wedded** *vt* casar // *vi* casar-se // *n*: **the newly-~s** os recém-casados *mpl*.

**we'd** [wi:d] = **we had; we would.**

**wedded** ['wɛdɪd] *pt*, *pp of* **wed.**

**wedding** ['wɛdɪŋ] *n* casamento, núpcias *fpl*; **silver/golden** ~ **bodas** *fpl* de prata/de ouro; ~ **day** *n* dia *m* do casamento; ~ **night** noite *f* de núpcias; ~ **dress** *n* vestido de noiva; ~ **present** *n* presente *m* de casamento; ~ **ring** *n* anel *m* or aliança de casamento.

**wedge** [wɛdʒ] *n* (*of wood etc*) cunha, calço; (*of cake*) fatia // *vt* (*pack tightly*) socar, apertar.

**wedlock** ['wɛdlɔk] *n* matrimônio, casamento.

**Wednesday** ['wɛdnzdɪ] *n* quarta-feira.

**wee** [wiː] *adj* (*Scottish*) pequeno, pequenino.

**weed** [wiːd] *n* erva daninha // *vt* capinar, mondar; ~**killer** *n* herbicida *m*.

**week** [wiːk] *n* semana; ~**day** *n* dia *m* da semana; ~**end** *n* fim *m* de semana; ~**ly** *adv* semanalmente // *adj* semanal // *n* semanário.

**weep** [wiːp] *pt, pp* **wept** *vt/i* chorar; ~**ing willow** *n* salgueiro chorão.

**weigh** [weɪ] *vt/i* pesar; **to** ~ **down** *vt* sobrecarregar; (*fig: with worry*) deprimir, acabrunhar; **to** ~ **up** *vt* ponderar, avaliar; ~**bridge** *n* báscula automática.

**weight** [weɪt] *n* peso; **to lose/put on** ~ emagrecer/engordar; ~**lessness** *n* ausência de peso; ~**lifter** *n* levantador *m* de pesos; ~**y** *adj* pesado, importante.

**weir** [wɪə*] *n* represa, açude *m*.

**weird** [wɪəd] *adj* misterioso, estranho.

**welcome** ['wɛlkəm] *adj* bem-vindo // *n* acolhimento, recepção *f* // *vt* dar as boas-vindas; (*be glad of*) receber com alegria; **you're** ~ de nada; **welcoming** *adj* acolhedor(a); (*speech*) de boas-vindas.

**weld** [wɛld] *n* solda // *vt* soldar, unir; ~**er** *n* (*person*) soldador *m*; ~**ing** *n* soldagem *f*, solda.

**welfare** ['wɛlfɛə*] *n* bem-estar *m*; (*social aid*) assistência social; ~ **state** *n* país auto-financiador da sua assistência social.

**well** [wɛl] *n* poço; (*pool*) nascente *f* // *adv* bem // *adj*: **to be** ~ estar bem (de saúde) // *excl* bem!, puxa!; **as** ~ também; **as** ~ **as** assim como; ~ **done!** está bem feito!; **get** ~ **soon!** melhoras!; **to do** ~ ir or sair-se bem; **to** ~ **up** *vi* brotar, manar.

**we'll** [wiːl] = **we will, we shall.**

**well:** ~**-behaved** *adj* bem educado, bem comportado; ~**-being** *n* bem-estar *m*; ~**-built** *adj* (*person*) robusto; ~**-deserved** *adj* bem merecido; ~**-developed** *adj* bem desenvolvido; ~**-dressed** *adj* bem vestido; ~**-heeled** *adj* (*col: wealthy*) rico; ~**-informed** *adj* bem informado, versado.

**wellingtons** ['wɛlɪŋtənz] *n* (*also:* **wellington boots**) botas *fpl* de plástico até os joelhos.

**well:** ~**-known** *adj* (*person*) conhecido, famoso; ~**-mannered** *adj* bem-educado; ~**-meaning** *adj* bem intencionado; ~**-off** *adj* próspero, rico; ~**-read** *adj* lido, versado; ~**-to-do** *adj* abastado; ~**-wisher** *n* simpatizante *m/f.*

**Welsh** [wɛlʃ] *adj* galês/galesa // *n* (*LING*) galês *m*; ~**man/woman** *n* galês/galesa *m/f.*

**went** [wɛnt] *pt* of **go.**

**wept** [wɛpt] *pt, pp* of **weep.**

**were** [wəː*] *pt* of **be.**

**we're** [wɪə*] = **we are.**

**weren't** [wəːnt] = **were not.**

**west** [wɛst] *n* oeste *m* // *adj* ocidental, do oeste // *adv* para o oeste *or* ao oeste; **the W**~ *n* o Oeste, o Ocidente; ~**erly** *adj* (*situation*) ocidental; (*wind*) oeste; ~**ern** *adj* ocidental // *n* (*CINEMA*) filme *m* de "far-west"; **W**~ **Germany** *n* Alemanha Ocidental; **W**~ **Indies** *npl* Antilhas *fpl*; ~**ward(s)** *adv* para o oeste.

**wet** [wɛt] *adj* (*damp*) úmido; (~ *through*) molhado, encharcado; (*rainy*) chuvoso; **to get** ~ molhar-se; "~ **paint**" "tinta fresca"; **to be a** ~ **blanket** (*fig*) ser um desmancha-prazeres; ~**ness** *n* umidade *f*; ~ **suit** *n* roupa de mergulho.

**we've** [wiːv] = **we have.**

**whack** [wæk] *vt* bater; ~**ed** *adj* (*col: tired*) morto, esgotado.

**whale** [weɪl] *n* (*ZOOL*) baleia.

**wharf** [wɔːf], pl **wharves** [wɔːvz] n cais m inv.

**what** [wɔt] excl quê!, como! // det que // pron (interrogative) que, o que; (relative, indirect: subject, object) o que, a que; ~ **are you doing?** o que é que você está fazendo?; **I saw ~ you did** eu vi o que você fez; ~ **a mess!** que bagunça!; ~ **is it called?** como se chama?; ~ **about me?** e eu?; ~**ever** det: ~**ever book you choose** qualquer livro que você escolha // pron: **do** ~**ever is necessary** faça tudo o que for preciso; **no reason** ~**ever** or ~**soever** nenhuma razão seja qual for, em absoluto; **nothing** ~**ever** nada em absoluto.

**wheat** [wiːt] n trigo.

**wheel** [wiːl] n roda; (AUT: also: **steering** ~) volante m; (NAUT) roda do leme // vt (pram etc) empurrar // vi (also: ~ **round**) girar, dar voltas, virar-se; ~**barrow** n carrinho de mão; ~**chair** n cadeira de rodas; ~**house** n casa do leme.

**wheeze** [wiːz] n respiração f difícil, chiado // vi respirar ruidosamente.

**when** [wɛn] adv quando // conj quando; (whereas) ao passo que; **on the day** ~ **I met him** no dia em que o conheci; ~**ever** conj quando, quando quer que; (every time that) sempre que.

**where** [wɛə*] adv onde // conj onde, aonde; **this is** ~ aqui é onde; ~**abouts** adv (por) onde // n: **nobody knows his** ~**abouts** ninguém sabe o seu paradeiro; ~**as** conj uma vez que, ao passo que; ~**ver** [-ˈɛvə*] adv onde quer que; (interrogative) onde?; ~**withal** n recursos mpl, meios mpl.

**whet** [wɛt] vt afiar; (appetite) abrir; (desire) despertar.

**whether** [ˈwɛðə*] conj se; **I don't know** ~ **to accept or not** não sei se aceito ou não; ~ **you go or not** quer você vá quer não.

**which** [witʃ] det (interrogative) que, qual; ~ **one of you?** qual de vocês?; ~ **picture do you want?** que quadro você quer? // pron (interrogative) qual; (relative: subject, object) que, o que, o qual, etc; **I don't mind** ~ não me importa qual; **the apple** ~ **is on the table** a maçã que está sobre a mesa; **the chair on** ~ **you are sitting** a cadeira na qual você está sentado; **he said he knew,** ~ **is true** ele disse que sabia, o que é verdade; **in** ~ **case** em cujo caso; ~**ever** det: **take** ~**ever book you prefer** pegue o livro que preferir; ~**ever book you take** qualquer livro que você pegue.

**whiff** [wif] n baforada, cheiro.

**while** [wail] n tempo, momento // conj durante; (as long as) enquanto; (although) embora; **for a** ~ durante algum tempo.

**whim** [wim] n capricho, veneta.

**whimper** [ˈwimpə*] n (weeping) choradeira; (moan) lamúria // vi choramingar, soluçar.

**whimsical** [ˈwimzikl] adj (person) caprichoso, de veneta; (look) excêntrico.

**whine** [wain] n (of pain) gemido; (of engine) zunido // vi gemer, zunir; (dog) ganir.

**whip** [wip] n açoite m; (for riding) chicote m; (Brit: POL) líder m da bancada // vt chicotear; (snatch) apanhar de repente; ~**ped cream** n creme m batido, chantilly m; ~**round** n coleta (Pt: -ct-).

**whirl** [wəːl] n remoinho // vt fazer rodar, rodopiar // vi girar; (leaves, water etc) fazer um remoinho; ~**pool** n remoinho; ~**wind** n furacão m, remoinho.

**whirr** [wəː*] vi zumbir.

**whisk** [wisk] n (CULIN) batedeira // vt bater; **to** ~ **sth away from sb** arrebatar algo de alguém; **to** ~ **sb away** or **off** levar rapidamente alguém.

**whisker** [ˈwɪskəˈ] n: ~s (of animal) bigodes mpl; (of man) suíças fpl.

**whisk(e)y** [ˈwɪskɪ] n uísque m.

**whisper** [ˈwɪspəˈ] n sussurro, murmúrio; (rumour) rumor m; (fig) confidência // vi sussurrar, murmurar; (fig) segredar.

**whist** [wɪst] n uíste m.

**whistle** [ˈwɪsl] n (sound) assobio; (object) apito // vi assobiar.

**white** [waɪt] adj branco, alvo; (pale) pálido // n branco; (of egg) clara; ~**collar worker** n empregado de escritório; ~ **lie** n mentira inofensiva or social; ~**ness** n brancura; ~ **paper** n (POL) livro branco; ~**wash** n (paint) cal f // vt caiar; (fig) encobrir.

**whiting** [ˈwaɪtɪŋ] n, pl inv (fish) pescada-marlonga.

**Whitsun** [ˈwɪtsn] n Pentecostes m.

**whittle** [ˈwɪtl] vt aparar; **to ~ away, ~ down** reduzir gradualmente.

**whizz** [wɪz] vi zunir; **to ~ past** or by passar a toda velocidade; ~ **kid** n (col) prodígio.

**who** [huː] pron (relative) que, o qual etc, quem; (interrogative) quem?; ~**ever** pron: ~**ever finds it** quem quer que or seja quem for que o encontre; **ask** ~**ever you like** pergunte a quem quiser; ~**ever he marries** não importa com quem se case.

**whole** [həʊl] adj (complete) todo, inteiro; (not broken) intacto // n (total) total m; (sum) conjunto; **the ~ of the town** toda a cidade, a cidade inteira; **on the ~, as a ~** como um todo, no conjunto; ~**hearted** adj sincero; ~**sale** n venda por atacado // adj por atacado; (destruction) em grande escala; ~**saler** n atacadista m/f; ~**some** adj saudável, sadio; **wholly** adv totalmente, completamente.

**whom** [huːm] pron que, o qual, quem; (interrogative) quem?

**whooping cough** [ˈhuːpɪŋkɔf] n coqueluche f, tosse f terrível.

**whopper** [ˈwɔpəˈ] n (lie) lorota; **it was a ~** era enorme; **whopping** adj (col: big) imenso.

**whore** [hɔːˈ] n (col: pej) prostituta.

**whose** [huːz] det: ~ **book is this?** de quem é este livro?; **the man ~ son you rescued** o homem cujo filho você salvou; **the girl ~ sister you were speaking to** a menina com cuja irmã você estava falando // pron: ~ **is this?** de quem é isto?; **I know ~ it is** eu sei de quem é.

**why** [waɪ] adv porque; (interrogative) por quê?, por que razão? // excl ora essa!, bem!; **tell me ~** diga-me (o) porquê.

**wick** [wɪk] n mecha, pavio.

**wicked** [ˈwɪkɪd] adj malvado, perverso.

**wicker** [ˈwɪkəˈ] n (also: ~**work**) (trabalho de) vime m.

**wicket** [ˈwɪkɪt] n (CRICKET) arco.

**wide** [waɪd] adj largo; (broad) extenso, amplo; (region, knowledge) vasto; (choice) variado; **it is 4 metres ~** tem 4 metros de largura // adv: **to open ~** abrir totalmente; **to shoot ~** atirar longe do alvo; ~**awake** adj bem acordado; (fig) vivo, esperto; ~**ly** adv (different) extremamente; **it is ~ly believed that...** há uma convicção generalizada de que...; **widen** vt alargar; ~**ness** n largura; (breadth) extensão f; ~ **open** adj (eyes) arregalado; (door) aberto de par em par, escancarado; ~**spread** (belief etc) difundido, comum.

**widow** [ˈwɪdəʊ] n viúva; ~**ed** adj viúvo; ~**er** n viúvo.

**width** [wɪdθ] n largura.

**wield** [wiːld] vt (sword) brandir, empunhar; (power) exercer.

**wife** [waɪf], pl **wives** [waɪvz] n mulher f, esposa.

**wig** [wɪg] n peruca.

**wiggle** ['wɪgl] vt menear, agitar // vi menear, agitar-se.

**wild** [waɪld] adj (animal) selvagem; (plant) silvestre; (rough) violento, furioso; (idea) disparatado, extravagante; (person) louco, insensato; ~s npl regiões fpl selvagens, terras fpl virgens; ~**erness** ['wɪldənɪs] n ermo, sertão m; ~**life** n animais e plantas selvagens; ~**ly** adv (roughly) violentamente; (foolishly) loucamente; (rashly) desenfreadamente.

**wilful** ['wɪlful] adj (person) teimoso, voluntarioso; (action) deliberado, intencional; (obstinate) obstinado; (child) teimoso.

**will** [wɪl] auxiliary vb: he ~ **come** ele virá // vt, pt, pp **willed**: **to ~ sb to do sth** desejar que alguém faça algo; **he ~ed himself to go on** reuniu grande força de vontade para continuar // n vontade f; (testament) testamento; ~**ing** adj (with goodwill) disposto, pronto; (submissive) complacente; ~**ingly** adv de bom grado, de boa vontade; ~**ingness** n boa vontade f, prontidão f.

**willow** ['wɪləu] n salgueiro.

**will power** n força de vontade.

**wilt** [wɪlt] vi murchar, definhar.

**wily** ['waɪlɪ] adj esperto, astuto.

**win** [wɪn] n (in sports etc) vitória f; (vb: pt, pp **won**) vt ganhar, vencer; (obtain) conseguir, obter // vi ganhar; **to ~ over**, ~ **round** vt conquistar.

**wince** [wɪns] vi encolher-se, estremecer.

**winch** [wɪntʃ] n guincho.

**wind** [wɪnd] n vento; (MED) gases mpl, flatulência; (breath) fôlego // (vb: [waɪnd], pt, pp **wound**) vt enrolar, bobinar; (wrap) envolver; (clock, toy) dar corda a // vi (road, river) serpentear // vt [wɪnd] (take breath away from) deixar sem fôlego; **to ~ up** vt (clock) dar corda

a; (debate) rematar, concluir; ~**break** n quebra-ventos msg; ~**fall** n golpe m de sorte; ~**ing** ['waɪndɪŋ] adj (road) sinuoso, tortuoso; ~ **instrument** n (MUS) instrumento de sopro; ~**mill** n moinho de vento.

**window** ['wɪndəu] n janela; (in shop etc) vitrina, vitrine f; (Pt) montra; ~ **box** n jardineira (no peitoril da janela); ~ **cleaner** n (person) limpador m de janelas; ~ **ledge** n peitoril m da janela; ~ **pane** n vidraça, vidro; ~**sill** n peitoril m, soleira.

**windpipe** ['wɪndpaɪp] n traquéia.

**windscreen** ['wɪndskriːn], **windshield** ['wɪndʃiːld] (US) n pára-brisa; ~ **washer** n lavador m de pára-brisa; ~ **wiper** n limpador m de pára-brisa.

**windswept** ['wɪndswɛpt] adj varrido pelo vento.

**windy** ['wɪndɪ] adj com muito vento, batido pelo vento; **it's** ~ está ventando; (Pt) faz vento.

**wine** [waɪn] n vinho; ~ **cellar** n adega; ~ **glass** n cálice m (de vinho); ~ **list** n lista de vinhos; ~ **merchant** n vinhateiro; ~ **tasting** n degustação f de vinhos.

**wing** [wɪŋ] n (gen) asa; (of building) ala; (AUT) aleta, pára-lamas m inv; ~**s** npl (THEATRE) bastidor msg; ~**er** n (SPORT) ponta, extremo.

**wink** [wɪŋk] n piscadela // vi piscar o olho; (light etc) piscar.

**winner** ['wɪnə*] n vencedor(a) m/f.

**winning** ['wɪnɪŋ] adj (team) vencedor(a); (goal) decisivo; ~**s** npl lucros mpl, ganhos mpl; ~ **post** n meta de chegada.

**winter** ['wɪntə*] n inverno // vi hibernar; ~ **sports** npl esportes mpl de inverno.

**wintry** ['wɪntrɪ] adj glacial, invernal.

**wipe** [waɪp] n: **to give sth a** ~ limpar algo com um pano // vt limpar; **to ~ off** vt remover esfregando; **to ~ out** vt (debt) liquidar; (memory) apagar; (destroy) exterminar.

**wire** ['waɪə*] n arame m; (ELEC) fio (elétrico); (TEL) telegrama m // vt (house) instalar a rede elétrica (Pt: -ct-); (also: **~ up**) conectar; (TEL) telegrafar para // vi passar um telegrama.

**wireless** ['waɪəlɪs] n rádio.

**wiring** ['waɪərɪŋ] n instalação f elétrica (Pt: -ct-).

**wiry** ['waɪərɪ] adj nervoso.

**wisdom** ['wɪzdəm] n sabedoria, sagacidade f; (good sense) bom senso; (care) prudência; **~ tooth** n dente m do siso.

**wise** [waɪz] adj sábio; (sensible) sensato; (careful) prudente.

**...wise** [waɪz] suff: **time~** com relação ao tempo.

**wisecrack** ['waɪzkræk] n graça, piada.

**wish** [wɪʃ] n (desire) desejo // vt desejar; (want) querer; **best ~es** (on birthday etc) parabéns mpl, felicidades fpl; **with best ~es** (in letter) cumprimentos; **to ~ sb goodbye** despedir-se de alguém; **he ~ed me well** me desejou boa sorte; **to ~ to do/sb to do sth** querer fazer/que alguém faça algo; **to ~ for** desejar; **it's ~ful thinking** é mais desejo do que realidade.

**wisp** [wɪsp] n mecha, tufo; (of smoke) fio.

**wistful** ['wɪstful] adj pensativo.

**wit** [wɪt] n (wittiness) presença de espírito, engenho; (intelligence) entendimento; (person) espirituoso/a.

**witch** [wɪtʃ] n bruxa; **~craft** n bruxaria.

**with** [wɪð, wɪθ] prep com; **red ~ anger** vermelho de raiva; **the man ~ the grey hat** o homem do chapéu cinza; **to be ~ it** (fig: aware) estar a par da situação; (: fashionable) estar

na moda; **I am ~ you** (I understand) compreendo.

**withdraw** [wɪθ'drɔː] (irr: like draw) vt tirar, remover // vi retirar-se; (go back on promise) voltar atrás; **to ~ money (from the bank)** retirar dinheiro (do banco); **~al** n retirada; **~n** adj (person) reservado, introvertido.

**wither** ['wɪðə*] vi murchar; **~ed** adj murcho.

**withhold** [wɪθ'həuld] (irr: like hold) vt (money) reter; (decision) adiar; (permission) negar; (information) esconder.

**within** [wɪð'ɪn] prep dentro de // adv dentro; **~ reach** ao alcance da mão; **~ sight of** ao alcance da vista, à vista; **~ the week** antes do fim da semana.

**without** [wɪð'aut] prep sem.

**withstand** [wɪθ'stænd] (irr: like stand) vt resistir a, opor-se a.

**witness** ['wɪtnɪs] n (person) testemunha; (evidence) testemunho // vt (event) testemunhar, presenciar; (document) legalizar; **~ box, ~ stand** (US) n banco das testemunhas.

**witticism** ['wɪtɪsɪzm] n observação f espirituosa, chiste m.

**witty** ['wɪtɪ] adj espirituoso, engenhoso.

**wives** [waɪvz] pl of **wife**.

**wizard** ['wɪzəd] n feiticeiro, mago.

**wk** abbr of **week**.

**wobble** ['wɔbl] vi oscilar; (chair) balançar.

**woe** [wəu] n dor f, mágoa.

**woke** [wəuk], **woken** ['wəukən] pt, pp of **wake**.

**wolf** [wulf], pl **wolves** [wulvz] n lobo.

**woman** ['wumən], pl **women** n mulher f; **~ly** adj feminino.

**womb** [wuːm] n (ANAT) matriz f, útero.

**women** ['wɪmɪn] pl of **woman**.

**won** [wʌn] pt, pp of **win**.

**wonder** ['wʌndə*] n maravilha, prodígio; (feeling) espanto // vi: to ~ whether perguntar-se a si mesmo se; to ~ at admirar-se de; to ~ about pensar sobre or em; it's no ~ that não é de admirar que; ~ful adj maravilhoso; ~fully adv esplendidamente.

**won't** [wəunt] = will not.

**woo** [wu:] vt (woman) namorar, cortejar.

**wood** [wud] n (timber) madeira; (forest) floresta, bosque m; ~ carving n escultura em madeira, entalhe m; ~ed adj arborizado; ~en adj de madeira; (fig) inexpressivo; ~pecker n pica-pau m; ~wind n (MUS) instrumentos mpl de sopro de madeira; ~work n carpintaria; ~worm n carcoma, caruncho.

**wool** [wul] n lã f; to pull the ~ over sb's eyes (fig) enganar alguém, vender a alguém gato por lebre; ~len, ~en (US) adj de lã; ~lens npl artigos mpl de lã; ~ly, ~y (US) adj de lã, coberto de lã; (fig: ideas) confuso.

**word** [wə:d] n palavra; (news) notícia; (message) aviso // vt (express) expressar; (document) redigir; in other ~s em outras palavras; to break/keep one's ~ faltar à palavra/cumprir a promessa; ~ing n redação (Pt: -cç-) f.

**wore** [wɔ:*] pt of wear.

**work** [wə:k] n (gen) trabalho; (job) emprego, trabalho; (ART, LITERATURE) obra // vi trabalhar; (mechanism) funcionar; (medicine) surtir efeito, ser eficaz // vt (wood etc) talhar; (mine etc) explorar; (machine) fazer trabalhar, manejar; (cause) fazer, produzir; to be out of ~ estar desempregado; ~s n (factory) fábrica sg // npl (of clock, machine) mecanismo sg; to ~ loose vi (part) soltar-se, desprender-se;

(knot) afrouxar-se; to ~ on vt fus trabalhar em, dedicar-se a; (principle) basear-se em; to ~ out vi (plans etc) dar certo, surtir efeito // vt (problem) resolver; (plan) elaborar, formular; does it ~ out? está dando resultado?; it ~s out at £100 monta or soma a 100 libras; to get ~ed up exaltar-se; ~able adj (solution) viável; ~er n trabalhador a m/f, operário/a; ~ing class n proletariado, classe f operária; ~ing-class adj do proletariado, da classe operária; in ~ing order em funcionamento; ~man n operário, trabalhador m; ~manship n (art) acabamento; (skill) habilidade f, ~shop n oficina; ~to-rule n paralisação f de trabalho extraordinário.

**world** [wə:ld] n mundo // cmp mundial; to think the ~ of sb (fig) ter alguém em alto conceito; ~ly adj mundano; ~-wide adj mundial, universal.

**worm** [wə:m] n verme m; (earth~) minhoca, lombriga.

**worn** [wɔ:n] pp of wear // adj usado; ~-out adj (object) gasto; (person) esgotado, exausto.

**worried** ['wʌrid] adj preocupado.

**worry** ['wʌri] n preocupação f // vt preocupar, inquietar // vi preocupar-se, afligir-se; ~ing adj inquietante, preocupante.

**worse** [wə:s] adj, adv pior, inferior // n o pior; a change for the ~ uma mudança para pior; worsen vt/i piorar; ~ off (fig): you'll be ~ off this way assim você ficará pior que nunca.

**worship** ['wə:ʃip] n culto; (act) adoração f // vt adorar, venerar; Your W~ (to mayor) vossa Excelência; (to judge) senhor Juiz; ~per n devoto/a, venerador(a) m/f.

**worst** [wə:st] adj (a/a) pior // adv pior // n o pior; at ~ na pior das hipóteses.

**worth** [wɔːθ] *n* valor *m*, mérito // *adj:* **to be** ~ valer; **it's** ~ **it** vale a pena; ~**less** *adj* sem valor; (*useless*) inútil; ~**while** *adj* (*activity*) que vale a pena; (*cause*) de mérito, louvável.

**worthy** [wɔːðɪ] *adj* (*person*) merecedor/a, respeitável; (*motive*) justo; ~ **of** digno de.

**would** [wud] *auxiliary vb:* **she** ~ **come** ela viria; **he** ~ **have come** ele teria vindo; ~ **you like a biscuit?** você quer um biscoito?; **he** ~ **go on Mondays** costumava ir às segundas-feiras; ~-**be** *adj* (*pej*) aspirante, que pretende ser.

**wound** [waund] *pt, pp of* **wind** // *n* [wuːnd] ferida // *vt* [wuːnd] ferir.

**wove** [wəuv], **woven** [ˈwəuvən] *pt, pp of* **weave**.

**wrangle** [ˈræŋgl] *n* briga // *vi* brigar.

**wrap** [ræp] *n* (*stole*) xale *m*; (*cape*) capa // *vt* (*also:* ~ **up**) embrulhar; ~**per** *n* envoltório, invólucro; (*of book*) capa; ~**ping paper** *n* papel *m* de embrulho.

**wrath** [rɔːθ] *n* cólera, ira.

**wreath** [riːθ], *pl* ~**s** [riːðz] *n* (*funeral* ~) coroa; (*of flowers*) grinalda.

**wreathe** [riːð] *vt* trançar, cingir.

**wreck** [rɛk] *n* naufrágio; (*ship*) restos *mpl* do naufrágio; (*pej: person*) ruína, caco // *vt* destruir, danificar; (*fig*) arruinar, arrasar; ~**age** *n* restos *mpl*; (*of building*) escombros *mpl*.

**wren** [rɛn] *n* (*ZOOL*) carriça.

**wrench** [rɛntʃ] *n* (*TECH*) chave *f* inglesa; (*tug*) puxão *m* // *vt* arrancar; **to** ~ **sth from sb** arrancar algo de alguém.

**wrestle** [ˈrɛsl] *vi:* **to** ~ (**with sb**) lutar (com *or* contra alguém); **wrestler** *n* lutador *m*; **wrestling** *n* luta romana; **wrestling match** *n* partida de luta romana.

**wretched** [ˈrɛtʃɪd] *adj* desventurado, infeliz.

**wriggle** [ˈrɪgl] *n* (*gen*) contorção *f* // *vi* (*gen*) retorcer-se, contorcer-se.

**wring** [rɪŋ], *pt, pp* **wrung** *vt* torcer, espremer; (*wet clothes*) torcer; (*fig*): **to** ~ **sth out of sb** arrancar à força algo de alguém.

**wrinkle** [ˈrɪŋkl] *n* ruga, prega // *vt* franzir // *vi* enrugar-se.

**wrist** [rɪst] *n* pulso; ~**watch** *n* relógio *m* de pulso.

**writ** [rɪt] *n* mandado judicial; **to issue a** ~ **against sb** demandar judicialmente alguém.

**write** [raɪt], *pt* **wrote**, *pp* **written** *vt/i* escrever; **to** ~ **down** *vt* escrever; (*note*) anotar; **to** ~ **off** *vt* (*debt*) cancelar; (*depreciate*) reduzir; **to** ~ **out** *vt* escrever por extenso; **to** ~ **up** *vt* redigir; ~-**off** *n* perda total; **the car is a** ~-**off** o carro virou sucata *or* está destroçado; **writer** *n* escritor/a *m/f.*

**writhe** [raɪð] *vi* contorcer-se.

**writing** [ˈraɪtɪŋ] *n* escrita; (*hand-*~) caligrafia, letra; (*of author*) obra; **in** ~ por escrito; ~ **paper** *n* papel *m* para escrever.

**written** [ˈrɪtn] *pp of* **write.**

**wrong** [rɔŋ] *adj* (*bad*) errado, mau; (*unfair*) injusto; (*incorrect*) errado, equivocado; (*not suitable*) impróprio, inconveniente // *adv* mal, erroneamente // *n* mal *m*; (*injustice*) injustiça // *vt* ser injusto com; (*hurt*) ofender; **you are** ~ **to do it** você se engana ao fazê-lo; **you are** ~ **about that, you've got it** ~ você está enganado sobre isso; **to be in the** ~ não ter razão; **what's** ~? que se passa com você?, o quê que há?; **to go** ~ (*person*) desencaminhar-se; (*plan*) não ser bem sucedido; (*machine*) sofrer uma avaria; ~-**ful** *adj* injusto; ~-**ly** *adv* injustamente.

**wrote** [rəut] *pt of* **write**.

**wrought** [rɔ:t] *adj*: ~ **iron** ferro forjado.

**wrung** [rʌŋ] *pt, pp of* **wring**.

**wry** [raɪ] *adj* (smile) irônico; **to make a** ~ **face** fazer uma careta.

**wt.** *abbr of* **weight**.

# X

**Xmas** [ˈɛksməs] *n abbr of* **Christmas**.

**X-ray** [eksˈreɪ] *n* radiografia; ~**s** *npl* raios *mpl* X // *vt* radiografar, tirar uma chapa.

**xylophone** [ˈzaɪləfəun] *n* xilofone *m*.

# Y

**yacht** [jɒt] *n* iate *m*; ~**ing** *n* (sport) iatismo; **yachtsman** *n* iatista *m/f*.

**Yank** [jæŋk] *n* (pej) ianque *m/f*.

**yap** [jæp] *vi* (dog) ganir.

**yard** [jɑ:d] *n* pátio, quintal *m*; (measure) jarda; ~**stick** *n* (fig) critério, padrão *m*.

**yarn** [jɑ:n] *n* fio; (tale) história inverossímil.

**yawn** [jɔ:n] *n* bocejo // *vi* bocejar.

**yd.** *abbr of* **yard(s)**.

**year** [jɪə*] *n* ano; **to be 8** ~**s old** ter 8 anos; ~**ly** *adj* anual // *adv* anualmente.

**yearn** [jə:n] *vi*: **to** ~ **for sth** ansiar *or* suspirar por algo; ~**ing** *n* ânsia, desejo ardente.

**yeast** [ji:st] *n* levedura, levedo.

**yell** [jɛl] *n* grito, berro // *vi* gritar, berrar.

**yellow** [ˈjɛləu] *adj, n* amarelo.

**yelp** [jɛlp] *n* latido // *vi* latir.

**yes** [jɛs] *adv, n* sim *m*.

**yesterday** [ˈjɛstədɪ] *adv, n* ontem *m*; **the day before** ~ anteontem.

**yet** [jɛt] *adv* ainda // *conj* porém, no entanto; **it is not finished** ~ ainda não está acabado; **the best** ~ o melhor até agora; **as** ~ até agora, ainda.

**yew** [ju:] *n* teixo.

**Yiddish** [ˈjɪdɪʃ] *n* (i)ídiche *m*.

**yield** [ji:ld] *n* produção *f*; (AGR) colheita; (COMM) rendimento // *vt* (gen) produzir; (profit) render // *vi* render-se, ceder; (US: AUT) ceder.

**yoga** [ˈjəugə] *n* ioga.

**yog(h)ourt, yog(h)urt** [ˈjəugət] *n* iogurte *m*.

**yoke** [jəuk] *n* canga, cangalha; (pair of oxen) junta; (on shoulders) balancim *m*; (fig) jugo // *vt* unir, ligar.

**yolk** [jəuk] *n* gema (do ovo).

**yonder** [ˈjɒndə*] *adv* além, acolá.

**you** [ju:] *pron* (subject) tu, você; (: pl) vós, vocês; (direct object) te, o/a; (: pl) vos, as/as; (indirect object) te, lhe; (: pl) vos, lhes; (after preposition) ti, você; (: pl) vós, vocês; (polite form) o senhor/a senhora; (: pl) os senhores/as senhoras; **with** ~ contigo, com você; convosco, com vocês; com o senhor *etc*; (one): ~ **never know a** gente nunca sabe; (impersonal): ~ **can't do that** isso não se faz.

**you'd** [ju:d] = **you had**; **you would**.

**you'll** [ju:l] = **you will**, **you shall**.

**young** [jʌŋ] *adj* jovem, moço; (Pt) novo // *npl* (of animal) filhotes *mpl*, crias *fpl*; (people): **the** ~ a mocidade *fsg*, a juventude *fsg*; ~**er** *adj* (brother etc) mais novo; ~**ish** *adj* bem novo; ~**ster** *n* jovem *m/f*, moço/a, broto.

**your** [jɔ:*] *adj* teu/tua, seu/sua; (pl) vosso, seu/sua; (formal) do senhor/da senhora.

**you're** [juə*] = **you are**.

**yours** [jɔːz] *pron* teu/tua, seu/sua; (*pl*) vosso, seu/sua; (*formal*) do senhor/da senhora; ~ **is blue** o teu/a tua é azul; **is it** ~? é teu *etc*?; ~ **sincerely** *or* **faithfully** atenciosamente.

**yourself** [jɔːˈsɛlf] *pron* (*subject*) tu mesmo, você mesmo; (*direct/indirect object*) te, se; (*after prep*) ti mesmo, si mesmo; (*formal*) o senhor mesmo/a senhora mesma; **yourselves** *pl pron* (*subject*) vós mesmos, vocês mesmos; (*direct/indirect object*) vos, se; (*formal*) os senhores mesmos/as senhoras mesmas.

**youth** [juːθ] *n* mocidade *f*, juventude *f*; (*young man: pl* ~s [juːðz]) jovem *m*; ~**ful** *adj* juvenil; ~ **hostel** *n* albergue *m* da juventude.

**you've** [juːv] = **you have.**

**Yugoslav** [ˈjuːɡəʊˈslɑːv] *adj*, *n* iugoslavo/a; ~**ia** *n* Iugoslávia.

**Yuletide** [ˈjuːltaɪd] *n* época natalina *or* do Natal.

## Z

**zany** [ˈzeɪnɪ] *adj* tolo, bobo.

**zeal** [ziːl] *n* zelo, fervor *m*; ~**ous** [ˈzɛləs] *adj* zeloso, entusiasta.

**zebra** [ˈziːbrə] *n* zebra; ~ **crossing** *n* faixa para atravessar.

**zenith** [ˈzɛnɪθ] *n* zênite *m*, apogeu *m*.

**zero** [ˈzɪərəu] *n* zero.

**zest** [zɛst] *n* vivacidade *f*, entusiasmo.

**zigzag** [ˈzɪgzæg] *n* ziguezague *m* // *vi* ziguezaguear.

**zinc** [zɪŋk] *n* zinco.

**Zionism** [ˈzaɪənɪzm] *n* sionismo; **Zionist** *n* sionista *m/f*.

**zip** [zɪp] *n* (*also:* ~ **fastener**, ~**per**) fecho ecler // *vt* (*also:* ~ **up**) fechar o fecho ecler de, subir o fecho ecler de; ~ **code** *n* (*US*) código postal.

**zodiac** [ˈzəudiæk] *n* zodíaco.

**zombie** [ˈzɒmbɪ] *n* (*fig*): **like a** ~ como um zumbi.

**zone** [zəun] *n* zona, região *f*.

**zoo** [zuː] *n* (jardim *m*) zoológico.

**zoological** [zuəˈlɔdʒɪkl] *adj* zoológico.

**zoologist** [zuːˈɔlədʒɪst] *n* zoólogo/a.

**zoology** [zuːˈɔlədʒɪ] *n* zoologia.

**zoom** [zuːm] *vi*: **to** ~ **past** passar zunindo; ~ **lens** *n* zoom *m*, zum *m*.

# PORTUGUÊS - INGLÊS
# PORTUGUESE - ENGLISH

## A

**a** (a + o = ao; a + a = à; a + os = aos; a + as = às) *prep* (*lugar*) at, in, on; (*direção*) to, towards; (*tempo*) at; à direita/esquerda on the right/left; ao lado de beside, at the side of; **~ que horas?** at what time?; **às 5 horas** at 5 o'clock; **à hora** on time; **aos 15 anos** at 15 years of age; **ao vê-lo** when I saw him; **~ cavalo/pé** on horseback/foot; **~ negócios** on business; (*maneira*): **à força** by force; (*sucessão*): **dia ~ dia** day by day; **pouco ~ pouco** little by little; **~ como é?** how much is it?; **~ Cr$2000 o quilo** Cr$2000 a kilo; (*com verbo*): **começou ~ nevar** it started to snow; **aprender ~ falar** to learn to speak; (*com infinitivo = gerúndio*): **~ correr** running // *art* the // *pron* her; (*você*) you; (*coisa*) it; **~ do chapéu azul** the girl/woman in the blue hat.

**(a)** *abr de* **assinado** signed.

**¹aba** *f* (*chapéu*) brim; (*casaco*) tail; (*montanha*) foot.

**abacaxi** [abakaˈʃi] *m* (*Br*) pineapple.

**abade/adessa** [aˈbadʒi/abaˈdesa] *m* abbot // *f* abbess; **abadia** *f* abbey.

**abafadiço/a** [abafaˈdʒisu/a] *adj* stifling; (*ar*) stuffy; (*fig*) tempered; **abafar** *vt* to suffocate; (*col*) to pilfer // *vi* to choke; **abafar-se** *vr* to wrap up, keep warm.

**abaixar** [abajˈʃax] *vt* to lower; (*preço*) to reduce; (*luz, som*) to turn down; **~-se** *vr* to stoop.

**abaixo** [aˈbajʃu] *adv* down; **~ de** *prep* below, under; **~ o governo!** down with the government!; **morro ~** downhill; **rio ~** downstream; **mais ~** further down; **~ e acima** up and down; **~ assinado** undersigned; **deitar ~** to bring down.

**abaixo-assinado** *m* (*documento*) petition.

**abajur** [abaˈʒux] *m* (*Br*) lamp(-shade).

**abalado/a** *adj* loose, shaky; (*fig*) upset // *f* flight.

**abalançar-se** [abalãˈsaxsɪ] *vr* to venture.

**abalar** *vt* to shake; (*fig*) to upset // *vi* to shake; (*fugir*) to run off; **~-se** *vr* to be moved.

**abalizado/a** *adj* eminent, distinguished; (*opinião*) reliable.

**abalo** *m* (GEO) earthquake; (*comoção*) shock; (*ação*) shaking.

**abanar** *vt* to shake, wag; (*com leque*) to fan.

**abandalhar** [abãdaˈʎax] *vt* to debase.

**abandonar** *vt* (*deixar*) to leave, desert; (*repudiar*) to reject; (*renunciar*) to abandon, give up; (*descuidar*) to neglect; **~-se** *vr* to abandon o.s. to; **abandono** *m* (*ato*) desertion; (*estado*) neglect.

**abarcar** [abaxˈkax] *vt* (*abranger*) to include; (*conter*) to enclose; (*monopolizar*) to monopolize.

**abarrotado/a** *adj* full; (*lugar*) crowded, crammed; **abarrotar** *vt* to fill up; (*gente*) to crowd, cram; **abarrotar-se** *vr* to overeat.

**abastado/a** *adj* wealthy; **abastança** *f* abundance, surfeit.

**abastardar** *vt* to degrade; (*corromper*) to corrupt; **~-se** *vr* to become corrupt.

**abastecer** [abaʃteˈsex] *vt* to supply; (*motor*) to fuel; (AUTO) to fill up; (AER) to refuel; **~-se de** to stock up with; **abastecimento** *m* supply; (*comestíveis*) provisions *pl*; (*ato*) supplying; **abastecimentos** *mpl* supplies.

**aba'ter** *vt* (*derrubar*) to knock down; (*diminuir*) to reduce, lessen; **abatido/a** *adj* depressed, downcast; **abatimento** *m* (*força*) weakness; (*preço*) reduction; (*prostração*) depression; **fazer um abatimento** to give a discount.

**abaulado/a** [abaw'ladu/a] *adj* convex; (*estrada*) cambered; **abaular-se** *vr* to bulge.

**ab'cesso** *m* tumour; (*dentes*) abscess.

**abdicação** [abdʒika'sãw] *f* abdication; **abdicar** *vt/i* to abdicate.

**ab'dômen** *m* abdomen.

**á-bê-'cê** *m* alphabet; (*fig*) rudiments *pl*; **o ~ da cozinha** the ABC of cooking.

**abeirar** [abej'rax] *vt* to bring near; **~-se** *vr*: **~-se de** to draw near to.

**abelha** [a'beʎa] *f* bee; **~-mestra** *f* queen bee.

**abençoar** [abẽ'swax] *vt* to bless.

**aberração** [abexa'sãw] *f* aberration; (*erro*) error.

**a'berto/a** *pp irr de* **abrir** // *adj* open; (*livre*) clear; (*desprotegido*) exposed; (*sincero*) candid, frank // *f* opening; (*clareira*) glade; (*intervalo*) break; **abertura** *f* opening; (*FOTO*) aperture; (*ELET*) socket; (: *US*) outlet; (*ranhura*) gap, crevice.

**a'beto** *m* fir tree.

**abis'mado/a** *adj* astonished.

**a'bismo** *m* abyss, chasm; (*fig*) depths *pl*.

**abjeção** [abʒe'sãw] (*Pt*: **-cç-**) *f* degradation; **abjeto/a** (*Pt*: **-ct-**) *adj* abject; (*vil*) mean.

**abnegação** [abnega'sãw] *f* self-denial; **abnegado/a** *adj* unselfish; **abnegar** *vt* to renounce.

**a'bóbada** *f* vault; (*telhado*) arched roof.

**a'bóbora** *f* pumpkin.

**abolição** [aboli'sãw] *f* abolition;

**abolir** *vt* to abolish, suppress.

**abominação** [abomina'sãw] *f* abomination; **abominar** *vt* to loathe, detest.

**abo'nar** *vt* to guarantee; (*dinheiro*) to advance; **~-se** *vr* to boast; **abono** *m* guarantee; (*JUR*) bail; (*louvor*) praise; **abono de família** child benefit; **em abono da verdade** to be absolutely honest.

**abor'dar** *vt* (*NÁUT*) to board; (*pessoa*) to approach; (*assunto*) to broach, tackle.

**aborígene** [abo'riʒɛni] *adj* native, aboriginal // *m/f* native, aborigine.

**aborrecer** [aboxe'sex] *vt* (*enfadar*) to annoy; (*maçar*) to bore; **~-se** *vr* to get annoyed; (*entediar-se*) to get bored; **aborrecido/a** *adj* annoying, boring; **que aborrecido!** how annoying!; **aborrecimento** *m* dislike; (*enfado*) boredom; **que aborrecimento!** what a nuisance!

**abor'tar** *vi* to miscarry, abort // *vt* to abort; **aborto** *m* (*MED*) miscarriage; (*forçado*) abortion.

**aboto'ar** [abo'twax] *vt* to button // *vi* (*BOT*) to bud.

**abra'çar** *vt* to hug; (*abranger*) to include; **~-se** *vr* to embrace; **ele abraçou-se a mim** he embraced me; **abraço** *m* embrace, hug; **com um abraço** (*carta*) with best wishes.

**abran'dar** *vt* to reduce; (*suavizar*) to soften; **~ a marcha** (*AUTO*) to slow down // *vi* to diminish; (*acalmar*) to calm down.

**abranger** [abrã'ʒex] *vt* to include, comprise; (*alcançar*) to reach.

**abra'sar** *vt* to burn; (*desbastar*) to erode; (*polir*) to polish // *vi* to be on fire; **~-se** *vr* to be consumed with passion.

**abre-'latas** (*Pt*) *m inv* can *ou* tin opener.

**abre'viar** *vt* to abbreviate; (*encurtar*) to shorten; (*texto*) to abridge; **abreviatura** *f* abbreviation; (*resumo*) précis.

**abri'dor de lata** *m* (*Br*) can *ou* tin opener.

**abri'gar** *vt* to shelter; (*proteger*) to protect; **~-se** *vr* to take shelter; **abrigo** *m* shelter, cover; **abrigo anti-nuclear** anti-nuclear shelter.

**abril** [a'briw] *m* April.

**a'brir** *vt* to open; (*fechadura*) to unlock; (*vestuário*) to unfasten; (*torneiras*) to turn on; (*ELET*, *TV*, *RÁDIO*) to switch on; **~ caminho** to force a way through // *vi* to open (up).

**abrogação** [abroga'sãw] *f* repeal, annulment; **abrogar** *vt* to repeal, annul.

**abrolho** [a'bro\u028eu] *m* thorn; **~s** *mpl* (*fig*) troubles.

**a'brupto/a** *adj* abrupt; (*repentino*) sudden; (*íngreme*) steep.

**absente'ísta** *m/f* absentee.

**absen'tismo** *m* absenteeism.

**ab'side** *f* apse; (*relicário*) shrine.

**absolu'tismo** *m* absolutism; **absolutista** *adj*, *m/f* absolutist; **absoluto/a** *adj* absolute; (*puro*) pure.

**absol'ver** *vt* to absolve; (*JUR*) to acquit; **absolvição** *f* absolution; (*JUR*) acquittal.

**absorção** [abzox'sãw] *f* absorption; **absorto/a** *pp irr de* absorver // *adj* absorbed, engrossed; **absorver** *vt* to absorb; **absorver-se**: **absorver-se em** to concentrate on.

**abstêmio/a** [ab'temju/a] *adj* abstemious; (*álcool*) teetotal // *m/f* abstainer, teetotaller.

**abstenção** [abʃtẽ'sãw] *f* abstention; **abstencionista** *adj*, *m/f* abstainer; **abster-se** *vr*: **abster-se de** to abstain *ou* refrain from.

**absti'nência** *f* abstinence; (*jejum*) fasting.

**abstração** [abʃtra'sãw] (*Pt*: **-cç-**) *f* abstraction; (*concentração*) concentration; **abstrair** *vt* to abstract; (*omitir*) to omit; (*separar*) to separate; **abstrair-se** *vr* to become distracted; **abstrato/a** (*Pt*: **-ct-**) *adj*

abstract; (*distraído*) absent-minded.

**ab'surdo/a** *adj* absurd // *m* nonsense.

**abu'lia** *f* apathy.

**abundância** [abũ'dãsja] *f* abundance; **abundante** *adj* abundant; **abundar** *vi* to abound.

**abu'sar** *vi* (*exceder-se*) to go too far; **~ de** to abuse; **abuso** *m* abuse; (*JUR*) indecent assault; **abuso de confiança** breach of trust.

**a'butre** *m* vulture.

**a.C.** *abr de* **antes de Cristo** B.C.

**a/c** *abr de* **ao cuidado de** c/o.

**aca'bado/a** *adj* finished; (*esgotado*) worn out; (*fig*) masterly; **acabamento** *m* finish.

**aca'bar** *vt* (*terminar*) to finish, complete; (*levar a cabo*) to accomplish; (*aperfeiçoar*) to complete; (*consumir*) to use up; (*rematar*) to finish off // *vi* to finish, end, come to an end; **~ com** to put an end to; **~ de chegar** to have just arrived; **~ por** to end (up) by; **~-se** *vr* (*terminar*) to be over; (*prazo*) to expire; (*esgotar-se*) to run out; **acabou-se!** that's enough!, it's all over!

**acabrunhado/a** [akabru'ɲadu/a] *adj* (*abatido*) depressed; (*envergonhado*) ashamed; **acabrunhar** *vt* (*entristecer*) to distress; (*abater*) to overwhelm.

**acade'mia** *f* academy; **acadêmico/a** *adj*, *m/f* academic.

**açafrão** [asa'frãw] *m* saffron.

**a'caime** *m* (*Pt*) muzzle.

**acaju** [aka'ʒu] *m* mahogany.

**acalen'tar** *vt* to rock to sleep; (*esperanças*) to cherish.

**acal'mar** *vt* to calm // *vi* (*vento etc*) to abate; **~-se** *vr* to calm down.

**acalo'rado/a** *adj* heated; **acalorar** *vt* to heat; (*fig*) to inflame; **acalorar-se** *vr* (*fig*) to get heated.

**acampa'mento** *m* camping; (*MIL*) camp, encampment; **acampar** *vi* to camp.

**acanhado/a** [aka'ɲadu/a] *adj* shy; (*estreito*) cramped, narrow; **acanhamento** *m* shyness; **acanhar-se** *vr* to be shy, become shy.

**ação** [a'sãw] *f* (Pt: **-çç-**) action; (*ato*) act, deed; (*movimento*) action; (MIL) battle; (*enredo*) plot; (JUR) lawsuit; (COM) share; ~ **ordinária/preferencial** ordinary/preference share; ~ **de graças** thanksgiving.

**acarear** *vt* to confront.

**acariciar** [akari'sjax] *vt* to caress; (*fig*) to cherish.

**acarretar** *vt* to result in, bring about.

**acaso** *m* chance, accident; **por** ~ by chance; **ao** ~ at random; **encontrar alguém por** ~ to meet sb by chance.

**acastanhado/a** [akaʃta'ɲadu/a] *adj* brownish; (*cabelo*) auburn.

**acatamento** *m* respect; (*deferência*) deference; **acatar** *vt* (*respeitar*) to respect; (*honrar*) to honour; (*lei*) to obey.

**acautelar** *vt* to warn; ~**-se** *vr* to be cautious; ~**-se contra** to guard against; **acautele-se!** watch out!

**aceder** *vi*: ~ **a** to agree to, accede to.

**aceitação** [asejta'sãw] *f* acceptance; (*aprovação*) approval; **aceitar** *vt* to accept; **aceitável** *adj* acceptable.

**aceite** [a'sejtʃi] (Pt: *pp irr de* **aceitar**) // *adj* accepted // *m* acceptance; **aceito/a** *pp irr de* **aceitar**.

**aceleração** [aselera'sãw] *f* acceleration; (*pressa*) haste; **acelerado/a** *adj* (*rápido*) quick; (*apressado*) hasty; **acelerador** *m* accelerator.

**acelerar** *vt/i* to accelerate; ~ **o passo** to go faster.

**acenar** *vi* (*com a mão*) to wave; (*com a cabeça*) to nod.

**acende dor** *m* lighter; **acender** *vt* (*cigarro, fogo*) to light; (*luz*) to switch on; (*pôr fogo em*) to set fire

to; (*fig*) to excite, inflame.

**aceno** *m* sign, gesture; (*com a mão*) wave; (*com a cabeça*) nod.

**acento** *m* accent; (*de intensidade*) stress; (*sotaque*) accent; **acentuação** *f* accentuation; (*ênfase*) stress; **acentuado/a** *adj* (*sílaba*) stressed; (*saliente*) conspicuous; **acentuar** *vt* (*marcar com acento*) to accent; (*salientar*) to stress, emphasize.

**acepipe** *m* tit-bit, delicacy; (Pt:) ~**s** *mpl* hors d'œuvres.

**acerca**: ~ **de** *prep* about, concerning.

**acercar-se** *vr*: ~ **de** to approach, draw near to.

**acérrimo/a** *adj* (*muito acre*) very bitter; (*defensor*) staunch.

**acertado/a** *adj* (*certo*) right, correct; (*sensato*) sensible; **acertar** *vt* (*ajustar*) to put right; (*relógio*) to set; **acertar o caminho** to find the right way // *vi* to get it right, be right; (*adivinhar*) to guess right; **acertar no alvo** to hit the mark; **acertar com** to hit upon.

**acervo** *m* heap; (JUR) estate; **um** ~ **de** a lot of.

**aceso/a** [a'sezu/a] *pp irr de* **acender** // *adj* (*luz, gás, TV*) on; (*fogo*) alight; (*excitado*) excited.

**acessível** *adj* accessible; (*pessoa*) approachable; **acesso** *m* access, entry; (MED) fit, attack; **um acesso de cólera** a fit of anger; **via de acesso** access road.

**acessório/a** *adj* accessory // *m* accessory.

**acetona** *f* nail varnish remover; (QUÍM) acetone.

**achado** [a'ʃadu] *m* find, discovery; (*pechincha*) bargain; (*sorte*) godsend.

**achaque** [a'ʃaki] *m* ailment.

**achar** [a'ʃax] *vt* (*descobrir*) to find, discover; (*pensar*) to think; **acho que sim** I think so; ~**-se** *vr*: ~**-se doente** to feel ill, be ill.

**achatar** [aʃa'tax] vt to squash, flatten.

**ache'gar-se** vr: ~ **a/de** to approach, get closer to.

**aci'cate** m spur; (fig) incentive.

**aciden'tado/a** adj (terreno) rough; (viagem) eventful; (vida) chequered // m/f injured person.

**aciden'tal** adj accidental; **acidente** m accident; (acaso) chance; (MED) fit; **por acidente** by accident.

**acidez** [asi'deʒ] f acidity; **ácido/a** adj acid; (azedo) sour // m acid.

**a'cima** adv above; (para cima) up; **rio** ~ up river; **passar rua** ~ to go up the street; **mais** ~ higher up // prep: ~ **de** above; (além de) beyond; ~ **de 1000 cruzeiros** more than 1000 cruzeiros.

**a'cinte** m provocation // adv deliberately, on purpose; **acintosamente** adv on purpose.

**acionado/a** [asju'nadu/a] (Pt: **-cc-**) pp de **acionar** // m/f (JUR) defendant; ~**s** mpl gestures; **acionar** (Pt: **-cc-**) vt to set in motion; (máquina) to drive, operate; (JUR) to sue.

**acionista** [asju'niʃta] (Pt: **-cc-**) m/f shareholder.

**acir'rar** vt to incite, stir up.

**aclamação** [aklama'sãw] f acclamation; (ovação) applause; **aclamar** vt to acclaim; (aplaudir) to applaud.

**aclaração** [aklara'sãw] f clarification; (explicação) explanation; **aclarar** vt to explain, clarify // vi to clear up; **aclarar-se** vr to become clear.

**aclimação** [aklima'sãw] f acclimatization; **aclimar** vt to acclimatize; **aclimar-se** vr to become acclimatized.

**'aço** m (metal) steel.

**acoco'rar-se** vr to squat, crouch.

**a'code** etc vb ver **acudir**.

**acoi'mar** vt (multar) to fine;

(censurar) to blame; (tachar) to brand.

**acoi'tar** vt to shelter, give refuge to.

**açoitar** [asoj'tax] vt to whip, lash; **açoite** m whip, lash.

**aco'lá** adv over there.

**acolchoado/a** [akoʎ'wadu/a] adj quilted // m quilt; **acolchoar** vt (costurar) to quilt; (forrar) to pad; (estofar) to upholster.

**acolhedor(a)** [akoʎe'dox(ra)] adj welcoming; (hospitaleiro) hospitable; **acolher** vt to welcome; (abrigar) to shelter; (aceitar) to accept; **acolher-se** vr to shelter; **acolhida** f, **acolhimento** m (recepção) reception, welcome; (refúgio) refuge.

**acome'ter** vt (atacar) to attack, assault; **acometimento** m (ataque) attack.

**acomodação** [akomoda'sãw] f accommodation; (arranjo) arrangement; (adaptação) adaptation; **acomodar** vt (alojar) to accommodate; (arrumar) to arrange; (tornar cômodo) to make comfortable; (adaptar) to adapt.

**acompanha'mento** m attendance; (cortejo) procession; (MÚS) accompaniment; (CULIN) side dish; **acompanhante** m/f companion; (MÚS) accompanist; **acompanhar** vt to accompany, go along with; (MÚS) to accompany.

**aconchegado/a** [akõʃe'gadu/a] adj snug, cosy; **aconchegar** vt to bring near; **aconchegar-se** vr to snuggle.

**acondiciona'mento** m packaging; **acondicionar** vt to condition; (empacotar) to pack; (embrulhar) to wrap (up).

**aconselhar** [akõseʎ'ʎax] vt to advise; ~**-se** vr: ~**-se com** to consult; **aconselhável** adj advisable.

**aconte'cer** vi to happen, occur; **acontecimento** m event.

**acor'dar** vt (despertar) to wake (up), awaken; (provocar) to arouse // vi (despertar) to wake up.

**acorde** [a'kɔrdʒi] m chord.

**a'cordo** m agreement; **de ~** agreed; **estar de ~** to agree; **de ~ com** (pessoa) in agreement with; (documento) in accordance with.

**A'çores** mpl: **os ~** the Azores.

**acor'rer** vi to come running; (acudir) to come to sb's aid.

**acos'sar** vt (perseguir) to pursue; (atormentar) to harass, torment.

**acosta'mento** m hard shoulder; (US) berm.

**acos'tar** vt to lean against; (NÁUT) to bring alongside; **~-se** vr to lean back; (deitar-se) to lie down.

**acostu'mado/a** adj (habituado) used, accustomed; (habitual) usual, customary; **acostumar** vt to accustom; **acostumar-se** vr: **acostumar-se a** to get used to.

**acotove'lar** vt to jostle; **~-se** vr to jostle.

**açougue** [a'sogi] m butcher's (shop); **açougueiro** m butcher.

**acovar'dar-se** vr (desanimar) to lose courage; (amedrontar-se) to flinch, cower.

**'acre** adj (amargo) bitter; (violento) severe, harsh; (fig) biting.

**acredi'tar** vt to believe; (COM) to credit; (afiançar) to guarantee // vi: **~ em** to believe in; **acreditável** adj credible.

**acrescen'tar** vt (aumentar) to increase; (ajuntar) to add; **acréscimo** m (aumento) increase; (elevação) rise.

**acrian'çado/a** adj childish.

**a'crílico** m acrylic.

**acriso'lar** vt to refine, purify.

**acroba'cia** f acrobatics pl; (prova) stunt; **~s aéreas** fpl stunt flying; **acrobata** m/f acrobat.

**a'çúcar** m sugar; **açucarar** vt to sugar; (adoçar) to sweeten; **açucareiro** m (vaso) sugar bowl.

**açude** [a'sudʒi] m dam.

**acu'dir** vi (acorrer) to come running; (ir em socorro) to go to help; (responder) to reply, respond; **~ a** come to the aid of.

**açu'lar** vt (incitar) to incite; **~ um cachorro contra alguém** to set a dog on sb.

**acumulação** [akumula'sãw] f accumulation; (montão) heap; **acumulador** m accumulator, (ELET) battery; **acumular** vt to accumulate; (armazenar) to store; (reunir) to collect.

**acusação** [akuza'sãw] f accusation, charge; (JUR) prosecution; **acusar** vt to accuse; (revelar) to reveal; (culpar) to blame; **acusar o recebimento de** to acknowledge receipt of.

**a'cústica** f acoustics pl.

**a'daga** f dagger.

**adágio** [ada'ʒju] m adage; (MÚS) adagio.

**a'damascado/a** adj (cor, sabor) apricot.

**adaptabili'dade** f adaptability.

**adaptação** f adaptation; **adaptar** vt (modificar) to adapt; (acomodar) to fit; **adaptar-se** vr: **adaptar-se a** to adjust to, fit in with.

**a'dega** f cellar.

**adejar** [ade'ʒax] vt (asas) to flap // vi to flutter; **~ sobre** to hover over.

**adelga'çado/a** adj thin; (aguçado) pointed; **adelgaçar** vt (rarefazer) to attenuate; (terminar em ponta) to taper; **adelgaçar-se** vr to grow thin.

**ade'mais** adv (além disso) besides, moreover.

**a'dentro** adv inside, in; **mata ~** into the woods.

**a'depto/a** m/f follower, adherent.

**adequado/a** [ade'kwadu/a] adj (suficiente) adequate; (apropriado) appropriate, suitable; **adequar** vt to adapt, make suitable.

**adere'çar** vt to adorn, decorate; **~-se** vr to dress up; **adereço** m adornment; **adereços** *mpl* (*teatro*) stage props.

**ade'rência** *f* adherence; **aderente** *adj* adherent, sticking // *m/f* (*partidário*) supporter; **aderir** *vi* to adhere; (*colar*) to stick.

**adesão** [adeˈzãw] *f* adhesion; (*patrocínio*) support; **adesivo/a** *adj* adhesive, sticky // *m* adhesive tape; (*MED*) sticking plaster.

**ades'trado/a** *adj* skilful, skilled; **adestrar** *vt* to train, instruct; (*cavalo*) to break in.

**adeus** [aˈdewʃ] *excl* goodbye!; **dizer** ~ to say goodbye, bid farewell; ~**inho** *excl* bye!

**adia'mento** *m* postponement; (*de uma sessão*) adjournment.

**adian'tado/a** *adj* advanced; (*relógio*) fast; (*col*: *atrevido*) fresh, insolent; **chegar** ~ to arrive ahead of time; **pagar** ~ to pay in advance.

**adianta'mento** *m* advancement, progress; (*dinheiro*) advance payment; **adiantar** *vt* to advance; (*relógio*) to put forward; **não adianta** (*nada*) it's no use (at all).

**adi'ante** *adv* (*na frente*) in front; (*para a frente*) forward, onward; **mais** ~ further on; (*no futuro*) later on; ~**!** (*continue!*) go on!

**adi'ar** *vt* to postpone, put off; (*uma sessão*) to adjourn.

**adição** [adʒiˈsãw] *f* addition; (*MAT*) sum; **adicionar** *vt* to add.

**a'dicto/a** *adj*: ~ **a** addicted to; (*dedicado*) devoted to.

**a'dido** *m* attaché.

**adinheirado/a** [adʒiɲejˈradu/a] *adj* wealthy, rich.

**adita'mento** *m* addition.

**adivinhação** [adʒiviɲaˈsãw] *f* (*destino*) fortune-telling; (*conjectura*) guessing; **adivinhar** *vt/i* (*conjecturar*) to guess; (*ler a sorte*) to foretell; **adivinhar o pensamento de alguém** to read sb's mind; **adivinho/a** *m/f* fortune-teller.

**adja'cente** *adj* adjacent.

**adje'tivo** *m* adjective.

**adjudicação** [adʒudʒkaˈsãw] *f* grant; (*de contratos*) award; (*JUR*) decision; **adjudicar** *vt* to award, grant.

**ad'junto/a** *adj* joined, attached // *m/f* assistant.

**administração** [adminiʃtraˈsãw] *f* administration; (*direção*) management; (*comissão*) board; **administrador(a)** *m/f* administrator; (*diretor*) director; (*gerente*) manager; **administrar** *vt* to administer, manage; (*governar*) to govern.

**admiração** [admiraˈsãw] *f* (*assombro*) wonder; (*estima*) admiration; **ponto de** ~ (*Pt*) exclamation mark; **admirado/a** *adj* astonished, surprised.

**admi'rar** *vt* to admire; ~**-se** *vr*: ~**-se de** to be astonished at, be surprised at; **não me admiro!** I'm not surprised; **admirável** *adj* (*assombroso*) amazing.

**admissão** [admiˈsãw] *f* admission; (*consentimento para entrar*) admittance; (*escola*) intake.

**admi'tir** *vt* (*aceitar*) to admit; (*permitir*) to allow; ~ **um empregado** to engage an employee.

**admoestação** [admwɛʃtaˈsãw] *f* warning; (*censura*) reprimand.

**adoção** [adoˈsãw] (*Pt*: -**pç**-) *f* adoption.

**ado'çar** *vt* (*com açúcar*) to sweeten; (*abrandar*) to soften; (*pacificar*) to pacify.

**adoe'cer** *vi* to fall ill; ~ **de/com** to fall ill with // *vt* to make ill.

**adoi'dado/a** *adj* crazy.

**adoles'cente** *adj*, *m/f* adolescent.

**ado'rar** *vt* to adore; (*venerar*) to worship; **adorável** *adj* adorable.

**adorme'cer** *vi* to fall asleep; (*entorpecer-se*) to go numb; **adormecido/a** *adj* sleeping // *m/f* sleeper.

**ador'nar** *vt* to adorn, decorate;

**adorno** *m* (*enfeite*) adornment.

**ado'tar** (*Pt*: **-pt-**) *vt* to adopt; **adotivo/a** (*Pt*: **-pt-**) *adj* (*filho*) adopted.

**adquirir** [adkɪ'rɪx] *vt* to acquire; (*obter*) to obtain.

**a'drede** *adv* on purpose, deliberately.

**'adro** *m* church forecourt; (*em volta da igreja*) churchyard.

**aduana** [ad'wana] *f* customs (house); **aduaneiro/a** *adj* customs // *m* customs officer.

**adu'bar** *vt* to manure; (*comida*) to season, spice; **adubo** *m* (*fertilizante*) fertilizer; (*comida*) seasoning.

**adulação** [adula'sãw] *f* flattery; **adulador(a)** *adj* flattering // *m/f* flatterer; **adular** *vt* to flatter.

**adulteração** [adultera'sãw] *f* adulteration; (*contas*) falsification; **adulterador(a)** *m/f* adulterator; **adulterar** *vt* (*vinho*) to adulterate; (*contas*) to falsify // *vi* to commit adultery.

**adul'tério** *m* adultery; **adúltero/a** *m* adulterer // *f* adulteress.

**a'dulto/a** *adj* adult, grown up // *m/f* adult.

**a'dusto/a** *adj* (*chamuscado*) scorched; (*ressequido*) parched; (*queimado*) burnt.

**adven'tício/a** *adj* (*casual*) accidental; (*estrangeiro*) foreign // *m/f* (*estrangeiro*) foreigner; (*intruso*) upstart.

**ad'vento** *m* advent, arrival; **o A~** Advent.

**ad'vérbio** *m* adverb.

**adver'sário** *m* adversary, opponent, enemy.

**adversi'dade** *f* adversity, misfortune; **adverso/a** *adj* adverse, contrary.

**adver'tência** *f* warning; (*conselho*) advice.

**adver'tido/a** *adj* prudent; (*informado*) well advised; **advertir** *vt* to warn; (*avisar*) to advise;

(*chamar a atenção a*) to draw attention to.

**advo'gado** *m* lawyer; **advogar** *vt* (*promover*) to advocate; (*JUR*) to plead // *vi* to practise law.

**aéreo/a** [a'ɛrju/a] *adj* air, aerial; **ataque ~** air raid; **Força A~a** Air Force; **por via ~a** by air mail.

**aeromoço/a** [aero'mosu/a] (*Br*) *m* steward // *f* air hostess.

**aero'nave** *f* aircraft.

**aero'porto** *m* airport.

**a'fã** *m* (*ardor*) eagerness; (*trabalho*) exertion; (*ânsia*) anxiety.

**afabili'dade** *f* friendliness, courtesy.

**afadi'gar** *vt* to tire (out); **~-se** *vr* to tire o.s. (out), get tired.

**afa'gar** *vt* (*acariciar*) to caress, fondle; (*cabelo*) to stroke; (*alisar*) to smooth (down).

**afa'mado/a** *adj* renowned, famous, celebrated.

**afanoso/a** [afa'nozu/a] *adj* laborious; (*meticuloso*) painstaking.

**afas'tado/a** *adj* (*distante*) remote; (*ausente*) away; (*isolado*) secluded; **manter-se ~** to keep to o.s.; **afastamento** *m* removal, withdrawal; (*distância*) distance.

**afas'tar** *vt* (*retirar*) to remove; (*apartar*) to keep off, keep away; (*desviar*) to deflect, turn; **~-se** *vr* (*ir-se embora*) to move away, go away; (*desviar-se*) to turn, swerve; **~-se do assunto** to stray from the subject.

**a'fável** *adj* courteous, genial.

**afa'zer** *vt* to accustom; **~-se** *vr*: **~-se a** to get used to.

**afa'zeres** *mpl* business *sg*; (*dever*) duties, tasks; **~ domésticos** household chores.

**afeição** [afej'sãw] *f* (*amor*) affection, fondness; (*dedicação*) devotion; **afeiçoado/a** *adj* (*amoroso*) fond; (*devotado*) devoted // *m/f* friend.

**afeiçoar-se** [afej'swax-si] *vr*: **~ a**

(*tomar gosto por*) to take a liking to.

**afeito/a** [a'fejtu/a] *adj*: ~ **a** accustomed to, used to.

**aferi'dor** *m* (*de pesos e medidas*) inspector; (*verificador*) checker; (*instrumento*) gauge; **aferir** *vt* (*medir*) to gauge; (*verificar*) to check, inspect; (*comparar*) to compare.

**afer'rado/a** *adj* obstinate, stubborn.

**afer'rar** *vt* (*prender*) to secure; (*NÁUT*) to anchor; (*agarrar*) to grasp; ~**-se** *vr*: ~**-se a** to cling to.

**afetação** [afeta'sãw] (*Pt*: **-cç-**) *f* affectation; **afetado/a** (*Pt*: **-cç-**) *adj* (*vaidoso*) conceited, affected; **afetar** (*Pt*: **-cç-**) *vt* to affect; (*fingir*) to pretend, feign.

**a'feto** (*Pt*: **-cç-**) *pp irr de* **afetar** // *adj* affectionate; ~ **a** fond of // *m* affection, fondness; **afetuoso/a** (*Pt*: **-cç-**) *adj* affectionate, tender.

**afi'ado/a** *adj* sharp; (*pessoa*) knowing.

**afian'çar** *vt* (*JUR*) to stand bail for; (*garantir*) to guarantee.

**afi'ar** *vt* to sharpen.

**aficio'nado/a** *m/f* fan, enthusiast.

**afigu'rar-se** *vr* to seem, appear; **afigura-se-me que** it seems to me that.

**afilhado/a** [afi'Aadu/a] *m* godson // *f* goddaughter.

**afili'ar** *vt* to affiliate, admit; ~**-se** *vr*: ~**-se a** (*ser inscrito*) to join.

**afim** [a'fĩ] *adj* (*semelhante*) similar; (*consangüíneo*) akin, related // *m/f* relative, relation.

**afinação** [afina'sãw] *f* (*MÚS*) tuning, harmony.

**afi'nado/a** *adj* in tune.

**afi'nal** *adv* at last, finally; ~ **de contas** after all.

**afi'nar** *vt* (*MÚS*) to tune // *vi* (*adelgaçar*) to taper.

**a'finco** *m* tenacity, persistence.

**afini'dade** *f* affinity.

**afirmação** [afixma'sãw] *f* affirmation; (*declaração*) statement; **afirmar** *vt/i* to affirm, assert; (*declarar*) to declare; **afirmativo/a** *adj* affirmative.

**afive'lar** *vt* to buckle.

**afi'xar** *vt* (*cartazes*) to stick, post.

**aflição** [afli'sãw] *f* affliction; (*ansiedade*) anxiety; (*angústia*) distress; (*agonia*) grief.

**afligir** [afli'ʒix] *vt/i* to distress; (*inquietar*) to worry; ~**-se** *vr*: ~**-se de** to worry about; **aflito/a** *pp irr de* **afligir** // *adj* distressed, upset, anxious.

**aflu'ência** *f* abundance; (*corrente copiosa*) great flow; (*concorrência*) crowd; **afluente** *adj* copious // *m* tributary.

**afluir** [a'flwix] *vi* to flow; (*concorrer*) to congregate.

**afo'gado/a** *adj* drowned // *m* drowned man // *f* drowned woman.

**afoga'dor** *m* (*Br*: *AUTO*) choke.

**afo'gar** *vt* to drown // *vi* (*AUTO*) to stall; ~**-se** *vr* to drown, be drowned.

**a'fogo** *m* suffocation; (*aflição*) anguish, affliction; (*pressa*) haste.

**a'fora** *prep* except, apart from // *adv*: **rua** ~ down the street.

**afor'rar** *vt* (*roupa*) to line; (*poupar*) to save; (*liberar*) to free.

**afortu'nado/a** *adj* fortunate, lucky.

**'África** *f* Africa; ~ **do Sul** South Africa; **africano/a** *adj, m/f* African.

**a'fronta** *f* insult, affront; **afrontar** *vt* to insult; (*ofender*) to offend.

**afrouxar** [afro'ʃax] *vt* (*desapertar*) to slacken; (*soltar*) to loosen // *vi* (*soltar-se*) to come loose.

**afugentar** [afuʒẽ'tax] *vt* to drive off, put to flight.

**afun'dar** *vt* (*submergir*) to sink; (*cavidade*) to deepen; ~**-se** *vr* to sink.

**agachar-se** [aga'ʃax-sɪ] *vr* (*acaçapar-se*) to crouch, squat; (*curvar-se*) to stoop; (*fig*) to cringe.

**agar'rar** vt to seize, grasp; ~**-se**
vr: ~**-se a** to cling to, hold on to.

**agasalho/a** [agaza'ʎadu/a] adj
cosy, snug; (abrigado) sheltered;
**agasalhar** vt (abrigar) to shelter;
(acolher) to welcome; **agasalhar-se**
vr to wrap o.s. up; **agasalho** m wrap,
warm clothing.

**agas'tar** vt to irritate; ~**-se** vr:
~**-se com** to get angry with.

**agatanhar** [agata'ɲax] vt to
scratch.

**agência** [a'ʒẽsja] f agency;
(escritório) office; ~ **de correio**
(Br) post office; ~ **de viagens**
travel agency.

**agenci'ar** vt to negotiate for;
(procurar) to obtain.

**agenda** [a'ʒẽda] f agenda;
(caderneta) diary.

**agente** [a'ʒẽtʃi] m agent; (de
polícia) policeman.

**ágil** [a'ʒiw] adj agile, nimble, active;
**agilidade** f agility.

**agiota** [a'ʒiɔta] m/f stockjobber;
(usurário) moneylender; (inte-
resseiro) speculator.

**agir** [a'ʒix] vi (atuar) to act;
(proceder) to behave; ~ **bem/mal**
to do right/wrong.

**agitação** [aʒita'sãw] f agitation;
(perturbação) disturbance; (inquietação) unrest.

**agi'tado/a** adj agitated, disturbed;
(inquieto) restless; (mar) rough;
**agitar** vt to agitate, disturb;
(sacudir) to shake; (a cauda) to wag;
(mexer) to stir; (os braços) to swing,
wave; **agitar-se** vr to get upset;
(mar) to get rough.

**aglomeração** [aglomera'sãw] f
gathering; (multidão) crowd;
**aglomerado** m: **aglomerado urbano**
city; **aglomerar** vt to heap up, pile
up; **aglomerar-se** vr (multidão) to
crowd together.

**ago'nia** f agony, anguish; (ânsia da
morte) death throes pl.

**agoni'zante** adj dying // m/f dying

person; **agonizar** vi to be dying;
(afligir-se) to agonize.

**a'gora** adv now; ~ **mesmo** right
now; (há pouco) a moment ago;
**desde** ~ from now on; **por** ~ for
the present; **até** ~ so far, up to now
// excl: ~! come now!, (Pt) I don't
believe it!; **e** ~ ? now what? // conj
now.

**a'gosto** m August.

**agourar** [ago'rax] vt to predict,
foretell; **agouro** m omen.

**agra'ciar** vt (condecorar) to
decorate.

**agra'dar** vt to please; **isso me
agrada** I like it; ~**-se** vr: ~**-se de** to
like, to be pleased with; **agradável**
adj pleasant.

**agrade'cer** vt to thank, be grateful
for; ~ **alguma coisa a alguém** to
thank sb for sth; **agradecido/a** adj
grateful, thankful; **mal agradecido**
ungrateful; **agradecimento** m gratitude; **agradecimentos** mpl thanks.

**a'grado** m (satisfação) satisfaction;
(gorjeta) small gift.

**a'grário/a** adj agrarian.

**agravação** [agrava'sãw] (Pt) f
aggravation; (piora) worsening;
**agravamento** (Br) m aggravation;
**agravante** adj aggravating // f
aggravating circumstances pl;
**agravar** vt to aggravate, make
worse; (ofender) to offend // vi
(piorar) to worsen; (JUR) to lodge an
appeal.

**a'gravo** m (afronta) offence; (JUR)
appeal.

**agre'dir** vt to attack, assault.

**agre'gado/a** m/f (lavrador)
tenant farmer; (Br) living-in
servant, retainer // m aggregate,
sum total; **agregar** vt (juntar) to
collect; (acrescentar) to add.

**agressão** [agre'sãw] f aggression;
(ataque) attack; (assalto) assault;
**agressivo/a** adj aggressive.

**a'greste** adj rural, rustic; (terreno)

wild, uncultivated; (*rude*) rough;
**agrestia** *f* roughness.

a**grícola** *adj* agricultural.

**agricul'tor** *m* farmer; **agricultura**
*f* agriculture, farming.

**agri'doce** *adj* bittersweet.

**agrilhoar** [agriʎo'ax] *vt* to chain;
(*escravizar*) to enslave.

**agrono'mia** *f* agronomy,
agriculture; **agrônomo** *m*
agricultural expert.

**agru'par** *vt* to group; ~**-se** *vr* to
group together.

**a'grura** *f* bitterness.

**água** ['agwa] *f* water; ~s *fpl* (*mar*)
sea *sg*; (*chuvas*) rain *sg*; (*maré*)
tides; ~ **abaixo** downstream; ~
**acima** upstream; ~ **benta** holy
water; ~ **calcária** hard water; ~
**corrente** running water; ~ **doce**
fresh water; ~ **leve** soft water; ~
**mineral** mineral water; ~
**oxigenada** peroxide; ~ **potável**
drinking water; ~ **salgada** salt
water; **fazer** ~ (*NÁUT*) to leak; ~**s
paradas são as mais fundas** still
waters run deep; ~ **passada não
move moinho** let bygones be
bygones.

**aguaceiro** [agwa'sejru] *m* (*chuva*)
heavy shower, downpour; (*com
vento*) squall.

**água-de-colônia** ['agwa dʒi
kɔ'lonja] *f* eau-de-cologne.

a**'guado/a** *adj* watery.

**água-fur'tada** *f* garret, attic.

**água-marinha** ['agwa-ma'riɲa] *f*
aquamarine.

**aguar** [ag'wax] *vt* to water; (*diluir*)
to dilute.

**aguar'dar** *vt* to wait for, await;
(*contar com*) to expect // *vi* to wait.

**aguar'dente** *m* brandy; (*Br*) rum,
cachaça.

**agua'rela** *f* watercolour.

**aguar'rás** *f* turpentine.

**agu'çar** *vt* (*afiar*) to sharpen; ~ **a
vista** to keep one's eyes peeled.

agu'**deza** *f* sharpness; (*perspicácia*)
perspicacity; (*som*) shrillness;

**agudo/a** *adj* sharp; (*divertido*) witty,
penetrating; (*som*) shrill; (*intenso*)
acute.

**aguentar** [agwẽ'tax] *vt* to tolerate,
stand, put up with; (*apoiar*) to
support // *vi* to last; ~**-se** *vr* to bear
up.

**aguerrido/a** [age'xidu/a] *adj*
warlike, bellicose; (*corajoso*)
courageous.

**águia** ['agja] *f* eagle; (*fig*) genius //
*m* (*Br*) cheat, rogue.

**aguilhada** [agi'ʎada] *f* goad;
**aguilhão** *m* (*espora*) spur, goad;
(*espigão*) spike; (*de inseto*) sting;
(*estímulo*) stimulus, incentive;
**aguilhoar** *vt* to goad, stimulate.

**agulha** [a'guʎa] *f* (*de coser, tricô*)
needle; (*NÁUT*) compass; (*estrada de
ferro*) points *pl*; (: *US*) switch;
**trabalho de** ~ needlework.

**agulheiro** [agu'ʎejru] *m* (*estojo*)
needle-case; (*almofada*) pin cushion;
(*fabricante*) needle-maker.

**agulheta** [agu'ʎeta] *f* (*bico*) nozzle.

**ai** [aj] *excl* (*suspiro*) oh!; (*dor*) ouch!;
~ **de mim!** poor me! // *m* (*suspiro*)
sigh; (*gemido*) groan.

**aí** [a'i] *adv* there; (*nessa ocasião*)
then; **por** ~ (*em lugar
indeterminado*) somewhere over
there, thereabouts; **espera** ~! wait!,
hang on a minute!

**aia** ['aja] *f* (*que educa crianças*)
nursemaid, nanny; (*preceptora*)
governess.

a**'inda** *adv* still, yet; (*mesmo*) even;
~ **agora** just now; ~ **assim** even so,
nevertheless; ~ **bem** fortunately,
it's a good thing; ~ **por cima** on top
of all that, in addition; ~ **não** not yet
// *conj*: ~ **que** even if; ~ **quando**
even though, even when.

**aio** ['aju] *m* mentor.

**aipo** ['ajpu] *m* celery.

**airado/a** [aj'radu/a] *adj* (*frívolo*)

frivolous; (*leviano*) dissolute; **estar ~ (Br)** to have a chill.

**airoso/a** [aj'rozu/a] *adj* graceful, elegant; (*decoroso*) decent.

**ajaular** [aʒaw'lax] *vt* to cage (up).

**ajeitar** [aʒej'tax] *vt* (*adaptar*) to fit, adjust; (*arranjar*) to arrange, fix; **~-se** *vr* to adapt.

**ajoelhado/a** [aʒwɛ'ʎadu/a] *adj* kneeling; (*fig*) humbled; **ajoelhar-se** *vr* to kneel (down).

**ajuda** [a'ʒuda] *f* help, aid, assistance; (*subsídio*) grant, subsidy; **sem ~** unaided; **prestar ~ a alguém** to lend sb a hand; **~ de custo** allowance.

**ajudante** [aʒu'dãtʃi] *m* assistant, helper; (*MIL*) adjutant; **~ de campo** aide-de-camp; **ajudar** *vt* to help, aid, assist.

**ajuizado/a** [aʒwi'zadu/a] *adj* (*sensato*) sensible; (*sábio*) wise; (*prudente*) discreet; **ajuizar** *vt* to judge; (*supor*) to suppose.

**ajunta'mento** *m* (*reunião*) meeting, gathering; **ajuntar** *vt* (*unir*) to join, add; (*dinheiro*) to save up; (*documentos*) to attach; (*reunir*) to gather.

**ajustagem** [aʒuʃ'taʒẽ] *f* (*Br: TEC*) adjustment.

**ajusta'mento** *m* adjustment; (*liquidação de contas*) settlement; **ajustar** *vt* (*regular*) to adjust, fit; (*arranjar*) to fix; (*conta, disputa*) to settle; (*motor*) to tune; (*acomodar*) to fit; **ajustar um preço** to agree on a price; **ajustar-se** *vr*: **ajustar-se a** to conform to; **ajuste** *m* (*acordo*) agreement; (*liquidação*) settlement; (*adaptação*) adjustment.

**'ala** *f* (*fileira*) row, file; (*passagem*) aisle; (*edifício, exército, ave*) wing.

**alagação** [alaga'sãw] *f* flooding; **alagamento** *m* flooding; (*arrasamento*) destruction; **alagar** *vt* to inundate, flood // *vi* to flood.

**alambi'cado/a** *adj* (*estilo*) pretentious; **alambicar-se** *vr*

(*estilo*) to become affected; **alambique** *m* still, retort.

**ala'meda** *f* (*avenida*) avenue; (*arvoredo*) grove.

**'álamo** *m* poplar.

**a'lar** *vt* to haul, heave.

**a'larde** *m* (*ostentação*) ostentation; (*jactância*) boasting; **fazer ~ de** to flaunt, show off; **alardear** *vt* to show off.

**alarga'mento** *m* enlargement; **alargar** *vt* (*ampliar*) to extend; (*fazer mais largo*) to widen, broaden; (*afrouxar*) to loosen, slacken.

**ala'rido** *m* (*clamor*) outcry; (*tumulto*) uproar.

**a'larma** *f* alarm; (*susto*) panic; (*tumulto*) tumult; (*vozearia*) outcry; **dar o sinal de ~** to raise the alarm; **~ de roubo** burglar alarm; (*fogo*) fire alarm; **alarmante** *adj* alarming; **alarmar** *vt* to alarm; **alarmar-se** *vr* to be frightened.

**a'larme** *m* = **alarma**.

**alas'trado/a** *adj*: **~ de** strewn with; **alastrar** *vt* (*espalhar*) to scatter; (*disseminar*) to spread; (*lastrar*) to ballast; **alastrar-se** *vr* (*epidemia, rumor*) to spread.

**ala'vanca** *f* lever; (*pé-de-cabra*) crowbar; **~ de mudanças** gear lever.

**al'barda** *f* pack-saddle.

**alber'gar** *vt* (*hospedar*) to provide lodging for; (*abrigar*) to shelter; (*sentimentos*) to harbour; **~-se** *vr* (*hospedar-se*) to take lodging; (*refugiar-se*) to take shelter; **albergue** *m* (*estalagem*) inn; (*refúgio*) hospice, shelter; **albergue para jovens** youth hostel; **albergueiro** *m* innkeeper.

**albufeira** [awbu'fejra] *f* lagoon.

**'álbum** *m* album; **~ de recortes** scrapbook.

**'alça** *f* (*asa*) handle; (*argola*) ring; (*fusil*) sight.

**alcácer** [aw'kasex] *m* fortress.

**alcachofra** [awka'ʃofra] f artichoke.

**alca'çuz** m licorice.

**al'çada** f (jurisdição) jurisdiction; (competência) competence; **isso não é da minha ~** that is beyond my control.

**alcan'çar** vt (chegar a) to reach, arrive at; (estender) to hand, pass; (obter) to obtain, get; (atingir) to attain; (compreender) to understand // vi (atingir) to reach.

**al'cance** m reach; (competência) power, competence; (compreensão) understanding; (de tiro, visão) range; **ao ~ de** within reach/range of; **ao ~ da voz** within earshot; **de grande ~** of great consequence; **fora do ~ da mão** out of reach; **fora do ~ de alguém** beyond sb's grasp.

**alcan'til** m crag, precipice; **~ado/a** adj (íngreme) steep; (penhascoso) craggy.

**alçapão** [awsa'pãw] m trapdoor; (arapuca) (bird-)trap.

**alça'prema** f (alavanca) crowbar.

**al'çar** vt to lift (up); (edificar) to erect; **~-se** vr to get up, rise; (revoltar-se) to revolt.

**alcatéia** [awka'teja] f (de lobos) pack; (de ladrões) gang.

**alca'tifa** f carpet.

**alcatrão** [awka'trãw] m tar.

**álcool** ['awkwɔl] m alcohol; **alcoólico/a** adj, m/f alcoholic.

**Alcorão** [awko'rãw] m Koran.

**alcoviteiro/a** [awkovi'tejru/a] m pimp // f procuress.

**alcunha** [aw'kuɲa] f nickname.

**aldeão/aldeã** [awdʒi'ãw/awdʒi'ã] m/f villager; **aldeia** f village.

**al'draba** f (Pt: tranqueta) latch; (de bater) door knocker; **aldrabão** m (Pt: vigarista) swindler; **aldrabar** vt to cheat, swindle.

**alecrim** [alɛ'kri] m rosemary.

**alegação** [alɛga'sãw] f allegation; **alegar** vt to allege; (JUR) to plead.

**alego'ria** f allegory.

**ale'grar** vt (tornar feliz) to cheer (up), gladden; (ambiente, etc) to brighten up; (animar) to liven (up); **~-se** vr to be glad; (embriagar-se) to get merry ou tight; **alegre** adj (jovial) cheerful; (contente) happy, glad; (cores) bright; (embriagado) merry, tight.

**ale'gria** f joy, happiness.

**ale'grete** m (canteiro) flowerbed.

**aleijado/a** [alej'ʒadu/a] adj crippled, disabled // m/f cripple; **aleijar** vt (mutilar) to maim.

**aleitação** [alejta'sãw] f, **aleitamento** [alejta'mẽtu] m nursing; (amamentação) suckling; **aleitamento materno** breast feeding; **aleitar** vt (criar a leite) to nurse; (amamentar) to suckle.

**aleivosia** [alejvo'zia] f (traição) treachery; (calúnia) slander; **aleivoso/a** adj (desleal) treacherous; (calunioso) slanderous.

**além** [a'lẽj] adv (lá ao longe) over there; (mais adiante) further on; **mais ~** further // prep: **~ de** beyond; (no outro lado de) on the other side of; (para mais de) over; (ademais de) besides; **~ disso** moreover; **~ mar** overseas.

**Alemanha** [alɛ'maɲa] f Germany; **~ Ocidental/Oriental** West/East Germany; **alemão/mã** adj, m/f German; **os alemães** mpl the Germans // m (língua) German.

**alen'tado/a** [alẽ'tadu/a] adj (valente) valiant; (grande) great; (volumoso) substantial.

**alenta'dor/a** [alẽta'dor/a] adj encouraging; **alentar** vt to encourage; **alentar-se** vr to cheer up.

**a'lento** m (fôlego) breath; (ânimo) courage; **dar ~ a** to encourage; **tomar ~** to draw breath.

**alergia** [alɛr'ʒia] f allergy; **alérgico/a** adj allergic.

**a'lerta** adv on the alert // m alert.

**alfa'beto** m alphabet.

**alface** [aw'fasɪ] f lettuce.

**alfaia** [aw'faja] f (*móveis*) furniture; (*utensílio*) utensil; (*enfeite*) ornament.

**alfaiate** [awfa'jatʃi] m tailor.

**al'fândega** f customs pl, customs house.

**alfarra'bista** m (*negociante*) second-hand book seller.

**alfa'vaca** f basil.

**alfa'zema** f lavender.

**alferes** [aw'fɛreʃ] m (MIL) second-lieutenant; (NÁUT) ensign.

**alfi'nete** m pin; ~s mpl pin money; ~ de segurança safety pin.

**al'fombra** f carpet.

**alforges** [aw'xɔbra] mpl (*saco*) saddle-bags.

**al'forra** f (*doença vegetal*) rust.

**alfo'rreca** f jellyfish.

**'alga** f seaweed; (BOT) alga.

**algara'via** f (*árabe*) Arabic language; (*confusão de vozes*) hubbub; (*linguagem confusa*) gibberish.

**alga'rismo** m numeral, digit.

**alga'zarra** f uproar, racket.

**'álgebra** ['awʒebra] f algebra.

**algemas** [aw'ʒemaʃ] fpl handcuffs.

**algeroz** [awʒe'rɔʃ] m guttering.

**algibe** [aw'ʒibi] m cistern.

**'algo** adv somewhat, rather // pron something; (*qualquer coisa*) anything.

**algodão** [awgo'dãw] m cotton; ~ hidrófilo cotton wool.

**alguém** [aw'gẽj] pron someone, somebody; anyone, anybody; ~ quer falar com ela someone wants to speak to her; tem (Br)/há (Pt) ~ aqui? is there anybody here?

**algum(a)** [aw'gũ/guma] adj some, any // pron some, one; ~ dia one day; ~ a vez sometime; ~ tempo for a while; ~a coisa something; (*negativa*) de modo ~ in no way; coisa ~a nothing.

**al'gures** adv somewhere.

**alheio/a** [a'ʎeju/a] adj (*de outrem*) someone else's; (*estranho*) alien;

(*estrangeiro*) foreign; (*impróprio*) inappropriate; ~ a foreign to.

**alho** ['aʎu] m garlic; ~-porro m leek.

**a'li** adv there; por ~ over there; (*direção*) that way; até ~ up to there; ~ por (*tempo*) round about; de ~ por diante from then on; ~ dentro in there.

**ali'ado/a** adj allied // m/f ally.

**ali'ança** f alliance; (*anel*) wedding ring; aliar vt to ally; aliar-se vr to make an alliance.

**ali'ás** adv (*além disso*) besides; (*de outro modo*) otherwise; (*contudo*) nevertheless; (*diga-se de passagem*) incidentally; (*ou seja*) I mean.

**'álibi** m alibi.

**ali'cate** m pliers pl.

**alicerce** [ali'sɛxsi] m (*de edifício*) foundation; (*base*) base.

**aliciar** [alis'jax] vt (*seduzir*) to entice; (*subornar*) to bribe.

**alienação** [aljena'sãw] f alienation; (*de bens*) transfer (of property); ~ mental insanity; alienado/a adj (*demente*) insane; (*bens*) transferred // m/f lunatic.

**ali'gátor** m alligator.

**aligeirar** [aliʒej'rax] vt (*tornar leve*) to lighten; (*apressar*) to quicken; (*mitigar*) to alleviate.

**alimentação** [alimẽta'sãw] f (*alimentos*) food; (*ação*) feeding; (*nutrição*) nourishment; (ELET) supply; alimentar vt (*dar alimento*) to feed; alimentar-se vr: alimentar-se de to feed on; alimento m food; (*nutrição*) nourishment; alimentos mpl (JUR) alimony.

**alínea** [a'linja] f (*parágrafo*) paragraph; (*subdivisão de artigo*) sub-heading.

**ali'nhado/a** adj elegant.

**alinhamento** [aliɲa'mẽtu] m alignment; alinhar vt to align, line up; alinhar-se vr (*enfileirar-se*) to form a line.

**alinha'var** vt (*costura*) to tack.

**alinho** [a'liɲu] m (alinhamento) alignment; (elegância) neatness.

**ali'sar** vt (tornar liso) to smooth; (madeira) to plane.

**alista'mento** m enlistment; **alistar** vt (arrolar) to enrol; (MIL) to recruit; **alistar-se** vr to enlist.

**alivi'ar** vt (mitigar) to alleviate; (carga etc) to lighten; (pessoa) to relieve; **alívio** m relief, alleviation.

**'alma** f soul; (pessoa) person; (animação) liveliness; (caráter) character.

**almejar** [awme'ʒax] vt to long for, yearn for.

**almiran'tado** m admiralty; **almirante** m admiral.

**almo'çar** vi to have lunch // vt: ~ **peixe** to have fish for lunch; **almoço** m lunch; **pequeno almoço** (Pt) breakfast.

**almo'creve** m mule driver.

**almo'fada** f cushion; (Pt) (travesseiro) pillow.

**al'môndega** f meat ball.

**a'lô** excl (Br: TEL) hullo.

**alojamento** [aloʒa'mẽtu] m accommodation; (habitação) housing; (MIL) billet; **alojar** vt to lodge; (MIL) to billet; **alojar-se** vr to stay.

**alon'gar** vt (fazer longo) to lengthen; (prazo) to extend; (prolongar) to prolong; ~**se** vr (sobre um assunto) to dwell.

**al'pendre** m (telheiro) shed; (pórtico) porch.

**'Alpes** mpl: os ~ the Alps.

**alpi'nismo** m mountaineering, climbing; **alpinista** m/f mountaineer, climber.

**al'piste** m bird seed.

**alquebrar** [awke'brax] vt (enfraquecer) to weaken // vi (curvar) to stoop, be bent double.

**alqueive** [aw'kejvi] m fallow land.

**alquimia** [awki'mia] f alchemy.

**'alta** f ver alto.

**altaneiro/a** [awta'nejru/a] adj (soberbo) proud.

**al'tar** m altar; ~**-mor** m high altar.

**alteração** [awtera'sãw] f (mudança) alteration; (desordem) disturbance; (falsificação) falsification; **alterar** vt (mudar) to alter; (falsificar) to falsify; **alterar-se** vr (mudar-se) to become altered; (enfurecer-se) to get angry, lose one's temper.

**alter'nar** vt/i to alternate; ~**se** vr to alternate; (por turnos) to take turns; **alternativo/a** adj alternative; (ELET) alternating // f alternative; **alterno/a** adj alternate.

**al'teza** f (altura) height; (título) highness.

**altisso'nante** adj high-sounding.

**alti'tude** f altitude.

**altivez** [awtʃi'veʒ] f (arrogância) haughtiness; (nobreza) loftiness; **altivo/a** adj (arrogante) haughty; (elevado) lofty.

**'alto/a** adj (elevado) high; (de grande estatura) tall; (som) high, sharp; (GEO) upper; ~**a noite** dead of night // adv (som) loudly, aloud // excl halt! // m (topo) top, summit; (elevação) height; (parada) halt, stop; **do** ~ from above; ~**s** mpl heights // f (de preços) rise; (de hospital) discharge; (sociedade) high society; ~**a fidelidade** high fidelity, hi-fi.

**alto-fa'lante** m loudspeaker.

**al'tura** f height; (momento) point, juncture; (altitude) altitude; (profundidade) depth; (de um som) pitch; **nesta** ~ at the moment; **ter 1.80 metros de** ~ to be 1.80 metres tall; **estar à** ~ **de** (ser capaz de) to be up to.

**a'lude** m avalanche.

**alu'dir** vi: ~**a** to allude to, hint at.

**alu'gar** vt (tomar de aluguel) to rent, hire; (dar de aluguel) to let, rent out; ~**se** vr to let; **aluguel** m, **aluguer** (Pt) m (ação) renting, hiring; (preço) rent.

**aluir** [al'wix] vt (abalar) to shake;

(*derrubar*) to demolish; (*arruinar*) to ruin // *vi* to collapse; (*ameaçar ruína*) to crumble.

**alumi'ar** *vt* to light (up); (*ilustrar*) to enlighten // *vi* (*brilhar*) to shine.

**alu'mínio** *m* aluminium.

**a'luno/a** *m/f* pupil, student; ~ **externo** day pupil; ~ **interno** boarder.

**alusão** [alu'zãw] *f* allusion.

**alu'sivo/a** *adj* allusive; (*alegórico*) suggestive.

**aluvião** [aluvi'ãw] *f* (GEO) alluvium; (*enchente*) flood.

**alvejar** [awve'ʒax] *vt* (*tomar como alvo*) to aim at; (*branquear*) to whiten, bleach.

**alvena'ria** *f* masonry.

**al'véolo** [aw'veolu] *m* (*ger*) cavity; (*de dentes*) socket.

**alvi'trar** *vt* to propose, suggest; **alvitre** *m* opinion.

**'alvo/a** *adj* (*cor*) white; (*puro*) pure // *m* target; **atingir o** ~ to hit the mark.

**alvo'rada** *f* dawn; **alvorecer** *vi* to dawn.

**alvoro'çar** *vt* (*agitar*) to stir up; (*entusiasmar*) to excite; ~**-se** *vr* to get excited; **alvoroço** *m* (*agitação*) commotion; (*entusiasmo*) enthusiasm.

**al'vura** *f* (*brancura*) whiteness; (*pureza*) purity.

**'ama** *f* (*de leite*) (wet) nurse; (*governanta*) governess.

**amabili'dade** *f* kindness; (*simpatia*) friendliness.

**amachucar** [amaʃu'kax] *vt* to crush.

**maci'ar** *vt* (*tornar macio*) to soften.

**a'mado/a** *m/f* beloved, sweetheart; **amador** *m* (*entusiasta*) enthusiast; (*não profissional*) amateur.

**amadure'cer** *vt/i* (*frutos*) to ripen; (*fig*) to mature.

**'âmago** *m* (*centro*) heart, core;

(*medula*) pith; (*essência*) essence.

**amainar** [amaj'nax] *vi* (*tempestade*) to abate; (*cólera*) to calm down.

**amaldiçoar** [amawdʒis'wax] *vt* to curse, swear at.

**amalga'mar** *vt* to amalgamate; (*combinar*) to fuse, blend.

**amamen'tar** *vt* to breast-feed.

**amaneirado/a** [amanej'radu/a] *adj* (*afetado*) affected; (*presumido*) conceited.

**amanhã** [ama'ɲã] *adv* tomorrow; ~ **de manhã** tomorrow morning; ~ **de tarde** tomorrow afternoon; ~ **à noite** tomorrow night; **depois de** ~ the day after tomorrow // *m* tomorrow.

**amanhar** [ama'ɲax] *vt* (*cultivar*) to cultivate; (*preparar*) to prepare.

**amanhecer** [amaɲe'sex] *vi* (*alvorecer*) to dawn; (*encontrar-se pela manhã*) to be at daybreak; **amanhecemos em Paris** we were in Paris at daybreak // *m* dawn; **ao** ~ at daybreak.

**amanho** [a'maɲu] *m* (*cultivo*) cultivation; (*arranjo*) arrangement; ~**s** *mpl* tools.

**aman'sar** *vt* (*animais*) to tame; (*cavalos*) to break in; (*aplacar*) to placate // *vi* to grow tame.

**a'mante** *m/f* lover; (*apreciador*) enthusiast, lover; **amar** *vt* to love, be in love with.

**amare'lado/a** *adj* yellowish; (*pele*) sallow; **amarelo/a** *adj* yellow // *m* yellow.

**amar'gar** *vt* to make bitter; (*fig*) to embitter; **amargo/a** *adj* · bitter; **amargura** *f* bitterness.

**amar'rar** *vt* (*prender*) to tie (up); (*NÁUT*) to moor.

**amas'sar** *vt* (*pão*) to knead; (*misturar*) to mix; (*amachucar*) to crush.

**a'mável** *adj* (*afável*) kind.

**ama'zona** *f* horsewoman // *m*: **o A~s** (GEO) the Amazon; **Amazônia**

f: a Amazônia the Amazon region.

**ambição** [ambi'sãw] f ambition;
**ambicionar** vt (ter ambição de) to
aspire to; (desejar) to crave for;
**ambicioso/a** adj ambitious.

**ambidestro/a** adj ambidextrous.

**ambiente** [ambi'ẽtʃi] m
atmosphere; (meio) environment //
adj surrounding; **meio ~**
environment; **temperatura ~** room
temperature.

**ambigüidade** [ambigwi'dadʒi] f
ambiguity; **ambíguo/a** adj
ambiguous.

**'âmbito** m (extensão) compass;
(campo de ação) scope, range.

**'ambos** adj pl both; ~ **nós** both of
us.

**ambu'lância** f ambulance.

**ambu'lante** adj walking; (errante)
wandering; **vendedor ~** street
seller // m pedlar, street seller.

**ambu'latório** m outpatient
department.

**ame'aça** f threat; **ameaçar** vt to
threaten.

**amedron'tar** vt to scare,
intimidate; ~**-se** vr to be frightened.

**ameigar** [amej'gax] vt to caress;
(tornar meigo) to soften.

**amêijoa** [a'mejʒwa] f mussel.

**ameixa** [a'mejʃa] f plum; (passa)
prune.

**amém** [a'mẽj] excl amen.

**a'mêndoa** f almond; **amendoim** m
peanut.

**ameni'dade** f wellbeing;
**amenidades** fpl light conversation.

**ameni'zar** vt (abrandar) to soften;
(tornar agradável) to make
pleasant; (facilitar) to ease;
**ameno/a** adj (agradável) pleasant;
(suave) mild, gentle.

**A'mérica** f America; ~ **do**
**Norte/do Sul** North/South America;
~ **Central/Latina** Central/Latin
America; **americano/a** adj, m/f
American.

**amesquinhar** [ameʃki'ɲax] vt to

belittle; ~**-se** vr (humilhar-se) to
belittle o.s.; (tornar-se avarento) to
become stingy.

**ames'trar** vt (adestrar) to train;
(um cavalo) to break in.

**ami'anto** m asbestos.

**a'mido** m starch.

**ami'gável** adj amicable.

**a'mígdala** f tonsil; **amigdalite** f
tonsilitis.

**a'migo/a** adj (amistoso) friendly;
**ser ~ de** to be friends with // m/f
friend.

**ami'mado/a** adj (acariciado)
petted; (amimalhado) spoilt.

**amimalhar** [amima'ʎax] vt (uma
criança) to spoil; **amimar** vt to pet,
pamper; (amimalhar) to spoil.

**amis'toso/a** adj friendly, cordial
// m (jogo) friendly.

**amiudar** [amju'dax] vt/i to repeat;
~ **as visitas** to make frequent
visits; **amiúde** adv often, frequently.

**ami'zade** f (relação) friendship;
(simpatia) friendliness; **fazer ~s** to
make friends.

**amnésia** [am'nɛzja] f amnesia.

**'amo** m (patrão) master;
(proprietário) owner.

**amodor'rado/a** adj drowsy;
**amodorrar-se** vr to become drowsy.

**amoe'dar** vt (cunhar) to mint.

**amofi'nar** vt to vex; ~**-se** vr to
fret (over).

**amolação** [amowa'sãw] f nuisance,
annoyance; **amolante** adj (Br)
annoying; **amolar** vt (afiar) to
sharpen; (enfadar) to annoy.

**amol'dar** vt to mould; ~**-se** vr;
~**-se a** (conformar-se) to conform
to; (acostumar-se) to get used to.

**amole'cer** vt (ger) to soften; (o
coração) to melt; (abrandar-se) to
relent.

**amolga'dura** f dent; **amolgar** vt
(entalhar) to dent; (esmagar) to
crush.

**a'mônia** f, **amo'níaco** m
ammonia.

**amonto'ar** vt to pile up, accumulate; ~ **riquezas** to amass a fortune.

**a'mor** m love; (amante) lover; **fazer** ~ to make love; ~ **próprio** self-esteem; (orgulho) conceit; **por** ~ **de** for the sake of.

**a'mora** f mulberry; ~ **preta** blackberry; (Pt): ~ **silvestre** blackberry.

**amorda'çar** vt to gag.

**amo'roso/a** adj loving, affectionate.

**amor-perfeito** [amox-pex'fejtu] m pansy.

**amortalhar** [amoxta'ʎax] vt (um defunto) to shroud; (fig) to enshroud.

**amortece'dor** m shock-absorber; **amortecer** vt (ger) to deaden // vi to weaken, fade; **amortecido/a** adj deadened; (enfraquecido) weak.

**amortização** [amɔrtisa'sãw] f payment in instalments.

**amos'tra** f sample.

**amoti'nar** vi to rebel, mutiny.

**ampa'rar** vt (proteger) to protect; (abrigar) to shelter; (apoiar) to support; ~**-se** vr: ~**-se em/contra** (apoiar-se) to lean on/against; **amparo** m (apoio) support; (proteção) protection.

**am'père** m (Br) ampere, amp.

**ampliação** [amplia'sãw] f (aumento) enlargement; (extensão) extension; **ampliar** vt (aumentar) to enlarge.

**amplificação** [amplifika'sãw] f (aumento) enlargement; (som) amplification; **amplificador** m amplifier; **amplificar** vt to amplify.

**ampli'tude** f (TEC) amplitude; (espaço) spaciousness; (extensão) extent; **amplo/a** adj (vasto) ample, spacious; (numeroso) numerous.

**am'pola** f (na pele) blister; (MED) ampoule.

**ampu'tar** vt to amputate.

**amu'ado/a** adj sulky; **amuar** vi to sulk; **amuo** m sulkiness.

**anacro'nismo** m anachronism.

**ana'far** vt to fatten (up).

**ana'grama** m anagram.

**anais** [a'najʃ] mpl annals.

**analfabe'tismo** m illiteracy; **analfabeto/a** adj, m/f illiterate.

**anali'sar** vt to analyse; **análise** f analysis; **analista** m/f analyst; **analítico/a** adj analytical.

**analogia** [analo'ʒia] f analogy; **análogo** adj analogous.

**a'nás** m (Pt) pineapple.

**anão/anã** [a'nãw/a'nã] m/f dwarf.

**anarquia** [anax'kia] f anarchy; **anarquista** f/f anarchist.

**a'nátema** m anathema.

**anato'mia** f anatomy.

**'anca** f (de pessoa) hip; (de animal) rump.

**ancho/a** [a'ʃu] adj (largo) broad; (vaidoso) conceited.

**anchova** [a'ʃova] f anchovy.

**ancião/anciã** [ãsi'ãw/ãsi'ã] adj old, ancient // m old man; (de uma tribo) elder // f old woman.

**ancinho** [ã'sinu] m rake.

**'âncora** f (NÁUT) anchor; (apoio) prop, support; **ancoradouro** m anchorage; **ancorar** vt/vi to anchor.

**anda'dura** f gait.

**andaime** [ã'dajmi] m (ARQ) scaffolding.

**anda'mento** m (progresso) progress; (movimento) movement; (direção) course; (MÚS) tempo; **em** ~ in progress.

**an'dar** vi to go; (ir a pé) to walk; (máquina) to work; (viajar) to travel; (progredir) to progress; (estar) ~ **triste** to be sad; ~ **a pé/a cavalo** to go on horseback; ~ **de trem/de avião** to travel by train/by plane; **anda!** come on! // m (modo de caminhar) gait; (pavimento) floor, storey (of building); (Br): ~ **térreo** ground floor.

**'Andes** *mpl*: os ~ the Andes.

**andorinha** [ãdo'rɪɲa] *f* (*pássaro*) swallow.

**andrajos** [ã'draʒuʃ] *mpl* rags; **andrajoso/a** *adj* ragged, tattered.

**ane'dota** *f* anecdote.

**anel** [a'nɛw] *m* ring; (*elo*) link; (*de cabelo*) curl; ~ **de casamento** wedding ring; ~**ado/a** *adj* curly.

**ane'lante** *adj* (*ansioso*) yearning.

**ane'lar** *vt* to long for // *vi*: ~ **por** to long for; **anelo** *m* longing, craving.

**ane'mia** *f* anaemia; **anêmico/a** *adj* anaemic.

**anes'tésico** *m* (MED) anaesthetic.

**ane'xar** *vt* to annex; (*juntar*) to attach; **anexo/a** *pp irr de* **anexar** // *adj* attached // *m* annexe.

**anfíbio/a** [ã'fɪbju/a] *adj* amphibious.

**anfiteatro** [ãfitʃi'atru] *m* amphitheatre; (*teatro*) dress circle.

**anfitrião/anfitriã** [ãfitri'ãw/ ãfitri'ã] *m* host // *f* hostess.

**angari'ar** *vt* (*obter*) to obtain; (*atrair*) to attract; ~ **votos** to canvass.

**angina** [ã'ʒina] *f* (MED) ~ **de garganta** inflammation of the throat; ~ **de peito** angina (pectoris).

**An'gola** *f* Angola; **angolano/a**, **angolense** *adj. m/f* Angolan.

**'angra** *f* inlet, cove.

**angu'lar** *adj* angular; **ângulo** *m* angle; (*canto*) corner.

**an'gústia** *f* (*ansiedade*) anxiety; (*aflição*) anguish; **angustiado/a** *adj* (*ansioso*) anxious; (*atribulado*) troubled; **angustiar** *vt* to distress; **angustioso/a** *adj* distressing.

**anho** [ˈaɲu] *m* lamb.

**anil** [a'nɪw] *m* (*cor*) indigo; (*lavagem de roupa*) blue powder.

**anilha** [a'nɪʎa] *f* (*aro*) ring; (*pia*) washer.

**anilho** [a'nɪʎu] *m* (*ilhó*) eyelet.

**animação** [anima'sãw] *f* (*viveza*)

liveliness; (*movimento*) bustle; **animado/a** *adj* (*vivo*) lively; (*alegre*) cheerful; **animador(a)** *adj* encouraging // *m/f* (*Br: TV*) presenter.

**animadversão** [animadvex'sãw] *f* (*ódio*) hatred, dislike; (*repreensão*) criticism; (*censura*) censure.

**animal** [ani'maw] *adj* animal; (*sensual*) sensual // *m* animal; (*bruto*) brute; ~ **de estimação** pet animal.

**ani'mar** *vt* (*dar vida*) to liven up; (*encorajar*) to encourage; ~**-se** *vr* (*alegrar-se*) to cheer up; ~**-se a** (*resolver-se*) to resolve to.

**'ânimo** *m* (*coragem*) courage; (*espírito*) spirit; (*intenção*) intention; **recobrar** ~ to pluck up courage; (*alegrar-se*) to cheer up; **perder o** ~ to lose heart // *excl* cheer up!

**animosi'dade** *f* (*hostilidade*) animosity; (*amargura*) bitterness.

**ani'moso/a** *adj* (*corajoso*) courageous.

**aninhar** [ani'ɲax] *vt* (*agasalhar*) to shelter // *vi* to nest; ~**-se** *vr* (*aconchegar-se*) to nestle.

**aniquilação** [anikila'sãw] *f* annihilation; **aniquilar** *vt* to annihilate; (*destruir*) to destroy.

**a'nis** *m* aniseed.

**anis'tia** (Pt: **-mn-**) *f* amnesty.

**aniver'sário** *m* anniversary; ~ **de casamento** wedding anniversary; ~ **de nascimento** birthday.

**anjo** [ˈãʒu] *m* angel; ~ **da guarda** guardian angel.

**'ano** *m* year; ~ **bissexto** leap year; ~ **econômico** financial year; **Feliz A~ Novo!** Happy New Year!; **o** ~ **passado** last year; **o** ~ **que vem** next year; **por** ~ per annum; **fazer** ~**s** to have a birthday; **ter dez** ~**s** to be ten (years old).

**anoitecer** [anoite'sex] *vi* to grow dark; **ao** ~ at nightfall.

**anojar** [ano'ʒax] *vt* (*enjoar*) to sicken; (*molestar*) to annoy; ~**-se**

*vr:* ~**-se de** to become sick of.
**anoma'lia** *f* anomaly; **anômalo/a**
*adj* anomalous.
**anoni'mato** *m* anonymity;
**anônimo/a** *adj* anonymous; (*COM*)
**sociedade anônima** limited
company; (*US*) stock company.
**anor'mal** [-aw] *adj* abnormal.
**anotação** [anɔta'sãw] *f*
(*comentário*) annotation; (*nota*)
note; **anotar** *vt* (*apontar*) to note
down; (*esclarecer*) to annotate.
**'ânsia** *f* (*ansiedade*) anxiety;
(*anelo*) longing; **ter** ~**s** (*de vômito*)
to feel sick.
**ansi'ar** *vi:* ~ **por** (*desejar alguma
coisa*) to yearn for; (*anelar por
fazer*) to long to; **ansiedade** *f*
(*angústia*) anxiety; (*desejo*)
eagerness; **ansioso/a** *adj* (*aflito*)
anxious; (*desejoso*) eager.
**anta'gônico/a** *adj* antagonistic;
(*rival*) opposing; **antagonismo** *m*
(*hostilidade*) antagonism; (*oposição*)
opposition; **antagonista** *m/f*
antagonist; (*adversário*) opponent.
**an'tártico/a** *adj* antarctic // *m*
Antarctic.
**'ante** *prep* (*na presença de*) before;
(*em vista de*) in view of, faced with.
**ante'braço** *m* forearm.
**antece'dência** *f* (*prioridade*)
priority; (*precedência*) precedence;
**com** ~ in advance; **antecedente** *adj*
(*prévio*) previous; (*precedente*)
preceding // *m* antecedent;
**antecedentes** *mpl* record *sg*,
background *sg*; **anteceder** *vt* to
precede, go before.
**antecipação** [ãtɛsipa'sãw] *f*
anticipation; (*pagamento*) advance
payment; **com um mês de** ~ a
month in advance; **antecipadamente** *adv* in advance, beforehand;
**pagar antecipadamente** to pay in
advance.
**anteci'par** *vt* to anticipate,
forestall; (*adiantar*) to bring
forward; (*prognosticar*) to expect;

**antecipo** *m* advance payment.
**antemão** [ãntɛ'mãw] *adv:* **de** ~
beforehand.
**an'tena** *f* (*BIO*) antenna, feeler;
(*TEL*) aerial.
**ante'nome** *m* Christian name;
(*título*) title.
**anteontem** [ãtɛ'õtẽ] *adv* the day
before yesterday.
**antepa'rar** *vt* (*defender*) to shield;
(*proteger*) to protect.
**ante'paro** *m* (*proteção*) screen.
**antepas'sados** *mpl* ancestors.
**ante'por** *vt* (*pôr antes*) to put
before.
**anteri'or** *adj* (*prévio*) previous;
(*antigo*) former; (*de posição*) front;
~**idade** *f* (*prioridade*) priority;
(*precedente*) precedent.
**'antes** *adv* before; (*primeiro*) first;
(*ao contrário*) rather; **quanto** ~ as
soon as possible // *prep:* ~ **de**
before; ~ **de partir** before leaving;
~ **do tempo** ahead of time; ~ **de
tudo** above all // *conj:* ~ **que**
before.
**anti'ácido/a** *adj* antacid // *m*
antacid.
**antia'éreo/a** *adj* anti-aircraft;
**abrigo** ~ air-raid shelter.
**antibi'ótico/a** *adj* antibiotic // *m*
antibiotic.
**antici'clone** *m* anticyclone.
**anti'clímax** *m* anticlimax.
**anticoncepcio'nal** *m* contraceptive.
**anticongelante** [ãtʃikõʒɛ'lãtʃi] *m*
antifreeze.
**an'tídoto** *m* antidote.
**antigalha** [ãtʃi'gaʎa] *f* (*de valor*)
antique; (*de pouco valor*) junk.
**antiga'mente** *adv* (*noutro tempo*)
formerly; (*no passado*) in the past;
**antigo/a** *adj* (*velho*) old, ancient;
(*anterior*) former; (*de estilo*)
antique.
**antiguidade** [ãtʃigi'dadʒi] *f*
antiquity, ancient times; (*de
emprego*) seniority; ~**s**

(*monumentos*) ancient monuments; (*artigos*) antiques.

**antilhano/a** [ātʃi'ʌanu/a] *adj, m/f* West Indian; **Antilhas** *fpl:* **as Antilhas** the West Indies.

**an'tílope** *m* antelope.

**antipa'tia** *f* antipathy, dislike; **antipático/a** *adj* unpleasant; (*pessoa*) disagreeable.

**antiquado/a** [āti'kwadu/a] *adj* antiquated; (*fora de moda*) out of date, old-fashioned.

**anti-se'mítico/a** *adj* anti-Semitic.

**anti-'séptico/a** *adj* antiseptic // *m* antiseptic.

**anti-social** [-sosj'aw] *adj* antisocial.

**antítese** [ā'tʃitɛz] *f* antithesis.

**antojar** [āto'ʒax] *vt* to imagine, fancy; **antojo** *m* (*capricho*) fancy; (*desejo extravagante*) craving.

**antolhos** [ā'toʎuʃ] *mpl* (*pala*) eyeshade; (*de cavalo*) blinkers; (*desejos*) fancies, whims.

**antologia** [ātolo'ʒia] *f* anthology.

**'antro** *m* cave, cavern; (*de animal*) lair; (*ladrões etc*) den.

**antro'pófago** *m/f* cannibal.

**antropolo'gia** *f* anthropology; **antropólogo/a** *m/f* anthropologist.

**anu'al** *adj* annual, yearly.

**anu'ário** *m* yearbook.

**anui'dade** *f* annuity.

**anu'ir** *vi:* **~ a** to agree to; **~ com** to comply with.

**anulação** [anula'sãw] *f* (*revogação*) annulment; (*cancelamento*) cancellation; **anular** *vt* (*invalidar*) to annul; (*revogar*) to rescind // *m* ring finger.

**anunci'ante** *m* (*COM*) advertiser; **anunciar** *vt* to advertise; (*noticiar*) to report; **anúncio** *m* (*COM*) advertisement; (*declaração*) announcement; (*cartaz*) poster; **anúncio luminoso** neon sign.

**anuvi'ar** *vt* (*nublar*) to cloud; (*obscurecer*) to darken; **~-se** *vr* to

cloud over; (*obscurecer-se*) to grow dark.

**an'verso** *m* (*moeda*) obverse.

**an'zol** *m* fish-hook; **cair no ~** to swallow the bait, be tricked.

**ao** [aw] = **a + o**, *ver* **a**.

**aonde** [a'õdʒi] *adv* where . . . to; **~ vai?** where are you going (to)?

**aos** [awʃ] = **a + os**, *ver* **a**.

**Ap.** *abr de* **apartamento** apartment.

**apadrinhar** [apadri'ɲax] *vt* (*ser padrinho*) to act as godfather to; (: *de noivo*) to be best man to; (*proteger*) to protect; (*patrocinar*) to support.

**apa'gado/a** *adj* (*fogo*) out, extinguished; (*luz elétrica*) (switched) off; (*escuro*) dark; (*indistinto*) faint; **apagar** *vt* (*fogo*) to put out, extinguish; (*luz elétrica*) to switch off; **apagar-se** *vr* to go out.

**apaixonado/a** [apajʃo'nadu/a] *adj* passionate; (*parcial*) biased; (*entusiástico*) keen; **ele está ~ por ela** he is mad about her; **ele é ~ pelo tênis** he's crazy about tennis; **apaixonar-se** *vr:* **apaixonar-se por** to fall passionately in love with.

**apale'ar** *vt* to beat (with a stick).

**apalpa'dela** *f* touch; **andar às ~s** to grope one's way; **apalpar** *vt* to touch, feel; (*MED*) to examine.

**apanhar** [apa'ɲax] *vt* (*pegar*) to catch; (*agarrar*) to seize; (*levar*) to take; (*colher*) to pick; (*juntar*) to gather; **~ em erro** to catch out; (*Pt*): **~ uma constipação**, (*Br*): **~ um resfriado** to catch a cold.

**apaniguado/a** [apani'gwadu/a] *m/f* (*partidário*) follower; (*protegido*) favourite.

**a'para** *f* (*de madeira*) shaving; (*de papel*) clipping; (*limalha*) filing.

**apara'dor** *m* sideboard.

**apara-'lápis** *m* (*Pt*) pencil sharpener.

**apa'rar** *vt* (*cabelo, unhas*) to trim, cut; (*árvore*) to prune; (*lápis*) to sharpen; (*o que cai, se tira*) to catch; (*pancada*) to parry; (*alisar*) to smooth out.

**apa'rato** *m* pomp, show.

**apare'cer** *vi* to appear; (*apresentar-se*) to turn up; (*ser publicado*) to be published; ~ **em casa de alguém** to drop in on sb, call on sb; **aparecimento** *m* appearance; (*publicação*) publication.

**aparelhado/a** [apareˈʎadu/a] *adj* (*preparado*) ready, prepared; (*madeira*) planed; **aparelhar** *vt* (*preparar*) to prepare, get ready; (*arrear*) to saddle, harness; (NÁUT) to rig; **aparelhar-se** *vr* to get ready.

**aparelho** [apaˈreʎu] *m* apparatus; (*equipamento*) equipment; (*pesca*) tackle, gear; (*utensílio*) utensil; (*máquina*) machine; (*Br: fone*) telephone; ~ **de gesso** plaster cast; ~ **de chá** tea set; ~ **de rádio/TV** radio/TV set.

**apa'rência** *f* appearance; (*aspecto*) aspect; **na** ~ apparently; **manter as** ~**s** to keep up appearances; **sob a** ~ **de** under the guise of.

**aparen'tado/a** *adj* related; **bem** ~ well connected.

**aparen'tar** *vt* (*fingir*) to feign, pretend; (*parecer*) to look, seem; ~**-se** *vr*: ~**-se com** to become related to.

**apa'rente** *adj* apparent.

**apari'ção** [apariˈsãw] *f* (*visão*) apparition; (*fantasma*) ghost.

**a'paro** *m* (*de caneta*) (pen) nib.

**apart.** *abr* de **apartamento**

**apar'tado/a** *adj* (*remoto*) secluded; (*distante*) distant; **apartamento** *m* apartment, flat.

**apar'tar** *vt* (*separar*) to separate; (*pôr de lado*) to set aside; ~**-se** *vr* (*separar-se*) to separate; ~**-se de** (*afastar-se*) to go away from; ~**-se do assunto** to digress.

**a'parte** *m* (*teatro*) aside.

**apascen'tar** *vt* to bring to pasture, graze.

**apa'tia** *f* apathy; **apático/a** *adj* apathetic; (*indiferente*) indifferent.

**apavo'rado/a** *adj* terror-stricken; **apavorar** *vt* to terrify.

**apaziguamento** [apazigwaˈmẽtu] *m* appeasement; (*pacificação*) pacification; **apaziguar** *vt* to appease; (*pacificar*) to pacify; **apaziguar-se** *vr* to calm down.

**apeadeiro** [apiaˈdejru] *m* (*trem*) stop, halt.

**ape'ar-se** *vr*: ~ **de** (*cavalo*) to dismount from.

**ape'dido** *m* (*Br*) newspaper article, statement or advertisement published at request of, or paid for by, the author.

**apedrejar** [apedreˈʒax] *vt* to stone.

**ape'gado/a** *adj* attached; **apegar-se** *vr*: **apegar-se a** (*aderir*) to stick to, cling to; (*afeiçoar-se*) to become devoted to; **apego** *m* (*afeição*) fondness, attachment.

**apela'ção** [apelaˈsãw] *f* appeal; **apelante** *m/f* (JUR) appellant; **apelar** *vi* to appeal; (JUR) **apelar da sentença** to appeal against the sentence.

**apeli'dar** *vt* (*chamar*) to name; (*Pt: dar um apelido*) to give a surname to; (*dar a alcunha de*) to nickname; ~**-se** *vr*: ~**-se de** to go by the name of; **apelido** *m* (*nome de família*) surname; (*alcunha*) nickname.

**a'pelo** *m* appeal.

**a'penas** *adv* (*unicamente*) only; (*mal*) hardly, scarcely // *conj* (*logo que*) as soon as; ~ **tinha partido quando . . .** no sooner had he left when . . .

**apêndice** [aˈpẽdʒisi] *m* appendix; (*anexo*) supplement; **apendicite** *f* appendicitis.

**aperce'ber-se** *vr*: ~ **de** to notice, see.

**aperfeiçoamento** [aperfejswamêtu] *m* (*perfeição*) perfection; (*melhoramento*) improvement; **aperfeiçoar** *vt* to perfect; (*melhorar*) to improve; **aperfeiçoar-se** *vr* to improve o.s.

**aperi'tivo** *m* aperitif.

**aperreação** [apexia'sãw] *f* (*opressão*) harassment; **aperreado/a** *adj* (*vexado*) harassed; **estar aperreado** (*sem dinheiro*) to be hard up; **aperrear** *vt* to dog, harass.

**aper'tado/a** *adj* (*roupa*) tight; (*estreito*) narrow; (*sem dinheiro*) hard up.

**aper'tar** *vt* (*espremer*) to squeeze; (*unir muito*) to pack together; (*segurar*) to grip; (*comprimir*) to press; ~ **a mão a** to shake hands with; ~ **o passo** to speed up // *vi* (*estreitar*) to narrow; (*sapatos*) to pinch, be tight.

**a'perto** *m* (*pressão*) pressure; (*situação difícil*) trouble, jam; **um** ~ **de mão** handshake.

**ape'sar** *prep*: ~ **de** in spite of, despite; ~ **disso** nevertheless.

**apete'cer** *vt*: (*Pt*) **apetece-me ir ao cinema** I feel like going to the cinema; **apetecível** *adj* (*tentador*) tempting; (*desejável*) desirable.

**apetite** [ape'titʃi] *m* appetite; (*desejo*) desire; (*ambição*) ambition; **apetitoso/a** *adj* appetizing; (*tentador*) tempting.

**apetrechar** [apetre'ʃax] *vt* to fit out, equip.

**ápice** ['apis] *m* (*cume*) summit, top; (*vértice*) apex; **num** ~ (*Pt*) in a trice.

**apiedar-se** [apje'dax-si] *vr*: ~ **de** (*ter piedade*) to pity; (*compadecer-se*) to take pity on.

**apimen'tado/a** *adj* (*picante*) peppery; (*fig*) spicy; **apimentar** *vt* to pepper, spice.

**apinhado/a** [apiˈɲadu/a] *adj* crowded; **apinhar** *vt* (*ajuntar*) to heap together; **apinhar-se** *vr*

(*aglomerar-se*) to crowd together.

**api'tar** *vi* to whistle; **apito** *m* whistle.

**apla'car** *vt* to placate // *vi* to calm down; ~**-se** *vr* to calm down.

**aplainar** [aplaj'nax] *vt* to plane.

**apla'nar** *vt* (*alisar*) to smooth; (*nivelar*) to level; (*dificuldades*) to smooth over.

**aplaudir** [aplaw'dʒix] *vt* to applaud; **aplauso** *m* applause; (*elogio*) praise; (*aprovação*) approval.

**aplicação** [aplikaˈsãw] *f* application; (*esforço*) effort; (*costura*) appliqué; (*da lei*) enforcement; **aplicado/a** *adj* hard-working.

**apli'car** *vt* to apply; ~ **uma lei** to enforce a law; ~**-se** *vr*: ~**-se a** to devote o.s. to, apply o.s. to; **aplicável** *adj* applicable, relevant.

**apo'dar** *vt* (*troçar*) to taunt, mock; (*alcunhar*) to nickname; ~ **alguém de ladrão** to call so a thief.

**apode'rar-se** *vr*: ~ **de** to seize, take possession of.

**a'podo** *m* ˌ(*alcunha*) nickname; (*mofa*) taunt, jeer.

**apodre'cer** *vt* to rot; (*corromper*) to corrupt // *vi* to rot, decay; **apodrecimento** *m* rottenness, decay; (*fig*) corruption.

**apogeu** [apo'ʒew] *m* (*ASTRO*) apogee; (*fig*) summit, height.

**apoiado/a** [apoˈjadu/a] *adj* supported; (*autorizado*) approved; (*encostado*) leaning // *m* (*aplauso*) applause; (*aprovação*) approval.

**apoi'ar** *vt* (*sustentar*) to support; (*fig*) to back up; (*basear*) to base; (*uma moção*) to second; ~**-se** *vr*: ~**-se em** to lean on, rest on; **apoio** *m* prop, support; (*fig*) backing, approval.

**apólice** [aˈpɔlis] *f* (*certificado*) policy, certificate; (*ação*) share, bond; ~ **de seguro** insurance policy.

**apologia** [apolo'ʒia] *f* (*elogio*)

eulogy; (*defesa*) defence.

**aponta'dor** *m* (Br: *apara-lápis*) pencil sharpener; (*capataz*) overseer.

**aponta'mento** *m* (*nota*) note; (*de uma reunião*) minute; (*esquema*) draft.

**apon'tar** *vt* (*fusil*) to aim; (*indicar*) to point out to; (*dedo*) to point; (*anotar*) to note down; (*fazer ponta*) to sharpen // *vi* (*aparecer*) to begin to appear; (*brotar*) to sprout; ~ **para** (*fazer pontaria*) to aim at; ~! take aim!

**apoquentar** [apokẽ'tax] *vt* (*afligir*) to worry; (*aborrecer*) to annoy, pester; ~**-se** *vr* to worry.

**aporre'ar** *vt* to beat.

**aporri'nhar** *vt* to pester, annoy.

**a'pós** *prep* after; (*atrás de*) behind // *adv* afterwards.

**aposen'tado/a** *adj* retired; **ficar** ~ to be retired, be pensioned off; **aposentar** *vt* (*reformar*) to retire, pension off; **aposentar-se** *vr* (*reformar-se*) to retire; (*hospedar-se*) to take lodgings.

**apo'sento** *m* (*quarto*) room; (*alojamento*) lodging.

**a'pósito/a** *adj* apposite, appropriate // *m* (*penso*) dressing.

**apos'sar-se** *vr*: ~ **de** to take possession of, seize.

**a'posta** *f* bet; **apostar** *vt* to bet // *vi*: **apostar em** to bet on.

**a'póstolo** *m* apostle.

**a'póstrofe** *f* apostrophe, invocation.

**a'póstrofo** *m* apostrophe.

**apote'ose** *f* apotheosis.

**apouca'do/a** [apo'kadu/a] *adj* (*mesquinho*) mean, base; (*escasso*) scanty.

**apouca'mento** *m* humiliation; **apoucar** *vt* (*rebaixar*) to humiliate; (*diminuir*) to lessen; (*desdenhar*) to belittle; **apoucar-se** *vr* to belittle o.s., underrate o.s.; (Br: *emagrecer*) to waste away.

**apra'zar** *vt* (*combinar*) to arrange, fix // *vi*: **apraz-me fazer isto** I like doing this.

**apreça'dor(a)** *m/f* valuer; **apreçar** *vt* to value, price.

**apreciação** [apresia'sãw] *f* appreciation; (*estimação*) estimation; **apreciar** *vt* to appreciate; (*estimar*) to value; (*gostar de*) to enjoy; **apreciativo/a** *adj* appreciative.

**apreci'ável** [-ew] *adj* appreciable; (*estimável*) estimable; **apreço** *m* (*estima*) esteem, regard; (*consideração*) consideration; **em apreço** in question.

**apreender** [apriẽ'dex] *vt* to apprehend; (*tomar*) to seize; (*entender*) to understand, grasp.

**apreensão** [apriẽ'sãw] *f* (*percepção*) perception; (*tomada*) seizure, arrest; (*receio*) apprehension; **apreensivo/a** *adj* apprehensive.

**apregoar** *vt* to proclaim, announce; (*mercadorias*) to cry.

**apren'der** *vt* to learn; ~ **de cor** to learn by heart // *vi*: to learn; ~ **a ler** to learn to read.

**aprendiz** [aprẽ'dʒiʃ] *m* apprentice; (*principiante*) beginner; ~**agem** *f* apprenticeship.

**apresar** [apre'zax] *vt* to take prisoner, capture.

**apresentação** [aprezẽta'sãw] *f* presentation; (*de pessoas*) introduction; (*porte pessoal*) bearing, appearance; **carta de** ~ letter of introduction; **apresentar** *vt* (*expor*) to present, show, exhibit; (*pessoas*) to introduce; **quero apresentar-lhe** may I introduce you to; **apresentar-se** *vr* (*aparecer*) to appear, turn up; **apresentar-se a** to introduce o.s. to.

**apres'sado/a** *adj* hurried, hasty; **estar** ~ to be in a hurry; **apressar** *vt* to hurry, hasten; **apressar-se** *vr* to hurry (up).

**apressu'rar** vt to hurry, hasten; ~-se vr to hurry (up).

**apres'tar** vt (aparelhar) to equip, fit out; (aprontar) to get ready; ~-se vr to get ready; **aprestos** mpl (equipamento) equipment, gear; (preparativos) preparations.

**aprisio'nado/a** adj imprisoned; **aprisionamento** m imprisonment; **aprisionar** vt (cativar) to capture; (encarcerar) to imprison.

**apron'tar** vt to get ready, prepare; ~-se vr: ~-se para to get ready to.

**apropriação** [aprɔpria'sãw] f appropriation; (tomada) seizure.

**apropri'ado/a** adj appropriate, suitable.

**apropri'ar** vt to appropriate; ~-se vr: ~-se de to seize, take possession of.

**aprovação** [aprɔva'sãw] f approval; (louvor) praise; (exame) pass; **aprovado/a** adj approved; **ser aprovado num exame** to pass an exam; **aprovar** vt to approve of; (exame) to pass // vi to pass.

**aproveita'mento** m use, utilization; (adiantamento) progress.

**aproveitar** [aprovej'tax] vt (tirar proveito) to profit by; (não desperdiçar) to take advantage of; (utilizar) to use // vi (Pt) to be of use; **não aproveita** it's no use; ~-se vr: ~-se de to make good use of, avail o.s. of; ~-se ao máximo de to make the most of.

**aprovisiona'mento** m supply, provision; **aprovisionar** vt to supply.

**aproximação** [aprosima'sãw] f (estimativa) approximation; (chegada) approach; (proximidade) nearness, closeness; **aproximado/a** adj (cálculo) approximate; (perto) nearby.

**aproximar** [aprosi'max] vt to bring near; (aliar) to bring together; ~-se vr: ~-se de (acercar-se) to approach, come near.

**apru'mado/a** adj vertical; (altivo)

upright; **aprumo** m vertical position; (confiança) assurance, aplomb; (altivez) haughtiness.

**aptidão** [aptʃi'dãw] f aptitude, ability; (jeito) knack; **exame de ~** aptitude test; **~ física** physical fitness.

**'apto/a** adj apt; (idôneo) suitable; (capaz) capable.

**apunhalar** [apuɲa'lax] vt to stab.

**apu'pada** f (insulto) boo, jeer; **apupar** vt (vaiar) to boo, jeer at; (buzinar) to hoot at; **apupos** mpl hooting.

**apu'rado/a** adj (escolhido) select; (fino) refined, fine.

**apu'rar** vt (purificar) to purify, refine; (aperfeiçoar) to perfect; (descobrir) to find out; (verificar) to verify; (dinheiro) to raise, get; (votos) to count; (caldo) to thicken.

**a'puro** m (elegância) refinement, elegance; (miséria) hardship, difficulty; **estar em ~s** to be in a jam.

**aquarela** [akwa'rela] f water-colour.

**aquário** [a'kwarju] m aquarium; (zodíaco) Aquarius.

**aquarte'lar** vt (MIL) to billet, quarter.

**a'quático/a** adj aquatic, water.

**aquecedor(a)** [akese'dox(ra)] adj warming // m heater.

**aquecer** [ake'sex] vt to heat, warm; ~-se vr to grow warm, heat up; **aquecimento** m heating; **aquecimento central** central heating.

**aquedar** [ake'dax] vt to calm, quieten.

**aqueduto** [ake'dutu] m aqueduct.

**aquele, aquela, aqueles, aquelas** [a'keli, a'kɛla, a'kelif, a'kɛlaf] adj that, (pl) those // pron that one, (pl) those; **sem mais aquela(s)** without more ado.

**aquém** [a'kẽj] adv on this side; ~

de on this side of; (*abaixo de*) beneath.

**aquentar** [akẽ'tax] *vt* to warm, heat; ~**-se** *vr* to get warm.

**aqui** [a'ki] *adv* (*lugar*) now; **eis** ~ here is/are, here you have; **por** ~ **e por ali** here and there; **por** ~ hereabouts; (*nesta direção*) this way; ~ **mesmo** right here; **daqui em diante** from now on; **daqui a uma semana** a week from now.

**aquietar** [akie'tax] *vt* to calm, quieten; ~**-se** *vr* to calm down.

**aquilatar** [akila'tax] *vt* (*metais*) to value; (*avaliar*) to evaluate.

**aquilo** [a'kilu] *pron* that (thing); ~ **que** what.

**aquisição** [akizi'sãw] *f* acquisition.

**aquoso/a** [a'kwozu/a] *adj* aqueous.

**ar** /a/ *m* air; (*semelhança*) look, appearance, aspect; (*aragem*) breeze; (*Pt: AUTO*) choke; ~ **condicionado** air conditioning; **ao** ~ **livre** in the open air; **tomar** ~ to go out, get some air; ~**es** *mpl* airs; (*clima*) climate *sg*; **dar-se** ~**es** to put on airs.

**'ara** *f* altar.

**'árabe** *adj, m/f* Arab // *m* (*língua*) Arabic.

**a'rábico/a** *adj, m/f* Arabian.

**a'rado** *m* plough.

**aragem** [a'raʒẽj] *f* breeze.

**a'rame** *m* wire; ~ **farpado** barbed wire.

**aranha** [a'raɲa] *f* spider.

**a'rar** *vt* to plough.

**arauto** [a'rawtu] *m* herald.

**arbitra'gem** *f* arbitration; (*esporte*) refereeing; **arbitrar** *vt* to arbitrate; (*esporte*) to referee; (*adjudicar*) to award.

**arbitrarie'dade** *f* arbitrariness; (*ato*) arbitrary act; (*capricho*) capriciousness; **arbitrário/a** *adj* arbitrary; (*caprichoso*) wilful.

**ar'bítrio** *m* (*decisão*) decision; (*resolução*) will; **ao** ~ **de** at the

discretion of; **livre** ~ free will.

**'árbitro** *m* (*juiz*) arbiter; (*JUR*) arbitrator; (*futebol*) referee; (*tênis*) umpire.

**ar'busto** *m* shrub, bush.

**'arca** *f* (*caixa*) chest; (*cofre*) coffer; ~ **de Noé** Noah's Ark.

**ar'cada** *f* (*série de arcos*) arcade; (*arco*) arch, span.

**arcaico/a** [ax'kajku/a] *adj* archaic; (*antiquado*) antiquated.

**arcanjo** [ax'kãʒu] *m* archangel.

**ar'car** *vt*: ~ **com** (*responsabilidades*) to shoulder.

**arce'bispo** *m* archbishop.

**'arco** *m* (*ARQ*) arch; (*MIL, MÚS*) bow; (*ELET, MAT*) arc; (*barril*) hoop.

**arco-'íris** *m* rainbow.

**ar'dente** *adj* burning; (*intenso*) fervent; (*apaixonado*) ardent; **arder** *vi* to burn; (*de um golpe*) to smart; (*de uma picada*) to sting; **arder em cólera** to burn with rage; **arder por** to desire passionately.

**ar'dido/a** *adj* (*fermentado*) rancid, sour; (*picante*) hot.

**ar'dil** *m* trick, ruse; ~**oso/a** *adj* cunning.

**ar'dor** *m* (*paixão*) ardour, passion; ~**oso/a** *adj* ardent.

**ar'dósia** *f* slate.

**árduo/a** [ˈaxdwu/a] *adj* arduous; (*difícil*) hard, difficult.

**área** [ˈarja] *f* area; (*esporte*) penalty area; ~ **de serviço**) (*pátio*) yard.

**areia** [aˈreja] *f* sand; ~ **movediça** quicksand.

**arejado/a** [areˈʒadu/a] *adj* aired, ventilated; **arejar** *vt* to air, ventilate; **arejar-se** *vr* to get some fresh air.

**a'rena** *f* (*contenda*) arena; (*circo*) ring.

**a'renga** *f* harangue; (*invectiva*) tirade; **arengar** *vt/i* to harangue.

**are'noso/a** *adj* sandy.

**arenque** [aˈrẽki] *m* herring.

**a'resta** *f* edge; (*saliência*) ridge.

**ar'fada** *f* (*ofego*) gasp; (*NÁUT*) pitching; **arfar** *vi* (*ofegar*) to pant, gasp for breath; (NÁUT) to pitch.

**arga'massa** f mortar; **argamassar** vt to plaster, apply mortar to.

**Argélia** [ax'ʒɛlja] f Algeria; **argelino/a** adj, m/f Algerian.

**argentino/a** [axʒē'tʃinu/a] adj Argentinian; (prateado) silvery, silver // m/f Argentinian // f: **A~a** Argentina.

**argento-vivo** [axʒētu-'vivu] m quicksilver.

**argila** [ax'ʒila] f clay.

**ar'gola** f ring; ~ **da porta** doorknocker; ~**s** fpl (brincos) hooped earrings; **argolada** f trap, knock.

**argúcia** [ax'gusja] f (sutileza) subtlety; (agudeza) astuteness; (piada) witticism; **arguciar** vi to quibble.

**argueiro** [ax'gejru] m (grânulo) speck; (coisa insignificante) trifle; **fazer de um ~ um cavaleiro** (Pt) to make a mountain out of a molehill.

**argüente** [ax'gwētʃi] m/f accuser; **argüido** m accused.

**argüir** [ax'gwix] vt to accuse; ~ **de** to accuse of; ~ **por** to blame for (Pt) vi to argue; (suplicar) to plead; (examinar) to test, examine.

**argumentação** [axgumēta'sãw] f argument, controversy; **argumentador(a)** adj argumentative // m/f arguer.

**argumen'tar** vt/i to argue; **argumento** m (disputa) argument; (de obra) plot, theme; (sumário) summary; **como argumento** as an example.

**ar'guto/a** adj (sutil) subtle; (astuto) shrewd.

**ari'ano/a** adj, m/f Aryan.

**aridez** [ari'deʒ] f (secura) dryness; (falta de interesse) dullness; **árido/a** adj (seco) arid, dry; (maçante) dull, boring.

**aristo'cra'cia** f aristocracy; **aristocrata** m/f aristocrat; **aristocrático/a** adj aristocratic.

**arit'mético/a** adj arithmetical // f arithmetic.

**arlequim** [axle'kĩ] m harlequin; (teatro) buffoon.

**'arma** f arm, weapon; ~ **branca** cold steel; ~ **de fogo** firearm; ~**s** fpl (brasão) coat of arms; (profissão militar) military career; **passar pelas** ~**s** to shoot, execute.

**armação** [axma'sãw] f (armadura) body, frame; (pesca) tackle; (equipamento) equipment; (navio) rigging.

**armadilha** [axma'dʒiʎa] f trap, snare.

**ar'mado/a** adj armed; (TEC) reinforced // f fleet, navy.

**arma'dor** m (tapeceiro) upholsterer; (NÁUT) chandler; shipowner; (agente de funerais) undertaker.

**arma'dura** f armour; (ELET) armature; (CONSTR) framework.

**arma'mento** m (armas) armament, weapons; (NÁUT) equipment.

**ar'mar** vt to arm; (barraca) to pitch; (um aparelho) to set up; (preparar) to prepare; (NÁUT) to fit out; ~ **uma briga com** to pick a quarrel with; ~ **uma armadilha** to set a trap; ~ **cavaleiro** to knight.

**arma'ria** f (MIL) armoury; (heráldica) heraldry.

**ar'mário** m cupboard; (de roupa) wardrobe, closet.

**armazém** [axma'zēj] m (loja) store; (depósito) warehouse; ~ **de secos e molhados** grocery store; **armazenagem** f storage; **armazenar** vt to store; (provisões) to stock.

**armeiro** [ax'mejru] m gunsmith.

**'aro** m (argola) ring; (de óculos) rim; (de porta) frame; ~**s** mpl outskirts.

**a'roma** f aroma, fragrance; **aromático/a** adj aromatic, fragrant.

**arpão** [ax'pãw] m harpoon; **arpoar** vt to harpoon.

**arquear** [axkⁱ'ax] vt to arch; (emperrar) to camber; ~-se vr to bend, arch; (entortar-se) to warp.

**arqueiro** [ax'kejru] m archer; (goleiro) goalkeeper.

**arquejar** [axke'ʒax] vi to pant, wheeze; **arquejo** m panting, gasping.

**arqueologia** [axkiolo'ʒia] f archaeology; **arqueólogo/a** m/f archaeologist.

**arquétipo** [ax'kɛtʃipu] m archetype.

**arquibancada(s)** f(pl) stalls.

**arquiteto/a** [axkiˈtɛtu/a] (Pt: -ct-) m/f architect; **arquitetura** (Pt: -ct-) f architecture.

**arquivar** [axkiˈvax] vt (depositar) to file; (registrar) to record; **arquivo** m archive; (móvel) filing cabinet.

**arraˈbaldes** mpl suburbs.

**arraia** [aˈxaja] f (peixe) ray; ~ miúda masses pl, rabble.

**arraiˈal** m (povoação) village; (Pt: festa) fair.

**arraiˈgado/a** adj deep-rooted; (fig) ingrained; **arraigar** vi to root; **arraigar-se** vr (enraizar-se) to take root; (estabelecer-se) to settle.

**arrais** [aˈxajʃ] m (NÁUT) skipper.

**arranˈcada** f (puxão) pull, jerk; (partida) get-away; (investida) charge; **arrancar** vt (extrair) to pull up, pull out; (arrebatar) to snatch (away); (fig) to extract // vi to start (off); **arrancar-se** vr to run off; **arranco** m (puxão) pull, jerk; (partida) sudden start.

**arranha-céu** [axaɲa-ˈsɛw] m skyscraper.

**arranhadura** [axaɲaˈdura] f, **arranhão** [axaˈɲãw] m scratch; **arranhar** vt to scratch.

**arranjar** [axãˈʒax] vt (organizar) to arrange; (arrumar) to tidy (up); (conseguir) to get; (consertar) to repair; (conciliar) to settle; ~ um emprego to get a job; ~-se vr (arrumar-se bem) to get by; (preparar-se) to get ready; ~-se

**sem** to do without; **arranjo** m (disposição) arrangement; (negociata) deal.

**arranque** [aˈxãki] m (AUTO) starter.

**ˈarras** fpl (penhor) surety; (doação) dowry.

**arraˈsar** vt (demolir) to demolish; (derrubar) to raze, level; (estragar) to ruin; (humilhar) to browbeat; ~-se vr (humilhar-se) to humble o.s.

**arrasˈtado/a** adj (rasteiro) crawling; (demorado) dragging; (voz) drawling.

**arrastão** [axasˈtãw] m tug, jerk; (rede) dragnet; **arrastar** vt to drag (along); (vento) to sweep (along); (impelir) to drive; **arrastar a asa** a to court // vi to trail; **arrastar-se** vr to crawl; (fig) to grovel; **arrasto** m (ação) dragging; (rede) trawl-net; (TEC) drag.

**arrazoado** [axaˈzwadu] m (JUR) defence; **arrazoar** vt to argue for (a cause) // vi to discuss; (discutir) to argue.

**arreˈar** vt (cavalo etc) to harness.

**arrebaˈtado/a** adj (impetuoso) rash, impetuous; (elevado) entranced; **arrebatamento** m (impetuosidade) impetuosity; (enlevo) ecstasy.

**arrebaˈtar** vt (agarrar) to snatch (away); (levar) to carry off; (enlevar) to entrance; (enfurecer) to enrage; ~-se vr (entusiasmar-se) to be entranced.

**arrebenˈtado/a** adj (falido) broke; (estafado) worn out; **arrebentar** vi (estourar) to explode, burst; **arrebentar-se** vr to be done for.

**arrebiˈtado/a** adj turned-up; (nariz) snub; **arrebitar** vt to turn up.

**arrebol** [axeˈbɔw] m red sky.

**arreˈcada** f earring.

**arrecadação** [axekadaˈsãw] f (de impostos etc) collection; (depósito) storehouse; (custódia) custody;

**arrecadador** m (de impostos) tax collector; **arrecadar** vt (impostos etc) to collect.

**arrecife** [axe'sɪfɪ] m reef.

**arre'dar** vt to move away, move back; **não ~ pé** not to move, to stand one's ground; **~-se** vr to withdraw.

**arre'dio/a** adj (cachorro) stray; (gado) runaway, stray; (solitário) solitary; (insociável) unsociable.

**arredon'dar** vt to round (off); **~ a conta** to make a round sum.

**arre'dores** mpl suburbs; (cercanias) outskirts.

**arrefe'cer** vt to cool // vi to cool (off).

**arrega'çar** vt (mangas) to roll up; (calças) to turn up.

**arrega'lar** vt to goggle.

**arreganhar** [axega'ɲax] vt (dentes) to bare (one's teeth).

**arreios** [a'xejuʃ] mpl harness sg.

**arre'lia** f (zanga) annoyance; **arreliar** vt to annoy; **arreliar-se** vr to get angry.

**arreman'gar** vt to roll up; **~-se** vr (aprontar-se) to get ready.

**arrema'tar** vt (rematar) to conclude; (comprar) to buy by auction; (vender) to sell by auction.

**arreme'dar** vt to mimic; **arremedo** m mimicry.

**arremes'sar** vt to throw, hurl; **~-se** vr to hurl o.s.; **arremesso** m (lançamento) throw.

**arreme'ter** vt to lunge; **~ contra** (acometer) to attack, assail; **arremetida** f attack, onslaught.

**arrenda'dor(a)** m landlord // f landlady.

**arrenda'mento** m (ação) renting; (contrato) lease; (preço) rent; **arrendar** vt (dar em arrendamento) to let; (alugar) to rent, hire; **arrendatário/a** m/f tenant.

**arrepanhar** [axepa'ɲax] vt (arregaçar) to tuck up); (enrugar) to crease; (arrebatar) to snatch; (economizar) to hoard.

**arrepen'der-se** vr to repent; (mudar de opinião) to change one's mind; **~ de** to regret, be sorry for; **arrependimento** m repentance, regret.

**arrepi'ar** vt (amedrontar) to horrify; (cabelo etc) to cause to stand on end; (peixe) to salt; **~-se** vr (sentir calafrios) to shiver; (cabelo) to stand on end; **isso me arrepia** it gives me goose flesh.

**arre'pio** m shiver; (de frio) chill; **isso me dá ~s** it gives me the creeps; **ao ~** the wrong way, against the grain.

**ar'resto** m (JUR) seizure, confiscation.

**arreve'sado/a** adj (obscuro) obscure; (intricado) intricate; **arrevesar** vt (pôr ao revés) to turn inside out/upside down; (complicar) to complicate.

**arri'ar** vt (baixar) to lower; (depor) to lay down // vi (afrouxar) to yield; (desistir) to give up; **~-se** vr (cair) to fall; (vergar) to sag.

**ar'riba** adv (acima) up, upward(s); (adiante) onward(s).

**arriba'ção** [axiba'sãw] f (Br: aves) migration; **arribar** vi (recuperar-se) to recuperate.

**arri'mar** vt to support; **~-se** vr: **~-se a** (apoiar-se) to lean against; **arrimo** m support, prop; **arrimo de família** breadwinner.

**arris'cado/a** adj (obscuro) risky; (audacioso) daring; **arriscar** vt to risk; (pôr em perigo) to endanger, jeopardize; **arriscar-se** vr to take a risk.

**arri'vista** m/f (oportunista) opportunist.

**arro'char** [axo'ʃax] vt (apertar) to tighten up // vi (ser exigente) to be demanding; **arrocho** m squeeze; (fig) predicament.

**arro'gância** f arrogance,

haughtiness; **arrogante** adj arrogant, haughty.

**arro¹gar** vt to attribute; ~**-se** vr to appropriate for o.s.; (atribuir-se) to attribute to o.s.

**arroio** [a¹xoju] m stream.

**arrojado/a** [axo¹ʒadu/a] adj (temerário) rash; (ousado) daring; **arrojar** vt (lançar) to hurl; **arrojar-se** vr: **arrojar-se a** (arremessar-se) to hurl o.s. into; (ousar) to dare to.

**arrojo** [a¹xoʒu] m (ousadia) boldness.

**arrola¹mento** m enrolment; (lista) list; **arrolar** vt to enrol.

**arromba¹dor** m burglar; **arrombamento** m burglary, breaking and entry; **arrombar** vt (abrir à força) to break into.

**arros¹tar** vt to confront, face (up to).

**arro¹tar** vt/i to belch; (alardear) to boast (of).

**arrote¹ar** vt (terreno) to clear; (: cultivar) to cultivate; (educar) to educate.

**arrouba¹mento** m ecstasy, rapture; **arroubar** vt to enrapture, entrance; **arroubo** m ecstasy, rapture.

**arroz** [a¹xoʒ] m rice; ~ **doce**, ~ **de leite** rice pudding; **arrozal**, ~ m rice field.

**arru¹aça** f street riot.

**arru¹ela** f (TEC) washer.

**arru¹gar** vt to wrinkle, crease.

**arrui¹nar** vt to ruin; (destruir) to destroy; (estragar) to spoil // vi (estragar-se) to get spoiled, go bad; ~**-se** vr to be ruined.

**arrulhar** [axu¹ʎax] vi (pombos) to coo; **arrulho** m (pombos) cooing.

**arruma¹ção** [axuma¹sãw] f (arranjo) arrangement; (de um quarto etc) tidying up; (de malas) packing; **arrumar** vt (pôr em ordem) to put in order, arrange; (um quarto etc) to tidy up; (malas) to pack; (obter) to get, secure.

**arse¹nal** m (MIL) arsenal; ~ **de Marinha** naval dockyard.

**¹arte** f (ger) art; (habilidade) skill; (ofício) trade, craft; (astúcia) cunning.

**arte¹fato** (Pt: **-ct-**) m (manufactured) article; (arqueológico) artefact; ~**s de couro** leather goods, leatherware sg.

**arteirice** [axtej¹risi] f cunning, guile; **arteiro/a** adj artful, cunning.

**artéria** [ax¹tɛrja] f (ANAT) artery.

**artesa¹nato** m craftwork, crafts.

**artesão/artesã** [axte¹zãw, axte¹zã] m artisan, craftsman // f craftswoman.

**¹ártico/a** adj Arctic // m: **o A~** the Arctic.

**articulação** [axtʃikula¹sãw] f articulation; (MED) joint; **articulado/a** adj articulated, jointed; **articular** vt (pronunciar) to articulate; (ligar) to join together.

**articu¹lista** m/f newspaper writer, columnist.

**ar¹tículo** m (ANAT) knuckle; (artigo) article.

**artífice** [ax¹tʃifis] m craftsman; (inventor) inventor // f craftswoman.

**artifício** [axtʃi¹fisju] m (habilidade) skill, art; (astúcia) cunning; **artificioso/a** adj (hábil) skilful; (astucioso) artful.

**ar¹tigo** m article; ~ **de fundo** leading article, editorial; ~**s** mpl goods.

**artilharia** [axtʃiʎa¹ria] f artillery; **artilheiro** m gunner, artilleryman.

**artimanha** [axtʃi¹maɲa] f (ardil) stratagem; (astúcia) cunning.

**ar¹tista** m/f (pintor etc) artist; (de teatro etc) artist; **artístico/a** adj artistic.

**ar¹trite** f (MED) arthritis.

**arvo¹rar** vt (erguer) to raise; (bandeira) to hoist.

**árvore** f tree; (TEC) axle, shaft; **arvoredo** m grove.

**as** art ver **a**.

**às** = **a** + **as**, ver **a**.

**ás** m ace.

**'asa** f wing; (de xícara etc) handle.

**asbesto** [az'bɛstu] m asbestos.

**ascen'dência** f (antepassados) ancestry; (domínio) ascendency, sway; **ascendente** adj rising, upward // m (antepassado) ancestor; (domínio) ascendency.

**ascen'der** vi (subir) to rise, ascend; ~ **a** to amount to; **ascensão** f ascent; (fig) rise; **dia da Ascensão** Ascension Day.

**ascen'sor** m (US) elevator; (Brit) lift.

**as'ceta** m/f ascetic.

**'asco** m loathing, revulsion; **dar** ~ to be revolting, disgust.

**áscua** ['aʃkwa] f (brasa) ember; (chispa) spark.

**as'falto** m asphalt.

**asfixia** [aʃfik'sia] f suffocation; **asfixiar** vt, **asfixiar-se** vr to suffocate.

**Ásia** ['azja] f Asia; **asiático/a** adj, m/f Asian.

**asi'lar** vt to give refuge to; ~**-se** vr to take refuge; **asilo** m (refúgio) refuge; (estabelecimento) home, asylum.

**asma** ['aʒma] f asthma.

**asneira** [aʒ'nejra] f (tolice) stupidity; (conversa tola) nonsense.

**'asno** m donkey; (fig) ass.

**'aspa** f (cruz) cross; ~**s** fpl (chifres) horns; (sinais ortográficos) inverted commas.

**as'pargo** m asparagus.

**as'pecto** m (aparência) appearance; (característica) feature; (ponto de vista) point of view; **ter bom** ~ to look well.

**aspe'reza** f roughness; (severidade) harshness; (rudeza) abruptness.

**aspergir** [aʃpex'ʒix] vt to sprinkle.

**'áspero/a** adj rough; (severo) harsh; (difícil) tough; (rude) abrupt.

**as'perso/a** pp irr de **aspergir** // adj scattered.

**aspiração** [aʃpira'sãw] f aspiration; (inalação) inhalation; (desejo) longing.

**aspi'rador** m: ~ **de pó** vacuum cleaner.

**aspi'rante** m/f applicant, candidate; (MIL) cadet.

**aspi'rar** vt to breathe in; (sorver) to suck in; (LING) to aspirate // vi: ~ **a** to aspire to.

**aspi'rina** f aspirin.

**asqueroso/a** [aʃke'rozu/a] adj disgusting, revolting.

**assadeira** [asa'dejra] f pan; **assado/a** adj roasted; **carne assada** roast beef // m roast; **assadura** f (skin-)rash.

**assal'tante** m/f assailant; (arrombador) burglar; **assaltar** vt (atacar) to attack, raid; (assediar) to besiege; (uma casa) to break into; **assalto** m (ataque) attack, raid; (a um banco etc) hold-up; (boxe) round; (a uma casa) burglary, break-in.

**assanhado/a** [asa'ɲadu/a] adj (enfurecido) furious; (irrequieto) restless; (sexualmente) ~ excited, aroused; **assanhar** vt to enrage, infuriate; (irritar) to inflame; (agitar) to stir up; (sexualmente) to tease, excite; **assanhar-se** vr to fly into a rage.

**as'sar** vt to roast; (na grelha) to grill.

**assassi'nar** vt to murder, kill; (POL) to assassinate; **assassinato** m, **assassínio** m murder, killing, assassination; **assassino/a** m/f murderer, killer; (político) assassin.

**assaz** [a'saʃ] adj enough, sufficient // adv (suficientemente) sufficiently; (muito) quite, rather.

**asse'ado/a** adj (limpo) clean; (aspecto) tidy; (esmerado) neat; **assear** vt to clean, tidy (up).

**assedi'ar** vt (sitiar) to besiege; (importunar) to pester; **assédio** m seige; (*insistência*) insistence.

**assegu'rar** *vt* (*tornar seguro*) to secure; (*garantir*) to ensure; (*afirmar*) to assure; ~-**se** *vr*: ~-**se de** to make sure of.

**asseio** [a'seju] *m* (*limpeza*) cleanliness; (*esmero*) neatness.

**assembléia** [asẽ'blɛja] *f* assembly; (*reunião*) meeting.

**assemelhar** [aseme'λax] *vt* to liken, compare; ~-**se** *vr* (*ser semelhante*) to be alike; ~-**se a** to resemble, look like.

**assen'tado/a** *adj* (*baseado*) based; (*firme*) fixed, secure; (*combinado*) agreed.

**assenta'dor** *m* (*registrador*) registrar; (*de tijolos*) bricklayer; **assentamento** *m* registration.

**assen'tar** *vt* (*fazer sentar*) to seat; (*colocar*) to place; (*estabelecer*) to establish; (*anotar*) to note down; (*decidir*) to decide upon; (*determinar*) to fix, settle // *vi* (*basear-se*) to base; (*ficar bem*) to suit; (*pó etc*) to settle; ~-**se** *vr* to sit down; **assente** *pp irr de* assentar // *adj* agreed; decided.

**assenti'mento** *m* assent, agreement; **assentir** *vi* to agree.

**as'sento** *m* (*móvel*) chair; (*de veículo etc*) seat; (*anotação*) entry, record; (*base*) base; (*ANAT*) bottom; (*residência*) residence.

**asses'sor(a)** *m/f* adviser.

**asses'tar** *vt* to aim, point.

**asseve'rar** *vt* to affirm, assert.

**assiduidade** [asidwi'dadʒi] *f* assiduousness, diligence; **assíduo/a** *adj* diligent; (*incessante*) constant.

**assim** [a'sĩ] *adv* (*deste modo*) like this, in this way, thus; (*portanto*) therefore; (*igualmente*) likewise; ~ **so-so**; ~ **mesmo** in any case; ~ **ou assado** in one way or another; **e** ~ **por diante and so on** // *conj*: ~ **como** as well as; ~ **que** (*logo que*) as soon as.

**assimilação** [asimila'sãw] *f*

assimilation; **assimilar** *vt* to assimilate; (*apreender*) to take in; (*assemelhar*) to compare.

**assina'lado/a** *adj* (*marcado*) marked; (*notável*) notable; (*célebre*) eminent; **assinalar** *vt* (*marcar*) to mark; (*distinguir*) to distinguish; (*especificar*) to point out.

**assi'nante** *m/f* (*de jornal etc*) subscriber; **assinar** *vt* (*nome*) to sign; (*jornal etc*) to subscribe to; (*fixar*) to fix; (*conferir*) to assign; **assinatura** *f* (*nome*) signature; (*de jornal etc*) subscription; (*teatro*) season ticket.

**assis'tência** *f* (*presença*) attendance, presence; (*público*) audience; (*auxílio*) aid, assistance.

**assis'tente** *adj* assistant // *m/f* (*pessoa presente*) spectator, onlooker; (*ajudante*) assistant.

**assis'tir** *vt* to attend, assist // *vi*: ~ **a** to attend, be present at.

**asso'ar** *vt*: ~ **o nariz** to blow one's nose; ~-**se** *vr* (*Pt*) to blow one's nose.

**assobi'ar** *vi* to whistle; **assobio** *m* whistle; (*instrumento*) whistle; (*de vapor*) hiss.

**associação** [asosia'sãw] *f* association; (*organização*) society; (*parceria*) partnership; **associado/a** *adj*, *m/f* associate, member; (*sócio*) partner; **associar** *vt* to associate; **associar-se** *vr* (*COM*) to form a partnership; **associar-se a** to associate with.

**assola'dor(a)** *adj* devastating; **assolar** *vt* to devastate.

**asso'mar** *vi* (*aparecer*) to appear; ~ **a** (*subir*) to climb to the top of.

**assombração** [asobra'sãw] *f* (*pavor*) dread; (*fantasma*) ghost; **assombrado/a** *adj* (*sombrio*) shady; (*casa*) haunted; **assombrar** *vt* (*assustar*) to frighten, startle; (*maravilhar*) to astonish; (*fantasma*) to haunt; **assombrar-se** *vr* to be amazed; **assombro** *m* (*espanto*) fright; (*pasmo*) astonishment; (*maravilha*) marvel; **assombroso/a** *adj* (*espantoso*) astonishing, amazing.

**assu'mir** *vt* to assume // *vi* to take office.

**assun'tar** *vt* (*prestar atenção*) to pay attention to; (*verificar*) to find out // *vi* (*considerar*) to consider.

**as'sunto** *m* (*tema*) subject, matter; (*enredo*) plot.

**assusta'diço/a** *adj* shy, timorous; **assustar** *vt* to frighten, scare, startle; **assustar-se** *vr* to be frightened.

**'astro** *m* star.

**astrologia** [aʃtrolo'ʒia] *f* astrology; **astrólogo/a** *m/f* astrologer.

**astronauta** [aʃtro'nawta] *m/f* astronaut.

**astro'nave** *f* spacecraft.

**astrono'mia** *f* astronomy; **astrônomo** *m* astronomer.

**as'túcia** *f* cunning; (*ardil*) trickery; **astuto/a** *adj* astute; (*esperto*) cunning.

**'ata** (*Pt:* **-ct-**) *f* (*de reunião*) minutes *pl*.

**ataca'dista** *m/f* wholesaler.

**ata'cador** *m* (*de sapato etc*) lace.

**ata'cante** *adj* attacking // *m/f* attacker, assailant // *m* (*futebol*) forward; **atacar** *vt* to attack.

**ata'dura** *f* bandage.

**atalaia** [ata'laja] *m* watchman // *f* (*posto de observação*) lookout post; (*sentinela*) lookout, sentry.

**atalhar** [ata'ʎax] *vt* (*impedir*) to prevent; (*deter*) to stop; (*abreviar*) to shorten // *vi* (*tomar um atalho*) to take a short cut; **atalho** *m* (*caminho*) short cut; (*estorvo*) obstacle.

**ataque** [a'taki] *m* attack; ~ **aéreo** air raid; ~ **cardíaco** heart attack.

**a'tar** *vt* to tie (up), fasten; **não** ~ **nem desatar** to waver.

**atare'fado/a** *adj* busy.

**atarra'cado/a** *adj* stocky.

**atascadeiro** [ataʃka'dejru] *m* bog; **atascar-se** *vr* to get bogged down.

**ataúde** [ata'udʒi] *m* coffin.

**atavi'ar** *vt* to adorn, decorate; ~**se** *vr* to get dressed up; **atavio** *m* adornment; (*vestes*) attire.

**a'té** *prep* (*Pt:* + a): (*lugar*) up to, as far as; (*tempo etc*) until, till; ~ **agora** up to now; ~ **certo ponto** to a certain extent; ~ **já** ou ~ **logo** see you soon // *conj:* ~ **que** until // *adv* even.

**ate'ar** *vt* (*fogo*) to kindle; (*fig*) to incite, inflame; ~ **fogo a** to set light to; ~**se** *vr* (*fogo*) to blaze; (*paixões*) to flare up.

**ate'ísmo** *m* atheism.

**atemori'zar** *vt* to frighten; (*intimidar*) to intimidate.

**atenção** [atẽ'sãw] *f* attention; (*cortesia*) courtesy; (*bondade*) kindness; **prestar** ~ to pay attention; **chamar a** ~ to attract attention; **chamar a** ~ **de alguém** to tell sb off // *excl* be careful!

**atenci'oso/a** *adj* (*atento*) attentive; (*cortês*) considerate.

**aten'der** *vt* to attend (to); (*deferir*) to grant; (*telefone etc*) to answer // *vi* (*estar atento*) to pay attention.

**aten'tado** *m* (*ataque*) attack; (*crime*) crime; (*contra a vida de alguém*) attempt on sb's life; **atentar** *vt* (*empreender*) to undertake // *vi* to make an attempt; **atentar a/em/para** to pay attention to.

**a'tento/a** *adj* (*atencioso*) attentive; (*cortês*) considerate.

**atenuação** [atenwa'sãw] *f* reduction, lessening; **atenuante** *adj* extenuating // *m* extenuating circumstances; **atenuar** *vt* (*diminuir*) to reduce, lessen.

**aterra'dor(a)** *adj* terrifying.

**aterragem** [ate'xaʒẽj] *f* (*Pt:* AER) landing.

**ater'rar** *vt* (*atemorizar*) to terrify; (*cobrir com terra*) to cover with earth // *vi* (*Pt:* AER) to land.

**aterrissagem** [atexisaˈʒeʒ] *f* (*Br*: AER) landing; **aterrissar** *vi* (*Br*: AER) to land.

**aterrorizar** *vt* to terrorize.

**atestado/a** *adj* certified // *m* certificate; (JUR) testimony; **atestar** *vt* (*certificar*) to certify; (*testemunhar*) to bear witness.

**ateu/atéia** [aˈtew/aˈteja] *adj, m/f* atheist.

**atiçador** *m* (*utensílio*) poker; (*pessoa*) instigator; **atiçar** *vi* (*fogo*) to poke; (*incitar*) to incite.

**atilado/a** *adj* (*esperto*) clever.

**atinar** *vt* (*acertar*) to guess correctly // *vi* to be right; ~ **com** (*solução*) to find.

**atingir** [atʃĩˈʒix] *vt* (*chegar*) to reach; (*interessar*) to affect, concern; (*obter*) to attain; (*compreender*) to understand, grasp; (*abranger*) to cover; **atingível** *adj* attainable.

**atirador** *m* marksman; ~ **de tocaia** sniper.

**atirar** *vt* (*lançar*) to throw, fling, hurl // *vi* (*arma*) to shoot; ~ **com** to throw off; ~-**se** *vr*: ~-**se a** (*lançar-se a*) to hurl o.s. at.

**atitude** *f* attitude; (*postura*) position, posture.

**ativar** (*Pt*: **-ct-**) *vt* to activate, set in motion; (*apressar*) to hasten; **atividade** (*Pt*: **-ct-**) *f* activity.

**ativo/a** (*Pt*: **-ct-**) *adj* active; (*vivo*) lively // *m* (COM) assets *pl*.

**atlântico/a** *adj* Atlantic // *m*: **o A**~ the Atlantic.

**atlas** *m* atlas.

**atleta** *m/f* athlete; **atletismo** *m* athletics *sg*.

**atmosfera** *f* atmosphere.

**ato** (*Pt*: **-ct-**) *m* act; (*ação*) action; (*cerimônia*) ceremony; (*teatro*) act; ~ **falho** Freudian slip; ~ **público** public ceremony; **em** ~ **contínuo** right away; **no mesmo** ~ at the same time.

**à-toa** [aˈtoa] *adj* worthless; **mulher** ~ woman of easy virtue // *adv* to no purpose.

**atoleiro** [atoˈlejru] *m* quagmire; (*fig*) quandary, fix.

**atômico/a** *adj* atomic; **atomizador** *m* atomizer; **átomo** *m* atom.

**atônito/a** *adj* astonished, amazed.

**ator** (*Pt*: **-ct-**) *m* actor.

**atordoado/a** *adj* dazed; **atordoador/a** *adj* stunning; **atordoamento** *m* dizziness; **atordoar** *vt* to daze, stun.

**atormentador/a** *adj* tormenting // *m/f* tormentor; **atormentar** *vt* to torment; (*amolar*) to tease; (*importunar*) to plague.

**atração** [atraˈsãw] (*Pt*: **-cç-**) *f* attraction.

**atracar** *vt/i* (NÁUT) to moor.

**atraente** *adj* attractive.

**atraiçoado/a** [atrajsˈwadu/a] *adj* (*traído*) betrayed; (*desleal*) treacherous; **atraiçoar** *vt* to betray.

**atrair** *vt* to attract; (*atenção*) to catch.

**atrapalhação** [atrapaʎaˈsãw] *f* (*confusão*) confusion; (*embaraço*) embarrassment; **atrapalhar** *vt* (*confundir*) to confuse; (*embaraçar*) to embarrass; **atrapalhar-se** *vr* to get confused.

**atrás** *adv* (*lugar*) behind; (*movimento*) back, backwards; (*tempo*) previously // *prep*: ~ **de** behind, after.

**atrasado/a** *adj* (*em atraso*) behind; (*país etc*) backward; (*relógio etc*) slow; (*tarde*) late; (*pagamento*) overdue; **atrasar** *vt* (*fazer demorar*) to delay; (*impedir*) to hold back // *vi* (*relógio etc*) to be slow; **atrasar-se** *vr* (*ficar para trás*) to fall behind; (*chegar tarde*) to be late; **atraso** *m* delay; (*de país etc*) backwardness; **em atraso** in arrears; **chegar com atraso** to arrive late.

**atrativo/a** (*Pt*: **-ct-**)

attractive // m attraction, appeal; ~s mpl charms.

**atra've's** adv across // prep: ~ de (de lado a lado) across; (pelo centro de) through.

**atraves'sar** vt (cruzar) to cross; (pôr ao través) to put ou cause through; (traspassar) to pass through; (impedir) to block; ~-se vr (na garganta etc) to get stuck.

**atreito/a** [a'trejtu/a] adj (inclinado) inclined, prone; (acostumado) accustomed.

**atre'lar** vt (cão) to put on a leash; (cavalo) to harness.

**atre'ver-se** vr: ~ a (ousar) to dare to; **atrevido/a** adj (petulante) impudent; (corajoso) bold; **atrevimento** m (ousadia) boldness; (insolência) insolence.

**atribuição** [atribwi'sãw] f attribution; (privilégio) privilege; **atribuições** fpl rights, powers; **atribuir** vt to attribute; (conferir) to confer.

**atribu'lar** vt to trouble, distress; ~-se vr to be distressed.

**atri'buto** m attribute; (qualidade) characteristic.

**'átrio** m hall; (pátio) courtyard.

**a'trito** m (fricção) friction; (desentendimento) disagreement, difference.

**atriz** [a'triʒ] (Pt: -ct-) f actress.

**atroa'dor(a)** adj deafening; **atroar** vt to shake; (aturdir) to stun // vi (retumbar) to reverberate, thunder.

**atrocidade** [atrosi'dadʒi] f atrocity; (fig) outrage.

**atropela'mento** m (pedestre) running over; **atropelar** vt (derrubar) to knock down; (passar por cima) to run over; (empurrar) to jostle; **atropelo** m bustle, scramble; (confusão) confusion.

**atroz** [a'trɔʃ] adj (cruel) merciless; (espantoso) atrocious.

**atuação** [atwa'sãw] (Pt: -ct-) f acting; (ação) action.

**atu'al** (Pt: -ct-) adj present(-day), current; (efetivo) actual; ~**idade** (Pt: -ct-) f present (time); **na** ~**idade** nowadays, these days; ~**idades** fpl news sg.

**atuali'zar** (Pt: -ct-) vt to modernize, update.

**atual'mente** (Pt: -ct-) adv now, nowadays.

**atu'ar** (Pt: -ct-) vi to act; ~ **sobre** to influence.

**atu'ário** (Pt: -ct-) m clerk; (COM) actuary.

**atulhar** [atu'ʎax] vt (encher) to fill up; (meter) to stuff.

**atum** [a'tũ] m tuna fish.

**atu'rar** vt (suportar) to endure, put up with // vi to endure, last.

**atur'dido/a** adj dazed; (fig) astounded; **aturdir** vt to stun; (fig) to bewilder.

**audácia** [aw'dasja] f boldness; (insolência) insolence; **audaz** adj daring; (insolente) insolent.

**audição** [awdʒi'sãw] f audition; (concerto) recital.

**audiência** [awdʒi'ẽsja] f audience; (de tribunal) session, hearing.

**auditor** [awdʒi'tox] m (juiz) judge; (ouvinte) listener; **auditório** m (ouvintes) audience; (recinto) auditorium.

**auge** ['awʒi] m climax.

**augurar** [awgu'rax] vt (felicidades) to wish; (ser de bom/mau augúrio) to augur (well/ill); **augúrio** m omen.

**aula** ['awla] f (Pt: sala) classroom; (lição) lesson, class.

**aumentar** [awmẽ'tax] vt (ger) to increase; (ampliar) to extend; (com binóculo etc) to magnify // vi to increase; **aumento** m increase; (preços) rise; (ampliação) enlargement; (crescimento) growth.

**aura** ['awra] f aura.

**áureo/a** ['awrju/a] adj golden.

**auréola** [aw'rεola] f halo.

**aurora** [aw'rrora] f dawn.

**ausência** [aw'zẽsja] f absence; (*falta*) lack.

**ausen'tar-se** vr to go/stay away; **ausente** adj absent // m/f missing person.

**austeri'dade** f austerity; **austero/a** adj austere.

**aus'tral** adj authentic.

**Aus'trália** f Australia; **australiano/a** adj, m/f Australian.

**'Áustria** f Austria; **austríaco/a** adj, m/f Austrian.

**autenti'car** vt to authenticate; **autêntico/a** adj authentic.

**auto** ['awtu] m (*documento*) document, report; (*automóvel*) car; **~s** mpl (*JUR: processo*) legal proceedings; (*documentos*) legal papers.

**autobiogra'fia** f autobiography.

**autocarro** [awto'kaxu] m (*Pt*) bus.

**autóctone** [aw'tɔktonɪ] adj indigenous // m/f native, aborigine.

**autodefesa** [awtode'feza] f self-defence.

**autodeterminação** [awtodetɛxmina'sãw] f self-determination.

**autodo'mínio** m self-control.

**auto-escola** [awto-ɪs'kɔla] f driving school.

**auto-es'trada** f motorway.

**auto'mático/a** adj automatic.

**automobi'lismo** m motoring; (*esporte*) motor car racing.

**automóvel** [awto'mɔvɛl] m (*Brit*) motor car; (*US*) automobile.

**autono'mia** f autonomy; (*político*) self government; **autônomo/a** adj autonomous.

**au'tor(a)** m author; (*de um crime*) perpetrator; (*JUR*) plaintiff // f authoress.

**auto-re'trato** m self-portrait.

**autori'dade** f authority.

**autorização** [awtorɪza'sãw] f authorization; **autorizar** vt to authorize.

**auto-serviço** [awto-sex'vɪsu] m self-service.

**auto-sufici'ência** f self-sufficiency.

**auxiliar** [awsɪlɪ'ax] adj auxiliary // m/f assistant // vt to help; **auxílio** m help, assistance.

**Av** abr de **avenida** avenue.

**aval** [a'vaw] m guarantee; (*COM*) surety.

**avalancha** [ava'lãʃa] f avalanche.

**avaliação** [avalɪa'sãw] f (*cálculo*) valuation, estimate; (*apreciação*) assessment, evaluation; **avaliar** vt (*calcular*) to estimate; (*apreciar*) to assess, evaluate.

**avan'çada** f advance; **avançar** vt to move forward; (*exceder*) to exceed // vi to advance; **avançar o sinal** to drive through a red light; **avanço** m advancement; (*progresso*) progress.

**avantajado/a** [avãta'ʒadu/a] adj (*corpulento*) stout.

**ava'rento/a** adj (*cobiçoso*) greedy; (*mesquinho*) mean // m/f miser; **avareza** f (*cobiça*) greed; (*mesquinhez*) meanness.

**ava'ria** f damage; (*TEC*) breakdown; **avariar** vt to damage // vi to suffer damage; (*TEC*) to break down.

**a'varo/a** adj (*cobiçoso*) greedy; (*mesquinho*) mean // m/f miser.

**'ave** f bird; **~ de rapina** bird of prey.

**aveia** [a'veja] f oats pl.

**ave'lã** f hazelnut.

**ave'nida** f avenue.

**aven'tal** [-aw] m apron; (*de criança*) pinafore.

**aven'tar** vt (*uma idéia etc*) to put forward.

**aven'tura** f adventure; (*proeza*) exploit; **aventurado/a** adj daring; **aventurar** vt (*ousar*) to risk, venture; **aventurar-se** vr: **aventurar-se a** to dare to; **aventureiro/a** adj rash // m/f adventurer.

**averiguação** [averɪgwa'sãw] f

investigation, inquiry; **averiguar** vt (*inquirir*) to investigate, ascertain; (*verificar*) to verify.

**a'vesso/a** adj (*contrário*) contrary // m wrong side, reverse; **ao** ~ inside out // fpl: **às** ~**as** (*inverso*) upside down; (*oposto*) the wrong way round.

**avestruz** [aveʃ'truʃ] m ostrich.

**ave'zar** vt to accustom; ~-**se** vr: ~-**se a** to get used to.

**aviação** [avia'sãw] f aviation, flying.

**avi'ado/a** adj (*executado*) ready; (*apressado*) hurried.

**avia'dor(a)** m aviator, airman // f airwoman.

**avia'mentos** mpl materials, supplies.

**avião** [avi'ãw] m aeroplane; ~ **a jato** jet; ~ **de caça** fighter.

**avi'ar** vt (*receita médica*) to make up.

**avidez** [avi'deʒ] f (*cobiça*) greediness; (*desejo*) eagerness; **ávido/a** adj (*cobiçoso*) greedy; (*desejoso*) eager.

**avil'tar** vt to debase; ~-**se** vr to demean o.s.

**avina'grado/a** adj sour, tasting of vinegar.

**a'vir-se** vr (*conciliar-se*) to reach an understanding; (*arranjar-se*) to manage; (*harmonizar-se*) to get along; **lá se avenha!** that's your problem!

**avi'sar** vt (*advertir*) to warn; (*informar*) to tell, notify; **aviso** m (*comunicação*) notice; (*advertência*) warning; (*conselho*) advice.

**avis'tar** vt to glimpse, catch sight of; ~-**se** vr: ~-**se com** (*ter entrevista*) to have an interview with.

**avi'var** vt (*animar*) to rouse; (*intensificar*) to intensify, heighten; (*apressar*) to hurry (up) // vi to revive, recover.

**aviven'tar** vt (*reviver*) to revive;

(*reanimar*) to revitalize.

**avizinhar-se** [avizi'ɲaxsi] vr (*aproximar-se*) to approach, come near.

**'avo** m: **um doze** ~**s** one twelfth.

**avô/avó** [a'vo/a'vɔ] m grandfather // f grandmother; **avós** mpl grandparents.

**avo'engos** mpl ancestors.

**a'vulso/a** adj separate, detached // m single copy.

**avul'tado/a** adj large, bulky; **avultar** vt to enlarge, expand // vi (*sobressair*) to stand out; (*aumentar*) to increase.

**axila** [ak'sila] f armpit.

**axioma** [asi'oma] m axiom.

**a'záfama** f bustle; (*pressa*) hurry.

**a'zar** m (*acaso*) chance, fate; (*desgraça*) misfortune.

**a'zedo/a** adj (*sabor*) sour; (*amargo*) bitter; (*fig*) irritable; **azedume** m (*sabor*) sourness; (*acrimônia*) bitterness; (*fig*) irritability.

**azeite** [a'zejtʃi] m oil.

**azeitona** [azej'tona] f olive.

**azenha** [a'zeɲa] f water mill.

**azeviche** [aze'viʃi] m jet.

**azevinho** [aze'viɲu] m holly.

**a'zia** f heartburn.

**azi'ago/a** adj (*de mau agouro*) ominous; (*infausto*) ill-fated.

**azinhaga** [azi'ɲaga] f (*country*) lane.

**azinheira** [azi'ɲejra] f holm-oak.

**'azo** m (*oportunidade*) opportunity; (*pretexto*) pretext; **dar** ~ **a** to give occasion to.

**a'zoto** m nitrogen.

**azougado/a** [azo'gadu/a] adj (*inquieto*) restless; (*vivo*) lively; (*esperto*) sharp-witted, shrewd; **azougue** m quicksilver; (*QUÍM*) mercury.

**a'zul** adj blue; ~ **celeste** sky blue; ~ **marinho** navy blue.

**azulejo** [azu'leʒu] m (*glazed*) tile.

# B

**ba'bá** f (regular) babysitter.

**'baba** f saliva, dribble; **babador** m, **babadouro** m bib.

**babar** [ba'bax] vt to dribble on; ~**-se** vr to dribble; **babeiro** m (Pt) bib.

**babugem** [ba'buʒẽ] f foam, froth; (restos) left-overs pl.

**bacalhau** [baka'ʎaw] m (dried) cod.

**bacana** [ba'kãna] adj inv (col) great, cool, amazing.

**bacharel** [baʃa'rɛw] m bachelor, graduate; **bacharelar-se** vr to graduate.

**ba'cia** f basin, bowl; (ANAT) pelvis.

**baço/a** ['basu/a] adj dull; (metal) tarnished // m (ANAT) spleen.

**bactéria** [ba'ktɛrja] f germ, bacterium; ~**s** fpl bacteria pl.

**'báculo** m staff; (de bispo) crosier.

**badalar** [bada'lax] vt/i (sino) to ring, peal; **badalo** m clapper.

**bafejar** [bafe'ʒax] vt (aquecer com o bafo) to blow on, breathe on; (fortuna) to smile upon.

**ba'fio** m musty smell.

**'bafo** m (hálito) (bad) breath; **baforada** f (fumaça) puff.

**'baga** f (fruta) berry; (gota) drop.

**ba'gaço** m (de frutos) pulp; (Pt: cachaça) brandy.

**bagageiro** [baga'ʒejru] m luggage compartment; (Pt) porter; **bagagem** f baggage, luggage.

**baga'tela** f trinket; (fig) trifle.

**'bago** m (fruto) berry; (uva) grape; (de chumbo) pellet.

**bagulho** [ba'guʎu] m (lixo) trash.

**ba'gunça** f (confusão) mess, shambles.

**ba'ía** f bay.

**bai'lado** m dance; (balé) ballet; **bailarino/a** m/f (professional)

dancer/ballerina; **baile** m dance; (formal) ball.

**bainha** [ba'ĩɲa] f (de arma) sheath; (de costura) hem.

**baioneta** [bajo'neta] f bayonet; ~ **calada** fixed bayonet.

**bairro** ['bajxu] m district, suburb.

**baixa** ['bajʃa] f (abaixamento) decrease; (redução de preço) reduction, fall; (diminuição) drop; (em combate) casualty; (do serviço) discharge; **dar** ~ to be discharged.

**baixada** [baj'ʃada] f lowland.

**baixa-mar** [bajʃa-'max] f low tide.

**baixar** [baj'ʃax] vt (preço, voz, persianas) to lower; (descer) to take down; ~ **a cabeça** to bow // vi to go/come down; (temperatura, preço) to drop, fall; ~ **à enfermaria** to go into hospital; **baixinho** adv (em voz baixa) softly, quietly; (em segredo) secretly.

**baixo/a** ['bajʃu/a] adj low; (pessoa) short, small; (raso) shallow; (chulo) common; (metal) base // adv low; (em posição baixa) low down; (voz) softly; **em** ~ below, downstairs; **para** ~ down, downwards // prep: **por** ~ **de** under, underneath // m (MÚS) bass; (parte inferior) bottom.

**'bala** f bullet; (Pt: doce) sweet; **balaço** m gunshot.

**ba'lada** f ballad.

**ba'lança** f scales pl; ~ **comercial** balance of trade; (ASTRO) **B**~ Libra.

**balan'çar** vt (fazer oscilar) to swing; (pesar) to weigh (up) // vi (oscilar) to swing; (em cadeira) to rock; ~**-se** vr to swing; (navio) to roll.

**ba'lanço** m (movimento) swinging; (brinquedo) swing; (de navio) rolling; (COM : registro) balance (sheet); (: verificação) audit; **em** ~ uncertain.

**balão** [ba'lãw] m balloon.

**ba'lar** vi to bleat.

**balaus'trada** f balustrade.

**balbuciar** [bawbu'sıax] *vt/i* to stammer, stutter; (*falar de modo confuso*) to babble.

**balbúrdia** [baw'buxdʒja] *f* uproar, bedlam.

**balcão** [baw'kãw] *m* balcony; (*de loja*) counter; (*teatro*) circle; **balconista** *m/f* shop-assistant.

**balda** *f* defect, fault; **baldadamente** *adv* in vain; **baldado/a** *adj* unsuccessful, fruitless; **baldar** *vt* to frustrate, foil.

**balde** ['bawdʒı] *m* bucket, pail; **baldeação** *f* transfer; **baldear** *vt* (*líquido*) to decant; (*transferir*) to transfer.

**bal'dio/a** *adj* fallow, uncultivated // *m* waste land.

**baleeira** [bali'ejra] *f* whaleboat; **baleeiro** *m* whaler; **baleia** *f* whale.

**ba'lido** *m* bleating; (*um só*) bleat.

**ba'liza** *f* (*estaca*) post; (*bóia*) buoy; (*luminosa*) beacon; (*esporte*) goal.

**balne'ário** *m* spa, bathing resort.

**ba'lofo/a** *adj* (*fofo*) fluffy; (*inchado*) puffed up.

**balouçar** [balo'sax] *vt/i* (*Pt*) to swing, sway; **baloiço** *m*, **balouço** *m* (*de criança*) swing; (*ação*) swinging.

**balsa** ['bawsa] *f* raft; (*barca*) ferry.

**'bálsamo** *m* balsam, balm.

**'báltico/a** *adj* Baltic // *m*: **o B~** the Baltic.

**balu'arte** *m* rampart, bulwark.

**'bamba** *m/f*, *adj* expert.

**'bambo/a** *adj* slack, loose.

**bambole'ar** *vt* to swing // *ii* (*pessoa*) to sway, totter; (*coisa*) to wobble.

**bam'bu** *m* bamboo.

**ba'nana** *f* banana; **bananeira** *f* banana tree.

**'banca** *f* (*de trabalho*) bench; (*escritório*) office; (*jogo*) bank; ~ **de jornais** newsstand; **bancada** *f* row of seats.

**ban'cário/a** *adj* bank, banking // *m/f* banker.

**bancar'rota** *f* bankruptcy; **ir à** ~ to go bankrupt.

**'banco** *m* (*assento*) bench; (*COM*) bank; ~ **de areia** sandbank; ~ **de coral** coral reef.

**'banda** *f* (*músicos, grupo, lista*) band; (*lado*) side; (*cinto*) sash; ~ **desenhada** (*Pt*) cartoon; **à** ~ to one side; **pôr de** ~ to put aside.

**bandeira** [bã'dejra] *f* flag; (*estandarte*) banner; **bandeirante** *m* pioneer; **bandeirinha** *m* (*esporte*) linesman.

**bandeja** [bã'deʒa] *f* tray.

**ban'dido** *m* bandit, outlaw.

**'bando** *m* band; (*grupo*) group; (*de malfeitores*) gang; (*de ovelhas*) flock; (*de gado*) herd.

**bandoleiro** [bãdo'lejru] *m* robber, bandit.

**banha** ['bana] *f* fat; (*de porco*) lard.

**banhar** [ba'nax] *vt* (*dar banho a*) to bath; (*mergulhar*) to dip; (*lavar*) to wash, bathe; ~**-se** *vr* (*em banheira*) to have a bath; (*no mar*) to bathe, go for a swim; **banheira** *f* bath; **banheiro** *m* bathroom; (*Pt*) lifeguard; **banhista** *m/f* bather.

**banho** ['banu] *m* (*na banheira*) bath; (*de mar*) bathe; (*mergulho*) dip; (*de tinta*) coating; ~ **de sol** sunbathing; ~ **de chuveiro** shower; **tomar** ~ to have a bath; (*de chuveiro*) to have a shower; ~**s de casamento** marriage banns.

**banho-maria** [banu-ma'rıa] *m* (*CULIN*) bain-marie, steamer.

**ba'nir** *vt* to banish.

**banqueiro** [bã'kejru] *m* banker; (*diretor*) bank manager.

**banquete** [bã'ketʃı] *m* banquet, feast.

**ban'zar** *vt* to surprise, astonish // *vi* to ponder, muse.

**banzé** [bã'zɛ] *m* (*col*) rumpus, racket.

**baque** ['bakı] *m* thud, thump; (*contratempo*) disaster.

**bar** m bar; (*estabelecimento*) public house, pub.

**bara'funda** f uproar, tumult.

**baralhar** [bara'ʎaʃ] vt (*cartas*) to shuffle; (*fig*) to mix up, confuse; **baralho** m pack of cards.

**barão** [ba'rãw] m baron.

**ba'rata** f cockroach.

**barate'ar** vt to cut the price of; (*menosprezar*) to belittle; **barato/a** adj cheap, inexpensive // adv cheaply.

**'barba** f beard; ~s fpl whiskers; **fazer a** ~ to have a shave.

**bar'bante** m string.

**barbari'dade** f barbarity, cruelty; (*disparate*) nonsense; **que** ~**!** good heavens!; **barbarismo** m barbarism; **bárbaro/a** adj (*cruel*) cruel, savage; (*grosseiro*) rough, crude; (*bacana*) great // m/f barbarian.

**barba'tana** f fin.

**barbea'dor** m razor; (*elétrico*) shaver; **barbearia** f barber's (shop); **barbeiro** m barber.

**'barca** f barge; (*de travessia*) ferry; **barcaça** f barge.

**'barco** m boat; (*grande*) ship; ~ **a motor** motorboat; ~ **a vela** sailing boat; ~ **de remos** rowing boat.

**'bardo** m bard, poet.

**barganha** [bax'gaɲa] f barter, swap; **barganhar** vt to swap.

**barla'vento** m (*NÁUT*) windward; **a** ~ to windward.

**ba'rômetro** m barometer.

**baro'nesa** f baroness.

**barqueiro** [bax'kejru] m boatman.

**'barra** [baxa] f bar, rod; (*faixa*) strip; (*traço*) stroke; (*alavanca*) lever.

**bar'raca** f (*tenda*) tent; (*de feira*) stall; (*de madeira*) hut; **barracão** m (*tenda*) marquee; (*de madeira*) shed.

**barragem** [ba'xaʒẽj] f (*represa*) dam; (*impedimento*) barrier.

**bar'ranco** m ravine, gully.

**barreira** [ba'xejra] f barrier;

(*cerca*) fence; ~ **do som** sound barrier.

**bar'rento/a** adj muddy.

**bar'rete** (*Pt*) m cap.

**barri'cada** f barricade.

**bar'riga** f belly; ~ **da perna** calf; **fazer** ~ to bulge.

**barril** [ba'xiw] m barrel, cask.

**'barro** m clay; (*lama*) mud.

**bar'roco/a** [-axo-] adj baroque; (*ornamentado*) extravagant.

**bar'rote** m beam.

**barulhento/a** [baru'ʎẽtu/a] adj noisy, rowdy; **barulho** m (*ruído*) noise, row; (*tumulto*) din, rumpus.

**base** ['bazi] f base; (*fig*) basis; **sem** ~ groundless; **basear** vt to base; **basear-se** vr: **basear-se em** to be based on.

**básico/a** ['baziku/a] adj basic.

**basquete** [baʃ'kɛtʃi] m, **basquete'bol** m basketball.

**bas'tante** adj (*suficiente*) enough; (*muito*) quite a lot (of) // adv (*suficientemente*) enough; (*muito*) quite.

**bastão** [baʃ'tãw] m stick.

**bas'tar** vi to be enough, be sufficient; ~ **para** to be enough to; ~**-se** vr to be self-sufficient; **basta!** (that's) enough!

**bas'tardo/a** adj, m/f bastard.

**basti'dor** m frame; ~**es** mpl (*teatro*) wings; **nos** ~**es** behind the scenes.

**'basto/a** adj (*espesso*) thick; (*denso*) dense.

**'bata** f (*roupão de mulher*) dressing gown; (*de médico*) overall.

**batalha** [ba'taʎa] f battle; **batalhão** m battalion; **batalhar** vi to battle, fight.

**ba'tata** f potato; ~ **doce** sweet potato; ~**s fritas** chips; (*US*) French fries; **batatinha frita** f crisps pl.

**batedeira** [bate'dejra] f beater; (*elétrico*) mixer; (*de manteiga*) churn; **batedor** m beater; (*polícia*) escort; (*no críquete*) batsman.

**'bátega** *f* downpour.

**ba'tente** *m* doorpost; (*aldrava*) knocker; (*col*) job; **no ~** at work.

**bate-'papo** *m* chat.

**ba'ter** *vt* (*derrotar, dar pancadas em*) to beat; (*horas*) to strike; (*o pé*) to stamp; (*trigo*) to thresh; (*porta*) to slam; (*explorar*) to search; (*ovos*) to beat; **~ uma chapa** to take a picture; **~ palmas** to clap; **~ a carteira de alguém** to pick sb's pocket; **~ um papo** to have a chat // *vi:* **~ à porta** to knock at the door; **~-se** *vr* to fight.

**bate'ria** *f* battery; (*MÚS*) percussion; **~ de cozinha** kitchen utensils *pl*.

**ba'tido/a** *adj* beaten; (*gasto*) worn, shabby // *m:* **~ de leite** (*Pt*) milkshake // *f* beat; (*da porta*) slam; (*à porta*) knock; (*da polícia*) raid; (*colisão*) bump; (*bebida*) brandy cocktail.

**ba'tina** *f* (*REL*) cassock.

**ba'tismo** (*Pt: -pt-*) *m* baptism, christening; **batizar** (*Pt: -pt-*) *vt* to baptize, christen; (*vinho*) to dilute.

**'batom** *m* lipstick.

**ba'tucada** *f* dance percussion group.

**ba'tuta** *f* baton.

**ba'ú** *m* trunk.

**baunilha** [baw'niʎa] *f* vanilla.

**ba'zar** *m* bazaar.

**ba'zófia** *f* boasting, bragging.

**beatifi'car** *vt* to beatify, bless; **beato/a** *adj* blessed // *f* overpious woman; (*hipócrita*) hypocrite.

**bebê** [be'be] (*Pt: -é*) *m* baby.

**bebedeira** [bebe'dejra] *f* (*estado de bêbedo*) drunkenness; **tomar uma ~** to get drunk; **bêbedo/a** *adj, m/f* drunk; **bebedor/a** *m/f* drinker; (*ébrio*) drunkard; **bebedouro** *m* drinking fountain.

**be'ber** *vt* to drink; (*absorver*) to drink up, soak up // *vi* to drink; **bebida** *f* drink.

**beco** ['beku] *m* alley, lane; **~ sem saída** cul-de-sac.

**bedelho** [be'deʎu] *m* latch; **meter o ~ em** to poke one's nose into.

**beiço** ['bejsu] *m* lip; **fazer ~** to pout; **beiçudo/a** *adj* thick-lipped.

**beija-flor** [bejʒa-'flɔʃ] *m* hummingbird.

**beijar** [bej'ʒax] *vt* to kiss; **~-se** *vr* to kiss (one another); **beijo** *m* kiss.

**beira** ['bejra] *f* (*borda*) edge; (*do rio*) bank; (*orla*) border; **~ do telhado** eaves; **à ~ de** on the edge of; (*ao lado de*) beside, by; (*fig*) on the verge of.

**beira-mar** [bejra-'max] *f* seaside.

**beirar** [bej'rax] *vt* (*ficar ao lado de*) to be at the edge of; (*caminhar ao lado de*) to skirt.

**beisebol** [bejsɨ'bɔw] *m* baseball.

**belas-artes** [bɛlaz-'axtʃ̩s] *fpl* fine arts.

**beldade** [bew'dadʒi] *f*, **beleza** [be'leza] *f* beauty; **que beleza!** how lovely!

**belga** ['bɛwga] *adj, m/f* Belgian; **Bélgica** *f* Belgium.

**beliche** [be'liʃi] *m* bunk.

**beliscão** [belɨʃ'kãw] *m* pinch; **beliscar** *vt* to pinch, nip; (*a comida*) to nibble.

**'belo/a** *adj* beautiful, lovely.

**bem** [bẽj] *adv* well; (*muito*) very; (*certamente*) quite; (*cheirar*) good, nice; **~ ali** right there; **~ duas horas** a good two hours // *conj:* **~ como** as well as // *m* (*ventura, utilidade*) good; (*amado*) love; **o ~ público** public welfare; **bens** *mpl* goods; **bens de consumo** consumer goods.

**bem-aven'turado/a** *adj* fortunate.

**bem-criado/a** [bẽj-kri'adu/a] *adj* well-bred, well-mannered.

**bem-disposto/a** [bẽj-dɨʃ'poʃtu/a] *adj* in a good mood.

**bem-estar** [bẽj-ɨʃ'tax] *m* comfort, well-being.

**bem-me-quer** [bẽj-me-'kex] *m* daisy.

**bem-vindo/a** [bẽj-'vĩdu/a] *adj* welcome.

**bênção** ['bẽsãw] *f* blessing; **bendito/a** *adj* blessed; **bendizer** *vt* (*louvar*) to praise; (*abençoar*) to bless.

**benefi'cência** *f* (*bondade*) kindness; (*caridade*) charity.

**benefici'ar** *vt* (*favorecer*) to benefit; (*melhorar*) to improve; **benefício** *m* (*proveito*) benefit, profit; (*favor*) favour; **benéfico/a** *adj* (*benigno*) beneficial; (*generoso*) generous; (*favorável*) favourable.

**bene'mérito/a** *adj* (*digno*) worthy; (*ilustre*) distinguished // *m/f* (*pessoa distinta*) distinguished person.

**bene'plácito** *m* consent, approval.

**benevo'lência** *f* benevolence, kindness; **benévolo/a** *adj* benevolent, kind.

**benfeitor(a)** [bẽfej'tox(ra)] *m* benefactor // *f* benefactress.

**ben'gala** *f* walking stick.

**benigni'dade** *f* kindness; **benigno/a** *adj* (*bondoso*) kind; (*agradável*) pleasant; (*MED*) benign.

**benquisto/a** [bẽ'kiʃtu/a] *adj* well-loved, well-liked.

**bens** *mpl ver* **bem**.

**'bento/a** *pp irr de* **benzer** // *adj* holy.

**benzedeiro/a** [bẽzi'dejru/a] *m* sorcerer // *f* sorceress.

**ben'zer** *vt* to bless; **~-se** *vr* to cross o.s.

**'berço** *m* cradle; (*lugar de nascimento*) birthplace.

**berin'jela** [berĩ'ʒela] *f* aubergine; (*US*) eggplant.

**ber'rante** *adj* flashy, gaudy.

**ber'rar** *vi* to bellow; (*criança*) to bawl.

**besouro** [be'zoru] *m* beetle.

**'besta** *adj* (*tolo*) stupid // *f* (*animal*) beast; (*pessoa*) fool, ass; ~ **de carga**

beast of burden; ~ **fera** wild beast.

**besteira** [bes'tejra] *f* nonsense, rubbish; **dizer ~s** to talk nonsense.

**besti'al** [-aw] *adj* bestial; (*repugnante*) repulsive; **~idade** *f* bestiality, brutality.

**besun'tar** *vt* to smear, daub.

**beter'raba** [-exa-] *f* beetroot.

**be'tume** *m* asphalt; (*para colar vidros*) putty.

**bexiga** [be'ʃiga] *f* (*órgão*) bladder; (*doença*) smallpox; **~s** *fpl* (*sinais*) pock marks.

**bezerro/a** [be'zexu/a] *m* calf // *f* heifer.

**'Bíblia** *f* Bible; **bíblico/a** *adj* biblical.

**bibliogra'fia** *f* bibliography.

**biblio'teca** *f* library; (*estante*) bookcase; **bibliotecário/a** *m/f* librarian.

**'bica** *f* spout; (*Pt*) black coffee (expresso); **estar na ~** to be about to happen.

**bi'cada** *f* peck; **bicar** *vt* to peck; (*comida*) to pick at.

**bicha** ['biʃa] *f* (*lombriga*) worm; (*Pt:* fila) queue; (*Br:* homosexual) gay.

**bicho** ['biʃu] *m* animal; (*inseto*) insect, bug; (*calouro*) fresher; **matar o ~** to wet one's whistle.

**bici'cleta** *f* bicycle; (*col*) bike; **andar de ~** to cycle.

**'bico** *m* (*de ave*) beak; (*ponta*) point; (*de chaleira*) spout; (*boca*) mouth; (*de pena*) nib; (*do peito*) nipple; (*de gás*) jet; **calar o ~** to shut up.

**bi'dê** [-e] (*Pt:* **-é** [-ɛ]) *m* bidet.

**bi'ela** *f* piston rod.

**'bife** *m* (beef) steak.

**bifurcação** [bifuxka'sãw] *f* fork; **bifurcar-se** *vr* to fork, divide.

**'bígamo/a** *adj* bigamous // *m/f* bigamist.

**bi'gode** *m* moustache.

**bi'gorna** *f* anvil.

**bijuteria** [biʒute'ria] *f* jewellery.

**bilha** ['biʎa] *f* (*Pt*) jug, jar.

**bilhar** [biˈʎax] m (jogo) billiards sg.

**bilhete** [biˈʎetʃi] m (entrada, loteria) ticket; (cartinha) note; ~ **de ida** single ticket; ~ **de ida e volta** return ticket; ~ **postal** postcard; ~ **de plataforma** platform ticket; **bilheteira** f (Pt) ticket office; **bilheteiro/a** m/f ticket seller; **bilheteria** f ticket office; booking office; (teatro) box office.

**bilíngüe** [biˈlĩgwi] adj bilingual.

**bilioso/a** adj bilious, liverish; **bílis** m bile; (fig) bad temper.

**bimensal** [-aw] adj twice-monthly.

**binóculo** m binoculars pl; (para teatro) opera glasses pl.

**biografia** f biography; **biógrafo/a** m/f biographer.

**biologia** f biology; **biologista** m/f biologist.

**biombo** m (tapume) screen.

**birra** [ˈbixa] f (teima) wilfulness, obstinacy; (aversão) aversion; **ter ~ com** to dislike, detest.

**bis** excl encore!

**bisagra** f hinge.

**bisavô/ó** [bizaˈvo/ɔ] m great-grandfather // f great-grandmother.

**bisbilhotar** [biʒbiʎoˈtax] vt/i to pry into // vi to gossip; **bisbilhotice** f gossip.

**biscoito** [biʃˈkojtu] m biscuit, (US) cracker.

**bisonho/a** [biˈzoɲu/a] adj inexperienced // m raw recruit.

**bispado** m bishopric; **bispo** m bishop.

**bissexto/a** [biˈseʃtu/a] adj: **ano ~** leap year.

**bisturi** m scalpel.

**bitola** f gauge; (padrão) pattern; (estalão) standard.

**bivacar** vi to bivouac; **bivaque** m bivouac.

**bizarria** [-axi-] f (galantaria) gallantry; (elegância) elegance; (pompa) pomp; **bizarro/a** adj (nobre) gallant; (elegante) elegant, handsome; (esquisito) bizarre.

**blandícia** f endearment; (carícia) caress.

**blasfemar** vt/i to blaspheme, curse; **blasfêmia** f blasphemy; (ultraje) swearing; **blasfemo/a** adj blasphemous // m/f blasphemer.

**blindado/a** adj armoured; **blindagem** f armour(-plating).

**bloco** m block; (político) bloc; (de escrever) writing pad; (de carnaval carnival troupe; ~ **de cilindros** cylinder block.

**bloquear** [blokiˈax] vt to blockade; **bloqueio** m blockade.

**blusa** f (de mulher) blouse; ~ **de lã** cardigan, pullover; **blusão** m jacket.

**boa** f boa constrictor // adj ver **bom**.

**boate** f nightclub.

**boato** m rumour.

**bobagem** [boˈbaʒẽ] f, **bobice** [boˈbisi] f silliness, nonsense; **deixe de bobagens!** stop being silly!

**bobina** f (para fio) bobbin; (ELET) coil; (foto) spool.

**bobo/a** adj silly, daft // m/f fool; **fazer-se de ~** to act the fool // m (de corte) jester.

**boca** [ˈboka] f mouth; (abertura) opening, entrance; **à ~ pequena** in whispers; **de ~ aberta** open-mouthed, amazed.

**bocadinho** [bokaˈdʒiɲu] m (pouco tempo) a little while; (pouquinho) a little bit; **bocado** m (quantidade na boca) mouthful, bite; (pedaço) piece, bit; (de tempo) a short while.

**bocal** [boˈkaw] m (de vaso) mouth; (de aparelho) mouthpiece; (de cano) nozzle.

**boçal** [boˈsaw] adj stupid, ignorant.

**bocejar** [boseˈʒax] vi to yawn; **bocejo** m yawn.

**bochecha** [boˈʃeʃa] f cheek.

**boda** f wedding; ~**s** fpl wedding anniversary sg; ~**s de prata/ouro** silver/golden wedding sg.

**bode** [ˈbɔdʒi] m goat; ~ **expiatório** scapegoat.

**bo'dega** *f* tavern; (*coisa sem valor*) rubbish.

**bofe'tada** *f* slap; **bofetão** *m* punch.

**boi** [boj] *m* ox.

**bóia** ['bɔja] *f* buoy; (*col*) meal.

**bo'iada** *f* herd of cattle.

**boião** [bo'jãw] *m* jar, pot.

**boiar** [bo'jax] *vt/i* to float.

**boico'tar** *vt* to boycott; **boicote** *m* boycott.

**boieiro** [bɔ'jejru] *m* herdsman.

**boina** ['bojna] *f* beret.

**'bojo** *m* (*saliência*) bulge; (*capacidade*) ability; **bojudo/a** *adj* bulging; (*barrigudo*) pot-bellied.

**bola** ['bɔla] *f* ball; ~ **de futebol** football; ~ **de gude** marble; ~ **de sabão** soap bubble; **ora** ~ **s!** rubbish!

**bolacha** [bo'laʃa] *f* biscuit; (*col: bofetada*) slap.

**bo'lar** *vt* to think up.

**boléia** [bo'leja] *f* driver's seat; (*Pt*): **dar uma** ~ to give a lift.

**boletim** [bole'tʃĩ] *m* report; ~ **meteorológico** weather forecast.

**bolha** ['bɔʎa] *f* (*na pele*) blister; (*de ar, sabão*) bubble.

**boliche** [bo'liʃi] *m* (*jogo*) bowling, skittles *sg.*

**'Bolívia** *f* Bolivia; **boliviano/a** *adj, m/f* Bolivian.

**bolo** ['bolu] *m* cake; **dar o** ~ to fail to turn up.

**bolor** [bo'lox] *m* mould; (*nas plantas*) mildew; (*bafio*) mustiness.

**bo'lota** *f* acorn.

**bolsa** ['bowsa] *f* (*saco*) bag; (*para dinheiro*) purse; (*de estudos*) grant; (*com*) stock exchange.

**'bolso** *m* pocket.

**bom/boa** [bõ/'boa] *adj* good; (*bondoso*) nice, kind; (*MED*) well; (*tempo*) fine; **um** ~ **quarto de hora** a good quarter of an hour; **essa é boa!** that's a good one!; **metido numa boa** in a tight spot; **essa é boa!** that's a good one!; **metido numa boa** (*col*) to be doing fine; **boa-noite** (*ao encontrar-se*) goodnight; **boa-tarde** good

afternoon, good evening; **boas vindas!** welcome! // *excl:* ~ **! right!**

**'bomba** *f* (*MIL*) bomb; (*TEC*) pump; ~ **atômica** *or* **fumaça/relógio** atomic/smoke/time bomb; ~ **de gasolina** petrol station; ~ **de incêndio** fire engine; **levar** ~ (*em exame*) to fail.

**bombarde'ar** *vt* to bomb, bombard; (*fig*) to bombard; **bombardeio** *m* bombing, bombardment.

**bombe'ar** *vt* to pump.

**bombeiro** [bõ'bejru] *m* fireman; (*encanador*) plumber; **o corpo de** ~**s** fire brigade.

**bombom** [bõ'bõ] *m* sweet.

**bom'bordo** *m* (*NÁUT*) port.

**bo'nança** *f* (*no mar*) fair weather; (*fig*) calm.

**bon'dade** *f* goodness, kindness; **tenha a** ~ **de vir** would you please come.

**'bonde** *m* (*Br*) tram.

**bon'doso/a** *adj* kind, good.

**bo'né** *m* (*chapéu*) cap.

**bo'neca** *f* doll.

**bo'nina** *f* (*Pt*) daisy.

**bo'nito/a** *adj* (*belo*) pretty; (*agradável*) nice // *m* (*peixe*) tunny.

**boquiaberto/a** [bokia'bɛxtu/a] *adj* dumbfounded, gaping.

**boquilha** [bo'kiʎa] *f* cigarette holder.

**borboleta** [boxbo'leta] *f* butterfly; **borboletear** *vi* to flutter, flit.

**borbotão** [boxbo'tãw] *m* gush, spurt; **sair aos borbotões** to gush out; **borbotar** *vt* to pour forth // *vi* to gush out.

**borbulhar** [boxbu'ʎax] *vi* (*líquido fervendo*) to bubble; (*brotar*) to sprout; (*jorrar*) to gush out.

**'borco** *m:* **de** ~ (*coisa*) upside down; (*pessoa*) face down.

**'borda** *f* edge; (*do rio*) bank; **à** ~ **de** on the edge of.

**bor'dado** *m* embroidery.

**bordão** [box'dãw] *m* staff; (*MÚS*)

bass string; (*arrimo*) support.

**bor'dar** *vt* to embroider.

**bordejar** [boxde'ʒax] *vi* (*NÁUT*) to tack; (*cambalear*) to stagger; **bordo** *m* (*ao bordejar*) tack; (*de navio*) side; **a bordo** on board.

**'borla** *f* tassel.

**bor'nal** *m* haversack.

**'borra** [-ɔxa] *f* dregs *pl*.

**borracha** [bo'xaʃa] *f* rubber.

**borracho/a** [bo'xaʃu/a] *adj* drunk // *m/f* drunk(ard).

**borrador** [boxa'dox] *m* (*caderno*) note book; (*COM*) day book.

**borralho** [bo'xaʎu] *m* embers *pl*; (*fig*) hearth, fireside.

**borrão** [bo'xãw] *m* (*escritura*) rough draft; (*mancha*) blot; (*esboço*) sketch; **borrar** *vt* to blot; (*riscar*) to cross out; (*pintar*) to daub.

**bor'rasca** *f* storm; (*no mar*) squall; **borrascoso/a** *adj* stormy.

**bor'rego** *m* (*Pt*) lamb.

**borri'far** *vt* to sprinkle // *vi* (*chuviscar*) to drizzle; **borrifo** *m* spray; (*chuvisco*) drizzle.

**bosque** [ˈbɔʃki] *m* wood, forest.

**bosquejar** [boʃke'ʒax] *vt* to sketch; **bosquejo** *m* sketch.

**'bossa** *f* (*inchaço*) swelling; (*no crânio*) bump; (*corcova*) hump; **ter ~ para** to have an aptitude for.

**'bosta** *f* dung.

**'bota** *f* boot; **~s de borracha** wellingtons.

**bota-'fora** *f* (*despedida*) send-off; (*de navio*) launching.

**botânico/a** [bo'tãniku/a] *adj* botanical // *m/f* botanist // *f* botany.

**botão** [bo'tãw] *m* button; (*flor*) bud.

**bo'tar** *vt* to put, place; (*Pt: lançar*) to throw; **~ fora** to throw away; **~ a língua** to stick out one's tongue; **~ ovos** to lay eggs.

**'bote** *m* (*barco*) boat; (*com arma*) thrust; (*salto*) spring; **de um ~ at** one stroke.

**botequim** [bote'kĩ] *m* bar, café.

**bo'tica** *f* pharmacy, chemist's (shop); **boticário/a** *m/f* pharmacist, chemist.

**botija** [bo'tiʒa] *f* (earthenware) jug.

**'boto/a** *adj* (*embotado*) blunt; (*rombo*) dull, stupid.

**botoeira** [bo'twejra] *f* button-hole.

**boxe** [ˈbɔksi] *m* boxing; **~ador** *m* boxer.

**bra'beza** *f* wildness; **brabo/a** *adj* (*cavalo*) wild; (*feroz*) fierce.

**'braça** *f* (*NÁUT*) fathom.

**bra'çada** *f* armful; (*natação*) stroke.

**bracejar** [brase'ʒax] *vi* to wave one's arms about.

**'braço** *m* arm; (*trabalhador*) hand; **~ direito** (*fig*) right-hand man; **a ~s com** struggling with; **de ~s cruzados** with arms folded; (*fig*) without lifting a finger; **de ~ dado** arm-in-arm.

**bra'dar** *vi* to shout, yell; **brado** *m* shout, yell.

**braguilha** [bra'giʎa] *f* flies *pl*.

**bra'mido** *m* bellow, roar; **bramir** *vi* to bellow, roar.

**'branco/a** *adj* white // *f* white woman // *m* white man; (*espaço*) blank; **em ~** (in) blank; **brancura** *f* whiteness.

**bran'dir** *vt* to brandish.

**'brando/a** *adj* (*mole*) soft; (*meigo*) gentle, mild; **brandura** *f* (*moleza*) softness; (*mansidão*) gentleness, mildness; **branduras** *fpl* (*carícias*) caresses.

**branquear** [brãki'ax] *vt* to whiten; (*caiar*) to whitewash; (*alvejar*) to bleach // *vi* to turn white.

**'brasa** *f* hot coal; **em ~** red-hot; **estar sobre ~s** to be on tenterhooks.

**brasão** [bra'zãw] *m* coat of arms; (*fig*) glory.

**braseiro** [bra'zejru] *m* brazier.

**Bra'sil** [-iw] *m* Brazil; **brasileiro/a** *adj, m/f* Brazilian.

**bra'vata** *f* bravado, boasting;

**bravatear** *vi* to boast, brag.

**braveza** [bra'veza] *f* (*ferocidade*) fierceness; (*coragem*) courage.

**bra'vio/a** *adj* (*selvagem*) wild, untamed.

**'bravo/a** *adj* (*corajoso*) brave; (*furioso*) angry; (*tempestuoso*) rough, stormy // *m* brave man // *excl*: ~! well done!; **bravura** *f* courage, bravery.

**'breca** *f*: **com a** ~ ! damn it!; **ser levado da** ~ to be naughty.

**bre'car** *vt* (*carro*) to stop; (*reprimir*) to curb // *vi* to brake.

**brecha** ['brɛʃa] *f* breach; (*abertura*) opening; (*dano*) damage; (*meio de escapar*) loophole.

**brejeiro/a** [bre'ʒejru/a] *adj* naughty, mischievous.

**brejo** ['brɛʒu] *m* marsh, swamp.

**brenha** ['brɛɲa] *f* (*mata*) dense wood; (*enredamento*) tangle, maze.

**'breque** *m* (*freio*) brake.

**breu** [brew] *m* tar, pitch; **escuro como** ~ pitch black.

**'breve** *adj* short; (*leve*) light; (*rápido*) brief; **em** ~ soon, shortly; **para ser** ~ to be brief; **até** ~ see you soon.

**brevi'dade** *f* brevity, shortness.

**'briga** *f* (*luta*) fight; (*disputa*) quarrel.

**bri'gada** *f* brigade.

**brigão/ona** [bri'gãw/ona] *adj* quarrelsome // *m/f* brawler, trouble-maker; **brigar** *vi* (*lutar*) to fight; (*disputar*) to quarrel; (*destoar*) to clash.

**brilhante** [bri'ʎãtʃi] *adj* brilliant // *m* diamond; **brilhar** *vi* to shine; **brilho** *m* (*luz viva*) brilliance; (*esplendor*) splendour; (*nos sapatos*) shine.

**brincadeira** [brĩka'dejra] *f* (*divertimento*) fun; (*gracejo*) joke; **deixe de** ~s! stop fooling!; **fora de** ~ joking apart; **de** ~ for fun; **brincalhão/hona** *adj* playful // *m/f* joker, teaser.

**brin'car** *vi* (*divertir-se*) to play, have fun; (*gracejar*) to joke; **estou brincando** I'm only kidding; ~ **de soldados** to play (at) soldiers; **brinco** *m* (*jóia*) earring; (*brincadeira*) play, fun; (*brinquedo*) toy.

**brin'dar** *vt* (*beber*) to drink a toast to; (*presentear*) to give a present to; **brinde** *m* (*saudação*) toast; (*presente*) gift, present.

**brinquedo** [brĩ'kedu] *m* toy.

**'brio** *m* (*orgulho*) pride; (*coragem*) courage; (*ânimo*) spirit; **brioso/a** *adj* (*valente*) brave; (*orgulhoso*) proud.

**'brisa** *f* breeze.

**bri'tânico/a** *adj* British // *m/f* Briton.

**'broca** *f* drill; **brocar** *vt* to drill, bore.

**brocha** ['brɔʃa] *f* (*prego*) tack.

**broche** ['brɔʃi] *m* brooch.

**brochura** [bro'ʃura] *f* (*de livro*) binding; (*folheto*) brochure, pamphlet.

**'brócoli** (*Pt*: **'brócolos**) *m* broccoli *sg*.

**'bronco/a** *adj* (*tosco*) rough; (*ignorante*) ignorant, rough; (*rude*) coarse // *f*: **dar uma** ~ a to tell off.

**bronquite** [brõ'kitʃi] *f* bronchitis.

**'bronze** *m* bronze; ~**ado/a** *adj* (*da cor do bronze*) bronze; (*pelo sol*) suntanned // *m* suntan.

**bronze'ar** *vt* to tan; ~**-se** *vr* to get a tan.

**broquear** [brɔki'ax] *vt* to drill, bore.

**bro'tar** *vt* to produce // *vi* (*manar*) to flow; (*BOT*) to sprout; (*nascer*) to spring up; **broto** *m* bud; (*fig*) youngster.

**'broxa** *f* (*large*) paint brush.

**bruços** [brusu']: **de** ~ *adv* face down.

**'bruma** *f* mist, haze; **brumoso/a** *adj* misty, hazy.

**bru'nido/a** *adj* polished; **brunir** *vt* to polish.

**'brusco/a** *adj* brusque; *(áspero)* rough; *(súbito)* sudden.

**bru'tal** [-aw] *adj* brutal; **~idade** *f* brutality.

**'bruto/a** *adj* brutish; *(grosseiro)* coarse; *(diamante)* uncut; *(petróleo)* crude; *(peso)* gross; **em ~** raw, in the rough // *m* brute.

**bruxa** ['bruʃa] *f* witch; *(velha feia)* hag; **~ria** *f* witchcraft.

**Bruxelas** [bru'ʃelaʃ] *f* Brussels.

**bruxo** ['bruʃo] *m* magician, wizard.

**bruxulear** [bruʃuli'ax] *vi* to flicker.

**bucha** ['buʃa] *f* wad; **~ de pão** hunk of bread.

**bucho** ['buʃu] *m* stomach.

**'buço** *m* down.

**bu'dismo** *m* Buddhism.

**'bufar** *vi* to puff, pant; *(com raiva)* to snort.

**bufê** [bu'fe] *m*, **bu'fete** *m (móvel)* sideboard; *(restaurante)* snack bar, buffet bar.

**'bufo/a** *adj* burlesque // *m* puff; *(palhaço)* buffoon.

**bugiganga** [buʒi'gãga] *f* trinket; **~s** *fpl* knicknacks.

**bugio** [bu'ʒu] *m* monkey, ape.

**bujão** [bu'ʒãw] *m (TEC)* cap; **~ de gas** gas cylinder.

**'bula** *f (REL)* papal bull; *(MED)* directions for use.

**'bulbo** *m* bulb.

**'bule** *m (de chá/café)* tea/coffee pot.

**bulha** ['buʎa] *f (ruído)* row, noise.

**bu'lício** *m (agitação)* bustle; *(sussurro)* rustling; **buliçoso/a** *adj (vivo)* lively; *(movediço)* restless; *(desenvolto)* boisterous.

**bu'lir** *vt* to move // *vi* to move, stir; **~ em** to touch, meddle with.

**'bunda** *f (col)* bottom, backside.

**buquê** [bu'ke] *m* bouquet.

**bu'raco** *m* hole; *(de agulha)* eye.

**burburejar** [buxbure'ʒax] *vi (água etc)* to bubble.

**burguês/guesa** [bux'geʃ/'geza] *adj* middle-class, bourgeois;

**burguesia** *f* middle class, bourgeoisie.

**bu'ril** *m* chisel; **burilar** *vt* to chisel.

**'burla** *f* trick, fraud; *(zombaria)* mockery; **burlar** *vt (enganar)* to cheat; *(defraudar)* to swindle; *(a lei)* to evade.

**burocra'cia** *f* bureaucracy; *(excessiva)* red tape; **burocrata** *m/f* bureaucrat.

**burra** ['buxa] *f (cofre)* safe; *(animal)* she-donkey; **burrice** *f (estupidez)* stupidity; *(asneira)* silliness; **burro** *m* donkey; *(pessoa)* silly ass, idiot; **burro/a** *adj* stupid.

**'busca** *f* search; **em ~ de** in search of; **buscar** *vt* to look for, search for; **ir buscar** to fetch, go for; **mandar buscar** to send for.

**'bússola** *f* compass.

**'busto** *m* bust.

**bu'zina** *f* horn; **buzinada** *f* toot, hoot; **buzinar** *vi* to toot, hoot.

**'búzio** *m (concha)* conch; *(corneta)* horn.

# C

**cá** *adv* here, over here; **para ~** this way; **para lá e para ~** back and forth.

**caa'tinga** *f (Br)* scrub(-land).

**ca'baça** *f* gourd.

**ca'bal** [-aw] *adj (perfeito)* perfect; *(completo)* complete; *(exato)* exact.

**ca'bala** *f (maquinação)* conspiracy, intrigue; **cabalar** *vt (votos etc)* to canvass (for) // *vi* to plot.

**ca'bana** *f* hut, shack.

**caba'ré** *m (boate)* night club.

**ca'beça** *f (ANAT)* head; *(inteligência)* intelligence; *(parte mais alta)* top // *m* leader, head.

**cabe'çada** *f (pancada com cabeça)* butt; *(inclinação da cabeça)* nod;

(*asneira*) blunder; **dar ~s** to nod.

**cabeçalho** [kabe'saʌu] *m* (*de jornal*) headline; (*de livro*) title page; (*título*) title.

**cabecear** [kabesi'ax] *vt* (*futebol*) to head // *vi* to nod.

**cabeceira** [kabe'sejra] *f* (*de cama*) head; (*de sepultura*) headstone.

**cabe'çudo/a** *adj* (*teimoso*) obstinate.

**cabeleira** [kabe'ʌejra] *f* head of hair; (*postiça*) wig; **cabeleireiro/a** *m/f* hairdresser; **cabelo** *m* hair; **cabeludo/a** *adj* hairy.

**ca'ber** *vi* (*poder entrar*) to fit, go; **cabe a você falar com ele** it is up to you to speak to him; **cabe-me dizer que** I have to say that; **não cabe aqui fazer comentários** this is not the time or place to comment.

**ca'bide** *m* (*móvel*) rack; (*gancho*) peg; (*guarda-roupa*) coat hanger.

**cabi'mento** *m* suitability; **ter ~** to be acceptable.

**ca'bine** *f* cabin; **~ do piloto** (*AER*) cockpit; **~ telefônica** telephone booth.

**cabisbaixo/a** [kabɪʃ'bajʃu/a] *adj* dispirited, crestfallen.

**'cabo** *m* (*extremidade*) end; (*de faca, vassoura etc*) handle; (*corda*) rope; (*elétrico etc*) cable; (*GEO*) cape; (*MIL*) corporal; **ao ~ de** at the end of; **de ~ a rabo** from end to end; **levar a ~** to carry out; **dar ~ de** to put an end to.

**ca'boclo/a** *m/f* (*Br*) (*cariboca*) half-breed // *m* (*sertanejo*) backwoodsman; (*habitante do sertão*) peasant(-farmer).

**cabo'grama** *m* cable(gram).

**'cabra** *f* goat; **~ cega** blind man's buff // *m* (*Br*) (*mulato*) half-caste; (*capanga*) hired gunhand.

**cabreiro/a** [ka'brejru/a] *adj* (*col*) suspicious.

**ca'bresto** *m* (*de cavalos*) halter.

**cabri'ola** *f* leap.

**ca'brito** *m* (*ger*) kid.

**cabrocha** [ka'brɔʃa] *f* mulatto girl.

**'caça** *f* (*ger*) hunting; (*busca*) hunt; (*animal*) quarry, game; **à ~ de** in pursuit of // *m* (*AER*) fighter (plane); **caçada** *f* (*jornada de caçadores*) hunting trip; (*produto de caça*) kill; **caçador/a** *m/f* hunter // *m* (*MIL*) rifleman.

**ca'camba** *f* (*balde*) bucket.

**caça-'minas** *m* minesweeper.

**ca'çar** *vt* to hunt; (*com espingarda*) to shoot.

**cacarejar** [kakare'ʒax] *vi* (*galinhas etc*) to cackle.

**caça'rola** *f* (*sauce*)pan.

**cacau** [ka'kaw] *m* cocoa; (*BOT*) cacao.

**cacete** [ka'setʃi] *adj* tiresome, boring // *m/f* bore // *m* club, stick.

**cachaça** [ka'ʃasa] *f* (*white*) rum.

**cachecol** [kaʃe'kɔw] *m* neck scarf.

**cachimbo** [ka'ʃĩbu] *m* pipe.

**cacho** ['kaʃu] *m* bunch; (*de cabelo*) curl, ringlet.

**cachoeira** [kaʃ'wejra] *f* waterfall.

**cachopa** [ka'ʃopa] *f* (*Pt*) girl, lass; **cachopo** *m* (*Pt*) lad.

**cachorra** [ka'ʃoxa] *f* bitch; (*Pt*) (*female*) puppy; **cachorrinho/a** *m/f* puppy; **cachorro** *m* dog; (*Pt*) puppy; (*filhote de animal*) cub; (*patife*) rascal; **cachorro quente** hot dog.

**cacimba** [ka'sĩba] *f* (*poço*) waterhole; (*chuva miúda*) drizzle.

**cacique** [ka'sikɪ] *m* chief; (*mandachuva*) local boss.

**'caco** *m* bit, fragment.

**caço'ar** *vt* to mock, ridicule // *vi* to joke, jest.

**caçoula** [ka'sola] *f* pan; (*vaso*) dish.

**'cacto** *m* cactus.

**ca'çula** *m/f* youngest child.

**'cada** *adj inv* each; (*todo*) every; **~ qual** each one; **~ semana** each week; **~ vez mais** more and more; **~ vez mais barato** cheaper and cheaper.

**cada'falso** *m* (*forca*) gallows; (*andaime*) scaffold.

**ca'dastro** m (*registro*) register; (*de criminosos*) criminal record.

**ca'dáver** m corpse, dead body.

**ca'dê** adv (col) ~...? where's ...?, what's happened to ...?

**cade'ado** m padlock.

**cadeia** [ka'deja] f chain; (*prisão*) prison; (*rede*) network.

**cadeira** [ka'dejra] f (*móvel*) chair; ~ **de rodas** wheelchair; ~s fpl (ANAT) hips.

**ca'dela** f (*cão*) bitch.

**ca'dência** f cadence; (*ritmo*) rhythm.

**cader'neta** f (*de apontamentos*) notebook; (*registro de alunos*) school register; (*de banco*) passbook; **caderno** m exercise book.

**ca'dete** m cadet.

**cadu'car** vi (*documentos*) to lapse, expire; (*pessoa*) to become senile; **caduco/a** adj (*nulo*) invalid, expired; (*decrépito*) decrepit.

**cafa'jeste** m/f (col) rogue, yob, thug.

**ca'fé** m coffee; (*estabelecimento*) café; ~ **da manhã** (Br) breakfast; **é** ~ **pequeno** it's child's play; **cafeeiro** m coffee plant; **cafeicultor** m coffee-grower; **cafeteira** f (*vaso*) coffee pot; (*máquina*) percolator; **cafezal** m coffee plantation; **cafezinho** m small black coffee.

**ca'fona** adj in bad taste // m/f person of bad taste.

**'cágado** m turtle.

**cai'ar** vt to whitewash.

**'caiba** etc vb ver **caber.**

**cãibra** ['kãjbra] f (MED) cramp.

**ca'ído/a** adj (*abatido*) dejected.

**caimão** [kaj'mãw] m alligator.

**cai'mento** m (*vestido*) hang, fall.

**cai'pira** m/f peasant, yokel.

**caipi'rinha** f cocktail of *cachaça*, lemon and sugar.

**ca'ir** vi to fall (down); (*acontecer*) to take place, occur; ~ **bem** to suit, go well with; ~ **em si** to come to one's senses; ~ **de cama** to fall sick; ~ **de**

**quatro** to land on all fours.

**cais** [kajʃ] m (NÁUT) quay; (Pt: FERRO) platform.

**caixa** ['kajʃa] f box; (*cofre*) safe; (*de uma loja*) cashdesk; ~ **de mudanças** (AUTO) gear box; ~ **econômica** savings bank; ~ **postal** P.O. box; ~ **de correio** letter box // m/f (COM: *pessoa*) cashier.

**caixão** [kaj'ʃãw] m large box; (*ataúde*) coffin.

**caixeira** [kaj'ʃejra] f saleswoman; **caixeiro** m salesman; **caixeiro viajante** commercial traveller.

**caixilho** [kaj'ʃiʌu] m (*moldura*) frame.

**caixote** [kaj'ʃɔtʃi] m packing case; ~ **do lixo** (Pt) dustbin; (US) garbage can.

**cajado** [ka'ʒadu] m staff, crook.

**caju** [ka'ʒu] m cashew nut; ~**eiro** m cashew tree.

**cal** f lime; (*para caiar*) whitewash.

**calabouço** [kala'bosu] m dungeon.

**ca'lado/a** adj silent, quiet // f (NÁUT) draught; **pela** ~ **a** stealthily; **na** ~ **a da noite** in the dead of night.

**cala'frio** m shiver; **ter** ~**s** to shiver.

**cala'mar** m squid.

**calami'dade** f calamity, disaster; **calamitoso/a** adj disastrous.

**calão** [ka'lãw] m: (*baixo*) ~ (Br) bad language; (Pt) slang.

**ca'lar** vt (*não dizer*) to keep quiet about; (*impor silêncio*) to silence; **cala a boca!** shut up! // vi, ~**-se** vr to keep silent.

**calça'deira** f shoehorn.

**calçado/a** adj (*rua*) paved // m footwear // f (*rua*) roadway; (Br: *passeio*) pavement; (US) sidewalk.

**calcanhar** [kawka'nax] m (ANAT) heel.

**calção** [kaw'sãw] m, pl **calções** [kaw'sõjʃ] shorts pl; ~ **de banho** swimming trunks pl.

**cal'car** vt (*pisar em*) to tread on; (*espezinhar*) to trample (on).

**cal'çar** vt (*sapatos, luvas*) to put on; (*pavimentar*) to pave.

**'calças** fpl trousers; (*US*) pants; ~ **curtas** shorts; **calcinhas** fpl panties.

**'cálcio** m calcium.

**'calço** m (*cunha*) wedge.

**calcula'dor** m calculator; **calcular** vt (*MAT*) to calculate // vi to make calculations; (*supor*) to reckon, guess; **cálculo** m calculation; (*MAT*) calculus; (*MED*) stone.

**'calda** f (*de doze*) syrup; **caldear** vt (*ligar metais*) to weld, fuse.

**caldeira** [kaw'dejra] f (*CULIN*) boiling pan, kettle; (*TEC*) boiler.

**caldeirada** [kawdej'rada] f (*Pt: guisado*) fish stew.

**caldeirão** [kawdej'rãw] m cauldron; **caldeiro** m (*balde*) bucket.

**'caldo** m (*sopa*) soup; (*de fruta*) juice.

**calefação** [kalefa'sãw] (*Pt: -cç-*) f heating.

**calejado/a** [kale'ʒadu/a] adj hardened; (*fig*) experienced.

**calen'dário** m calendar.

**calha** ['kaʎa] f (*sulco*) channel; (*para água*) gutter.

**calhar** [ka'ʎax] vi (*convir*) to be suitable, fit; (*acontecer*) to happen; **se** ~ (*Pt*) perhaps, maybe.

**calhau** [ka'ʎaw] m stone, pebble.

**cali'brar** vt to gauge, calibrate; **calibre** m (*de cano*) bore, calibre; (*fig*) calibre.

**'cálice** m (*copinho*) wine glass; (*REL*) chalice.

**'cálido/a** adj warm.

**calma** ['kawma] f (*serenidade*) calm; (*calor*) heat; **conservar/perder a** ~ to keep/lose one's temper // excl: ~! take it easy!

**calmante** [kaw'mãtʃi] adj soothing // m (*MED*) sedative; **calmo/a** adj calm, tranquil.

**'calo** m callus; (*no pé*) corn.

**ca'lor** m heat; (*agradável*) warmth.

**calo'ria** f calorie; **caloroso/a** adj warm; (*entusiástico*) enthusiastic.

**ca'lota** f (*AUTO*) hubcap.

**ca'lote** m (*dívida*) bad debt; (*trapaça*) swindle; **calotear** vt (*trapacear*) to swindle.

**calouro/a** [ka'loru/a] m/f (*EDUC*) fresher; (: *US*) freshman; (*noviço*) novice.

**ca'lúnia** f slander; **calunioso/a** adj slanderous.

**calvície** [kaw'visi] f baldness; **calvo/a** adj bald.

**'cama** f bed; ~ **de solteiro** single bed; ~ **de casal** double bed.

**cama'da** f layer; (*de tinta*) coat.

**'câmara** f (*ger*) chamber; (*FOTO*) camera; ~ **de ar** (*de pneu*) inner tube; ~ **municipal** (*Br*) town council; (*Pt*) town hall; **em** ~ **lenta** in slow motion.

**cama'rada** m/f comrade; (*companheiro*) companion; ~**gem** f comradeship.

**camarão** [kama'rãw] m shrimp.

**camarilha** [kama'riʎa] f clique; (*política*) lobby group.

**camarim** [kama'rĩ] m (*teatro*) dressing room.

**cama'rote** m (*NÁUT*) cabin; (*teatro*) box.

**cam'bada** f bunch, gang.

**cambaio/a** [kam'baju/a] adj (*de pernas*) bow-legged.

**cambale'ante** adj staggering; **cambalear** vi to stagger, reel.

**cambalhota** [kamba'ʎota] f somersault.

**cambi'ante** adj changing, variable // m (*cor*) shade; **cambiar** vt to change; (*trocar*) to exchange // vi: **cambiar de idéia** to change one's mind; **câmbio** m (*dinheiro etc*) exchange; (*preço de câmbio*) rate of exchange; **câmbio livre** free trade; **câmbio negro** black market.

**cam'bista** m (*de dinheiro*) money

changer; (Br: de ingressos) (ticket-)tout.

**ca'melo** m camel; (fig) dunce.

**came'lô** m street pedlar.

**camião** [kamɪˈãw] (Pt) m lorry; (US) truck.

**caminhada** [kamɪˈɲada] f walk; **caminhante** m/f walker; (transeunte) pedestrian.

**caminhão** [kamɪˈɲãw] (Br) m lorry; (US) truck.

**caminhar** [kamɪˈɲax] vi (andar) to go; (ir a pé) to walk; (distâncias) to travel.

**caminho** [kaˈmɪɲu] m (direção) way; (vereda) road, path; (Pt): ~ **de ferro** railway; (US) railroad; **a meio** ~ halfway (there); **em** ~ **on the** way, en route; **caminhonete** m (AUTO) van.

**camio'neta** (Pt) f (para passageiros) coach; (comercial) van.

**ca'misa** f shirt; ~ **de dormir** nightshirt; ~ **de Vênus** condom, sheath; **camiseta** f vest.

**cami'sola** f (Br) nightdress; (Pt: pulôver) sweater.

**'campa** f (de sepultura) gravestone; (sino) bell.

**campainha** [kampaˈɪɲa] f bell.

**cam'pal** [-paw] adj: **batalha** ~ pitched battle; **missa** ~ open-air mass.

**campa'nário** m (torre) church tower, steeple; (aldeia) parish.

**campanha** [kamˈpaɲa] f (MIL etc) campaign; (planície) plain.

**campeão/campeã** [kampɪˈãw/kampɪˈã] m/f champion; **campeonato** m championship.

**cam'pestre** adj rural, rustic.

**cam'pina** f prairie, grassland.

**cam'pismo** m camping; **parque de** ~ campsite; **campista** m/f camper.

**'campo** m (ger) field; (fora da cidade) countryside; (de esporte) ground; (acampamento) camp; (alcance) sphere, scope; (de tênis) court; **em** ~ **aberto** in the open; **pôr**

**em** ~ to bring into play.

**campo'nês/esa** m countryman; (agricultor) farmer // f countrywoman; **campônio/a** adj, m/f (pej) yokel, country bumpkin.

**camuflagem** [kamuˈflaʒẽ] f camouflage; **camuflar** vt to camouflage.

**camun'dongo** m (Br) mouse.

**ca'murça** f chamois (leather).

**'cana** f cane; (col: cadeia) jail; (de açúcar) sugar cane; ~ **de pesca** (Pt) fishing rod.

**Cana'dá** m Canada; **canadense** adj, m/f Canadian.

**ca'nal** m (ger) channel; (de navegação) canal; (ANAT) duct.

**canalha** [kaˈnaʎa] f rabble, mob // m/f wretch, scoundrel.

**canalização** [kanalizaˈsãw] f (água) plumbing; (gás) piping; (eletricidade) wiring; **canalizador** m (Pt) plumber; **canalizar** vt to channel; (colocar canos) to lay pipes.

**ca'nário** m canary.

**ca'nastra** f (big) basket; (jogo) canasta.

**canavi'al** m cane field.

**canção** [kãˈsãw] f song; ~ **de ninar** lullaby.

**can'cela** f gate.

**cancela'mento** m cancellation; **cancelar** vt to cancel; (invalidar) to annul.

**'câncer** m cancer.

**cancioneiro** [kãsɪoˈnejru] m song book.

**candeeiro** [kãdʒiˈejru] m (Br) oil-lamp ou gas-lamp; (Pt) lamp.

**cande'labro** m (castiçal) candlestick; (lustre) chandelier.

**can'dente** adj white hot; (fig) inflamed.

**candi'dato** m candidate; **candidatura** f candidature.

**candidez** [kãdʒiˈdeʒ] f (inocência) innocence; **cândido/a** adj (ingênuo) naive; (inocente) innocent; (branco) white; **candura** f (*simplicidade*) simplicity; (*inocência*) innocence.

**ca'neca** f mug, tankard.

**ca'nela** f (*especiaria*) cinnamon; (ANAT) shin.

**ca'neta** f pen; ~ **esferográfica** ballpoint pen; **caneta-tinteiro** f fountain pen.

**cangaceiro** [kãga'sejru] m (Br) bandit.

**cangu'ru** m kangaroo.

**cânhamo** ['kaɲamu] m hemp.

**canhão** [ka'ɲãw] m (MIL) cannon; (GEO) canyon.

**canhoto/a** [ka'ɲotu/a] adj left-handed // m/f left-handed person // m (de cheque) stub.

**ca'niço/a** adj (col) skinny // m reed.

**ca'nícula** f height of the summer; **canicular** adj hot, sultry.

**ca'nil** [-nɪw] m kennel.

**cani'vete** m penknife.

**canja** ['kãʒa] f (sopa) chicken soup; (col) cinch, pushover.

**can'jica** f maize porridge.

**'cano** m pipe; (tubo) tube; (de arma de fogo) barrel; ~ **de esgoto** sewer.

**ca'noa** f canoe.

**can'saço** m tiredness, weariness; **cansado/a** adj tired, weary; (aborrecido) fed up.

**can'sar** vt (fatigar) to tire; (irritar) to irritate; (entediar) to bore // vi, ~**-se** vr (ficar cansado) to get tired; **cansativo/a** adj tiring; (tedioso) tedious; **canseira** f (cansaço) weariness; (trabalho árduo) toil.

**can'tar** vt to sing // m song.

**'cântaro** m water jug.

**cantaro'lar** vt to hum.

**canteira** f quarry; **canteiro** m stonemason; (de flores) flower bed.

**can'tiga** f ballad; (conto) tale; ~ **de ninar** lullaby.

**can'til** [-tɪw] m canteen, flask.

**can'tina** f canteen.

**'canto** m (ângulo) corner; (canção)

song; **aos quatro** ~**s** to the four corners of the earth; **de** ~ edgeways.

**can'tor(a)** m/f singer.

**canu'dinho** m straw.

**ca'nudo** m tube; (canudinho) straw.

**cão** [kãw] m, pl **cães** [kãjʃ] dog; (de arma de fogo) hammer.

**caos** ['kaoʃ] m chaos; **caótico/a** adj chaotic.

**'capa** f (roupa) cape; (de livro) cover; (envoltório) wrapper.

**capa'cete** m helmet.

**capacho** [ka'paʃu] m door mat; (fig) toady.

**capaci'dade** f capacity; (aptidão) ability, competence.

**ca'par** vt to castrate, geld.

**capataz** [kapa'taʃ] m foreman.

**capaz** [ka'paʃ] adj able, capable.

**ca'pela** f chapel; **capelão** m (REL) chaplain.

**ca'peta** m devil.

**capim** [ka'pĩ] m grass.

**capi'tal** [-taw] adj capital, principal // m capital, funds pl // f (cidade) capital; ~**ismo** m capitalism; ~**ista** m/f capitalist.

**capitane'ar** vt to command, head; **capitania** f captaincy; **capitania do porto** port authority; **capitão** m, pl **capitães** captain.

**capitulação** [kapitula'sãw] f capitulation, surrender.

**ca'pítulo** m chapter.

**ca'pô** m (AUTO) bonnet, (US) hood.

**capoeira** [kap'wejra] f (Pt) hencoop; (mata) brushwood; (jogo) foot-fighting dance.

**ca'pota** f (coberta de automóvel) hood, top.

**capo'tar** vi to overturn, capsize.

**ca'pote** m (capa) cloak; (sobretudo) overcoat.

**capricho** [ka'prɪʃu] m whim, caprice; (teimosia) obstinacy; (apuro) care; **caprichoso/a** adj capricious; (variável) changeable; (com apuro) meticulous.

**cap'tar** vt (atrair) to win; (rádio) to pick up; (águas) to collect, dam up; (apanhar) to catch; **captura** f capture; **capturar** vt to capture, seize.

**capuz** [ka'puʒ] m hood.

**cáqui** ['kaki] adj khaki.

**'cara** f (de pessoa) face; (de disco) side; (de moeda) face; (aspeto) appearance; **ter boa ~** to look well; **~ ou coroa?** heads or tails?; **ser a ~ de** (col) to be the spitting image of; **ter ~ de** to look (like); **dar de cara com** to bump into // m (col) guy // f (col) girl.

**cara'bina** f rifle.

**cara'col** [-ow] m snail; (de cabelo) curl.

**carac'teres** pl of **caráter**.

**caracte'rístico/a**      adj characteristic // f characteristic, feature; **caracterização** f characterization; (de ator) make-up; **caracterizar** vt to characterize, typify.

**cara'dura**      adj barefaced, shameless.

**cara'melo** m caramel; (bala) sweet; (US) candy.

**caranguejo** [karã'geʒu] m crab.

**cara'paça** f shell.

**carapau** [kara'paw] m (peixe) jack-fish; (fig) skinny person, beanpole.

**carapinha** [kara'piɲa] f curly hair.

**cara'puça** f cap; **se a ~ serve** if the cap fits.

**ca'ráter** m, pl **carac'teres** character; (BIO) characteristic.

**cara'vana** f caravan.

**carboni'zar** vt to carbonize; (queimar) to char; **carbono** m carbon.

**carbura'dor** m carburettor.

**car'caça** f (esqueleto) carcass; (armação) frame; (de navio) hull.

**carce'reiro** ['kaxseɾi] m prison; (fig) hell.

**carcereiro** m jailer, warder.

**car'comido/a**      adj worm-eaten; (fig) rotten.

**car'dápio** m (Br) menu.

**cardeal** [kaxd͡ʒi'aw] adj cardinal // m cardinal.

**cardí'aco/a** adj cardiac.

**cardi'nal** adj cardinal.

**'cardo** m thistle.

**car'dume** m (peixes) shoal.

**ca'reca** adj bald.

**carecer** [kare'sex] vi: **~ de** (ter falta) to lack; (precisar) to need; **carência** f (falta) lack, shortage; (necessidade) need; (privação) deprivation; **carente** adj wanting; (pessoa) needy.

**cares'tia**      f expensiveness; (encarecimento) high prices pl; (escassez) scarcity.

**ca'reta** f grimace; (máscara) mask; **fazer uma ~** to pull a face.

**'carga** f (peso) load; (de um navio) cargo; (ato de carregar) loading; (ELET) charge; (dever) duty; (MIL) attack, charge; (reabastecimento) refill; **voltar à ~** to insist.

**'cargo** m (responsabilidade) duty, responsibility; (função pública) office.

**carica'tura** f (desenho) cartoon; (imitação cômica) caricature; **caricaturista** m/f cartoonist.

**ca'rícia** f caress.

**cari'dade** f charity; (bondade) kindness; (esmola) alms pl.

**cárie** ['kaɾi] f (MED) caries; (de dente) tooth decay.

**ca'ril** [-w] m curry.

**carim'bar** vt to stamp; (no correio) to postmark; **carimbo** m rubber stamp; (postal) postmark.

**carinho** [ka'riɲu] m affection, fondness; (carícia) caress; **fazer ~** to caress; **carinhoso/a** adj affectionate.

**cari'oca** adj of Rio de Janeiro // m/f native of Rio de Janeiro // m (Pt: café) type of weak coffee.

**carita'tivo/a** adj charitable.

**carmesin** [kaxme'sĩ] adj crimson.

**carnal** [kax'naw] adj carnal; **primo** ~ first cousin.

**carnaval** [kaxna'vaw] m carnival.

**carne** ['kaxni] f flesh; (CULIN) meat; ~ **moída** minced meat; **em** ~ **e osso** in flesh and blood.

**carneiro** [kax'nejru] m sheep; (macho) ram.

**carniça'ria** f (matança) slaughter; (açougue) butcher's shop; **carniceiro/a** adj (cruel) cruel; **carnificina** f slaughter; **carnívoro/a** adj carnivorous.

**car'nudo/a** adj plump, fleshy; (col) beefy.

**'caro/a** adj dear, expensive; (estimado) dear; **sair** ~ to cost a lot // adv dear.

**carochinha** [karo'ʃiɲa] f: **conto da** ~ fairy tale.

**ca'roço** m (de frutos) stone; (endurecimento) lump.

**ca'rola** m/f (col) sanctimonious person, obsessive churchgoer.

**ca'rona** f (Br: viagem gratuita) lift; **viajar de** ~ to hitchhike.

**carpinta'ria** f carpentry; **carpinteiro** m carpenter; (de teatro) stagehand.

**carranca** [ka'xa-] f frown, scowl; **carrancudo/a** adj surly; (soturno) sullen; (semblante) scowling.

**carra'pato** m (insecto) tick; (pessoa) hanger-on.

**car'rasco** m executioner; (fig) tyrant.

**carre'gado/a** adj loaded, laden; (semblante) sullen; (céu) dark; **carregador** m porter; **carregamento** m (ação) loading; (carga) load, cargo.

**carre'gar** vt (veículo, arma) to load; (levar) to carry; (bateria) to charge; (sobrecarregar) to burden; (Pt: apertar) to press.

**carreira** [ka'xejra] f (ação de correr) run, running; (competição) race; (curso) course; (profissão)

career; (trilha) track, route; (fileira) row; (pista de corridas) track, course; **às** ~**s** in a hurry.

**car'reta** f cart; (de artilharia) carriage.

**carreteiro** [kaxe'tejru] m cart driver.

**carretel** [kaxe'tew] m spool, reel.

**carril** [ka'xiw] m (de ferro) rail; (sulco de rodas) rut, track.

**carrilhão** [kaxi'ʎãw] m chime.

**carrinha** [ka'xiɲa] f (Pt) f van.

**carrinho** [ka'xiɲu] m small cart; ~ **de criança** - pram; ~ **de mão** wheelbarrow.

**carro** ['kaxo] m (automóvel) car; (de bois) cart; (de mão) handcart, barrow; (RAIL, TEC) carriage; (caminhão) truck; ~ **de corrida** racing car; ~ **esporte** sports car; **carroça** f cart, waggon.

**carroce'ria** [kaxo-] f (AUTO) bodywork.

**carruagem** [kaxu'aʒẽ] f carriage, coach.

**'carta** f letter; (de jogar) card; (mapa) chart; (diploma) diploma; (constituição) charter; ~ **aérea** airmail letter; ~ **registrada** registered letter; ~ **de crédito** letter of credit; ~ **de direção** driving licence; **dar as** ~**s** to deal.

**cartão** [kax'tãw] m (Pt: material) cardboard; (bilhete) card; ~ **de visita** (calling) card; ~ **postal** postcard; ~ **de crédito** credit card.

**car'taz** m poster; (US) bill; **ter** ~ to have a good reputation.

**carteira** [kax'tejra] f (móvel) desk; (para dinheiro) wallet; (num banco) department; ~ **de identidade** identity card; ~ **de motorista/ chofer** driving licence.

**carteiro** [kax'tejru] m postman.

**cartilagem** [kaxtʃi'laʒẽ] f (ANAT) cartilage.

**carto'liana** f (material) card.

**car'tório** m registry; (arquivo) archive.

**cartucheira** [kaxtu'ʃejra] f cartridge belt; **cartucho** m cartridge; (saco de papel) packet.

**caruncho** [ka'ruɲu] m (insecto) woodworm; (podridão) rot.

**carvalho** [kax'vaʎu] m oak.

**carvão** [kax'vãw] m coal; (de madeira) charcoal; **carvoeiro** m (comerciante) coal merchant.

**'casa** f house; (lar) home; (COM) firm; ~ **de botão** buttonhole; ~ **de câmbio** exchange bureau; ~ **de pensão** boarding house; ~ **de saúde** hospital; ~ **da moeda** mint; **em** ~ (at) home; **fora de** ~ out.

**ca'saca** f dress coat; (col) tails pl; **virar a** ~ to become a turncoat; **casaco** m coat.

**casal** [ka'zaw] m (par) married couple.

**casa'mento** m marriage; (boda) wedding; **casar** vt to marry; (combinar) to match (up); **casar-se** vr to get married; (harmonizar-se) to combine well.

**'casca** f (de árvore) bark; (de banana) skin; (de ferida) scab; (de laranja) peel; (de nozes, ovos) shell; (de milho) husk.

**cascalho** [kaʃ'kaʎu] m (pedra britada) gravel; (na praia) shingle; (entulho) rubble.

**cascão** [kaʃ'kãw] m crust; (sujeira) grime.

**cas'cata** f waterfall.

**casca'vel** m (serpente) rattlesnake.

**'casco** m (crânio) skull; (pele da cabeça) scalp; (de animal) hoof; (de navio) hull; (para bebidas) empty bottle.

**casebre** [ka'zebri] m hovel, shack.

**caseiro/a** [ka'zejru/a] adj (produtos) home-made; (pessoa) home-loving // m tenant.

**ca'serna** f barracks pl.

**cas'murro/a** adj moody, introverted.

**'caso** m case; ~ **amoroso** love affair // conj in case, if; **em** ~ **de** in case (of); **em todo** ~ in any case; **fazer pouco** ~ **de** to belittle; **não fazer** ~ **de** to ignore; (não fazer questão de) not to be fussy about; **vir ao** ~ to be relevant.

**'caspa** f dandruff.

**cas'sete** m cassette.

**cas'sino** m casino.

**'casta** f case; (estirpe) lineage.

**castanheira** [kaʃta'nejra] f chestnut tree; **castanho/a** adj brown // f chestnut; **castanha de caju** cashew nut; **castanha-do-pará** f Brazil nut.

**castanholas** [kaʃta'nɔlaʃ] fpl castanets.

**cas'telo** m castle.

**casti'çal** [-aw] m candlestick.

**cas'tiço/a** adj (de boa casta) of good stock, pedigree.

**casti'dade** f chastity.

**casti'gar** vt to punish; (admoestar) to reprimand; (corrigir) to correct; **castigo** m punishment; (penalidade) penalty.

**'casto/a** adj chaste, pure.

**cas'tor** m beaver.

**cas'trado/a** adj castrated // m eunuch; **castrar** vt to castrate.

**casual** [kaz'waw] adj accidental; (fortuito) fortuitous; ~**idade** f chance; (acidente) accident; **por** ~**idade** by chance, accidentally.

**ca'sulo** m (de sementes) pod; (de insectos) cocoon.

**'cata** f: **à** ~ **de** in search of.

**cata'clismo** m cataclysm.

**catalisa'dor** m catalyst.

**catalo'gar** vt to catalogue; **catálogo** m catalogue; **catálogo telefônico** telephone directory.

**cata'plasma** f poultice.

**cata'pora** f (Br) chickenpox.

**ca'tar** vt to look for, search for; (piolho) to delouse; (recolher) to collect, gather.

**cata'rata** f (cascata) waterfall; (MED) cataract.

**ca'tarro** *m* catarrh; *(constipação)* cold.

**ca'tástrofe** *f* catastrophe.

**cata-'vento** *m* weathercock.

**cate'cismo** [kate'sɪ3mu] *m* catechism.

**cate'dral** [-aw] *f* cathedral.

**cate'drático/a** *m/f* professor.

**catego'ria** *f* category; *(social)* rank; *(qualidade)* quality; **de alta** ~ first rate; **categórico/a** *adj* categorical.

**ca'tinga** *m/f* *(pessoa)* miser // *f* stench, stink.

**cati'vante** *adj* captivating; **cativar** *vt* *(capturar)* to capture; *(escravizar)* to enslave; *(fascinar)* to captivate; *(encantar)* to charm; **cativeiro** *m* captivity; *(escravidão)* slavery; *(cadeia)* prison; **cativo/a** *m/f* *(escravo)* slave; *(prisioneiro)* prisoner.

**catoli'cismo** [katoli'sɪ3mu] *m* catholicism; **católico/a** *adj*, *m/f* catholic.

**ca'torze** *num* fourteen.

**catur'rice** [katu'xɪsɪ] *f* obstinacy.

**cau'ção** [kaw'sãw] *f* security, guarantee; **prestar** ~ to give bail; **sob** ~ on bail.

**caucho** ['kawʃu] *m* *(árvore)* gum tree; *(borracha)* rubber.

**caucio'nar** [kawsjo'nax] *vt* to guarantee, stand surety for; *(JUR)* to stand bail for.

**cauda** ['kawda] *f* tail; *(de vestido)* train; *(retaguarda)* rear.

**cau'dal** *m* *(dum rio)* flow; *(torrente)* torrent; *(cachoeira)* waterfall; **caudaloso/a** *adj* *(abundante)* abundant; *(rio)* torrential.

**caudilho** [kaw'dʒiʎu] *m* leader, chief.

**caule** ['kauli] *m* stalk, stem.

**causa** ['kawza] *f* cause; *(motivo)* motive, reason; *(JUR)* lawsuit, case; **por** ~ **de** on account of; **causar** *vt* to cause, bring about.

**cau'tela** *f* caution; *(senha)* ticket; ~ **de penhor** pawn ticket; **cauteloso/a** *adj* cautious, wary.

**'cava** *f* *(cova)* pit; *(de manga)* armhole.

**ca'vaco** *m* *(lenha)* firewood; *(estilha)* splinter; *(conversa)* chat.

**ca'vala** *f* mackerel.

**cava'ria** *f* *(MIL)* cavalry; *(equitação)* horsemanship; *(instituição medieval)* chivalry.

**cava'riça** *f* stable.

**cavaleiro** [kava'lejru] *m* rider, horseman; *(cavalheiro)* gentleman; *(medieval)* knight.

**cava'lete** *m* stand; *(FOTO)* tripod; *(de pintor)* easel; *(de mesa)* trestle; *(do violino)* bridge.

**cavalheiresco/a** [kava-ʎej'reʃku/a] *adj* gentlemanly; *(brioso)* chivalrous; **cavalheiro** *m* gentleman; *(na dança)* partner.

**cavalinho** [kava'liɲu] *m*: ~ **de pau** rocking horse; ~**-de-judeu** *m* dragonfly; ~**-do-mar** *m* sea horse.

**ca'valo** *m* horse; *(xadrez)* knight; *(cartas)* jack; **a** ~ on horseback; **50** ~**s-vapor** 50 horsepower.

**ca'var** *vt* to dig; ~ **a vida** to earn one's living // *vi* *(animal)* to burrow; *(fig)* to delve.

**'cave** *f* *(Pt)* wine-cellar.

**caveira** [ka'vejra] *f* skull.

**ca'verna** *f* cavern.

**cavi'dade** *f* cavity.

**cavilha** [ka'viʎa] *f* *(de madeira)* peg, dowel; *(de metal)* bolt.

**'cavo/a** *adj* *(oco)* hollow; *(côncavo)* concave; **cavouco** *m* ditch, trench; **cavouqueiro** *m* navvy.

**caxumba** [ka'ʃumba] *f* mumps *pl*.

**c/c** *abr* **de conta corrente** current account.

**cear** [si'ax] *vt* to have for supper // *vi* to dine.

**ce'bola** *f* onion; *(bolho)* bulb.

**cece'ar** [sesi'ax] *vi* to lisp; **ceceio** *m* lisp.

**ce'der** *vt* to give up; *(entregar)* to

hand over; ~ **o passo** to give way // *vi* to give in, concede; (*afrouxar*) to slacken.

**cedilha** [se'dʒiʎa] *f* cedilla.

**cedo** ['sedu] *adv* early; (*prematuramente*) prematurely; (*em breve*) soon; **mais ~ ou mais tarde** sooner or later; **o mais ~ possível** as soon as possible.

**'cedro** *m* cedar.

**'cédula** *f* (*moeda-papel*) banknote; (*US*) bill; (*eleitoral*) ballot paper; (*declaração de dívida*) I.O.U.; **~ de identidade** identity card.

**C.E.E.** *abr de* **Comunidade Econômica Europeia** E.E.C.

**ce'gar** *vt* to blind; (*ofuscar*) to dazzle; **cego/a** *adj* blind // *m* blind man // *f* blind woman; **às cegas** blindly.

**cegonha** [se'goɲa] *f* stork.

**cegueira** [se'gejra] *f* blindness; (*ignorância*) ignorance.

**ceia** ['seja] *f* evening meal.

**ceifa** ['sejfa] *f* (*colheita*) harvest; **ceifar** *vt* to reap, harvest; (*vidas*) to slaughter; **ceifeiro/a** *m/f* reaper.

**'cela** *f* cell.

**celebração** [selebra'sãw] *f* celebration; **celebrar** *vt* to celebrate; (*comemorar*) to commemorate; (*exaltar*) to praise.

**célebre** ['sɛlebrɪ] *adj* famous, well known; **celebridade** *f* celebrity.

**celeiro** [se'lejru] *m* granary; (*depósito*) barn.

**ce'leste** *adj* celestial, heavenly.

**celiba'tário/a** *adj* unmarried; (*solteiro*) single // *m* bachelor // *f* spinster; **celibato** *m* celibacy.

**celo'fane** [selo'fanɪ] *m* cellophane.

**'célula** *f* (*BIO*, *ELET*) cell.

**celu'lar** *adj* cellular.

**cem** [sẽ] *num* hundred.

**cemi'tério** *m* cemetery, graveyard.

**'cena** *f* scene; (*palco*) stage; **em ~** on the stage; **levar a ~** to stage; **cenário** *m* (*decoração teatral*) scenery; (*cinema*) scenario; (*de um acontecimento*) scene, setting.

**ce'nógrafo/a** *m/f* (*teatro*) set designer.

**cenoura** [se'nora] *f* carrot.

**'censo** *m* census.

**cen'sor** *m* censor; (*crítico*) critic; **censura** *f* (*POL etc*) censorship; (*repreensão*) censure, criticism; **censurar** *vt* (*reprovar*) to censure; (*filme, livro etc*) to censor; **censurável** *adj* blameworthy, reprehensible.

**cen'tavo** *m* cent.

**centeio** [sẽ'teju] *m* rye.

**centelha** [sẽ'teʎa] *f* spark; (*fig*) flash.

**cen'tena** *f* hundred; **às ~s** in hundreds; **centenário/a** *adj* centenary // *m/f* centenarian // *m* centenary, centennial.

**cen'tésimo/a** *adj* hundredth // *m* hundredth part.

**cen'tígrado** *m* centigrade.

**cen'tímetro** *m* centimetre.

**'cento** *m*: **aos ~s** in hundreds; **por ~** per cent.

**centopeia** [sẽto'peja] *f* centipede.

**cen'tral** [-aw] *adj* central // *f* (*de polícia etc*) head office; ~ **telefônica** telephone exchange; ~ **elétrica** (*electric*) power station; **~ização** *f* centralization; **~izar** *vt* to centralize; **centro** *m* centre, middle.

**'cepa** *f* (*cepo*) stump.

**'cepo** *m* (*toco*) stump; (*toro*) log.

**'cera** *f* wax.

**'cerca** *f* (*de madeira, arame*) fence; (*cerca viva*) hedge; (*terreno*) plot // *prep*: ~ **de** (*mais ou menos*) nearly, about.

**cer'cado** *m* enclosure, pen.

**cerca'nias** *fpl* (*arredores*) outskirts; (*vizinhança*) neighbourhood *sg*.

**cer'car** *vt* to enclose; (*pôr cerca em*) to fence in; (*rodear*) to surround; (*MIL*) to besiege.

**cercear** [sɛxsɪ'ax] vt (*cortar pela base*) to cut at the root; (*liberdade*) to curtail, restrict.

**'cerco** m encirclement; (*lugar cercado*) enclosure; (MIL) siege; **pôr ~ a** to besiege.

**cere'al** [-aw] m cereal.

**'cérebro** m brain; (*fig*) intelligence.

**cereja** [se'reʒa] f cherry; **cerejeira** f cherry tree.

**cerimónia** [seri'mɔnja] f ceremony; **sem ~** informal; (*descortês*) rude, offhand; **sem mais ~s** without more ado; **cerimonial** adj ceremonial // m etiquette; **cerimonioso/a** adj ceremonious.

**cerração** [sɛxa'sãw] f (*nevoeiro*) fog.

**cer'rado/a** adj shut, closed; (*denso*) dense, thick // m enclosure; (*vegetação*) scrub(-land); **cerrar** vt to close, shut.

**certame** [sex'tami] m (*combate*) fight; (*concurso*) contest, competition; (*discussão*) discussion.

**certeiro/a** [sex'tejru/a] adj (*tiro*) well aimed; (*acertado*) correct.

**cer'teza** f certainty; **com ~** certainly, surely; **ter ~ de** to be certain of.

**certidão** [sextʃi'dãw] f certificate.

**certifi'cado** m (*garantia*) certificate.

**certifi'car** vt to certify; (*assegurar*) to assure; **~-se** vr: **~-se de** to make sure of.

**'certo/a** adj certain, sure; (*exato*) correct, right; (*combinado*) agreed; (*um, algum*) a certain; **por ~** certainly; **ao ~** for certain; **está ~** okay.

**cerveja** [sex'veʒa] f beer; **~ria** f (*fábrica*) brewery; (*bar*) bar, public house.

**'cervo/a** m (*espécie*) deer; (*macho*) stag // f hind.

**cerzi'dura** f darning; **cerzir** vt to darn.

**cessão** [sɛ'sãw] f (*cedência*)

surrender; (*transferência*) transfer.

**ces'sar** vi to cease, stop; **sem ~** continually.

**'cesta** f basket; **cesto** m small basket; (*com rampa*) hamper; **cesto de vigia** (NÁUT) crow's nest.

**ceticismo** [setʃi'siʒmu] (Pt: **-pt-**) m scepticism; **cético/a** (Pt: **-pt-**) adj sceptical // f sceptic.

**cetim** [se'tʃĩ] m satin.

**'cetro** (Pt: **-pt-**) m sceptre.

**céu** m sky; (REL) heaven; (*boca*) roof.

**'ceva** f (*ação*) fattening; (*comida para animais*) feed; (*isca*) bait.

**ce'vada** f barley.

**ce'var** vt (*engordar*) to fatten; (*alimentar*) to feed; (*engodar*) to bait; **~-se** vr (*saciar-se*) to satisfy o.s.; (*engordar*) to get fat.

**chá** [ʃa] m tea; (*reunião*) tea party.

**cha'cal** [-aw] m jackal.

**'chácara** f (*granja*) farm; (*casa de campo*) country house.

**chacinar** [ʃasi'nax] vt (*matar*) to slaughter.

**cha'cota** f (*trova*) humorous song; (*zombaria*) mockery; **chacotear** vi: **chacotear de** to make fun of.

**chafariz** [ʃafa'riʒ] m fountain.

**cha'furdar** vi to wallow.

**'chaga** f (MED) sore; (: *na boca*) ulcer; (*fig*) wound.

**cha'lé** m chalet.

**chaleira** [ʃa'lejra] f kettle; (*bajulador*) crawler, toady.

**'chama** f flame; **em ~s** on fire.

**cha'mada** f call; (MIL) roll call; (*num livro*) note; **chamamento** m call; (*convocação*) summons sg.

**cha'mar** vt to call; (*telefone*) to ring, phone; (*atenção*) to attract; **mandar ~** to summon, send for // vi to call (out); **~-se** vr to be called; **chamo-me João** my name is John.

**chamariz** [ʃama'riʒ] m decoy; (*pio*) bird call; (*fig*) lure.

**chami'né** f chimney; (*de navio*) funnel.

**champanha** [ʃam'paɲa] *m* champagne.

**cham'pu** *m* shampoo.

**chamus'car** *vt* to scorch, singe.

**chan'cela** *f* seal, official stamp; **chancelaria** *f* chancellery.

**chantagem** [ʃan'taʒẽ] *f* blackmail; **chantagista** *m/f* blackmailer.

**chão** [ʃãw] *m* ground; (*terra*) soil.

**'chapa** *f* (*placa*) plate; (*eleitoral*) list; ~ **de matrícula** (*Pt*: AUTO) number plate.

**chapela'ria** *f* (*loja*) hatshop; **chapéu** *m* hat.

**chapinha** [ʃa'piɲa] *f*: ~ **de garrafa** bottle top.

**chapinhar** [ʃapi'ɲax] *vi* to splash.

**cha'rada** *f* (*quebra-cabeça*) puzzle.

**'charco** *m* stagnant pond.

**charlatão** [ʃaxla'tãw] *m* impostor; (*curandeiro*) quack.

**char'neca** *f* moor, heath.

**charrua** [ʃa'xua] *f* (*Pt*: *arado*) plough.

**cha'ruto** *m* cigar.

**chas'sis** *m* (AUTO, ELET) chassis.

**chateação** [ʃatʃia'sãw] *f* (*maçada*) bore; **chatear** *vt* to bother, annoy; (*aborrecer*) to bore; **chatice** *f* (*Pt*) nuisance; **chato/a** *adj* (*plano*) flat, level; (*maçante*) tiresome // *m/f* bore.

**chave** ['ʃavi] *f* key; (ELET) switch; ~ **de porcas** spanner; ~ **inglesa** (monkey) wrench; ~ **de fenda** screwdriver; **chaveiro** *m* (*utensílio*) key ring.

**'chávena** (*Pt*) *f* cup.

**'chefe** *m* head, chief; (*patrão*) boss; ~ **de turma** foreman; ~ **de estação** stationmaster; **chefia** *f* leadership; **chefiar** *vt* to lead.

**che'gada** *f* arrival.

**che'gado/a** *adj* (*próximo*) near; (*íntimo*) close, intimate.

**che'gar** *vt* (*aproximar*) to bring near // *vi* to arrive; (*ser suficiente*) to be enough; **chega!** that's enough!; ~ **a** (*atingir*) to reach; (*conseguir*)

to manage (to); ~**-se** *vr*: ~**-se a** to approach.

**cheia** ['ʃeja] *f* flood.

**'cheio/a** *adj* full, filled; (*repleto*) full up; (*farto*) fed up; ~ **de si** self-important.

**cheirar** [ʃej'rax] *vt* to smell // *vi*: ~ **a** to smell of; **cheiro** *m* smell; **cheiroso/a** *adj* scented.

**'cheque** *m* cheque; (*US*) check; (*xadrez*) check; ~ **cruzado** crossed cheque; ~ **em branco** blank cheque; ~**-mate** *m* checkmate.

**chi'ar** *vi* to squeak; (*porta*) to creak; (*vapor*) to hiss; (*fritura*) to sizzle.

**chi'bata** *f* (*vara*) cane.

**chicle** ['ʃikli] (*Pt*) *m*, **chic'lete** *m* (chewing) gum.

**chi'cória** *f* chicory.

**chi'cote** *m* whip; **chicotear** *vt* to whip, lash.

**'chifre** *m* (*corno*) horn.

**'Chile** *m* Chile; **chileno/a** *adj*, *m/f* Chilean.

**chilre'ar** *vi* to chirp, twitter; **chilreio** *m* chirping; **chilro** *m* chirping.

**chimpan'zé** *m* chimpanzee.

**'China** *f* China.

**chi'nela** *f*, **chi'nelo** *m* slipper.

**chinês/esa** [ʃi'neʃ/eza] *adj*, *m/f* Chinese.

**'chique** *adj* stylish, chic.

**chiqueiro** [ʃi'kejru] *m* pigsty.

**'chispa** *f* spark; **chispada** *f* (*Br*) dash; **chispar** *vi* to sparkle; (*correr*) to dash.

**'chita** *f* printed cotton, calico.

**choça** ['ʃosa] *f* shack, hut.

**chocalhar** [ʃoka'ʎax] *vt/i* to rattle; **chocalho** *m* (*MÚS, brinquedo*) rattle; (*para animais*) bell.

**cho'car** *vt* (*incubar*) to hatch, incubate; (*ofender*) to shock, offend // *vi* (*carros*) to collide, crash; ~**-se** *vr* (*ofender-se*) to be shocked.

**chocho/a** ['ʃoʃu/a] *adj* hollow, empty.

choco'late *m* chocolate.

cho'fer *m* driver.

chofre ['ʃofrɪ] *m*: de ~ all of a sudden.

'chope *m* draught beer.

'choque *m* (*abalo*) shock; (*colisão*) collision; (*MED, ELET*) shock; (*impacto*) impact; (*AUTO*) crash; (*conflito*) clash, conflict.

choramin'gar *vi* to whine, whimper; **choramingas** *m/f* crybaby.

chorão/rona [ʃoˈrãw/rona] *m/f* crybaby // *m* (*BOT*) weeping willow; **chorar** *vt/i* to weep, cry; **choroso/a** *adj* tearful.

choupana [ʃoˈpana] *f* shack, hut.

'choupo *m* poplar.

chouriço [ʃoˈrɪsu] *m* (*Br*) black pudding; (*Pt*) spicy sausage.

cho'ver *vi* to rain; ~ a cântaros to rain cats and dogs.

chu'lé *m* foot odour.

chum'bar *vt* to fill with lead; (*soldar*) to solder; (*rede*) to weight with lead // *vi* (*Pt: reprovar*) to fail; **chumbo** *m* lead; (*de caça*) gunshot; **cor de chumbo** leaden.

chu'par *vt* to suck; (*absorver*) to absorb; (*parasitar*) to sponge on.

chu'peta *f* (*para criança*) dummy; (*US*) pacifier.

chur'rasco *m* barbecue.

chu'tar *vt* to kick // *vi* to shoot; **chute** *m* kick, shot; **chuteira** *f* football boot.

'chuva *f* rain; ~**-de-pedra** *f* hailstorm; **chuveiro** *m* shower; **chuviscar** *vi* to drizzle; **chuvisco** *m* drizzle; **chuvoso/a** *adj* rainy.

Cⁱᵃ *abr de* **companhia** Co., company.

cicatriz [sikaˈtrɪʃ] *f* scar.

ciciar [sɪsɪˈax] *vi* to whisper; (*rumorejar*) to murmur.

cic'lismo *m* cycling; **ciclista** *m/f* cyclist.

'ciclo *m* cycle.

ci'clone *m* cyclone.

cidadão/cidadã [sidaˈdãw/ sidaˈdã] *m/f* citizen; **cidade** *f* town; (*grande*) city; **cidadela** *f* citadel.

ciência [sjˈensja] *f* science; (*erudição*) knowledge; **ciente** *adj* aware, informed; **científico/a** *adj* scientific; **cientista** *m/f* scientist.

'cifra *f* (*escrita secreta*) cipher; (*algarismo*) number, figure; **cifrão** *m* dollar sign.

ci'frar *vt* to write in code.

ci'gano/a *adj, m/f* gypsy.

ci'garra [-axa] *f* cicada; (*ELET*) buzzer.

cigarreira [sigaˈxejra] *f* (*estojo*) cigarette case; **cigarro** *m* cigarette.

ci'lada *f* (*emboscada*) ambush; (*armadilha*) trap; (*embuste*) trick.

ci'líndrico/a *adj* cylindrical; **cilindro** *m* cylinder; (*rolo*) roller.

'cima *f*: **de ~ para baixo** from top to bottom; **para ~** up // *prep*: **em ~ de on top of**; **por ~ de** over; **cimeira** *f* (*Pt*) summit.

cimen'tar *vt* to cement; (*fig*) to strengthen; **cimento** *m* cement; (*fig*) foundation; **cimento armado** reinforced concrete.

'cimo *m* top, summit.

'cinco *num* five.

ci'nema *m* cinema, movies *pl*.

cingir [sĩˈʒix] *vt* (*pôr à cintura*) to fasten round one's waist; (*cercar*) to encircle, ring; ~**se** *vr*: ~**se a** (*restringir-se*) to restrict o.s. to; (*chegar-se*) to keep close to, hug.

'cínico/a *adj* cynical; (*impudico*) shameless // *m/f* cynic; **cinismo** *m* cynicism; (*impudência*) shamelessness.

cinqüenta [sĩˈkwenta] *num* fifty.

'cinta *f* (*banda*) sash; (*de mulher*) girdle.

cinti'lar *vi* to sparkle, glitter.

'cinto *m* belt; (*faixa*) sash; ~ **de segurança** safety belt; (*AUTO*) seatbelt.

cin'tura *f* waist; (*linha*) waistline.

**'cinza** f ash, ashes pl; **cinzeiro** m ashtray.

**cin'zel** [-ɛw] m chisel; **cinzelar** vt to chisel; (gravar) to carve, engrave.

**cin'zento/a** adj grey.

**cioso/a** [sɪ'ozu/a] adj (zeloso) zealous.

**ci'pó** m liana, creeper.

**ci'preste** m cypress (tree).

**cipri'ota** adj, m/f Cypriot.

**'circo** m circus.

**circuito** [sɪx'kwitu] m circuit; **curto** ~ short circuit.

**circulação** [sɪxkula'sãw] f circulation; (trânsito) movement; **circular** adj circular, round // f (carta) circular // vi to circulate; (trânsito) to move, flow; **circulem!** move on!; **círculo** m circle.

**circunci'dar** vt to circumcise; **circuncisão** f circumcision; **circunciso/a** adj circumcised.

**circunfe'rência** f circumference.

**circun'flexo/a** adj circumflex // m circumflex.

**circun'screver** vt to circumscribe, limit.

**circunspeção** [sɪxkunʃpe'sãw] (Pt: **-cç-**) f circumspection; **circunspeto/a** adj cautious; (sisudo) serious.

**circun'stância** f circumstance; **circunstanciado/a** adj detailed.

**circun'stante** m/f onlooker, bystander; ~s mpl audience.

**cir'rose** [-ɪxo-] f cirrhosis.

**cirurgia** [sɪrux'ʒɪa] f surgery; ~ **plástica/estética** plastic surgery; **cirurgião** m surgeon.

**cisão** [sɪ'zãw] f (divisão) split, division; (desacordo) disagreement.

**cisma** ['sɪʒma] m schism // f worry; (suspeita) suspicion; **cismar** vi to worry; (LITER: fantasiar) to daydream; (Br: suspeitar) to suspect.

**cisne** ['sɪʒnɪ] m swan.

**cis'terna** f cistern, tank.

**'cisto** m cyst.

**citação** [sɪta'sãw] f quotation; (JUR)

summons sg; **citar** vt to quote; (JUR) to summon.

**ciúme** [sɪ'umɪ] m jealousy; **ter** ~**s de** to be jealous of; **ciumento/a** adj jealous.

**ci'vil** [-ɪw] adj civil; (cortês) polite // m/f civilian; ~**idade** f politeness.

**civilização** [sɪvɪlɪza'sãw] f civilization; **civilizar** vt to civilize.

**ci'vismo** m public spirit.

**cla'mar** vt to clamour for // vi to cry out, clamour; **clamor** m outcry, uproar; **clamoroso/a** adj noisy.

**clandes'tino/a** adj clandestine; (ilegal) underground.

**'clara** f white of egg.

**clarabóia** [klara'bɔja] f skylight.

**clarão** [kla'rãw] m (cintilação) flash; (claridade) gleam.

**clare'ar** vi (o dia) to dawn; (o tempo) to clear up, brighten up.

**clareira** [kla'rejra] f (na mata) clearing.

**cla'reza** f (nitidez) clarity; **claridade** f (luz) brightness; **clarificação** f clarification; **clarificar** vt to clarify.

**clarim** [kla'rĩ] m bugle.

**clari'nete** m clarinet; (pessoa) clarinetist.

**'claro/a** adj (gen) clear; (luminoso) bright; (côr) light; (evidente) clear, evident // m (na escrita) space; (clareira) clearing // adv clearly; **às claras** openly // excl of course!

**'classe** f class; ~ **média/operária** middle/working class.

**'clássico/a** adj classical; (fig) classic.

**classificação** [klasɪfɪka'sãw] f classification; **classificar** vt to classify.

**claustro** ['klawʃtru] m cloister.

**cláusula** ['klawzula] f clause.

**'clava** f (pau) club.

**'clave** f (MÚS) clef.

**cla'vícula** f collar bone.

**cle'mência** f mercy; **clemente** adj merciful.

**cleptoma'níaco/a** _m/f_ kleptomaniac.

**'clérigo** _m_ clergyman; **clero** _m_ clergy.

**cli'ché** _m_ (FOTO) plate; (chavão) cliché.

**cli'ente** _m_ client; (loja) customer; (de médico) patient; **clientela** _f_ clientele; (loja) customers _pl_; (de médico) patients _pl_.

**'clima** _m_ climate.

**'clínico/a** _adj_ clinical // _m_ doctor // _f_ clinic; (particular) practice.

**'clipe** _m_ clip; (para papéis) paper clip.

**clo'rídrico/a** _adj_ hydrochloric.

**cloro'fórmio** _m_ chloroform.

**'clube** _m_ club.

**coabi'tar** _vi_ to live together, cohabit.

**coação** [koa'sãw] (Pt: **-cç-**) _f_ coercion.

**coa'dor** _m_ strainer.

**coagir** [koa'ʒix] _vt_ to coerce, compel.

**coagu'lar** _vt/i_ to coagulate; (sangue) to congeal, clot; **~-se** _vr_ to congeal; **coágulo** _m_ clot.

**coalhar** [koa'ʎax] _vt/i_ (leite) to curdle; **~-se** _vr_ to curdle.

**coalizão** [koali'zãw] _f_ coalition.

**co'ar** _vt_ (líquido) to strain.

**coa'xar** _vi_ to croak.

**cobaia** [ko'baja] _f_ guinea pig.

**co'berto/a** _pp de_ **cobrir** // _adj_ covered // _f_ cover, covering; (NÁUT) deck; **cobertor** _m_ blanket; **cobertura** _f_ covering; (telhado) roof; (apartamento) penthouse.

**cobiça** [ko'bisa] _f_ greed; (desejo) desire; **cobiçar** _vt_ to covet; **cobiçoso/a** _adj_ covetous.

**'cobra** _f_ snake.

**cobra'dor** _m_ — collector; (transporte) conductor; **cobrança** _f_ collection.

**co'brar** _vt_ to collect; (cheque) to cash; (preço) to charge; (reaver) to get back.

**'cobre** _m_ copper.

**co'brir** _vt_ to cover; (ocultar) to hide, conceal; (proteger) to protect.

**co'cada** _f_ coconut sweet.

**co'çar** _vt_ to scratch; **~-se** _vr_ to scratch o.s.; **não ter tempo para se ~** to have no time to spare.

**cócegas** ['kɔsɛgaʃ] _fpl_ **fazer ~** to tickle; **tenho ~ nos pés** my feet tickle.

**'coche** _m_ (carruagem) coach.

**cochichar** [koʃi'ʃax] _vi_ to whisper.

**cochi'lar** _vi_ to snooze, doze.

**'coco** _m_ coconut.

**'cócoras** _fpl_: **de ~** squatting.

**côdea** ['kodja] (Pt) _f_ (de pão) crust; (de queijo) rind.

**'código** _m_ code.

**codor'niz** _f_ quail.

**coelho** ['kweʎu] _m_ rabbit.

**coerção** [koex'sãw] _f_ coercion, compulsion.

**coe'rência** _f_ coherence; **coerente** _adj_ coherent.

**coesão** [koe'zãw] _f_ cohesion.

**coetâneo/a** [koe'tanju/a] _adj_ contemporary.

**coexis'tência** _f_ coexistence; **coexistir** _vi_ to coexist.

**'cofre** _m_ safe; (caixa) strongbox.

**cogitar** [koʒi'tax] _vt/i_ to contemplate.

**cogu'melo** _m_ mushroom; **~ venenoso** toadstool.

**coibição** [koibi'sãw] _f_ restraint, restriction; **coibir** _vt_ to restrain; **coibir de** to restrain from; **coibir-se** _vr_: **coibir-se de** to abstain from.

**coice** ['kojsi] _m_ kick; (de arma) recoil; **dar ~s** to kick.

**coinci'dência** _f_ coincidence; **coincidir** _vi_ to coincide; (concordar) to agree.

**coisa** ['kojza] _f_ thing; (assunto) affair; **~ de** about.

**coitado/a** [koj'tadu/a] _adj_ poor, wretched; **~ !** poor thing!

**coito** ['kojtu] _m_ intercourse, coitus.

**'cola** f glue, gum; (rabo) tail; (Br: cópia) crib.

**colaboração** [kolabura'sãw] f collaboration; **colaborar** vi to collaborate.

**co'lapso** m collapse; ~ **cardíaco** heart failure.

**co'lar** vt to stick, glue; (vinho) to clarify; (Br: copiar) to crib; ~ **grau** to graduate // m necklace; ~**inho** m collar.

**'colcha** f bedspread; **colchão** m mattress.

**col'chete** m clasp, fastening; (parêntese) square bracket; ~ **de gancho** hook and eye; ~ **de pressão** press stud.

**coleção** [kole'sãw] (Pt: -cç-) f collection; **colecionar** (Pt: -cc-) vt to collect.

**co'lega** m/f colleague.

**co'légio** [ko'lεʒju] m college; (escola) (private) school.

**'cólera** f (ira) anger; (fúria) rage; (MED) cholera; **colérico/a** (irado) angry; (furioso) furious // m/f (MED) cholera patient.

**co'leta** (Pt: **-ct-**) f collection; **coletar** (Pt: -ct-) vt to tax.

**co'lete** m waistcoat; (US) vest; (de senhora) corset; ~ **de forças** straitjacket; ~ **de salvação** life jacket; (US) life preserver.

**coletivi'dade** (Pt: **-ct-**) f community; **coletivo/a** (Pt: -ct-) adj collective, joint.

**colheita** [ko'ʎejta] f harvest; (produto) crop.

**co'lher** [ko'ʎex] vt (recolher) to gather, pick; (prender) to catch.

**co'lher** [ko'ʎex] f spoon; **colherada** f spoonful; **colherão** m ladle.

**coli'bri** m hummingbird.

**'cólica** f colic.

**co'lidir** vi: ~ **com** to collide with, crash into.

**coligação** [koliga'sãw] f coalition; **coligir** [koli'ʒix] vt to collect.

**co'lina** f hill.

**colisão** [koli'zãw] f collision, crash.

**col'mar** vt to thatch.

**colmeia** [kow'meja] f beehive.

**colmilho** [kow'mɪʎu] m (dente) eye tooth; (de elefante) tusk; (de cão) fang.

**'colo** m (pescoço) neck; (peito) bosom; (regaço) lap; **no** ~ on one's lap, in one's arms.

**colocação** [koloka'sãw] f placing; (emprego) job, position; **colocar** vt to place, position; (empregar) to find a job for; (COM) to market.

**Co'lômbia** f Colombia; **colombiano/a** adj, m/f Colombian.

**'cólon** m colon.

**co'lônia** f colony.

**colonização** [koloniza'sãw] f colonization; **colonizador(a)** adj colonizing // m/f colonist, settler; **colonizar** vt to colonize; **colono** m settler; (cultivador) farmer.

**colóquio** [ko'lokju] m conversation; (congresso) conference.

**colo'rido** m colouring, colour; **colorir** vt to colour; (fig) to disguise.

**co'luna** f column; (pilar) pillar; ~ **vertebral** spine.

**com** [kõ] prep with; (apesar de) in spite of; ~ **que** so, and so; ~ **que então!** so!

**co'madre** f (mexeriqueira) gossip, crony; **minha** ~ the godmother of my child ou the mother of my godchild.

**coman'dante** m commander; (MIL) commandant; (NÁUT) captain; **comandar** vt to command; **comando** m command; **comando a distância** remote control.

**com'bate** m combat, fight; (fig) battle; **combatente** m/f combatant; **combater** vt to fight, combat // vi to fight.

**combinação** [kõbina'sãw] f combination; (QUÍM) compound; (acordo) arrangement; (plano) scheme; (roupa) slip; **combinar** vt to

**combine;** (arranjar) to arrange; **combinado!** agreed!

**comboio** [kõ'boju] m (Pt) train; (de navios) convoy.

**combustão** [kobuʃ'tãw] f combustion; **combustível** m fuel.

**começar** [kome'sax] vt/i to begin, start, commence; **começo** m beginning, start.

**co'média** f comedy; (teatro) play, drama; **comediante** m (comic) actor // f (comic) actress.

**come'dido/a** adj moderate; (prudente) prudent; (discreto) discreet; **comedir-se** vr to control o.s.

**comemoração** [komemora'sãw] f commemoration, celebration; **comemorar** vt to celebrate, commemorate.

**comen'tar** vt to comment on; **comentário** m comment, remark; (análise) commentary.

**co'mer** vt to eat (up); (damas, xadrez) to take, capture // vi to eat; **dar de ~ a** to feed; **~-se** vr: **~-se (de)** to be consumed with.

**comerci'al** adj commercial; (relativo ao negócio) business cmp; **comerciante** m/f trader, merchant; **comerciar** vi to trade, do business; **comércio** m commerce; (tráfico) trade; (negócio) business; (fig) dealings pl.

**comes'tível** adj edible // mpl: ~s foodstuff.

**co'meta** m comet.

**come'ter** vt to commit; **cometimento** m undertaking, commitment.

**comichão** [komi'ʃãw] f itch, itching.

**comício** [ko'misju] m meeting; (assembléia) assembly.

**'cômico/a** adj comic(al) // m comedian; (de teatro) actor.

**co'mida** f (alimento) food; (refeição) meal.

**co'migo** pron with me; with myself.

**comilão/lona** [komi'lãw/lona] adj greedy // m/f glutton.

**comissão** [komi'sãw] f commission; (comitê) committee; **comissário** m commissioner; (COM) agent; **comissário de bordo** purser.

**comi'tê** m committee.

**comi'tiva** f retinue.

**'como** adv as; (assim como) like; (de que maneira) how; ~? what?, I beg your pardon?; ~ **assim?** how come?; ~ **que morto as if dead** // excl what!; ~ **não!** of course! // conj (porque) as, since; (quando) when; ~ **se** as if; ~ **quer que** however; **seja ~ for** be that as it may.

**comoção** [komo'sãw] f (confusão) commotion; ~ **nervosa** shock.

**comodi'dade** f (conforto) comfort; (conveniência) suitability; **cômodo/a** adj (confortável) comfortable; (conveniente) convenient; (próprio) suitable // m (aposento) room // f chest of drawers; (US) bureau.

**comove'dor(a)** adj moving, touching; **comover** vt to move; **comover-se** vr to be moved; **comovido/a** adj moved, touched.

**com'pacto/a** adj (comprimido) compact; (espesso) thick; (sólido) solid.

**compade'cer** vt (ter compaixão de) to pity; (tolerar) to bear; ~-se vr: ~-se **de** to be sorry for, pity; **compadecido/a** adj sympathetic; **compadecimento** m sympathy; (piedade) pity.

**com'padre** m (col: companheiro) buddy, pal, crony; **meu** ~ the godfather of my child ou the father of my godchild.

**compaixão** [kõpaj'ʃãw] m (piedade) compassion, pity; (misericórdia) mercy.

**companheiro/a** [kõpa'ɲejru/a] m/f (colega) friend; (col) buddy, mate; ~ **de trabalho** fellow-worker; ~ **de viagem** fellow traveller.

**companhia** [kõpaˈɲia] f (COM) company, firm; (convivência) company; **fazer ~ a alguém** to keep sb company; **em ~ de** accompanied by, along with.

**comparação** [kõparaˈsãw] f comparison; **comparar** vt (cotejar) to compare; **comparar a** to liken to; **comparar com** to compare with; **comparar-se** vr: **comparar-se com** to bear comparison with; **comparativo/a** adj comparative; **comparável** adj comparable.

**compare'cer** vi to appear, show up; **~ a uma reunião** to attend a meeting; **comparecimento** m (presença) attendance.

**com'parsa** m/f (teatro) extra; (cúmplice) accomplice.

**compartilhar** [kõpaxtʃiˈʎax] vt (partilhar) to share; **~ de** (participar de) to share in, participate in; **~ com alguém** to share with sb.

**comparti'mento** m (divisão de móvel/veículo) compartment; (aposento) room; **compartir** vt (dividir) to share out.

**compas'sado/a** adj (medido) measured; (moderado) moderate; (cadenciado) regular.

**com'passo** m (instrumento) a pair of compasses; (MÚS) time; (ritmo) beat; **dentro do ~** in time with the music; **fora do ~** out of time.

**compatibili'dade** f compatibility; **compatível** adj compatible.

**compatri'ota** m fellow countryman, compatriot // f fellow countrywoman.

**compe'lir** vt to force, compel.

**com'pêndio** m (sumário) compendium; (livro de texto) text book.

**compenetração** [kõpenetraˈsãw] f conviction; **compenetrar-se** vr (convencer-se) to be convinced.

**compensação** [kõpẽsaˈsãw] f compensation; (de cheques) clearance; **em ~** on the other hand; **compensar** vt (reparar o dano) to make up for, compensate for; (equilibrar) to offset, counterbalance; **compensatório/a** adj compensatory.

**compe'tência** f (habilidade) competence; (aptidão) ability; **competente** adj (capaz) competent; (idôneo) suitable.

**competição** [kõpetʃiˈsãw] f (rivalidade) competition; (desafio) contest; **competidor(a)** m/f competitor, contestant.

**compe'tir** vi to compete; (ser da competência de) to be one's responsibility; **compete-lhe decidir** it is up to you to decide; **~ com** (rivalizar) to compete with, rival; **competitivo/a** adj competitive.

**compla'cência** f complaisance; **complacente** adj obliging.

**compleição** [kõplejˈsãw] f (estatura) build; (temperamento) temperament, disposition.

**complemen'tar** adj complementary; **complemento** m complement.

**completa'mente** adv completely, quite.

**comple'tar** vt (concluir) to complete, finish; (atingir) to reach; **~ dez anos** to be ten; **completo/a** adj complete; (cheio) full (up) // m whole; **por completo** completely.

**complexi'dade** f complexity; **complexo/a** adj complex; (difícil) complicated // m complex.

**complicação** [kõplikaˈsãw] f complication; (dificuldade) difficulty; **complicado/a** adj complicated; **complicar** vt to complicate, make difficult; **complicar-se** vr to become complicated; (enredo) to thicken.

**compo'nente** adj, m component.

**com'por** vt (MÚS) to compose; (discurso, livro) to write; (arranjar) to arrange; (aliviar) to settle;

(*imprensa*) to set; ~**-se** *vr* (*tranquilizar-se*) to calm down; ~**-se de** to be made up of, be composed of.

**com'porta** *f* floodgate; (*de canal*) lock; ~**s** *fpl* wiles.

**comporta'mento** *m* behaviour; (*conduta*) conduct; **mau** ~ (*de criança*) misbehaviour; (*de adulto*) misconduct.

**compor'tar** *vt* (*suportar*) to put up with, bear; (*conter*) to hold; ~**-se** *vr* (*portar-se*) to behave; (*ter bons modos*) to behave o.s.; ~**-se mal** (*criança*) to misbehave, behave badly.

**composição** [kõpozi'sãw] *f* composition; (*imprensa*) type-setting; (*conciliação*) compromise; **compositor(a)** *m/f* composer; (*imprensa*) typesetter.

**com'posto/a** *adj* (*sério*) serious; (*de muitos elementos*) composite, compound; ~ **de** made up of, composed of // *m* compound.

**compos'tura** *f* composure.

**com'pota** *f* jam; (*US*) fruit preserve; ~ **de laranja** marmalade.

**'compra** *f* purchase; (*suborno*) bribe; **fazer** ~**s** to go shopping; **comprador(a)** *m/f* buyer, purchaser; **comprar** *vt* to buy, purchase; (*subornar*) to bribe.

**compreender** [kõpriẽ'dex] *vt* (*entender*) to understand; (*conter em si*) to be comprised of, consist of; **compreensão** *f* understanding, comprehension; **compreensível** *adj* understandable, comprehensible; **compreensivo/a** *adj* understanding.

**compressão** [kõpre'sãw] *f* compression.

**com'prido/a** *adj* long; **ao** ~ lengthways; **comprimento** *m* length.

**compri'mido/a** *adj* compressed // *m* (*pílula*) pill; (*pastilha*) tablet; **comprimir** *vt* to compress; (*apertar*) to squeeze; (*condensar*) to condense.

(*arriscar*) to endanger, jeopardize; (*empenhar*) to pledge; ~**-se** *vr*: ~**-se a** to undertake to, promise to; ~**-se com uma moça** to promise to marry a girl.

**compro'misso** *m* (*promessa*) promise; (*obrigação*) obligation; (*hora marcada*) appointment; (*encontro*) engagement, commitment; (*acordo*) agreement; **sem** ~ without obligation.

**comprovação** [kõprova'sãw] *f* proof; (*provas*) evidence; (*ADMIN*) receipt, voucher; **comprovar** *vt* to prove; (*confirmar*) to confirm.

**compul'sivo/a** *adj* compulsive; **compulsório/a** *adj* compulsory.

**compunção** [kõpũ'sãw] *f* compunction.

**computação** [kõputa'sãw] *f* computation; **computador(a)** *adj* (*que faz cômputos*) computing; (*que calcula*) calculating // *m* computer; **computar** *vt* to compute; (*calcular*) to calculate; (*contar*) to count; **cômputo** *m* computation.

**comum** [ko'mũ] *adj* (*de todos*) common; (*habitual*) ordinary, usual // *m* the usual thing; **o** ~ **é partirmos às 8** we usually set off at 8; **fora do** ~ unusual.

**comun'gar** *vi* to take communion; ~ **em** (*participar em*) to share; ~ **com** (*unir-se*) to commune with; **comunhão** *f* communion; (*REL*) Holy Communion; **comunhão de bens** joint ownership.

**comunicação** [komunika'sãw] *f* communication; (*informações*) information; (*mensagem*) message; **comunicado** *m* report; (*oficial*) communiqué.

**comuni'car** *vt* (*informar*) to report; (*transmitir*) to pass on, communicate; (*revelar*) to make known; (*unir*) to join // *vi*

---

**compromete'dor(a)** *adj* compromising.

**comprome'ter** *vt* to compromise;

(estabelecer comunicação) to communicate.

**comuni'dade** f community.

**comu'nismo** m communism; **comunista** adj, m/f communist.

**comu'tar** vt (JUR) to commute; (trocar) to exchange.

**'côncavo/a** adj concave; (cavado) hollow // m hollow.

**conce'ber** vt (ger) to conceive; (imaginar) to conceive of, imagine // vi to become pregnant.

**conce'der** vt (permitir) to allow; (outorgar) to grant; (admitir) to admit; (dar) to give.

**concei'ção** [kõsej'sãw] f Immaculate Conception.

**conceito** [kõ'sejtu] m (idéia) concept, idea; (fama) reputation; (opinião) opinion; **conceituado/a** adj well thought of, highly regarded.

**concelho** [kõ'seʎu] m (administração) council; (município) district.

**concentração** [kõsẽtra'sãw] f concentration; **concentrado/a** adj concentrated // m concentrate.

**concen'trar** vt to concentrate; (atenção) to focus; (reunir) to bring together; ~**-se** vr: ~**-se em** to concentrate on.

**concepção** [kõsep'sãw] f (geração) conception; (noção) idea, concept; (opinião) opinion.

**concer'tar** vt (arranjar) to fix, put right; (combinar) to settle; (opiniões) to reconcile; (uma disputa) to settle // vi: ~ **em** (concordar) to agree to.

**con'certo** m (espetáculo) concert; (composição) concerto; (acordo) agreement, harmony.

**concessão** [kõse'sãw] f concession; (permissão) permission; (doação) grant; **concessionário** m concessionaire.

**concha** ['kõʃa] f (moluscos) shell; (para líquidos) ladle; (para farinha) scoop.

**conchavar** [kõʃa'vax] vi (conluiarse) to conspire.

**conciliação** [kõsilia'sãw] f (acordo) compromise; (harmonização) reconciliation; **conciliador/a** adj conciliatory // m/f conciliator; **conciliar** vt (reconciliar) to reconcile; **conciliatório/a** adj conciliatory.

**concílio** [kõ'siliu] m (REL) council.

**con'ciso/a** adj brief, concise.

**conci'tar** vt (estimular) to stir up, arouse; (incitar) to incite.

**conclu'dente** adj (categórico) conclusive; (merecendo fé) convincing.

**concluir** [kõ'klwix] vt (terminar) to end, conclude // vi (deduzir) to conclude; **conclusão** f (término) end; (dedução) conclusion; **chegar a uma conclusão** to come to a decision; **conclusivo/a** adj conclusive; (final) final.

**concor'dância** f (acordo) agreement; (harmonia) harmony; **concordar** vi to agree; **não concordo!** I disagree!; **concórdia** f (harmonia) harmony; (acordo) agreement; (paz) peace.

**concor'rência** f (competição) competition; **concorrente** m/f (competidor) competitor; **concorrer** vi (competir) to compete; **concorrer para** (contribuir) to contribute to.

**concreti'zar** vt to make real; ~**-se** vr (sonho) to come true; (ambições) to be realized.

**con'creto/a** adj concrete; (verdadeiro) real; (sólido) solid // m concrete; ~ **armado** reinforced concrete.

**concupiscência** [kõkupiˈsẽsja] f (desejo de bens) greed; (apetite sexual) lust.

**con'curso** m (competição) competition.

**concussão** [kõku'sãw] f concussion.

**condão** [kõ'dãw] m (dom) talent;

(*poder misterioso*) magic power; **varinha de** ~ magic wand.
**'conde** *m* count.
**condecoração** [kõdekora'sãw] *f* (*insígnia*) decoration; (*medalha*) medal; **condecorar** *vt* (*dar uma insígnia*) to decorate.
**condenação** [kõdena'sãw] *f* condemnation; (*JUR*) conviction; ~ **eterna** damnation; **condenar** *vt* to condemn; (*JUR*: *sentenciar*) to sentence; (*JUR*: *declarar culpado*) to convict.
**condescen'dência** *f* acquiescence, tolerance; **condescender** *vi* (*concordar*) to agree; (*ceder*) to give in; **condescender a/em** to condescend to, deign to.
**con'dessa** *f* countess.
**condição** [kõdʒi'sãw] *f* condition; (*social*) status; **ter** ~ **para** to be fit to, be able to; **com a** ~ **de que** on condition that, provided that; **condições** *fpl* terms, conditions; **pôr em condições** to put in order.
**condicionado/a** [kõdʒisjo'nadu/a] *adj* conditioned; **ar** ~ air conditioning; **condicional** *adj* conditional; **condicionamento** *m* conditioning.
**con'digno/a** *adj* (*adequado*) fitting; (*merecido*) due.
**condimen'tar** *vt* to season; **condimento** *m* seasoning.
**condi'zente** *adj*: ~ **com** in keeping with; **condizer** *vi*: **condizer com** to match, go well together; **não condizer** to clash.
**condo'er-se** *vr*: ~ **com** to sympathize with; **condolência** *f* condolence.
**condução** [kõdu'sãw] *f* (*ato de conduzir*) driving; (*transporte*) transport; (*física*) conduction; **carta de** ~ (*Pt*) driving licence.
**con'duta** *f* behaviour; **má** ~ misbehaviour.
**con'duto** *m* (*tubo*) tube; (*cano*) pipe; (*canal*) channel.

**condu'tor** *m* (*MÚS*: *ELET*) conductor; (*de veículo*) driver; (*guia*) guide; (*chefe*) leader; **conduzir** *vt* (*Pt*: *veículo*) to drive; (*levar*) to lead; (*guiar*) to guide; (*negócio*) to manage; (*física*) to conduct; **conduzir-se** to behave.
**'cônego** *m* (*REL*) canon.
**conexão** [konɛk'sãw] *f* connection.
**confecção** [kõfɛk'sãw] *f* making; **roupa de** ~ ready-made clothes *pl*; **confecções** *fpl* manufacturing *sg*; **confeccionar** *vt* (*fazer*) to make; (*fabricar*) to manufacture.
**confederação** [kõfedera'sãw] *f* confederation; (*liga*) league.
**confede'rar** *vt* to unite; ~-**se** *vt* to form an alliance.
**confeitar** [kõfej'tax] *vt* (*bolo*) to ice; **confeitaria** *f* sweet shop, confectioner's; (*US*) candy store; **confeiteiro/a** *m/f* confectioner.
**confe'rência** *f* conference; (*discurso*) lecture; **conferencista** *m* (*que fala*) speaker; **conferente** *m* (*verificador*) checker.
**confe'rir** *vt* (*verificar*) to check; (*outorgar*) to grant; (*título*) to confer // *vi*: ~ **com** (*discutir*) to confer with; (*estar certo*) to tally.
**confes'sar** *vt* to confess; ~ **alguém** (*REL*) to hear sb's confession; ~-**se** *vr* to confess; ~-**se culpado** (*JUR*) to plead guilty; **confessionário** *m* confessional; **confessor** *m* confessor.
**con'fetes** *mpl* confetti.
**confi'ado/a** *adj* familiar; (*col*) cheeky.
**confi'ança** *f* confidence; (*fé*) faith; (*atrevimento*) familiarity; **de** ~ reliable; **digno de** ~ trustworthy.
**confi'ar** *vt* to entrust // *vi*: ~ **em** (*fiar*) to trust; (*contar*) to confide in; (*esperar*) to hope; ~-**se** *vr* to trust.
**confi'dência** *f* secret; **em** ~ in confidence; **confidencial** *adj* confidential; **confidente** *m* confidant // *f* confidante.

**configuração** [kõfiguraˈsãw] *f* configuration; (*forma*) shape, form; **configurar** *vt* to shape, form; **configurar-se** *vr* to take shape.

**confi'nar** *vt* (*limitar*) to limit; (*encerrar*) to confine // *vi*: ~ **com** to border on; **~-se** *vr*: **~-se a** to confine o.s. to; **confins** *mpl* limits, boundaries.

**confirmação** [kõfirmaˈsãw] *f* confirmation; **confirmar** *vt* to confirm; **confirmar-se** *vr* (REL) to be confirmed; (*realizar-se*) to come true.

**confiscação** [kõfiʃkaˈsãw] *f* confiscation, seizure; **confiscar** *vt* to confiscate, seize.

**confissão** [kõfiˈsãw] *f* confession.

**conflagração** [kõflagraˈsãw] *f* conflagration, blaze; **conflagrar** *vt* to inflame, set alight.

**con'flito** *m* (*luta*) conflict; (*guerra*) war; (*combate*) fight; **entrar em ~ com** to clash with.

**conflu'ente** *m* tributary; **confluir** *vi* to flow together.

**conformação** [kõfoxmaˈsãw] *f* (*resignação*) resignation; **conformado/a** *adj* resigned.

**confor'mar** *vt* (*formar*) to form; **~-se** *vr*: **~-se com** to resign o.s. to.

**con'forme** *adj*: ~ **com** in agreement with // *prep* according to, as // *conj* (*logo que*) as soon as.

**conformi'dade** *f* agreement; **em ~ com** in accordance with; **conformista** *m/f* conformist.

**confor'tar** *vt* (*consolar*) to comfort, console; **confortável** *adj* comfortable; **conforto** *m* comfort.

**confranger** [kõfrãˈʒex] *vt* (*afligir*) to torment; **~-se** *vr* to be distressed; **confrangido/a** *adj* distressed, upset.

**confra'ria** *f* fraternity; brotherhood; **confraternizar** *vi* to fraternize.

**confron'tar** *vt* (*acarear*) to confront; (*cotejar*) to compare;

~**-se** *vr* to face each other.

**confun'dir** *vt* (*não distinguir*) to confuse, mistake; (*embaralhar*) to mix up; (*perturbar*) to confuse; ~ **com** to mistake for; **~-se** *vr* to get mixed up, become confused.

**confusão** [kõfuˈzãw] *f* (*tumulto, falta de clareza*) confusion; (*perplexidade*) bewilderment; **que ~!** what a muddle!; **confuso/a** *adj* (*misturado*) jumbled, mixed up; (*perturbado*) confused, bewildered.

**congelação** [kõʒelaˈsãw] *f* (Pt) (*frio*) freezing; (*solidificação*) congealing; **congelador** *m* freezer, deep freeze; **congelamento** *m* freezing; (ECON) freeze; **congelar** *vt* (*gelar*) to freeze; (*solidificar*) to congeal; **congelar-se** *vr* to freeze.

**con'gênito/a** *adj* congenital.

**congestão** [kõʒeʃˈtãw] *f* congestion; **congestionado/a** *adj* (*olhos*) bloodshot; (*rosto*) flushed; **congestionar-se** *vr* to flush, go red.

**conglomeração** [kõglomeraˈsãw] *f* conglomeration; **conglomerado** *m* conglomerate; **conglomerar** *vt* to heap together; **conglomerar-se** *vr* (*unir-se*) to join together, group together.

**congraça'mento** *m* confraternization.

**congratu'lar** *vt*: ~ **alguém por** to congratulate sb on; **~-se** *vr*: **~-se com alguém por ter ganho** to congratulate sb on winning.

**congregação** [kõgregaˈsãw] *f* (REL) congregation; (*reunião*) gathering; **congregar** *vt* to assemble; **congregar-se** *vr* to assemble, gather together.

**congres'sista** *m* congressman // *f* congresswoman; **congresso** *m* congress.

**conhaque** [koˈnaki] *m* cognac, brandy.

**conhecer** [koɲeˈsex] *vt* to know; (*estar consciente de*) to be aware of; ~**-se** *vr* to get to know one another;

**quero conhecê-la** I want to get to know her; **conheci-o no ano passado** I met him last year; **que eu conheça não** not to my knowledge; **conhecido/a adj** known; (*célebre*) well-known // *m/f* acquaintance.

**conhecimento** [koɲesi'mẽtu] *m* (*erudição*) knowledge; (*compreensão*) understanding; (*COM*) bill of lading; **levar ao ~ de alguém** to bring to sb's notice; **ter ~ de** to be aware of; **tomar ~ de** to look into.

**coni'vente** *adj* conniving; **ser ~ em** to connive in.

**conjetura** [kõʒe'tura] (*Pt:* -**ct**-) *f* conjecture, guessing; **fazer ~ sobre** to guess (at).

**conjugal** [kõʒu'gaw] *adj* conjugal; **vida ~** married life; **conjugar** *vt* (*verbo*) to conjugate; (*unir*) to join; **conjugar-se** *vr* to join together; **cônjuge** *m* husband // *f* wife.

**conjunção** [kõʒũ'sãw] *f* (*união*) union; (*LING*) conjunction.

**conjun'tivo** *m* (*Pt:* LING) subjunctive.

**con'junto/a** *adj* joint; **em ~ together** // *m* (*totalidade*) whole; (*coleção*) collection; (*equipe*) team; (*músicos*) group; (*roupa*) outfit.

**conjun'tura** *f* (*situação*) situation; (*momento*) juncture.

**conjuração** [kõʒura'sãw] *f* plot, conspiracy; **conjurado/a** *m/f* conspirator.

**conju'rar** *vt* (*maquinar*) to plot // *vi*: ~ **contra** to plot against.

**co'nosco** (*Pt:* -**nn**-) *pron* with us.

**conquanto** [kõ'kwãtu] *conj* although, though.

**conquista** [kõ'kiʃta] *f* (*vitória*) conquest; (*da ciência*) achievement; **conquistar** *vt* (*subjugar*) to conquer; (*ganhar*) to win, gain; **conquistar uma pessoa** to win a person over.

**consagração** [kõsagra'sãw] *f* (*REL*) consecration; (*homenagem*) acclaim; (*elogio*) praise;

**consagrado/a** *adj* (*estabelecido*) established.

**consangüíneo/a** [kõsã'gwiniu/a] *adj* related by blood // *m/f* blood relation.

**consciência** [kõ'sjẽsja] *f* (*moral*) conscience; (*percepção*) awareness; (*senso de responsabilidade*) conscientiousness; **em sã ~** in all conscience; **estar em paz com a ~** to have a clear conscience; **conscioncioso/a** *adj* conscientious.

**consciente** [kõsi'ẽtʃi] *adj* conscious; **cônscio/a** *adj* aware.

**consecução** [kõseku'sãw] *f* attainment.

**conseguinte** [kõse'gĩtʃi] *adj*: **por ~ therefore.**

**conseguir** [kõse'gix] *vt* (*obter*) to get, obtain; ~ **fazer** to manage to do, succeed in doing; **não ~ fazer** to fail to do.

**conselheiro** [kõse'ʎejru] *m* (*que aconselha*) counsellor, adviser; (*POL*) councillor.

**conselho** [kõ'seʎu] *m* advice; (*opinião*) opinion; (*corporação*) council; ~ **de guerra** court martial; **C~ de ministros** (*POL*) Cabinet.

**con'senso** *m* consensus; (*acordo*) agreement.

**consenti'mento** *m* consent, permission; **consentir** *vt* (*admitir*) to allow, permit; (*aprovar*) to agree to // *vi*: **consentir em** to agree to.

**conseqüência** [kõse'kwẽsja] *f* (*resultado*) consequence, result; (*importância*) importance; **por ~ therefore**, consequently; **em ~ de** because of; **conseqüente** *adj* consequent.

**conser'tar** *vt* to mend, repair.

**con'serva** *f* (*fruta*) preserve; (*em vinagre*) pickle; **fábrica de ~s** cannery; **conservação** *f* conservation; (*vida, alimentos*) preservation; **conservado/a** *adj* (*fruta*) preserved; (*pessoa*) well-preserved; (*em vinagre*) pickled;

**conservado em lata** tinned, canned.

**conserva'dor(a)** adj conservative // m/f (POL) conservative; **conservar** vt (preservar) to preserve, maintain; (reter, manter) to keep, retain; **conservar-se** vr to keep; **conservatório** m conservatoire.

**considera'ção** [kõsidera'sãw] f consideration; (estima) esteem; (reflexão) thought; **tomar em ~** to take into account; **considerado/a** adj respected, well thought of.

**conside'rar** vt/i to consider, to think about, reflect on; **considerável** adj (importante) important; (grande) large, considerable.

**consigna'ção** [kõsigna'sãw] f consignment; **consignar** vt (enviar mercadorias) to send, dispatch; (: por navio) to ship; (dedicar) to dedicate.

**con'sigo** pron (m) with himself; (f) with herself; (pl) with themselves; (com você) with you // vb ver **conseguir**.

**consis'tência** f consistency; (firmeza) firmness; (estabilidade) stability.

**consis'tente** adj (sólido) solid; (espesso) thick; **consistir** vi: **consistir em** to be made up of, consist of.

**conso'ante** f consonant // prep according to // conj as; **~ prometera** as he had promised.

**consola'ção** [kõsola'sãw] f consolation; **consolar** vt to console; **consolar-se** vr (receber consolação) to console o.s.; (animar-se) to cheer up.

**conso'nância** f (harmonia) harmony; (concordância) agreement.

**consorci'ar** vt to join // vi: **~ a** to unite with; **consórcio** m (união) partnership; (COM) consortium.

**conspícuo/a** [kõʃ'pikwu/a] adj conspicuous.

**conspira'ção** [kõʃpira'sãw] f plot, conspiracy; **conspirador(a)** m/f plotter, conspirator; **conspirar** vt to plot // vi to plot, conspire.

**cons'tância** f (perseverança) perseverance; (lealdade) faithfulness; **constante** adj (invariável) constant, continual; (inalterável) firm; **constante de** consisting of.

**cons'tar** vi: **~ que** (ser evidente que) to be obvious that; **~ de** to consist of; (estar escrito) to be written; **não me constava que ...** I was not aware that ... .

**consta'tar** vt (verificar) to verify; (comprovar) to prove.

**constela'ção** [kõʃtela'sãw] f constellation; (grupo) cluster; **constelado/a** adj (estrelado) starry.

**consterna'ção** [kõʃtexna'sãw] f (desalento) dismay; (desolação) distress; **consternado/a** adj (desalentado) dismayed.

**constipa'ção** [kõʃtʃipa'sãw] (Pt) f cold; **constipado/a** adj: **estar constipado** to have a cold; **constipar-se** vr to catch a cold.

**constituci'onal** adj constitutional; **constituição** f constitution.

**constitu'ir** [kõʃtʃi'twix] vt (formar) to constitute, make up; (estabelecer) to establish, set up; (nomear) to appoint; **~-se** vr: **~-se em** to set o.s. up as.

**constrangedor(a)** [kõʃtranʒe'dox(ra)] adj restricting; **constranger** vt (impedir) to restrict; (compelir) to force, compel; **constrangimento** m (aperto) restriction; (violência) force; (timidez) restraint.

**constru'ção** [kõʃtru'sãw] f building, construction; **construir** vt to build, construct; **construtivo/a** adj constructive; **construtor(a)** m/f builder, constructor.

**consuetudinário/a** [kõswetudʒi'narju/a] adj (JUR) usual, customary.

'cônsul m consul; consulado m consulate; consular adj consular; consulesa f lady consul; (esposa) consul's wife.

con'sulta f (médica) consultation; livro de ~ reference book; horas de ~ consulting hours.

consul'tar vt (médico) to consult; (obra) to refer to; ~ alguém sobre to ask sb's opinion about; consultivo/a adj advisory; consultor(a) m/f adviser, consultant; consultório m surgery.

consumação [kõsuma'sãw] f (acabamento) completion; (realização) fulfilment; (bebida/comida) minimum order; consumado/a adj (perfeito) perfect; (completo) complete.

consu'mar vt (completar) to complete; (realizar) to fulfil, carry out.

consumi'dor(a) adj, m/f consumer; consumir vt to consume; (devorar) to eat away; (gastar) to use up; consumir-se vr to waste away.

con'sumo m consumption; artigos de ~ consumer goods.

'conta f (cálculo) count; (em bar, restaurante) bill; (fatura) invoice; (COM) account; (de colar) bead; (responsabilidade) responsibility; à ~ de to the account of; ajustar ~s com to settle an account with; ~ corrente current account; fazer de ~ que to pretend that; levar em ~ to take into account; por ~ própria on one's own account; prestar ~s de to account for; sem ~ countless; não é da sua ~ it's none of your business.

contabili'dade f book-keeping, accountancy; (departamento) accounts department.

con'tado/a adj (números) counted; (história) told, related; dinheiro de

~ (Pt) cash payment; contador(a) m/f (COM) accountant; (narrador) story-teller // m (TEC. medidor) meter; contadoria f audit department; contagem f (de números) counting; (escore) score.

contagiar [kõtaʒi'ax] vt to infect; ~-se vr to become infected; contágio m infection; contagioso/a adj contagious; (col) catching.

conta-'gotas m inv dropper.

contami'nar vt to contaminate; (contagiar) to infect; (viciar) to corrupt.

con'tanto que conj provided that.

conta-quilómetros [kõta-kilometruʃ] (Pt) m speedometer; (US) odometer.

con'tar vt (números) to count; (narrar) to tell; (propor) to intend; (pesar) to count, matter; ~ com to count on, depend on; (esperar) to expect; ~ dois anos to be two years old.

con'tato (Pt: -ct-) m contact; (toque) touch; pôr-se em ~ com to get in touch with, contact.

contemplação [kõtẽpla'sãw] f contemplation; contemplar vt to contemplate; (olhar) to gaze at // vi to meditate; contemplar-se vr to look at o.s.

contempo'râneo/a adj, m/f contemporary.

contempori'zar vi (transigir) to compromise; (ganhar tempo) to play for time.

contenção [kõtẽ'sãw] f (contenda) quarrel, dispute; (refreio) restriction, containment; contenda f quarrel, dispute.

conta'mento m (felicidade) happiness; (satisfação) contentment; contentar vt (dar prazer) to please; (dar satisfação) to content; contentar-se vr to be satisfied; contente adj (alegre) happy; (satisfeito) pleased, satisfied,

**contento** m: **a contento** satisfactorily.

**con'ter** vt (encerrar) to contain, hold; (refrear) to restrain, hold back; **~-se** vr to restrain o.s.

**contestação** [kõtʃta'sãw] f challenge; (negação) denial;

**contestar** vt (contrariar) to dispute, contest, question; (impugnar) to challenge; **contestável** adj questionable.

**conteúdo** [kõtʃi'udu] m contents pl.

**contexto** [kõ'teʃtu] m context.

**con'tido/a** adj contained; (reprimido) restrained, held back.

**con'tigo** prep with you.

**contiguidade** [kõtʃigwi'dadʒi] f proximity; **contiguo/a** adj: **contiguo a** next to; (próximo) neighbouring, nearby.

**conti'nência** f chastity; (militar) salute; **fazer ~ a** to salute; **continente** adj chaste // m continent.

**contingência** [kõtʃĩ'ʒẽsja] f eventuality; **contingente** adj uncertain; (condicional) conditional // m quota; (MIL) contingent; (COM) contingency, reserve.

**continuação** [kõtʃinwa'sãw] f continuation.

**contin'uar** vt to continue, carry on // vi: **~ a falar** to go on talking, keep on talking; **continue!** carry on!; **continuidade** f continuity.

**contínuo/a** [kõ'tʃinwu/a] adj (persistente) continual; (sem interrupção) continuous // m office boy.

**con'tista** m/f story writer; **conto** m story, tale; (Pt: dinheiro) 1000 escudos; **conto-do-vigário** m confidence trick.

**contorção** [kõtox'sãw] f contortion; (dos músculos) twitch; **contorcer** vt to twist; **contorcer-se** vr to writhe.

**contor'nar** vt (rodear) to go round; (ladear) to skirt; **contorno** m

(da terra) contour; (da cara) profile; (de um esboço) outline.

**'contra** prep against; (em troca de) in exchange for; (ao contrário de) contrary to.

**contra-almi'rante** m rear-admiral.

**contra-a'taque** m counterattack.

**contrabalan'çar** vt to counterbalance; (compensar) to compensate.

**contraban'dista** m/f smuggler; **contrabando** m smuggling; (artigos) contraband.

**contração** [kõtra'sãw] (Pt: -cç-) f contraction.

**contradição** [kõtradʒi'sãw] f contradiction; **contradizer** vt to contradict; (negar) to deny.

**contrafação** [kõtrafa'sãw] (Pt: -cç-) f falsification; (assinatura) forgery; **contrafazer** vt (reproduzir) to copy; (imitar) to imitate; (falsificar) to counterfeit.

**contrafeito/a** [kõtra'fejtu/a] adj (acanhado) uneasy; (embaraçado) self-conscious.

**contra'forte** m buttress.

**contra'ir** vt to contract; (doença) to catch; (hábito) to form; **~ matrimônio** to get married; **~-se** to shrink.

**contra'mestre/tra** m/f (fábrica, oficina) supervisor // m (NÁUT) boatswain.

**contra'peso** m counterbalance.

**contra'por** vt (opor) to oppose; **~ a** to set against; **~-se vr** to be in opposition.

**contraprodu'cente** adj counter-productive, self-defeating.

**contra-revolução** [kõtra-xevolu'sãw] f counter-revolution.

**contrari'ar** vt (contradizer) to contradict; (frustrar) to frustrate; (aborrecer) to annoy; (desapontar) to disappoint; **contrariedade** f (aborrecimento) annoyance, vexation.

**con'trário/a** adj (oposto) contrary; (desfavorável) unfavourable, adverse; **pelo ~** on the contrary // m/f adversary

**contra-'senso** m nonsense.

**contras'tar** vt to oppose // vi to contrast; **contraste** m contrast; (oposição) opposition.

**contra'tante** adj contracting // m/f contractor; **contratar** vt (serviços) to contract; (empregar) to engage.

**contra'tempo** m (contrariedade) setback; (aborrecimento) disappointment.

**con'trato** m contract; (acordo) agreement.

**contraven'ção** f [kõtravẽ'sãw] contravention, violation.

**contribui'ção** f [kõtribwi'sãw] contribution; (imposto) tax; **contribuinte** m/f contributor; (que paga impostos) taxpayer; **contribuir** vt to contribute // vi (pagar impostos) to pay taxes.

**contris'tar** vt (entristecer) to sadden; (afligir) to distress; **~-se** vr to become sad.

**contro'lar** vt to control; **controle** m control.

**contro'vérsia** f controversy; (discussão) debate; **controverso/a** adj controversial.

**con'tudo** conj nevertheless, however.

**contu'mácia** f obstinacy; (JUR) contempt of court; **contumaz** adj obstinate, stubborn.

**contun'dente** adj bruising; (argumento) cutting; **instrumento ~** blunt instrument; **contundir** vt to bruise.

**contuba'ção** f [kõtuxba'sãw] f disturbance, unrest; (motim) riot; **conturbado/a** adj disturbed; **conturbar** vt to disturb; (amotinar) to stir up.

**contu'são** f [kõtu'zãw] f bruise; **contuso/a** adj bruised.

**convales'cença** f convalescence; **convalescer** vi to convalesce.

**convali'dar** vt (tornar válido) to validate.

**conven'ção** f [kõvẽ'sãw] f convention; (acordo) agreement.

**conven'cer** vt to convince; (persuadir) to persuade; **~-se** vr: **~-se de** to be convinced about.

**convencio'nal** adj conventional.

**conveni'ência** f convenience; **conveniente** adj convenient, suitable; (vantajoso) advantageous.

**con'vênio** m (reunião) convention; (acordo) agreement; (pacto) pact.

**con'vento** m (de freiras) convent; (de frades) monastery.

**con'versa** f conversation; **~ fiada** idle chatter; **conversação** f (ato) conversation.

**conver'são** f [kõvɛx'sãw] f conversion.

**conver'sar** vi to talk, converse.

**conversibili'dade** f convertibility; **conversível** adj convertible // m (automóvel) convertible.

**conver'ter** vt to convert; **~-se** vr to be converted; **convertido/a** adj converted // m/f convert.

**con'vés** m (NÁUT) deck.

**con'vexo/a** adj convex.

**convic'ção** f [kõvik'sãw] f conviction; (certeza) certainty; **convicto/a** adj (convencido) convinced; (réu) convicted.

**convi'dado/a** adj invited // m/f guest; **convidar** vt to invite; **convidativo/a** adj attractive.

**convin'cente** adj convincing.

**con'vir** vi (ser conveniente) to suit, be convenient; (ficar bem) to be appropriate.

**con'vite** m invitation.

**convi'vência** f living together; (familiaridade) familiarity, intimacy; **conviver** vi (viver em comum) to live together; (ter familiaridade) to be on familiar terms; **convívio** m (viver em comum) living together; (familiaridade) familiarity.

**convo'car** vt to summon, call upon; (reunião) to call, convene.

**convulsão** [kõvul'sãw] f convulsion; (fig) upheaval; **convulsionar** vt (abalar) to shake; (excitar) to stir up; **convulso/a** adj shaking.

**cooperação** [koopera'sãw] f cooperation; **cooperar** vi to cooperate; **cooperativo/a** adj cooperative // f (COM) cooperative.

**coordenação** [kooxdena'sãw] f coordination; **coordenar** vt to coordinate.

**'copa** f (duma árvore) top; (dum chapéu) crown; (compartimento) pantry; (taça) cup; ~s fpl (naipes) hearts.

**'cópia** f copy; **tirar ~ de** to duplicate; **copiadora** f (máquina) duplicating machine; (loja) photocopying shop; **copiar** vt to copy.

**copi'oso/a** adj abundant, numerous.

**copo** ['kɔpu] m (vaso) glass.

**coqueiro** [ko'kejru] m (BOT) coconut tree.

**coqueluche** [koke'luʃi] f (MED) whooping cough.

**cor** f colour; ~**-de-rosa** pink; **de ~** coloured; (de memória) by heart.

**coração** [kora'sãw] m (ANAT) heart; (medula) core; (coragem) courage; (bondade) kindness; **de bom ~** kind-hearted; **de todo o ~** wholeheartedly.

**co'rado/a** adj ruddy.

**coragem** [ko'raʒẽ] f courage; (atrevimento) nerve; **corajoso/a** adj courageous.

**co'rar** vt (tingir) to dye; (roupa) to bleach (in the sun) // vi (ruborizar-se) to blush; (tornar-se branco) to bleach.

**cor'cel** m steed.

**cor'cova** f hump; **corcovar** vi (cavalo) to buck; **corcunda** m/f hump; (pessoa) hunchback.

**'corda** f (cabo) rope, line; (de relógio) spring; **dar ~ em** to wind up; **roer a ~** to go back on one's word; ~**s vocais** vocal chords.

**cordão** [kox'dãw] m string, twine; (ELET) lead; (fileira) row; ~ **de sapato** shoestring.

**cordeiro** [kox'dejru] m lamb; (fig) sheep.

**cordel** [kox'dew] m string; **literatura de ~** pamphlet literature.

**cordial** [koxdʒi'jaw] adj cordial // m (bebida) cordial; ~**idade** f warmth, cordiality.

**coreogra'fia** f choreography; **coreógrafo/a** m/f choreographer.

**co'reto** m bandstand.

**co'risco** m (faísca) flash.

**co'rista** m/f chorister // f (no teatro) chorus girl.

**corja** ['kɔxʒa] f (Pt: canalha) rabble; (bando) gang.

**cor'neta** f cornet; (MIL) bugle // m bugler; **corneteiro** m bugler; **cornetim** m (MÚS) french horn.

**'coro** m chorus; (conjunto de cantores) choir.

**co'roa** f crown; (de flores) garland; (Br: col) fogey, old timer; **coroação** f coronation; **coroar** vt to crown; (premiar) to reward.

**coro'nel** [-ew] m colonel.

**coronha** [ko'rɔɲa] f (de um fuzil) butt; (de um revólver) handle.

**'corpo** m body; (MIL) corps sg; ~ **diplomático** diplomatic corps sg; ~ **de bombeiros** fire brigade; **lutar a ~ a ~** to fight hand to hand.

**corpu'lência** f stoutness; **corpulento/a** adj stout.

**correção** [koxe'sãw] (Pt: **-cç-**) f correction; (exatidão) correctness; (castigo) chastisement; **casa de ~** reformatory.

**corre'diço/a** *adj* sliding // *f* (*cortina*) curtain.

**corre'dor(a)** *m/f* runner // *m* (*passagem*) corridor, passageway; (*cavalo*) racehorse.

**correia** [ko'xeja] *f* strap; (*de máquina*) belt; (*para cachorro*) leash.

**correio** [ko'xeju] *m* mail, post; (*local*) Post Office; (*pessoa*) courier; (*carteiro*) postman; **~ aéreo** air mail; **pôr no ~** to post.

**cor'rente** *adj* (*águas*) running; (*fluente*) flowing; (*comum*) usual, common; (*ano etc*) present // *f* current; (*cadeia*) chain; **~ de ar** draught.

**cor'rer** *vt* to run; (*viajar por*) to travel across; (*cortina*) to draw; (*examinar*) to search; (*expulsar*) to drive out; (*perseguir*) to pursue // *vi* to run; (*líquido*) to flow, run; (*o tempo*) to elapse.

**correspon'dência** *f* correspondence; **correspondente** *adj* (*que corresponde*) corresponding; (*apropriado*) appropriate // *m* correspondent.

**correspon'der** *vi*: **~ a** (*ser apropriado*) to suit, be suitable for; (*ser igual*) to match (up to); (*retribuir*) to reciprocate; **~-se com** *vr* to correspond with.

**cor'reto/a** (*Pt*: **-ct-**) *adj* correct; (*conduta*) proper.

**corre'tor** *m* broker; **~ de fundos/de bolsa** stockbroker.

**cor'rido/a** *adj* (*envergonhado*) ashamed; (*expulso*) driven out; (*gasto*) hackneyed // *f* (*ato de correr*) running; (*certame*) race; **~a de cavalos** horse race; **campo de ~as** race course; **~a de touros** bull fight.

**corrigir** [koxi'ʒix] *vt* to correct; (*censurar*) to reprimand.

**corrimão** [koxi'mãw] *m* handrail.

**corriqueiro/a** [koxi'kejru/a] *adj* hackneyed.

**corroboração** [koxobora'sãw] *f* confirmation; **corroborar** *vt* to corroborate, confirm.

**corrom'per** *vt* to corrupt; (*alimentos*) to turn bad; (*adulterar*) to adulterate.

**corrução** [koxu'sãw] (*Pt*: **-pç-**) *f* corruption; (*decomposição*) decay, rot; **corrupto/a** *adj* corrupt; (*podre*) rotten.

**cor'sário** *m* (*homem*) pirate; (*navio*) privateer.

**'Córsega** *f* Corsica.

**corta'dura** *f* (*corte*) cut; (*entre montes*) gap; **cortante** *adj* cutting; **cortar** *vt* to cut; (*eliminar*) to cut out; (*água etc*) to cut off; **cortar a palavra a alguém** to interrupt sb // *vi* to cut; (*encurtar caminho*) to take a short cut.

**'corte** *m* cut; (*roupa*) style; (*gume*) cutting edge; (*ferroviário*) cutting; **~ de cabelo** haircut // *f* (*de um monarca*) court; (*namoro*) courtship; **fazer a ~ a alguém** to court sb; **~s** *fpl* (*Pt*) parliament.

**cortejo** [kox'teʒu] *m* (*procissão*) procession; (*cumprimentos*) greetings *pl*.

**cor'tês** *adj* polite; **cortesão/tesã** *adj* courtly // *m* courtier // *f* courtesan; **cortesia** *f* politeness.

**cor'tiça** *f* (*matéria*) cork.

**cor'tiço** *m* (*habitação*) slum tenement.

**cor'tina** *f* curtain; (*biombo*) screen.

**coruja** [ko'ruʒa] *f* owl.

**corus'car** *vi* to sparkle, glitter.

**'corvo** *m* crow.

**co'ser** *vt/i* to sew, stitch.

**cos'mético/a** *adj* cosmetic // *m* cosmetic.

**cosmopo'lita** *adj* cosmopolitan.

**'cospe** *etc vb ver* **cuspir**.

**'costa** *f* coast, shore; **~s** *fpl* back; **dar as ~s a** to turn one's back on.

**cos'tado** *m* back; **dos quatro ~s** through and through.

**coste'ar** *vt* (*rodear*) to go round;

(*gado*) to round up // *vi* to follow the coast.

**cos'tela** *f* rib.

**coste'leta** *f* chop, cutlet; **~s** *fpl* (*suíças*) side-whiskers.

**costu'mado/a** *adj* (*usual*) usual; **costumar** *vt* (*habituar*) to accustom // *vi* to be accustomed to, be in the habit of; **costumava dizer ...** he used to say ....

**cos'tume** *m* custom, habit; (*traje*) costume; **de ~** usual(ly); **~s** *mpl* behaviour, conduct; **costumeiro/a** *adj* usual, habitual.

**cos'tura** *f* sewing, needlework; (*sutura*) seam; **sem ~** seamless; **costurar** *vt/i* to sew; **costureira** *f* dressmaker.

**'cota** *f* (*quinhão*) quota, share; (GEO) height.

**cotação** [kota'sãw] *f* (*de preços*) list, quotation; (*consideração*) esteem; **~ bancária** bank rate.

**cotejar** [kote'ʒax] *vt* to compare; **cotejo** *m* comparison.

**cotidi'ano/a** *adj* daily.

**'coto** *m* (*do corpo*) stump; (*de uma vela etc*) stub.

**coto'velo** *m* (ANAT) elbow; (*curva*) bend; **falar pelos ~s** to talk non-stop.

**'coube** *etc vb ver* **caber.**

**couraça** [ko'rasa] *f* (*para o peito*) breastplate; (*de navio etc*) armour-plate; **couraçado** *m* (Pt) battleship.

**couro** ['koru] *m* leather; (*de um animal*) hide; **~ cabeludo** scalp.

**couve** ['kovi] *f* cabbage; **~-flor** *f* cauliflower.

**cova** ['kɔva] *f* (*escavação*) pit; (*caverna*) cavern; (*sepultura*) grave.

**co'varde** *adj* cowardly // *m/f* coward.

**coveiro** [ko'vejru] *m* gravedigger.

**co'vil** *m* den, lair.

**covinha** [ko'viɲa] *f* dimple.

**coxa** ['kɔʃa] *f* thigh; **coxear** *vi* to limp, hobble.

**coxia** [ko'ʃia] *f* (*passagem*) aisle, gangway.

**coxo/a** ['koʃu/a] *adj* lame.

**co'zer** *vt* to cook; (*em água*) to boil; (*ao forno*) to bake; **~ a bebedeira** to sleep it off // *vi* to cook; **cozido** *m* stew.

**cozinha** [ko'ziɲa] *f* (*compartimento*) kitchen; (*arte*) cookery; (*modo de cozinhar*) cuisine; **cozinhar** *vt/i* to cook; **cozinheiro/a** *m/f* cook.

**C.P.** *abr de* **Caminhos de Ferro Portugueses** Portuguese State Railway.

**Cr$** *abr de* **cruzeiro** cruzeiro.

**'crânio** *m* skull.

**craque** ['kraki] *m/f* ace, expert // *m* (*jogador de futebol*) soccer star.

**'crasso/a** *adj* crass.

**cra'tera** *f* crater.

**cra'var** *vt* (*prego etc*) to drive (in); (*pedras*) to set; (*com os olhos*) to stare at.

**craveiro** [kra'vejru] *m* (BOT) carnation.

**cravelha** [kra've/a] *f* (MÚS) tuning peg.

**'cravo** *m* (*prego*) nail; (*flor*) carnation.

**'creche** *f* crèche.

**credi'tar** *vt* to give credit to, loan; **'crédito** *m* credit; **a crédito** on credit; **digno de crédito** reliable.

**'credo** *m* creed // *excl* (Pt) heavens!

**cre'dor(a)** *adj* worthy, deserving // *m* creditor.

**creduli'dade** *f* credulity; **crédulo/a** *adj* credulous.

**'creio** *etc vb ver* **crer.**

**cremalheira** [krema'/ejra] *f* (*trilho*) rack.

**cre'mar** *vt* to cremate; **crematório** *m* crematorium.

**'creme** *adj* cream-coloured // *m* cream; (*doce*) custard; **~ dental** toothpaste; **cremoso/a** *adj* creamy.

**'crença** *f* belief.

**cren'dice** f superstition.

**'crente** adj believing // m/f believer.

**crepitação** [krɛpitaˈsãw] f crackling; **crepitar** vi to crackle.

**crepuscu'lar** adj twilight; **crepúsculo** m dusk, twilight.

**crer** vt/i to think, believe; **~ em** to believe in.

**cres'cente** adj growing; (forma) crescent // m crescent; **crescer** vi to grow; (aumentar) to increase; (medrar) to thrive; **crescido/a** adj (pessoa) grown up; (grande) large; **crescimento** m growth; (aumento) increase.

**'crespo/a** adj (cabelo) curly; (áspero) rough; (água) choppy, rough.

**cre'tino** m cretin, imbecile.

**'cria** f (animal) baby animal, young; **criação** f creation; (de animais) raising, breeding; (educação) upbringing; (animais domésticos) livestock.

**cria'dor(a)** adj creative // m/f creator // m: **~ de gado** cattle breeder.

**cri'ança** f child.

**cri'ar** vt to create; (crianças) to bring up; (animais) to raise, breed; (produzir) to produce; (amamentar) to suckle, nurse; **criativo/a** adj creative; **criatura** f creature; (indivíduo) individual.

**'crime** m crime; **criminal** adj criminal.

**crimi'noso/a** adj, m/f criminal.

**'crina** f mane.

**cri'oulo/a** adj creole // m/f creole; (Br: negro) black (person).

**cri'sálida** f chrysalis.

**'crise** f crisis; (escassez) shortage; (MED) attack, fit.

**'crisma** f (REL) confirmation; (óleo) holy oil.

**cris'mar** vt (REL) to confirm; **~-se** vr (REL) to be confirmed.

**cri'sol** [-ɔw] m crucible; (fig) test.

**cris'par** vt (contrair) to contract; **~-se** vr to twitch.

**'crista** f (de monte) crest; (de galo) cock's comb.

**cris'tal** [-aw] m crystal; **~izar** vi to crystallize.

**cristan'dade** f Christianity; **cristão/cristã** adj, m/f, pl **-ãos** Christian.

**cristia'nismo** m Christianity; **Cristo** m Christ; (crucifixo) crucifix.

**cri'tério** m (norma) criterion; (juízo) judgement.

**'crítica** f criticism; (artigo) critique; (conjunto de críticos) critics pl; **criticar** vt to criticize; (um livro) to review; **crítico/a** adj critical // m critic.

**cri'var** vt (com balas) to riddle; (de perguntas, de insultos) to bombard with.

**crível** [ˈkrivew] adj credible.

**'crivo** (Pt) m sieve.

**cro'chê** m crochet.

**croco'dilo** m crocodile.

**'cromo** m chrome.

**'crônico/a** adj chronic // f chronicle; (coluna de jornal) newspaper column; **cronista** m/f (de jornal) columnist; (historiógrafo) chronicler.

**crono'logia** f chronology; **cronológico/a** adj chronological.

**croquete** [kroˈkɛtʃi] m croquette.

**cro'qui** m sketch.

**'crosta** f crust; (MED) scab.

**cru/'crua** adj raw; (não refinado) crude; (ignorante) green.

**crucificação** [krusifikaˈsãw] f crucifixion; **crucificar** vt to crucify; **crucifixo** m crucifix.

**cruel** [kruˈew] adj cruel; **~dade** f cruelty.

**cru'ento/a** adj (sanguinolento) bloody; (cruel) cruel.

**'crupe** m (MED) croup.

**cruz** f cross; **~ gamada** swastika; **C~ Vermelha** Red Cross; **cruzado/a** adj crossed // m crusader; (moeda) cruzado // f crusade.

**cruza'dor** m (navio) cruiser.

**cruza'mento** m (de estradas) crossing; (mestiçagem) cross breeding; **cruzar** vt to cross; (os braços) to fold; (NÁUT) to cruise; **cruzar-se** vr to cross; (pessoas) to pass by each other.

**cruzeiro** [kru'zejru] m (cruz) (monumental) cross; (moeda) cruzeiro; (viagem de navio) cruise.

**cru'zeta** f (régua T) T square; (Pt: cabide) coat hanger.

**'cuba** f vat; (TEC) reservoir.

**'Cuba** f Cuba; **cubano/a** adj, m/f Cuban.

**'cúbico/a** adj cubic; **cubículo** m cubicle; **cubo** m cube; (de roda) hub.

**'cuco** m cuckoo.

**cueca** ['kwɛka] f (para homens) underpants; ~s (Pt: para mulheres) panties.

**cueiro** [ku'ejru] m nappy.

**cuidado** [kwi'dadu] m care; (preocupação) worry; **aos** ~ **de** in the care of; **ter** ~ to be careful // excl: ~! watch out!; **cuidadoso/a** adj careful.

**cuidar** [kwi'dax] vi: ~ **de** to take care of, look after; ~**-se** vr to look after o.s.

**cujo** ['kuʒu] pron (de quem) whose; (de que) of which.

**cu'latra** f (de arma) breech.

**culi'nário/a** adj culinary // f cookery.

**culpa** ['kulpa] f fault; (JUR) guilt; **ter** ~ **de** to be to blame for; **por** ~ **de** because of; ~**bilidade** f guilt; **culpado/a** adj guilty // m/f culprit.

**culpar** [kuw'pax] vt to blame; (acusar) to accuse; ~**-se** vr to take the blame; **culpável** adj guilty.

**cultivar** [kuwtʃi'vax] vt to cultivate; **cultivo** m cultivation.

**culto/a** ['kuwtu/a] adj (que tem cultura) cultured; (civilizado) civilized // m (homenagem)

worship; (religião) cult; **cultura** f culture; (da terra) cultivation; (polidez) refinement; **cultural** adj cultural.

**'cume** m top, summit; (fig) climax.

**'cúmplice** m/f accomplice; **cumplicidade** f complicity.

**cumprimen'tar** vt (saudar) to greet; (dar parabéns) to congratulate; **cumprimento** m (realização) fulfilment; (saudação) greeting; (elogio) compliment; **cumprimentos** mpl best wishes.

**cum'prir** vt (desempenhar) to carry out; (promessa) to fulfil; (anos) to reach // vi (convir) to be necessary; ~ **a palavra** to keep one's word; **fazer** ~ to enforce; ~**-se** vr to be fulfilled.

**'cúmulo** m heap, pile; (auge) height; **é o** ~! that's the limit!

**cunha** ['kuɲa] f wedge; (pistolão) connections pl.

**cunhado/a** [ku'ɲadu/a] m brother-in-law // f sister-in-law.

**cunhar** [ku'ɲax] vt (moedas) to mint; (palavras) to coin.

**cupim** [ku'pĩ] m termite.

**'cúpula** f (ARQ) dome.

**'cura** f (ato de curar) cure; (tratamento) treatment; (de carnes etc) curing, preservation // m priest; **curandeiro** m (feiticeiro) healer, medicine man; (charlatão) quack.

**cu'rar** vt (doença) to cure; (ferida) to treat, heal; (carne etc) to cure, preserve; ~**-se** vr to get well; **curativo/a** adj medicinal // m (tratamento) treatment; (penso) dressing.

**cu'ringa** m (cartas) joker.

**curiosi'dade** f curiosity; (objeto raro) curio; **curioso/a** adj curious // m/f snooper, inquisitive person.

**curral** [ku'xaw] m pen, enclosure.

**cur'rículo** m curriculum; **curriculum vitae** m curriculum vitae.

**cur'sar** vt (aulas) to attend; (cursos) to follow.

**cur'sivo** m (tipografia) script.

**'curso** m course; (direção) direction; **em** ~ (ano etc) current; (processo) in progress.

**cur'tir** vt (couro) to tan; (tornar rijo) to toughen up; (padecer) to suffer, endure; (col) to enjoy.

**'curto/a** adj short, brief; (entendimento) narrow; **de** ~**a vista** (míope) short-sighted.

**curto-circuito** [kuxtu-six'kwitu] m short circuit.

**'curva** f curve, bend; **curvar** vt to bend, curve; **curvar-se** vr (abaixar-se) to stoop; **curvatura** f curvature.

**cu'spir** vi to spit.

**'custa** f cost, expense; ~**s** fpl (JUR) costs; **à** ~ **de** at the expense of; **custar** vi to cost; (ser difícil) to be difficult; **custar caro** to be expensive; **custear** vt to bear the cost of.

**'custo** m cost, price; **a** ~ with difficulty; **a todo** ~ at all costs.

**cus'tódia** f custody.

**cus'toso/a** adj costly; (difícil) difficult.

**cutela'ria** f knife-making; **cutelo** m cleaver, carving knife; **cutilada** f cut, slash.

**'cútis** f (pele) skin; (fez) complexion.

# D

**da** = **de** + **a**, ver **de**.

**'dádiva** f (donativo) donation; (oferta) gift; **dadivoso/a** adj generous.

**'dado/a** pp **de dar** given // m (jogo) die; (fato) fact; ~**s** mpl (jogo) (fatos) data // ~ **que** conj supposing that, given that.

**da'í** adv (= **de** + **aí**) (desse lugar)

from there; (desse momento) from then; ~ **a um mês** a month later; ~ **por/em diante** from then on.

**da'li** adv (= **de** + **ali**) from there.

**dal'tônico/a** [dawt-] adj colour-blind; **daltonismo** m colour blindness.

**'dama** f lady; (xadrez, cartas) queen; ~**s** fpl draughts; (US) checkers.

**da'masco** m (fruta) apricot; (tecido) damask; **damasqueiro** m apricot tree.

**danação** [dana'sãw] f damnation; (travessura) mischief, naughtiness; **danado/a** adj (condenado) damned; (zangado) furious, angry; (menino) mischievous, naughty; **cão danado** mad dog.

**'dança** f (ger) dance; **dançar** vi to dance; **dançarino/a** m/f dancer; **danceteria** f disco(theque).

**danifi'car** vt (objeto) to damage; **daninho/a** adj harmful; **dano** m (moral) harm; (a um objeto) damage; (a uma pessoa) hurt, injury; **danoso/a** adj (a uma pessoa) harmful; (a uma coisa) damaging.

**'dantes** adv before, formerly.

**da'quele/da'quela** = **de** + **aquele/aquela**, ver **aquele**.

**daqui** [da'kı] adv (= **de** + **aqui**) (deste lugar) from here; (deste momento) from now; ~ **a pouco** soon, in a little while; ~ **a uma semana** in a week's time; ~ **em diante** from now on.

**da'quilo** = **de** + **aquilo**, ver **aquilo**.

**dar** vt to give; (cartas) to deal; (golpes, horas) to strike; ~ **à luz** to give birth to; ~ **gritos** to shout; ~ **uma volta/um passeio** to go for a walk // vi: ~ **certo** to turn out right; ~ **com** (encontrar) to meet, come across; (porta) to slam; ~ **de comer/beber** a to feed/give a drink to; ~ **em** (pessoa) to hit, beat up; (lugar) to come to, get to; ~ **para**

look onto; ~ **parte de** to report; ~ **por** to notice; **dá licença?** may I?; ~**-se** *vr* (*acontecer*) to happen; ~**-se a** (*dedicar-se a*) to devote o.s. to; ~**-se bem com** to get on well with; ~**-se por vencido** to admit defeat; **não me dou bem com o clima** the climate doesn't suit me; **pouco se me dá** I don't care.

**'dardo** *m* dart; (*grande*) spear.

**das** = **de** + **as**, *ver* **da**.

**'data** *f* date; (*época*) time; **de longa** ~ of long standing; **datar** *vt* to date // *vi*: **datar de** to date from.

**datilogra'far** (*Pt:* **-ct-**) *vt* to type; **datilografia** (*Pt:* **-ct-**) *f* typing; **datilógrafo/a** (*Pt:* **-ct-**) *m/f* typist.

**de** (*de* + *o* = *do*; *de* + *a* = *da*; *de* + *os* = *dos*; *de* + *as* = *das*) *prep* of, from; **venho ~ São Paulo** I come from São Paulo; **a casa ~ João** John's house; **um romance ~ a** novel by; **tirar a tampa ~** to take the lid off; **o infeliz do homem** the poor man; **um vestido ~ seda** a silk dress; **perto ~** near to; **longe ~** far from; ~ **manhã** in the morning; ~ **dia** by day; **vestido ~ branco** dressed in white; **um homem ~ cabelo comprido** a man with long hair; ~ **dois em dois dias** every other day; ~ **trem** by train.

**dê** *etc vb ver* **dar.**

**deão** [dʒi'ãw] *m* dean.

**debaixo** [de'baʃu] *adv* below, underneath // *prep*: ~ **de** under, beneath.

**de'balde** *adv* in vain.

**deban'dada** *f* stampede; **em** ~ in confusion; **debandar** *vt* to put to flight // *vi* to scatter.

**de'bate** *m* (*discussão*) debate; (*disputa*) argument; **debater** *vt* to debate; (*discutir*) to discuss; **debater-se** *vr* to struggle.

**debe'lar** *vt* to put down, suppress.

**debi'car** *vt* (*caçoar*) to make fun of.

**débil** ['dɛbiw] *adj, pl* **'débeis**

(*pessoa*) weak, feeble; (*luz*) dim, faint // *m*: ~ **mental** mental defective, moron; **debilidade** *f* weakness; (*luz*) dimness; **debilitar** *vt* to weaken; **debilitar-se** *vr* to become weak, weaken.

**debique** [de'biki] *m* mockery, ridicule.

**debi'tar** *vt* to debit; (*ELET*) to supply; **débito** *m* debit.

**debo'chado/a** *adj* mocking // *m/f* mocking person; **debochar** *vt* to mock, make fun of.

**debruçar-se** [debru'sax-si] *vr* (*inclinar-se*) to bend over; ~ **na janela** to lean out of the window.

**debrum** [de'brū] *m* hem.

**debulha** [de'buʎa] *f* (*trigo*) threshing; **debulhar** *vt* (*grão*) to thresh; (*descascar*) to shell; **debulhar-se** *vr*: **debulhar-se em lágrimas** to burst into tears.

**debu'tar** *vi* to appear for the first time, make one's début.

**'década** *f* decade.

**deca'dência** *f* decadence; **decadente** *adj* decadent.

**deca'ir** *vi* (*cair*) to fall; (*declinar*) to decline; (*cair em decadência*) to decay.

**decalcar** [-kaw'kax] *vt* to trace; (*fig*) to copy; **decalque** *m* tracing.

**de'cano** *m* (*membro*) oldest member.

**decan'tar** *vt* (*líquido*) to decant; (*purificar*) to purify; (*celebrar*) to sing the praises of.

**decapi'tar** *vt* to behead, decapitate.

**decência** [de'sēsja] *f* decency.

**decênio** [de'senju] *m* decade.

**de'cente** *adj* decent; (*limpo*) clean.

**dece'par** *vt* to cut off, chop off.

**decepção** [desep'sãw] *f* disappointment; **decepcionar** *vt* to disappoint, let down.

**de'certo** *adv* certainly.

**deci'dido/a** *adj* (*resoluto*) determined; (*resolvido*) decided.

**deci'dir** vt (determinar) to decide; (solucionar) to resolve; ~**se** vr: ~**se a** to make up one's mind to; ~**se por** to decide on, go for.

**deci'frar** vt to decipher; (adivinhar) to unravel.

**deci'mal** [-maw] adj decimal // m (número) decimal; **décimo/a** adj tenth // m tenth.

**decisão** [desi'zãw] f (sentença) decision; (capacidade de decidir) decisiveness, resolution; **decisivo/a** adj decisive.

**declamação** [deklama'sãw] f (poema) recitation; (pej) ranting; **declamar** vt/i (poemas) to recite; (pej) to rant.

**declaração** [deklara'sãw] f declaration; (depoimento) statement; ~ **de amor** proposal; **declarar** vt (anunciar) to declare; (designar) to state; **declarar-se** vr to declare o.s.

**declinação** [deklina'sãw] f (LING) declension.

**decli'nar** vt (recusar) to decline, refuse; (nomes) to give // vi (sol) to sink; ~ **de fazer** to decline to do.

**de'clive** m slope, incline.

**decolagem** [deko'laʒẽ] f (avião) take-off; **decolar** vi to take off.

**decomposição** [dekõpozi'sãw] f (apodrecimento) decomposition; (análise) dissection; **decompor** vt (analisar) to analyse; **decompor-se** vr to rot, decompose.

**decoração** [dekora'sãw] f decoration; (teatral) scenery; **decorar** vt to decorate; (aprender) to learn by heart; **decorativo/a** adj decorative.

**de'coro** m (decência) decency; (dignidade) decorum; **decoroso/a** adj decent, respectable.

**decor'rer** vi (tempo) to pass; (acontecer) to take place, happen; ~ **de** (originar-se) to result from.

**deco'tado/a** adj (roupa) low-necked; **decotar** vt (vestido) to cut

low; **decote** m (vestido) low neckline.

**decre'scente** adj decreasing, diminishing; **decrescer** vi to decrease, diminish; **decréscimo** m decrease, decline.

**decre'tar** vt to decree, order; **decreto** m decree, order.

**decupli'car** vt to multiply by ten.

**de'curso** m (tempo) course; **no** ~ **de** in the course of, during.

**de'dal** m thimble; (quantidade) thimbleful.

**dedeira** [de'dejra] f (MÚS) plectrum.

**dedicação** [dedʒika'sãw] f dedication; (devotamento) devotion.

**dedi'car** vt (poema) to dedicate; (tempo, atenção) to devote; ~**se** vr: ~**se a** to devote o.s. to; **dedicatória** f (de obra) dedication.

**dedilhar** [dedʒi'ʎax] vt (instrumento) to finger; (violão) to strum.

'**dedo** m finger; (do pé) toe; ~ **anular** ring finger; ~ **indicador** index finger; ~ **mínimo** little finger; ~ **polegar** thumb.

**dedução** [dedu'sãw] f deduction; **deduzir** vt to deduct // vi (concluir) to deduce, infer.

**defa'sado/a** adj out of step; **defasagem** f discrepancy.

**defecção** [defek'sãw] f defection; (deserção) desertion; **defectivo/a** adj faulty, defective; (LING) defective.

**defeito** [de'fejtu] m defect, flaw; **pôr** ~ **s em** to find fault with; **com** ~ broken, out of order; **defeituoso/a** adj defective, faulty.

**defen'der** vt (ger, Jur) to defend; (proteger) to protect; ~**se** vr: ~**se de** to stand up against.

**defen'sável** adj defensible; **defensiva** f defensive; **ficar na defensiva** to be on the defensive; **defensor(a)** m/f defender; (JUR) defending counsel.

**defe'rência** f (*condescendência*) deference; (*respeito*) respect.

**deferi'mento** m (*aprovação*) approval; (*concessão*) granting; **deferir** vt (*atender a*) to approve; (*conferir*) to grant, bestow // vi (*concordar*) to concede; (*acatar*) to defer.

**de'fesa** f defence; (*JUR*) counsel for the defence // m (*futebol*) back.

**deficiência** [defisi'ēsja] f deficiency; **deficiente** adj (*carente*) deficient, lacking; (*imperfeito*) defective.

**'déficit** m deficit.

**definhar** [defi'nax] vt to waste away // vi (*consumir-se*) to waste away; (*murchar*) to wither.

**definição** [defini'sāw] f definition; **definido/a** adj (*demarcado*) defined; (*determinado*) definite; **definir** vt (*demarcar*) to define; (*interpretar*) to explain; (*estabelecer*) to establish.

**defini'tivo/a** adj (*absoluto*) definite; (*categórico*) definitive; (*final*) final.

**deflação** [defla'sāw] f deflation.

**deformação** [defoxma'sāw] f (*alteração*) alteration; (*desfiguração*) distortion; **deformar** vt to deform; (*deturpar*) to distort; **deformar-se** vr to become deformed; **deformidade** f deformity.

**defraudação** [defrawda'sāw] f fraud; (*de dinheiro*) embezzlement; **defraudar** vt (*dinheiro*) to embezzle; (*uma pessoa*) to swindle; **defraudar alguém de alguma coisa** to cheat sb of sth.

**defron'tar** vt to face // vi: ~ **com** to face; (*dar com*) to come face to face with; ~**-se** vr to face each other.

**de'fronte** adv opposite, facing; ~ **de** prep opposite, facing.

**defu'mado/a** adj smoked; **defumar** vt (*presunto*) to smoke.

**de'funto/a** adj dead, deceased // m/f dead person.

**degelar** [deʒe'lax] vt to defrost, thaw // vi to thaw out; **degelo** m thaw.

**degeneração** [deʒenera'sāw] f degeneration; (*moral*) degeneracy; **degenerar** vt to corrupt // vi to degenerate; **degenerar-se** vr to become depraved.

**deglu'tir** vt/i to swallow.

**dego'lar** vt (*pessoa*) to behead, decapitate; (*pescoço*) to cut the throat of.

**degradação** [degrada'sāw] f degradation; **degradar** vt to degrade, debase; **degradar-se** vr to demean o.s.

**degrau** [de'graw] m step; (*de escada de mão*) rung.

**degre'dar** vt to exile; **degredo** m exile.

**degustação** [deguʃta'sāw] f tasting, sampling; **degustar** vt to taste; (*vinho*) to sip.

**'dei** etc vb ver **dar**.

**deificar** [deifi'kax] vt to deify.

**dei'tado/a** pp de **deitar** // adj (*estendido*) lying down; (*na cama*) in bed.

**deitar** [dej'tax] vt (*estender*) to lay down; (*na cama*) to put to bed; (*colocar*) to put, place; (*lançar*) to cast; (*Pt: líquido*) to pour; ~ **sangue** (*Pt*) to bleed; ~ **abaixo** to knock down, flatten; ~ **a correr** to start running; (*Pt*): ~ **uma carta** to post a letter; (*Pt*): ~ **fora** to throw away/out; ~**-se** vr to lie down; (*na cama*) to go to bed.

**deixa** [ˈdejʃa] f (*teatro*) cue.

**deixar** [dej'ʃax] vt (*ger*) to leave; (*abandonar*) to abandon; (*permitir*) to let, allow; ~ **de lado** to set aside; ~ **cair** to drop // vi: ~ **de** (*parar*) to stop; (*não fazer*) to fail to; **não posso** ~ **de ir** I must go; **não posso** ~ **de rir** I can't help laughing.

**'dela** = **de** + **ela**, ver **ela**.

**dela'tar** *vt* to denounce, inform on; (*revelar*) to reveal; **delator(a)** *m/f* informer.

**'dele = de + ele,** *ver* **ele.**

**delegação** [delega'sãw] *f* delegation.

**dele'cia** *f* office; ~ **de polícia** police station; **delegado/a** *m/f* delegate, representative; **delegar** *vt* to delegate.

**deleitar** [delej'tax] *vt* to delight; ~**se** *vr*: ~**se com** to enjoy, delight in; **deleite** *m* delight; **deleitoso/a** *adj* delightful.

**dele'tério/a** *adj* harmful.

**delfim** [dew'fĩ] *m* dolphin.

**delgado/a** [dew'ga¹-] *adj* thin; (*esbelto*) slim, slender; (*fino*) fine.

**deliberação** [delibera'sãw] *f* deliberation; (*decisão*) decision.

**delibe'rar** *vt* to decide, resolve // *vi* to ponder.

**delica'deza** *f* delicacy; (*cortesia*) kindness; **delicado/a** *adj* delicate; (*frágil*) fragile; (*leve*) light; (*sensível*) sensitive.

**de'lícia** *f* delight; (*prazer*) pleasure; **delicioso/a** *adj* delightful; (*comida, bebida*) delicious.

**delimitação** [delimita'sãw] *f* demarcation; **delimitar** *vt* to delimit.

**deline'ar** *vt* (*esboçar*) to outline; (*planejar*) to plan out.

**delinquência** [deli'kwẽsja] *f* delinquency; **delinquente** *adj, m/f* delinquent, criminal; **delinquir** *vi* to commit an offence.

**deli'rante** *adj* delirious; **delirar** *vi* (*com febre*) to be delirious; (*de ódio, prazer*) to go mad, wild; **delírio** *m* (*MED*) delirium; (*êxtase*) ecstasy; (*excitação*) excitement.

**de'lito** *m* (*crime*) crime; (*pecado*) offence; **apanhar em flagrante** ~ to catch red-handed.

**de'longa** *f* delay; **sem mais** ~**s** without more ado.

**delta** ['dɛwta] *f* delta.

**dema'gogo** *m* demagogue.

**demais** [de'majʃ] *adv* (*em demasia*) too much; (*muitíssimo*) very much // *pron*: **o** ~ the rest (of it); **os** ~ *mpl* the rest (of them); **por** ~ too much; **já é** ~ ! this is too much!; **é bom** ~ it is too good.

**de'manda** *f* (*JUR*) lawsuit; (*disputa*) claim; (*ECON*) demand; **em** ~ **de** in search of; **demandar** *vt* (*JUR*) to sue; (*buscar*) to search for; (*exigir*) to demand.

**demão** [de'mãw] *f* (*tinta*) coat, layer.

**demarcação** [demaxka'sãw] *f* demarcation; **demarcar** *vt* (*delimitar*) to demarcate; (*fixar*) to mark out.

**dema'sia** *f* excess, surplus; (*imoderação*) lack of moderation; **em** ~ too much, in excess; **demasiado/a** *adj* too much; (*pl*) too many // *adv* too much.

**de'mência** *f* insanity, madness; **demente** *adj* crazy, demented.

**demissão** [demi'sãw] *f* dismissal; **pedido de** ~ resignation; **pedir** ~ to resign; **demitir** *vt* to dismiss; (*col*) to sack, fire; **demitir-se** *vr* to resign.

**'demo** *m* devil.

**democra'cia** *f* democracy; **democrata** *m/f* democrat; **democrático/a** *adj* democratic.

**demolição** [demoli'sãw] *f* demolition; **demolir** *vt* to demolish, knock down; (*fig*) to destroy.

**demo'níaco/a** *adj* devilish; **demônio** *m* devil, demon.

**demonstração** [demõʃtra'sãw] *f* (*lição prática*) demonstration; (*de amizade*) show, display; (*prova*) proof; **demonstrar** *vt* (*ensinar*) to demonstrate; (*provar*) to prove; (*mostrar*) to show; **demonstrativo/a** *adj* demonstrative.

**de'mora** *f* delay; (*parada*) stop; **sem** ~ at once, without delay.

**demo'rar** *vt* to delay, slow down // *vi* (*permanecer*) to stay; (*tardar a* *vir*) to be late; ~ **a chegar** to be a long time coming; **vai ~ muito?** will it take long?; ~**-se** *vr* to stay too long, linger.

**dene'grir** *vt* to blacken; (*difamar*) to denigrate.

**den'goso/a** *adj* (*criança*) whining; (*mulher*) coquettish, coy; (*choraminguento*) whimpering.

**deno'dado/a** *adj* brave, daring.

**denominação** [denomina'sãw] *f* (REL) denomination; (*título*) name.

**deno'tar** *vt* (*mostrar*) to show, indicate; (*significar*) to signify.

**densi'dade** *f* density; **denso/a** *adj* (*cerrado*) dense; (*espesso*) thick; (*compacto*) compact; (*fig*) heavy.

**den'tado/a** *adj* serrated // *f* bite; **dentadura** *f* (set of) teeth; (*artificial*) dentures *pl*; **dental** *adj* dental.

**'dente** *m* tooth; (*de animal*) fang; (*de elefante*) tusk; (*de alho*) clove; ~ **abalado** loose tooth; ~ **postiço** false tooth; **falar entre os ~s** to mutter, mumble.

**dente-de-le'ão** *m* dandelion.

**denti'frício** *m* toothpaste.

**den'tista** *m/f* dentist.

**'dentro** *adv* inside; **aí** ~ in there // *prep*: ~ **de** inside; (*tempo*) within; ~ **de dois dias** in/within two days; ~ **em breve** soon, shortly; ~ **em pouco** soon, before long; **de** ~ **para fora** inside out.

**de'núncia** *f* denunciation; (*acusação*) accusation; **denunciar** *vt* to denounce; inform against; (*revelar*) to reveal.

**depa'rar** *vt* (*revelar*) to reveal; (*fazer aparecer*) to present // *vi*: ~ **com** to come across, meet.

**departa'mento** *m* department.

**depe'nar** *vt* to pluck.

**depen'dência** *f* dependence; (*edificação*) annexe; (*colonial*) dependency; **dependente** *m/f* dependent; **depender** *vi*: **depender de** to depend on.

**dependu'rar** *vi* to hang.

**depi'lar** *vt* to remove hair from; **depilatório** *m* hair-remover.

**deplo'rar** *vt* to deplore; (*lamentar*) to regret; **deplorável** *adj* deplorable; (*lamentável*) regrettable.

**depoimento** [depoj'mẽtu] *m* testimony, evidence.

**depois** [de'pojʃ] *adv* afterwards, next // *prep*: ~ **de** after; ~ **de comer** after eating.

**de'por** *vt* (*rei*) to depose; (*governo*) to overthrow // *vi* (JUR) to testify.

**deportação** [depoxta'sãw] *f* deportation; **deportar** *vt* to deport.

**deposição** [depozi'sãw] *f* deposition; (*governo*) overthrow.

**deposi'tar** *vt* to deposit; (*voto*) to cast; ~ **confiança em** to place one's confidence in; ~**-se** *vr* (*líquido*) to form a deposit; **depositário/a** *m/f* trustee // *m* (*fig*) confidant /*f* (*fig*) confidante.

**de'pósito** *m* deposit; (*armazém*) warehouse, depot; (*de lixo*) dump; (*reservatório*) tank; ~ **de bagagens** left-luggage office.

**depravação** [deprava'sãw] *f* depravity, corruption; **depravar** *vt* to deprave, corrupt; (*estragar*) to ruin; **depravar-se** *vr* to become depraved.

**depre'car** *vt* to beg for, pray for // *vi* to plead.

**depreciação** [depresja'sãw] *f* depreciation; **depreciar** *vt* (*desvalorizar*) to devalue; (*desdenhar*) to belittle; **depreciar-se** *vr* to depreciate, lose value.

**depredação** [depreda'sãw] *f* depredation; **depredar** *vt* to pillage, plunder.

**de'pressa** *adv* fast, quickly; (*com pressa*) in a hurry; **vamos** ~ let's hurry.

**depressão** [depre'sãw] *f* (ger) depression; **deprimido/a** *adj* depressed, low; **deprimir** *vt* depress; **deprimir-se** vr to get depressed.

**depuração** [depura'sãw] f purification; **depurar** vt to purify.

**depu'tado/a** m/f deputy; (agente) agent; (político: US) Representative; (: Brit) Member of Parliament, M.P.

**'dera** etc vb ver **dar**.

**de'riva** f drift; **ir à** ~ to drift; **ficar à** ~ to be adrift.

**derivação** [deriva'sãw] f derivation; **derivar** vt (desviar) to change the course of; (LING) to derive // vi (ir à deriva) to drift; **derivar-se** vr (palavra) to be derived; (ir à deriva) to drift.

**derradeiro/a** [dɛxa'dejro/a] adj last, final.

**derrama'mento** m spilling; (sangue, lágrimas) shedding; **derramar** vt to spill; (sangue, lágrimas) to shed; (espalhar) to scatter; **derramar-se** vr to pour out; (correr) to flow; **derrame** m (MED) discharge; (de sangue) haemorrhage.

**derre'dor** adv/prep: **em** ~ (de) around.

**derre'ter** vt to melt; **~-se** vr to melt; (neve) to thaw.

**derri'bar** vt ver **derrubar**.

**derro'cada** f downfall; (ruína) collapse.

**der'rota** f defeat, rout; (NÁUT) route; **derrotar** vt (vencer) to defeat; (em jogo) to beat.

**derru'bar** vt to knock down; (destruir) to destroy; (demolir) to pull down.

**desaba'far** vt (sentimentos) to give vent to // vi to let off steam.

**desaba'lado/a** adj (excessivo) excessive; (precipitado) headlong.

**desa'bar** vi to fall, tumble down.

**desabotoar** [dɛzabot'wax] vt to unbutton.

**desa'brido/a** adj rude, brusque.

**desabro'char** vi (flores) to open, bloom.

**desabu'sado/a** adj (sem preconceitos) unprejudiced; (atrevido) impudent.

**desaca'tar** vt to disregard; (desprezar) to scorn; **desacato** m (falta de respeito) disrespect; (desprezo) disregard.

**desa'certo** m mistake, blunder.

**desacor'dado/a** adj unconscious.

**desa'cordo** m (falta de acordo) disagreement; (desarmonia) discord.

**desacostu'mado/a** adj unaccustomed.

**desacredi'tado/a** adj discredited; **ficar** ~ to lose one's reputation; **desacreditar** vt to discredit; **desacreditar-se** vr to lose one's reputation.

**desafia'dor/a** adj challenging; (pessoa) defiant // m/f challenger; **desafiar** vt (propor combate) to challenge; (afrontar) to defy.

**desafi'nado/a** adj out of tune; **desafinar** vt (atrapalhar) to spoil // vi to play out of tune.

**desa'fio** m challenge; (Pt: esporte) match, game.

**desafo'gado/a** adj (desimpedido) clear; (desembaraçado) untroubled; **desafogar** vt (libertar) to free; (desapertar) to relieve; (desabafar) to give vent to; **desafogo** m (alívio) relief; (folga) leisure.

**desafo'rado/a** adj rude, insolent; **desaforo** m insolence, abuse.

**desafortu'nado/a** adj unfortunate, unlucky.

**desa'fronta** f (satisfação) redress; (vingança) revenge.

**desagra'dar** vt to displease, offend; **desagradável** adj unpleasant.

**desa'grado** m displeasure.

**desagra'var** vt (insulta) to make amends for; (pessoa) to make amends to; **~-se** vr to avenge o.s.; **desagravo** m amends pl.

**desagregação** [dezagrɛga'sãw] f

(*separação*) separation; (*dissolução*) disintegration; **desagregar** vt (*desunir*) to break up, split; (*separar*) to separate; **desagregar-se** vr (*desunir-se*) to break up, split; (*separar-se*) to separate.

**desa'guar** vt to drain // vi to flow.

**desai'roso/a** adj (*desajeitado*) awkward, clumsy; (*deselegante*) inelegant.

**desajeitado/a** [dɛzaʒej'tadu/a] adj clumsy, awkward.

**desajuizado/a** [dɛzaʒwi'zadu/a] adj foolish, unwise.

**desalen'tado/a** adj disheartened; **desalentar** vt to discourage; (*deprimir*) to depress; **desalento** m discouragement.

**desalinhado/a** [dɛzali'nadu/a] adj untidy, disorderly; **desalinho** m untidiness.

**desal'mado/a** [-awm-] adj cruel, inhuman.

**desalojar** [dɛzalo'ʒax] vt (*expulsar*) to oust; **~-se** vr to move out.

**desamar'rar** vt to untie // vi (*NÁUT*) to cast off.

**desa'mor** m dislike; (*desprezo*) disdain.

**desampa'rado/a** adj (*abandonado*) abandoned; **desamparar** vt to abandon.

**desan'dar** vi: **~ a correr** to break into a run; **~ a chorar** to burst into tears.

**desani'mado/a** adj (*pessoa*) depressed, downhearted; (*festa*) dull; **desanimar** vt (*desalentar*) to discourage; (*deprimir*) to depress; **desanimar-se** vr to lose heart; **desânimo** m depression; (*desalento*) dejection.

**desanuvi'ado/a** adj unclouded, clear; **desanuviar** vt to clear; **desanuviar-se** vr to clear up; (*cabeça*) to put one's mind at rest.

**desapaixonado/a** [dɛza-pajʃu'nadu/a] adj dispassionate.

**desapare'cer** vi to disappear, vanish; **desaparecido/a** adj lost, missing // m missing person; **desaparecimento** m disappearance; (*falecimento*) death; (*perda*) loss.

**desape'gado/a** adj indifferent, detached; **desapegar** vt to detach; **desapego** m indifference, detachment.

**desaperce'bido/a** adj (*desprevenido*) unprepared; (*desguarnecido*) unequipped.

**desaper'tar** vt (*desabotoar*) to unfasten; (*afrouxar*) to loosen.

**desapie'dado/a** adj pitiless, ruthless.

**desaponta'mento** m disappointment; **desapontar** vt to disappoint.

**desapropri'ar** vt (*bens*) to expropriate; (*pessoa*) to dispossess.

**desapro'var** vt (*reprovar*) to disapprove of; (*censurar*) to object to.

**desaproveitado/a** [dɛzaprovej'tadu/a] adj wasted; (*terras*) undeveloped.

**desarma'mento** m disarmament; **desarmar** vt to disarm; (*desmontar*) to dismantle; (*bomba*) to defuse.

**desarmo'nia** f discord.

**desarraigar** [dɛzaxajˈgax] vt to uproot.

**desarranjado/a** [dɛzaxãˈʒadu/a] adj (*intestino*) upset; (*TEC*) out of order; **desarranjar** vt (*transtornar*) to upset, disturb; (*estragar*) to mess up; **desarranjo** m (*desordem*) disorder; (*enguiço*) breakdown; (*col*) diarrhoea.

**desarru'mado/a** adj untidy, messy; (*TEC*) out of order; **desarrumar** vt to disarrange; (*mala*) to unpack.

**desarticu'lado/a** adj dislocated; **desarticular** vt (*osso*) to dislocate.

**desassos'sego** m (*inquietação*) disquiet; (*perturbação*) restlessness.

**desas'trado/a** adj (*funesto*)

disastrous; (*sem graça*) awkward, clumsy; **desastre** *m* disaster; (*acidente*) accident; (*de avião*) crash; **desastroso/a** *adj* disastrous.

**desa'tar** *vt* (*botão*) to unfasten; (*nó*) to undo, untie // *vi*: ~ **a chorar** to burst into tears; ~ **a rir** to burst out laughing.

**desaten'der** *vt* (*não fazer caso de*) to pay no attention to, ignore; (*desprezar*) to be discourteous to // *vi*: ~ **a** to ignore.

**desati'nado/a** *adj* crazy, wild; **desatinar** *vi* to behave foolishly; **desatino** *m* (*loucura*) madness; **ato de desatino** folly, foolishness.

**desa'vença** *f* (*briga*) quarrel; (*discórdia*) disagreement; **em ~ at** loggerheads.

**desavergonhado/a** [deza-vexgo'nadu/a] *adj* insolent, impudent, shameless.

**desa'vir-se** *vr*: ~ **com** to fall out with.

**desbarata'mento** *m* (*derrota*) defeat; (*desperdício*) waste; **desbaratar** *vt* to ruin; (*desperdiçar*) to waste, squander; (*vencer*) to defeat.

**desbas'tar** *vt* (*cabelo, plantas*) to thin (out); (*vegetação*) to trim; (*fig*) to polish.

**desbo'tar** *vt* to discolour // *vi* to fade; ~**-se** *vr* to fade.

**desbrava'dor(a)** *m/f* explorer; **desbravar** *vt* (*terras desconhecidas*) to explore.

**desca'bido/a** *adj* (*impróprio*) improper; (*inoportuno*) inappropriate.

**descal'çar** *vt* (*sapatos*) to take off; ~**-se** *vr* to take off one's shoes; **descalço/a** *adj* barefoot.

**desca'mar** *vt* (*peixe*) to scale.

**descam'pado** *m* open country.

**descan'sado/a** *adj* (*tranqüilo*) calm, quiet; (*vagaroso*) slow; **fique ~** don't worry; **descansar** *vt* to rest; (*apoiar*) to lean // *vi* (*repousar*) to

rest, relax; **descansar em** (*confiar*) to trust; **descanso** *m* (*repouso*) rest; (*alívio*) relief; (*folga*) break; (*recreio*) relaxation; **sem descanso** without a pause.

**desca'rado/a** *adj* cheeky, impudent; **descaramento** *m* cheek, impudence.

**des'carga** *f* unloading; (*vaso sanitário*) flushing; (*MIL*) volley; (*ELET*) discharge; **dar ~** to flush the toilet.

**descar'nado/a** *adj* scrawny, skinny.

**descaro'çar** *vt* (*semente*) to seed; (*fruto*) to stone, core; (*algodão*) to gin.

**descarregadouro** [deʃka-xega'doru] *m* wharf; **descarregamento** *m* unloading; (*ELET*) discharge; **descarregar** *vt* (*carga*) to unload; (*ELET*) to discharge; (*aliviar*) to relieve; (*raiva*) to give vent to.

**descarrilha'mento** *m* derailment; **descarrilhar** *vt* to derail // *vi* to run off the rails; (*fig*) to go off the rails.

**descar'tar** *vt* to discard; ~**-se de** to get rid of.

**descasca'dor** *m* peeler; **descascar** *vt* (*fruta*) to peel; (*ervilhas*) to shell; (*repreender*) to tear a strip off // *vi*: **o feijão descascou** the skin came off the beans; **a cobra descascou** the snake shed its skin.

**descen'dência** *f* descendants *pl*, offspring *pl*; **descendente** *adj* descending, going down // *m/f* descendant; **descender** *vi*: **descender de** to descend from.

**descentrali'zar** *vt* to decentralize.

**descer** [deʃ'sex] *vt* (*escada*) to go/come down; (*bagagem*) to take down // *vi* (*saltar*) to get off; (*baixar*) to go/come down; ~ **a pormenores** to get down to details.

**descer'rar** vt (abrir) to open; (revelar) to reveal, disclose.

**descida** [deʃ'sida] f descent; (declive) slope; (abaixamento) fall, drop.

**desclassifi'car** vt (eliminar) to disqualify; (desacreditar) to discredit.

**desco'berto/a** adj discovered; (nu) bare, naked; (exposto) exposed; a ~ openly; pôr em ~ (conta) to overdraw // f discovery; (invenção) invention; **descobridor(a)** m/f discoverer; (explorador) explorer; **descobrimento** m discovery.

**desco'brir** vt (tirar cobertura) to uncover; (revelar) to reveal, show; (encontrar) to discover, find; (avistar) to discern; (petróleo) to strike; ~-se vr to take off one's hat.

**desco'lar** vt to unstick; (separar) to detach, remove.

**descolo'rir** vt to discolour // vi to fade.

**descompas'sado/a** adj (exagerado) out of all proportion; (ritmo) out of step.

**descom'por** vt (desordenar) to disturb, upset; (afrontar) to abuse; (censurar) to scold, tell off; **descomposto** adj (aspeto) improperly dressed; (transtornado) upset; **descompostura** f (desordem) disarray; (censura) dressing-down.

**descompri'mir** vt to decompress.

**descomu'nal** [-aw] adj (fora do comum) unusual; (colossal) huge, enormous.

**desconcer'tado/a** adj (embaraçado) disconcerted; (em desordem) out of order; **desconcertar** vt (atrapalhar) to confuse, baffle; **desconcertar-se** vr to get upset; **desconcerto** m (desordem) disorder, disarray; (discordância) disagreement.

**desco'nexo/a** adj (desunido) disconnected, unrelated; (incoerente) incoherent.

**desconfi'ado/a** adj suspicious, distrustful // m/f suspicious person; **desconfian'ça** f suspicion, distrust; **desconfiar** vi (julgar) to suspect; **desconfiar de alguém** to distrust sb.

**descon'forme** adj disagreeing, at variance.

**descon'forto** m discomfort; (aflição) distress.

**descongela'mento** m thawing; **descongelar** vt (degelar) to thaw out; **descongelar-se** vr (derreter-se) to melt.

**desconhecer** [deʃkoɲe'sex] vt (ignorar) not to know; (não reconhecer) not to recognise; (um benefício) not to acknowledge; (não admitir) not to accept; **desconhecido/a** adj unknown // m/f stranger; **desconhecimento** m ignorance.

**desconjun'tado/a** adj disjointed; (ossos) dislocated; **desconjuntar** vt (ossos) to dislocate; **desconjuntar-se** vr to come apart.

**desconso'lado/a** adj miserable, disconsolate; **desconsolar** vt to sadden, depress; **desconsolar-se** vr to despair.

**descon'tar** vt (abater) to deduct; (não levar em conta) to discount; (não fazer caso) to make light of.

**descontenta'mento** m discontent; (desgosto) displeasure; **descontentar** vt (desgostar) to displease; (lei) to go against; (pessoa) to upset; **descontente** adj (não satisfeito) dissatisfied; (infeliz) discontented.

**des'conto** m discount; **com ~** at a discount.

**descontro'lar-se** vr (situação) to get out of control; (pessoa) to lose one's self-control.

**desco'rar** vt to discolour // vi to pale, fade.

**descor'tês** adj rude, impolite; **descortesia** f rudeness, impoliteness.

**desco'ser** (Pt) vt (descosturar) to unstitch; (rasgar) to rip apart; ~-se vr to come apart at the seams.

**descostu'rar** (Br) vt ver descoser.

**des'crédito** m discredit.

**des'crença** f disbelief, incredulity; **descrente** adj sceptical // m/f sceptic; **descrer** vt to disbelieve // vi: **descrer de** to disbelieve in.

**descre'ver** vt to describe; **descrição** f description; **descritivo/a** adj descriptive; **descrito/a** pp de descrever.

**descuidado/a** [dɛʃkwi'dadu/a] adj careless; **descuidar** vt to neglect // vi: **descuidar de** to neglect, disregard; **descuido** m (falta de cuidado) carelessness; (negligência) neglect; (erro) oversight, slip; **por descuido** inadvertently.

**des'culpa** f (escusa) excuse; (perdão) pardon; **pedir ~s de alguma coisa a alguém** to apologise to sb for sth.

**descul'par** vt (justificar) to excuse; (perdoar) to pardon, forgive; **~ alguma coisa a alguém** to forgive sb for sth; **~-se** vr to apologize; **desculpe!** (I'm) sorry, I beg your pardon; **desculpável** adj excusable.

**'desde** prep from, since; **~ então** from that time, ever since; **~ há muito** for a long time (now); **~ já** at once, right now // conj: **~ que** since.

**desdém** [dɛʒ'dẽ] m scorn, disdain; **desdenhar** vt to scorn, disdain; **desdenhoso/a** adj disdainful, scornful.

**desden'tado/a** adj toothless.

**des'dita** f (desventura) misfortune; (infelicidade) unhappiness.

**desdi'zer** vt to contradict; **~-se** vr to go back on one's word.

**desdo'brar** vt (abrir) to unfold; (tropas) to deploy; (bandeira) to unfurl; **~-se** vr to unfold; (pessoa) to

work hard, make a big effort.

**des'douro** m tarnish, stain.

**dese'jar** [dese'ʒax] vt to want, desire; **~ ardentemente** to long for; **que deseja?** what would you like?; **desejável** adj desirable; **desejo** m wish, desire.

**desejoso/a** [deze'ʒozu/a] adj: **~ de alguma coisa** wishing for sth; **~ de fazer** anxious to do, keen to do.

**desemaranhar** [dɛzimara'ɲax] vt to disentangle; (decifrar) to unravel.

**desembainhar** [dɛzẽbajˈɲax] vt to unsheathe; (espada) to draw.

**desembara'çado/a** adj (livre) free, clear; (desinibido) uninhibited, free and easy.

**desembara'çar** vt (livrar) to free; (desenredar) to disentangle; **~-se** vr to lose one's inhibitions; **~-se de** to get rid of; **desembaraço** m (viveza) liveliness; (facilidade) ease; (confiança) self-assurance.

**desemba'rcar** vt (carga) to unload; (passageiros) to put on shore // vi to land, disembark; **desembarque** m landing, disembarkation.

**desemboca'dura** f river mouth; **desembocar** vi: **desembocar em** (rio) to flow into; (rua) to lead into.

**desembol'sar** vt to spend; **desembolso** m expenditure.

**desembre'ar** vt (AUTO) to declutch.

**desembrulhar** [dɛzẽbru'ʎax] vt to unwrap; (esclarecer) to clear up.

**desempaco'tar** vt to unpack.

**desem'pate** m: **partida de ~** (jogo) play-off, decider.

**desempe'nar** vt (endireitar) to straighten; **~-se** vr to stand up straight.

**desempenhar** [dɛzẽpe'ɲax] vt (cumprir) to carry out, fulfil; **~ um papel** to play a part; **desempenho** m (cumprimento) fulfilment; (teatro) performance.

**desemper'rar** vt to loosen.

**desempre'gado/a** *adj* unemployed // *m/f* unemployed person; **desempregar-se** *vr* to lose one's job; **desemprego** *m* unemployment.

**desenrade'ar** *vt* to unleash; (*despertar*) to provoke, trigger off // *vi* (*chuva*) to pour; **~-se** *vr* to break loose; (*tempestade*) to burst, break out.

**desencai'xado/a** *adj* misplaced; **desencaixar** *vt* to force out of joint; (*deslocar*) to dislodge, gouge out; **desencaixar-se** *vr* to become dislodged.

**desencaminhar** [dezẽkamiˈnax] *vt* to lead astray; (*dinheiro*) to embezzle; **~-se** *vr* to go astray.

**desencan'tar** *vt* to disenchant; (*desiludir*) to disillusion.

**desen'cargo** *m* fulfilment; **~ de consciência** clearing of one's conscience; **desencarregar-se** *vr* (*obrigação*) to discharge o.s.

**desenfasti'ar** *vt* to amuse; (*convalescente*) to restore sb's appetite; **~-se** *vr* to amuse o.s.

**desenfre'ado/a** *adj* unruly, wild.

**desenga'nar** *vt* to disillusion; (*de falsas crenças*) to put sb wise, to open sb's eyes; **~-se** *vr* (*sair de erro*) to realize the truth; (*desiludir-se*) to become disillusioned; **desengano** *m* disillusionment; (*desapontamento*) disappointment.

**desengon'çado/a** *adj* unhinged; (*mal-seguro*) rickety; (*pessoa*) ungainly.

**desengre'nado/a** *adj* out of gear.

**desenhar** [dezeˈnax] *vt* to draw; (*TEC*) to design; **~-se** (*figurar-se*) to take shape; **desenhista** *m/f* (*TEC*) designer; **desenho** *m* drawing; (*modelo*) design; (*esboço*) sketch; (*plano*) plan; **desenho animado** cartoon.

**desenlace** [dezeˈlasi] *m* outcome.

**desenre'dar** *vt* to disentangle; (*mistério*) to unravel; **~-se** *vr* to

extricate o.s.; **desenredo** *m* untangling.

**desenro'lar** *vt* to unroll; (*narrativa*) to develop; **~-se** *vr* to unfold.

**desenten'der** *vt* (*não entender*) to misunderstand; **~-se** *vr*: **~-se com** to fall out with; **desentendido/a** *adj*: **fazer-se de desentendido** to pretend not to understand; **desentendimento** *m* misunderstanding.

**desenter'rar** *vt* (*cadáver*) to exhume; (*tesouro*) to dig up; (*descobrir*) to bring to light.

**desento'ado/a** *adj* discordant; (*desafinado*) out of tune.

**desentranhar** [dezẽtraˈnax] *vt* to disembowel; (*arrancar*) to draw out.

**desentu'pir** *vt* to unblock.

**desen'volto/a** *adj* (*desembaraçado*) self-assured, confident; (*desinibido*) uninhibited; **desenvoltura** *f* (*desembaraço*) self-confidence.

**desenvol'ver** *vt* to develop; (*desembrulhar*) to unwrap; **~-se** *vr* to develop; **desenvolvimento** *m* development; (*crescimento*) growth.

**desequilibra'do/a** [dezikiliˈbradu/a] *adj* unbalanced.

**deserção** [dezexˈsãw] *f* desertion; **desertar** *vt* to desert, abandon // *vi* to desert; **deserto/a** *adj* (*desabitado*) deserted; (*solitário*) lonely // *m* desert.

**desespe'rado/a** *adj* desperate; (*furioso*) furious; **desesperança** *f* despair.

**desespe'rar** *vt* to drive to despair; **~-se** *vr* to despair; **desespero** *m* despair, desperation; (*raiva*) fury.

**desfaça'tez** *f* impudence, cheek.

**desfal'car** *vt* to embezzle.

**desfale'cer** *vt* (*enfraquecer*) to weaken // *vi* (*enfraquecer*) to weaken; (*desmaiar*) to faint.

**desfalque** [dʒfˈawki] *m* embezzlement, misappropriation.

**desfavo'rável** *adj* unfavourable.

**desfa'zer** vt (desmanchar) to undo; (dúvidas) to dispel; (agravo) to redress; ~-se vr (desaparecer) to vanish; (derreter-se) to melt; ~-se de (livrar-se) to get rid of.

**desfechar** [deʃfe'ʃax] vt (disparar) to fire; (setas) to shoot; (golpe) to deal; (insultos) to hurl // vi (tempestade) to break; **desfecho** m ending, outcome.

**desfeito/a** [deʃ'fejtu/a] pp de **desfazer** // adj (desmanchado) undone; (dissolvido) dissolved; (derrotado) destroyed; (contrato) broken // f affront, insult.

**desfe'rir** vt (golpe) to strike; (sons) to emit; (lançar) to throw.

**desfi'ar** vt to unweave, unravel; ~-se vr to become frayed.

**desfigu'rar** vt (adulterar) to distort; (tornar feio) to disfigure.

**desfiladeiro** [deʃfila'dejru] m (de montanha) pass.

**desfi'lar** vi to march past, parade past; **desfile** m parade, procession.

**des'forra** f (vingança) revenge; (reparação) redress; **tirar** ~ to get even.

**desfru'tar** vt (deliciar-se com) to enjoy; (parasitar) to sponge on; **desfrute** m (deleite) enjoyment; (zombaria) ridicule, mockery.

**desgalhar** [dɛ:ʒga'ʎax] vt to prune.

**desgar'rado/a** adj lost; (navio) off course; **desgarrar-se** vr: **desgarrar-se de** to stray from.

**desgas'tar** vt to wear away, erode; ~-se vr to become worn away; **desgaste** m wear and tear.

**desgos'tar** vt (desagradar) to displease; (contrariar) to annoy // vi: ~ **de** to dislike; ~-se vr: ~-se **de** to lose one's liking for; ~-se **com** to take offence at; **desgosto** m (desprazer) displeasure; (pesar) sorrow; (mágoa) pain.

**des'graça** f (desventura) misfortune; (miséria) misery; (desfavor) disgrace; (desastre)

disaster; **desgraçado/a** adj (infeliz) poor, unfortunate; (pobre) poor, miserable // m/f wretch.

**desgrenhado/a** [dɛ:ʒgre'ɲadu/a] adj dishevelled, tousled.

**desidratação** [dezidrata'sãw] f dehydration; **desidratar** vt to dehydrate.

**designação** [dezigna'sãw] f (indicação) designation; (nomeação) appointment; (escolha) choice; **designar** vt to designate; (nomear) to name, appoint.

**designio** [de'ziʒniu] m (propósito) purpose.

**desigual** adj (terreno) uneven; (combate) unequal.

**desilu'dir** vt (desenganar) to disillusion; (causar decepção a) to disappoint; ~-se vr to lose one's illusions; **desilusão** f disillusionment, disenchantment.

**desimpe'dido/a** adj free; **desimpedir** vt (obstáculo) to clear away.

**desinchar** [dezin'ʃax] vt (orgulho) to deflate; (MED) to reduce the swelling of; ~-se vr to become less swollen.

**desinfecção** [dezinfe'sãw] f disinfection; **desinfetante** (Pt: -ct-) adj, m disinfectant; **desinfetar** (Pt: -ct-) vt to disinfect.

**desintegração** [dezintegra'sãw] f disintegration, break-up; **desintegrar** vt to separate; **desintegrar-se** vr to disintegrate, fall to pieces.

**desinteres'sado/a** adj disinterested, dispassionate, impartial; **desinteressar-se** vr: **desinteressar-se de** to lose interest in; **desinteresse** m (falta de interesse) lack of interest.

**desis'tir** vi to give up; ~ **de fumar** to stop smoking.

**desle'al** [-aw] adj disloyal; ~**dade** f disloyalty.

**desleixo** [deʒ'lejʃu] m (negligência)

carelessness; (*pessoa*) slovenliness.
**desli'gado/a** adj (*eletricidade*) off;
(*pessoa*) **estar ~** to be miles away;
**desligar** vt (*TEC*) to disconnect;
(*desatar*) to unfasten, undo; (*soltar*)
to release; (*luz*, *TV*) to switch off;
(*telefone*) to hang up; **não desligue**
(*TEL*) hold the line.
**desli'zar** vi to slide; (*por acidente*)
to slip; (*passar de leve*) to glide;
**deslize** m (*lapso*) lapse;
(*escorregadela*) slip.
**deslo'car** vt (*mover*) to move;
(*afastar*) to remove; (*articulação*) to
dislocate.
**deslumbra'mento** m dazzle;
(*fascinação*) fascination;
**deslumbrar** vt to dazzle;
(*maravilhar*) to amaze; (*fascinar*) to
fascinate.
**deslus'trar** vt to tarnish;
(*manchar*) to sully.
**desmaiado/a** [deʒmaˈjadu/a] adj
(*sem sentidos*) unconscious; (*pálido*)
faint; **desmaiar** vi (*desfalecer*) to
faint; (*descorar*) to turn pale;
**desmaio** m (*desfalecimento*) faint;
(*desalento*) dejection.
**desma'mar** vt to wean.
**desmancha-prazeres** [deʒ-
manʃaˈprazerɪʃ] m/f kill-joy,
spoilsport.
**desmanchar** [dezmanˈʃax] vt
(*costura*) to undo; (*contrato*) to
break; (*noivado*) to break off; **~-se**
vr (*costura*) to come undone.
**desmante'lar** vt (*demolir*) to
demolish; (*desmontar*) to dismantle,
take apart.
**desmasca'rar** vt to unmask.
**desmaze'lado/a** adj slovenly,
untidy.
**desme'dido/a** adj excessive.
**desmen'tido** m (*negação*) denial;
(*contradição*) contradiction;
**desmentir** vt (*contradizer*) to
contradict; (*negar*) to deny.
**desmere'cer** vt (*não merecer*)
not to deserve; (*rebaixar*) to belittle.

**desmesu'rado/a** adj immense,
enormous.
**desmio'lado/a** adj brainless.
**desmon'tar** vt (*máquina*) to take
to pieces // vi (*do cavalo*) to
dismount, get off.
**desmorali'zar** vt to demoralize.
**desmoro'nar** vt to knock down //
vi to collapse.
**desna'tar** vt to skim.
**desneces'sário/a** adj unnecessary.
**des'nível** m difference in levels.
**desnorte'ado/a** adj (*perturbado*) bewildered, confused;
(*desorientado*) off course;
**desnortear** vt to throw off course;
(*embaraçar*) to bewilder;
**desnortear-se** vr to lose one's way;
(*perturbar-se*) to become confused.
**desnu'dar** vt to strip; **~-se** vr to
undress.
**desnutrição** [deʒnutriˈsãw] f
malnutrition.
**desobede'cer** vt to disobey;
**desobediência** f disobedience.
**desobri'gar** vt to free from doing,
excuse from doing.
**desocu'pado/a** adj (*casa*) empty,
vacant; (*disponível*) free; (*sem
trabalho*) unemployed; **desocupar** vt
(*casa*) to vacate.
**desodo'rante** m deodorant.
**desolação** [dezolaˈsãw] f (*de um
lugar*) desolation; (*fig*) grief;
**desolado/a** adj (*lugar*) desolate;
(*fig*) distressed; **desolar** vt (*afligir*)
to distress.
**deso'nesto/a** adj (*sem honestidade*)
dishonest; (*impudico*) indecent.
**des'onra** f (*desonrar*) disgrace; **desonrar** (*infamar*) to
disgrace; (*mulher*) to seduce;
**desonrar-se** vr to disgrace o.s.
**desordem** [dezˈoxdẽ] f disorder,
confusion; **em ~** (*casa*) untidy.
**desorgani'zar** vt to disorganize;
(*dissolver*) to break up.
**desorientação** [dezorĩetaˈsãw]

**f** bewilderment, confusion; **desorientar** vt (desnortear) to throw off course; (perturbar) to confuse; **desorientar-se** vr (perder-se) to lose one's way.

**deso'ssar** vt (galinha) to bone.

**de'sova** f laying (of eggs); **desovar** vt to lay; (peixe) to spawn.

**despachar** [deʃpa'ʃax] vt (expedir) to dispatch, send off; (atender) to deal with; (matar) to kill; **~-se** to hurry (up); **despacho** m (remessa) dispatch; (decisão) decision.

**desparafu'sar** vt to unscrew.

**despeda'çar** vt (quebrar) to smash; (rasgar) to tear apart.

**despe'dida** f (adeus) farewell; (de trabalhador) dismissal.

**despe'dir** vt (de emprego) to dismiss, sack; (mandar embora) to send away; **~-se** vr: **~-se de** to say goodbye to.

**despe'gar** vt to take off; **~-se** vr: **~-se de** to go off, lose one's liking for; **despego** m detachment, indifference.

**despeitado/a** [deʃpej'tadu/a] adj spiteful; (ressentido) resentful; **despeito** m spite; **a despeito de** in spite of, despite.

**despejar** [deʃpe'ʒax] vt (água) to pour; (esvaziar) to empty; (inquilino) to evict; **despejo** m (de casa) eviction; **quarto de despejo** junk room.

**despen'car** vi to fall down, tumble down.

**despenhadeiro** [deʃpeɲa'dejro] m cliff, precipice.

**des'pensa** f larder.

**desperce'bido/a** adj unnoticed.

**desperdi'çar** vt to waste; (dinheiro) to squander; **desperdício** m waste.

**desperta'dor** m alarm clock; **despertar** vt (pessoa) to wake; (suspeitas) to arouse; (reminiscências) to revive; (apetite) to

whet // vi to wake up, awake; **desperto/a** adj awake.

**des'pesa** f expense.

**des'pido/a** adj (nu) naked, bare; (livre) free.

**des'pir** vt (roupa) to take off; (pessoa) to undress; (despojar) to strip; **~-se** vr to undress.

**despis'tar** vt to throw off the track, mislead.

**despo'jado/a** adj (pessoa) unambitious; (lugar) spartan, basic; **despojar** vt (privar) to strip; **despojo** m loot, booty; **despojos mortais** mortal remains.

**despon'tar** vi to emerge; **ao ~ do dia** at daybreak.

**des'porto** m sport.

**despo'sado/a** adj, m/f newly-wed; **desposar** vt to marry; **desposar-se** vr to get married.

**'déspota** m despot; **despotismo** m despotism.

**despovo'ado/a** adj uninhabited // m wilderness; **despovoar** vt to depopulate.

**despre'gar** vt to take off, detach; **~ os olhos de** to take one's eyes off; **~-se** vr to free o.s.

**despren'der** vt (soltar) to loosen; (desatar) to unfasten; (emitir) to emit; **~-se** vr (botão) to come off; (cheiro) to be given off.

**despreocu'pado/a** adj carefree, unconcerned.

**despretensi'oso/a** adj unpretentious, modest.

**despreve'nido/a** adj unprepared, unready; **apanhar ~** to catch unawares.

**despre'zar** vt (não prezar) to despise, disdain; (recusar) to reject; **desprezível** adj despicable; **desprezo** m scorn, contempt; **dar ao desprezo** to ignore.

**desproporção** [deʃpropox'sãw] f disproportion; **desproporcionado/a** adj disproportionate; (desigual) unequal; **desproporcional** adj disproportionate.

**desproposi'tado/a** adj (absurdo) preposterous; **despropósito** m nonsense.

**despro'vido/a** adj deprived; ~ **de** without.

**desquitar-se** [deʃkiˈtax-si] vr to get a legal separation; **desquite** m legal separation.

**desre'grado/a** adj (desordenado) disorderly, unruly; (devasso) immoderate; **desregrar-se** vr to run riot.

**desrespeitar** [deʒxeʃpejˈtax] vt to disrespect; **desrespeito** m disrespect; **desrespeitoso/a** adj disrespectful.

**'desse** etc vb ver **dar** // = **de** + **esse**.

**desse'car** vt to dry up; ~**se** vr to dry up.

**desta'cado/a** adj outstanding; **destacamento** m (MIL) detachment.

**desta'car** vt (MIL) to detail; ~ **alguma coisa** to make sth stand out; (fig) to emphasize sth; ~**se** vr to stand out; (pessoa) to be outstanding.

**destam'par** vt to take the lid off.

**desta'par** vt (descobrir) to uncover; (abrir) to open.

**destaque** [deʃˈtaki] m distinction; **pessoa de** ~ notable person.

**'deste** etc = **de** + **este**, ver **este**.

**deste'mido/a** adj fearless, intrepid.

**destempe'rar** vt (diluir) to dilute, weaken; (perturbar) to upset.

**dester'rar** vt (exilar) to exile; (fig) to banish; **desterro** m exile.

**destilação** [deʃtʃilaˈsãw] f distillation; **destilar** vt to distil; **destilaria** f distillery.

**desti'nar** vt to destine; ~ **dinheiro para** to set aside money for; ~**se** vr: ~**se a** to be intended for, be addressed to; **destinatário/a** m/f addressee.

**des'tino** m (fortuna) destiny, fate; (finalidade) purpose; (lugar) destination; **com** ~ **a** bound for; **sem** ~ (direção) [adj] aimless; (adv) aimlessly.

**destituição** [deʃtʃitwiˈsãw] f (demissão) dismissal; **destituir** vt (demitir) to dismiss; **destituir de** (privar de) to deprive of.

**desto'ante** adj (som) discordant; (opiniões) diverging; **destoar** vi (som) to jar; (não condizer) to be out of keeping.

**destran'car** vt to unbolt.

**destra'var** vt to unlatch.

**des'treza** f (habilidade) skill; (agilidade) dexterity.

**destrin'çar** vt (desenredar) to unravel; (esmiuçar) to treat in detail.

**'destro/a** adj (hábil) skilful; (ágil) agile; (não canhoto) right-handed.

**destro'çar** vt (derrotar) to destroy; (quebrar) to smash, break; (arruinar) to ruin, wreck; **destroço** m destruction; **destroços** mpl wreckage sg; (pedaços) pieces.

**des'tronar** vt to depose.

**destruição** [deʃtrwiˈsãw] f destruction; **destruidor(a)** adj destructive; **destruir** vt to destroy.

**desu'mano/a** adj inhuman; (bárbaro) cruel.

**desunião** [dezunjˈãw] f disunity; (separação) separation; **desunir** vt (separar) to separate; (TEC) to disconnect; (fig) to cause a rift between.

**desu'sado/a** adj (não usado) disused; (incomum) unusual; **desuso** m disuse; **em desuso** out of use.

**desvairado/a** [deʒvajˈradu/a] adj (louco) crazy, demented; (desorientado) bewildered; **desvairar** vt to drive mad.

**desva'lido/a** adj (desamparado) helpless; (miserável) destitute; **desvalorizar** vt to devalue;

**desvalorizar-se** *vr* to undervalue o.s.

**desvane'cer** *vt* (*tornar orgulhoso*) to make vain; **~-se** *vr* to vanish; **desvanecido/a** *adj* faded; (*vaidoso*) vain.

**desvantagem** [dɛʒvɐnˈtaʒẽ] *f* disadvantage.

**desva'rio** *m* madness, folly.

**desve'lar** *vt* (*revelar*) to unveil, reveal; **~-se** *vr* (*ter cuidado*) to be solicitous; **desvelo** *m* (*vigilância*) vigilance; (*cuidado*) devotion.

**desven'dar** *vt* (*tirar a venda*) to remove the blindfold from; (*revelar*) to disclose.

**desven'tura** *f* (*desgraça*) misfortune; (*infelicidade*) unhappiness; **desventurado/a** *adj* (*desgraçado*) unfortunate; (*infeliz*) unhappy // *m* (*infeliz*) wretch.

**desvi'ar** *vt* (*veículo*) to divert; (*um golpe*) to ward off; (*dinheiro*) to embezzle; **~ os olhos** to look away; **~-se** *vr* (*afastar-se*) to turn away; **~-se de** (*evitar*) to avoid; **~-se do assunto** to digress; **desvio** *m* diversion, detour; (*curva*) bend; (*fig*) deviation; (*de dinheiro*) embezzlement; (*FERRO*) siding.

**desvirtu'ar** *vt* (*fatos*) to misrepresent.

**detalhar** [detaˈʎax] *vt* to (give in) detail; **detalhe** *m* detail.

**detenção** [detẽˈsɐ̃w] *f* detention; **deter** *vt* (*fazer parar*) to stop; (*prender*) to arrest, detain; (*documento*) to keep; **deter-se** *vr* to stop.

**detergente** [detɛxˈʒẽtʃi] *m* detergent, soap powder.

**deterioração** [deteriɔraˈsɐ̃w] *f* deterioration; **deteriorar** *vt* to spoil, damage; **deteriorar-se** *vr* to deteriorate; (*relações*) to worsen.

**determinação** [detɛxminaˈsɐ̃w] *f* (*firmeza*) determination; (*decisão*) decision.

**determi'nar** *vt* (*fixar*) to

---

determine, settle; (*decretar*) to order; (*resolver*) to decide (on); (*causar*) to cause.

**detes'tar** *vt* to hate, detest; **detestável** *adj* horrible, hateful.

**dete'tive** *vt* (*Pt:* -**ct**-) *m* detective.

**de'tidamente** *adv* carefully, thoroughly; **detido/a** *adj* (*preso*) under arrest; (*minucioso*) thorough.

**deto'nar** *vi* to detonate, go off.

**de'trás** *adv* behind // *prep*: **~ de** behind; **por ~** (*from*) behind.

**detri'mento** *m*: **em ~ de** to the detriment of.

**de'trito** *m* debris *sg*, remains *pl*, dregs *pl*.

**detur'par** *vt* (*desfigurar*) to disfigure; (*viciar*) to corrupt; (*adulterar*) to pervert, adulterate.

**deus(a)** [dews(a)] *m* god; **D~ me livre!** God forbid!; **Graças a D~** thank goodness; **se D~ quiser** God willing; **meu D~!** good Lord // *f* goddess.

**deus-dará** [dewʒ-daˈra] *adv*: **viver ao ~** to live from hand to mouth.

**deva'gar** *adv* slowly; **~inho** *adv* nice and slowly.

**devane'ar** *vt* to imagine, dream of // *vi* to daydream; (*divagar*) to wander, digress; **devaneio** *m* daydream.

**de'vassa** *f* investigation, inquiry.

**devassidão** [devasiˈdɐ̃w] *f* debauchery; **devasso/a** *adj* dissolute // *m* lecher.

**devas'tar** *vt* (*destruir*) to devastate; (*arruinar*) to ruin.

**'deve** *m* (*débito*) debit; (*coluna*) debit column; **devedor(a)** *adj* owing // *m/f* debtor.

**de'ver** *m* duty // *vt* to owe // *vi* (*suposição*) **deve** (*de*) **estar doente** he must be ill; (*obrigação*) **devo partir às oito** (*have to*) I must go at eight; **você devia ir ao médico** (*ought to*) you should go to the doctor; **ele devia ter vindo** (*ought to have*) he should have come; **que**

**devo fazer?** what shall I do?

de'veras adv really, indeed.

devida'mente adv properly, duly; **devido a** due to, owing to; **no devido tempo** in due course.

devido/a adj proper;

devoção [devo'sãw] f devotion.

devolução [devolu'sãw] f devolution; (restituição) return; **devolver** vt to give back, return; (COM) to refund.

devo'rar vt to devour, eat up.

devo'tar vt to devote; ~-se vr: ~-se a to devote o.s. to; devoto/a adj devout // m/f devotee.

'dez num ten.

de'zembro m December.

de'zena f: uma ~ ten; (dias) ten days.

dezenove [dezi'nɔvi] (Pt: deza'nove) num nineteen.

dezesseis [dezi'sejʃ] (Pt: deza'sseis) num sixteen.

dezessete [dezi'setʃi] (Pt: deza'ssete) num seventeen.

dezoito [de'zojtu] num eighteen.

**D.F.** (Br) abr de **Distrito Federal** ≈ capital (city).

'dia m day; (claridade) daylight; ~ a ~ day by day; (jornal) daily (paper); ~ de folga day off; ~ útil weekday; andar em ~ to be up-to-date; de ~ by day; hoje em ~ nowadays; mais ~ menos ~ sooner or later; no outro ~ on the next day; todos os ~s every day.

dia'bético/a adj, m/f diabetic.

di'abo m devil; dos ~s fiendish; que ~! damn it!; por que ...? why the devil ...?; diabólico/a adj diabolical; diabrete m imp.

dia'brura f prank; ~s fpl mischief sg.

dia'fragma m diaphragm.

diagnosti'car vt to diagnose; diagnóstico m diagnosis.

dia'leto (Pt: -ct-) m dialect.

di'álogo m dialogue; (conversa) talk, conversation.

dia'mante m diamond.

di'âmetro m diameter.

di'ante adv in front // prep: ~ de before; (na frente de) in front of; **daqui em** ~ from now on; **e assim por** ~ and so on; **para** ~ forward; **dianteiro/a** adj front // f front, vanguard; **tomar a dianteira** to get ahead.

diaposi'tivo m (FOTO) slide.

di'ário/a adj daily // m diary; (jornal) daily (paper); (COM) accounts book; ~ **de bordo** log book // f (de hotel) daily rate.

diarréia [dʒia'xeja] f diarrhoea.

'dica f (col) hint.

dicção [dʒik'sãw] f diction.

dicionário [dʒisjo'narju] m dictionary.

'diesel adj: motor a ~ diesel motor.

di'eta f diet; fazer ~ to go on a diet.

difamação [dʒifama'sãw] f (escrita) libel; (falada) slander; difamar vt to slander, libel.

dife'rença f difference; diferente adj different.

dife'rir vi: ~ de to differ from.

di'fícil [dʒi'fisjw] adj difficult, hard; dificilmente adv with difficulty; (apenas) hardly; dificuldade f difficulty; (aperto) trouble; **em dificuldades** in trouble; dificultar vt to make difficult; (complicar) to complicate.

difte'ria f diphtheria.

difun'dir vt (luz) to shed, cast; (espalhar) to spread; (notícia) to broadcast.

'diga etc vb ver dizer.

digerir [dʒiʒe'rix] vt to digest; digestão f digestion.

'digital [-aw] adj: impressão ~ fingerprint; dígito m digit.

dig'nar-se vr: ~ de to deign to, condescend to; dignidade f dignity; (função) rank; digno/a adj (merecedor) worthy; (nobre) dignified.

**'digo** etc vb ver **dizer.**

**digressão** [dɪgrɛ'sãw] f digression.

**dilace'rar** vt to tear to pieces, lacerate.

**dilatação** [dʒɪlata'sãw] f dilation; **dilatar** vt to dilate, expand; (prolongar) to prolong; (retardar) to delay.

**di'lema** m dilemma.

**diligência** [dʒɪlɪ'ʒẽsja] f diligence; (pesquisa) inquiry; (veículo)
- stagecoach; **diligente** adj hardworking, industrious.

**diluir** [dʒɪl'wɪx] vt to dilute.

**di'lúvio** m flood.

**dimensão** [dʒɪmẽ'sãw] f dimension; **dimensões** fpl measurements.

**diminuição** [dʒɪmɪnwɪ'sãw] f reduction; **diminuir** vt to reduce // vi to grow less, diminish; **diminuto/a** adj minute, tiny.

**Dina'marca** f Denmark; **dinamarquês/quesa** adj Danish // m/f Dane.

**di'nâmico/a** adj dynamic; **dinamismo** m (fig) energy, drive.

**dinami'tar** vt to blow up; **dinamite** f dynamite.

**'dínamo** m dynamo.

**dinas'tia** f dynasty.

**dinheiro** [dʒɪ'nejru] m money; ~ **de contado** (Pt) ready cash; ~ **miúdo** small change; **sem** ~ (col) penniless, broke.

**di'ploma** m diploma.

**diploma'cia** f diplomacy; **diplomata** m/f diplomat; **diplomático/a** adj diplomatic; (discreto) tactful.

**dique** ['dʒɪkɪ] m dam; (GEO) dike.

**direção** [dʒɪre'sãw] (Pt: -cç-) f direction; (endereço) address; (AUTO) steering; (administração) management; (comando) leadership; (diretoria) board of directors; **em** ~ **a** towards.

**di'rei** etc vb ver **dizer.**

**direito/a** [dʒɪ'rejtu/a] adj right-

hand; (reto) straight; (justo) right, just // m (prerrogativa) right; (JUR) law; **ter** ~ **a** to have a right to; ~**s** mpl (alfandegários) duties; (de autor) royalties; **livre de** ~**s** duty-free // f (mão) right hand; (lado) right-hand side; (política) right wing; **mantenha-se à** ~**a** (AUTO) keep to the right!; **à** ~**a** on the right // adv (em linha reta) straight; (bem) right.

**di'reto/a** (Pt: -ct-) adj (reto) straight; (contato) direct; **trem/comboio** ~ through train; **transmissão** ~**a** (TV) live broadcast; **diretor(a)** (Pt: -ct-) adj directing, guiding // m/f (COM) director; (de jornal) editor; (MÚS) conductor // m headmaster // f headmistress.

**dirigir** [dʒɪrɪ'ʒɪx] vt to direct; (COM) to manage, run; (veículo) to drive; (atenção) to turn; ~**se** vr: ~**se a** (falar com) to speak to, address; (lugar) to go to, head for.

**diri'mir** vt (anular) to annul, cancel; (dúvida) to settle, clear up.

**discagem** [dʒɪ'kaʒẽ] f (TEL) dialling; ~ **direta** direct dialling; **discar** vi to dial.

**disci'plina** f discipline; **disciplinar** vt to discipline.

**dis'cípulo/a** m/f disciple; (aluno) pupil.

**'disco** m disc; (MÚS) record; (de telefone) dial; ~ **voador** flying saucer.

**discor'dar** vi to disagree; **discórdia** f discord, strife.

**discor'rer** vi (falar) to talk, reason; (vaguear) to stroll around.

**disco'teca** f record-library; (danceteria) discotheque; (col) disco.

**discre'pância** f discrepancy; (desacordo) disagreement; **discrepar** vi: **discrepar de** to differ from.

**dis'creto/a** adj discreet;

(*modesto*) modest; (*prudente*) shrewd; **discrição** f discretion, good sense.

**discrimi'nar** vt to discriminate; (*distinguir*) to discern; ~ **entre** to discriminate between.

**discur'sar** vi (*em público*) to make a speech; (*falar*) to speak; **discurso** m speech; (LING) discourse.

**discussão** [diʃkuˈsãw] f (*debate*) discussion, debate; (*contenda*) argument.

**disfar'çar** vt to disguise; **disfarce** m disguise; (*máscara*) mask.

**dis'forme** adj deformed, hideous.

**dispa'rar** vt to shoot, fire // vi (*arma*) to go off; (*correr*) to shoot off, bolt.

**dispara'tado/a** adj silly, absurd; **disparate** m nonsense, rubbish; (*erro*) blunder.

**dis'pêndio** m expenditure; (*fig*) loss.

**dis'pensa** f exemption; (REL) dispensation; **dispensar** vt (*desobrigar*) to excuse; (*prescindir de*) to do without; (*conferir*) to grant.

**disper'sar** vt to disperse.

**displicência** [diʃpliˈsensja] f (Br: descuido) negligence, carelessness; **displicente** adj careless.

**dispo'nível** adj available; **dispor** vt (*arranjar*) to arrange; (*colocar em ordem*) to put in order // vi: **dispor de** (*usar*) to have the use of; (*ter*) to have, own; **dispor-se** vr: **dispor-se a** to be prepared to, be willing to; **não disponho de tempo para ...** I can't afford the time to ...

**disposição** [dispoziˈsãw] f (*arranjo*) arrangement; (*humor*) disposition; (*intento*) intention; **à sua ~** at your disposal.

**disposi'tivo** m (*mecanismo*) gadget, device.

**dis'posto/a** adj (*arranjado*) arranged, ready; (*inclinado a*) disposed, willing; **estar bem ~** to be in a good mood; **sentir-se ~ a fazer** to feel like doing.

**dis'puta** f dispute, argument; **disputar** vt to dispute; (*lutar por*) to fight over; **disputar uma corrida** to run a race // vi (*discutir*) to quarrel, argue; (*competir*) to compete.

**'disse** etc vb ver **dizer.**

**disse'car** vt to dissect.

**dissemi'nar** vt to disseminate; (*espalhar*) to spread.

**dissensão** [disenˈsãw] f dissension, discord.

**dissertação** [disextaˈsãw] f dissertation; (*ensaio*) thesis; (*discurso*) lecture; **dissertar** vi to speak.

**dissi'dente** adj, m/f dissident.

**dissimulação** [disimulaˈsãw] f (*fingimento*) pretence; (*disfarce*) disguise; **dissimular** vt (*ocultar*) to hide; (*fingir*) to pretend // vi to dissemble.

**dissipação** [disipaˈsãw] f waste, squandering; **dissipar** vt (*dispersar*) to disperse, dispel; (*malgastar*) to squander, waste; **dissipar-se** vr to vanish.

**dissolução** [disoluˈsãw] f (*dissolvência*) dissolving; (*libertinagem*) debauchery; **dissoluto/a** adj dissolute, debauched.

**dissol'ver** vt (*solver*) to dissolve; (*dispersar*) to disperse; (*motim*) to break up.

**dissua'dir** vt to dissuade; ~ **alguém de fazer** to talk sb out of doing, dissuade sb from doing.

**dis'tância** f distance; **a grande ~** far away; **à ~ de 3 quilómetros** 3 kilometres away; **distanciar** vt (*afastar*) to distance, set apart; (*colocar por intervalos*) to space out; **distanciar-se** vr to move away; **distante** adj distant, far-off; (*fig*) aloof; **distar** vi to be far away; **o aeroporto dista 10 quilómetros da**

**cidade** the airport is 10 kilometres away from the city.

**distinção** [dʒiʃtʃĩ'sãw] f (*diferença*) difference; (*em exame*) distinction; (*honraria*) honour.

**distinguir** [dʒiʃtʃĩ'gix] vt (*diferenciar*) to distinguish, differentiate; (*avistar*) to make out; **~-se** vr to stand out; **distintivo/a** adj distinctive // m (*insígnia*) badge; (*emblema*) emblem; **distinto/a** adj (*diferente*) different; (*eminente*) distinguished; (*claro*) distinct.

**distração** [dʒiʃtra'sãw] (Pt: **-cç-**) f (*alheamento*) absent-mindedness; (*divertimento*) pastime; (*descuido*) oversight; **distraído/a** adj absent-minded; (*não atento*) inattentive; **distrair** vt (*tornar desatento*) to distract; (*divertir*) to amuse; **distrair-se** vr to amuse o.s.

**distribuição** [dʒiʃtribwi'sãw] f distribution; (*de cartas*) delivery; **distribuir** vt to distribute; (*repartir*) to share out; (*cartas*) to deliver.

**dis'trito** m district; **~ eleitoral** constituency.

**dis'túrbio** m disturbance.

**di'tado** m dictation; (*provérbio*) saying.

**dita'dor** m dictator; **ditadura** f dictatorship.

**di'tame** m (*da consciência*) dictate; (*regra*) rule; **ditar** vt to dictate; (*impor*) to impose.

**'dito/a** pp de **dizer**; **~ e feito** no sooner said than done // m: **~ espirituoso** witticism.

**di'tongo** m diphthong.

**di'toso/a** adj (*feliz*) happy; (*venturoso*) lucky.

**di'urno/a** adj day.

**diva'gar** vi (*vaguear*) to wander; **~ do assunto** to wander off the subject, digress.

**divergência** [dʒivex'ʒẽsja] f divergence; (*desacordo*) disagreement.

**diversão** [dʒivex'sãw] f

(*divertimento*) amusement; (*passatempo*) pastime.

**diversi'dade** f diversity; **diversificar** vt to diversify // vi to vary; **diverso/a** adj (*diferente*) different; (*pl*) various // pron: **diversos** some, several.

**diver'tido/a** adj amusing, funny; **divertimento** m amusement, entertainment; **divertir** vt to amuse, entertain; **divertir-se** vr to enjoy o.s., have a good time.

**'dívida** f debt; (*obrigação*) indebtedness; **contrair ~s** to run into debt.

**divi'dir** vt to divide; (*despesas*) to share; **~-se** vr to divide, split up.

**di'visa** f (*emblema*) emblem; (*frase*) slogan; (MIL) stripe; **~s** fpl foreign exchange/currency.

**divisão** [dʒivi'zãw] f division; (*discórdia*) dissension.

**divi'sar** vt (*avistar*) to see, make out.

**divisório/a** [dʒivi'zorju/a] adj (*linha*) dividing // f partition.

**divorci'ar** vt to divorce; **~-se** vr to get divorced; **divórcio** m divorce.

**divul'gar** vt (*notícias*) to spread; (*segredo*) to divulge; **~-se** vr to leak out.

**di'zer** vt (*exprimir*) to say; (*contar*) to tell; (*falar*) to speak, talk; **~ bem com** to go well with; **por assim ~** so to speak; **quer ~** that is to say; **querer ~** to mean; **~-se** vr to claim to be; **diz-se que** it is said that // m (*dito*) saying.

**do** = **de** + **o**.

**dó** m (*lástima*) pity; (MÚS) do; **ter ~ de** to have pity on.

**doação** [doa'sãw] f donation, gift; **doar** vt to donate, give.

**'dobra** f pleat; (*de calças*) turn-up; **dobradiço/a** adj flexible // f hinge.

**do'brar** vt (*duplicar*) to double; (*papel*) to fold; (*joelho*) to bend; (*esquina*) to turn, go round // vi (*duplicar-se*) to double; (*sino*) to toll;

(*vergar*) to bend; **~-se** vr to double (up); **dobre** adj (*fig*) two-faced; **dobro** m double.

**'doca** f dock.

**doce** ['dosɪ] adj sweet; (*terno*) gentle // m sweet.

**docente** [do'sētʃɪ] adj teaching; **o corpo ~** teaching staff.

**dócil** ['dosɪw] adj docile.

**documentação** [dokumēta'sãw] f documentation; (*documentos*) papers pl; **documento** m document.

**do'cura** f sweetness; (*brandura*) gentleness.

**doença** [do'ēsa] f illness; **doente** adj ill, sick // m/f sick person; (*cliente*) patient; **doentio/a** adj (*pessoa*) sickly; (*clima*) unhealthy; (*curiosidade*) morbid.

**do'er** vi to hurt, ache; (*pesar*) to grieve; **~-se** vr to be offended.

**doidice** [doj'dʒisɪ] f, **doideira** [doj'dejra] f madness, foolishness; **doido/a** adj mad, crazy; **doido por** mad/crazy about // m madman // f madwoman.

**dois** [dojʃ] num two.

**'dólar** m dollar.

**'dolo** m fraud.

**dolo'rido/a** adj painful, sore; (*fig*) sorrowful.

**dom** [dõ] m gift; (*aptidão*) talent, knack; **o ~ da palavra** the gift of the gab.

**do'mar** vt to tame.

**domesti'cado/a** adj domesticated; (*domado*) tame; **doméstico/a** adj domestic, household.

**domicílio** [domɪ'silju] m home, residence.

**dominação** [domɪna'sãw] f domination; **dominante** adj dominant; (*predominante*) predominant; **dominar** vt to dominate; (*reprimir*) to overcome // vi to dominate, prevail; **dominar-se** vr to control o.s.

**do'mingo** m Sunday.

**do'mínio** m (*poder*) power; (*dominação*) control; (*território*) domain; (*esfera*) sphere; **~ próprio** self-control.

**'dona** f (*proprietária*) owner; **~ de casa** housewife.

**'donde** (Pt) adv from where; **~ vem?** where do you come from?

**'dono** m (*proprietário*) owner; (*chefe*) boss.

**dor** f ache; (*aguda*) pain; (*fig*) grief, sorrow; **~ de cabeça** headache; **~ de dentes** toothache.

**dor'mir** vi to sleep; **~ a sono solto** to sleep soundly; **~ como uma pedra** to sleep like a log; **hora de ~** bedtime; **dormitar** vi to doze; **dormitório** m bedroom; (*coletivo*) dormitory.

**'dorso** m back.

**dos = de + os.**

**dosagem** [do'zaʒẽ] m dosage; **dose** f dose; **dose excessiva** overdose.

**dotação** [dota'sãw] f endowment, allocation; **dotado/a** adj gifted; **dotado de** endowed with; **dotar** vt (*favorecer*) to endow; (*a filha*) to give a dowry to; **dote** m dowry; **dotes** mpl gifts.

**'dou** vb ver **dar.**

**dourado/a** [do'radu/a] adj golden; (*com camada de ouro*) gilt, gilded; **dourar** vt to gild.

**dou'tor(a)** m/f doctor; (*licenciado*) graduate; **doutorado** m doctorate.

**doutrina** [do'trɪna] f doctrine.

**doze** ['dozɪ] num twelve.

**dragão** [dra'gãw] m dragon; (*MIL*) dragoon.

**'drama** m (*teatro*) drama; (*peça*) play; **~turgo** m playwright, dramatist.

**dre'nar** vt to drain.

**'droga** f drug; (*fig*) rubbish; **drogado/a** m/f drug addict; **drogaria** f chemist's shop.

**dto** abr de **direito** on the right.

**'duas** num ver **dois.**

**'dúbio/a** *adj* dubious; *(vago)* uncertain.

**dublagem** [duˈblaʒẽ] *f (filme)* dubbing; **dublar** *vt* to dub.

**ducha** [ˈduʃa] *f (banho)* shower; *(MED)* douche.

**duelo** [ˈdwelu] *m* duel.

**'duna** *f* dune.

**dupli'car** *vt (repetir)* to duplicate // *vi (dobrar)* to double.

**duque/duquesa** [ˈduki/duˈkeza] *m* duke // *f* duchess.

**duração** [duraˈsãw] *f* duration; **de pouca ∼** short-lived; **duradouro/a** *adj* lasting.

**du'rante** *prep* during; **∼ uma hora** for an hour.

**du'rar** *vi* to last; **durável** *adj* lasting.

**'durex** *adj*: **fita ∼** ® adhesive tape, sellotape.

**du'reza** *f* hardness; *(severidade)* harshness; **duro/a** *adj* hard; *(som)* harsh; *(resistente)* tough.

**'durmo** *vb ver* **dormir.**

**'dúvida** *f* doubt; **sem ∼** no doubt; **duvidar** *vt* to doubt // *vi* to be uncertain; *(hesitar)* to hesitate; **duvidoso/a** *adj (incerto)* doubtful; *(indeciso)* hesitant; *(suspeito)* suspicious.

**du'zentos/as** *num* two hundred.

**'dúzia** *f* dozen.

# E

**e** [i] *conj* and; **∼ a bagagem?** what about the luggage?

**é** *etc vb ver* **ser.**

**'ébano** *m* ebony.

**'ébrio/a** *adj* drunk // *m* drunkard.

**ebulição** [ebuliˈsãw] *f* boiling; *(fig)* ferment.

**eclesi'ástico/a** *adj* ecclesiastical, church // *m* clergyman.

**e'clipse** *m* eclipse.

**e'clusa** *f (de canal)* lock;

*(comporta)* floodgate; *(represa)* dam.

**'eco** *m* echo; **ter ∼** to catch on.

**ecologia** [ekoloˈʒia] *f* ecology.

**econo'mia** *f* economy; *(ciência)* economics *pl*; **∼s** *fpl* savings; **econômico/a** *adj (barato)* cheap; *(que consome pouco)* economical; *(pessoa)* thrifty; *(COM)* economic; **caixa econômica** savings bank; **economista** *m/f* economist.

**edição** [edʒiˈsãw] *f (publicação)* publication; *(conjunto de exemplares)* edition.

**edi'fício** *m* building.

**edi'tar** *vt* to publish.

**e'dito** *(Pt: -ct-) m* edict, decree.

**edi'tor(a)** *adj* publishing; **casa ∼a** publishing firm // *m* publisher // *f* publishers *pl*; **editorial** *adj* publishing // *m* editorial.

**edredom** [edreˈdõ] *m* eiderdown.

**educação** [edukaˈsãw] *f (ensino)* education; *(criação)* upbringing; *(de animais)* training; *(maneiras)* good manners *pl*; **educar** *vt (criar)* to bring up; *(instruir)* to educate; *(animal)* to train.

**efeito** [eˈfejtu] *m* effect, result; **fazer ∼** to work; **com ∼** indeed.

**eferve'scente** *adj (bebida)* effervescent; *(col)* fizzy.

**efetiva'mente** *(Pt: -ect-) adv* really, in fact; **efetivo/a** *(Pt: -ct-) adj* effective; *(real)* actual, real; *(funcionário)* holding permanent civil service post // *m (COM)* liquid assets *pl*; **efetuar** *(Pt: -ct-) vt* to carry out.

**efi'cácia** *f (de pessoa)* efficiency; *(de tratamento)* effectiveness; **eficaz** *adj (pessoa)* efficient; *(tratamento)* effective.

**eficiência** [efisiˈẽsja] *f* efficiency; **eficiente** *adj* efficient, competent.

**egípcio/a** [eˈʒipsju/a] *adj, m/f* Egyptian; **Egito** *(Pt: -pt-) m* Egypt.

**ego'ísmo** *m* selfishness, egoism;

**egoísta** *adj* selfish, egoistic // *m/f* egoist.

**egrégio/a** [e'grɛʒju/a] *adj* distinguished.

**e'gresso** *m* (*preso*) ex-prisoner; (*frade*) former monk; (*universidade*) graduate.

**égua** ['ɛgwa] *f* mare.

**'ei-lo** *etc* = **eis-lo** + **o**, *ver* **eis**.

**eira** ['ejra] *f* (*Pt*) threshing floor; **sem ~ nem beira** down and out; **eirado** *m* terrace.

**eis** [ejʃ] *adv* here is, here are *pl*; **~ aí** there is, there are *pl*.

**ei'vado/a** *adj* contaminated; (*fig*) full.

**eixo** ['ejʃu] *m* (*de rodas*) axle; (*MAT*) axis; (*de máquina*) shaft; **~ de transmissão** drive shaft.

**ela** ['ɛla] *pron* (*pessoa*) she; (*coisa*) it; (*com prep: pessoa*) her; (: *coisa*) it; **~s** *fpl* they; (*com prep*) them.

**elaboração** [elabora'sãw] *f* (*de uma teoria*) working out; (*preparo*) preparation; **elaborar** *vt* (*preparar*) to prepare; (*fazer*) to make.

**elastici'dade** *f* elasticity; (*flexibilidade*) suppleness; **elástico/a** *adj* elastic; (*flexível*) flexible; (*colchão*) springy // *m* elastic band.

**ele** ['eli] *pron* he; (*coisa*) it; (*com prep: pessoa*) him; (: *coisa*) it; **~s** *mpl* they; (*com prep*) them.

**ele'fante/ta** *m/f* elephant.

**ele'gância** *f* elegance; **elegante** *adj* elegant; (*da moda*) fashionable.

**eleger** [ele'ʒe] *vt* (*por votação*) to elect; (*escolher*) to choose.

**elegia** [ele'ʒia] *f* elegy.

**elegível** [ele'ʒivew] *adj* eligible.

**eleição** [elej'sãw] *f* (*por votação*) election; (*escolha*) choice; **eleito/a** *pp irr de* **eleger** (/ *adj* (*por votação*) elected; (*escolhido*) chosen; **eleitor(a)** *m/f* voter; **eleitorado** *m* electorate.

**elemen'tar** *adj* (*simples*) elementary; (*fundamental*) basic, fundamental; **elemento** *m* element;

(*parte*) component; **elementos** *mpl* rudiments.

**e'lenco** *m* (*lista*) list; (*de atores*) cast.

**eletrici'dade** (*Pt*: **-ct-**) *f* electricity; **eletricista** (*Pt*: **-ct-**) *m/f* electrician; **elétrico/a** (*Pt*: **-ct-**) *adj* electric // *m* (*Pt*) tram; **eletrizar** (*Pt*: **-ct-**) *vt* to electrify; (*fig*) to thrill.

**e'letro...** (*Pt*: **-ct-**) *pref* electro...; **~cutar** *vt* to electrocute; **eletrodo** *m* electrode; **~domésticos** *mpl* (electrical) household appliances; **eletrônico/a** *adj* electronic // *f* electronics *sg*.

**elevação** [eleva'sãw] *f* (*ARQ*) elevation; (*aumento*) rise; (*ato*) raising; (*altura*) height; **elevador** *m* lift, elevator; **elevar** *vt* (*levantar*) to lift up; (*preço*) to raise; (*exaltar*) to exalt; **elevar-se** *vr* to rise.

**elimi'nar** *vt* to remove, eliminate.

**'elite** *f* elite.

**'elo** *m* link.

**elogiar** [eloʒi'ax] *vt* to praise; **elogio** *m* praise.

**eloquência** [elo'kwɛsja] *f* eloquence; **eloquente** *adj* eloquent; (*persuasivo*) persuasive.

**em** [ẽ] (*em* + *o* = *no*; *em* + *a* = *na*; *em* + *essa* = *nessa*; *em* + *os* = *nos*; *em* + *as* = *nas*) *prep in*; (*sobre*) on; **~ casa** at home; **~ São Paulo** in São Paulo; **nessa altura** at that time; **~ breve** soon; **nessa ocasião** on that occasion; **tudo aconteceu ~ 6 dias** it all happened in/within six days.

**emagrecer** [imagre'sex] *vt* to make thin // *vi* to grow thin; (*mediante regime*) to slim.

**ema'nar** *vi*: **~ de** to come from, emanate from.

**emanci'par** *vt* to emancipate; **~-se** *vr* to come of age.

**emaranhar** [imara'nax] *vt* to tangle; (*complicar*) to complicate;

~-se *vr* to get entangled; (*fig*) to get mixed up.

**embaci'ado/a** *adj* dull; (*vidro*) misted.

**embaixada** [ẽbaj'ʃada] *f* embassy; **embaixador(a)** *m* ambassador // *f* ambassadress; **embaixatriz** *f* ambassador's wife.

**embaixo** [ẽbaj'ʃu] *adv* = **em + baixo**, *ver* **baixo**.

**embalagem** [ẽba'laʒẽ] *f* packing; **embalar** *vt* to pack; (*balançar*) to rock.

**embalsa'mar** *vt* (*perfumar*) to perfume; (*cadáver*) to embalm.

**embara'çar** *vt* (*impedir*) to hinder; (*complicar*) to complicate; (*perturbar*) to embarrass; ~-se *vr* to become embarrassed; **embaraço** *m* (*estorvo*) hindrance; (*atrapalhação*) embarrassment.

**embarcação** [ẽbaxka'sãw] *f* vessel; **embarcadiço/a** *adj* seafaring // *m* seafarer.

**embarca'douro** *m* wharf; **embarcar** *vt* to embark, put on board; (*mercadorias*) to ship, stow // *vi* to go on board, embark.

**em'bargo** *m* (*de navio*) embargo; (*JUR*) seizure; (*impedimento*) impediment; **sem** ~ nevertheless.

**embarque** [ẽ'baxki] *m* (*de pessoas*) embarkation; (*de mercadorias*) shipment.

**embasba'cado/a** *adj* gaping, open-mouthed.

**embate** [ẽ'batʃi] *m* clash; (*choque*) shock.

**embatu'car** *vt* to dumbfound.

**embe'ber** *vt* to soak up, absorb; ~-se *vr*: ~-se em to become absorbed in.

**embi'car** *vi* (*tropeçar*) to stumble; (*NÁUT*) to enter port, dock; (*fig*) ~ **para** to head for; ~ **com** to have an argument with.

**embir'rar** *vi* to sulk; ~ **em** to persist in; ~ **com** to dislike.

**em'blema** *m* emblem; (*na roupa*) badge.

**emboca'dura** *f* (*de rio*) mouth; (*MÚS*) mouthpiece; (*de freio*) bit.

**'êmbolo** *m* piston.

**em'bora** *conj* though, although; **ir-se** ~ to go away.

**embor'car** *vt* to turn upside down.

**embor'nal** [-aw] *m ver* **bornal**.

**embos'cada** *f* ambush.

**embo'tar** *vt* (*lâmina*) to blunt; (*fig*) to deaden, dull.

**embreagem** [ẽbri'aʒẽ] *f* (*AUTO*) clutch.

**embria'gar** *vt* to make drunk, intoxicate; ~-se *vr* to get drunk; **embriaguez** *f* drunkenness; (*fig*) rapture.

**embrião** [ẽbri'ãw] *m* embryo.

**embro'mar** *vt* (*adiar*) to postpone, put off; (*enganar*) to deceive.

**embrulhada** [ẽbru'ʎada] *f* muddle, mess; **embrulhar** *vt* (*pacote*) to wrap; (*complicar*) to complicate; (*estômago*) to upset; **embrulhar-se** *vr* to get into a muddle; **embrulho** *m* (*pacote*) package, parcel; (*confusão*) mix-up.

**embu'çar** *vt* to disguise; **embuço** *m* hood; (*disfarce*) disguise.

**embur'rar** *vi* to sulk.

**em'buste** *m* (*engano*) deception; (*ardil*) trick; **embusteiro/a** *adj* deceitful // *m/f* cheat; (*mentiroso*) liar; (*impostor*) impostor.

**embu'tido/a** *adj* (*armário*) built-in.

**e'menda** *f* correction; (*JUR*) amendment; **emendar** *vt* (*corrigir*) to correct; (*reparar*) to mend; (*injustiças*) to make amends for; (*JUR*) to amend; **emendar-se** *vr* to mend one's ways.

**e'menta** *f* (*Pt*) menu.

**emergência** [imex'ʒẽsja] *f* (*nascimento*) emergence; (*crise*) emergency; **emergir** *vi* to emerge, appear; (*submarino*) to surface.

**emigração** [emigra'sãw] *f*

emigration; (aves) migration; **emigrado/a** adj, m/f emigrant; **emigrar** vi to emigrate; (aves) to migrate.

**emi'nência** f eminence; (altura) height; **eminente** adj eminent, distinguished; (GEO) high.

**emissão** [emi'sãw] f emission; (rádio) broadcast; (de moeda) issue; **emissor(a)** adj (moeda-papel) issuing // m (rádio) transmitter // f (estação) broadcasting station; (empresa) broadcasting company; **emitir** vt (som) to give out; (cheiro) to give off; (moeda) to issue; (rádio) to broadcast; (opinião) to express.

**emoção** [emo'sãw] f emotion; (excitação) excitement; **emocional** adj emotional; **emocionante** adj (comovente) moving; (excitante) exciting; **emocionar** vt (comover) to move; (perturbar) to upset; (excitar) to excite, thrill.

**emoldurar** vt to frame.

**empacotar** vt to pack, wrap up.

**em'pada** f pie.

**empalidecer** vi to turn pale.

**empa'nar** vt (ocultar) to obscure; (embaciar) to dim; (metal) to tarnish; (vidro) to steam up; (CULIN) to batter.

**empanturrar-se** vr to gorge o.s.

**empa'par** vt to soak; ~-se vr to get soaked.

**emparelhar** [ẽpare'ʎax] vt to pair; (equiparar) to match // vi: ~ **com** to be equal to.

**empa'tar** vt (embaraçar) to hinder; (dinheiro) to tie up; (no jogo) to draw, tie; **empate** m (no jogo) draw; (no xadrez) stalemate; (em negociações) deadlock.

**empavo'nar-se** vr to strut.

**empe'cilho** m obstacle; (col) snag.

**empeder'nido/a** adj hardhearted.

**empe'nar** vt (curvar) to warp, bend.

**empenhar** [ẽpe'ɲax] vt (objeto) to

pawn; (palavra) to pledge; (empregar) to exert; (compelir) to oblige; ~-se vr: ~-se em fazer to strive to do, do one's utmost to do; **empenho** m (de um objeto) pawning; (palavra) pledging; (insistência) determination.

**empi'nado/a** adj (direito) upright; (cavalo) rearing; (colina) steep; **empinar** vt to raise, uplift; (ressaltar) to thrust out; (papagaio) to fly; (copo) to empty.

**em'plastro** m (MED) plaster.

**empobre'cer** vt to impoverish // vi to become poor; **empobrecimento** m impoverishment.

**em'pola** f (na pele) blister; (de água) bubble; **empolado/a** adj covered with blisters; (estilo) pompous, bombastic.

**empol'gante** adj exciting; **empolgar** vt to excite; (agarrar) to grasp, seize; (a atenção) to grip.

**em'pório** m (mercado) market; (armazém) department store.

**empreende'dor(a)** adj enterprising // m/f entrepreneur; **empreender** vt to undertake; **empreendimento** m undertaking.

**empre'gado/a** m/f employee; (em escritório) clerk; (doméstico) servant; **empregar** vt (pessoa) to employ; (coisa) to use; **empregar-se** vr to get a job; **emprego** m (ocupação) job; (uso) use.

**empreiteiro** [ẽprej'tejru] m contractor.

**em'presa** f undertaking; (COM) enterprise, firm.

**empres'tado/a** adj on loan; **pedir** ~ to borrow; **emprestar** vt to lend; **empréstimo** m loan.

**empunhar** [ẽpu'ɲax] vt to grasp, seize.

**empurrão** [ẽpu'xãw] m push, shove; **aos empurrões** jostling; **empurrar** vt to push, shove.

**emude'cer** vt to silence // vi to be silent/quiet.

**emu'lar** vt to emulate.

**enamo'rado/a** adj (encantar) enchanted; (apaixonado) in love.

**encabe'çar** vt to head.

**encabu'lado/a** adj (envergonhado) embarrassed; (acanhado) shy.

**encadea'mento** m (série) chain; (conexão) link; **encadear** vt to chain together, link together.

**encadernação** [ĕkadexna'sãw] f binding; **encadernar** vt to bind.

**encaixar** [ĕkaj'ʃax] vt (colocar) to fit in, set in; (inserir) to insert // vi to fit; **encaixe** m (ato) fitting; (ranhura) groove; (buraco) socket; **encaixotar** vt to pack into boxes.

**en'calço** [-'kawsu] m pursuit; **ir no ~ de** to pursue.

**enca'lhado/a** adj stranded; (mercadoria) unsaleable.

**encalhar** [ĕka'ʎax] vi (embarcação) to run aground.

**encaminhar** [ĕkami'ɲax] vt (dirigir) to direct; (no bom caminho) to put on the right path; **~-se** vr: **~-se para/a** to set out for/to.

**encana'dor** m plumber; **encanamento** m plumbing.

**encane'cido/a** adj grey; (cabelo) white.

**encan'tado/a** adj delighted; **encantador(a)** adj delightful, charming // m enchanter // f enchantress; **encantamento** m (magia) spell; (fascinação) charm; **encantar** vt (enfeitiçar) to bewitch; (cativar) to charm; (deliciar) to delight; **encanto** m (delícia) delight; (fascinação) charm.

**encapo'tar** vt to cloak, conceal.

**encaraco'lar** vt/i to curl; **~-se** vr to curl up.

**enca'rar** vt to face; (olhar) to look at.

**encarce'rar** vt to imprison.

**encare'cer** vt (subir o preço) to raise the price of; (louvar) to praise; (exagerar) to exaggerate // vi to go up in price, get dearer; **encarecimento** m (preço) increase.

**en'cargo** m (responsabilidade) responsibility; (ocupação) job, assignment; (oneroso) burden.

**encar'nado/a** adj red, scarlet.

**encarquilhado/a** [ĕkaxkɪ'ɹadu/a] adj (fruta) wizened; (rosto) wrinkled.

**encarre'gado/a** adj: **~ de** in charge of // m/f person in charge; **~ de negócios** chargé d'affaires // m (de operários) foreman.

**encarre'gar** vt: **~ alguém de alguma coisa** to put sb in charge of sth; **~-se** vr: **~-se de fazer** to undertake to do.

**encarrilhar** [ĕkaxɪ'ʎax] vt to put back on the rails; (fig) to put on the right track.

**ence'nar** vt (teatro) to stage; (exibir) to show.

**ence'rar** vt to wax.

**encer'rar** vt (confinar) to shut in, lock up; (conter) to contain; (concluir) to close.

**ence'tar** vt to start, begin.

**enchente** [ĕ'ʃētʃi] f flood; **encher** vt to fill (up); **encher de/com** to fill up with; **encher-se** vr to fill up; **enchimento** m filling.

**enchova** [ĕ'ʃova] f anchovy.

**enciclo'pédia** f encyclopaedia.

**enco'berto/a** pp de **encobrir** // adj (escondido) concealed; (céu) overcast; **encobrir** vt to conceal, hide.

**encoleri'zar** vt to irritate, annoy; **~-se** vr to get angry.

**encolher** [ĕko'ʎex] vt to draw up; (os ombros) to shrug // vi to shrink; **~-se** vr (acanhar-se) to cringe.

**enco'menda** f order; **feito de ~** made to order, custom-made; **encomendar** vt to order; **encomendar alguma coisa a alguém** to order sth from sb.

**encon'trar** vt (achar) to find; (inesperadamente) to come across, meet; (dar com) to bump into // vi: ~ **com** to bump into; ~**-se** vr (achar-se) to be; (ir ter com) to meet; **encontro** m (de pessoas) meeting; (MIL) encounter; **ir (vir) ao encontro de** to go and meet; (aspirações) to meet, fulfil; **ir (vir) de encontro a** to go against, run contrary to.

**encorajar** [ẽkora'ʒax] vt to encourage.

**encor'pado/a** adj stout; (vinho) full-bodied; (tecido) closely-woven.

**en'costa** f slope.

**encos'tar** vt: (o cabelo) to lean against; ~**-se** vr: ~**-se em** to lean against; (deitar-se) to lie down; **encosto** m (arrimo) support; (de cadeira) back.

**encres'par** vt (o cabelo) to curl; (penas) to ruffle; ~**-se** vr (água) to curl; (o mar) to get choppy.

**encruzilhada** [ẽkruzi'ʎada] f crossroads sg.

**encur'tar** vt to shorten.

**endere'çar** vt (carta) to address; (encaminhar) to direct; **endereço** m address.

**endia'brado/a** adj devilish; (travesso) mischievous.

**endinhei'rado/a** adj rich, wealthy, well-off.

**endirei'tar** [ẽdʒirej'tax] vt (objeto) to straighten; (retificar) to put right; (fig) to straighten out; ~**-se** vr to straighten up.

**endivi'dar-se** vr to run into debt.

**endoidecer** [ẽdojde'sex] vt to madden; ~**-se** vr to go mad.

**endos'sar** vt to endorse; **endosso** m endorsement.

**endure'cer** vt/i to harden; ~**-se** vr (fig) to become callous; **endurecido/a** adj hardened; (fig) callous.

**energia** [enex'ʒia] f (vigor) energy, drive; (TEC) power, energy; **enérgico/a** adj energetic, vigorous.

**enevo'ado/a** adj misty, hazy.

**enfa'dar** vt (entediar) to bore; (incomodar) to annoy; ~**-se** vr: ~**-se de** to get tired of; ~**-se com** (aborrecer-se) to get fed up with; **enfado** m annoyance; **enfadonho/a** adj (cansativo) tiresome; (aborrecido) boring.

**'enfase** f emphasis, stress.

**enfasti'ado/a** adj bored; **enfastiar** vt (cansar) to weary; (aborrecer) to bore; **enfastiar-se** vr: **enfastiar-se de/com** (cansar-se) to get tired of; (aborrecer-se) to get bored with.

**en'fático/a** adj emphatic.

**enfeitar** [ẽfej'tax] vt to decorate; ~**-se** vr to dress up; **enfeite** m decoration.

**enfeitiçar** [ẽfejtʃi'sax] vt to bewitch, cast a spell on.

**enferma'ria** f (hospital) infirmary; (sala) ward; **enfermeiro/a** m male nurse // f nurse; **enfermidade** f illness; **enfermo/a** adj ill, sick // m/f sick person, patient.

**enferru'jar** vt to rust, corrode; ~**-se** vr to go rusty.

**enfe'zar** vt to stunt; (enfadar) to make angry; ~**-se** vr to become angry.

**enfi'ada** f (de pérolas) string; (fila) row; **de** ~ at a stretch; **enfiar** vt (agulha) to thread; (pérolas) to string together; (vestir) to slip on // vi: **enfiar para** to head for; **enfiar-se** vr: **enfiar-se em** to slip into.

**enfim** [ẽ'fĩ] adv finally, at last; (em suma) in short.

**enfor'car** vt to hang; ~**-se** vr to hang o.s.

**enfraquecer** [ẽfrake'sex] vt to weaken // vi to grow weak.

**enfren'tar** vt (encarar) to face;

(*confrontar*) to confront; (*arrostar*) to face up to.

**enfure'cer** vt to infuriate; **~-se** vr to get furious.

**enga'nar** vt to deceive; (*desonrar*) to seduce; **~-se** vr (*cair em erro*) to be wrong, be mistaken; (*iludir-se*) to deceive o.s.; **~-se de paletó** to get the wrong coat; **engano** m (*error*) mistake; (*ilusão*) deception; (*logro*) trick; **enganoso/a** adj (*mentiroso*) deceitful; (*artificioso*) fake; (*conselho*) misleading; (*aspecto*) deceptive.

**engarrafa'mento** m (*trânsito*) traffic jam; **engarrafar** vt to bottle.

**engas'gar** vt/i to choke.

**engas'tar** vt (*jóias*) to set, mount; **engaste** m setting, mounting.

**enga'tar** vt (*vagões*) to couple, hitch up; (*AUTO*) to put into gear.

**engelhar** [ēʒeˈʎax] vt/i (*a pele*) to wrinkle; (*plantas*) to shrivel up.

**engen'drar** vt to engender; (*fig*) to produce.

**engenharia** [ēʒeɲaˈria] f engineering; **engenheiro** m engineer.

**engenho** [ēˈʒeɲu] m (*talento*) talent; (*destreza*) skill; (*máquina*) machine; (*moenda*) mill; **engenhoso/a** adj clever, ingenious.

**englo'bar** vt to include.

**engo'dar** vt to lure, entice; **engodo** m (*para peixe*) bait; (*para pessoas*) lure, enticement.

**engo'lir** vt to swallow.

**engo'mar** vt to starch; (*passar*) to iron.

**en'gonço** m hinge.

**engor'dar** vt to fatten // vi to put on weight, get fat.

**engra'çado/a** adj funny, amusing.

**engra'dado** m crate.

**engrande'cer** vt (*aumentar*) to enlarge; (*elevar*) to elevate // vi to grow; **~-se** vr (*elevar-se*) to rise; (*ilustrar-se*) to become great.

**engraxa'dor** m (*Pt*) shoe shiner;

**engraxar** vt to polish; **engraxate** m shoe shiner.

**engrenagem** [ēgreˈnaʒē] f (*AUTO*) gear; **engrenar** vt (*AUTO*) to put into gear.

**engros'sar** vt/i (*sopa*) to thicken; (*inchar*) to swell; (*aumentar*) to increase.

**enguia** [ēˈgia] f eel.

**enguiçar** [ēgiˈsax] vi (*máquina*) to break down; **enguiço** m (*má sorte*) bad luck; (*empecilho*) snag; (*desarranjo*) breakdown.

**engulho** [ēˈguʎu] m nausea.

**e'nigma** m enigma; (*mistério*) mystery.

**enjau'lar** vt to cage, cage up.

**enjeitado/a** [ēʒeiˈtadu/a] m/f foundling, waif; **enjeitar** vt (*rejeitar*) to reject; (*abandonar*) to abandon.

**enjo'ado/a** adj sick; (*enfastiado*) bored; **enjoar** vt to make sick // vi to be sick; **enjôo** m sickness.

**enla'çar** vt (*atar*) to tie, bind; (*abraçar*) to hug; (*unir*) to link, join; **~-se** vr to be linked; **enlace** m link, connexion; (*casamento*) marriage, union.

**enlame'ar** vt to cover in mud; (*reputação*) to besmirch.

**enla'tar** vt to can, tin.

**enle'ar** vt (*atar*) to bind; (*envolver*) to entangle; (*confundir*) to confuse, perplex; **enleio** m (*enredo*) entanglement; (*confusão*) confusion.

**enle'var** vt (*deleitar*) to enrapture; (*absorver*) to absorb; **enlevo** m (*êxtase*) rapture; (*deleite*) delight.

**enlouquecer** [ēlokeˈsex] vt to drive mad // vi to go mad.

**enlu'tado/a** adj in mourning; **enlutar-se** vr to go into mourning.

**enobre'cer** vt to ennoble.

**eno'jado/a** adj annoyed, fed up; **enojar** vt to disgust, sicken; **enojar-se** vr to be annoyed.

**e'norme** adj enormous; huge; **enormidade** f enormity.

**enove'lar** *vt* to wind into a ball; (*enrolar*) to roll up.

**enquadrar** [ẽkwa'drax] *vt* to fit, assimilate.

**enquanto** [ẽ'kwãtu] *conj* while; ~ **isso** meanwhile; **por** ~ for the time being; ~ **ele não vem** until he comes.

**enraive'cer** *vt* to enrage.

**enrai'zar** *vi* to take root.

**enra'scada** *f* tight spot, predicament.

**enre'dar** *vt* (*emaranhar*) to entangle; (*complicar*) to complicate; ~**-se** *vr* to get entangled; **enredo** *m* (*de uma obra*) plot; (*intriga*) intrigue.

**enrege'lado/a** *adj* (*congelado*) frozen; (*muito frio*) freezing.

**enriquecer** [ẽxike'sex] *vt* to enrich; ~**-se** *vr* to get rich.

**enro'lar** *vt* to roll up; (*agasalhar*) to wrap up // *vi* (*col*) to waffle; ~**-se** *vr* to roll up; (*agasalhar-se*) to wrap up.

**enros'car** *vt* (*torcer*) to twist, wind (round); ~**-se** *vr* to coil up.

**enrouquecer** [ẽxoke'sex] *vt* to make hoarse // *vi* to go hoarse.

**enru'gar** *vt* (*pele*) to wrinkle; (*testa*) to furrow; (*tecido*) to crease; ~**-se** *vr* to crease.

**ensaiar** [ẽsa'jax] *vt* (*provar*) to test, try out; (*treinar*) to practise; (*teatro*) to rehearse; **ensaio** *m* (*prova*) test; (*tentativa*) attempt; (*treino*) practice; (*teatro*) rehearsal; (*literário*) essay; **ensaio e erro** trial and error.

**ensangüentar** [ẽsãgwẽ'tax] *vt* to stain with blood.

**ense'ada** *f* inlet, cove; (*baía*) bay.

**ensejo** [ẽ'seʒu] *m* chance, opportunity.

**ensimes'mar-se** *vr* to be lost in thought.

**ensi'nar** *vt* to teach; ~ **alguém a patinar** to teach sb to skate; **ensino**

*m* teaching, tuition; (*educação*) education.

**enso'pado/a** *adj* soaked // *m* stew; **ensopar** *vt* to soak, drench.

**ensurdece'dor/a** *adj* deafening; **ensurdecer** *vt* to deafen // *vi* to go deaf.

**entabu'lar** *vt* (*negociação*) to start, open; (*empreender*) to undertake; (*assunto*) to broach; (*conversa*) to strike up.

**enta'lar** *vt* (*encravar*) to wedge, jam; (*fig*) to put in a fix.

**entalhar** [ẽta'ʎax] *vt* to carve; **entalhe** *m* groove, notch; **entalho** *m* woodcarving.

**en'tanto** *adv* meanwhile // *conj* (*todavia*) however, nevertheless; **no** ~ (*adv*) meanwhile; (*conj*) yet, however.

**então** [ẽ'tãw] *adv* then; **até** ~ up to that time; **desde** ~ ever since; **e** ~? well then?

**'ente** *m* being.

**ente'ado/a** *m* stepson // *f* stepdaughter.

**enten'der** *vt* (*perceber*) to understand; (*pensar*) to think; (*querer dizer*) to mean; **dar a** ~ to imply; **no meu** ~ in my opinion; ~ **de música** to know about music; ~**-se** *vr* (*compreender-se*) to understand one another; ~**-se com alguém** to get along with sb.

**enten'dido/a** *adj*: ~ **em** (*conhecedor*) good at; **bem** ~ that is // *m* expert; (*gír*) homosexual, gay; **entendimento** *m* (*intelecto*) intellect; (*compreensão*) understanding; (*juízo*) sense.

**enterne'cer** *vt* to move, touch; ~**-se** *vr* to be moved.

**enter'rar** *vt* to bury; (*faca*) to plunge; **enterro** *m* burial; (*funeral*) funeral.

**ente'sar** *vt* to stiffen; (*esticar*) to stretch; ~**-se** *vr* to stiffen.

**enti'dade** *f* (*ser*) being;

(*corporação*) body; (*coisa que existe*) entity.

**entoação** [ĕtoaˈsãw] *f* intonation; **entoar** *vt* (*cantar*) to chant.

**entonte'cer** *vt* to make dizzy // *vi* to become/get dizzy.

**entor'nar** *vt* to spill; (*fig: copo*) to drink a lot.

**entorpe'cente** *m* narcotic; **entorpecer** *vt* (*paralisar*) to numb, stupefy; (*retardar*) to slow down; **entorpecimento** *m* numbness; (*torpor*) lethargy.

**en'torse** *f* sprain.

**entor'tar** *vt* (*curvar*) to bend; (*empenar*) to warp; ~ **os olhos** to squint.

**en'trado/a** *adj* (Pt): ~ **em anos** elderly // *f* (*ato*) entry; (*lugar*) entrance; (TEC) inlet; (*de casa*) doorway; (*começo*) beginning; (*bilhete*) ticket; (CULIN) entrée; (*pagamento inicial*) down payment.

**entra'nhado/a** *adj* deep-rooted; **entranhar-se** *vr* to penetrate; **entranhas** *fpl* bowels, entrails; (*sentimentos*) feelings; (*centro*) heart.

**en'trar** *vi* to go/come in, enter; ~ **para um clube** to join a club; ~ **em vigor** to come into force; **deixar** ~ to let in; ~ **bem** (*gir*) to get into trouble.

**entra'var** *vt* to obstruct, impede.

**'entre** *prep* (*dois*) between; (*mais de dois*) among(st); ~ **si** to o.s.

**entrea'berto/a** *adj* half-open; (*porta*) ajar; **entreabrir** *vt* to half open; **entreabrir-se** *vr* (*flores*) to open up.

**entrecho'car-se** *vr* to collide, crash; (*fig*) to clash.

**en'trega** *f* (*de mercadorias*) delivery; (*a alguém*) handing over; (*rendição*) surrender; **pagamento contra** ~ C.O.D., cash on delivery; **pronta** ~ speedy delivery; **entregar** *vt* (*dar*) to hand over; (*mercadorias*) to deliver; (*ceder*) to give up;

**entregar-se** *vr* (*render-se*) to give o.s. up; (*dedicar-se*) to devote o.s.; **entregue** *pp irr de* **entregar**.

**entrela'çar** *vt* to entwine.

**entrelinha** [ĕtreˈliɲa] *f*: **ler nas** ~**s** to read between the lines.

**entreme'ar** *vt* to intermingle.

**entreolhar-se** [ĕtrioˈʎax-si] *vr* to exchange glances.

**entre'tanto** *adv* meanwhile; **no** ~ in the meantime // *conj* however.

**entreteni'mento** *m* entertainment; (*distração*) pastime; **entreter** *vt* (*divertir*) to entertain, amuse; (*manter*) to keep up; (*esperanças*) to cherish; **entreter-se** *vr* (*divertir-se*) to amuse o.s.; (*ocupar-se*) to occupy o.s.

**entre'vado/a** *adj* paralysed, crippled; **entrevar** *vt* to paralyse, cripple.

**entre'ver** *vt* to glimpse, catch a glimpse of.

**entre'vista** *f* interview; **entrevistar** *vt* to interview; **entrevistar-se** *vr* to have an interview.

**entriste'cer** *vt* to sadden, grieve; ~**-se** *vr* to feel sad.

**entronca'mento** *m* junction.

**en'trudo** *m* (Pt) carnival; (REL) Shrovetide.

**entulho** [ĕˈtuʎu] *m* rubble, debris sg.

**entupi'mento** *m* blockage; **entupir** *vt* to block, clog; **entupir-se** *vr* to become blocked.

**entusias'mar** *vt* to fill with enthusiasm; (*animar*) to excite; ~**-se** *vr* to get excited; **entusiasmo** *m* enthusiasm; (*júbilo*) excitement; **entusiasta** *adj* enthusiastic // *m/f* enthusiast.

**enume'rar** *vt* to enumerate.

**enunci'ar** *vt* to express, state.

**envaidecer** [ĕvajdeˈsex] *vt* to make conceited; ~**-se** *vr* to become conceited.

**envelhecer** [ẽveʎe'sex] vt to age // vi to grow old, age.

**enve'lope** m envelope.

**envenena'mento** m poisoning; ~ **do sangue** blood poisoning; **envenenar** vt to poison; (fig) to corrupt.

**envere'dar** vi: ~ **por um caminho** to follow a road; ~ **para** to head for.

**enverga'dura** f (asas, velas) spread; (avião) wingspan; (fig) scope; **de grande** ~ large-scale.

**envergonhado/a** [ẽvexgo'naðu/a] adj ashamed; (tímido) shy; **envergonhar** vt to shame; (degradar) to disgrace; **envergonhar-se** vr to be ashamed.

**envi'ado/a** m/f envoy, messenger; **enviar** vt to send.

**envidra'çar** vt to glaze.

**en'vio** m sending; (expedição) despatch; (remessa) remittance; (de mercadorias) consignment.

**enviuvar** [ẽvju'vax] vi to be widowed.

**en'volto/a** pp irr de **envolver**; **envolver** vt (embrulhar) to wrap (up); (cobrir) to cover; (comprometer) to involve; (nos braços) to embrace; **envolver-se** vr (intrometer-se) to become involved; (cobrir-se) to wrap o.s. up.

**enxada** [ẽ'ʃada] f hoe.

**enxa'drista** m/f chess player.

**enxaguar** [ẽʃag'wax] vt to rinse.

**enxame** [ẽ'ʃami] m swarm.

**enxaqueca** [ẽʃa'keka] f migraine.

**enxergão** [ẽʃɛx'gãw] m (straw) mattress.

**enxer'gar** vt (avistar) to catch sight of; (divisar) to make out; (notar) to observe, see.

**enxer'tar** vt to graft; (fig) to incorporate.

**enxó** [ẽ'ʃo] m adze.

**enxofre** [ẽ'ʃofri] m sulphur.

**enxota-'moscas** m (Pt) fly swatter; **enxotar** vt (expulsar) to drive out.

**enxoval** [ẽʃo'vaw] m (de noiva) trousseau; (de recém-nascido) layette.

**enxovalhar** [ẽʃova'ʎax] vt (manchar) to stain; (amarrotar) to crumple; (reputação) to blacken; ~**se** vr to disgrace o.s.

**enxuga'dor** m clothes drier; **enxugar** vt to dry.

**enxur'rada** f (de água) torrent; (fig) spate.

**enxuto/a** [ẽ'ʃutu/a] adj dry; (magro) slim.

**'épico/a** adj epic // m epic poet.

**epide'mia** f epidemic; **epidêmico/a** adj epidemic.

**Epifa'nia** f Epiphany.

**epilep'sia** f epilepsy.

**e'pílogo** m epilogue.

**episco'pado** m bishopric.

**epi'sódio** m episode.

**e'pístola** f epistle; (carta) letter.

**epi'táfio** m epitaph.

**'época** f time, period; (da história) age, epoch; **naquela** ~ at that time; ~ **da colheita** harvest time; **fazer** ~ to be epoch-making.

**epopéia** [epo'pɛja] f epic.

**equa'dor** m equator; E~ m Ecuador.

**e'quânime** adj fair; (caráter) unbiased, neutral.

**eqüidade** [ekwi'dadʒi] f equity.

**equilibrar** [ekili'brax] vt to balance; ~**se** vr to balance; **equilíbrio** m balance, equilibrium.

**equipa** [e'kipa] f (Pt) team.

**equipa'mento** m equipment, kit; **equipar** vt (navio) to fit out; (prover) to equip.

**equipa'rar** vt (comparar) to compare; ~**se** vr: ~**se a** to equal.

**equipe** [e'kipi] f (Br) team.

**equitação** [ekita'sãw] f (ato) riding; (arte) horsemanship.

**eqüitativo/a** [ekwita'tʃivu/a] adj fair, equitable.

**equivalente** [ekɪvaˈlẽtʃi] *adj* equivalent // *m* equivalent; **equivaler** *vi*: **equivaler a** to be the same as, equal.

**equivoˈcado/a** *adj* mistaken, wrong; **equivocar-se** *vr* to make a mistake, be wrong; **equívoco/a** *adj* ambiguous // *m* (*engano*) mistake.

**'era** *etc vb ver* **ser** // *f* era, age.

**eˈrário** *m* exchequer.

**ereˈmita** *m/f* hermit; **eremitério** *m* hermitage.

**eˈreto/a** (*Pt:* -**ct**-) *adj* upright, erect.

**erguer** [exˈgex] *vt* (*levantar*) to raise, lift; (*edificar*) to build, erect; **~-se** *vr* to rise; (*pessoa*) to stand up.

**eriˈçado/a** *adj* bristling; (*cabelos*) on end; **eriçar-se** *vr* to bristle; (*cabelos*) to stand on end.

**'ermo/a** *adj* (*solitário*) lonely; (*desabitado*) uninhabited // *m* wilderness.

**eˈrótico/a** *adj* erotic; **erotismo** *m* eroticism.

**erˈrado/a** *adj* wrong, mistaken; **errante** *adj* wandering; **errar** *vt* (*o alvo*) to miss; (*a conta*) to get wrong; **errar o caminho** to lose one's way // *vi* (*vaguear*) to wander, roam; (*enganar-se*) to be wrong, make a mistake.

**'erro** *m* mistake; **salvo** ~ unless I am mistaken; ~ **de imprensa** misprint; ~ **de pronúncia** mispronunciation; **errôneo/a** *adj* wrong, mistaken; (*falso*) false, untrue.

**erudição** [eruczˈisãw] *f* erudition, learning; **erudito/a** *adj* learned, scholarly // *m* scholar.

**erupção** [erupˈsãw] *f* eruption; (*na pele*) rash; (*fig*) outbreak.

**'erva** *f* (*relva*) grass; (*MED*) herb; (*daninha*) weed.

**ervilha** [exˈviʎa] *f* pea.

**esbafoˈrido/a** *adj* breathless, panting.

**esbanjar** [ɪʒbãˈʒax] *vt* to squander, waste.

**esbarˈrar** *vi*: ~ **em** to bump into; (*obstáculo*) to come up against; **~-se** *vr* to jostle one another.

**esbelˈtez** *f*, **esbelˈteza** *f* slenderness; (*elegância*) elegance **esbelto/a** *adj* (*fino*) slender; (*pessoa*) slim; (*elegante*) elegant.

**esboˈçar** *vt* to sketch; (*delinear*) to outline; **esboço** *m* (*desenho*) sketch; (*primeira versão*) draft.

**esbugalhado/a** [ɪʒbugaˈʎadu/a] *adj*: **olhos** ~**s** goggle eyes; **esbugalhar-se** *vr* to goggle, boggle.

**esc** *abr de* (*Pt*) **escudo**.

**escabeche** [ɛʃkaˈbeʃi] *m* (*tempero*) marinade, sauce of spiced vinegar and onion; **em** ~ pickled.

**escaˈbroso/a** *adj* (*áspero*) rough, rugged; (*indecoroso*) indecent.

**escachar** [ɪʃkaˈʃax] *vt* to split open.

**esˈcada** *f* (*dentro da casa*) staircase, stairs *pl*; (*fora da casa*) steps *pl*; (*de mão*) ladder; ~ **de caracol** spiral staircase; ~ **de incêndio** fire escape; ~ **rolante** escalator; **escadaria** *f* staircase.

**escafanˈdrista** *m/f* deep-sea diver.

**esˈcala** *f* scale; (*NÁUT*) port of call; (*parada*) stop; **fazer** ~ **em** to call at; **sem** ~ non-stop.

**escaˈlada** *f* (*de guerra*) escalation.

**escalão** [ɛʃkaˈlãw] *m* step; (*MIL*) echelon; **escalar** *vt* (*montanha*) to climb; (*muro*) to scale.

**escalˈdar** *vt* to scald; **~-se** *vr* to scald o.s.

**escalˈfar** *vt* (*Pt: ovos*) to poach.

**esˈcama** *f* (*de peixe*) scale; (*de tinta*) flake; **escamar** *vt* to scale.

**escamoteˈar** *vt* (*furtar*) to pinch, pilfer; (*empalmar*) to make disappear (by sleight of hand).

**escancaˈrado/a** *adj* wide open.

**escandaliˈzar** *vt* to shock; **~-se** *vr* to be shocked; (*ofender-se*) to be offended; **escândalo** *m* scandal;

(*indignação*) outrage; **fazer um escândalo** to make a scene; **escandaloso/a** *adj* shocking, scandalous.

**escangalhar** [ɛʃkãgaˈʎax] *vt* to break, smash (up); (*a saúde*) to ruin; **~-se** *vr* to get broken.

**escaninho** [ɛʃkaˈniɲu] *m* (*na secretária*) pigeonhole.

**escanteio** [ɛʃkãˈteju] *m* (*futebol*) corner.

**esca'par** *vi*: **~ a/de** to escape from; **deixar ~** (*uma oportunidade*) to miss; (*palavras*) to blurt out; **~ por um triz** to have a narrow escape; **~-se** *vr* to run away, flee.

**es'cape** *m* (*de gases*) leak; (*AUTO*) exhaust.

**escara'muça** *f* skirmish.

**escaravelho** [ɛʃkaraˈveʎu] *m* beetle.

**escar'late** *adj* scarlet; **escarlatina** *f* scarlet fever.

**escarne'cer** *vt* to mock, make fun of; **escárnio** *m* mockery; (*desprezo*) derision.

**escar'pado/a** *adj* steep.

**escarrapa'char-se** *vr* to sprawl.

**escar'rar** *vt* to spit (up) // *vi* to spit; **escarro** *m* phlegm, spit.

**escasse'ar** *vt* to skimp on // *vi* to become scarce; **escassez** *f* (*falta*) shortage; **escasso/a** *adj* (*carente*) scarce; (*raro*) rare.

**escavação** [ɛʃkavaˈsãw] *f* digging, excavation; **escavar** *vt* to excavate.

**esclare'cer** *vt* (*iluminar*) to light up; (*mistério*) to clear up, explain; **~-se** *vr* to become clear, be explained; **esclarecimento** *m* explanation.

**escoadouro** [ɛʃkoaˈdoru] *m* drain; (*cano*) drainpipe; **escoar** *vt* to drain off // *vi* to drain away; **escoar-se** *vr* to seep out.

**esco'cês/esa** *adj* Scottish // *m* Scot, Scotsman // *f* Scotswoman; **Escócia** *f* Scotland.

**es'col** *m* best; **de ~** of excellence.

**es'cola** *f* school; **~ superior** college; **escolar** *adj* school // *m* pupil, schoolboy // *f* schoolgirl.

**escolha** [iʃˈkoʎa] *f* choice; **escolher** *vt* to choose, select.

**escolho** [iʃˈkoʎu] *m* reef; (*obstáculo*) obstacle; (*risco*) pitfall.

**es'colta** *f* escort; **escoltar** *vt* to escort.

**es'combros** *mpl* ruins, debris *sg*.

**esconde-es'conde** *m* hide-and-seek; **esconder** *vt* to hide, conceal; **esconder-se** *vr* to hide; **esconderijo** *m* hiding place; (*de bandidos*) hideout; **escondidas** *fpl*: **às escondidas** secretly.

**esconju'rar** *vt* (*o Demônio*) to exorcize; (*afastar*) to keep off; (*amaldiçoar*) to curse // *vi* (*suplicar*) to beg.

**es'copo** *m* aim, purpose.

**es'cora** *f* prop, support; (*cilada*) ambush.

**es'cória** *f* (*de metal*) dross; **a ~ da humanidade** the scum of the earth.

**escoriação** [ɛʃkorjaˈsãw] *f* abrasion, scratch.

**escorpião** [iʃkoxpiˈãw] *m* scorpion; (*ASTRO*) Scorpio.

**escorrega'dela** *f* slip; (*erro*) mistake, slip; **escorregadi(ç)o/a** *adj* slippery; **escorregar** *vi* to slip; (*errar*) to slip up; (*decorrer*) to slip by.

**escor'rer** *vt* (*fazer correr*) to drain (off); (*verter*) to pour out // *vi* (*pingar*) to drip; (*correr em fio*) to trickle.

**esco'teiro** *m* scout.

**escotilha** [ɛʃkoˈtiʎa] *f* hatch, hatchway.

**es'cova** *f* brush; **~ de dentes** toothbrush; **escovar** *vt* to brush.

**escra'vatura** *f* (*tráfico*) slave trade; (*escravidão*) slavery; **escravidão** *f* slavery; **escravizar** *vt* to enslave; **escravo/a** *adj* captive // *m/f* slave.

**escre'vente** *m/f* clerk; **escrever**

*vt/i* to write; **escrever à máquina** to type; **escrevinhar** *vt* to scribble.

**es'crito/a** *pp de* **escrever** // *adj*: ~ **à mão** handwritten // *m* piece of writing; **dar por** ~ to put in writing // *f* writing; (*pessoal*) handwriting; **escritor(a)** *m/f* writer; (*autor*) author.

**escri'tório** *m* office; (*em casa*) study.

**escri'tura** *f* (*JUR*) deed; (*caligrafia*) handwriting; **as Sagradas E~s** the Scriptures.

**escrituração** [eʃkritura'sãw] *f* book-keeping; **escriturar** *vt* (*contas*) to register, enter up; (*documento*) to draw up; **escriturário/a** *m/f* clerk/clerkess.

**escrivaninha** [eʃkriva'niɲa] *f* writing desk.

**escrivão/vã** [eʃkri'vãw/vã] *m/f* registrar, recorder.

**es'crúpulo** *m* scruple; (*inquietação da consciência*) prick of conscience; **sem** ~ unscrupulous; **escrupuloso/a** *adj* scrupulous; (*cuidadoso*) careful.

**escru'tínio** *m* (*votação*) poll; (*apuração de votos*) counting; (*exame atento*) scrutiny; ~ **secreto** secret ballot.

**escudeiro** [eʃku'dejru] *m* squire.

**es'cudo** *m* shield; (*moeda*) Portuguese coin.

**esculhambação** [eʃkuʎãba'sãw] *f* (*col*) mess; **esculhambado/a** *adj* (*descuidado*) shabby, slovenly; (*estragado*) messed up, knackered; **esculhambar** *vt* to mess up; (*criticar*) to criticise, give stick.

**escul'pir** *vt/i* to carve; (*gravar*) to engrave.

**escul'tor(a)** *m* sculptor // *f* sculptress; **escultura** *f* sculpture.

**es'cuma** *f* (*NÁUT*) schooner.

**es'cuma** *f* (*NÁUT*) foam; (*em cerveja*) froth.

**es'curas** *fpl*: **às** ~ in the dark.

**escure'cer** *vt* to darken, get dark;

**ao** ~ at dusk; **escuridão** *f* (*trevas*) darkness; **escuro/a** *adj* (*sombrio*) dark; (*dia*) overcast; (*pessoa*) swarthy; (*negócios*) shady // *m* darkness.

**es'cusa** *f* excuse; **escusado/a** *adj* unnecessary; **é escusado fazer isso** there's no need to do that; **escusar** *vt* (*desculpar*) to excuse, forgive; (*não precisar de*) not to need; **escusar-se** *vr* (*desculpar-se*) to apologise; **escusar-se de fazer** to refuse to do.

**escu'tar** *vt* to listen to // *vi* to listen, hear.

**esface'lar** *vt* (*destruir*) to destroy.

**esfaimado/a** [iʃfaj'madu/a] *adj* famished, ravenous.

**esfal'far** *vt* to tire out, exhaust; ~**se** *vr* to tire o.s. out.

**esfaquear** [iʃfaki'ax] *vt* to stab.

**esfarra'pado/a** *adj* ragged, in tatters; **esfarrapar** *vt* to tear to pieces.

**es'fera** *f* sphere; (*globo*) globe; **esférico/a** *adj* spherical.

**esfero'gráfica** *m* ballpoint pen.

**esfinge** [eʃ'fĩʒi] *f* sphinx.

**esfo'lar** *vt* to skin; (*arranhar*) to graze; (*cobrar demais a*) to overcharge, fleece.

**esfome'ado/a** *adj* famished, starving.

**esfor'çado/a** *adj* (*enérgico*) energetic; (*forte*) strong; (*valoroso*) brave; **esforçar-se para** to try hard to, strive to; **esforço** *m* effort; (*coragem*) courage; (*TEC*) stress; **fazer esforços** to try hard.

**esfre'gar** *vt* to rub; (*com água*) to scrub.

**esfri'ar** *vt* to cool, chill; ~**se** *vi* to grow cold; (*fig*) to cool off.

**esfu'mar** *vt* to tone down, soften; ~**se** *vr* to fade away.

**esgalhar** [iʒga'ʎax] *vt* to prune.

**esga'nado/a** *adj* (*sufocado*) choked; (*voraz*) greedy; (*avaro*) grasping; **esganar** vt to strangle, choke.

**esgarava'tar** vt (arranhar) to scratch; (fig) to delve into.

**esgo'tado/a** adj (exausto) exhausted; (consumido) used up; (livros) out of print; **os ingressos estão ~s** the tickets are sold out; **esgotamento** m exhaustion; **esgotar** vt (vazar) to drain, empty; (consumir) to use up; (cansar) to exhaust; **esgotar-se** vr (cansar-se) to become exhausted; (mercadorias) to be sold out.

**es'goto** m drain; (público) sewer.

**es'grima** f (esporte) fencing; **esgrimir** vi to fence.

**esgueirar-se** [izgej'rax-si] vr to slip away, sneak off.

**esguelha** [iʒ'geʎa] f slant; **de ~** obliquely, sideways.

**esguichar** [ɛʒgi'ʃax] vt to squirt // vi to squirt out.

**esguio/a** [ɛʒ'giu/a] adj (pessoa) lanky; (pessoa, objeto) slender.

**esma'gar** vt to crush; (vencer) to overpower.

**es'malte** m enamel; (de unhas) nail varnish.

**esme'rado/a** adj careful, neat; (bem acabado) polished.

**esme'ralda** f emerald.

**esme'rar-se** vr to do one's best; **esmero** m (great) care.

**esmigalhar-se** [ɛʒmiga'ʎax-si] vr to crumble.

**esmiuçar** [ɛʒmiu'sax] vt (pão) to crumble; (examinar) to examine in detail.

**'esmo** m: **andar a ~** to walk aimlessly; **falar a ~** to prattle.

**esmo'er** vt to munch, chew.

**es'mola** f alms pl; (col) thrashing; **pedir ~s** to beg.

**esmore'cer** vt to discourage // vi (desanimar-se) to lose heart.

**es'nobe** adj snobbish; (col) stuck-up // m/f snob; **esnobismo** m snobbery.

**esp'acial** [-aw] adj spatial, space; **nave ~** space-ship.

**es'paço** m space; (tempo) period; **~ para 3 pessoas** room for 3 people; **a ~s** from time to time; **espaçoso/a** adj spacious, roomy.

**es'pada** f sword; **~s** fpl (no baralho) spades; **espadarte** m swordfish.

**es'pádua** f shoulder blade.

**espairecer** [ɛʃpajre'sex] vt to amuse, entertain; **~-se** vr to relax.

**espal'dar** m (chair) back.

**espalhafato** [ɛʃpaʎa'fatu] m din, commotion.

**espalhar** [iʃpa'ʎax] vt to scatter, spread (around); (luz) to shed.

**espana'dor** m duster; **espanar** vt to dust.

**espan'car** vt to beat up, thrash.

**espanhol(a)** [ɛʃpa'ɲol(a)] adj Spanish // m/f Spaniard // m (língua) Spanish.

**espan'talho** m scarecrow; **espantar** vt (causar medo a) to frighten; (admirar) to amaze, astonish; (afugentar) to frighten away; **espantar-se** vr (admirar-se) to be amazed; (assustar-se) to be frightened; **espanto** m (medo) fright, fear; (admiração) amazement; **espantoso/a** adj (admirável) amazing; (assustador) frightening.

**espara'drapo** m (sticking) plaster.

**espargir** [ɛʃpax'ʒix] vt (líquido) to sprinkle; (flores) to scatter; (luz) to shed.

**esparra'mar** vt (líquido) to splash; (espalhar) to scatter.

**es'pasmo** m spasm, convulsion.

**espaven'tar** vt to frighten; **espavorir** vt to terrify.

**especi'al** [-jaw] adj special; **em ~** especially; **~idade** f (particularidade) speciality; (ramo de atividades) specialisation; **~ista** m/f specialist; (perito) expert;

~**-izar-se** vr: ~**-izar-se em** to specialize in.

**especia'ria** f spice.

**es'pécie** [eʃˈpɛsi] f (BIO) species sg; (tipo) sort, kind; **causar** ~ to take aback; **pagar em** ~ to pay in kind.

**especifi'car** vt to specify; **específico/a** adj specific.

**es'pécime** m specimen.

**especi'oso/a** adj (argumento) specious; (enganoso) deceptive.

**especta'dor/a** m/f (testemunha) onlooker; (ao futebol) spectator; (no teatro) member of the audience; ~**es** mpl audience sg.

**es'pectro** m ghost, phantom; (FÍSICA) spectrum.

**especu'lar** vi to speculate.

**espelho** [eʃˈpeʎu] m mirror; (fig) model; ~ **retrovisor** (AUTO) rearview mirror.

**espe'lunca** f (caverna) den; (local sujo) hovel; (casa de jogo) gambling den.

**es'pera** f (demora) wait; (expectativa) expectation; **à** ~ **de** waiting for; **à minha** ~ waiting for me; **esperança** f (confiança) hope; (expectativa) expectation; **esperar** vt (aguardar) to wait for; (desejar) to hope for; (contar com) to expect // vi to wait; (desejar) to hope; (contar com) to expect; **espero que sim/não** I hope so/not; **fazer alguém esperar** to keep sb waiting.

**es'perma** m sperm.

**espertalhão/lhona** [eʃpertaˈʎãw/ʎona] m/f crook, swindler; **esperteza** f cleverness, cunning; **esperto/a** adj clever.

**es'pesso/a** adj thick; **espessura** f thickness.

**espetacu'lar** (Pt: **-ct-**) adj spectacular; **espetáculo** (Pt: **-ct-**) m (teatral) show; (vista) sight; (cena ridícula) spectacle; **dar espetáculo** to make a spectacle of o.s.

**espe'tar** vt (carne) to put on a spit; (cravar) to stick; (fixar) to fix;

**espetinho** m skewer; **espeto** m spit.

**espia** [eʃˈpia] m/f, **espião** [eʃˈpiãw] m/f spy; **espiar** vt (observar) to watch for; (uma ocasião) to watch out for // vi to spy, watch.

**espichar** [eʃpiˈʃax] vt (couro) to stretch out; (pescoço) to stick out // vi (deitar-se) to stretch out; (col: morrer) to kick the bucket.

**es'piga** f (de milho) ear; **espigueiro** m granary.

**espi'nafre** m spinach.

**espin'garda** f shotgun, rifle; ~ **de ar comprimido** air rifle.

**espinha** [eʃˈpiɲa] f (de peixe) bone; (na pele) pimple; (coluna vertebral) spine; **espinhar** vt (picar) to prick; (irritar) to irritate, annoy.

**espinheiro** [eʃpiˈɲejru] m bramble bush; **espinhento/a** adj pimply; **espinho** m thorn; (de animal) spine; **espinhoso/a** adj (planta) prickly, thorny; (fig) difficult; (problema) thorny.

**espionagem** [eʃpioˈnaʒẽ] f spying, espionage; **espionar** vt to spy on // vi to spy, snoop.

**espi'ral** [-aw] adj f, f spiral.

**es'pírita** m/f spiritualist.

**es'pírito** m spirit; (álcool) spirits pl; **E~ Santo** Holy Spirit; **espirituoso/a** adj (vivo) lively; (dito) witty.

**espir'rar** vi to sneeze; (jorrar) to spurt out; (riso) to burst out; **espirro** m sneeze.

**es'plêndido/a** adj splendid; **esplendor** m splendour.

**espo'leta** f (de arma) fuse.

**espoli'ar** vt to plunder; **espólio** m (herança) estate, property; (roubado) booty, spoils pl.

**esponja** [eʃˈpõʒa] f sponge; (parasita) sponger.

**espon'sais** mpl (contrato) engagement sg; (cerimônia) wedding ceremony sg.

**espon'tâneo/a** adj spontaneous.

**es'pora** f spur.

**espo'rádico/a** adj sporadic.

**esporão** [ɛʃpo'rãw] m (de galo) spur; (ARQ) buttress; **esporear** vt (picar) to spur on; (fig) to incite.

**es'porte** m sport; **esportista** [ɛʃpoɾ'tʃista] m / f sportsman // f sportswoman; **esportivo/a** adj sporting.

**espo'sar** vt to marry; (causa) to defend; **esposo/a** m husband // f wife.

**espraiar** [ɛʃpra'jaɾ] vt/i to spread; (dilatar) to expand.

**espreguiçar-se** [ɛʃpregi'saχ-si] vr to stretch.

**espreitar** [ɛʃprej'taχ] vt (espiar) to spy on; (observar) to observe, watch.

**espre'mer** vt (fruta) to squeeze; (roupa molhada) to wring out.

**es'puma** f foam; (de cerveja) froth, head; (de sabão) lather; **espumante** adj frothy, foamy; (vinho) sparkling.

**es'púrio/a** adj spurious, bogus.

**esquadra** [ɛʃ'kwadra] f (NÁUT) fleet; (MIL) squadron; (da polícia) police station.

**esquadrão** [ɛʃkwa'dɾãw] m, **esquadrilha** [ɛʃkwa'dɾiʎa] f squadron.

**esquadrinhar** [ɛʃkwadɾi'ɲaχ] vt to scrutinize.

**esquadro** [ɛʃ'kwadru] m set square.

**esqualidez** [ɛʃkwali'deʒ] f squalor; **esquálido/a** adj squalid, filthy.

**esquecer** [ɛʃke'seχ] vt/i to forget; **~se** vr: **~se de** to forget; **esquecidiço/a** adj forgetful; **esquecido/a** adj forgotten; (esquecidiço) forgetful; **esquecimento** m (falta de memória) forgetfulness; (olvido) oblivion.

**esque'leto** m skeleton; (arcabouço) framework.

**es'quema** m (resumo) outline; (plano) scheme; (esboço) diagram.

**esquen'tar** vt to heat (up), warm (up).

**esquerdo/a** [ɛʃ'kexdu/a] adj left //

f left; **à ~ a de** on the left.

**esqui** [ɛʃ'ki] m (patim) ski; (esporte) skiing; **~ aquático** water skiing; **esquiar** vi to ski.

**esquilo** [ɛʃ'kilu] m squirrel.

**esquina** [ɛʃ'kina] f corner.

**esquisito/a** [ɛʃki'situ/a] adj strange, odd.

**esquivar-se** [ɛʃki'vax-si] vr: **~ de** to escape from, get away from; **esquivo/a** adj aloof, standoffish.

**esq°** abr ver **esquerdo**.

**esse, essa, esses, essas** ['esi, 'εsa, 'esiʃ, 'εsaʃ] adj, pron (sg) that; (pl) those.

**es'sência** f essence; **essencial** adj essential // m: **o essencial** the main thing.

**estabele'cer** vt to establish, set up; **~se** vr to establish o.s., set o.s. up; **estabelecimento** m establishment; (casa comercial) business.

**estabili'dade** f stability.

**es'tábulo** m cow-shed.

**es'taca** f post, stake; **estacada** f (defensiva) stockade; (fileira de estacas) fencing.

**estação** [ɛʃta'sãw] f station; (do ano) season; **~ balneária** seaside resort; **~ rodoviária** coach station.

**esta'car** vt to prop up // vi to stop short, halt.

**estaciona'mento** m (ato) parking; (lugar) parking place; **estacionar** vt to park // vi to park; (não mover) to remain stationary; **estacionário/a** adj (veículo) stationary; (COM) slack.

**es'tada** f stay.

**es'tádio** m stadium.

**esta'dista** m statesman // f stateswoman; **estado** m state; **estado civil** marital status; **em bom estado** in good condition; **estado maior** staff; **Estados Unidos (da América)** United States (of America), U.S.A.

**esta'far** vt to tire out, fatigue; **~se** vr to tire o.s. out.

**esta'fermo** m (Pt) scarecrow; (col) nincompoop.

**estagiário/a** [eʃtaʒɪ'arju/a] m/f probationer; (professor) student teacher; (médico) junior doctor; **estágio** m (de professor) probationary period; **fazer um estágio** (como professor) to be a student teacher; (como médico) to be a junior doctor; (aprendizado) to be on an apprenticeship.

**estagnação** [eʃtagna'sãw] f stagnation; **estagnado/a** adj stagnant; **estagnar-se** vr to stagnate.

**estalagem** [eʃta'laʒẽ] f inn.

**esta'lar** vt (quebrar) to break; (os dedos) to snap // vi (fender-se) to split; (crepitar) to crackle; (uma guerra) to break out; ~ **de fome** to be dying of hunger.

**estaleiro** [eʃta'lejru] m shipyard.

**esta'lido** m, **esta'lo** m (do chicote) crack; (dos dedos) snap; (dos lábios) smack; ~ **de trovão** thunderclap; (de foguete) bang.

**es'tampa** f (figura impressa) print; (ilustração) picture; **estampado/a** adj printed // m (tecido) print; **estampar** vt (imprimir) to print; (marcar) to stamp.

**estam'pido** m bang.

**estampilha** [eʃtam'piʎa] f (TESOURO) stamp.

**estan'car** vt (sangue) to staunch; (fazer cessar) to stop; (a sede) to quench // vi (esgotar) to run dry; ~-**se** vr (parar) to stop.

**es'tância** f (fazenda) ranch, farm; (versos) stanza; ~ **hidromineral** spa resort; **estancieiro** m rancher, farmer.

**estan'darte** m standard, banner.

**estanho** [eʃ'taɲu] m (metal) tin.

**estanque** [eʃ'tãki] adj watertight.

**es'tante** f (armário) bookcase; (suporte) stand.

**es'tar** vi (estado temporário) to be; ~ **fazendo**, (Pt): ~ **a fazer** to be

doing; ~ **bem** to be all right; **está bem** OK; ~ **bem com** to be on good terms with; ~ **calor/frio** (o tempo) to be hot/cold; ~ **com fome/sede/medo** to be hungry/thirsty/afraid; ~ **doente** to be ill; ~ **em casa** to be in; ~ **na hora de fazer** to be time to do; ~ **para conversas** to be in the mood for talking; ~ **para fazer** to be about to do; ~ **por alguma coisa** to be in favour of sth; ~ **por fazer** to be still to be done.

**es'tático/a** adj static // f (TEC) static.

**esta'tística** f statistic; (ciência) statistics sg.

**estati'zar** vt to nationalize.

**es'tátua** f statue.

**esta'tura** f stature; (altura) height.

**esta'tuto** m (JUR) statute; (de cidade) bye-law; (de associação) rule.

**es'tável** adj stable.

**este** [eʃtʃi] m east.

**este, esta, estes, estas** [ˈeʃtʃi, ˈeʃta, ˈeʃtʃiʃ, ˈeʃta] adj (sg) this; (pl) these // pron this one; (pl) these.

**e'steio** m prop, support; (NÁUT) stay.

**esteira** [eʃ'tejra] f mat; (de navio) wake; (rumo) path.

**es'teja** etc vb ver **estar**.

**esten'der** vt to extend; (mapa) to spread out; (massa) to roll out; (roupa molhada) to hang out; ~ **a mão** to hold out one's hand; ~ **a mesa** to lay the table; ~-**se** vr (dilatar-se) to stretch; (epidemia) to spread; (no chão) to lie down.

**esteno-dacti'lógrafo/a** m/f shorthand typist; **estenografia** f shorthand.

**es'tepe** m spare tyre.

**es'terco** m manure, dung.

**es'tereo...** pref stereo; ~**fônico/a** adj stereophonic; (col) stereo; ~**tipar** vt to stereotype; **estereótipo** m stereotype.

**es'téril** [-rɪw] adj sterile; (fig) futile.

**ester'lino/a** adj sterling; **libra** ~**a** a pound sterling // m sterling.

**es'tético/a** adj aesthetic // f aesthetics sg; (beleza) beauty.

**es'teve** vb ver **estar**.

**esti'agem** f dry season; **estiar** vi (não chover) to stop raining; (o tempo) to clear up.

**esti'bordo** m starboard.

**esti'car** vt (uma corda) to stretch, tighten; (a perna) to stretch out, ~**-se** vr to stretch out.

**es'tigma** m (marca) mark, scar; (fig) stigma; ~**tizar** vt (marcar) to brand; (fig) to stigmatize.

**estilha'çar** vt to splinter; (despedaçar) to shatter; **estilhaço** m fragment, chip, splinter.

**es'tilo** m style; (TEC) stylus.

**es'tima** f esteem; (afeto) affection; **estimação** f (respeito) esteem, estimation; (afeição) affection; **animal de estimação** pet animal; **estimar** vt (apreciar) to appreciate; (avaliar) to value; (ter estima a) to have a high regard for; (calcular aproximadamente) to estimate; **estimatura** f estimate.

**estimu'lante** adj stimulating // m stimulant; **estimular** vt to stimulate; (excitar) to excite; (animar) to encourage; **estímulo** m stimulus; (ânimo) encouragement; (incitamento) provocation.

**es'tio** m summer.

**estipulação** [eʃtʃipula'sãw] f stipulation; (condição) condition; **estipular** vt to stipulate.

**esti'rar** vt to stretch (out); ~**-se** vr to stretch.

**es'tirpe** f stock, lineage.

**es'tive** etc vb ver **estar**.

**esto'cada** f stab, thrust.

**esto'car** vt to stock.

**estofa'dor** m upholsterer; **estofar** vt to upholster; (acolchoar) to pad, stuff; **estofo** m (tecido) material; (para acolchoar) padding, stuffing.

**es'tóico** adj stoic(al); (impassível) impassive.

**estojo** [eʃ'toʒu] m case; ~ **de unhas** manicure set; ~ **de ferramentas** tool kit.

**e'stola** f stole.

**es'tólido/a** adj stupid.

**es'tômago** m stomach; **ter** ~ **para** to tolerate.

**estonte'ar** vt to stun, daze.

**estoque** [eʃ'tɔki] m (COM) stock.

**es'tore** m (Pt) blind.

**es'tória** f story.

**estorninho** [eʃtoɾ'niɲu] m starling.

**estor'var** vt to hinder, obstruct; (fig) to bother, disturb; ~ **alguém de fazer** to prevent sb from doing; **estorvo** m hindrance, obstacle; (fig) bother, nuisance.

**estourar** [eʃto'ɾax] vi to explode; (pneu) to burst; (escândalo) to blow up; **estouro** m explosion; **ser um estouro** (col) to be great.

**estou'vado/a** adj rash, foolhardy.

**es'trábico/a** adj cross-eyed; **estrabismo** m squint.

**es'trada** f road; (Br): ~ **de ferro** railway; (US) railroad; (Br): ~ **de rodagem** motorway; (US) freeway; ~ **de terra** dirt road.

**es'trado** m (tablado) platform.

**estra'gar** vt (uma festa) to spoil; (arruinar) to ruin, wreck; (desperdiçar) to waste; **estrago** m (destruição) destruction; (desperdício) waste; (dano) damage; **os estragos da guerra** the ravages of war.

**estrangeiro/a** [eʃtɾã'ʒeɾu/a] adj foreign // m/f foreigner; **no** ~ abroad.

**estrangula'dor** m strangler; (TEC) throttle; **estrangulamento** m (AUTO) bottleneck; **estrangular** vt to strangle, choke.

**estranhar** [eʃtɾa'ɲax] vt to be surprised at; ~ **os visitantes** to be shy with visitors; **estranhei o clima** the climate did not agree with me;

**estranho/a** adj strange, odd; (influências) outside // m (desconhecido) stranger; (de fora) outsider.

**estratagema** [eſtrataˈʒema] m (MIL) stratagem; (ardil) trick.

**estra·tégia** f strategy; **estratégico/a** adj strategic.

**es·trato** m layer, stratum.

**estre·ar** vt (vestido, peça) to wear/put on for the first time; (veículo) to use for the first time; (filme) to show for the first time.

**estrebuchar** [eſtrebuˈʃax] vi to struggle; (ao morrer) to shake (in death throes).

**estréia** [eſˈtreja] f (de artista) debut; (de uma peça) first night; (abertura) opening; **é a ~ do meu carro** it's the first time I've used my car.

**estreitar** [eſtrejˈtax] vt (reduzir) to narrow; (roupa) to take in; (abraçar) to hug // vi (estrada) to narrow; **~-se** vr (rua) to narrow; **(laços de amizade)** to deepen; **estreiteza** f narrowness; (de roupa) tightness; **estreiteza de pontos de vista** narrowmindedness; **estreito/a** adj narrow; (apertado) tight; (saia) straight; (amizade) close // m strait.

**es·trela** f star; **estrelado/a** adj (céu) starry; (ovo) fried; **estrela-do-mar** f starfish; **estrelar** vt (ovos) to fry.

**estreme·cer** vt (sacudir) to shake // vi (vibrar) to shake; (tremer) to tremble; (horrorizar-se) to shudder; **estremecimento** m (sacudida) shaking, trembling; (tremor) tremor; (amizade) deep friendship.

**es·trépito** m din, racket; (fig) fuss; **estrepitoso/a** adj noisy, rowdy; (fig) sensational.

**es·tria** f groove.

**estri·bar** vt to base; **~-se** vr: **~-se em** to be based on.

**estribilho** [eſtriˈbiʎu] m (MÚS) chorus; (na conversa) catchphrase.

**es·tribo** m (de cavalo) stirrup; (degrau) step; (plataforma) platform; (apoio) support.

**estri·dente** adj (penetrante) shrill, piercing; (dissonante) grating.

**es·trito/a** adj (rigoroso) strict; (restrito) restricted.

**es·trofe** f stanza.

**estron·dar** vi to boom; (fig) to resound; **estrondo** m (de trovão) rumble; (de armas) din; **estrondo sônico** sonic boom.

**estropi·ar** vt (aleijar) to maim, cripple; (fatigar) to wear out, exhaust; (texto) to mutilate; (pronunciar mal) to mispronounce.

**es·trume** m manure.

**estru·tura** f structure.

**estu·ário** m estuary.

**estu·dante** m/f student; **estudantil** adj student; **estudar** vt to study.

**es·túdio** m studio.

**estudi·oso/a** adj studious; **estudo** m study.

**es·tufa** f (fogão) stove, heater; (de plantas) greenhouse; **estufadeira** f (Pt) stewpot; **estufado** m (Pt) stew.

**es·tulto/a** adj foolish, silly.

**estupefação** [eſtupefaˈsãw] (Pt: **-çç-**) f numbness; (fig) amazement, astonishment; **estupefato/a** (Pt: **-ct-**) adj (entorpecido) numb; (pasmado) speechless.

**estu·pendo/a** adj wonderful; (col) fantastic, terrific.

**estupi·dez** f stupidity; (asneira) piece of nonsense; **estúpido/a** adj stupid, silly // m/f idiot.

**estu·prar** vt to rape; **estupro** m rape.

**estuque** [eſˈtuki] m stucco; (massa) plaster.

**es·túrdia** f prank, silliness.

**estur·rar** vt (torrar) to scorch; (queimar) to burn.

**esvae·cer-se** vr to fade away, vanish.

**esva·ir-se** vr to vanish, disappear; **~ em sangue** to lose a lot of blood.

**esvazi'ar** vt to empty.

**esvoa'çar** vi to flutter.

**e'tapa** f (fase) stage.

**eterni'dade** f eternity; **eterno/a** adj eternal.

**'ético/a** adj ethical // f ethics pl.

**etiqueta** [etʃi'keta] f (maneiras) etiquette; (rótulo) label, tag.

**'étnico/a** adj ethnic.

**eu** [ew] pron I.

**E.U.A.** abr de **Estados Unidos da América** U.S.A., United States of America.

**eucaristia** [ewkarɪʃ'tʃia] f Holy Communion.

**eufe'mismo** m euphemism.

**eufo'ria** f euphoria.

**Eu'ropa** f Europe; **europeu/péia** adj, m/f European.

**euta'násia** f euthanasia.

**evacu'ar** vt to evacuate; (sair de) to leave; (MED) to discharge // vi to defecate.

**eva'dir** vt to evade; (col) to dodge; ~-se vr to escape.

**evangelho** [evã'ʒeʎu] m gospel; **evangélico/a** adj evangelical.

**evaporação** [evapora'sãw] f evaporation; **evaporar** vt/i to evaporate // vi (desaparecer) to vanish; **evaporar-se** vr (desaparecer) to vanish.

**evasão** [eva'sãw] f escape, flight; (fig) evasion; **evasivo/a** adj evasive // f excuse.

**e'vento** m (acontecimento) event; (eventualidade) eventuality; **eventual** adj fortuitous, accidental; **eventualidade** f eventuality.

**evi'dência** f evidence, proof; **evidenciar** vt (comprovar) to prove; (mostrar) to show; **evidenciar-se** vr to be evident, be obvious; **evidente** adj obvious, evident.

**evi'tar** vt to avoid; (impedir) to prevent.

**evo'car** vt to evoke; (o passado) to recall.

**evolução** [evolu'sãw] f

(desenvolvimento) development; (MIL) manoeuvre; (movimento) movement; (BIO) evolution; **evoluir** vi to evolve.

**exacer'bar** vt (irritar) to irritate, annoy; (agravar) to aggravate, worsen.

**exage'rar** vt/i to exaggerate; **exagero** m exaggeration.

**exalar** [eza'lax] vt (odor) to give off.

**exal'tado/a** adj (fanático) fanatical; (apaixonado) overexcited; **exaltar** vt (elevar) to exalt; (louvar) to praise; (excitar) to excite; (irritar) to annoy; **exaltar-se** vr (excitar-se) to get worked up; (arrebatar-se) to get carried away.

**exame** [ɪ'zami] m examination, exam; **fazer um** ~ to take an exam; **examinar** vt to examine.

**exangue** [ɪ'zãgi] adj (sem sangue) bloodless; (exausto) exhausted.

**exantema** [ɪzan'tema] m (MED) rash.

**exaspe'rar** vt to exasperate; ~-se vr to get exasperated.

**exatidão** [ɪzatʃi'dãw] f (Pt: -ct-) f (precisão) accuracy; (perfeição) correctness; **exato/a** adj (Pt: -ct-) adj (certo) right, correct; (preciso) exact.

**exaurir** [ɪzaw'rix] vt (esgotar) to exhaust, drain; ~-se vr (cansar-se) to become exhausted; (águas) to run dry; **exausto/a** pp irr de **exaurir** // adj exhausted.

**exceção** [ɪʃsɛ'sãw] f (Pt: -pç-) f exception.

**exceder** [ɪʃsɛ'dex] vt to exceed; (superar) to surpass; ~ **em peso/brilho** to outweigh/outshine; ~-se vr (exagerar) to overdo; (cansar-se) to overdo things.

**exce'lência** f excellence; **por** ~ par excellence; **Vossa E**~ Your Excellency; **excelente** adj excellent.

**excentrici'dade** f eccentricity; **excêntrico/a** adj, m/f eccentric.

**excepcio'nal** [-aw] *adj* (*extraordinário*) exceptional; (*especial*) special.

**exces'sivo/a** *adj* excessive; **excesso** *m* excess; (*COM*) surplus.

**ex'ceto** (*Pt*: **-pt**) *prep* except for, apart from; **excetuar** (*Pt*: **-pt**) *vt* to except, make an exception of.

**excitação** [ɛʃita'sãw] *f* excitement; **excitado/a** *adj* excited; (*estimulado*) aroused; **excitar** *vt* to excite; (*estimular*) to arouse; **excitar-se** *vr* to get excited.

**exclamação** [ɛʃklama'sãw] *f* exclamation; **exclamar** *vi* to exclaim.

**excluir** [ɛʃ'klwix] *vt* to exclude; (*deixar fora*) to leave out, shut out; **exclusivo/a** *adj* exclusive; **para uso exclusivo de** for the sole use of.

**excomun'gar** *vt* to excommunicate.

**excursão** [ɛʃkux'sãw] *f* trip, outing; (*em grupo*) excursion; **~ a pé** hike, **excursionista** *m/f* tourist; (*para o dia*) day-tripper; (*a pé*) hiker.

**execução** [ezeku'sãw] *f* execution; (*de música*) performance; **executante** *m/f* player, performer; **executar** *vt* to execute; (*MÚS*) to perform.

**execu'tivo/a** *adj*, *m/f* executive; **executor(a)** *m* executor; (*verdugo*) executioner.

**exemplar** [izẽ'plax] *adj* exemplary // *m* model, example; (*BIO*) specimen; (*livro*) copy; **exemplo** *m* example; **por exemplo** for example, for instance.

**exéquias** [i'zɛkjaʃ] *fpl* funeral rites.

**exercer** [izer'sex] *vt* to exercise; (*influência*, *pressão*) to exert; (*função*) to perform; (*profissão*) to practise; **exercício** *m* (*ginástica*) exercise; (*de medicina*) practice; (*MIL*) drill; (*COM*) financial year; **exercitar** *vt* (*profissão*) to practise; (*direitos*, *músculos*) to exercise; (*adestrar*) to train.

**exército** [i'zexsitʊ] *m* army.

**exibição** [izibi'sãw] *f* display; **exibir** *vt* to show, display; **exibir-se** *vr* to show off.

**exigência** [izi'ʒẽsja] *f* demand; **exigente** *adj* demanding; **exigir** *vt* to demand.

**exíguo/a** [e'zigwu/a] *adj* (*diminuto*) small; (*escasso*) scanty.

**exilado/a** [ezi'ladu/a] *adj* exiled // *m/f* exile; **exilar** *vt* to exile; (*pessoa indesejável*) to deport; **exilar-se** *vr* to go into exile; **exílio** *m* exile; (*forçado*) deportation.

**exímio/a** [e'zimju/a] *adj* (*eminente*) famous, distinguished; (*excelente*) excellent.

**eximir** [ezi'mix] *vt*: **~ de** to exempt from; **~-se** *vr*: **~-se de** to avoid, shun.

**existência** [ezi'tẽsja] *f* existence; (*ser*) being; **existir** *vi* to exist, be.

**êxito** ['ezitu] *m* (*resultado*) result; (*bom sucesso*) success; **ter ~** to succeed, be successful; **não ter ~** to fail, be unsuccessful.

**exonerar** [ezone'rax] *vt* (*demitir*) to dismiss; **~ de uma obrigação** to free from an obligation.

**exorcismar** [ezoxsiʒ'max] *vt* to exorcise; **exorcismo** *m* exorcism; **exorcizar** *vt* to exorcise.

**exortação** [ezoxta'sãw] *f* exhortation; (*advertência*) warning; **exortar** *vt* (*animar*) to urge on; (*aconselhar*) to advise.

**exótico/a** [e'zotʃiku/a] *adj* exotic.

**expandir** *vt* to expand; (*vela*) to unfold; (*espalhar*) to spread; **~-se** *vr* (*dilatar-se*) to expand; **~-se com alguém** to be frank with sb; **expansão** *f* expansion, spread; (*de alegria*) effusiveness; **expansivo/a** *adj* (*pessoa*) outgoing.

**expecta'tiva** *f* (*esperança*) expectation; (*perspectiva*) prospect.

**expedição** [ɛʃpedʒi'sãw] *f* (*viagem*) expedition; (*de* *mercadorias*) despatch; (*por navio*) shipment.

**expediente** [ɛʃpe'dȝetʃi] *m* expedient; (*serviço*) day's work; (*correspondência*) correspondence; (*horas*) ~ **do escritório** office hours *pl*; **expedir** *vt* (*enviar*) to send, despatch; (*decreto*) to issue.

**expe'dito/a** *adj* prompt, speedy.

**expe'lir** *vt* (*invasor*) to expel; (*fazer sair*) to throw out.

**experi'ência** *f* (*prática*) experience; (*prova*) experiment, test; **em** ~ on trial.

**experimen'tado/a** *adj* (*perito*) experienced; (*testado*) tried; (*provado*) tested; **experimentar** *vt* (*comida*) to taste; (*vestido*) to try on; (*pôr à prova*) to try out, test; (*conhecer pela experiência*) to experience; (*sofrer*) to suffer, undergo; **experimento** *m* (*científico*) experiment.

**expi'ar** *vt* to atone for.

**expi'rar** *vt* (*ar*) to exhale, breathe out // *vi* (*morrer*) to die; (*terminar*) to end.

**expla'nar** *vt* to explain.

**explica'ção** [ɛʃplɨka'sãw] *f* explanation; (*Pt*: *lição*) private lesson; **explicar** *vt* to explain.

**expli'cito/a** *adj* explicit, clear.

**explo'dir** *vi* to explode, blow up.

**explora'ção** [ɛʃplora'sãw] *f* (*de um país*) exploration; (*abuso*) exploitation; (*de uma fábrica*) running; **explorar** *vt* (*região*) to explore; (*mina*) to work, run; (*ferida*) to probe; (*enganar*) to exploit; (*uma situação*) to make the most of.

**explosão** [ɛʃplo'zãw] *f* explosion, blast; (*fig*) outburst; **explosivo/a** *adj* explosive; (*pessoa*) hot-headed // *m* explosive.

**ex'por** *vt* to expose; (*a vida*) to risk; (*teoria*) to explain; (*mercadorias*) to display; (*quadros*) to exhibit; ~**se** *vr* to expose o.s.

**exporta'ção** [ɛʃpoxta'sãw] *f* (*ato*) export(ing); (*mercadorias*) exports *pl*; **exportador(a)** *adj* exporting // *m/f* exporter; **exportar** *vt* to export.

**exposi'ção** [ɛʃpozi'sãw] *f* (*exibição*) exhibition; (*explicação*) explanation; (*declaração*) statement; (*narração*) account; (*FOTO*) exposure; **expositor(a)** *m/f* exhibitor.

**expres'são** [ɛʃpre'sãw] *f* expression; **expressar** *vt* to express; **expresso/a** *adj* (*manifesto*) definite, clear; (*ordem, carta*) express // *m* express.

**expri'mir** *vt* to express; ~**se** *vr* to express o.s.

**expropri'ar** *vt* to dispossess, expropriate.

**expug'nar** *vt* to take by storm.

**expulsão** [ɛʃpul'sãw] *f* expulsion; **expulsar** *vt* to expel; (*inimigo*) to drive out; (*botar fora*) to throw out.

**expur'gar** *vt* to expurgate.

**'êxtase** *m* ecstasy.

**extensão** [ɛʃtẽ'sãw] *f* extension; (*de uma empresa*) expansion; (*terreno*) expanse; (*tempo*) length, duration; (*alcance*) extent; **extenso/a** *adj* (*amplo*) wide; (*comprido*) long; **por extenso** in full.

**extenuado/a** [ɛʃten'wadu/a] *adj* (*esgotado*) worn out; **extenuante** *adj* exhausting; (*debilitante*) debilitating; **extenuar** *vt* to exhaust; (*debilitar*) to weaken.

**exteri'or** *adj* (*de fora*) outside, exterior; (*aparência*) outward; (*comércio*) foreign // *m* (*da casa*) outside; (*aspecto*) outward appearance; **do** ~ (*do estrangeiro*) from abroad.

**extermi'nar** *vt* (*inimigo*) to wipe out, exterminate; (*acabar com*) to do away with; **extermínio** *m* extermination, wiping out.

**exter'nato** *m* day school; **externo/a** *adj* external; (*aparente*) outward; **aluno externo** day pupil.

**extinguir** [ɛʃtĩ'gix] *vt* (*fogo*) to put

out, extinguish; (*um povo*) to wipe
out; (*sede*) to quench; ~-**se** *vr* (*fogo,
luz*) to go out; (*BIO*) to become
extinct; **extinto/a** *adj* (*fogo*)
extinguished; (*língua*) dead;
(*animal*) extinct; **extintor** *m* (*fire*)
extinguisher.

**extir'par** *vt* (*desarraigar*) to
uproot; (*corrupção*) to eradicate.

**extorquir** [εʃtoxˈkix] *vt* to extort;
**extorsão** *f* extorsion.

**'extra** *adj* extra // *m/f* extra
person; (*teatro*) extra.

**extração** [εʃtraˈsãw] (*Pt*: **-cç-**) *f*
extraction; (*de loteria*) draw.

**extra'ir** *vt* to extract, take out.

**extraordi'nário/a** *adj*
extraordinary; (*despesa*) extra;
(*reunião*) special; **horas ~as**
overtime *sg*.

**extrater'restre** *adj* extra-
terrestrial.

**ex'trato** (*Pt*: **-ct-**) *m* extract;
(*resumo*) summary; (*banco*)
statement.

**extrava'gância** *f* (*prodigalidade*)
extravagance; **extravagante** *adj*
(*pródigo*) extravagant; (*roupa*)
outlandish; (*conduta*) wild.

**extrava'sar** *vi* to overflow.

**extravi'ado/a** *adj* lost, missing;
**extraviar** *vt* (*perder*) to mislay;
(*pessoa*) to lead astray; (*dinheiro*) to
embezzle // *vi* to get lost; **extraviar-
se** *vr* to get lost; **extravio** *m* (*perda*)
loss; (*roubo*) embezzlement; (*fig*)
deviation.

**extre'mado/a** *adj* (*coragem*)
outstanding.

**extremi'dade** *f* extremity; (*do
dedo*) tip; (*fim*) end; (*orla*) edge;
**extremo/a** *adj* extreme; (*longe*) far.

**extre'moso/a** *adj* fond, loving.

**extrover'tido/a** *m/f* extrovert.

**exube'rância** *f* exuberance;
**exuberante** *adj* (*abundante*)
abundant, plentiful; (*animado*)
exuberant.

**exumar** [εzuˈmax] *vt* (*corpo*) to
exhume; (*fig*) to dig up.

**ex-voto** [es-ˈvotu] *m* votive offering.

# F

**'fábrica** *f* factory; ~ **de conservas**
cannery.

**fabricação** [fabrikaˈsãw] *f*
manufacture; (*produção*)
production; **fabricante** *m/f*
manufacturer; **fabricar** *vt* to
manufacture, make; (*inventar*) to
fabricate.

**'fábula** *f* fable; (*conto*) tale; (*Br*)
fortune; **fabuloso/a** *adj* fabulous.

**'faca** *f* knife; **facada** *f* stab, cut.

**façanha** [faˈsaɲa] *f* exploit, deed.

**facção** [fakˈsãw] *f* faction;
**faccioso/a** *adj* factious.

**face** [ˈfasi] *f* (*rosto*) face; (*bochecha*)
cheek; **em ~ de** in view of; **fazer ~
a** to face up to.

**fachada** [faˈʃada] *f* facade, front.

**facho** [ˈfaʃu] *m* torch.

**fácil** [ˈfasiw] *adj* easy; **facilidade** *f*
ease; (*jeito*) dexterity; **facilitar** *vt* to
facilitate, make easy; (*fornecer*) to
provide.

**fa'cínora** *m* criminal.

**'faço** *etc vb ver* **fazer**.

**'facto** *m* (*Pt*) fact; **de ~** in fact.

**facul'dade** *f* faculty; (*poder*)
power; **facultar** *vt* (*permitir*) to
allow; (*conceder*) to grant;
**facultativo/a** *adj* optional // *m*
doctor.

**'fada** *f* fairy.

**fa'dado/a** *adj* fated, destined,
doomed; **bem ~** fortunate; **fadar** *vt*
to destine; (*condenar*) to doom.

**fa'diga** *f* fatigue; (*trabalho*) toil.

**fa'dista** *m/f* singer of 'fado' // *m*
ruffian; (*ocioso*) layabout // *f*
prostitute; **fado** *m* fate; (*canção*)
traditional song of Portugal.

**fagueiro/a** [fa'gejru/a] *adj* (*encantador*) sweet; (*contente*) happy.

**fagulha** [fa'guʎa] *f* spark.

**faia** ['faja] *f* beech (tree).

**faina** ['fajna] *f* toil, work; (*tarefa*) task.

**faisão** [faj'sãw] *m* pheasant.

**fa'ísca** *f* spark; (*brilha*) flash; **faiscar** *vi* to sparkle; (*cintilar*) to flash.

**faixa** ['fajʃa] *f* (*cinta*) belt; (*tira*) strip; (*área*) zone; (AUTO: *pista*) lane.

**fa'juto/a** *adj* (*col*) kitsch.

**fala** *f* speech; (*conversa*) conversation; (*dito*) remark; **chamar às ~s** to call to account; **sem ~** speechless.

**falácia** [fa'lasja] *f* fallacy.

**fala'dor(a)** *adj* talkative // *m/f* chatterbox; **falante** *adj* garrulous, talkative.

**fa'lar** *vt/i* to speak, talk; **~ com** to talk to; **por ~ em** speaking of; **sem ~ em** apart from; **pelos cotovelos** to talk one's head off.

**falaz** [fa'laʃ] *adj* deceptive, misleading; (*falso*) false.

**falcão** [faw'kãw] *m* falcon.

**fale'cer** *vi* to die; (*faltar*) to be lacking; **falecido/a** *adj* dead // *m/f* deceased; **falecimento** *m* death.

**fa'lência** *f* bankruptcy; **abrir ~** to declare o.s. bankrupt; **levar à ~** to bankrupt.

**falhar** ['fa/ax] *vi* to fail; (*não acertar*) to miss; (*errar*) to be wrong; **falho/a** *adj* faulty // *f* (*defeito*, Geo *etc*) fault; (*lacuna*) omission.

**fa'lido/a** *adj*, *m/f* bankrupt; **falir** *vi* (*COM*) to go bankrupt.

**fal'sário/a** [faw-] *m/f* forger; **falsear** *vt* to forge, falsify; **falsidade** *f* falsehood; (*fingimento*) pretence; (*engano*) deceit.

**falsifi'car** *vt* to forge, falsify; (*adulterar*) to adulterate; (*desvirtuar*) to misrepresent;

**falso/a** *adj* false; (*fraudulento*) dishonest; (*errôneo*) wrong; **pisar em falso** to miss one's step, put a foot wrong.

**'falta** *f* (*carência*) absence; (*ausência*) absence; (*defeito*) fault; (*futebol*) foul; **por/na ~ de** for lack of; **sem ~** without fail; **ter ~ de** to lack, be in need of; **fazer ~** to be lacking, be needed.

**fal'tar** *vi* (*escassear*) to be lacking, be wanting; (*falhar*) to fail; **~ ao trabalho** to be absent from work; **~ à palavra** to break one's word; **falta pouco para ...** it won't be long until ...

**falto/a** *adj* lacking, deficient.

**fama** *f* (*renome*) fame; (*reputação*) reputation; **ter ~ de generoso** to be said to be generous.

**fa'mélico/a** *adj* starving.

**fa'mília** *f* family; **familiar** *adj* (*da família*) family *cmp*; (*conhecido*) familiar; **familiaridade** *f* familiarity; (*sem-cerimónia*) informality.

**fa'minto/a** *adj* hungry; (*fig*) eager.

**fa'moso/a** *adj* famous.

**fa'nático/a** *adj* fanatical // *m/f* fanatic; **fanatismo** *m* fanaticism.

**fanfarrão/rona** [fãfa'xãw/'xona] *adj* boastful // *m/f* braggart; (*valentão*) bully.

**fani'quito** *m* fit of nervousness.

**fanta'sia** *f* fantasy; (*imaginação*) imagination; (*capricho*) fancy; (*traje*) fancy dress; **fantasiar** *vt* to imagine // *vi* to daydream; **fantasiar-se** *vr* to dress up.

**fan'tasma** *m* ghost; (*alucinação*) illusion; (*ameaça*) spectre; **fantástico/a** *adj* fantastic; (*ilusório*) imaginary; (*incrível*) unbelievable.

**fantoche** [fã'tɔʃi] *m* puppet.

**'farda** *f* uniform.

**'fardo** *m* bundle; (*carga*) load; (*fig*) burden.

**fa'rei** *etc vb ver* **fazer.**

**farejar** [fare'ʒax] *vt* to smell (out), sniff (out); (*procurar*) to seek;

(*adivinhar*) to sense // *vi* to sniff.

**farfalhar** [faxfaˈʎax] *vi* to rustle; (*fanfarrear*) to boast; **farfalhice** *f* showiness; **farfalhudo/a** *adj* ostentatious.

**farinha** [faˈrɪɲa] *f* (*manioc*) flour.

**farmacêutico/a** [farmaˈsewtʃiku/a] *adj* pharmaceutical // *m/f* chemist, pharmacist; **farmácia** *f* chemist's (shop), pharmacy.

**'faro** *m* sense of smell; (*fig*) flair.

**fa'rofa** *f* (*CULIN*) side dish based on manioc flour.

**fa'rol** [-ow] *m* lighthouse; (*AUTO*) headlight; ~**eiro** *m* lighthouse keeper; (*col*) braggart; ~**etes traseiros** *mpl* rear lights.

**'farpa** *f* barb; (*estilha*) splinter; (*rasgão*) tear; **farpado/a** *adj* barbed.

**'farra** *f* binge, spree.

**far'rapo** *m* rag; (*pedaço*) tatter.

**'farsa** *f* farce; **farsante** *m/f* joker.

**far'tar** *vt* to satiate, fill up; (*enfastiar*) to tire, sicken; ~**-se** *vr* to gorge o.s.; ~**-se de** (*cansar-se*) to get fed up with; **farto/a** *adj* full, satiated; (*abundante*) plentiful; (*cansado*) fed up; **cabeleira farta** full head of hair, shock of hair.

**fartum** [faxˈtũ] *m* stench.

**far'tura** *f* abundance, plenty.

**fas'cículo** *m* (*de publicação*) instalment.

**fasci'nante** *adj* fascinating; **fascinar** *vt* to fascinate; (*encantar*) to charm.

**fas'cismo** *m* fascism; **fascista** *adj*, *m/f* fascist.

**fase** [ˈfazi] *f* phase; (*etapa*) stage.

**fastidi'oso/a** *adj*, **fasti'ento/a** *adj* tedious; (*enfadonho*) annoying.

**fas'tígio** [faʃˈtʒiju] *m* peak, summit; (*fig*) height.

**fas'tio** *m* lack of appetite; (*repugnância*) disgust; (*tédio*) boredom.

**fatal** [faˈtaw] *adj* fatal; (*decisivo*) fateful; (*inevitável*) inescapable;

~**idade** *f* (*destino*) fate; (*desgraça*) disaster.

**fa'tia** *f* slice.

**fa'tídico/a** *adj* fateful.

**fati'gante** *adj* tiring; (*aborrecido*) tiresome; **fatigar** *vt* to tire; (*aborrecer*) to bore; **fatigar-se** *vr* to get tired.

**'fato** *m* fact; (*sucesso*) event; (*Pt: traje*) suit; **de** ~ in fact, really.

**fa'tor** (*Pt: -ct-*) *m* factor; (*agente*) agent.

**'fátuo/a** *adj* (*vão*) fatuous.

**fa'tura** (*Pt: -ct-*) *f* bill, invoice; **faturar** (*Pt: -ct-*) *vt* to invoice.

**'fava** *f* (*broad*) bean; **mandar alguém às** ~**s** to send sb packing.

**fa'vela** *f* slum, shanty town.

**fa'vor** *m* favour; **a** ~ **de** in favour of; **em** ~ **de** on behalf of; **por** ~ please; **faça o** ~ **de ...** would you be so good as to ..., kindly ...; ~**ecer** *vt* to favour; (*beneficiar*) to benefit; ~**ito/a** *adj*, *m/f* favourite.

**faxina** [faˈʃina] *f* (*gravetos*) brushwood; (*limpeza*) cleaning (up); **faxineira** *f* (*pessoa*) cleaner.

**fa'zenda** *f* farm; (*de café*) plantation; (*de gado*) ranch; (*propriedade*) property; (*pano*) cloth, fabric; (*ECON*) treasury, exchequer; **fazendeiro** *m* (*de café*) plantation-owner; (*de gado*) rancher, ranch-owner.

**fa'zer** (*ger*) *m* to make; (*executar*) to do; (*TEC*) to produce, manufacture; (*obrigar*) to force, compel // *vi* (*portar-se*) to act, behave; ~**-se** *vr* (*tornar-se*) to become; ~**-se de** to pretend to be; ~ **água** to leak; ~ **as vezes de** to replace; ~ **anos** to celebrate one's birthday; ~ **caso de** to take notice of; ~ **com que** to cause, see to it that; ~ **de** to act as; ~ **perguntas** to ask (questions); ~ **bem/mal** to act rightly/wrongly; **faz frio/calor** it's cold/hot; **faz um ano** a year ago; **faz um ano que** it is a year since; **não**

**faz mal** never mind; **tanto faz** it's all the same.

**'fé** f faith; (*crença*) belief; (*confiança*) trust; **de boa/má** ~ in good/bad faith; **dar** ~ **de** (*notar*) to notice; (*testificar*) to bear witness to.

**feal'dade** f ugliness.

**'febre** f fever; (*fig*) excitement; ~ **do feno** hay fever; ~ **amarela** yellow fever; ~ **palustre** malaria; **febril** adj feverish.

**fe'chado/a** adj shut, closed; **noite** ~**a** well into the night.

**fechadura** [feʃa'dura] f (*porta*) lock.

**fechar** [fe'ʃax] vt to close, shut; (*concluir*) to finish, conclude; (*luz, torneira*) to turn off; ~ **à chave** to lock // vi to close (up), shut; ~**se** vr to close, shut; (*pessoa*) to withdraw.

**fecho** ['feʃu] m fastening; (*trinco*) latch; (*término*) close, closing; ~ **ecler** zip fastener.

**'fécula** f starch.

**fecun'dar** vt to fertilize, make fertile; **fecundo/a** adj fertile; (*produtivo*) fruitful.

**fe'der** vi to stink.

**federação** [federa'sãw] f federation.

**fede'ral** adj federal.

**fe'dor** m stench; **fedorento/a** adj stinking.

**feição** [fej'sãw] f form, shape; (*caráter*) nature; (*modo*) manner; **à** ~ favourably; **feições** fpl (*face*) features.

**feijão** [fej'ʒãw] m beans pl.

**feio/a** ['feju/a] adj ugly; (*ameaçador*) grim; **fazer** ~ to make a bad impression.

**feira** ['fejra] f fair; (*mercado*) market.

**feitiçaria** [fejtʃisa'ria] f witchcraft, magic; **feiticeiro/a** adj bewitching, enchanting // m wizard // f witch; **feitiço** m charm, spell.

**feitio** [fej'tʃu] m shape, pattern;

(*caráter*) nature, manner; (*TEC*) workmanship.

**feito/a** ['fejtu/a] pp de **fazer** // adj (*terminado*) finished, ready; ~! agreed!; ~ **a** hand-made; **homem** ~ grown man // m act, deed; (*façanha*) feat; **de** ~ in fact.

**feitor(a)** [fej'tox(ra)] m/f administrator; (*capataz*) supervisor.

**feixe** ['fejʃi] m bundle, bunch; (*TEC*) beam.

**fel** ['fɛw] m bile, gall; (*fig*) bitterness.

**felici'dade** f happiness; (*sorte*) good luck; (*êxito*) success; ~**s** fpl congratulations; **felicitações** fpl congratulations, best wishes; **felicitar** vt to congratulate.

**fe'liz** adj happy; (*afortunado*) fortunate; (*próspero*) successful.

**fel'pudo/a** adj fuzzy, downy.

**feltro** ['fewtru] m felt.

**'fêmea** f (*BIO, BOT*) female; (*mulher*) woman; **feminino/a** adj feminine; (*BIO*) female.

**fenda** f slit, crack; (*GEO*) fissure; **fender** vt/i to split, crack.

**fene'cer** vi to die; (*terminar*) to come to an end.

**'feno** m hay.

**fenome'nal** [-aw] adj phenomenal; (*espantoso*) amazing; (*pessoa*) brilliant; **fenômeno** m phenomenon.

**'féretro** m (*andor*) bier.

**feri'ado** m holiday; **férias** fpl holidays, vacation sg; **de férias** on holiday.

**fe'rida** f wound, injury; (*ofensa*) insult; **ferir** vt to injure, wound; (*ofender*) to offend.

**fermen'tar** vt to ferment; (*fig*) to excite // vi to ferment; **fermento** m yeast; **fermento em pó** baking powder.

**'fero/a** adj fierce // f wild animal; (*fig: pessoa cruel*) beast; (*pessoa irascível*) hot-tempered person; (*pessoa talentosa*) dab-hand, whizz kid; **ferocidade** f fierceness, ferocity; **feroz** adj fierce, ferocious; (cruel) cruel.

**fer'rado/a** adj (cavalgadura) shod; (sem saída) done for; ~ **no sono** sound asleep; **ferradura** f horseshoe.

**ferra'menta** f tool; (caixa de ferramentas) tool kit.

**ferrão** [feˈxãw] m goad; (de inseto) sting.

**fer'rar** vt to spike; (cavalo) to shoe; (gado) to brand; ~**se** vr (col) to make a mess of, bungle, botch.

**ferreiro** [feˈxejru] m blacksmith.

**ferrenho/a** [feˈxeɲu/a] adj inflexible; (fig) stubborn.

**'férreo/a** adj iron; (duro) hard; (fig) intransigent.

**fer'rete** m branding iron; (fig) stigma.

**'ferro** m iron; ~ **de passar** iron; ~ **batido** wrought iron; ~ **fundido** cast iron; ~ **velho** scrap metal; **de** ~ (pessoa) sturdy; **a** ~ **e fogo** at all costs; ~**s** mpl shackles, chains.

**ferrolho** [feˈxoʎu] m (trinco) bolt.

**ferro'via** f railway; (US) railroad.

**ferrugem** [feˈxuʒẽ] f rust; (BOT) blight.

**fértil** [ˈfɛxtʃiw] adj fertile, fruitful; **fertilidade** f fertility; (abundância) fruitfulness; **fertilizante** m fertilizer // **fertilizar** vt to fertilize.

**fer'vente** adj boiling; (fervoroso) fervent; **ferver** vt to boil // vi to boil; (espumar) to seethe; (fig) to rage; **fervilhar** vi (ferver) to simmer; (pulular) to swarm.

**fer'vor** m fervour; ~**oso/a** adj zealous, fervent.

**'festa** f (reunião) party; (conjunto de ceremônias) festival; **dia de** ~ public holiday; ~**s** fpl caresses; **boas** ~**s** (Natal) Merry Christmas; (ano novo) Happy New Year; **festejar** vt (celebrar) to celebrate; (acolher) to welcome, greet; (acariciar) to caress; **festejo** m (festividade)

festivity; (carícias) caresses pl.

**festim** [fɛʃˈtʃĩ] m (banquete) banquet; (festa particular) party.

**festi'val** [-aw] m festival; **festividade** f festivity; **festivo/a** adj festive; **dia festivo** public holiday.

**fe'tiche** m fetish.

**'fétido/a** adj (malcheiroso) foul; (podre) rotten.

**'feto** m (MED) foetus; (BOT) fern.

**feudal** [fewˈdaw] adj feudal; ~**ismo** m feudalism.

**fevereiro** [feveˈrejru] m February.

**fez** vb ver **fazer**.

**'fezes** fpl (borra) dregs; (excremento) excrement sg.

**fiação** [fjaˈsãw] f spinning; (fábrica) textile mill.

**fi'ado/a** adj (a crédito) on credit; **comprar/vender** ~ to buy/sell on credit // f (fileira) row, line.

**fia'dor(a)** m/f (JUR) guarantor; (COM) backer.

**fi'ambre** m cold meat; (presunto) ham.

**fiança** [fjˈãsa] f surety, guarantee; (JUR) bail; **prestar** ~ **por** to stand bail for.

**fi'apo** m thread.

**fi'ar** vt (algodão etc) to spin; (confiar) to entrust; (vender a crédito) to sell on credit; ~**se em** to trust.

**fi'asco** m fiasco.

**'fibra** f fibre.

**fi'car** vi (permanecer) to stay, remain; (sobrar) to be left; (tornar-se) to become; (estar situado) to be; (durar) to last; (amprar) to wait; ~ **escuro** to grow dark; ~ **cego/surdo** to go blind/deaf; ~ **com** (guardar) to keep; ~ **com raiva/medo** to get angry/frightened; ~ **de** to agree to; ~ **por fazer** to be still to be done; ~ **bom** to recover; ~ **bem** to suit; **esta saia não fica bem para você** that skirt doesn't suit you.

**ficção** [fikˈsãw] f fiction.

**ficha** [ˈfiʃa] f token; (de fichário)

(index) card; (fig) record; (ELET) plug; **fichar** vt to file, index; **fichário** m (móvel) filing cabinet; (caixa) card index; (caderno) file; **ficheiro** m (Pt) ver **fichário**.

**fictício/a** [fik'tʃisju/a] adj fictitious.

**fi'dalgo** m nobleman.

**fide'digno/a** adj trustworthy.

**fideli'dade** f (lealdade) loyalty; (exatidão) exactness; **fiel** adj (leal) faithful; (exato) accurate; (que não falha) reliable.

**'figa** f talisman; **duma ~** damned; **fazer ~s a** to exorcise, give a thumb between two fingers to.

**'fígado** m liver; **de maus ~s** bad-tempered, vindictive.

**'figo** m fig; **figueira** f fig tree.

**fi'gura** f figure; (forma) form, shape; (gramática) figure of speech; (aspecto) appearance; **figurante** m/f (cinema) extra; **figurão** m V.I.P.; **figurar** vi (fazer parte) to figure, appear.

**'fila** f row, line; (fileira de pessoas) queue; **em ~** in a row; **fazer ~** to form a line, queue.

**filan'tropo** m philanthropist.

**fi'lar** vt (agarrar) to seize; (col: pedir/obter gratuitamente) to scrounge.

**filate'lia** f philately.

**fi'lé** m (bife) steak; (peixe) fillet.

**fi'leira** f file, row, line; **~s** fpl military service.

**fi'lete** m fillet; (de parafuso) thread.

**filho/a** ['fiʎu/a] m son; **~ da mãe** son of a gun, creep; **~s** mpl children; (de animais) young // f daughter; **filhote** m young; (cachorro) pup(py).

**fili'al** [-jaw] f (sucursal) branch.

**Fili'pinas** fpl: **as ~** the Philippines.

**filmagem** [fiw'maʒẽ] f filming; **filmar** vt to film; **filme** m film.

**filoso'fia** f philosophy; **filósofo/a** m/f philosopher.

**filtrar** [fiw'trax] vt to filter; **~-se** vr (líquidos) to filter; (infiltrar-se) to infiltrate; **filtro** m (TEC) filter.

**fim** [fĩ] m end; (motivo) aim, purpose; **a ~ de** in order to; **por ~** finally; **ter por ~** to aim at; **no ~ das contas** after all; **pôr ~ a** to put an end to; **sem ~** endless; **~ de semana** weekend.

**'fímbria** f (franja) fringe; (de vestido) hem.

**fi'nado/a** adj, m/f deceased.

**final** [fi'naw] adj final, last // m end; (MÚS) finale; **~izar** vt to finish, conclude.

**fi'nanças** fpl finance sg; **financeiro/a** adj financial // m financier; **financiamento** m financing; **financiar** vt to finance; **financista** m/f financier.

**fi'nar-se** vr (consumir-se) to waste away; (morrer) to die.

**fin'car** vt (cravar) to drive in; (fixar) to fix.

**fin'dar** vt/i to end, finish.

**fi'neza** f fineness; (gentileza) kindness.

**fingimento** [fiʒĩ'mẽtu] m pretence; **fingir** vt (inventar) to invent, make up; (simular) to feign // vi to pretend; **fingir-se** vr: **fingir-se de** to pretend to be.

**finlan'dês/esa** adj Finnish // m/f Finn // m (língua) Finnish; **Finlândia** f Finland.

**'fino/a** adj (ger) fine; (delgado) slender; (educado) polite; (astuto) shrewd; (som, voz) shrill; **finório/a** adj crafty, sly; **finura** f fineness; (magreza) slenderness; (elegância) finesse.

**'fio** m thread; (BOT) fibre; (ELET) wire; (telefônico) line; (de líquido) trickle; (gume) edge.

**'firma** f (assinatura) signature; (COM) firm, company.

**fir'mar** vt (tornar firme) to secure, make firm; (assinar) to sign; (estabelecer) to establish; (basear) to base; **~-se** vr: **~-se em** (basear-se) to rest on, be based on; **firme** adj firm; (estável) stable; (sólido) solid; (constante) steady; (cor) fast; **firmeza** f firmness; (estabilidade) stability; (constância) steadiness.

**fis'cal** [-aw] m supervisor; (aduaneiro) customs officer; (de impostos) tax inspector; **~izar** vt (supervisionar) to supervise; (examinar) to inspect, check.

**fis'gar** vt to catch; (enfeitiçar) to captivate.

**'físico/a** adj physical // m/f (cientista) physicist // m (corpo) physique // f physics sg.

**'fita** f (tira) strip, band; (de seda, algodão) ribbon, tape; (filme) film; (para máquina de escrever) ribbon; (magnética, adesiva) tape; **~** **métrica** tape measure; **~ elástica** rubber band.

**fi'tar** vt (com os olhos) to stare at, gaze at; **fito/a** adj fixed // m aim, intention.

**fi'vela** f buckle.

**fixar** [fik'saʃ] vt to fix; (pegar) to stick, fasten; (data) to set; (atenção) to concentrate on; (estabelecer) to fix; **~ os olhos em** to stare at; **~ residência** to set up house, settle down; **~-se** vr: **~-se em** to notice; **fixo/a** adj fixed; (firme) firm; (permanente) permanent; (cor) fast.

**fiz** etc vb ver **fazer**.

**fla'grante** adj flagrant; **apanhar em ~** to catch red-handed.

**flame'jante** adj flaming; **flamejar** vi to blaze.

**fla'nela** f flannel.

**'flash** m (FOTO) flash.

**flauta** [flawta] f flute.

**flecha** [fleʃa] f arrow.

**fleugma** [flewma] f, **'fleuma** f phlegm.

**fle'xível** adj flexible.

**'floco** m (de neve) snowflake; **~ de milho** cornflake.

**flor** f flower; (o melhor) cream,

pick; **em ~** in bloom; **a fina ~** the elite; **a ~ de** on the surface of; **~-escente** adj (BOT) in flower; (próspero) flourishing; **~escer** vi (BOT) to flower; (prosperar) to flourish.

**flo'resta** f forest.

**flu'ência** f fluency; **fluente** adj fluent; **fluido/a** adj fluid // m fluid; **fluir** vi to flow.

**fluores'cente** adj fluorescent; **lâmpada ~** fluorescent light.

**flutu'ar** vi to float.

**fluxo** ['fluksu] m (corrente) flow; (ELET) flux; **~grama** f flow chart.

**'foca** f (animal) seal.

**focali'zar** vt to focus (on).

**focinho** [fo'siɲu] m snout.

**'foco** m focus; (farol) light.

**'fofo/a** adj soft, spongy.

**fogão** [fo'gãw] m stove, cooker.

**foge** etc vb ver **fugir**.

**'fogo** m fire, (fig) ardour; **~s de artifício** fireworks; **a ~ lento** on a low flame; **à prova de ~** fireproof; **abrir ~** to open fire; **pôr ~ a** to set fire to; **pegar ~** to catch fire; **fazer ~** to make a fire.

**fo'goso/a** adj fiery.

**fogo-'fátuo** m will-o'-the-wisp.

**fogueira** [fo'gejra] f bonfire; **morrer na ~** to be burnt at the stake.

**foguete** [fo'getʃi] m rocket.

**foi** vb ver **ir** ou **ser**.

**foice** ['fojsi] f scythe.

**fol'clore** m folklore; **folclórico/a** adj folkloric.

**'fole** m bellows sg.

**'fôlego** m breath; (folga) breathing space; **perder o ~** to lose one's breath.

**'folga** f (descanso) rest, break; (espaço livre) clearance; **dia de ~** rest day; **folgado/a** adj (pessoa) easy going; (roupa) loose, slack; **folgar** vt to loosen, slacken // vi (descansar) to rest, relax; (divertir-

*se*) to have fun, amuse o.s.; **folgar em** to enjoy.

**folha** ['foʎa] f leaf; (*de papel, de metal*) sheet; (*página*) page; (*de faca*) blade; ~ **de estanho** tinfoil; **folhagem** f foliage; **folhear** vt to leaf through; **folheto** m booklet, pamphlet.

**fo'lia** f revelry, merriment.

**'fome** f hunger; (*escassez*) famine; (*avidez*) longing; **passar** ~ to go hungry; **ter** ~ to be hungry.

**fomen'tar** vt to instigate, promote; **fomento** m (MED) fomentation; (*estímulo*) promotion.

**'fone** m telephone, phone; (*peça do telefone*) receiver.

**'fonte** f (*nascente*) spring; (*chafariz*) fountain; (*origem*) source; (ANAT) temple; **de** ~ **limpa** from a reliable source.

**for** etc vb ver **ir** ou **ser**.

**'fora** adv out, outside // prep (*exceto*) apart from; ~ **de** outside; ~ **de si** beside o.s. // excl: ~! get out!

**foragido/a** [fora'ʒidu/a] adj, m/f (*fugitivo*) fugitive.

**forasteiro/a** [foraʃ'tejru/a] adj (*alheio*) alien // m/f stranger; (*de outro país*) foreigner.

**'forca** f gallows pl.

**força** ['foxsa] f (*energia física*) strength; (TEC, ELET) power; (*esforço*) effort; (*coerção*) force; **à** ~ by force; **à** ~ **de** by dint of; **dar (uma)** ~ **a** to back up, encourage; **fazer** ~ to try (hard); **por** ~ of necessity.

**for'cado** m pitchfork.

**forçado/a** [fox'sadu/a] adj forced; (*afetado*) false; **forçar** vt to force; (*olhos, voz*) to strain; **forçar-se a** to force o.s. to; **forcejar** vi (*esforçar-se*) to strive; (*lutar*) to struggle; **forçoso/a** (*necessário*) necessary; (*vigoroso*) forceful.

**forja** ['foxʒa] f forge; **forjar** vt to forge.

**'forma** f form, shape; (*molde*) mould; (*maneira*) manner, way; (MED) fitness; **desta** ~ in this way; **de tal** ~ **que** in such a way that; **de qualquer** ~ anyway; **da mesma** ~ likewise; **de outra** ~ otherwise.

**formação** [foxma'sãw] f formation; (*antecedentes*) background; **formado/a** adj (*modelado*) formed; **ser formado de** to consist of // m/f graduate.

**formal** [fox'maw] adj formal; ~**idade** f formality.

**formão** [fox'mãw] m chisel.

**for'mar** vt to form; (*constituir*) to constitute, make up; (*educar*) to train, educate; ~**-se** vr (*tomar forma*) to form; (EDUC) to graduate; **formatura** f (MIL) formation; (EDUC) graduation.

**formi'dável** adj (*temível*) formidable; (*extraordinário*) tremendous, great, excellent.

**for'miga** f ant; **formigar** vi (*ser abundante*) to abound; (*sentir comichão*) to itch; **formigueiro** m ants' nest; (*multidão*) throng, swarm.

**for'moso/a** adj (*belo*) beautiful; (*esplêndido*) superb; **formosura** f beauty.

**'fórmula** f formula; **formular** vt to formulate; **formular votos** to express one's hopes/wishes; **formulário** m form.

**fornalha** [fox'naʎa] f furnace.

**forne'cer** vt to supply, provide.

**'forno** m (CULIN) oven; (TEC) furnace; **alto** ~ blast furnace.

**'foro** m forum; (JUR) Court of Justice; ~**s** mpl privileges; **de** ~ **íntimo** personal, private.

**forra** ['foxa] f: **ir à** ~ (col) to get one's own back.

**forragem** [fo'xaʒẽ] f fodder.

**for'rar** vt (*cobrir*) to cover; (: *interior*) to line; (*de papel*) to paper; **forro/a** adj freed // m (*cobertura*) covering; (*teto*) ceiling; (*roupa*) lining.

**fortale'cer** vt to strengthen; **fortaleza** f strength; (*coragem*) fortitude; (*forte*) fortress; **ser uma fortaleza** to be as strong as an ox; **forte** adj strong; (*pancada*) hard; (*chuva*) heavy; (*comida*) rich; (*som*) loud // adv strongly; (*som*) loud(ly) // m (*fortaleza*) fortress; **fortificar** vt to fortify.

**fortuito/a** [fox'twitu/a] adj accidental.

**for'tuna** f (*sorte*) fortune, (good) luck; (*riqueza*) fortune, wealth.

**'fosco/a** adj (*sem brilho*) dull; (*opaco*) opaque.

**'fósforo** m (*QUÍM*) phosphorous; (*pau de fósforo*) match.

**'fossa** f pit.

**'fóssil** [-siw] m, pl **'fósseis** fossil.

**'fosso** m trench, ditch; (*de uma fortaleza*) moat.

**'foto** f photo.

**foto'cópia** f photocopy; **fotocopiadora** f photocopier; **fotocopiar** vt to photocopy.

**fotogra'far** vt to photograph; **fotografia** f photography; (*uma foto*) photography; **fotógrafo/a** m/f photographer.

**foz** f river mouth.

**fração** [fra'sãw] (*Pt*: **-cç-**) f fraction.

**fracas'sar** vi to fail; **fracasso** m failure.

**'fraco/a** adj weak.

**'frade** m (*REL*) friar; (: *monge*) monk.

**'fraga** f crag, rock.

**fra'gata** f (*NÁUT*) frigate.

**frágil** ['fraʒiw] adj, pl **frágeis** ['fraʒejs] (*débil*) fragile; (*quebradiço*) breakable; **fragilidade** f fragility; (*de uma pessoa*) frailty.

**frag'mento** m fragment.

**fra'grância** f (*aroma*) fragrance; (*perfume*) perfume; **fragrante** adj fragrant.

**'fralda** [-awda] f (*da camisa*) shirt tail; (*para bebê*) nappy; (: *US*) diaper; (*de montanha*) foot.

**frambo'esa** f raspberry.

**França** ['frãsa] f France; **francês/esa** adj French // m (*língua*) French; (*pessoa*) Frenchman // f Frenchwoman.

**'franco/a** adj (*sincero*) frank; (*isento*) free; **entrada** ~**a** free admission; ~ **de porte** post paid // m franc.

**frangalho** [frã'gaʎu] m (*trapo*) rag, tatter; (*pessoa*) wreck; **em** ~**s** in tatters.

**'frango** m chicken.

**franja** ['frãʒa] f fringe.

**franquear** [frãki'ax] vt (*caminho*) to clear; (*isentar de imposta*) to exempt from duties.

**franqueza** [frã'keza] f frankness.

**franquia** [frã'kia] f (*para cartas*) postage; (*isenção*) exemption.

**fran'zir** vt (*preguear*) to pleat; (*enrugar*) to wrinkle, crease; (*sobrancelhas*) to frown; (*lábios*) to curl.

**fraqueza** [fra'keza] f weakness.

**'frasco** m flask.

**'frase** f sentence; ~ **feita** set phrase.

**fra'tura** (*Pt*: **-ct-**) f fracture, break.

**fraude** ['frawdʒi] f fraud, deception; **fraudulento/a** adj fraudulent.

**fre'ar** (*Br*) vt (*conter*) to curb, restrain (*f* o *veículo*) to brake.

**freguês/guesa** [fre'geʃ/'geza] m/f (*cliente*) customer; (*Pt*) parishioner; **freguesia** f (*clientes*) customers pl; (*Pt*) parish.

**frei** [frej] m friar, monk; (*título*) Brother.

**freio** ['freju] m (*veículo*) brake; (*cavalo*) bridle; (*bocado do freio*) bit; (*fig*) check; ~ **de mão** handbrake.

**freira** ['frejra] f nun.

**freixo** ['frejʃu] m (*BOT*) ash.

**fre'mente** adj (*que estremece*)

trembling; (*violento*) raging; **fremir**
*vi* (*bramar*) to roar; (*tremer*) to
tremble; **frémito** *m* (*rumor*)
murmur; (*vibração*) tremor;
(*bramido*) roaring; (*emoção*) thrill;
**frémito cardíaco** palpitation (of the
heart).

**frene'si** *m* frenzy; **frenético/a** *adj*
frantic, frenzied.

'**frente** *f* (*de objeto*) front; (*rosto*)
face; (*fachada*) facade; ~ **a** ~ face
to face; **em** ~ **de** opposite; **à** ~ **de**
at the front of; **para a** ~ ahead,
forward.

**freqüência** [fre'kwɛsja] *f*
frequency; **com** ~ often, frequently;
**freqüentar** *vt* to frequent, attend
regularly; **freqüente** *adj* frequent.

'**fresco/a** *adj* (*frio*) cool; (*novo*)
fresh; (*col: efeminado*) camp // *m*
(*ar*) fresh air; (*arte*) fresco // *f:*
**tomar a** ~**a** to get some fresh air;
**frescura** *f* freshness; (*frialdade*)
coolness; (*col: pieguice*) slush; **que**
**frescura!** how fussy/stuffy!

'**fresta** *f* gap, slit.

**fre'tar** *vt* (*alugar*) to hire, charter;
**frete** *m* (*carregamento*) freight,
cargo; (*tarifa*) freightage.

**frial'dade** *f* coldness; (*indiferença*)
indifference, coolness.

**fricção** [frik'sãw] *f* friction; (*ato*)
rubbing; (*MED*) massage.

**frieira** [fri'ejra] *f* chilblain.

**fri'eza** *f* coldness; (*indiferença*)
coolness.

**frigideira** [friʒi'dejra] *f* frying pan;
**frigir** *vt* to fry; **no frigir dos ovos**
when it comes down to it.

**frigo'rífico** *m* refrigerator, (*col*)
fridge; (*congelador*) freezer.

**frincha** ['frĩʃa] *f* chink, slit.

'**frio/a** *adj* cold // *m* coldness; **estou**
**com** ~ I'm cold; **faz** ~**/está**
**fazendo** ~ it's cold.

**fri'sar** *vt* (*encrespar*) to curl;
(*salientar*) to emphasise.

**fri'tar** *vt* to fry; **frito/a** *adj* fried;
(*col*) **estar frito** to be done for.

'**frívolo/a** *adj* frivolous.

**fronha** ['froɲa] *f* pillowcase.

**frontão** [frõ'tãw] *m* gable.

'**fronte** *f* (*ANAT*) forehead, brow.

**fronteira** [frõ'tejra] *f* frontier,
border; **fronteiriço** *adj* frontier *cmp*.

'**frota** *f* fleet.

**frouxo/a** ['froʃu/a] *adj* loose, slack;
(*fraco*) weak; (*indolente*) lax; (*col:
impotente*) impotent.

**frus'trar** *vt* to frustrate.

'**fruta** *f* fruit; **fruteira** *f* fruit bowl;
**frutífero/a** *adj* (*proveitoso*) fruitful;
(*árvore*) fruit-bearing; **fruto** *m* (*BOT*)
fruit; (*resultado*) result, product; **dar**
**fruto** to bear fruit.

'**fuga** *f* flight, escape; (*de gás etc*)
leak; **fugaz** *adj* fleeting; **fugir** *vi* to
flee, escape; **fugitivo/a** *adj*, *m/f*
fugitive.

**fui** *vb ver* **ir** *ou* **ser**.

**fu'lano/a** *m/f*-so-and-so.

'**fulcro** *m* fulcrum.

**ful'gor** *m* brilliance.

**fuligem** [fu'liʒẽ] *f* soot.

**fulmi'nante** *adj* (*devastador*)
devastating; (*palavras*) scathing.

**fu'maça** *f* (*de fogo*) smoke; (*de
gás*) fumes *pl*; **fumador** *m/f* (*Pt*)
smoker; **fumante** *m/f* smoker;
**fumar** *vt/i* to smoke.

'**fumo** *m* (*Pt: de fogo*) smoke; (*Pt:
de gás*) fumes *pl*; (*Br: tabaco*)
tobacco; ~**s** *mpl* conceit.

**função** [fũ'sãw] *f* function; (*ofício*)
duty; (*papel*) role; (*espetáculo*)
performance; **funcionamento** *m*
functioning, working; **pôr em**
**funcionamento** to set going, start;
**funcionar** *vi* to function; (*máquina*)
to work, run.

**funcio'nário/a** *m/f* official;
(*público*) civil servant.

'**funda** *f* sling; (*MED*) truss.

**fundação** [fũda'sãw] *f* foundation;
**fundamental** *adj* fundamental,
basic; **fundamentar** *vt* (*argumento*)
to substantiate; (*basear*) to base;
**fundamento** *m* (*CONSTR*) foundation;

(*motivo*) motive; **sem fundamento** groundless; **fundar** vt to establish, found; (*basear*) to base.

**funde'ar** vi to anchor.

**fundição** [fundʒi'sãw] f fusing; (*fábrica*) foundry; **fundir** vt to fuse; (*metal*) to smelt, melt down; (*COM*) to merge; (*em molde*) to cast; **fundir a cuca** to set one's head spinning; **fundir-se** vr (*derreter-se*) to melt; (*confundir-se*) to merge, fuse.

**'fundo/a** adj deep; (*fig*) profound // m (*do mar*) bottom; (*profundidade*) depth; (*base*) basis; (*parte traseira*) back; (*de quadro*) background; (*de dinheiro*) fund; **a ~** deep(ly), thorough(ly); **no ~** in essence; **~s** mpl (*COM*) funds.

**'fúnebre** adj funeral cmp, funereal; **funeral** m funeral; **funerário/a** adj funeral cmp; **casa funerária** undertakers pl.

**fu'nesto/a** adj (*fatal*) fatal; (*infausto*) disastrous.

**fun'gar** vt/i to sniff.

**fu'nil** [-nɪw] m funnel.

**furação** [fura'kãw] m hurricane.

**furão** [fu'rãw] m ferret.

**fu'rar** vt (*perfurar*) to bore, perforate; (*penetrar*) to penetrate; (*frustrar*) to foil; **~ uma greve** to break a strike.

**furgão** [fux'gãw] m van; **furgoneta** f (*Pt*) van.

**'fúria** f fury, rage; **furibundo/a** adj furious; **furioso/a** adj furious.

**'furo** m hole; (*num pneu*) puncture; (*de reportagem*) scoop.

**fu'ror** m fury, rage; **fazer ~** to be all the rage.

**fur'tar** vt/i to steal; **~-se** vr: **~-se a** to avoid, evade; **furtivo/a** adj furtive, stealthy; **furto** m theft.

**fu'rúnculo** m (*MED*) boil.

**fusão** [fu'zãw] f fusion; (*aliança*) union, merger; (*derretimento*) melting.

**'fusco/a** adj dark, dusky.

**fu'sível** [-ɪvew] m (*ELET*) fuse.

**'fuso** m (*TEC*) spindle; **~ horário** time zone.

**fusti'gar** vt (*espancar*) to beat; (*açoitar*) to flog, whip; (*castigar*) to punish.

**fute'bol** m football; **~ de salão** five-a-side football; **~ totó** table football.

**fútil** ['futʃiw] adj futile; (*insignificante*) trivial; **futilidade** f triviality.

**fu'trica** f gossip.

**fu'turo/a** adj future // m future.

**fu'zil** [-ɪw] m (*arma*) rifle; **fuzilar** vt to shoot.

# G

**ga'bar** vt to praise; **~-se** vr: **~-se de** to boast about.

**gabar'dina** f, (*Pt*) **gabar'dine** f raincoat; (*pano*) gabardine.

**gabi'nete** m (*COM*) office; (*escritório*) study; (*de ministros*) cabinet.

**ga'bola** adj boastful.

**'gado** m livestock; (*reses*) cattle.

**gafanhoto** [gafa'ɲotu] m grasshopper, locust.

**gaguejar** [gage'ʒax] vi to stammer, stutter.

**gai'ato/a** adj mischievous.

**gaiola** [ga'jola] f (*para pássaro*) cage; (*cadeia*) jail.

**gaita** ['gajta] f: **~ de boca** harmonica; **~ de foles** bagpipes pl.

**gaivota** [gaj'vota] f seagull.

**gajo** [ga'ʒu] m (*Pt: col*) guy, fellow.

**'gala** f (*traje*) full dress; (*festa*) gala.

**ga'lã** m (*ator*) leading man; **galantear** vt to court; woo; **galanteio** m wooing.

**galão** [ga'lãw] m (*MIL*) stripe; (*medida*) gallon; (*Pt: café*) white coffee.

**ga'láxia** m galaxy.

**ga'lé** f (*NÁUT*) galley // m galley slave.

**ga'lego/a** adj Galician // m/f (*col*) foreigner.

**ga'lera** f (*NÁUT*) galley.

**gale'ria** f gallery; (*varanda*) veranda.

**'Gales** m: **País de ~** Wales; **galês/esa** adj Welsh //m Welshman; (*língua*) Welsh // f Welshwoman.

**gal'gar** vt (*saltar*) to leap over; (*subir*) to climb up.

**gal'go** greyhound.

**galhardia** f (*elegância*) elegance; (*valor*) bravery; (*galantaria*) dash.

**galheteiro** [gaʎe'tejru] m cruet stand.

**galho** ['gaʎu] m (*de árvore*) branch; (*galhada*) antler; (*gir*) hassle, problem; **quebrar um/o ~** to patch it up, sort it out.

**galinha** [ga'liɲa] f hen; (*covarde*) coward; **galo** m cock, rooster; (*inchação*) bump.

**galo'par** vi to gallop; **galope** m gallop.

**galvani'zar** vt to galvanize.

**'gama** f (*MÚS*) scale; (*fig*) range; (*animal*) doe; **gamo** m (fallow) deer.

**'gana** f (*desejo*) craving, desire; (*ódio*) hate; **ter ~s de** to have a good mind to.

**gancho** ['gãʃu] m hook.

**gan'grena** f gangrene.

**ganhador(a)** [gaɲa'dox(ra)] adj winning // m/f winner.

**ganha-pão** [gaɲa-'pãw] m living, livelihood.

**ganhar** [ga'ɲax] vt to win; (*salário*) to earn; (*adquirir*) to gain, get; (*um lugar*) to reach; **~ a vida** to earn a living // vi (*vencer*) to win; **ganho/a** pp de ganhar // m (*lucro*) profit, gain; **ganhos** mpl (*ao jogo*) winnings.

**ga'nir** vi to yelp, squeal.

**'ganso/a** m gander // f goose.

**garagem** [ga'raʒẽ] f garage.

**garan'tia** f guarantee; **garantir** vt

to guarantee; (*responsabilizar-se por*) to vouch for.

**garatujar** [garatu'ʒax] vt to scribble, scrawl.

**'garbo** m (*elegância*) elegance; **garboso/a** adj (*enérgico*) dashing; (*elegante*) elegant.

**garço/a** ['gaxsu/a] adj bluish green // f heron.

**'garfo** m fork.

**gargalhada** [gaxga'ʎada] f burst of laughter; **rir às ~s** to roar with laughter.

**gar'ganta** f (*ANAT*) throat; (*GEO*) gorge, ravine.

**gargarejar** [gaxgare'ʒax] vi to gargle; **gargarejo** m (*ato*) gargling; (*líquido*) gargle.

**garim'peiro** m prospector.

**ga'roa** f drizzle; **garoar** vi to drizzle.

**ga'roto/a** m youngster, kid; (*Pt: café*) coffee with milk // f girl.

**'garra** f claw; (*de ave*) talon; **~s** fpl (*posse*) clutches.

**gar'rafa** f bottle; **~ térmica** thermos flask.

**gar'rido/a** adj (*elegante*) smart; (*brilhante*) bright.

**garrulice** [gaxu'lisi] f chatter, prattle; **gárrulo/a** adj (*palrador*) chattering, prattling; (*ave*) talkative.

**ga'rupa** f (*de cavalo*) hindquarters pl; (*alforje*) saddle pack; (*moto*) back seat.

**'gás** m gas; **~ lacrimogêneo** tear gas.

**gaso'lina** f petrol; (*US*) gas(oline); **posto de ~** petrol station; (*US*) gas station.

**ga'sosa** f (*Pt*) fizzy drink; (*US*) soda pop.

**gas'tar** vt (*dinheiro*, *tempo*) to spend; (*energias*) to use up; (*deteriorar*) to wear out; (*desperdiçar*) to waste; **~-se** vr (*deteriorar-se*) to wear out; **gasto/a** pp de gastar // adj (*dinheiro*, *tempo*, *energias*) spent; (*frase*) trite;

(deteriorado) worn out // m (despesa) expenditure; (quebra) waste; **gastos** mpl expenses; (custo) costs.

**gatilho** [ga'tʃiʎu] m trigger.

**gatinhar** [gatʃi'ɲax] vi to crawl; **gatinhas** fpl: **andar de gatinhas** (Br) to go on all fours.

**'gato/a** m cat; (de carpinteiro) clamp; (gatuno) thief; ~ **montês** wildcat // f cat; **andar de ~as** (Pt) to go on all fours.

**ga'tuno** m thief.

**ga'veta** f drawer.

**gavião** [gavi'ãw] m hawk.

**'gaza** f, **'gaze** f gauze.

**ga'zeta** f (jornal) newspaper, gazette; **fazer ~** to play truant.

**geada** [ʒi'ada] f frost.

**geladeira** [ʒela'dejra] f refrigerator; (US) icebox; **gelado/a** adj frozen // m (Pt : sorvete) ice cream; **gelar** vt (congelar) to freeze; (vinho etc) to chill // vi to freeze.

**gelatina** [ʒela'tʃina] f gelatine.

**geléia** [ʒe'lɛja] f jelly; (US) jello; (compota) jam.

**geleira** [ʒe'lejra] f (GEO) glacier.

**gelo** ['ʒelu] m ice; **quebrar o ~** to break the ice.

**gelosia** [ʒelo'zia] f (estore) blind; (janela) lattice window.

**gema** ['ʒema] f (de ovo) yolk; (pedra preciosa) gem; (BOT) bud; **ser da ~** to be genuine.

**gêmeo/a** ['ʒemju/a] adj, m/f twin.

**gemer** [ʒe'mex] vi to groan, moan; **gemido** m groan, moan.

**genebra** [ʒe'nebra] f (Pt: gim) gin.

**general** [ʒene'raw] m (MIL) general; ~**idade** f generality; ~**ização** f generalization; ~**izar** vi to generalize; ~**izar-se** vr to become general, spread.

**gênero** ['ʒeneru] m (espécie) type, kind; (literatura) genre; (BIO) genus; (gramática) gender; ~**s** mpl goods; (alimentícios) foodstuffs.

**generosi'dade** f generosity;

generoso/a adj generous.

**gênese** ['ʒenɛz] f origin, beginning.

**ge'nética** f genetics sg.

**gengibre** [ʒẽ'ʒibri] m ginger.

**gengiva** [ʒẽ'ʒiva] f (ANAT) gum.

**genial** [ʒeni'aw] adj inspired; (idéia) brilliant; (prazenteiro) cheerful; **gênio** m (temperamento) nature; (humor) temper; (pessoa inspirada) genius; **de bom gênio** good-natured; **de mau gênio** bad-tempered.

**genro** ['ʒẽxu] m son-in-law.

**gente** ['ʒẽtʃi] f (pessoas) people pl; ~ **grande** grown-ups pl; **tem ~ batendo à porta** there's somebody knocking at the door; **ser ~** (ter importância) to be somebody; **a ~** (indeterminado) we, one.

**gentil** [ʒẽ'tʃiw] adj (esbelto) graceful; (cortês) polite; ~**eza** f (delicadeza) kindness; (elegância) elegance.

**gentio/a** [ʒẽ'tʃiu/a] adj, m/f heathen.

**genuíno/a** [ʒen'winu/a] adj genuine.

**geografia** f geography.

**geologia** f geology.

**geometria** f geometry.

**geração** [ʒera'sãw] f (da família) generation; (formação) creation; (produção) production; **gerador(a)** adj productive // m/f (produtor) producer // m (TEC) generator.

**geral** [ʒe'raw] adj general; **em** ~ generally; **o** ~ **dos homens** most men; ~**mente** adv generally, usually.

**gerar** [ʒe'rax] vt (produzir) to produce; (eletricidade) to generate; **gerência** [ʒe'rẽsja] f management; **gerente** m manager; **gerir** vt to manage, run.

**germe** ['ʒexmi] m (embrião) embryo; (micróbio) germ; (fig) origin; **germinar** vi (semente) to germinate; (fig) to develop.

**gesso** ['ʒesu] m plaster (of Paris).

**gesticular** vi to make gestures,

gesture; **gesto** m gesture.
**giba** ['ʒiba] f hump; (NÁUT) jib.
**gi'gante/a** adj gigantic, huge // m giant.
**gi'lete** f (lâmina) razor blade; (aparelho) razor.
**gim** [ʒĩ] m gin.
**ginásio** [ʒi'nazju] m (para ginástica) gymnasium; (escola) secondary school; **ginástica** f gymnastics sg.
**ginja** ['ʒĩʒa] f (fruta) morello cherry; **ginjinha** f cherry brandy.
**gira-discos** [ʒira-'dʒiʃkus] m (Pt) record-player.
**gi'rafa** f giraffe.
**girar** [ʒi'rax] vt/i to turn, rotate; (como pião) to spin.
**girassol** [ʒira'sɔw] m sunflower.
**gira'tório/a** adj revolving.
**gíria** ['ʒiria] f (calão) slang; (jargão) jargon.
**giro** ['ʒiru] m turn; **dar um ~** to go for a walk; (em veículo) to go for a spin; (Pt): **que ~ !** terrific!
**giz** [ʒiʃ] m chalk.
**glacê** [gla'se] m icing.
**glaci'al** [-ʒaw] adj icy.
**'glândula** f gland.
**glo'bal** [-aw] adj (total) total, entire; **preço ~** overall price; **globo** m globe.
**'glória** f glory; **gloriar-se** vr: **gloriar-se de** to boast of; **glorificar** vt to glorify; **glorioso/a** adj glorious.
**'glosa** f comment; **glosar** vt to comment on; (criticar) to criticize; (conta) to cancel; (contestar) to take issue with, query.
**glos'sário** m glossary.
**glutão/tona** [glu'tãw/tona] adj greedy // m/f glutton.
**go'ela** f gullet; (garganta) throat.
**goi'aba** f guava.
**gol** [gow] m goal; **marcar um ~** to score a goal.
**'gola** f collar; **~ rulê** polo neck.
**gole** ['gɔli] m gulp, swallow; **de um só ~** at one gulp.
**goleiro** [go'lejru] m goalkeeper.

**golfar** [gow'fax] vt (vomitar) to spit up; (emitir) to throw out // vi to spurt out.
**golfe** ['gowfi] m golf; **campo de ~** golf course; **golfista** m/f golfer.
**'golfo** m gulf.
**golpe** ['gowpi] m blow; (de mão) smack; (de punho) punch; **~ de estado** coup d'état; **de um só ~** at a stroke; **golpear** vt to beat, hit; (com navalha) to stab; (com o punho) to punch.
**'goma** f (cola) gum, glue; (de roupa) starch.
**'gomo** m (de laranja) slice.
**gonzo** m hinge.
**go'rar** vt to frustrate, thwart // vi to fail, go wrong.
**'gordo/a** adj (pessoa) fat; (gordurento) greasy; (carne) fatty; **gordura** f fat; (derretida) grease; (obesidade) fatness; **gordurento/a** adj (ensebado) greasy; (gordo) fatty; **gorduroso/a** adj (cabelo) greasy, oily.
**go'rila** m gorilla.
**gorjear** [goxʒi'ax] vi to chirp, twitter; **gorjeio** m twittering, chirping.
**gorjeta** [gor'ʒeta] f tip, gratuity.
**gorro** m cap; (boina) beret.
**gos'tar** vi: **~ de** to like; **~ mais de** to prefer; **gosto** m taste; (prazer) pleasure; **a seu gosto** to one's liking; **de bom/mau gosto** in good/bad taste; **gostoso/a** adj (comida) tasty; (ambiente) pleasant; (delicioso) lovely, gorgeous // f (col: mulher) cracker.
**'gota** f drop; (de suor) bead; **~ a ~** drop by drop; **goteira** f (cano) gutter; (buraco) leak; **gotejar** vi to drip.
**'gótico/a** adj Gothic.
**governa'dor(a)** m/f governor; **governar** vt (um país) to govern, rule; (dirigir) to manage; (barco) to steer; **governo** m (do país)

government; (*controle*) contrôl; (*NÁUT*) steering; **governo da casa** housekeeping.

**go'zado/a** *adj* funny; **gozar** *vt* to enjoy; (*col*) to make fun of // *vi* to enjoy o.s.; (*col: sexo*) to come, have an orgasm; **gozar de** to enjoy; (*Pt: rir*) to make fun of; **gozo** *m* (*prazer*) pleasure; (*uso*) enjoyment, use.

**Grã-Bretanha** [grã-bre'taɲa] *f* Great Britain.

**graça** ['grasa] *f* grace; (*elegância*) charm; (*gracejo*) joke; (*humor*) wit; **de ~** free, for nothing; **sem ~** dull, boring; **ter ~** to be funny; **~s a** thanks to; **gracejar** *vi* to joke; **gracejo** *m* joke; **gracioso/a** *adj* charming; (*divertido*) funny.

**grade** ['gradʒi] *f* (*no chão*) grating; (*grelha*) grill; (*de embalagem*) crate; (*na janela*) bars *pl*.

**'grado/a** *adj* .(*importante*) important // *m*: **de bom/mau ~** willingly/unwillingly.

**graduação** [gradwa'sãw] *f* graduation; (*divisão*) division; (*posição*) rank; **curso de ~** degree course; **gradual** *adj* gradual; **graduar** *vt* to graduate; **graduar-se** *vr* to graduate.

**'gráfico/a** *adj* graphic // *m* (*MAT*) graph; (*diagrama*) diagram, chart.

**grã-fino/a** [grã-'finu/a] *m/f* aristocrat; (*col*) snob.

**gra'fite** *f* (*lápis*) lead; (*escritura*) graffiti.

**gralha** ['graʎa] *f* jay; (*Pt*) rook.

**'grama** *m* (*peso*) gramme // *f* (*capim*) grass; **gramado** *m* lawn; **gramar** *vt* to plant/sow with grass; (*Pt: col*) to be fond of // *vi* (*Pt: col*) to cry out.

**gra'mática** *f* grammar.

**grampe'ar** *vt* to staple; (*Br: TEL*) to bug; **grampo** *m* staple; (*no cabelo*) hairgrip; (*de carpinteiro*) clamp.

**'grana** *f* (*col*) money, dough.

**gra'nada** *f* (*MIL*) shell; (*pedra*) garnet; **~ de mão** hand grenade.

**'grande** *adj* big, large; (*alto*) tall; (*fig*) great; **grandeza** *f* (*tamanho*) size; (*fig*) greatness; **grandioso/a** *adj* magnificent, grand.

**gra'nel** *m* granary; **a ~** (*COM*) in bulk.

**gra'nito** *m* (*GEO*) granite.

**gra'nizo** *m* hail; **chover ~** to hail.

**granja** ['grãʒa] *f* farm; (*de galinhas*) chicken farm.

**granjear** [grãʒi'ax] *vt* (*simpatia, amigos*) to win, gain.

**grão** ['grãw] *m*, *pl* **grãos** ['grãwʃ] grain; (*semente*) seed; (*de café*) bean.

**gras'nar** *vi* (*corvo*) to caw; (*pato*) to quack; (*rã*) to croak.

**gratidão** [gratʃi'dãw] *f* gratitude.

**gratificação** [gratʃifika'sãw] *f* (*gorjeta*) tip; (*bônus*) bonus; **gratificante** *adj* rewarding; **gratificar** *vt* (*dar gorjeta*) to tip.

**'grátis** *adv* free, for nothing.

**'grato/a** *adj* (*agradável*) pleasant; **ficar ~ a alguém por** (*agradecido*) to be grateful to sb for.

**gratuito/a** [gra'twitu/a] *adj* (*grátis*) free; (*infundado*) gratuitous.

**grau** [graw] *m* (*ger*) degree; (*nível*) level; (*escolar*) class.

**gravação** [grava'sãw] *f* (*em madeira*) carving; (*TEC*) recording; **gravador** *m* tape recorder.

**gra'var** *vt* (*madeira*) to carve; (*metal*) to engrave; (*na memória*) to fix; (*TEC*) to record.

**gra'vata** *f* tie; **~ borboleta** bow tie.

**grave** ['gravi] *adj* (*sério*) serious; (*trágico*) grave.

**'grávida** *adj* pregnant.

**gravi'dade** *f* gravity.

**gravi'dez** *f* pregnancy.

**gra'vura** *f* (*em madeira*) engraving; (*estampa*) print.

**graxa** ['graʃa] *f* (*para sapatos*) polish; (*lubrificante*) grease.

**'grego/a** *adj*, *m/f* Greek.

**grei** [grej] *f* (*rebanho*) flock; (*congregação*) congregation.

**grelha** ['grɛʎa] f grill; (de fornalha) grate; **grelhado/a** adj grilled // m (prato) grill; **grelhar** vt to grill.

**'grêmio** m (associação) guild; (clube) club.

**'greta** f crack; **gretado/a** adj cracked.

**'greve** f strike; **fazer ~** to go on strike; **~ de fome** hunger strike; **~ branca** go-slow; **grevista** m/f striker.

**gri'fado/a** adj in italics; **grifar** vt to italicize; (sublinhar) to underline; (fig) to emphasize.

**grilhão** [gri'ʎãw] m chain; **grilhões** mpl (fig) fetters.

**'grilo** m cricket; (AUTO) squeak; (col) problem; **qual é o ~ ?** what's the matter?

**grim'par** vi to climb; (AUTO) to seize up.

**gri'nalda** f garland.

**gri'par-se** vr to catch flu; **gripe** f flu, influenza.

**grisalho/a** adj (cabelo) grey.

**'grita** f uproar; **gritante** adj glaring, gross, blatant; **gritar** vt/i to shout, yell; **gritaria** f shouting, din; **grito** m shout; (de expressão) scream; (de dor) cry; (de animal) call; **dar um grito** to cry out.

**groselha** [gro'zɛʎa] f (red)currant.

**grosseiro/a** [gro'sejru/a] adj (incivil) rude; (piada) crude; **grosseria** f rudeness; **fazer uma grosseria** to be vulgar.

**'grosso/a** adj (denso) thick; (áspero) rough; (voz) deep; **a ~ modo** roughly // m (do exército) the main body; **o ~ de** the bulk of // f gross; **grossura** f thickness.

**gro'tesco/a** adj grotesque.

**'grua** f (MEC) crane.

**gru'dar** vt/i to glue, stick; **grude** f glue.

**grunhido** [gru'ɲidu] m grunt; **grunhir** vi (porco) to grunt; (tigre) to growl; (resmungar) to grumble.

**'grupo** m group; (TEC) unit, set; **~ sanguíneo** blood group.

**'gruta** f grotto.

**guarda** ['gwaxda] f (polícia) policewoman; (vigilância) guarding; (de objeto) safekeeping; **estar de ~** to be on guard; **pôr-se em ~** to be on one's guard // m (MIL) guard; (polícia) policeman.

**guarda-chuva** [gwaxda-'ʃuva] m umbrella.

**guarda-'costas** m inv (NÁUT) coastguard boat; (capanga) bodyguard.

**guardanapo** [gwaxda'napu] m napkin.

**guardar** [gwax'dax] vt to guard; (conservar) to keep; (vigiar) to watch over; **~ silêncio** to keep quiet; **~-se** vr (defender-se) to protect o.s.; **~-se de** (acautelar-se) to guard against.

**guarda-redes** [gwaxda-'xedʒis] m (Pt) goalkeeper.

**guarda-roupa** [gwaxda-'xopa] m (armário) wardrobe; (público) cloakroom.

**guarda-'sol** m sunshade, parasol.

**guarida** [gwa'rida] f refuge.

**guarnecer** [gwaxne'sex] vt (prover) to provide; (MIL) to garrison; (adornar) to trim; **guarnição** f (MIL) garrison; (NÁUT) crew; (de roupa) trimming; (CULIN) garnish.

**'gude** m (jogo) marbles pl; **bola de ~** marble.

**guelra** ['gelra] f (de peixe) gill.

**guerra** ['gexa] f war; (luta) struggle; **~ nuclear** nuclear warfare; **~ fria** cold war; **fazer ~** to wage war; **após ~** post-war; **guerrear** vi to wage war; **guerreiro/a** adj (lutando) fighting; (belicoso) warlike // m warrior; **guerrilha** f (luta) guerrilla warfare; (tropa) guerrilla band; **guerrilheiro/a** adj, m/f guerrilla.

**guia** ['gia] f (conselho) guidance;

(COM) permit, bill of lading // m guide; (livro) guidebook; **guiar** vt (orientar) to guide; (AUTO) to drive; (avião) to pilot; **guiar-se** vr: **guiar-se por** to go by.

**guidão** [giˈdãw] m handlebar.

**guilhotina** [giʎoˈtʃina] f guillotine.

**guinada** [giˈnada] f (NÁUT) lurch; (virada) swerve; (dor) sharp pain.

**guin'char** vt (carro) to tow.

**guincho** [ˈgĩʃu] m (de animal, rodas) squeal; (de pessoa) shriek.

**guin'dar** vt to hoist, lift; (fig) to raise, promote; **guindaste** m hoist, crane.

**'guisa** f: a ~ **de** like, by way of.

**gui'sado** m stew.

**gui'tarra** f guitar.

**'gula** f gluttony, greed; **guloseima** f delicacy, titbit; **guloso/a** adj greedy.

**'gume** m cutting edge; (fig) sharpness.

**gutu'ral** adj guttural.

# H

NB: initial H is always silent in Portuguese.

**h** abr de **hora** hour.

**há** vb ver **haver**.

**'hábil** [-iw] adj, pl **'hábeis** (inteligente) clever; (competente) capable; (destro) able, skilful; **habilidade** f (destreza) skill, ability; (inteligência) cleverness; **habilidoso/a** adj skilful, clever.

**habilitação** [abilitaˈsãw] f (aptidão) eligibility, qualification; **habilitações** fpl (JUR) documentary evidence sg; (conhecimentos) qualifications pl; **habilitar** vt to prepare.

**habitação** [abitaˈsãw] f dwelling, residence; (BIO) habitat; **habitante** m/f inhabitant; **habitar** vt (viver em) to live in; (povoar) to inhabit // vi to live.

**'hábito** m habit; (social) custom; **habitual** adj usual.

**habitu'ar** vt: ~ **alguém a** to get sb used to, accustom sb to; ~**-se** vr: ~**-se a** to get used to.

**'haja** etc vb ver **haver**.

**'hálito** m breath.

**ham'búrguer** m hamburger.

**harmo'nia** f harmony; (paz) peace; (acordo) agreement; **harmonioso/a** adj harmonious.

**'harpa** f harp.

**'hasta** f: ~ **pública** auction.

**'haste** f (de bandeira) flagpole; (TEC) shaft, rod; **hastear** vt to raise, hoist.

**haurir** [awˈrix] vt (esgotar) to drain, exhaust; (aspirar) to inhale; (beber) to suck up.

**ha'ver** vb auxiliar to have // vb impessoal: **há** there is, (pl) there are; **há muita gente** there are a lot of people; **deve ~** there must be; **há cinco dias que não o vejo** I haven't seen him for five days; **há um ano que ela chegou** it's a year since she came; **há muito tempo** long ago; ~ **de** (futuro): **há de ver** you will see; **haja o que houver** come what may; **o que é que há?** what's the matter? // m (COM) credit; **haveres** mpl property sg, possessions.

**hec'tare** m hectare.

**hedi'ondo/a** adj vile, revolting; (crime) heinous.

**'hei** vb ver **haver**.

**hélice** [ˈɛlis] f propeller.

**heli'cóptero** m helicopter.

**hemis'fério** m hemisphere.

**hemorragia** [emoxaˈʒia] f haemorrhage; ~ **nasal** nosebleed.

**hemor'roidas** *fpl* haemorroids, piles.

**'hera** *f* ivy.

**he'rança** *f* inheritance; (*fig*) heritage.

**her'dade** *f* (*Pt*) large farm.

**her'dar** *vt:* ~ **de** to inherit from; ~ **a** to bequeath to; **herdeiro/a** *m* heir // *f* heiress.

**herege** [e're3i] *m/f* heretic; **heresia** *f* heresy; **herético/a** *adj* heretical.

**her'mético/a** *adj* airtight.

**herói** [e'roj] *m* hero; **heróico/a** *adj* heroic; **heroina** *f* heroine; **heroísmo** *m* heroism.

**'herpes** *m* herpes *sg*.

**hesitação** [ezita'sãw] *f* hesitation; **hesitar** *vi* to hesitate.

**heterossexual** [eteroseks'wal] *adj* heterosexual.

**hi'ato** *m* (*intervalo*) interval, gap; (*LING*) hiatus.

**'híbrido/a** *adj* hybrid.

**hidráulico/a** [i'drawliku/a] *adj* hydraulic; **instalação** ~**a** waterworks *sg*.

**hidravião** [idravi'ãw] *m* seaplane.

**hidre'létrico/a** (*Pt:* **-ct-**) *adj* hydroelectric.

**'hidro...** *pref* hydro..., water...; **hidrófilo/a** *adj* absorbent; **hidrofobia** *f* rabies *sg*; **hidrogênio** *m* hydrogen.

**hiena** ['jena] *f* hyena.

**hierarquia** [jerax'kia] *f* hierarchy.

**'hífen** *m* hyphen.

**higiene** [i'3jeni] *f* hygiene; **higiênico/a** *adj* (*MED*) hygienic, sanitary; **papel higiênico** toilet paper.

**'hino** *m* hymn; ~ **nacional** national anthem.

**hipertensão** [ipextẽ'sãw] *f* high blood pressure.

**'hípico/a** *adj* (*atr*) horse; **hipismo** *m* horse racing.

**hip'nose** *f* hypnosis; **hipnotisar** *vt* to hypnotize.

**hipocri'sia** *f* hypocrisy; **hipócrita** *adj* hypocritical // *m/f* hypocrite.

**hi'pódromo** *m* racecourse.

**hipo'teca** *f* mortgage.

**hipótese** [i'potez] *f* hypothesis; **na** ~ **de** in the event of; **em** ~ **alguma** under no circumstances; **hipotético/a** *adj* hypothetical.

**hirto/a** ['ixtu/a] *adj* stiff, rigid.

**his'pânico/a** *adj* Hispanic.

**histe'ria** *f* hysteria.

**his'tória** *f* (*o passado*) history; (*conto*) story, tale; (*mentira*) fib; ~ **da carochinha** nursery tale; **historiador(a)** *m/f* historian; **histórico/a** *adj* historical; (*fig*) historic; **historieta** *f* anecdote, very short story.

**hoje** ['o3i] *adv* today; (*atualmente*) now(adays); ~ **à noite** tonight; ~ **de manhã** this morning; **de** ~ **a uma semana** in a week's time; **de** ~ **em diante** from now on; ~ **em dia** nowadays.

**holan'dês/esa** *adj* Dutch // *m* Dutchman; (*língua*) Dutch // *f* Dutchwoman.

**holo'fote** *m* searchlight.

**homem** ['omẽ] *m* man; (*a humanidade*) mankind; ~ **do povo** man in the street; ~ **de bem** honest man; ~ **de estado** statesman; ~ **de negócios** businessman; ~**-rã** *m* frogman.

**homenagem** [ome'na3ẽ] *f* (*feudal*) homage; (*respeito*) honour, respect.

**homi'cida** *adj* (*pessoa*) homicidal // *m/f* murderer; **homicídio** *m* murder; **homicídio involuntário** manslaughter.

**homizi'ado/a** *adj* in hiding // *m/f* fugitive; **homiziar** *vt* (*dar abrigo*) to shelter; (*esconder*) to hide.

**homossexual** [omoseks'wal] *adj* homosexual; (*col*) gay // *m* homosexual.

**honesti'dade** *f* honesty; (*decência*) decency; (*pureza*) purity, virtue; **honesto/a** *adj* (*íntegro*) honest; (*virtuoso*) virtuous.

**hono'rário/a** adj honorary // mpl: ~s fees.

**'honra** f honour; (castidade) virtue; **em ~ de** in honour of; **honradez** f honesty; (de pessoa) integrity; **honrado/a** adj honest; (respeitado) honourable; **honrar** vt to honour; **honroso/a** adj honourable.

**hóquei** ['ɔkej] m hockey.

**'hora** f (ger) time; (específica) hour; **~ de dormir** bedtime; **~s vagas** spare time; **a que ~s?** when?, at what time?; **que ~s são?** what time is it?; **são duas ~s** it's two o'clock; **bem na ~** just in time; **chegar na ~** to be on time; **dar ~s** to strike the hour; **de última ~** last-minute; **fazer ~** to kill time; **marcar ~** to make an appointment; **meia ~** half an hour; **altas ~s** in the small hours; **na ~ "H"** in the nick of time; **horário/a** adj hourly; **100 km horários** 100 kilometres an hour // m timetable.

**horizon'tal** adj horizontal; **horizonte** m horizon.

**ho'róscopo** m horoscope.

**hor'rendo/a** adj horrendous, frightful; **horripilante** adj horrifying, hair-raising; **horripilar** vt to horrify; **horrível** adj awful, horrible.

**hor'ror** m horror; **que ~!** how awful!; **~izar** vt to horrify, frighten; **~izar-se** vr to be horrified; **~oso/a** adj ghastly, appalling.

**'horta** f vegetable garden; **~liças** fpl vegetables.

**hortelã** [ɔxte'lã] f mint; **~ pimenta** peppermint.

**hortelão/loa** [ɔxte'lãw/loa] m/f (Pt) (market) gardener.

**hospedagem** [ofpe'daʒẽ] f lodging; **hospedar** vt to put up, lodge; **hospedar-se** vr to stay, lodge; **hospedaria** f inn; **hóspede** m (amigo) guest; (estrangeiro) lodger; **hospedeiro/a** adj hospitable, welcoming // m (de hospedaria)

landlord; (em casa) host // f landlady; (em casa) hostess.

**hospi'tal** m hospital.

**hospitaleiro/a** [ofpita'lejru/a] adj hospitable; **hospitalidade** f hospitality.

**'hóstia** f Host, wafer.

**hos'til** adj hostile; **~idade** f hostility.

**ho'tel** m hotel; **~eiro/a** adj hotel cmp // m hotelier; **rede ~eira** hotel chain.

**'houve** etc vb ver **haver.**

**humani'dade** f (os homens) man(kind); (compaixão) humanity; **humanitário/a** adj humanitarian; (benfeitor) humane; **humano/a** adj human; (bondoso) humane.

**'húmido/a** adj (Pt) ver **úmido.**

**humil'dade** f humility; **humilde** adj humble; (pobre) poor; **humilhação** f humiliation; **humilhar** vt to humiliate.

**hu'mor** m (disposição) mood, temper; (graça) humour; **de bom/mau ~** in a good/bad mood; **~ismo** m humour; **~ístico/a** adj humorous.

**'húngaro/a** adj, m/f Hungarian.

# I

**iate** ['jatʃi] m yacht; **iatismo** m yachting.

**i'bérico/a** adj, m/f Iberian; **ibero-americano** adj, m/f Ibero American.

**içar** [i'sax] vt to hoist, raise.

**icterícia** [ikte'risja] f jaundice.

**'ida** f going, departure; **~ e volta** round trip, return.

**i'dade** f age; **ter cinco anos de ~** to be five (years old); **de meia ~** middle-aged; **de menor ~** under age; **a I~ Média** the Middle Ages.

**ide'al** [-aw] adj (perfeito) ideal; (imaginário) imaginary // m ideal;

**~ista** *m/f* idealist; **~izar** *vt* to idealize; (*planejar*) to devise, create.

**ide'ar** *vt* (*imaginar*) to imagine, think up; **idéia** *f* idea; (*mente*) mind; **mudar de idéia** to change one's mind; **não ter idéia** to have no idea; **não faço idéia** I can't imagine.

**'idem** *pron* ditto.

**i'dêntico/a** *adj* identical; **identidade** *f* identity; **carteira de identidade** identity card; **identificação** *f* identification; **identificar** *vt* to identify; **identificar-se** *vr:* **identificar-se com** to identify with.

**ideologia** [ideolo'ʒia] *f* ideology; **ideológico/a** *adj* ideological.

**idi'oma** *m* language.

**idi'ota** *adj* idiotic // *m/f* idiot; **idiotice** *f* idiocy.

**i'dólatra** *adj* idolatrous // *m* idolater // *f* idolatress; **idolatrar** *vt* to idolize; **idolatria** *f* idolatry; **ídolo** *m* idol.

**idoneidade** [idonej'dadʒi] *f* suitability; (*competência*) competence; **~ moral** moral probity; **idôneo/a** *adj* (*conveniente*) suitable, fit; (*pessoa*) able, capable.

**i'doso/a** *adj* elderly, old.

**ignição** [igni'sãw] *f* ignition.

**igno'mínia** *f* disgrace, ignominy; **ignominioso/a** *adj* ignominious.

**igno'rado/a** *adj* (*desconhecido*) unknown; (*obscuro*) obscure; **ignorância** *f* ignorance; **ignorante** *adj* ignorant, uneducated // *m/f* ignoramus; **ignorar** *vt* not to know, be unaware of; **ignoto/a** *adj* (*lit*) unknown.

**igreja** [i'greʒa] *f* church.

**igual** [i'gwaw] *adj* equal; (*superfície, temperatura*) even; **em partes iguais** in equal parts; **ser ~ a** to be the same as, be like // *m/f* equal; **igualar** *vt* (*fazer igual*) to make equal; (*nivelar*) to level // *vi:* **igualar a** to be equal to, be the

same as; **igualdade** *f* (*paridade*) equality; (*uniformidade*) evenness, uniformity.

**igualha** [i'gwaʎa] *f:* **gente de minha ~** my equals; **da mesma ~** of the same ilk.

**iguaria** [igwa'ria] *f* (*CULIN*) delicacy.

**ilação** [ila'sãw] *f* inference, deduction.

**ile'gal** [-aw] *adj* illegal.

**ile'gítimo/a** *adj* illegitimate.

**ilegível** [ile'ʒivew] *adj* illegible.

**i'leso/a** *adj* unhurt.

**ilha** [i'ʎa] *f* island.

**ilharga** [i'ʎaxga] *f* (*ANAT*) side; (*de animal*) flank.

**i'lhéu/i'lhoa** *m/f* islander.

**i'lícito/a** *adj* illicit.

**ilimi'tado/a** *adj* unlimited.

**i'lógico/a** *adj* illogical; (*absurdo*) absurd.

**ilu'dir** *vt* (*enganar*) to deceive; (*a lei*) to evade; **~-se** *vr* to deceive o.s.

**iluminação** [ilumina'sãw] *f* lighting; (*fig*) enlightenment; **iluminar** *vt* to light up; (*fig*) to enlighten.

**ilusão** [ilu'zãw] *f* illusion; (*quimera*) delusion; (*burla*) trick; **~ de ótica** optical illusion; **ilusionista** *m/f* conjurer; **ilusório/a** *adj* (*enganoso*) deceptive.

**ilustração** [ilustra'sãw] *f* (*figura*) illustration; (*saber*) learning; **ilustrado/a** *adj* (*com gravuras*) illustrated; (*instruído*) learned; **ilustrar** *vt* (*com gravuras*) to illustrate; (*instruir*) to instruct; (*explicar*) to explain; **ilustrar-se** *vr* (*distinguir-se*) to excel; (*instruir-se*) to inform o.s.; **ilustre** *adj* famous, illustrious.

**ímã** *m* magnet.

**imagem** [i'maʒẽ] *f* image; (*semelhança*) likeness; (*visual*) picture; **imaginação** *f* imagination; **imaginar** *vt* to imagine; (*supor*) to suppose; **imaginário/a** *adj* imaginary; **imaginativo/a** adj imaginative.

**ima'turo/a** adj immature; (*fruta*) unripe.

**imba'tível** adj invincible.

**imbe'cil** adj stupid // m/f imbecile, half-wit; ~**idade** f stupidity.

**imbri'car** vt, ~-**se** vr to overlap.

**imbuir** [ˈibwix] vt: ~ **de** (*sentimentos*) to imbue with.

**imediações** [imedjaˈsõjʃ] fpl vicinity sg, neighbourhood sg.

**imediata'mente** adv immediately, right away; **imediato/a** adj immediate; (*seguinte*) next; **imediato a** next to; **de imediato** straight away // m second-in-command.

**imensi'dade** f immensity; **imenso/a** adj immense, huge.

**imere'cido/a** adj undeserved.

**imigração** [imigraˈsãw] f immigration; **imigrante** adj, m/f immigrant; **imigrar** vi to immigrate.

**imiscuir-se** [imiʃˈkwix-si] vr to meddle, interfere.

**imitação** [imitaˈsãw] f imitation, copy; **imitar** vt to imitate, copy.

**imobi'liário/a** adj property cmp; (*US*) real estate // f estate agency.

**imo'lar** vt to sacrifice.

**imo'ral** adj immoral.

**imor'tal** adj immortal; ~**izar** vt to immortalize.

**i'móvel** adj (*parado*) motionless, still; (*não movediço*) immovable // m property.

**impaciência** [impasˈjɛsja] f impatience; **impacientar-se** vr to lose one's patience; **impaciente** adj impatient; (*inquieto*) anxious.

**im'pacto** m impact.

**impalu'dismo** m malaria.

**'ímpar** adj (*números*) odd.

**imparci'al** [-jaw] adj fair, impartial; ~**idade** f impartiality.

**im'pávido/a** adj (*lit*) fearless, intrepid.

**impe'cável** [-avew] adj perfect, impeccable.

**impe'dido/a** adj hindered; (*estrada*) blocked; (*futebol*) offside // m (*MIL*) batman; **impedir** vt (*obstruir*) to obstruct; (*estrada*) to block; (*movimento*) to impede; **impedir alguém de fazer** to prevent sb from doing.

**impe'lir** vt to drive (on); (*obrigar*) to force, impel.

**impene'trável** [-avew] adj impenetrable; (*fig*) incomprehensible.

**impeni'tente** adj unrepentant.

**impen'sado/a** adj (*imprevidente*) thoughtless; (*sem cálculo*) unpremeditated; (*imprevisto*) unforeseen.

**impera'dor** m emperor; **imperar** vi to reign, rule; (*fig*) to prevail.

**imperativo/a** adj (*urgente*) imperative // m necessity; **imperatriz** f empress.

**impercep'tível** [-ivew] adj imperceptible; (*diminuto*) slight.

**imperdo'ável** [-avew] adj unforgivable, inexcusable.

**impere'cível** [-ivew] adj imperishable.

**imperfeição** [impɛxfejˈsãw] f imperfection; (*falha*) flaw; **imperfeito/a** adj imperfect; (*inacabado*) unfinished; (*defeituoso*) faulty.

**imperi'al** [-jaw] adj imperial; ~**ismo** m imperialism.

**impe'rícia** f (*inabilidade*) incompetence; (*inexperiência*) inexperience.

**im'pério** m empire; **imperioso/a** adj (*dominador*) domineering; (*urgente*) pressing, urgent.

**imperme'ável** [-avew] adj impervious; (*à água*) waterproof // m raincoat.

**imperti'nência** f impertinence; (*despropósito*) irrelevance; **impertinente** adj (*alheio*) irrelevant; (*insolente*) impertinent.

**impessoal** [ɪmpɛs'waw] *adj* impersonal.

**ímpeto** *m* (*TEC*) impetus; (*furor*) force; (*de cólera*) surge, rush; **agir com** ~ to act on impulse.

**impetuosi'dade** *f* impetuosity; (*veemência*) vehemence; **impetuoso/a** *adj* (*pessoa*) headstrong, impetuous; (*ato*) rash, hasty.

**impie'dade** *f* irreverence; (*crueldade*) cruelty.

**impla'cável** [-avew] *adj* (*pessoa*) unforgiving; (*destino, doença*) relentless.

**impli'car** *vt* (*envolver*) to implicate; (*dar a entender*) to imply; ~ **com** (*contender*) to pick a quarrel with; ~-**se** *vr* (*meter-se*) to get involved.

**im'plícito** *adj* implicit; (*subentendido*) implied.

**implo'rar** *vt* to beg, implore.

**impo'nente** *adj* impressive, imposing.

**impopu'lar** *adj* unpopular.

**im'por** *vt* to impose; (*respeito*) to command; ~-**se** *vr* to make one's influence felt.

**importa'ção** [ɪmpoxta'sãw] *f* (*ato*) importing; (*mercadorias*) imports *pl*; **importa'dor(a)** *adj* import *cmp* // *m/f* importer.

**impor'tância** *f* importance; (*de dinheiro*) sum, amount; **não tem** ~ it doesn't matter, never mind; **importante** *adj* important // *m* : **o importante** the main/important thing; **importar** *vt* (*COM*) to import; (*trazer*) to bring in // *vi* to matter, be important; **não me importo** I don't care; **não importa!** never mind!; **importar em** to add up to, amount to.

**im'porte** *m* (*total*) amount; (*custo*) cost.

**importu'nar** *vt* to bother, annoy; **importuno/a** *adj* (*maçante*) annoying; (*inoportuno*) inopportune.

**impossibili'dade** *f* impossibility; **impossibilitar** *vt* to make impossible; **impossível** *adj* impossible; (*insuportável*) insufferable.

**im'posto/a** *pp de* **impor** // *m* tax; ~ **de renda** income tax; ~ **predial** rates *pl*.

**impos'tor** *m* impostor; **impostura** *f* deception.

**impo'tência** *f* impotence; **impotente** *adj* impotent; (*fraco*) powerless.

**imprati'cável** *adj* impracticable.

**impre'ciso/a** *adj* vague.

**impreg'nar** *vt* to impregnate.

**im'prensa** *f* (*a arte*) printing; (*máquina, jornalistas*) press; (*casa*) printer's.

**imprescin'dível** [-d͡ʒivew] *adj* essential, indispensable.

**impres'são** [ɪmpre'sãw] *f* (*sensação*) impression; (*imprensa*) printing; (*marca*) imprint; ~ **digital** fingerprint; **impressionante** *adj* impressive; (*comovente*) moving; **impressionar** *vt* (*afetar*) to impress; (*comover*) to move // *vi* to be impressive; **impresso/a** *pp irr de* **imprimir** // *adj* printed // *m* (*para preencher*) form; (*folheto*) leaflet; **impressos** *mpl* printed matter; **impressor** *m* printer; **impressora** *f* printing machine.

**impre'visto/a** *adj* unexpected, unforeseen.

**impri'mir** *vt* to print; (*marca*) to stamp; (*infundir*) to instil; ~-**se** *vr* to be stamped, be impressed.

**'ímprobo/a** *adj* (*desonesto*) dishonest; (*árduo*) arduous.

**improce'dente** *adj* groundless, unjustified.

**improdu'tivo/a** *adj* unproductive.

**improfícuo/a** [ɪmpro'fɪkwu/a] *adj* useless, futile.

**impro'pério** *m* insult.

**improprie'dade** *f* (*inoportunidade*) unsuitability; (*incorreção*) incorrectness, impropriety; **impróprio/a** *adj* (*inadequado*) unsuitable; (*errado*) wrong; (*conduta*) improper.

**impro'vável** [-avew] *adj* unlikely.

**improvi'dência** *f* (*imprudência*) rashness; (*descuido*) carelessness; **improvidente** *adj* (*esbanjador*) thriftless; (*negligente*) careless.

**improvi'sado/a** *adj* improvised, impromptu; **improvisar** *vt/i* to improvise; (*teatro*) to ad-lib; **improviso** *m* impromptu talk; **de improviso** suddenly; **falar de improviso** to talk off the cuff.

**impru'dência** *f* imprudence; (*irreflexão*) rashness; **imprudente** *adj* (*irrefletido*) rash.

**impu'dência** *f* impudence; (*col*) cheek; **impudente** *adj* (*sem-vergonha*) shameless; (*descarado*) impudent; (*lascivo*) lewd.

**impu'dico/a** *adj* (*sem-vergonha*) shameless; (*lascivo*) lewd.

**impug'nar** *vt* (*refutar*) to refute; (*opor-se a*) to oppose.

**impulsio'nar** *vt* (*impelir*) to drive, impel; (*estimular*) to urge.

**impul'sivo/a** *adj* impulsive; **impulso** *m* (*ímpeto*) thrust, push; (*estímulo*) urge, impulse.

**im'pune** *adj*; **~mente** *adv* with impunity; **impunidade** *f* impunity.

**impu'reza** *f* impurity; (*despudor*) indecency; **impuro/a** *adj* impure; (*sensual*) lewd.

**imputação** [imputa'sãw] *f* accusation; **imputar** *vt* (*atribuir*) to attribute; **imputar alguma coisa a alguém** to blame sb for sth; **imputável** *adj* attributable.

**imun'dícia** *f* filth; **imundo/a** *adj* filthy.

**i'mune** *adj*: **~ a** immune to/from; **imunidade** *f* immunity.

**imu'tável** [-avew] *adj* fixed, unalterable, unchanging.

**inaba'lável** [-avew] *adj* unshakeable.

**in'ábil** [-abıw] *adj* (*desajeitado*) clumsy; (*incapaz*) incapable; **inabilidade** *f* (*incompetência*) incompetence; (*falta de destreza*) clumsiness; **inabilitar** *vt* (*incapacitar*) to incapacitate; (*em exame*) to disqualify.

**inabi'tável** *adj* uninhabitable.

**inaca'bável** *adj* interminable, unending.

**inação** [ina'sãw] (*Pt*: **-cç-**) *f* (*inércia*) inactivity; (*irresolução*) indecision.

**inaceitável** [ınasej'tavew] *adj* unacceptable.

**inaces'sível** *adj* inaccessible.

**inadequado/a** [ınade'kwadu/a] *adj* (*impróprio*) unsuitable.

**inadmis'sível** *adj* inadmissible.

**inadquirível** [ınadkı'rıvew] *adj* unobtainable.

**inadver'tência** *f* oversight; **inadvertido/a** *adj* unintentional.

**ina'lar** *vt* to inhale, breathe in.

**inalte'rável** *adj* unchangeable; (*impassível*) imperturbable.

**inanição** [ınanı'sãw] *f* starvation.

**inani'mado/a** *adj* (*morto*) lifeless; (*sem vida*) inanimate.

**inaptidão** [ınaptʃı'dãw] *f* inability; **inapto/a** *adj* (*incapaz*) unfit, incapable; (*inadequado*) unsuited.

**inatingível** [ınatʃĩ'ʒıvew] *adj* unattainable.

**inativi'dade** (*Pt*: **-ct-**) *f* inactivity; (*de funcionário*) unemployment, redundancy; **inativo/a** (*Pt*: **-ct-**) *adj* inactive; (*inerte*) inert; (*aposentado*) retired.

**i'nato/a** *adj* innate, inborn.

**inaudito/a** [ınaw'dʒıtu/a] *adj* unheard-of.

**inauguração** [ınawgura'sãw] *f* inauguration; (*de exposição*) opening; **inaugurar** *vt* to inaugurate; (*exposição*) to open.

**incalcu'lável** *adj* incalculable.

**incan'sável** adj tireless, untiring.

**incapaci'dade** f (inaptidão) incapacity; (incompetência) incompetence; **incapacitar** vt (inabilitar) to make unfit; (estropiar) to disable; **incapaz** adj : **incapaz de fazer** unable to do, incapable of doing; **incapaz para** unfit for.

**inçar** ['tsax] vt to infest.

**incauto/a** [ɪŋ'kawtu/a] adj (imprudente) rash; (crédulo) unsuspecting.

**incendi'ar** vt to set fire to; (fig) to inflame; ~**se** vr to catch fire; **incendiário/a** adj incendiary; (fig) inflammatory // m/f agitator; **incêndio** m fire; **incêndio premeditado** arson.

**in'censo** m incense.

**incen'tivo** m incentive.

**incer'teza** f uncertainty; (dúvida) doubt; **incerto/a** adj uncertain; (duvidoso) doubtful.

**inces'sante** adj incessant.

**inchado/a** [ɪ'ʃadu/a] adj swollen; (fig) conceited; **inchar** vt to swell; (inflar) to blow up // vi to swell; **inchar-se** vr to swell (up); (fig) to become conceited.

**inci'dente** m incident.

**incine'rar** vt to burn; (cadáver) to cremate.

**incisão** [ɪnsi'zãw] f (corte) cut; (MED) incision; **incisivo/a** adj cutting, sharp; (fig) incisive // m incisor.

**incitação** [ɪnsita'sãw] f, **incita'mento** m incitement; **incitar** vt to incite; (instigar) to rouse.

**inci'vil** adj rude, ill-mannered.

**incle'mência** f harshness, rigour; (tempo) inclemency; **inclemente** adj severe, harsh; (tempo) inclement.

**inclinação** [ɪklina'sãw] f (propensão) inclination; (da terra) slope; (simpatia) liking; ~ **da cabeça** nod; **inclinado/a** adj : **estar**

**inclinado/pouco inclinado a** to be inclined/loath to; **inclinar** vt (objeto) to tilt; (cabeça) to nod; (conversa) to turn // vi (terra) to slope; (objeto) to tilt; **inclinar para** (propensão) to incline towards; **inclinar-se** vr (objeto) to tilt; (dobrar o corpo) to bow, stoop.

**'ínclito/a** adj illustrious, renowned.

**incluir** ['kluix] vt to include; (conter) to incorporate; (pôr dentro) to enclose; **inclusão** f inclusion.

**inclusive** [ɪklu'zivi] adj inclusive // prep including; (até) up to // adv inclusively; **incluso/a** adj included; (em carta) enclosed.

**incoerente** [ɪkoe'rẽtʃi] adj incoherent.

**in'cógnito/a** adj unknown // adv incognito // f unknown quantity; (MAT) unknown.

**inco'lor** adj colourless.

**incólume** ['kolumɪ] adj safe and sound; (ileso) unharmed.

**incomensu'rável** adj immense.

**incomo'dar** vt (molestar) to bother, trouble; (irritar) to annoy; ~**se** vr to bother, put o.s. out; **não se incomode!** never mind!; **incômodo/a** adj (desconfortável) uncomfortable; (importuno) annoying; (inoportuno) inconvenient // m (indisposição) ailment; (maçada) nuisance, trouble; (amolação) inconvenience.

**incompa'rável** adj incomparable.

**incompatibili'dade** f incompatibility; **incompatível** adj incompatible.

**incompe'tência** f incompetence; **incompetente** adj incompetent.

**incom'pleto/a** adj incomplete, unfinished.

**incompreen'sível** adj incomprehensible.

**incomuni'cável** adj (preso) in solitary confinement.

**inconce'bível** adj inconceivable; (incrível) incredible.

**inconcili'ável** adj irreconcilable; (incompatível) incompatible.

**inconclu'dente** adj inconclusive.

**incondicio'nal** [-aw] adj unconditional; (apoio) wholehearted; (partidário) staunch.

**inconfi'dência** f disloyalty; (JUR) treason; **inconfidente** adj disloyal // m conspirator.

**inconfun'dível** [-dʒivew] adj unmistakeable.

**incongru'ente** adj incongruous.

**inconsciência** [ĩkõ'sjẽsja] f unconsciousness; (irreflexão) thoughtlessness; **inconsciente** adj unconscious; (involuntário) unwitting; (irresponsável) irresponsible.

**inconseqüente** [ĩkõse'kwẽtʃi] adj inconsistent; (contraditório) illogical.

**inconsis'tente** adj (contraditório) inconsistent; (fraco) weak.

**incons'tante** adj fickle.

**incontes'tável** adj undeniable.

**inconti'nência** f (sensual) licentiousness; (MED) incontinence; **incontinente** adj (sensual) licentious; (MED) incontinent.

**inconveni'ência** f unsuitability, inappropriateness; (descortesia) impoliteness; **inconveniente** adj (impróprio) unsuitable, inappropriate; (indecoroso) impolite // m difficulty, problem; **qual é o inconveniente?** what's wrong with it?

**incorpo'rar** vt to incorporate; (juntar) to add; (COM) to merge; **~-se** vr: **~-se a/em** to join.

**incorreção** [ĩkoxe'sãw] (PT: **-cç-**) f (erro) inaccuracy.

**incor'rer** vi: **~ em** to incur.

**incor'reto/a** (PT: **-ct-**) adj (errado) wrong, incorrect; (pessoa) bad-mannered; (ação) improper.

**incorri'gível** [ĩkoxi'ʒivew] adj incorrigible.

**incorru'tível** (PT: **-pt-**) adj incorruptible.

**increduli'dade** f incredulity; (ceticismo) scepticism; **incrédulo/a** adj incredulous; (cético) sceptical // m/f sceptic.

**incre'mento** m (desenvolvimento) growth; (acréscimo) increase.

**incrível** [ĩ'krivew] adj incredible.

**incru'ento/a** adj (lit) bloodless.

**incrus'tar** vt to encrust; (inserir) to inlay.

**incuba'dora** f incubator; **incubar** vt (ovos) to incubate; (plano) to hatch.

**incul'car** vt to impress (upon sb); (aconselhar) to recommend.

**incul'par** vt (censurar) to blame; (acusar) to accuse.

**in'culto/a** adj (pessoa) uncultured, uneducated; (terreno) uncultivated.

**incum'bir** vt: **~ alguém de** to put sb in charge of // vi: **~ a alguém** to be sb's duty; **~-se vr: ~-se de** to undertake, take charge of.

**incu'rável** adj incurable.

**incursão** [ĩkux'zãw] f (invasão) raid, attack; (penetração) foray.

**incu'tir** vt to instil, inspire.

**indagação** [ĩdaga'sãw] f (pesquisa) investigation; (busca) search; (JUR) inquiry; **indagar** vt (investigar) to investigate; (averiguar) to ascertain // vi: **indagar de** to inquire about.

**inde'cente** adj indecent, improper; (obsceno) obscene.

**indecisão** [ĩdesi'zãw] f indecision; (hesitação) hesitation; **indeciso/a** adj (irresoluto) undecided, hesitant; (indistinto) vague.

**indeco'roso/a** adj indecent, improper.

**indefe'rido/a** adj refused, rejected; **indeferir** vt (desatender) to reject; (requerimento) to turn down.

**inde'feso/a** adj undefended; (fraco) defenceless.

**indefi'nido/a** adj indefinite; (vago) vague, undefined.

**inde'lével** [-ew] adj indelible.

**indenização** [ɪndeniˈsãw] (Pt: -mn-) f compensation; (COM) indemnity; **indenizar** (Pt: -mn-) vt (compensar) to compensate; (gastos) to reimburse // vi: **indenizar de** to compensate for.

**indepen'dência** f independence; **independente** adj independent; (auto-suficiente) self-sufficient.

**indese'jável** adj undesirable.

**'India** f India; **indiano/a** adj, m/f Indian.

**indicação** [ɪndʒikaˈsãw] f indication; (sinal) sign; (sugestão) hint; (de termômetro) reading; **indicador** m indicator; (TEC) gauge; (dedo) index finger; (ponteiro) pointer; **indicar** vt (mostrar) to show, indicate; (apontar) to point to; (termômetro) to register.

**índice** [ˈɪndʒisɪ] m (de livro) index; (dedo) index finger.

**indício** [ɪnˈdʒisju] m (sinal) sign; (vestígio) trace; (sugestão) clue.

**indife'rença** f indifference; (apatia) apathy; **indiferente** adj indifferent; (apático) apathetic; **isso me é indiferente** it's all the same to me.

**indígena** [ɪnˈdʒiʒena] adj, m/f native; (índio) Indian.

**indigência** [ɪndʒiˈʒesja] f poverty; (fig) lack, need.

**indigestão** [ɪndʒiʒeʃˈtãw] f indigestion; **indigesto/a** adj indigestible; (aborrecido) dull, boring.

**indignação** [ɪndʒignaˈsãw] f indignation; **indignado/a** adj indignant; **indignar** vt to anger, incense; **indignar-se** vr: **indignar-se com** to get indignant about.

**indigni'dade** f indignity; (ultraje) outrage; **indigno/a** adj (não merecedor) unworthy; (desprezível) disgraceful, despicable.

**'indio/a** adj, m/f (da América) Indian.

**indi'reto/a** (Pt: -ct-) adj indirect;

(olhar) sidelong; (procedimento) roundabout // f insinuation.

**indis'creto/a** adj indiscreet; (sem tato) tactless; **indiscrição** f indiscretion; (falta de diplomacia) tactlessness; (ato) blunder, gaffe.

**indiscu'tível** adj indisputable.

**indispen'sável** adj essential, vital // m essentials pl.

**indispo'nível** adj unavailable.

**indis'por** vt to disturb, upset; (saúde) to make ill; **~-se** vr: **~-se com um amigo** to fall out with a friend; **indisposição** f sickness; **indisposição gástrica** stomach upset; **indisposto/a** adj (doente) unwell, poorly.

**indis'tinto/a** adj indistinct; (vago) vague.

**individual** [ɪndʒiviˈdwaw] adj individual; **indivíduo** m individual, person.

**indi'zível** adj (extraordinário) unspeakable; (indescritível) indescribable.

**in'dócil** [-ɪw] adj (rebelde) unruly, wayward; (incontentável) difficult, restless.

**'índole** f (temperamento) nature; (tipo) sort, type.

**indo'lência** f laziness, indolence.

**indo'mável** [-avew] adj (animal) untameable; (coragem) indomitable; (criança) unmanageable, unruly; **indómito/a** adj untamed, wild.

**indulgência** [ɪnduwˈʒesja] f (clemência) forgiveness; (perdão) pardon; (REL) indulgence.

**indul'tar** vt to pardon; (JUR) to reprieve; **indulto** m pardon; (anistia) amnesty; (REL) dispensation.

**in'dústria** f industry; **industrial** adj industrial // m/f industrialist; **industrioso/a** adj (laborioso) hard-working, industrious; (hábil) clever, skilful.

**indu'zir** vt to induce; **~ a** to

persuade to; ~ **em erro** to lead astray.

**in'édito/a** adj (livro) unpublished; (incomum) unheard of, rare.

**ine'fável** adj indescribable.

**inefi'caz** adj ineffective; (inútil) useless; **ineficiência** f inefficiency.

**ine'gável** adj (lit) undeniable.

**inelu'tável** adj inescapable, inevitable.

**i'népcia** f ineptitude; **inepto/a** adj inept, incompetent.

**inequívoco/a** [ineˈkivoku/a] adj (evidente) clear; (inconfundível) unmistakeable.

**i'nércia** f (torpor) lassitude, lethargy; (FÍSICA) inertia.

**ine'rente** adj inherent.

**in'erme** adj (lit: não armado) unarmed; (desprotegido) defenceless.

**in'erte** adj still, motionless; (FÍSICA) inert.

**inesgo'tável** adj inexhaustible; (superabundante) boundless, abundant.

**inespe'rado/a** adj unexpected, unforeseen.

**inesquecível** [ineʒkeˈsivew] adj unforgettable.

**inesti'mável** adj invaluable.

**inevi'tável** adj inevitable.

**inexatidão** [inezatʃiˈdãw] (Pt: -**ct**-) f inaccuracy; **inexato/a** (Pt: -**ct**-) adj inaccurate.

**inexpug'nável** adj (fortaleza) impregnable; (invencível) invincible.

**infa'lível** adj infallible; (inevitável) inevitable.

**in'fame** adj (notório) notorious; (detestável) vile, shocking; **infâmia** f (má fama) notoriety; (desonra) disgrace; (vileza) villainy.

**in'fância** f infancy, childhood.

**infanta'ria** f infantry.

**in'fante** m (filho dos reis) prince; (soldado) foot soldier; **infantil** adj (ingênuo) childlike; (pueril) childish;

(para crianças) children's cmp.

**infati'gável** adj untiring.

**infausto/a** [ˈfawʃtu/a] adj unlucky.

**infecção** [ifekˈsãw] f infection; (contaminação) contamination; **infeccionar** vt (ferida) to infect; (contaminar) to contaminate; **infeccioso/a** adj infectious.

**infelici'dade** f unhappiness; (desgraça) misfortune; **infeliz** adj (triste) unhappy; (infausto) unfortunate; (sem sorte) unlucky; **infelizmente** adv unfortunately.

**inferi'or** adj (em valor) inferior; (mais baixo) lower // m inferior, subordinate; ~**idade** f inferiority.

**infe'rir** vt to infer, deduce.

**in'ferno** m hell.

**infes'tar** vt (bandidos) to overrun; (ratos) to infest.

**infe'tar** (Pt: -**ct**-) vt to infect, contaminate.

**infideli'dade** f infidelity, unfaithfulness; (REL) disbelief; **infiel** adj (desleal) disloyal; (marido) unfaithful; (texto) inaccurate // m/f unbeliever.

**'ínfimo/a** adj lowest.

**infini'dade** f infinity; **uma** ~ **de** countless; **infinito/a** adj infinite // m infinity.

**inflação** [iflaˈsãw] f inflation; **inflacionário/a** adj inflationary.

**infla'mar** vt (MED) to inflame; (fig) to excite; ~**-se** vr to catch fire; (avermelhar-se) to go red; (fig) to get excited.

**in'flar** vt to inflate, blow up; ~**-se** vr to swell (up).

**infle'xível** adj stiff, rigid; (fig) unyielding.

**infligir** [ifliˈʒix] vt: ~ **alguma coisa a alguém** to inflict sth upon sb.

**influ'ência** f influence; **influenciar** vt to influence; **influente** adj influential.

**influir** [ˈfluix] vi: ~ **em** to influence, have an influence on.

**influxo** [iˈfluksu] *m* influx; (*preamar*) high tide.

**informação** [ifoxmaˈsãw] *f* (*comunicação*) report; (*MIL*) intelligence; (*JUR*) inquiry; **informações** *fpl* information *sg*; **pedir informações sobre** to ask about, inquire about.

**informal** [ifoxˈmaw] *adj* informal.

**informante** [ifoxˈmãtʃi] *m* informant; (*JUR*) informer; **informar** *vt* to inform; **informar alguém de** to let sb know about // *vi*: **informar de** to report on, tell about; **informar-se** *vr*: **informar-se de** to find out about, inquire about.

**informe** *adj* shapeless // *m* report, statement.

**infortúnio** *m* misfortune.

**infração** [ifraˈsãw] (*Pt*: **-cç-**) *f* breach, infringement; (*futebol*) foul; **~ de trânsito** traffic offence; **infrator(a)** (*Pt*: **-ct-**) *m/f* offender, law breaker.

**infringir** [ifrĩˈʒix] *vt* to infringe, contravene.

**infrutífero/a** *adj* fruitless.

**infundado/a** *adj* groundless, unfounded.

**infundir** *vt* to infuse; (*terror*) to strike; (*incutir*) to instil.

**ingente** [iˈʒẽtʃi] *adj* huge, enormous.

**ingenuidade** [iʒenwiˈdadʒi] *f* (*simplicidade*) ingenuousness; **ingênuo/a** *adj* (*inocente*) ingenuous.

**ingerência** [iʒeˈrẽsja] *f* interference.

**ingerir** [iʒeˈrix] *vt* to ingest; (*engolir*) to swallow.

**Inglaterra** *f* England; **inglês/esa** *adj* English // *m* Englishman; (*língua*) English // *f* Englishwoman.

**ingratidão** [igratʒiˈdãw] *f* ingratitude; **ingrato/a** *adj* (*mal agradecido*) ungrateful; (*desagradável*) unpleasant.

**ingrediente** *m* ingredient.

**íngreme** *adj* steep.

**ingressar** *vi*: **~ em** to enter, go into; (*um clube*) to join; **ingresso** *m* (*entrada*) entry; (*admissão*) admission; (*bilhete*) ticket.

**inhaca** [iˈɲaka] *f* (*fedor*) stink; (*má sorte*) bad luck.

**inibir** *vt* to inhibit; **~ de** to prevent from.

**inicial** [-jaw] *adj* initial, first // *f* initial; **iniciar** *vt* to initiate; (*começar*) to begin, start; **iniciativa** *f* initiative; **início** *m* beginning; **de/no início** at first.

**inimigo/a** *adj*, *m/f* enemy; **inimizade** *f* enmity, hatred.

**iníquo/a** [iˈnikwa/a] *adj* iniquitous.

**injeção** [ĩʒeˈsãw] (*Pt*: **-cç-**) *f* injection; **injetado/a** (*Pt*: **-ct-**) *adj* (*olhos*) bloodshot; **injetar** (*Pt*: **-ct-**) *vt* to inject.

**injúria** [ĩˈʒurja] *f* (*insulto*) insult; (*agravo*) offence; (*dano*) harm; **injuriar** *vt* (*insultar*) to insult; (*causar dano*) to harm; **injurioso/a** *adj* insulting; (*ofensivo*) offensive.

**injustiça** [ĩʒuʃˈtʃisa] *f* injustice; **injusto/a** *adj* unfair, unjust.

**inocência** *f* innocence; **inocente** *adj* innocent; (*ingênuo*) simple, naïve // *m/f* (*idiota*) simpleton.

**inocular** *vt* to inoculate.

**inócuo/a** [iˈnokwu/a] *adj* harmless.

**inofensivo/a** *adj* harmless, inoffensive.

**inopinado/a** *adj* unexpected.

**inoportuno/a** *adj* inconvenient, inopportune.

**inóspito/a** *adj* inhospitable.

**inovação** [inovaˈsãw] *f* innovation; **inovar** *vt* to innovate.

**inoxidável** *adj*: **aço ~** stainless steel.

**inquebrantável** [ĩkebrãˈtavew] *adj* unbreakable; (*amizade*) firm.

**inquérito** [ĩˈkɛritu] *m* inquiry; (*JUR*) inquest.

**inquietação** [ĩkjetaˈsãw] *f* (*preocupação*) anxiety, uneasiness; (*agitação*) restlessness; **inquietar** *vt* to worry, disturb; **inquietar-se** *vr* to worry, bother; **inquieto/a** *adj* (*ansioso*) anxious, worried; (*agitado*) restless.

**inquilino/a** [ĩkɪˈlinu/a] *m/f* tenant.

**inquirição** [ĩkɪrɪˈsãw] *f* (*indagação*) investigation; (*inquisição*) interrogation; (*JUR*) cross-examination; **inquirir** *vt* (*JUR*) to cross-examine // *vi* to enquire.

**insaciável** [ĩsasˈjavew] *adj* insatiable.

**insa'lubre** *adj* unhealthy.

**insani'dade** *f* madness, insanity.

**insatis'feito/a** *adj* dissatisfied, unhappy.

**inscre'ver** *vt* to inscribe; (*aluno*) to enrol, register; **~-se** *vr* to enrol; **inscrição** *f* (*legenda*) inscription; (*em escola*) enrolment, registration.

**insegu'rança** *f* insecurity; **inseguro/a** *adj* insecure.

**insensa'tez** *f* folly, madness; **insensato/a** *adj* unreasonable, foolish.

**insensibili'dade** *f* insensitivity; (*indiferença*) callousness; **insensível** *adj* insensitive; (*dormente*) numb; (*despropositado*) nonsensical.

**inse'rir** *vt* to insert, put in.

**inseti'cida** (*Pt*: **-ct-**) *m* insecticide; **inseto** (*Pt*: **-ct-**) *m* insect.

**insidi'oso/a** *adj* insidious.

**in'signe** *adj* distinguished, eminent.

**in'sígnia** *f* (*sinal distintivo*) badge; (*emblema*) emblem; (*bandeira*) ensign.

**insignifi'cante** *adj* insignificant.

**insinuação** [ĩsĩnwaˈsãw] *f* insinuation; (*sugestão*) hint; **insinuante** *adj* ingratiating; **insinuar** *vt* to insinuate, imply; **insinuar-se** *vr*: **insinuar-se por/entre** to slip into; **insinuar-se na confiança de alguém** to worm one's way into sb's confidence.

**in'sípido/a** *adj* insipid.

**insis'tência** *f* insistence;

(*obstinação*) persistence; **insistir** *vi*: **insistir em** (*perseverar*) to persist in; (*exigir*) to insist on; (*fig*: *sublinhar*) to stress.

**inso'frido/a** *adj* impatient, restless.

**insolação** [ĩsolaˈsãw] *f*: **pegar uma ~** to get sunstroke.

**inso'lência** *f* insolence; **insolente** *adj* insolent.

**in'sólito/a** *adj* unusual.

**inso'lúvel** *adj* insoluble.

**insol'vência** *f* insolvency.

**inson'dável** *adj* unfathomable.

**in'sônia** *f* insomnia.

**in'sosso/a** *adj* unsalted; (*sem sabor*) tasteless.

**inspeção** [ĩʃpɛˈsãw] (*Pt*: **-cç-**) *f* inspection, check; **inspecionar** (*Pt*: **-cc-**) *vt* (*oficialmente*) to inspect; (*observar*) to examine; (*conferir*) to check; **inspetor(a)** (*Pt*: **-ct-**) *m/f* inspector.

**inspiração** [ĩʃpɪraˈsãw] *f* inspiration; **inspirar** *vt* to inspire; (*MED*) to inhale; **inspirar-se** *vr* to be inspired.

**instalação** [ĩʃtalaˈsãw] *f* installation; **~ hidráulica** waterworks *sg*; **instalar** *vt* (*equipamento*) to install; (*estabelecer*) to set up; **instalar-se** *vr* (*numa cadeira*) to install o.s.; (*alojar-se*) to settle in.

**in'stância** *f* (*pedido urgente*) urgent request; (*pedido insistente*) entreaty, adjuration; (*JUR*) **tribunal de primeira ~** magistrate's court; **em última ~** as a last resort.

**instan'tâneo/a** *adj* instant, instantaneous // *m* (*FOTO*) snapshot; **instante** *m* instant, moment; **nesse instante** just a moment ago.

**in'star** *vt* to urge; **~ com alguém para que faça algo** to urge sb to do sth // *vi* (*estar iminente*) to be imminent, be about to happen; (*ser urgente*) to be urgent; (*insistir*) to insist.

**instaurar** [inʃtawˈrax] *vt* to establish, set up.

**in'stável** *adj* unstable; (*tempo*) unsettled.

**insti'gar** *vt* (*incitar*) to urge; (*provocar*) to provoke.

**in'stinto** *m* instinct; **por ~** instinctively.

**instituição** [inʃtʃitwiˈsãw] *f* institution; **instituir** *vt* to institute; (*fundar*) to establish, found; **instituto** *m* (*escola*) institute; (*instituição*) instituiton.

**instrução** [inʃtruˈsãw] (*Pt*: **-cç-**) *f* instruction; (*erudição*) learning; **instruído/a** *adj* educated; **instruir** *vt* to instruct; (*adestrar*) to train; (*educar*) to teach.

**instru'mento** *m* instrument; (*ferramenta*) implement.

**instru'tor(a)** (*Pt*: **-ct-**) *m* instructor; (*esporte*) coach // *f* instructress.

**insubordi'nado/a** *adj* unruly; **insubordinar-se** *vr* to rebel; (*NÁUT*) to mutiny.

**insuficiência** [insufiʃˈjèsja] *f* shortage; (*MED*) deficiency; **insuficiente** *adj* (*não bastante*) insufficient.

**insu'flar** *vt* to blow up, inflate; (*fig*) to instil.

**insu'lar** *vt* (*TEC*) to insulate.

**insu'lina** *f* insulin.

**insul'tar** *vt* to insult; **insulto** *m* insult.

**insupe'rável** *adj* (*árduo*) insurmountable; (*excelente*) unsurpassable.

**insupor'tável** *adj* unbearable.

**insurgente** [insurˈʒètʃi] *adj* rebellious // *m/f* rebel; **insurgir-se** *vr* to rebel, revolt; **insurreição** *f* rebellion, insurrection.

**insuspeito/a** *adj* (*não suspeito*) unsuspected; (*imparcial*) impartial.

**insusten'tável** *adj* untenable.

**intangível** [intãˈʒivew] *adj* intangible.

**in'tato/a** (*Pt*: **-ct-**) *adj* intact; (*ileso*) unharmed; (*fig*) untouched.

**inte'gral** [-aw] *adj* whole; **pão ~** wholemeal bread // *f* (*MAT*) integral; **integrar** *vt* to unite, combine; (*MAT, RAÇAS*) to integrate.

**integri'dade** *f* integrity; **íntegro/a** *adj* entire; (*reto*) upright, honest.

**inteiramente** [intejraˈmètʃi] *adv* entirely, completely.

**inteirar** [intejˈrax] *vt* (*completar*) to complete; **~ alguém de** to inform sb about/of; **~-se** *vr*: **~-se de** to find out about; **inteireza** *f* entirety; (*integridade*) integrity; **inteiro/a** *adj* (*total*) whole, entire; (*ileso*) unharmed; (*não quebrado*) undamaged.

**inte'lecto** *m* intellect; **intelectual** *adj, m/f* intellectual.

**inteligência** [inteliˈʒèsja] *f* intelligence; **inteligente** *adj* intelligent, clever; **inteligível** *adj* intelligible.

**intem'périe** *f* bad weather.

**intenção** [intèˈsãw] *f* intention; **segundas intenções** ulterior motives; **ter a ~ de** to intend to; **intencionado/a** *adj*: **bem intencionado** well-meaning; **mal intencionado** ill-intentioned; **intencional** *adj* intentional, deliberate.

**inten'dência** *f* (*Pt*) management, administration.

**intensi'dade** *f* intensity; **intenso/a** *adj* intense; (*emoção*) deep; (*impressão*) vivid.

**inten'tar** *vt* to try, attempt; (*JUR*) **~ uma ação contra** to sue; **intento** *m* aim, purpose.

**interca'lar** *vt* to insert.

**inter'câmbio** *m* (*troca*) exchange.

**interce'der** *vi*: **~ por** to intercede on behalf of; **intercessão** *f* intercession.

**interco'stal** *adj, pl* **interco'stais** (*MED*) intercostal.

**interdição** [ɪntexdʒɪ'sãw] *f* prohibition, ban; **interditado/a** *adj* prohibited, forbidden; **interdito/a** *adj* prohibited, forbidden // *m* prohibition, ban; (*JUR*) injunction.

**interes'sante** *adj* interesting; **interessar** *vt* to interest, be of interest to; **interessar-se** *vr*: **interessar-se em/por** to take an interest in, be interested in; **interesse** *m* interest; (*próprio*) self-interest; (*proveito*) advantage; **no interesse de** for the sake of; **interesseiro/a** *adj* self-seeking.

**interfe'rência** *f* interference; **interferir** *vi*: **interferir em** to interfere in; (*rádio*) to jam.

**ínterim** [ˈīterĩ] *m* interim; **nesse ~** in the meantime.

**inte'rino/a** *adj* temporary, interim.

**interi'or** *adj* inner, inside; (*COM*) domestic, internal // *m* inside, interior; (*coração*) heart; (*do país*) **no ~** inland, in the country; **Ministério do I ~** Home Office.

**interjeição** [ɪntexʒej'sãw] *f* interjection.

**intermedi'ário/a** *adj* intermediary // *m* (*COM*) middleman; **intermédio** *m* intermediary; (*intervenção*) intervention; **por intermédio de** by means of, through; (*pessoa*) through the intervention of.

**intermi'nável** *adj* endless.

**intermissão** [ɪntexmi'sãw] *f* interval; **intermitente** *adj* intermittent.

**internacio'nal** *adj* international.

**inter'nar** *vt* to intern; (*aluno*) to put into boarding school; (*doente*) to put into hospital; **internato** *m* boarding school; **interno/a** *adj* internal, interior; (*do país*) domestic // *m/f* (*aluno*) boarder; (*em hospital*) intern.

**interpe'lar** *vt* to challenge; (*pessoa*) to question.

**inter'por** *vt* to put in, interpose; **~-se** *vr* to intervene.

**interpretação** [ɪntexpreta'sãw] *f* interpretation; (*teatro*) performance; **interpretar** *vt* to interpret; (*um papel*) to play, perform; **intérprete** *m/f* interpreter; (*teatro*) performer, artist.

**interrogação** [ɪntexoga'sãw] *f* questioning, interrogation; **ponto de ~** question mark; **interrogar** *vt* to question, interrogate; **interrogatório** *m* cross-examination.

**interrom'per** *vt* to interrupt; (*parar*) to stop; (*ELET*) to cut off; **~-se** *vr* to break off, pause; **interrupção** *f* interruption; (*intervalo*) break; **interruptor** *m* (*ELET*) switch.

**interseção** [ɪntexse'sãw] (*Pt*: **-cç-**) *f* intersection.

**interur'bano/a** *adj*: **telefonema ~** trunk call.

**inter'valo** *m* interval; (*descanso*) break; **a ~s** every now and then.

**intervenção** [ɪntexvẽ'sãw] *f* intervention; (*MED*) operation; **intervir** *vi* to intervene; (*tomar parte*) to participate.

**intes'tino/a** *adj* (*interno*) internal; (*nacional*) domestic // *m* intestine.

**inti'mar** *vt* to announce; (*JUR*) to summon; **~ alguém a fazer** to order sb to do.

**intimi'dade** *f* intimacy; (*vida privada*) private life; (*familiaridade*) familiarity; **íntimo/a** *adj* intimate; (*sentimentos*) innermost; (*amigo*) close; (*vida*) private; **no íntimo** at heart // *m/f* close friend.

**intole'rância** *f* intolerance; **intolerável** *adj* intolerable, unbearable.

**intoxicação** [ɪntɔksika'sãw] *f* poisoning.

**intransigente** [ɪntrãsi'ʒẽtʃi] *adj* uncompromising; (*rígido*) strict.

**intransi'tável** *adj* impassable.

**intrepi'dez** f courage, bravery; **intrépido/a** adj daring, intrepid.

**intri'cado/a** adj intricate.

**in'triga** f intrigue; (enredo) plot; (Pt) : ~ **amorosa** love affair; **intrigante** m/f troublemaker // adj intriguing; **intrigar** vt to intrigue.

**in'trínseco/a** adj intrinsic.

**introdução** [introdu'sãw] f introduction; **introduzir** vt to introduce; (prego) to insert; **introduzir-se** vr to get into.

**intromer'ter-se** vr to interfere, meddle; **intrometido/a** adj interfering; (col) nosey // m/f busybody.

**intrujão** [intru'ʒãw] m swindler; **intrujar** vt to trick, swindle.

**in'truso/a** m/f intruder.

**intuição** [intwi'sãw] f intuition; **intuito** m (intento) intention; (fim) aim, purpose.

**intumescência** [intume'sẽsja] f swelling; **intumescer-se** vr to swell (up); **intumescido/a** adj swollen.

**inume'rável** adj, **i'número/a** adj countless, innumerable.

**inundação** [inunda'sãw] f (enchente) flood; (ato) flooding; **inundar** vt to flood; (fig) to inundate.

**inusi'tado/a** adj unusual.

**inútil** [i'nutʃiw] adj useless; (esforço) futile; **ser** ~ to be of no use, be no good; **inutilidade** f uselessness; **inutilizar** vt to make useless, render useless; **inutilizar-se** vr to become useless; **inutilmente** adv in vain.

**inva'dir** vt to invade.

**in'válido/a** adj, m/f invalid.

**invari'ável** adj invariable; (constante) constant.

**invasão** [inva'zãw] f invasion; **invasor(a)** adj invading // m/f invader.

**inveja** [in've3a] f envy; (ciúme) jealousy; **invejar** vt to envy; (cobiçar: bens) to covet // vi to be envious; **invejoso/a** adj envious.

**invenção** [invẽ'sãw] f invention; **inventar** vt to invent; (uma história) to make up.

**inven'tário** m inventory.

**inven'tiva** f inventiveness; **inventor(a)** m/f inventor.

**in'verno** m winter.

**invero'símil** adj unlikely, improbable.

**inversão** [invex'sãw] f reversal, inversion; (COM) investment; **inverso/a** adj inverse; (oposto) opposite; (ordem) reverse; **ao inverso de** contrary to; **inversor(a)** m/f (COM) investor; **inverter** vt (COM) to invest; (mudar) to alter; (colocar às avessas) to turn upside down, invert; **inverter a marcha** (AUTO) to reverse.

**in'vés** m wrong side; **ao** ~ on the contrary; **ao** ~ **de** contrary to.

**investigação** [investʃiga'sãw] f investigation; (estudo) research; **investigar** vt to investigate; (examinar) to examine; (estudar) to research into.

**investi'mento** m investment; **investir** vt to invest; **investir contra** (atacar) to attack; **investir alguém no cargo de presidente** to install sb in the presidency // vi : **investir com** to set upon, attack.

**in'victo/a** adj unconquered.

**invi'sível** adj invisible.

**invo'car** vt to invoke, call on.

**in'vólucro** m (cobertura) covering; (envoltório) wrapping.

**iodo** [ˈjodu] m iodine.

**ioga** [ˈjɔga] f yoga.

**iogurte** [joˈgurtʃi] m yogurt.

**ir** vi to go; ~ **a cavalo/a pé** to ride/walk; ~ **de avião/de carro** to fly/drive; (Pt) ~ **ter com** to meet; ~ **bem** to be all right; (harmonizar) to go well; ~ **buscar** to fetch, go and get; ~ **falando** to keep on talking; ~ **melhor** (de saúde) to be feeling better; ~ **morrendo** to be dying; **como vai?** how are you?;

~-se *vr* : ~-se embora to go away.

**'ira** *f* anger, rage; **irado/a** *adj* angry, irate.

**Irã** ['irã] *m* Iran; **iraniano/a** *adj, m/f* Iranian.

**ira'scível** *adj* irritable, short-tempered.

**'íris** *m* iris.

**Ir'landa** *f* Ireland; **irlandês/esa** *adj* Irish // *m* Irishman; (*língua*) Irish // *f* Irishwoman.

**irmã** [ix'mã] *f* sister; **irmanar** *vt* to join together, unite; **irmandade** *f* brotherhood; (*confraternidade*) fraternity; **irmão** *m* brother.

**iro'nia** *f* irony; **irônico/a** *adj* ironic(al).

**'irra!** *excl* (Pt) damn!

**irradi'ar** *vt* (*luz*) to radiate; (*espalhar*) to spread; (*rádio*) to broadcast, transmit // *vi* to radiate; (*rádio*) to be on the air; ~-se *vr* (*propagar-se*) to spread; (*rádio*) to be transmitted.

**irre'al** *adj* unreal.

**irreconcili'ável** *adj* irreconcilable.

**irrefle'tido/a** *adj* rash, thoughtless.

**irremedi'ável** *adj* (*sem remédio*) incurable; (*sem esperança*) hopeless.

**irresis'tível** *adj* irresistible; (*desejo*) overwhelming.

**irrespon'sável** *adj* irresponsible.

**irri'gar** *vt* to irrigate.

**irri'sório/a** *adj* derisory, ludicrous.

**irri'tar** *vt* to irritate; (*agastar*) to annoy; ~-se *vr* to get angry, get annoyed.

**'isca** *f* (*pesca*) bait; (*fig*) lure, bait.

**isenção** [izẽ'sãw] *f* exemption; **isentar** *vt* to exempt; (*livrar*) to free; **isento/a** *adj* (*dispensado*) exempt; (*livre*) free.

**Is'lã** *m* Islam.

**Is'lândia** *f* Iceland.

**iso'lado/a** *adj* (*separado*) isolated;

(*solitário*) lonely; **isolamento** *m* isolation; (*MED*) isolation ward; (*ELET*) insulation; **isolar** *vt* to isolate; (*ELET*) to insulate.

**isqueiro** [iʃ'kejru] *m* (cigarette) lighter.

**Isra'el** *m* Israel; **israelense** *adj, m/f* Israeli.

**'isso** *pron* that, that thing; ~ **mesmo** exactly; **por** ~ therefore, so; **só** ~? is that all?

**'istmo** *m* isthmus.

**'isto** *pron* this, this thing; ~ **é** that is, namely.

**I'tália** *f* Italy; **italiano/a** *adj, m/f* Italian.

**i'tálico** *m* italics *pl*.

**itine'rário** *m* (*plano*) itinerary; (*caminho*) route; (*livro*) guidebook.

**Iugoslávia** [jugoʃ'lavia] *f* Yugoslavia.

# J

**já** [ʒa] *adv* (*de antemão*) already; (*agora*) now; (*sem demora*) right now, at once; (*num tempo próximo*) soon; **até** ~ (good)bye; **desde** ~ from now on; **é para** ~ it won't be a minute; ~ **esteve na Inglaterra?** have you ever been to England?; ~ **não** no longer, no more; ~ **não vem** he doesn't come any more; ~ **que** now that, since; ~ **se vê** of course; ~ **vou** I'm coming.

**jaça** ['ʒasa] *f* fault, imperfection.

**jaca'ré** *m* alligator.

**jacente** [ʒa'sẽtʃi] *adj* lying; (*herança*) unclaimed.

**jacinto** [ʒa'sĩtu] *m* hyacinth.

**jac'tância** *f* boasting; **jactar-se** *vr* : **jactar-se de** to boast about.

**ja'ez** *m* harness; (*categoria*) sort.

**jaguar** [ʒa'gwax] *m* jaguar.

**ja'gunço** *m* hired gun(man), bandit.

**ja'leco** *m* jacket.

**jamais** [ʒa'majʃ] *adv* never; (*com palavra negativa*) ever; **ninguém ~ veio** nobody ever came.

**ja'manta** *f* juggernaut.

**janeiras** [ʒa'nejraʃ] *fpl* (*canções*) carols; (*presentes*) New Year's gifts.

**janeiro** [ʒa'nejru] *m* January.

**ja'nela** *f* window.

**jan'gada** *f* raft, float.

**ja'nota** *m* dandy.

**'janta** *f* dinner.

**jan'tar** *m* supper; (*ceia*) dinner // *vt* to have for supper // *vi* to dine.

**Japão** [ʒa'pãw] *m* Japan; **japonês/esa** *adj, m/f* Japanese.

**jaqueta** [ʒa'keta] *f* jacket.

**jardim** [ʒax'dʒĩ] *m* garden; **~ zoológico** zoo; **~-de-infância** *m* kindergarten; **jardineiro/a** *m/f* gardener // *f* (*móvel*) flower-stand; (*ônibus*) open bus; (*professora*) kindergarten teacher.

**jargão** [ʒax'gãw] *m* (*gíria profissional*) jargon.

**'jarra** *f* jar.

**jar'rete** *m* hamstring.

**'jarro** *m* jug.

**jasmim** [ʒa'mĩ] *m* jasmine.

**jato** ['ʒatu] (*Pt*: **-ct-**) *m* jet; (*líquido*) gush; (*luz*) stream.

**jaula** ['ʒawla] *f* cage.

**java'li** *m* wild boar.

**ja'zer** *vi* to lie; **jazigo** *m* grave; (*monumento*) tomb; (*GEO*) deposit.

**jeito** ['ʒejtu] *m* (*maneira*) way, manner; (*aspecto*) appearance; (*propensão*) skill, knack; **a ~** conveniently, handily; **falta de ~** clumsiness; **ter ~ de** to look like; **jeitoso/a** *adj* (*hábil*) skilful; (*elegante*) handsome; (*apropriado*) suitable.

**jejuar** [ʒe'ʒwax] *vi* to fast; **jejum** *m* fast.

**jerarquia** [ʒerax'kia] *f* ver **hierarquia**.

**je'rico** *m* donkey; **idéia de ~** stupid idea.

**je'suíta** *m* Jesuit; **Jesus** *m* Jesus.

**jibóia** [ʒi'bɔja] *f* boa (constrictor).

**'jipe** *m* jeep.

**joalheiro** [ʒoa'ʎejru] *m* jeweller; **joalheria** *f* jeweller's (shop).

**joão-ninguém** [ʒwãw-nĩ'gẽj] *m* (a) nobody.

**jo'coso/a** *adj* jocular, humorous.

**joelho** [ʒo'eʎu] *m* knee; **de ~s** kneeling.

**joga'dor(a)** *m/f* player; (*jogador de azar*) gambler; **jogar** *vt* to play; (*fazer apostas*) to gamble; (*atirar*) to fling, throw; **jogo** *m* play; (*partida*) game; (*de azar*) gamble; **jogo de palavras** pun, play on words; **em jogo** at stake.

**jóia** ['ʒɔja] *f* jewel.

**jor'nada** *f* (*viagem*) day's journey; (*dia de trabalho*) working day.

**jor'nal** *m* newspaper; **~ falado** news bulletin; **~eiro** *m* (da) labourer; **~ista** *m/f* journalist, newspaperman // *f* newspaperwoman.

**jor'rar** *vi* to gush, spurt out; **jorro** *m* jet; (*fig*) stream, flood.

**jovem** ['ʒɔvẽ] *adj* young // *m* young man, youth // *f* young woman, girl.

**jovi'al** *adj* jovial, cheerful.

**'juba** (*de leão*) mane.

**jubilação** [ʒubila'sãw] *f* jubilation; (*aposentadoria*) retirement; **jubilar** *vt* (*aposentar*) to retire, pension off // *vi* to rejoice; **jubilar-se** *vr* to retire.

**jubileu** [ʒubi'lew] *m* jubilee.

**'júbilo** *m* rejoicing.

**judeu/judia** [ʒu'dew/ʒu'dʒja] *adj* Jewish // *m* Jew // *f* Jewess; **judiação** *f* maltreatment; **judiaria** *f* (*crueldade*) ill treatment.

**judica'tura** *f* (*cargo*) office of judge; (*magistratura*) judicature; **judicial** *adj*, **judiciário/a** *adj* judicial; **judicioso/a** *adj* judicious, wise.

**'jugo** *m* yoke; (*fig*) oppression.

**juiz(a)** [ʒu[i]za] *m/f* judge // *m* (*árbitro*) referee; **juizo** *m* judgement; (*parecer*) opinion; (*siso*) common sense; **Juízo Final** Day of Judgement, doomsday; **perder o juízo** to lose one's mind.

**julga'mento** *m* judgement; (*audiência*) trial; (*sentença*) sentence; **julgar** *vt* to judge; (*achar*) to think.

**julho** ['ʒuʎu] *m* July.

**ju'mento/a** *m/f* donkey.

**junco** *m* reed, rush.

**junho** ['ʒuɲu] *m* June.

**juntar** *vt* to join, connect; (*ajuntar*) to bring together, unite; **junto/a** *adj* joined; (*chegado*) near; **ir juntos** to go together; **junto a/de** near/next to // *f* (*comissão*) board, committee, commission; (*articulação*) joint; **juntura** *f* join; (*articulação*) joint.

**'jura** *f* oath; **jurado/a** *m/f* juror; **juramento** *m* oath, vow; **jurar** *vt/i* to swear.

**júri** ['ʒuri] *m* jury.

**ju'rídico/a** *adj* legal.

**jurisdição** [ʒuriʒdʒi'sãw] *f* jurisdiction; **jurisprudência** *f* jurisprudence; **jurista** *m/f* jurist.

**'juro** *m* (ECON) interest.

**justeza** [ʃuʃ'teza] *f* rightness; (*precisão*) exactness, precision.

**justiça** [ʃuʃ'tʃisa] *f* justice; (*eqüidade*) fairness; **com** ~ justly, fairly.

**justiceiro/a** [ʒuʃtʃi'sejru/a] *adj* upright; (*equitativo*) impartial.

**justificação** [ʒuʃtʃifika'sãw] *f* justification; **justificar** *vt* to justify.

**justo/a** ['ʒuʃtu/a] *adj* just, fair, right; (*exato*) exact; (*apertado*) tight.

**juve'nil** [-iw] *adj* youthful; **juventude** *f* youth; (*jovialidade*) youthfulness; (*jovens*) young people *pl*.

# L

**L** *abr de* **Largo** (*endereços*) Square.

**lá** *adv* there; ~ **fora** outside; ~ **em baixo** down there; **por** ~ (*direção*) that way, over there; (*situação*) over there.

**lã** [lã] *f* wool.

**laba'reda** *f* flame; (*fig*) ardour.

**'lábia** *f* lip; **ter** ~ to have the gift of the gab.

**labi'rinto** *m* labyrinth, maze.

**la'bor** *m* work, labour.

**labora'tório** *m* laboratory.

**labori'oso/a** *adj* (*diligente*) hard-working; (*árduo*) laborious.

**la'buta** *f* toil, drudgery; **labutar** *vi* to toil; (*esforçar-se*) to struggle, strive.

**'laca** *f* lacquer.

**lacaio** [la'kaju] *m* lackey.

**la'çar** *vt* to bind, tie; **laço** *m* knot; (*laçada*) bow; (*armadilha*) snare; (*fig*) bond, tie.

**la'cônico/a** *adj* laconic.

**la'craia** *f* centipede.

**la'crar** *yt* to seal (with wax).

**la'crau** *m* scorpion.

**lacre** *m* sealing wax.

**lacri'moso/a** *adj* tearful.

**'lácteo/a** *adj* milky; **via** ~**a** Milky Way.

**la'cuna** *f* gap; (*omissão*) omission.

**ladainha** [lada'iɲa] *f* litany.

**lade'ar** *vt* (*flanquear*) to flank.

**ladeira** [la'dejra] *f* slope, hillside.

**la'dino/a** *adj* cunning, crafty.

**'lado** *m* side; (MIL) flank; (*rumo*) direction; **ao** ~ **de** beside; **de** ~ sideways; **pôr de** ~ to set aside; **por outro** ~ on the other hand; **de um** ~ **para outro** back and forth.

**'ladra** *f* thief.

**ladrão** [la'drãw] *m* thief, robber.

**la'drar** *vi* to bark.

**ladrilho** [la'driʎu] *m* tile.

**la'gar** m fruit press.

**la'garta** f caterpillar.

**la'garto** m lizard.

**'lago** m lake; **lagoa** f pool, pond.

**la'gosta** f lobster; **lagostim** m crayfish.

**'lágrima** f tear; (*gota*) drop.

**la'guna** f lagoon.

**laia** ['laja] f kind, sort, type.

**laivo** ['lajvu] m (*mancha*) stain; (*nódoa*) spot; ~s mpl smattering.

**laje** f paving stone, flagstone; **lajear** vt to pave.

**lama** f mud; ~**çal** m quagmire, mud patch; ~**cento/a** adj muddy.

**lambão/bona** [lam'bãw/'bona] adj greedy, gluttonous; (*desmazelado*) sloppy.

**lam'ber** vt to lick.

**lamen'tar** vt to lament; (*sentir*) to regret; **lamentável** adj regrettable; (*deplorável*) deplorable; **lamento** m lament; (*gemido*) moan.

**'lâmina** f (*chapa*) sheet; (*placa*) plate; (*de faca*) blade.

**'lâmpada** f lamp; ~ **elétrica** light bulb; **lampião** m lantern; (*de rua*) street lamp.

**lança** f lance, spear.

**lançadeira** [lãsa'dejra] f shuttle.

**lança'mento** m throwing; (*NÁUT, COM*) launching; **lançar** vt to throw, fling; (*NÁUT, COM*) to launch; (*MED*) to vomit; **lance** m (*acontecimento*) incident; (*crise*) emergency; (*aventura*) exploit; (*impulso*) fit; (*esporte*) stroke, shot; (*leilão*) bid; (*de escada*) flight.

**lancha** ['lãʃa] f launch; ~ **torpedeira** torpedo boat.

**lanche** ['lãʃi] m snack.

**langui'dez** f languor, listlessness; **lânguido/a** adj languid; (*sem energia*) listless.

**la'nhar** vt to slash, gash; (*fig: estropiar*) to murder; **lanho** m slash, gash.

**lan'terna** f lantern.

**la'nudo/a** adj woolly; **lanugem** f down, fluff.

**'lapa** f (*abrigo*) cave, grotto.

**la'pela** f lapel.

**lapi'dar** vt (*apedrejar*) to stone; (*jóias*) to cut; (*aperfeiçoar*) to polish, refine; **lápide** f tombstone.

**'lápis** m pencil; **lapiseira** f propelling pencil; (*caixa*) pencil case.

**'lapso** m lapse; (*de tempo*) interval; (*erro*) slip.

**lar** m hearth, fireside; (*casa*) home.

**laranja** [la'rãʒa] f orange; **laranjada** f orangeade; **laranjal** m orange grove; **laranjeira** f orange tree.

**la'rápio** m thief.

**lareira** [la'rejra] f hearth, fireside.

**'larga** f : **a** ~ lavishly, generously; **dar** ~**s a** to give free rein to; **largada** f (*corrida*) start; **largar** vt to let go of, release; (*conceder*) to concede, give up // vi to leave, depart.

**'largo/a** adj wide, broad; (*amplo*) extensive; **ao** ~ **a** a distance, far off; **fazer-se ao** ~ to put out to sea; **passar de** ~ **sobre** to overlook, ignore; **mede 5 metros de** ~ it is 5 metres wide // m (*praça*) square; **largueza** f liberality; **largura** f width, breadth.

**laringe** [la'rĩʒi] f larynx.

**larva** f larva, grub.

**lasca** f (*de madeira*) splinter, chip; (*de pedra*) chip; (*fatia*) slice.

**lascivo/a** [la'sivʊ/a] adj lewd.

**lassidão** [lasi'dãw] f, **lassi'tude** f lassitude, weariness.

**'lástima** f pity, compassion; (*desgraça*) misfortune; **lastimar** vt to lament; **lastimar-se** vr to complain, be sorry for o.s.; **lastimoso/a** adj (*lamentável*) pitiful; (*plangente*) mournful.

**'lastro** m ballast.

**'lata** f tin, can; (*material*) tin-plate;

~ **de lixo** rubbish bin; (*US*) garbage can.

**la'tada** *f* trellis.

**latão** [la'tãw] *m* brass.

**'látego** *m* whip.

**latejar** [late'ʒax] *vi* to throb; beat; **latejo** *m* throbbing, beat.

**la'tente** *adj* latent, hidden.

**late'ral** *adj* side, lateral // *f* (*futebol*) sideline // *m* (*futebol*) throw-in.

**la'tido** *m* bark(ing), yelp(ing).

**lati'fúndio** *m* large estate.

**latim** [la'tʃĩ] *m* (*LING*) Latin; **gastar o seu** ~ to waste one's breath.

**la'tino/a** *adj* Latin; ~-**americano/a** *adj, m/f* Latin-American.

**la'tir** *vi* to bark, yelp.

**lati'tude** *f* latitude; (*largura*) breadth; (*fig*) scope.

**'lato/a** *adj* broad.

**latrocínio** [latro'sinju] *m* armed robbery.

**laudo** ['lawdu] *m* (*JUR*) decision, findings *pl*.

**laure'ado/a** *adj* honoured // **laureate**; **laurel** *m* laurel wreath; (*fig*) prize, reward.

**lauto/a** ['lawtu/a] *adj* sumptuous; (*abundante*) lavish, abundant.

**'lava** *f* lava.

**la'vabo** *m* washbasin; **lavadora** *f* washing machine; **lavadouro** *m* washing place.

**lavagem** [la'vaʒẽ] *f* washing; (*restos*) slops *pl*; ~ **a seco** dry cleaning; ~ **cerebral** brainwashing; **lavanderia** *f* laundry; **lavar** *vt* to wash; **lavar a seco** to dry clean.

**lavoura** [la'vora] *f* tilling; (*agricultura*) farming; (*terreno*) plantation.

**'lavra** *f* ploughing; (*mina*) mine; **ser da** ~ **de** to be the work of; **lavrador** *m* farmer; **lavrar** *vt* to work; (*esculpir*) to carve; (*redigir*) to draw up.

**laxante** [la'ʃãtʃi] *adj, m* laxative.

**leal** [li'aw] *adj* loyal; ~**dade** *f* loyalty.

**leão** [le'ãw] *m* lion.

**'lebre** *f* hare.

**lecionar** [lɛsjo'nax] (*Pt*: **-cc-**) *vt* to teach, instruct.

**legação** [lega'sãw] *f* legation; **legado** *m* envoy, legate; (*herança*) legacy, bequest.

**le'gal** *adj* legal, lawful; (*col*) great, fine; ~**idade** *f* legality, lawfulness; ~**izar** *vt* to legalize; (*autenticar*) to authenticate.

**le'gar** *vt* to bequeath, leave; **legatário/a** *m/f* legatee.

**legenda** [le'ʒẽda] *f* inscription; (*letreiro*) caption; (*cinema*) subtitle.

**legião** [le'ʒjãw] *f* legion.

**legislação** [leʒiʒla'sãw] *f* legislation; **legislar** *vi* to legislate.

**legiti'mar** *vt* to legitimize; **legítimo/a** *adj* legitimate; (*justo*) rightful; (*autêntico*) genuine.

**le'gível** [le'ʒivew] *adj* legible, readable.

**légua** ['lɛgwa] *f* league.

**le'gume** *m* vegetable.

**lei** [lej] *f* law; (*regra*) rule; (*metal*) standard.

**leigo/a** ['lejgu/a] *adj* (*REL*) lay, secular; (*fig*) ignorant // *m* layman.

**leilão** [lej'lãw] *m* auction.

**'leio** *etc vb ver* **ler**.

**leitão** [lej'tãw] *m* sucking pig.

**leite** ['lejtʃi] *m* milk; ~ **em pó** powdered milk; ~ **desnatado** skimmed milk; ~ **de magnésia** milk of magnesia; **leiteira** *f* (*para ferver*) milk pan; (*para servir*) milk jug; **leiteria** *f* dairy.

**'leito** *m* (*gen*) bed; (*camada*) layer.

**lei'tor(a)** *m/f* reader; **leitura** *f* reading.

**'lema** *m* motto; (*POL*) slogan.

**lem'brança** *f* recollection, memory; (*presente*) souvenir; ~**s** *fpl*: ~**s a sua mãe!** regards to your mother!; **lembrar** *vt* (*fazer recordar*) to remind; (*ter memória de*) to recall; **lembrar-se** vr : **lembrar-se de** to remember.

**'leme** m rudder; (NÁUT) helm; (fig) control.

**lenço** m handkerchief; (de pescoço) headscarf.

**len'çol** [-ow] m sheet; **em maus lençóis** in a fix.

**'lenda** f legend; **lendário/a** adj legendary.

**'lêndea** f (piolho) nit.

**lenha** ['leɲa] f firewood; **~dor** m woodcutter; **lenho** m (madeiro) log; (material) timber.

**leni'tivo/a** adj soothing // m palliative; (alívio) relief.

**lente** f lens sg; **~s de contato** fpl contact lenses.

**lentidão** [lětʃi'dãw] f slowness.

**lentilha** [lě'tʃiʎa] f lentil.

**'lento/a** adj slow.

**le'oa** f lioness.

**leo'pardo** m leopard.

**'lepra** f leprosy; **leproso/a** adj leprous // m/f leper.

**leque** ['lɛki] m fan.

**ler** vt to read.

**'lerdo/a** adj slow, sluggish; (tolo) dull, stupid.

**lés** m : **de ~ a ~** (Pt) from one end to the other.

**lesão** [le'zãw] f lesion; (fig) injury; (JUR) violation; **lesar** vt to injure; (JUR) to violate.

**'lésbica** f lesbian.

**lesma** f slug; (fig) sluggard.

**leso/a** adj injured, wounded; (tolhido) paralytic, palsied; (idiota) daft; (prejudicado) wronged; **crime de ~a majestade** high treason.

**'leste** m east.

**le'tal** [-aw] adj lethal.

**letargia** [letax'ʒia] f lethargy.

**le'tivo/a** (Pt: -**ct**-) adj school cmp; **ano ~** academic year.

**'letra** f letter; (caligrafia) handwriting; (de canção) lyrics pl; **~ de câmbio** (COM) bill of exchange; **~ de imprensa** print; **ao**

**pé da ~** literally, word for word; **letrado/a** adj learned, erudite // m/f scholar.

**letreiro** [let'rejru] m sign, notice; (inscrição) inscription; (legenda) caption.

**léu** [lɛw] m: **ao ~** (à vontade) at random, aimlessly.

**'leva** f (NÁUT) weighing anchor; (MIL) levy; (alistamento) recruitment.

**le'vado/a** adj mischievous.

**levanta'mento** m lifting, raising; (revolta) uprising, rebellion; (arrolamento) survey.

**levan'tar** vt to lift, raise; (apanhar) to pick up; (suscitar) to arouse; **~ vôo** (AER) to take off; **~-se** to get up, stand up; (rebelar-se) to rebel.

**le'vante** m east; (revolta) revolt.

**le'var** vt to take; (portar) to bear, carry; (tirar) to take away; (tempo) to pass, spend; (roupa) to wear; **~ a mal** to take amiss; **~ a cabo** to carry out; **~ adiante** to go ahead with; **~ uma vida feliz** to lead a happy life; **~ em conta** to take into account.

**'leve** adj light; (insignificante) slight; (ao) **de ~** lightly, softly.

**le'vedo** m, **leve'dura** f yeast.

**levian'dade** f frivolity; **leviano/a** adj frivolous; (inconstante) fickle.

**'léxico** m dictionary, lexicon.

**le'zíria** f (Pt) marshland.

**lha(s) = lhe + a(s).**

**lhaneza** [ʎa'neza] f frankness; (singeleza) simplicity; (afabilidade) amiability; **lhano/a** adj frank; (simples) straightforward; (amável) amiable.

**lhe** pron (a ele) to him; (a ela) to her; (a você) to you; **~s** pl (a eles/elas) to them; (a vocês) to you.

**lho(s) = lhe + o(s).**

**'lia** f dregs pl, sediment.

**li'ame** m tie, bond.

**liba'nês/esa** adj Lebanese; **Líbano** m : **o Líbano** the Lebanon.

**li'belo** m satire, lampoon; (JUR) formal indictment.

**li'bélula** f dragonfly.

**libe'ral** adj generous; (tolerante) liberal // m/f liberal; **~idade** f liberality; **~ismo** m liberalism.

**libe'rar** vt to free, release.

**liber'dade** f freedom; **~ condicional** probation; **~ sob palavra** parole; **pôr em ~** to set free; **libertador** m liberator; **libertar** vt to free.

**liber'tino/a** adj loose-living // m/f libertine.

**li'berto/a** pp irr de **libertar**.

**libidi'noso/a** adj lecherous, lustful.

**'libra** f pound; **~ esterlina** pound sterling; **L~** (ASTRO) Libra.

**li ção** [li'sãw] f lesson.

**licença** [li'sẽsa] f (ger) licence; (US) license; (permissão) permission; (MIL) leave; **em ~** on leave; **com ~** excuse me; **dá ~?** may I?; **licenciado/a** m/f graduate; **licenciar** vt to license; **licenciar-se** vr (EDUC) to graduate; **licenciatura** f degree.

**licenci'oso/a** adj licentious.

**liceu** [li'sew] m (Pt) secondary school.

**licitação** [lisita'sãw] f auction; **licitante** m/f bidder; **licitar** vt (pôr em leilão) to put up for auction.

**'lícito/a** adj lawful; (justo) fair, just; (permissível) permissible.

**li'cor** m liqueur; (líquido) liquor.

**'lida** f toil; **lidar** vi to toil; (lutar) to strive, struggle.

**'liga** f league; (de meias) garter, suspender; (QUÍM) alloy.

**ligação** [liga'sãw] f connection; **ligado/a** adj (TEC) connected; (luz, rádio etc) on.

**liga'dura** f bandage; (MÚS) ligature.

**li'gar** vt to tie, bind; (unir) to join, connect; (abrir) to switch on; **~ importância a** to pay attention to;

**~ para** to telephone, ring up.

**ligeireza** [liʒei'reza] f lightness; (rapidez) swiftness; (agilidade) nimbleness; **ligeiro/a** adj light; (de importância) slight; (rápido) quick, swift; (ágil) nimble.

**li'lás** adj, m lilac.

**'lima** f (BOT) lime; (ferramenta) file.

**limão** [li'mãw] m lemon.

**li'mar** vt to file; (fig) to polish.

**limeira** [li'mejra] f lime tree.

**limi'ar** m threshold.

**limitação** [limita'sãw] f limitation, restriction; **limitar** vt to limit, restrict; **limitar-se** vr : **limitar-se a** to limit o.s. to; **limitar-se com** to border on; **limite** m limit, boundary.

**'limo** m (BOT) water weed; (lodo) slime.

**limoeiro** [lim'wejru] m lemon tree.

**limonada** f lemonade.

**limpa'dor** m : **~ de pára-brisas** windscreen wiper; (US) windshield wiper; **limpar** vt to clean; (enxugar) to wipe; (polir) to shine, polish; (fig) to clean up; **limpeza** f cleanliness; (esmero) neatness; (ato) cleaning; (fig) clean-up.

**'limpo/a** pp irr de **limpar** // adj (COM) net, clear; (fig) pure; **passar a ~** to make a fair copy; **tirar a ~** to find out the truth about, clear up.

**'lince** m lynx; **ter olhos de ~** to have eyes like a hawk.

**linchar** [lĩ'ʃax] vt to lynch.

**'lindo/a** adj pretty, lovely; (fig) fine.

**língua** ['lĩgwa] f tongue; (linguagem) language; **dar com a ~ nos dentes** to let the cat out of the bag; **estar na ponta da ~** to be on the tip of one's tongue.

**linguado** [lĩ'gwadu] m (peixe) sole.

**linguagem** [lĩ'gwaʒẽ] f language; (falada) speech.

**linguarudo/a** [lĩgwa'rudu/a] adj gossiping.

**língüeta** [lĩ'gweta] f (balança) pointer; (fechadura) bolt.

**lingüiça** [lɪ'gwisa] f sausage.

**lingüista** [lɪ'gwiʃta] m/f linguist; **lingüística** f linguistics sg.

**linha** ['liɲa] f line; (fio) cord, thread; (ELET) cable, wire; (fila) row; ~ **de montagem** assembly line; ~ **reta** straight line.

**linhaça** [lɪ'ɲasa] f linseed.

**linhagem** [lɪ'ɲaʒẽ] f lineage.

**linho** ['liɲu] m linen; (planta) flax.

**li'nóleo** m linoleum.

**líquen** ['likɛn] m lichen.

**liquidação** [likida'sãw] f liquidation; (venda) clearance sale; **liquidar** vt to liquidate; (conta) to settle; **líquido/a** adj liquid, fluid; (COM) net // m liquid.

**'lira** f lyre; (moeda) lira; **lírico/a** adj -lyric(al).

**'lírio** m lily.

**li'rismo** m lyricism.

**Lis'boa** f Lisbon; **lisboeta** adj Lisbon cmp // m/f inhabitant ou native of Lisbon.

**liso/a** adj smooth; (tecido) plain; (cabelo) straight.

**lisonja** [li'zõʒa] f flattery; **lisonjear** vt to flatter; **lisonjeiro/a** adj flattering.

**'lista** f list; (listra) stripe; (tira) strip; (Pt: menu) menu; ~ **telefônica** telephone directory.

**'listra** f stripe.

**lite'rário/a** adj literary; **literato** m (escritor) writer; **literatura** f literature.

**liti'gar** vt to contend, fight // vi to go to law; **litígio** m (JUR) lawsuit; (contenda) dispute.

**'lito'ral** [-aw] adj coastal // m coast, seaboard.

**'litro** m litre; (US) liter.

**'lívido/a** adj livid.

**livra'mento** m release; ~ **condicional** parole; **livrar** vt to release, liberate; (salvar) to save; **Deus me livre!** Heaven forbid; **livrar-se** vr to escape; **livrar-se de** to get rid of.

**livra'ria** f bookshop.

**'livre** adj free; (lugar) unoccupied; (desimpedido) clear, open; (natural) spontaneous; **ao ar** ~ in the open air; ~ **de impostos** tax-free.

**livreiro** [liv'rejru] m bookseller; **livro** m book; **livro de bolso** pocket-sized book; **livro de consulta** reference book; **livro de mercadorias** stock book; **livro de cheques** (Pt) cheque book; (US) check book.

**lixa** ['liʃa] f sandpaper; (unhas) nail-file; (peixe) dogfish.

**lixo** ['liʃu] m rubbish; (US) garbage.

**lobisomem** [lobi'sõmẽ] m werewolf; **lobo** m wolf; **lobo-marinho** m sea-lion.

**lobri'gar** vt to glimpse.

**'lóbulo** m ear lobe.

**locação** [loka'sãw] f lease.

**local** [lo'kaw] adj local // m site, place; ~**idade** f (zona) locality; (sítio) location; ~**izar** vt to locate; (situar) to place.

**loção** [lo'sãw] f lotion.

**locomoção** [lokomo'sãw] f locomotion; **locomotiva** f railway engine, locomotive.

**locução** [loku'sãw] f (frase) expression.

**'lodo** m mud, slime.

**lógico/a** ['lɔʒika/a] adj logical // f logic.

**'logo** adv (imediatamente) right away, at once; (após) then; (mais tarde) later; ~, ~ straightaway, without delay; ~ **mais** in a while, shortly; ~ **no começo** right at the start // conj so; ~ **que** as soon as; **até** ~! cheerio!

**lo'grar** vt to achieve; (obter) to get, obtain; (alcançar) to attain; ~ **fazer** to manage to do.

**'logro** m enjoyment; (engano) fraud.

**loiro/a** ['lojru/a] adj ver **louro/a**.

**loja** ['lɔʒa] f shop; (maçônica) lodge; **lojista** m/f shopkeeper.

**'lomba** f ridge; (ladeira) slope;

**lombada** f (de animal) back; (de livro) spine; **lombar** adj lumbar; **lombo** m back; (pedaço de carne) loin.

**'lona** f canvas.

**'Londres** m London; **londrino/a** adj London cmp // m/f Londoner.

**longe** ['lōʒi] adv far, far away; **ao ~** in the distance; **de ~** from afar; **~ dos olhos, ~ do coração** out of sight, out of mind // prep : **~ de** far from // mpl : **~s** (indícios) traces; **longínquo/a** adj distant, remote.

**longitude** [lōʒi'tudʒi] f (GEO) longitude; **longo/a** adj long; **ao longo de** along, alongside.

**lontra** f otter.

**loquaz** [lo'kwaʃ] adj talkative.

**lotação** [lota'sãw] f capacity; (vinho) blending; **~ completa/esgotada** (teatro) sold out.

**'lote** m (porção) portion, share; (grupo) batch; (leilão) lot; (terreno) plot; **loteria** f lottery.

**louça** ['losa] f china; (conjunto) crockery; **~ de barro** earthenware; **lavar a ~** to do the washing up.

**louça'nia** f elegance.

**louco/a** ['loku/a] adj crazy, mad; **~ varrido** raving mad; **~ de** mad with; **~ por** crazy about // m/f lunatic, mad person; **loucura** f madness; (ato) crazy act.

**louro/a** ['loru/a] adj blond, fair // m laurel; (CULIN) bay leaf.

**lousa** ['loza] f flagstone; (tumular) gravestone; (quadro-negro) blackboard; (portátil) slate.

**louva-a-deus** [lova-a-'dɛwʃ] m inv praying mantis.

**lou'var** vt to praise; **louvável** adj praiseworthy; **louvor** m praise.

**lua** ['lua] f moon; **estar no mundo da ~** to have one's head in the clouds; **lua-de-mel** f honeymoon; **luar** m moonlight.

**lubrifi'cante** m lubricant; **lubrificar** vt to lubricate.

**luci'dez** f lucidity, clarity; **lúcido/a** adj lucid.

**'lúcio** m (peixe) pike.

**lu'crar** vt (aproveitar) to profit from/by; (gozar) to enjoy // vi to gain; **lucro** m gain; (COM) profit.

**ludibri'ar** vt to dupe, deceive; (escarnecer) to mock, deride.

**lu'fada** f gust (of wind).

**lu'gar** m place; (espaço) space, room; (ocasião) opportunity; **em ~ de** instead of; **dar ~ a** to give rise to; **~ comum** commonplace; **em primeiro ~** in the first place; **em todo ~** everywhere; **~ejo** m village.

**'lúgubre** adj mournful; (escuro) gloomy.

**'lula** f squid.

**'lume** m fire; (luz) light; **trazer a ~** to bring to light; **vir a ~** to become known; **dar a ~** to publish.

**lumi'nária** f lamp, lantern; **~s** fpl illuminations; **luminoso/a** adj luminous, bright; (claro) clear.

**lu'nar** adj lunar // m (na pele) mole.

**lu'neta** f eye-glass; (telescópio) telescope.

**'lupa** f magnifying glass.

**lupa'nar** m brothel.

**'lúpulo** m (BOT) hop.

**lusco-'fusco** m (anoitecer) dusk; (amanhecer) daybreak; (luz) twilight.

**lusi'tano/a** adj, **'luso/a** adj Portuguese, Lusitanian.

**lus'trar** vt to polish, clean; **lustre** m gloss, sheen; (fig) lustre; (luminária) chandelier; **lustro** m polish, shine; (tempo) lustrum, five-year period.

**'luta** f fight, struggle; (contenda) contest; **~ livre** wrestling; **lutar** vi to fight, struggle; (luta livre) to wrestle.

**'luto** m mourning; (dó) grief; **de ~** in mourning.

**'luva** f glove; **assentar como uma ~** to fit like a glove; **~s** fpl (*recompensa*) reward *sg*.

**luxo** ['luʃu] *m* luxury; **de** ~ **de** luxe; **poder dar-se o** ~ **de** to afford; **luxuoso/a** *adj* luxurious; **luxúria** *f* lust; (*BOT*) lushness.

**luz** *f* light; **dar à** ~ to give birth to; **sair à** ~ to be published; **à** ~ **de** in view of; ~**idio/a** *adj* shining, glossy; **luzir** *vi* to shine, gleam; (*fig*) to be successful.

**Lx.a** *abr de* Lisboa.

# M

**ma** *pron* = **me** + **a**.

**má** *adj ver* **mau**.

'**maca** *f* stretcher.

**maçã** [ma'sã] *f* apple; ~ **do rosto** cheekbone.

**macacão** [maka'kãw] *m* (*de trabalhador*) overalls *pl*; (*da moda*) jump-suit.

**ma'caco** *m* monkey; (*MEC*) jack.

**ma'çada** *f* (*pancada*) blow with a club; (*coisa sem interesse*) bore; (*coisa enfadonha*) nuisance.

**maca'dame** *m* tarmac.

**maça'dor(a)** *adj* (*Pt*) (*sem interesse*) boring; (*cansativo*) tedious.

**maça'neta** *f* knob.

**ma'çante** *adj* (*Br*) *ver* **maçador(a).**

**mação** [ma'sãw] *m* (*maçom*) (free)mason.

**macaquear** [makake'ax] *vt* to imitate, ape.

**ma'çar** *vt* to bore.

**macarrão** [maka'xãw] *m* macaroni; (*ger*) pasta.

**machado** [ma'ʃadu] *m* axe.

**machão** [ma'ʃãw] *m* tough guy, he-man; (*mulher*) butch woman.

**machete** [ma'ʃetʃi] *m* machete.

**macho** ['maʃu] *adj* male; (*fig*) virile, manly // *m* male.

**machucar** [maʃu'kax] *vt* to crush; (*contusão*) to bruise; (*cereais*) to mash; (*ferir*) to injure, hurt.

**macio/a** [ma'siu/a] *adj* (*espesso*) thick; **ouro** ~ solid gold; **uma dose** ~**a** a massive dose // *m* (*GEO*) massif.

**macieira** [masi'ejra] *f* apple tree.

**maciento/a** [masi'lẽtu/a] *adj* gaunt, haggard.

**macio/a** [ma'siu/a] *adj* (*brando*) soft; (*liso*) smooth.

'**maço** *m* (*de folhas*) bundle; (*de cigarros*) packet.

**maçona'ria** *f* freemasonry.

**má-cria'ção** [ma-kria'sãw] *f* rudeness, bad manners *pl*.

**'mácula** *f* stain, blemish.

**ma'cumba** *f* black magic, voodoo.

**madeira** [ma'dejra] *f* wood; (*pau*) stick; ~ **compensada** plywood; **de** ~ wooden; ~**s** *fpl* (*MÚS*) woodwind // *m* Madeira wine; **madeiro** *m* (*lenho*) log; (*viga*) beam.

**madeixa** [ma'dejʃa] *f* (*de cabelo*) lock; ~**s** *fpl* tresses.

**ma'draço/a** *adj* idle // *m/f* loafer, idler.

**ma'drasta** *f* stepmother.

'**madre** *f* (*freira*) nun; (*superiora*) mother superior.

**madres'silva** *f* honeysuckle.

**madrinha** [ma'drɪɲa] *f* godmother.

**madru'gada** *f* (*early*) morning; (*alvorada*) dawn, daybreak; **duas horas da** ~ two in the morning; **madrugador(a)** *m/f* early riser; (*fig*) early bird; **madrugar** *vi* to get up early; (*fig*) to get ahead; (*aparecer cedo*) to be early.

**madu'rar** *vt/i* (*fruta*) to ripen; (*fig*) to mature; **madureza** *f* (*fruta*) ripeness; (*pessoa*) maturity; **maduro/a** *adj* (*fruta*) ripe; (*fig*) mature.

**mãe** [mãj] *f* mother.

**maestro/maestrina** [ma'ɛʃtru/mae'ʃtrina] *m* (*compositor*) composer; (*de orquestra*) conductor

**// f** (*de orquestra*) conductress.
**maga'refe** *m* (*Pt*) butcher, slaughterer.
**maga'zine** *m* magazine; (*armazém*) store.
**magia** [ma'ʒia] *f* magic; **mágico/a** *adj* magic // *m/f* magician.
**magis'tério** *m* (*ensino*) teaching; (*profissão*) teaching profession; (*professorado*) teachers *pl*.
**magis'trado** *m* magistrate; **magistral** *adj* magisterial; (*fig*) masterly; **magistratura** *f* magistracy.
**mag'nânimo/a** *adj* magnanimous.
**mag'nata** *m*, **mag'nate** *m* magnate, tycoon.
**mag'nético/a** *adj* magnetic; **magnetizar** *vt* to magnetize; (*fascinar*) to mesmerize.
**mag'nífico/a** *adj* splendid, magnificent.
**magni'tude** *f* magnitude; **magno/a** *adj* (*grande*) great; (*importante*) important.
**'mago** *m* magician; **os reis ~s** the Three Wise Men, the Three Kings.
**'mágoa** *f* (*tristeza*) sorrow, grief; (*fig: desagrado*) hurt; **magoado/a** *adj* hurt; (*fig*) to hurt, injure; **magoar** *vt* (*ferir*) to hurt, injure; (*fig*) to hurt, wound.
**magrinho/a** [ma'grɪɲu/a] *adj* thin; (*pej*) skinny; **magro/a** *adj* (*pessoa*) thin; (*carne*) lean.
**maio** [maju] *m* May.
**maiô** [ma'jo] *m* swimsuit.
**maionese** [majo'nɛzɪ] *f* mayonnaise.
**maior** [ma'jɔx] *adj* (*comparativo: de tamanho*) bigger; (*: de importância*) greater; (*superlativo: de tamanho*) biggest; (*: superior*) greatest; **~ de idade** of age, adult; **~ de 21 anos** over 21 // *m* adult; **~al** *m* chief, leader.
**maioria** [majo'ria] *f* majority; **a ~ de** most of; **maioridade** *f* adulthood;

**atingir a maioridade** to come of age.
**mais** [majʃ] *adv* more; (*com palavra negativa ou interrogativa*) any more // *adj* more; (*superlativo*) most // *m*: **o ~** the rest // *prep* plus, as well as; **~ de** more than; **~ nada** nothing else; **~ dois** two more; **~ ou menos** more or less; **~ uma vez** once more; **a ~** too much; **alguém/ninguém ~** somebody/ nobody else; **cada vez ~** more and more; **por ~ que** however much; **quanto ~ ganha, ~ gasta** the more he earns, the more he spends.
**mai'sena** *f* cornflower.
**maiúscula** [ma'juʃkula] *f* capital letter.
**majes'tade** *f* majesty; **majestoso/a** *adj* majestic.
**ma'jor** *m* (*MIL*) major.
**mal** *m*, *pl* **'males** (*maldade*) evil; (*dano*) harm; (*MED*) illness; (*desgraça*) trouble, misfortune; **falar ~ de** to speak ill of; **fazer ~ a** to harm, hurt; **fazer ~ em** to be wrong to; **levar a ~** to take offence at; **não faz ~** never mind // *adv* badly; (*dificilmente*) hardly; **estar ~** to be ill // *conj* (*logo que*) **~ chegaram tiveram de partir** no sooner had they arrived than they had to leave.
**'mala** *f* suitcase; **~s** *fpl* luggage *sg*; **fazer as ~s** to pack.
**malaba'rismo** *m* juggling; **malabarista** *m/f* juggler.
**malan'dragem** *f* (*preguiça*) idleness; (*velhacaria*) villainy, double-dealing; **malandro/a** *adj* idle // *m/f* (*patife*) spiv, rogue, scoundrel; (*preguiçoso*) idler, layabout.
**ma'lária** *f* malaria.
**mal-arru'mado/a** *adj* untidy.
**malbara'tar** *vt* (*dissipar*) to squander, waste.
**malcri'ado/a** *adj* ill-mannered, rude.

**mal'dade** f evil, wickedness.

**maldição** [mawdʒi'sãw] f curse; **maldito/a** adj damned, accursed; **maldizente** m/f slanderer; **maldizer** vt to curse.

**mal'doso/a** adj wicked; (fig) malicious.

**maledicência** [maledʒi'sẽsja] f slander; **maledicente** m/f slanderer.

**ma'léfico/a** adj (pessoa) malicious; (coisa) harmful, injurious.

**mal-enten'dido/a** adj misunderstood // m misunderstanding.

**mal-es'tar** m (doença) indisposition, discomfort; (inquietação) uneasiness.

**ma'leta** f small suitcase, grip.

**malevolência** [malevo'lẽsja] f malice, spite; **malévolo/a** adj malicious, spiteful.

**malfa'dado/a** adj unlucky.

**malfeito/a** [mal'fejtu/a] adj poorly made; (disforme) misshapen; (injusto) wrong, unjust; **malfeitor** m malefactor; (facínora) criminal.

**malha** ['maʎa] f mesh; (no tricô) stitch; (suéter) sweater; (de ginástica) leotard; **artigos de ~** knitwear; **~ perdida** ladder, run.

**malhado/a** [ma'ʎadu/a] adj spotted, mottled, dappled.

**malhar** [ma'ʎar] vt (cereais) to thresh; (bater) to beat, strike; (fig) to deride, knock.

**malho** ['maʎu] m (maço) mallet; (grande) sledgehammer.

**mal-humo'rado/a** adj grumpy, sullen.

**malícia** [ma'lisja] f (má índole) wickedness; (astúcia) slyness; (esperteza) cleverness; (brejeirice) mischievousness; (intenção: maldosa) spite(fulness); (: satírica) sarcasm; **malicioso/a** adj wicked; (astuto) sly; (brejeiro) mischievous; (sarcástico) spiteful, sarcastic.

**maligni'dade** f malice, spite; (MED) malignancy; **maligno/a** adj

(maléfico) evil, malicious; (danoso) harmful; (MED) malignant.

**malmequer** [mawme'kex] m marigold.

**malo'grado/a** adj (frustrado) abortive, frustrated; (sem êxito) unsuccessful; (infeliz) unlucky; **malograr** vt (planos) to spoil, upset; (frustrar) to thwart, frustrate; **malograr-se** vr (planos) to fail through; (fracassar) to fail; **malogro** m failure.

**ma'lote** m (small) case; (serviço) express courier.

**mal-pas'sado/a** adj underdone; (bife) rare.

**malquerença** [mawke'rẽsa] f ill will, enmity.

**mal'quisto/a** adj disliked; (odiado) hated.

**malsão/sã** [maw'sãw/'sã] adj (doentio) sickly; (insalubre) unhealthy; (nocivo) harmful.

**'malta** f (Pt) gang, mob; (col) lot.

**'malte** m malt.

**maltrapilho/a** [mawtra'piʎu/a] adj in rags, ragged // m/f ragamuffin.

**maltra'tar** vt to ill-treat; (insultar) to abuse; (estragar) to ruin, damage.

**ma'luco/a** adj crazy, daft // m madman // f madwoman; **maluquice** f madness; (bobagem) silliness.

**mal'vado/a** adj wicked.

**malversação** [mawvexsa'sãw] f (dinheiro) embezzlement; **malversar** vt (administrar mal) to mismanage; (dinheiro) to embezzle, misappropriate.

**'mama** f breast; **mamadeira** f feeding bottle.

**mamãe** [ma'mãj] f mum, mummy.

**mamão** [ma'mãw] m papaya.

**ma'mar** vt to suck; (fig) to take in; (empresa) to milk (dry); **mamilo** m nipple.

**'mana** f sister.

**ma'nada** f herd, drove.

**manancial** [manã'sjaw] *m* spring; (*fig*) source.

**man'car** *vt* to cripple // *vi* to limp.

**mancebo** [mã'sebu] *m* young man, youth.

**mancha** ['mãʃa] *f* (*nódoa*) stain; (*na pele*) mark, spot; (*em pintura*) blotch; **sem ~** (*reputação*) spotless; **manchar** *vt* (*sujar*) to dirty; (*enodoar*) to stain, mark.

**'manco/a** *adj* crippled, lame; (*defeituoso*) defective, faulty.

**man'dado** *m* (*ordem*) order; (*JUR*) writ, injunction; **~ de prisão/busca** warrant for arrest/search warrant; **mandamento** *m* order, command; (*REL*) commandment; **mandante** *m* instigator.

**mandão/dona** [mã'dãw/'dona] *adj* bossy, domineering // *m/f* bossy person.

**man'dar** *vt* (*ordenar*) to order; (*enviar*) to send; **~ buscar/chamar** to send for; **~ embora** to send away; **~ fazer um vestido** to have a dress made; **~ que alguém faça/~ alguém fazer** to tell sb to do // *vi* to be in charge.

**manda'tário** *m* (*delegado*) delegate; (*representante*) representative, agent; **mandato** *m* (*autorização*) mandate; (*ordem*) order.

**man'díbula** *f* jaw.

**man'dinga** *f* witchcraft.

**mandi'oca** *f* cassava, manioc.

**'mando** *m* (*comando*) command; (*poder*) power; **a ~ de** by order of.

**mandrião/driona** [mãdri'ãw/dri'ona] *adj* (*Pt*) lazy // *m/f* idler, lazybones *sg*; **mandriar** *vi* to idle, loaf about.

**maneira** [ma'nejra] *f* (*modo*) way; (*estilo*) style, manner; **à ~ de** like; **de ~ que** so that; **de ~ alguma** not at all; **~s** *fpl* manners.

**manejar** [mane'ʒax] *vt* (*instrumento*) to handle; (*máquina*)

to work; **manejável** *adj* manageable; **manejo** *m* handling.

**manequim** [mane'kĩ] *m* model; (*boneco*) dummy.

**ma'neta** *adj* one-handed.

**'manga** *f* sleeve; (*fruta*) mango; (*filtro*) filter; (*mangueira*) hose; (*aguaceiro*) cloudburst.

**man'gar** *vi*: **~ com/de** to tease, make fun of.

**mangue** ['mãgı] *m* mud-flat, swamp; (*planta*) mangrove.

**mangueira** [mã'gejra] *f* hose(pipe); (*árvore*) mango tree.

**manha** ['maɲa] *f* (*malícia*) guile, craftiness; (*ardil*) trick; (*mau hábito*) habit; (*choro*) whining.

**manhã** [ma'ɲã] *f* morning; **de ~** in the morning.

**manhoso/a** [ma'ɲozu/a] *adj* (*ardiloso*) crafty, sly; (*esperto*) smart, clever; (*choroso*) whining.

**ma'nia** *f* (*MED*) mania; (*obsessão*) obsession, craze; (*paixão*) passion.

**mania'tar** *vt* to tie the hands of; (*algemar*) to handcuff.

**manicômio** [mani'komju] *m* asylum, mental hospital.

**mani'cura** *f*, **mani'cure** *f* (*tratamento*) manicure; (*pessoa*) manicurist.

**manie'tar** *vt ver* **maniatar.**

**manifestação** [manifeʃta'sãw] *f* demonstration, display; (*expressão*) expression, declaration; (*política*) demonstration; **manifestar** *vt* (*revelar*) to show, display; (*declarar*) to express, declare; **manifestar-se** *vr* to appear; (*patentear-se*) to be obvious, be evident; **manifesto/a** *adj* obvious, clear // *m* manifesto.

**manilha** [ma'niʎa] *f* (*ceramic*) drain-pipe.

**manipu'lar** *vt* to manipulate; (*manejar*) to handle.

**mani'vela** *f* (*ferramenta*) crank.

**manjar** [mã'ʒar] *m* food, dish; (*iguaria*) delicacy, titbit; (*Br*) coconut and milk pudding; ~ **branco** blancmange.

**manjedoura** [mãʒeˈdora] f manger, crib.

**manjericão** [mãʒeriˈkãw] m basil.

**'mano** m brother.

**ma'nobra** f manoeuvre; (de trens) shunting; (fig) trick; **manobrar** vt to manoeuvre; (acionar) to operate, work // vi to manoeuvre; (fazer funcionar) to work; (planejar) to scheme.

**manquejar** [mãˈkeʒax] vi to limp.

**mansão** [mãˈsãw] f mansion; (morada) residence.

**mansidão** [mãsiˈdãw] f gentleness, meekness; **manso/a** adj (brando) gentle; (águas) calm; (animal) tame.

**'manta** f (cobertor) blanket; (xale) shawl; (de viajar) travelling rug.

**manteiga** [mãˈtejga] f butter; **manteigueira** f butter dish.

**man'ter** vt to maintain; (uma família) to support; (a palavra) to keep; (princípios) to abide by; **~-se** vr (sustentar-se) to support o.s.; (permanecer) to remain; (agüentar) to hold on; **~-se firme** to stand firm.

**mantilha** [mãˈtiʎa] f mantilla; (véu) veil.

**manti'mentos** mpl provisions.

**'manto** m cloak; (de cerimônia) robe.

**manual** [manˈwaw] adj manual // m handbook; (compêndio) manual.

**manufa'tura** (Pt: **-ct-**) f manufacture; (fábrica) factory.

**manus'crito/a** adj handwritten // m manuscript.

**manuse'ar** vt (manejar) to handle; (livro) to leaf through.

**manutenção** [manuteˈsãw] f maintenance.

**mão** [mãw] f, pl irr: **mãos** [mãws] hand; (de animal) paw; (de pintura) coat; **à ~** by hand; (perto) at hand; **feito à ~** handmade; **contra a ~** on the wrong side of the road; **dar a ~**

a to shake hands with; **de mãos dadas** hand in hand; **de segunda ~** second-hand; **pôr mãos à obra** to set to work; **ter uma ~ (boa) para** to be good at.

**mão-de-obra** [mãw-dʒi-ˈɔbra] f (trabalho) workmanship; (trabalhadores) labour.

**'mapa** m map; (gráfico) chart.

**maquilagem** [makiˈlaʒẽ] f make-up; (ato) making up; **maquilar-se** vr to put on one's make-up.

**máquina** [ˈmakina] f machine; (de trem) engine; (fig) machinery; ~ **de calcular** calculator; ~ **fotográfica/de filmar** camera; ~ **de escrever** typewriter; ~ **de lavar roupa** washing-machine.

**maquinação** [makinaˈsãw] f machination, plot.

**maquinal** [makiˈnaw] adj mechanical, automatic; **maquinaria** f machinery; **maquinismo** m mechanism; (máquinas) machinery; **maquinista** m engine driver.

**'mar** m sea; **em alto ~** on the high seas; **por ~** by sea; **cair no ~** to fall overboard; **fazer-se ao ~** to set sail.

**maracu'já** m passionflower; (fruto) passion fruit.

**ma'rasmo** m debilitation; (caquexia) wasting away; (apatia) apathy.

**mara'tona** f marathon.

**maravilha** [maraˈviʎa] f marvel, wonder; **às mil ~s** wonderfully; **maravilhar** vt to amaze, astonish; **maravilhar-se** vr: **maravilhar-se de** to be astonished at, be amazed at; **maravilhoso/a** adj marvellous, wonderful.

**'marca** f mark; (COM) make, brand; (carimbo) stamp; ~ **de fábrica** trademark; **marcação** f marking; (em jogo) scoring; (de instrumento) reading; (teatro) action; **marcar** vt to mark; (animal) to brand; (delimitar) to demarcate; (observar) to keep an eye on; (hora, data) to fix, set; (*Pt: discar*) to dial; (*num jogo*) to score; **marcar uma consulta** to make an appointment.

**marceneiro** [maxse'nejru] *m* cabinet-maker, joiner.

**marcha** ['maxʃa] *f* (a *pé*) walking; (*em cortejo*) march; (*de acontecimentos*) course; (*passo*) pace, step; (*AUTO*) gear; ~ **à ré** reverse (gear); **pôr-se em** ~ to set off; **marchar** *vi* (*ir*) to go; (*andar a pé*) to walk; (*MIL*) to march.

'**marco** *m* landmark; (*de janela*) frame; (*fig*) frontier.

**março** ['maxsu] *m* March.

**ma'ré** *f* tide; ~ **alta/baixa** high/low tide; **marear** *vt* to make seasick // *vi* to be seasick.

**marechal** [mare'ʃaw] *m* marshal.

**marfim** [max'fĩ] *m* ivory.

**marga'rida** *f* daisy.

**marga'rina** *f* margarine.

**margem** ['maxʒẽ] *f* (*borda*) edge; (*do rio*) bank; (*de impresso*) margin; (*fig: tempo*) time; (: *lugar*) space; **à** ~ **de** alongside; **dar** ~ **a** to give an opportunity to.

**ma'ricas** *m* (*col*) queer, gay.

**ma'rido** *m* husband.

**marinheiro** [mari'ɲejru] *m* seaman, sailor; **marinho/a** *adj* sea, marine // *f* navy; (*pintura*) seascape; **marinha mercante** merchant navy.

**mari'ola** *m* messenger; (*patife*) scoundrel // *f* wrapped tablet of banana candy.

**mari'onete** *f* puppet.

**mari'posa** *f* moth; (*col*) prostitute.

**ma'risco** *m* shellfish.

**ma'rítimo/a** *adj* sea, maritime; **pesca** ~**a** sea fishing.

**marme'lada** *f* quince jam; (*col*) double-dealing; **marmelo** *m* quince.

**mar'mita** *f* (*vaso*) pot.

'**mármore** *m* marble; **marmóreo/a** *adj* marble.

**ma'roto/a** *m/f* rogue, rascal; (*criança*) naughty boy/girl.

**marquês/quesa** [max'keʃ/'keza] *m* marquis // *f* marchioness.

**mar'reco** *m* duck.

**Mar'rocos** *m* Morocco.

**marrom** [ma'xõ] *adj* brown.

**marroquim** [maxo'kĩ] *m* morocco leather.

'**marte** *m* Mars.

**marte'lar** *vt* to hammer (on); **martelo** *m* hammer.

'**mártir** *m* martyr; **martírio** *m* martyrdom; (*fig*) torment.

**marujo** [ma'ruʒu] *m* sailor.

**marulhar** [maru'ʎax] *vi* (*agitar-se*) to surge; (*de encontro a alguma coisa: forte*) to crash, pound; (: *brando*) to lap; (*produzir ruído*) to roar; **marulho** *m* surge; (*agitação*) tossing; (*fig*) noise, hubbub.

**mar'xista** *adj*, *m/f* Marxist.

**mas** *conj* but // *pron* = **me + as**.

**mas'car** *vt* to chew.

'**máscara** *f* mask; **sob a** ~ **de** under the guise of; **mascarado/a** *adj* masked; **mascarar** *vt* to mask; disguise.

**mascu'lino/a** *adj* masculine; (*BIO*) male; **roupa** ~**a** a men's clothes *pl*.

**mas'morra** *f* dungeon.

**masoquista** [mazo'kiʃta] *m/f* masochist.

'**massa** *f* (*física*) mass; (*de tomate*) paste; (*CULIN*) dough; as ~**s** the masses; **em** ~ en masse; **~ de vidraceiro** putty.

**massa'crar** *vt* to massacre; **massacre** *f* massacre.

**massagem** [ma'saʒẽ] *f* massage.

**mas'sudo/a** *adj* bulky; (*espesso*) thick.

**masti'gar** *vt* to chew; (*palavras*) to mumble, mutter.

**mastim** [maʃ'tĩ] *m* watchdog.

'**mastro** *m* (*NÁUT*) mast; (*para bandeira*) flagpole.

**mastur'bar-se** *vr* to masturbate.

'**mata** *f* forest, wood.

**mata-bicho** [mata-'biʃu] *m* tot of brandy, snifter.

**mata-borrão** [mata-bo'xãw] *m* blotting paper.

**mata'dor(a)** *m/f* killer // *m* (*em tourada*) matador; **matadouro** *m* slaughterhouse.

**mata'gal** *m* bush; (*brenha*) thicket, undergrowth.

**ma'tança** *f* massacre; (*de reses*) slaughter(ing); **matar** *vt* to kill; (*a sede*) to quench; (*aula*) to skip; **matar-se** *vr* to kill o.s.

**'mate** *adj* matt // *m* (*chá*) maté tea; **xeque ~** checkmate.

**mate'mático/a** *adj* mathematical // *m/f* mathematician // *f* mathematics *sg*, maths *sg*.

**ma'téria** *f* matter; (*TEC*) material; (*escolar: assunto*) subject; **em ~ de** on the subject of.

**materi'al** *adj* material; (*corporal*) physical // *m* material; (*TEC*) equipment; **~ humano** manpower; **~ismo** *m* materialism; **~ista** *adj* materialistic // *m/f* materialist.

**matéria-'prima** *f* raw material.

**mater'nal** *adj* motherly, maternal; **escola ~** nursery school; **maternidade** *f* motherhood, maternity; (*hospital*) maternity hospital; **materno/a** *adj* motherly, maternal; (*língua*) mother.

**matilha** [ma'tʃiʎa] *f* (*cães*) pack; (*chusma*) rabble.

**mati'nal** *adj* morning.

**ma'tiz** *m* shade; (*combinação de cores*) blend (of colours); **matizar** *vt* (*colorir*) to tinge, colour; (*combinar cores*) to blend.

**'mato** *m* scrubland, bush; (*floresta*) forest; (*o campo*) country.

**ma'traca** *f* rattle; **falar como uma ~** to talk nineteen to the dozen; **matraquear** *vi* to rattle, clatter; (*tagarelar*) to chatter, rabbit on.

**matreiro/a** [ma'trejru/a] *adj* cunning, crafty.

**ma'trícula** *f* (*lista*) register; (*inscrição*) registration; (*pagamento*) enrolment fee; (*Pt: AUTO*)

registration number; (*US*) license plate number; **chapa de ~** numberplate; (*US*) license plate; **matricular** *vt*, **matricular-se** *vr* to enrol, register.

**matri'mônio** *m* marriage.

**ma'triz** *f* (*MED*) womb; (*fonte*) source; (*molde*) mould; (*COM*) head office; **igreja ~** mother church.

**maturi'dade** *f* maturity.

**matu'tino/a** *adj* morning // *m* morning paper.

**mau/má** [maw/ma] *adj* bad; (*malvado*) evil, wicked.

**mau-olhado** [maw-o'ʎadu] *m* evil eye.

**mavi'oso/a** *adj* tender, soft; (*som*) sweet.

**maxila** [mak'sila] *f*, **maxi'lar** *m* jawbone.

**máxime** ['maksimɛ] *adv* especially.

**máximo/a** ['masimu/a] *adj* (*maior que todos*) greatest; **o ~ cuidado** the greatest of care // *m* maximum; (*o cúmulo*) peak; **no ~** at most // *f* maxim, saying.

**maxixe** [ma'ʃiʃi] *m* gherkin; (*Br: dança*) 19th-century dance.

**ma'zela** *f* (*ferida*) sore spot; (*doença*) illness; (*fig*) blemish.

**me** *pron* (*direto*) me; (*indireto*) (to) me; (*reflexivo*) (to) myself.

**me'ada** *f* skein, hank.

**me'ado** *m* middle; **em ~(s) de Julho** in mid-July.

**me'cânico/a** *adj* mechanical; **broca ~a** power drill // *m* mechanic // *f* (*ciência*) mechanics *sg*; (*mecanismo*) mechanism; **mecanismo** *m* mechanism.

**mecha** ['meʃa] *f* (*de vela*) wick; (*cabelo*) tuft; (*tingida*) highlight; (*MED*) swab; **mechar** *vt* (*cabelo*) to put highlights in.

**'meço** *etc* *vb* *ver* **medir**.

**medalha** [me'daʎa] *f* medal.

**'média** *f* average; **em ~** on average.

**mediação** [medʒia'sãw] *f*

mediation; **por ~ de** through; **medianeiro** m mediator; **mediano/a** adj medium, average; (*mediocre*) mediocre.

**medi'ante** prep by (means of), through; **mediar** vt to mediate (for) // vi (ser mediador) to mediate; **a distância que medeia entre** the distance between.

**medicação** [medʒikaˈsãw] f treatment; **medicamento** m medicine.

**medição** [medʒiˈsãw] f measurement.

**medi'cina** f medicine; **médico/a** adj medical // m/f doctor.

**me'dida** f measure; (*medição*) measurement; (*prudência*) prudence; **à ~ que** while, as; **tomar ~s** to take steps; **tomar as ~s de** to measure; **feito sob ~** made to measure; **medidor m: medidor de pressão** pressure gauge; **medidor de gás** gas meter.

**'médio/a** adj (*lugar*) middle, mid; (*no meio-termo*) medium; (*mediano*) average // f average.

**me'díocre** adj mediocre; **mediocridade** f mediocrity.

**me'dir** vt to measure; (*pesar*) to weigh up; (*avaliar*) to judge // vi to measure; **~-se** vr (*competir*) to vie.

**medi'tar** vt (*pensar em*) to think over // vi to meditate.

**mediter'râneo/a** adj Mediterranean // m: **o M~** the Mediterranean.

**'médium** m (*pessoa*) medium.

**'medo** m fear; **com ~** afraid; **ter ~ de** to be afraid of; **medonho/a** adj terrible, awful.

**me'drar** vi to thrive, flourish.

**me'droso/a** adj (com medo) frightened; (*tímido*) timid.

**me'dula** f marrow.

**me'dusa** f jellyfish.

**meia** ['meja] f stocking // adj ver **meio**; **~-calça** f tights pl; (US) panty hose.

**meia-i'dade** f middle age.

**meia-noite** [meja-ˈnojtʃi] f midnight.

**meigo/a** ['mejgu/a] adj gentle; (*voz*) sweet; **meiguice** f gentleness, sweetness.

**meio/a** ['meju/a] adj half; **~ quilo** half a kilo; **uma hora e ~** a half past one // adv half, rather; **~ morto** half-dead // m (*ponto*) middle; (*ambiente*) environment; (*método*) means pl, way; **cortar ao ~** to cut in half.

**meio-dia** [meju-ˈdʒia] m midday, noon.

**mel** m honey; **melaço** m molasses pl; **melado/a** adj (cor) honey-coloured; (*pegajoso*) sticky // m (*melaço*: US) molasses; (: Brit) treacle.

**melancia** [melãˈsia] f watermelon.

**melan'cólico/a** adj sad, melancholy.

**melão** [meˈlãw] m melon.

**me'lena** f long hair; (*juba*) mane.

**melhor** [meˈʎɔx] adj, adv (*comparativo*) better; (*superlativo*) best; **~ que nunca** better than ever; **quanto mais ~** the more the better; **seria ~ começarmos** we had better begin; **tanto ~** so much the better; **melhora f, melhoramento** m improvement; **melhorar** vt to improve, make better // vi to improve, get better.

**meli'ante** m scoundrel; (*vagabundo*) tramp.

**melin'drar** vt to offend, hurt; **~-se** vr to take offence, be hurt; **melindroso/a** adj (*sensível*) sensitive, touchy; (*problema, situação*) tricky.

**melo'dia** f melody; (*composição*) tune.

**melo'drama** m melodrama; **melodramático/a** adj melodramatic.

**me'loso/a** adj sweet; (fig) corny.

**'melro** m blackbird.

**'membro** m member; (do corpo) limb; **membrudo/a** adj big; (fig) robust.

**memo'rando** m (aviso) note; (COM: comunicação) memorandum.

**me'mória** f memory; **de ~** by heart; **~s** fpl (de autor) memoirs.

**menção** [mē'sãw] f mention, reference; **~ honrosa** honours, distinction; **fazer ~ de sair** to make as if to leave, begin to leave; **mencionar** vt to mention.

**mendi'cância** f begging; **mendigar** vt to beg for // vi to beg; **mendigo/a** m/f beggar.

**mene'ar** vt (corpo, cabeça) to shake; (quadris) to swing; **meneio** m (balanço) swaying.

**me'nino/a** m boy // f girl; (olhos): **~ a dos olhos** pupil.

**menopausa** [meno'pawza] f menopause.

**me'nor** adj (mais pequeno: comparativo) smaller; (: superlativo) smallest; (mais jovem: comparativo) younger; (: superlativo) youngest; (o mínimo) the least, slightest; (de idade) under age; **não tenho a ~ idéia** I haven't the slightest idea // m/f juvenile, young person; **~ abandonado** abandoned child.

**'menos** adj (comparativo: sg) less; (: pl) fewer; (superlativo: sg) least; (: pl) fewest // adv (comparativo) less; (superlativo) least // prep except // m: **o ~** the least; **a ~ (faltando)** missing; **a ~ que** unless; **ao/pelo/quando ~** at least; **mais ou ~ more or less; **de/que** less than.

**menospre'zar** vt to underrate; (desprezar) to despise, scorn; **menosprezo** m contempt, disdain.

**mensageiro/a** [mēsa'ʒejru/a] adj, m/f messenger; **mensagem** f message.

**men'sal** adj monthly; **~idade** f monthly payment; **~mente** adv monthly.

**menstruação** [mēʃtrua'sãw] f period, menstruation; **menstruar** vi to menstruate, have a period; **mênstruo** m period, menstruation.

**men'tal** adj mental; **~idade** f mentality; (a mente) mind; **mente** f mind; **de boa mente** willingly.

**mente'capto/a** adj mad, crazy // m/f fool, idiot.

**men'tir** vi to lie; **mentira** f lie; (ato) lying; **parece mentira que** it seems incredible that; **mentiroso/a** adj lying; (enganoso) deceitful // m/f liar.

**me'nu** m menu.

**mer'cado** m market; **M~ Comum** Common Market; **~ negro/paralelo** black market; **mercador** m merchant, trader; **mercadoria** f commodity; **mercadorias** fpl goods.

**mer'cante** adj, m/f merchant; **mercantil** adj mercantile, commercial.

**mercê** [mex'se] f (favor) favour; (perdão) mercy; **à ~ de** at the mercy of.

**mercearia** [mexsea'ria] f grocer's (shop); **merceeiro** m grocer.

**merce'nário/a** adj, m mercenary.

**mer'cúrio** m mercury.

**merecer** [mere'sex] vt to deserve, merit; (valer) to be worth // vi to deserve; **merecido/a** adj deserved; (justo) just, due; **merecimento** m desert; (valor, talento) merit.

**me'renda** f snack; (no campo) picnic; **~ escolar** free school meal; **merendar** vi to have as a snack // vi to have a snack; **merendeira** f (funcionária) dinner-lady; (lancheira) lunch-bag/box.

**merengue** [me'rēgi] m meringue.

**mergulhar** [mexgu'ʎax] vt to dip in, immerse // vi (para nadar) to dive; (penetrar) to plunge; **mergulho** m dip(ping), immersion; (em natação) dive.

**meridio'nal** adj southern.

**'mérito** m merit; (valor) worth, value.

**'mero/a** adj mere.

**'mês** m month; (salário) month's pay.

**'mesa** f table; (COM) board; **pôr/tirar a ~** to lay/clear the table.

**me'sada** f monthly allowance; (criança) pocket-money.

**'mescla** f mixture; **mesclar** vt to mix (up); (cores) to blend.

**me'seta** f plateau, tableland.

**'mesmo/a** adj same; **eu ~** I myself; **este ~ homem** this very man; **ele ~ o fez** he did it himself; **o Rei ~** the King himself; **continuar na ~a** to be just the same; **dá no ~** or **na ~** it's all the same // m: **o ~** the same (thing) // adv (até) even; **aqui/agora/hoje ~** right here/right now/this very day; **~ que** even if; **é ~** it's true; **isso ~!** exactly!

**mesquinho/a** [meʃ'kiɲu/a] adj (avaro) mean, miserly.

**mesquita** [meʃ'kita] f mosque.

**messias** [me'sias] m Messiah.

**mes'tiço/a** adj half-caste, of mixed race; (animal) crossbred // m/f half-caste; (animal) half-breed.

**'mestre/'mestra** adj master-cmp; **chave mestra** master key; **obra mestra** masterpiece // m master; (chefe: de fábrica) manager; (: de operários) foreman; **de ~** masterful, masterly // f (professora) mistress; **mestria** f mastery; (habilidade) expertise; **com mestria** to perfection.

**me'sura** f (cumprimento) bow; (cortesia) courtesy.

**'meta** f (corrida de cavalos) finishing post; (regata) finishing line; (gol) goal; (alvo) aim; (fim) end.

**me'tade** f half; (meio) middle; **~ de uma laranja** half an orange.

**me'táfora** f metaphor.

**me'tal** m, pl **me'tais** metal; **~ sonante** hard cash; **metais** (MÚS)

brass sg; **metálico/a** adj (som) metallic; (de metal) metal; **~urgia** f metallurgy.

**mete'oro** m meteor.

**me'ter** vt (colocar) to put; (implicar) to involve; (introduzir) to introduce; **~ na cabeça** to take it into one's head; **~-se** vr (esconder-se) to hide; (intrometer-se) to get involved in; **~ na cama** to get into bed; **~-se com** (provocar) to pick a quarrel with; **~-se a médico** to set o.s. up as a doctor.

**me'tódico/a** adj methodical; **método** m method.

**metralhadora** [metraʎa'dora] f sub-machine gun.

**'métrico/a** adj metric; **metro** m metre; (US) meter.

**me'trô** m (Br), **'metro** m (Pt) (FERRO) underground; (US) subway.

**me'trópole** f metropolis; (capital) capital; **metropolitano/a** adj metropolitan // m (FERRO) underground; (US) subway.

**meu/minha** [mew/'miɲa] adj my; **um amigo ~** a friend of mine // pron mine.

**mexer** [me'ʃex] vt (mover) to move; (a cabeça) to nod, shake; (misturar) to mix, stir; (ovos) to scramble // vi (mover) to move; **~ em** to meddle with; **~ com** (comerciar) to deal in; (provocar) to annoy, tease; **~-se** vr to move, budge; (apressar-se) to get a move on; **mexa-se!** get going!, budge yourself!

**mexericar** [meʃeri'kax] vi to gossip; **mexeriqueiro/a** adj gossiping // m/f gossip, busybody.

**mexicano/a** [meʃi'kanu/a] adj, m/f Mexican; **México** m Mexico.

**mexido/a** [me'ʃidu/a] adj (papéis) mixed up; (agitado) restless; **ovos ~s** scrambled eggs // f mess, disorder.

**mexilhão** [meʃi'ʎãw] m mussel.

**mezinha** [me'ziɲa] f home-made remedy.

**mi'ar** vi to miaow; **miau** m miaow.

**mi'cróbio** m germ, microbe.

**micro'fone** m microphone.

**micro'onda** f microwave.

**micros'cópio** m microscope.

**migalha** [mi'gaʎa] f crumb; ~s fpl scraps.

**migração** [migra'sãw] f migration; **migrar** vi to migrate; **migratório/a** adj migratory; **aves migratórias** birds of passage.

**mijar** [mi'ʒax] vi to urinate; ~-**se** vr to wet o.s.

**mil** num thousand; **dois** ~ two thousand.

**mi'lagre** m miracle; **milagroso/a** adj miraculous.

**milha** ['miʎa] f mile.

**milhão** [mi'ʎãw] m million.

**milhar** [mi'ʎax] m thousand.

**milharal** [miʎa'raw] m maize field; **milho** m maize; (US) corn.

**mi'lícia** f (MIL) militia; (: vida) military life; (: força) military force.

**mi'límetro** m millimetre; (US) millimeter.

**milio'nário/a** adj, m/f millionaire.

**mili'tante** adj, m/f militant; **militar** adj military // m soldier // vi (POL) to be an active member.

**mim** [mĩ] pron me; (reflexivo) myself.

**mi'mado/a** adj (acariciado) petted; (amimalhado) spoilt; **mimar** vt to pamper, spoil; **mimo** m (presente) gift; (carícia) caress sg; (de criança) spoiling; (coisa delicada) delicacy; **mimoso/a** adj (delicado) delicate; (terno) tender, loving, sweet; (acustumado a mimos) spoilt.

**'mina** f mine; (fig: de riquezas) gold mine; (: de informações) mine of information; **minar** vt to mine; (fig) to undermine; **mineiro/a** adj mining; (de Minas Gerais) from Minas Gerais // m miner; **mineral** adj mineral // m mineral; **minério** m ore.

**'míngua** f: à ~ **de** for want of; **minguante** adj waning // f wane, decline; **quarto minguante** (ASTRO) last quarter; **minguar** vi (diminuir) to decrease, dwindle; (faltar) to run short.

**minha** ['miɲa] adj, pron ver **meu**.

**minhoca** [mi'ɲɔka] f (earth)worm.

**minia'tura** adj, f miniature.

**'mínimo/a** adj minimum; **a** ~**a atenção** the slightest attention // m minimum, least; **no** ~ at least.

**minissaia** [mini'saja] f miniskirt.

**minis'tério** m ministry; **M**~ **do Exterior/da Fazenda** Foreign Office/Treasury; **ministro** m minister.

**mino'rar** vt to lessen, reduce; **minoria** f minority.

**minuci'oso/a** adj (individuo) thorough; (explicação) detailed.

**mi'núsculo/a** adj minute, tiny; **letra** ~**a** small letter.

**mi'nuta** f (rascunho) rough draft; (CULIN) à ~ cooked to order.

**mi'nuto** m minute.

**mi'olo** m (de pão) inside; (polpa) pulp; (de maçã) core; ~**s** mpl (fig) brains.

**míope** ['mjɔpi] adj short-sighted; **miopia** f short-sightedness.

**'mira** f (de fuzil) sight; (objetivo) aim, purpose; **à** ~ **de** on the lookout for; **ter em** ~ to keep an eye on.

**mi'rada** f look; **miradouro** m viewpoint, belvedere.

**miragem** [mi'raʒẽ] f mirage.

**mira'mar** m sea view.

**mi'rante** m viewpoint, belvedere.

**mi'rar** vt to look at; (observar) to watch; (fig: apontar para) to aim at; ~ **para** to look onto; ~-**se** vr to look at o.s.

**mir'rar** vt/i, **mir'rar-se** vr to wither, dry up.

**misce'lânea** f miscellany; (fig) mixture.

**mise'rável** adj (lastimável) miserable, wretched; (avaro) stingy, mean; (insignificante) paltry; (lugar) squalid; (infame) despicable // m (indigente) wretch; (coitado) poor thing; (perverso) rotter; **miséria** f (estado lastimável) misery; (pobreza) poverty; (avareza) stinginess; **uma miséria** (dinheiro) a pittance; **misericórdia** f (compaixão) pity, compassion; (graça) mercy.

**'missa** f (REL) mass.

**missão** f (mis'sãw) f mission.

**'misse** f beauty queen.

**'míssil** ['misjw] m missile.

**missio'nário** m missionary.

**mis'ter** m (trabalho) occupation, job; (profissão) profession; (propósito) purpose; **ser ~** to be necessary.

**mis'tério** m mystery.

**'místico/a** adj, m/f mystic.

**'misto/a** adj mixed; (confuso) mixed up // m mixture; **misto-quente** m toasted cheese and ham sandwich.

**mis'tura** f (ato) mixing; (conjunto) mixture; (QUÍM) compound; **misturar** vt to mix, blend; **misturar-se** vr: **misturar-se com** to mix in with, mingle with.

**'mito** m myth.

**miudezas** [mju'dezaʃ] fpl minutiae; (bugigangas) odds and ends; **miúdo/a** adj (pequeno) tiny, minute; (cuidadoso) thorough; **dinheiro miúdo** small change // m/f (Pt: criança) youngster, kid; **miúdos** mpl (dinheiro) change sg; (de aves) giblets.

**mixórdia** [mi'ʃɔxdʒia] f mess, jumble.

**mo** pron = **me + o**.

**mó** f (de moinho) millstone; (para afiar) grindstone; **moagem** f grinding.

**mobi'lar** vt (Pt) to furnish; **mobília** f furniture; **mobiliar** vt (Br) to furnish; **mobiliário** m furnishings pl.

**mobili'zar** vt to mobilize.

**'moça** f ver **moço**.

**moção** [mo'sãw] f motion.

**mochila** [mo'ʃila] f rucksack.

**mocho/a** ['moʃu/a] adj hornless // m (ave) owl.

**mocidade** [mosi'dadʒi] f youth; (os moços) young people; **moço/a** adj young; (da juventude) youthful // m young man, lad; **moço de bordo** ordinary seaman; **moço de cavalariça** groom // f girl, young woman.

**'moda** f fashion; (estilo) style; **estar na ~** to be in fashion, be all the rage; **fora da ~** old-fashioned; **sair da ~** to go out of fashion.

**mode'lar** vt to model; **modelo** m model; (costura) pattern.

**mode'rado/a** adj moderate; (clima) mild; **moderar** vt to moderate; (violência) to control, restrain; (velocidade) to reduce; **moderar-se** vr to calm down.

**moderni'zar** vt to modernize; **moderno/a** adj modern; (atual) present-day; **modernoso/a** adj newfangled.

**mo'déstia** f modesty; **modesto/a** adj modest; (simples) simple, plain.

**'módico/a** adj moderate; (preço) reasonable.

**modifi'car** vt to modify, alter.

**mo'dismo** m idiom.

**mo'dista** f dressmaker.

**'modo** m (maneira) way, manner; (LING) mood; (MÚS) mode; **~s** mpl manners; **~ de pensar** way of thinking; **de ~ que** so (that); **de nenhum** in no way; **de qualquer ~** anyway, anyhow; **tenha ~s!** behave yourself!

**mo'dorra** f (sonolência) drowsiness; (letargia) lethargy.

**mo'eda** f (uma) coin; (dinheiro) money; **uma ~ de 10p** a 10p piece;

~ **corrente** currency; **pagar na mesma** ~ to give tit for tat.

**mo'er** *vt* (*café*) to grind; (*cana*) to crush; (*bater*) to beat; (*cansar*) to tire out.

**mo'far** *vi* to get mouldy; ~ **de** to mock, scoff at.

**mo'fino/a** *adj* (*covarde*) cowardly; (*doentio*) sickly; (*avarento*) stingy.

**'mofo** *m* (BOT) mould; (*cheiro*) mustiness.

**'mogno** *m* mahogany.

**mo'ído/a** *pp de* **moer** // *adj* (*café*) ground; (*carne*) minced; (*cansado*) tired out; **moinho** *m* mill; (*de café*) grinder.

**moita** ['mojta] *f* thicket.

**'mola** *f* (TEC) spring.

**mo'lar** *m* molar (tooth).

**mol'dar** *vt* to mould; (*metal*) to cast; **molde** *m* mould; (*de papel*) pattern; (*fig*) model; **moldura** *f* (*de pintura*) frame.

**'mole** *adj* (*macio, fofo*) soft; (*fraco*) weak, flabby; (*fácil*) easy; (*pessoa*) easy-going, soft, listless.

**mo'lécula** *f* molecule.

**moles'tar** *vt* to bother; (*desgostar*) to annoy; (*incomodar*) to put out; ~**-se** *vr* (*aborrecer-se*) to be annoyed; (*magoar-se*) to be hurt; **moléstia** *f* (*doença*) illness; **molesto/a** *adj* (*incômodo*) troublesome; (*aborrecido*) annoying; (*molestado*) troubled.

**molhado/a** [mo'ʎadu/a] *adj* wet, damp; **molhar** *vt* (*umedecer*) to wet; (: *de leve*) to moisten, dampen; (*meter*) to dip; **molhar-se** *vr* to get wet.

**molhe** ['moʎi] *m* (Pt) jetty; (*cais*) wharf, quay.

**molho** ['moʎu] *m* (*de chaves*) bunch; (*de trigo*) sheaf; (CULIN) sauce; (: *de salada*) dressing; (: *de carne*) gravy; **pôr de** ~ to soak.

**momen'tâneo/a** *adj* momentary; **momento** *m* moment; (TEC) momentum; **a todo momento** constantly; **de um momento para outro** suddenly; **no momento em que** just as.

**mo'narca** *m/f* monarch, ruler; **monarquia** *f* monarchy.

**mo'nástico/a** *adj* monastic.

**monção** [mõ'sãw] *f* monsoon.

**mon'dar** *vt* (Pt: *ervas daninhas*) to weed; (*árvores*) to prune; (*fig*) to weed out.

**monge** ['mõʒi] *m* monk; **monja** *f* nun.

**'mono/a** *m/f* monkey, ape.

**mono'pólio** *m* monopoly; **monopolizar** *vt* to monopolize.

**monoto'nia** *f* monotony; **monótono/a** *adj* monotonous.

**'monstro/a** *adj* monster; (*fig*) fantastic // *m* monster; **monstruoso/a** *adj* monstrous.

**'monta** *f:* **de pouca** ~ trivial, of little account.

**montagem** [mõ'taʒẽ] *f* assembly; (ARQ) erection; (*cinema*) montage; (*teatro*) production.

**montanha** [mõ'taɲa] *f* mountain; ~**-russa** *f* roller coaster; **montanhês/esa** *adj* mountain // *m/f* highlander; **montanhoso/a** *adj* mountainous.

**mon'tante** *m* total, sum.

**montão** [mõ'tãw] *m* heap, pile.

**mon'tar** *vt* (*subir a*) to mount, get on; (*cavalgar*) to ride; (*peças*) to assemble, put together; (*loja, máquina*) to set up // *vi:* ~ **a/em** (*animal*) to get on; (*cavalgar*) to ride; (*despesa*) to come to; **montaria** *f* (*caçada*) hunting; (*cavalgadura*) mount; (*sela*) side-saddle.

**'monte** *m* hill; (*montão*) heap, pile; (*de gente*) crowd.

**'montra** *f* (Pt) shop window.

**monumen'tal** [-taw] *adj* monumental; (*fig*) magnificent, splendid; **monumento** *m* monument.

**mo'rada** *f* home, residence; (Pt: *endereço*) address; **morador(a)** *m/f* (*de casa*) resident; (*de casa alugada*) tenant; (*habitante*) inhabitant.

**moral** [mo'raw] *adj* moral // *f* (*ética*) ethics *pl*; (*conclusão*) moral // *m* morale; ~**izar** *vt* to moralize.

**mo'rango** *m* strawberry.

**mo'rar** *vi* to live, reside.

**'mórbido/a** *adj* (*malsão*) unhealthy; (*doente*) sickly.

**morcego** [mɔx'segu] *m* (BIO) bat.

**mor'cela** *f* black pudding.

**mor'daça** *f* (*de animal*) muzzle; (*fig*) gag; **mordaz** *adj* biting; (*corrosivo*) caustic; (*sarcástico*) scathing.

**morde'dura** *f* bite; **morder** *vt* to bite; (*penetrar em*) to bite into; (*corroer*) to corrode; **morder a língua** to bite one's tongue; **morder-se** *vr*: **morder-se de inveja** to be green with envy.

**mo'reno/a** *adj* dark(-skinned); (*de cabelos*) brunette // *f* brunette; (*cor*) brown.

**mor'fina** *f* morphine.

**mor'gado/a** *m* (*Pt: herdeiro*) heir; (*filho mais velho*) eldest son; (*propriedade*) entailed estate // *f* heiress.

**mori'bundo/a** *adj* dying.

**morigerado/a** [moriʒe'radu/a] *adj* upright.

**morma'cento/a** *adj* sultry.

**mor'mente** *adv* chiefly, especially.

**'morno/a** *adj* lukewarm, tepid.

**mo'roso/a** *adj* slow, sluggish.

**mor'rer** *vi* to die; (*luz, cor*) to fade; (*fogo*) to die down; (AUTO) to stall; ~ **por** to be mad about; ~ **de rir** to die laughing.

**'morro** *m* hill.

**morta'dela** *f* salami.

**mor'tal** *adj* mortal; (*letal*) deadly.

**mortalha** [mox'taʎa] *f* shroud.

**mortali'dade** *f* mortality; **mortandade** *f* slaughter; **morte** *f* death.

**morteiro** [mox'tejru] *m* mortar.

**mortiço/a** [mox'tʃisu/a] *adj* (*morrediço*) dying; (*embaciado*) dull; (*desanimado*) lifeless; (*luz*) dimming; **mortífero/a** *adj* deadly, lethal; **mortificar** *vt* (*torturar*) to torture; (*afligir*) to annoy, torment.

**'morto/a** *pp irr de matar* ou **morrer** // *adj* (*cor*) dull; (*exausto*) exhausted; (: *col*) done in; **estar** ~ to be dead; **ser** ~ to be killed; **estar** ~ **de inveja** to be green with envy; **estar** ~ **por**, **estar** ~ **de vontade de** to be dying to // *m* dead man; (*cadáver*) corpse, dead body // *f* dead woman.

**mos** *pron* = **me** + **os**.

**mosaico** [mo'sajku] *m* mosaic.

**'mosca** *f* fly.

**Moscou** [moʃ'ko] *m* Moscow.

**mosquiteiro** [moʃki'tejru] *m* mosquito net; **mosquito** *m* mosquito.

**'mossa** *f* dent; (*fig*) impression.

**mos'tarda** *f* mustard.

**mosteiro** [moʃ'tejru] *m* monastery; (*de monjas*) convent.

**'mosto** *m* (*vinho*) must.

**'mostra** *f* (*exibição*) display; (*sinal*) sign, indication; **dar** ~**s de** to show signs of; ~**dor** *m* (*de relógio*) face, dial; **mostrar** *vt* to show; (*mercadorias*) to display; (*provar*) to prove; **mostrar-se** *vr* to appear, seem.

**'mote** *m* (*frase*) motto; (*tema*) theme.

**motejar** [mote'ʒax] *vt* to taunt, mock // *vi*: ~ **de** (*gracejar*) to jeer at, make fun of; **motejo** *m* mockery, derision; (*dito*) joke.

**motim** [mo'tʃĩ] *m* riot, revolt; (*militar*) mutiny.

**moti'var** *vt* (*causar*) to cause, bring about; (*estimular*) to motivate; **motivo** *m* (*causa*) cause, reason; (*fim*) motive; (MÚS) motif.

**'moto** *m*: **de** ~ **próprio** of one's own accord.

**'moto** *f*, **motoci'cleta** *f*, **moto'ciclo** (*Pt*) *m* motorbike; **motoneta** *f* (*motor-*)scooter; **motoniveladora** *f* bulldozer.

**mo'tor/mo'triz** adj driving // m motor, engine; ~ **de arranque** starter (motor); ~ **de explosão interno** internal combustion engine; **motorista** m/f driver; **motorizado/a** adj motorized.

**mouco/a** ['moku/a] adj deaf, hard of hearing.

**move'diço/a** adj easily moved; (instável) unsteady; **areia** ~**a** quicksand; **móvel** adj movable // m (peça de mobília) piece of furniture; **móveis** mpl furniture sg; **bens móveis** personal property.

**mo'ver** vt to move; (cabeça) to shake; (causar) to cause; (acionar) to drive; ~ **uma ação** to start a lawsuit; ~**se** vr to move; **movimento** m movement; (TEC) motion; (na rua) activity, bustle.

**mu'ar** m/f mule.

**'muco** m mucus.

**muçulmano/a** [musul'manu/a] adj, m/f Moslem.

**mu'dança** f change; (de casa) move; (AUTO) gear; **mudar** vt to change; (deslocar) to move // vi (ave) to moult; **mudar de roupa/de conversa** to change clothes/the conversation; **mudar de casa** to move (house); **mudar-se** vr (de casa) to move (away); (transformar-se) to change.

**'mudo/a** adj dumb; (calado, cinema) silent; (telefone) dead.

**mugir** [mu'ʒix] vi (vaca) to moo, low.

**muito/a** ['mwĩtu/a] adj a lot of; (em frase negativa ou interrogativa: sg) much, (: pl) many // adv a lot; (+ adjetivo) very; ~ **admirado** (+ comparativo) ~ **melhor** a lot/much/far better; (de tempo) long; ~ **depois** long after; **há** ~ a long time ago; ~**as vezes** often; **por** ~ **que** however much // pron a lot; (em frase negativa ou interrogativa) much.

**'mula** f mule.

**mu'lato/a** adj, m/f mulatto.

**mu'leta** f crutch; (fig) support.

**mulher** [mu'ʎex] f woman; (esposa) wife.

**'multa** f fine; **levar uma** ~ to get fined; **multar** vt to fine.

**multidão** [multʃi'dãw] f (grande afluência) crowd; **uma** ~ **de** (muitos) lots of.

**multilate'ral** adj multilateral.

**multipli'car** vt (MAT) to multiply; (aumentar) to increase.

**mun'dano/a** adj worldly; **mundial** adj worldwide; (guerra, recorde) world // m (campeonato) world championship; **o mundial de futebol** the World Cup.

**'mundo** m world; **todo o** ~ everybody; **um** ~ **de** lots of, a great many; **correr** ~ to see the world.

**munheca** [mu'ɲeka] f wrist.

**munição** [muni'sãw] f (de armas) ammunition; (chumbo) shot; (MIL) munitions pl, supplies pl.

**município** [muni'sipju] m town council, corporation; (cidade) town; (condado) county.

**mu'nir** vt: ~ **de** to provide with, supply with.

**muralha** [mu'raʎa] f (de fortaleza) rampart; (muro) wall.

**murchar** [mur'ʃax] vt (BOT) to wither // vi (BOT) to wither, wilt; (fig) to fade.

**murmuração** [muxmura'sãw] f muttering; (maledicência) gossiping; **murmurar** vi (segredar) to murmur, whisper; (queixar-se) to mutter, grumble; (água) to ripple; (folhagem) to rustle; **murmúrio** m whispering; (queixa) grumbling; (água) rippling; (folhagem) rustling; (maledicência) gossiping.

**'muro** m wall.

**'murro** m punch, sock.

**'músculo** m muscle.

**museu** [mu'sew] m museum.

**'musgo** m moss; **musgoso/a** adj mossy.

**musi'cal** [-kaw] adj, m musical; **músico/a** adj musical // m/f musician // f music.

**mutação** [muta'sãw] f change, alteration; (BIO) mutation.

**muti'lar** vt to mutilate; (pessoa) to maim.

**mutu'ário** m borrower; **mútuo/a** adj mutual // m loan.

# N

**na = em + a.**

**'nabo** m turnip.

**nação** [na'sãw] f nation.

**'nácar** m mother-of-pearl; (cor) pink, pinky.

**nacio'nal** [-naw] adj national; ~**idade** f nationality; ~**ismo** m nationalism; ~**ista** m/f nationalist; ~**izar** vt to nationalize.

**'naco** m piece, chunk.

**'nada** pron nothing; **não dizer** ~ to say nothing, not to say anything // m nothingness; (pessoa) nonentity // adv not at all, in no way; **antes de mais** ~ first of all; **de/por** ~! not at all!

**nada'dor(a)** m/f swimmer; **nadar** vi to swim.

**'nádegas** fpl buttocks.

**'nado** m: ~ **de peito** breaststroke; ~ **de costas** backstroke; **a** ~: **atravessar a** ~ to swim across.

**naipe** ['najpi] m (cartas) suit (of cards); (categoria) order.

**namo'rado/a** m boyfriend // f girlfriend; **namorar** vt (ser namorado de) to be going out with, court, woo; **namoricar** vt to flirt with; **namoro** m courtship; (amistade) relationship.

**não** [nãw] adv not; (resposta) no; ~ **sei** I don't know; ~ **muito** not much; ~ **só ... mas também** not only ... but

also; **agora** ~ not now // excl: ~! no!

**não-** pref: ~**alinhado/a** adj non-aligned; ~**conformista** adj, m/f nonconformist.

**narci'sista** adj narcissistic; **narciso** m (BOT) narcissus; (pessoa) vain man; **narciso-dos-prados** m daffodil.

**nar'cótico/a** adj, m narcotic.

**nari'gudo/a** adj big-nosed; **narina** f nostril; **nariz** m nose; **meter o nariz em** to poke one's nose into; **torcer o nariz para** to turn one's nose up at.

**narração** [naxa'sãw] f narration; (relato) account; **narrar** vt to narrate, recount; **narrativo/a** adj narrative // f narrative; (história) story.

**nas = em + as.**

**nasal** [na'zaw] adj nasal; ~**ização** f nasalization.

**nascença** [na'sẽsa] f birth; (fig) origin; **nascente** adj nascent // m East, Orient // f (fonte) spring.

**nas'cer** vi to be born; (plantas) to sprout; (o sol) to rise // m: ~ **do sol** sunrise; **nascido/a** adj born; **nascimento** m birth; (fig) origin; (estirpe) descent.

**'nata** f (CULIN) cream.

**natação** [nata'sãw] f swimming.

**natal** [na'taw] adj (relativo ao nascimento) natal; (lugar) native; **cidade** ~ home town; **terra** ~ birthplace // m: N~ Christmas; ~**ício/a** adj: **aniversário** ~**ício** birthday // m birthday; ~**idade** f: **índice de** ~**idade** birth rate; **natividade** f nativity.

**na'tivo/a** adj native; (natural) natural // m/f native.

**'NATO** (Pt) f NATO, ver OTAN.

**'nato/a** adj born.

**natu'ral** [-naw] adj natural // m (nativo) native; (índole) nature; ~**idade** f naturalness; ~**ização** f naturalization; ~**izar-se** vr to become naturalized; ~**mente** adv naturally.

**natu'reza** f nature; (espécie) kind, type; ~ **morta** still life; **por** ~ by nature.

**nau** [naw] f ship; (de guerra) warship; **naufragar** vi to be shipwrecked; (fig: malograr-se) to fail; **naufrágio** m shipwreck; (fig) failure; **náufrago/a** m/f castaway, shipwrecked person.

**náusea** ['nawsea] f nausea; **sentir** ~**s** to feel sick; **nauseabundo/a** adj, **nauseante** adj nauseating, sickening.

**náutico/a** ['nawtʃiku/a] adj nautical // f seamanship.

**navalha** [na'vaʎa] f (de barba) razor; (faca) knife.

**'nave** f (de igreja) nave; (navio) ship; ~ **espacial** spaceship.

**navega'ção** [navega'sãw] f navigation, sailing; ~ **aérea** air traffic; ~ **costeira** coastal shipping; **navegador** m navigator; **navegar** vt (navio) to sail; (avião) to fly // vi (viajar em navio) to sail (: em avião) to fly; (dirigir o rumo) to navigate; **navegável** adj navigable.

**na'vio** m ship; ~ **a vela** sailing boat; ~ **de carreira** liner; ~ **de guerra** warship; ~ **petroleiro** oil tanker.

**'nazi** (Pt) adj, m/f, **na'zista** (Br) adj, m/f Nazi.

**ne'blina** f fog, mist; **nebuloso/a** adj foggy, misty; (céu) cloudy; (fig) vague // f (ASTRO) nebula.

**neces'sário/a** adj necessary; **necessidade** f need, necessity; (pobreza) poverty, need; **ter necessidade de** to need; **necessitado/a** adj needy, poor; **necessitar** vt to need, require // vi to be in need.

**necrologia** [nɛkrolo'ʒɪa] f obituary column; **necrológio** m obituary; **necrópole** f cemetery; **necrotério** m mortuary; (US) morgue.

**'néctar** m nectar.

**'nédio/a** adj (luzidio) glossy, sleek; (rechonchudo) plump.

**neerlandês/esa** [neexlã'deʃ/eza] adj Dutch // m Dutchman // f Dutchwoman; **Neerlândia** f the Netherlands pl.

**ne'fando/a** adj atrocious, heinous.

**ne'fasto/a** adj (de mau agouro) ominous; (trágico) tragic.

**ne'gaça** f lure, bait; **negacear** vt (atrair) to entice; (provocar) to provoke.

**nega'ção** [nega'sãw] f negation; (recusa) refusal, denial; **negar** vt (recusar) to refuse; (desmentir) to deny; **negar-se** vr: **negar-se a** to refuse to; **negativo/a** adj negative // m (TEC, FOTO) negative // f (LING) negative; (recusa) denial; **negável** adj deniable.

**negligência** [negli'ʒēsja] f negligence, carelessness; **negligente** adj negligent, careless.

**negocia'ção** [negosia'sãw] f negotiation; (transação) transaction; **negociante** m businessman; (comerciante) merchant // f businesswoman; **negociar** vt/i (diplomacia etc) to negotiate; (comerciar) to trade; **negociável** adj negotiable.

**ne'gócio** [ne'gɔsju] m (COM) business; (transação) deal, transaction; (col: coisa) thing; (assunto) affair, business; **homem de** ~**s** businessman; **a** ~**s** on business.

**negreiro/a** [ne'grejru] m/f slave-trader.

**'negro/a** adj black; (medonho) dreadful // m black man, Negro // f black woman, Negress; **negrura** f blackness.

**nem** [nēj] conj nor, neither; ~ **sequer** not even; ~ **que** not even if; ~ **bem** hardly; ~ **um só** not a single one; ~ **estuda** ~ **trabalha** he neither studies nor works.

**ne'nê** m, **ne'ném** m baby.

**nenhum(a)** [ne'nu/'numa] *adj* no, not any // *pron* (*nem um só*) none, not one; (*de dois*) neither.

**ne'núfar** *m* water lily.

**neologismo** [neolo'ʒiʒmu] *m* neologism.

**neozelan'dês/esa** *adj* New Zealand *cmp* // *m/f* New Zealander.

**'nervo** *m* (ANAT) nerve; (*fig*) energy, strength; **~sidade** *f* nervousness; (*energia nervosa*) nervous energy; **~sismo** *m* (*nervosidade*) nervousness; (*irritabilidade*) irritability.

**nervoso/a** *adj* nervous; (*irritável*) irritable; (*excitável*) excitable; **nervudo/a** (Pt) *adj* (*robusto*) robust.

**néscio/a** ['nɛsju/a] *adj* (*ignorante*) ignorant; (*insensato*) foolish.

**'nessa = em + essa**.

**'nesse = em + esse**.

**'neto/a** *m* grandson; **~s** *mpl* grandchildren // *f* granddaughter.

**neuralgia** [newraw'ʒia] *f* neuralgia; **neurose** *f* neurosis; **neurótico/a** *adj*, *m/f* neurotic.

**neutrali'dade** *f* neutrality; **neutralizar** *vt* to neutralize; (*anular*) to counteract; **neutro/a** *adj* neuter.

**nêutron** ['newtrõ] *m* neutron.

**ne'vada** *f* snowfall; **nevar** *vi* to snow; **nevasca** *f* snowstorm; **neve** *f* snow.

**'névoa** *f* fog, mist; **nevoeiro** *m* thick fog.

**nexo** ['nɛksu] *m* connection, link; **sem ~** disconnected, incoherent.

**Nica'rágua** *f* Nicaragua; **nicaragüense** *adj*, *m/f* Nicaraguan.

**nicho** ['niʃu] *m* niche.

**'nimbo** *m* (GEO) halo; (*nuvem*) rain cloud.

**'nímio/a** *adj* excessive.

**ni'nar** *vt* to sing to sleep.

**ninguém** [nĩ'gẽĩ] *pron* nobody, no-one; **não vi ~** I saw no-one, I didn't see anybody; **~ mais** nobody else.

**ninhada** [nĩ'ɲada] *f* brood.

**ninharia** [nĩɲa'ria] *f* (*bagatela*) trifle.

**ninho** ['niɲu] *m* (*de aves*) nest; (*toca*) lair; (*lar*) home.

**níquel** ['nikɛw] *m* nickel; **niquelar** *vt* (TEC) to nickel-plate.

**'nisso, 'nisto = em + isso, isto**.

**niti'dez** *f* (*clareza*) clarity; (*brilho*) brightness; (*imagem*) sharp. **nítido/a** *adj* bright; (*limpo*) clear.

**ni'trato** *m* nitrate.

**nitrogênio** [nitro'ʒenju] *m* nitrogen.

**'nível** *m* level; **~ de vida** standard of living; **~ do mar** sea level; **ao ~ de** level with; **nivelar** *vt* (*terreno etc*) to level; (*arrasar*) to flatten; **nivelar-se com** to be equal to.

**no = em + o**.

**nó** *m* knot; (*de uma questão*) crux; **~ corredio** slipknot; **~ na garganta** lump in the throat; **~s dos dedos** knuckles.

**'nobre** *adj*, *m* noble; **nobreza** *f* nobility.

**noção** [no'sãw] *f* notion; **~ vaga** inkling.

**nocivo/a** [no'sivu/a] *adj* harmful.

**noc'tâmbulo** *m* (*sonâmbulo*) sleepwalker.

**'nódoa** *f* spot; (*mancha*) stain.

**nogueira** [no'gejra] *f* (*árvore*) walnut tree; (*madeira*) walnut.

**noitada** [noj'tada] *f* (*noite inteira*) whole night; (*noite de divertimento*) a night out; **noite** *f* night; **à/de noite** at night.

**noivado** [noj'vadu] *m* (*compromisso de casamento*) engagement; **noivo/a** *m* (*prometido*) fiancé; (*recém-casado*) bridegroom; **noivos** *mpl* (*prometidos*) engaged couple; (*recém-casados*) newlyweds // *f* (*prometida*) fiancée; (*recém-casada*) bride.

**nojento/a** [no'ʒetu/a] *adj* nauseating, disgusting; **nojo** *m* (*náusea*) nausea; (*repulsão*) loathing; (*luto*) mourning.

**'no-la** = nos + a; **no-lo** = nos + o; **no-las** = nos + as; **no-los** = nos + os.

**'nome** *m* name; (*fama*) fame; (LING) noun; ~ **de batismo** Christian name; **em** ~ **de** in the name of; **nomeação** *f* nomination; (*para um cargo*) appointment; **nomeada** *f* fame; **nomeadamente** *adv* namely; **nomear** *vt* to nominate; (*conferir um cargo*) to appoint; (*dar nome a*) to name; **nomenclatura** *f* nomenclature.

**'nono/a** *adj* ninth.

**'nora** *f* daughter-in-law; (*Pt: de tirar água*) waterwheel.

**nor'deste** *m* northeast; **o** N~ Northeast; **nordestino/a** *adj* northeastern // *m/f* Northeasterner.

**'nórdico/a** *adj* Nordic.

**'norma** *f* standard, norm; (*regra*) rule; **como** ~ as a rule.

**normal** [nox'maw] *adj* normal; (*natural*) natural, usual; **nomeada** *f* normality; ~**izar-se** *vr* to return to normal.

**noro'este** *adj* northwest, northwestern // *m* northwest.

**'norte** *adj* northern, north // *m* north; (*fig:* direção) bearing, direction.

**norte-ameri'cano/a** *adj, m/f* (North) American.

**Noruega** [nor'wega] *f* Norway; **norueguês/esa** *adj, m/f* Norwegian.

**nos** [nuʃ] *pron* (*direto*) us; (*indireto*) us, to us, for us; (*reflexivo*) ourselves; (*recíproco*) to each other // = **em** + **os**.

**nós** [nɔʃ] *pron* we; ~ **mesmos** ourselves; **para** ~ for us.

**'nosso/a** *adj our* // *pron* ours; **um amigo** ~ a friend of ours.

**nostalgia** [noʃtal'ʒia] *f* nostalgia; (*saudades da pátria etc*) homesickness.

**'nota** *f* note; (*escolar*) mark; (*conta*) bill; (*cédula*) banknote; **digno de** ~ noteworthy; ~**bilidade** *f* notability; (*pessoa*) notable; ~**ção** *f* notation.

**no'tar** *vt* (*reparar em*) to notice, note; **é de** ~ **que** it is to be noted that; **fazer** ~ to call attention to; ~**-se** *vr* to be obvious.

**no'tário** *m* notary.

**no'tável** *adj* notable, remarkable.

**notícia** [no'tʃisja] *f* (*informação*) piece of news; ~**s** *fpl* news *sg*; **pedir** ~**s de** to inquire about; **ter** ~**s de** to hear from; **noticiar** *vt* to announce, report; **noticiário** *m* (*de jornal*) news section; (*cinema*) newsreel; (*rádio etc*) news bulletin.

**notificação** [notʃifika'sãw] *f* notification; **notificar** *vt* to notify, inform.

**notorie'dade** *f* renown, fame; **notório/a** *adj* well-known, evident.

**no'turno/a** (*Pt: -ct-*) *adj* nocturnal, nightly // *m* (*trem*) night train.

**'nova** *f* piece of news; ~**s** *fpl* news *sg*.

**nova'mente** *adv* again.

**no'vato/a** *adj* inexperienced, raw // *m/f* (*principiante*) beginner, novice; (EDUC) fresher.

**'nove** *num* nine; ~**centos/as** *num* nine hundred.

**no'vela** *f* short novel, novella; (*rádio, televisão*) soap-opera.

**no'velo** *m* (*bola de fio*) ball of thread.

**no'vembro** *m* November.

**no'venta** *num* ninety.

**noviciado** [novis'jadu] *m* (REL) novitiate; **noviço** *m* (REL) novice.

**novi'dade** *f* novelty; (*notícia*) piece of news; **sem** ~ without incident; ~**s** *fpl* news *sg*.

**novilho/a** [no'viʎu/a] *m* young bull // *f* heifer.

**'novo/a** *adj* new; (*jovem*) young; (*adicional*) further; **de** ~ again // *f* ver **nova**.

**noz** f walnut, nut; ~ **moscada** nutmeg.

**nu'nua** adj naked, bare; ~ **em pelo** stark naked // m/f nude.

**nu'blado/a** adj cloudy, overcast; **nublar** vt to darken; **nublar-se** vr to cloud over.

**'nuca** f nape (of the neck).

**nucle'ar** adj nuclear; **núcleo** m nucleus sg; (centro) centre.

**nu'dez** f nakedness, nudity; **nudismo** m nudism.

**nuli'dade** f nullity, invalidity; (pessoa) nonentity; **nulo/a** adj null, void; (inepto) inept.

**numeração** [numera'sãw] f numbering, numbers pl; **numeral** m numeral; **numerar** vt to number; (contar) to enumerate, count.

**nume'rário** m cash, money.

**nu'mérico/a** adj numerical; **número** m number; (de jornal) issue; **sem número** countless; **numeroso/a** adj numerous.

**'nunca** adv never; ~ **mais** never again; **como** ~ as never before; **quase** ~ hardly ever.

**núpcias** ['nupsiaʃ] fpl nuptials, wedding sg.

**nutrição** [nutri'sãw] f nutrition; **nutrido/a** adj (bem alimentado) well-nourished; (robusto) robust; **nutrimento** m nourishment; **nutrir** vt to nourish, feed; (proteger) to nurture; (alentar) to encourage; **nutritivo/a** adj nourishing.

**nuvem** ['nuvẽj] f cloud; (insetos) swarm; **pôr nas nuvens** to praise to the skies; **cair das nuvens** (espantar-se) to be astounded.

# O

**o** art ver **a.**

**oásis** [o'asiʃ] m oasis.

**obcecação** [obseka'sãw] f

obfuscation; (obstinação) obstinacy; **obcecar** vt to blind.

**obedecer** [obede'sex] vi: ~ **a** to obey; **obediência** f obedience; **obediente** adj obedient.

**obesidade** f obesity; **obeso/a** adj obese.

**óbice** ['ɔbisi] m obstacle.

**'óbito** m demise, death.

**objeção** [obʒe'sãw] (Pt: **-cç-**) f objection; **pôr objeções a** to object to; **objetar** (Pt: **-ct-**) vt to object.

**obje'tivo/a** (Pt: **-ct-**) adj objective // m objective, aim; **sem** ~ aimlessly.

**ob'jeto** (Pt: **-ct-**) m (coisa) object; (causa) motive; (propósito) aim.

**oblíquo/a** [o'blikwu/a] adj oblique, slanting; (olhar) sidelong.

**obo'é** m oboe.

**'obra** f (ger) work; (ARQ) building, construction; (teatro) play; ~ **prima** masterpiece; **em** ~**s** under repair; **O**~**s Públicas** Public Works; **obrar** vt to work; (produzir) to produce; (causar) to cause, bring about // vi to act, work; **obreiro/a** adj working // m/f worker.

**obrigação** [obriga'sãw] f obligation, duty; (COM) bond; **obrigado/a** adj (compelido) obliged, compelled; (agradecido) grateful // excl: **obrigado!** thanks!; **obrigar** vt to oblige, compel; **obrigar-se** vr: **obrigar-se a fazer algo** to undertake to do sth; **obrigatório/a** adj compulsory, obligatory.

**obsceni'dade** f obscenity; **obsceno/a** adj obscene.

**obscure'cer** vt to obscure; ~**-se** vr to get dark; **obscuridade** f obscurity; (falta de luz) darkness; **obscuro/a** adj dark; (fig) obscure.

**obse'dar** vt, **obsedi'ar** vt to obsess.

**obsequiar** [obseki'ax] vt (presentear) to give presents to; (tratar com agrados) to treat kindly; **obséquio** m favour, kindness;

**obsequioso/a** *adj* obliging, courteous.

**observação** [obsεxva'sãw] *f* observation; (*comentário*) remark, comment; **observador(a)** *adj* observant // *m/f* observer; **observância** *f* observance; **observar** *vt* to observe; (*notar*) to notice; **observatório** *m* observatory.

**obsessão** [obsε'sãw] *f* obsession.

**obso'leto/a** *adj* obsolete.

**obs'táculo** *m* obstacle; (*dificuldade*) hindrance, drawback.

**obs'tante:** **não** ~ *conj* nevertheless, however // *prep* in spite of, notwithstanding.

**obs'tar** *vi*: ~ **a** to hinder, obstruct; (*opor-se*) to oppose.

**obs'tetra** *m/f* obstetrician; **obstetrícia** *f* obstetrics *sg*; **obstétrico/a** *adj* obstetric.

**obstinação** [obʃtʃina'sãw] *f* obstinacy; **obstinado/a** *adj* obstinate, stubborn; **obstinar-se** *vr* to be obstinate; **obstinar-se em** (*porfiar em*) to persist in.

**obstrução** [obʃtru'sãw] *f* obstruction; **obstruir** *vt* to obstruct; (*impedir*) to impede.

**obtenção** [obtẽ'sãw] *f* acquisition; (*consecução*) attainment; **obter** *vt* to obtain, get; (*ganhar*) to gain.

**obturação** [obtura'sãw] *f* (*dum dente*) filling; **obturador** *m* (*FOTO*) shutter; **obturar** *vt* to stop up, plug; (*dente*) to fill.

**ob'tuso/a** *adj* (*ger*) obtuse; (*pessoa*) thick, slow, dull.

**'óbvio/a** *adj* obvious.

**ocasião** [okazi'ãw] *f* (*oportunidade*) opportunity, chance; (*momento*) occasion, time; (*causa*) cause; **ocasionar** *vt* to cause, bring about.

**o'caso** *m* (*do sol*) sunset; (*ocidente*) the west; (*decadência*) decline.

**oceano** [ose'anu] *m* ocean.

**ocidental** [osidẽ'taw] *adj* western; **ocidente** *m* west.

**ócio** ['osju] *m* (*folga*) leisure, rest;

(*preguiça*) idleness; **ociosidade** *f* idleness; **ocioso/a** *adj* idle.

**'oco/a** *adj* hollow, empty; (*fútil*) vain, futile // *m* hollow.

**ocorrência** [oko'xẽsja] *f* incident, event; (*circunstância*) circumstance; **ocorrer** *vi* to happen, occur; (*vir ao pensamento*) to come to mind.

**ocu'lar** *adj* ocular; **oculista** *m/f* optician; **óculo** *m* spyglass; **óculos** *mpl* glasses, spectacles; **óculos de proteção** goggles.

**ocul'tar** *vt* to hide, conceal; **oculto/a** *adj* (*escondido*) hidden; (*desconhecido*) unknown; (*secreto*) secret.

**ocupação** [okupa'sãw] *f* occupation; **ocupado/a** *adj* (*pessoa*) busy; (*lugar*) occupied; (*telefone*) engaged; **ocupar** *vt* to occupy; **ocupar-se** *vr*: **ocupar-se de/com/em** to concern o.s. with; (*cuidar*) to look after.

**odi'ar** *vt* to hate; **ódio** *m* hate, hatred; **odioso/a** *adj* hateful; (*mau*) nasty.

**o'dor** *m* smell; ~**ífero/a** *adj* fragrant.

**'odre** *m* wineskin.

**'oeste** *m* west.

**ofe'gante** *adj* breathless, panting; **ofegar** *vi* to pant, puff.

**ofen'der** *vt* to offend; (*ferir*) to hurt, injure; ~**-se** *vr* to take offence; **ofensa** *f* (*injúria*) insult, abuse; (*lesão*) injury; **ofensivo/a** *adj* offensive; (*agressivo*) aggressive // *f* (*MIL*) offensive.

**ofere'cer** [ofere'seʃ] *vt* to offer, present; (*propor*) to propose; ~**-se** *vr* (*ocorrer*) to occur; (*pessoa*) to offer o.s., volunteer; **oferecimento** *m* offer; **oferta** *f* (*oferecimento*) offer; (*dádiva*) gift; **a oferta e a demanda** (*COM*) supply and demand.

**oficial** [ofis'jaw] *adj* official // *m* official; (*MIL*) officer.

**ofi'cina** *f* workshop; ~ **mecânica** garage.

**ofício** [o'fisju] m (profissão)
profession, trade; (REL) service;
(carta) official letter; **bons ~s** good
offices; **oficioso/a** adj (de fontes
oficiais) unofficial.

**of'tálmico/a** adj ophthalmic.

**ofus'car** vt (obscurecer) to darken;
(deslumbrar) to dazzle.

**oitava/a** [ɔj'tavu/a] adj eighth // m
eighth; **oitenta** num eighty; **oito** num
eight; **oitocentos/as** num eight
hundred.

**o'lá** excl hello!

**ola'ria** f pottery.

**ole'ado** m oil cloth.

**oleiro** [o'lejru] m potter; (de tijolos)
brickmaker.

**'óleo** m (lubricante) oil; ~
**combustível** fuel oil; ~ **de rícino**
castor oil; **pintura a** ~ oil painting;
**oleoso/a** adj oily; (gorduroso)
greasy.

**ol'fato** m sense of smell.

**olhada** [o'ʎada] f glance, look; **olhar**
vt to look at; (observar) to watch;
(ponderar) to consider; (cuidar de)
to look after; **olhar fixamente** to
stare at // vi to look; **olhar para** to
look at; **olhar por** to look after;
**olhar-se** vr (pessoas) to look at one
another // m look, glance; **olhar
fixo** stare.

**olheiras** [o'ʎejras] fpl dark rings
under the eyes.

**olho** ['oʎu] m eye; (vista) eyesight; **a**
~**s vistos** before one's very eyes; ~
**por** ~ an eye for an eye; **num abrir
e fechar de** ~**s** in a flash; **não
pregar** ~ not to sleep a wink; **ver
com bons** ~**s** to approve of.

**oligarquia** [oligar'kia] f oligarchy.

**olim'píada** f: **as O~s** the
Olympics.

**oli'val** m, **oli'vedo** m olive grove;
**oliveira** f olive tree.

**ol'meiro** m, **'olmo** m elm.

**o'lor** m fragrance; ~**oso/a** adj
fragrant.

**olvi'dar** vt to forget.

**om'breira** f (de porta) doorpost;
(de roupa) shoulder pad.

**'ombro** m shoulder; **encolher os**
~**s/dar de** ~ to shrug one's
shoulders.

**ome'leta** (Pt) f, **ome'lete** f
omelette; (US) omelet.

**omissão** [omi'sãw] f (falta)
omission; (descuido) neglect;
**omisso/a** adj (negligente)
neglectful; **omitir** vt to omit.

**omo'plata** f shoulder blade.

**onça** ['ɔsa] f (peso) ounce; (animal)
jaguar; ~**parda** f puma.

**'onda** f wave; ~ **sonora/luminosa**
sound/light wave; ~ **curta/
média/longa** short/medium/long
wave; ~ **de calor** heat wave; **ir na**
~ to be taken in.

**'onde** adv where // conj where, in
which; **por** ~ through which; **por**
~? which way?; ~ **quer que**
wherever.

**onde'ado/a** adj wavy // m
(cabelo) wave; **ondeante** adj
waving, undulating; **ondear** vt to
wave // vi to wave; (água) to ripple;
(serpear) to meander, wind;
**ondulação** f undulation; **ondulado/a**
adj wavy; **ondulante** adj waving,
undulating.

**one'rar** vt to burden, weigh down;
**oneroso/a** adj onerous.

**'ônibus** (Br) m bus.

**onipo'tência** (Pt: **omn-**) f
omnipotence; **onipotente** (Pt: **omn-**)
adj omnipotent.

**o'nívoro/a** (Pt: **omn-**) adj
omnivorous.

**'ônix** m onyx.

**ontem** ['õtẽ] adv yesterday; ~ **à
noite** last night; ~ **à tarde**
yesterday afternoon.

**'ONU** f abr de **Organização das
Nações Unidas** UNO, United
Nations Organization.

**'onze** num eleven.

**o'paco/a** adj opaque; (obscuro)
dark.

**o'pala** f opal; (tecido) fine muslin.

**opção** [op'sãw] f option, choice; (preferência) first claim, right.

**'ópera** f opera; ~ **bufa** comic opera.

**operação** [opera'sãw] f operation; (COM) transaction; **operador(a)** m/f operator; (cirurgião) surgeon; (num cinema) projectionist; (dum filme) camera operator; **operar** vt (produzir) to produce, bring about; (MED) to operate on // vi (agir) to act, function; **operar-se** vr (suceder) to take place; (MED) to have an operation.

**ope'rário/a** adj working; classe ~a working class // m/f worker.

**opi'nar** vt (julgar) to think // vi (dar o seu parecer) to express an opinion; **opinião** f opinion.

**'ópio** m opium.

**o'píparo/a** adj (lit) splendid, lavish.

**opo'nente** adj opposing // m/f opponent; **opor** vt to oppose; (resistência) to put up, offer; **opor-se** vr (fazer objeção) to object; (resistir) to resist.

**oportuni'dade** f opportunity; **oportunismo** m opportunism; **oportunista** m/f opportunist; **oportuno/a** adj (momento) opportune, right; (conveniente) convenient, suitable.

**oposição** [pozi'sãw] f opposition; **em** ~ **a** against; **oposto/a** adj (contrário) opposite; (em frente) facing, opposite; (antagônico) opposed, contrary.

**opressão** [opre'sãw] f oppression; **opressivo/a** adj oppressive; **opressor(a)** m/f oppressor; **oprimir** vt to oppress.

**o'próbrio** m (infâmia) ignominy; (lit: desonra) shame.

**op'tar** vi (escolher) to choose; ~ **por** to opt for.

**opu'lência** f opulence; **opulento/a** adj opulent.

**o'púsculo** m pamphlet, booklet.

**'ora** adv now; **de** ~ **em diante** from now on; **por** ~ for the time being // conj now; (pois bem) well; ~ **sim**, ~ **não** first yes, then no // excl well now!; ~ **essa!** the very idea!, come off it!; ~ **bem** now then; ~ **viva!** hello there!

**oração** [ora'sãw] f (reza) prayer; (discurso) speech; (LING) sentence.

**o'ráculo** m oracle.

**ora'dor(a)** m/f (aquele que fala) speaker; (pregador) preacher.

**o'ral** adj oral.

**orango'tango** m orang-utan.

**o'rar** vi (REL) to pray.

**'orbe** m orb, sphere; **órbita** f orbit.

**orçamento** [oxsa'mẽtu] m (finanças) budget; (avaliação) estimate.

**ordeiro/a** [ox'dejru/a] adj peaceable, law-abiding.

**ordem** ['oxdẽ] f (ger) order; (mandado) command; ~ **do dia** agenda; **de primeira** ~ first-rate; **por** ~ in order, in turn; **até nova** ~ until further notice; **pôr em** ~ to arrange, tidy; **às suas ordens** at your service.

**ordenação** [oxdena'sãw] f (REL) ordination; (lei) decree.

**orde'nado/a** adj (posto em ordem) in order; (metódico) orderly // m salary, wages pl.

**orde'nança** m (MIL) orderly // f (regulamento) ordinance.

**orde'nar** vt to arrange, put in order; ~**-se** vr (REL) to be ordained.

**orde'nhar** [oxde'ɲax] vt to milk.

**ordi'nário/a** adj ordinary; (comum) usual; (medíocre) mediocre; (mal-educado) coarse, vulgar; **de** ~ usually.

**orelha** [o'reʎa] f (ANAT) ear; (aba) flap; **orelhão** m open telephone kiosk.

**orfa'nato** m orphanage; **órfão/órfã** m/f orphan.

**or'gânico/a** adj organic;

**organismo** m organism; (entidade) organization.

**orga'nista** m/f organist.

**organização** [oxganiza'sãw] f organization; **organizar** vt to organize.

**órgão** ['oxgãw] m organ.

**or'gasmo** m orgasm.

**orgia** [ox'ʒia] f orgy.

**orgulhar-se** [oxgu'ʎax-si] vr: ~ de to be proud of; **orgulho** m pride; (arrogância) arrogance; **orgulhoso/a** adj proud; (soberbo) haughty.

**orientação** [orĩẽta'sãw] f (direção) direction; (posição) position; (tendência) tendency; (EDUC) training, guidance.

**orien'tal** adj eastern.

**orien'tar** vt (situar) to orientate; (dirigir) to direct; (informar) to guide; ~**-se** vr to get one's bearings.

**ori'ente** m: O~ the East; **Extremo** O~ Far East; O~ **Médio/Próximo** Middle/Near East.

**orifício** [ori'fisju] m hole, opening.

**origem** [o'riʒẽ] f (procedência) origin; (ascendência) lineage, descent; **lugar de** ~ birthplace; **original** adj (novo) original; (estranho) strange, odd; **originalidade** f originality; **originar** vt to originate, start; **originar-se** vr to arise; **originário/a** adj (proveniente) native.

**ori'undo/a** adj (procedente) arising from; (natural) native of.

**'orla** f (borda) edge, border; (de roupa) hem; (faixa) strip; ~ **marítima** seafront.

**ornamen'tar** vt to decorate, adorn; **ornamento** m adornment, decoration; **ornar** vt to adorn, decorate; **ornato** m (adorno) ornament; (ornamento) decoration.

**ornitologia** [oxnitolo'ʒia] f ornithology; **ornitologista** m/f ornithologist.

**orquestra** [ox'kɛʃtra] f orchestra;

~ **de câmara/sinfônica** chamber/symphony orchestra.

**orquídea** [ox'kidea] f orchid.

**ortodo'xia** f orthodoxy; **ortodoxo/a** adj orthodox.

**ortogra'fia** f spelling.

**ortope'dia** f orthopaedics sg.

**orvalhar** [ox'va/ax] vt to sprinkle with dew; **orvalho** m dew.

**os** art ver **a**.

**oscilação** [osila'sãw] f (movimento) oscillation; (flutuação) fluctuation; (vacilação) hesitation; **oscilar** vi (balançar-se) to sway, swing; (hesitar) to hesitate.

**'osso** m bone; (dificuldade) predicament; **um** ~ **duro de roer** a hard nut to crack; **ossudo/a** adj bony.

**osten'sivo/a** adj ostensible, apparent.

**ostentação** [oʃtẽta'sãw] f ostentation; (exibição) display, show; **ostentar** vt to show; (alardear) to show off, flaunt; **ostentoso/a** adj ostentatious, showy.

**'ostra** f oyster.

**ostra'cismo** m ostracism.

**'OTAN** f abr de **Organização do Tratado do Atlântico Norte** NATO, North Atlantic Treaty Organization.

**'ótico/a** (Pt: **-pt-**) adj optical // m/f optician // f optics sg.

**'ótimo/a** (Pt: **-pt-**) adj excellent, splendid // excl great!, super!

**ou** [o] conj or; ~ **este** ~ **aquele** either this one or that one; ~ **seja** in other words.

**'ouço** etc vb ver **ouvir**.

**ourela** [o'rela] f edge, border.

**ouriço** [o'risu] m (europeu) hedgehog; (do Brasil) coendou; (casca) shell; (col: animação) riot; ~ **do mar** sea urchin.

**ourives** [o'rivef] m inv (fabricante) goldsmith; (vendedor) jeweller; ~**aria** f (arte) goldsmith's art; (loja) jeweller's (shop); **ouro** m gold;

(*cartas*) diamonds; **de ouro** golden; **ouropel** *m* tinsel.

**ousa'dia** *f* daring; **ousar** *vt/i* to dare.

**outeiro** [o'tejru] *m* hill.

**ou'tono** *m* autumn.

**ou'trora** *adv* formerly.

**ou'torga** *f* granting, concession; **outorgar** *vt* (*dar*) to grant; (*conceder*) to concede.

**outrem** [o'trẽ] *pron inv* (*sg*) somebody else; (*pl*) other people.

**outro/a** ['otru/a] *adj* (*sg*) another; (*pl*) other / *pron* another (one); **~s** others; **~a coisa** something else; **qualquer** any other; **de ~ modo/de ~a maneira** otherwise; **~ tanto** the same again.

**ou'trora** *adv* formerly; (*antigamente*) a long time ago.

**outrossim** [otro'sĩ] *adv* likewise, moreover.

**ou'tubro** *m* October.

**ouvido** [o'vidu] *m* (ANAT) ear; (*sentido*) hearing; **de ~ by ear; dar ~s a** to listen to; **ouvinte** *m/f* listener; **ouvir** *vt* to hear; (*escutar*) to listen to; (*missa*) to attend; **ouvir dizer que ...** to hear that ...; **ouvir falar de** to hear of.

**ovação** [ova'sãw] *f* ovation, acclaim.

**o'val** *f* oval; **ovalado/a** *adj* oval.

**o'vário** *m* ovary.

**ovelha** [o've/ʎa] *f* sheep.

**'ovo** *m* egg; **~s cozidos duros** hard-boiled eggs; **~s escalfados** (*Pt/*) **poché** (*Br*) poached eggs; **~s estrelados/fritos** fried eggs; **~s mexidos** scrambled eggs; **~s quentes** soft-boiled eggs; **ovulação** *f* ovulation; **óvulo** *m* ovum.

**oxalá** [oʃa'la] *excl* if only it were so!, some hope! / *conj* let's hope; **if only ...!; ~ ele venha hoje!** let's hope he comes today!

**oxidação** [oksida'sãw] *f* oxidation; (*ferrugem*) rusting; **óxido** *m* oxide; **óxido de carbônio** carbon monoxide; **oxigenar** *vt* to

oxygenate; (*cabelo*) to bleach; **oxigênio** *m* oxygen.

**o'zônio** *m* ozone.

# P

**pá** *f* shovel; (*de remo, hélice*) blade; **~ de lixo** dustpan; **~ mecânica** bulldozer / *m* (*Pt*) pal, mate.

**pa'cato/a** *adj* (*pessoa*) peace-loving; (*lugar*) peaceful.

**pachorren'to/a** [paʃo'xẽtu/a] *adj* slow, sluggish.

**paciência** [pas'jẽsja] *f* patience; (*perseverança*) endurance; (*cartas*) patience; **ter ~** to be patient; **~!** we'll just have to put up with it; **paciente** *adj* patient; (*resignado*) resigned // *m/f* patient.

**pacificação** [pasifika'sãw] *f* pacification; **pacificar** *vt* to pacify, calm (down); **pacificar-se** *vr* to calm down; **pacífico/a** *adj* (*pessoa*) peace-loving; (*sossegado*) peaceful; **Oceano Pacífico** Pacific Ocean; **pacifismo** *m* pacifism; **pacifista** *m/f* pacifist.

**'paço** *m* palace; (*fig*) court.

**pa'cote** *m* packet; (*embrulho*) parcel.

**'pacto** *m* pact; (*ajuste*) agreement; **pactuar** *vt* to agree on // *vi* to make a pact *ou* an agreement.

**pada'ria** *f* bakery, baker's (shop).

**padecer** [pade'sex] *vt* to suffer; (*suportar*) to put up with, endure; **padecimento** *m* suffering; (*dor*) pain.

**padeiro** [pa'dejru] *m* baker; (*entregador de pão*) breadman.

**padrão** [pa'drãw] *m* (*oficial*) standard; (*medida*) gauge; (*modelo*) pattern; (*modelo*) model; **~ da vida** standard of living.

**pa'drasto** *m* stepfather; **padre** *m* priest; **O Santo Padre** the Holy

Father; **padrinho•** *m* (REL) god-father; (*de noivo*) best man; (*de duelo*) second; (*fig*) sponsor.

**padroeiro/a** [padro'ejru/a] *m* patron; (*santo*) patron saint // *f* patroness; (*santa*) patron saint.

**padronização** [padroniza'sãw] *f* standardization; **padronizar** *vt* to standardize.

**'paga** *f* payment; (*soldo*) pay; **em ~ de** in return for; **~dor(a)** *adj* paying // *m/f* (*quem paga*) payer; (*de soldada*) pay clerk; (*de banco*) teller; **~mento** *m* payment.

**pagão/pagã** [pa'gãw/pa'gã] *adj, m/f* pagan.

**pa'gar** *vt* to pay; (*compras, pecados*) to pay for; (*o que devia*) to pay back; (*recompensar*) to reward; **~ a prestações** to pay by hire purchase ou in instalments; **~ à vista** (*Br*)/**a pronto** (*Pt*) to pay on the spot, pay at the time of purchase; **~ dinheiro** (*Br*)/**de contado** (*Pt*) to pay cash; **a ~** unpaid.

**página** ['pa‚ʒina] *f* (*folha*) page.

**'pago/a** *pp de* **pagar** // *adj* paid; (*fig*) even // *m* pay.

**pa'gode** *m* pagoda; (*fig*) fun, high jinks *pl*.

**pai** [paj] *m* father; **~s** *mpl* parents.

**painel** [paj'nɛw] *m* (*numa parede*) panel; (*quadro*) picture; (*AUTO*) dashboard; (*de avião*) instrument panel.

**paio** ['paju] *m* pork sausage.

**paiol** [pa'jɔw] *m* storeroom; (*celeiro*) barn; (*de pólvora*) powder magazine; **~ de carvão** coal bunker.

**pairar** [paj'rax] *vi* to hover; (*embarcação*) to lie to.

**país** [pa'iʃ] *m* country; (*região*) land; **~ encantado** fairyland; **~ natal** native land; **paisagem** *f* scenery; (*o campo*) countryside; (*pintura*) landscape; **paisano/a** *adj* civilian // *m/f* (*não militar*) civilian;

(*compatriota*) fellow countryman; **paisana** (*soldado*) in civvies; (*policial*) in plain clothes.

**paixão** [paj'ʃãw] *f* passion; **paixoneta** *f* crush.

**pajem** ['pa‚ʒẽ] *m* (*moço*) page.

**'pala** *f* (*de boné*) peak; (*em automóvel*) sun visor; (*de vestido*) yoke.

**palácio** [pa'lasju] *m* palace; **~ da justiça** courthouse.

**pala'dar** *m* taste.

**pala'dino** *m* (*medieval, fig*) champion.

**palanque** [pa'lãki] *m* (*estrado*) stand.

**pa'lavra** *f* word; (*fala*) speech; (*promessa*) promise; (*direito de falar*) right to speak; **~!** honestly!; **~s cruzadas** crossword (puzzle); **cortar a ~ a alguém** to cut sb short; **dirigir a ~ a** to address; **em poucas ~s** briefly; **pedir a ~** to ask permission to speak; **palavrão** *m* (*obsceno*) swearword; **palavreado** *m* babble, gibberish; (*loquacidade*) smooth talk.

**'palco** *m* (*teatro*) stage.

**pa'lerma** *adj* silly, stupid; (*col*) daft // *m/f* fool.

**pales'tino/a** *adj, m/f* Palestinian // *f*: **P~a** Palestine.

**pa'lestra** *f* (*conversa*) chat, talk; (*conferência*) talk.

**pa'leta** *f* palette.

**pale'tó** *m* coat, jacket.

**palha** ['paʎa] *f* straw; (*fig*) trifle; **por dá cá aquela ~** (*Pt*) for no obvious reason.

**palhaço** [pa'ʎasu] *m* clown.

**palheiro** [pa'ʎejru] *m* hayloft; (*monte de feno*) haystack; **palhoça** *f* thatched hut.

**pali'ar** *vt* (*disfarçar*) to disguise, gloss over; (*atenuar*) to mitigate, extenuate; **paliativo/a** *adj* palliative.

**pali'çada** *f* fence; (*militar*) stockade; (*para torneio*) enclosure;

**pali'dez** *f* paleness; **pálido/a** *adj* pale.

**'pálio** *m* canopy.

**pali'tar** *vt* to pick // *vi* to pick one's teeth.

**pa'lito** *m* stick; (*para os dentes*) toothpick.

**'palma** *f* (*folha*) palm leaf; (*da mão*) palm; **bater ~s** to clap; **palmada** *f* slap; **palmeira** *f* palm tree; **palmo** *m* (hand) span; **palmo a palmo** inch by inch.

**pal'pável** *adj* tangible; (*fig*) obvious.

**'pálpebra** *f* eyelid.

**palpitação** [pawpita'sãw] *f* beating, throbbing; **palpitacões** *fpl* palpitations; **palpitante** *adj* beating, throbbing; (*fig: emocionante*) thrilling; (*: de interesse atual*) sensational; **palpitar** *vi* (*coração*) to beat; (*comover-se*) to shiver; **palpite** *m* (*intuição*) hunch; (*turfe*) tip.

**pal'rar** *vi* to chatter, prattle.

**pa'lude** *m* marsh, swamp; **paludismo** *m* malaria; **palustre** *adj* (*terra*) marshy; (*aves*) marsh-dwelling.

**Pana'má** *m* Panama; **panamenho/a** *adj* Panamanian.

**'pança** *f* belly, paunch.

**pan'cada** *f* (*no corpo*) blow, hit; (*choque*) knock; (*relógio*) stroke; **~ d'água** downpour; **dar uma ~ com a cabeça** to bang one's head; **dar ~ em alguém** to hit sb; **levar uma ~** to get hit.

**pan'cudo/a** *adj* fat, potbellied.

**'pândega** *f* merrymaking, good time.

**pan'deiro** *m* tambourine.

**pa'nela** *f* (*de barro*) pot; (*de metal*) pan; **~ de pressão** pressure cooker.

**pan'fleto** *m* pamphlet.

**'pânico/a** *adj* panic; **em ~** panic-stricken.

**panificação** [panifika'sãw] *f* (*fabricação*) bread-making;

(*padaria*) bakery; **panificadora** *f* baker's.

**'pano** *m* cloth; (*teatro*) curtain; (*largura de tecido*) width; (*de parede*) panel; (*mancha no corpo*) blemish; **~ de cozinha** dishcloth; **~ de pratos** teacloth; **~ de pó** duster.

**pano'rama** *m* (*vista*) view; (*fig: observação*) survey.

**panqueca** [pã'kɛka] *f* pancake.

**panta'nal** [-aw] *m* swampland; **pântano** *m* marsh, swamp; **pantanoso/a** *adj* marshy, swampy.

**pan'tera** *f* panther.

**panto'mima** *f* pantomime.

**pão** [pãw] *m*, *pl* **pães** [pãjʃ] bread; **um ~** a loaf; **~ de carne** meat loaf; **~ de forma** sliced loaf; **~ caseiro** home-made bread; **~ torrado** toast; **ganhar o ~** to earn a living; **~de-ló** *m* sponge cake; **~zinho** *m* roll.

**'papa** *m* Pope // *f* (*cozida*) mush, pap; **não ter ~s na língua** to be outspoken, not to mince one's words.

**papagaio** [papa'gaju] *m* parrot; (*de papel*) kite.

**papai** [pa'paj] *m* dad, daddy; **P~ Noel** Santa Claus, Father Christmas.

**pa'palvo** *m* simpleton.

**papa-'moscas** *f* *inv* (*BIO*) flycatcher.

**papari'car** *vt* to pamper; **paparicos** *mpl* (*mimos*) pampering *sg*.

**pa'pel** *m* paper; (*no teatro*) part, role; **fazer um ~** to play a part; **~ aéreo** airmail paper; **~ carbono/de embrulho** carbon paper/wrapping paper; **~ de escrever/de alumínio** writing paper/tinfoil; **~ higiênico** toilet paper; **~ de parede** wallpaper; **~ de seda/transparente** tissue paper/tracing paper; **~ usado** waste paper; **~ada** *f* pile of papers; (*burocracia*) red tape.

**papelão** [pape'lãw] *m* cardboard; (*fig*) fiasco; **papelaria** *f* stationer's (shop); **papelzinho** *m* scrap of paper.

**'papo** *m* (*de ave*) crop; **bater** ~ to chat, have a chat.

**papoula** [pa'pola] *f* poppy.

**paquete** [pa'ketʃi] *m* steamship.

**par** *adj* (*igual*) equal; (*número*) even // *m* pair; (*casal*) couple; (*pessoa na dança*) partner; (*nobre*) peer; **abrir de** ~ **em** ~ to open wide; **sem** ~ incomparable; **abaixo de** ~ (COM, GOLFE) below below par.

**'para** *prep* for; (*direção*) to, towards; **bom** ~ **comer** good to eat; ~ **não ser ouvido** so as not to be heard; ~ **quê?** what for?, why?; **ir** ~ **São Paulo** to go to São Paulo; **ir** ~ **casa** to go home; ~ **com** (*atitude*) towards; **de lá** ~ **cá** since then; ~ **a semana** next week; **estar** ~ to be about to // *conj*: ~ **que** so that, in order that.

**parabéns** [para'bẽʃ] *mpl* congratulations; (*aniversário*) happy birthday; **dar** ~ **a** to congratulate.

**pa'rábola** *f* parable; (MAT) parabola.

**pára-'brisa** *m* windscreen; (US) windshield.

**pára-choques** [para-'ʃɔkiʃ] *m inv* (AUTO: *exterior*) bumper; (: *interior*) shock absorber.

**pa'rada** *f* stop; (COM) stoppage; (*militar, colegial*) parade.

**paradeiro** [para'dejru] *m* whereabouts; (COM) slump.

**para'doxo** *m* paradox.

**para'fina** *f* paraffin.

**pa'ráfrase** *f* paraphrase.

**para'fusar** *vt* to screw in // *vi*: ~ (*meditar*) to ponder; **parafuso** *m* screw.

**paragem** [pa'raʒẽ] *f* stop; (Pt): ~ **de eléctrico** tram stop; **paragens** *fpl* (*lugares*) places, parts.

**pa'rágrafo** *m* paragraph.

**para'íso** *m* paradise.

**paralele'pípedo** *m* paving stone.

**para'lelo/a** *adj* parallel // *m* (GEO,

*comparação*) parallel // *f* parallel line; ~**as** *fpl* (*esporte*) parallel bars.

**para'lisar** *vt* to paralyse; (*trabalho*) to bring to a standstill; ~**se** *vr* to become paralysed; (*fig*) to come to a standstill; **paralisia** *f* paralysis; **paralítico/a** *adj, m/f* paralytic.

**para'mento** *m* (*adorno*) ornament; ~**s** *mpl* (*vestes*) vestments; (*de igreja*) hangings.

**paramili'tar** *adj* paramilitary.

**para'nóico/a** *adj, m/f* paranoid, paranoiac.

**parapeito** [para'pejtu] *m* (*muro*) wall, parapet; (*da janela*) windowsill.

**pára-quedas** [para-'kedaʃ] *m inv* parachute; **a pára-quedista** *m/f* parachutist // *m* (MIL) paratrooper.

**pa'rar** *vi* to stop; (*ficar*) to stay // *vt* to stop; **fazer** ~ (*deter*) to stop; ~ **na cadeia** to end up in jail; ~ **de fazer** to stop doing.

**pára-raios** [para-'xajoʃ] *m inv* lightning conductor.

**para'sita** *adj* parasitic // *m* parasite; **parasito** *m* parasite.

**parceiro/a** [pax'fejru/a] *m/f* partner.

**par'cela** *f* piece, bit; (*de terra*) plot.

**parce'ria** *f* partnership.

**parci'al** *adj* (*eclipse*) partial; (*juiz*) biased; ~**idade** *f* (*preconceito*) bias, prejudice; (*paixão*) partiality; (*partido*) party, faction.

**'parco/a** *adj* (*escasso*) scanty; (*que economiza*) thrifty.

**par'dal** *m* sparrow.

**'pardo/a** *adj* (*cinzento*) grey; (*castanho*) brown.

**pare'cer** *m* (*opinião*) opinion; **de bom** ~ good-looking // *vi* (*ter a aparência de*) to look, seem; (*ter semelhança com*) to look like, seem like; ~**se com** to look alike, resemble each other; ~**se com o pai** to take after one's father; **ao que parece** apparently; **parece-me que** I think that, it seems to me that; **que lhe parece?** what do you think?; **parecido/a** adj alike, similar; **parecido com** like.

pa'**rede** f wall; (greve) strike.

pa**relha** [pa'reʎa] f (de cavalos) team; (par) pair; (de pessoas) couple.

pa'**rente/a** m/f relative, relation; **parentela** f relations pl; **parentesco** m relationship, (fig) connection.

pa'**rêntese** m parenthesis; (na escrita) bracket.

pari'**dade** f (igualdade) equality; (de câmbio) parity.

pa'**rir** vt to give birth to // vi to give birth; (mulher) to have a baby.

parlamen'**tar** adj parliamentary; **parlamento** m parliament.

'**pároco** m parish priest.

pa'**ródia** f parody; **parodiar** f (imitar) to copy; (fazer paródia de) to mimic, parody.

pa**róquia** [pa'rɔkja] f (REL) parish; **paroquiano/a** m/f parishioner.

paro'**xismo** m fit, attack; **~s mpl** death throes.

**parque** ['paxkı] m (de caça) reserve; (público) park; **~ industrial** industrial estate; **~amento** m (Pt) parking.

par'**reira** f trellised vine.

'**parte** f part; (quinhão) share; (lado) side; (papel) role; **~ interna** inside; **a maior ~ de** most of; **a maior ~ das vezes** most of the time; **à ~** (separadamente) apart; (além de) apart from; **em grande ~** to a great extent; **em ~ alguma** nowhere; **por toda (a) ~** everywhere; **pôr de ~** to set aside; **tomar ~ em** to take part in; **dar ~ de** to inform of.

par**teira** [pax'tejra] f midwife.

participa**ção** [paxtʃɪsipa'sãw] f participation; (comunicação) announcement, notification; **~ nos lucros** profit-sharing; **participante** m/f participant; **participar** vt to

announce, notify of // vi: **participar de** (tomar parte) to participate in, take part in; (compartilhar) to share in.

parti'**cípio** m participle.

particu'**lar** adj (especial) particular, special; (privativo, pessoal) private // m particular; **em ~** in private; **~es** mpl details; **~izar** vt (especificar) to specify; (detalhar) to give details of; **~izar-se** vr to distinguish o.s.; **~mente** adv privately.

parti'**dário/a** adj partisan // f (esporte) supporter, follower; (POL) partisan.

par'**tido/a** adj broken // m (POL) party; (para casamento) catch; (em jogo) handicap; **tirar ~ de** to profit from; **tomar o ~ de** to side with // f (saída) departure; (esporte) game, match; (COM. quantidade) lot; (: remessa) shipment; (em corrida) start; **perder a ~a** to lose.

par**tilha** [pax'tʃiʎa] f share; **partilhar** vt to share; (distribuir) to share out.

par'**tir** vt (quebrar) to break; (dividir) to divide, split // vi (pôr-se a caminho) to set off, set out; (ir-se embora) to leave, go away; **~ de** (começar) to start; (originar) to arise from; **~-se** vr (quebrar-se) to break; **a ~ de** (starting) from.

'**parto** m (chñd)birth; **estar em trabalho de ~** to be in labour.

'**parvo/a** adj stupid, silly // m/f fool, idiot; **parvoíce** f silliness, stupidity.

'**Páscoa** f Easter; (dos judeus) Passover.

pas'**mado/a** adj amazed, astonished; **pasmar** vt to amaze, astonish; **pasmar-se** vr: **pasmar-se com** to be amazed at.

pas'**palho** m simpleton.

pas**quim** [pa'kĩ] m (jornal) satirical newspaper.

**'passa** f (de uva) raisin; (de ameixa) prune.

**pas'sada** f (passo) step; **dar uma ~ em** to call in at.

**passadeira** [pasa'dejra] f (tapete) stair carpet; (mulher) ironing woman.

**passa'diço/a** adj passing // f (NÁUT) bridge.

**pas'sado/a** adj (decorrido) past; (antiquado) old-fashioned; (fruto) bad; (peixe) off; **o ano ~** last year; **bem ~a** (carne) well done // m past.

**passa'dor** m (coador) strainer; (filtro) filter; (de macarrão) colander; (de cabelo) pin, grip.

**passageiro/a** [pasa'ʒejru/a] adj (transitório) passing; (local) busy // m passenger.

**passagem** [pa'saʒẽ] f passage; (preço de condução) fare; (bilhete) ticket; **~ de nível** level crossing; **~ de ida e volta** return ticket; (US) round trip ticket; **~ subterrânea** subway; **~ de pedestres** pedestrian crossing; **de ~** in passing.

**passa'porte** m passport.

**pas'sar** vt to pass; (ponte, rio) to cross; (exceder) to go beyond, exceed; (coar: farinha) to sieve; (: líquido) to strain; (: café) to percolate; (a ferro) to iron; (tarefa) to set; (telegrama) to send; (o tempo) to spend; (bife) to cook; (a outra pessoa) to pass on; **~ por cima** to overlook // vi to pass; (na rua) to go past; (tempo) to go by; (fruta) to go off; (terminar) to be over; (ser admissível) to pass; (mudar) to change; **~ bem de saúde)** to be well; **como está passando?** how are you?; **não ~ de** to be only; **~ sem** to do without; **~ por casa de** to call in on; **~ pela cabeça a** to occur to; **~ a ser** to become; **~-se** vr (acontecer) to go on, happen; (desertar) to go over; (tempo) to go by.

**passa'rela** f footbridge; (para modelos) catwalk.

**'pássaro** m bird.

**passa'tempo** m pastime; (diversão) amusement; **como ~** for fun.

**pas'sável** adj passable, so-so, all right.

**'passe** m (licença) pass.

**passe'ar** vt to take for a walk; (exibir) to show off // vi to go for a walk; **~ a cavalo** to go for a ride; **passeata** (marcha coletiva) protest march; **passeio** m walk; (calçada) pavement; **dar um passeio** to go for a walk; **um passeio de automóvel** drive.

**pas'sivo/a** adj passive // m (COM) liabilities (pl).

**'passo** m (pé; medida) pace; (ruído dos passos) footstep; (sinal de pé) footprint; **apertar o ~** to hurry up; **a cada ~** constantly; **ceder o ~** to give way; **dar um ~** to take a step; **marcar o ~** to mark time.

**'pasta** f paste; (de couro) briefcase; (de cartolina) folder; (de ministro) portfolio; **~ dentifrícia/de dentes** toothpaste.

**pastagem** [pa'taʒẽ] f pasture; **pastar** vt to graze on // vi to graze.

**pas'tel** m pie; (desenho) pastel drawing; **~aria** f (loja) cake shop; (comida) pastry.

**pastilha** [pa'tiʎa] f (MED) tablet; (doce) pastille; (TEC: informática) chip.

**'pasto** m (erva) grass; (terreno) pasture; **casa de ~** (Pt) cheap restaurant, diner.

**pas'tor(a)** m shepherd; (REL) clergyman, pastor // f shepherdess.

**'pata** f (pé de animal) foot, paw; (ave) duck; **meter a ~** to put one's foot in it; **patada** f kick.

**pata'mar** m (de escada) landing.

**pa'tente** adj obvious, evident // f (COM) patent; (MIL: título) commission; **altas ~s** high-ranking

officers; **patentear** vt to show,
reveal; (COM) to patent; **patentear-se** vr to be shown, be evident.

**pa'terno/a** adj fatherly, paternal;
casa ~a family home.

**pa'teta** adj stupid, daft // m/f idiot.

**pa'tético/a** adj pathetic, moving.

**pa'tíbulo** m gallows.

**pa'tife** m scoundrel, rogue.

**patim** [pa'tʃĩ] m skate; ~ **de rodas**
roller skate; **patinação** f skating;
(lugar) skating rink; **patinar** vi to
skate; (AUTO: derrapar) to skid.

**patinhar** [patʃi'ɲax] vi (como um
pato) to dabble; (em lama) to splash
about, slosh.

**'pátio** m (de uma casa) patio,
backyard; (espaço cercado de
edifícios) courtyard; (de escola)
playground; (MIL) parade ground; ~
**de recreio** playground.

**'pato** m duck; (macho) drake.

**patranha** [pa'traɲa] f fib, story.

**patrão** [pa'trãw] m (COM) boss;
(dono de casa) master;
(proprietário) landlord; (NÁUT)
skipper.

**'pátria** f native land, homeland.

**patri'mônio** m (herança)
inheritance; (fig) heritage; (bens)
property.

**patri'ota** m/f patriot; **patriótico/a**
adj patriotic; **patriotismo** m
patriotism.

**pa'troa** f (mulher do patrão) boss's
wife; (dona de casa) lady of the
house; (proprietária) landlady.

**patroci'nar** vt to sponsor; (apoiar)
to support; **patrocínio** m spon-
sorship, backing.

**patrulha** [pa'truʎa] f patrol.

**patus'cada** f good time, spree;
**andar em** ~s to live it up.

**pau** [paw] m (madeira) wood; (vara)
stick; (viga) beam; de ~ wooden; ~
**de bandeira** flagpole; **a meio** ~
(bandeira) at half-mast; ~s mpl
(cartas) clubs; **levar** ~ (em exame)
to fail.

**pa'ul** m marsh, swamp.

**pau'lada** f blow (with a stick).

**paulatina'mente** adv gradually;
**paulatino/a** adj slow, gradual.

**paulifi'car** vt to annoy, bother.

**pau'pérrimo/a** adj poverty-
stricken.

**pausa** ['pawza] f pause; (intervalo)
break; (descanso) rest; **pausado/a**
adj (lento) slow; (sem pressa)
leisurely; (cadenciado) measured.

**pauta** ['pawta] f (linha) (guide)line;
(MÚS) staff; (lista) list; (folha) ruled
paper; (indicações) guidelines; **sem**
~ (papel) plain; **pautado/a** adj
(papel) ruled.

**pavão/voa** [pa'vãw/'voa] m
peacock // f peahen.

**pavilhão** [pavi'ʎãw] m (tenda)
tent; (de madeira) hut; (em
exposição) stand; (bandeira) flag; ~
**de isolamento** isolation ward.

**pavi'mento** m (chão, andar) floor;
(da rua) road surface.

**pa'vio** m wick.

**pavone'ar** vt (ostentar) to show off
// vi (caminhar) to strut; ~**se** vr to
show off.

**pa'vor** m dread, terror; **ter** ~ **de** to
be terrified of; ~**oso/a** adj dreadful,
terrible;

**paz** f peace; (sossego) peacefulness;
**fazer as** ~**es** to make up, be friends
again.

**pé** m (de pessoa) foot; (da mesa) leg;
(fig: base) footing; (de alface) head;
(milho, café) plant; **ir a** ~ to walk,
go on foot; **ao** ~ **de** near, by; **a água**
**dá** ~ (natação) you can touch the
bottom; **em** ~ standing (up); **em** ~
**de guerra** on a war footing; **pôr-se**
**em** ~ to stand up.

**peão** [pi'ãw] m (Pt) pedestrian;
(MIL) foot soldier; (xadrez) pawn;
(trabalhador) farm labourer.

**'peça** f (pedaço) piece; (AUTO) part;
(aposento) room; (logro) trick;
(teatro) play; (serviço) pago por ~
piecework; ~ **de roupa** garment.

pe'cado *m* sin; **pecador(a)** *m/f* sinner, wrongdoer; **pecaminoso/a** *adj* sinful; **pecar** *vi* to sin; (*cometer falta*) to do wrong; **pecar por excesso de zelo** to be overzealous.

pechincha [pe'ʃĩʃa] *f* (*vantagem*) godsend; (*coisa barata*) bargain; **pechinchar** *vi* to bargain, haggle.

'peço *etc vb ver* pedir.

peçonha [pe'soɲa] *f* poison.

pecu'ária *f* cattle-raising.

peculi'ar *adj* (*especial*) special, peculiar; (*particular*) particular.

pe'cúlio *m* (*acumulado*) savings *pl*; (*bens*) wealth.

pe'daço *m* piece, bit; **esperar um ~** to wait a bit; **aos ~s** in pieces.

pedágio [pe'daʒju] *m* (*pagamento*) toll; (*posto*) tollbooth.

pe'dal *m* pedal; **pedalar** *vt* to pedal // *vi* to pedal; (*andar de bicicleta*) to cycle.

pe'dante *adj* pedantic // *m/f* pedant.

pederneira [pedex'nejra] *f* flint.

pedes'tal *m* pedestal.

pe'destre *m* pedestrian.

pedi'atra *m/f* paediatrician; (*US*) pediatrician; **pediatria** *f* paediatrics (*sg*); (*US*) pediatrics (*sg*).

pedi'curo/a *m/f* chiropodist; (*US*) podiatrist.

pe'dido *m* (COM) order; (*solicitação*) request; **~ de casamento** proposal (of marriage); **~ de demissão** resignation; **~ de informação** inquiry.

pedinchar [pedĩ'ʃax] *vt* to beg for // *vi* to beg.

pe'dir *vt* to ask for; (COM: *comida*) to order; (*demandar*) to demand; **~ alguma coisa a alguém** to ask sb for sth // *vi* to ask; **~ a alguém que faça** to ask sb to do; **~ desculpa** to apologize; **~ emprestado** to borrow; **~ 100 cruzeiros por algo** to ask 100 cruzeiros for sth; **~ para vir** to ask to come.

'pedra *f* stone; (*rochedo*) rock; (de

granizo) hailstone; (*de açúcar*) lump; **~ de amolar** grindstone; **pedregal** *m* stony ground; **pedregoso/a** *adj* stony, rocky; **pedreira** *f* quarry; **pedreiro** *m* stonemason.

pedre'gulho *m* gravel.

pega ['pɛga] *f* (*briga*) quarrel // *f* ['pega] magpie; (Pt: *moça*) bird; (: *meretriz*) tart.

pegada [pe'gada] *f* (*do pé*) footprint; (*no futebol*) save; (*vestígio*) track, trace.

pega'diço/a *adj* (*viscoso*) sticky; (MED) infectious, catching; **pegado/a** *adj* (*colado*) stuck; (*unido*) together; **a casa pegada** the house next door.

pe'gar *vt* (*selos*) to stick (on); (*agarrar*) to take hold of; (*doença, fogo, fugitivo, peixe*) to catch; **ir ~** (*buscar*) to go and get; (*compreender*) to take in; **~ um emprego** to get a job; **~ uma rua** to take a street; **~ fogo a** to set fire to // *vi* (*aderir*) to stick; (*planta*) to take; (*moda*) to catch on; (*doença*) to be contagious; (*motor*) to start; **~ em** (*segurar*) to grab, pick up; **~ com** (*casa*) to be next door to; **~ a fazer** to start to do; **~-se** *vr* (*aderir*) to stick; (*brigar*) to have a fight, quarrel.

peitilho [pej'tʃiʎu] *m* shirt front; **peito** *m* (ANAT) chest; (*de ave, mulher*) breast; (*fig*) courage; **dar o peito a um bebê** to breastfeed a baby.

peitoril [pejto'riw] *m* windowsill.

peixaria [pejʃa'ria] *f* fishmonger's; **peixe** *m* fish; **peixeiro/a** *m* fishmonger // *f* fishwife.

pe'jar-se *vr* to be ashamed; **pejo** *m* shame; **ter pejo** to be ashamed.

pejora'tivo/a *adj* pejorative.

'pela = por + a.

pe'lado/a *adj* (*sem pele*) skinned; (*sem pêlo*) shorn; (*fruta*) peeled; (*nu*) bare; (*sem dinheiro*) broke.

**'pélago** m (mar alto) high seas pl, ocean; (abismo) depths pl; (fig) abyss.

**pe'lar** vt (tirar a pele) to skin; (tirar o pêlo) to cut the hair of; (fruta) to peel; (fig) to fleece; **~-se** vr: **~-se por** to be crazy about, adore.

**'pelas** = por + as.

**pele** ['pelɪ] f skin; (couro) leather; (como agasalho) fur (coat).

**peleja** [pele'ʒa] f (luta) fight; (briga) quarrel; **pelejar** vi (lutar) to fight; (discutir) to quarrel; **pelejar pela paz** to struggle for peace.

**pele-vermelha** [pelɪ-vex'meʎa] m/f redskin.

**pe'lica** f kid (leather).

**peli'cano** m pelican.

**pe'lícula** f film; (de pele) film of skin.

**pe'lintra** adj (Pt) shabby; (pobre) penniless.

**'pelo** = por + o.

**'pêlo** m hair; (de animal) fur, coat; **em ~** stark naked; **montar em ~** to ride bareback.

**'pelos** = por + os.

**pelotão** [pelo'tãw] m platoon, squad.

**pe'lúcia** f plush.

**pe'ludo/a** adj hairy.

**'pena** f (pluma) feather; (de caneta) nib; (escrita) writing; (castigo) punishment; (sofrimento) suffering; (piedade) pity; (mágoa) grief, sadness; **~ capital** capital punishment; **cumprir ~** to serve a term in jail; **que ~!** what a shame!; **ter ~ de** to feel sorry for; **valer a ~** to be worthwhile; **não vale a ~** it's not worth it; **sob ~ de** under penalty of.

**pe'nal** adj penal; **~idade** f penalty; (castigo) punishment; **impor uma ~idade a** to penalize.

**'pênalti** m (futebol) penalty.

**pe'nar** vt to grieve // vi to suffer.

**pen'dência** f dispute, quarrel.

**pen'dente** adj (pendurado)

hanging; (por decidir) pending; (inclinado) sloping; **~ de** (dependente) dependent on // m pendant.

**pen'der** vt to hang // vi to hang; (estar para cair) to sag, droop; **~ de** (estar pendurado) to hang from; **~ para** (inclinar) to lean towards; (ter tendência para) to tend to; **~ a** (estar disposto a) to be inclined to.

**'pêndulo** m pendulum.

**pendu'rado/a** adj hanging; **pendurar** vi: **pendurar de** to hang from.

**pe'nedo** m rock, boulder.

**peneira** [pe'nejra] f (da cozinha) sieve; (do jardim) riddle; **peneirar** vt to sift, sieve; (chover) to drizzle.

**pe'netra** m/f gate-crasher; **penetração** f (ato) penetration, entering; (perspicácia) insight, sharpness; **penetrante** adj (olhar) searching; (ferida) deep; (pessoa) sharp; (som) penetrating; piercing; **penetrar** vt (entrar: com dificuldade) to get into, penetrate; (: em segredo) to steal into; (espada) to pierce; (compreender) to understand.

**penha** ['peɲa] f (rocha) rock; (penhasco) cliff; **penhasco** m cliff, crag.

**penhor** [pe'ɲox] m pledge; **casa de ~es** pawnshop; **dar em ~** to pawn; **~adamente** adv gratefully; **~ado/a** adj pawned; **penhorar** vt (dar em penhor) to pledge, pawn; (pegar) to confiscate; (fig) to put under an obligation.

**penici'lina** f penicillin.

**pe'nínsula** f peninsula; **peninsular** adj peninsular.

**'pênis** m penis.

**peni'tência** f (contrição) penitence; (expiação) penance; **penitenciária** f prison, penitentiary; **penitente** adj repentant // m/f penitent.

**pe'noso/a** adj (assunto,

*tratamento*) painful; (*trabalho*) hard.

**pen'sado/a** *adj* deliberate, intentional; **pensador(a)** *m/f* thinker; **pensamento** *m* thought; (*ato*) thinking; (*mente*) thought, mind; (*opinião*) way of thinking; (*idéia*) idea.

**pensão** [pẽ'sãw] *f* (*casa*) boarding house; (*comida*) board; ~ **completa** full board; ~ **de aposentadoria** (retirement) pension.

**pen'sar** *vi* to think; (*imaginar*) to imagine; ~ **em** to think of/about; ~ **fazer** (*ter intenção*) to intend to do, be thinking of doing; ~ **sobre** (*meditar*) to ponder over // *vt* (*ferimento*) to dress; **pensando bem** on second thoughts; ~ **alto** to think out loud; **pensativo/a** *adj* thoughtful, pensive.

**pensio'nista** *m/f* pensioner; (*que mora em pensão*) boarder.

**'penso** *m* (*tratamento*) treatment, care; (*Pt: de ferimento*) dressing.

**'pente** *m* comb; ~**adeira** *f* dressing table; ~**ado** *m* (*arranjo de cabelo*) hairdo; (*estilo*) hair style; **pentear** *vt* to comb; (*arranjar o cabelo*) to do, style; **pentear-se** *vr* (*com um pente*) to comb one's hair; (*arranjar o cabelo*) to do one's hair.

**pente'costes** *m* Whitsuntide.

**pente-'fino** *m* fine-tooth comb.

**penugem** [pe'nuʒẽ] *f* (*de ave*) down; (*pêlo*) fluff.

**pe'núltimo/a** *adj* last but one.

**pe'numbra** *f* (*ao cair da tarde*) twilight, dusk; (*sombra*) shadow; (*meia-luz*) half-light.

**pe'núria** *f* poverty.

**pe'pino** *m* cucumber.

**pe'pita** *f* (*de ouro*) nugget.

**pequenez** [peke'neʒ] *f* smallness; (*infância*) infancy; (*fig: mesquinhez*) meanness; **pequeno/a** *adj* small, little // *m* boy // *f* girl; (*namorada*) girlfriend.

**Pequim** [pe'kĩ] *m* Peking.

**'pêra** *f* pear.

**pe'ralta** *adj* naughty // *m* dandy, fop; (*menino*) naughty child.

**pe'rante** *prep* before, in the presence of.

**per'calço** *m* (*dificuldade*) difficulty; (*estorvo*) drawback; (*transtorno*) hitch.

**perce'ber** *vt* (*por meio dos sentidos*) to perceive; (*compreender*) to understand; (*ver*) to see; (*um som*) to hear; (*ver ao longe*) to make out; (*dinheiro: receber*) to receive.

**percentagem** [pexsẽ'taʒẽ] *f* percentage.

**percepção** [pexsep'sãw] *f* perception; (*compreensão*) understanding; **perceptível** *adj* perceptible, noticeable; (*som*) audible.

**percevejo** [pexse've ʒu] *m* (*inseto*) bug; (*prego*) drawing pin.

**percor'rer** *vt* (*viajar por*) to travel (across/over); (*passar por*) to go through, traverse; (*investigar*) to search through; **percurso** *m* (*espaço percorrido*) distance (covered); (*trajeto*) route; (*viagem*) journey; **fazer o percurso entre** to travel between.

**percussão** [pexku'sãw] *f* (*MÚS*) percussion; **percutir** *vt* to strike.

**'perda** *f* loss; (*dano*) damage; (*desperdício*) waste.

**perdão** [pex'dãw] *m* pardon, forgiveness; ~**!** sorry!

**per'der** *vt* (*ficar sem*) to lose; (*o tempo*) to waste; (*trem, oportunidade*) to miss // *vi* to lose; ~**se** *vr* (*extraviar-se*) to get lost; (*arruinar-se*) to be ruined; (*desaparecer*) to disappear; **perdição** *f* perdition, ruin; **perdido/a** *adj* lost; (*imoral*) depraved; **perdido por** (*apaixonado*) desperately in love with.

**perdigão** [pexdʒi'gãw] *m* (*macho*) partridge.

**perdigueiro** [pexdʒi'gejru] *m*

(*cachorro*) pointer, setter.

**per'diz** *f* partridge.

**perdo'ar** *vt* (*desculpar*) to forgive, pardon; (*justificar*) to excuse; (*dívida*) to spare.

**perdu'lário/a** *adj* wasteful // *m/f* spendthrift.

**perdu'rar** *vi* (*durar muito*) to last a long time; (*continuar a existir*) to still exist.

**pere'cer** *vi* to perish; (*morrer*) to die; (*acabar*) to come to nothing.

**peregrinação** [peregrɪna'sãw] *f* (*viagem*) long tour, travels *pl*; (REL) pilgrimage; **peregrinar** *vi* (*viajar*) to travel; (REL) to go on a pilgrimage; **peregrino/a** *adj* (*estranho*) strange; (*de beleza rara*) exquisite; (*raro*) rare // *m/f* pilgrim.

**pereira** [pe'rejra] *f* pear tree.

**peremp'tório/a** *adj* (*final*) final, (*decisivo*) decisive.

**perene** [pe'renɪ] *adj* (*perpétuo*) everlasting; (BOT) perennial.

**perfa'zer** *vt* (*completar o número de*) to make up.

**perfeição** [pexfej'sãw] *f* perfection; **perfeitamente** *adv* perfectly // *excl*: **perfeitamente!** exactly!; **perfeito/a** *adj* perfect; (*completo*) complete.

**per'fídia** *f* treachery; **pérfido/a** *adj* treacherous.

**per'fil** *m* (*do rosto*) profile; (*silhueta*) silhouette, outline; (ARQ) (*cross*) section; **de ~** in profile; **perfilar** *vt* (*soldados*) to line up; (*aprumar*) to straighten up; **perfilar-se** *vr* to stand to attention.

**perfu'mar** *vt*, **perfu'mar-se** *vr* to put perfume on; **perfume** *m* perfume; (*cheiro*) scent.

**perfura'dor(a)** *m* borer, drill; (*de papel*) punch // *f* punch machine; **perfurar** *vt* (*o chão*) to drill a hole in; (*papel*) to punch (a hole in); **perfuratriz** *f* drill.

**pergaminho** [pexga'mɪɲu] *m* parchment; (*diploma*) diploma.

**per'gunta** *f* question; **fazer uma ~ a alguém** to ask sb a question; **perguntar** *vt* to ask; (*interrogar*) to question; **perguntar alguma coisa a alguém** to ask sb sth // *vi*: **perguntar por alguém** to ask after sb; **perguntar-se** *vr* to wonder.

**perícia** [pe'rɪsja] *f* (*conhecimento*) expertise; (*destreza*) skill; **pericial** *adj* expert.

**perife'ria** *f* periphery; (*da cidade*) outskirts *pl*; **periférico/a** *adj* peripheral; **estrada periférica** ring road // *m* (INFORMÁTICA) peripheral.

**pe'rífrase** *f* circumlocution.

**pe'rigo** *m* danger; **correr ~** to be in danger; **perigoso/a** *adj* dangerous; (*arriscado*) risky.

**peri'ódico/a** *adj* periodic; (*chuvas*) occasional; (*doença*) recurrent // *m* (*revista*) magazine, periodical; (*jornal*) (news)paper; **período** *m* period; (*estação*) season; **período letivo** term (*time*).

**peripécia** [perɪ'pɛsja] *f* unexpected event, incident.

**periquito** [perɪ'kɪtu] *m* parakeet.

**peri'scópio** *m* periscope.

**pe'rito/a** *adj*: **~ em** (*destro*) skilful at, clever at; (*sabedor*) expert at // *m/f* expert; **~ em matéria de** expert in.

**perju'rar** *vi* to commit perjury; **perjúrio** *m* perjury; **perjuro/a** *m/f* perjurer.

**permanecer** [pexmane'sex] *vi* (*num lugar*) to stay; (*continuar a ser*) to remain, keep; **~ parado** to keep still; **permanência** *f* (*estada*) stay; (*constância*) permanence; (*continuidade*) continuance; **permanente** *adj* (*dor*) constant; (*cor*) fast; (*residência*, *pregas*) permanent // *m* (*cartão*) pass // *f* perm.

**permeio** [pex'meju] *adv*: **de ~ in** between.

**permissão** [pexmɪ'sãw] *f* permission, consent; **permitir** *vt* to allow, permit; (*conceder*) to grant; **permitir a alguém fazer** to let sb do, allow sb to do.

**per'muta** f (*troca*) exchange; (*de coisas colecionadas*) swap, swapping; **permutação** f (MAT) permutation; (*troca*) exchange; **permutar** vt to exchange; (*col*) to swap.

**'perna** f leg.

**pernicioso/a** [pɛxnɪsɪ'ozu/a] adj (*nocivo*) harmful; (*mau*) bad; (MED) malignant.

**per'nil** m (*de animal*) haunch; (CULIN) leg.

**pernoi'tar** vi to spend the night.

**'pérola** f pearl.

**pero'rar** vi to make a speech, hold forth.

**perpas'sar** vi to pass by.

**perpendicu'lar** adj perpendicular; **ser ~ a** to be at right angles to.

**perpetração** [pexpetra'sãw] f perpetration; **perpetrar** vt to perpetrate, commit.

**perpe'tuar** vt to perpetuate; **perpetuidade** f eternity; **perpétuo/a** adj perpetual; (*eterno*) eternal; **prisão perpétua** life imprisonment.

**perplexi'dade** f confusion, bewilderment; **perplexo/a** adj (*confuso*) bewildered, puzzled; (*indeciso*) uncertain.

**perquirir** [pexki'rix] vt to probe, investigate.

**perscru'tar** vt to scrutinize, examine.

**perseguição** [pexsegi'sãw] f pursuit; (REL, POL) persecution; **perseguidor(a)** m/f pursuer; (REL, POL) persecutor; **perseguir** vt (*seguir*) to pursue; (*moça*) to chase after; (REL) to persecute; (*importunar*) to harass, pester.

**perseve'rança** f (*insistência*) persistence; (*constância*) perseverance; **perseverante** adj persistent; **perseverar** vi to

persevere; **perseverar em** (*conservar-se firme*) to persevere in; **perseverar corajoso** to remain brave; **perseverar em erro** to keep on doing wrong.

**persi'ana** f Persian blind.

**persig'nar-se** vr to cross o.s.

**persis'tente** adj persistent; **persistir** vi to persist; **persistir em** to persist in; **persistir calado** to keep quiet.

**personagem** [pexso'naʒẽ] m/f famous person, celebrity; (*teatro*) character; **personalidade** f personality.

**perspec'tiva** f (*na pintura*) perspective; (*panorama*) view; (*probabilidade*) prospect; **em ~** expected, in prospect.

**perspi'cácia** f insight, perceptiveness; **perspicaz** adj (*que observa*) observant; (*que vê bem*) keen-sighted; (*fig*) shrewd.

**persuadir** [pexswa'dʒix] vt to persuade; (*convencer*) to convince; **~ alguém de que/alguém a fazer** to persuade sb that/sb to do; **~-se** vr to convince o.s., make up one's mind; **persuasão** f persuasion; (*convicção*) conviction.

**perten'cente** adj belonging; **~ a** (*pertinente*) pertaining to; **pertencer** vi: **pertencer a** to belong to; (*referir-se*) to concern; **pertences** mpl (*de uma pessoa*) belongings.

**perti'nácia** f obstinacy; **pertinaz** adj (*persistente*) persistent; (*obstinado*) obstinate; **pertinente** adj (*referente*) relevant; (*apropriado*) appropriate.

**'perto/a** adj nearby // adv (*não longe*) near; **~ da casa** near ou close to the house; **conhecer de ~** to know very well; **de ~** closely; **~ de 100 cruzeiros** about 100 cruzeiros.

**perturbação** [pextuxba'sãw] f (*angústia*) distress; (*desordem*) upset; (MED) trouble; (POL) disturbance; **perturbado/a** adj upset; (desvairado) delirious; **perturbar** vt (o sossego) to disturb; (pessoa) to upset, trouble.

**pe'ru** m turkey.

**Pe'ru** m Peru; **peruano/a** adj, m/f Peruvian.

**perversão** [pexvex'sãw] f perversion; **perversidade** f perversity; **perverso/a** adj perverse; (malvado) wicked; **perverter** vt (corromper) to corrupt, pervert; **pervertido/a** adj perverted // m/f pervert.

**pesa'delo** m nightmare.

**pe'sado/a** adj heavy; (trabalho) hard; (estilo) dull, boring; (andar) slow; (piada) coarse; (comida) stodgy; (ar) sultry.

**pêsames** ['pesamiʃ] mpl condolences, sympathy sg.

**pe'sar** vt to weigh; (fig) to weigh up // vi to weigh; (ser pesado) to be heavy; (influir) to carry weight; (causar mágoa) to hurt, grieve; ~ **sobre** (recair) to fall upon; **em que pese despite**; ~**oso/a** adj (triste) sorrowful, sad; (arrependido) regretful, sorry.

**'pesca** f (ato) fishing; (os peixes) catch; **ir à** ~ to go fishing; **pescada** f whiting; ~**dor(a)** m fisherman // f fisherwoman; ~**dor à linha** angler; **pescar** vt (peixe) to fish for; (tentar apanhar) to fish for; (retirar como que pescando) to fish out; (um marido) to catch, get // vi to fish; (Br: col) to understand.

**pes'coço** m neck.

**'peso** m weight; (ônus) burden; (prestígio) importance; ~ **bruto/líquido** gross/net weight; **em** ~ in full force.

**pesqueiro/a** [peʃ'kejru/a] adj fishing.

**pesquisa** [peʃ'kiza] f inquiry, investigation; (científica) research; ~ **de mercado** market research.

**'pêssego** m peach.

**pessi'mista** adj pessimistic // m/f pessimist; **péssimo/a** adj very bad, awful.

**pes'soa** f person; ~**s** fpl people; **em** ~ personally; **pessoal** adj (particular, íntimo) personal; (individual) individual // m personnel pl, staff pl; (col) people, folk.

**pes'tana** f eyelash; **pestanejar** vi to blink; (piscar) to wink.

**'peste** f (epidemia) epidemic; (bubônica) plague; (fig) pest, nuisance; **pestífero/a** adj (nocivo) noxious, poisonous; **pestilência** f plague; (epidemia) epidemic.

**'peta** f lie; (col) fib.

**'pétala** f petal.

**petição** [peti'sãw] f (rogo) request; (documento) petition; **peticionário/a** m/f petitioner; (JUR) plaintiff.

**petis'car** vt to nibble at, peck at // vi to have a nibble; **petisco** m savoury, titbit.

**pe'tiz** m (Pt) boy.

**petrechos** [pe'treʃuʃ] mpl equipment sg; (MIL) stores, equipment; (da cozinha) utensils.

**petrifi'car** vt (de medo) to petrify; (tornar duro) to harden; (assombrar) to stupefy; ~**-se** vr to be petrified.

**petroleiro/a** [petro'lejru/a] adj oil cmp, petroleum cmp // m (navio) oil tanker; **petróleo** m oil, petroleum; **petróleo bruto** crude oil.

**petu'lância** f impertinence; (col) cheek; **petulante** adj impudent, cheeky.

**peúga** ['pjuga] f (Pt) sock.

**pevide** [pe'vidɨ] f (Pt: de melão) seed; (: de maçã) pip.

**p. ex.** abr de **por exemplo** e.g. (for example).

**'pia** f wash basin; (da cozinha) sink; ~ **batismal** font.

**pi'ada** f joke.

**pia'nista** m/f pianist; **piano** m piano.

**pião** [pɪ'ãw] m (brinquedo) top.

**pi'ar** vi to cheep; (coruja) to hoot.

**picadeiro** [pɪka'dejru] m (circo) ring.

**pica'dinho** m mince.

**'picado/a** adj (por agulha) pricked; (por abelha) stung; (por cobra, mosquito) bitten; (irritado) cross // m (carne) mince // f (de agulha) prick; (de abelha) sting; (de mosquito, cobra) bite; (de avião) dive; (de navalha) stab; (atalho) path, trail.

**pi'cante** adj (tempero) hot; (piada) risqué, blue; (comentário) saucy.

**pica-pau** [pɪka-'paw] m woodpecker.

**pi'car** vt (agulha) to prick; (abelha) to sting; (mosquito) to bite; (pássaro) to peck; (um animal) to goad; (carne) to mince; (papel) to shred; (fruta) to chop up; (irritar) to nettle; (a língua) to burn // vi (a isca) to take the bait; (produzir coceira) to sting; **~-se** vr to be offended.

**pica'resco/a** adj comic, ridiculous.

**pica'reta** f pickaxe.

**'pícaro/a** adj crafty, cunning.

**pi'carra** f shale.

**'pico** m (de arma) peak; (espinho) thorn; (Pt: um pouco) a bit; **mil e ~** just over a thousand; **meio-dia e ~** just after midday.

**pico'lé** m iced lolly.

**pico'tar** vt to perforate.

**pic'tórico/a** adj pictorial.

**piedade** [pɪe'dadʒɪ] f (devoção) piety; (compaixão) pity; **ter ~ de** to have pity on; **piedoso/a** adj (REL) pious; (compassivo) merciful.

**piegas** [pɪ'egaʃ] adj inv sentimental; (col) soppy // m/f softy; **pieguice** f sentimentality.

**pigarrear** [pɪgaxɪ'ax] vi to clear one's throat; **pigarro** m (col) a frog in one's throat.

**pig'mento** m pigment.

**pigmeu/pigméia** [pɪg'mɛw/ pɪg'meja] m/f pigmy.

**pilão** [pɪ'lãw] m crusher; (rural) mortar; **pilar** vt to pound, crush // m pillar.

**pilha** [ˈpɪʎa] f (eletroquímica) battery; (monte) pile, heap; (informática) stack.

**pilhagem** [pɪ'ʎaʒẽ] f (ato) pillage; (objetos) plunder, booty; **pilhar** vt (saquear) to plunder, pillage; (conseguir) to get (hold of); (roubar) to rob; (apanhar) to catch.

**pilhéria** [pɪ'ʎɛrja] f joke; **pilheriar** vi to joke, jest.

**pilotagem** [pɪlo'taʒẽ] f flying; **escola de ~** flying school; **pilotar** (avião) to fly; (navio) to steer; **piloto** m (de avião) pilot; (de navio) first mate; (motorista) (racing) driver; (chama) pilot light; **piloto automático** automatic pilot.

**'pílula** f pill; **a ~ anticoncepcional** the pill.

**pi'menta** f (CULIN) pepper; **~-do-reino** f black pepper; **pimentão** m (BOT) pepper; **pimentão verde** green pepper; **pimenteira** f pepper plant.

**pimpão/pona** [pɪ'pãw/'pona] adj (Pt) smart, flashy // m/f show-off.

**pimpolho** [pɪ'poʎu] m (rebento) shoot; (criança) youngster.

**pinaco'teca** f art gallery.

**pi'náculo** m pinnacle, summit.

**pinça** [ˈpɪsa] f (pequena) tweezers pl; (de casa) tongs pl; (MED) forceps pl.

**pi'náculo** m summit, peak.

**pincel** [pɪ'sɛw] m brush; (para pintar) paintbrush; **~ de barba** shaving brush; **~ada** f (brush) stroke.

**'pinga** f (gota) drop; (Pt: trago) drink; (cachaça) rum; **pingar** vi to drip; (começar a chover) to start to rain.

**pingente** [pĩˈʒẽtʃi] *m* pendant; (*brinco*) earring.

**'pingo** *m* (*gota*) drop; (*ortografia*) dot; ~ **de gente** (*col*) scrap of nothing.

**pingue-pongue** [pĩgɪˈpõgɪ] *m* ping-pong.

**pingüim** [pĩˈgwĩ] *m* penguin.

**pinha** [ˈpiɲa] *f* pine cone; **pinhal** *m* pine wood; **pinheiro** *m* pine (tree); **pinho** *m* pine.

**'pino** *m* (*peça*) pin; **a** ~ upright; **o sol está a** ~ the sun is at its height.

**'pinta** *f* (*mancha*) spot; (*aparência*) appearance, looks *pl*.

**pin'tar** *vt* to paint; (*descrever*) to describe; ~**se** *vr* to put on one's make-up // *vi* to paint; (*col*) to appear, turn up; ~ **o sete** to paint the town red.

**pintarroxo** [pĩtaˈxoʃu] *m* linnet; (*Pt*) robin.

**'pinto** *m* chick.

**pin'tor(a)** *m/f* painter; **pintura** *f* painting; (*do rosto*) make-up; (*quadro*) picture; **pintura a óleo** oil painting; **pintura rupestre** cave painting.

**'pio/a** *adj* (*devoto*) pious; (*caridoso*) charitable // *m* cheep, chirp.

**piolho** [piˈoʎu] *m* louse.

**pioneiro/a** [pioˈnejru/a] *adj* pioneering // *m* pioneer.

**pi'or** *adj, adv* (*comparativo*) worse; (*superlativo*) worst // *m*: **o** ~ worst of all; **piora** *f* worsening; **piorar** *vt* to make worse, worsen // *vi* to get worse.

**'pipa** *f* barrel, cask; (*de papel*) kite.

**pipa'rote** *m* (*com o dedo*) flick.

**pique** [ˈpiki] *m* (*lança*) pike; (*sabor*) piquancy; (*jogo*) hide and seek; **a** ~ vertically, steeply; **a** ~ **de** on the verge of; **ir a** ~ to sink.

**piquenique** [pikeˈniki] *m* picnic; **fazer** ~ to have a picnic.

**piquete** [piˈketʃi] *m* (*MIL*) squad; (*em greve*) picket.

**pi'râmide** *f* pyramid.

**pi'rata** *m* pirate; (*sedutor*) lady-killer; ~**ria** *f* piracy.

**pires** [ˈpiriʃ] *m inv* saucer.

**piri'lampo** *m* glow worm.

**pirotec'nia** *f* pyrotechnics *sg*, art of making fireworks.

**pirueta** [piˈrweta] *f* pirouette.

**piru'lito** *m* lollipop.

**pi'sada** *f* (*passo*) footstep; (*rastro*) footprint; **pisar** *vt* (*andar por cima de*) to tread on; (*uvas*) to tread, press; (*esmagar, subjugar*) to crush; (*café*) to pound // *vi* (*andar*) to step, tread; (*acelerar*) to put one's foot down.

**pisca'dela** *f* (*involuntária*) blink; (*sinal*) wink; **pisca-piscas** *fpl* (*AUTO*) indicators; **piscar** *vt* to blink; (*dar sinal*) to wink; (*estrelas*) to twinkle.

**pis'cina** *f* swimming pool; (*col*) baths *pl*; (*para peixes*) fish pond.

**'piso** *m* floor.

**'pista** *f* (*vestígio*) track, trail; (*indicação*) clue; (*de corridas*) track; (*de aviões*) runway; (*de equitação*) ring; (*de estrada*) lane; (*de dança*) (dance) floor.

**pistão** [piʃˈtãw] *m* piston.

**pis'tola** *f* (*arma*) pistol; (*para tinta*) spray gun.

**pi'tada** *f* (*porção*) pinch.

**pi'tar** *vt/i* to smoke; **piteira** *f* cigarette-holder.

**pi'toresco/a** *adj* picturesque.

**'placa** *f* plate; (*AUTO*) number plate; (*: US*) license plate; ~ **de sinalização** roadsign.

**placi'dez** *f* peacefulness, serenity; **plácido/a** *adj* (*sereno*) calm; (*manso*) placid.

**plagiar** [plaʒiˈax] *vt* to plagiarize; **plágio** *m* plagiarism.

**plaina** [ˈplajna] *f* (*instrumento*) plane.

**'plana** *f*: **de primeira** ~ first-class.

**plana'dor** *m* glider.

**pla'nalto** *m* tableland, plateau.

**pla'nar** *vi* to glide.

**plane'ar** (*Pt*) *vt*, **plane'jar** *vt* to

plan; (edifício) to design.

**pla'neta** m planet.

**plangente** [plã'ʒetʃi] adj plaintive, mournful.

**planície** [pla'nisi] f plain.

**planifi'car** vt (programar) to plan out; (uma região) to make a plan of.

**'plano/a** adj (terreno) flat, level; (liso) smooth // m (projeto, mapa) plan; (MAT) plane; ~ diretor master plan; em primeiro/em último ~ in the foreground/background.

**'planta** f (BIO) plant; (do pé) sole; (plano) plan.

**plantação** [plãta'sãw] f (ato) planting; (terreno) planted land; **plantar** vt (um vegetal) to plant; (semear) to sow; (casas) to put up; (estabelecer) to set up; **plantar-se** vr to plant o.s., stand.

**pla'nura** f plain.

**plaquê** [pla'ke] m (Pt) gold plate.

**plas'mar** vt to mould, shape.

**'plástico/a** adj plastic // m plastic // f modelling.

**plata'forma** f platform.

**'plátano** m plane tree.

**platéia** [pla'teja] f (teatro etc) stalls pl.

**pla'tina** f platinum; **platinado/a** adj platinum; **platinados** cmp; **loura platinada** platinum blonde // mpl: **platinados** points.

**plausível** [plaw'zivɛw] adj credible, plausible.

**'plebe** f common people, populace; **plebeu/béia** adj plebeian // m/f pleb; **plebiscito** n referendum, plebiscite.

**'plectro** m (MÚS) plectrum.

**pleitear** [plejt∫i'ax] vt (JUR: causa) to plead; (contestar) to contest; **pleito** m lawsuit, case; (fig) dispute.

**ple'nário/a** adj plenary; **plenilúnio** m full moon; **plenitude** f plenitude, fullness; **pleno/a** adj full; (completo) complete; em pleno dia in broad daylight.

**pleurisia** [plewri'zia] f pleurisy.

**'plinto** m plinth.

**'pluma** f feather; **plumagem** f plumage.

**plu'ral** [-aw] adj, m plural.

**pluto'crata** adj plutocratic // m/f plutocrat.

**plu'tônio** m plutonium.

**pluvi'al** [-jaw] adj pluvial, rain cmp.

**pneu** ['pnew] m tyre; (US) tire; ~mático/a adj pneumatic // m tyre; (US) tire.

**pneumonia** [pnewmo'nia] f pneumonia.

**pó** [pɔ] m (partículas) powder; (sujeira) dust; ~ de arroz face powder.

**'pobre** adj poor // m/f poor person; os ~s the poor; **pobreza** f poverty.

**poça** ['posa] f puddle, pool; ~ de sangue pool of blood.

**poção** [po'sãw] f potion.

**pocilga** [po'siwga] f pigsty.

**poço** ['posu] m (de água) well; (de mina) shaft.

**'poda** f pruning; ~deira f pruning knife; **podar** vt/i to prune.

**po'der** vt (ser capaz de) to be able to, be capable of, can; (ter o direito de) to be allowed to, may; **pode ser que** it may be that; **não pode deixar de fazer isso** he can't help doing it; **até não mais** ~ with all one's might; **não posso com ele** I cannot cope with him // m power; (autoridade) authority; ~ aquisitivo purchasing power; **poderio** m might, power; **poderoso/a** adj mighty, powerful.

**'podre** adj rotten, putrid; (fig) rotten, corrupt; **podridão** f decay, rottenness.

**poeira** [po'ejra] f dust; **poeirento/a** adj dusty.

**po'ema** m poem.

**po'ente** m west; (do sol) setting.

**poesia** [poe'zia] f poetry; (poema) poem; **poeta** m poet; **po'ético/a** adj poetic; **poetisa** f poetess.

**pois** [pojʃ] adv well (then);

(*portanto*) so; (*Pt: assentimento*) yes; ~ **bem**/~ **então** well then; ~ **é** that's right; ~ **não!** (*Br*) of course!; ~ **não?** (*Pt*) isn't it?, aren't you?, didn't they? etc // *conj* as, since, because.

**po'laco/a** (*Pt*) *adj* Polish // *m/f* Polo // *m* (*língua*) Polish.

**po'lar** *adj* polar; **~idade** *f* polarity; **~izar** *vt* to polarize.

**'poldro/a** *m* colt // *f* filly.

**pole'gada** *f* inch; **polegar** *m* thumb.

**poleiro** [po'lejru] *m* perch.

**po'lêmica** *f* controversy, dispute.

**'pólen** *m* pollen.

**po'lia** *f* pulley.

**po'lícia** *f* police, police force // *m* (*Pt*) policeman, constable; **agente de** ~ police constable; ~ **rodoviária** traffic police; **policial** *adj* police *cmp*; **novela** *ou* **romance policial** detective story // *m* (*Br*) policeman, constable // *f* (*Br*) policewoman.

**poli'dez** *f* good manners *pl*, politeness; **polido/a** *adj* (*lustrado*) polished, shiny; (*cortês*) well-mannered, polite.

**poli'éster** *m* polyester.

**poli'glota** *adj, m/f* polyglot.

**poli'mento** *m* (*lustração*) polishing; (*finura*) refinement.

**'pólio** *f*, **poliomielite** [poliomie'litʃi] *f* polio(myelitis).

**po'lir** *vt* to polish.

**poli'técnica** *f* (*escola*) polytechnic.

**po'lítico/a** *adj* political; (*astuto*) crafty // *m/f* politician // *f* (*ramo sg*; *programa*) policy; (*astúcia*) cunning.

**'pólo** *m* (*GEO, ELET*) pole; (*esporte*) polo; ~ **aquático** water polo.

**polo'nês/esa** *adj* Polish // *m/f* Pole // *m* (*língua*) Polish.

**'polpa** *f* pulp.

**poltrão/trona** [pol'trãw/'trona]

*adj* cowardly // *m/f* coward // *f* armchair, easy chair.

**poluição** [polwi'sãw] *f* pollution; **poluir** *vt* to pollute.

**polvilhar** [powvi'ʎax] *vt* to sprinkle, powder; **polvilho** *m* powder.

**'polvo** *m* octopus.

**'pólvora** *f* gunpowder.

**po'mada** *f* pomade, ointment; (*vaidade*) vanity.

**po'mar** *m* orchard.

**'pomba** *f* dove; **pombal** *m* dovecote; **pombo** *m* pigeon.

**'pomo** *m* (*fruto*) fruit; ~ **de discórdia** bone of contention; ~**-de-Adão** *m* Adam's apple.

**'pompa** *f* pomp, ceremony; **pomposo/a** *adj* ostentatious, pompous.

**poncho** ['põʃu] *m* poncho, cape.

**ponderação** [põdera'sãw] *f* consideration, meditation; **ponderado/a** *adj* prudent, well-considered; **ponderar** *vt* to consider, weigh up // *vi* to meditate, muse.

**'ponho** *etc vb ver* **pôr**.

**'ponta** *f* point, tip; (*extremidade*) end; (*um pouco*) touch; ~ **esquerda** (*futebol*) outside-left; ~ **de cigarro** cigarette end; **na** ~ **da língua** on the tip of one's tongue; **na(s)** ~**(s) dos pés** on tiptoe; **ponta-cabeça** *f*: **de ponta-cabeça** upside down; **pontada** *f* (*dor*) twinge.

**pontão** [põ'tãw] *m* pontoon.

**ponta'pé** *m* kick; **dar** ~ **em** to kick.

**ponta'ria** *f* aim; **fazer** ~ to take aim.

**ponte** ['põtʃi] *f* (*ger*) bridge; ~ **aérea** air shuttle, airlift; ~ **levadiça** drawbridge; ~ **suspensa/pênsil** suspension bridge.

**ponte'ado/a** *adj* stippled, dotted // *m* stipple; **pontear** *vt* (*pontilhar*) to dot, stipple; (*dar pontos*) to sew, stitch.

**ponteiro/a** [põ'tejru/a] *m*

(*indicador*) pointer; (*de relógio*) hand; (*MÚS. plectro*) plectrum // f ferrule, tip.

**pontia'gudo/a** adj sharp, pointed.

**pontifi'cado** m pontificate; **pontífice** m pontiff, Pope.

**pontilhar** [põtʃiʎ´ʌx] vt to dot, stipple; **linha pontilhada** dotted line.

**pontinha** [põ'tʃiɲɐ] f (*um pouco*) bit, touch.

**'ponto** m point; (*sinal*) dot, speckle; (*pontuação*) full stop; (*jogo*) point; (*objetivo*) aim, object; (*teatro*) prompter; (*lugar*) spot, place; ~ **morto** (*AUTO*) neutral; **em** ~ prompt, on the dot; ~ **e vírgula** semicolon; ~ **de interrogação/exclamação** question/exclamation mark; ~ **de vista** point of view; ~ **de táxi** (Br) taxi stand; **até certo** ~ to a certain extent.

**pontuação** [põtwa'sãw] f punctuation.

**pontual** [põ'twaw] adj punctual; ~**idade** f punctuality.

**pon'tuar** vt to punctuate.

**'popa** f stern, poop; **à** ~ astern, aft.

**pope'lina** f poplin.

**popu'laça** f mob, rabble; **população** f population; **popular** adj (*estimado*) popular; (*do povo*) of the people; (*comum*) common, current; **popularidade** f popularity; **popularizar** vt to popularize, make popular; **popularizar-se** vr to become popular.

**pôquer** ['pɔkex] m (*jogo*) poker.

**por** [pox] (*por + o = pelo; por + a = pela; por + os = pelos; por + as = pelas*) prep (*a fim de*) in order to; (*a favor de*) for; (*por causa de*) out of, because of, from; (*meio*) by; (*troca*) (in exchange) for; (*através de*) through, by; **soubemos disso** ~ **carta** we learnt about it by letter; **viemos pelo parque** we came through the park; **pelas duas horas** at two o'clock; ~ **aqui** this way; ~

**isso** therefore; ~ **cento** per cent; ~ **mais difícil que seja** however difficult it is; ~ **Deus!** for heaven's sake!; ~ **escrito** in writing; ~ **fora/~ dentro** outside/inside; ~ **exemplo** for example; ~ **ano** yearly; ~ **mês** monthly; ~ **semana** weekly; ~ **dia** daily; **está** ~ **acontecer** it is about to happen, it is yet to happen; ~ **que** (Br) why; ~ **quê?** (Br) why?

**pôr** [pox] vt to put; (*colocar*) to place; (*roupas*) to put on; (*dúvidas*) to raise; (*ovos*) to lay; ~ **furioso** to infuriate; ~ **de lado** to set aside; ~**-se** vr (*sol*) to set; ~**-se de pé** to stand up; ~**-se a caminho** to set off.

**porão** [po'rãw] m (NÁUT) hold; (*casa*) basement.

**porção** [pox'sãw] f portion, piece; **uma** ~ a lot of.

**porca'ria** f filth; (*fig*) mess; (*coisa ruim*) rubbish // excl ~! damn!

**porce'lana** f porcelain, china.

**'porco/a** adj filthy // m (BIO) pig, hog; (*carne*) pork // f (BIO) sow; (TEC) nut; **porco-espinho** m porcupine; **porco-montês** m wild boar.

**porém** [po'rẽ] conj however, nevertheless.

**por'fia** f (*altercação*) dispute, wrangle; (*obstinação*) stubbornness, obstinacy; **porfiado/a** adj (*disputado*) hotly disputed; (*obstinado*) stubborn, obstinate; **porfiar** vt (*questionar*) to dispute; **porfiar em** (*obstinar-se*) to persist in.

**porme'nor** m detail; ~**izar** vt to detail.

**pornogra'fia** f pornography; **pornográfico/a** adj pornographic.

**'poro** m pore; **poroso/a** adj porous.

**porquanto** [pox'kwãtu] conj since, seeing that.

**porque** ['poxke] conj because, since; (*interrogativo*: Pt) why;

**porquê** adv why; **porquê?** (Pt) why? // m reason, motive.

**'porta** f (dum edifício) door, doorway; (dum jardim) gate; ~ **giratória** revolving door; a ~s **fechadas** behind closed doors.

**porta-aviões** [pɔxta-aviˈõjʃ] m inv aircraft carrier.

**porta-chaves** [pɔxta-ˈʃavɪʃ] m inv key-holder.

**porta'dor(a)** m/f bearer; **ao** ~ (COM) payable to bearer.

**portagem** [pɔxˈtaʒẽ] f (Pt) toll.

**por'tal** [-aw] m doorway.

**porta'ló** m (NÁUT) gangway.

**porta-luvas** m inv (AUTO) glove compartment.

**porta-'malas** m inv (AUTO) boot; (US) trunk.

**porta-moedas** [pɔxta-ˈmwedaʃ] (Pt) m purse.

**por'tanto** conj so, therefore.

**por'tar** vt to carry; ~-**se** vr to behave.

**porta'ria** f (dum edifício) entrance hall; (recepção) reception desk; (do governo) edict, decree.

**porta-seios** [pɔxta-ˈsejuʃ] m inv bra, brassiere.

**portátil** [pɔxˈtatʃiw] adj portable.

**porta-'voz** m (pessoa) spokesman // f (pessoa) spokeswoman.

**'porte** m (transporte) transport; (custo) freight charge, carriage; (NÁUT) tonnage, capacity; (atitude) bearing; ~ **pago** post paid.

**porteiro/a** [pɔxˈtejru/a] m/f caretaker.

**por'tento** m wonder, marvel; **portentoso/a** adj amazing, marvellous.

**'pórtico** m porch, portico.

**portinhola** [pɔxtʃiˈɲɔla] f (de carruagem) door.

**'porto** m (do mar) port, harbour; (vinho) port; P~ Oporto; ~ **de escala** port of call.

**português/guesa** [pɔxtu-

geʃ/ˈgeza] adj, m/f Portuguese // m (língua) Portuguese.

**por'vir** m future.

**pôs** vb ver **pôr.**

**po'sar** vi (FOTO) to pose.

**pós-da'tar** vt to postdate.

**pós-es'crito** m postscript.

**posição** [poziˈsãw] f (lugar) position; (social) standing, status.

**positi'vo/a** adj, m positive.

**pos'por** vt to put after; (adiar) to postpone.

**pos'sante** adj powerful, strong.

**posse** [ˈpɔsɪ] f possession, ownership; ~s fpl possessions, belongings; **tomar** ~ to take office; **tomar** ~ **de** to take possession of; **possessão** f possession; **possessivo/a** adj possessive; **possesso/a** adj possessed, crazed.

**possibili'dade** f possibility; (oportunidade) chance; ~s fpl means; **possibilitar** vt to make possible, permit; **possível** adj possible, feasible; **fazer todo o possível** to do one's best.

**'posso** etc vb ver **poder.**

**possuidor(a)** [poswiˈdox(a)] m/f owner, possessor; **possuir** vt to own, possess; (usufruir) to enjoy; (posto) to hold.

**'posta** f (pedaço) piece, slice; (correio) post, mail; **postal** adj postal // m postcard.

**'poste** m pole, post.

**poster'gar** vt (adiar) to postpone.

**posteri'dade** f posterity.

**posteri'or** adj (mais tarde) subsequent, later; (traseiro) rear, back // m posterior, bottom; ~**mente** adv later, subsequently.

**postiço/a** [pɔʃˈtʃisu/a] adj false, artificial; **dentes** ~s false teeth.

**'posto/a** pp de **pôr** // adj put, placed; **sol** ~ sunset // m post, position; (emprego) job; ~ **de gasolina** service/petrol station // conj: ~ **que** although.

**postu'lado** m postulate,

assumption; **postular** vt (pedir) to request.

**'póstumo/a** adj posthumous.

**pos'tura** f (posição) posture, position; (atitude) attitude.

**po'tassa** f potash; **potássio** m potassium.

**po'tável** adj drinkable; **água** ~ drinking water.

**'pote** m jug, pitcher; **chover a** ~ (Pt) to rain cats and dogs.

**potência** [po'tẽsja] f power, strength; (nação) power; **potencial** adj potential, latent // m potential; **potente** adj powerful, potent.

**'potro/a** m (cavalo) colt, foal // f filly, foal.

**pouca-vergonha** [poka-vex'gona] f shameful behaviour, disgrace.

**pouco/a** ['poku/a] adj (sg) little; (pl) few // adv not much, little // m a little; **há** ~ **tempo** a short time ago; ~**as vezes** rarely; ~ **a** ~ gradually, little by bit; **por** ~ almost; **aos** ~**s** gradually; ~**chino/a** adj: **um** ~**chinho/a** (Pt) very little // m a little bit.

**pou'par** vt to save; (economizar) to economize on; (vida) to spare.

**pousada** [po'zada] f inn, resting place; **pousar** vt to place, set down; (mão) to rest, place // vi to rest; (pássaros) to perch.

**'povo** m people; (raça) people, race; **póvoa** f (aldeia) village, hamlet; **povoação** f (vila) town, settlement; (habitantes) population; (ato de povoar) settlement, colonization; **povoado/a** adj populated // m village, settlement; **povoar** vt (de habitantes) to people, populate; (de animais etc) to stock.

**praça** ['prasa] f (largo) square; (mercado) market; (soldado) soldier; **sentar** ~ to enlist; ~ **de touros** bull ring; ~ **forte** stronghold.

**'prado** m meadow, grassland; (Br: hipódromo) racecourse.

**'praga** f (maldição) curse; (coisa importuna) pest, plague; (desgraça) calamity.

**prag'mático/a** adj (prático) pragmatic.

**praguejar** [prage'ʒax] vt/i to curse.

**praia** ['praja] f beach, seashore.

**prancha** ['prãʃa] f plank; (NÁUT) gangplank.

**prante'ar** vt to mourn // vi to weep; **pranto** m weeping.

**'prata** f silver; **prateado/a** adj silver-plated; (brilhante) silvery.

**prateleira** [prate'lejra] f (de livros) shelf.

**prati'cante** adj practising // m/f apprentice; **praticar** vt (fazer) to practise, perform; (crime) to commit, perpetrate; **praticável** adj practical, feasible; **prático/a** adj practical // m/f expert // m (NÁUT) pilot // f (ato de praticar) practice; (experiência) experience, knowhow; (costume) habit, custom.

**'prato** m (louça) plate, dish; (comida) dish; (coberta) course; ~**s** mpl (MÚS) cymbals.

**praxe** ['praksi] f custom, usage.

**prazenteiro/a** [prazẽ'tejru/a] adj cheerful, pleasant; **prazer** m pleasure; **muito prazer em conhecê-lo** pleased to meet you.

**'prazo** m term, period; (vencimento) expiry date, time limit; **a curto/longo** ~ short-/long-term; **comprar a** ~ to buy on hire purchase ou in instalments.

**prea'mar** m (Br) high tide, high water.

**pre'âmbulo** m preamble, introduction.

**pre'cário/a** adj precarious, insecure.

**preca'tado/a** adj cautious; **precatar-se** vr to take precautions, be careful; **quando mal se precata** when least expected.

**precaução** [prekaw'sãw] f precaution.

**preca'ver-se** *vr* to be on one's guard; (*guardar-se*) to take precautions; **precavido/a** *adj* cautious.

**prece** [ˈprɛsi] *f* prayer.

**prece'dência** *f* precedence; **preceder** *vt* to precede.

**preceito** [preˈsejtu] *m* precept, ruling; **preceituar** *vt* to decree, prescribe.

**precep'tor** *m* tutor, instructor.

**preciosidade** [presjoziˈdadʒi] *f* (*qualidade*) preciousness; (*coisa*) treasure; **preciosismo** *m* preciosity; **precioso/a** *adj* (*valioso*) precious, valuable; (*afetado*) over-refined.

**precipício** [presiˈpisju] *m* precipice; (*fig*) abyss.

**precipitação** [presipitaˈsãw] *f* haste; (*imprudência*) rashness; **precipitado/a** *adj* hasty; (*imprudente*) rash; **precipitar** *vt* (*apressar*) to hurry, precipitate; (*lançar*) to hurl down; **precipitar-se** *vr* to hurry.

**precisão** [presiˈzãw] *f* (*exatidão*) precision, exactness; (*falta*) need, necessity; **precisar** *vt* (*especificar*) to specify, state in detail; (*faltar*) to want, need; **preciso ir** I have to go // *vi*: **precisar de** to need; **preciso/a** *adj* (*exato*) precise, exact; (*necessário*) necessary, imperative; **é preciso ir** you must go.

**pre'claro/a** *adj* famous, illustrious.

**preço** [ˈpresu] *m* price; (*custo*) cost; (*valor*) value; **~ por atacado** *or* **de varejo** wholesale/retail price; **~ de ocasião** bargain price; **~ de venda** sale price.

**precoce** [preˈkɔsi] *adj* precocious; (*antecipado*) early; **precocidade** *f* (*talento*) precociousness.

**preconce'bido/a** *adj* preconceived; **preconceito** *m* prejudice, bias.

**preconi'zar** *vt* to extol.

**precur'sor(a)** *m/f* (*predecessor*) precursor, forerunner; (*mensageiro*) herald.

**preda'dor** *m* predator; **predatório/a** *adj* predatory.

**predeces'sor** *m* predecessor.

**predesti'nado/a** *adj* predestined.

**predetermi'nado/a** *adj* predetermined.

**predi'al** *adj* property *cmp*, real-estate *cmp*; **imposto ~** domestic rates.

**predição** [predʒiˈsãw] *f* prediction, forecast.

**predileção** [predʒileˈsãw] *f* (*Pt*: **-cç-**) *f* preference, predilection; **predileto/a** (*Pt*: **-ct-**) *adj* favourite.

**'prédio** *m* building; **~ de apartamentos** block of flats.

**predis'por** *vt* to predispose.

**predi'zer** *vt* to predict, forecast.

**predomi'nância** *f* predominance, prevalence; **predominar** *vi* to predominate, prevail; **predomínio** *m* predominance, supremacy.

**preeminência** [priemiˈnẽsja] *f* pre-eminence, superiority; **preeminente** *adj* pre-eminent, superior.

**preencher** [priẽˈʃex] *vt* (*minuta*) to fill in/out, complete; (*necessidade*) to fulfil, meet.

**pré-fabri'cado/a** *adj* prefabricated.

**prefácio** [preˈfasju] *m* preface.

**prefeito** [preˈfejtu] *m* mayor; **prefeitura** *f* town hall.

**prefe'rência** *f* preference; **de ~** preferably; **preferir** *vt* to prefer; **preferível** *adj* preferable.

**pre'fixo** *m* (*LING*) prefix.

**'prega** *f* pleat, fold.

**prega'dor** *m* preacher; **pregão** *m* proclamation, cry; **pregões** *mpl* marriage banns; **pregar** *vt/i* (*um sermão*) to preach; (*anunciar*) to proclaim.

**pregar** [preˈgax] *vt* (*com prego*) to nail; (*fixar*) to pin, fasten; (*cosendo*) to sew; **~ uma peça** to play a trick

**~ os olhos em** to fix one's eyes on; **não ~ olho** not to sleep a wink; **prego** *m* nail.

**pregoeiro** [pre'gwejru] *m* · (*proclamador*) town crier; (*num leilão*) auctioneer.

**preguear** [pregi'ax] *vt* to pleat, fold.

**preguiça** [pre'gisa] *f* laziness; (*animal*) sloth; **preguiçoso/a** *adj* lazy.

**preia-mar** [preja-'max] *f* (*Pt*) high tide, high water.

**preito** ['prejtu] *m* homage, tribute; **render ~ a** to pay homage to.

**prejudi'car** *vt* to damage, prejudice; **prejuízo** *m* (*dano*) damage, harm; (*parcialidade*) prejudice.

**pre'lado** *m* prelate.

**preleção** [prelε'sãw] (*Pt*: **-cç-**) *f* lecture.

**prelimi'nar** *adj* preliminary // *f* (*partida*) preliminary.

**'prelo** *m* (printing) press; **no ~** in the press.

**pre'lúdio** *m* (*prólogo*) prelude; (*Mús*) overture.

**prema'turo/a** *adj* premature.

**premedi'tado/a** *adj* premeditated; **premeditar** *vt* to premeditate.

**pre'mente** *adj* pressing; **premer** *vt* to press; (*espremer*) to squeeze.

**premi'ado/a** *adj* prize-winning; **premiar** *vt* to award a prize to; (*pagar*) to reward; **prêmio** *m* prize; (*seguros*) premium.

**pre'mir** *vt ver* **premer**.

**pre'missa** *f* premise.

**'prenda** *f* gift, present; (*em jogo*) forfeit; **~s** *fpl* talents, accomplishments; **prendado/a** *adj* gifted, talented.

**prende'dor** *m* fastener; **~ de roupa** clothes peg; **~ de papéis** paper clip; **prender** *vt* (*pregar*) to fasten, fix; (*capturar*) to arrest, capture; (*agarrar*) to catch, seize;

**prender-se** *vr* to get caught, stick.

**prenhe** ['preɲi] *adj* pregnant; **prenhez** *f* pregnancy.

**pre'nome** *m* first name, Christian name.

**'prensa** *f* (*ger*) press; **prensar** *vt* to press, compress.

**prenunci'ar** *vt* to predict, foretell; **prenúncio** *m* forewarning, sign.

**preocupação** [preokupa'sãw] *f* (*envolvimento*) preoccupation; (*inquietação*) worry, concern; **preocupar** *vt* (*absorver*) to preoccupy; (*inquietar*) to worry; **preocupar-se** *vr*: **preocupar-se com** to worry about, be worried about.

**preparação** [prepara'sãw] *f* preparation; **preparar** *vt* to prepare, arrange; **preparar-se** *vr*: **preparar-se para** to prepare to ou for; **preparativos** *mpl* preparations, arrangements.

**preponde'rância** *f* preponderance, predominance.

**preposição** [prepozi'sãw] *f* preposition.

**prerroga'tiva** *f* prerogative, privilege.

**'presa** *f* (*na guerra*) spoils *pl*; (*vítima*) prey; (*dente de animal*) fang.

**pres'bita** *adj* long-sighted.

**presbi'tério** *m* presbytery.

**presbi'tia** *f*, **presbi'tismo** *m* long-sightedness.

**presciência** [pre'sjεsja] *f* foreknowledge, foresight; **presciente** *adj* far-sighted, prescient.

**prescin'dir** *vi*: **~ de algo** to do without sth; **prescindível** *adj* dispensable.

**prescre'ver** *vt* to prescribe // *vi* to expire; **prescrição** *f* order, rule.

**presença** [pre'zẽsa] *f* presence; (*comparecimento*) attendance; (*porte*) bearing, air; **~ de espírito** presence of mind; **presenciar** *vt* to witness, be present at; **presente** *adj* present; **ter presente** to bear in mind // m (oferta) gift, present; (tempo) present; (LING) present (tense); **os presentes** those present; **presentemente** adv at present.

**pre'sépio** m Nativity scene, crib.

**preservação** [prezexva'sãw] f preservation; **preservar** vt to preserve, protect; **preservativo** m preservative; (anticoncepcional) sheath.

**presi'dência** f (de um país) presidency; (de uma assembléia) chairmanship, presidency; **assumir a ~** to take the chair; **presidente** m (de um país) president; (de uma assembléia) chairman, president.

**presidi'ário** m convict; **presídio** m (prisão) military prison; (praça de guerra) fortress.

**presi'dir** vt to preside over // vi to preside.

**presilha** [pre'ziʎa] f fastener.

**'preso/a** adj (em prisão) imprisoned; (capturado) under arrest, captured; (atado) bound, tied // m/f prisoner.

**'pressa** f haste, hurry; (rapidez) speed; (urgência) urgency; **à(s) ~(s)** hurriedly; **dar-se ~** to hurry (up); **estar com ~** to be in a hurry.

**pressagiar** [presa'ʒjax] vt to foretell, presage; **presságio** m omen, sign.

**pressão** [pre'sãw] f pressure; **~ sangúínea** blood pressure.

**pressenti'mento** m premonition, presentiment; **pressentir** vt to sense, have a premonition of.

**pressu'posto** m (conjetura) presupposition.

**pressu'roso/a** adj (apressado) hurried, in a hurry; (zeloso) keen, eager.

**prestação** [presta'sãw] f instalment; **prestamista** m/f moneylender; (comprador) person paying hire purchase; **prestar** vt to give, render; (servir) to be of use;

(emprestar) to lend; **prestar-se** vr: **prestar-se a** to be suitable for; **prestar atenção** to pay attention; **prestar juramento** to take an oath; **não presta para nada** it's absolutely useless.

**prestes** ['prɛʃtʃiʃ] adj inv ready, about; **~ a partir** about to leave; **presteza** f (prontidão) willingness, promptness; (agilidade) nimbleness, agility.

**prestidigitação** [preʃtʃi-diʒita'sãw] f sleight of hand, conjuring, magic tricks; **prestidigitador** m conjurer, magician.

**pre'stígio** m (reputação) prestige, reputation; **prestigioso/a** adj prestigious, eminent.

**'préstimo** m use, usefulness; **sem ~** useless, worthless; **~s** mpl favours, services.

**presu'mido/a** adj vain, self-important; **presumir** vt to presume, suppose; (entender) to assume; **presunção** f (suposição) presumption; (vaidade) conceit, self-importance; **presunçoso/a** adj vain, self-important.

**pre'sunto** m (cured) ham.

**preten'dente** m/f claimant; (candidato) candidate, applicant; (galanteador) suitor; **pretender** vt (desejar) to want to; (tencionar) to intend; (esperar conseguir) to hope to get; **pretensão** f (reivindicação) claim; (vaidade) pretention; (aspiração) aim, aspiration; **pretensões** fpl (presunção) pretentiousness; **pretensioso/a** adj pretentious.

**prete'rir** vt to ignore, disregard.

**pre'térito/a** adj past, bygone // m (LING) preterite.

**pre'texto** [pre'teʃtu] m pretext, excuse; **a ~ de** on the pretext of.

**pretidão** [pretʃi'dãw] f blackness, darkness; **preto/a** adj black; **pôr o preto no branco** to put it down in writing // *m* black man, Negro // *f* black woman, Negress.

**prevalecer** [prevale'sex] *vi* to prevail, predominate; **~ sobre** to outweigh; **~-se** *vr*: **~-se de** (*aproveitar-se*) to take advantage of.

**prevari'car** *vi* (*faltar ao dever*) to fail in one's duty; (*proceder mal*) to misbehave.

**prevenção** [preve̍'sãw] *f* (*ato de evitar*) prevention; (*preconceito*) prejudice; (*cautela*) caution; **prevenido/a** *adj* (*cauteloso*) cautious, wary; (*avisado*) forewarned; **prevenir** *vt* (*evitar*) to prevent; (*avisar*) to warn; (*antecipar-se*) to anticipate; (*preparar*) to prepare; **prevenir-se** *vr* (*acautelar-se*) to take precautions; (*equipar-se*) to equip o.s.; **preventivo/a** *adj* preventive.

**pre'ver** *vt* to foresee.

**previa'mente** *adv* previously.

**previ'dência** *f* (*previsão*) foresight; (*precaução*) precaution; **~ social** social welfare.

**'prévio/a** *adj* previous, prior; (*preliminar*) preliminary.

**previsão** [previ'zãw] *f* (*antevisão*) foresight; (*prognóstico*) forecast; **~ meteorológica** weather forecast; **previsto/a** *adj* foreseen.

**pre'zado/a** *adj* esteemed; (*numa carta*) dear; **prezar** *vt* to value highly, esteem; **prezar-se** *vr* (*ter dignidade*) to have self-respect; **prezar-se de** (*orgulhar-se*) to pride o.s. on.

**pri'mado** *m* (*primazia*) primacy; **primar** *vi* to excel, stand out.

**pri'mário/a** *adj* primary.

**prima'vera** *f* spring; (*planta*) primrose.

**pri'maz** *m* primate; **primazia** *f* primacy; (*prioridade*) priority; (*superioridade*) superiority.

**primeiro/a** [pri'mejru/a] *adj* first; (*fundamental*) fundamental, prime; **~ ministro** prime minister; **em ~**

**lugar** first of all // *adv* first // *f* (*AUTO*) first gear.

**primi'tivo/a** *adj* primitive; (*original*) original.

**'primo/a** *m/f* cousin; **~ co-irmão** first cousin; **~ segundo** second cousin // *m* (*número*) prime number.

**primo'génito/a** *adj* first-born.

**pri'mor** *m* excellence, perfection; **com ~** to perfection; **é um ~** it's perfect.

**primordial** [-ox'dʒjaw] *adj* (*original*) original; (*principal*) principal, fundamental.

**primo'roso/a** *adj* excellent, exquisite.

**prin'cesa** *f* princess.

**princi'pado** *m* principality.

**princi'pal** [-aw] *adj* principal, main // *m* (*chefe*) head, principal.

**príncipe** ['prĩsipi] *m* prince.

**principi'ante** *m* beginner; **principiar** *vt* to begin.

**princípio** [prĩ'sipju] *m* (*começo*) beginning, start; (*origem*) origin; (*moral*) principle; **~s** *mpl* rudiments; **no ~** in the beginning; **por ~** on principle.

**pri'or** *m* (*sacerdote*) parish priest; (*de convento*) prior.

**priori'dade** *f* priority.

**prisão** [pri'zãw] *f* (*encarceramento*) imprisonment; (*cadeia*) prison, jail; (*detenção*) arrest; **ordem de ~** warrant for arrest; **~ perpétua** life imprisonment; **~ de ventre** constipation; **prisioneiro/a** *m/f* prisoner.

**'prisma** *f* prism.

**privação** [priva'sãw] *f* deprivation; (*penúria*) want, hardship; **privacidade** *f* privacy; **privações** *fpl* hardship *sg*; **privado/a** *adj* (*particular*) private; (*carente*) deprived; **privar** *vt* to deprive // *vi*: **privar com** to be on intimate terms with; **privativo/a** *adj* peculiar to; (*particular*) private.

**privilegiado/a** [prɪvɪleʒɪˈadu/a] *adj* privileged; (*distinto*) distinguished; **privilégio** *m* privilege.

**pró** [prɔ] *adv* for, in favour // *m* advantage; **os ~s e os contras** the pros and cons.

**'proa** *f* prow, bow; (*fig*) conceit.

**probabi'lidade** *f* probability, likelihood; **~s** *fpl* odds; **segundo todas as ~s** in all probability.

**probi'dade** *f* integrity, uprightness.

**pro'blema** *m* problem; **problemático/a** *adj* problematic.

**'probo/a** *adj* honest.

**proce'dência** *f* (*origem*) origin, source; **procedente** *adj* (*oriundo*) derived from, rising from; (*lógico*) logical; **proceder** *vi* (*ir adiante*) to proceed; (*comportar-se*) to act, behave; (*JUR*) to take legal action; **proceder a** to carry out; **proceder de** to originate from, arise from // *m* conduct; **procedimento** *m* (*comportamento*) conduct, behaviour; (*processo*) procedure; (*JUR*) legal action, trial.

**procela** [proˈsɛla] *f* storm, tempest; **proceloso/a** *adj* stormy.

**proces'sar** *vt* (*proceder contra*) to take proceedings against, prosecute; (*verificar*) to check, verify; **processo** *m* process; (*procedimento*) procedure; (*JUR*) lawsuit, legal proceedings.

**procissão** [prosɪˈsãw] *f* procession.

**proclamação** [proklamaˈsãw] *f* proclamation; **proclamar** *vt* to proclaim.

**procriação** [prokrɪaˈsãw] *f* procreation; **procriar** *vt/i* to procreate.

**pro'cura** *f* search; (*COM*) demand; **em ~ de** in search of; **~ção** *f* power of attorney; (*documento*) letter of attorney; **por ~ção** by proxy; **~dor** *m* (*advogado*) attorney; (*mandatário*) agent; **P~dor Geral**

da República Attorney General; **procurar** *vt* (*buscar*) to look for, seek; (*esforçar-se*) to try to, aim at; (*ir visitar*) to call on, go and see.

**prodigali'zar** *vt* (*gastar excessivamente*) to squander; (*dar com profusão*) to lavish.

**prodígio** [proˈdʒiʒu] *m* prodigy; **prodigioso/a** *adj* prodigious, marvellous.

**'pródigo/a** *adj* (*perdulário*) wasteful; (*generoso*) lavish; **filho ~** prodigal son.

**produção** [produˈsãw] *f* production; (*volume de produção*) output; (*produto*) product; **produtividade** *f* productivity; **produtivo/a** *adj* productive; (*rendoso*) profitable; **produto** *m* product; (*produção*) production; (*renda*) proceeds *pl*, profit; **produtos alimentícios** foodstuffs; **produzir** *vt* to produce; (*ocasionar*) to cause, bring about.

**proemi'nência** *f* prominence; (*protuberância*) protuberance; **proeminente** *adj* prominent.

**pro'eza** *f* exploit, feat.

**profanação** [profanaˈsãw] *f* sacrilege, profanation; **profanar** *vt* to desecrate, profane; **profano/a** *adj* profane; (*secular*) secular // *m* layman // *f* laywoman.

**profecia** [profeˈsia] *f* prophecy.

**profe'rir** *vt* to utter; **~ um discurso** to make a speech.

**profes'sar** *vt* (*declarar*) to profess // *vi* (*REL*) to take religious vows; **professor(a)** *m/f* teacher; **professor titular** (*Br*)/**catedrático** (*Pt*) university professor; **professorado** *m* (*professores*) teaching staff; (*classe*) teaching profession.

**pro'feta** *m* prophet; **profetizar** *vt/i* to prophesy, predict.

**proficiência** [profɪsɪˈɛsja] *f* proficiency, competence; **proficiente** *adj* proficient, competent.

**profícuo/a** [proˈfikwu/a] *adj* useful, advantageous.

**profissão** [profi'sãw] f (*ofício*)
profession; (*declaração*)
declaration; **profissional** adj
professional.

**pro'fundas** fpl depths;
**profundidade** f depth; **tem 4 metros
de profundidade** it is 4 metres deep;
**profundo/a** adj deep; (*complexo*)
profound.

**profusão** [profu'zãw] f profusion,
abundance; **profuso/a** adj
(*abundante*) profuse, abundant.

**progénie** [pro'ʒeni] (*Pt*:
**progénie** [-e-]) f (*ascendência*)
lineage; (*prole*) offspring, progeny;
**progenitor** m ancestor; (*pai*) father.

**prognosti'car** vt to predict,
forecast // vi (MED) to make a
prognosis; **prognóstico** m
prediction, forecast; (MED)
prognosis.

**pro'grama** m programme; (TEC,
*informática*) program;
**programação** f program(m)ing;
**programar** vt to program(me),
schedule.

**progre'dir** vi to progress, make
progress; **progressista** adj, m/f
progressive; **progressivo/a** adj
progressive; (*gradual*) gradual;
**progresso** m progress.

**proibição** [proibi'sãw] f
prohibition, ban; **proibir** vt to
prohibit, forbid; **"proibido fumar"**
"no smoking".

**projeção** [proʒe'sãw] (*Pt*: **-cç-**) f
projection; (*arremesso*) throwing;
(*proeminência*) prominence;
**projetar** (*Pt*: **-ct-**) vt (*ger*) to
project; (*arremessar*) to throw;
(*planejar*) to plan; **projetar-se** vr
(*lançar-se*) to hurl o.s.; (*sombra etc*)
to fall; (*delinear-se*) to stand out;
(*prolongar-se*) to stretch; **projétil**
(*Pt*: **-ct-**) m projectile, missile; (MIL)
missile; **projetista** (*Pt*: **-ct-**) m/f
planner; (*engenheiro projetista*)
designer; **projeto** (*Pt*: **-ct-**) m plan,
project; **projeto de lei** bill; **projetor**

(*Pt*: **-ct-**) m (*cinema*) projector;
(*holofote*) searchlight.

**prol** m advantage; **em ~ de** on
behalf of, for the benefit of.

**'prole** f offspring, progeny.

**proletari'ado** m proletariat;
**proletário/a** adj, m/f proletarian.

**proliferação** [prolifera'sãw] f
proliferation; **proliferar** vi to
proliferate; **prolífico/a** adj prolific.

**prolixo/a** [pro'liksu/a] adj long-
winded, tedious.

**'prólogo** m prologue.

**prolongação** [prolõga'sãw] f
extension; **prolongado/a** adj
prolonged; **prolongamento** m
extension; **prolongar** vt (*tornar mais
longo*) to extend, lengthen; (*adiar*)
to prolong; **prolongar-se** vr to
extend.

**pro'messa** f promise;
**prometedor(a)** adj promising;
**prometer** vt to promise // vi (*ter
potencial*) to show promise;
**prometido/a** adj promised // m
fiancé // f fiancée.

**promiscuidade** [promiʃ-
kwi'dadʒi] f (*mistura desordenada*)
disorder, confusion; (~ *sexual*)
promiscuity; **promíscuo/a** adj
(*misturado*) disorderly, mixed up;
(*comportamento sexual*)
promiscuous.

**promissão** [promi'sãw] f promise;
**terra da ~** Promised Land;
**promissor(a)** adj promising.

**promoção** [promo'sãw] f
promotion; (COM) publicity
(campaign).

**promon'tório** m headland,
promontory.

**promo'tor(a)** adj promoting // m
promoter; (JUR) prosecutor; ~
**público** public prosecutor;
**promover** vt (*dar impulso a*) to
promote; (*causar*) to cause; (*elevar
a cargo superior*) to promote.

**promul'gar** vt (*lei etc*) to

promulgate; (*tornar público*) to declare publicly.

**pro'nome** *m* pronoun.

**prontidão** [prõtʃi'dãw] *f* (*estar preparado*) readiness; (*rapidez*) promptness, speed; **pronto/a** *adj* (*preparado*) ready; (*rápido*) quick, speedy; (*sem dinheiro*) broke // *adv* promptly // *excl*: **pronto!** right!, that's it!; **pronto-socorro** *m* emergency hospital.

**prontuário** [prõ'twarju] *m* (*manual*) handbook; (*policial*) record.

**pro'núncia** *f* pronunciation; (*JUR*) indictment; **pronunciamento** *m* proclamation, pronouncement; **pronunciar** *vt* to pronounce; (*discurso*) to make, deliver; (*JUR*) to indict; **pronunciar mal** to mispronounce; **pronunciar-se** *vr* (*expressar opinião*) to express one's opinion.

**propagação** [propaga'sãw] *f* propagation; **propaganda** *f* (*política*) propaganda; (*COM*) advertising; **propagar** *vt* to propagate.

**propensão** [propẽ'sãw] *f* inclination, tendency; **propenso/a** *adj* inclined; **ser propenso a** to be inclined to, have a tendency to.

**propiciar** [propisi'ax] *vt/i* (*tornar favorável*) to favour; (*proporcionar*) to provide; **propício/a** *adj* (*favorável*) favourable, propitious; (*adequado*) adequate.

**pro'pina** *f* (*gorjeta*) tip; (*Pt: cota*) fee.

**pro'por** *vt* to propose, put forward; (*um problema*) to pose; **~-se** *vr* (*pretender*) to intend.

**proporção** [propox'sãw] *f* proportion; **proporções** *fpl* dimensions; **proporcionado/a** *adj* proportionate; **proporcionar** *vt* (*dar*) to provide, give; (*adaptar*) to adjust, adapt.

**proposição** [propozi'sãw] *f* proposition, proposal.

**pro'pósito** *m* purpose, aim; **a ~** by the way; (*oportunamente*) suitably; **a ~ de** with regard to; **de ~** on purpose.

**pro'posta** *f* proposal; (*oferecimento*) offer.

**propria'mente** *adv* properly, exactly; **~ dito** strictly speaking.

**proprie'dade** *f* property; (*direito de proprietário*) ownership; (*particularidade*) attribute, quality; (*o que é apropriado*) appropriateness, propriety; **~ imobiliária** real estate; **proprietário/a** *m* owner, proprietor; (*de casa alugada*) landlord; (*de jornal*) publisher // *f* owner; (*de estalagem etc*) landlady.

**'próprio/a** *adj* own, of one's own; (*mesmo*) very, selfsame; (*conveniente*) proper; (*caraterístico*) characteristic; (*depois de pronome*) -self; **eu ~** I myself; **ele ~** he himself; **mora em casa ~a** he lives in a house of his own; **por si ~** of one's own accord; **o ~ homem** the very man.

**propulsão** [propul'sãw] *f* propulsion; **~ a jato** jet propulsion; **propulsor(a)** *adj* propelling // *m* propellor.

**prorrogação** [proxoga'sãw] *f* extension; (*COM*) deferment; (*JUR*) stay; **prorrogar** *vt* to extend, prolong.

**prorrom'per** *vi* to burst out, break out.

**'prosa** *f* prose; (*conversa*) chatter; (*tagarelice*) boasting, bragging; **ter boa ~** to have the gift of the gab; **prosador(a)** *m/f* prose writer; **prosaico/a** *adj* prosaic; (*trivial*) dull, humdrum.

**proscénio** [pro'senju] *m* proscenium.

**proscre'ver** *vt* to prohibit, ban; (*expulsar*) to banish, exile; **proscrição** *f* proscription;

(*proibição*) prohibition, ban; (*desterro*) exile; **proscrito** *m* (*criminoso*) outlaw; (*desterrado*) exile.

**pro'sélito** *m* convert.

**pros'pecto** *m* (*vista*) outlook, prospect; (*impresso*) prospectus; **prospector** *m* prospector.

**prospe'rar** *vi* to prosper, thrive; **prosperidade** *f* prosperity; (*bom êxito*) success; **próspero/a** *adj* prosperous, thriving; (*bem sucedido*) successful; (*favorável*) favourable.

**prossecução** [proseku'sãw] *f* (*Pt*) continuation; **prosseguimento** *m* continuation; **prosseguir** *vt* (*continuar*) to continue, carry on with; (*seguir*) to follow // *vi* to continue, go on.

**prostituição** [proʃtitwi'sãw] *f* prostitution; **prostituir** *vt* to prostitute; **prostituir-se** *vr* (*desonrar-se*) to debase o.s.; (*tornar-se prostituta*) to become a prostitute; **prostituta** *f* prostitute.

**prostração** [proʃtra'sãw] *f* prostration; (*cansaço*) exhaustion; (*desalento*) dejection; **prostrar** *vt* (*derrubar*) to knock down, throw down; (*enfraquecer*) to tire out; **prostrar-se** *vr* to prostrate o.s.; (*humilhar-se*) to humble o.s.

**protago'nista** *m/f* protagonist.

**proteção** [prote'sãw] (*Pt*: **-cç-**) *f* protection; (*amparo*) support, backing; **protecionismo** (*Pt*: **-cc-**) *m* protectionism; **proteger** *vt* to protect; **protegido/a** *adj* protected // *m* protégé *f* protégée.

**prote'ína** *f* protein.

**prote'lar** *vt* to postpone, put off.

**protes'tante** *adj, m/f* Protestant; **protestantismo** *m* Protestantism; **protestar** *vt* to protest; (*declarar*) to declare, affirm // *vi* to protest, object; **protesto** *m* (*queixa*) protest; (*declaração*) affirmation.

**protetor(a)** [prote'tox(ra)] (*Pt*:

**-ct-**) *adj* protective, protecting // *m/f* protector.

**proto'colo** *m* protocol.

**pro'tótipo** *m* prototype.

**'prova** *f* proof; (*ensaio*) test, trial; (*EDUC: exame*) examination; (*sinal*) sign; (*de comida, bebida*) taste; (*de roupa*) fitting; (*tipografia*) proof; à ~ on trial; à ~ **de bala/fogo/água** bulletproof/fireproof/waterproof; **pôr à** ~ to put to the test; **provação** *f* (*sofrimento*) hardship, suffering; **provar** *vt* (*comprovar*) to prove; (*comida*) to taste; (*roupa*) to try on // *vi* to try.

**pro'vável** *adj* probable, likely.

**prove'dor(a)** *m/f* (*fornecedor*) provider; (*COM*) supplier.

**proveito** [pro'vejtu] *m* (*ganho*) profit; (*vantagem*) advantage; **em** ~ **de** for the benefit of; **tirar** ~ **de** to benefit from; **proveitoso/a** *adj* profitable, advantageous.

**proveniência** [proven'ɛsja] *f* source, origin; **proveniente** *adj*: **proveniente de** coming from, originating from.

**pro'ver** *vt* (*fornecer*) to provide, supply; (*vaga*) to fill // *vi*: ~ **a** to take care of, see to.

**pro'vérbio** *m* proverb.

**pro'veta** *f* test tube.

**provi'dência** *f* providence; ~**s** *fpl* measures, steps; **tomar** ~**s** to take steps; **providenciar** *vt* (*prover*) to provide; (*tomar providências*) to take steps, arrange // *vi* (*tomar providências*) to make arrangements; (*prover*) to make provision; **providenciar para que** to see to it that; **providente** *adj* provident; (*prudente*) prudent, careful.

**pro'vido/a** *adj* (*fornecido*) supplied, provided; (*cheio*) full up, fully stocked.

**'próvido/a** *adj* provident; (*prudente*) prudent, careful.

**provi'mento** m: dar ~ (JUR) to grant a petition.

**pro'víncia** f province; **provinciano/a** adj provincial.

**pro'vir** vi: ~ de to come from, derive from.

**provisão** [provi'zãw] f (abastecimento) provision, supply; **provisões** fpl provisions; **provisório/a** adj provisional, temporary.

**provocação** [provoka'sãw] f provocation; **provocador(a)** adj, **provocante** adj provocative, provoking; **provocar** vt to provoke; (ocasionar) to cause; (atrair) to tempt, attract; (estimular) to rouse, stimulate.

**proximi'dade** f proximity, nearness; ~s fpl neighbourhood, vicinity.

**próximo/a** ['prosimu/a] adj (perto) near, close; (seguinte) next; (vizinho) neighbouring; ~ a/de near to, close to; futuro ~ near, coming // m fellow man.

**pru'dência** f (sabedoria) wisdom; (cautela) care, prudence; **prudente** adj sensible, prudent.

**'prumo** m plumb line; (NÁUT) lead; a ~ perpendicularly, vertically.

**pru'rido** m (comichão) itch; (fig) yearning, desire.

**pseudônimo** [psew'donimu] m pseudonym.

**psicanálise** [psika'nalizi] f psychoanalysis; **psicanalítico/a** adj psychoanalytic(al).

**psicologia** [psikolo'ʒia] f psychology; **psicológico/a** adj psychological; **psicólogo/a** m/f psychologist; **psicopata** m/f psychopath; **psicose** f psychosis.

**psiquiatra** [psiki'atra] m/f psychiatrist; **psiquiatria** f psychiatry; **psiquiátrico/a** adj psychiatric.

**pua** f sharp point; (de broca) bit; (de galo de briga) spur.

**puber'dade** f puberty.

**publicação** [publika'sãw] f publication; **publicar** vt (editar) to publish; (divulgar) to divulge; (proclamar) to announce; (popularizar) to make well known; **publicidade** f publicity; (COM) advertising; **publicitário/a** adj publicity cmp; (COM) advertising cmp; **público/a** adj public // m public (cinema, teatro etc) audience.

**'púcaro** m (Pt) jug, mug.

**'pude** etc vb ver **poder**.

**'púdico/a** adj bashful, shy.

**pudim** [pu'dʒĩ] m pudding; ~-**flã** (Pt) m crème caramel.

**pu'dor** m bashfulness, modesty; **atentado ao** ~ indecent assault.

**puerícia** [pue'risja] f childhood; **puericultura** f child care; **pueril** adj puerile; **puerilidade** f childishness, foolishness.

**pugilato** [puʒi'latu] m boxing, fighting; **pugilismo** m boxing; **pugilista** m boxer.

**'pugna** f fight, struggle; **pugnar** vi (lutar) to struggle; (pelejar) to fight.

**pujança** [pu'ʒãsa] f vigour, strength; (de vegetação) vigorous growth; **na** ~ **da vida** in the prime of life; **pujante** adj vigorous, powerful.

**pu'lar** vi to jump, leap; ~ **de alegria** to jump for joy.

**'pulga** f flea; **pulgão** m greenfly.

**pulha** ['puʎa] m rat, creep.

**pulmão** [pul'mãw] m lung; **pulmonar** adj pulmonary, lung cmp.

**'pulo** m leap, jump; **dar** ~**s de contente** to be delighted; **dar um** ~ **até** to pay a flying visit to; **aos** ~**s** by leaps and bounds; **de um** ~ at one bound.

**pu'lôver** m pullover.

**'púlpito** m pulpit.

**pulsação** [pulsa'sãw] f pulsation, beating; (MED) pulse; **pulsar** vi (palpitar) to pulsate, throb.

**pulseira** [pul'sejra] f bracelet.

**'pulso** m (ANAT) wrist; (MED) pulse; (fig) vigour, energy; **obra de ~** work of great importance; **homem de ~** energetic man; **tomar o ~ de alguém** to take sb's pulse.

**pulu'lar** vi to swarm, teem.

**pulveriza'dor** m (para líquidos etc) spray, spray gun; **pulverizar** vt to pulverize; (reduzir a pó) to grind; (líquido) to spray.

**punção** [pũ'sãw] m (instrumento) punch // f (MED) puncture.

**pundo'nor** m dignity, self-respect.

**pungente** [pũ'ʒẽtʃi] adj (acre) sharp, pungent; (doloroso) painful.

**punguista** [pũ'gista] m pickpocket.

**'punha** etc vb ver **pôr**.

**pu'nhado** m handful.

**punhal** [pu'ɲaw] m dagger; **~ada** f stab.

**punho** ['puɲu] m fist; (de manga) cuff; (de espada) hilt; **de seu próprio ~** in one's own handwriting.

**punição** [puni'sãw] f punishment; **punir** vt to punish.

**'pupilo/a** m (tutelado) ward; (aluno) pupil // f (ANAT) pupil; (tutelada) ward.

**pu'rê** m (tutelado) purée; **~ de batatas** mashed potatoes.

**pu'reza** f purity; (nitidez) clarity.

**'purga** f (MED) purgative; **purgação** f purge; (purificação) purification; **purgante** m purgative; **purgar** vt to purge; (purificar) to purify; **purgativo/a** adj, m purgative; **purgatório** m purgatory.

**purificação** [purifika'sãw] f purification; **purificar** vt to purify; (refinar) to refine; **purista** m/f purist; **puritanismo** m puritanism; **puritano/a** adj (atitude) puritanical; (seita) puritan // m/f (REL) puritan; **puro/a** adj pure; (límpido) clear; (limpo) clean; (verdadeiro) genuine; (completo) complete, absolute; (casto) chaste.

**'púrpura** f purple; **purpúreo/a** adj (cor) crimson.

**puru'lento/a** adj festering, suppurating.

**pus** m pus, matter.

**pus** etc vb ver **pôr**.

**pusi'lânime** adj fainthearted; (covarde) cowardly.

**'puta** f whore, prostitute.

**putrefação** [putrefa'sãw] (Pt: **-cç-**) f rotting, putrefaction; **pútrido/a** adj putrid, rotten.

**puxa'dor** [puʃa'dox] m handle, knob; **puxão** m tug, jerk; **puxar** vt to pull; (sacar) to pull out; (provocar) to provoke; (assunto) to bring up; **puxar a** to take after; **puxa-saco** m creep, crawler, toady.

# Q

**quadra** ['kwadra] f (de rua) block; (estrofe) quatrain; (campo de esportes) court; (período) time, period; (jogos) four; **quadrado/a** adj 'square; (fig) stupid // m 'square; **quadrar** vt to square, make square // vi: **quadrar a** (ser conveniente) to suit; (adaptar-se) to fit, agree with; **quadriculado/a** adj (desenho decorativo) checkered; **papel quadriculado** squared paper.

**quadril** [kwa'driw] m hip, haunch.

**quadrilha** [kwa'driʎa] f gang; (dança) square dance.

**quadro** ['kwadru] m (pintura) painting; (lista) list; (tabela) chart, table; (TEC: painel) panel; (pessoal) staff; (teatro) scene; **~ de avisos** bulletin board; **~ negro** blackboard; **~ de reserva** (MIL) reserve list.

**'quádruplo/a** adj quadruple.

**qual** [kwaw] pron, pl **quais** [kwajʃ] which; **~ deles** which of them; **o ~** which; (pessoa: sujeito) who; (pessoa: objeto) whom; **seja ~** for whatever/whichever it may be; **cada ~** each one; **~ é?/~ é** é a tua?

what are you up to? // conj as, like;
~ **seja** such as; **tal** ~ just like //
excl nonsense!; ~ **nada!/** o quê!
no such thing!

**qualidade** [kwali'dadʒi] f quality;
**na** ~ **de** in the capacity of.

**qualificação** [kwalifika'sãw] f
qualification; **qualificado/a** adj
qualified; **qualificar** vt to qualify;
**qualificar de/como** to classify as,
regard as; **qualificar-se** vr to
qualify.

**qualquer** [kwaw'kex] adj, pl
**quais'quer** [kwaj'kex] any //
pron any; (pessoa) anyone, anybody;
~ **dos dois** either; ~ **outro** any
other; ~ **dia** any day; ~ **que seja**
whichever it may be; (pessoa)
whoever it may be; **um disco** ~ any
record at all, any record you like.

**quando** ['kwãdu] adv when // conj
when; (interrogativo) when?; (se) if,
even if; (ao passo que) whilst; **ainda**
~ even though; ~ **muito** at most;
~ **menos** at least; ~ **quer que**
whenever; **de** ~ **em** ~/**de vez em**
~ now and then; **desde** ~? how
long?, since when?; ~ **mais não**
**seja** if for no other reason.

**quantia** [kwã'tʃia] f sum, amount;
**quantidade** f quantity, amount.

**quanto/a** ['kwãtu/a] adj, pron all
that, as much as; (interrogativo: sg)
how much? (: pl) **quantos/as** how
many? // adv: ~ **tempo?** how long?;
~ **custa?** how much does it cost?;
~ **a as** regards; ~ **a mim** as for me;
~ **antes** as soon as possible; ~
**mais cedo melhor** the sooner the
better; ~ **mais trabalha, mais**
**ganha** the more he works, the more
he earns; **tudo** ~ everything that, as
much as; ~ **sofria!** how he suffered!

**quão** [kwãw] adv how.

**quarenta** [kwa'rẽta] num forty.

**quarentão** [kwarẽ'tãw] m man in
his forties.

**quaren'tena** f quarantine.

**quaren'tona** f woman in her
forties.

**quaresma** [kwa'reʒma] f Lent.

**quarta-feira** ['kwaxta-fejra] f
Wednesday; ~ **de cinzas** Ash
Wednesday.

**quarteirão** [kwaxtej'rãw] m (de
casas) block; (número) quarter-
century.

**quartel** [kwax'tɛw] m (MIL)
barracks sg; (quarta parte) quarter;
(um século) quarter-century;
~**general** m headquarters pl.

**quarteto** [kwax'tetu] m (MÚS)
quartet.

**quarto/a** ['kwaxtu/a] adj fourth //
m (quarta parte) quarter;
(aposento) room; (MIL) watch;
(anca) haunch; ~ **de banho**
bathroom; ~ **de dormir** bedroom;
~ **de casal** double bedroom; ~ **de**
**solteiro** single room;
**crescente/minguante** (ASTRO)
first/last quarter // f quarter; (de
cântaro) pitcher; (MÚS) fourth.

**quartzo** ['kwaxtsu] m quartz.

**quase** ['kwazi] adv almost, nearly.

**quatro** ['kwatru] num four;
~**centos/as** num four hundred.

**que** [ki] pron (sujeito) who, that;
(: coisa) which, that; (complemento)
whom, that; (: coisa) which, that;
(interrogativo: coisa) what?, which?;
**o** ~ (coisa) what; (pessoa) he who;
(interrogativo) what?, which?;
**não** other than, but; **nada** ~ **fazer**
nothing to do; ~ **nem** (BR: col) like
// conj that // adj which, what; ~
**jornal?** what newspaper?; ~ **pena!**
what a pity!; **do** ~ than; **mais do** ~
**pensa** more than you think; **não há**
**nada** ~ **fazer** there's nothing to be
done.

**quê** [ke] m something;
(complicação) complication; **tem**
**seus** ~**s** it has its drawbacks; **não**
**tem de** ~ don't mention it; **para** ~?
what for?; **por** ~? why?

**quebra** ['kebra] f break, rupture;

(COM) bankruptcy; **de** ~ as a bonus, extra; ~**-cabeça** m puzzle, problem; (jogo) jigsaw puzzle; **quebradiço/a** adj fragile, breakable; **quebrado/a** adj (partido) broken; (cansado) exhausted; (COM) bankrupt // (vertente) slope; (barranco) ravine, gully; (curva) bend.

**quebra-'galho** adj inv makeshift //m stopgap.

**quebra-gelo** [kebra-'ʒelu] m (NÁUT) icebreaker.

**quebra-luz** [kebra-'luʃ] m lampshade.

**quebra-mar** [kebra-'max] m breakwater, sea wall.

**quebra-nozes** [kebra-'noziʃ] m inv nutcrackers pl.

**quebrantar** [kebrã'tax] vt (quebrar) to break; (debilitar) to weaken, wear out; ~**-se** vr (tornar-se fraco) to grow weak; **quebranto** m (fraqueza) weakness; (mau-olhado) blight, evil eye.

**quebrar** [ke'brax] vt (romper) to break; (debilitar) to weaken // vi (COM) to go bankrupt; ~**-se** vr (romper-se) to get broken.

**queda** ['keda] f fall; (decadência) decline; (ruína) downfall; (tendência) inclination; ~**-d'água** f waterfall.

**queijada** [kej'ʒada] f cheesecake; (coletivo) a lot of cheese; **queijo** m cheese.

**queima** ['kejma] f burning; (COM) clearance sale; **queimado/a** adj burnt; (zangado) angry; **queimada do sol** sunburnt; **queimadura** f burn; **queimadura do sol** sunburn; **queimar** vt to burn, scorch; (com líquido) to scald; (bronzear a pele) to tan; (murchar) to wither; (mercadorias) to sell cheaply // vi to burn; (estar quente) to be burning hot; **queimar-se** vr (pessoa) to burn o.s.; (incendiar-se) to burn down; (zangar-se) to get angry; ~**-roupa** f:

à ~**-roupa** point-blank; (MIL) at point-blank range.

**'queixa** etc vb ver **quexer.**

**queixa** ['kejʃa] f complaint; (lamentação) lament; (gemido) moan.

**queixada** [kej'ʃada] f (de animal) jaw.

**queixar-se** [kej'ʃax-sɪ] vr to complain; (soltar gemidos) to wail; ~ **de** to complain about.

**queixo** ['kejʃu] m (barba) chin; (maxilar) jaw; **de** ~ **caído** open-mouthed.

**queixoso/a** [kej'ʃozu/a] adj complaining; (magoado) doleful // m (JUR) plaintiff; **queixume** m complaint; (lamentação) lament; (gemido) moan.

**quem** [kẽj] pron who, whom; (interrogativo) who?, whom?; ~ **quer que** whoever; **seja** ~ **for** whoever it may be; **de** ~ whose; ~ **é?** who is it?, who is there?

**quente** ['kẽtʃi] adj hot; (fig) fiery, ardent; **quentura** f heat, warmth.

**quer** [kex] conj either, or; ~ **chova** ~ **não** whether it rains or not; ~ **queiras**, ~ **não** whether you like it or not; **onde** ~ **que** wherever; **quando** ~ **que** whenever; **quem** ~ **que** whoever.

**querela** [ke'rɛla] f dispute; (JUR) complaint, accusation; **querelado** m (JUR) defendant; **querelador(a)** m/f, **querelante** m/f (JUR) plaintiff; **querelar** vt (JUR) to prosecute, sue // vi: **querelar contra/de** (queixar-se) to lodge a complaint against; **querelar-se** vr to complain.

**querença** [ke'rẽsa] f liking, affection.

**querer** [ke'rex] vt (desejar) to want, wish; (ter afeição) to be fond of; ~ **bem a** to love; ~ **mal a** to hate; ~ **dizer** to mean; **sem** ~ unintentionally; **querido/a** adj dear // m/f darling.

**quermesse** [kex'mɛsɪ] f church fête.

**querosene** [kero'zenɪ] m kerosene oil.

**quesito** [ke'zɪtu] m (questão) query, question; (requesito) requirement.

**questão** [keʃ'tãw] f (pergunta) question, inquiry; (assunto) matter, question; (contenda) dispute, quarrel; **fazer ~ de** to insist on; **questionar** vi to question, argue // vt to question, call into question; **questionário** m questionnaire.

**quiçá** [kɪ'sa] adv perhaps.

**quieto/a** [kɪ'etu/a] adj still, quiet; **quietude** f calm, tranquillity.

**quilate** [kɪ'latʃɪ] m carat; (fig) excellence.

**quilha** [ˈkɪʎa] f (NÁUT) keel; ~ **corrediça** centreboard.

**quilo** [ˈkɪlu] m kilo; ~**grama** m kilogramme; **quilômetro** m kilometre; ~**watt** m kilowatt.

**quimera** [kɪˈmɛra] f chimera; **quimérico/a** adj fantastic.

**químico/a** [ˈkɪmɪku/a] adj chemical // m/f chemist // f chemistry.

**quina** [ˈkɪna] f (canto) corner; (em jogos) five; **de ~** edgeways; (US) edgewise.

**quinhão** [kɪˈɲãw] m share, portion.

**quinhentista** [kɪɲeˈtʃɪʃta] adj sixteenth century cmp; **quinhentos/as** num five hundred.

**quinina** [kɪˈnina] f quinine.

**quinquagenário/a** [kwɪkwaˈʒeˈnarju/a] adj in his/her fifties.

**quinquilharias** [kɪˈkɪʎaˈɾiaʃ] fpl odds and ends; (miudezas) knick-nacks, trinkets.

**quinta-feira** [kɪˈtaˈfejra] f Thursday.

**quintal** [kɪˈtaw] m back yard; (jardim) back garden.

**quinteiro** [kɪˈtejru] m (Pt) farmer.

**quinto/a** [ˈkɪtu/a] adj, m fifth // f estate; (terreno cultivado) farm.

**quinze** [ˈkɪzɪ] num fifteen; **duas e ~**

a quarter past two; ~ **para as sete** a quarter to seven; **quinzena** f fortnight; (salário) fortnight's wages.

**quiosque** [kɪˈɔʃkɪ] m (Pt: com jornais) newsstand; (: com comida/bebida) food/drink stand.

**quiromante** [kɪroˈmãtʃɪ] m/f palmist, fortune teller.

**'quis** etc vb ver **querer**.

**quisto** [ˈkɪʃtu] m cyst.

**quitação** [kɪtaˈsãw] f (de dívidas) discharge, remission; (recibo) receipt.

**quitanda** [kɪˈtãda] f (loja) grocer's (shop); **quitandeiro** m (numa loja) grocer; (vendedor de hortaliças) greengrocer.

**quitar** [kɪˈtax] vt (dívida) to pay off; (desquitar-se) to separate from; **quite** adj (livre) free; (com um credor) squared up; (igualado) even.

**quociente** [kwoˈsjẽtʃɪ] m quotient; ~ **de inteligência, (Q.I.)** intelligence quotient, (I.Q.).

**quota** [ˈkwota] f quota; (porção) share, portion.

**quotidiano/a** [kwotʃiˈdʒjanu/a] adj (usual) everyday.

# R

**R** abr de **Rua** street.

**rã** f frog.

**ra'bada** f (rabo) tail; (fig) tail end.

**raba'nada** f (fatia) French toast.

**raba'nete** m radish.

**ra'bino** m rabbi.

**rabis'car** vt (escrever mal, às pressas) to scribble // vi to doodle; (escrever mal) to scribble.

**'rabo** m (cauda) tail; (col) bottom; ~**de-cavalo** m ponytail.

**rabu'gento/a** adj sulky, grumpy.

**'raça** f race; (de animal) breed; **de**

~ thoroughbred; (*pessoa*) of character, of breeding.

**ração** [xa'sãw] f ration.

**racha** ['xaʃa] f (*fenda*) split; (*greta*) crack /// m (col) scrap.

**rachador** [xaʃa'dox] m woodcutter; **rachadura** f (*fenda*) crack; **rachar** vt (*objeto, despesas*) to split; (*lenha*) to chop // vi, **rachar-se** vr to split; (*cristal*) to crack; **frio de rachar** bitter cold.

**racial** [xa'sjaw] adj racial.

**raciocinar** [xasjosi'nax] vi to reason; **raciocínio** m reasoning; **racional** adj rational; **racionalizar** vt to rationalize.

**racionamento** [xasjona'mẽtu] m rationing; **racionar** vt (*distribuir*) to ration out; (*limitar a venda de*) to ration.

**racismo** [xa'sɪʒmu] m racialism, racism; **racista** adj, m/f racist.

**ra'dar** m radar.

**radiação** [xadʒia'sãw] f radiation; (*raio*) ray; **radiador** m radiator; **radiante** adj radiant; (*de alegria*) overjoyed.

**radical** [xadʒi'kaw] adj radical // m radical; (LING) root; **radicar-se** vr to take root; (*fixar residência*) to settle down.

**rádio** ['xadʒju] m radio; (QUÍM) radium; **radioamador** m radio ham.

**radioa'tivo/a** (Pt: **-ct-**) adj radioactive.

**radiodifusão** [xadʒjodʒifu'zãw] f broadcasting; **radiodifusora** f radio station; **radioemissora** f radio broadcasting station.

**radiogra'far** vt to X-ray; **radiografia** f X-ray.

**radio'grama** m cablegram.

**radiojornal** [xadʒjoʒux'naw] m radio news.

**radi'oso/a** adj radiant, brilliant; (*fig:* radiante) radiant; (: alegre) overjoyed.

**radiotera'pia** f radiotherapy.

**radiouvinte** [xadʒjo'vĩtʃi] m/f listener.

**ra'gu** m stew, ragoût.

**raia** ['xaja] f (*risca*) line; (*fronteira*) boundary; (*limite*) limit; (*de corrida*) track; (*peixe*) ray, skate; **chegar às ~s** to reach the limit; **raiado/a** adj striped.

**raiar** [xa'jax] vi (*brilhar*) to shine; (*madrugada*) to dawn; (*aparecer*) to appear.

**rainha** [xa'iɲa] f queen.

**raio** ['xaju] m (*de sol*) ray; (*de luz*) beam; (*de roda*) spoke; (*relâmpago*) flash of lightning; (*distância*) range; (MAT) radius; **~s X** X-rays.

**raiva** ['xajva] f rage, fury; (MED) rabies sg; **ter ~ de** to hate; **raivoso/a** adj furious; (MED) rabid, mad.

**raiz** [xa'iʃ] f root; (*origem*) source; **~ quadrada** square root; **criar raízes** to put down roots.

**rajada** [xa'ʒada] f (*vento*) gust; (*de tiros*) burst.

**ra'lado/a** adj: **pão ~** breadcrumbs pl; **ralador** m grater; **ralar** vt (*coco*) to grate; (*pão*) to crumble; (*fig*) to annoy.

**ra'lé** f the common people, rabble.

**rale'ar** vt/i to thin out.

**ralhar** [xa'ʎax] vi to scold; **~ com alguém** to tell sb off.

**'ralo/a** adj thin, sparse // m (*de regador*) rose, nozzle; (*ralador*) grater.

**'rama** f branches pl, foliage; **em ~** raw; **pela ~** superficially; **ramada** f branches pl, foliage; **ramagem** f branches pl, foliage; **ramal** m (FERRO) branch line; (*telefônico*) extension; (AUTO) branch (road).

**ramalhete** [xama'ʎetʃi] m bouquet, posy.

**ramifi'car-se** vr to branch out; **ramo** m branch; (*profissão, negócios*) line; (*de flores*) bunch; **Domingo de Ramos** Palm Sunday.

**'rampa** f ramp; (*ladeira*) slope.

**ran'çar** vi to go rancid.

**rancheiro** [xã'ʃejru] m cook; **rancho** m (grupo) group, band; (cabana) hut; (MIL) mess.

**ran'cor** m (ressentimento) bitterness; (ódio) hatred; ~**oso/a** adj bitter, resentful; (odiento) hateful.

**ran'çoso/a** adj rancid; (cheiro) musty.

**ranger** [xã'ʒex] vi to creak // vt: ~**os dentes** to grind one's teeth; **rangido** m creak.

**ranho** ['xaɲu] m (col) snot; **ranhoso/a** adj (col) snotty.

**ranhura** [xa'ɲura] f groove; (para moeda) slot.

**ra'núnculo** m buttercup.

**rapace** [xa'pasi] adj rapacious // f bird of prey; **rapacidade** f rapacity, rapaciousness.

**rapadeira** [xapa'dejra] f scraper.

**rapa'pé** m bowing and scraping; (lisonja) flattery.

**ra'par** vt to scrape; (barbear) to shave; (o cabelo) to crop; ~**alguém** (roubar) to steal from sb; (col) to pinch from sb.

**rapa'riga** f (Pt) girl; (Br) young woman.

**ra'paz** m boy; (col) lad; ~**iada** f (grupo) gang of lads.

**ra'pé** m snuff.

**rapi'dez** f speed, rapidity; **rápido/a** adj quick, fast // adv fast, quickly // m (trem) express.

**ra'pina** f robbery; **ave de** ~ bird of prey.

**ra'poso/a** m/f (fig) crafty person // m fox // f vixen.

**rap'sódia** f rhapsody.

**rap'tar** vt to kidnap; **rapto** m kidnapping; **raptor** m kidnapper.

**raqueta** [xa'keta] f, **raquete** [xa'ketʃi] f (de tênis) racquet; (de pingue-pongue) bat.

**raquítico/a** [xa'kitʃiku/a] adj (franzino) stunted, puny; (fig) poor, feeble; **raquitismo** m rickets sg.

**rara'mente** adv rarely, seldom; **rarear** vt to make scarce // vi to become scarce; (cabelos) to thin; **raridade** f rarity; **raro/a** adj rare; (ralo) thin // adv rarely, seldom.

**ra'sante** adj (vôo) low-flying.

**ra'sar** vt (nivelar) to level; (tocar de leve: a pele) to graze; (: as ondas) to skim; (encher) to fill to the brim; ~**se** vr to fill up.

**rascunhar** [xaʃku'ɲax] vt to draft, make a rough copy of; **rascunho** m rough copy, draft.

**ras'gado/a** adj (roupa) torn, ripped; (cumprimentos) effusive; (gesto) generous; **rasgão** m tear, rip; **rasgar** vt to tear, rip; (destruir) to tear up, rip up; **rasgar-se** vr to split; **rasgo** m (rasgão) tear, rip; (risco) stroke; (ação) feat; (ímpeto) burst; (da imaginação) flight.

**'raso/a** adj (liso) flat, level; (sapato) flat; (não fundo) shallow; (baixo) low; **soldado** ~ private.

**'raspa** f (de madeira) shaving; (de metal) filing; ~**deira** f scraper; **raspão** m scratch, graze; **tocar de raspão** to graze; **raspar** vt (limpar, tocar) to scrape; (alisar) to file; (ferir) to graze; (arranhar) to scratch; (pêlos) to shave; (apagar) to rub out; **raspar-se** vr to clear off, sneak off.

**rasteiro/a** [xaʃ'tejru/a] adj (que se arrasta) crawling; (planta) creeping; (de pouca altura) low-lying; (ordinário) common // f (pessoa) trip; **dar uma** ~**a em** to trip up; **rastejar** vi (com dificuldade) to crawl; (furtivamente) to creep.

**rastilho** [xaʃ'tʃiʎu] m (de pólvora) fuse.

**'rasto** m (vestígio) trace; (sinal) sign; (pista) track, trail; **andar de** ~**s** to crawl; **levar de** ~**s** to drag along.

**ratão** m rat; **ratazana** f rat.

**rate'ar** vt (dividir) to share // vi (motor) to break down.

**ratifi'car** vt to confirm, ratify.

**'rato** m rat; (Pt: *rato pequeno*) mouse; (*ladrão*) thief; ~ **de biblioteca** bookworm; ~**eira** f rat trap; (*pequena*) mousetrap.

**razão** [xa'zãw] f (*juízo, motivo*) reason; (*bom senso*) common sense; (*raciocínio, argumento*) reasoning, argument; (*conta*) account; (MAT) ratio // m (COM) ledger; **à** ~ **de** at the rate of; **em** ~ **de** on account of; **dar** ~ **a alguém** to support sb; **ter** ~/**não ter** ~ to be right/be wrong; **razoar** vi (*raciocinar*) to reason; (*falar*) to talk; **razoável** adj reasonable; (*moderado, justo*) fair.

**r/c** (Pt) abr de **rés-do-chão** ground floor; (Pt) first floor.

**ré** f ver **réu**; (AUTO) reverse gear; **dar marcha a** ~ to reverse, back up.

**reabastecer** [xiabaʃte'sex] vt (AUTO) to refuel; (*mercadorias*) to restock.

**reabili'tar** vt (*restituir*) to restore the reputation of; (*condenado*) to rehabilitate.

**rea'brir** vt to reopen.

**reação** [xia'sãw] (Pt: **-çç-**) f reaction; ~ **em cadeia** chain reaction; **reacionário/a** adj reactionary; **reagir** vi to react; **reagir a** (*resistir*) to resist; (*protestar*) to rebel against.

**re'al** adj real; (*de rei*) royal.

**realçar** [xeaw'sax] vt to accentuate, emphasize; (fig, com maquilagem) to highlight; **realce** m (*destaque*) emphasis; (*mais brilho*) highlight; **dar realce a** to enhance.

**realejo** [xea'leʒu] m barrel organ.

**rea'leza** f royalty.

**realidade** [xeali'dadʒi] f reality; **na** ~ really, in fact.

**realimentação** [xealimẽta'sãw] f (ELET) feedback.

**realização** [xealiza'sãw] f fulfilment; (de projeto) execution, carrying out; (transformação em

dinheiro) conversion into cash; **realizar** vt (um objetivo) to achieve; (projeto) to carry out; (ambições) to fulfill; (reunião) to hold; (negócios) to transact; **realizar-se** vr (acontecer) to take place; (sonhos) to come true.

**realmente** [xeaw'mẽtʃi] adv really, actually.

**reani'mar** vt to revive; (encorajar) to encourage; ~**se** vr (pessoa) to cheer up.

**reaparecer** [xeapare'sex] vi to reappear.

**rea'tar** vt (continuar) to resume, take up again; (nó) to retie.

**rea'tor** (Pt: **-ct-**) m reactor.

**rea'ver** vt to recover, get back.

**rebaixa** [xe'bajʃa] f reduction; (tornar mais baixo) to lower; (o preço de) to lower the price of; (humilhar) to put down, humiliate // vi to drop; **rebaixar-se** vr to demean o.s.

**rebanho** [xe'baɲu] m (de carneiros, fig) flock; (de gado, elefantes) herd.

**rebarba'tivo/a** adj (pessoa) disagreeable, unpleasant.

**rebate** [xe'batʃi] m (sinal) alarm; (COM) discount; ~ **falso** false alarm; **rebater** vt (um golpe) to ward off; (acusações) to refute; (COM) to discount; (futebol) to kick back.

**rebe'lar-se** vr to rebel, revolt; **rebelde** adj rebellious; (indisciplinado) unruly, wild // m/f rebel; **rebeldia** f rebelliousness; (fig: obstinação) stubbornness; (: oposição) defiance; **rebelião** f rebellion.

**rebentão** [xebẽ'tãw] m offshoot; (criança) offspring; **rebentar** vi (guerra) to break out; (brotar) to sprout; **rebentar de alegria** to burst with happiness; **rebento** m shoot; (filho) offspring.

**rebite** [xe'bitʃi] m (TEC) rivet.

**rebo'ar** vi to resound, echo.

**reboca'dor** m (embarcação)

tug(boat); (de paredes) plasterer; **rebocar** vt (paredes) to plaster; (veículo mal estacionado) to tow away; (dar reboque a) to tow; **reboco** m plaster.

**rebo'lar** vt (os quadris) to swing // vi, ~-**se** vr to roll over; (bambolear-se) to sway; (fig) to work hard.

**re'bolo** m (mó) grindstone; (cilindro) cylinder.

**reboque** [xe'bɔki] m (ato) tow; (cabo) towrope; **carro ~** trailer; **a ~** in tow.

**re'bordo** m rim, edge.

**rebu'çado** m (Pt) sweet; (US) candy.

**rebu'liço** m commotion, hubbub.

**rebus'cado/a** adj affected; **rebuscar** vt (buscar) to search carefully for.

**re'cado** m (mensagem) message; **mandar ~** to send word; **menino de ~s** errand boy.

**reca'ída** f relapse.

**recalci'trante** adj recalcitrant.

**reca'mado/a** adj embroidered.

**recambiar** [xekã'bjax] vt to send back.

**re'canto** m (lugar aprazível) corner, nook; (esconderijo) hiding place.

**recapitu'lar** vt to sum up, recapitulate.

**reca'tado/a** adj (modesto) modest; (reservado) reserved; **recatar-se** vr to become withdrawn; (ocultar-se) to hide; **recato** m (modéstia) modesty.

**recauchutado/a** [xekaw-ʃu'tadu/a] adj: **pneumático ~** (AUTO) retread, remould.

**recear** [xese'ax] vt to fear // vi to be afraid.

**recebe'dor(a)** m/f receiver; (de impostos) collector; **receber** vt to receive; (hóspedes) to take in; (convidados) to entertain; (acolher bem) to welcome // vi to entertain, have guests; **recebimento** m (Br)

reception; (de uma carta) receipt; **acusar o recebimento de** to acknowledge receipt of.

**receio** [xe'seju] m fear.

**receita** [xe'sejta] f (renda) income; (do Estado) revenue; (MED) prescription; (culinária) recipe; **receitar** vt to prescribe.

**recém** [xe'sẽ] adv recently, newly; ~-**chegado/a** m/f newcomer; ~-**nascido/a** m/f newborn child.

**recen'der** vt: ~ **um cheiro** to give off a smell // vi to smell; ~ **a** to smell of.

**recenseamento** [xesẽsɪa'mẽtu] m census; **recensear** vt to take a census of.

**recente** [xe'sẽtʃɪ] adj recent; (novo) new, fresh.

**receoso/a** [xese'ozu/a] adj (medroso) frightened, fearful; (tímido) timid, shy.

**recepção** [xesɛp'sãw] f reception; (de uma carta) receipt; (Pt): **acusar a ~ de** to acknowledge receipt of; **recepcionista** m/f receptionist.

**recep'táculo** m receptacle.

**recep'tar** vt to receive; **receptivo/a** adj receptive; (acolhedor) welcoming; **receptor** m (TEC) receiver.

**recheado/a** [xeʃi'adu/a] adj (ave) stuffed; (empada, bolo) filled; (cheio) full, crammed; **recheio** m (para carne assada) stuffing; (de empada, de bolo) filling; (o conteúdo) contents pl.

**rechonchudo/a** [xeʃõ'ʃudu/a] adj chubby, plump.

**re'cibo** m (documento) receipt.

**reci'diva** f recurrence.

**recife** [xe'sifɪ] m reef.

**re'cinto** m (espaço fechado) enclosure; (lugar) area.

**recipiente** [xesɪpɪ'ẽtʃɪ] m container, receptacle.

**recipro'car** vt (trocar) to exchange; **recíproco/a** adj reciprocal.

**'récita** f (teatral) performance;
**recitação** f recitation; **recital** m
recital; **recitar** vt (declamar) to
recite.

**reclamação** [xeklama'sãw] f
(queixa) complaint; (protesto)
protest; (JUR) claim; **reclamante**
m/f claimant; **reclamar** vt (exigir)
to demand; (herança) to claim // vi:
**reclamar contra** to complain about;
**reclame** m, **reclamo** m (anúncio)
advertisement; (queixa) complaint.

**recli'nar** vt, **recli'nar-se** vr to
rest, lean; (deitar-se) to lie down.

**reclusão** [xeklu'jãw] f (isolamento)
seclusion; (encarceramento) imprisonment; (prisão) prison.

**reco'brar** vt to recover, get back;
**~-se** vr to recover.

**recolher** [xeko'ʎeʀ] vt (dados,
mensalidades) to collect; (gado,
roupa) to bring in; (juntar) to gather
together; (abrigar) to give shelter
to; (notas antigas) to withdraw;
**~-se** vr (ir para casa) to go home;
(deitar-se) to go to bed; (retrair-se)
to withdraw; (concentrar-se) to
meditate; **recolhido/a** adj (lugar)
secluded; (retraído) withdrawn;
**recolhimento** m (vida retraída)
retirement; (contemplação) meditation.

**recomendação** [xekomẽda'sãw] f
recommendation; (conselho) advice;
(advertência) warning; **recomendações** fpl regards; **recomendar** vt
(aconselhar) to recommend, advise;
**recomendar alguém a alguém** to
remember sb to sb, give sb's
regards to sb.

**recom'pensa** f (prêmio) reward;
(indenização) recompense;
**recompensar** vt (premiar) to
reward; (indenizar) to compensate
for.

**recom'por** vt (reorganizar) to
reorganize; (restabelecer) to
restore.

**reconcili'ar** vt to reconcile; **~-se**

vt to become reconciled.

**re'côndito/a** adj (escondido)
hidden; (ignorado) unknown.

**reconfor'tar** vt to invigorate;
**~-se** vr to be invigorated.

**reconhecer** [xekoɲe'seʀ] vt to
recognize; (admitir) to realise,
admit; (MIL) to reconnoitre;
(assinatura) to witness;
**reconhecido/a** adj recognized;
(agradecido) grateful, thankful;
**reconhecimento** m recognition;
(gratidão) gratitude; (MIL)
reconnaissance.

**reconquista** [xekõ'kiʃta] f
reconquest.

**reconside'rar** vt/i to reconsider.

**reconstituinte** [xekõʃtʃi'twĩtʃi] m
tonic.

**reconstru'ir** vt to rebuild,
reconstruct.

**recordação** [xekoxda'sãw] f
(reminiscência) memory; (coisa)
souvenir, memento; **recordar** vt
(lembrar) to remember; **recordar-
se** vr: **recordar-se de** to remember.

**re'corde** adj inv record cmp // m
record; **em tempo ~** in record time;
**bater um ~** to break a record.

**recor'rer** vi: **~ a** (para socorro) to
run to, turn to; (valer-se) to resort
to; **~ da sentença** (JUR) to appeal
against the sentence.

**recor'tar** vt to cut out; **~-se** vr to
be silhouetted; **recorte** m (ato)
cutting out; (de jornal) cutting,
clipping; **álbum de recortes**
scrapbook.

**recos'tar** vt to lean, rest; **~-se** vr
to lean back; (deitar-se) to lie down.

**recreação** [xekrea'sãw] f fun,
recreation; **por sua alta ~** just for
fun; **recrear** vt to entertain, amuse;
**recrear-se** vr to have fun;
**recreativo/a** adj recreational;
**recreio** m recreation;
(divertimento) amusement, fun;
**hora do recreio** break; (escola)

playtime; **viagem de recreio** trip, outing.

**recri'ar** vt to recreate.

**recrimina'ção** [xekrımına'sãw] f recrimination; **recriminar** vt to reproach, reprove.

**recrudes'cência** f worsening; **recrudescer** vi to grow worse, worsen; **recrudescimento** m worsening.

**re'cruta** m/f recruit; **~mento** m recruitment.

**récua** ['xɛkwa] f (de mulas) pack, train; (de cavalos) drove.

**recu'ar** vt/i to move back.

**recuperação** [xekupera'sãw] f recovery; **recuperar** vt to recover; (tempo perdido) to make up for; (reabilitar) to rehabilitate; **recuperar-se** vr: **recuperar-se de** to recuperate from.

**re'curso** m resort; (JUR) appeal; **~s** mpl (meios) means; (: financeiros) resources; **em último ~** as a last resort.

**re'cusa** f refusal; (negação) denial; **recusar** vt (não aceitar) to refuse; (negar) to deny; (rejeitar) to reject; **recusar-se** vr: **recusar-se a** to refuse to.

**redação** [xeda'sãw] (Pt: **-cç-**) f (escolar) composition, essay; (de jornal) editing; (redatores) editorial staff; (lugar) editorial office.

**redargüir** [xedax'gwix] vi to retort.

**reda'tor(a)** (Pt: **-ct-**) m/f journalist; (revisor) editor; **~-chefe** m/f editor in chief.

**rede** ['xedʒi] f net; (de salvamento) safety net; (de cabelos) hairnet; (de dormir) hammock; (cilada) trap; (FERRO. TEC) network.

**'rédea** f rein; **dar ~ larga a** to give free rein to.

**redemoinho** [xedemo'iɲu] m ver **remoinho**.

**redenção** [xedẽ'sãw] f redemption;

**redentor(a)** adj redeeming // m/f redeemer.

**redigir** [xedʒi'ʒix] vt (escrever) to compose, write.

**re'dil** m (Pt) sheepfold.

**redo'brar** vt to fold again; (aumentar) to increase; (sinos) to ring out // vi (aumentar) to increase; (sinos) to ring out.

**redon'deza** f roundness; (arredores) vicinity; **redondo/a** adj round; (gordo) plump.

**re'dor** m: **ao/em ~ (de)** around, round about.

**redução** [xedu'sãw] f reduction; (MED: ossos) setting.

**redun'dância** f redundancy; **redundar** vi: **redundar em** (resultar em) to result in.

**re'duto** m stronghold.

**redu'zido/a** adj reduced; (limitado) limited; (pequeno) small; **reduzir** vt to reduce; (dinheiro) to convert; (MED) to set; (abreviar) to abridge; **reduzir-se** vr: **reduzir-se a** to be reduced to.

**reembolsar** [xiẽbol'sax] vt to reimburse; (depósito) to refund; **reembolso** m refund, repayment; **reembolso postal** cash on delivery, C.O.D.

**refa'zer** vt (fazer novamente) to redo, repeat; (consertar) to repair, fix; (restaurar) to restore; (nutrir) to build up; **~-se** vr (MED) to recover.

**re'fego** m (dobra) fold; (num vestido) pleat.

**refeição** [xefej'sãw] f meal.

**refei'tório** m dining hall, refectory.

**refém** [xe'fẽ] m hostage.

**refe'rência** f reference; **com ~ a** with reference to, about.

**referen'dar** vt to countersign, endorse.

**referendum** [xefe'rẽdũ] m (POL) referendum.

**refe'rente** adj: **~ a** concerning, regarding.

**refe'rido/a** adj aforesaid, already mentioned; **referir** vt (contar) to relate, tell; **referir-se** vr: **referir-se a** to refer to.

**refeste'lar-se** vr (recostar-se) to stretch out, lean back; (comprazer-se) to enjoy o.s.

**refi'nado/a** adj refined; (completo) absolute; **refinamento** m refinement; **refinar** vt to refine; (fig) to perfect, polish; **refinaria** f refinery.

**refle'tido/a** (Pt: **-ct-**) adj reflected; (prudente) thoughtful; **refletir** (Pt: **-ct-**) vt (espelhar) to reflect; (som) to echo; **refletir em** (pensar) to consider, think about; **refletir-se** vr to be reflected; **refletor(a)** (Pt: **-ct-**) adj reflecting // m reflector.

**reflexão** [xeflɛk'sãw] f reflection; (contemplação) thought, contemplation; **reflexivo/a** adj reflexive.

**re'flexo/a** adj (luz) reflected; (ação) reflex // m reflection; (MED) reflex; (cópia) copy.

**refluxo** [xe'fluksu] m ebb.

**refo'gado** m (tempero) sautéed seasonings; (prato) stew; **refogar** vt to stew in seasoning.

**refor'çado/a** adj strengthened; (forte) strong; (ARQ) reinforced; **reforçar** vt (fazer mais forte) to strengthen; (revigorar) to invigorate; **reforçar-se** vr to grow stronger; **reforço** m reinforcement.

**re'forma** f (agrária) reform; (ARQ) renovation; (REL) reformation; (aposentadoria) retirement; **reformado/a** adj (Pt: MIL) retired; **reformar** vt (ARQ) to rebuild, renovate; (modificar) to change, alter; (aposentar) to retire; (sentença) to commute; **reformar-se** vr (militar) to retire; (prisioneiro) to reform, mend one's ways.

**reforma'tório** m approved school, borstal.

**refrão** [xe'frãw] m (cantado) refrain; (provérbio) saying.

**refra'tário/a** (Pt: **-ct-**) adj (desobediente) difficult, unmanageable; (TEC) heat-resistant.

**refre'ar** vt (frear) to check; (dominar) to restrain; ~ **a língua** to mind one's language, mince one's words; ~**se** vr to restrain o.s.

**re'frega** f fight.

**refres'cante** adj refreshing; **refrescar** vt (refrigerar) to cool; (restaurar) to refresh // vi to cool down; **refrescar-se** vr to be refreshed; **refresco** m (bebida) cool drink.

**refrigerador** [xefriʒera'dox] m refrigerator; (col) fridge; **refrigerante** m cool drink, soft drink; **refrigerar** vt to keep cool; (consolar) to comfort, console; **refrigério** m solace, consolation.

**refugiado/a** [xefuʒi'adu/a] m/f refugee; **refugiar-se** vr to take refuge, seek shelter; **refúgio** m refuge.

**re'fugo** m waste, rubbish; (US) garbage; (coisa inútil) reject.

**reful'gência** f brilliance; **refulgir** vi to shine out.

**refun'dir** vt (ouro) to recast; (escrito) to revise; ~**se** vr (derreter-se) to melt.

**refutação** [xefuta'sãw] f refutation; **refutar** vt to refute.

**reg** abr de **regimento, regular.**

**reg°** abr de **regulamento.**

**'rega** f watering; (irrigação) irrigation.

**re'gaço** m (colo) lap.

**rega'dor** m watering can.

**rega'lado/a** adj (encantado) delighted; (confortável) comfortable // adv comfortably; **regalar** vt (causar prazer) to delight; **regalar alguém com algo** to give sb sth, present sb with sth; **regalar-se** vr (divertir-se) to enjoy o.s.; (alegrar-se) to be delighted.

**rega'lia** f privilege.

re'galo m (presente) present; (prazer) pleasure, treat.

re'gar vt (aguar) to water; (molhar) to sprinkle; (comida) to wash down.

re'gata f regatta.

regate'ar vt (o preço) to haggle over, bargain for // vi to haggle; regateio m haggling.

re'gato m brook, stream.

regência [xe'ʒẽsja] f regency; (LING) government; (MÚS) conducting.

regeneração [xeʒenera'sãw] f regeneration; regenerar vt to regenerate; (prisioneiro) to reform.

regente [xe'ʒẽtʃi] m (POL) regent; (de orquestra) conductor; (de banda) leader; reger vt to govern, rule; (orquestra) to conduct; reger uma cadeira (EDUC) to hold a chair.

região [xe'ʒjãw] f region.

re'gime m (POL) regime; (de motor) speed, (dieta) diet; fazer ~ to go on a diet.

regi'mento m (MIL) regiment; (regras) regulations pl, rules pl.

régio/a ['xɛʒju/a] adj (real) royal; (digno do rei) regal.

regional [xeʒjo'naw] adj regional.

registra'dor(a) (Pt: regista'dor(a)) m/f registrar, recorder; caixa registradora cash register; registrar (Pt: registar) vt to register, record; registro (Pt: registo) m (ato) registration; (livro) register; (contador) meter; (MÚS) range; registro civil registry office.

'rego m (para água) ditch; (de arado) furrow.

regozi'jar vt to gladden, cheer up; ~-se vr to be delighted, rejoice; regozijo m joy, delight.

'regra f rule; sair da ~ to step out of line; em ~ as a rule, usually; ~s fpl (MED) periods.

regres'sar vi to come ou go back, return; regresso m return.

régua ['xɛgwa] f ruler; ~ de calcular slide rule.

regueira [xe'gejra] f drainage ditch.

regula'dor(a) adj regulating // m regulator; regulamento m rules pl, regulations pl.

regu'lar adj regular; (estatura) average, medium; (normal) normal, usual; (razoável) not bad // vt (regrar) to control; (regularizar) to regulate; (ajustar) to adjust // vi to function; ~-se vr: ~-se por to be guided by; regularidade f regularity; ~idade f regularity; ~izar vt (pôr em ordem) to sort out, settle; (regular) to regularize.

rei [xej] m king.

reimpri'mir vt to reprint.

reinado [xej'nadu] m reign; reinar vi to reign; (fig) to prevail.

reincidir [xeĩsi'dʒix] vi to relapse.

reino ['xejnu] m kingdom.

reinte'grar vt (em emprego) to reinstate; (reconduzir) to return, restore.

reite'rar vt/i to reiterate, repeat.

reitor [xej'tox] m (pároco) rector; (de uma universidade) vice-chancellor; (US) president.

reivindi'car vt (exigir) to claim.

rejeição [xeʒej'sãw] f rejection; rejeitar vt to reject; (recusar) to refuse.

rejuvenes'cer vt to rejuvenate // vi to be rejuvenated; ~-se vr to be rejuvenated.

relação [xela'sãw] f relation; (ligação) connection, relationship; (MAT) ratio; (lista) list; com/em ~ a regarding, with reference to; relações públicas public relations, P.R.; relacionar vt (pôr em lista) to make a list of; (ligar) to connect; relacionar-se vr: relacionar-se com (ligar-se) to be connected with, have to do with; (conhecer) to become acquainted with.

re'lâmpago m lightning; (clarão) flash of lightning; passar como um ~ to flash past; relampaguear vi, relampejar vi to flash;

**relampagueava** the lightning flashed.

**re'lance** m glance; **olhar de ~** to glance at.

**rela'tar** vt to give an account of.

**rela'tivo/a** adj relative.

**re'lato** m (relatório) account, report; (história) story; **relatório** m report.

**relaxação** [xelaʃa'sãw] f relaxation; (desleixo) slovenliness; **relaxado/a** adj relaxed; (frouxo) slack; (desleixado) slovenly, sloppy; **relaxamento** m relaxation; (desleixo) slovenliness; **relaxar** vt (afrouxar) to loosen, relax; (moderar) to moderate // vi (afrouxar) to slacken; (enfraquecer) to weaken; **relaxar-se** vr (afrouxar-se) to relax; (desleixar-se) to become lax; **relaxe** m relaxation.

**rele'gar** vt to relegate.

**re'lento** m: **ao ~** out of doors.

**reles** ['xɛliʃ] adj inv common, vulgar.

**rele'vante** adj outstanding, notable; **relevar** vt (tornar saliente) to emphasize; (atenuar) to relieve; (desculpar) to pardon, forgive; **relevo** m relief; (fig) prominence, importance; **pôr em relevo** to emphasize.

**reli'cário** m reliquary, shrine.

**religião** [xeli'ʒãw] f religion; **religioso/a** adj religious // m monk // f nun.

**relinchar** [xelĩ'ʃax] vi to neigh; **relincho** m (som) neigh; (ato) neighing.

**relíquia** [xe'likja] f relic; **~ de família** family heirloom.

**relógio** [xe'lɔʒu] m clock; (de gás) meter; **~ despertador** alarm clock; **~ de pulso** (wrist)watch; **relojoeiro** m watchmaker.

**relu'tância** f reluctance.

**relu'zente** adj brilliant, shining; **reluzir** vi to gleam, shine.

**'relva** f grass; (terreno gramado)

lawn; **relvado** m (Pt) lawn.

**rem** abr de **remetente** sender.

**remanes'cente** adj leftover // m surplus; (de comida) leftovers pl.

**re'manso** m stillness, quiet; (água) backwater.

**re'mar** vt/i to row.

**rema'tado/a** adj (concluído) completed; (fig) complete; **rematar** vt to finish off; **remate** m (fim) end, conclusion; (acabamento) finishing touch; (ARQ) coping; (cume) peak.

**remedi'ado/a** adj comfortably off; **remediar** vt (emendar) to put right, repair; **remédio** m (medicamento) medicine; (recurso) remedy; (ajuda) help; (JUR) recourse; **não tem remédio** it can't be helped; **que remédio?** what else can one do?

**reme'lento/a** adj bleary-eyed.

**remen'dar** vt to mend; (com pano) to patch; **remendo** m repair; (de pano) patch. •

**re'messa** f (COM) shipment, dispatch; (de dinheiro) remittance; **remetente** m/f (de carta) sender; (COM) shipper; **remeter** vt (expedir) to send, dispatch; (dinheiro) to remit; (entregar) to hand over; **remeter-se** vr: **remeter-se a** (referir-se) to refer to.

**reme'xer** vt (papéis) to rummage through; (líquidos) to stir (up); (misturar) to mess about.

**reminiscência** [xemini'sẽsja] f reminiscence.

**re'mir** vt (coisa penhorada, REL) to redeem; (livrar) to free; (compensar) to make up for; **~-se** vr (pecador) to redeem o.s.

**remissão** [xemi'sãw] f (perdão) forgiveness; (compensação) payment; (num livro) cross-reference.

**re'misso/a** adj remiss, careless.

**re'mível** adj redeemable.

**'remo** m (de embarcação) oar; (esporte) rowing.

**remo'çar** vt to rejuvenate; ~-**se** vr to be rejuvenated.

**remo'inho** m (ato) whirling, swirling; (na água) eddy, whirlpool; (de vento) whirlwind.

**remon'tar** vt (elevar) to raise; (tornar a armar) to re-assemble; ~ **o vôo** to soar // vi (recuar) to go back; (em cavalo) to remount.

**remoque** [xe'moki] m gibe, taunt; **remoquear** vt to taunt.

**remor'der** vt (morder) to bite again and again; (atormentar) to distress, torture; (cismar em) to brood over.

**re'morso** m remorse.

**re'moto/a** adj remote, far off.

**remo'ver** vt (mover) to move; (transferir) to transfer; (demitir) to dismiss; (retirar) to remove.

**remuneração** [xemunera'sāw] f remuneration; (pagamento) payment; **remunerador/a** adj remunerative; **remunerar** vt to remunerate; (premiar) to reward.

**'rena** f reindeer.

**re'nal** adj renal, kidney cmp.

**renascença** [xena'sēsa] f rebirth; (fig) revival; **a R** ~ the Renaissance; **renascer** vi to be reborn; (fig) to be revived.

**'renda** f income; (nacional) revenue; (tecido) lace; ~ **bruta/líquida** gross/net income; **imposto de** ~ income tax; **rendado/a** adj lace-trimmed; (com aspecto de renda) lacy // m lacework.

**rendeiro/a** [xē'dejru/a] m/f tenant // f lacemaker.

**ren'der** vt (produzir) to produce, yield; (preço) to fetch; (graças) to give; (guarda) to relieve // vi (dar lucro) to pay; ~-**se** vr (capitular) to surrender; **rendição** f surrender; **rendido/a** adj subdued; **rendimento** m (renda) income; (lucro) profit; (juro) interest; (produtividade) productivity; output; (duma máquina) efficiency; **rendoso/a** adj profitable.

**rene'gado/a** adj, m/f renegade; **renegar** vt (renunciar) to renounce; (detestar) to hate; (trair) to betray; (negar) to deny.

**renhido/a** [xe'ɲidu/a] adj hard-fought; (batalha) bloody.

**reni'tência** f obstinacy; **renitente** adj obstinate, stubborn.

**re'nome** m fame, renown; **de** ~ renowned.

**renovação** [xenova'sāw] f renewal; (ARQ) renovation; **renovador de ar** ventilator; **renovar** vt to renew; (restaurar) to renovate // vi to be renewed.

**re'novo** m sprout, shoot.

**rentabili'dade** f profitability.

**rente** ['xētʃi] adj (cabelo) close-cropped; (casa) nearby // adv close.

**renúncia** [xe'nūsja] f renunciation; (de cargo) resignation; **renunciar** vt to give up, renounce // vi to resign.

**reorgani'zar** vt to reorganize.

**reparação** [xepara'sāw] f (conserto) mending, repairing; (fig) amends pl; **reparar** vt (consertar) to repair; (forças) to restore; (compensar) to compensate for, make amends for; (observar) to notice // vi: **reparar em** to notice; **não repare em** pay no attention to; **repare em** (olhar) look at; **reparo** m (conserto) repair; (crítica) criticism; (observação) observation; (ajuda) help; (defesa) defence.

**repartição** [xepartʃi'sāw] f (ato) distribution; (COM) department, office; **repartir** vt (distribuir) to distribute; (dar em porções) to share out; **repartir-se** vr (dividir-se) to spread.

**repas'sar** vt (passar de novo) to go over again; (lição) to revise, go over.

**repatri'ar** vt to repatriate; ~-**se** vr to go back home.

**repelão** [xepe'lãw] *m* push, shove; **de ~** brusquely.

**repe'lente** *adj*, *m* repellent; **repelir** *vt* to drive away, repel.

**re'pente** *m* outburst; **de ~** suddenly; **repentino/a** *adj* sudden.

**repercussão** [xepexku'sãw] *f* repercussion; **repercutir** *vt* (*som*) to echo // *vi* (*som*) to reverberate, echo; **repercutir-se** *vr*: **repercutir-se (em)** to have repercussions (on).

**reper'tório** *m* (*lista*) list; (*coleção*) collection, catalogue; (*de livro*) index; (*teatro*) repertoire.

**repetição** [xepetʃi'sãw] *f* repetition; **repetido/a** *adj* repeated; **repetidas vezes** repeatedly, again and again; **repetir** *vt* to repeat; (*vestido*) to wear again; **repetir-se** *vr* to be repeated.

**repi'car** (*sinos*) to ring; (*carne*) to mince; (*legumes*) to chop // *vi* (*sinos*) to ring (out).

**repim'pado/a** *adj* (*refestelado*) lolling; (*satisfeito*) full up.

**repique** [xe'piki] *m* peal.

**repi'sar** *vt* (*assunto*) to repeat (: *insistir*) to harp on; (*uvas*) to tread.

**re'pleto/a** *adj* replete, full up.

**'réplica** *f* (*cópia*) replica; (*contestação*) reply, retort; **replicar** *vt* to answer, reply to // *vi* to reply, answer back.

**repolho** [xe'poʎu] *m* cabbage.

**repon'tar** *vi* (*aparecer*) to appear.

**re'por** *vt* to put back, replace.

**reportagem** [xepox'taʒẽ] *f* (*ato*) reporting; (*noticiário*) report; (*repórteres*) reporters *pl*; **reportar** *vt* (*o pensamento*) to take back; **reportar-se** *vr*: **reportar-se a** to refer to; **repórter** *m/f* reporter.

**reposteiro** [xepoʃ'tejru] *m* (*de porta*) curtain.

**repou'sar** *vi* to rest; **repouso** *m* rest.

**repreender** [xepriẽ'dex] *vt* to reprimand; (*col*) to tell off;

**repreensão** *f* rebuke, reprimand **repreensível** *adj* reprehensible.

**re'presa** *f* dam.

**repre'sália** *f* reprisal.

**representação** [xeprezẽta'sãw] *f* representation; (*escrita*) petition (*teatro*) performance; **represen tante** *m* representative; **represen tativo/a** *adj* representative **representar** *vt* to represent (*teatro*) to play; **representar un anjo** to play the part of an angel // *vi* (JUR: *queixa*) to make complaint.

**repressão** [xepre'sãw] *f* repression; **reprimir** *vt* to repress (*lágrimas*) to keep back.

**'réprobo/a** *adj*, *m/f* reprobate.

**reprodução** [xeprodu'sãw] *f* reproduction; **reproduzir** *vt* tc reproduce; (*repetir*) to repeat **reproduzir-se** *vr* to breed, multiply (*repetir-se*) to be repeated.

**reprovação** [xeprova'sãw] *f* disapproval; (*em exame*) failure **reprovar** *vt* (*condenar*) to disapprove of; (*aluno*) to fail.

**'réptil** *m* reptile.

**'repto** *m* challenge, provocation.

**re'pública** *f* republic **republicano/a** *adj*, *m/f* republican.

**repudi'ar** *vt* to repudiate, reject; (*esposa*) to divorce; (*abandonar*) to disown; **repúdio** *m* rejection.

**repug'nância** *f* repugnance; **repugnante** *adj* repugnant repulsive; **repugnar** *vt* (*enojar*) to be repugnant to // *vi* to be repulsive; **repugnar a alguém** to disgust sb.

**re'pulsa** *f* (*ato*) rejection; (*sentimento*) repugnance; (*fig*) rebuff; (*física*) repulsion; **repulsivo/a** *adj* repulsive.

**reputação** [xeputa'sãw] *f* reputation; **reputar** *vt* to consider regard as.

**repuxar** [xepu'ʃax] *vt* (*puxar*) to tug; (*esticar*) to pull tight; **repuxo** *m* (*de água*) fountain; (*de arma*) kick, recoil.

**requebrado** [reke'bradu] *m* (*rebolado*) swing, sway; **requebrar** *vt* (*menear*) to wiggle, swing; **requebrar-se** *vr* to wiggle, swing.

**requeijão** [xekej'sãw] *m* cottage cheese.

**requeimar** [xekej'max] *vt* (*fogo*) to scorch; (*sol*) to burn; (*picar*) to burn.

**requentar** [xekē'tax] *vt* to reheat, warm up.

**requerente** [xeke'rētʃi] *m/f* (*JUR*) petitioner; **requerer** *vt* (*emprego*) to apply for; (*pedir*) to request, ask for; (*exigir*) to require, call for; (*JUR*) to petition for; **requerimento** *m* application; (*pedido*) request; (*petição*) petition.

**requintado/a** [xekĩ'tadu/a] *adj* refined, elegant; **requinte** *m* refinement, elegance; (*cúmulo*) height.

**requisição** [xekizi'sãw] *f* request, demand; **requisitar** *vt* to make a request for; (*MIL*) to requisition; **requisito** *m* requirement.

**requisitório** [xekizi'torju] *m* official indictment.

**rês** [xeʃ] *f* head of cattle; **reses** *fpl* cattle, livestock *sg.*

**rescindir** *vt* (*contrato*) to rescind.

**rés-do-chão** [xɛʒdu'ʃãw] (*Pt*) *m* (*andar térreo*) ground floor; (*US*) first floor.

**resenha** [xe'zeɲa] *f* (*relatório*) report; (*resumo*) summary; **resenhar** *vt* (*livro*) to review.

**reserva** *f* reserve; (*para hotel, fig*) reservation; **reservado/a** *adj* reserved; (*retraído*) standoffish; **reservar** *vt* (*guardar*) to keep back; (*mesa*) to book, reserve; **reservar-se** *vr* to save o.s.; **reservatório** *m* (*lago*) reservoir.

**resfolegar** *vi* to pant.

**resfriado/a** [xef'jadu] *adj*: **estar ~** to have a cold // *m* cold, chill; **resfriar** *vt* to cool, chill // *vi*, **resfriar-se** *vr*

(*pessoa*) to catch (a) cold.

**resgatar** *vt* (*prisioneiro*) to ransom; (*salvar*) to rescue; (*retomar*) to get back, recover; (*dívida*) to pay off; (*remir*) to redeem; **resgate** *m* (*livramento*) rescue, recovery; **pagar um resgate** to pay a ransom.

**resguardar** [xeʒgwax'dax] *vt* to protect; **~-se** *vr*: **~-se** to guard against; **resguardo** *m* protection; (*cuidado*) care.

**residência** *f* house, residence; **residente** *adj*, *m/f* resident; **residir** *vi* to live, reside.

**resíduo** [xe'zdwu] *m* residue.

**resignação** [xezigna'sãw] *f* resignation; **resignado/a** *adj* resigned; **resignar-se** *vr*: **resignar-se com** to resign o.s. to.

**resina** *f* resin.

**resistência** *f* resistance; (*de atleta*) stamina; **resistente** *adj* resistant; (*calçado*) hard-wearing, strong; **resistente a traças** mothproof; **resistir** *vi*: **resistir a** (*não ceder*) to resist; (*sobreviver*) to survive; **resistir ao uso** to wear well; (*durar*) to last.

**resma** *f* ream.

**resmungar** *vt/i* to mutter, mumble.

**resolução** [xezolu'sãw] *f* resolution; (*coragem*) courage; (*de um problema*) solution; **resoluto/a** *adj* resolute.

**resolver** *vt* (*problema*) to solve; (*questão*) to resolve; (*decidir*) to decide // *vi*: **~ em** (*transformar*) to turn into; **~-se** *vr*: **~-se a** (*decidir*) to make up one's mind to, decide to.

**respectivo/a** *adj* respective.

**respeitar** [xɛʃpej'tax] *vt* to respect; **respeitável** *adj* (*venerável*) respected; (*digno de respeito*) respectable; (*importante*) considerable; **respeito** *m* respect; **a respeito de/com respeito a** as to, as regards; **dizer respeito a** to concern; **faltar ao respeito a** to be rude to; **respeitos** *mpl* regards; **respeitoso/a** *adj* respectful.

**respin'gar** *vt/i* to splash, spatter.

**respiração** [xeʃpira'sãw] *f* breathing; (*hálito*) breath; (MED) respiration; **respirador** *m* respirator; **respirar** *vt/i* to breathe; (*folgar*) to have a respite; **respiro** *m* (*abertura*) vent.

**resplande'cente** *adj* resplendent; **resplandecer** *vi* to gleam, shine (out); **resplendor** *m* brilliance; (*fig*) splendour; (: *fama*) glory.

**respondão/dona** [xeʃpõ'dãw/'dona] *adj* cheeky, insolent; **responder** *vt* to answer // *vi* to answer; **responder por** to be responsible for, answer for.

**responsabili'dade** *f* responsibility; **responsabilizar-se** *vr*: **responsabilizar-se por** to take responsibility for, take charge of; **responsável** *adj*: **responsável por** responsible for // *m* person responsible *ou* in charge.

**res'posta** *f* answer, reply.

**resquício** [xeʃ'kisju] *m* (*vestígio*) trace.

**res'saca** *f* (*refluxo*) undertow; (*contra o litoral*) surf; (*fig*) hangover.

**ressaibo** [xe'sajbu] *m* (*mau sabor*) unpleasant taste; (*fig*) trace.

**ressal'tar** *vt* to emphasize // *vi* to stand out.

**res'salva** *f* (*proteção*) safeguard; (MIL) exemption certificate; (*correção*) correction; (*restrição*) qualification.

**ressar'cir** *vt* (*pagar*) to compensate; (*compensar*) to compensate for; ~ **alguém de** to compensate sb for.

**resse'car** *vt*, **resse'car-se** *vr* to dry up.

**ressen'tido/a** *adj* (*ofendido*) hurt, resentful; **ressentimento** *m* resentment; **ressentir-se** *vr*:

**ressentir-se de** (*ser ofendido*) to resent, be hurt by; (*sofrer*) to suffer from, feel the effects of.

**ressequido/a** [xesɛ'kidu/a] *adj* parched; (*seco*) dried up.

**resso'ar** *vi* to resound; (*ecoar*) to echo; **ressonância** *f* resonance; (*eco*) echo.

**ressurgimento** [xesuxʒi'mẽtu] *m* resurgence, revival.

**ressurreição** [xesuxej'sãw] *f* resurrection.

**ressusci'tar** *vt* to revive, resuscitate.

**restabele'cer** *vt* to re-establish, restore; ~**-se** *vr* to recover, recuperate.

**res'tante** *m* rest; **restar** *vi* to remain, be left; **não lhe resta nada** he has nothing left; **resta-me comprar o chapéu** I still have the hat to buy.

**restauração** [xeʃtawra'sãw] *f* restoration; (*dente*) filling.

**restaurante** [xeʃtaw'rãtʃi] *m* restaurant.

**restaurar** [xeʃtaw'rax] *vt* to restore; (*recuperar*) to recover; (*renovar*) to renew.

**'réstia** *f* (*de cebolas*) string; (*luz*) ray.

**restituição** [xeʃtʃitwi'sãw] *f* restitution, return; (*dinheiro*) repayment; **restituir** *vt* to return, give back; (*dinheiro*) to repay; (*restaurar*) to restore; (*repor*) to put back.

**'resto** *m* rest, remainder; **de** ~ besides; ~**s** *mpl* remains, scraps.

**restolho** [xeʃ'toʎu] *m* stubble; (*fig*) remains pl.

**restrição** [xeʃtri'sãw] *f* restriction; **restringir** *vt* to restrict; (*diminuir*) to reduce; **restrito/a** *adj* restricted; (*diminuído*) reduced.

**resul'tado** *m* result; **dar** ~ to succeed; **resultar** *vi* to result; (*evidenciar-se*) to turn out to be.

**resu'mido/a** *adj* abbreviated,

abridged; (*curto*) concise; **resumir** *vt* to abbreviate; (*simbolizar*) to epitomize; (*sintetizar*) to sum up; (*reduzir*) to reduce; **resumir-se** *vr*: **resumir-se a** to consist in/of; **resumo** *m* summary, résumé; **em resumo** in short, briefly.

**resva'lar** *vt* to slide, slip.

**retaguarda** [xcta'gwaxda] *f* rearguard; (*posição*) rear.

**retalhar** [xeta'ʎax] *vt* to cut up; (*separar*) to divide; (*despedaçar*) to shred; (*ferir*) to slash; **retalho** *m* piece; (*sobra*) scrap, shred; (*Pt*): **vender a retalho** to sell retail; **colcha de retalhos** patchwork quilt.

**retar'dar** *vt* to hold up, slow down; (*atrasar*) to postpone; **retardatário/a** *m/f* latecomer.

**retenção** [xetẽ'sãw] *f* retention; **reter** *vt* (*guardar*) to retain; (*deter*) to stop, detain; **reter-se** *vr* to restrain o.s.

**rete'sar** *vt* to tighten; (*esticar*) to stretch.

**reti'cência** *f* reticence, reserve; ~s *fpl* suspension points; **reticente** *adj* reticent.

**retidão** [xetʃi'dãw] (*Pt*: **-ct-**) *f* rectitude; (*justeza*) soundness; (*de linha*) straightness.

**retifica'dor** (*Pt*: **-ct-**) *m* rectifier; **retifi'car** (*Pt*: **-ct-**) *vt* to rectify.

**reti'nir** *vi* (*ferros*) to clink; (*campainha*) to ring, jingle; (*ressoar*) to resound.

**reti'rada** *f* withdrawal, retreat; **bater em** ~ to beat a retreat; **retirado/a** *adj* isolated; (*recluso*) solitary; **retirar** *vt* to withdraw; (*retratar*) to take back // *vi* to withdraw, retire; (*MIL*) to retreat; **retiro** *m* retreat.

**'reto/a** (*Pt*: **-ct-**) *adj* straight; (*vertical*) upright; (*justo*) fair; (*honesto*) honest, upright // *m* rectum.

**reto'car** *vt* (*pintura*) to touch up;

(*aperfeiçoar*) to perfect; **retoque** *m* finishing touch.

**retorcer** [xetox'sex] *vt* to twist; ~**se** *vr* to wriggle, writhe.

**re'tórica** *f* rhetoric.

**re'torno** *m* return; (*COM*) barter, exchange.

**retorquir** [xetox'kix] *vi* to retort, reply.

**retrac'tar** *vt* (*Pt*) to retract, recant.

**retraído/a** *adj* retracted; (*fig*) reserved, timid; **retraimento** *m* withdrawal; (*contração*) contraction; (*fig*) timidity, shyness; **retrair-se** *vr* to withdraw, retire; (*recuar*) to draw back.

**retratação** [xetrata'sãw] (*Pt*: **-ct-**) *f* retraction; **retratar** *vt* (*fazer o retrato*) to portray, depict; (*retirar*) to retract, recant; **retrato** *m* portrait; (*FOTO*) photo; (*sósia*) spitting image.

**retribuição** [xctribwi'sãw] *f* reward, recompense; (*pagamento*) remuneration; **retribuir** *vt* to reward, recompense; (*corresponder*) to requite; (*pagar*) to remunerate; (*hospitalidade*) to return.

**retroce'der** *vi* to retreat, fall back; (*decair*) to decline.

**retru'car** *vi* to retort, reply.

**retum'bância** *f* resonance; **retumbar** *vi* to resound, echo; (*ribombar*) to rumble, boom.

**réu/ré** [xɛw/xɛ] *m/f* defendant; (*culpado*) culprit, criminal; ~ **de morte** condemned man.

**reumatismo** [xcwma'tʃiʒmu] *m* rheumatism.

**reunião** [xiu'njãw] *f* meeting; (*ato*) reunion; **reunir** *vt* to bring together; (*juntar*) to join, unite; **reunir-se** *vr* to meet, gather together.

**revelação** [xevela'sãw] *f* revelation; (*FOTO*) development; **revelar** *vt* to reveal; (*mostrar*) to show; (FOTO) to develop; **revelar-se** vr to turn out to be.

**reve'lia** f default; **à ~ by** default; **~ de** without the knowledge or consent of.

**re'ver** vt to see again; (examinar) to scrutinize; (revisar) to check, revise.

**reverde'cer** vt/i to turn green again.

**reve'rência** f reverence, respect; (ato) bow; (: de mulher) curtsey; **reverenciar** vt to revere, venerate; (obedecer) to obey; **reverendo/a** adj venerable // m priest, clergyman; **reverente** adj reverent, reverential.

**reversão** [xevex'sãw] f reversion; **reversível** adj reversible; **reverso** m reverse; (oposto) opposite; **o reverso da medalha** (fig) the other side of the coin.

**re'vés** m reverse; (infortúnio) setback, mishap; **ao ~ on** the contrary; **ao ~ de** contrary to; **de ~** obliquely, aslant; (olhar) askance.

**reves'tir** vt to put on; (tapar) to cover; **~-se** vr: **~-se de** (assumir) to assume, take on.

**reve'zar** vt to relieve // vi to take turns, rotate; (alternar) to alternate.

**revigo'rar** vt to refresh, reinvigorate.

**revi'rada** f about-turn, change of direction; **revirar** vt to turn round; (atrapalhar) to throw into confusion; **revirar os olhos** to roll one's eyes; **reviravolta** f about-turn, U-turn.

**revisão** [xevi'zãw] f revision; **~ de provas** proofreading; **revisar** vt to revise; (rever) to check; **revisor** m (FERRO) ticket inspector; (de provar) proofreader.

**re'vista** f (ger) review; (MIL) inspection; (publicação) journal, magazine; (teatro) revue; **passar em ~** to review; (inspecionar) to inspect, go over.

**revo'gar** vt to revoke, repeal; (anular) to cancel.

**re'volta** f revolt, revolution; **revoltar** vt to disgust; **revoltar-se** vr to rebel, revolt; **revolto/a** pp irr de **revolver** // adj turbulent; (agitado) troubled; (cabelo) dishevelled; (mar) rough; (desarrumado) untidy.

**revolução** [xevolu'sãw] f revolution; **revolucionar** vt to revolutionize; **revolucionário/a** adj, m/f revolutionary.

**revol'ver** vt (mexer) to stir; (olhos) to roll // vi (girar) to revolve, rotate.

**re'vólver** m revolver, gun.

**re'zar** vt (missa) to say // vi to pray.

**'ria** f estuary, river mouth.

**riacho** [ri'aʃu] m stream, brook.

**ri'balta** f (teatro) footlights pl.

**ribanceira** [xibã'sejra] f (margem) steep river bank; (rampa) steep slope; (precipício) cliff.

**ribeira** [xi'bejra] f riverside; (riacho) stream; **ribeirão** m (Br) stream; **ribeirinho/a** adj riverside cmp; **ribeiro** m brook, stream; (US) creek.

**ribom'bar** vi to rumble, boom; (ressoar) to resound.

**ricaço** [xi'kasu] m plutocrat, very rich man.

**rícino** ['xisinu] m castor-oil plant; **óleo de ~** castor oil.

**'rico/a** adj rich, wealthy; (abundante) fertile; (opulento) sumptuous; (Pt: lindo) beautiful; (: excelente) splendid.

**ridiculari'zar** vt, **ridiculi'zar** vt to ridicule; **ridículo/a** adj ridiculous.

**'rifa** f raffle, lottery.

**rifão** [xi'fãw] m proverb, saying.

**ri'far** vt to raffle; (col: abandonar) to dump.

**rigidez** [xiʒi'deʃ] f rigidity, stiffness; (austeridade) severity, strictness; (inflexibilidade) inflexibility; **rígido/a** adj rigid, stiff; (fig) strict, severe.

**ri'gor** m rigidity; (severidade) harshness, severity; (exatidão) precision; a ~ strictly speaking; de ~ essential, obligatory; **no** ~ **do inverno** in the depths of winter; ~**oso/a** adj rigorous; (severo) harsh; (exigente) demanding; (minucioso) precise, accurate.

**rijo/a** ['xiʒu/a] adj tough, hard; (rigoroso) cruel, severe; (robusto) sturdy, strong.

**rim** [xĩ] m kidney; **rins** mpl small of the back sg.

**'rima** f rhyme; (poema) verse, poem; **rimar** vt to put into verse // vi to rhyme; **rimar com** to agree with, tally with.

**'rímel** ® m máscara.

**rinchar** [xĩ'ʃax] vi to neigh, whinny.

**rinoceronte** [xinɔse'rõtʃi] m rhinoceros.

**'rio** m river.

**'ripa** f lath, slat.

**riqueza** [xi'keza] f wealth, riches pl; (qualidade) richness; (fartura) abundance; (fecundidade) fertility.

**rir** vi to laugh; ~ **de** to laugh at; **risada** f (riso) laughter; (gargalhada) guffaw.

**'risca** f stroke; (decor) stripe; (cabelo) parting; **à** ~ to the letter, exactly; **riscar** vt to score, mark; (apagar) to score out; (desenhar) to draw, trace; (acender) to light; **risco** m scratch; (desenho) drawing, sketch; (perigo) risk.

**ri'sível** adj laughable, ridiculous; **riso** m laughter; (gargalhada) laugh; **risonho/a** adj laughing, smiling; (contente) cheerful, happy.

**'ríspido/a** adj (rude) sharp, curt; (áspero) harsh.

**'riste** m: **em** ~ (dedo) pointing; (orelhas) pointed.

**'rítmico/a** adj rhythmic(al); **ritmo** m rhythm.

**'rito** m rite; (seita) cult; **ritual** adj, m ritual.

**ri'val** adj, m/f rival; ~**idade** f

rivalry; ~**izar** vt to rival // ~**izar com** to compete with; vie with.

**rixa** ['xiʃa] f quarrel, fight.

**robuste'cer** vt to strengthen; ~**-se** vr to become stronger; **robusto/a** adj strong, robust.

**'roça** f plantation; (mato) clearing; (campo) country; **roçado** m clearing; **roçar** vt (terreno) to clear; (atritar) to graze // vi: **roçar em/por** to graze, brush against; **roceiro** m (lavrador) peasant; (caipira) country bumpkin.

**rocha** ['xɔʃa] f rock; (penedo) crag; **rochedo** m crag, cliff.

**'roda** f wheel; (círculo) circle; (grupo) ring; ~ **dentada** cog(wheel); **alta** ~ high society; **em/à** ~ **de** round, around; **rodagem** f: **estrada de rodagem** trunk/major road; **rodar** vt (fazer girar) to turn, spin; (rolar) to roll // vi to roll; (girar) to turn; (AUTO) to drive; **roda-viva** f bustle, commotion.

**rode'ar** vt to go round; (circundar) to encircle, surround; **rodeio** m circumlocution; (subterfúgio) subterfuge; (gado) round-up; **fazer rodeios** to beat about the bush; **sem rodeios** plainly, frankly.

**ro'dela** f (pedaço) slice.

**'rodo** m rake; a ~ in abundance.

**rodopi'ar** vi to whirl around, swirl.

**roedor(a)** [xoe'dox(a)] adj gnawing // m rodent; **roer** vt to gnaw, nibble; (enferrujar) to corrode.

**ro'gado** pp de **rogar**; **fazer-se de** ~ to play hard to get; **rogar** vi to ask, request; **rogar a alguém que** . . . to beg sb to . . .; **rogo** m request; **a rogo de** at the request of.

**rol** m roll, list.

**'rola** f (turtle-)dove.

**ro'lar** vt/i to roll.

**rol'dana** f pulley.

**roldão** [xol'dãw] m confusion; **de** ~ headlong, pell-mell.

**ro'leta** f roulette; (borboleta) turnstile.

**rolha** ['xoʎa] f cork; (fig) gag (on free speech).

**ro'liço/a** adj plump, chubby.

**'rolo** m (de papel etc) roll; (cilindro) roller.

**'Roma** f Rome.

**ro'mã** f pomegranate.

**romagem** [xo'maʒẽ] f pilgrimage.

**ro'mance** m (novela) novel; (conto) story; (amor) romance; ~ policial detective story; **romanceado/a** adj exaggerated, fanciful; **romancista** m/f novelist.

**ro'mânico/a** adj (LING) Romance; (ARQ) romanesque; **romano/a** adj, m/f Roman.

**ro'mântico/a** adj romantic; **romantismo** m romanticism.

**roma'ria** f (peregrinação) pilgrimage; (festa) festival.

**'rombo** m (abertura) opening, hole; (MAT) rhombus; (desfalque) embezzlement.

**romeiro/a** [xo'mejru/a] m/f pilgrim.

**ro'meno/a** adj, m/f Rumanian // m (língua) Rumanian.

**rom'pante** m (arrogância) arrogance; (impetuosidade) rashness, impetuousness.

**rom'per** vt/i to break; (rasgar) to tear; (relações) to break off; **rompimento** m breaking; (fenda) break; (interrupção) rupture, breaking-off.

**ron'car** vi (ressonar) to snore; (estrondar) to roar.

**'ronco** m (de sono) snore; (de motor) roar; (grunhir) grunt.

**'ronda** f patrol, beat; **fazer a ~** to go the rounds; **rondar** vt to patrol, go the rounds of; (vaguear) to prowl, hang around // vi to prowl about, lurk.

**ronqueira** [xõ'kejra] f wheeze.

**ronrom** [xõ'xõ] m purring; **ronronar** vi to purr.

**roque** ['xɔki] m (xadrez) rook, castle; (MÚS) rock.

**ror** m: **um ~ de** (col) a lot of, loads of.

**rosa** ['xɔza] f rose // adj rose-coloured, pink; **rosado/a** adj rosy, pink; **~-dos-ventos** f inv compass.

**ro'sário** m rosary.

**rosbife** [xɔʒ'bifi] m roast beef.

**'rosca** f spiral, coil; (de parafuso) thread; (pão) ring-shaped loaf.

**roseira** [xo'zejra] f rosebush.

**roséola** [xo'zeola] f rash.

**ros'nar** vi (murmurar) to mutter, mumble; (cão) to growl, snarl.

**ros'sio** m (Pt) large square.

**'rosto** m (cara) face; (frontispício) title page.

**'rota** f route, course.

**rotação** [xota'sãw] f rotation.

**roteiro** [xo'tejru] m (itinerário) itinerary; (ordem) schedule; (guia) guidebook; (de filme) script.

**ro'tina** f routine; **rotineiro/a** adj routine.

**'roto/a** pp irr de **romper** // adj broken; (rasgado) torn.

**'rótula** f (ANAT) kneecap.

**'rótulo** m label, tag.

**roubar** [xo'bax] vt to steal, rob; ~ **algo a alguém** to steal sth from sb; **roubo** m theft, robbery.

**rouco/a** ['roku/a] adj hoarse.

**roupa** ['xopa] f clothes pl, clothing; ~ **de baixo**, ~ **branca** underclothes pl, underwear; ~ **de cama** bedclothes pl, bed linen; **~gem** f clothes pl, apparel; (fig) appearance; **roupão** m dressing gown.

**rouquidão** [xoki'dãw] f hoarseness.

**rouxinol** [xoʃi'nɔl] m nightingale.

**roxo/a** ['xoʃu/a] adj purple, violet.

**'rua** f street // excl: ~! get out!, clear off!

**ru'béola** f (MED) German measles.

**ru'bi** m ruby.

**ru'bor** m blush; (fig) shyness, bashfulness; **~izar** vi to blush.

**ru'brica** f (*título*) rubric, title; (*teatro*) stage directions pl; (*firma*) signed initials pl; **rubricar** vt to initial.

**'ruço/a** adj grey, dun.

**'rude** adj rough, unpolished; **rudeza** f roughness, crudity.

**rudi'mento** m rudiment; **~s** mpl rudiments, first principles.

**ru'ela** f lane, alley.

**ru'far** vt (*tambor*) to beat.

**rufião** [xuˈfjãw] m pimp.

**'ruga** f (*na pele*) wrinkle; (*na roupa*) crease.

**'rúgbi** m rugby.

**rugido** [xuˈʒidu] m roar; **rugir** vi to roar, bellow.

**ru'goso/a** adj (*pele*) wrinkled; (*roupa*) creased.

**ru'ído** [ˈxwidu] m noise, din; **ruidoso/a** adj noisy.

**ruim** [xuˈĩ] adj (*malvado*) wicked, evil; (*inútil*) useless; (*ordinário*) awful; (*mau*) bad.

**ru'ína** [ˈxwina] f (*restos*) ruin; (*decadência*) downfall, destruction; **ruindade** [xwĩˈdadʒi] f wickedness, evil.

**ruir** [xuˈix] vi to collapse, go to ruin.

**ruivo/a** [ˈxwivu/a] adj red-haired // m/f redhead.

**rum** m rum.

**rumi'nar** vt/i to ruminate, chew the cud; (*fig*) to meditate, ponder.

**'rumo** m course, bearing; **~ a** bound for; **sem ~** adrift.

**ru'mor** m (*ruído*) noise; (*notícia*) rumour, report; **~ejar** vi to murmur; (*folhas*) to rustle; (*água*) to ripple.

**rup'tura** f break, rupture.

**ru'ral** adj rural, rustic.

**rusga** f (*briga*) quarrel, row.

**'russo/a** adj, m/f Russian // m (*língua*) Russian.

**'rústico/a** adj rustic, (*rude*) rough, crude.

**ruti'lar** vi to shine, glitter.

# S

**S.** abr de **Santo/Santa/São** Saint.

**sã** adj ver **são.**

**'sábado** m Saturday.

**sabão** [saˈbãw] m soap.

**sabe'dor(a)** adj (*consciente*) aware, informed; **sabedoria** f (*razão*) wisdom; (*sensatez*) common sense; (*erudição*) learning.

**sa'ber** vt (*ter conhecimento de*) to know; (*ter capacidade para*) to know how to, be able to; **~ de cor e salteado** to know off by heart; **ele sabe nadar?** can he swim? // vi to taste; **~ a** to taste of // m knowledge, learning; **a ~** namely; **sabichão/chona** m/f know-it-all, smart aleck; **sábio/a** adj wise, learned // m/f scholar, learned person.

**sabo'nete** m toilet soap.

**sa'bor** m taste, flavour; **ao ~ de** at the mercy of; **saborear** vt to relish, savour; **~oso/a** adj tasty, delicious.

**sabota'dor** m saboteur; **sabotagem** f sabotage; **sabotar** vt to sabotage.

**sabugueiro** [sabuˈgejru] m elder, elderberry.

**sabur'rento/a** adj (*língua*) furry.

**'saca** f sack, bag.

**sa'car** vt to take out, pull out; (*dinheiro*) to withdraw; (*esporte*) to serve; (*col*) to understand.

**saca'rina** f saccharine; (*US*) saccharin.

**saca-rolhas** [saka'-xoʎaʃ] m inv corkscrew.

**sacer'dócio** [sasexˈdosju] m priesthood; **sacerdote** m priest.

**saciar** [saˈsjax] vt (*satisfazer*) to satisfy; (*fartar*) to satiate; (*sede*) to quench.

**'saco** m sack, bag; **~ de dormir** sleeping bag; **encher o ~ a** (*Br: col*) to annoy, pester // *excl*: ~! (*Br*: *col*) damn!.

**sacra'mento** *m* sacrament.

**sacrifi'car** *vt* to sacrifice; **sacrifício** *m* sacrifice.

**sacrilégio** [sakri'lɛʒu] *m* sacrilege; **sacrílego/a** *adj* sacrilegious.

**sacristão** [sakri'ʃtãw] *m* sacristan, sexton; **sacristia** *f* sacristy; **sacro/a** *adj* sacred; (*santo*) holy.

**sacudi'dela** *f* shake, jolt; **sacudido/a** *adj* shaken; (*movimento*) rapid, quick; **sacudir** *vt* to shake, jolt.

**sa'dio/a** *adj* healthy; (*saudável*) wholesome.

**sa'fado/a** *adj* (*gasto*) worn out; (*descarado*) shameless, barefaced // *m* rogue; **safar** *vt* (*extrair*) to pull out; **safar-se** *vr* to escape.

**sa'fira** *f* sapphire.

**'safra** *f* harvest; (*produto*) crop.

**sagacidade** [sagasi'dadʒi] *f* shrewdness; (*astúcia*) cleverness; **sagaz** *adj* shrewd, clever.

**sa'grado/a** *adj* sacred, holy.

**saguão** [sa'gwãw] *m* (*pátio*) yard, patio; (*entrada*) foyer, lobby.

**saia** ['saja] *f* skirt.

**saibro** ['sajbru] *m* gravel.

**sa'ída** *f* (*porta*) exit, way out; (*partida*) departure; (*venda*) outlet, sale; **de** ~ firstly; **sair** *vi* (*ir para fora*) to go out; (*vir para fora*) to come out; (*partir*) to leave, depart; (*pessoa*) to go out; **sair bem** to turn out well, be successful; **sair de** to leave; **sair-se** *vr*: **sair-se bem/mal de** to be successful/unsuccessful in.

**sal** *m* salt; (*graça*) wit, sparkle.

**'sala** *f* (large) room; (*num edifício público*) hall; (*numa casa*) lounge, drawing room; ~ **de espera** waiting room; ~ **de estar** living room.

**sa'lada** *f* salad; (*fig*) confusion, mix up.

**salão** [sa'lãw] *m* large room, hall; **de**

~ (*jogos*) indoor; (*anedota*) proper, acceptable.

**sa'lário** *m* wages *pl*, salary.

**sal'dar** *vt* (*contas*) to settle; **saldo** *m* balance; (*sobra*) surplus; (*fig*) result.

**saleiro** [sa'lejru] *m* salt cellar; **salgado/a** *adj* salty, salted; (*picante*) saucy, risqué; **salgar** *vt* to salt.

**salgueiro** [sal'gejru] *m* willow; ~ **chorão** weeping willow.

**sali'ência** *f* prominence, projection; **salientar** *vt* to point out; (*acentuar*) to stress, emphasise; **saliente** *adj* jutting out, prominent; (*evidente*) clear, conspicuous; (*importante*) outstanding.

**salitre** [sa'litri] *m* saltpetre, nitre.

**sa'liva** *f* saliva; (*cuspe*) spittle.

**salmão** [sal'mãw] *m* salmon.

**'salmo** *m* psalm.

**salmoura** [saw'mora] *f* brine, pickle.

**sa'lobro/a** *adj* salty, brackish.

**saloio** [sa'loju] *m* (*Pt*: *camponês*) country bumpkin.

**salpi'car** *vt* to splash; (*polvilhar*) to sprinkle.

**'salsa** *f* parsley.

**salseira** [sawsejra] *f* sauce boat.

**salsicha** [saw'siʃa] *f* sausage.

**sal'tar** *vt* to jump (over), leap (over) // *vi* to jump, leap; (*mergulhar*) to dive; (*omitir*) to skip, miss out; ~ **à vista** to be obvious.

**salteador** [sawtʃja'dox] *m* highwayman.

**saltim'banco** *m* charlatan.

**salti'tar** *vt* (*brincar*) to skip.

**'salto** *m* jump, leap; (*mergulho*) dive; (*de calçado*) heel; ~ **em altura** high jump; **dar um** ~ to jump, leap; ~**-mortal** *m* somersault.

**salubre** [sa'lubri] *adj* healthy, salubrious.

**salu'tar** *adj* salutary, beneficial.

**'salva** *f* salvo, salute; (*de palmas*) round; (*bandeja*) tray, salver; (*BOT*) sage.

**salvação** [sawva'sãw] f salvation; **salvador** m saviour; **salvados** mpl salvage; (COM) salvaged goods.

**sal'var** vt (livrar) to save, rescue; (objetos, de ruína) to salvage; **salva-vidas** m inv (bóia) lifebuoy; (pessoa) lifeguard; **barco salva-vidas** lifeboat; **salvo/a** adj safe; **a salvo** in safety; **pôr-se a salvo** to run to safety // prep except, save; **todos salvo ele** all except him; **salvo-conduto** m safe-conduct.

**'samba** f samba; **sambar** vi to dance the samba.

**sa'nar** vt to cure; (remediar) to remedy; **sanatório** m sanatorium; **sanável** adj curable; (remediável) remediable.

**sanção** [sã'sãw] f sanction; **sancionar** vt to sanction; (autorizar) to authorize.

**san'dália** f sandal.

**san'dice** f foolishness, lunacy.

**sanduíche** [sand'wiʃi] f sandwich.

**saneamento** [sanja'mẽtu] m sanitation; **sanear** vt (corrupção) to clean up; (drenar) to drain.

**sa'nefa** f pelmet.

**san'grar** vt/i to bleed; **sangrento/a** adj bloody; (manchado de sangue) bloodstained.

**sangue** ['sãgi] m blood; **~-frio** m cold-bloodedness; **sanguessuga** f leech, bloodsucker; **sanguinário/a** adj bloodthirsty, cruel; **sanguíneo/a** adj sanguine; (atr) blood-; (tez) ruddy; **vaso sanguíneo** blood vessel.

**sanha** ['sana] f rage, fury.

**sani'dade** f (saúde) healthiness; **sanita** f (Pt) toilet, lavatory; **sanitário/a** adj hygienic, sanitary; **vaso sanitário** toilet, lavatory (bowl).

**santi'dade** f holiness, sanctity; **sua S~** His Holiness (the Pope); **santificar** vt to sanctify, make holy.

**'santo/a** adj holy, sacred; **dia ~** holy day; **todo o ~ dia** the whole day long // m/f saint; **santuário** m shrine, sanctuary.

**são/sã** [sãw/sã] adj (sadio) healthy, sound; (salubre) wholesome; **~ e salvo** safe and sound.

**sapa'ria** f shoe shop; **sapateiro** m shoemaker, cobbler; **sapato** m shoe.

**sa'peca** adj forward, flirtatious.

**sapi'ência** f wisdom, learning.

**'sapo** m toad.

**saque** [saki] m (COM) draft, bill; (esporte) serve; (pilhagem) plunder, pillage; **saquear** vt to pillage, plunder.

**sara'banda** f (dança) saraband.

**saracote'ar** vi to shake one's hips.

**saraiva** [sa'rajva] f hail; **saraivada** f hailstorm; **saraivar** vi to hail.

**sa'rampo** m measles pl.

**sarapin'tado/a** adj spotted, speckled.

**sa'rar** vt to cure, heal // vi to recover, be cured.

**sarau** [sa'raw] m soirée, social evening.

**'sarça** f (BOT) bramble (bush).

**sar'casmo** m sarcasm; **sarcástico/a** adj sarcastic.

**'sarda** f freckle.

**sardinha** [sax'dʒina] f sardine; **como ~ em lata** (apertado) like sardines.

**sar'dônico/a** adj sardonic, sarcastic.

**sargento** [sax'ʒẽtu] m sergeant.

**sarilho** [sa'riʎu] m winch, reel; (fig) confusion, mix up.

**sarja** ['saxʒa] f (tecido) serge.

**sarjeta** [sax'ʒeta] f gutter.

**'sarna** f scabies sg.

**'sarro** m (de vinho) tartar, deposit; **tirar um ~** (col) to pet, neck.

**Sa'tã** m, **Sata'nás** m Satan, the Devil.

**satélite** [sa'tɛlitʃi] m satellite; (fig) hanger-on.

**'sátira** f satire.

**satisfação** [satʃiʃfa'sãw] f satisfaction; (*recompensa*) reparation; **satisfazer** vt to satisfy.

**satu'rar** vt to saturate, soak.

**saudação** [sawda'sãw] f greeting.

**saudade** [saw'dadʒi] f (*desejo ardente*) longing, yearning; (*lembrança nostálgica*) homesickness, nostalgia; **ter ~s de** (*desejar*) to long for; (*sentir falta de*) to miss; **deixar ~s** to be greatly missed; **dá ~s a Maria** give Mary my regards.

**saudar** [saw'dax] vt (*cumprimentar*) to greet; (*dar as boas vindas*) to welcome.

**saudável** [saw'davew] adj healthy, wholesome; **saúde** f health; (*brinde*) toast; **beber à saúde de** to drink to, toast; **casa de saúde** hospital; **vender saúde** to be bursting with health.

**saudoso/a** [saw'dozu/a] adj (*nostálgico*) nostalgic; (*da família ou terra natal*) homesick; (*de uma pessoa*) longing.

**sauna** ['sawna] f sauna.

**sazo'nado/a** adj ripe, mature.

**se** [si] conj if, whether; **~ bem que** even though // pron (*ger*) oneself; (*m*) himself; (*f*) herself; (*coisa*) itself; (*você*) yourself; (*vocês*) yourselves; (*eles/elas*) themselves; (*reciprocamente*) each other; **diz~ que ...** it is said that ...; **sabe~ que** it is known that ... .

**sé** [sɛ] f cathedral; **Santa S~** Holy See.

**sê** [se] vb ver **ser**.

**seara** [si'ara] f (*campo de cereais*) wheat ou corn field; (*campo cultivado*) tilled field.

**sebe** ['sɛbi] f (Pt) fence; **~ viva** hedge.

**se'bento/a** adj (*sujo*) dirty, filthy; (*gordurento*) greasy.

**'sebo** m fat, tallow; (*livraria*) secondhand bookshop.

**'seca** adj ver **seco**.

**'seca'dor** m drier.

**seção** [se'sãw] (Pt: **-cç-**) f section.

**se'car** vt to dry; (*tornar murcho*) to parch // vi to dry (up); (*plantas*) to wither.

**secessão** [sese'sãw] f secession.

**'seco/a** adj (*árido*) arid; (*alimentos*) dried; (*ríspido*) curt, brusque; (*desejoso*) eager; **pôr em ~** (*embarcação*) to run aground // f (*estiagem*) drought // mpl: **~s e molhados** groceries; **armazém de ~s e molhados** grocery store.

**secre'taria** f (*local*) general office, secretary's office; (*ministério*) ministry; **secretário/a** m/f secretary// f (*mesa*) writing desk.

**se'creto/a** adj m secret.

**sec'tário/a** adj sectarian // m/f follower; **sectarismo** m sectarianism.

**secu'lar** adj (*leigo*) secular, lay; (*muito antigo*) age-old; **século** m (*cem anos*) century; (*época*) age.

**secun'dar** vt (*apoiar*) to support, back up.

**secun'dário/a** adj secondary.

**se'cura** f dryness; (*fig*) coldness.

**'seda** f silk; **papel de ~** tissue paper; **bicho da ~** silkworm.

**seda'tivo/a** adj, m sedative.

**sede** ['sedʒi] f thirst; (*fig*) craving; **ter ~** to be thirsty; **matar a ~** to quench one's thirst // f ['sɛdʒi] f (*de empresa, instituição*) headquarters sg; (*de governo*) seat; (*REL*) see, diocese.

**seden'tário/a** adj sedentary.

**se'dento/a** adj thirsty; (*fig*) eager, avid.

**sedição** [sedʒi'sãw] f sedition; **sedicioso/a** adj seditious.

**sedi'mento** m sediment.

**sedução** [sedu'sãw] f seduction; (*atração*) allure, charm; **sedutor(a)** adj seductive; (*tentador*) alluring // m/f seducer; **seduzir** vt to seduce; (*fascinar*) to fascinate, entice; (*desencaminhar*) to lead astray.

**'sega** f harvest, reaping; **~deira** f (foice) scythe; (máquina) harvester; **~dor** m harvester, reaper; **segar** vt (ceifar) to harvest, reap.

**seg'mento** m segment; (divisão) section.

**segre'dar** vt to whisper; **segredo** m secret; (silêncio, sigilo) secrecy; (discrição) discretion; **em segredo** in private.

**segregação** [segrega'sãw] f segregation; **segregar** vt to segregate, separate.

**seguido/a** [se'gidu/a] adj following; (contínuo) continuous, consecutive; **três dias ~s** three days running; **em ~a** (depois) afterwards, next; (imediatamente) immediately, right away; **seguidor(a)** m/f follower.

**seguimento** [segi'mẽtu] m continuation; **dar ~ a** to proceed with; **em ~ de** after; **seguinte** adj next, following; **seguir** vt to follow; (vir depois) to come after; (perseguir) to pursue; (continuar) to continue // vi to follow (on); (continuar) to continue, carry on; **logo a seguir** next; **seguir-se** vr to follow, ensue; (resultar) to result.

**segunda-feira** [segũda-'fejra] f Monday.

**se'gundo/a** adj second; **~ tempo** (futebol) second half // prep according to // conj as; **~ disse** as he said, from what he said // m second // f (MÚS) second; (AUT) second (gear); **de ~a** second-rate; **de ~a mão** second-hand.

**segura'mente** adv surely.

**segu'rança** f safety; (proteção) security; (confiança) confidence; (certeza) certainty; **com ~** assuredly; **segurar** vt (tornar seguro) to secure, fix; (agarrar) to seize, take hold of; (garantir) to guarantee, ensure; (COM) to insure; **seguro/a** adj (livre de perigo) safe; (livre de risco) secure; (certo)

certain, sure; (firme) firm, secure; (confiável) reliable; (avaro) stingy; (tempo) settled // m (COM) insurance; **seguro de vida** life insurance; **apólice de seguro** insurance policy; **fazer seguro** to take out an insurance policy.

**sei** vb ver **saber.**

**seio** ['seju] m breast, bosom; (âmago) heart; (~ paranasal) sinus; **no ~ de** in the heart of.

**seis** [sejs] num six; **~centos/as** num six hundred.

**seita** ['sejta] f sect.

**seiva** ['sejva] f sap; (fig) vigour, vitality.

**seixo** ['sejʃu] m pebble.

**seja** etc vb ver **ser.**

**'sela** f saddle.

**se'lar** vt (carta) to stamp; (pôr selo em) to mark with a seal, stamp; (cavalo) to saddle; (fechar) to shut, seal; (concluir) to conclude; (confirmar) to confirm.

**seleção** [sele'sãw] (Pt: -cç-) f selection, choice; (equipe) team, squad; **selecionado** (Pt: -cc-) m (equipe) team; **selecionar** (Pt: -cc-) vt to select, choose.

**se'letivo/a** (Pt: -ct-) adj selective; **seleto/a** (Pt: -ct-) adj select, choice // f anthology.

**selim** [se'lĩ] m saddle.

**'selo** m (postal, estampilha) stamp; (carimbo, sinete) seal.

**'selva** f jungle, forest.

**selvagem** [sɛw'vaʒẽ] adj (silvestre) wild; (feroz) savage, fierce; (não domesticado) wild.

**sem** [sẽ] prep without.

**se'máforo** m (AUTO) traffic lights pl; (FERRO) signal.

**se'mana** f week; **semanal** adj weekly; **semanário** m weekly (publication).

**sem'blante** m face; (fig) appearance, look.

**seme'ar** vt to sow; (fig) to spread; (espalhar) to scatter.

**semelhança** [seme'ʎãsa] *f* similarity, resemblance; **a ~ de** like; **semelhante** *adj* similar, resembling; (*tal*) such // *m* fellow creature; **semelhar** *vi* to seem like, resemble.

**'sêmen** *m* semen.

**se'mente** *f* seed; **sementeira** *f* sowing, spreading.

**semes'tral** *adj* half-yearly; **semestre** *n* six months; (*EDUC*) semester.

**semicírculo** [semi'sıxkulu] *m* semicircle.

**semiconsciente** [semicõ'sjêtʃi] *adj* semiconscious.

**semifi'nal** *f* semifinal; **~ista** *m/f* semifinalist.

**semi'nário** *m* (*EDUC, congresso*) seminar; (*REL*) seminary.

**sempi'terno/a** *adj* everlasting, eternal.

**sempre** ['sêpri] *adv* always; (*na verdade*) really, actually; (*ainda*) still, yet; **você ~ vai?** (*Pt*) are you still going?; **para ~** forever; **~ que** whenever; **como ~** as always; **a história de ~** the same old story; **para todo o ~** for ever and ever; **quase ~** nearly always.

**sem-vergonha** [sê-vex'goɲa] *m/f* (*pessoa*) shameless person; **sem-vergonhice** *f* shamelessness.

**se'nado** *m* senate; **senador(a)** *m/f* senator.

**senão** [se'nãw] *conj* otherwise, if not; (*mas sim*) but, but rather; **~ quando** when suddenly; **~ que/também** but also // *m* flaw, defect.

**'senda** *f* path.

**senha** ['seɲa] *f* (*sinal*) sign; (*palavra de passe*) password; (*recibo*) receipt, voucher; (*Pt: bilhete*) ticket, voucher.

**senhor(a)** [se'ɲox(ra)] *m* (*homem*) man; (*cavalheiro*) gentleman; (*feudal*) lord; (*dono*) owner; (*tratamento*) Mr.; (*tratamento respeitoso*) sir; (*: carta*) **Ilustríssimo (Il.<sup>mo</sup>) S~**; (*Pt*) **Excelentíssimo (Ex.<sup>mo</sup>) S~**; **Dear Sir; Nosso S~** Our Lord; **o ~** you; **~ de si** cool, collected // *f* (*mulher*) lady; (*esposa*) wife; (*tratamento*) Mrs.; (*tratamento respeitoso*) madam; (*: carta*) **Excelentíssima (Ex.<sup>ma</sup>) S~a** Dear Madam; **Nossa S~a** Our Lady; **a ~a** you.

**senho'ria** *f* (*proprietária*) landlady; **senhorial** *adj* (*atr*) manor-, manorial; **senhoril** *adj* lordly; **senhorinha** *f ver* **senhorita; senhorio** *m* (*autoridade*) domination, control; (*proprietário*) landlord; **senhorita** *f* Miss; (*mulher jovem*) young lady.

**se'nil** *adj* senile; **~idade** *f* senility.

**sensabo'ria** *f* (*insipidez*) insipidity, dullness; (*col*) unpleasantness.

**sensação** [sẽsa'sãw] *f* sensation, feeling; **causar ~** to cause a sensation; **sensacional** *adj* sensational.

**sensa'tez** *f* good sense; **sensato/a** *adj* sensible, level-headed.

**sensibilidade** [sẽsibili'dadʒi] *f* sensitivity, sensibility; **sensibilizar** *vt* to touch, move; **sensibilizar-se** *vr* to be moved; **sensitivo/a** *adj* psychic; **sensível** *adj* sensitive; (*perceptível*) perceptible; (*considerável*) considerable; **sensivelmente** *adv* perceptibly, markedly.

**'senso** *m* sense; (*juízo*) judgement; **~ comum** *ou* **bom ~** common sense; **sensual** *adj* sensual, sensuous.

**sen'tar** *vt* to seat // *vi* to sit; **~-se** *vr* to sit down.

**sen'tença** *f* (*JUR*) sentence; **sentenciar** *vt* (*julgar*) to pass judgement on; (*pronunciar sentença*) to sentence.

**sen'tido/a** *adj* (*magoado*) grieved, sorrowful; (*triste*) sad // *excl*: **~!** attention! // *m* sense; (*significação*) sense, meaning; (*direção*) direction;

~ **único** (*sinal*) one-way; **perder/recobrar os** ~**s** to lose/recover consciousness; **em certo** ~ in a sense; **sem** ~ meaningless.

**sentimen'tal** *adj* sentimental; ~**ismo** *m* sentimentalism; **sentimento** *m* sentiment, feelings *pl*; (*pesar*) grief; **sentimentos** *mpl* condolences.

**senti'nela** *f* sentry, guard; **estar de** ~ to be on guard duty; **render** ~ to relieve the guard.

**sen'tir** *vt* to feel; (*perceber*) to perceive, sense; (*lamentar*) to regret; (*ressentir-se*) to be offended by; ~ **a falta de** to miss // *vi* (*ter sensibilidade*) to feel; (*ter pesar*) to grieve; ~**se** *vr* to feel; (*imaginar-se*) to imagine o.s. to be, feel like.

**sen'zala** *f* slave quarters.

**separação** [separa'sãw] *f* separation; (*parede*) partition; **separado/a** *adj* separate, separated; **em separado** separately, apart; **separar** *vt* to separate; (*dividir*) to divide; **separar-se** *vr* to separate; (*dividir-se*) to be divided; (*afastar-se*) to leave, depart; **separata** *f* offprint; **separatismo** *m* separatism.

**'séptico/a** *adj* septic.

**se'pulcro** *m* tomb; **sepultar** *vt* (*enterrar*) to bury; (*esconder*) to hide, conceal; **sepultura** *f* grave, tomb.

**sequaz** [se'kwaʃ] *m* (*seguidor*) follower, adherent.

**sequela** [se'kwela] *f* sequel; (*consequência*) consequence.

**sequência** [se'kwẽsja] *f* sequence, succession.

**sequer** [se'kɛʀ] *adv* at least; **nem** ~ not even.

**sequestra'dor(a)** *m/f* sequestrator; (*raptor*) kidnapper; (*de avião etc*) hijacker; **seqüestrar** *vt* (*bens*) to seize, confiscate; (*raptar*) to kidnap; (*avião etc*) to hijack;

**seqüestro** *m* seizure; (*rapto*) abduction, kidnapping.

**sequioso/a** [ski'ozu/a] *adj* (*sedento*) thirsty; (*desejoso*) eager.

**séquito** ['sɛkitu] *m* retinue, suite.

**ser** *vi* to be; ~ **de** (*provir de*) to be from, come from; (*feito de*) to be made of; (*pertencer*) to belong to; **a não** ~ **que** unless; **pode** ~ it may be; **que horas são?** what time is it?; **é uma hora** it is one o'clock; ~ **feito de** to have become of; **o que é feito dele?** what has become of him?; **seja... seja....** whether... or....; **ou seja** that is to say; **era uma vez** once upon a time; **será que...?** I wonder if...? // *m* being.

**serão** [se'rãw] *m* (*trabalho noturno*) night work; (*horas extraordinárias*) overtime; (*sarau*) evening party; **fazer** ~ to work overtime.

**sereia** [se'reja] *f* (*sirena*) siren; (*figura mitológica*) mermaid.

**sere'nar** *vt* (*acalmar*) to calm (down) // *vi* (*tornar-se sereno*) to calm down; ~**se** *vr* to grow calm; **serenidade** *f* calmness, tranquillity; **sereno/a** *adj* calm; (*tempo*) fine, clear // *m* (*relento*) damp night air; (*chuva*) drizzle; **no sereno** in the open.

**seri'ado/a** *adj* in a series, serialised // *m* (*filme*) serial; **série** *f* series *sg*; (*seqüência*) sequence, succession; (*EDUC*) grade; (*categoria*) category; **em série** (*filme etc*) serial *cmp*; **produção em série** mass production.

**seriedade** [serje'dadʒ] *f* seriousness; (*aplicação*) diligence; (*honradez*) honesty, sincerity.

**se'ringa** *f* syringe.

**serin'gal** *m* rubber plantation; **seringalista** *m* rubber plantation owner; **seringueira** *f* rubber tree; **seringueiro** *m* rubber tapper.

**'sério/a** *adj* serious; (*sincero*) sincere, honest; (*aplicado*) diligent;

a ~ seriously; **levar a** ~ to take seriously.

**sermão** [sex'mãw] *m* sermon.

**se'rôdio/a** *adj* late, belated.

**serpeante** [sɛxpi'ãtʒi] *adj* wriggling, (*fig*) winding, meandering; **serpear** *vi* (*como serpente*) to wriggle; (*fig*) to wind, meander; **serpente** *f* snake; (*pessoa*) snake in the grass; **serpentear** *vi ver* **serpear**.

**serpen'tina** *f* (*conduto*) coil; (*fita de papel*) streamer.

**'serra** *f* (*montanha*) mountain range; (*TEC*) saw; **subir a** ~ to lose one's temper; **serragem** *f* (*pó*) sawdust.

**serralheiro** [sɛxa'ʎejru] *m* locksmith.

**serra'nia** *f* mountain range; **serrano/a** *adj* highland // *m/f* highlander.

**ser'rar** *vt* to saw, cut; **serraria** *f* sawmill.

**sertanejo/a** [sɛxta'neʒu/a] *adj* rustic, country // *m/f* inhabitant of the backlands // *m* backwoodsman; **sertão** *m* backlands, bush (country).

**ser'vente** *m/f* (*criado*) servant; (*operário*) assistant; ~ **de pedreiro** bricklayer's labourer.

**servi'çal** *adj* obliging, helpful // *m/f* (*criado*) servant; (*trabalhador*) wage earner; **serviço** *m* service; (*de chá etc*) set; **serviço ativo** (*MIL*) active duty; **serviço doméstico** housework; **serviço militar** military service; **serviços públicos** public utilities; **prestar serviço** to help, be of help; **estar de serviço** to be on duty.

**servidão** [sexvi'dãw] *f* servitude, serfdom; **servido/a** *adj* served; (*usado*) worn; **servido de** (*provido*) supplied with, provided with; **está servido almoçar?** would you care to join us for lunch?; **servidor** *m* (*criado*) servant; (*funcionário*) employee; **servil** *adj* servile; **servir**

*vt* to serve // *vi* to serve; (*ser útil*) to be useful; (*ajudar*) to help; (*ficar bem*) to suit; **servir-se vr** (*tomar para si*) to serve o.s.; **servir-se de** to use, make use of; **servo/a** *m/f* (*feudal*) serf; (*criado*) servant.

**sessão** [sɛ'sãw] *f* session; (*reunião*) meeting; (*de cinema*) showing.

**ses'senta** *num* sixty.

**'sesta** *f* siesta, nap.

**'seta** *f* arrow, dart.

**sete** ['sɛtʃi] *num* seven; ~**centos/as** *num* seven hundred.

**se'tembro** *m* September.

**se'tenta** *num* seventy.

**setentrio'nal** *adj* northern.

**'sétimo/a** *adj* seventh.

**se'tor** (*Pt*: **-ct-**) *m* sector.

**seu/sua** [sew/'sua] *adj* (*dele*) his; (*dela*) her; (*duma coisa*) its; (*deles, delas*) their; (*de você, vocês*) your // *pron* (*dele*) his; (*dela*) hers; (*deles, delas*) theirs; (*de você, vocês*) yours.

**severi'dade** *f* severity, harshness; **severo/a** *adj* severe, harsh.

**sevícias** [se'visjaʃ] *fpl* (*maus tratos*) ill treatment; (*desumanidade*) inhumanity, cruelty.

**'sexo** *m* sex.

**sexta-feira** [sɛʃta-'fejra] *f* Friday; **S**~ **Santa** Good Friday.

**sexto/a** ['sɛʃtu/a] *adj* sixth.

**sexual** [sɛks'waw] *adj* sexual; ~**idade** *f* sexuality.

**sezão** [se'zãw] *f* (*febre*) (intermittent) fever; (*malária*) malaria.

**s.f.f.** *abr de* **se faz favor** please.

**si** *pron* oneself; (*m*) himself; (*f*) herself; (*coisa*) itself; (*você*) yourself, you; (*vocês*) yourselves; (*pl*) themselves.

**siamês/esa** [sia'meʃ/eza] *adj* Siamese.

**sibi'lar** *vi* to hiss; (*assobiar*) to whistle.

**si'cário** *m* hired assassin.

**si'crano** *m* what's-his-name, so-and-so.

**siderúrgico/a** [sɪdeˈruxʒɪku/a] *adj* iron and steel *cmp*: **usina** ~**a** steel works // *f* the steel industry.

**sidra** *f* cider.

**sifão** [sɪˈfãw] *m* syphon; (*soda*) soda.

**siga** *etc vb ver* **seguir.**

**sigilo** [sɪˈʒɪlu] *m* secret; (*silêncio*, *segredo*) secrecy; **guardar** ~ **sobre** to keep secret; ~**oso/a** *adj* secret.

**signatário** *m* signatory.

**significação** [sɪgnɪfikaˈsãw] *f* significance; **significado** *m* meaning; **significar** *vt* to mean, signify; **significativo/a** *adj* significant; **signo** *m* sign.

**sigo** *vb ver* **seguir.**

**sílaba** *f* syllable.

**silenciar** *vt* (*pessoa*) to silence; (*escândalo*) to hush up // *vi* to remain silent; **silêncio** *m* silence, quiet; **silencioso/a** *adj* silent, quiet // *m* (AUTO) silencer.

**silhueta** [sɪˈʎweta] *f* silhouette.

**silício** [sɪˈlisju] *m* silicon.

**silo** *m* silo.

**silva** *f* bramble bush.

**silvar** *vi* to hiss; (*assobiar*) to whistle.

**silvestre** [sɪlˈvɛʃtrɪ] *adj* wild.

**sim** [sĩ] *adv* yes; **creio que** ~ I think so; **isso** ~ that's it!; **pelo** ~, **pelo não** just in case; **claro que** ~ of course // *m* consent; **dar o** ~ to consent.

**simbólico/a** *adj* symbolic; **simbolismo** *m* symbolism; **simbolizar** *vt* to symbolise; **símbolo** *m* symbol.

**simetria** *f* symmetry; **simétrico/a** *adj* symmetrical.

**similar** *adj* similar; ~**idade** *f* similarity.

**simpatia** *f* (*inclinação*) liking; (*afeto*) affection; (*afinidade*) affinity, fellow feeling; **simpático/a** *adj* (*agradável*) nice, pleasant; (*amável*) kind; **simpatizante** *adj* sympathising // *m/f* sympathiser; **simpatizar** *vi*: **simpatizar com** to take a liking to;

(*causa*) to sympathise with.

**simples** [ˈsɪplɪʃ] *adj inv* simple; (*único*) single; (*de fácil compreensão*) simple, easy; (*mero*) mere, simple; (*ingênuo*) naïve; **simplicidade** *f* simplicity; (*ingenuidade*) naïveté; (*modéstia*) plainness; (*naturalidade*) naturalness; **simplificar** *vt* to simplify; **simplório/a** *adj* gullible // *m/f* fool, simpleton.

**simulação** [sɪmulaˈsãw] *f* simulation; (*fingimento*) pretence, sham; **simulacro** *m* (*imitação*) imitation; (*fingimento*) pretence, sham; (*ídolo*) idol; **simulado/a** *adj* simulated, pretend; **simular** *vt* to simulate.

**simultaneamente** [sɪmultaniaˈmẽtʃɪ] *adv* simultaneously; **simultâneo/a** *adj* simultaneous.

**sina** *f* fate, destiny.

**sinagoga** *f* synagogue.

**sinal** *m*, *pl* **sinais** [sɪˈnajʃ] sign, signal; (*da pele*) mole, birthmark; (*indício*) indication; (*presságio*) omen; (*penhor*) deposit, guarantee; ~ **de tráfego** traffic light; ~ **rodoviário** road sign; **fazer** ~ to signal; **dar de** ~ to give as a deposit; ~**eira** *f* traffic signal; ~**eiro** *m* (FERRO) signalman; ~**ização** *f* (*ato*) signalling; (*para motoristas*) traffic signs *pl*; (FERRO) signals *pl*; ~**izar** *vi* to signal.

**sinceridade** [sĩseriˈdadʒɪ] *f* sincerity; **sincero/a** *adj* sincere.

**síncope** [ˈsĩkopɪ] *f* faint, fainting fit.

**sincronizar** *vt* to synchronize.

**sindical** *adj* union *cmp*, trade union *cmp*; ~**ista** *m/f* trade unionist; **sindicato** *m* (*de trabalhadores*) trade union; (*financeiro*) syndicate; **síndico** *m* (*de condomínio*) manager; (*de massa falida*) receiver.

**sineiro** [sɪˈnejru] *m* bell-ringer; (*fabricante*) bellmaker.

**sinfo'nia** f symphony; **sinfônico/a** adj symphonic.

**singeleza** [sĩʒe'leza] f (simplicidade) simplicity; **singelo/a** adj simple.

**sin'grar** vt to sail.

**singu'lar** adj singular; (extraordinário) exceptional; (bizarro) odd, peculiar; ~**idade** f strangeness, peculiarity; ~**izar** vt (distinguir) to single out; ~**izar-se** vr to stand out, distinguish o.s.

**sinis'trado** m injured party; **sinistro/a** adj left; (fig) sinister // m disaster, accident.

**'sino** m bell.

**si'nônimo/a** adj synonymous // m synonym.

**sinopse** [si'nɔpsɪ] f synopsis.

**'sinta** etc vb ver **sentir**.

**sintaxe** [sĩ'tasɪ] f syntax.

**'síntese** f synthesis; **em** ~ in short; **sintético/a** adj (resumido) summarized; (artificial) synthetic; **sintetizar** vt to synthesize; (resumir) to summarize.

**sin'toma** m symptom; **sintomático/a** adj symptomatic.

**sintoni'zar** vt (rádio) to tune (in) // vi: ~ **com** to get on with.

**sinuosidade** [sɪnwozi'dadɪ] f (ondulação) winding; **sinuoso/a** adj winding, wavy.

**si'rena** f siren.

**si'ri** m crab.

**'sirvo** vb ver **servir**.

**'siso** m good sense; **dente do** ~ wisdom tooth.

**sis'tema** m system; (método) method; **sistemático/a** adj systematic.

**si'sudo/a** adj serious, sober.

**siti'ar** vt to besiege, lay siege to; **sítio** m (lugar) place, location; (MIL) siege; (propriedade rural) small farm.

**situação** [sɪtwa'sãw] f situation, position; (posição social) standing; **situado/a** adj situated; **estar situado** to be situated; **situar** vt (pôr) to place, put; (edifício) to situate, locate.

**só** [sɔ] adj (desacompanhado) alone; (único) single; (solitário, desamparado) solitary, alone; **um** ~ only one; **a** ~**s** alone // adv only, just; **não** ~ ... **mas também** ... not only ... but also ...

**soalheiro/a** [swaˈʎejru/a] adj sunny // f heat of the sun // m sunny spot.

**soalho** ['swaʎu] m (wooden) floor.

**so'ar** vi to sound; (cantar) to sing; (horas) to strike; ~ **a** to sound like, seem like.

**sob** prep under; ~ **pena de** on pain of; ~ **minha palavra** on my word; ~ **juramento** on oath; ~ **emenda** subject to correction.

**'sobe** etc vb ver **subir**.

**sobejar** [sobeˈʒax] vi (superabundar) to be more than enough, abound; (restar) to be left over; **sobejo/a** adj abundant; (imenso) immense // mpl: **sobejos** remains, leftovers.

**sobera'nia** f sovereignty; **soberano/a** adj sovereign; (fig) supreme // m/f sovereign.

**so'berbo/a** adj (arrogante) haughty, arrogant; (magnífico) magnificent, splendid // f haughtiness, arrogance.

**'sobra** f surplus, remnant; **de** ~ spare, extra; (demasiado) in abundance; **ficar de** ~ to be left over; ~**s** fpl leftovers, remains.

**sobra'çar** vt (levar debaixo do braço) to carry under one's arm.

**so'brado** m (andar) floor; (casa) house (of two or more storeys).

**sobrance'ar** vt to tower above; **sobranceiro/a** adj (acima de) lofty, towering; (proeminente) prominent; (arrogante) haughty, arrogant.

**sobrancelha** [sobrã'seʎa] f eyebrow; **franzir as** ~**s** to frown.

**so'brar** vi to be left over, remain;

**ficar sobrando** (*pessoa*) to be left out; **sobram-me cinco** I have five left.

**sobre** ['sobrɪ] *prep* on; (*por cima de*) above, over; (*acima de*) on top of, above; (*a respeito de*) about, concerning; (*além de*) as well as, besides.

**sobreaviso** [sobrɪa'vizu] *m*: **de ~** alert, on one's guard.

**sobre'capa** *f* (*de livro*) cover.

**sobre'carga** *f* (*carga excessiva*) excess load, overloading; **sobrecarregar** *vt* (*carregar em demasia*) to overload; (*oprimir*) to oppress.

**sobrecenho** [sobre'seɲu] *m* frown, scowl.

**sobre-hu'mano/a** *adj* superhuman.

**sobreiro** [so'brejru] *m* cork oak.

**sobrele'var** *vt* (*exceder em altura*) to tower above, rise above; (*levantar*) to raise; (*dominar*) to overcome // *vi* (*destacar-se*) to stand out; **~-se** *vr* to stand out.

**sobremaneira** [sobrema'nejra] *adv* exceedingly, extraordinarily.

**sobre'mesa** *f* dessert.

**sobre'modo** *adv* exceedingly.

**sobrenatu'ral** *adj* supernatural.

**sobrenome** [sobre'nomi] *m* surname, family name.

**sobrepe'liz** *f* surplice.

**sobre'por** *vt* (*pôr em cima*) to put on top of, lay on top; (*adicionar*) to add; (*antepor*) to put first, value more; **~-se** *vr*: **~-se a** (*pôr-se sobre*) to cover, go on top of; (*sobrevir*) to follow, succeed; (*fig*) to overcome.

**sobrepujar** [sobrepu'ʒax] *vt* (*exceder em altura*) to rise above; (*superar*) to excel, surpass; (*vencer*) to overcome.

**sobrescri'tar** *vt* to address; **sobrescrito** *m* (*envelope*) envelope; (*endereço*) address.

**sobressa'ir** *vi* to stand out.

**sobressa'lente** *adj* spare, surplus // *m* spare.

**sobressal'tar** *vt* (*surpreender*) to startle; (*atemorizar*) to frighten; **~-se** *vr* to be startled; **sobressalto** *m* shock; (*susto*) scare, shock; **de sobressalto** suddenly.

**sobretaxa** [sobre'taʃa] *f* surcharge.

**sobre'tudo** *m* overcoat // *adv* above all, especially.

**sobre'vir** *vi* (*suceder*) to occur, arise; **~ a** (*seguir*) to follow (on from).

**sobrevi'vência** *f* survival; **sobrevivente** *adj* surviving // *m/f* survivor; **sobrevi'ver** *vi* to survive; **sobreviveu ao seu pai** he survived his father.

**sobriedade** [sobrje'dadʒɪ] *f* sobriety, soberness; (*comedimento*) moderation, restraint.

**sobrinho/a** [so'briɲu/a] *m* nephew // *f* niece.

**'sóbrio/a** *adj* sober; (*moderado*) moderate, restrained.

**sobrolho** [so'broʎu] *m* eyebrow; **~ carregado** scowl; **carregar o ~** to scowl; **franzir o ~** to frown.

**so'capa** *f*: **à ~** furtively, on the sly.

**so'car** *vt* (*esmurrar*) to hit, strike; (*calcar*) to crush, pound.

**soca'var** *vt* (*escavar*) to excavate.

**social** [so'sjaw] *adj* social; (*pessoa*) sociable; **~ismo** *m* socialism; **~ista** *adj, m/f* socialist; **~izar** *vi* to socialize; **sociável** *adj* sociable.

**sociedade** [sosje'dadʒɪ] *f* society; (*COM*) company; **~ anônima** joint-stock *ou* limited company; **sócio** *m* (*COM*) partner, associate; (*membro dum clube*) member; **sócio comanditário** (*COM*) silent partner.

**sociologia** [sosjolo'ʒia] *f* sociology; **sociológico/a** *adj* sociological; **sociólogo/a** *m/f* sociologist.

**'soco** *m* (*golpe*) blow, punch.

**soço'brar** *vt* (*afundar*) to sink, wreck // *vi* (*naufragar*) to sink, founder.

**socor'rer** vt to help, assist; (salvar) to rescue; ~-se vr: ~-se de to resort to, have recourse to; **socorro** m help, assistance; **ir em socorro de** to come to the aid of; **primeiros socorros** first aid sg // excl: **socorro!** help!

**'soda** f (cáustica) caustic soda; (para bebidas) soda water.

**so'fá** m sofa, settee; ~-**cama** m studio couch.

**so'fisma** m sophism; (col) trick; **sofismar** vt to swindle, cheat.

**'sôfrego/a** adj (ávido) greedy; (impaciente) impatient.

**so'frer** vt (padecer) to suffer; (agüentar) to bear, put up with; (experimentar) to go through, experience // vi to suffer; **sofrido/a** adj long-suffering, patient; **sofrimento** m suffering; (paciência) endurance; **sofrível** adj bearable; (razoável) passable, moderate.

**'sogro/a** m father-in-law // f mother-in-law.

**soja** ['sɔʒa] f soya.

**sol** m sun; (luz) sunshine, sunlight; **ao/no** ~ in the sun; **fazer** ~ to be sunny; **de** ~ **a** ~ from dawn to dusk.

**'sola** f (de calçado ou pé) sole.

**sola'par** vt (escavar) to dig into; (fig: arruinar) to undermine, destroy.

**so'lar** adj solar // m manor house.

**sola'vanco** m jolt, bump; **andar aos** ~s to jog along.

**'solda** f solder.

**sol'dado** m soldier; ~ **raso** private soldier; ~ **de chumbo** toy soldier.

**solda'dor** m welder; **soldar** vt to solder, weld; (fig) to unite, amalgamate.

**'soldo** m (MIL) pay.

**soleira** [so'lejra] f (duma porta) doorstep, threshold.

**solene** [so'lɛni] adj solemn; **solenidade** f solemnity; **solenizar** vt to solemnize.

**sole'trar** vt to spell out; (ler devagar) to read out slowly.

**solha** ['soʎa] f plaice.

**solicitação** [solisita'sãw] f request; **solicitações** fpl (apelo) inducement sg, appeal sg; **solicitar** vt to ask for, seek; (emprego) to apply for.

**so'lícito/a** adj (diligente) diligent; (prestimoso) helpful; **solicitude** f great care; (boa vontade) concern, thoughtfulness.

**solidão** [soli'dãw] f solitude, isolation; (sem amigos, parentes etc) loneliness; (lugar) wilderness, desert.

**solidariedade** [solidarje'dadʒi] f solidarity; **solidário/a** adj (manifestando simpatia) sympathetic; (partilhando responsabilidade) jointly responsible; **solidarizar-se** vr to sympathize.

**soli'dez** f solidity, strength; **sólido/a** adj solid.

**solilóquio** [soli'lɔkju] m soliloquy.

**so'lista** m/f soloist.

**soli'tário/a** adj lonely, solitary // m hermit; (jóia) solitaire.

**'solo** m (terreno) ground, earth; (MÚS) solo.

**sol'tar** vt (tornar livre) to set free; (desatar) to loosen, untie; (afrouxar) to slacken, loosen; (emitir) to emit; (grito, risada) to let out; ~-**se** vr (desprender-se) to come loose; (escapar) to escape.

**solteiro/a** [sol'tejru/a] adj unmarried, single // m bachelor // f single woman, spinster; **solteirona** f old maid.

**'solto/a** pp irr de **soltar** // adj loose; (livre) free; (sozinho) alone; à ~**a** freely; **verso** ~ blank verse; **intestino** ~ loose bowels, diarrhoea; **dormir a sono** ~ to sleep like a log; **soltura** f looseness; (liberdade) release, discharge.

**solução** [solu'sãw] f solution.

**solu'çar** vi (chorar) to sob; (MED) to hiccup.

**solucionar** [solusjo'nax] *vt* to solve.

**so'luço** *m* (*pranto*) sob; (*MED*) hiccup.

**so'lúvel** *adj* soluble.

**solvência** *f* solvency; **solver** *vt* (*resolver*) to solve; (*pagar*) to pay.

**som** [sõ] *m* sound; (*MÚS*) tone; (*Br: col: equipamento*) hi-fi, stereo; **sem tom nem** ~ without rhyme or reason; **ao** ~ **de** (*MÚS*) to the accompaniment of.

**'soma** *f* sum, total; **somar** *vt* (*adicionar*) to add (up); (*chegar a*) to add up to, amount to // *vi* to add up.

**'sombra** *f* shadow; (*como proteção*) shade; (*fantasma*) ghost; (*indício*) trace, sign; (*capanga*) henchman, bodyguard; **à** ~ **de** in the shade of; (*sob a proteção de*) under the protection of; **fazer** ~ **a** to outshine; **nem por** ~**s** not a chance; **sem** ~ **de dúvida** without a shadow of a doubt; **sombreado/a** *adj* shady; **sombrear** *vt* to shade; **sombrinha** *f* parasol, sunshade; (*Br*) lady's umbrella; **sombrio/a** *adj* (*escuro*) shady, dark; (*triste*) gloomy.

**'some** *etc vb ver* **sumir.**

**so'menos** *adj* inferior, poor; **de** ~ **importância** unimportant.

**somente** [so'mẽtʃi] *adv* only, merely; **tão** ~ only.

**'somos** *vb ver* **ser.**

**sonambu'lismo** *m* sleepwalking; **sonâmbulo/a** *adj* sleepwalking // *m/f* sleepwalker.

**so'nata** *f* sonata.

**'sonda** *f* (*instrumento*) plummet, sounding lead; (*MED*) probe; (*de petróleo*) drill; **sondagem** *f* (*NÁUT*) sounding; (*para petróleo*) drilling; (*para minerais*) boring; (*de opinião, mercado*) survey; **sondar** *vt* (*NÁUT*) to sound, probe; (*explorar*) to explore, probe; (*opinião etc*) to sound out, take a survey of.

**so'neca** *f* nap, snooze.

**sone'gar** *vt* (*ocultar*) to conceal, withhold; (*surripiar*) to steal, pilfer; (*deixar de pagar*) to dodge.

**so'neto** *m* sonnet.

**sonhador(a)** [soɲa'dox(ra)] *adj* dreamy, dreaming // *m/f* dreamer; **sonhar** *vi* to dream; **sonhar com** to dream about; **sonho** *m* dream; (*CULIN*) doughnut; **sonho acordado** daydream.

**'sono** *m* sleep; **estar com** ~ /**ter** ~ to be sleepy; **pegar no** ~ to fall asleep; ~**lência** *f* drowsiness; ~**lento/a** *adj* sleepy, drowsy.

**so'noro/a** *adj* sonorous; (*ressonante*) resonant, resounding.

**'sonso/a** *adj* sly, artful.

**'sopa** *f* soup; (*coisa fácil*) pushover, cinch; **em** ~ soaked.

**so'papo** *m* slap, cuff.

**so'pé** *m* foot, bottom.

**sopeira** [so'pejra] *f* (*CULIN*) soup dish.

**sope'sar** *vt* (*tomar o peso de*) to weigh in one's hand; (*equilibrar*) to balance in one's hand; (*agüentar o peso de*) to bear, support.

**sopi'tar** *vt* (*fazer dormir*) to make sleepy; (*acalmar*) to calm (down), appease; (*debilitar*) to weaken; (*conter*) to curb, repress.

**so'prar** *vt* to blow; (*encher de ar*) to blow up; (*apagar um fogo, vela etc*) to blow out; (*dizer em voz baixa*) to whisper // *vi* to blow; **sopro** *m* blow, puff; (*de vento*) gust; (*hálito*) breath; (*no coração*) murmur; **instrumento de sopro** wind instrument.

**sórdido/a** *adj* sordid; (*sujo*) dirty; (*obsceno*) indecent, dirty; (*mesquinho*) miserly.

**'sorna** *adj* (*Pt*) lazy; (*maçador*) pestering // *f* (*preguiça*) laziness, sluggishness // *m/f* (*pessoa*) idler.

**'soro** *m* (*MED*) serum; (*do leite*) whey.

**'sóror** *f* (*REL*) sister.

**sorrateiro/a** [soxa'tejru/a] *adj* sly, sneaky.

**sorri'dente** adj smiling; **sorrir** vi to smile; **sorriso** m smile.

**sorte** ['sɔxtʃi] f (fortuna) luck; (casualidade) chance; (destino) fate, destiny; (condição) lot; (género) sort, kind; **desta** ~ so, thus; **de** ~ **que** so that; **dar** ~ to bring good luck; **tentar a** ~ to try one's luck; **ter** ~ to be lucky; **tirar a** ~ to draw lots; ~ **grande** big prize; **sortear** vt to draw lots for; (rifar) to raffle; (MIL) to draft; **sorteio** m draw; (rifa) raffle; (MIL) draft.

**sor'tido/a** adj (abastecido) supplied, stocked; (variado) varied, assorted.

**sortilégio** [soxtʃi'lɛʒu] m (bruxaria) sorcery; (encantamento) charm, fascination.

**sorti'mento** m assortment, stock; **sortir** vt (abastecer) to supply, stock; (variar) to vary, mix.

**sorum'bático/a** adj gloomy, melancholy.

**sorvedouro** [soxve'doru] m whirlpool; (abismo) chasm.

**sor'ver** vt to sip; (inalar) to inhale; (tragar) to swallow up; (absorver) to soak up, absorb; **sorvete** m ice cream; **sorvo** m sip.

**'sósia** m/f double; (col) spitting image.

**soslaio** [soʒ'laju] adv: **de** ~ sideways, obliquely; **olhar algo de** ~ to squint at sth.

**sosse'gado/a** adj peaceful, calm; **sossegar** vt to calm, quieten // vi to rest; **sossego** m peacefulness, calm.

**sotaina** [so'tajna] f cassock, soutane.

**sótão** ['sɔtãw] m attic, loft.

**sotaque** [so'taki] m (fala) accent.

**sota'vento** m (NÁUT) lee; **a** ~ to leeward.

**soter'rar** vt to bury.

**so'turno/a** adj sad, gloomy.

**sou** vb ver **ser**.

**'soube** etc vb ver **saber**.

**soutien** [su'tʃã] m bra(ssiere).

**'sova** f beating, thrashing.

**so'vaco** m armpit.

**so'var** vt (golpear) to beat, thrash; (massa) to knead.

**so'vela** f awl.

**sovi'ético/a** adj, m/f Soviet.

**so'vina** m/f miser, skinflint.

**sozinho/a** [sɔ'ziɲu/a] adj (all) alone, by oneself.

**Sr.** abr de **senhor** Mr.

**Sr.ª** abr de **senhora** Mrs.

**Sr.ia** abr de **senhorita** Miss.

**sua** ['sua] adj, pron ver **seu**.

**su'ado/a** adj hard-earned; **suar** vi to sweat, perspire // vt to slave over, strive for.

**suave** ['swavɪ] adj (brando) soft; (benigno) mild; (terno) gentle; (sem dificuldades) smooth; (encantador) suave; **suavidade** f (brandura) softness; (ternura) gentleness; (amenidade) mildness; (encanto) charm; **suavizar** vt to soften.

**subal'terno/a** adj inferior, subordinate // m (MIL) subaltern.

**subarren'dar** vt (Pt) to sublet.

**subconsciência** [subcõ'sjẽsja] f subconscious; **subconsciente** adj, m subconscious.

**subdesenvol'vido/a** adj underdeveloped; **subdesenvolvimento** m underdevelopment.

**'súbdito** (Pt) m ver **súdito**.

**subenten'der** vt to understand, assume.

**su'bido/a** adj (alto) high, lofty; (nobre) noble // f ascent, climb; (ladeira) slope; (de preços) rise; **subir** vi to go up, ascend, climb; (preços) to rise; **subir a** (montar) to mount, get on to // vt (ladeira) to raise; (uma ladeira) to climb, go up.

**'súbito/a** adj sudden; **de** ~ suddenly.

**subjetivo/a** [subʒɛ'tʃivu/a] (Pt: -ct-) adj subjective.

**subjugar** [subʒu'gax] vt to subjugate, subdue; (dominar) to overpower.

**sublevação** [subleva'sãw] f (up)rising, revolt; **sublevar** vt to stir up in revolt; **sublevar-se** vr to revolt, rebel.

**sublime** [su'blimɪ] adj sublime, noble.

**sublinhar** [subli'ɲax] vt (pôr linha debaixo de) to underline; (destacar) to emphasise, stress.

**sublocatário** m sub-tenant.

**submarino/a** adj underwater // m submarine.

**submergir** [submex'ʒix] vt, **submergir-se** vr to submerge.

**submeter** vt (subjugar) to subdue; (entregar) to submit; **~-se** vr: **~-se a** to submit to; (operação) to undergo.

**submissão** [submi'sãw] f submission; **submisso/a** adj submissive, docile.

**subordinar** vt to subordinate.

**subornar** vt to bribe; **suborno** m bribery.

**sub-reptício/a** [sub-xɛp'tʃisju/a] adj surreptitious.

**subscrever** vt (assinar) to sign; (concordar) to agree with; **~-se** vr to sign one's name; **subscrição** f subscription.

**subsecretário/a** m/f under-secretary.

**subseqüente** [subse'kwẽtʃi] adj subsequent, following.

**subsidiário/a** adj subsidiary // f (COM) subsidiary (company); **subsídio** m subsidy; (ajuda) aid; **subsídios** mpl data, information.

**subsistência** f (sustento) subsistence; (meio de vida) livelihood.

**substância** f substance; **substantivo/a** adj substantive // m noun.

**substituir** [subʃtʃi'twix] vt to substitute, replace; **substituto/a** adj, m/f substitute.

**subterfúgio** [subtex'fuʒju] m subterfuge, trick.

**subterrâneo/a** adj subterranean, underground.

**subtil** (Pt) adj ver **sutil**.

**subtítulo** m subtitle.

**subtrair** vt (furtar) to steal, embezzle; (deduzir) to subtract.

**suburbano/a** adj suburban; **subúrbio** m suburb.

**subvenção** [subvẽ'sãw] f subsidy, grant; **subvencionar** vt to subsidize.

**subversivo/a** adj, m/f subversive; **subverter** vt to subvert.

**sucata** f scrap metal.

**sucedâneo/a** [suse'danju/a] adj substitute // m (substância) substitute.

**suceder** vi (acontecer) to happen, occur; **~ a** (acontecer a) to befall; (seguir) to succeed, follow; **sucedido/a** adj: **bem sucedido** successful // m event, occurrence; **sucessão** f succession; **sucessivo/a** adj successive; **sucesso** m event, occurrence; **sucessor(a)** m/f successor.

**súcia** ['susja] f gang, band.

**sucinto/a** [su'sĩtu/a] adj concise, succinct.

**suco** m (Br) juice; **suculento/a** adj succulent, juicy.

**sucumbir** vi to render) to succumb, yield; (morrer) to die, perish.

**sucursal** f (COM) branch.

**sudário** m shroud.

**sudeste** [su'dɛʃtʃi] adj southeast // m the South East.

**súdito** (Pt: **-bd-**) m (de rei etc) subject.

**sudoeste** [sud'wɛʃtʃi] adj southwest // m the South West.

**Suécia** ['swɛsja] f Sweden; **sueco/a** adj Swedish // m/f Swede // m (língua) Swedish.

**sueste** ['swɛʃtʃi] adj southeast // m the South East.

**suéter** ['swɛtɛx] m sweater.

**suficiência** [sufis'jẽsja] f (quantidade suficiente) sufficiency;

(*aptidão*) competence; **suficiente** *adj* sufficient, enough.

**sufixo** [su'fiksu] *m* suffix.

**sufo'cante** *adj* (*calor*) sweltering, oppressive; **sufocar** *vt/i* to suffocate, choke.

**sufrágio** [su'fraʒu] *m* suffrage, vote.

**su'gar** *vt* to suck; (*fig*) to extort.

**sugerir** [suʒe'rix] *vt* to suggest; **sugestão** *f* suggestion; (*indireta*) hint.

**suíças** ['swisaʃ] *fpl* sideburns.

**suicida** [swi'sida] *m/f* suicidal person; (*morto*) suicide, a person who has committed suicide; **suicidar-se** *vr* to commit suicide; **suicídio** *m* suicide.

**suíço/a** ['swisu/a] *adj*, *m/f* Swiss // *f*: S~a Switzerland.

**suíno** ['swinu] *m* pig, hog.

**sujar** [su'ʒax] *vt* to soil, dirty.

**sujeição** [suʒei'sãw] *f* subjection; **sujeitar** *vt* to subdue, subject; **sujeitar-se** *vr* to submit; **sujeito/a** *adj* subjected; (*exposto*) subject, liable // *m* (*LING*) subject; (*homem*) guy, fellow // *f* (*mulher*) woman.

**sujidade** [suʒi'dadʒi] *f* (*estado*) dirtiness; (*porcaria*) filth, dirt; **sujo/a** *adj* dirty, filthy.

**sul** *adj inv* south, southern // *m* the south.

**sul'car** *vt* to plough; **sulco** *m* (*rego de arado*) furrow; (*ruga*) wrinkle.

'**suma** *f* summary; **em** ~ in short.

**suma'mente** *adv* extremely.

**su'mário/a** *adj* (*breve*) brief, concise; (*JUR*) summary // *m* summary.

**sumiço** [su'misu] *m* disappearance; **dar** ~ **a** to spirit away; **levar** ~ to disappear.

**su'mido/a** *adj* faint, indistinct; (*olhos*) sunken; (*voz*) low.

**sumidouro** [sumi'doru] *m* (*esgoto*) drain.

**su'mir** *vt* (*submergir*) to submerge;

(*esconder*) to hide; ~**-se** *vr* to disappear, vanish.

'**sumo** *m* (*Pt*) juice.

'**sumo/a** *adj* extreme; (*superior*) supreme.

'**sumula** *f* summary.

'**sunga** *f* swimming trunks; (*suporte*) jock strap, athletic support.

**suntuoso/a** [sũ'twozu/a] (*Pt*: **-umpt-**) *adj* sumptuous.

**su'or** *m* sweat, perspiration.

**superaquecer** [superake'sex] *vi* to overheat.

**supe'rar** *vt* (*dominar*) to overcome; (*exceder*) to exceed, surpass; **superávit** *m* (*COM*) surplus.

**superestru'tura** *f* superstructure.

**superficial** [supexfis'jaw] *adj* superficial; **superfície** *f* (*parte externa*) surface; (*extensão*) area.

**su'pérfluo/a** *adj* superfluous, unnecessary.

**superinten'dente** *m* superintendent, supervisor.

**superi'or** *adj* (*melhor*) superior; (*mais elevado*) higher; ~ **a** above; (*além de*) beyond // *m* superior; (*REL*) superior, abbot; **superiora** *f* mother superior.

**superla'tivo/a** *adj* superlative // *m* superlative.

**supermer'cado** *m* supermarket.

**superpo'tência** *f* superpower.

**superpovoado/a** *adj* [supexpov'wadu/a] *adj* overpopulated.

**superprodução** [supexprodu'sãw] *f* overproduction.

**super'sônico/a** *adj* supersonic.

**superstição** [supexstʃi'sãw] *f* superstition; **supersticioso/a** *adj* superstitious.

**supervi'sar** *vt*, **supervisio'nar** *vt* to supervise.

**suplan'tar** *vt* to supplant, supersede.

**suple'mento** *m* supplement.

**su'plente** *m/f* substitute.

**'súplica** f supplication, plea;
**suplicante** m supplicant; (JUR)
plaintiff; **suplicar** vt to plead, beg.
**suplício** [su'plɪsju] m torture.
**su'por** vt to suppose.
**supor'tar** vt to hold up, support;
(tolerar) to bear, tolerate;
**suportável** adj bearable, tolerable;
**suporte** m support, stand.
**suposição** [supozi'sãw] f
supposition, presumption; **suposto/a**
adj supposed, would-be // f
assumption.
**supre'macia** f supremacy;
**supremo/a** adj supreme, highest.
**supressão** [supre'sãw] f
suppression; (omissão) omission.
**supri'mento** m supply.
**supri'mir** vt to suppress; (omitir)
to omit, delete.
**su'prir** vt to supply, provide;
(substituir) to make up for, take the
place of.
**sur'dina** f (MÚS) mute; **em** ~
stealthily, on the quiet.
**'surdo/a** adj deaf; (som) muffled,
dull // m/f deaf person; ~-**mudo/a**
adj deaf and dumb // m/f deaf-mute.
**surgir** [sux'ʒix] vi (emergir) to
emerge, appear; (sair) to come out,
emerge; (levantar-se) to arise.
**surpreendente** [suxpriẽ'dẽtʃi] adj
surprising, amazing; **surpreender** vt
to surprise, amaze; (pegar de
surpresa) to take unawares;
**surpresa** f surprise; **de surpresa** by
surprise.
**'surra** f beating, thrashing;
**surrado/a** adj worn out; **surrar** vt to
beat, thrash; (couro) to tan, cure.
**sur'tir** vt to produce, bring about;
~ **bem** to turn out well.
**suscetível** [suse'tʃivew] adj,
**susceptível** [suscp'tʃivew] adj
susceptible.
**suscitar** [susi'tax] vt to excite, stir
up; ~ **dúvidas** to raise doubts.
**suspeitar** [suʃpej'tax] vt/i to
suspect; (desconfiar) to distrust;

**suspeito/a** adj suspect, suspicious //
f suspicion; **suspeitoso/a** adj
distrustful, suspicious.
**suspen'der** vt (pendurar) to hang;
(interromper) to suspend, stop;
(adiar) to adjourn, defer; **suspensão**
f suspension; (interrupção) interruption, stoppage; **suspensórios** mpl
braces; (US) suspenders.
**suspicácia** [suʃpi'kasja] f distrust,
suspicion; **suspicaz** adj (suspeito)
suspect; (desconfiado) suspicious.
**suspi'rar** vi to sigh; ~ **por algo** to
long for sth; **suspiro** m sigh; (doce)
meringue.
**sussur'rar** vt/i to whisper;
**sussurro** m whisper.
**sus'tância** f (força) strength;
(comida) nourishment.
**sus'tar** vt/i to stop.
**susten'tar** vt to sustain; (objeto) to
hold up, support; (manter) to
maintain; **sustento** m food,
sustenance; **suster** vt to support,
hold up; (reprimir) to restrain, hold
back.
**'susto** m fright, scare.
**su'til** (Pt: -bt-) adj subtle; (fino)
fine, delicate; ~**eza** f subtlety;
(finura) fineness, delicacy.

# T

**ta** = te + a.
**tabaca'ria** f tobacconist's (shop);
**tabaco** m tobacco.
**ta'bela** f table, chart; (lista) list; **por**
~ indirectly.
**tabelião** [tabeli'jãw] m notary
public.
**ta'berna** f tavern, bar;
**taberneiro/a** m/f (dono) publican.
**tabique** [ta'biki] m partition.
**ta'blado** m stage, platform.
**ta'bu** adj, m taboo.

**'tábua** f (*madeira*) plank, board; (*MAT*) list, table.

**tabule:ro** [tabu'leʒru] m tray; (*xadrez*) board.

**tabu'leta** f (*letreiro*) sign, signboard.

**'taça** f cup.

**tacanho/a** [ta'kaɲu/a] adj mean, niggardly; (*de idéias curtas*) narrow-minded.

**tacha** ['taʃa] f (*prego*) tack; **tachar** vt to find fault with; **tachar de** to brand as.

**'tácito/a** adj tacit, implied; **taciturno/a** adj taciturn, reserved.

**'taco** m (*de bilhar*) cue; (*de golfe, hóquei*) club, stick; (*bucha*) plug, wad.

**taga'rela** adj talkative; // m/f chatterbox; **tagarelar** vi to chatter, gossip; **tagarelice** f chat, chatter, gossip.

**taipa** ['tajpa] f mud wall.

**tal** adj such; ~ **e coisa** this and that; **um ~ de Sr. X** a certain Mr. X; **que ~?** what do you think?; (*Pt*) how are things?; ~ **pai,** ~ **filho** like father, like son // adv so, as; ~ **como** just as; ~ **qual** just so, just as it is // pron such a thing.

**'tala** f (*MED*) splint.

**ta'lante** m: **a seu** ~ at will.

**talão** [ta'lãw] m (*de recibo*) stub; ~ **de cheques** cheque book.

**'talco** m talc; **pó de** ~ (*Pt*) talcum powder.

**ta'lento** m talent; (*aptidão*) ability.

**talha** ['taʎa] f (*corte*) carving; (*vaso*) pitcher; (*NÁUT*) tackle; **talhada** f slice.

**talhão** [ta'ʎãw] m plot, patch.

**talhar** [ta'ʎar] vt to cut, slice; (*esculpir*) to carve // vi (*coalhar*) to curdle; **talhe** m cut, shape.

**talher** [ta'ʎex] m item of cutlery; (*lugar*) place (at table); ~**es** mpl cutlery.

**talho** ['taʎu] m (*corte*) cutting,

slicing; (*Pt: açougue*) butcher's (shop).

**'talo** m stalk, stem; (*ARQ*) shaft.

**talude** [ta'ludʒi] m slope, incline.

**tal'vez** adv perhaps, maybe; ~ **tenha razão** maybe you're right.

**ta'manco** m clog, wooden shoe.

**tamanho/a** [ta'maɲu/a] adj so big, so great // m size; **em** ~ **natural** life-size.

**'tâmara** f (*fruto*) date.

**também** [tã'bẽj] adv also, too, as well; (*aliás*) besides.

**tam'bor** m drum; **tamboril** m, **tamborim** m tambourine.

**'tampa** f lid; (*de garrafa*) cap; **tampão** m cover; (*rolha*) stopper, plug.

**'tanga** f loincloth; **estar de** ~ (*col*) to be broke.

**tanger** [tã'ʒex] vt (*MÚS*) to play; (*sinos*) to ring; (*cordas*) to pluck; ~ **a** (*dizer respeito*) to concern; **no que tange a** as regards, with respect to.

**tange'rina** f tangerine.

**tangível** [tã'ʒivew] adj tangible.

**tanoeiro** [tan'wejru] m cooper.

**tanque** ['tãki] m (*reservatório, MIL*) tank.

**'tanto/a** adj (*sg*) so much; (: + *interrogativa/negativa*) as much; (*pl*) so many; (: + *interrogativa/negativa*) so many; **vinte e** ~**s** twenty-odd; ~ **como** as much as // adv so much; ~ **melhor/pior** so much the better/the more's the pity; ~ **se me dá** it's all the same to me; ~ **... como ...** both ... and ...; ~ **mais ... quanto mais ...** the more ... the more ....

**tão** [tãw] adv so; ~ **rico quanto** as rich as; ~**-só** adv only.

**'tapa** f slap.

**ta'par** vt to cover; (*garrafa*) to cork.

**tapeça'ria** f tapestry, wall hanging.

**tapete** [ta'petʃi] m carpet, rug.

**tapume** [ta'pumi] m fencing, boarding; (*cerca viva*) hedge.

**taquigrafia** [takigra'fɪa] *f* shorthand.

**tar'dança** *f* delay, slowness; **tardar** *vi* to delay, be slow; (*chegar tarde*) to be late; **sem mais tardar** without delay; **ele tardou a vir** he was long in coming // *vt* to delay; **tarde** *f* (*dia*) afternoon; (*quase noite*) evening // *adv* late; **tardinha** *f* late afternoon; **tardio/a** *adj* late.

**ta'refa** *f* task, job.

**ta'rifa** *f* tariff.

**ta'rimba** *f* bunk; (*fig*) army life; **ter ~** to be an old hand; **tarimbado/a** *adj* experienced.

**tartamude'ar** *vi* to stammer, stutter; **tartamudo/a** *m/f* stammerer, stutterer.

**tarta'ruga** *f* turtle.

**tas** = **te** + **as**.

**'tasca** *f* (*Pt*) cheap eating place.

**'tático/a** (*Pt*: **-ct-**) *adj* tactical // *f* tactics *pl*.

**'tato** (*Pt*: **-ct-**) *m* (*sentido*) touch; (*prudência*) tact.

**ta'tu** *m* armadillo.

**tatuagem** [ta'twaʒẽ] *f* tattoo.

**tauromaquia** [tawroma'kɪa] *f* bullfighting.

**tavão** [ta'vãw] *m* horsefly.

**taxa** ['taʃa] *f* (*imposto*) tax; (*preço*) fixed price, fee; **~ de câmbio** exchange rate; **~ de juros** interest rate; **taxar** *vt* (*fixar o preço de*) to fix the price of; (*lançar impostos sobre*) to tax.

**'táxi** *m* taxi, cab.

**'tcheco/a** *adj, m/f* Czech; **Tcheco-Eslováquia** *f* Czechoslovakia.

**te** *pron* you.

**tear** [tʃi'ax] *m* loom.

**teatral** [tʃia'traw] *adj* theatrical; **teatro** *m* theatre; (*US*) theater; (*obras*) plays *pl*, dramatic works *pl*.

**tecelão/lã** [tʃise'lãw/'lã] *m/f* weaver; **tecer** *vt* to weave; (*fig*) to contrive, devise; **tecido** *m* cloth, material; (*MED*) tissue.

**tecla** *f* (*MÚS, máquina de escrever*)

key; **teclado** *m* keyboard.

**'técnico/a** *adj* technical // *m/f* technician; (*especialista*) expert // *f* technique.

**'tédio** *m* tedium; (*aborrecimento*) boredom; **tedioso/a** *adj* tedious; (*aborrecido*) boring.

**teia** ['teja] *f* web; (*enredo*) intrigue, plot; **~ de aranha** spider's web.

**teimar** [tej'max] *vi*: **~ em** to insist on; (*persistir*) to persist in; **teimoso/a** *adj* obstinate, persistent.

**teixo** ['tejʃu] *m* yew.

**'tela** *f* (*tecido*) fabric, material; (*de pintar*) canvas; (*cinema, televisão*) screen.

**tele-...** [tɛlɛ] *pref* tele-...; **~comando** *m* remote control; **~comunicação** *f* telecommunications *pl*; **~térico** *m* cable car; **~fonar** *vt/i* to telephone, ring; (*col*) to ring; **~fone** *m* phone, telephone; **~fonema** *m* phone call; **~fônico/a** *adj* telephone *cmp*; **~fonista** *m/f* telephonist; **~grafar** *vt/i* to telegraph, wire; **~grama** *m* telegram, cable; **~guiado/a** *adj* remote-controlled; **~impressor** *m* teleprinter; **telêmetro** *m* rangefinder; **~objetiva** (*Pt*: **-ct-**) *f* telephoto lens; **~pático/a** *adj* telepathic; **~scópio/a** *adj* telescopic; **~scópio** *m* telescope; **~spetador(a)** (*Pt*: **-ct-**) *m/f* viewer; **~tipista** *m/f* teletypist; **~tipo** *m* teletype; **~visão** *f* television; **~visar** *vt* to televise; **~visor** *m* (*aparelho*) television (set), TV (set).

**telex** ['tɛlɛks] *m* telex.

**telha** ['teʎa] *f* tile; **ter uma ~ de menos** to have a screw loose; **telhado** *m* roof; **telhudo/a** *adj* crazy.

**'tema** *m* theme; (*assunto*) subject.

**te'mer** *vt* to fear, be afraid of.

**teme'rário/a** *adj* reckless, foolhardy; **temeridade** *f* recklessness, foolhardiness.

**teme'roso/a** *adj* fearful, afraid;

**temível** *adj* fearsome, terrible; **temor** *m* fear, dread.

**'têmpera** *f* (*de metais*) tempering; (*caráter*) temperament; (*pintura*) distemper, tempera; **temperado/a** *adj* (*metal*) tempered; (*clima*) temperate; **temperamento** *m* temperament, nature; **temperar** *vt* (*metal*) to temper, harden; (*comida*) to season.

**tempera'tura** *f* temperature.

**tem'pero** *m* seasoning, flavouring.

**tempestade** [tẽpeʃ'tadʒi] *f* storm, tempest; ~ **em copo de água** a storm in a teacup; **tempestuoso/a** *adj* stormy; (*fig*) tempestuous.

**'templo** *m* temple; (*igreja*) church.

**'tempo** *m* (*no relógio*) time; (*meteorológico*) weather; (*gramática*) tense; **bom/mau** ~ fine/bad weather; **a** ~ **on** time; **ao mesmo** ~ at the same time; **de** ~ **em** ~ from time to time; **no** ~ **da onça/há muito** ~ a long time ago; **levar** ~ to take time; **temporada** *f* season; (*espaço*) spell; **temporal** *adj* secular, worldly // *m* storm, gale; **temporário/a** *adj* temporary, provisional.

**tenaci'dade** *f* tenacity; **tenaz** *adj* tenacious; (*teimoso*) stubborn // *f* tongs *pl*.

**tencio'nar** *vt/i* to intend, plan.

**'tenda** *f* (*barraca*) tent; (*de mercado*) stall.

**ten'dência** *f* tendency, inclination; **tendencioso/a** *adj* tendentious, biassed; **tender** *vi* to tend to, have a tendency to.

**tene'broso/a** *adj* dark, gloomy.

**tenente** [te'nẽtʃi] *m* lieutenant.

**'tênia** *f* tapeworm.

**'tênis** *m* tennis; **tenista** *m/f* tennis player.

**'tenro/a** *adj* tender; (*brando*) soft; (*delicado*) delicate; (*novo*) young.

**tensão** [tẽ'sãw] *f* (*ger*) tension; (*pressão*) pressure, strain; (*rigidez*) tightness; (*TEC*) stress; (*ELET.*

*voltagem*) voltage; **tenso/a** *adj* tense; (*sob pressão*) under stress, strained.

**'tenta** *f* (*MED*) probe.

**tentação** [tẽta'sãw] *f* temptation.

**ten'táculo** *m* tentacle.

**tenta'dor(a)** *adj* tempting; (*sedutor*) inviting // *m* tempter // *f* temptress; **tentar** *vt/i* (*intentar*) to try, attempt; (*seduzir*) to tempt, entice; **tentativa** *f* try, attempt.

**tente'ar** *vt* (*sondar*) to probe; (*apalpar*) to grope (for).

**'tento** *m* attention, care; (*casino*) chip; (*ponto*) point; (*futebol*) goal.

**tênue** ['tenui] *adj* tenuous; (*fino*) thin; (*delicado*) delicate; **tenuidade** *f* tenuousness.

**teologia** [tʃiolo'ʒia] *f* theology; **teólogo** *m* theologian.

**te'or** *m* (*conteúdo*) tenor; (*sentido*) meaning, drift; (*norma*) system; (*QUIM*) grade.

**teo'ria** *f* theory; **teórico/a** *adj* theoretical.

**'tépido/a** *adj* tepid, lukewarm.

**ter** *vt* to have; (*na mão*) to hold; (*considerar*) to consider; (*conter*) to hold, contain; (*possuir*) to have, possess; ~ **fome** to be hungry; ~ **frio/calor** to be cold/hot; ~ **razão** to be right; **ela tem 5 anos** she is 5 years old; **tem 10 metros de largura** it is 10 metres wide; ~ **que/de** to have to, must; ~ **o que dizer/fazer** to have something to say/do; ~ **a ver com** to concern, have to do with; **tem telefone aqui?** is there a phone here?; **ir** ~ **com** (*Pt*) to (go and) meet; ~**-se** *vr* : ~**-se por** to consider o.s.

**terça-feira** [tɛxsa-'fejra] *f* Tuesday; ~ **gorda** Shrove Tuesday.

**terceiro/a** [tex'sejru/a] *adj* third; **terço** *m* third (part).

**tergiversar** [tɛxʒivex'sax] *vi* to prevaricate, evade the issue.

**ter'mal** *adj* thermal; **termas** *fpl* spa *sg*, hot springs.

**terminação** [tɛxmina'sãw] *f*
(*LING*) ending; **terminal** *adj*
terminal // *m* (*de rede*, *ELET*)
terminal; **terminantemente** *adv*
categorically, expressly; **terminar**
*vt/i* to finish, end; **término** *m* (*fim*)
end, termination.

**termite** [tɛx'mitʃi] *f* termite.

**termo** *m* (*fim*) end, termination;
(*limite*) limit, boundary; (*prazo*)
period; (*vocábulo*) term, expression;
~ **médio** average; **pôr** ~ **a** to put
an end to.

**ter'mômetro** *m* thermometer.

**terno/a** *adj* gentle, tender // *m*
(*de pessoas*) trio, threesome; (*em
cartas*) three; (*roupa*) suit; **ternura** *f*
gentleness, tenderness.

**terra** *f* (*mundo*) earth, world;
(*pátria*) homeland; (*solo*) ground;
(*terreno*) soil, earth; ~ **firme** dry
land; **terraço** *m* terrace; **terramoto**
*m* (*Pt*) earthquake; **terreiro** *m* yard,
square; **terremoto** *m* earthquake.

**ter'reno** *m* ground, land; (*porção
de terra*) plot of land; (*GEO*) terrain;
(*terra*) soil; **térreo/a** *adj* ground
level *cmp*; **andar térreo** (*Br*)
ground floor; (*US*) first floor;
**terrestre** *adj* terrestrial, land *cmp*;
(*mundano*) worldly.

**ter'rina** *f* tureen.

**terri'tório** *m* territory; (*distrito*)
district, region.

**ter'rível** *adj* terrible, dreadful;
**terror** *m* terror, dread; **terrorismo**
*m* terrorism; **terrorista** *m/f*
terrorist.

**ter'túlia** *f* gathering of friends.

[…]
[…] (*proposição*)
[…]
[…] tense, taut;
[…] (*imóvel*)
[…] ~ to be
[…]
[…] scissors *pl*; (*fig*)
[…] of scissors.

**tesoureiro/a** [tezo'rejru/a] *m/f*
treasurer; **tesouro** *m* treasure; (*COM*)
treasury, exchequer.

**'testa** *f* brow, forehead; **à** ~ **de** at
the head of; ~**-de-ferro** *f*
figurehead, dummy.

**testa'mento** *m* will, testament;
**Velho/Novo T**~ Old/New Testament.

**teste** ['tɛʃtʃi] *m* test, exam.

**testemunha** [tɛʃtʃi'muɲa] *f*
witness; ~ **ocular** eyewitness;
**testemunhar** *vi* to testify // *vt* to
give evidence of, reveal;
**testemunho** *m* evidence, testimony;
**dar testemunho** to give evidence.

**tes'tudo/a** *adj* big-headed; (*fig*)
stubborn, headstrong.

**'teta** *f* teat, nipple.

**'teto** (*Pt*: -**ct**-) *m* ceiling; (*telhado*)
roof.

**'tétrico/a** *adj* gloomy, dismal;
(*horrível*) horrible, frightening.

**teu/tua** [tew/'tua] *adj* your // *pron*
yours.

**'teve** *vb ver* **ter**.

**te'vê** *f* telly.

**'têxtil** *m*, *pl* **têxteis** textile.

**texto** ['tejʃtu] *m* text.

**tex'tura** *f* texture.

**texugo** [tʃi'ʃugu] *m* badger.

**tez** *f* complexion; (*pele*) skin.

**ti** *pron* you.

**'tia** *f ver* **tio**.

**'tíbia** *f* shinbone.

**tibi'eza** *f* tepidness; (*fig*) half-
heartedness; **tíbio/a** *adj* tepid,
lukewarm; (*fig*) unenthusiastic.

**'tifo** *m* typhoid, typhus.

**tigela** [tʃi'ʒela] *f* bowl.

**tigre** ['tʃigri] *m* tiger; **tigresa** *f*
tigress.

**tijolo** [tʃi'ʒolu] *m* brick.

**til** *m* tilde.

**timão** [tʃi'mãw] *m* (*NÁUT*) helm,
tiller.

**timbre** ['tʃimbri] *m* insignia,
emblem; (*selo*) stamp; (*MÚS*) tone,
timbre.

**timi'dez** f shyness, timidity; **tímido/a** adj shy, timid.

**timoneiro** [tʃimo'nejru] m helmsman, coxswain.

**'tímpano** m eardrum; (MÚS) kettledrum.

**tina** f (banheira) tub; (vasilha) vat.

**tingir** [tʃĩ'ʒix] vt to dye; (fig) to tinge.

**'tinha** etc vb ver **ter**.

**ti'nir** vi to jingle, tinkle.

**'tino** m (juízo) discernment, judgement; (intuição) intuition; **perder o ~** to lose one's senses; **ter ~ para algo** to have a flair for sth.

**'tinta** f (de pintar) paint; (de escrever) ink; (para tingir) dye, stain; (vestígio) hint, touch; **tinteiro** m inkwell; **tinto/a** adj dyed, stained; **vinho tinto** red wine; **tintura** f dye; (vestígio) hint, touch; **tinturaria** f dyer's; (lavandaria) launderette; (: a seco) dry-cleaners.

**'tio/a** m uncle // f aunt.

**'típico/a**     adj    typical, characteristic; **tipo** m (ger) type; (de imprensa) print; (classe) kind; (homem) guy, chap; **tipografia** f printing, typography; (estabelecimento) printing office, printer's; **tipógrafo** m printer.

**tique** ['tʃiki] m habit, idiosyncrasy; (MED) twitch, tic.

**'tira** f strip; (Br: col) cop.

**tiracolo** m: **a ~** slung from the shoulder.

**'tirada** f (de caminho, tempo) stretch; **tiragem** f (dum livro) edition.

**tira-'manchas** m inv stain remover.

**tira'nia** f tyranny.

**ti'rano/a** adj tyrannical // m tyrant.

**tirante** [tʃi'rãtʃi] m (de arreio) trace; (MEC) driving rod; (viga) tie beam // prep except; **tirar** vt (retirar) to remove, take away; (sacar) to take out, draw; (puxar) to

pull; (roupa) to take off, take off; **sem tirar nem pôr** exactly, precisely; **tirar uma fotografia** to take a photograph.

**tiri'tar** vi to shiver.

**'tiro** m (disparo) shot; (ato de disparar) shooting, firing; (de bois) team; **~ ao alvo** target practice; **sair o ~ pela culatra** (fig) to backfire.

**tirocínio** [tʃiro'sinju] m apprenticeship, training.

**tiroteio** [tʃiro'teju] m shooting, exchange of shots.

**'tísico/a** adj consumptive // f consumption.

**tis'nar** vt to smudge; (enegrecer) to blacken.

**títere** ['tʃiteri] m puppet.

**titube'ar** vi (cambalear) to totter, stagger; (vacilar) to hesitate.

**titu'lar** adj titular // m holder; (POL) minister // vt to title; **título** m title; (COM) bond, certificate; (universitário) degree; **a título de** by way of, as.

**'tive** etc vb ver **ter**.

**to** = **te** + **o**.

**'toa** f towrope; **à ~** at random.

**to'ada** f tune, melody; (boato) rumour.

**toalha** [to'aʎa] f towel; **~ de mesa** tablecloth.

**to'ar** vi to sound, resound.

**'toca** f burrow, hole; (refúgio) hiding place.

**toca-'discos** m inv (Br) record-player.

**tocante** [to'kãtʃi] adj moving, touching; **no ~ a** regarding, concerning; **tocar** vt to touch, feel; (MÚS) to play; (campainha) to ring; (comover) to move, touch; **pelo que me toca** as far as I am concerned; **tocar em algo** to touch upon sth.

**'toco** m tree stump; (cigarro

**toda'via** adv yet, still, however.

**'todo/a** adj all; (qualquer) entire; (cada) e

**velocidade** at full speed; **~a a gente** (*Pt*), **~ o mundo** (*Br*) everyone, everybody; **em ~a a parte** everywhere; **~s nós** all of us; **~s os dias** *ou* **~ dia** every day; **~ o dia** all day // *m* whole; **ao ~** altogether; **de ~** completely; **todos** *mpl* everybody *sg*, everyone *sg*; **~poderoso/a** *adj* almighty, all-powerful // *m* : **o T~-poderoso** the Almighty.

**'toga** *f* toga; (*EDUC*) gown.

**toicinho** [toj'siɲu] *m* bacon fat.

**tojo** ['tɔʒu] *m* gorse.

**'toldo** *m* awning, sun blind.

**toleima** [to'lejma] *f* folly, stupidity.

**tole'rância** *f* (*liberalidade*) broadmindedness, tolerance; (*indulgência*) toleration, forbearance; **tolerante** *adj* broadminded, understanding; **tolerar** *vt* (*permitir*) to tolerate, allow; (*aguentar*) to put up with, bear; **tolerável** *adj* (*admissível*) tolerable, bearable; (*admissível*) passable.

**tolher** [to'ʎex] *vt* to impede, hinder.

**tolice** [to'lisi] *f* stupidity, foolishness; **tolo/a** *adj* foolish, mad, stupid.

**tom** [tõ] *m* tone; (*inflexão*) intonation; (*cor*) shade.

**to'mada** *f* capture; (*ELET*) socket; **tomar** *vt* to take; (*capturar*) to capture, seize; (*decisão*) to make; (*bebida*) to take, have; **tomar-se** *vr*: **tomar-se de** to be overcome with.

**tomate** [to'matʃi] *m* tomato.

**tom'bar** *vi* to fall down, tumble down // *vt* to knock down, knock over; (*conservar um edifício*) to list; **tombo** *m* (*queda*) tumble, fall; (*registro*) archives *pl*, records *pl*.

**tomilho** [to'miʎu] *m* thyme.

**'tomo** *m* tome, volume.

**'tona** *f* surface; **vir à ~** to come to the surface; (*fig*) to come to light.

**to'nel** *m* cask, barrel.

**tone'lada** *f* ton; **tonelagem** *f* tonnage.

**'tônico/a** *adj* tonic; **nota ~a**

keynote; **acento ~** stress // *f* tonic; **tonificante** *adj* invigorating.

**toninha** [to'niɲa] *f* porpoise.

**'tono** *m* air, melody; (*TEC*) tone.

**ton'teira** *f* (*tontice*) nonsense; (*vertigem*) dizziness; **tontice** *f* stupidity, nonsense; **tonto/a** *adj* stupid, silly; (*zonzo*) dizzy, lightheaded; **às tontas** impulsively; **tontura** *f* dizziness, lightheadedness.

**to'par** *vt* to meet, come across; (*col*) to fancy, agree to; **você topa um sorvete?** do you fancy an ice cream?; **~ com** to meet, come across.

**tope** ['tɔpi] *m* (*cimo*) summit, top.

**'tópico/a** *adj* topical // *m* topic; (*tema*) subject.

**'topo** *m* (*cimo*) top, summit; (*extremidade*) end, extremity.

**toque** ['tɔki] *m* (*contato*) touch, contact; (*instrumento musical*) playing; (*campainha*) ringing; (*corneta*) bugle call; (*vestígio*) trace, touch.

**toranja** [to'rãʒa] *f* grapefruit.

**torção** [tox'sãw] *m* twist, twisting; (*MED*) sprain.

**torce'dura** *f* twist; (*torção*) sprain; **torcer** *vt* to twist; (*direção*) to turn; (*produzir torção em*) to sprain; (*desvirtuar*) to distort, misconstrue; (*esporte*) to support; **torcer-se** *vr* to squirm, writhe.

**torcida** [tox'sida] *f* (*mecha*) wick; (*esporte*: *ato de torcer*) supporting; (: *adeptos*) supporters.

**'tordo** *m* thrush.

**tor'menta** *f* storm.

**tor'mento** *m* torment, torture; (*angústia*) anguish.

**tormen'toso/a** *adj* stormy, tempestuous.

**tor'nado** *m* tornado.

**tor'nar** *vi* (*voltar*) to return, go back; **~ a fazer algo** to do sth again // *vt* to render, make; **~-se** *vr* to become.

**torne'ar** vt to turn (on a lathe), shape.

**torneio** [tox'neju] m tournament.

**torneira** [tox'nejra] f tap; (US) faucet.

**torniquete** [toxni'ketʃi] m (MED) tourniquet.

**'torno** m lathe; **em ~ de** around, about.

**torno'zelo** m ankle.

**torpe** ['toxpi] adj obscene, vile.

**tor'pedo** m torpedo.

**tor'peza** f obscenity, vileness.

**tor'rada** f toast; **torradeira** f toaster.

**torrão** [toˈxãw] m turf, sod; (terra) soil, land; (de açúcar) lump; **~ natal** native land.

**tor'rar** vt (pão) to toast; (café) to roast; (plantação) to parch.

**torre** ['toxi] f tower; (duma igreja) steeple, tower; (xadrez) castle, rook; **~ de vigia** watchtower.

**torrefação** [toxefaˈsãw] (Pt: **-cç-**) f coffee-roasting house.

**torrente** [toˈxẽtʃi] f torrent.

**tor'resmo** m crackling.

**'tórrido/a** adj torrid.

**'torta** f pie, tart.

**'torto/a** adj twisted, crooked; **a ~ e a direito** recklessly, indiscriminately; **tortuoso/a** adj winding.

**tor'tura** f torture; (fig) anguish, agony; **torturar** vt to torture; (fig) to torment.

**torvelinho** [toxveˈliɲu] m (vento) whirlwind; (água) whirlpool.

**tos = te + os.**

**tosão** [toˈzãw] m fleece; **tosar** vt (ovelha) to shear; (cabelo) to crop.

**'tosco/a** adj rough, unpolished; (grosseiro) coarse, crude.

**tosquiar** [toʃkiˈax] vt (ovelha) to shear, clip.

**tosse** ['tosi] f cough; **~ convulsa** ou **comprida** whooping cough; **tossir** vi to cough.

**'tosta** f (Pt) toast; **~ mista** toasted cheese and ham sandwich;

**tostado/a** adj toasted; (pelo sol) tanned; **tostar** vt to toast; **tostar-se** vr to get tanned, get sunburnt.

**to'tal** adj total, complete // m total; **~idade** f totality, entirety; **~itário/a** adj totalitarian.

**touca** ['toka] f bonnet; (de freira) veil.

**touca'dor** m (penteadeira) dressing table.

**toupeira** [toˈpejra] f mole; (fig) numbskull, idiot.

**tou'rada** f bullfight; **tourear** vi to fight (bulls); **touro** m bull; **pegar a touro à unha** to take the bull by the horns; **praça de touros** bullring.

**'tóxico/a** adj poisonous, toxic; **toxicómano/a** m/f drug addict.

**trabalhador(a)** [trabaʎaˈdox(ra)] adj hard-working, industrious // m/f worker, labourer; **trabalhar** vi to work, labour; (máquina) to work, function // vt (máquina) to work, operate; (o solo) to till, work; **trabalhista** adj labour; **Partido Trabalhista** Labour Party; **trabalho** m work, labour; (emprego) occupation, job; **trabalho braçal** manual work; **trabalhos forçados** hard labour, forced labour; **trabalhoso/a** adj laborious, arduous.

**'traça** f moth.

**tra'çado** m sketch, plan.

**tração** [traˈsãw] (Pt: **-cç-**) f traction, pull.

**tra'çar** vt to draw; (delinear) to trace, outline; **traço** m (linha) line, dash; (de lápis) stroke; (vestígio) trace, vestige; (caráter) feature, trait.

**tradição** [tradʒiˈsãw] f tradition; **tradicional** adj traditional.

**tradução** [traduˈsãw] f translation; **tradutor(a)** m/f translator; **traduzir** vt to translate.

**'tráfego** m (trânsito) traffic.

**trafi'cante** m/f trafficker, dealer; **traficar** vi to trade, deal; **tráfico** m traffic.

**tra'gar** vt to swallow; (fumaça) to inhale; (suportar) to tolerate.

**tragédia** [tra'ʒedʒja] f tragedy; **trágico/a** adj tragic; **tragicomédia** f tragicomedy.

**'trago** m mouthful, gulp; (dose) shot // vb ver **trazer**.

**traição** [traj'sãw] f treason, treachery; (deslealdade) betrayal, disloyalty; **traiçoeiro/a** adj treacherous; (infiel) disloyal; **traidor(a)** m traitor // f traitress.

**traineira** [traj'nejra] f trawler.

**tra'ir** vt to betray, be disloyal to.

**trajar** [tra'ʒax] vt to wear; ~**se** vr: ~**se de preto** to be dressed in black; **traje** m dress, clothes pl; **traje de banho** bathing costume; **traje de noite** evening gown; **traje a rigor** evening dress; **traje de passeio** informal dress.

**trajeto** [tra'ʒetu] (PT: **-ct-**) m course, path; **trajetória** (PT: **-ct-**) f trajectory, path.

**tralha** ['traʎa] f fishing net; (col) junk.

**'trama** f (tecido) woof; (enredo) scheme, plot; **tramar** vt (tecer) to weave; (intrigar) to scheme, plot.

**trambolhão** [trambo'ʎãw] m tumble, heavy fall; **andar aos trambolhões** to stumble along; **trambolho** m encumbrance.

**trâmite** ['tramitʃi] m path; (fig) course; ~**s** mpl (fig) procedure sg; (JUR) channels.

**tramóia** [tra'mɔja] f (fraude) swindle, trick; (trama) plot, scheme.

**tramon'tana** f Pole star; **perder a** ~ to lose one's bearings.

**trampolim** [trampo'lĩ] m trampoline; (de piscina) diving board; (fig) springboard.

**trampoli'nagem** f trick, swindle; **trampolineiro** m trickster, swindler; **trampolinice** f trick, swindle.

**'tranca** f (de uma porta) bolt.

**'trança** f (cabelo) lock; (galão) braid; ~**s** fpl plaits.

**tran'car** vt (porta) to bar, bolt.

**tranqüilidade** [trãkwili'dadʒi] f tranquillity; (paz) peacefulness; (calma) calm; **tranqüilizar** vt to calm, quieten; **tranqüilo/a** adj tranquil; (quieto) quiet; (calmo) calm; (pacífico) peaceful.

**'transa** f (Br: namoro) affair.

**transação** [trãza'sãw] (PT: **-cç-**) f transaction, deal.

**tran'sado/a** adj: **bem** ~ well made.

**transat'lântico/a** adj transatlantic // m (transatlantic) liner.

**transbor'dar** vi to overflow; **transbordo** m (de viajantes) change, transfer.

**transcor'rer** vi to elapse, go by.

**transe** ['trãzi] m ordeal; (lance) plight; **a todo** ~ at all costs.

**transeunte** [trãzi'jũtʃi] m/f passerby, pedestrian.

**transfe'rir** vt to transfer.

**transfigu'rar** vt to transfigure, transform.

**transformação** [trãʃfoxma'sãw] f transformation; **transformador** m (ELET) transformer; **transformar** vt to transform, change.

**'trânsfuga** m (desertor) deserter; (político) renegade, turncoat.

**transfusão** [trãʃfu'zãw] f transfusion; ~ **de sangue** blood transfusion.

**transgre'dir** vt to transgress, infringe; **transgressão** f transgression, infringement.

**transição** [trãzi'sãw] f transition, change.

**tran'sido/a** adj numb, benumbed.

**transigente** [trãzi'ʒetʃi] adj willing to compromise; **transigir** vi to compromise, make concessions.

**transi'tar** vt (percorrer) to go through // vi: ~ **por** to move about/through; **transitável** adj (caminho) passable; **transitivo/a** adj (LING) transitive; **trânsito** m transit, passage; (na rua: veículos:

traffic; (: *pessoas*) flow; **transitório/a** *adj* transitory, passing.

**transmissão** [trãʃmiˈsãw] *f* (*RÁDIO, TV*) transmission, broadcast; (*transferência*) transfer; **transmitir** *vt* (*RÁDIO, TV*) to broadcast, transmit; (*transferir*) to transfer.

**transparente** [trãʃpaˈrɛtʃi] *adj* transparent; (*roupa*) seethrough; (*evidente*) clear, obvious.

**transpirar** *vi* (*suar*) to perspire, sweat; (*divulgar-se*) to become known, transpire.

**transplantar** *vt* to transplant; **transplante** *m* transplant.

**transpor** *vt* to cross over, span; (*inverter*) to transpose.

**transportar** *vt* (*levar*) to transport, carry; (*enlevar*) to entrance, enrapture; **~-se** *vr* to be entranced; **transporte** *m* transport, conveyance; (*COM*) haulage; (*contas*) amount carried forward; (*êxtase*) rapture, delight.

**transtornar** *vt* to upset; **~-se** *vr* to get upset; **transtorno** *m* upset, disturbance.

**transversal** *adj* transverse, cross.

**transviado/a** [trãʒviˈadu/a] *adj* wayward, erring; **transviar** *vt* to lead astray; **transviar-se** *vr* to go astray.

**trapaça** *f* swindle, fraud; **trapaceiro/a** *adj* crooked, cheating // *m/f* swindler, cheat.

**trapalhada** [trapaˈʎada] *f* confusion, mix up; **trapalhão/lhona** *m/f* bungler, blunderer.

**'trapo** *m* rag, cloth.

**traquéia** [traˈkeja] *f* windpipe.

**traquinas** [traˈkinaʃ] *adj inv* mischievous.

**tra'rei** *etc vb ver* **trazer**.

**trás** *prep, adv* after, behind; **para ~** backwards; **por ~ de** behind; **traseiro/a** *adj* back, rear // *m* (*ANAT*) bottom, behind // *f* rear.

**trasladar** *vt* to remove, transfer; (*copiar*) to transcribe; **traslado** *m*

(*cópia*) copy; (*deslocamento*) removal, transference.

**traspassar** *vt* (*atravessar*) to cross; (*penetrar*) to pierce, penetrate; (*exceder*) to exceed, overstep; (*transferir*) to transmit, transfer; (*Pt: sublocar*) to sublet; **traspasse** *m* transfer; (*sublocação*) sublease, sublet.

**traste** [ˈtrastʃi] *m* (*ger*) piece of junk; (*móvel*) old piece of furniture; (*fig*) rogue, rascal.

**tra'tado** *m* treaty, pact; (*obra*) treatise.

**trata'mento** *m* treatment; (*título*) title.

**tratante** [traˈtãtʃi] *m* crook, swindler.

**tra'tar** *vt* to treat; (*tema*) to deal with, cover; **~ com** (*COM*) to deal with; **~ de** (*assunto*) to discuss, attend to; **~ por** to address as; **de que se trata?** what is it about?; **trata-se de** it is a question of; **tratável** *adj* treatable; (*afável*) approachable, amenable; **trato** *m* (*tratamento*) treatment; (*contrato*) agreement, contract; **maus tratos** ill-treatment.

**tra'tor** (*Pt:* **-ct-**) *m* tractor.

**trautear** [trawˈtʃjar] *vt* to hum; (*col*) to annoy, pester // *vi* to hum.

**travão** [traˈvãw] *m* (*Pt*) brake; **travar** *vt* (*roda*) to lock; (*iniciar*) to engage in; (*conversa*) to strike up; **travar amizade com** to become friendly with, make friends with // *vi* to brake.

**trave** [ˈtravi] *f* beam, crossbeam; (*esporte*) crossbar.

**tra'vés** *m* slant, incline; **de ~** across, sideways; **olhar de ~** to look sideways (at); **travessa** *f* crossbeam, crossbar; (*rua*) lane, alley; **travessão** *m* (*de balança*) bar, beam; (*pontuação*) dash.

**travesseiro** [traveˈsejru] *m* pillow; **consultar o ~** to sleep on it, think it over.

**traves'sia** f (viagem) journey, crossing.

**tra'vesso/a** adj mischievous, naughty; (atravessado) cross, transverse; **travessura** f mischief, prank.

**'travo** m bitterness, sourness.

**tra'zer** vt to bring; (roupa) to wear; (causar) to bring about, cause; ~ à **memória** to bring to mind.

**trecho** ['treʃu] m (extrato) passage; (parte) stretch.

**trégua** ['trɛgwa] f truce; (descanso) respite, rest.

**treinar** [trej'nax] vt, **treinar-se** vr to train; **treino** m training.

**'trela** f (correia) lead, leash; (col: conversa) chat; **dar ~ a** to chat with; (encorajar) to lead on.

**trem** [trẽʒ] m train; **trens** mpl (col) gear sg, belongings pl; (Pt: carruagem) carriage, coach; ~ **de carga** freight train; ~ **correio** mail train; ~ **de cozinha** kitchen utensils pl; ~ **de aterrissagem** (avião) landing gear.

**treme'dal** m bog, quagmire.

**tremeli'car** vi to tremble, shiver.

**tremelu'zir** vi to twinkle, glimmer.

**tre'mendo/a** adj (formidável) tremendous, enormous; (terrível) terrible, awful; **tremer** vi to shudder, quake; **tremor** m tremor, trembling.

**trempe** ['trẽpi] f tripod.

**tremu'lar** vi (bandeira) to flutter, wave; (luz) to glimmer, flicker; **trêmulo/a** adj shaky, trembling.

**'trena** f tape-measure.

**tre'nó** m sledge, sleigh.

**trens** mpl ver **trem**.

**trepadeira** [trepa'dejra] f creeper, climbing plant; **trepar** vt to climb // vt/i (col) to screw.

**trepidação** [trepida'sãw] f shaking; **trepidar** vi to tremble, shake.

**três** num three.

**tresan'dar** vt (fazer andar para trás) to turn back; (transtornar) to upset // vi to stink, reek.

**tresloucado/a** [treʒlo'kadu/a] adj crazy, deranged.

**tresmalhar** [treʒma'ʎax] vt (deixar fugir) to let escape; (dispersar) to scatter, disperse // vi to stray.

**trespassar** vt ver **traspassar**; **trespasse** m ver **traspasse**.

**'trevas** fpl darkness sg; (estupidez) ignorance.

**'trevo** m clover.

**treze** ['trezi] num thirteen.

**tre'zentos/as** num three hundred.

**triangular** [trjãgu'lax] adj triangular; **triângulo** m triangle.

**'tribo** f tribe.

**tribulação** [tribula'sãw] f tribulation, affliction.

**tri'buna** f platform, rostrum; (REL) pulpit; **tribunal** m court; (comissão) tribunal.

**tribu'tar** vt (impor impostos a) to tax; (render) to render; **tributo** m tribute.

**tri'cô** m knitting; **tricotar** vt/i to knit.

**'trigo** m wheat; **trigueiro/a** adj dark, swarthy.

**tri'lar** vt to warble, trill.

**trilhado/a** [tri'ʎadu/a] adj (pisado) well-worn, well-trodden; **trilhar** vt (vereda) to tread, wear; **trilho** m rail; (vereda) path, track.

**trimestre** [tri'mɛʃtri] m (período) term, quarter; (pagamento) quarterly payment.

**tri'nado** m warbling, singing.

**tri'ncar** vt to crunch; (morder) to bite // vi to crunch.

**trinchar** [trĩ'ʃax] vt to carve.

**trincheira** [trĩ'ʃejra] f (escavação) trench; (barreira) barrier.

**'trinco** m latch.

**trindade** [trĩ'dadʒi] f trinity; ~**s** fpl angelus sg.

**'trinta** num thirty.

**'trio** m trio.

**'tripa** f gut, intestine; **~s** fpl bowels, guts; (CULIN) tripe sg; **comer à ~ forra** to gorge o.s.; **fazer das ~s coração** to pluck up courage.

**tri'pé** m tripod.

**tripulação** [tripula'sãw] f crew; **tripulante** m crew member; **tripular** vt to man.

**'trismo** m lockjaw.

**triste** ['triʃtʃi] adj sad, unhappy; (sombrio) miserable, wretched; **tristeza** f sadness, unhappiness; (mágoa) melancholy.

**tritu'rar** vt (moer) to grind; (argumento) to destroy, tear to pieces.

**triunfar** [triũ'fax] vi to triumph, win; **triunfo** m victory, triumph.

**trivi'al** adj (comum) common(place), ordinary; (insignificante) trivial, trifling.

**triz** m: **por um ~** by the skin of one's teeth; **escapar por um ~** to have a narrow escape.

**'troca** f exchange, swap; **em ~ de** in exchange for.

**'troça** f ridicule, mockery; **fazer ~ de** to make fun of.

**troca'dilho** m pun, play on words.

**tro'car** vt to exchange, swap; (substituir) to change, replace; **~ dinheiro** to change money.

**tro'çar** vt to ridicule, make fun of; **trocista** m/f joker, wag.

**'troco** m (dinheiro) change; (réplica) retort, rejoinder; **a ~ de** in exchange for.

**'troço** m (pedaço) piece, portion; (Br: coisa inútil) thingummyjig; (: coisa) thing.

**troféu** [tro'fɛw] m trophy.

**'tromba** f (de elefante) trunk; (de outro animal) snout; **~-d'água** f waterspout.

**trom'beta** f (MÚS) trumpet, bugle; **trombone** m (MÚS) trombone; **trompa** f (MÚS) horn.

**tronchar** [trõ'fax] vt to cut off, chop off.

**'tronco** m (de árvore) trunk; (de corpo) torso, trunk; (de família) lineage; (: fig) stock.

**'trono** m throne.

**'tropa** f troop, gang; (MIL) troop; (exército) army; **ir para a ~** (Pt) to join the army.

**trope'çar** vi to stumble, trip; (fig) to blunder; **~ em dificuldades** to meet with difficulties; **tropeço** m obstacle, hindrance; **pedra de tropeço** stumbling block.

**'trôpego/a** adj shaky, unsteady.

**tro'pel** m (ruído) uproar, tumult; (confusão) confusion, throng; (estrépito de pés) stamping of feet; **tropelia** f tumult, confusion.

**tropi'cal** adj tropical; **trópico** m tropic.

**tro'tar** vi to trot; **trote** m trot.

**trouxa** ['trofa] f bundle of clothes; (col: pessoa) sucker.

**'trouxe** etc vb ver **trazer**.

**'trova** f ballad, folksong; **~dor** m troubador, minstrel.

**trovão** [tro'vãw] m clap of thunder; **trovejar** vi to thunder; **trovoada** f thunderstorm; **trovoar** vi to thunder.

**truão** [tru'ãw] m clown, buffoon.

**truci'dar** vt to butcher, slaughter.

**trun'car** vt to chop off, cut off; (texto) to mutilate.

**'trunfo** m trump card.

**truque** ['truki] m (ardil) trick, dodge; (publicitário) gimmick.

**'truta** f trout.

**tu** pron (Pt) you; **tua** adj, pron ver **teu**.

**tubarão** [tuba'rãw] m shark.

**tu'bérculo** m tuber.

**tuberculose** [tubɛxku'lɔzi] f tuberculosis, T.B.

**'tubo** m tube, pipe; **~ de ensaio** test tube.

**tu'cano** m toucan.

**'tudo** pron all, everything; **~ quanto**

everything that; **antes de** ~ first of all.

**tufão** [tu'fãw] *m* typhoon, hurricane.
**'tufo** *m* tuft.

**tu'gúrio** *m* (*cabana*) hut, shack; (*refúgio*) shelter.

**tulha** ['tuʎa] *f* (*arca*) bin, store; (*celeiro*) granary.

**tu'lipa** *f* tulip.

**'tumba** *f* (*sepultura*) tomb; (*lápide*) tombstone.

**tu'mido/a** *adj* (*dilatado*) swollen.

**tu'mor** *m* tumour.

**tu'multo** *m* tumult, uproar; **tumultuar** *vt* to rouse, incite; **tumultuoso/a** *adj* tumultuous; (*revolto*) stormy.

**'tunda** *f* thrashing, beating; (*fig*) dressing-down.

**túnel** *m* tunnel.

**'túnica** *f* tunic.

**'turba** *f* throng, crowd; ~ **multa** mob.

**turbante** [tux'bãtʃi] *m* turban.

**tur'bar** *vt* (*escurecer*) to darken, cloud; (*perturbar*) to upset, perturb; ~**-se** *vr* (*inquietar-se*) to be troubled *ou* upset.

**turbilhão** [tuxbi'ʎãw] *m* (*de vento*) whirlwind; (*de água*) whirlpool.

**turbu'lência** *f* turbulence; **turbulento/a** *adj* turbulent, stormy.

**'turco/a** *adj* Turkish // *m/f* Turk // *m* (*língua*) Turkish.

**'turfa** *f* peat.

**túrgido/a** ['tuxʒidu/a] *adj* swollen, bloated.

**tu'rismo** *m* tourism; (*indústria*) tourist industry; **turista** *m/f* tourist; **turístico/a** *adj* tourist *cmp*.

**'turma** *f* group, gang; (*turno*) shift.

**'turno** *m* shift, period of work; **por** ~**s** alternately, by turns, in turn.

**Turquia** [tux'kia] *f* Turkey.

**'turra** *f* (*disputa*) argument, dispute; **andar às** ~**s** to be at loggerheads.

**tur'var** *vt* (*tornar opaco*) to cloud, obscure; (*escurecer*) to darken; ~**-se** *vr* to become clouded; **turvo/a**

*adj* (*opaco*) clouded, muddy.

**tu'tano** *m* (ANAT) marrow.

**tu'tela** *f* protection, guardianship; **tutelar** *adj* protecting, guardian; **anjo tutelar** guardian angel // *vt* to watch over, protect; **tutor(a)** *m/f* guardian.

**TV** *abr de* **televisão**.

# U

**'úbere** *m* udder.

**ubiqüidade** [ubikwi'dadʒi] *f* ubiquity; **ubíquo/a** *adj* ubiquitous.

**'ufa** *excl* whew!

**ufa'nar-se** *vr* to boast; ~ **de** to take pride in, pride o.s. on.

**'ufanismo** *m* (*Br*) boastful nationalism, chauvinism.

**uísque** ['wiʃki] *m* whisky; (*US*) whiskey.

**uivar** [wi'vax] *vi* to howl; **uivo** *m* howl.

**'úlcera** *f* ulcer; **ulcerar** *vi* to ulcerate.

**ulterior** [ulteri'ox] *adj* (*além*) further, farther; (*depois*) later, subsequent; ~**mente** *adv* later on, subsequently.

**ultima'ção** [ultʃima'sãw] *f* conclusion, finishing; **ultimamente** *adv* (*há pouco*) recently, lately; **ultimar** *vt* to finish, bring to a conclusion; **ultimar-se** *vr* to come to a conclusion; **ultimato** *m* ultimatum; **último/a** *adj* final, last; (*mais recente*) latest; (*fig*) final, extreme; **por último** finally; **a(s) última(s)** the latest news; **estar nas últimas** to be on one's last legs.

**ultrajar** [ultra'ʒax] *vt* to insult, offend; **ultraje** *m* insult, offence.

**ultra'mar** *m* overseas; (*tinta*) ultramarine; ~**ino/a** *adj* overseas *cmp*; (*azul*) ultramarine.

**ultrapas'sar** *vt* (*atravessar*) to

cross, go beyond; (*exceder*) to exceed, surpass; (*transgredir*) to overstep; (*AUTO*) to overtake.

**ultra-som** [ultra-'sõ] *m* ultrasound; **ultra-sônico/a** *adj* ultrasonic; (*MED*) ultrasound *cmp*; **ultra-sonografia** *f* ultrasound scanning.

**ulu'lar** *vi* to howl, wail.

**um(a)** [0/'uma] *art, pl* **uns/umas** [0s/'umas] (*sg*) a; (*antes de vogal ou 'h' mudo*) an; (*pl*) some // *num* one // *pron* one; ~ **e outro** both; ~ **a** ~ one by one; ~ **ao outro** one another; (*entre dois*) each other; **à uma** at the same time; (*aproximadamente*) ~ 5 about 5.

**um'bigo** *m* navel.

**um'bral** *m* (*limiar*) threshold.

**umede'cer** *vt* to moisten, wet; ~**se** *vr* to get wet; **umidade** *f* dampness; (*clima*) humidity; **úmido/a** *adj* wet, moist; (*roupa*) damp; (*clima*) humid.

**unânime** [u'nanimi] *adj* unanimous; **unanimidade** *f* unanimity.

**unção** [0'sãw] *f* anointing.

**undécimo/a** [0'dɛsimu/a] *adj* eleventh // *m* (*fração*) eleventh.

**ungir** [0'ʒiʀ] *vt* to rub with ointment; (*REL*) to anoint; **ungüento** *m* ointment.

**unha** ['uɲa] *f* nail; (*garra*) claw; **com** ~**s e dentes** tooth and nail; **ser** ~ **e carne com** to be hand in glove with; **unhada** *f* scratch.

**união** [uni'ãw] *f* union; (*ato*) joining; (*unidade*) unity; (*casamento*) marriage; (*TEC*) joint; **a U~ Soviética** the Soviet Union.

**unica'mente** *adv* only; **único/a** *adj* only; (*sem igual*) unique; (*só um*) single; **mão única** (*sinal*) one-way.

**uni'dade** *f* (*TEC*) unit; (*fig*) unity; **unido/a** *adj* joined, linked; (*fig*) united; **manter-se unidos** to stick together; **unificar** *vt* to unite; **unificar-se** *vr* to join together.

**uni'forme** *adj* uniform;

(*semelhante*) alike, similar; (*superfície*) even // *m* uniform; **uniformidade** *f* uniformity; **uniformizar** *vt* to standardize; (*pessoa*) to put into uniform; **uniformizar-se** *vr* to put on one's uniform.

**unila'teral** *adj* unilateral.

**u'nir** *vt* (*juntar*) to join together; (*pessoas, fig*) to unite; (*misturar*) to mix together; (*atar*) to tie together; ~**se** *vr* to join together.

**u'níssono** *m*: **em** ~ in unison.

**univer'sal** *adj* universal; (*geral*) general; (*mundial*) worldwide.

**universi'dade** *f* university; **universitário/a** *adj* university *cmp* // *m/f* (*professor*) lecturer; (*aluno*) university student.

**uni'verso** *m* universe.

**'uno/a** *adj* one, in one.

**un'tar** *vt* (*esfregar*) to rub; (*engordurar*) to grease, oil; (*bolo*) to rub with ointment; **unto** *m* fat, lard; **untuoso/a** *adj* greasy; **untura** *f* (*REL*) anointing; (*ungüento*) ointment.

**urânio** [u'ranju] *m* uranium.

**urbani'dade** *f* courtesy, politeness.

**urba'nismo** *m* town planning; **urbanização** *f* urbanization; **urbano/a** *adj* (*da cidade*) city, urban; (*cortês*) polite; **urbe** *f* city.

**ur'dir** *vt* (*tecer*) to weave; (*aranha*) to spin; (*fig: vingança*) to plot; (: *conspiração*) to hatch.

**urgência** [ux'ʒẽsja] *f* urgency; (*pressa*) speed, haste; **com toda** ~ as quickly as possible; **urgente** *adj* urgent; **entrega urgente** special delivery; **urgir** *vi* to be urgent; (*tempo*) to be pressing // *vt* (*tornar necessário*) to necessitate.

**u'rina** *f* urine; **urinar** *vi* to urinate, pass water.

**'urna** *f* urn; ~ **eleitoral** ballot box.

**ur'rar** *vt/i* to roar.

**'urso** *m* bear; **~-branco** *m* polar bear.

**URSS** [uexces'esi] *f*: **a ~** the USSR.

**urti'cária** *f* nettle rash; **urtiga** *f* nettle.

**uru'bu** *m* vulture.

**Uruguai** [uru'gwaj] *m*: **o ~** Uruguay; **uruguaio/a** *adj*, *m/f* Uruguayan.

**urze** ['uxzi] *m* heather.

**u'sado/a** *adj* used; (*roupa*) worn; (*gasto*) worn out; **~ a** (*acostumado*) accustomed to; (*uso*) usage; **usar** *vt* (*servir-se de*) to use; (*vestir*) to wear; (*gastar com o uso*) to wear out // *vi*: **usar de** to use.

**u'sina** *f* (*fábrica*) factory; (*de energia*) plant; (*de açúcar*) mill.

**'uso** *m* (*emprego*) use; (*utilização*) usage; (*prática*) practice; (*moda*) fashion; **usual** *adj* usual; (*comum*) common; **usuário** *m* user; **usuário do telefone** telephone subscriber.

**usufruir** [uzu'frwix] *vt* to enjoy the benefits of; **usufruto** *m* enjoyment; (*JUR*) usufruct.

**u'sura** *f* usury; **usurário** *m* usurer.

**usur'par** *vt* to seize; (*trono*) to usurp.

**utensílio** [ute'silju] *m* utensil.

**útero** *m* womb, uterus.

**'útil** *adj*, *pl* **úteis** ['utejʃ] useful; (*benéfico*) helpful; **dias úteis** weekdays, working days; **utilidade** *f* usefulness; (*vantagem*) advantage; **utilizar** *vt* to use; **utilizar-se** *vr*: **utilizar-se de** to make use of.

**uto'pia** *f* Utopia; **utópico/a** *adj* Utopian.

**'uva** *f* grape.

# V

**v** *abr de* **volt.**

**vá** *etc vb ver* **ir.**

**'vaca** *f* cow; **carne de ~** bɜef.

**va'cância** *f* vacancy; **vacante** *adj* vacant.

**vaci'lar** *vi* (*hesitar*) to hesitate.

**va'cina** *f* vaccine; **vacinar** *vt* to vaccinate.

**vacuidade** [vakwi'dadʒi] *f* emptiness.

**vacum** [va'kũ] *adj*: **gado ~** cattle.

**vácuo** ['vakwu] *m* vacuum; (*fig*) void; (*espaço*) space.

**vade'ar** *vt* to wade through.

**vadiação** [vadʒia'sãw] *f*, **vadiagem** [vadʒi'aʒẽ] *f* vagrancy; **vadiar** *vi* to lounge about; (*não trabalhar*) to idle about; **vadio/a** (*ocioso*) idle, lazy; (*errante*) wandering; (*vagabundo*) vagrant // *m* idler; (*vagabundo*) vagabond, vagrant.

**'vaga** *f* (*onda*) wave; (*vacância*) vacancy; (*lugar livre*) place.

**vagabun'dar** *vi* to wander about, roam about; **vagabundo/a** *adj* (*errante*) wandering; (*ocioso*) idle; (*barato*) cheap, worthless // *m/f* tramp.

**vagão** [va'gãw] *m* (*de passageiros*) carriage; (*de cargas*) wagon; **~-leito** *m* (*Pt*) sleeping car.

**va'gar** *vi* to wander about, roam about; (*barco*) to drift; (*ficar vago*) to be vacant; **~oso/a** *adj* slow; (*sem pressa*) leisurely.

**vagem** ['vaʒẽ] *f* green bean; (*invólucro*) pod.

**vagido** [va'ʒidu] *m* wail.

**vagina** [va'ʒina] *f* vagina.

**'vago/a** *adj* (*indeterminado*) vague; (*desocupado*) vacant, free; **horas ~as** spare time; **vaguear** *vi* to wander, roam; (*passear*) to ramble.

**vai** *etc vb ver* **ir.**

**'vaia** *f* booing; **vaiar** *vt/i* to boo, hiss.

**vaidade** [vaj'dadʒi] *f* vanity; (*futilidade*) futility; **vaidoso/a** *adj* vain, conceited.

**vaivém** [vaj'vẽj] *m* coming and going, to-and-fro; **vaivens** *mpl* (*fig*) ups and downs.

**'vala** f ditch; ~ **comum** common grave.

**vale** ['vali] m valley; (poético) vale; (escrito) voucher; ~ **postal** postal order; (reconhecimento de dívida) I.O.U.

**valentão/tona** [valẽ'tãw/'tona] adj tough // m/f bully; (col) show-off; **valente** adj brave; (forte) strong; **valentia** f courage, bravery; (proeza) feat.

**va'ler** vi (ser igual em valor, merecer) to be worth; (ser válido) to be valid; (ter valor) to count; (significar) to mean; (ser útil) to be useful; (socorrer) to help; ~ **a pena** to be worthwhile; **não vale a pena** it isn't worth it; ~ **por** (equivaler) to be equal to; **para** ~ (muito) very much, a lot; **vale dizer** in other words; ~-**se** vr: ~-**se de** to use, make use of.

**va'leta** f gutter.

**valete** [va'letʃi] m (no jogo) jack.

**va'lia** f value; **de** ~ valuable; **validade** f validity; **validar** vt to validate, make valid.

**'válido/a** adj valid; **valioso/a** adj valuable.

**va'lise** f case, grip.

**va'lor** m value, worth; (coragem) courage; (preço) price; (importância) importance; **dar** ~ **a** to value; **sem** ~ worthless; **no** ~ **de** to the value of; ~-**es** mpl (dum exame) marks; (COM) securities.

**valorização** [valoriza'sãw] f increased value; **valorizar** vt to value; (aumentar o valor) to raise the value of; **valorizar-se** vr to go up in value.

**valo'roso/a** adj brave.

**'valsa** f waltz.

**'válvula** f valve.

**vam'piro** m vampire.

**vanda'lismo** m vandalism; **vândalo** m vandal.

**vanglori'ar-se** vr: ~ **de** to boast of/about.

**vanguarda** [vã'gwaxda] f vanguard, forefront; (arte) avant-garde.

**vantagem** [vã'taʒẽ] f advantage; (ganho) profit, benefit; **vantajoso/a** adj advantageous; (lucrativo) profitable; (proveitoso) beneficial.

**vão/vã** [vãw/vã] adj (fútil) futile; **em** ~ in vain // m (intervalo) space; (abertura) opening.

**va'por** m steam, vapour; (navio) steamer; **cozer no** ~ to steam; ~**oso/a** adj steamy, misty; (transparente) transparent, seethrough.

**vaqueiro** [va'kejru] m cowboy, cowhand.

**'vara** f (pau) stick; (TEC) rod; (JUR) jurisdiction; (de porcos) herd; **salto de** ~ pole vault.

**va'randa** f verandah; (balcão) balcony.

**varão** [va'rãw] adj male // m man, male; (de ferro) rod.

**varapau** [vara'paw] m (pessoa) beanpole.

**va'rar** vt (furar) to pierce; (passar) to cross // vi to beach, run aground.

**varejeira** [vare'ʒejra] f bluebottle.

**varejista** [vare'ʒista] m/f retailer; **varejo** m (COM) retail trade; **loja de varejo** retail store.

**variação** [varia'sãw] f variation, change; **variado/a** adj varied, assorted; **variar** vt/i to vary; (mudar) to change; (diversificar) to diversify; **variável** adj variable.

**varicela** [vari'sɛla] f chicken pox.

**variedade** [varie'dadʒi] f variety; ~**s** fpl (teatro) variety show sg.

**varinha** [va'rina] f wand; ~ **de condão** magic wand.

**'vário/a** adj (diverso) varied; (pl) various, several; (COM) sundry.

**va'ríola** f smallpox.

**varizes** [va'rizi] fpl varicose veins.

**varo'nil** adj manly, virile.

**varrão** [va'xãw] m boar.

**var'rer** vt to sweep; (sala) to sweep

out; (folhas) to sweep up.
**várzea** ['vaxzja] f meadow, field.
**'vasa** f slime.
**vase'lina** f vaseline.
**vasilha** [va'zıʎa] f (para líquidos) jug; (para alimentos) dish, container; (barril) barrel.
**'vaso** m pot; (para flores) vase; (NÁUT) vessel; ~ **sanitário** toilet (bowl); ~ **sanguíneo** blood vessel.
**vassoura** [va'sora] f brush, broom.
**vastidão** [vaʃtʃi'dãw] f vastness, immensity; **vasto/a** adj vast, huge.
**vatici'nar** vt/i to foretell, prophesy; **vaticínio** m prophecy.
**vau** [vaw] m ford, river crossing; (NÁUT) beam.
**'vaza** f (no jogo) trick.
**vaza'mento** m leak.
**va'zante** f ebb tide.
**vazão** [va'zãw] f flow; (saída) outlet; **dar** ~ **a** (expressar) to give vent to; (COM) to clear; **vazar** vt (tornar vazio) to empty; (entornar) to spill; (verter) to pour out // vi to empty; (pouco a pouco) to leak; (a maré) to go out; **vazio/a** adj empty; (pessoa) empty-headed, frivolous // m vacuum; (espaço) void.
**veado/a** ['vjadu/a] m deer; (Br col) gay; **carne de** ~ venison // f hind.
**ve'dado/a** adj (proibido) forbidden; (fechado) enclosed; **vedar** vt (proibir) to ban, prohibit; (sangue) to stop the flow of; (burraco) to stop up.
**ve'deta** f (atriz) star; (NÁUT) speedboat.
**ve'dete** f (atriz) star.
**veemência** [vɪe'mēsja] f vehemence; (paixão) passion; (vigor) vigour; **veemente** adj vehement; (intenso) intense; (fervoroso) fervent.
**vegetação** [veʒeta'sãw] f vegetation; **vegetal** adj vegetable cmp, plant cmp // m vegetable; **vegetariano/a** adj, m/f vegetarian.

**veia** ['veja] f (MED, BOT) vein; **não estou com** ~ I'm not in the mood.
**ve'ículo** m vehicle; (fig: meio) means sg.
**veio** ['veju] m (de rocha) vein; (na mina) seam; (madeira) grain; (eixo) shaft // vb ver **vir**.
**'veja** etc vb ver **ver**.
**'vela** f candle; (AUTO) spark plug; (NÁUT) sail; **fazer-se à/de** ~ to set sail.
**ve'lar** vt (ocultar) to hide; (vigiar) to keep watch over; (um doente) to sit up with // vi (não dormir) to stay up; (vigiar) to keep watch.
**veleidade** [velej'dadʒı] f whim, fancy; (inconstância) fickleness.
**veleiro** [ve'lejru] m (navio) sailing ship.
**ve'leta** f weather vane.
**velhaco/a** [ve'ʎaku/a] adj crooked // m crook.
**velharia** [veʎa'ria] f (coisa) old-fashioned thing; **velhice** f old age; **velho/a** adj old // m old man // f old woman.
**velocidade** [velosi'dadʒı] f speed, velocity; (Pt: AUTO) gear; **velocímetro** m speedometer.
**ve'lódromo** m cycle track.
**ve'loz** adj fast.
**ve'ludo** m velvet; ~ **cotelê** corduroy.
**vence'dor(a)** adj winning // m/f winner, victor; **vencer** vt (num jogo) to beat; (dominar) to overcome, master // vi (num jogo) to win; (conseguir o seu fim) to win through; **vencer-se** vr (prazo) to run out; (promissória) to become due; **vencimento** m (COM) expiry; (data) expiry date; (salário) salary; **dar vencimento a** to cope with.
**'venda** f sale; (pano) blindfold; **à** ~ on sale, for sale.
**ven'dar** vt to blindfold.
**venda'val** m gale; (fig) tumult.
**ven'dável** adj marketable; **vendedor** m seller; **vender** vt to sell;

vender por atacado/a varejo to sell wholesale/retail; **vender fiado/a prestações** to sell on credit/in instalments; **vendilhão** m pedlar.

ve'neno m poison; (fig, de serpente) venom; **venenoso/a** adj poisonous; (fig) venomous.

venera'ção [venera'sãw] f reverence; **venerar** vt to revere; (REL) to worship.

ve'néreo/a adj venereal.

'venha etc vb ver **vir.**

'vênia f (desculpa) forgiveness; (licença) permission; **venial** adj venial, forgiveable.

'venta f nostril.

venta'nia f gale; **ventar** vi: venta the wind is blowing.

'ventas fpl nose sg.

ventila'ção [vẽt∫ila'sãw] f ventilation; **ventilador** m ventilator; (elétrico) fan; **ventilar** vt to ventilate; (roupa, sala) to air; (fig) to discuss.

'vento m wind; (brisa) breeze; ~inha f (cata-vento) weathercock; (grimpa) weather vane; ~sidade f flatulence, wind; **ventoso/a** adj windy.

'ventre m belly; (útero) womb.

ventríloquo [vẽ'trilokwu] m ventriloquist.

ven'tura f (boa sorte) luck; (felicidade) happiness; (destino) fortune.

ver vt to see; (olhar para) to look at // vi to see; ~-se vr (achar-se) to be, find o.s.; (duas pessoas) to meet; ~-se com to settle accounts with; a meu ~ in my opinion; **bem se vê que** it's obvious that; **já se vê** of course; **não tenho nada que ~ com isto** it is nothing to do with me, it is none of my concern.

veraci'dade f truthfulness.

verane'ar vi to spend the summer; **veraneio** m summer holidays pl; **verão** m summer.

ve'raz adj truthful.

'verba f (JUR) clause; (nota) note; (alocação de recursos) allocation, allowance; (quantia) sum; **verbal** adj verbal.

ver'bete m (num dicionário) entry.

'verbo m verb; **verboso/a** adj wordy, verbose.

ver'dade f truth; **na** ~ in fact; **é** ~ it's true; **verdadeiro/a** adj true; (genuíno) real.

'verde adj green; (fruta) unripe; (fig) immature // m green; ~jar vi to turn green; **verdor** m greenness; (BOT) greenery; (fig) inexperience.

ver'dugo m executioner.

ver'dura f (BOT) greenery; (cor verde) greenness; ~s fpl (CULIN) greens, green vegetables.

verea'dor m councillor; **vereança** f (cargo) office of councillor; (tempo) period of office.

ve'reda f path.

vere'dicto m verdict.

'verga f (vara) stick; (de metal) rod.

ver'gão [vex'gãw] m weal.

ver'gar vt (curvar) to bend // vi to bend; (com um peso) to sag.

vergas'tar vt to whip.

ver'gel [vex'ʒew] m orchard.

ver'gonha [vex'gona] f shame; (timidez) embarrassment; (honra) sense of shame; **é uma** ~ it's disgraceful; **ter** ~ **de** to be ashamed of; **ter** ~ **de fazer** to be ashamed of doing; (ser tímido) to be too shy to do; **sem** ~ cheeky, brazen; **vergonhoso/a** adj (infame) shameful; (indecoroso) disgraceful.

ver'gôntea f shoot; (fig) offspring.

ve'rídico/a adj true, truthful.

verifica'ção [verifika'sãw] f (exame) checking; (confirmação) verification; **verificar** vt to check; (confirmar) to verify; **verificar-se** vr (acontecer) to happen; (realizar-se) to come true.

'verme m worm.

vermelho/a [vex'meʎu/a] adj red.

**ver'mute** m vermouth.

**ver'náculo/a** adj, m vernacular.

**ver'niz** m varnish; (couro) patent leather; (fig) whitewash.

**veros'símil** adj (provável) likely, probable; (crível) credible.

**ver'rina** f violent attack, diatribe.

**ver'ruga** f wart.

**ver'sado/a** adj: ~ **em** clever at, good at.

**versão** [vex'zãw] f version; (tradução) translation; **versar** vi: **versar sobre** to be about, concern.

**ver'sátil** adj versatile.

**verse'jar** vt to write verses; **verso** m verse; (linha) line of poetry; (da página) other side, reverse; **vide verso** see over.

**ver'tente** f slope.

**ver'ter** vt to pour out; (por acaso) to spill; (traduzir) to translate; (lágrimas, sangue) to shed // vi: ~ **de** to spring from.

**verti'cal** adj (TEC) vertical; (de pé) upright, standing.

**'vértice** m apex.

**vertigem** [vex'tʃiʒẽ] f dizziness; **vertiginoso/a** adj dizzy, giddy; (velocidade) frenetic.

**'vesgo/a** adj cross-eyed.

**'vespa** f wasp.

**'véspera** f the day before; ~ **de** Natal Christmas Eve; ~**s** fpl (REL) vespers; **estar nas** ~**s de** to be about to; **vespertino/a** adj evening.

**'veste** f garment; (REL) vestment, robe; **vestiário** m (em casa) cloakroom; (esporte) changing room; (de ator) dressing room.

**vestibu'lar** m college entrance exam.

**ves'tíbulo** m hall(-way), vestibule; (teatro) foyer.

**ves'tido/a** adj dressed // m (roupa) dress; **vestidura** f (REL) robe.

**vestígio** [ves'tʃiʒju] m (pista) track; (sinal) sign, trace.

**ves'tir** vt (uma criança) to dress;

(pôr roupa) to put on; (trajar roupa) to wear; (comprar roupa para) to clothe; (fazer roupa para) to make clothes for // vi, ~**se** vr to dress; (de manhã) to get dressed; (fantasiar-se) to dress up; **vestuário** m clothing.

**ve'tar** vt to veto; (proibir) to forbid.

**vetera'no/a** adj, m/f veteran.

**veteri'nário/a** adj veterinary // m/f vet(erinary surgeon).

**'veto** m veto.

**ve'tusto/a** adj ancient; (honrado) time-honoured.

**véu** [vɛw] m veil.

**ve'xar** vt (molestar) to annoy, upset; (envergonhar) to put to shame; ~**se** vr to become ashamed.

**vez** f time; (turno) turn; **uma** ~ once; **alguma** ~ ever; **algumas** ~**es, às** ~**es** sometimes; ~ **por outra** sometimes; **cada** ~ **mais/menos** more and more/less and less; **desta** ~ this time; **de** ~ once and for all; **de** ~ **em quando** from time to time; **em** ~ **de** instead of; **fazer as** ~**es de** (pessoa) to stand in for; (coisa) to replace; **mais uma** ~ again, once more; **raras** ~**es** seldom; **uma** ~ **que** since.

**'via** f road, route; (meio) way; (documento) copy; ~ **férrea** railway line; **em** ~ **de** about to; **por** ~ **aérea** by air; **por** ~ **das dúvidas** just in case; **por** ~ **de regra** generally // prep via, by way of.

**viação** [via'sãw] f transport; (companhia de ônibus) bus/coach company.

**via'duto** m viaduct.

**viageiro/a** [via'ʒejru/a] adj travelling; **viagem** f journey, trip; **viajens** fpl travels; **viagem de ida e volta** return trip, round trip; **viagem de núpcias** honeymoon; **viajante** adj travelling // m traveller; (COM) commercial traveller; **viajar** vi to travel; **viandante** m traveller.

**via'tura** f vehicle.

**vi'ável** adj (fig) feasible; (MED) viable.

**'víbora** f viper.

**vibração** [vibra'sãw] f vibration; **vibrante** adj vibrant; (discurso) stirring; **vibrar** vt (brandir) to brandish; (fazer oscilar) to vibrate; (cordas) to strike // vi to vibrate, shake; (som) to echo.

**vicejar** [vise'ʒax] vi to flourish.

**vice-presidente** [visɪ-prezi'dẽtʃi] m vice president.

**vice-rei** [visɪ-'xej] m viceroy.

**vici'ado/a** adj addicted; (ar) foul // m/f addict; **um ~ em entorpecentes** a drug addict; **viciar** vt (criar vício em) to make addicted; (falsificar) to falsify; (estragar) to spoil; (corromper) to corrupt; **viciar-se** vr to become addicted; **vício** m vice; (defeito) failing; (costume) bad habit; (em entorpecentes) addiction; **vicioso/a** adj (defeituoso) defective; (círculo) vicious.

**vicissi'tude** f vicissitude; **~s** fpl ups and downs.

**vi'çoso/a** adj (plantas) luxuriant; (fig) exuberant.

**'vida** f life; (duração) lifetime; (fig) vitality; **com ~** alive; **ganhar a ~** to earn one's living; **modo de ~** way of life; **para toda a ~** forever; **sem ~** dull, lifeless.

**vi'deira** f grapevine.

**vi'draça** f window pane; **vidraçaria** f glazier's; (fábrica) glass factory; (conjunto de vidraças) glasswork; **vidraceiro** m glazier; **vidraria** f (fábrica) glass factory; (artigos) glassware; (arte) glassmaking; **vidreiro** m glazier, glassmaker; **vidro** m glass.

**vi'ela** f alley.

**vi'er** etc vb ver **vir**.

**vi'és** m slant; (costura) bias strip; **ao/de ~** diagonally.

**vi'este** vb ver **vir**.

**'viga** f beam; (de ferro) girder.

**vigarice** [viga'risɪ] f swindle.

**vi'gário** m vicar.

**viga'rista** m swindler, confidence trickster.

**vigência** [vi'ʒẽsja] f validity; **durante a ~ da lei** while the law is in force; **vigente** adj in force, valid.

**vigia** [vi'ʒia] f (ato) watching; (NAUT) porthole; **de ~** on watch // m night watchman; **vigiar** vt to watch, keep an eye on; (velar por) to keep watch over // vi to be on the lookout.

**vigi'lância** f vigilance; **vigilante** adj vigilant; (atento) alert.

**vi'gor** m energy; **em ~** in force; **entrar/pôr em ~** to take effect/put into effect; **vigorar** vi to be in force; **~oso/a** adj vigorous.

**vil** adj vile, low.

**'vila** f town; (casa) villa.

**vila'nia** f villainy; **vilão/vilã** m/f (patife) villain.

**vi'leza** f vileness; (ação) mean trick.

**vilipendi'ar** vt to revile; (desprezar) to despise.

**vim** vb ver **vir**.

**'vime** [vimɪ] m wicker.

**vi'nagre** m vinegar.

**'vinco** m (em tecido) crease; (sulco) furrow.

**'vínculo** m bond, tie.

**'vinda** f arrival; **dar as boas ~s** to welcome.

**vindi'car** vt to vindicate.

**vin'dima** f grape harvest; **vindimar** vt (fig) to harvest // vi to gather grapes.

**vindouro/a** [vĩ'doru/a] adj future, coming// **~s** mpl future generations.

**vinga'dor(a)** adj avenging // m/f avenger; **vingança** f vengeance, revenge; **vingar** vt to avenge // vi (ter êxito) to be successful; (crescer) to grow; **vingar-se** vr: **vingar-se de** to take revenge on

**vingativo/a** *adj* vindictive.

**'vinha** *vb ver* **vir**.

**vinha** ['vɪɲa] *f* vineyard; **vinhedo** *m* vineyard; **vinho** *m* wine; **vinícola** *adj inv* wine-producing.

**vi'nil** *m* vinyl.

**vinte** ['vɪtʃi] *num* twenty; **vintém** *m*: **sem vintém** penniless; **vintena** *f* twenty, a score.

**violação** [vɪola'sãw] *f* violation; **~ da lei** lawbreaking.

**violão** [vɪo'lãw] *m* guitar.

**vio'lar** *vt* to violate; *(a lei)* to break.

**vio'lência** *f* violence; **violentar** *vt* to force; *(mulher)* to rape; **violento/a** *adj* violent; *(intenso)* intense; *(furioso)* furious.

**vio'leta** *f* violet.

**vio'lino** *m* violin.

**vir** *vi* to come; **~ a ser** to become; **a semana que vem** next week; **~ abaixo** to collapse; **mandar ~** to send for; **o sol vinha nascendo** the sun was rising.

**viração** [vɪra'sãw] *f* breeze.

**vi'rada** *f* turning; *(momento de virar)* turning-point; *(guinada)* swerve; **viragem** *f* turn; *(fig)* swing; **virar** *vt* to turn; *(página)* to turn over; *(esquina)* to turn; *(bolsos)* to turn inside out; *(copo)* to empty; **virar de cabeça para baixo** to turn upside down // *vi (mudar)* to change; **virar do avesso** to turn inside out; **virar para** to face; **virar-se** *vr* to turn; *(voltar-se)* to turn round.

**vira'volta** *f* reversal, turnabout.

**virgem** ['vɪrʒẽ] *adj (puro)* pure; *(não usado)* unused; *(: cassete)* blank // *f* virgin.

**'vírgula** *f* comma; *(decimal)* point.

**vi'ril** *adj* virile.

**virilha** [vɪ'riʎa] *f* groin.

**virili'dade** *f* virility.

**virtualmente** [vɪxtwal'mẽtʃi] *adv* virtually.

**virtude** [vɪx'tudʒi] *f* virtue; **em ~ de** owing to, because of; **virtuoso/a**

*adj* virtuous // *m* virtuoso.

**viru'lência** *f* virulence; **virulento/a** *adj* virulent.

**'vírus** *m* virus.

**visão** [vɪ'zãw] *f* vision; *(MED)* eyesight; **visar** *vt (um alvo)* to aim at; *(ter em vista)* to have in view; *(documento)* to stamp.

**'visco** *m* mistletoe; *(fig)* bait.

**vis'conde** *m* viscount.

**vis'coso/a** *adj* sticky, viscous.

**viseira** [vɪ'zejra] *f* visor.

**visibili'dade** *f* visibility.

**visio'nário/a** *adj, m/f* visionary.

**vi'sita** *f* visit, call; *(pessoa)* visitor; **fazer uma ~** to visit; **ter ~s** to have company; **~ de médico** flying visit; **visitar** *vt* to visit, call on; *(inspecionar)* to inspect.

**visível** [vɪ'zivew] *adj* visible.

**vislum'brar** *vt* to glimpse, catch a glimpse of; **vislumbre** *m (sinal)* glimpse; *(idéia)* hint, inkling.

**'visto/a** *pp de* **ver** // *adj* seen; **~ que** since; **está ~ que** of course // *m (em passaporte)* visa; *(em documento)* stamp // *f* sight; *(MED)* eyesight; *(panorama)* view; *(braguilha)* fly; **à ~ de** in view of; **~a curta** shortsightedness; **pagamento à ~** a cash payment; **conhecer de ~a** to know by sight; **dar na ~a** to be striking; **dar uma ~a de olhos em** to glance at; **fazer ~a grossa a** to turn a blind eye to; **pôr à ~a** to show; **ter em ~a** to have in mind.

**visto'ria** *f* inspection.

**vis'toso/a** *adj* handsome, eye-catching.

**vi'tal** *adj* vital; *(essencial)* essential; **~ício/a** *adj* for life; **~idade** *f* vitality.

**vita'mina** *f* vitamin.

**vi'tela** *f* calf; *(carne)* veal.

**viticul'tura** *f* vine growing.

**'vítima** *f* victim.

**vi'tória** *f* victory, win; **vitorioso/a** *adj* winning, victorious.

**'vítreo/a** adj (feito de vidro) glass; (com o aspeto de vidro) glassy; **vitrina** f, **vitrine** f shop window; (armário) glass case.

**vi'trola** f gramophone.

**vitupe'rar** vt (insultar) to insult, abuse; **vitupério** m (insulto) abuse.

**viuvez** [vju'veʒ] f widowhood; **viúvo/a** adj widowed // m widower // f widow.

**'viva** m cheer; ~! hurray!; ~ o rei! long live the king!

**vivaci'dade** f vivacity; (energia) vigour; **vivaz** adj (animado) lively.

**viveiro** [vi'vejru] m nursery.

**vi'venda** f (casa) residence.

**vi'ver** vi to live; ~ **de pão/de seu trabalho** to live on bread/by one's work.

**'víveres** mpl provisions.

**vivifi'car** vt to give life to.

**vivissecção** [vivisek'sãw] f vivisection.

**'vivo/a** adj alive, living; (cheiro) strong; (cor) bright; (animado) lively // m: **os** ~**s** the living; **televisionar ao** ~ to televise live.

**vizinhança** [vizi'ɲãsa] f neighbourhood; **vizinho/a** adj neighbouring; (perto) nearby // m/f neighbour.

**voa'dor/a** adj flying; (veloz) swift; **voar** vi to fly; (explodir) to blow up, explode; **fazer voar (pelos ares)** (dinamitar) to blow up, blast.

**vocabu'lário** m vocabulary; **vocábulo** m (palavra) word; (termo) term.

**vocação** [voka'sãw] f vocation, calling.

**vo'cal** adj vocal.

**você** [vo'se] pron you.

**vocife'rar** vt/i to shout, yell.

**'vodca** f vodka.

**'voga** f (NÁUT) rowing; (moda) fashion; (popularidade) popularity; **em** ~ popular, fashionable.

**vo'gal** f (LING) vowel // m/f (votante) voting member.

**vo'gar** vi to row; (boiar) to float; (importar) to matter; (estar na moda) to be popular.

**vo'lante** adj (móvel) mobile // m (AUTO) steering wheel; (motorista) driver; (impresso para apostas) betting slip.

**vo'látil** adj volatile.

**voleibol** [volej'bɔw] m volleyball.

**volição** [voli'sãw] f volition.

**volt** m volt.

**'volta** f turn; (regresso) return; (curva) bend, curve; (circuito) lap; (passeio) stroll; (resposta) retort; **passagem de ida e** ~ return ticket; (US) round trip ticket; **dar uma** ~ to go for a walk; **estar de** ~ to be back; **na** ~ **do correio** by return (post); **por** ~ **de** about, around.

**voltagem** [vol'taʒẽ] f voltage.

**vol'tar** vt to turn // vi to return, go/come back; ~ **a fazer** to do again; ~ **a si** to come to; ~**se** vr to turn; (ir de regresso) to turn back.

**volubili'dade** f fickleness.

**vo'lume** m (livro, som) volume; (tamanho) bulk; (pacote) package; **volumoso/a** adj bulky, big; (som) loud.

**volun'tário/a** adj voluntary // m/f volunteer.

**voluntari'oso/a** adj headstrong.

**voluptuoso/a** [volup'twozu/a] adj voluptuous.

**vo'lúvel** adj fickle, changeable.

**vol'ver** vt to turn // vi to go/come back.

**vomi'tar** vt/i to vomit; (fig) to pour out; **vômito** m (ato) vomiting; (efeito) vomit.

**von'tade** f will; (desejo) wish; **má** ~ ill will; **à** ~ (as much) as you like; **com** ~ with pleasure; **esteja à** ~ make yourself at home; **ter** ~ **de** feel like doing.

**vôo** (Pt: **voo**) ['vou] m flight; **levantar** ~ to take off.

**voragem** [vo'raʒẽ] f abyss, gulf; (turbilhão) whirlpool.

**vo'raz** *adj* voracious, greedy.

**vórtice** ['vɔxtʃisɪ] *m* whirlpool; (*de ar*) whirlwind.

**vós** [vɔʃ] *pron* you.

**vos** [vuʃ] *pron* you, to you.

**'vosso/a** *adj* your // *pron*: (**o**) ~ yours.

**votação** [vota'sãw] *f* vote, ballot; (*ato*) voting; **votante** *m/f* voter; **votar** *vt* (*eleger*) to vote for; (*dedicar*) to devote; (*prometer*) to make a vow of // *vi* to vote; **votar-se** *vr*: **votar-se a** to dedicate o.s. to; **voto** *m* vote; (*promessa*) vow; **fazer votos por** to wish for; **fazer votos que** to hope that.

**vou** *vb ver* **ir.**

**vovô** [vo'vo] *m* grandad.

**vovó** [vo'vɔ] *f* grandma.

**voz** *f* voice; (*grito*) cry; (*boato*) rumour; **a meia** ~ in a whisper; **dar** ~ **de prisão a alguém** to tell sb he is under arrest; **de viva** ~ orally; **ter** ~ **ativa** to be an authority; **em** ~ **alta** aloud; ~**earia** *f*, ~**eario** *m* shouting, hullabaloo.

**vulcão** [vul'kãw] *m* volcano.

**vul'gar** *adj* (*comum*) common, (*reles*) cheap; ~**idade** *f* commonness; (*ação*) vulgarity; ~**izar** *vt* to popularize; (*abandalhar*) to cheapen; **vulgo** *m* common people *pl* // *adv* commonly known as.

**vulne'rável** *adj* vulnerable.

**'vulto** *m* (*corpo*) figure, form; (*volume*) mass; (*fig*) importance; (*pessoa importante*) important person.

---

# X

Initial x is pronounced [ʃ].

**xá** [ʃa] *m* shah.

**'xácara** *f* ballad.

---

**xa'drez** *m* (*jogo*) chess; (*tabuleiro*) chessboard; (*tecido*) checked cloth // *adj* check(ered).

**xale** ['ʃalɪ] *m* shawl.

**xam'pu** *m* shampoo.

**xa'rá** *m* namesake.

**xaro'pada** *f* cough syrup; (*col*) boring talk; **xarope** *m* syrup.

**xelim** [ʃe'lĩ] *m* shilling.

**xenofo'bia** *f* xenophobia.

**xeque** ['ʃɛkɪ] *m* (*xadrez*) check; ~**-mate** *m* checkmate.

**xere'tar** *vi* to poke one's nose in.

**xe'rez** *m* sherry.

**'xícara** *f* cup.

**xilo'fone** *m* xylophone.

**xin'gar** *vt* (*insultar*) to abuse; ~ **alguém de algo** to call sb sth.

**xis** *m* (*letter*) x.

**xixi** [ʃi'ʃi] *m*: **fazer** ~ to wee, have a wee.

**xo'dó** *m* flirting; (*pessoa*) sweetheart.

---

# Z

**'zaga** *f* (*futebol*) fullback position; **zagueiro** *m* fullback.

**'zanga** *f* (*cólera*) anger; (*irritação*) annoyance; **zangado/a** *adj* angry; (*aborrecido*) annoyed.

**zangão** [zã'gãw] *m* (*inseto*) drone.

**zan'gar** *vt* to annoy, irritate; ~**-se** *vr* (*aborrecer-se*) to get annoyed; ~**-se com** to get cross with.

**za'rolho/a** *adj* blind in one eye.

**Zé** *abr de* **José** Joe.

**'zebra** *f* zebra; (*fig*) silly ass; (*jogo*) collapse, surprise result.

**zela'dor** *m* caretaker; **zelar** *vt* to look after; **zelo** *m* devotion, zeal; **zeloso/a** *adj* zealous; (*diligente*) hard-working.

**zênite** ['zenitʃi] *m* zenith.

**zé-povinho** [zɛ-po'viɲu] *m* the man

in the street; (*o povo*) the masses *pl*;
(*ralé*) riffraff.

**'zero** *m* zero, nothing; (*esporte*) nil;
~ **à esquerda** nonentity, a nobody.

**ziguezague** [zigı-'zagı] *m* zigzag.

**'zinco** *m* zinc; **folha de** ~
corrugated iron.

**'zíper** *m* zip.

**zo'ar** *vi* to buzz, drone.

**zo'díaco** *m* zodiac.

**zom'bar** *vi* : ~ **de** to make fun of;
**zombaria** *f* mockery, ridicule.

**'zona** *f* area; (*parte*) part; (*GEO*)
zone.

**'zonzo/a** *adj* dizzy.

**zôo** ['zou] *m* zoo; **zoológico/a** *adj*

zoological; **jardim zoológico** zoo;
**zoólogo** *m* zoologist.

**'zorra** *f* (*col*) mess.

**zum** *m* zoom.

**zum'bido** *m* buzz(ing); (*de tráfego*)
hum; **zumbir** *vi* to buzz; (*motor*) to
hum.

**zu'nido** *m* (*vento*) whistling;
(*inseto*) whir, buzz; **zunir** *vi* (*vento*)
to whistle; (*seta*) to whizz; (*bala*) to
zip; (*inseto*) to buzz.

**zunzum** [zũ'zũ] *m* buzz(ing); (*boato*)
rumour.

**zur'rapa** *f* rough wine; (*col*) plonk.

**zur'rar** *vi* to bray.

# PORTUGUESE VERB TABLES

*1* Gerund. *2* Imperative. *3* Present. *4* Imperfect. *5* Preterite. *6* Future.
*7* Present subjunctive. *8* Imperfect subjunctive. *9* Future subjunctive.
*10* Past participle. *11* Pluperfect. *12* Personal infinitive.

*Etc* indicates that the irregular root is used for all persons of the tense, e.g.
**ouvir:** *7* ouça, ouças, ouça, ouçamos, ouçais, ouçam.

**abrir** *10* aberto

**acudir** *2* acode *3* acudo, acodes, acode, acodem

**aderir** *3* adiro *7* adira

**aduzir** *2* aduz *3* aduzo, aduzes, aduz

**advertir** *3* advirto *7* advirta *etc*

**afear** *2* afeia *3* afeio, afeias, afeia, afeiam *7* afeie *etc*

**agir** *3* ajo *7* aja *etc*

**agradecer** *3* agradeço *7* agradeça *etc*

**agredir** *2* agride *3* agrido, agrides, agride, agridem *7* agrida *etc*

**AMAR** *1* amando *2* ama, amai *3* amo, amas, ama, amamos, amais, amam *4* amava, amavas, amava, amávamos, amáveis, amavam *5* amei, amaste, amou, amámos, amastes, amaram *6* amarei, amarás, amará, amaremos, amareis, amarão *7* ame, ames, ame, amemos, ameis, amem *8* amasse, amasses, amasse, amássemos, amásseis, amassem *9* amar, amares, amar, amarmos, amardes, amarem *10* amado *11* amara, amaras, amara, amáramos, amáreis, amaram *12* amar, amares, amar, amarmos, amardes, amarem

**ansiar** *2* anseia *3* anseio, anseias, anseia, anseiam *7* anseie *etc*

**aprazer** *2* apraz *3* aprazo, aprazes, apraz *5* aprouve *etc* *8* aprouvesse *etc* *9* aprouver *etc* *11* aprouvera *etc*

**apreçar** *7* aprece *etc*

**arrancar** *7* arranque *etc*

**arruinar** *3* arruina *3* arruino, arruinas, arruina, arruinam *7* arruine, arruines, arruine, arruinem

**aspergir** *3* aspirjo *7* aspirja *etc*

**averiguar** *7* averigúe, averigúes, averigúe, averigúem

**boiar** *2* bóia *3* bóio, bóias, bóia, bóiam *7* bóie, bóies, bóie, bóiem

**bulir** *2* bole *3* bulo, boles, bole, bolem

**caber** *3* caibo *5* coube *etc* *7* caiba *etc* *8* coubesse *etc* *9* couber *etc*

**cair** *2* cai *3* caio, cais, cai, caimos, cais, caem *4* caia *etc* *5* caí, caiste *7* caia *etc* *8* caísse *etc*

**cobrir** *3* cubro *7* cubra *etc* *10* coberto

**colorir** *3* coluro *7* colura *etc*

**compelir** *3* compilo *7* compila *etc*

**crer** *2* crê *3* creio, crês, crê, cremos, credes, crêem, *5* cri, creste, creu, cremos, crestes, creram *7* creia *etc*

**cuspir** *3* cuspo, cospes, cospe, cospem

**dar** *3* dou, dás, dá, damos, dais, dão *5* dei, deste, deu, demos, destes, deram *7* dê, dês, dê, demos, deis, dêem *8* desse *etc* *9* der *etc* *11* dera *etc*

**delir** *3* dilo *7* dila *etc*

279

**demolir** 3 demulo 7 demula *etc*

**denegrir** 2 denigre 3 denigro, denigres, denigre, denigrem 7 denigra *etc*

**despir** 3 dispo 7 dispa *etc*

**dizer** 3 diz (dize) 3 digo, dizes, diz, dizemos, dizeis, dizem 5 disse *etc* 6 direi *etc* 7 diga *etc* 8 dissesse *etc* 9 disser *etc* 10 dito

**doer** 3 dói 3 doo, dóis, dói

**dormir** 3 durmo 7 durma *etc*

**escrever** 10 escrito

**ESTAR** 2 está 3 estou, estás, está, estamos, estais, estão 4 estava *etc* 5 estive, estiveste, esteve, estivemos, estivestes, estiveram 7 esteja *etc* 8 estivesse *etc* 9 estiver *etc* 11 estivera *etc*

**explodir** 3 expludo 7 expluda *etc*

**extorquir** 3 exturco 7 exturca *etc*

**FAZER** 3 faço 5 fiz, fizeste, fez, fizemos, fizestes, fizeram 6 farei *etc* 7 faça 8 fizesse *etc* 9 fizer *etc* 10 feito 11 fizera *etc*

**ferir** 3 firo 7 fira *etc*

**flectir** 3 flito 7 flita *etc*

**fluir** 3 fluo, fluis, flui, fluimos, fluís, fluem

**fremir** 3 frimo 7 frima *etc*

**fruir** 3 fruo, fruis, frui, fruimos, fruís, fruem

**fugir** 2 foge 3 fujo, foges, foge, fogem 7 fuja *etc*

**ganhar** 10 ganho

**gastar** 10 gasto

**gerir** 3 giro 7 gira *etc*

**haver** 2 há 3 hei, hás, há, havemos, haveis, hão 4 havia *etc* 5 houve, houveste, houve, houvemos, houvestes, houveram 7 haja *etc* 8 houvesse *etc* 9 houver *etc* 11 houvera *etc*

**ir** 1 indo 2 vai 3 vou, vais, vai, vamos, ides, vão 4 ia *etc* 5 fui, foste, foi, fomos, fostes, foram 7 vá, vás, vá

vamos, vades, vão 8 fosse, fosses, fosse, fôssemos, fôsseis, fossem 9 for *etc* 10 ido 11 fora *etc*

**jazer** 3 jazo, jazes, jaz

**ler** 2 lê 3 leio, lês, lê, lemos, ledes, lêem 5 li, leste, leu, lemos, lestes, leram 7 leia *etc*

**medir** 3 meço 7 meça *etc*

**mentir** 3 minto 7 minta *etc*

**ouvir** 3 ouço 7 ouça *etc*

**pagar** 10 pago

**parar** 3 pára 3 paro, paras, pára

**parir** 3 pára, paras, pára

**pecar** 7 peque *etc*

**pedir** 3 peço 7 peça *etc*

**perder** 3 perco 7 perca *etc*

**poder** 3 posso 5 pude, pudeste, pôde, pudemos, pudestes, puderam 7 possa *etc* 8 pudesse *etc* 9 puder *etc* 11 pudera *etc*

**polir** 3 pule 3 pulo, pules, pule, pulem 7 pula *etc*

**pôr** 1 pondo 2 põe 3 ponho, pões, põe, pomos, pondes, põem 4 punha *etc* 5 pus, puseste, pôs, pusemos, pusestes, puseram 6 porei *etc* 7 ponha *etc* 8 pusesse *etc* 9 puser *etc* 10 posto 11 pusera *etc*

**premir** 2 prime 3 primo, primes, prime, primem 7 prima *etc*

**preferir** 3 prefiro 7 prefira *etc*

**prevenir** 2 previne 3 previno, prevines, previne, previnem 7 previna *etc*

**prover** 2 provê 3 provejo, provês, provê, provemos, provedes, provêem 5 provi, proveste, proveu, provemos, provestes, proveram 7 proveja *etc* 8 provesse *etc* 9 prover *etc*

**provir** 2 provém 3 provenho, provéns, provém, provimos, provindes, provêm 4 provinha *etc* 5 provim, provieste, proveio, proviemos, proviestes, provieram

7 provenha etc 8 proviesse etc 9
provier 10 provindo 11 proviera
etc

**querer** 3 quero, queres, quer 5 quis,
quiseste, quis, quisemos,
quisestes, quiseram 7 queira etc 8
quisesse etc 9 quiser etc 11 quisera
etc

**repetir** 3 repito 7 repita etc

**requerer** 3 requeiro, requeres,
requer 7 requeira etc

**retorquir** 3 retorço 7 retorça etc

**reunir** 2 reúne 3 reúno, reúnes,
reúne, reúnem 7 reúna etc

**rir** 2ri 3rio, ris, ri, rimos, rides, riem
5 ri, riste, riu, rimos, ristes, riram
7 ria etc

**saber** 3 sei, sabes, sabe, sabemos,
sabeis, sabem 5 soube, soubeste,
soube, soubemos, soubestes,
souberam 7 saiba etc 8 soubesse
etc 9 souber etc 11 soubera etc

**seguir** 3 sigo 7 siga etc

**sentir** 3 sinto 7 sinta etc

**ser** 2sê 3sou, és, é, somos, sois, são 4
era etc 5 fui, foste, foi, fomos,
fostes, foram 7 seja etc 8 fosse etc
9 for etc 11 fora etc

**servir** 3 sirvo 7 sirva etc

**subir** 2 sobe 3 subo, sobes, sobe,
sobem

**suster** 2sustém 3 sustenho, sustens,
sustém, sustemos, sustendes,
sustêm 5 sustive, sustiveste,
sustive, sustivemos, sustivestes,
sustiveram 7 sustenha etc

**ter** 2 tem 3 tenho, tens, tem, temos,
tendes, têm 4 tinha etc 5 tive,
tiveste, teve, tivemos, tivestes,
tiveram 6 terei etc 7 tenha etc 8
tivesse etc 9 tiver etc 11 tivera etc

**torcer** 3 torço 7 torça etc

**tossir** 3 tusso 7 tussa etc

**trair** 2 trai 3 traio, trais, trai,
traímos, traís, traem 7 traia etc

**trazer** 2(traze) 3traz 7trago, trazes,

traz 5 trouxe, trouxeste, trouxe,
trouxemos, trouxestes, trouxeram
6 trarei etc 7 traga etc 8 trouxesse
etc 9 trouxer etc 11 trouxera etc

**UNIR** 1unindo 2une, uni 3 uno,
unes, une, unimos, unis, unem 4
unia, unias, unia, uníamos,
uníeis, uniam 5 uni, uniste, uniu,
unimos, unistes, uniram 6 unirei,
uniras, unirá, uniremos, unireis,
unirão 7una, unas, una, unamos,
unais, unam 8 inisse, unisses,
unisse, uníssemos, unísseis,
unissem 9 unir, unires, unir,
unirmos, unirdes, unirem 10
unido 11 unira, uniras, unira,
uniramos, unireis, uniram 12
unir, unires, unir, unirmos,
unirdes, unirem

**valer** 3 valho 7 valha etc

**ver** 2vê 3vejo, vês, vê, vemos, vedes,
vêem 4 via etc 5 vi, viste, viu,
vimos, vistes, viram 7 veja etc 8
visse etc 9 vir etc 10 visto 11 vira
etc

**vir** 1 vindo 2 vem 3 venho, vens,
vem, vimos, vindes, vêm 4 vinha
etc 5 vim, vieste, veio, viemos,
viestes, vieram 7 venha etc 8 viesse
etc 9 vier etc 10 vindo 11 viera etc

**VIVER** 1 vivendo 2 vive, vivei 3
vivo, vives, vive, vivemos, viveis,
vivem 4 vivia, vivias, vivia,
vivíamos, vivíeis, viviam 5 vivi,
viveste, viveu, vivemos, vivestes,
viveram 6 viverei, viverás, viverá,
viveremos, vivereis, viverão 7
viva, vivas, viva, vivamos, vivais,
vivam 8 vivesse, vivesses, vivesse,
vivêssemos, vivêsseis, vivessem 9
viver, viveres, viver, vivermos,
viverdes, viverem 10 vivido 11
vivera, viveras, vivera, vivêramos,
vivêreis, viveram 12 viver,
viveres, viver, vivermos, viverdes,
viverem

# VERBOS IRREGULARES EM INGLÊS

| present | pt | pp | present | pt | pp |
|---------|-----|-----|---------|-----|-----|
| arise | arose | arisen | cut | cut | cut |
| awake | awoke | awaked | deal | dealt | dealt |
| be (am, is, are; being) | was, were | been | dig | dug | dug |
| | | | do (3rd person; he/she/it/does) | did | done |
| bear | bore | born(e) | | | |
| beat | beat | beaten | draw | drew | drawn |
| become | became | become | dream | dreamed, dreamt | dreamed, dreamt |
| befall | befell | befallen | | | |
| begin | began | begun | drink | drank | drunk |
| behold | beheld | beheld | drive | drove | driven |
| bend | bent | bent | dwell | dwelt | dwelt |
| beseech | besought | besought | eat | ate | eaten |
| beset | beset | beset | fall | fell | fallen |
| bet | bet, betted | bet, betted | feed | fed | fed |
| bid | bid | bid | feel | felt | felt |
| bind | bound | bound | fight | fought | fought |
| bite | bit | bitten | find | found | found |
| bleed | bled | bled | flee | fled | fled |
| blow | blew | blown | fling | flung | flung |
| break | broke | broken | fly | flew | flown |
| breed | bred | bred | forbid | forbade | forbidden |
| bring | brought | brought | forego | forewent | foregone |
| build | built | built | foresee | foresaw | foreseen |
| burn | burnt, burned | burnt, burned | foretell | foretold | foretold |
| | | | forget | forgot | forgotten |
| burst | burst | burst | forgive | forgave | forgiven |
| buy | bought | bought | forsake | forsook | forsaken |
| can | could | (been able) | freeze | froze | frozen |
| cast | cast | cast | get | got | got, (US) gotten |
| catch | caught | caught | | | |
| choose | chose | chosen | give | gave | given |
| cling | clung | clung | go (goes) | went | gone |
| come | came | come | | | |
| cost | cost | cost | grind | ground | ground |
| creep | crept | crept | grow | grew | grown |

282

| present | pt | pp | present | pt | pp |
|---------|-----|-----|---------|-----|-----|
| hang | hung, hanged | hung, hanged | read | read | read |
| | | | rend | rent | rent |
| have | had | had | rid | rid | rid |
| hear | heard | heard | ride | rode | ridden |
| hide | hid | hidden | ring | rang | rung |
| hit | hit | hit | rise | rose | risen |
| hold | held | held | run | ran | run |
| hurt | hurt | hurt | saw | sawed | sawn |
| keep | kept | kept | say | said | said |
| kneel | knelt, kneeled | knelt, kneeled | see | saw | seen |
| | | | seek | sought | sought |
| know | knew | known | sell | sold | sold |
| lay | laid | laid | send | sent | sent |
| lead | led | led | set | set | set |
| lean | leant, leaned | leant, leaned | shake | shook | shaken |
| | | | shall | should | – |
| leap | leapt, leaped | leapt, leaped | shear | sheared | shorn, sheared |
| learn | learnt, learned | learnt, learned | shed | shed | shed |
| | | | shine | shone | shone |
| leave | left | left | shoot | shot | shot |
| lend | lent | lent | show | showed | shown |
| let | let | let | shrink | shrank | shrunk |
| lie (lying) | lay | lain | shut | shut | shut |
| | | | sing | sang | sung |
| light | lit, lighted | lit, lighted | sink | sank | sunk |
| | | | sit | sat | sat |
| lose | lost | lost | slay | slew | slain |
| make | made | made | sleep | slept | slept |
| may | might | – | slide | slid | slid |
| mean | meant | meant | sling | slung | slung |
| meet | met | met | slit | slit | slit |
| mistake | mistook | mistaken | smell | smelt, smelled | smelt, smelled |
| mow | mowed | mown, mowed | sow | sowed | sown, sowed |
| must | (had to) | (had to) | | | |
| pay | paid | paid | speak | spoke | spoken |
| put | put | put | speed | sped, speeded | sped, speeded |
| quit | quit, quitted | quit, quitted | spell | spelt, | spelt, |

283

| present | pt | pp | present | pt | pp |
|---|---|---|---|---|---|
| | spelled | spelled | **swim** | swam | swum |
| **spend** | spent | spent | **swing** | swung | swung |
| **spill** | spilt, | spilt, | **take** | took | taken |
| | spilled | spilled | **teach** | taught | taught |
| **spin** | spun | spun | **tear** | tore | torn |
| **spit** | spat | spat | **tell** | told | told |
| **split** | split | split | **think** | thought | thought |
| **spoil** | spoiled, | spoiled, | **throw** | threw | thrown |
| | spoilt | spoilt | **thrust** | thrust | thrust |
| **spread** | spread | spread | **tread** | trod | trodden |
| **spring** | sprang | sprung | **wake** | woke, | woken, |
| **stand** | stood | stood | | waked | waked |
| **steal** | stole | stolen | **waylay** | waylaid | waylaid |
| **stick** | stuck | stuck | **wear** | wore | worn |
| **sting** | stung | stung | **weave** | wove, | woven, |
| **stink** | stank | stunk | | weaved | weaved |
| **stride** | strode | stridden | **wed** | wedded, | wedded, |
| **strike** | struck | struck, | | wed | wed |
| | | stricken | **weep** | wept | wept |
| **strive** | strove | striven | **win** | won | won |
| **swear** | swore | sworn | **wind** | wound | wound |
| **sweep** | swept | swept | **wring** | wrung | wrung |
| **swell** | swelled | swollen, | **write** | wrote | written |
| | | swelled | | | |

# OS NÚMEROS

# NUMBERS

| | | |
|---|---|---|
| um(a)/primeiro(a) | 1 | one/first |
| dois (duas)/segundo(a) | 2 | two/second |
| três/terceiro(a) | 3 | three/third |
| quatro/quarto(a) | 4 | four/fourth |
| cinco/quinto(a) | 5 | five/fifth |
| seis/sexto(a) | 6 | six/sixth |
| sete/sétimo(a) | 7 | seven/seventh |
| oito/oitavo(a) | 8 | eight/eighth |
| nove/nono(a) | 9 | nine/ninth |
| dez/décimo(a) | 10 | ten/tenth |
| onze/décimo(a) primeiro(a) | 11 | eleven/eleventh |
| doze/décimo(a) segundo(a) | 12 | twelve/twelfth |
| treze/décimo(a) terceiro(a) | 13 | thirteen/thirteenth |
| catorze/décimo(a) quarto(a) | 14 | fourteen/fourteenth |
| quinze/décimo(a) quinto(a) | 15 | fifteen/fifteenth |
| dezesseis/décimo(a) sexto(a) | 16 | sixteen/sixteenth |
| dezessete/décimo(a) sétimo(a) | 17 | seventeen/seventeenth |
| dezoito/décimo(a) oitavo(a) | 18 | eighteen/eighteenth |
| dezenove/décimo(a) nono(a) | 19 | nineteen/nineteenth |
| vinte/vigésimo(a) | 20 | twenty/twentieth |
| vinte e um(a) | 21 | twenty-one |
| vinte e dois (duas) | 22 | twenty-two |
| trinta | 30 | thirty |
| trinta e um(a) | 31 | thirty-one |
| trinta e dois (duas) | 32 | thirty-two |
| quarenta | 40 | forty |
| quarenta e um(a) | 41 | forty-one |
| cinqüenta | 50 | fifty |
| cinqüenta e um(a) | 51 | fifty-one |
| sessenta | 60 | sixty |
| sessenta e um(a) | 61 | sixty-one |
| setenta | 70 | seventy |
| setenta e um(a) | 71 | seventy-one |
| setenta e dois (duas) | 72 | seventy-two |
| oitenta | 80 | eighty |
| oitenta e um(a) | 81 | eighty-one |
| noventa | 90 | ninety |
| noventa e um(a) | 91 | ninety-one |
| cem, cento/centésimo(a) | 100 | a hundred, one hundred/hundredth |

| | | |
|---|---|---|
| cento e um(a) | 101 | a hundred and one |
| duzentos(as) | 200 | two hundred |
| duzentos(as) e um(a) | 201 | two hundred and one |
| trezentos(as) | 300 | three hundred |
| trezentos(as) e um(a) | 301 | three hundred and one |
| quatrocentos(as) | 400 | four hundred |
| quinhentos(as) | 500 | five hundred |
| seiscentos(as) | 600 | six hundred |
| setecentos(as) | 700 | seven hundred |
| oitocentos(as) | 800 | eight hundred |
| novecentos(as) | 900 | nine hundred |
| mil/milésimo(a) | 1000 | a thousand, one thousand/ thousandth |
| mil e dois (duas) | 1002 | a thousand and two |
| cinco mil | 5000 | five thousand |
| um milhão | 1,000,000 | a million, one million |

## Exemplos / Examples

| Exemplos | Examples |
|---|---|
| mil novecentos e oitenta e cinco | 1985 |
| cento e duas mulheres | 102 women |
| cem por cento | 100% |
| Carlos quinto | Charles V |
| a página 7 | page 7 |
| no dia 7 (de Maio) | on the 7th (of May) |
| mora no número 7 | he lives at number 7 |
| chegou em sétimo | he came in 7th |
| 1º (1ª), 2º (2ª), 3º (3ª), 4º (4ª), 5º (5ª) | 1st, 2nd, 3rd, 4th, 5th |

**N.B.** In Portuguese the ordinal numbers from 1 to 10 are commonly used; from 11 to 20 they are used in front of the noun; above 20 they are rarely used and are replaced by the cardinal numbers.

| A HORA | THE TIME |
|---|---|
| que horas são? | what time is it? |
| é/são | it's ou it is |
| a que horas? | (at) what time? |
| a/as | at |
| meia-noite | midnight |
| uma da manhã | one (o'clock) (a.m. ou in the morning), 1 a.m. |
| uma e dez | ten past one |
| uma e quinze | a quarter past one, one fifteen |
| uma e vinte | twenty past one |
| uma e meia | half past one, one thirty |
| quinze para as duas | a quarter to two, one forty-five |
| dez para as duas | ten to two, one fifty |
| meio-dia | twelve (o'clock), midday, noon |
| uma da tarde | one (o'clock) (p.m. ou in the afternoon) |
| sete da tarde, dezenove | seven (o'clock) (p.m. ou at night) |
| nove e meia da noite, vinte e uma e meia | nine thirty (p.m. ou at night) |
| meio-dia e quinze | twelve fifteen (a.m.), a quarter past midday |
| meia-noite e dez | ten past twelve (p.m.), ten past midnight |